The Encyclopedia of Sculpture

Volume One

Board of Advisers

The Encyclopedia of Sculpture

Volume One
A–F

Antonia Boström, editor

Fitzroy Dearborn
New York • London

Published in 2004 by
Fitzroy Dearborn
An imprint of the Taylor & Francis Group
29 West 35th Street
New York, NY 10001

Published in Great Britain by
Fitzroy Dearborn
An imprint of the Taylor & Francis Group
11 New Fetter Lane
London EC4P 4EE

10 9 8 7 6 5 4 3 2 1

Library of Congress Cataloging-in-Publication Data

The encyclopedia of sculpture / Antonia Boström, editor.
　　p. cm.
Includes bibliographical references and index.
ISBN 1-57958-248-6 (set : alk. paper)—ISBN 1-57958-428-4 (vol. 1 : alk. paper)—ISBN 1-57958-429-2
(vol. 2 : alk. paper)—ISBN 1-57958-430-6 (vol. 3 : alk. paper) 1. Sculpture, Modern—20th century—
Encyclopedias. I. Title: The encyclopedia of sculpture. II. Boström, Antonia.
NB198.E53 2004
735′.23′03—dc22

2003015677

Printed in the United States on acid-free paper.

Contents

ACKNOWLEDGMENTS

The Board of Advisers has been crucial in helping to winnow down an unwieldy series of headings into a coherent but comprehensive selection of entries, and I wish to thank them warmly: Sergei Androssov; Charles Avery, Peter Barnet, Sarah Bassett, Thomas Cummins, Penelope Curtis, Jan Fontein, Norbert Jopek, Donald F. McCallum, Stig Miss, Robert Morkot, Elsie Peck, William Peck, David Penney, Anthony Radcliffe, Frits Scholten, R.R.R. Smith, Richard Stone, Marjorie Trusted, Philip Ward-Jackson, Ian Wardropper, Paul Williamson, and Dorothy Wong. The long list of contributors to *The Encyclopedia of Sculpture*, as well as commentators on the project, have further assisted in shaping the final list and have highlighted its lacunae, while also contributing to its realization.

At Fitzroy Dearborn Publishers I have been assisted to an invaluable degree by Commissioning Editors, Carol Burwash, Christy Prahl, and Steve Laurie, without whose expert and infinitely good-humored collaboration at every stage of the creation and editing of this work, these three volumes might not have taken shape. At Routledge I have been assisted by Development Editor Lynn M. Somers, whose diligence helped bring this project to fruition. I thank them all warmly for their forbearance. Daniel Kirkpatrick at a very early stage in the concept of this book, and George Walsh and Paul Schellinger at later stages, had faith in the value of this book, and have been encouraging in the face of adversity. Aimée Marcereau has sensitively and imaginatively selected the large number of accompanying illustrations. My colleagues at The Detroit Institute of Arts have been supportive of this project and the staff of the DIA library most helpful in my bibliographical queries, for which I thank them. My greatest debt of gratitude is to Dean Baker, without whose support during the long genesis of this book I might have despaired, and finally to Olivia and Anna Boström Baker, who sat with me during its last stages, sweet and constant companions.

Antonia Boström

INTRODUCTION

The subject of *The Encyclopedia of Sculpture*—sculpture, in all its manifestations and interpretations—has been treated in a wide range of art-historical and technical formats. Until the development of this project, however, sculpture had not yet been awarded its own discrete encyclopedia, and this three-volume reference work aims to change that situation.

From the outset of the project the objective has been to consider the subject of sculptural achievement in its broadest chronological, historical, technical, and international contexts. During the conception and planning stages the project profited from the advice of an experienced and insightful board of advisers (see Acknowledgments) and from many scholars and contributors who have highlighted the omissions or oversights in the initial selection of headings. Of course no book, no matter the number of volumes, can purport to cover the entirety of a subject as vast as sculpture, but it is felt that, on the whole, this encyclopedia contributes a rich, comprehensive, and well-balanced reference work that is truly the first of its kind. Originally planned as a two-volume work, the final publication has expanded to three solidly illustrated volumes. With a total of 763 entries, the resulting text marries the most crucial element of standard survey texts (the images) with the critical scholarship, for which the Routledge Reference texts are historically known.

The entries appear in alphabetical order and explore the subject of sculpture from the viewpoints of history, criticism, theory, production, training, and conservation, as well as from the more traditional approaches of biography and critical analysis of individual works of art. In addition, extensive country surveys treat the subject from a regional aspect, which is especially appropriate where individual sculptors are unidentifiable, or where a style is associated with an entire region or school. A complete *Alphabetical List of Entries* is provided and followed by a *Thematic List of Entries*, the latter of which facilitates access to the contents, particularly for students and librarians. These thematic categories include *Artist Biographies*, with a subcategory of *Works* entries by the individual artists (for instance, Brancusi, Constantin; and *Bird in Space*); *Works, Monuments, and Sites* (for church complexes or monuments for which the artist is unknown, etc.); *Styles and Periods* (such as Neoclassicism and Romanticism); *Geographies* (both countries and regions); *Materials, Forms, and Techniques* (such as Caryatid, Precious Metals); and *Critical Concerns* (Collecting and Patronage, Women Sculptors).

In terms of format, biographical essays detail the artistic developments and contributions of individual sculptors, and then follow with a brief biographical sketch and a list of the sculptor's selected works, including dates of construction, materials used, and current locations. Works entries begin with informative data—dates of construction, materials used, current locations, and dimensions of the work, and then follow with a discussion of the work in its context. Some major sculptors receive more than one work essay (for instance, Donatello, Bernini, or Rodin), and other minor sculptors not given their own entries are discussed in general regional or historical survey essays. Reference to these sculptors, as well as to many important terms and concepts, may be found in the extensive index at the end of the third volume. Throughout the body of the encyclopedia there are also many *See also* sections that direct the reader to discussions of these sculptors, terms, and concepts. A *Further Reading* section follows every entry to point the invested reader toward studies that augment the introductory information to which an encyclopedia entry is inevitably limited. While the selection of artists and individual sculptures and monuments was arduously compiled, taking into consideration historically essential figures and their works of canonical stature, care was taken to augment this conventional approach with lesser-known and -studied artists who are germane to the critical study that such an encyclopedia offers.

Style and period entries provide broad, historical summaries and analyses of the subject. Entries such as *Gothic Sculpture, Modernism*, and *Minimalism* are likely not only to treat a number of artists and works that could not be represented by individual entries but to examine stylistic developments, trends, social contexts, and studies relevant to particular pedagogies. Other topic entries such as *Garden Sculpture, Forgeries and Deceptive Restorations, Natabori, Tomb Sculpture*, and *Conservation* provide a fuller understanding of the history and practice of sculpture, its materials, techniques, processes, and forms. Though *The Encyclopedia of Sculpture* inevitably reflects the enormous wealth of research on the sculptural achievements of Europe and the Americas, diligent efforts were made to give due coverage to sculpture in Asia and Africa, and this is reflected in the considerable length of those country survey essays. Their *Further Reading* lists lead the reader to more in-depth and comprehensive studies.

The illustrations were meticulously researched and selected with several aims, primarily to illustrate works of the contributing authors' choices. In some cases, the editors' selections were predicated on the availability of images from museums and collectors, copyright issues, and reproduction issues. The illustration captions were deliberately written to be concise and avoid repeating information that can be found within the accompanying essays. Care was taken to comply with all of the rights and reproductions requirements of the participating organizations and institutions. In the case of images from particular museum collections such as The Museum of Modern Art, New York, New York, and The Detroit Institute of Arts, Detroit, Michigan those museums require specific information that lengthened the captions considerably.

Throughout these volumes the editorial approach, while imposing strict standards for coverage and format, has allowed the voices of the contributors to speak in individual entries, allowing for a more personal and varied tone, as well as reflecting a range of art-historical and critical approaches. Fitzroy Dearborn Publishers and Routledge, an imprint of Taylor and Francis, are committed to offering what should become a seminal work in the field of sculpture.

Alphabetical List of Entries

ALPHABETICAL LIST OF ENTRIES

THEMATIC LIST OF ENTRIES

Artist Biographies

Aaltonen, Wäinö
Adam Family
Agostino di Duccio
Aleijadinho (Antônio Francisco Lisboa)
Algardi, Alessandro
Amadeo, Giovanni Antonio
Ammanati, Bartolomeo
Andre, Carl
Anguier, François
Anguier, Michel
Antelami, Benedetto
Antico (Pier Jacopo Alari Bonacolsi)
Antinous
Antokol'sky, Mark Matveyevich
Archipenko, Alexander Porfirevich
Arman (Fernandez)
Arnolfo di Cambio
Arp, Jean (Hans)
Artemision Zeus (Poseidon)
Aspetti, Tiziano

Bacon, John
Balkenhol, Stephan
Bandinelli, Baccio
Bandini, Giovanni (Giovanni dell'Opera)
Banks, Thomas
Barlach, Ernst
Bartholdi, Frédéric-Auguste
Bartolini, Lorenzo
Barye, Antoine-Louis
Begarelli, Antonio
Belling, Rudolf
Bellmer, Hans
Benedetto da Maiano
Bernhardt, Sarah
Bernini, Gianlorenzo
Bernini, Pietro
Berruguete, Alonso
Bertaux, Madame Léon
Bertoldo di Giovanni
Bertos, Francesco

Beuys, Joseph
Bienaime, Luigi
Bistolfi, Leonardo
Boccioni, Umberto
Bonazza, Antonio
Bontemps, Pierre
Borobudur
Bossuit, Francis van
Botero, Fernando
Bouchardon, Edmé
Bourdelle, Émile-Antoine
Bourgeois, Louise
Bracci, Pietro
Brancusi, Constantin
Brecheret, Victor
Broecke, Willem van den (Paludanus)
Brokof, Ferdinand Maximilian
Brüggmann, Hans
Buon Family
Bushnell, John
Busti, Agostino (Bambaia)
Butler, Reg

Caffà, Melchiorre
Caffiéri Family
Calder, Alexander
Campagna, Girolamo
Cano, Alonso
Canova, Antonio
Carlo di Cesare del Palagio
Caro, Anthony
Carpeaux, Jean-Baptiste
Carrier-Belleuse, Albert-Ernest
Cellini, Benvenuto
Certosa di Pavia
César (César Baldacchini)
Chantrey, Sir Francis (Legatt)
Chinard, Joseph
Christo and Jeanne-Claude
Cibber, Caius Gabriel
Claudel, Camille
Clésinger, (Jean-Baptiste) Auguste

xix

THEMATIC LIST OF ENTRIES

Styles and Periods

Countries and Geographies

Materials, Forms, and Techniques

Critical Concerns

A

WÄINÖ AALTONEN 1894–1966 *Finnish*

Wäinö Aaltonen was perhaps the most important Finnish sculptor of the 20th century. With a career coinciding with the development of the Finnish republic, he won a number of public commissions, such as allegorical figures for the senate and statues of the composer Jean Sibelius (1936), which formally contributed to the celebration of Finland's political and cultural accomplishments.

Public admiration for Aaltonen's work seems to have rested on a realistic approach to his subjects. Of Aaltonen, Hugo Otava once remarked that he "fuses the achievements of classicism and realism into a new, totally modern form of art" (see Pfäffli, 1994). Aaltonen's style softened the recognizable muscled versions of Soviet sculpture that were prominent during this period of Finland's struggle for cultural independence. Aaltonen was thus able to develop works that satisfied both national needs and the individual needs of the subjects. Aaltonen's numerous portrait heads reveal this balance and illustrate the artist as essentially a symbolic realist. His ability not only to create a likeness to many of his well-known subjects, but also to capture the essence of these individuals has contributed to Aaltonen's recognition as one of the greatest European sculptors of the 20th century.

After completing his education at the Turku School of Fine Arts in 1915 in Finland, Aaltonen admitted he knew little of the history of art. In the early 1920s he took his first overseas trip to Germany and Italy, during which time he was exposed to Classical sculpture. The classic Italian sculptures, such as Michelangelo's *Moses* (*ca.* 1515), least impressed him. However, during this visit to Italy he studied current trends in contemporary art and associated himself with Italian Futurists, such as F.T. Marinetti, calling on all artists to "create the future!!! And make it so beautiful that it is accessible to everybody" (see Kangas, 1994).

One of Aaltonen's most widely celebrated sculptures is the statue *Paavo Nurmi Running*, commissioned in 1924. Nurmi was a contemporary athletic hero and is considered one of the best long-distance runners of all time. His success spanned the 1920s, soon after Finland gained independence. Although Nurmi modeled for the artist, Aaltonen decided not to create a realistic portrait of Finland's greatest athlete. Instead, he combined Nurmi's features with aesthetic ones. For instance, although Nurmi used the entire sole of his foot when running, Aaltonen's statue appears to be running on its toes, which gives the image a more dynamic smoothness strongly associated with the Futurists' aesthetic ideals. The nude athlete clearly draws on Classical Greek Olympic subjects.

Aaltonen's *Maiden in Black Granite* (1920) portrays a standing nude woman. The subject's eroticism gives way to the Classical purity of the female form. Lacking arms, she is positioned as if in midstep, with her right knee bent. Aaltonen framed her legs with granite so that she seems to be stepping out of the stone, thus recalling Michelangelo's unfinished sculptures. This sculpture exemplifies the classicism of Aaltonen's early 20th-century modernity.

In 1925, during a trip to Paris and London, Aaltonen studied these cities' museum collections of Egyptian, Greek, and Chinese art. After the civil war many of Finland's artists looked to Classical military and heroic themes for their inspiration. Yet for Aaltonen this trip proved once again how influential contemporary art was to his work. His *Aleksis Kivi* of 1930–39 incorporates a number of exaggerated cubic forms that make up this sculptural portrait of Finland's national writer, playwright, and creator of the country's modern literary language. Aaltonen's experimentation with Cubism lasted only a short time as he continued to develop a regional variant of an international style.

The bronze memorial to Kivi, unveiled in 1939, shows a contemplative Kivi sitting with his left arm draped over the back of the chair in an almost melancholic pose. Aaltonen borrowed the author's features from a portrait painted by A.E. Forsell but modeled the sitting figure after a painting Aaltonen himself completed of a sitting woman in 1926. The author sits in a chair under which Aaltonen included reliefs inspired by Kivi's writing: "My heart sings, Swing and The seven brothers flee Impivaara." This memorial demonstrates Aaltonen's exceptional ability to combine physical resemblance with an unaffected realistic form, a Classical tradition that predominated Finnish monumental works throughout much of the 20th century.

In 1930 Aaltonen won the sculpture competition for the Helsinki parliament's assembly chamber. Aaltonen submitted a proposal consisting of five allegorical figures, *Settler*, *Intellectual Work*, *Future*, *Faith*, and *Harvester*, to answer to the competition's theme of "Work and the Future." Although four figures are men, *Future* consists of a nude woman and child; the finished work represents the stylistic ideals of the 1930s. Some critics have said that Aaltonen styled his nude figures in a Classical manner to answer to the contemporary desire to show Finns as Westerners, not Mongols.

The success of this allegorical group sculpture led Aaltonen to create in 1945 a second version of the Mother and Child/Future figure to adorn the entryway of the Federation of Mother and Child Homes and Shelter, Helsinki. He depicted this figure, much more expressly Classical, as a nude torso facing away from the viewer or visitor to the building. Its location lends to it intriguing symbolism, and the torso represents the delicateness of happiness in motherhood. The naked and hurt female turns away as if hiding her pain. In contrast, the child she holds reaches out to the viewer in pure innocence and unscathed trust.

Throughout the 1940s Aaltonen continued to become a much more political voice in the Finnish art circle, signing a manifesto along with many other leading cultural figures who intended to unite several extreme rightist groupings to form a new fascist-style organization. During the postwar years, the artist had a steadily growing school of sculptors studying under him who helped him to complete numerous large-scale public works. His outdoor war memorials across Finland play a large role in nationalism and have deep meaning for the country's citizens.

Aaltonen's later work shows the artist's ability to combine various styles in a single monument, as is evident in a bronze relief from the 1950s the artist donated to the University of Helsinki that is housed in the reading room of the main library. The relief depicts a group of scholars engaged in various academic activities, centered by a profiled seated woman reading. Aaltonen used friends and acquaintances as models for this group relief. Most remarkable is the combination of Classical and modern forms and sketchlike Expressionism. The artist also combined both high and low relief, adding to the dynamic of the composition.

Although Aaltonen drew inspiration from contemporary art movements in Europe throughout much of his career, the 1960s found the artist distributing harsh criticism of the contemporary art scene. Like many of his European contemporaries, he believed the starting point for all artists should always be nature. Without this basis, Aaltonen believed, the artist achieves mere decoration.

In 1958 the Soviet Academy of Arts elected Aaltonen as an honorary member. Recognized for his influence on Finland's cultural and political successes, he provided inspiration for generations of the country's artists. During a time when Finland was caught between two superpowers, viewers saw Aaltonen and his works, many of which still dot the country's landscape, as a symbol of confidence and outright optimism.

KATHY HORNBROOK

Biography

Born in Marttila (St. Mårtens), Finland, Russian Empire, 8 March 1894. Father a tailor; enrolled at Turku School of Fine Arts in Finland; studied sculpture there and assisted sculptor Aarre Aaltonen (no relation), 1910–15; traveled to Italy and had first encounter with classic Italian sculpture, 1923; to France and London, 1925. Awarded honorary title of professor at Helsinki University, 1940; retrospective at Turku Art Museum, 1961. Died in Helsinki, Finland, 30 May 1966.

Selected Works

1917–20 *Granite Boy*; granite; Athenaeum Art Museum, Helsinki, Finland
1917–22 *Little Wader*; marble; private collection
1924 *Wader*; marble; Athenaeum Art Museum, Helsinki, Finland
1925 *Girl's Head*; gilded wood; Athenaeum Art Museum, Helsinki, Finland

1925   *Paavo Nurmi Running*; bronze; Turku, Finland
1930–39 *Aleksis Kivi*; bronze; Railway Station Square, Helsinki, Finland
1961   *Genius montanus I*; bronze; Maaria Cemetery, near Turku, Finland

Further Reading

Jakobson, Max, *Finland in the New Europe*, Westport, Connecticut: Praeger, 1998
Kangas, Matthew, "Wäinö Aaltonen: Museum of Finnish Art," *Sculpture* 13 (November/December 1994)
Pfäffli, Heidi, *Wäinö Aaltonen: 1894–1966*, Turku, Finland: Wäinö Aaltonen Museum, 1994
Valkonen, Markku, *The Golden Age of Finnish Art, 1850–1907*, translated by Michael Wynne-Ellis, Porvoo, Finland: Werner Söderström Osakeyhtiö, 1992

ABSTRACT EXPRESSIONISM

Sculpture at mid century in both the United States and Europe developed on the whole through its intimate historical ties with Cubism and Constructivism, binding together pictorial tendencies of abstraction, the organic, the expressive, as well as a visual language of existentialism and primitivism. The emergence of Abstract Expressionist sculpture, in part, would not be conceivable without its parallel movement in painting, often called the New York School and epitomized by the large-scale, gestural action paintings of European émigrés Willem de Kooning, Mark Rothko, Arshile Gorky, and Adolf Gottlieb, in addition to fellow American painters Jackson Pollock, Franz Kline, Clyfford Still, Barnett Newman, and others. The Abstract Expressionist credo for painters and sculptors considered style to be an attribute of a deep and mystical content; monumental expressivity became the index of existential yearning in which metaphor supplanted any previous importance placed on the subject, the literary, or the narrative. Personal mythology usurped religion and the power of the artist to represent the heretofore unrepresentable took center stage in the drama of art and life.

In Barnett Newman's epistolic essay of 1948, "The Sublime is Now," he advanced a rhetorical argument in which abstract secular painting would replace the spiritual or religious art of past history. He insisted that the modern artists "are creating images whose reality is self-evident and which are devoid of the props and crutches that evoke associations with outmoded images, both sublime and beautiful" (see Newman, 1948). Freed of the need to represent an external reality dependent upon history, mythology, nostalgia, legend, or memory, the artist could search, find, and reveal internal truths—an internal reality that Newman argued would dominate the pictorial and plastic traditions of the previous centuries.

Some of the first manifestations of such a sculpture were evident in early 20th century experiments with Constructivism, Bauhaus technology, and the machine aesthetic, such as Lázsló Moholy-Nagy's *Light-Space Modulator* (1921–30), or Naum Gabo's experimental *Kinetic Construction: Vibrating Spring* (1920). While these ingenious excursions into an industrial revolution freed sculpture from the figurative, the following generation of American sculptors eschewed what they called the Constructivists' fetish of technology. Modern sculptors such as Julio González and Pablo Picasso had as early as the mid 1930s began to use materials such as wrought iron and steel to construct three-dimensional work that was vaguely representational but primarily abstract in feeling and form. Gonzáles's early forays into welded metal sculpture, a technical and media innovation, would profoundly shape the ideas of David Smith and Anthony Caro in the United States and England, respectively. As Clement Greenberg, the preeminent critic of Abstract Expressionism presciently noted in 1948, the new sculpture possessed an inherent "self-sufficiency" due to the flexibility of its medium, which was "freed" from the confines of illusionism and representation. Inventive sculptural materials such as wire, steel, alloys, glass, and iron—the tools of the blacksmith or the welder—resulted in the modernist "reduction" that allowed sculpture to become almost exclusively visual in its essence (see Greenberg, 1961).

The search for an Abstract Expressionist idiom in sculpture relied on a similar process as did painting and collage work of the time. Underlying much of Abstract Expressionist sculpture was a vitalist, truth-to-materials aesthetic, borrowed in part from Modernists such as Constantin Brancusi, but fully reworked in the hands of an experienced welder such as David Smith, whose lyrical steel and bronze abstractions evoked spontaneous, live gestures or drawings in space. Pieces such as *Blackburn: Song of an Irish Blacksmith* (1949–50) and *Australia* (1951) imbued the industrial and even brutal materials with a poetry that Smith related to sources as disparate as the individualism of James Joyce, the honest working spirit of his blue-collar youth, and the flowing linearity of Action painting. Suggestive of Miróesque biomorphic painted shapes, the organicism of Adolf Gottlieb's pictographs, and the powerful totems of African and Oceanic cultures, Smith's sculpture seemed to derive less from a sculptural tradition from that of painting and the primitive. The metal Smith used possessed little of art history; the artist was drawn to its contemporary associations such as "power, structure, movement, progress, suspension, destruction, brutality" (see Hunter et al.,

2000). Smith's later pieces of the 1960s—his *Cubi* and *Tank Totem* series—perhaps best suggested a complete embrace of abstraction with their architectural scale, powerfully reductive shapes, and light-reflective, wire-brushed and burnished surfaces.

The artists who created the closest sculptural equivalents to Jackson Pollock's painted webs included Ibram Lassaw, the son of Russian-Jewish parents born in Egypt, who moved to New York as a child to study the art and theories of Bauhaus artists such as Moholy-Nagy, Brancusi, Gonzáles and others; Herbert Ferber, a New York sculptor whose models included the German Expressionists, Ernst Barlach, Aristide Maillol, and the "Negro sculpture" in the Paris Musée de l'Homme; and Seymour Lipton, a self-taught sculptor who tended toward a formal dialectic of opposites, such as curving and planar forms, interior and exterior hollows, and folding and unfolding sheaths of bronze and steel. In works such as Lassaw's *Clouds of Magellan*, a welded bronze and steel relief that replaces the mass of more conventional sculptural processes with an investigation of materials in space, the artist used an oxyacetylene torch to spontaneously weld weblike constellations of geometric shapes with flexible wires and rods that appear to float and vibrate in relation to each other.

In Ferber's *Cage* (1954) he transforms the ponderousness of lead into a delicately writhing organic form, seemingly alive with exuberance and emotion. *Cage*'s graceful linear C-shapes, serpentine S-curves, and boomerang-inspired spears suggest a primal rather than a decorative nature. Seymour Lipton's *Imprisioned Figure* (1948), a vertical wood and sheet-lead construction that stands on a low base suggests the quirky, biomorphic abstraction of Surrealism and the existentialism of Alberto Giacometti's postwar sculptures but without any direct reference to the figure. Lipton stopped carving in wood and began to sculpt sheets of monel metal that he bent and hammered into shapes that evoked abstract animal and plantlike forms. The sculptures were often patinated with nickel, silver, or bronze, creating contrasting shimmering and matte surfaces that emphasized the tactile and the visual quality of the forms. Works such as *Moby Dick* reflect Lipton's interest in the myriad relationships between the dense material and balance, stability, and movement.

Direct welding, in fact, proved to be the Abstract Expressionist sculptor's answer to the linear gesture of New York School painting. The organic, seemingly weightless calligraphy of such Abstract Expressionist sculpture lent itself to the diminished role of the pedestal, as sculptors began to consider how environmental and architectural scale had shifted the role of sculpture from something that represented nature to a concrete yet metaphysical presence built upon and expressed through the essential components of matter. Ferber described the new sculpture as one of "extension" rather than solid mass: "It resembles the open summits of Gothic towers more than the statues of Gothic portals. Its aesthetic body is the relationship of solids and spaces which define each other. Space is not displaced, the mark of traditional sculpture; rather it is pierced and held in tension" (see Ferber, 1954). This sculpture of extension, therefore, did not begin with the idea of carving out from a surface or a center; rather, it abandoned the notion of surface altogether for a kinetic, energetic process that pushed and pulled materials in space through a complex choreography of sculptural techniques. The kinetic mobile sculptures of Alexander Calder, for example, reflected such a displacement of mass for linear and aerial movement predicated on the delicacy and flexibility of materials such as wire, metal, and steel. Likewise, the spearlike totem figures Louise Bourgeois carved in soft wood in 1947–49 shared Abstract Expressionism's commitment to symbolic meaning. Bourgeois's totem sculptures (which she termed *personages*) retained the mysticism of African power figures while at the same time eschewing aspects of Western style for emotional content.

Concurrent to American Abstract Expressionism, a movement termed L'Art Informel emerged in Paris during the 1940s and 1950s that relied on a similar sense of physical spontaneity, roughly modeled expressive forms, and the reduction of subject matter. This broad term for French postwar expressionism in painting and sculpture rejected the geometric and certainly by 1950 oppressive language of Cubism in favor of an intuitive, free, undisciplined art, or what French critic Michel Tapié called "un art autre" (another art). L'Art Informel found a dominant presence in painting in the works of Pierre Soulages, Alberto Burri, and Georges Mathieu; although European sculptors such as Zoltan Kemeny, Eduardo Chillida, and Arnaldo Pomodoro created assemblage-based works forged in iron, steel, copper, bronze, zinc, and other metals. For each of these artists, the monumental and economical means of construction evoked a powerful sense of presence, or object-like character of the work. Using an intricate balance of rectangular, square, and spherical solid horizontal and vertical masses, punctuated by spatial voids, artists such as the Spanish sculptor Chillida created a concrete parallel to the great painted swaths of Franz Kline or the writhing strokes of Pollock's heroic drip paintings. As in the pictorialism of Abstract Expressionism, European postwar sculpture struggled to find and reveal the essential qualities of its medium while at the same time, conveying a sense of poetry, metaphor, and the sublime.

LYNN M. SOMERS

Further Reading

Ferber, Herbert, "On Sculpture," *Art in America*, 42/4 (1954)

Fineberg, Jonathan, *Art Since 1940: Strategies of Being*, New Jersey: Prentice Hall, 2000

Goldwater, Robert, *What Is Modern Sculpture?* New York: The Museum of Modern Art, 1969

Greenberg, Clement, "The New Sculpture (1948)," *Art and Culture: Critical Essays*, Boston, Massachusetts: Beacon Press, 1961

Hunter, Sam, John Jacobus and Daniel Wheeler, *Modern Art*, 3rd revised edition, New Jersey and New York: Prentice Hall and Harry Abrams, 2000

Krauss, Rosalind, *Passages in Modern Sculpture*, London: Thames and Hudson, and New York: Viking, 1977

Newman, Barnett, "The Sublime is Now," *Tiger's Eye*, 6 (1948)

Phillips, Lisa, *The Third Dimension: Sculpture of the New York School*, New York: Whitney Museum of American Art, 1984

Sandler, Irving, *The New York School: The Painters and Sculptors of the Fifties*, New York: Harper and Row, 1978

ACADEMIES AND ASSOCIATIONS

Training sculptors in the art of stone has always been closely associated with masons working on site or in family workshops. The training system for stoneworkers was a practical experience, often beginning with a young relative or apprentice assisting in an established workshop. First, he received the most menial tasks and with practice and mastery became entrusted with more demanding branches of the craft, passing to the status of assistant and associate until his skills developed sufficiently for him to be acknowledged as a master in his own right, fit to train others. This article concentrates on the major changes in systems of training young sculptors in western Europe from the Middle Ages to the present day.

Sculptors were categorized into three basic levels of proficiency. First, the master was acknowledged by his peers to have demonstrated the highest ability in the craft: a member of the local guild, he was bound by its regulations but allowed by the guild to run his own workshop, accept commissions, and employ long- and short-term staff, and he was entitled to train apprentices and to give less formal instruction to fee-paying pupils. Before admittance into the guild, a master might have to prove that he had studied his craft for a given number of years and was fully conversant with his craft.

The apprentice was formally indentured in boyhood, before qualified witnesses, to an established master. He learned his craft through a program of practical work that was regularly supervised and finally judged by guild representatives. An apprenticeship fee was paid to the guild by the boy's family. His few privileges usually included his own bed. He was forbidden to divulge any trade secrets about the technicalities of his craft or to pass on any information that he gleaned from discussions at the masons' lodge. An apprentice was bound for three to six years before he could apply to become a master of the guild.

The third category was the journeyman, a trained and qualified sculptor, not usually a master of a guild but able to be employed by a master to do piecework, sometimes of a highly skilled kind, at daily rates. A journeyman had some rights to short-term contracts and requirements of notice. Sometimes towns required journeymen to leave the town where they had trained and work elsewhere for a minimum period. A journeyman could apply for membership in a guild and set up his own workshop if he complied with the stringent local guild rules concerning citizenship, fees, and the production of work of sufficient quality.

Guilds were sworn associations of tradesmen based in individual towns, and they defined and controlled a particular area of technical competence. By the 15th century a city could have dozens of different guilds, and social, religious, and economic structures revolved around their rules and activities. As Christian associations, each had its own patron saint whose feast day it celebrated: for example, St. Joseph represented the carpenters' guild and St. Luke both the painters and the sculptors. Guild members met for church festivals and an annual feast.

The organization within each guild was elaborate, with a constitution, rules, and statutes. Officials or consuls implemented the legal statutes, cared for sick and bereaved members, monitored the training of apprentices, rigorously maintained standards of work and levels of payment, and supervised the securing of patronage and the production of works of art. Masons' lodges provided storage areas for tools and materials and meeting rooms where administrative matters were conducted and where technical issues and financial disputes might be resolved.

Guilds protected local workers from outside competition, regulated relationships between rival workshops in the same city, and legislated against the growth of large, powerful workshops that could challenge the authority of the guild. Carvers at Ulm, for instance, were not permitted to solicit work, and the guild closely supervised their purchase of materials. Guilds also limited the numbers of apprentices that a master could take on, for these young assistants formed an invaluable source of semiskilled, cheap labor that could unfairly tip the balance of competition between workshops. Masters could engage a specified number of journeymen qualified in their own craft but became liable to a fine if they gave piecework to outsiders or hired anyone not properly trained. The guild discouraged and limited the purchase of imported materials and often supervised the extraction and transport of high-quality stone and wood.

Large guilds and confraternities often financed city projects and controlled the employment of sculptors on the works under their patronage. During the Renaissance, when commissions to produce statues or stained-glass windows for a large-scale civic building were distributed among the city guilds by corporate committees, lively competition ensued between rival trades to engage the best sculptors and to produce the most beautiful work.

Most sculptors belonged to an appropriate local guild: stoneworkers joined the guild of masons, bronze masters the brass-making guild, and carvers of wood a carpenters' guild. Workers in fine metal might enroll in the goldsmiths' guild. In Florence one of the earliest guilds to be established was that of the Comacine, or master builders, which incorporated the skills of architecture, painting, and sculpture. On the other hand, in 15th-century northern Europe, wood sculptors were clearly distinguished from joiners, masons, and goldsmiths. Guilds flourished from the 12th to the 16th centuries and had considerable power, protecting their members and setting standards of professional competence.

The guild often defined and limited the nature of the tools used or the materials in which a sculptor could work. For example, brass workers could not work in wood, nor could members of the woodworking guilds cast statues in metal. This sort of regulation proved problematic in the production of polychrome statues and retables, which required the members of joiners', painters', and sculptors' guilds to work in close cooperation. Through careful consultation, guild officials from different cities established formal divisions of responsibility and expertise. The claim of a master to supervise a project that involved both painters and carvers usually rested on whether the polychrome statue or retable was begun and completed entirely on his premises.

Guild records reveal the efforts of members of one guild to subject members of other guilds to its control for financial advantage. In 1514–16, for example, members of the painters' guild in Strasbourg tried to establish statutes that would allow them to employ sculptor journeymen, which would have given painters control over the carving of figural and decorative work on altars in addition to the execution of polychromatic work. Although similar arrangements had operated earlier in Basel and Munich, members of the sculptors' guild naturally resisted it.

The power of the guilds to control or prevent the subcontracting of subsidiary craftsmen from other guilds by workshops that produced polychrome statues and retables varied from city to city. Riemenschneider, for example, employed without hindrance three specialist stonemasons in 1508 to create sandstone replicas of his wooden statues. In towns with strong guilds, the local guild in essence prevented a journeyman carver from another town from setting up his own workshop, insisting on his establishing citizenship, paying a large entry fee, and submitting an elaborate, expensive masterpiece. This careful control resulted in the perpetuation of a highly conservative style.

Workshop arrangements remained hierarchical during the Renaissance. The master engaged and supervised apprentices and assistants whose work was usually identified under his name. Master sculptors occasionally entered into temporary partnerships as particular commissions required; for example, legal contracts between Donatello and Michelozzo have been found. The right half of Filarete's bronze relief (1440–45), on the inside of the doors for Old St. Peter's Basilica in Rome, illustrates the formal relationship between master and assistants: three assistants form a line, in order of seniority, behind a named master sculptor. Masters organized commissions for the workshop, drew up project designs, and supervised all aspects of the work, documentation, and pay.

This workshop arrangement did not end with the guild system. As late as the 19th century, Jean-Antoine Houdon (trained by Michel-Ange Slodtz) achieved an impressive output of casts and versions of his work through his masterful organization of subordinate apprentices, assistants, pupils, technicians, stone carvers, modelers, and foundrymen. He supervised three establishments: a studio in the artisans' quarter of Paris, a bronze-casting foundry nearby, and a separate studio for specialist work in terracotta, plaster, and marble. He claimed to have revived the art of bronze casting in France by constructing the furnaces, training workmen, and learning the craft through experimentation. He trained the sculptor Pierre-Phillippe Thomire as his foundryman and used bronze-casting activities as a subject of study for his students.

Early instruction manuals for the student sculptor are rare and do not seem intended as a substitute for direct teaching. An exception to this is book 3 of the 12th-century manual by Theophilus, *De diversis artibus*, which contains instructions on bronze casting sufficiently detailed to be used as a practical aid, or the diagrams in Villard de Honnecourt's sketchbook, which he recommends as templates for designs of stone structures such as elaborate pinnacles. Some early copies of Cennino Cennini's 14th-century text on painting, *Il libro dell arte*, include basic instructions on how to make a life mask and cast one's own figure that are insufficient as a practical guide. More significant is Leon Battista Alberti's *De statua*, his important treatise on the principles and practice of sculpture from the 1460s. In it he explains how to carve an accurate full-scale representation from two-dimensional designs and urges sculptors to study human anatomy. Lorenzo Ghiberti's *Commentari*, written during the last years of his life (*d.* 1455), takes Alberti's theoretical ideas forward in a more practical manner, discussing relief and freestanding statuary, whereas Averlino Filarete's *Trattato dell'architettura* (1461–62) continues to emphasize the role of sculpture in relation to architecture.

From the early 16th century, technical information on sculptural methods becomes more common, as in Pomponio Gaurico's treatise on sculpture of about 1500–1504, and could have been used by practicing carvers. Few are as detailed as Vannuccio Biringuccio's seminal treatise *De la pirotechnica* (1540), however, which provided the first published account of metallurgical practice. He describes the procedures he employed in molding reliefs using the lost-wax process. He defines the nature of metal ores, claims to have closely observed firsthand the processes of metal smelting, working, and casting, and peppers the text with practical tips. Despite containing much material on working precious metals, Biringuccio's text is not mentioned by Benvenuto Cellini, the more famous sculptor, who wrote his influential technical texts on goldsmithing and sculpture from 1565. These describe Cellini's innovations in striking medals, as well as the technical methods more generally employed by goldsmiths and sculptors in 16th-century Italy and were published in a truncated form in 1568. His autobiography, the *Vita di Benvenuto Cellini*, begun about 1558, had limited circulation until its publication in 1728. It contains abundant advice on large-scale bronze-casting techniques and makes clear the important role of assistants in the foundry. How far these texts were used as teaching tools is not clear. Gradually, drawing manuals and texts on sculpture techniques proliferated and became common in the 18th century. The most comprehensive and important descriptive and illustrated manual on arts, crafts, and trades was certainly the *Encyclopédie*, published by Denis Diderot between 1751–72.

The first academies of art developed in Italy in the 15th century among the humanist literati, rather than practicing artisans, and were concerned with philosophical debate about art in the manner of Plato's academy rather than with technical training. Sculpture was central to these early Renaissance academies. Poggio Bracciolini termed his private collection of antique sculpture his "academy," and about 1490 Lorenzo de'

Medici selected sculptor Bertoldo di Giovanni to instruct budding artists in an institution in Florence, where, according to Vasari, Lorenzo had identified a shortage of sculptors. These students had the unusual opportunity to draw from the Medici collection of antique sculpture under Bertoldo's supervision. Some sculptors offered opportunities within their own premises for students to draw from casts and sculpture in a discursive group. The most famous of these studio groups is that of the sculptor Baccio Bandinelli, who was recorded, in 1531, with a group of artists drawing from a statuette, in an engraving by Agostino dei Musi. Unlike many guild systems, these groups did not restrict members to any one material division of artistic activity but encouraged exchange of views across subject boundaries.

In the 16th century artists, particularly aspiring painters and sculptors, saw association with such academies as a way to raise the status of the artist from craftsman to educated professional. Sculpture, painting, and architecture were distinguished as liberal rather than mechanical arts. Academies recognized drawing as the central concern of all branches of the visual arts, and in 1563 the Accademia del Disegno, which came to control artistic judgment in Florence, was formally constituted. Michelangelo, the joint head of this academy, defined *disegno* not as the manual activity of copying but as the visible expression of an abstract idea, the difficult activity of an intellectual. Sculpture was debatably superior to painting because, lacking realistic color, it did not unworthily try to imitate reality but rather sought to express a concept.

The Accademia del Disegno and later the short-lived Accademia di San Luca, which was established under Zucarro's presidency in Rome in 1593 under the protection of Grand Duke Cosimo I de Medici, set up structures independent of the guilds and took on many guild functions, such as administration of contracts, quality control, and the teaching of young artists. Competitive drawing from casts of Classical sculpture and from the life model (considered to be the essential aspect of all art training) under the direction of a sequence of academic staff became a standard feature of academic curricula.

In the 17th century academies proliferated in Europe and took on the role of practical training in addition to providing a liberal education for painters and sculptors. Outside Italy, 17th-century sculptors often studied anatomy with medical students and gained knowledge of Classical models by drawing from private collections of miscellaneous casts and copies of antique statues. Practicing artists in Italy, Spain, the Netherlands, England, and Scotland set up academies that provided teaching in the liberal arts or instruction in life drawing, but these academies invariably lacked the necessary long-term public or crown funding and were short lived.

In France, however, the crown founded the most systematic and centralized of these institutions, the Académie Royale de Peinture et de Sculpture, in 1648 in a deliberate effort to establish painting and sculpture as liberal arts requiring theoretical learning in addition to mechanical skill. Under the direction of Charles Le Brun, the French academy gained control over the education, training, and patronage of artists from the guilds in a deliberate development of the propaganda program of Louis XIV. This move precipitated a long-term power struggle with the French guilds, who saw guildsmen's ability to develop expertise in the higher branches of a particular craft diminished and their status demoted. A particular grievance was the exclusive right of the academy to hold life-drawing classes; ambitious stone carvers in stonemasons' workshops employed on projects that involved figural imagery were not permitted to attend the classes. This denigration of guild craftsmanship intensified when the academy established a hierarchy of subject matter based on the primacy of the human figure. The structures and membership of the academy in Paris were strictly separate from those of the stone carvers' guild.

Education programs provided for training young sculptors at most academies were only available for a few hours a day. During the rest of the day, students carved or modeled under the supervision of an established academician at his studio in an arrangement closely paralleling the guild apprentice system. Many major sculptor academicians, such as Etienne-Maurice Falconet and Guillaume I Coustou, continued to run large dynastic studio workshops. By 1663 an academician could teach up to six pupils and had to provide a certificate for each one who applied for admission to one of the two academy classes. Students, except sons of academicians, paid a small fee for classes. According to a set timetable, students drew from drawings, from casts, and eventually from the life model. In addition, professors gave a program of lectures on anatomy, perspective, and geometry. An analytical approach to judging works of art, which used measurements of Classical statues as the basis of a canon of perfect proportions, dominated all teaching in the Paris academy. Charles Le Brun's influential *Methode pour apprendre a dessiner les passions* (Lecture on Expression, 1698) presented prototypes of major states of emotion to students of painting and sculpture so that they could recognize the intention of major works of art such as the *Laocoön* and emulate them in their own works. The great prize for absorbing these lessons was the Prix de Rome—the opportunity to study Classical and Renaissance sculpture at its source in Rome. Prizewinners returning from Rome had to produce a *morceau de reception* of a set religious, allegorical, or Classical subjects before they qualified for admittance to the academy. Many of these pieces incorporated blatant royal propaganda or represented extreme states of emotion as expounded in Le Brun's instruction manuals on expression.

Many academies established in Europe in the 18th century, such as the Royal Academy founded in London in 1768, followed the French pattern. Each ran a curriculum of lectures, classes, prizes, and exhibitions firmly rooted in the idea that art could be taught through the application of systems and rules based on the Classical tradition. State art education in France changed after the French Revolution, but already in 1766 the economic significance of good design had been recognized when the École Gratuite de Dessin was founded as a school to train industrial workers in the utility of drawing.

Although much teaching for painters and sculptors revolved around drawing from casts of sculpture such as the *Apollo Belvedere* and the *Laocoön*, or from a life model, sculptors formed a minority of academicians and students in many 18th-century institutions. The first Council of the Royal Academy, London, comprised six painters, one sculptor, and one architect, although professors of anatomy, architecture, painting, and perspective were also appointed. The academy formed collections of casts of the greatest Classical sculptures and admitted students, some as young as 11 years old, for a decade of instruction. Although discipline was difficult to maintain among the younger members of the drawing class, awards, including a gold medal for sculpture or bas relief, were possible for those who persevered.

By the beginning of the 19th century, more than a hundred academies flourished. The academic curriculum for sculptors in some institutions is difficult to distinguish from that of painters, but a surviving timetable for the Berlin academy (Akademie der Kunste) in 1800 lists a series of alternative classes running in parallel, some of which were clearly intended for sculptors. On Mondays, for example, while painters studied "Drawing and Painting," sculptors took "Modeling: Antique (Plaster)." Other classes specifically for sculptors included instruction in perspective and architectural drawing. During the 19th century, alternative educational establishments, often associated with industry, began to reclaim the role of practical training from academies and reintegrated some areas of arts and crafts.

The definition of sculpture dramatically extended in scope during the 20th century, and training in many countries is currently in a transitional phase. In Europe and the United States, it is still possible to find object-based training in sculpture, and students usually begin their training after completing a general education; but conceptual and digital art is a preoccupation in many British institutions and has revolutionized teaching programs; in many British institutions, teaching programs for both painters and sculptors now include training in installations and the use of computers. In Germany students study with a particular individual, under the old professorial system. Similarly, in China state art institutions incorporate the tradition of training students to emulate the style of a particular master.

Training institutions in the United States offer a large range of programs for sculptors: many follow traditional undergraduate academic training programs within a tight modular system. While some are Postmodernist in emphasis, others are more arts-and-crafts based, and still others concentrate on technical rather than aesthetic issues. Postgraduates often receive considerable independence, with flexible access to specialized tutors. The most formal of art-college sculpture curricula in both the United States and Europe still follow traditional, carefully constructed patterns over a period of three or four years, in order to provide a good foundation for subsequent professional practice.

Sculpture schools are often separately administered sectors of large colleges, although many encourage students to develop interdisciplinary skills. The 20th-century development of Installation work has blurred lines between sculptors, architects, and painters. Some modular courses in the United States still emphasize the acquisition of basic technical skills, but many now explicitly stress defining and clarifying the personal expression of the individual student through discussion and experiment. Increasing student numbers are gradually eroding the effort to maintain a master-apprentice relationship in such schools.

In England students often take a year to attempt a wide variety of basic materials, tools, and techniques before enrolling in an undergraduate sculpture-training program. The primacy of competence in drawing remains central to many sculpture school curricula, but draftsmanship is seen in Renaissance terms, as a perceptual expressive activity—a source for sculptural ideas rather than simply a training in eye-to-hand transmission. Unlike Renaissance or academic training, students must often articulate their own aims and intentions at points during a course. They receive the opportunity to travel abroad, to discuss general artistic issues, and to consider their future professional practice. Academic humanities programs, reading tasks, and project-related visits to local resources encourage the student's wider education. Programs require a level of academic competence in addition to demonstrable technical skill and often base the final assessment of a student's competence on the presentation of an exhibition of work mounted by the student rather than an examination piece. Few prizes are now as lavish as the

Prix de Rome, but awards sometimes include financial support for foreign travel and further subsidized study. The standard of training in British institutions is regularly monitored against government benchmarks by government-appointed bodies or agreed interinstitutional appointees.

Some established sculptors consider studio teaching as an opportunity to extend their own learning. Jack Squiers, for example, described his studio-based employment at Cornell University beginning in 1965 as an ideal situation in which to completely change his approach to his own abstract work by teaching students to work from realistic human figures. Shared studio space provides a context of mutual support in a cooperative environment and can lead to multimedia experiments.

A minority of women sculptors practiced during all periods discussed, usually anonymously; the *Künstlerlexicon* by Ulrich Thieme and Becker (1907) was the first attempt at a comprehensive list. The barring of women from sculpture training on building sites (unless they were mortar mixers) or from the life classes in the academies until the late 19th century essentially excluded them from public recognition. Women who did train as sculptors usually trained in their family's workshops or had the financial resources to command instruction.

The heavy physical exertion required for stone-working made women's direct contributions in this medium rare, although problems surround any definition of "ownership" of the conception between a sculptural design in drawing or model form and its final artisan execution. Vasari mentions the nobly born and multitalented Properzia de'Rossi as a Bolognese sculptor of the Renaissance, but few other records of women artists specify that they were trained as sculptors of stone. Falconet employed two assistants in the 18th century, Anne Seymour Damer and Marie-Anne Collot, at court in St. Petersburg, principally to model portrait busts.

Throughout the 19th-century women continued to experience great difficulty receiving a thorough grounding in anatomy, figure drawing, perspective, and traditional historical composition, even after the Government Female School of Art and Design in England opened to them in 1843. Eleanor Coade, who exhibited figural sculpture as well as decorative carving at the Society of Artists from 1773 to 1780, appears to have gained her carving skills in the successful family firm, Coade and Sealey, which she ran and passed on to her daughter. Amelia Robertson Paton (Mrs. D.O. Hill) came from a family of artists and became an accomplished sculptor, but she was not permitted to enter the ranks of Academicians at Edinburgh in the 1840s. Susan Durant (1820/30–73) trained with Baron de Triqueti before 1847.

By 1877 in Paris it was possible for women art students who were able to attend Julien's private studio to work from the nude male model. Official training institutions such as the École des Beaux-Arts in Paris still excluded women, but provincial schools were not as rigid about admitting women as students. By 1887 the Royal Academy in London admitted women for modeling classes during the day but barred them from the evening class. It established a separate life-drawing class for females only in 1903.

The *Art Journal* of 1866 noted a colony of 12 women sculptors training in Rome; it was initiated by Harriet Hosmer of Massachusetts. Supported by her parents, Hosmer overcame institutional barriers by arranging private instruction in anatomy at a medical school. She received subsequent technical training from John Gibson. Edmonia Lewis could not persuade any male sculptor to train her and was instructed by Anne Whitney.

Paris remained an important center for the training and development of British and American women sculptors throughout the 20th century. Communities of artists working in the 1930s offered mutual support to women sculptors such as Barbara Hepworth. Art movements such as Surrealism and Abstraction shifted the focus of subject, scale, and medium in sculpture away from monumental projects in bronze and stone depicting the male nude, allowing wider public acceptance for training in sculpture as a suitable field for women. During the 20th century sculpture training slowly and gradually became made available to women in the pioneering major art institutions, such as the Leeds School of Art in England, on an equal basis with their male counterparts.

J. Patricia Campbell

See also **Bandinelli, Baccio; Coustou Family; Damer, Anne Seymour; Donatello; Falconet, Étienne-Maurice; Filarete; Gibson, John; Hosmer, Harriet; Houdon, Jean-Antoine; Installation;** *Laocoön and His Sons*; **Michelangelo; Michelozzo di Bartolomeo; Riemenschneider, Tilman; Rossi, Properzia de'; Slodtz, René-Michel [Michel-Ange]; Women Sculptors**

Further Reading

Alberti, Leon Battista, *On Painting, and On Sculpture: The Latin Texts of De Pictura and De Statua*, edited by Cecil Grayson, London: Phaidon, 1972

Barker, Emma, Nick Webb, and Kim Woods (editors), *The Changing Status of the Artist*, New Haven, Connecticut: Yale University Press, 1999

Baxandall, Michael, *The Limewood Sculptors of Renaissance Germany*, New Haven, Connecticut: Yale University Press, 1980

Chadwick, Whitney, *Women, Art, and Society*, New York and London: Thames and Hudson, 1990

Coldstream, Nicola, *Masons and Sculptors*, Toronto and Buffalo, New York: University of Toronto Press, and London: British Museum Press, 1991

Egbert, Virginia Wylie, *The Medieval Artist at Work*, Princeton, New Jersey: Princeton University Press, 1967

Félibien, André, *Conférences de l'Academie royale de peinture et de sculpture*, Paris: Leonard, 1669; reprint, Portland, Oregon: Collegium Graphicum, 1972

Gimpel, Jean, *Les bâtisseurs de cathedrals*, Paris: Seuil, 1958; as *The Cathedral Builders*, translated by Carl F. Barnes, Jr., New York: Grove Press, 1961

Goldstein, Carl, *Teaching Art: Academies and Schools from Vasari to Albers*, Cambridge and New York: Cambridge University Press, 1996

Graves, Algernon (compiler), *A Dictionary of Artists Who Have Exhibited Works in the Principal London Exhibitions of Oil Paintings from 1760–1880*, London, 1884; 3rd edition, as *A Dictionary of Artists Who Have Exhibited . . . from 1760 to 1893*, London: Graves, 1901; reprint, New York: Franklin, 1970

Montagu, Jennifer, *The Expression of the Passions: The Origin and Influence of Charles Le Brun's Conférence sur l'expression générale et particulière*, New Haven, Connecticut: Yale University Press, 1994

Perry, Gillian, and Colin Cunningham (editors), *Academies, Museums, and Canons of Art*, New Haven, Connecticut: Yale University Press, 1999

Pevsner, Nicolas, *Academies of Art, Past and Present*, Cambridge: Cambridge University Press, and New York: Macmillan, 1940

Risenhoover, Morris, and Robert T. Blackburn, *Artists as Professors: Conversations with Musicians, Painters, Sculptors*, Urbana: University of Illinois Press, 1976

Rockwell, Peter, *The Art of Stoneworking: A Reference Guide*, Cambridge and New York: Cambridge University Press, 1993

Seymour, Charles, *Sculpture in Italy, 1400–1500*, London and Baltimore, Maryland: Penguin, 1966

Swartwout, Robert Egerton, *The Monastic Craftsman: An Inquiry into the Services of Monks to Art in Britain and in Europe North of the Alps during the Middle Ages*, Cambridge: Heffer, 1932

Staley, John Edgcumbe, *The Guilds of Florence*, London and New York: Methuen, 1906; reprint, New York: Blom, 1967

Wittkower, Rudolf, *Sculpture: Processes and Principles*, New York: Harper and Row, and London: Allen Lane, 1977

ADAM FAMILY *French*

Lambert-Sigisbert Adam 1700–1759

Lambert-Sigisbert Adam attracted attention as a promising sculptor only four years after he arrived in Paris; the Duke d'Antin, *surintendant des bâtiments du roi* (the king's superintendent of buildings) sent him, together with Edme Bouchardon, as a *pensionnaire* (fellow) at the Académie de France in Rome, even before Lambert-Sigisbert won first prize at the Académie Royale in August 1723. As was requisite for sculptors in the French academy, Lambert-Sigisbert copied an antique in Rome for the king—in this case the *Ludovisi*

Mars, which critics greatly admired. Cardinal de Polignac, the French ambassador and an art collector, gave Lambert-Sigisbert his antique sculpture to restore and bought marble busts of *Neptune* and *Amphitrite* by the sculptor. Lambert-Sigisbert's talent allowed him to compete with Italian artists for important Roman commissions; according to French sources, critics first preferred his model for the Trevi fountain, although Nicolas Salvi received the commission. Lambert-Sigisbert also took part in the decoration of the richest chapel built in Rome in the first half of 18th century, the Chapel of Clement XII Corsini, Basilica of San Giovanni in Laterano, for which the sculptor carved one marble relief. On the strength of this work, Roman artists named Lambert-Sigisbert a member of the Accademia di San Luca. *Sorrow*, which he offered in acknowledgment, demonstrates his ability to portray extreme emotional force in a marble bust.

Lambert-Sigisbert gained much experience carving during his long stay in Rome, but although many considered his restorations to be as beautiful as the original antiques, the heads he added to the *Lycomede's Daughters* group are closer to the Rococo style than to the antique canon. Indeed, his work shows him to be sensitive above all to the quality of Baroque art. Gianlorenzo Bernini's influence on his works is constant; Lambert-Sigisbert's copy of the *Ludovisi Mars* includes Bernini's restorations. But he studied Michelangelo and Alessandro Algardi as well: the man drawing the curtain in the Corsini Chapel, for instance, recalls a figure on a relief of Algardi's Leo XI monument. Aware that Bouchardon and Lambert-Sigisbert were in part responsible for the new fame of the Académie de France, the Duke d'Antin allowed both the sculptors to remain in Rome for a lengthy period. Indeed, both played an important part in the Roman artistic community, earning reputations that were comparable to that of Pierre Legros II and Jean-Baptiste Théodon at the beginning of the century and that only Michel-Ange Slodtz and then Jean-Antoine Houdon would reach later. But in 1732 the two sculptors returned to France at the request of the king.

Upon Lambert-Sigisbert's return to France several high nobles of the court commissioned him to create garden sculpture decoration. He also paid particular attention to his career in the Académie Royale, being received as a member in 1737 on the basis of his *Neptune Calming the Waves*, which displays affinities with Bernini's *Neptune and Triton* (1620). Lambert-Sigisbert received the opportunity to realize in a large scale this same subject, which he had already studied in Rome for a marble bust and for the Trevi fountain model. His first well-known work in France was the central group of the Bassin de Neptune in Versailles, for which Jean-Baptiste Lemoyne and Edme Bouchardon created the lateral groups. The *Triumph of Neptune*

Lambert-Sigisbert Adam; *Neptune Calming the Waves*; Musée du Louvre, Paris

and Amphitrite, finished in 1740 with his brother's help, must be considered the most important manifestation of the French Baroque; its dynamic composition, multiplicity of details, and impression of force and movement reveal its opposition to Bouchardon's Fontaine de Grenelle. Lambert-Sigisbert's religious works, such as the statue of *St. Jerome* for the Invalides, show the same vigorous style. But his career was concentrated mostly on decorative sculpture. The best examples of these are the large groups *Fishing* and *Hunting* offered by Louis XV to Frederick the Great for the park of Schloss Sanssouci.

Lambert-Sigisbert created few portrait busts. Bouchardon received the commissions for these in Rome, and at the court of France Lambert-Sigisbert could not compete in this medium with rivals such as Lemoyne; Lambert-Sigisbert's *Louis XV as Apollo*, which he carved without a commission and set up in the castle of Choisy on his own initiative, failed to suit the king.

Owing to his ambitious character, Lambert-Sigisbert Adam had to withstand many critics. They accused him, for instance, of exaggerating carving effects in marble only to display his virtuosity. But some of these criticisms may simply reflect a change of taste. The French Baroque style reached its height through Lambert-Sigisbert's art, following the path first broken by the brothers Coustou, whereas Bouchardon's works helped to prepare the way toward Neoclassicism.

Nicolas-Sébastien Adam 1705–1778

Nicolas-Sébastien Adam, in contrast to his brother Lambert-Sigisbert, did not follow the traditional academic route to Rome: three years after he arrived in Paris, he accepted a commission for the Château de la Mosson, near Montpellier. In this way he earned enough money to reach Rome in 1726 and stay there for eight years without being a *pensionnaire*. Persuaded by Lambert-Sigisbert, Cardinal de Polignac employed Nicolas-Sébastien to restore antique sculpture, during which time the younger brother also studied in order to win a prize in the biblical relief competition of the Accademia di San Luca. According to Calmet, Nicolas-Sébastien left Rome in September 1734 after shipping the cardinal's antiques to France. There is evidence to suggest that he probably worked during these years for other collectors as well.

In France Nicolas-Sébastien received a commission to create a bas-relief for the Chapel of the Château, Versailles, the *Martyrdom of Ste. Victoire*. The relief's composition reveals the influence of the Roman Baroque, as do details such as the adolescent's gesture on the right, which recalls a figure of Angelo de Rossi's relief on the tomb of Alexander VIII. While helping his brother with the Bassin de Neptune, Nicolas-Sébastien worked independently for private commissions and for the bâtiments du roi.

According to Dezallier, in 1747 Frederick the Great of Prussia wanted Nicolas-Sébastien as his first sculptor, but Lambert-Sigisbert instead sent his younger brother, François-Gaspard-Balthasar. That same year Nicolas-Sébastien won the commission for the tomb of Queen Catharina Opalinska; the monument, finished in 1749 in Nancy, is one of the masterpieces of 18th-century French funerary art.

Nicolas-Sébastien began his career with the Académie Royale quite late: even though many thought he would never be able to carve the required *morceau de réception* (a piece submitted as part of the requirement for membership), he finished it, a *Prometheus* in marble, in 1762 and entered the academy. While his *morceau de réception* demonstrates his carving virtuosity, gained from his experience with antique statues, it also reveals in its diagonal composition the opposing spiral movements of the eagle's and Prometheus' bodies, the muscular tension, and the expression of Prometheus'

face that demonstrate his assimilation of the lessons of Roman Baroque art. He succeeded in creating a group that must be considered one of the masterpieces of the French Baroque style.

François-Gaspard-Balthasar Adam 1710–1761

François-Gaspard-Balthasar Adam was unusually young when he first journeyed to Rome, to which he traveled twice. Unlike his brothers, he left the paternal workshop to go in 1729 not to Paris but to Rome at the age of 19. In Rome he worked mainly with his brothers on the restoration of Cardinal de Polignac's antique sculpture; while there, he probably studied the great works of Antiquity and of the Renaissance and Baroque as well.

After his return to Paris he continued working with his brothers but also took part in academic competitions in order to return to Rome as *pensionnaire* (fellow) of the Académie de France. Little is known about his second stay in Rome; as the Académie de France did not have the resources to buy marble, it no longer asked sculptors to create a copy from the antique but only to draw or make clay models. Even though Lambert-Sigisbert tried to arrange a longer stay for his brother, François-Gaspard-Balthasar was forced to leave after nearly four years at the academy.

After two years in France, François-Gaspard-Balthasar left for Prussia, even though, according to Dezallier, Frederick the Great had asked not for him but for his brother Nicolas-Sébastien. There, François-Gaspard-Balthasar became the first sculptor of the king and took care of the decoration of Potsdam's Schloss Sanssouci. With the help of a Roman sculptor he called from Italy in 1748, he carved many mythological groups in marble for the castle that display a high technical mastery. One of the two portraits known to be by François-Gaspard-Balthasar, the statue *Maréchal Christoph von Schwerin*, demonstrates in its gesture the influence of Bartolomeo Ammanati's *Mars (ca. 1560)*, a statue the sculptor could have seen in Rome.

François-Gaspard-Balthasar created much decorative garden sculpture, for which he was perfectly suited, but his art, influenced by Lambert-Sigisbert's style, does not demonstrate any original creativity. He trained many artists in Germany, playing a significant part in spreading the French Baroque style to northern Europe. Nevertheless, it was mainly due to his career in Prussia that his brothers, whose works display greater artistic merit, did not completely overshadow François-Gaspard-Balthasar.

ANNE-LISE DESMAS

See also **Clodion (Claude Michel)**

Lambert-Sigisbert Adam

Biography

Born in Nancy, France, 10 October 1700. First son of Jacob-Sigisbert Adam, sculptor, and uncle of Sigisbert-François Michel and Claude Michel (called Clodion), both sculptors. Trained by father before moving to Paris, 1719, where probably studied in atelier of sculptor François Dumont; won first prize at Académie Royale de Peinture et de Sculpture, August 1723; *pensionnaire* of Académie de France, Rome, September 1723–April 1731; lived with youngest brother François-Gaspard in apartment near the Chiesa Nuova, 1732; left Rome, January 1733, returning to France through Florence, Bologna, and Venice; became sculptor of the king in Paris and Versailles; admitted (*agréé*) in Académie Royale de Peinture et de Sculpture, April 1733; received (*reçu*) as member, May 1737; appointed assistant professor, 1737, and professor, 1744. Member of Accademia di San Luca, Rome, 16 November 1732, and of Accademia Clementina, Bologna, 8 July 1735. Died in Paris, France, 12 May 1759.

Selected Works

1724–27 *Amphitrite*; marble; Schloss Charlottenburg, Berlin, Germany

1724–27 *Neptune*; marble; Schloss Charlottenburg, Berlin, Germany; terracotta: County Museum of Art, Los Angeles, California, United States

1729–32 (Heads of) *Lycomede's Daughters*; marble restorations; Sculpturensammlung, Potsdam, Germany

1730 *Ludovisi Mars* (copy from the antique); marble; Schloss Sanssouci, Potsdam, Germany

1730 Models for the Trevi fountain; wax (lost)

1732 *The Virgin Appearing to St. Andrew Corsini*; terracotta; Musée des Beaux-Arts, Nancy, France; marble relief: Corsini Chapel, Basilica of San Giovanni in Laterano, Rome, Italy

1733 *Sorrow*; marble; Accademia di San Luca, Rome, Italy

1734 Statues personifying *The Seine* and *The Marne*; stone; Park of Saint-Cloud, Hauts-de-Seine, France

1736 *Justice, History and Fame, Musique*, and *Painting and Poetry*; stucco; Hôtel de Soubise, Paris, France

1736–40 *Triumph of Neptune and Amphitrite*, for the Bassin de Neptune (with Nicolas-Sébastien); lead; Château, Versailles, Yvelines, France

1737 *Neptune Calming the Waves*; marble; Musée du Louvre, Paris, France

1738 *St. Adelaide Taking Leave of St. Odilo*; plaster; Chapel of the Château, Versailles, Yvelines, France; bronze: 1742, Chapel of the Château, Versailles, Yvelines, France

ca. 1741 *Louis XV as Apollo*; terracotta; Victoria and Albert Museum, London, England; marble version: 1745, private collection

1749 Statue groups of *Fishing* and *Hunting*; marble; Schloss Sanssouci park, Potsdam, Germany

1752 *Lyric Poetry*; marble; Musée du Louvre, Paris, France

1752 *St. Jerome* for the Invalides; marble; Church of Saint-Roch, Paris, France

Nicolas-Sébastien Adam

Biography

Born in Nancy, France, 22 March 1705. Also called Adam le Cadet. Second son of Jacob-Sigisbert Adam. Trained by father in Nancy; moved to Paris, 1721; worked in castle near Montpellier, France, 1724; went to Rome, 1726; stayed with brothers, Lambert-Sigisbert and François-Gaspard-Balthasar, in the Académie de France, until 1731; won second prize of first class in competition of Accademia di San Luca, 1728; lived alone in apartment inhabited by his brothers the year before near Chiesa Nuova, 1733; left Rome, September 1734, arriving in Paris one month later; worked in Versailles with brother Lambert-Sigisbert and on his own in Paris; worked for Stanislav Leszczynski, grand duke of Lorraine, 1747–52; admitted (*agréé*) in Académie Royale de Peinture et de Sculpture, January 1735, received (*reçu*) as member, June 1762, appointed assistant professor, 1763, and professor, 1768. Died in Paris, France, 27 March 1778.

Selected Works

1724–26 Decoration on the facade; stone; Château de la Mosson, near Montpellier, France

ca. 1726–35 *Clytie* and *Martyrdom of Iphigenia*; terracotta (lost)

1736 *Loves of the Gods*; stucco; Hôtel de Soubise, Paris, France

1736–40 *Triumph of Neptune and Amphitrite*, for the Bassin de Neptune (with Lambert-Sigisbert Adam); lead; Park of the Château, Versailles, Yvelines, France

1737 *Martyrdom of Ste. Victoire*; plaster (lost); bronze relief: 1743, Chapel of the Château, Versailles, Yvelines, France

1740 *Justice* and *Prudence*, for facade of the

Chambre des Comptes, Paris; stone (destroyed)

1745 *Religion Welcoming a Convert*; plaster; Church of Saint-Paul-Saint-Louis, Paris, France

1745 Vase with the *Attributes of Autumn*; marble; Metropolitan Museum of Art, New York City, United States

1747–49 Tomb of Queen Catharina Opalinska; marble, bronze; Church of Notre-Dame-de-Bon-Secours, Nancy, France

ca. 1753 Four reliefs of the *History of Apollo*; stone; Musée Carnavalet, Paris, France

ca. 1753 Statues of *Angelica and Medor, Diana,* and *Apollo*; stone; Musée de Picardie, Amiens, France

1762 *Prometheus*; marble; Musée du Louvre, Paris, France

1775–76 *Iris Attaching Her Wings* (completed by Clodion); marble; Versailles, Yvelines, France

François-Gaspard-Balthasar Adam

Biography

Born in Nancy, France, 23 May 1710. Youngest son of Jacob-Sigisbert Adam and youngest brother of Lambert-Sigisbert and Nicolas-Sébastien. Trained by father in Nancy; went to Rome to join brothers, 1729; stayed with them in the Académie de France until 1731, and with Lambert-Sigisbert in apartment near Chiesa Nuova, 1732; returned to France, 1733; studied and worked with brother Lambert-Sigisbert in Paris and Versailles; won second class medal for trimestral competition at the Académie Royale de Peinture et de Sculpture, 1734, and second prize, 1740; won first prize at Académie Royale de Peinture et de Sculpture, 1741; returned to Italy as a *pensionnaire* of Académie de France, in Rome, November 1742–July 1746; went to Prussia; remained there for rest of career; first sculptor of Frederick the Great in Potsdam, 1747–60; nominated member of Accademia del Disegno, Florence, July 1746. Died in Paris, France, 18 August 1761.

Selected Works

1748 *Apollo* and *Urania*; marble; Schloss Sanssouci, Potsdam, Germany

1749 *Zephyrus and Flora*; marble; terrace of Schloss Sanssouci, Potsdam, Germany

1750 *Cleopatra and the Asp*; marble; terrace of Schloss Sanssouci, Potsdam, Germany

1752 *Apollo Seated*; marble; park of Schloss Sanssouci, Potsdam, Germany

1753 *Diana* and *Juno*; marble; park of Schloss Sanssouci, Potsdam, Germany

1754 *Jupiter*; marble; park of Schloss Sanssouci, Potsdam, Germany

1755–65 *Chancellor Samuel de Cocceji* (finished by Sigisbert-François Michel); marble; Charlottenburg Castle, Berlin, Germany

1756 *Fire* (or *Vulcan*); marble; park of Schloss Sanssouci, Potsdam, Germany

1757–69 *Maréchal Christoph von Schwerin* (finished by Sigisbert-François Michel); marble; Staatliche Museen, Berlin, Germany

1758 *Earth* (or *Cybele*); marble; park of Schloss Sanssouci, Potsdam, Germany

1760 *Minerva*; marble; park of Schloss Sanssouci, Potsdam, Germany

Further Reading

Calmet, Augustin, *Bibliothèque lorraine, ou Histoire des hommes illustres*, Nancy, France: Leseure, 1751; reprint, Geneva: Slatkine, 1971 (on all the brothers)

Dézallier d'Argenville, Antoine-Joseph, *Vies des fameux architectes depuis la Renaissance des arts*, 2 vols., Paris: Debure l'Aîné, 1787; reprint, Geneva: Minkoff, 1972 (on all the brothers)

Fusco, Peter, "Lambert-Sigisbert Adam's 'Bust of Neptune,'" *Los Angeles County Museum of Art Bulletin* 21 (1976)

Fusco, Peter, "L.-S. Adam's Adieu to Rome," *Antologia di Belle Arti* 7/8 (1978)

Hodgkinson, Terence, "A Bust of Louis XV by Lambert Sigisbert Adam," *The Burlington Magazine* 94 (1952)

Levey, Michael, *Painting and Sculpture in France, 1700–1789*, New Haven, Connecticut: Yale University Press, 1993 (on all the brothers)

Polignac, François de, and Saskia Hüneke, "L'antiquité, prétexte ou modèle? L'invention des 'filles de Lycomède,'" in *La fascination de l'antique: 1700–1770: Rome découverte, Rome inventé* (exhib. cat.), Paris: Somogy, 1998 (on Lambert-Sigisbert Adam)

Seelig, Lorenz, "François-Gaspard Adams Stanbild des Feldmarschalls Schwerin," *Münchner Jahrbuch der bildenden Kunst* 27 (1976)

Souchal, François, "L'inventaire après décès du sculpteur Lambert-Sigisbert Adam," *Bulletin de la Société de l'histoire de l'art français* (1973)

ADELE D'AFFRY

See Marcello

AEGEAN SCULPTURE

In 1900 Sir Arthur Evans of Oxford University's Ashmolean Museum, taking the ancient story of King Minos on authority, named the ancient peoples that were occupying his archaeological investigations on

Crete at the time the "Minoans," after their ruler. It was an ethnic identity that would have been meaningless to the people who lived on Crete during the Bronze Age. Evans was following the lead of the German Heinrich Schleimann, who, a quarter century earlier, culturally identified the "Mycenaeans" by taking clues from the Homeric legends to make the great archaeological discoveries at ancient Troy in Asia Minor, and Mycenae on the Greek mainland. Others with professional and amateur archaeological ambitions followed, making connections among science, ancient stories, and on-site discoveries. Since these early excavations, archaeology has experienced a vivid century of growth, with the discovery of architectural wonders, dazzling frescoes, and intriguing artistic objects produced by Pre-classical Greek cultures.

Long before the Bronze Age cultures unearthed by Schleimann and Evans occupied the Aegean, late Neolithic transitions from nomadic hunter-gatherer to earth worker had been underway since the sixth millennium BCE, during which time efforts toward agriculture, pottery, and crude dwellings occurred. What military conquest and obsession with the afterlife were to the land-locked Mesopotamian and Egyptian cultures, sea commerce was to the Aegean world and its island settlers. Production of wine, grains, and olive oil formed the basis of highly lucrative trading activities. Economic success provoked maritime contacts and colonial settlements in mainland Greece, Asia Minor, the Levant, Egypt, Libya, and beyond. Nature proved bountiful, and it followed naturally that the earth was mother and nurturer—the Great Goddess. This in part explains the sudden appearance of a variety of figural sculpture that began to take notable form toward the end of the Neolithic era late in the 4th millennium BCE.

The Cyclades

With the waning of Neolithic culture and the onset of the Bronze Age (*ca.* 3000 BCE), around the time that the first city of Troy began to rise and Egypt was entering the stability of its Old Kingdom, remarkable developments in pottery, metals, and sculpture took place on a group of islands in the southern Aegean at the midpoint between Greece and Asia Minor. These are the Cyclades, a group of about 25 islands taking their name from the Greek *kyklos* (circle), which denotes their location around the smallest but most important of them, the island of Delos, only 3.2 square kilometers in size, sacred to Apollo and later the location of the Delian League treasury. The Cyclades are rich in obsidian, emery, and high-quality marble. The latter was especially important, because this material was skillfully and artistically formed into Europe's first great works of sculpture.

Before the onset of Modernism, Cycladic archaeological finds were deemed "grotesque" and "repulsively ugly," anathema to European tastes attuned to Johann Joachim Winckelmann's 18th-century idealism and the later refinements of 19th century Neoclassical sculpture. Changes in artistic sensibility brought about by Modernist sculptors such as Pablo Picasso, Constantin Brancusi, and Henry Moore prompted an appreciation for the aesthetics of reductiveness found in Preclassical art. In its extreme simplicity, Cycladic sculpture achieved masterpiece status and was an inspiration for the Modernist predilection for "significant form."

Before the Bronze Age, Neolithic figurines were commonly steatopygous, or chubby with exaggerated anatomic features—features that relate them to the earlier Paleolithic tradition originating with the Venus of Willendorf and continuing at Chatal Hüyük and on Malta. German scholarship of the mid 19th century concluded that the ancient civilizations viewed all of creation, the gods, and humanity as originating from a single female source and termed this entity "Magna Mater," the Great Goddess. Inanna—or Ishtar—in Mesopotamia, Isis in Egypt, Aphrodite and Demeter in Greece, and other female deities related to life, love, fecundity, and death derive their essential character from this universal feminine power. The Cycladic plank idols, most of them female figures ranging from a few centimeters to more than 2 meters in height, should be considered within the context of this tradition, but their actual function remains unknown.

With the availability of Bronze Age tools, marble could be more easily worked and a greater variety of forms produced. The plank idols, so called because of their flatness and general anthropomorphic reference, strike the viewer as humanly ideal depictions of nude figures, usually female, in strictly frontal, tiptoed poses. Because most were laid prone in simple cist graves, their function is assumed to be funerary. Their appearance, elusive and remote in the abstract treatment of physical features, recalls the slightly earlier Sumerian votive figures, such as those found at Tell Asmar. The upward-tilting heads perch atop long necks, and the lowered arms are folded across the abdomen. The left arm is usually positioned horizontally parallel above the right across the abdomen in a folded-arm gesture that both equally divides the upper torso and frames the breasts. Except for the pronounced nose, all facial features are absent, although remnants of color on many examples indicate that they were originally painted with eyes, necklaces, headbands, and other markings. An etched, inverted triangle denotes the pubic region of the female figures, and raised mounds depict breasts. Fingers and toes, if depicted, are represented by four incised horizontal or vertical lines, in keeping with the strict simplicity of the whole form.

Consistency in the general form of the plank idols suggests a canon developed that provided a manner of systematic production. A general equidistant division of the form at the neck, waist, and knees creates a balance and harmonious quadripartite form. Sculpting of the arms, legs, pubic area, breasts, and other details was obtained by chiseling or incising onto a flat marble slab that had been given the shape of a human contour. The whole was then smoothed by abrasive polishing, and paint was applied. The idea of a canon for the human figure was a pragmatic way of achieving harmony and ease of production, but it also connects these works to contemporary Egyptian sculptural practice, as well as to the later Classical order of Polykleitos.

Of the fewer male figurines that exist, the *Harpist* found on Keros is an outstanding example. Unlike the two-dimensional and stagnant gestures of the female figures, the *Harpist* forms an exquisite essay on form and space. The lyrical depiction of playing music activates the arms, and the figure's relative informality suggests connections with the living rather than the dead. In this it recalls the harpist on the contemporary Sumerian *Standard of Ur*, who plays his instrument within the context of royal banqueting in celebration of victory and peace.

Like the idols, the terracotta "frying pans" were found at gravesites, many on the island of Syros. Although they resemble cookware, there is no indication of their use in food preparation. Rather, suggested functions range from libation vessels, which would explain the 6 centimeter rim for containing water on the undecorated side, to predynastic Egyptian-type cosmetic palettes, or even mirrors. The "legs," pubic triangle, and womb-shaped body indicate ritual associations to the plank idols and also link them to the Great Goddess tradition. They are frequently incised with rows of connected spirals, often surrounding ships suggesting the cyclical journey from birth through life and into death.

Minoan

The 20th century had scarcely begun when news of another discovery was announced: Europe's first civilization, said to have existed somewhere toward the end of the 3rd millennium BCE on the largest and southernmost Aegean island of Crete, some 160 kilometers due south of the Cyclades. The archaeological excavation carried out by Evans was centered at Knossos on the northern coast. In addition to Schliemann's example, the interest that brought Evans to this location was his search for a lost language stimulated by engraved seals found there with markings he described as

"squiggles." These turned out to be the still-undeciphered hieroglyphic-like script now known as Linear A, in use on Crete from the 18th to the 15th centuries BCE.

The island's self-sufficiency and strategic location made it an important ancient crossroads. From the time of its earliest settlement by migrants from Mediterranean shores, maritime trade became the economic mainstay of Crete, exporting the prized grains, wine, olive oil, and ceramic ware in exchange for the metals and precious stones that the island lacked. The building of this economic status, along with the natural defense of the vast surrounding seas, provided the Minoan culture the luxury of relatively unrestrained pursuits in artistic expressions.

Images of feminine power inform Minoan artistic production from the earliest times. Excavations at the prepalatial settlement of Myrtos in southeastern Crete uncovered the *Goddess of Myrtos*, a terracotta work roughly contemporary with the marble idols of the Cyclades. This curious female-figure vase with a long, solid neck and head, hollow body, and breasts of raised clay pellets contains red paint applied for eyes, nipples, and the prominent pubic triangle. On the left hip of the womblike body, thin arms grasp a tiny vase that also functions as the pouring spout of the vessel. Its discovery in close proximity to both an altarlike structure in a shrine setting and a grain storage area, together with the water vessel held at the side, indicate a Great Goddess association, with the Great Goddess acting as provider and protector of these vital necessities of life.

Examples of the earliest true sculpture on Crete—that is, that not associated with vases—can be said to have developed in the protopalatial period that followed (2000–1700 BCE) in a group of small (approximately 10 to 23 cm) terracotta figurines found at Petsofas, a ritual mountain site, or "peak sanctuary," at the island's easternmost peninsula. Here were discovered votive-type worshiping figures exhibiting active, open gestures. A male figure, nude except for a codpiece and a prominent sheathed dagger at waist level, extends elbows horizontally with hands pulled to the chest, whereas the fully clothed female figure wears a prominent headdress and has arms extended and raised. The openness, freedom, and casual appearance of these examples anticipates the spirited attitude characteristic of mature Palace-period sculpture.

The bull is ubiquitous in Minoan art and legend. It was the earthly manifestation of the god Poteidan, probably the chief and most powerful deity of the Minoans. Poteidan (later called Poseidon by the Myscenaeans) held power over the sky, in the sea, and beneath the earth. In the later Classical legend, Zeus, with the captured Europa, fathered Minos, the great king of Knossos, by disguising himself as a bull. The powerful bull was central to geography, religious belief, and the art of the people of Crete.

The bull's violent pursuit and capture are the themes of the two exquisitely tooled gold *repoussé* (the method of producing relief metal by hammering and punching chiefly from behind) cups found at Vapheio near Sparta on the Greek mainland. Undoubtedly crafted by a Minoan palace artisan, these contain what has been considered the best Aegean representative images of both the bull and the human figure. They give anatomy and physical action careful attention, and the dynamic human-animal exchange is one of the highest achievements in Minoan relief sculpture. Evans's belief that the figure being gored is a woman is consistent with others who suggest that women and men participated equally in important social and religious rituals.

This is the case in bull jumping, a subject found throughout the range of Minoan sculpted media, from ceramics to semiprecious seal-stones (small utilitarian objects used to signify ownership, but which are also an important key to Minoan imagery in general). The imagery on these objects indicates that the bull jump was performed by both male and female acrobats with the help of grapplers and assistants. It was quite possibly part of a sacred rite of passage through which the human struggles with the divine in honor of the powerful Poteidan. The spirited *ciré perdue* (lost-wax) bronze from the British Museum stands approximately 14 centimeters high and is of remarkable quality. Here a bull leaper leans backward in full body extension. In arresting a moment in time, and in its reference to a field of action outside of itself, this work is unprecedented and would not find an equivalent until the Hellenistic period.

The most important and largest surviving sculpture produced by Minoan artisans is the group of three snake-wielding faience figures referred to as *Snake Goddesses*. They were discovered in the so-called Temple Repositories near the central court at Knossos. Full agreement on their identity as goddess figures, queens, or merely attendants has not been reached. They could well relate to Potnia, thought to be the most powerful Cretan goddess, whose symbol may have been the snake. Snake handling, then, could have been a deity-confronting activity similar to bull jumping. The tallest figure, with open hands at waist level, is approximately 34 centimeters high and stands symmetrically in a headdress echoed by the skirt, which is roughly twice its size. Two snakes coil about the figure, framing the bared breasts and wrapping around the outstretched arms, and a third snake rises to the top of the cone-shaped headdress. Faience, possibly the first synthetic material known, was produced in Egypt in predynastic times and brought to Crete early

in the 2nd millennium BCE. A mixture of quartz, glass, and copper resulting in a uniquely resplendent blue-green glaze, faience finds in the Minoan *Snake Goddesses* its greatest artistic achievement in the medium.

Mycenae

Sculptural production during the Mycenaean era was diminished and derivative. After 1600 BCE contact between Mycenae and Crete via the Cyclades for both military and commercial purposes was firmly established. Artifacts bearing distinct Minoan influence have been discovered in at least a dozen locations on the Greek mainland, including Mycenae, Argos, and Messina, the most prominent in power and wealth. Why these sites began their commanding ascendancy is still not known, but excavation of shaft graves and *tholos*, or circular, beehive-shaped tombs, have borne out Homer's epithet, "Mycenae, rich in gold," although much of this work appears to have been the product of Minoan artisans from Knossos working in Mycenae. The famous cups from Vapheio near Sparta, already discussed, are outstanding examples of this cultural exchange. In addition, many treasures found at the excavation site of Grave Circle A at Mycenae were actually produced by Minoan craftsmen employed on the mainland during this period of Minoan decline. Around 1500 BCE the volcanic eruption at Thera devastated Minoan outposts, including Knossos, and Mycenae assumed broader Aegean control.

The design of the famous limestone Lion Gate tympanum relief located in the triangular corbeled space above the post and lintel entry of Mycenae can be traced to Minoan seal-stones and earlier, to Mesopotamia and predynastic Egypt. Most scholars conclude that the animals carved in this stone relief are lions, although there is less agreement on the lions' sex. The heads, which are no longer intact, faced out toward those entering the gate and were probably of a more distinctive stone, although gold or bronze has also been suggested. It is largely agreed that the central symbolic column represents a deity whose image it was forbidden to depict. The tradition of animals flanking gateways is relatively common in the Mediterranean region, but this is the single Mycenaean example. One suggestion is that the carved relief was actually brought from elsewhere and installed here. Despite its elusive meaning, the gateway was visible throughout history and provided for the early Greeks, as it did for Schliemann, an imposing entry into the majestic courts of Agamemnon.

The remarkable ivory group found at Mycenae in 1939 of two embracing women tending a (possibly divine) child between them is given titles such as *Three Deities* or *Two Women with a Child*, indicating an uncertainty of the work's subject. Most agree that it "must surely have been made by a Cretan, or a Cretan-trained artist," and stylistic connections with ancient Near Eastern art have also been noted. Whatever its pedigree, it is the most humanly intimate and sensitive work produced in all of the Aegean. Within a century of its making, the Mycenaean culture had entered decline, and by the 12th century BCE, it totally disappeared from ancient Aegean history. The intimate attitude this work conveys is foreign to the cultures covered here. It would be a millennium before the forms anticipated by it received their full due.

JAMES SLAUSON

See also **Cretan Sculpture; Egypt, Ancient**

Further Reading

Castleden, Rodney, *Minoans: Life in Bronze Age Crete*, London and New York: Routledge, 1990

Doumas, Christos, *Cycladic Art: Ancient Sculpture and Pottery from the N.P. Goulandris Collection*, London: British Museum, 1983

Fitton, J. Lesley, *Cycladic Art*, London: British Museum, 1989; Cambridge, Massachusetts: Harvard University Press, 1990; 2nd edition, London: British Museum, 1999

Higgins, Reynold Alleyne, *Minoan and Mycenaean Art*, New York: Praeger, and London: Thames and Hudson, 1967; revised edition, London and New York: Thames and Hudson, 1997

Howland, Richard Hubbard (editor), *Mycenaean Treasures of the Aegean Bronze Age Repatriated*, Washington, D.C.: Society for the Preservation of the Greek Heritage, 1996

Hutton, R., "The Neolithic Great Goddess: A Study in Modern Tradition," *Antiquity* 71 (March 1997)

Marinatos, Spyridon, *Crete and Mycenae*, New York: Abrams, and London: Thames and Hudson, 1960

Mylonas, George E., *Polychrysoi Mykenai*, Athens: Ekdotike Athenon, 1983; as *Mycenae Rich in Gold*, Athens: Ekdotike Athenon, 1983

Preziosi, Donald, and Louise A. Hitchcock, *Aegean Art and Architecture*, Oxford: Oxford University Press, 1999

Taylour, William, *The Mycenaeans*, New York: Praeger, and London: Thames and Hudson, 1964; revised edition, New York and London: Thames and Hudson, 1983

Thimme, Jürgen (editor), *Kunst und Kultur der Kykladeninseln im 3. Jahrtausend v. Chr.*, Chicago: University of Chicago Press, 1977; as *Art and Culture of the Cyclades in the Third Millennium BC*, translated and edited by Pat Getz-Preziosi, Chicago: University of Chicago Press, 1977

Warren, Peter, *Myrtos: An Early Bronze Age Settlement in Crete*, London: Thames and Hudson, 1972

Warren, Peter, *The Aegean Civilizations*, London and Oxford: Elsevier, 1975; 2nd edition, Oxford: Phaidon, 1989

AFRICA: pre-20th CENTURY

Ashanti

During the 1470s Portuguese visitors to the coast of present-day Ghana found highly developed kingdoms displaying quantities of gold. This area of West Africa, named the Gold Coast by the Portuguese, became a magnet for Europeans over the next 400 years. North of the coast inland, a confederation of states consolidated under the leadership of the Ashanti at the beginning of the 18th century. Led by the king, the Ashanti expanded their territory, subduing other states and bringing them into the confederation. The Ashanti maintained their supremacy until a series of struggles with the British during the last quarter of the 19th century, during which the Ashanti lost their primacy and the king was deported. The Ashanti royal court located in the city of Kumasi has been restored, and the Ashanti king rules a politically diminished but artistically significant nation.

The Ashanti identify art within a variety of related contexts. In addition to its popular and secular uses, art focuses religious activities and serves as regalia of office. Visual imagery is matched to proverbs or other verbally expressive forms, establishing a linkage of verbal and visual elements that addresses traditional moral and ethical behavior, political and social ranking, allusions to God, or simple comments on the human condition.

Royal regalia identified with chieftaincy and statehood are a dominant form of Ashanti arts. The most important image for the Ashanti is the Golden Stool (*Sika Dua*), which symbolically binds the various states into the confederacy and represents the collective soul of the Ashanti people. State swords used for swearing oaths or as badges of office make up another class of regalia. Swords (*afena*) symbolize the power and authority of the king and the state; the figurative gold ornaments (*abosode*) attached to the swords refer to royal attributes. Carved wooden speaker's staffs (*okyeame poma*), with sculpted finials covered with gold leaf, identify advisors to the kings. The majority of Ashanti sculpture is allied with symbolism and proverb.

The best-known Ashanti sculptures are the small abstracted female figures known as *akua'ba*, literally, Akua's child or daughter. Women who desired a child would carry these *akua'ba*, which are named after Akua, an Ashanti woman who conceived a child after carrying such a figure. After a successful delivery the figure would be given to a shrine in appreciation or kept by the woman or perhaps given to the daughter as a toy. The *akua'ba* are also a paradigm of Ashanti aesthetics; the shape of the head refers to their concepts of beauty in idealized form. The head is a rounded and flattened disk shape with facial features delicately carved into the lower third of the face, emphasizing the broad expanse of forehead. The abstracted legless cylindrical torso has short stublike arms and a neck with rings carved into it. The figures are painted a glossy black and often have beads attached.

The most numerous Ashanti sculptures are small figurative and geometric weights cast in brass, long used in the gold trade, which date as early as the 15th century and continued to be used until the beginning of the 20th century. Based on Islamic sources from the western Sudan, they also share the corpus of proverbial and popular lore of other Ashanti sculpture. Islamic influence on the arts of the Ashanti also manifests itself in cast-bronze containers, known as *kuduo*, used to hold an individual's gold dust or other personal possessions. The *kuduo* were originally inspired by North African metalwork that followed trans-Saharan trade to the Ashanti; their decorated surfaces show the strong influence of Islamic decorative patterns and script. During the 18th or 19th century, figures representing chiefs or proverbial subject matter began to appear on the top or lid of the container. By the late 19th and early 20th centuries, *kuduo* fell out of use; they are now only objects of prestige.

Baga

The Baga are a small West African ethnic group living in a coastal area of swamps and inland waterways in Guinea bordering the Atlantic Ocean. They share cultural traditions and art forms with neighboring Nalu and Landuma and the dominant Susu people. While Baga is their original speech, the language of the neighboring Susu has become commonplace, and Baga art forms are often known in the West by their Susu titles. Examples of Baga sculpture have been documented from as early as the 19th century.

In the Baga's complex system of beliefs and initiations, deities are portrayed by dynamic examples of ritual regalia. As with other West African societies, art served to represent spirits during rites of passage and to validate initiations. The Baga used a variety of mask forms during initiations of young boys to adulthood and adults to higher knowledge and senior rank within the men's society. Perhaps the largest sculptural form in sub-Saharan Africa is a huge construction generally known by its Susu name *kaklimbe*. Rising six or more meters in height, it depicts the principal Baga male initiation spirit, Somtup. A giant bird head tops a massive construction covered with raffia and cloth, which is reportedly carried by 20 or more men who move the bird, make its head tilt down to acknowledge senior members, and terrify young initiates with bird cries.

A-Mantsho-na-Tshol, the first deity after Somtup, is characterized as a tall, twisting, and brightly colored snake spirit. A large headpiece carved from wood, it has geometric polychromatic patterns carved in shallow relief to imitate the patterns of a snake's skin, and

it sometimes has glass inserts for eyes. Identified by the Susu as *bansonyi*, it would dance either singly or in groups representing different lineage clusters of the village during initiations.

Among the best-known sculptures of the Baga are the large wooden masks known as *d'mba* or *nimba*, a Susu term. This monumental idealized female sculpture stands well over a meter in height and is made to rest on the head and shoulders of the dancer. When danced, the mask and male dancer would be covered with cloth and palm fiber, creating an elegant form about one-third again larger than a normal person. A female bust literally stands on four legs and is carried on the head of the dancer, who looks out through an opening between the figure's breasts. The large and elegantly carved head displays prominent facial features and strong emphasis on the medial hair crest. The *d'mba* functions as a shrine or dances during a wide range of ritual and social appearances. The voluptuous oiled female form of the mask refers to the concept of fertility and regeneration and to the establishment of culture and community.

The bird as icon is prominent in Baga sculpture, whether as a mask or as elegant shrine sculptures known as *a-Tshol* or *elek*. These sculptures, with a rounded base and a thin neck topped by a horizontal stylized bird's head with a long thin beak, worked to heal as a curative agent, identify wrongdoers, fight sorcery, and determine appropriate retribution for unacceptable social behavior.

Some of the most revered and important objects identified with male initiations among the Baga are the large drums, known as *timba*, played at the end of the initiation ritual. Caryatid figures, animals, or geometric forms support the barrel of the drum, which is polychromed. The sex of the supporting figure determines whether it is played by males or females during their initiation rituals.

Baule

The Baule are an Akan-speaking people living in the Ivory Coast within a complex region of cultural interchange reflecting differing traditions of language, social structure, and art. Various Mande neighbors have influenced the Baule in their mask forms and imagery. However, the social uses strictly reflect the Baule's cultural ethos.

As an Akan people, the Baule had a centralizing tendency, with chiefly prestige indicated by regalia and symbols of power and authority, which included gold-leaf-covered wooden staffs with carved finials, fly whisks, swords, crowns, and other ornaments used by the chief's counselors and spokesmen as objects of office and authority. Animals such as the leopard or elephant known for their fierceness and size, or the antelope for its quickness and guile, are visual metaphors for chiefly attributes.

Figurative statuary is some of the best known and most collected of Baule art. Finely carved male and female figures ranging in size from 20 to 60 centimeters are generally portrayed in a standing position of formal calmness, with arms close to the body and hands resting on the abdomen. Attention focuses on the head, with detailed face and neck scarification and elaborate hairstyles. The addition of gold leaf or jewelry often enhances the figures. Baule figure sculptures fall into two categories: the first represents spirits of the wild (asie usu) that live in the bush beyond village boundaries; the second are male and female figures that represent "spirit-world spouses" for their owners.

The asie usu, the spirits of the bush, are venerated by the Baule with offerings that often give the sculptures a rough surface or crusty patination. An anti-aesthetic aspect reflecting magical powers and special capacities is found in a monkey-shaped figure, called aboya, with a large head and underslung jaw.

The other group of Baule anthropomorphic sculptures, the "spirit-world spouses," are kept by their owners in personal shrines. The burnished figures reflect Baule ideas of beauty and aesthetics. The female (blolo bla) and male (blolo bian) figures exhibit youthful well-formed bodies, with much attention to details of hair and scarification, and are dressed in what is considered fashionable, and in recent times, European-style clothing.

The Baule have appropriated helmet- and face-mask forms from their Mande neighbors, using them in local contexts of ritual and representation. Helmet masks (bonu amuin) are composed of polyzoomorphic elements taken from animals prominent in everyday life or Baule myth, such as elephants, antelopes, warthogs, and buffalo. Most generally seen is a buffalo-mask bonu amuin dance, used to honor visiting dignitaries and during funerals honor senior men and former dancers of masks. Although identified with the sacred forest, they do not appear to have a well-defined religious or ritual function. Some of the masks are blackened, while others are brightly painted with red and white enamel paints. They are worn with a loose costume of raffia or woven grasses.

A second zoomorphic helmet mask, known as goli, first appeared among the Baule near the end of the 19th century, having originated among Mande-speaking neighbors, the Wan people. Goli constitutes a troupe of carved masks appearing as four male and female pairs that dance publicly for funerals, festivals, and simply as entertainment. One of the pairs of masks identified as kplekple consists of brightly painted flat disk-shaped masks with features carved in abstracted shallow relief. All goli masks are painted to embellish the sculptural form and to define the sex of the mask, red defining the male and black the female.

Some face masks (ngbla) portray a variety of animals, while others depict people in everyday tasks. Some ngbla can be described as portrait masks, appearing with the individual after whom the mask was carved.

Baule artists infuse utilitarian objects with the same skill and attention given to masks and figures. Sculpted doors, heddle pulleys used in weaving, gong beaters, chairs, and stools reflect not only skill but also a highly developed aesthetic sense of form and design.

Benin

When Portuguese visitors first made their way to what is now Nigeria in 1485, they came into contact with the Edo people of Benin, a highly advanced kingdom ruled by a semidivine king known as the Oba. As a military and political power, the early kingdom of Benin had a highly structured and powerful court located in the palace at Benin City where elaborate ceremonies took place in which numerous works of art served to honor the Oba and his predecessors and to purify the nation. The complex structure of the royal household included court functionaries and retainers as well as guilds of artists and craftsmen in service to the king and his court.

A significant artistic culture was already in place when Europeans first visited Benin. Oral history records that sculpture was part of Benin ceremonial and political life as early as the 13th century. Brass casting is said to have come to Benin through contact with the ancient Yoruba capital of Ife. It was also during this early period at Benin that the brass-caster's guild was established to provide sculptures for the Oba, who was the primary patron for their work. Brass or bronze sculptures and ivory carvings were restricted to those of the highest social order or to the king as a royal monopoly; even today some forms are reserved exclusively for the Oba.

Contact with the Portuguese in the late 15th century gave added impetus to an already flourishing art tradition. By the 17th century, artists were depicting Portuguese in ivory carvings, brass plaques, and figurative sculptures. New materials encouraged established sculptural traditions as brass bars were melted down to be used in the casting of memorial heads of the Obas and to provide sculpture for the numerous altars in the palace. During the early 19th century up to 30 altars may have been dedicated to previous Obas with brass memorial heads and brass or bronze sculptures on them. A European visitor noted at the end of the 17th century that there were 11 brass heads on one altar supporting elephant tusks. The brass memorial heads have been dated to as early as the 15th century and developed stylistically from naturalism to stylization in three distinct periods ending in the late 19th century. The commemorative altar heads of the Oba and the Iyoba (queen mother) grew in size and changed in ornamentation, which may reflect a natural development or the impact of continuing contact with Europeans with growing access to bronze and brass to cast larger and more ornate sculptures.

Some altar figures have been scientifically dated to the 14th century. Examples of altar sculptures include cast tableaux composed of multiple figures of either the Oba or the Iyoba with retinues of musicians or retainers and animals. Sculptures of elephants, leopards, birds, fish, serpents, and roosters are commonly found as individual figures or modeled on plaques. Bells, often with faces cast in relief on their sides, staffs, large ornamented rings, cups and containers, and bracelets, in addition to other objects, were also cast in bronze or brass. Royals, chiefs, and titleholders wore brass pendants and pectorals or small metal masks at the waist or on the left hip. Bracelets in either brass or ivory that included figures, animals, and complex patterns worked in relief on their sides serve as indicators of prestige.

An early 17th-century traveler to Benin mentions numerous galleries whose pillars were covered by cast-brass plaques showing warlike scenes and numerous portrayals of the Oba during ceremonies, as well as other nobility. These plaques may have appeared during first contacts with the Portuguese in the late 15th century; they seem to have fallen out of manufacture during the late 17th century and to have been removed from view during the 18th century. Approximately 800 to 900 plaques are known to survive complete or as fragments. The brass plaques served to catalogue costume, regalia, ceremony, and events at court during an important era for Benin. In addition to portrayals of the Oba and retainers at court, the numerous representations of Portuguese as advisors and warriors on the brass plaques attest to the presence and prominence of the Portuguese at Benin. A number of plaques include animals as the central motif. Other examples show a rider on a mule or horse, referring to contact with mounted peoples from the north or horses that the Portuguese brought with them. Often, plaques include background designs of simple quatrefoil patterns, slightly raised rosettes, or simple punctations.

Other Benin sculpture reflects a high quality of skill in ivory and wood carving. Ivory was a royal prerogative worked by members of the carver's guild for the Oba and close members at court. Artists carved elephant tusks fitted onto the memorial brass heads in relief with animal images and motifs that portray ceremonies and rituals at court or battles fought, representations of court functionaries, and prominent renderings of the Oba. Also found are representations of Portuguese in close alliance with Obas or chiefs. The Portuguese also commissioned ivory carvers to carve spoons, salt containers, and ivory trumpets to return with them to Portugal, perhaps an example of early "tourist" art.

As a result of British incursions during the 1897 war, much of Benin art fell out of use as the Oba was deported, the court at Benin lost its importance, and the guilds without patrons dispersed. Under the patronage of later Obas, the art traditions of Benin are being reestablished at court, where the guilds today both meet the needs of the royal court and serve a popular nontraditional tourist market.

Cameroon

Cameroon is a large country with mountainous terrain, broad savannas, and grasslands. The grasslands of southwest Cameroon are the most populated. There, a number of centralized kingdoms or chiefdoms have developed, each with distinctive individual art traditions. A constellation of these kingdoms, called the grasslands kingdoms and including Bamileke, Bamenda-Tikar, Bamum, Kom, and a number of smaller kingdoms, share common religious beliefs, political structures, and social institutions. These kingdoms have complex structures of relationships balancing the authority of the Fon (Foyn; the ruler, chief, or king) to various titleholders and secret men's associations. The Fon also serves to mediate between spirits, ancestors, and the living to ensure the continued well-being of the kingdom and people.

Grasslands art serves to indicate social status and rank; specific materials and symbols are used by individuals reflecting their station at court or in men's ceremonial and regulatory associations in which masks play an important role. The most prestigious imagery and material is reserved for the king and other nobility, diminishing in importance as one moves downward in rank. Certain artists and artisans served the king exclusively, working in materials reserved for the Fon; well-known artists from other kingdoms would be commissioned to sculpt objects for the king. Ranging from royal regalia of high prestige to objects of everyday usage, most objects were embellished with either simple designs or complex symbolic imagery of political icons or spiritual identity. Although they share common usage of symbols and images, the various grasslands kingdoms each developed their own style with identifiable traits. In addition, some kings developed reputations for their own artistry as sculptors. The advent of German colonization during the late 1880s brought new influences, with other patrons and new ideas.

Imposing in scale and impressive by their sculptural ornamentation, royal palaces demonstrate the power of the Fon and the wealth of the kingdom. Large palace doorways would be covered with openwork or relief carvings of human or animal figures rendering events from the Fon's life or that of earlier kings. Tall pillars supporting the thatched roof are carved in relief or in some instances as fully articulated figures reaching near-life-size proportions.

Architectural sculptures adorning the royal palaces have counterparts in the carved memorial figures of kings, their mothers, royal wives, court attendants, and a variety of animals symbolically identified with kingship. Carved life-size sculptures, at times covered with beadwork or thin sheet brass, represent the ruler and his family members. Sculpted figures act as backrests of large thronelike seats, with openwork carvings of human heads, spiders, leopards, chameleons, or elephants serving as the base of the royal seat. Tables, stools, bed frames, and containers serving the king and other notables also contain human and animal motifs. Large terracotta pipes used by kings or notables served as symbols of rank and royal regalia. Beadwork or metal placed on the pipe stems further embellished the pipes. Smaller pipes cast in bronze or carved from clay share similar iconographic imagery.

Not all grasslands art was dedicated to royal usage; small figures known as *mu po* are used by Bamileke healers and diviners to heal and forestall witchcraft.

Men's secret societies, which use both human and animal masks, are found in most of the states of the grasslands. In certain northern areas masks known as *kwifo* serve the king in exercising social control, while other masks owned by prominent lineages serve to counter the power of the king and to exercise social control. Worn on the top of the head, masks characterize elephants, buffalo, rams, bats, and birds, as well as human forms. Human masks have highly articulated headdresses composed of open-carved representations of hairstyles, bats, spiders, or buffalo horns. Abstraction of motifs such as the spider or frog results in highly stylized openwork superstructures of masks, while other masks are more literal in their presentation. Facial features are deeply carved with exaggerated features, with paint often applied to enhance features of the face and add to the dramatic effect. Some masks are covered with beaten copper (sheet) overlay or have cowry shells and human hair attached.

Dan

The Mande-speaking Dan people of northern Liberia and neighboring Guinea and the Ivory Coast migrated south from present Mali and today live in forested regions as agriculturists. Known for their numerous wooden masks and masquerades, the Dan share many cultural features, including a dynamic masking complex, with their Mano neighbors in Liberia and the We or Guere and Wobe in the Ivory Coast.

The Dan believe that spirits of the wild, known as *du*, manifest themselves in masks and masquerades. An individual instructed in a dream by *du* to dance a mask would commission a carver to create a mask. Dan masks are grouped in an assortment of forms, and each type of mask is named according to its appearance and function and differentiated by its carved form. The Dan have more than ten different mask types in forms ranging from naturalistic to abstract. Masks such as the oval-shaped "smiling mask"—*deangle* or *tangle*—have finely carved features and a shiny smooth black surface. Masks with geometrically abstracted features or grotesque exaggerations, such as *bugle* or *kaogle*, incite people to war, and a mask known as *zakpai*, with red cloth around the eyes, controls the use of fire during the dry season. *Glewa* masks, known for the abundance of their costume with elements of bells, cloth, feathers, and skirting supporting the carved wooden face mask, settle disputes, punish those judged guilty, and mediate the end of wars.

Known popularly as "passport" masks and locally named *ma go*, small head, or simply *ma*, small masks measuring only a few centimeters in length act as a personal talisman for a man, who speaks to it and makes offerings, or uses it to prove his membership in men's secret societies. Women sometimes also have *ma* masks to keep them connected to their family mask when they move to their husband's home.

Sculptures known as *lu me*, or "wooden person," are relatively uncommon sculptures commissioned by the Dan or Yacuba and can be more than 60 centimeters in height. *Lu me* are stylized portraits of real individuals that closely represent the hairstyle, body markings, and physiognomy of the person. These superb examples of Dan sculpture are the creation of well-known artists working in secret away from women and children. Small brass figures up to 20 centimeters tall, representing soldiers or people conducting everyday activities, began to be cast during the late 19th and early 20th centuries, apparently as prestige or aesthetic objects with no ritual use linked to them.

Other objects indicated the status of women. Sculpted human or animal heads form the end of the handle of large ladle-like spoons, up to 70 centimeters and larger in length. Other spoons, known as *wunkirle*, *wakemia*, or *wunkirmian*, are in the shape of a figure in which the oval spoon forms the body and the handle is in the form of human legs. Each spoon symbolizes the woman in her beauty as well as the spirit *du*, who assists her in her activities.

Fang

During migrations that took place in the late 18th and early 19th centuries, the Fang people moved to their present area, becoming part of a complex overlay of population of approximately 200,000, stretching from southern Cameroon through Equatorial Guinea and Gabon. Occupying a large geographical region over an extended period of time, the Fang have developed a cultural kinship with the various peoples in the region, resulting in a number of shared sculptural styles identified under the general rubric of Fang, although varying in detail and reflecting local stylistic traits.

The dense rain forest environment constrained the Fang to relatively small-scale social structures defined by the family lineage and an economic way of life dependent on transitional farming and hunting. Each lineage's ancestors were located in family shrines where memorials or reliquary boxes, known as *byeri*, containing their bones remained under the care of an elder known as the Esa. Sculpted figures that guarded the remains of Fang ancestors surmounted containers made of bark or woven basketry. Known as *eyema-o-byeri*, these guardian figures also served to witness and validate the initiation rituals of young men. Some Fang figures appear to be slightly crouched with legs bent in a seated position to rest on the container, while others have a narrow sticklike extension reaching downward from the buttocks, which enables the figures to perch on the edge of the *byeri* with their legs hanging over the side, held in place by the extension that fitted into the top of the container.

The Fang also employed sculpted freestanding wooden heads on simple plinths that fitted onto the reliquary containers. More often found among the northern Fang, the heads are seemingly contemporaneous with the guardian figures. A semicircle of braids or a flattened hairstyle opens to a large expanse of domed forehead emphasizing the heart-shaped face with a long and flattened nose ending in an underslung, prognathous jaw with a thin mouth and nearly absent chin. These facial features are ubiquitous in Fang sculpture. Sculptors carved the Fang heads and *eyema-o-byeri* sculptures from a heavy, dense wood, which continues to give off a dark resinous liquid over many years. This sticky black substance gives the heads and figures a shiny patination that enhances the sculpture's surface. In a practice predating European contact, artists used copper disks or metal inserts to depict eyes on the heads, with startling effect. Figures often had native copper bands around the arms and wrists; later artists used brass tacks to embellish details.

White-painted masks identified to the Ngil society are known for their elegant abstractions of the human face. While emphasizing its pure forms, the mask's white color also marks its spiritual identity. Ngil masks are often described as having a heart-shaped face because the facial features emphasize refined curves of the orbital ridges above the eyes and the prominent line of the long tapering nose, which ends above a square mouth, completing the abstraction of the face. The Ngil wore these masks, used for judicial and social control activities in searching out sorcerers, during initiations. The French banned them in 1910. A later development among the Fang was the appearance of a mask known as *ngontangan*, "the head of the young white girl," referring to early European women missionaries who arrived on the coast during the 19th century. The elegant forms and abstractions of the Ngil masks, although few in number, made them attractive to modern European artistic sensibilities, serving as models for a number of sculptors.

Kota

The Kota share language and culture with a constellation of smaller ethnic groups living in Gabon and along the western reaches of the Republic of the Congo, including the Ndassa, Wumbu, Sogho (Tsogho or Mitsogho), Shamaye, and Kwele peoples and the most prominent of the Kota subgroups, the Obamba and the Mahongwe (Osseyba). All have in common a set of sculptural forms and ceremonies in service to a cult practice known as Bwete.

The focal point of Bwete rituals are reliquary containers made of bark or basketry that hold magical objects or the bones of ancestors. Among the Kota, Bwete reliquaries would be grouped together under a small shelter in the village, gathering the different lineages and clans in symbolic union. Highly abstracted anthropomorphic guardian figures attach to the top of the Bwete reliquaries, depicting founders of the clan and important individuals. These figures also served to protect the relics from malicious actions of witches and malefactors. The geometric abstraction of the body repeats in the large, stylized heads. Adding to the visual impact, either copper or brass sheeting covers the heads.

Kota-Mahongwe (Ossyeba)

The Kota-Mahongwe, also identified as the Ossyeba, have the most stylistically abstracted Bwete reliquary figures, with concave spear-shaped heads. Copper or brass wire, flattened and worked into a patterned overlay to define the face, covers the wooden carving. A flat finlike projection from the face makes up the nose, and rounded metal disks make up the eyes. The most widely known reliquary figures in Gabon are those from the southern Kota-Obamba, which are known as *mbulu ngulu* (spirits of the dead). Obamba heads are oval, with slightly concave faces and elaborate hairstyles extending from the sides of the head. Ornamented with either copper or brass metal cladding over the face and coiffure, the figures attach to the reliquary containers by their lozenge-shaped body. Artists worked the metal sheeting with punches or pressure engraving to produce designs and patterns that in some instances may represent details of scarification. Some Kota figures are Janus-faced, with different features and details of hair and facial markings on either side.

The copper- or brass-clad reliquary figures are some of the earliest examples of sculpture noted by European travelers and colonial officials. Drawings of figures surmounting funerary bundles appeared as early as 1887 and 1888 in the journal *Le Tour du monde*. A reliquary figure from Gabon identified as Ondoumbo (Ndumba) acquired by the Museé d'Ethnographie du Trocadero in Paris early as 1884 is an example of early colonial collecting interest. The metal-covered reliquary figures were popular among European artists and collectors during the early 20th century, highly prized as embodying modern Western ideals of abstraction and sophisticated forms, as well as for the interesting combination of wood and metal.

Few masks exist among the Kota; Kota social structure allied to the strong presence of the Bwete ancestor cult constrained the development of a prominent masking complex. Nonetheless, Kota in the eastern region of Gabon in the province of Ogowe-Ivindo use masks measuring 40 to 80 centimeters, known as *emboli* or *mbuto*, during initiation ceremonies for young boys. The masks are also worn during antiwitchcraft rituals. The wooden helmet mask completely covers the wearer's head, with exaggerated hair crests surmounting a stylized human face. A crest running laterally from ear to ear crosses another at right angles stretching front to back.

Makonde

Makonde are Bantu-speaking people who today live in northern Mozambique and in southern Tanzania. Close to the Indian Ocean coast, both groups had contact with Islamized peoples along the East African coast, and the Tanzanian Makonde were under constant pressures from incursions of different peoples.

The volume of sculpture in museums attests to a vibrant artistic tradition active among the Makonde. The most noted sculptural forms are female figures used in the past and realistic helmet masks still in use today. The best known mask among the Makonde appears during initiations of boys coming to the village from the bush, accompanied by drums and initiated men. Called *lipiko* (plural, *mapiko*), it is a realistic helmet mask worn by men to instruct and intimidate young boys during rites of passage. Early examples of *mapiko* represent the head of a woman with human hair attached to the mask, a labret in her lips, and facial marks indicated by beeswax attached to the surface. A large cloth at the bottom of the mask hides the dancer's body.

As a rule the Makonde in the past were governed by clan elders. Wooden figures known as *masinamu* (singular, *lisinamu*) carved to represent the elders upon their death were used for the veneration of the ancestors, who were considered to be semidivine, and kept in clan houses, where an elder had responsibility for their care. Often carved out of light-colored wood, the figures reached up to 80 centimeters in height. Artists painted or carved patterns representing scarification or tattooing onto the figures, some of which had small bits of beeswax attached to depict raised body markings.

Other examples of Makonde sculpture include anthropomorphic body masks (*ndimu*), used in the past during boy's initiation ceremonies, and large drums (*likuti*), used to warn villagers of wild animals or danger from attack.

By the 1930s, as a result of colonial contact, the Makonde began to move from the carving of sculpture primarily for ritual purpose to the production of spirit figures for the nontraditional and export market by the 1970s.

Mangbetu

Sometime during the 18th century the Mangbetu migrated from central Sudan to their present area in the northeastern range of the rain forest of the Democratic Republic of Congo (former Zaire). Today the Mangbetu have a mixed forest economy of agriculture and fishing. In 1870 an early visitor to the Mangbetu royal court of King Munza marveled at the size of a reception hall that could hold a few thousand people. Europeans believed that the Mangbetu, colonized by 1891, were superior in their art and culture to others of the region.

The Mangbetu worked in a number of materials, carving wood and ivory, forging iron, and forming copper. Particularly known for their prestigious royal arts and dress, the Mangbetu nobility wore garments of superior craftsmanship decorated in geometric patterns that are also found on wood carving, metalwork, and ceramics. Regalia at court included harps with carved bodies and graceful heads, knives with sculpted handles, and anthropomorphic containers and pipes. Some of the best-known examples of Mangbetu sculpture are the human-headed ceramic pots, which share style and sensibility with wooden sculpture.

Association with Europeans, who were especially taken by the elegant upward sweep of the head capped by a flared coiffure so prominent on the sculptures, enhanced Mangbetu art production with the introduction of a new audience for their works. Only a few early figures can be firmly attributed to the Mangbetu. Figural sculpture dates to a tradition developed during the late 19th century as they came into contact with the Zande and other neighboring peoples, including the Barambo, Bua, Mamvu, and Bodu. As a result of the extensive cultural and artistic interchange with these other peoples, it is often difficult to fix a specific style to be known as Mangbetu.

The Mangbetu did not use or sculpt masks because of the high degree of centralization and art that was identified with the royal courts.

Nok

The earliest sculptures known in sub-Saharan Africa, terracotta sculptures dating as early as 500 BCE, come from a culture in central Nigeria known as Nok, found within a broad area bounded by the Benue and Kaduna Rivers. First identified at the village of Nok and subsequently recognized at a number of other widely scattered sites including Jemaa, Katsina Ala, and Taruga, numerous terracotta figures sharing similar stylistic traits attest to an extended sculptural tradition in force over time and distance. The first example identified by Bernard Fagg, at Nok in 1944, was a sculpted terracotta human head. Other Nok sculptures were discovered in alluvial deposits exposed as the result of local tin mining. Archaeological excavations indicate that the people of Nok were an Iron Age society with a rich sculptural tradition dating from approximately 500 BCE to sometime after 200 CE.

Figures range in size from a few centimeters in height to fragments of figures that if complete would have been more than life size. The smallest of the figures are modeled out of solid clay, while larger Nok sculptures are hollow, made by a coiling technique. As a result of the low firing temperature, these terracotta

sculptures are fragile, and surface details worked by incision or stamping are often lost through abrasion or damage. The sculptor would first shape the body and then add limbs, after which details of facial features, jewelry, hairstyle, and dress were affixed to the figure using a number of techniques.

Nok terracotta sculptures include human and animal figures. Artists sculpted animals such as elephants or monkeys individually while often working snakes in relief on pottery. Freestanding human figures are the most common, presented on a number of platforms ranging from stools or columnar supports to simple bases. Others simply rested directly on the ground in a number of positions. Some examples of Nok sculpture stand on pots similar in style to those found among a number of groups in northern Nigeria.

Nok figures wear elaborate costumes and bead necklaces, bracelets, and anklets in multiple layers. Both male and female figures wear a variety of intricate hairstyles; details of dress include skirts for women and loincloths or coverings for both men and women. Some female figures have smaller figures attached, similar to maternity figures widely known in sub-Saharan sculpture. Sculptors rendered terracotta figures either naturalistically or in stylized forms with exaggerated details, representing physical deformities that served symbolic ends representing deities or transformative beings.

Stylistic traits specifically identified with the Nok complex of sculpture include a particular treatment of the eye in which the lower half of the eye is represented as a triangular or semicircular shape with emphasis on the pupil. In addition, the heads of figures are proportionally larger than the bodies. Some details of Nok facial features were carved rather than simply modeled by hand and may represent a carving tradition present in Nok wooden sculpture, of which no remains have as yet been found.

The actual purpose of Nok sculpture is unclear, although posture and expression, dress, complexity of hairstyles, and details of jewelry or other adornment may indicate social differences. Equally, Nok figures may have served as memorial figures used at burials or as ancestral figures placed on altars.

Yoruba

The Yoruba of Nigeria and the Benin Republic are the single largest art-producing people of sub-Saharan Africa. Numbering approximately 25 million, they have a rich tradition of art dating to their founding sometime during the 10th century at the ancient Yoruba capital of Ife and later at Oyo (1680–1830). The Yoruba are an urban people living in numerous city-states headed by rulers who are thought to be semi-divine. The rulers and an elite population serve as patrons of the arts, commissioning the making of sculpture. Yoruba art ranges in scale from small carvings of figures and containers to larger architectural elements such as doors and pillars. Emerging from a deep philosophical system of aesthetics in service to cosmological and religious beliefs, Yoruba art portrays complex ideas in forms that are simple and elegantly direct. Yoruba artists strive to capture the essence of meaning in a form that balances message to sculptural representation and to incorporate traditional imagery with modern idioms. Therefore, Yoruba sculpture is always of its time as artists give age-old concepts new forms.

Sango, the fourth Yoruba king of Oyo, is venerated and honored through the use of carved dance wands carried by devotees and the images of kneeling female figures holding bowls (*arugba*) placed on altars to Sango. Other carved figures placed on altars hold wands or kneel; some carry children on their backs. Women followers of Sango carry the dance wands known as Ose Sango while singing praise songs and dancing. Altar figures and the Ose Sango dance wands share a common symbolic motif of shaped Neolithic stone axes either as a stylized headdress or finials on the wands.

Masking associations are prominent among the Yoruba, blending the drama of sculpted masks with music and singing. A masking tradition known as *egungun*, said to have originated in Oyo, dances to recognize the ancestral lineage and to celebrate and honor the living. The masks also appear at the funerals and initiations. *Egungun* masks are complex structures of carved headpieces and lavish cloth ensembles. Face masks, flat traylike forms, or helmet masks with rabbit features and prominent ears or assemblages of cloths or beaded panels cover the dancer. Among the western Yoruba, wooden headpieces known as *gelede* represent elderly women fondly called "our mothers." The masks dance to express the positive and negative forces that these mothers command and their influence on society. *Gelede* masks are carved either with a single face or human figure or with birds holding serpents in their beaks. Sculptures surmounting modern *gelede* masks imaginatively depict figures in modern dress riding motorcycles or automobiles. Massive helmet masks known as *epa* or *elefon* found among the northeastern Yoruba can be more than one meter in height. The mask is composed of two parts, a helmet with a face carved on it surmounted by a large superstructure of carved figures. Young men dance the *epa* to honor elders, warriors, and priests, whose multiple images are carved and embellished by painting on the super-

structure of the mask. When not being danced they are placed in shrines where they are venerated.

A divination cult known as Ifa is practiced throughout Yoruba society. Crucial to the act of divination is the sculpture that makes up the diviner's ritual equipment. Divination boards or trays (*opon Ifa*) are fashioned out of wood in round, rectangular, or semicircular shapes and carved in relief showing symbols of cosmological forces or humans in various activities. The diviner keeps the chain or palm nuts used for the divination in a cuplike container known as *agere Ifa*, carved in the round with images from Yoruba life and religion. Diviners use small ivory or wooden tappers called *iroke* at the beginning of Ifa divination to attract and greet the gods. Carved in the form of a kneeling female figure, *iroke* incorporate Yoruba concepts of supplication and respect.

Cult activity shapes much of Yoruba art, focusing ritual and religious ceremony on symbolic figures placed on altars or household shrines or kept as personal objects of veneration and power. Diviners use the figure of the god Eshu/Elegba, a divine messenger identified with the crossroads between the sprit and human world, as a messenger to the gods. The figure, which is found on shrines, wears a string of cowry shells and has an exaggerated hairstyle reaching back over his head. Other altar sculptures and figures characterize devotion and supplication of the gods by their kneeling postures. Still other small-scale sculptures known as *ibeji* represent deceased twins and are probably the most numerous of sculptures among the Yoruba.

The Yoruba create sculpture in a variety of media, including wood, terracotta, ivory, and bronze and iron metalwork. Bronze figures are prominent among members of the Osugbo or Ogboni society, made up of senior male and female elders. Bronze-cast figures known as *edan* are joined by a chain and worn over shoulders as badges of office or placed on the ground in front of the elders during judicial deliberations, funerals, and ceremonies in which rulers are installed in office. Larger bronze figures called *onile* honor all male and females of the Osugbo society and Ile, the earth goddess. A forged iron staff with a bird sculpture that itself may be surrounded by as many as 16 smaller birds represents Osanyin, the spirit of herbal medicine and healing.

Zande

The Zande (Azande) originated in the Sudan, migrating during the 18th century to southern Zaire, now the Democratic Republic of Congo, and the Central African Republic. Although agriculturists today, in the past they were a powerful warlike people led by the Avongara clan, expanding and assimilating defeated peoples together with their art and artisans into the larger fabric of Zande culture. Within a loose confederation, chiefs gave sculpted figures as gifts to other chiefs and later to European visitors as a form of aesthetic exchange. Artists held recognized positions in royal courts, and some towns were noted as carving centers during the colonial period.

Figural sculpture is identified with a secret society known as Mani, which formed to mitigate the power of the ruling clan during the 19th century. The Mani originated in the Central African Republic; membership was open to both men and women, who used small wooden sculptures (12–15 centimeters) known as *yanda* during annual ritual ceremonies. Beads or brass rings adorn some figures, while others have white powder placed over them. The style of *yanda* carved figures ranges from highly abstracted to anthropomorphic. The abbreviated arms and legs share similarities with figures of the neighboring Ngbaka or Ngbande.

The Zande sculpted musical instruments with anthropomorphic attributes. *Sanza* or *mbira*, thumb pianos, were the instruments of commoners; the elegant human-headed harps were courtly instruments. The warlike Zande also made their weapons of iron into abstracted sculptural forms with multiple blades, which were often covered with geometric markings.

Zimbabwe

The ruins of Great Zimbabwe form a complex of curved walls forming enclosures, open spaces, and a tower. Of monumental proportions, the stacked-stone structures were neither dwellings nor fortresses. However, for a period of time from approximately 1250 to sometime after 1450, Great Zimbabwe was the center of the great Shona kingdom. As the largest stone-building complex of the precolonial period in sub-Saharan Africa, it functioned as a ritual center for the Shona kingdom. The structures of Great Zimbabwe are divided by topography and function: the enclosure and tower of the upper elevation is known as Hill Ruin and a walled area below is called the Lower Homestead. The king lived near the upper buildings, and residences for the royal wives were close to the lower valley constructions.

Large soapstone carvings were found in enclosures, the most impressive being large birds up to one meter in height. Archaeologists discovered eight of these stylized birds within ritual or sacred precincts in both the upper and lower constructions. All of the birdlike forms are combinations of eagle and human features intermixed. Although each of the carvings is distinct, they are sufficiently close in style and form to suggest that a single carver made all eight. In Shona mythology the bird or eagle carries messages to the ancestors or the supreme deity.

Investigators also found bowl-shaped carvings in the Eastern Enclosure, close by the raised platform that supported six of the birds. With diameters ranging up to 60 centimeters, these soapstone bowls had raised sides reaching 10 centimeters in height. Most bowls contained some form of carving either in relief or inscribed onto the vertical surface of their sides. Abstracted geometric patterns predominated, while a lesser number had naturalistic representations. Interpreting the various abstracted motifs is problematic; it is even more difficult to ascribe meaning to the naturalistic figures. However, the abstracted geometrical designs have been catalogued with other Zimbabwe symbols representing snakes or water symbols.

Although other Zimbabwe culture sites have been identified, none have yielded either the monumental architecture or the sculpture of Great Zimbabwe, demonstrating its importance and authority as the center of the Shona kingdom. While Great Zimbabwe drew its power from the control of trade, it lost its prominence when trade lessened and was abandoned around 1450.

DANIEL MATO

Further Reading

Binet, Jacques, *Sociétés de danse chez les Fang du Gabon*, Paris: Office de la Recherche Scientifique et Technique Outre-mer, 1972

Fernandez, James W., "La statuaire Fang-Gabon," *African Arts* 8/1 (1974)

Fernandez, James W., *Fang Architectonics*, Philadelphia, Pennsylvania: Institute for the Study of Human Issues, 1977

Fernandez, James W., and R.L., "Fang Reliquary Art: Its Quantities and Qualities," *Cahiers d'études africaines* 15/5 (1975)

Perrois, Louis, *La statuaire fan, Gabon*, Paris: ORSTOM, 1972

Perrois, Louis, *Problèmes d'analyse de la sculpture traditonnelle du Gabon*, Paris: ORSTOM, 1977

Perrois, Louis, "Arts du Gabon: Les arts plastiques du Bassin de l'Ogooué," *Arts d'Afrique noire* 20 (winter 1979)

Perrois, Louis, *Arts ancestral du Gabon: Dans les collections du Musée Barbier-Mueller*, Geneva: Musée Barbier-Mueller, 1985; as *Ancestral Art of Gabon: From the Collections of the Barbier-Mueller Museum*, translated by Francine Farr, Geneva: The Barbier-Mueller Museum, 1985

Phillips, Tom (editor), *Africa: The Art of a Continent*, London: Royal Academy of Arts, and New York and Munich: Prestel, 1995

Roy, Christopher G., *Art and Life in Africa: Selections from the Stanley Collection, Exhibitions of 1985 and 1992*, Iowa City: University of Iowa Museum of Art, 1992

Schmalenbach, Werner (editor), *Afrikanische Kunst aus der Sammlung Barbier-Mueller, Genf*, Munich: Prestel, 1988; as *African Art from the Barbier-Mueller Collection, Geneva*, Munich: Prestel, 1988

Tessmann, Günter, *Die Pangwe*, 2 vols., Berlin: Wasmuth, 1913; reprint, 1 vol., New York: Johnson Reprint, 1972

AFRICA: 20TH-CENTURY–CONTEMPORARY

Sculpture produced in Africa in the 20th century had a demonstrable impact on world art and popular cultures. While the dichotomies of traditional/modern, old/new, and contemporary/Postmodern continued in African art, the term *contemporary art* in this text encompasses the diversity of art produced in Africa since 1900.

Africa was in contact with the rest of the world before the presumed discovery of the continent by European adventurers in the 15th century. Africa's interactions with the Western and Islamic worlds mean that the formal and contextual roles of the arts are more complex than is usually assumed in extant discourses. The issue of African independence and nationhood made the second half of the 20th century a period of unprecedented change in art practices in continental Africa. Independence and nationhood brought about freedom of visual directions, untold creative energy, and government commissions, as well as private patronage, for the modern sculptor. For instance, Nigerian sculptor Ben Enwonwu's sculpture of Queen Elizabeth II meant that by the time of independence, contemporary Nigerian sculpture enjoyed great visibility. As a result of nationhood and increased patronage, the range of subject and technique options open to Enwonwu and the other sculptors became marginal. The sculptures that are produced in modern-day Africa cannot easily be grouped into popular (commercial) art, academic (modern) art, and traditional (indigenous) art, as many writers commonly do. The continuing development of these artistic traditions, as diverse as the continent's inhabitants, remains widespread into the 21st century.

Africa, the second largest continent in the world, has approximately 760 million inhabitants with more than 3000 ethnic groups who speak more than 1000 languages. Arguably, one can also refer to as African artists those Arabs, Asians, Europeans, and other significant inhabitants who intermingle and work with the indigenous population. Archaeological studies suggest that the evolution of humankind started in Africa, at the Great Rift Valley, five million years ago. Regardless of whether this theory is valid, its acceptance by the Western world today has the result only of localizing Africa to less global prominence. The television image of Africa in the West still associates the continent with jungles and wild-game reserves; in the same manner museums construct collections of African art based mainly on the aesthetic traditions of precolonial African societies. Nonetheless, the preeminence of tradi-tional African art (mainly sculpture) in these museums is slowly giving way to acknowledgment of the diverse range of contemporary art in the continent. These indigenous traditions have had great influence on the constitution of European modernism as Western artists turned to African sculpture in search of new paradigms of representation in the first decade of the 20th century.

Within the same period that artists such as Pablo Picasso began to appropriate the formal elements of classical African sculptures, the Nigerian artist Aina Onabolu adopted a mimetic approach to art, thus nullifying the colonial misconception that African artists could not work in a naturalistic mode of representation. Within the first quarter of the century, under the impetus of a new cultural consciousness, African American artists began to view African sculpture as a shared heritage and used its formal solutions in their work. This process of reclamation, which intensified during the Harlem Renaissance, progressed throughout the 20th century, yielding new interpretations of age-old African aesthetic practices.

The history of international appropriation of African aesthetics is well known; less studied is the history of voluntary migration of continental Africans artists to the West in the 20th century. For instance, Oku Ampofo, a Ghanaian sculptor, traveled to Europe in 1932 to study art and medicine. The late 20th century saw an extensive rise in the number of African students, scholars, businesspeople, workers, and political refugees in the West, adding to the growth and visibilities of continental African communities. In most cases the expatriate African artists explore issues of cultural identity in relation to their host communities as well as their indigenous heritage.

The Harmon Foundation, a New York-based private organization that supported African American art, sponsored an exhibition of works by Enwonwu at Howard University in 1950. It was the first exhibition of contemporary African art in the United States.

After 1960 the emergence of independent African nations engendered a growth in art academies from which emerged numerous influential artists; the consequent periods of political freedom, prosperity, urbanization, political upheavals, economic downturns, and dictatorships lent credence to art that emerged from these institutions. The schools continued a tradition of cultural relevance espoused by earlier institutions such as the Makerere Art School, formed in the 1930s, which flourished for a long time as a principal center for modern art in the east. Other art schools in Addis Ababa, Khartoum, Abidjan, Dakar, and Zaria extended this initial focus into a militant affirmation of African identity in art. In line with the Negritude and Pan-Africanist ideals of the 1950s and 1960s that propagated uniqueness of the Africa culture, these premier schools forged a philosophy of cultural essence that is discernible in works of their early graduates and those of subsequent generations.

Contemporary African artists deploy varied styles and aesthetic orientation. For example, Vincent Kofi of Ghana used themes of Akan social and artistic terrains to sculpt figures in wood, bronze, cement, and stone. Kofi received art training in the indigenous and European contexts; his role as a teacher, artist, and writer influenced the directions of contemporary sculpture in Ghana. The sculptures of Amir Nour have also been influential. He drew from his memories of growing up in Sudan to create geometric forms. *Grazing at Shendi* (1969), an installation of 200 semispherical stainless steel tubes in a repeated shape but varying sizes immortalizes Nour's memories of watching goats grazing at his birthplace. *Grazing at Shendi* and more recent works, including the bronze *Spoon* (1975) and cold-rolled steel *Calabash 4* (1980) are impressive artworks whose timelessness transcends the cultural space that inspired their evolution.

In addition to the formal art schools, European art teachers and culture critics created workshop schools where they conducted informal training in art. Frank McEwan founded in 1957 the National Gallery Workshop School in Harare, Zimbabwe. From this school, and with the encouragement of McEwan, emerged a new tradition of stone carving known as Shona sculpture. These sculptures are generally of strong indigenous content, largely figurative, and monumental, owing to their peculiar modes of execution. Within the shared techniques and aesthetics of Zimbabwe stone sculptors, one can perceive the evolution of individual styles in the sculptures of Sylvester Mubayi, John Takawira, Joram Mariga, Richard Mteki, and Nicholas Mukomberanwa. The Zimbabwean National Gallery Workshop School, like the Nigerian Oshogbo Workshop School, has captivated the international art market.

Following the First World Festival of Negro Arts (1966) held in Senegal and the Festival of Arts and Culture (FESTAC 1977) held in Nigeria, which brought to African shores peoples of African descent from all over the world, the reclamation of aspects of African heritage grew stronger in the arts of the Africans. Across the continent popular tourist art and commercial sculptures, largely derived from traditional sculptures, have grown to be sources of income to the middle artists, or self-trained and/or popular commercial artists whose works occupy the terrain between the traditional and contemporary art of the academy. Lamidi Fakeye is a contemporary Nigerian sculptor who works in the indigenous style of classical Yoruba sculpture extracted from the ritual and secular contexts of village and palace commissions. An internationally acclaimed sculptor, Fakeye has held several important fellowships and was an artist-in-residence at Obafemi Awolowo University in Ife, Nigeria, among other places.

The end of the 20th century saw an increased movement to the West among African artists who accepted invitations for exhibitions, short-term art residencies, education, and work. The professional contacts and international exposure transformed the works of these sculptors, but critics still debate the degree of the effects of market forces, imported tools, and international aesthetic ideals on their works. The evidence of interchange is in every artistic tradition. It is thus inaccurate to refer to the sculptures of contemporary African artists as mere mimicry of Western artistic culture, just as it would be incorrect to read 20th-century Western Modernism as solely a provincial extension of traditional African aesthetic modes of representation; the two cultures have been symbiotic. Contemporary African art sprouts from radically divergent historical, sociocultural, and political trends akin to the continent. Between 1900 and 1960, African artists and scholars engaged in debates about matters of artistic, historical, political, and social import, and after many African nations became independent of direct colonial control, issues of decolonization of African art became primary to these debates. At the turn of the 21st century, the attention of African artists, scholars, and writers has remained focused on questions of artistic identity and cultural distinctiveness in relation to the continued dynamism of contemporary African visual culture.

El Anatsui is a Nigerian-based Ghanaian sculptor and prominent member of the University of Nigeria Nsukka's department of fine and applied arts, commonly referred to as the Nsukka School. Anatsui uses chain saws and pneumatic tools to inscribe ideographic images on wood, which he then chars with fire. Anatsui's themes reiterate the complexities of Africa's cultural history and the brutal episodes of colonial domination whose effects continue to affect contemporary existence in Africa. Some of Anatsui's former students, graduates of the Nsukka School, including such notable female artists as Ndidi Dike, one of the most significant artists to emerge from Nsukka School, have extended the slash-and-brand technique pioneered by Anatsui. Dike incorporates shells, metal objects, animal skins, and fibers into her branded-wood pieces. Her *Pennies and Palms* (1987) is a freestanding carved wood sculpture made up of four figures representing kidnapped people who are tied with ropes and who are on a forced march to the coast. The assemblage alludes to the century-long slave trade in Africa. Gender-sensitive issues foregrounded in sculptural assemblages of Dike and the complex metal ensembles of Sokari

Douglas-Camp attest to the changing roles of women in Africa. Douglas-Camp, based in England, draws from her childhood memories and later visits to her Kalabari-Nigerian homeland to create monumental figurative metal sculptures, often motorized to simulate cultural performances and events. Whereas Douglas-Camp's kinetic sculptures reflect the exuberance of indigenous Kalabari performances, the ceramic sculptures of Magdelene Odundo, a Kenyan artist, evoke a classical solidity of form in their elegant and burnished surfaces. By manipulating the physical qualities of clay, Odundo produces ceramic vessels whose ritualistic forms transcend their functions as containers.

South African township art, an urban art form associated with South African black artists, was a vehicle of indigenous resistance to the colonial order of South Africa's apartheid regimes. In the 1980s, in response to the government's ban on the creation of politically oriented art, anonymous community art projects known as "Peace Parks" became an alternative mode of public protest. Peace Parks were site-specific installations chiefly comprised of items derived from the cultural detritus of the urban landscape. The apartheid government frequently destroyed these installations. The demise of apartheid brought a new orientation to South African arts, which are now characterized by themes of multiculturalism and pluralism. Jackson Hlungwani is a self-taught Venda artist whose sculptures bear Christian messages. Andries Botha is a renowned white South African sculptor who, in his search for appropriate visual language, appropriates the grass-weaving traditions of Zulu women.

Sculptures executed in bronze, cement, stone, and even wood commissioned from both academy-trained and self-trained artists now adorn public spaces in African towns and cities. The inclusion of innovative works by the Ghanian carpenter and coffin maker Kane Kwei in major exhibitions of contemporary African art such as *Africa Explores* in New York City (1990) and *Magiciens de la Terre* in Paris (1991) attests to the changing discourse of African art. According to Olu Oguibe, Kwei's fantastic, designer caskets transcend the confines of carpentry and reflect the postmodern materiality of African artistic localities (see Oguibe and Enwezor, 1999). However, many African artists and critics seem to suggest that Eurocentric Postmodern art is ahistorical, is intellectually and conceptually sterile, and is of little importance to contemporary African sculpture. Despite this objection, some contemporary African artists, mostly those practicing in the Western world, attach their art to the contested terrains of Postmodernism. Oguibe's eclectic installations and Ike Ude's evocative body painting are unmistakably Postmodern.

Modern and contemporary African sculpture reflects the diversity and distinctive sensibilities of 20th-century African spaces. The practice of contemporary African sculptors echoes this diversity and its inherently dynamic nature, ensuring that it will continue to develop in positive directions.

BARTHOSA NKURUMEH

Further Reading

Beier, Ulli, *Contemporary Art in Africa*, New York: Praeger, and London: Pall Mall, 1968

Brown, Evelyn S., *Africa's Contemporary Art and Artists*, New York: Harmon Foundation, 1966

Fosu, Kojo, *20th-Century Art of Africa*, Zaria, Nigeria: Gaskiya, 1986; revised edition, Accra, Ghana: Artists Alliance, 1993

Kelly, Bernice (compiler), *Nigerian Artists: A Who's Who and Bibliography*, edited by Janet Stanley, London and New York: Zell, 1993

LaDuke, Betty, *Africa through the Eyes of Women Artists*, Trenton, New Jersey: Africa World Press, 1991

Mount, Marshall Ward, *African Art: The Years since 1920*, Bloomington: Indiana University Press, and Newton Abbot, Devon: David and Charles, 1973

Oguibe, Olu, and Okwui Enwezor (editors), *Reading the Contemporary: African Art from Theory to the Marketplace*, London: inIVA, and Cambridge, Massachusetts: MIT Press, 1999

Williamson, Sue, *Resistance Art of South Africa*, New York: St. Martin's Press, and London: Catholic Institute for International Relations, 1990

Younge, Gavin, *Art of the South African Townships*, New York: Rizzoli, and London: Thames and Hudson, 1988

AGOSTINO DI DUCCIO 1418–before 1498 *Italian*

For Agostino di Duccio, architectural activity was secondary to his sculptural work. In his chief architectural work, the Oratory of San Bernardino facade in Perugia (1457–61), the preeminence of the decorative conception of the architectural surface, which is wholly covered by reliefs, is clear. Moreover, the original polychromy of the reliefs, through the use of polychrome marbles and painting, makes evident the artist's priority in the pictorial effects, which were quite distinct from architectural concerns.

Agostino's activity as a sculptor raises a number of complex problems, mostly for the peculiarity of his style, which is difficult to relate to other styles with any real precision. There are also remarkable problems in determining his training, which eludes placement in Florentine workshops on both chronological and stylistic grounds. The reconstruction of his Venetian period is also problematic. It seems to have been of some importance for his training, and critics have associated him with some of the major local workshops, but without conclusive results.

The major problems for scholars surrounding Agostino are those of attributing nondocumented works and of distinguishing the master's hand from his collaborators in documented works. The difficulty of such determination is made more vexing by some variations in the quality level in Agostino's ascertained works. This confused situation has its origins in Giorgio Vasari's 16th-century *Lives of the Painters, Sculptors, and Architects*, wherein Agostino's figure is confused with that of other sculptors.

Agostino was the most important of the numerous Florentine sculptors working mostly outside Tuscany in the 15th century. His chief sculptural work was the interior decoration of the Tempio Malatestiano in Rimini, at the commission of Sigismondo Pandolfo Malatesta, Lord Rimini, who arranged the transformation of the medieval Church of San Francesco into a temple of personal glorification, renaming it the Tempio Malatestiano. He assigned the direction of the architectural renovation to Leon Battista Alberti. Alberti, who realized the facade of the new church, probably planned its entire renovation. It was perhaps still under Alberti's direction that the transformation of the interior was realized by the architect and medallist Matteo de' Pasti. The decorative plan also involved the renowned painters Piero della Francesca and Filippo Lippi, although the decoration is almost wholly sculptural.

The Tempio Malatestiano's sculptural decorative scheme is the most important from the Renaissance to have survived entirely. The decoration also carries great interest for its complex iconography, which is a typical product of a humanistic court culture. The astonishing feature of refined paganism that pervades these decorations was also the object of contemporaneous polemical reactions from the ecclesiastical hierarchy.

The sculptural decoration of the Tempio Maltestiano involves the six principal chapels of the church, three on each side. The plan provides a concentration of decoration on the entrance piers of each chapel, which are covered by reliefs, disposed on three sides in two or three tiers. A statue ornaments the altar of each chapel, and other reliefs appear on the walls. The two principal chapels, the Chapel of San Sigismondo and the Chapel of Isotta degli Atti, contain important funerary monuments of the patron and his mistress. The plan also provides some symmetry on the two sides of the church, between the opposite chapels.

The first and most important chapel to be realized was that of San Sigismondo. This structure represents open celebration of Lord Rimini through his patronymic saint, and the chapel is filled with Malatestian emblems and Sigismondo's portraits. The piers of the chapel rest on sculpted elephants in the round and are decorated by 12 reliefs representing *Virtues* and shield-bearing figures. Two reliefs on the opposite wall portray *Angels Drawing Curtains*.

The highest quality of sculpture has been recognized in the reliefs of the Chapel of the Planets, for the extraordinary invention of their schemes, particularly of the landscapes, such as the *Flood*. The piers are decorated with 18 reliefs representing planetary figures. The reliefs on the Chapel of Isotta degli Atti, also on the right side of the church, portray *Music-Making Children* and *Children Bearing Emblems*. It also contains the tomb of Isotta degli Atti, which is covered with reliefs.

On the opposite side of the church are the Chapel of the Martyrs (Chapel of the Sybils), with 12 reliefs representing *Prophets* and *Sybils*; the Chapel of the Guardian Angel (Chapel of the Infant Games), with 18 reliefs representing *Playing Children*; and the Chapel of San Gaudenzio (Chapel of the Liberal Arts), whose 18 reliefs portray the *Liberal Arts*.

It remains a puzzling problem to distinguish the extent of Agostino's role in the Tempio Malatestiano from that of his collaborators, most of whose names are uncertain. It is particularly problematic to define the role of Matteo de' Pasti, well known as a medallist and documented also as an architect, and who was probably also a superlative marble sculptor. Matteo was strictly connected with the Malatestian court and is documented together with Agostino as working at the Tempio Malatestiano.

Agostino was also renowned for marble and stucco reliefs representing the *Virgin and Child with Angels*. His oeuvre includes many of these compositions, with half-figures in both high and low relief. This type of sculpture, in which Agostino seems to have special-

Relief portrait from San Sigismondo, Tempio Malatestiano
© Alinari / Art Resource, NY

ized, was typical of 15th-century Florentine work-shops, popular for private devotion. Agostino's works in this genre present many problems of dating and in distinguishing originals from copies.

Agostino's work is almost entirely limited to reliefs, and it is in this technique that his stylistic characteristics have been defined. These include the predilection for low relief for very flat and ample forms, and for simplified figures, such as those seen in the reliefs of the Chapel of the Infant Games in the Tempio Malatestiano. The main feature of Agostino's style, however, is the constant play of linear games and undulating rhythms. The reliefs with *Angels Drawing Curtains* in the Chapel of San Sigismondo are beautiful examples of the most characteristic linear style of Agostino, with their virtuoso handling of curved and wavy elements.

Critics have often used the word "archaism" to define Agostino's peculiar style, although fixing any reference point of origin is difficult. Critics have also assessed the importance of Agostino's production, particularly the Tempio Malatestiano reliefs, as being marginal to major Tuscan artistic trends for the development of northern Italian sculpture.

FRANCESCA PELLEGRINO

Biography

Born in Florence, Italy, 1418. After father's death, enrolled in company of Giovanni da Tolentino until 1433; probably trained outside Florence in the circle of Michelozzo di Bartolommeo and Donatello; worked in Modena, 1442; banned from Florence, 1446–63; worked in Vienna, 1446–49, in Rimini, 1449–56, in Perugia, 1457–61, and in Bologna, 1462–63; returned to Florence, 1463; enrolled in the sculptor's guild and continued working in Florence until 1473; worked in Perugia, 1473–81. Died in Perugia, Italy, after 1481 and before 1498.

Selected Works

1442	Altar antependium with four scenes from the story of San Gimignano; marble (dismembered); Cathedral of Modena, Italy
1449–56	Interior sculptural decoration (with collaborators); marble; Tempio Malatestiano, Rimini, Italy
ca. 1457–61	Architectural plan and facade sculptural decoration; marble; Oratory of San Bernardino, Perugia, Italy
ca. 1460s	*Virgin and Child with Angels* (Auvilliers Madonna); marble; Musée du Louvre, Paris, France
ca.	*Virgin and Child with Angels*; marble;

1460s	Victoria and Albert Museum, London, England
ca. 1460s	*Virgin and Child with Angels*; stucco; Bode Museum, Berlin, Germany
ca. 1460s	*Virgin and Child with Angels*; stucco; Museo Nazionale del Bargello, Florence, Italy
ca. 1460s	*Virgin and Child with Angels*; stucco; Thyssen Collection, Lugano, Italy

Further Reading

Borsi, Franco, "The Tempio Malatestiano," in *Leon Battista Alberti*, by Borsi, Oxford: Phaidon, 1977

Hope, Charles, "The Early History of the Tempio Malatestiano," *Journal of Warburg and Courtauld Institutes* 55 (1992)

Janson, Horst W., "The Beginnings of Agostino di Duccio," *Art Bulletin* 29 (1942)

Janson, Horst W., "An Unpublished Florentine Early Renaissance Madonna," *Jahrbuch der Hamburger Kunstsammlungen* 2 (1966)

Kokole, Stanko, "Agostino di Duccio in the Tempio Malatestiano, 1449–1457: Challenges of Poetic Invention and Fantasies of Personal Style," (dissertation), Baltimore: Johns Hopkins University, 1997

Mitchell, Charles, "The Imagery of the Tempio Malatestiano," *Studi Romagnoli* 2 (1951)

Pasini, Pier Giorgio, "Agostino (di Antonio) di Duccio," in *The Dictionary of Art*, edited by Jane Turner, vol. 1, New York: Grove, and London: Macmillan, 1998

Pope-Hennessy, John, *An Introduction to Italian Sculpture*, 3 vols., London: Phaidon, 1963; 4th edition, 1996; see especially vol. 2, *Italian Renaissance Sculpture*

Pope-Hennessy, John, and Ronald Lightbrow, *Catalogue of Italian Sculpture in the Victoria and Albert Museum*, 3 vols., London: HMSO, 1964; see especially vol. 3

Seymour, Charles, *Sculpture in Italy, 1400 to 1500*, London and Baltimore, Maryland: Penguin, 1966

ALBASTER

See **Gypsum, Alabaster, and "Egyptian" Alabaster**

ALBERT MEMORIAL

Sir George Gilbert Scott (1811–1878)
1863–1876
iron structure, gilded metalwork, mosaic work, marble and bronze sculptures, polished stone
h. 53 m
Kensington Gardens, London, England

The Albert Memorial was the largest and most significant of the memorial tributes built in response to Prince Albert's death (14 December 1861). Queen Victoria's initiative of creating a Royal Mausoleum at Frogmore, a memorial chapel at Windsor, and a cairn at Balmoral was followed by commissions of many statues to the prince by numerous towns across England. The idea of erecting a memorial in London was promoted by the lord mayor, William Cubitt, who convened a public meeting on 14 January 1862. There it was agreed that a memorial should be created that would be "monumental and national in character," approved of by the queen, and paid for by the people. Consequently, an organizing committee, including Charles Eastlake, director of the National Gallery, having abandoned the initial proposal to erect a monolithic granite obelisk, invited several architects to submit ideas for a personal monument to the prince (and for a memorial hall, eventually built as a private speculation between 1867 and 1871). In July 1862 entries were received from P.C. Hardwick, J. Pennethorne, T. Donaldson, M.D. Wyatt, E. Barry, and George Gilbert Scott. All the proposals showed a statue of the prince in an architectural setting, and all of them except Scott's were designed in the Classical style. Scott's scheme, as he indicated in his *Explanatory Remarks on the Design Submitted for the Memorial*, was in the Gothic style because this was not only the greatest style (the Eleanor crosses of Edward I being "the most touching monuments ever erected in this country to a Royal Consort") but also the style most closely associated with Victorian England. Scott's design was chosen; later it was modified.

The Albert Memorial confirmed Scott's reputation as the leading British architect of his day working in the Gothic style. Wanting to create an enlarged, modern version of a 13th-century jewelers' shrine to house a statue of the prince, Scott looked back to medieval precedents such as the Shrine of the Three Kings at Cologne and of St. Elizabeth at Marburg. He doubtless also looked to certain recent British memorials that were composed of a Gothic canopy over a seated figure, such as George Meickle Kemp's Walter Scott Memorial in Edinburgh (1836) and Thomas Worthington's Albert Memorial in Manchester, plans for which were illustrated in *The Builder* of November 1862, although Scott never admitted such influences. To create the expensive and elaborate effect he desired, Scott employed several different polychrome materials in a novel way for the external decorations, including gilded metalwork (carried out by F. Skidmore of Coventry) and mosaic work (the images of *Sculpture, Architecture, Painting*, and *Poetry* being designed by J.R. Clayton of Clayton and Bell and executed by A. Salviati of Murano). To ensure the solidity of his vast construction, Scott relied on the most up-to-date advice of engineers and used cast iron, a material that was still relatively new in the 1860s, to create a flèche, around which he designed the structure. The result did not please everyone: Henry Cole, the first director of the South Kensington Museum, for example, complained in his *Memorandum on Crosses and Shrines in England* (1863) of the shrine's lack of scholarship and taste.

Apart from its sheer size, its elaborate and complex sculptural program ensured the Albert Memorial's place at the head of all commemorative monuments in Victorian England. The program was meant to speak symbolically of the prince's belief in the providential and educational role of the arts and sciences, as well as of his own participation in England's endeavor to spread such benefits throughout the world. Scott designed the *Frieze of Parnassus* on the podium to show the world's greatest poets, musicians, artists, sculptors, and architects; in doing so he recalled similar schemes, such as Paul Delaroche's *Hemicycle* in the École des Beaux-Arts, Paris, and James Barry's murals at the Royal Society of Arts, London. To carve the 169 figures, Scott chose H.H. Armstead and J.B. Philip. Above the podium Scott envisaged two main groups of sculpture illustrating the arts and sciences that Prince Albert had fostered; the queen chose the sculptors to execute the work. The lower group represents the continents, which Albert had helped to bring together at the Great Exhibition of 1851: *Asia* was carved by J.H. Foley, *Africa* by W. Theed (who had worked for Prince Albert at Osborne House, East Cowes, Isle of Wight, England), *Europe* by P. MacDowell, and *America* by J. Bell. The upper group of sculptures represents the industrial arts, which Albert had promoted as president of both the Royal Society of Arts from 1846 and the British Association for the Advancement of Science from 1859: *Manufacture, Agriculture, Commerce*, and *Engineering*. These sculptures were carved by, respectively, H. Weekes (who had produced the first bust of Queen Victoria after her succession), W. Calder-Marshall, H. Thornycroft, and J. Lawlor. In addition, smaller figures in bronze set higher up the shrine represent *Geometry, Astronomy, Chemistry*, and *Geology*, as well as *Physiology, Rhetoric, Medicine*, and *Philosophy*, which were designed by Armstead and Philip. Toward the top of the shrine, Scott planned bronze sculptures representing the religious virtues of *Faith, Hope, Charity*, and *Humility*, intertwined between *Fortitude, Prudence, Justice*, and *Temperance*, and he chose J.J. Redfern to execute them. Finally, at the pinnacle are two tiers of gilt-bronze angels, carved by Philip, the lower showing attitudes of resignation toward worldly honors, the upper aspiration toward heavenly glory. While producing their work, many of the sculptors experienced difficulties, either artistic (much of the allegory was thought to be incomprehensible or overdone and had to be reworked) or practical (many deadlines were broken because the campanella marble proved exceedingly tough to work or the sculptors were overstretched with other commissions).

Sir George Gilbert Scott, Albert Memorial, London, England
The Conway Library, Courtauld Institute of Art

Reactions to the Albert Memorial were mixed. When the queen officially unveiled the shrine on 1 July 1872, she remarked that it was "really magnificent," and the press was enthusiastic; when, however, the statue of Albert joined the complex, there was no ceremony and comparatively little press interest. Throughout the monument's construction, Scott had had to put up with criticism from outsiders (some who said that the monument lacked unity and harmony, others that it was, in constructional terms, an elaborate sham), as well as from the sculptors (many of whom felt underpaid). Scott himself may have become wearied by the bureaucracy of the undertaking, and by the fact that the executive committee obliged him to work alongside John Kelk (because Kelk's offer to pay for building the memorial at cost price had been accepted by the committee) and to accept the queen's choice of sculptor sometimes for idiosyncratic reasons (for instance, Thornycroft, on account of his impoverished state). Yet today the *Albert Memorial* is recognized as Scott's masterpiece and, as one of the best-loved landmarks in London, it was recently conserved (1995–98) to its original magnificence.

SUSANNA AVERY-QUASH

Further Reading

Bayley, Stephen, *The Albert Memorial: The Monument in Its Social and Architectural Context*, London: Scolar Press, 1981

Brooks, Chris, *The Albert Memorial*, London: English Heritage, Victorian Society, Westminster City Council, 1995

Cole, David, *The Work of Sir Gilbert Scott*, London: Architectural Press, 1980

Cunningham, Colin, "The Albert Memorial," in *Academies, Museums, and Canons of Art*, edited by Gill Perry and Cunningham, New Haven, Connecticut: Yale University Press, 1999

Ferriday, Peter, "Syllabus in Stone," *Architectural Review* 135 (1964)

Sir Gilbert Scott (1811–1878), Architect of the Gothic Revival (exhib. cat.), London: Victoria and Albert Museum, 1978

Read, Benedict, *Victorian Sculpture*, New Haven, Connecticut: Yale University Press, 1982

Scott, George Gilbert, *Personal and Professional Recollections by the Late R.A. George Gilbert Scott, Sir*, edited by G. Gilbert Scott, London: Low Marston Searle and Rivington, 1879; new edition, as *Personal and Professional Recollections*, Stamford, Lincolnshire: Watkins, 1995

Victorian Society, *Save Albert: A Conference on the History, Present State, and Future of the Albert Memorial*, London: Victorian Society, 1993

Within the shrine Scott planned a large sculpture of *Prince Albert*, and once again the queen chose the sculptor. She selected Carlo Marochetti, probably because the prince had admired his work. The production of this statue proved to be quite a protracted affair. Marochetti was asked to alter the design for an equestrian statue he had submitted in the spring of 1867 but instead sent in a barely revised version at the end of the year; then, on 29 December, he died. Foley, asked to produce a new design, submitted one showing the prince seated on a throne. This too received criticism: John Bell, for instance, maintained that it would be more appropriate to portray Prince Albert as a Christian knight kneeling in prayer. Even when the queen approved Foley's design in December 1860, further delays occurred because of the complexity of casting the statue's 1500 component parts and the deaths of both Foley (in August 1874) and of Henry Prince, the head of the foundry firm (in early 1875). The task of assembling the statue was left to Thomas Brock, an assistant to Foley. Thus it was only on 9 March 1876 that the bronze sculpture, gilded in triple-thickness gold, was erected inside the canopy, an act that marked the completion of the Albert Memorial. The project had taken nearly 15 years to complete and had cost £137,000. Scott, for his labors, received £5000 and a knighthood.

ALEIJADINHO (ANTÔNIO FRANCISCO LISBOA) *ca.* 1739–1814 *Brazilian*

The Baroque period in Brazil lasted throughout the colonial period, from the mid 16th to the end of the

18th century, and found its height in the gold and diamond mining province of Minas Gerais ("general mines"), a time and place so rich in poetry, architecture, painting, and sculpture that it has been identified as the *barroco mineiro* (Minas Baroque). Its leading artist was the singularly expressive sculptor Antônio Francisco Lisboa, known as Aleijadinho. This sobriquet means "little cripple," from the Portuguese word *aleijado* (crippled), and was given to the artist after he became handicapped in midlife.

Aleijadinho, who was of mixed race (not uncommon among colonial artisans), received his training from his Portuguese father, a leading local architect. Aleijadinho also learned drawing and carving from artists who collaborated with his father. Aleijadinho's father was an émigré, like many skilled workers who had emigrated to Minas Gerais and other parts of Brazil to advance their careers. Many clergy also came to Minas Gerais. The emerging society was organized in lay brotherhoods of religious orders. The building of richly decorated churches asserted social status and was also meant to help expiate for sins committed in the libertine frontier environment.

Aleijadinho worked primarily and initially in Ouro Prêto, the capital of Minas Gerais. As his fame grew, he and his staff were called to the surrounding towns, eventually even to the viceregal court at Rio de Janeiro. Aleijadinho worked mainly in wood, principally cedar, and soapstone (*pedra de sabão*). He was sensitive to his status as a bastard of mixed blood, but his contemporaries nonetheless recognized and keenly sought his talent.

It is sometimes difficult to authenticate works by Aleijadinho. As his fame spread, others copied him. Moreover, he worked in teams with others artists, and items were not individually signed. Receipts for bills are often the only way of authenticating a work. Before the onset of disease in 1777, probably leprosy, Aleijadinho had an effulgent, bohemian character; after the crippling disease, however, he turned morose and introverted. Although 1777 marked a change in the character and technique of his work, it did not witness a change in his productivity, which continued in intensity until shortly before his death at about the age of 80. Because of his handicaps, his three slaves had to carry him and attach the instruments for his sculpting to his gnarled hands and fingers. As his physical handicaps increased, he trained his slaves to carve for him, following his instructions.

Of the hundreds of statues, altars, pulpits, fonts, communion rails, and choral balustrades that Aleijadinho produced, he is most noted for his work on two structures: the Church of São Francisco de Assis in Ouro Prêto, and the pilgrimage complex at the Church of Bom Jesus do Matosinhos in Congonhas do Campo.

São Francisco is most representative of his church interiors, which feature a unity of composition and refinement of detail that convey the triumph and glory of faith and devotion. There is a sense of robust yet serene assurance. The elaborate arches and overhead sculpture of the main doorways contrast with the immediate surround of the building fronts, which are bare and white or light gray. This counterpoint of richness and spareness conveys a feeling of stark benevolence and dignified authority.

The stone and wooden statuary at the architectural complex of Congonhas do Campo is Aleijadinho's crowning achievement and gives expression to his acute suffering and austere spirituality. The complex follows a pattern typical of similar pilgrimage sites then existing in Catholic Europe. Entering the complex, one follows an ascending zigzag path (representing the path to Calvary), along which at each angular point is a sanctuary containing a life-size portrayal of a scene from the Way of the Cross. The painted wooden figures are extraordinarily natural, and one advances

Two of the Statues of the Twelve Prophets, Church of Bom Jesus do Matosinhos, Brazil
© Julia Waterlow; Eye Ubiquitous / CORBIS

along the route increasingly moved. The veins of a hand, the muscles of a leg, the drape of a robe, the reflection in a face are absorbingly conveyed. Most majestic is the first scene, that of the Last Supper of Christ and the Twelve Apostles. Most moving are the latter scenes, showing the flagellation and the crowning with thorns, the figure of Jesus bearing pain with subdued dignity.

Completing the way of the cross, one comes to a terrace of steps rising to the Church of Bom Jesus do Matosinhos. Twelve prophets rise on pedestals along the side walls of the steps. Their individualized and distinct faces and gestures, stark against the arching sky, convey a sense of power. One is struck by the serene firmness of their eyes and mouths and the urgency of their gestures. The clothing is a curious hybrid, the figures shod as they are in boots (having come from afar with their messages), wearing Old Testament robes that hang almost like contemporary frocks, and their heads crowned with imperious turbans. The head and body of each figure reinforces the prophets' declamations announcing the immediacy of God's Word. The path that the pilgrim has just encountered in the way of the Cross serves to confirm the veracity of these prophets' messages.

EDWARD A. RIEDINGER

Biography

Born in Ouro Prêto, Minas Gerais, Brazil, *ca.* 1739. Son of locally noted Portuguese architect, Manuel Francisco da Costa Lisboa, and one of his slaves. At baptism, he received his father's name and was manumitted; thereby he was able to be a free laborer but was unable to inherit his father's property; worked mainly in the province of Minas Gerais and in the towns of Ouro Prêto, São João, and Sabará; an anonymous disease, probably leprosy, left him handicapped, 1777; had one son, whom he trained to help him; confined to bed for the last two years of his life, he was nursed by his daughter-in-law, a midwife and the primary oral source of information on his life as recounted to Rodrigo José Ferreira Bretas. Died in Ouro Prêto, Brazil, 18 November 1814.

Selected Works

1766–94 Main altar and sanctuary; wood; Church of São Francisco de Assis, Ouro Prêto, Brazil

1796–99 64 life-size wooden statues for seven scenes in six sanctuaries of the Way of the Cross: *The Last Supper*, *Agony in the Garden*, *Betrayal*, *Flagellation*, *Crowning with Thorns*, *Road to Calvary*, *Crucifixion*; painted wood; Church of Bom Jesus do Matosinhos, Congonhas do Campo, Brazil

1800–05 Twelve Old Testament prophets; stone; Church of Bom Jesus do Matosinhos, Congonhas do Campo, Brazil

Further Reading

"Antônio Francisco Lisboa, 'O Aleijadinho,'" *Latin American Research Review* 2 (1974)

Bazin, Germain, *L'architecture religieuse baroque au Brésil*, 2 vols., São Paulo, Brazil: Museu de Arts, 1956–58

Bretas, Rodrigo José Ferreira, *Antônio Francisco Lisboa, o Aleijadinho*, Rio de Janeiro: Directoria do Patrimônio Histórico e Artístico Nacional, 1951

Costa, Lúcio, "Antônio Francisco Lisboa, o 'Aleijadinho,'" in *O universeo mágico do barroco brasileiro*, São Paulo, Brazil: SESI, 1998

Jorge, Fernando, *O Aleijadinho: Sua vida, sua obra, seu gênio*, 2nd edition, Rio de Janeiro: Buccini, 1961; 6th edition, São Paulo, Brazil: Difel, 1984

Laclette, René, *O Aleijadinho e suas doenças*, Rio de Janeiro: Cátedra, 1976

Machado, Lourival Gomes, and Eduardo Airosa, *Reconquista de Congonhas*, Rio de Janeiro: Ministerio da Educacão e Cultura, Institute Nacional do Livro, 1960

Mann, Hans, *The Twelve Prophets of Antonio Francisco Lisboa "O Aleijadinho"*, Rio de Janeiro: Ministerio da Educacão e Cultura, 1958

Oliveira, Myriam Andrade Ribeiro de, *Passos da paixão: O Aleijadinho* (bilingual Portuguese-English edition), Rio de Janeiro: Alumbramento, 1984

ALESSANDRO ALGARDI 1598–1654
Italian

Alessandro Algardi is one of the most important Italian sculptors of the Baroque period, second only to Gianlorenzo Bernini. He was trained first as a draftsman at Lodovico Carracci's Accademia degli Incaminati and then as a sculptor under Giulio Cesare Conventi. In 1622 he left his native Bologna for Mantua, where he entered the service of Duke Ferdinando Gonzaga. The duke recommended Algardi to his first patron in Rome, Cardinal Ludovico Ludovisi, when Algardi decided to visit the city in 1625.

Ludovisi employed Algardi to restore his collection of antique statuary, such as the *Torchbearer*. The *Torchbearer* is Algardi's first known marble sculpture, with all of his previous works having been executed in either stucco or clay. The tension between the figure's stance and its torso is typical of Algardi's approach to restoration; he would alter a figure's appearance to correct what he considered to be its limitations. Although Algardi continued throughout his career to work as a restorer, in 1628/29 he received his first commission for an original public work: two stucco figures representing saints Mary Magdalene and John the Evangelist. The heightened sense of emotion found in the *St. Mary Magdalene* shows Algardi's debt to Bernini's *St. Bibiana* (1624–26; Santa Bibiana, Rome), whereas the emphasis placed on its formal characteristics invites a comparison to François du Quesnoy's *St. Susanna* (1629–33; Church of Santa Maria di Loreto, Rome). This latter quality led contemporary critics such as Giovanni Pietro Bellori to place Algardi within a school of Classical artists who rejected the more flamboyant aspects of Baroque art.

In 1634 Algardi received his first commission for a monumental work, the tomb of Pope Leo XI (completed in 1644) in St. Peter's Basilica in Rome. The monument shows Leo XI enthroned above his urn and flanked by the allegorical figures of *Magnanimity* and *Liberality*. Algardi borrowed this design from Bernini's tomb of Urban VIII (1627–47), which is located in the same church. He departed from earlier papal tombs by artists like Guglielmo della Porta by representing the pope's image in marble instead of bronze. The monument was highly regarded by Algardi's contemporaries and became the standard model for later papal tombs such as Camillo Rusconi's tomb of Gregory XIII (1715–23; St. Peter's Basilica, Rome). Rusconi was the pupil of Ercole Ferrata, who some scholars believe carved one of the allegorical figures on Algardi's tomb.

Algardi received two other major commissions in 1634. The first was for the group *The Beheading of St. Paul* for the high altar of the Church of S. Paolo Maggiore in Bologna. Algardi modeled his design on Bolognese sculptural altarpieces executed in the round, but he rendered the work in marble instead of the traditional terracotta. The second commission was for *St. Philip Neri with an Angel*. Despite the highly dramatic character of its subject, the figures within the scene show little emotion. This same tendency appears in Algardi's portrait busts in this period, as in his bust for the tomb of Cardinal Giovanni Garzia Mellini, which emphasizes the sitter's physiognomy over his devotion. This sense of apathy became a standard feature of Algardi's work, reflecting his belief that the primary goal of the artist was to maintain artistic decorum, not to invoke emotion.

Through projects such as these, Algardi's reputation steadily increased, and under the pontificate of Innocent X he became the preferred artist of papal circles. One of his strongest supporters was the pope's nephew, Camillo Pamphilj, who assigned him the task of building and decorating the family estate, Villa Doria Pamphilj. Another major project from this period is the Fountain of St. Damasus, the first of a series of fountains designed by Algardi. Both contemporary and modern critics have commented on the fountain's small scale, which does not sufficiently meet the requirements of its site. Algardi solved this problem in his monumental relief *Pope Leo Driving Attila from Rome* (1646–53; St. Peter's Basilica, Rome) by altering the monument's design to coincide with its format instead of trying to make its format fit his design.

In 1648 Algardi received his most prestigious commission to date, a bronze statue representing Innocent X for the Palazzo dei Conservatori. Intended to commemorate the pope's building program, the sculpture was unveiled in 1650, which was designated by the Roman Catholic Church as a holy year. Despite a disastrous first casting that forced Algardi to leave the work somewhat unfinished, it was immediately considered to be a masterpiece, said to surpass even the work of Bernini, whose statue of Urban VIII (1635–40) had served as its model. Yet it is not the statue of Innocent X that represents the height of Algardi's mature style; rather, it is the high altar of the Church of S. Nicola da Tolentino that does so. Illustrating the vision and miraculous cure of St. Nicholas, the altarpiece shows the saint and the subjects of his vision in various states of relief and set within an unusual, curved niche. By using a curved niche, borrowed once again from contemporary Bolognese sculptors, Algardi solved the spatial problems inherent to relief sculpture, such as the distortion of figures when observed from certain viewpoints.

Such innovations continued to influence generations of artists after Algardi's death in 1654. Algardi's style is particularly evident in works executed by artists who served as his assistants, such as Ercole Ferrata's *Martyrdom of St. Emerenziana* (begun 1660; Church of Sant'Agnese in Agone, Rome) and Domenico Guidi's *Lamentation over the Body of Christ* (1667–76; Cappella Monte di Pietà, Rome). Both Ferrata and Guidi became prominent sculptors in their own right and used models and casts after Algardi's to train their own students. Algardi's fame reached its height in the 18th century when he was praised by Neoclassical critics for the simplicity and clarity of his designs, which inspired sculptors such as Rusconi and Edmé Bouchardon.

DAVID L. BERSHAD AND GABRIELLA SZALAY

See also **Bernini, Gianlorenzo; Ferrata, Ercole; Guidi, Domenico; Rusconi, Camillo**

Biography

Born in Bologna, Italy, 31 July 1598. Trained in Bologna at the Accademia degli Incaminati under Lodovico Carracci; took up sculpture, receiving instruction from Giulio Cesare Conventi; moved to Mantua, 1622; settled in Rome, 1625; received first commission for original public works, 1628; received first commission for monumental work, tomb of Pope Leo XI, 1634; became unofficial papal sculptor under Innocent X, 1640s. Member of the Accademia di San Luca, 1630; elected censor, 1633. Died in Rome, Italy, 10 June 1654.

Selected Works

1626	*Torchbearer*; marble; Museo delle Terme, Rome, Italy
1628–29	*St. John the Evangelist*; stucco; Bandini Chapel, San Silvestro al Quirinale, Rome, Italy
1628–29	*St. Mary Magdalene*; stucco; Bandini Chapel, San Silvestro al Quirinale, Rome, Italy
1634–38	*St. Philip Neri with an Angel*; marble; Church of Santa Maria in Vallicella, Rome, Italy
1634–44	Tomb of Pope Leo XI; marble; St. Peter's Basilica, Rome, Italy
1634–48	*The Beheading of St. Paul*; marble; Church of San Paolo Maggiore, Bologna, Italy
1637–38	Tomb of Giovanni Garzia Mellini; marble; Chapel of St. Nicholas of Tolentino, Church of Santa Maria del Popolo, Rome, Italy
1646–48	Fountain of St. Damasus; marble; Cortile San Damaso, Vatican, Rome, Italy
1646–53	*Pope Leo Driving Attila from Rome*; marble; St. Peter's Basilica, Rome, Italy
1648–50	*Pope Innocent X*; bronze; Palazzo dei Conservatori, Rome, Italy
1651–55	Altar of St. Nicholas of Tolentino; marble; Church of San Nicola da Tolentino, Rome, Italy

Further Reading

Cellini, Antonia Nava, *La scultura del Seicento*, Turin: UTET, 1982

Heimbürger Ravalli, Minna, *Alessandro Algardi scultore*, Rome: Istituto di Studi Romani, 1973

Montagu, Jennifer, "Alessandro Algardi's Altar of S. Nicola da Tolentino and Some Related Models," *The Burlington Magazine* 112 (1970)

Montagu, Jennifer, "Alessandro Algardi and the Statue of St. Philip Neri," *Jahrbuch der Hamburger Kunstsammlungen* 22 (1977)

Montagu, Jennifer, *Alessandro Algardi*, 2 vols., New Haven, Connecticut: Yale University Press, 1985

Raggio, Olga, "Alessandro Algardi e gli stucchi di Villa Pamphili," *Paragone* 251 (1971)

Seine, Harriet F., "The Tomb of Leo XI by Alessandro Algardi," *Art Bulletin* 60 (1978)

Wittkower, Rudolf, "Algardi's Relief of Pope Liberius Baptizing Neophytes," *Bulletin of the Minneapolis Institute of Arts* 49 (1960)

POPE LEO DRIVING ATTILA FROM ROME

Alessandro Algardi; (1598–1654)

1646–1653

marble

h. 7.5 m

St. Peter's Basilica, Rome, Italy

Alessandro Algardi's monumental relief *Pope Leo Driving Attila from Rome*, executed for the altar of Pope Leo I, depicts the encounter between St. Leo the Great and Attila the Hun in 452. According to the *Liber Pontificalis* and the *Chronicles* of St. Antoninus, Leo brought an end to Attila's invasion of Italy at this meeting. It was said that when he confronted Attila, Sts. Peter and Paul miraculously appeared in the sky, each carrying a sword and commanding the Huns to retreat. Algardi represents the moment in which the saints appear, visible only to Attila, who withdraws in terror.

The congregation of the Reverenda Fabricca di S. Pietro, charged with overseeing the commission, selected this subject because of its relevance to the life of Pope Leo and the papacy in general. Leo the Great, who wrote extensively on the theme of papal primacy, was the first pope to refer to himself as the successor of Peter. The legend of his encounter with Attila alludes to the absolute power of the papacy, which is represented by the two swords held by Peter and Paul and mentioned in the Gospel of Luke as symbols of the spiritual and worldly authority conferred upon Peter by Christ. The legend also establishes the pope as the earthly successor of Peter, who comes to defend his heir. Papal primacy was an issue of great debate in the first half of the 16th century, as the movement of Jansenism questioned the power and authority of the pope. Within this context, Leo's repulsion of Attila was intended to show that the papacy, and by extension the Roman Catholic Church, would overcome heresy, which was symbolized by the Huns.

Although the subject of the altarpiece was determined as early as 1626, it took nearly 30 years to complete. Its complicated history begins in 1626 when Urban VIII erected an altar dedicated to Leo I in the southwest corner chapel of St. Peter's Basilica. The same year that the altar was erected, Guido Reni was commissioned to paint its altarpiece. When nothing came of this commission, the project was passed on to the painter Giuseppe Cesari (Il Cavaliere d'Arpino), whose death in 1640 once again prevented its completion. The painter Giovanni Lanfranco then wrote to

Cardinal Franceso Barberini, one of the members of the congregation, asking for the assignment and providing some preliminary sketches for his approval. His petition was unsuccessful, and the project was abandoned. When Innocent X assumed the papal throne in 1644, he renewed efforts to complete the altarpiece in preparation for the upcoming jubilee in 1650. For a variety of reasons, including concern over conservation and papal image, it was determined that the altarpiece should be carved and not painted. Algardi's connection with papal circles, particularly with members of the congregation, ensured his selection for the project.

When Algardi began work on the altarpiece in January 1646, he was faced with a number of challenges. The foremost of these were the dimensions of the site, which were tall and narrow and did not accord well with the congregation's instructions to represent the expansive entourage of Attila and Leo. A preliminary terracotta model (*ca.* 1646; Museo Nazionale del Bargello, Florence) shows that Algardi had to reduce his composition at least once in order to comply with these dimensions. Another problem was the poor lighting in the chapel. According to Passeri, the artists were also concerned that their work would be compared with Raphael's fresco of the same subject (1513–14; Stanza d'Eliodoro, Vatican). Although Raphael's fresco certainly served as an important prototype, the congregation specifically instructed that Pope Leo be the focus of attention and be brought to the fore in order to facilitate devotion. Both of these characteristics are absent in Raphael's composition, which places greater emphasis on Attila and his vision.

These problems were resolved in part by altering the iconography traditionally associated with the repulsion of Attila. Instead of representing the pope and king on horseback, as did Raphael and Lanfranco, Algardi placed them on foot. This brought Leo and Attila into the immediate foreground and enabled Algardi to use the available space to greater advantage. Algardi also altered the general structure of the relief, departing from the Classical and Renaissance practice of representing all objects, regardless of their distance to the viewer, on the same picture plane. He instead divided the image into three distinct levels, consisting of high, medium, and low relief, to give an illusion of depth. Algardi also abandoned the rules of perspective, eliminating all fixed viewpoints and overlapping his figures. This technique is typical of his reliefs and was already evident in his first relief on the urn of St. Ignatius of Loyola (*ca.* 1629; Gesù, Rome). Outlines created by a running drill around some of the background figures in *Pope Leo Driving Attila from Rome* suggest that this approach was not wholly successful.

Pope Leo Driving Attila from Rome
© Scala / Art Resource, NY

Before Algardi, only a few artists, such as Pietro Bernini, had attempted to correct the spatial problems inherent in relief. This is partially because relief sculpture during this period was rare, and none of the existing examples were on the same scale as the altarpiece in question. As a result, Algardi's relief became highly influential and initiated a vogue for sculpted altarpieces. The plans for the Church of S. Agnese in Rome, for example, called for all of the altars to be decorated with sculptures, not paintings. Algardi's assistants, particularly Domenico Guidi who worked with him on *Pope Leo Driving Attila from Rome*, were instrumental in this resurgence of interest in sculpted altarpieces. Guidi's *Lamentation* (1659–76; Chapel of Monte di Pietà, Rome), for example, borrowed Algardi's technique of overlapping figures to create a sense of depth, but unlike Algardi, Guidi was not concerned with creating a coherent sense of space. This illustrates the fundamental difference between Algardi and other sculptors of the period, warranting the praise of one

39

contemporary who claimed that the relief deserved to "be put on a level with the antique."

DAVID L. BERSHAD AND GABRIELLA SZALAY

Further Reading

Bershad, David, "Domenico Guidi: Some New Attributions," *Antologia di Belle Arti* 1 (1977)

Giardini, Claudio, *Considerazioni intorno ad un modello per Attila*, Rome: Paleani, 1989

Lavagnino, Emilio, *Altari barocchi in Roma*, Rome: Bancodi Rome, 1959

Magnuson, Torgil, *Rome in the Age of Bernini*, 2 vols., Stockholm: Almqvist and Wiksell, 1982; Atlantic Highlands, New Jersey: Humanities Press, 1986

Montagu, Jennifer, *Alessandro Algardi*, 2 vols., New Haven, Connecticut: Yale University Press, 1985

Neumann, Enno, *Mehrfigurige Reliefs von Alessandro Algardi: Genese, Analyse, Ikonographie*, Frankfurt and New York: Peter Lang, 1985

Passeri, Giovanni Battista, *Vite de pittori, scultori, et architetti che anno lavarato in Roma, morte dal 1641 fino al 1673*, edited by Jacob Hess, Rome: Settari, 1772; reprint, Bologna, Italy: Forni, 1976

Preimesburger, Rudolf, "Eine Peripetie in Stein? Bemerkungen zu Alessandro Algardis Relief der Begegnung Leos des Grossen mit Attila," *Aachener Kunstblätter* 60 (1994)

Rice, Louise, *The Altars and Altarpieces of New St. Peter's (1621–1653)*, Cambridge and New York: Cambridge University Press, 1997

Schleier, Erich, "Drawings by Lanfranco for the Altar of St. Leo the Great in St. Peter's," *Master Drawings* 5 (1967)

Ullman, Walter, "Leo I and the Theme of Papal Primacy," *Journal of Theological Studies* 11/1 (1960)

ALTARPIECE: NORTHERN EUROPE

There is a distinction in meaning between the terms "altar" and "altarpiece." An altar (Latin *mensa* [table]) is the table or block at which the priest celebrates Mass and consecrates the bread and wine by which they become the Body and Blood of Christ, according to Roman Catholic doctrine based on the words of Jesus Christ in the Gospels. The altar is therefore a critical piece of furniture used in the celebration of the Mass. Altarpieces, in contrast, are optional additions of Christian imagery. Usually located behind the altar itself, altarpieces vary considerably in size, form, and subject. The earliest surviving altarpieces date back to the 12th century, and by the 15th century, altarpieces became such large productions that a workshop, guided by a master artisan who was aided by multiple assistants, would require a few years to complete just one.

The sources of altarpiece designs and subject matter appear to be closely related to antependiums, pieces of church furniture made of precious woven materials, painted tempera panels, relief sculpture in wood, metal, or stone, etc., that are placed in front of the altar.

Compositional elements common to both altarpieces and antependiums include columns, arcades, and tracery in addition to figurative work. An unusual example is found in the high altar in Cologne Cathedral. Surrounded with freestanding sculpture and an arcade with tracery, the Cologne altar shows similarities to other altarpieces (for example, the *Retable de Champmol* discussed below) as well as early antependiums. Apostles, Old Testament prophets, Christ, and the Virgin, to mention a few, are placed inside arches while tiny finials mimic the architectural ornament of a Gothic cathedral. The penchant for architectural forms, figurative scenes, and organic vegetation becomes a defining characteristic of altarpieces by the 15th century, particularly in Germany and the Low Countries.

The configuration of altarpieces varies from simple to complex. In its most simple form an altarpiece would have a central panel, either painted or sculpted, and perhaps a modest frame decorated with foliate or architectural ornament. Altarpieces from the 12th century have this sort of design—perhaps a single panel painted in tempera, high-relief sculpture carved into a stone slab, or *repoussé* metalwork (the method of producing relief metal by hammering and punching chiefly from behind). Altarpieces became more complex during the 15th century as more elements were added. Those altarpieces that opened and closed were called "winged" or "transformational" altarpieces (*Flügelaltar* or *Wandelaltar*). Wings were attached to the outside edge of the central panel and, since panels and wings were often painted on both sides, multiple "transformations" could be seen. The first transformation is the appearance with the outer wings closed. With the second transformation, the reverse sides of the outer wings are revealed along with the central inside panel. Dated to about 1399, the *Retable de Champmol* represents this type. The central panel (Latin *corpus*; German *Schrein*) is comprised of a shallow box to house sculpture. Carved in wood and gilded by the Flemish sculptor Jacques de Baerze, gables, pinnacles, and tracery designs provide the setting for the Crucifixion and adoration of the Magi. The two moveable wings, painted by Melchior Broederlam, open and close to reveal the central scene. The Champmol altarpiece represents a typical altarpiece configuration in which sculpture and painted panels are combined.

Combination altarpieces appear throughout Europe, yet they are more concentrated in the northernmost regions of Germany, Scandinavia, the Baltic, and the southern Netherlands. Lynn Jacobs has suggested that standardized altarpieces were carved in Brussels and Antwerp and sold at open fairs to international visitors (see Jacobs, 1989). Since they were not made for particular patrons, innovation in these altarpieces gave way to formulized designs of little artistic influence, despite rehearsed craftsmanship. Through export and trade, no doubt eased by the active Hanseatic League in the northernmost regions of Europe (in England and the Baltic), large numbers of such altarpieces were disseminated. Pattern books and single-leaf prints also influenced the design of carved altarpieces. Master HL, also known as the Master of the Breisach Altarpiece, is thought to be both an engraver and sculptor since his prints and three-dimensional works possess striking similarities. Prints and pattern books would have inspired sketches and designs (German *Visierung*) that were used to show the patron the overall design of the finished product. In particular, the engraver Master ES appears to have exerted significant influence on sculptural designs during the last quarter of the 15th century through the circulation of his prints.

Some altarpieces were entirely carved of wood. Known as *Schnitzaltar* (carved altar) in German, examples primarily appear in the Netherlands and Germany. The most celebrated German sculptors included Michael Pacher, Veit Stoss, and Tilman Riemenschneider (who was unique in avoiding polychromy in favor of monochrome and natural wood tones). Jan Borman the Elder and his Altarpiece of St. George is an impressive Netherlandish example. Deeply carved sculpture, placed inside a boxlike setting, is situated in the foreground, while a continuous row of elaborate, late Gothic arcades hang above like a theatrical curtain. Contained within one long rectangular composition that is itself divided into seven compartments (two wings and a corpus), scenes from the life of St. George run across the front in a continuous narrative format.

Artisans continued to make wooden altarpieces with wings, but after 1500, wingless, monumental limestone and marble altars became equally popular. This change from wood to marble corresponds to a change in style. The *Moritzbrunneraltar* carved in stone by Loy Hering not only shows a change in material and format, it also illustrates the dramatic shift from Gothic tracery and ornamentation carved of wood to the Italian-inspired curved hemicycles and classical columns carved in fine limestone. When Hering's altarpiece was carved in 1548, the forms of the Italian Renaissance had already become commonplace in northern Europe. Alongside Gothic pinnacles, pointed arches, and delicate tracery, the Italian-inspired smooth columns, Renaissance capitals, and a noticeable absence of Gothic ornamentation found common use in northern Europe during the 16th century.

During the Reformation and Baroque periods in northern Europe, carved altarpieces gave way to painted altarpieces like those found in Renaissance Italy. Tombs, epitaphs, and secular works of sculpture (such as fountains) also began to replace the graven images so detested by Protestants. Counter Reformation sculpture in northern Europe, especially in lower Germany and the Rhine-Meuse area of the Netherlands, appeared during the 16th century but only in the form of individual saints and not entire altarpieces. In fact, patronage of altarpieces was all but eliminated and, in their place, more fundamental themes such as depictions of the Last Supper, or even quotations from the Bible were called for instead.

KEVIN McMANAMY

See also **Antependium; Hering, Loy; Netherlands and Belgium; Pacher, Michael; Riemenschneider, Tilman**

Further Reading

Baxandall, Michael, *The Limewood Sculptors of Renaissance Germany*, New Haven, Connecticut: Yale University Press, 1980

Braun, Joseph, *Der christliche Altar in seiner geschichtlichen Entwicklung*, 2 vols., Munich: Alte Meister Guenther Koch, 1924

Humfrey, Peter, and Martin Kemp (editors), *The Altarpiece in the Renaissance*, Cambridge and New York: Cambridge University Press, 1990

Huth, Hans, *Künstler und Werkstatt der Spätgotik*, Augsburg, Germany: Filser, 1923; 2nd edition, Darmstadt, Germany: Wissenschaftliche Buchgesellschaft, 1967

Jacobs, Lynn F, "The Marketing and Standardization of South Netherlandish Carved Altarpieces: Limits on the Role of the Patron," *Art Bulletin* 72 (1989)

Reinle, Adolf, *Die Ausstattung deutscher Kirchen im Mittelaltar: Eine Einfürung*, Darmstadt, Germany: Wissenschaftliche Buchgesellschaft, 1988

Schmitt, Otto (editor), *Reallexikon zur deutschen Kunstgeschichte*, Stuttgart, Germany: Metzler, 1937

ALTARPIECE: SOUTHERN EUROPE

Any discussion of sculptured altarpieces in Italy from the Middle Ages through the Baroque period is, like that of many liturgical furnishings, conditioned by the issue of their survival. Altarpieces were among the most elaborate and expensive of church furnishings, but the liturgy did not, in fact, require their presence. Church directives necessitated that the altar be treated with the utmost cleanliness and respect; in order to reflect the highest honor, decorative enrichment of altars thus became the norm. Sculptured decoration in particular, inherently costly, admirably expressed the dignity of the altar in Christian worship.

Altarpiece development in southern Europe corresponded with a new liturgical focus: the increasing tendency of the priest to move to the front of the altar, with his back to the laity. When the priest celebrated Mass *versus populum*, facing the congregation from behind the table, the frontal (antependium) had constituted the major decoration of the altar. The priest's change of position obscured the front of the altar but conversely provided a new focal point for decorative enrichment. Placed at the back of or behind the altar, a panel with appropriate imagery emphasized the raising of the consecrated Host, the most dramatic moment of the Mass ritual.

Rectangular panels originally intended as altar frontals were sometimes moved to the back of the *mensa* (altar table) to serve as altarpieces. An early example of this type of adaptation, the *Pala d'Oro*, originally created (1102–18) as an antependium for the high altar of the Basilica of San Marco, Venice, was enlarged and moved in 1209 to its position above the altar table between the rear columns of the ciborium (stationary altar canopy). An elaborate gilded silver framework, set with precious stones and enclosing numerous enamels of holy figures and narrative scenes of Christ and St. Mark, dominates the San Marco altarpiece. Altarpieces began to appear regularly by the 12th century, and sculptors created rectangular panels in higher relief intended specifically as altarpieces. The silver retable in the Cathedral of Pistoia (1287), dedicated to St. James, displays multiple saints in niches, narrative reliefs, and Christ enthroned at the top in a *mandorla* (an almond-shaped aureole). Increasingly complex, altarpieces began to break the confines of a strict rectangular format. The most expensive were made of metal, but more commonly, sculptors used wood, marble, and other types of stone in sculptured altarpieces of the late Middle Ages. Parallel to contemporary 13th-century Tuscan painted retables (for example, the *Saint Francis* panel of 1235 in San Francesco, Pescia, Italy), altarpieces also developed with single figures of saints, carved in stone relief or freestanding in a tabernacle. The earliest of these can be found in Venice; indeed, northeastern Italy in general appears to have had a strong tradition of sculptured altarpieces.

By the 14th century, the new orders of mendicants, the Franciscans and Dominicans, began to commission altarpieces to decorate their newly built Gothic-style churches. Wider altar tables provided a stable base for larger sculpted marble or wood altarpieces, which often took the form of Gothic triptychs and polyptychs. Similar to contemporary examples in northern Europe, the high altar of the Church of S. Francesco in Bologna (1388–92), for instance, features a multistoried freestanding marble structure, crowned by a Crucifixion atop a tall central pinnacle, above a standing Virgin and Child. Multiple saints in niches flank a coronation of the Virgin, and a *predella* (carved panel at the base of the altarpiece) holds narrative scenes. In the Iberian Peninsula in the late Middle Ages, the *retablo* (high altarpiece) grew to enormous dimensions. Both Portugal and northern Spain were heavily influenced by the Franco-Flemish artists, and huge Gothic polychrome wood *retablos* remained the norm into the early 16th

century. The *retablo* of the Cathedral of Seville (1482) fills the wall of the sanctuary, and its rich wood polychrome and gilded carvings are divided into compartments and surrounded by an elaborate Gothic frame. In Portugal especially, the Gothic style was affected by the area of Iberian exploration: nautical motifs, seashells, and exotic animals enrich the decorative vocabulary of many altarpieces. Unlike Italy, wood remained the traditional medium for sculpted altarpieces in Spain and Portugal and was transmitted eventually to altarpieces for colonial churches in the Americas.

The long-standing Italian tradition of a ciborium over the altar gave birth to a new type of sculpted altarpiece in the 14th century. Andrea Orcagna's magnificent combination of sculptural decoration and architectural framework (1359) for the Florentine Church of Orsanmichele, his altar-tabernacle enshrining a miracle-working Madonna, provides a significant example of an Italian type that was to be transformed by *all'antica* (after the antique) decoration in the next century.

Sculptors in the 15th century invigorated altarpieces, among the first monuments to partake of Renaissance classicism, with the new architectural paradigm. Relief sculpture in particular underwent a transformation, all but eliminating the pictorial barrier between sculpture and painting. Creating an illusion of depth within a single field, artists sculpted altarpieces with rich *all'antica* frameworks and illusionistic narrative scenes, such as Antonio Rossellino's *Adoration of the Shepherds* (*ca.* 1470–75) in the Church of S. Anna dei Lombardi, Naples. Moreover, Donatello had provided a crucial precedent for sculptural versions of the *sacra conversazione* (grouping of the Madonna and Child with saints) type so prevalent in contemporary painted retables: the elaborate bronze altarpiece (*ca.* 1445–54) for the Basilica of Sant'Antonio in Padua, with multiple life-size, freestanding figures surrounding the Virgin and Child and boldly illusionistic narrative reliefs. Many artists, particularly in northern Italy, took their cue from Donatello's groundbreaking imagery, creating relief versions of the Virgin and Child surrounded by saints and united in a single field.

The 15th century had seen a new focus on the iconography of the Blessed Sacrament, and more complex altar structures were frequently designed to incorporate reservation of the Host. In the 16th century, Counter Reformation edicts proscribed Eucharistic reservation anywhere except the high altar (with rare pontifical exceptions), modifying and transforming altarpieces in the Roman Catholic world. This transition is dramatically demonstrated by a quattrocento monument, Vecchietta's free-standing bronze Eucharistic tabernacle crowned by a figure of the Risen Christ (*ca.* 1476), which was incorporated into the high altar of Siena Cathedral in 1532. After the Council of Trent, particularly, altarpieces of the Roman Church increased in size and uniformity of purpose. The design of later 16th-century altarpieces clearly reflects the Counter Reformation focus on Host reservation. An especially clear instance is found in the pontifical chapel of Sixtus V in the Basilica of Santa Maria Maggiore, Rome, where the altar is dedicated exclusively to the Blessed Sacrament. On the large, centralized altar, four angels hold aloft an elaborate tabernacle for the Blessed Sacrament (1589) in the form of a classical domed, octagonal *tempietto* (small temple), richly encrusted with figures and relief sculpture in gilt bronze and colored marble inlays.

In the same decade, the construction of the high altarpiece or *retablo* (finished in 1590) of the royal basilica of the Escorial in Spain, dedicated to St. Lawrence (and holding his and other saints' relics in the altar stone), reflects the contemporary imperative for Host reservation. In addition, it manifests the complex formal influences on Spanish sculptors. Although its massive size, rich colorism, and architectural format conform to the Iberian tradition of northern-influenced multistoried altarpieces, a new clarity of parts, the choice of media, and sculptural style attest to the assimilation of Italian classicism. In a niche in the first tier of the *retablo*, directly above the mensa, a huge central tabernacle of gilded bronze and jasper in the form of a *tempietto* provides an appropriate Counter Reformation focal point for the faithful. Set into the sanctuary wall and extending up to the vault, the altarpiece combines bronze sculpture and narrative paintings within an elaborate framework of marble and red jasper. Imposing it its visual impact, the entire structure is crowned by Pompeo Leoni's sculpture, a gilded bronze *Calvary*, set within a frame of classicizing columns and pediment.

Baroque altarpieces are the supreme statement of the sculpted altarpiece: architecture, sculpture, and painting merged to create a whole environment in which to meditate the meaning of the altar. The dignity of the altar found full expression in the glorious combining of media in works such as Gianlorenzo Bernini's altarpiece dedicated to the ecstatic vision of St. Teresa of Avila (1647–52) in the Cornaro Chapel at the Church of Santa Maria della Vittoria in Rome. Bernini blurred the line between the real and fictive space of the chapel and the altarpiece; an oval niche placed behind and above the altar, invited the viewer into a new, profoundly interactional experience.

Ultimately, the Counter Reformation religious orders, particularly the Jesuits, transferred the vivid, sculpted Baroque altarpiece to the New World. Indigenous customs sustained and reinvigorated the southern Baroque tradition: a spiritual vision manifested as a tangible physical presence, the unique legacy of the sculpted altarpiece.

KRISTEN VAN AUSDALL

See also **Bernini, Gianlorenzo; Donatello; Orcagna (Andrea di Cione); Rossellino, Bernardo and Antonio; Vecchietta (Lorenzo di Pietro)**

Further Reading

Braun, Joseph, *Der christliche Altar in seiner geschichtlichen Entwicklung*, 2 vols., Munich: Alte Meister Guenther Koch, 1924

Burckhardt, Jakob, "Das Altarbild," in *Beiträge zur Kunstgeschichte von Italien*, Basel, Switzerland: Lendorff, 1898; reprint, Basel: Schwabe, 1930; as *The Altarpiece in Renaissance Italy*, edited and translated by Peter Humfrey, Cambridge and New York: Cambridge University Press, 1988

Gardner, Julian, "Altars, Altarpieces, and Art History: Legislation and Usage," in *Italian Altarpieces, 1250–1550: Function and Design*, edited by Eve Borsook and Fiorella Superbi Gioffredi, Oxford: Clarendon Press, 1994

Hager, Hellmut, *Die Anfänge des italienischen Altarbildes: Untersuchungen zur Entstehungsgeschichte des toskanischen Hochaltarretabels*, Munich: Schroll, 1962

Humfrey, Peter, *The Altarpiece in Renaissance Venice*, New Haven, Connecticut: Yale University Press, 1993

Humfrey, Peter, and Martin Kemp (editors), *The Altarpiece in the Renaissance*, Cambridge and New York: Cambridge University Press, 1990

Ostrow, Steven, *Art and Spirituality in Counter-Reformation Rome: The Sistine and Pauline Chapels in S. Maria Maggiore*, Cambridge and New York: Cambridge University Press, 1996

Rice, Louise, *The Altars and Altarpieces of New St. Peter's: Outfitting the Basilica, 1621–1666*, Cambridge and New York: Cambridge University Press, 1997

GIOVANNI ANTONIO AMADEO
ca. 1447–1522 *Italian*

Giovanni Antonio Amadeo was the preeminent Lombard sculptor of the late 15th century and the greatest Lombard Renaissance architect. Born about 1447, he was apprenticed to Giovanni Solari from 1460 to 1466 to learn the arts of sculpture and drawing, thus beginning a lifelong association with the Solari family. Giovanni Solari, then more than 70 years old, had been a sculptor and later an architect of the Certosa di Pavia (Carthusian monastery in Pavia) and Milan Cathedral. His son, Guiniforte, succeeded him as architect of the Certosa and the Duomo, and his other son, Francesco, was an important sculptor for the Duomo and the Certosa. Amadeo married Guiniforte's daughter, and he learned from all three Solari men, inheriting and surpassing the Solarian eminence in Milanese sculpture and architecture.

Trained when the Renaissance movement toward naturalism and classicism was being established in

Lombard sculpture, Amadeo became the leading Lombard exponent of this style. As early as the pair of terracotta pilasters in the Portinari Chapel, he modeled in low relief naturalistic images of classically nude putti vivaciously climbing swags of fruit. These putti display a pictorial sense of existence in space, turning and extending their limbs in various directions without any distortion. In one image, a putto sits in profile in front of another who faces into the depth with his back turned. A similar perspectival virtuosity is displayed in the *Madonna and Child* relief in the Misericordia in Florence.

This pictorial sense of perspective is further developed in the *Annunciation* relief, the right-hand lunette of the terracotta lavabo in the small cloister of the Certosa di Pavia. The receding orthogonals are adjusted to look correct from a point of view below the base of the relief. This lavabo was a collaborative effort involving Francesco Solari and Amadeo, as were other terracottas in the small and large cloisters. Amadeo was also influenced by Vincenzo Foppa, whose frescoes in the Portinari Chapel exposed him to the most advanced pictorial and perspectival naturalism in Lombardy.

Nine corbels on the north side of the large cloister can be attributed to Amadeo. Part of a series of 130 corbels, each is decorated with the image of a saint, most carved by Cristoforo Mantegazza; those by Amadeo display a bolder sense of relief, and in their drapery they depart from Mantegazza's late Gothic curvilinearity to achieve an angular, crystalline effect. Amadeo again collaborated with Mantegazza in the keystones of the Certosa di Pavia.

The small cloister portal (signed), Amadeo's first masterpiece, displays mature perspectival and pictorial virtuosity. The lunette showing the Virgin and Child adored by saints and Carthusians builds up a convincing illusion of space by layering figures and varying relief height. The portal displays Classical elements, such as egg and dart moldings, nude putti, and an image of Hercules and Antaeus. Various figures on the portal display action, character, and emotion. Moreover, the portal has a rich iconographic program: the triumph of Christianity over paganism, the rooting of the history of salvation in the Gospels and the writings of the church fathers, the sorrows of the Passion, and the joy of souls in heaven.

The tomb of Medea Colleoni (signed) was commissioned by Bartolomeo Colleoni. Originally located in the sanctuary of the Church of S. Maria in Basella but later moved to the Colleoni Chapel, Bergamo, it combines secular elements, such as coats of arms and Medea's courtly dress, with religious images, such as the Man of Sorrows. The angel to the right of the Man of Sorrows is more powerfully expressive than any earlier figure by Amadeo and shows strong foreshort-

ening in low relief. Colleoni then entrusted Amadeo with his greatest early commissions, the Colleoni Chapel and the tomb of Bartolomeo Colleoni.

Between 1472 and 1499, Amadeo and others were intermittently involved with the altar of St. Joseph for the Milan Cathedral. Although this was subsequently dismembered, documents describe an elaborate monument that must have been one of the most important sculptural projects of the Milanese Renaissance.

A document of 1478 mentions four roundels of the church fathers for the Certosa *tiburio* (lantern tower), two by Amadeo, one by Cristoforo Mantegazza, and one by Antonio Mantegazza. Those representing St. Ambrose and St. Gregory have been identified as Amadeo's on the basis of style.

In the early 1480s, Amadeo was responsible for the production of several saints' shrines for Cremona, but these were executed largely by assistants who worked according to Amadeo's designs. The relief of St. Imerio Giving Alms, with its deep vanishing-point perspective and layers of gradually diminishing figures, was designed and largely executed by Amadeo.

In 1474 Amadeo was granted the right to make half of the facade of the Certosa di Pavia; the other half was given to Cristoforo and Antonio Mantegazza. He seems not to have begun the work immediately. Although he was heavily involved in the supervision and design of the facade, the only pieces that certainly display his execution are 16 of the socle medallions on the southern half of the facade and the reliefs depicting the history of the Carthusian order on the southern socle of the main portal. The medallions display a powerful classicism based on careful study of Roman coins. Whereas some of the medallions are designed to be seen from below, looking up at levels higher than the spectator's eye, Amadeo's portal reliefs display vanishing-point perspectives adjusted to be seen from above, looking down. These reliefs represent Amadeo's latest and most pictorial style, which includes atmospheric perspectives and figure compositions bustling with life and movement.

Amadeo's late style culminates in the Shrine of St. Lanfranco near Pavia. Although this work involved several assistants, a number of reliefs by Amadeo resemble those of the Certosa portal in their pictorial vivacity.

Gifted with prodigious talent, trained by the influential Solari, associated with the greatest Lombard Renaissance artists, and involved with the most important sculptural projects of his day, Amadeo helped initiate and lead to fruition the Renaissance movement in Lombard sculpture.

CHARLES MORSCHECK

See also **Certosa di Pavia; Mantegazza, Cristoforo and Antonio**

Biography

Born probably in Pavia, Italy, *ca.* 1447. Brother of Protasio, a painter, and Caterina, who married sculptor Lazzaro Palazzi in 1467. Apprenticed in Milan to architect and sculptor Solari, 1460–66; learned sculpture from both Giovanni Solari and son Francesco Solari; active at Certosa di Pavia, 1466–67, and later as a sculptor in marble and terracotta; produced sculpture for Bartolomeo Colleoni's family tombs, 1470s; received contract to execute half of facade of Certosa di Pavia, 1474, and worked there intermittently between 1474 and 1499; made contract with Antonio Mantegazza and Antonio della Porta (called Tamagnino), 1492, making them associates to finish Certosa di Pavia facade; supervised sculptural monuments for Cremona, Italy, early 1480s; chief architect of Milan Cathedral, 1490–1522. Died in Milan, Italy, 27 August 1522.

Selected Works

ca. 1465–68   *Madonna and Child*; marble; Misericordia, Florence, Italy

ca. 1465–68   Pilasters; terracotta; Portinari Chapel, Church of S. Eustorgio, Milan, Italy

ca. 1465–70   *Annunciation* relief; terracotta; small cloister, Certosa di Pavia, Pavia, Italy

ca. 1465–70   Nine corbels; Angera stone; large cloister, Certosa di Pavia, Pavia, Italy

ca. 1467–70   Three keystones; Angera stone; Certosa di Pavia, Pavia, Italy

ca. 1470   Small cloister portal; marble; Certosa di Pavia, Pavia, Italy

ca. 1470–75   Tomb of Medea Colleoni; marble; Colleoni Chapel, Church of S. Maria Maggiore, Bergamo, Italy

ca. 1470–77   Facade sculpture; marble; Colleoni Chapel, Church of S. Maria Maggiore, Bergamo, Italy

ca. 1470–77   Tomb of Bartolomeo Colleoni; marble; Colleoni Chapel, Church of S. Maria Maggiore, Bergamo, Italy

ca. 1470–80   *Coronation of the Virgin*; marble; Carmine Church, Pavia, Italy

ca. 1472–99   Reliefs and statues for the altar of St. Joseph, Milan Cathedral, Italy; marble (dismantled)

ca. 1475–85   Seated Virtue with heraldic shield; marble; Sacristy of Lavabo, Certosa di Pavia, Pavia, Italy

ca. 1475–78   St. Ambrose and St. Gregory roundels; Angera stone; Certosa di Pavia, Pavia, Italy

ca.   Sixteen socle medallions; marble; Certosa

1478–95   di Pavia, Pavia, Italy

ca. 1481–84   St. Imerio Giving Alms, for tomb of St. Imerio; marble; Cremona Cathedral, Italy

ca. 1496–1501   History of the Carthusian Order; marble; Certosa di Pavia, Pavia, Italy

ca. 1498–1507   Shrine of St. Lanfranco; marble; Church of St. Lanfranco, near Pavia, Italy

Further Reading

Bernstein, JoAnne G., "A Reconsideration of Amadeo's Style in the 1470's and 1480's and Two New Attributions," *Arte Lombarda* 13 (1968)

Castelfranchi Vegas, Liana, and Janice Shell (editors), *Giovanni Antonio Amadeo: Scultura e architettura del suo tempo*, Milan: Cisalpino, 1993

Malaguzzi Valeri, Francesco, *Giovanni Antonio Amadeo: Scultore e architetto lombardo (1447–1522)*, Bergamo, Italy: Istituto Italiano d'Arte Grafiche, 1904

Morscheck, Charles R., *Relief Sculpture for the Facade of the Certosa di Pavia, 1473–1499*, New York: Garland, 1978

Morscheck, Charles R., "Keystones by Amadeo and Cristoforo Mantegazza in the Church of the Certosa di Pavia," *Arte Lombarda* 69/70 (1984)

Morscheck, Charles R., "The Certosa Medallions in Perspective," *Arte Lombarda* 123 (1998)

Schofield, Richard V., and Janice Shell, "Amadeo, Giovanni Antonio," in *The Dictionary of Art*, edited by Jane Turner, New York: Grove, and London: Macmillan, 1996

TOMB OF BARTOLOMEO COLLEONI

Giovanni Antonio Amadeo (ca. 1447–1522)

ca. 1470–77

marble

h. 7.2 m

Colleoni Chapel, Church of S. Maria Maggiore, Bergamo, Italy

The tomb of Bartolomeo Colleoni is the finest sculptural example of Lombard Renaissance classicism and naturalism made before 1477 and the greatest masterpiece of Giovanni Antonio Amadeo's early period. The tomb must be understood in conjunction with the sculpture of the Colleoni Chapel made by Amadeo at about the same time.

Although Amadeo's authorship of the tomb and chapel is undisputed, documentation is scarce and indirect; therefore, attribution and dating of the component parts depend on inference and stylistic analysis. On 3 November 1469, Martino Benzoni and Cristoforo and Antonio Mantegazza made a contract to collaborate on a tomb for Colleoni, should they be offered the commission; apparently, Colleoni had not yet hired sculptors for the tomb. Colleoni's daughter Medea died on 6 March 1470, and Amadeo made her tomb shortly thereafter. Colleoni died 2 November 1475 and was entombed 4 January 1476. A ducal letter dated 10 December 1475 asks that Amadeo be paid 900 ducats owed him for work on the tomb. A January 1476 funeral oration for Colleoni names Amadeo as architect of the chapel. A document dated 20 February 1477 requests that Amadeo return to Bergamo to finish part of the chapel.

It is unclear whether the tomb and the chapel were two separate commissions or one. It is also not known exactly when either was finished or where the sculptures were carved. Many documents between 1471 and 1477 indicate that Amadeo was busy with other projects in Milan or Pavia, which suggests that the Colleoni sculptures were made in the region between Milan and Pavia, where marble could be economically shipped via water. The lighter, finished sculptures could be transported over land to Bergamo at considerable savings.

The tomb is extraordinarily large—approximately 3.5 meters wide and 7 meters tall—and is in a rich, courtly, antiquarian style. Two superimposed sarcophagi surmounted by a canopy resembling a triumphal arch are attached to a wall. The lower sarcophagus, in which Colleoni's remains were found in 1969, is supported by four square columns resting on pedestals from which lions emerge. This sarcophagus displays five scenes of the Passion interspersed with statuettes of Virtues. The socle of the lower sarcophagus contains a frieze of putti supporting heraldic shields and numismatic medallions. The upper sarcophagus portrays three Infancy scenes. The lower sarcophagus supports two standing statues, a seminude man (Hercules or Samson) and an armored warrior of dubious identity, and three seated warriors. On the upper sarcophagus stand two female figures, Judith and an armored woman, and a gilt wooden equestrian statue of Colleoni added by German sculptors in 1493.

The chapel facade is iconographically related to the tomb. The facade has ten Old Testament reliefs, from the creation of Adam to the sacrifice of Isaac, and four reliefs of the labors of Hercules. Numismatic medallions of Roman emperors decorate the socles of the corner pilasters and the spandrels above the windows, and on the corner pilasters, roundels of ancient heroes alternate with lozenges with heads of saints. Above the windows are busts of Julius Caesar and Trajan; inscriptions say "Divus Julius . . . imperavit annis V" (The Divine Julius ruled five years) and "Divus Traianus . . . imperavit annis XVIII" (The Divine Trajan ruled 18 years). A lead tablet found in the tomb says Colleoni "imperavit annis IIII et XX" (ruled 24 years); he was a general longer than both emperors combined. Above the central rose window is a statue variously

Giovanni Antonio Amadeo: Tomb of Bartolomeo Colleoni
© Alinari / Art Resource, NY

identified as Alexander the Great, St. Alexander (patron saint of Bergamo), and Colleoni himself. In the pediment of the doorway, God the Father presides. This imagery complements that of the tomb by depicting Colleoni as a brave and virtuous general, like the greatest heroes of antiquity. Moreover, Colleoni surpassed them in that he was a Christian. His equestrian statue on the tomb triumphs over the statues and medallions of ancient heroes. He salutes the altar, thus appearing as a champion of Christianity. The biblical reliefs on the facade and the tomb represent Christ's triumph over sin and death through grace and heroic sacrifice, implying that Colleoni merited eternal life through his faith and virtuous acts.

The tomb sculpture reveals several hands of execution. Most of the figural reliefs were carved by Amadeo and represent the apex of his early style. The end panels of the lower sarcophagus, the flagellation and Resurrection, were designed and carved by a hand commonly called the "Flagellation Master." The flagellation displays in flattened relief a fully developed Albertian perspective in which all orthogonals recede to a vanishing point at the eye level of the figure standing at the left. Everything diminishes rationally as it recedes into the depth, exhibiting a perspectival sophistication not reached by Amadeo until his works of the 1480s. The male figures on the tomb show several hands of execution, none of them certainly Amadeo's.

The most exquisite carving is in Amadeo's frieze of putti at eye level on the lower sarcophagus. These happy, playful putti are more completely pictorial and occupy space more convincingly than those in Amadeo's earlier works. They move and look about in all directions. Those in the background are flatter and smaller, so as to appear farther away, and they are skillfully foreshortened, with no distortion.

The Annunciation, Nativity, and Adoration of the Magi on the upper sarcophagus create a strong sense of pictorial naturalism. They were designed to be seen from below looking up. The foreground figures are as tall as the panels, but the vanishing points are located at about half the height of each panel. The heads of figures in the background are lower than those closer to us. The foreground figures on the upper sarcophagus are larger and in higher relief than those in the Passion scenes, in some places overlapping their frames. The way of the cross, Crucifixion, and lamentation on the lower sarcophagus display more and smaller figures and greater movement and expression. They are designed to be seen from the eye level of the spectator. Despite these differences, all of the New Testament reliefs on the front of the tomb are consistent with the progression of Amadeo's style in his earlier works.

CHARLES MORSCHECK

Further Reading

Bernstein, JoAnne G., "Milanese and Antique Aspects of the Colleoni Chapel: Site and Symbolism," *Arte Lombarda* 100 (1992)

Bernstein, JoAnne G., "Patronage, Autobiography, and Iconography: The Facade of the Colleoni Chapel," in *Giovanni Antonio Amadeo: Scultura e architettura del suo tempo,* edited by Janice Shell and Liana Castelfranchi Vegas, Milan: Cisalpino, 1993

Erben, Dietrich, *Bartolomeo Colleoni: Die künstlerische Repräsentation eines Condottiere im Quattrocento,* Sigmaringen, Germany: Thorbecke, 1996

Piel, Friedrich, *La Cappella Colleoni e il Luogo Pio della Pietà in Bergamo, Opera,* Bergamo, Italy: Luogo Pio della Pietà Bartolomeo Colleoni, 1975

Pope-Hennessy, John, *An Introduction to Italian Sculpture,* 3 vols., London: Phaidon, 1963; 4th edition, 1996; see especially vol. 2, *Italian Renaissance Sculpture*

Schofield, Richard, "Avoiding Rome: An Introduction to Lombard Sculptors and the Antique," *Arte Lombarda* 100 (1992)

Schofield, Richard, and Andrew Burnett, "The Decoration of the Colleoni Chapel," *Arte Lombarda* 126 (1999)

Schofield, Richard, Janice Shell and Grazioso Sironi, *Giovanni Antonio Amadeo: Documents/I documenti,* Como, Italy: New Press, 1989

Shell, Janice, "The Mantegazza Brothers, Martino Benzoni, and the Colleoni Tomb," *Arte Lombarda* 100 (1992)

AMBER

Amber is the fossilized sap of pinelike trees of the Tertiary period (*Pinus succinifera*) formed through sedimentation in the sea or in the ground. It is distinguished by its place of origin: sea or maritime amber and earth amber. The largest amber deposits lie in the Baltic region, in the area of East Prussia, and on the coasts of the North Sea. More rarely, it washes ashore or is otherwise found in the Mediterranean (Sicily) in the layers of what is known as the "blue earth." Trade with the "gold of the Baltic" developed along three trade routes following the most important river courses: the Elba-Moldavia-Danube-Rhine-Carnuntum-Aquileia; the Vistula-Danube-Volga-Black Sea; and the North Sea-Rhine-Rhone-Genoa. The color spectrum of amber ranges from white (bone amber) through several hues of yellow to dark brown. Interesting variations, whose popularity varies by region, arise from the differential distributions of transparent and opaque layers. While light amber was especially prized in the west, the Chinese preferred the transparent red amber from Burma; in other parts of the Orient, collectors sought especially clear yellow amber and cloudy, milky amber.

Artists have sculpted amber, which is easily rendered malleable by applying heat, through lathing, carving, and rubbing and working it with knives and engraving steel. The techniques are similar to those used for glass, ivory, and gems, which were usually sculpted by amber artists as well. Artists and collectors have used and prized amber as a precious stone for 10,000 years. It is the only raw material to have been a highly prized precious commodity over such a prodigious span of time, almost without interruption. The interest in amber dissipated with the scientific explanation of its origins by Friedrich Samuel Bock in Königsberg (Kaliningrad) in 1767. As with ivory, people have sometimes attributed magical powers to amber on the basis of its electrostatic attraction.

From the time of the Stone Age, artists processed amber primarily into jewelry and amulets. Little is known about medieval amber works; presumably, they were desirable and widely distributed items, as was the case in Antiquity and in the Renaissance and later. Amber chains have been discovered as burial gifts in the Rhineland from the Merovingian and Franconian dynasties; such chains consist of amber beads strung together in alternation with glass, clay, and even gold beads. Paternoster makers were organized into guilds beginning in 1260 (Paris; 1302 in Bruges and Lübeck); until the second half of the 15th century, they had the sole right to process the amber controlled and delivered by the Teutonic order. Gdansk developed alongside Königsberg into a center for amber artists. The order's archives contain reports about the *Hofbernsteinmeisters* (court amber masters) of the ducal court in Königsberg, who were also active as gilders and embossers. The oldest preserved figure is an enthroned Madonna from Lüneburg from the first half of the 15th century (Kestner Museum, Hannover). Charles V of France and the duke of Berry also owned amber figures. Through the support of Duke Albrecht of Prussia, the custodian of the laws regulating amber, amber acquired new uses after the Reformation with the production of secular luxury items (such as chess sets, boxes, cutlery, boxes, handles, and statuettes) corresponding to courtly tastes. Albrecht inherited the rights to the amber monopoly from the Teutonic order, which was secularized under the duchy of Prussia. Artists created portrait medallions either as collector's items or to be set into vessels. Most popular, however, were amber vessels (bowls, trophies, tankards), which in the 16th and 17th centuries exhibit unusually strict and simple forms, comparable to those of goldsmithing in Königsberg.

It became common in the 16th century to combine variously colored ambers and to join them with sharply contrasting materials—ivory, silver, and ebony. Such works became even more popular in the 17th century. The three-dimensional decoration of tankards became more and more elaborate to the point of preciosity through lavish fittings made of precious metals, sometimes with enamel inlays and pearls. In the first half of the 17th century came a new technique for working amber that would become the great standard. Georg Schreiber (Scriba) is considered to be its inventor. In this technique, the artist covered small thin plates of amber with fine relief and bound them together with the aid of slender metal threads. Artists created many vessels (for example, those found at Victoria and Albert Museum, London; Grünes Gewölbe, Dresden; Schatzkammer der Residenz, Munich) and jewelry boxes (Schatzkammer der Residenz, Munich; Staatliche Kunstsammlungen, Kassel; Kunsthistorisches Museum, Vienna) using this technique, in which light penetrates the transparent amber plates and makes them luminous. In another technique, incrustation, the artist mounted amber plates, some of which were engraved in fine intaglio on the back side, onto a wood carcass, allowing large objects made of many different pieces to be created, although these did not let any light in.

The large altars originating from workshops in Gdansk during the 17th and 18th centuries (Geistliche Schatzkammer, Vienna; Victoria and Albert Museum, London; Palazzo Pitti, Florence) masterfully demonstrate the various techniques and possibilities for combining amber in a wide variety of ways. Objects made of pure amber, however, were considered to be the showpieces, demonstrating the greatest artistic ability. The most beautiful multitiered boxes created at the close of the 17th century came from the hands of Michel Redlin and Christoph Maucher (Malbork). A second group of amber works is marked by their sculptural characteristics. The best-known master of these was Jakob Heise from Königsberg, who carved his fine figures in a characteristic static way with a high degree of detail (for example, his *Great Elector and His Wife*, 1654–63). Maucher worked with amber and ivory, and his compositions, some of which contain several figures, exhibit some clearly Baroque stylistic features (London, Victoria and Albert Museum; Berlin, Staatliche Sammlungen Preussischer Kulturbesitz; Vienna, Kunsthistorisches Museum).

In the 18th century, distinguished individual masters such as Jakob Dobbermann and the Labhardt brothers, Lorenz Spengler, and Wilhelm Krüger, who were active as ivory carvers at the courts in Kassel, Copenhagen, and Dresden, took over amber sculpting, which had been centralized in the area of Königsberg and Gdansk. Flemish sculptors apparently worked with amber as well (such as François du Quesnoy's *Sleeping Nymph*, 1625).

The greatest and most ambitious work made of amber was the legendary amber room in Tsarskoye Selo Palace near St. Petersburg, whose present location is still shrouded in mystery (it disappeared in 1945). In 1701 the Prussian king Frederick I commissioned the work from Gottfried Wolffram of Copenhagen. Two artists from Gdansk, Ernst Schacht and Gottfried Turow, continued the work, based on a design by Andreas Schlüter. In 1716 Czar Peter I received the costly interior as a gift from Elector Friedrich Wilhelm of Brandenburg.

At the start of the Rococo period, amber seems to have lost its fascination; its only noteworthy use was for bridal necklaces. Despite efforts to revive amber art at the world exhibitions at the beginning of the 20th century, artists did not find a modern answer to the great age of amber sculpting.

Outside Europe, artists in China used amber, preferably red Burmite, to create vessels, statuettes, and pendants. As early as the 5th century BC, the Chinese were aware of amber's botanical origin, but it surfaced in mythology later. It was probably sculpted since the 1st century CE.

SABINE HAAG

See also **du Quesnoy, François; Schlüter, Andreas**

Further Reading

Baer, Winfried, "Ein Bernsteinstuhl für Kaiser Leopold I.: Ein Geschenk des Kurfürsten Friedrich Wilhelm von Brandenburg," *Jahrbuch der Kunsthistorischen Sammlungen in Wien* 78 (1982)

Grimaldi, David, *Amber, Window to the Past*, New York: Abrams, 1996

Pelka, Otto, *Bernstein*, Berlin: Schmidt, 1920

Philippovich, Eugen von, "Bernstein," in *Antiquitäten, Kuriositäten: Ein Handbuch für Sammler und Liebhabler*, Braunschweig, Germany: Klinckhardt und Biermann, 1966

Reineking-von Bock, Gisela, *Bernstein: Das Gold der Ostsee*, Munich: Callwey Verlag, 1981

Rohde, Alfred, *Das Buch vom Bernstein*, Königsberg, Prussia: Ost-Europa-Verlag, 1937

Trusted, Marjorie, *Four Amber Statuettes by Christoph Maucher*, Munich: Pantheon III, 1984

Trusted, Marjorie, *Catalogue of European Ambers in the Victoria and Albert Museum*, London: Victoria and Albert Museum, 1985

AMBO

An ambo is a raised platform used for the reading or singing of scripture. Ambos were also used for the exposition of biblical texts by the priest and, on occasion, for other solemn ceremonial functions. Historically, ambos are related to the *bimah* of the ancient synagogue and the *bema* of the Syriac Church. The word *ambo* entered Latin from Greek and is probably derived from the Greek verb *anabainein* (to mount). Other words commonly used by early Christian and medieval authors in reference to the same (or similar) structures are *gradus* and *pulpitum* in the West and *bema* and *pyrgos* in the East. It is only in modern times that the term *ambo* (the reading platform) has been distinguished from the term *pulpit* (the platform or lectern used for delivering the homily).

Ambos are mentioned in many early Christian texts, including St. Augustine's *City of God*, Cyprian's *Epistles*, the Canons of Laodicea, the biography of St. Ambrose in *Vita S. Ambrosii a Paulino*, and the biography of St. John Chrysostom in *Historia Ecclesia* (by the Christian author Socrates). Both of the bishops, Augustine and Ambrose, mounted the ambo to preach on special occasions, and apparently John Chrysostom did so regularly. Still, these practices were considered exceptional because the bishop's cathedra was also employed for these functions.

The normal intended use of the ambo was for the reading or singing of the epistle and the gospel and the singing of the gradual (*Psalmus gradualis*). In most versions of the *Ordo Romanus* (a description of the Roman rite), for example, the liturgy of the word began with the subdeacon ascending the ambo to read the epistle. Next, the cantor ascended to sing the gradual and alleluia. Last, the deacon ascended to read the gospel, which was supported by the arm of the subdeacon. The gospel reading was accompanied by a solemn and complicated processional ceremony derived from the Byzantine rite.

It would appear that the standard architectural form of the ambo itself is also of Byzantine origin. Emperor Justinian I (527–565) is believed to have been responsible for the introduction of the ambo as a customary architectural feature in Western and North African churches. A grand but in other respects representative version of this Eastern type was the ambo erected in Hagia Sophia in Constantinople (present-day Istanbul, Turkey). No longer extant, the ambo was carefully described in a contemporary poem by Paulus Silentiarius, which was probably read to Justinian I on the occasion of the church's rededication. This ambo was an imposing structure placed slightly east of the center of the church along its central axis. It possessed two sets of stairs—one located at the east end and the other at the west end—both of which led to an elliptical platform supported by eight columns and surmounted by a canopy (ambos were ascended from the eastern stairs and descended from the western stairs, which were closer to the altar). It was adorned with candles and two crosses and elaborately decorated with inlaid ivory, silver, and semiprecious stones. Other similarly shaped ambos (but without the canopy) in Greece and Asia Minor include those at St. John at Ephesus and in the basilicas of Notion, Olympia, and Thasos.

The first known examples of ambos in Europe and North Africa also derive from the 6th century. They preserve this double-staired arrangement. One ambo in a church of Sabratha, Libya, even includes a canopy. In Ravenna, Italy, the cathedral and the Church of S. Agata both contained this sort of double-staired ambo. The ambo in the cathedral was composed of a walled staircase on either side of a parapeted platform and was decorated with sculptures of fish, ducks, doves, stags, peacocks, and lambs (it was reconstructed in 1913 according to a reliable 17th-century description). The ambo of S. Agata was created by hollowing out and retooling a segment of a large ancient marble column, a practice also used to create the ambo in Justinian's North African church of Lepcis Magna in Libya. Unlike their Eastern counterparts (and Lepcis Magna), in which the ambo stands in the center of the north–south axis, these Western ambos are set in the southern part of the nave and closer to the altar. This placement is repeated in all other Western churches with a single ambo, such as the Church of Santa Maria Antiqua in Rome and the plans for the Abbey of St. Gall, Switzerland.

In later churches, the ambo was usually attached to the southern wall of the lower choir. This southern placement would allow the deacon to read the gospel while facing north (toward the central axis of the church), as is prescribed in medieval ordinals.

In Italian churches with two ambos, one for the gospel reading and one for the epistle reading, the gospel

Ambo, from the Church of St. Agata *ca.* 556–559; Ravenna, Italy
The Conway Library, Courtauld Institute of Art

ambo is usually set to the south, whereas the epistle ambo usually takes the north side, even though this contradicts indications found in liturgical texts. Because most churches are oriented so that their apses face east, the gospel ambo is usually placed to the right and the epistle ambo to the left, such as at the churches of Santa Maria in Cosmedin and San Lorenzo fuori le Mura in Rome. At the Church of San Clemente in Rome, the gospel ambo occupies the left side because the church has a western orientation.

The gospel ambo—considered the more important of the two—is often distinguished from the epistle ambo by its larger size, richer decoration, and greater tendency to retain the double staircase from its Eastern ancestors. Common decorative elements include *cosmati* work (colorful mosaic inlay of stone and/or glass) or relief sculpture representing floral elements, animal symbols, or scenes from the life of Christ (in later examples). The gospel ambo often possesses a monumental candlestick—probably another adaptation of Byzantine tradition—such as that at San Clemente. In all three Roman churches mentioned, the epistle ambo possesses only one staircase. Single-staired ambos also exist in churches with only one ambo, such as in the Church of Santa Maria in Castel St. Elia, Nepi.

The hierarchy of the readings is also evident in French liturgical texts, which indicate that the cantor and subdeacon may not ascend to the summit of the ambo because this space is reserved for the deacon's gospel reading. The same kind of logic may account for other iconographic peculiarities, such as the double-decker, 12th-century pulpit-ambo at the Basilica of San Marco in Venice. The higher platform with its eagle lectern and canopy was presumably intended for the gospel reading and the lower platform for the singing of the gradual (or perhaps the epistle, though there exists a second single-leveled ambo on the other side of the church).

Although the Roman liturgy only requires, and indeed only mentions, one ambo, by the High Middle Ages it was probably felt to be liturgically clearer and perhaps more visually appealing to divide its function into two structures. Similarly, when preaching grew more common, the ambo's unofficial function as a podium for homilies and addresses was given its own separate architectural form, the pulpit.

MAIA WELLINGTON GAHTAN

See also **Cosmati; Pulpit**

Further Reading

Blaauw, Sible de, *Cultus et decor: Liturgia e architettura nella Roma tardoantica e medievale: Basilica Salvatoris, Sanctae Mariae, Sancti Petri*, 2 vols., Vatican City: Biblioteca Apostolica Vaticana, 1994

LeClercq, Henri, "Ambon," in *Dictionnaire d'archéologie chrétienne et de liturgie*, by Ferdinand Cabrol and LeClercq, Paris: Letouzey et Ané, 1924

Fleury, Georges Rohault de, *La messe: Études archéologiques sur ses monuments*, 8 vols., Paris: Morel, 1883

Hickley, Dennis, "The Ambo in Early Liturgical Planning—A Study with Special Reference to the Syrian *Bema*," *Heythrop Journal* 7 (1966)

Kazhdan, Alexander, "A Note on the 'Middle-Byzantine' Ambo," *Byzantion: Revue internationale des études Byzantines* 57 (1987)

Mathews, Thomas, "An Early Roman Chancel Arrangement," *Rivista di archeologia cristiana* 38 (1962)

Vrins, G.P., "De ambon: Oorsprong en verspreiding tot '600,' " in *Feestbundel F. Van der Meer*, Amsterdam and Brussels: Elsevier, 1966

Xydis, Stephen G., "The Chancel Barrier, Solea, and Ambo of Hagia Sophia," *Art Bulletin* 29 (1947)

BARTOLOMEO AMMANATI 1511–1592
Italian

Bartolomeo Ammanati determined at an early age to move beyond his master Baccio Bandinelli's teachings and to draw directly on Michelangelo's greatness. Once he left Bandinelli's shop, and after his decisive encounter with Jacopo Sansovino in Venice (*ca.* 1527–

32), which accentuated the impact of Michelangelo's style, the young Ammanati struck out to create a distinct style, one that would blend classicism and lyricism. He took from Michelangelo his grace, not his *terribilità* (immense force [of art]), perhaps because the latter would have led back to Bandinelli's harshest style. *God the Father* (1535–36), which Ammanati sculpted for the altar by Stagio Stagi in the Cathedral of Pisa, already shows Michelangelo's influence, as does the *Saint Nazarius* (1536–38) on the Sannazzaro tomb (designed by Giovanni Montorsoli) in the Church of Santa Maria del Parto in Naples. In the early 1540s the Nari tomb, in the Church of Santissima Annunziata in Florence, evinced Ammanati's development of a truly personal style, one that aimed to give a truthfulness and a sense of motion to the figures, which the artist presented in various attitudes, with their faces and hair richly and carefully crafted. Contemporary artists and the more cultivated members of the public praised the Nari tomb, which they took as an example of the new sculpture being produced in Florence and even as a source for some marble works by sculptors such as Benvenuto Cellini.

Around 1540 Ammanati was in Urbino, working for Francesco Maria della Rovere on a tomb and on the stucco decoration of the Villa Imperiale in Pesaro (nothing from these projects has survived). Shortly afterward the sculptor returned to Venice, where he collaborated with Sansovino on a sculptural decoration of the Marciana Library. In 1544 in Padua, Ammanati began working for Marco Mantova Benavides, a Classical scholar, jurisconsult, and counselor to Emperor Charles V. For the garden behind the Benavides palace, Ammanati created a triumphal arch, adorned with statues of *Apollo* and *Jupiter*, as well as a *Hercules* more than seven meters high, the tallest statue executed in the 16th century. He also executed the tomb of Marco Mantova Benavides in the Church of the Eremitani in Padua. While the tomb shows the influence of Michelangelo, the works Ammanati produced for the Benavides garden, centering on the colossal *Hercules*, demonstrate a link to ancient sculpture, per Benavides's request, and also attest to the sculptor's return to an aggressive expressiveness that harks back to Bandinelli.

Around 1546 Ammanati was working on three fountains (now lost) for Girolamo Gualdo, a patron in Vicenza. In 1548 he settled in Rome, through the good offices of Benavides. Here, the sculptor executed the tomb of Francesco Del Nero in the Church of Santa Maria sopra Minerva and came into close contact with Michelangelo and Giorgio Vasari. In 1550 they helped him obtain the commission for the fine sculptures on the tombs of Fabiano and Antonio del Monte (relatives of Pope Julius III) in the Church of San Pietro in Mont-

orio; although the architectural design of the tombs was Vasari's, Michelangelo had revised it. Ammanati also collaborated with Vasari and Giacomo da Vignola on the pope's Villa Giulia in Rome, creating the spectacular *Nymphaeum* behind the villa, adorned with caryatids and statues of the Tiber and Arno Rivers, and a fountain facing onto the Flaminian Way.

In 1555 Ammanati returned to Florence and began a fruitful relationship with Duke Cosimo I. Cosimo's growing impatience with Cellini and the elderly Bandinelli cleared the way for Ammanati. Backed by Vasari, he presented himself as an efficient artist capable of replacing Bandinelli after the latter's death in 1560. Ammanati's first project for Cosimo was the Juno fountain, meant to be placed in the Palazzo Vecchio on the wall facing Bandinelli's Audience Hall, in celebration of the grand duke's government. Ammanati organized the fountain (now in the Museo Nazionale del Bargello in Florence) on a novel ring-shaped plan and adorned it with huge allegorical statues of *Juno*, *Ceres*, *Temperance*, *Florence*, *Arno*, and *Hippocrene*. Although the conception reveals a typically Mannerist complexity and a courtly intellectualism, the statues— especially the standing figures of *Ceres* and *Temperance*—express motion and vivacity despite their bulk. A sketch attributable to Ammanati (now in the Casa Buonarroti in Florence) probably relates to his first design of the male figure of *Temperance*; its former attribution to Michelangelo confirms in a way the latter's great influence over Ammanati.

Ammanati's next projects were large bronzes: a neo-Hellenistic *Mars*, a *Hercules and Antaeus*, and a huge *Apennine*, the last two for the Villa Medicea di Castello near Florence. The Bandinelli influence reappears in all these sculptures, especially evident in the *Hercules and Antaeus*, although here Ammanati accentuated the realistic aspect, notably in the flailing limbs. His dependence on his early master's ideas and projects—doubtless reinforced by the patronage of the Medici, who were seeking to fill the gap left by Bandinelli—explains why Ammanati won the commission from the Medici for his masterpiece, the Neptune fountain in Florence.

Bandinelli's death also opened a new career for Ammanati as an architect and as master builder for the cathedral works of Florence Cathedral. As such, he restructured the Palazzo Pitti and completed in the cathedral the construction of Bandinelli's chancel; he also erected the beautiful tabernacles he himself had designed for a set of monumental statues of the apostles. His major architectural works also include the Santa Trinità Bridge, the Palazzo Grifoni and the Church of San Giovannino in Florence, and the Palazzo Pubblico in Lucca.

Ammanati's architectural commissions left him much less time for sculpting, which he now concentrated essentially on the complex Neptune fountain and its numerous bronzes cast after his designs by a series of artists. His last sculptures are the small bronze statuette of *Ops*, for Francesco I's *studiolo* (study) in the Palazzo Vecchio, and the tomb of Giovanni Boncompagni (1572) in the Camposanto in Pisa. An exercise in Mannerist elegance and geometry, the spiraling lines of the small, exquisite bronze *Ops*, encircled by animal figures, lead the viewer's eyes up to the ideal beauty of the figure's head and her sensual gesture.

The influence of the Jesuits in Florence precipitated a religious crisis in the aged Ammanati, which is documented in two letters, one to the Accademia del Disegno (1582), and the other to Grand Duke Ferdinando I de' Medici (*ca.* 1590). Both are full of Counter Reformation zeal and remorse for the nudity of some of his statues, in particular those on the fountains of Neptune and Juno.

FRANCESCO VOSSILLA

See also **Bandinelli, Baccio; Michelangelo**

Biography

Born in Settignano, near Florence, Italy, 18 June 1511. Family were stonecarvers. Apprenticed to Baccio Bandinelli in the 1520s, and probably worked with him in Rome, 1523–27; accused (together with Nanni di Baccio Bigio) of stealing Michelangelo's drawings and models, 1529, and left Florence for Venice; joined circle of Jacopo Sansovino, friend of painter Battista Franco and architect Girolamo Genga; obtained important commissions in Florence, Venice, Urbino, Padua, Vicenza, and Rome, 1529–48; set up shop in Rome, 1548, and encountered Michelangelo, Giorgio Vasari, and Vignola; with Vasari's aid, returned to Florence, 1555; worked for Cosimo I de' Medici as sculptor and architect; appointed master builder of Florence Cathedral. Founding member of Accademia del Disegno. Died in Florence, Italy, 13 April 1592.

Selected Works

ca. 1540–42	*Victory* for tomb of Mario Nari, Church of Santissima Annunziata, Florence, Italy; marble: Museo Nazionale del Bargello, Florence, Italy
1544–45	*Hercules*; stone; Benavides Garden, Padua, Italy
1544–47	Triumphal arch with statues of *Apollo* and *Jupiter*; Benavides Garden, Padua, Italy
ca. 1546	Tomb of Marco Mantova Benavides; marble and stone; Church of the Eremitani, Padua, Italy
ca. 1548	Tomb of Francesco Del Nero; marble; Church of Santa Maria sopra Minerva, Rome, Italy
1550–52	Tombs of Cardinal Antonio del Monte and Fabiano del Monte; marble; Church of San Pietro in Montorio, Rome, Italy
ca. 1552	*Nymphaeum*; marble and stone; Villa Giulia, Rome, Italy
1555–63	*Juno, Ceres, Temperance, Florence, Arno,* and *Hippocrene*, for Juno fountain; marble; Museo Nazionale del Bargello, Florence, Italy
ca. 1560	*Hercules and Antaeus*, for Fountain of Hercules in gardens at Villa Medicea di Castello, near Florence, Italy; bronze; Villa Medicea della Petraia, Florence, Italy
ca. 1560	*Mars*; bronze; Galleria degli Uffizi, Florence, Italy
ca. 1560–75	Neptune fountain; marble, bronze; Piazza della Signoria, Florence, Italy
1563–65	*Apennine*; marble; Villa Medicea di Castello, near Florence, Italy
ca. 1570–72	*Ops*; bronze; *studiolo* of Francesco I, Palazzo Vecchio, Florence, Italy
1572	Tomb of Giovanni Boncompagni; marble; Camposanto, Pisa, Italy

Further Reading

Davis, Charles, "The Tomb of Mario Nari for the SS. Annunziata in Florence: The Sculptor Bartolomeo Ammannati until 1544," *Mitteilungen des Kunsthistorischen Institutes in Florenz* 21 (1977)

Del Turco, Niccolò Rosselli, and Federica Salvi (editors), *Bartolomeo Ammannati: Scultore e architetto, 1511–1592*, Florence: Alinea, 1995

Fossi, Mazzino, *Bartolomeo Ammannati, architetto*, Naples: Morano, 1967

Heikamp, Detlef, "Ammanati's Fountain for the Sala Grande of the Palazzo Vecchio," in *Fons Sapientiae: Renaissance Garden Fountains*, edited by Elisabeth B. MacDougall, Washington: Dumbarton Oaks Trustees, 1978

Heikamp, Detlef, "Sulla scultura fiorentina fra Maniera e Controriforma," in *Magnificenza alla corte dei Medici: Arte a Firenze alla fine del Cinquecento*, edited by Cristina Acidini Luchinat et al., Milan: Electa, 1997

Kinney, Peter, *The Early Sculpture of Bartolomeo Ammanati*, New York: Garland, 1976

NEPTUNE FOUNTAIN

Bartolomeo Ammanati (1522–1592)

ca. 1560–1575

marble and bronze

h. 5.6 m

Piazza della Signoria, Florence, Italy

In the early 1550s Baccio Bandinelli was already working on the design of a fountain for the Piazza della Signoria in Florence, the primary setting for the exhibition of the Medici family's power. Bandinelli's fountain was to be dominated by the figure of Neptune, a subject that evoked Medicean Tuscany's aspiration to become a maritime power; Cosimo I dreamed of expanding into the central Mediterranean, starting by freeing the sea of North African pirates. The monument was to be enlivened by jets of water, an idea that was in vogue; all the great monarchs were building fountains to emphasize their power and dazzle their subjects.

From Giorgio Vasari and from Bandinelli's letters, we know that the idea for the fountain was born out of discussions between the sculptor and Eleonora of Toledo, Cosimo I's Spanish-born wife. Bandinelli's explicit references to fountains in Spanish Italy demonstrate the project's intended scope. In Eleonora's mind the model for the Neptune fountain was the idea her father, Don Pedro di Toledo, Charles V's viceroy in Naples, had had for beautifying Naples with the two monumental fountains (now destroyed) built after 1537 by Giovanni da Nola to extol Charles V's maritime policy. However, the proper artistic model was taken to be the Orion fountain in Messina (1547–51) by the Florentine sculptor and architect Giovan Angelo da Montorsoli. Charles V, a new Orion, stands over a three-pool structure symbolizing the Habsburgs' vast domains, which in that part of the Mediterranean had been pacified by the imperial campaigns against the Muslim pirates.

Bandinelli intended to surpass these imperial models; he conceived of a huge pool surmounted by a colossus at least as tall as the two giant statues already installed in the Piazza della Signoria, Michelangelo's *David* (1501–04; original now at the Galleria dell'Accademia, Florence) and Bandinelli's own *Hercules and Cacus* (1525–34; *in situ* at the Piazza della Signoria). His solution was similar to the one finally created, for which Bartolomeo Ammanati perhaps gained Medici approval by evoking Bandinelli's ideas. Bandinelli had not gone beyond a small model, although he did start carving a huge block of Carrara marble reserved for the purpose. Nonetheless, two small bronzes (Galleria Colonna, Rome; private collection) cast by his pupils are based on his last design. In both, Neptune faces left; Bandinelli's marble version would likely have looked left as well, toward the *David* and the *Hercules and Cacus*, as Ammanati's does. This solution would have worked only for the northeast corner of the Palazzo Vecchio; hence, the fountain's eventual location was probably already chosen in Bandinelli's day.

After Bandinelli's death in 1560, Ammanati was the most plausible candidate to build the fountain. Even before Bandinelli's death, Vasari had urged the impatient Cosimo I to assign the fountain to Ammanati. The Neptune and other fountains built at the time related to the construction of new aqueducts that revolutionized Florence's water supply; the piping extended as far as the Piazza della Signoria and into the Palazzo Vecchio. A porphyry fountain by Francesco del Tadda Ferrucci was to go in the courtyard of the Palazzo Vecchio, and Ammanati's Juno fountain in the Hall of the Five Hundred (Salone dei Cinquecento). Thus, the decoration of the palace and that of the piazza would echo each other in a rhetoric of indoor and outdoor spaces.

In 1560 the huge block of marble was set up beside the Loggia della Signoria, where Ammanati was preparing a large plaster model. Benvenuto Cellini eventually cajoled the grand duke into giving him permission to work on a model of his own under the loggia. Inspired by Cellini's tenacity, Vincenzo Danti, Giambologna, and Francesco Mosca prepared still other huge Neptunes. However, Cosimo I intended to choose only between Cellini's and Ammanati's models, as if their temporary installation under the loggia were a sign of the grand duke's esteem for these two sculptors. That Danti and Giambologna were not native Florentines also weighed against their chances of winning the commission for so prestigious a work. This seems

Neptune fountain
© Farrell Grehan / CORBIS

evident from Cosimo's refusal even to look at Giambologna's highly praised model; Cosimo had already decided to give Ammanati the job. It is possible that, after Bandinelli's death and without Cellini's interference, Cosimo may have immediately chosen Ammanati—a Florentine with an international reputation—to create two fountains, the Juno fountain inside the ducal palace and the Neptune on the adjacent piazza.

Having won the rigged competition, Ammanati began to carve the marble in 1561, and in 1565 the Neptune fountain was set up in the piazza for the occasion of Francesco de' Medici's marriage to Johanna of Austria. Because the nymphs and satyrs poised on the edge of the great octagonal pool were not ready yet, Ammanati put plaster versions in their place. The work started again under Francesco I and was completed in 1575, probably with changes. Ammanati had numerous assistants, including Andrea Calamech and Battista Fiammeri, but it is now considered unlikely that any of the expressive bronzes were by Giambologna or Vincenzo de' Rossi, as was once supposed.

To the contrary, the many bronze figures attest to Ammanati's inventiveness, which displays a modern sense of movement and plastic liveliness. The marble Neptune, on the other hand, is more stilted; the figure is checked by the motionless pose originally conceived by Bandinelli, but also by a gracefulness conditioned by Michelangelo's *David*. In fact, Ammanati avoided animating the god's aspect in a hypertrophic sense, as Bandinelli would have done, partly to capture the light through the stretches of muscle. Compared with Bandinelli's *Hercules and Cacus*, Neptune's musculature seems too flat to move his huge body.

Ammanati's creative effort is also evident from his attempt to "correct" the block of marble by adding extra pieces and skillfully hiding the joints. Also noteworthy are the pool and Neptune's chariot, drawn by splendid steeds and decorated with the signs of the zodiac and lion heads. Moreover, the use of variously colored blocks of marble gives a sumptuous and remarkably modern decorative effect.

The architectural and sculptural Neptune complex transformed the medieval site into a princely piazza. The fountain, aligned with the *David* and the *Hercules and Cacus*, ideally prolonged the entrance of the Palazzo Vecchio. Moreover, the eye of a viewer approaching from the northeast would now be directed not only toward the verticals of the austere palace or the arches of the loggia but toward the imposing and joyous spectacle of water jets and statuary at the corner of the ducal palace.

FRANCESCO VOSSILLA

See also **Bandinelli, Baccio; Cellini, Benvenuto**

Further Reading

De Filippis, Felice, *Piazze e fontane di Napoli*, Naples: Azienda Autonoma di Soggiorno Cura e Turismo, 1957

Ffolliott, Sheila, *Civic Sculpture in the Renaissance: Montorsoli's Fountain at Messina*, Ann Arbor, Michigan: UMI Research Press, 1984

Francini, Carlo, "Le settanta bocche della Fontana di Piazza," *Bollettino della Società di Studi Fiorentini* no. 0, Firenze: Alinea (1997) 1997

Heikamp, Detlef, "La fontana del Nettuno in Piazza della Signoria e le sue acque," in *Bartolomeo Ammanati: Scultore e architetto, 1511–1592*, edited by Niccolò Rosselli del Turco and Federica Salvi, Florence: Lucca 1994

Heikamp, Detlef, "Nettuno di Baccio Bandinelli (scheda n.ro 181)," in *Magnificenza alla corte dei Medici: Arte a Firenze alla fine del Cinquecento*, edited by Cristina Acidini Luchinat et al., Milan: Electa, 1997

Keutner, Herbert, "Un modello del Bandinelli per il Nettuno della fontana di Piazza della Signoria a Firenze," in *Scritti in onore di R. Salvini*, Florence: Sansoni, 1984

Kriegbaum, Friederich, "Der Neptunsbrunnen auf der Piazza Signoria," *Mitteilungen des Kunsthistorischen Institutes in Florenz* 3 (1919–32)

Poeschke, Joachim, *Die Skulptur der Renaissance in Italien*, vol. 2, *Michelangelo und seine Zeit*, Munich: Hirmer, 1992; as *Michelangelo and His World: Sculpture of the Italian Renaissance*, translated by Russell Stockman, New York: Abrams, 1996

Utz, Hildegard, "A Note on Ammanati's Apennine and on the Chronology of the Figures for His Fountain of Neptune," *The Burlington Magazine* 115 (1973)

Vossilla, Francesco, "L'altar maggiore di Santa Maria del Fiore di Baccio Bandinelli," in *Altari e committenza: Episodi a Firenze nell' età della controriforma*, edited by Cristina de Benedictis, Florence: Pontecorboli, 1996

CARL ANDRE 1935– *United States*

Carl Andre is by most accounts one of the leading sculptors of the late 20th century. His redefinition of sculpture as something at floor level, which can be walked on, tremendously broadened the traditional idea of sculpture as a vertical and precious object that stands at a distance from the viewer and contains a hidden or symbolic meaning.

The grandson of a bricklayer, Andre was born and raised in Quincy, Massachusetts, a town known for its granite quarries. These quarries, as well as the local tidal marshes and the nearby shipyards where huge, flat, steel plates laid about in all kinds of weather, comprised his early visual memories. He studied at Phillips Academy in Andover, Massachusetts, where the painters Maud and Patrick Morgan encouraged his artistic expression. At Kenyon College in Ohio, his teachers included the noted critic and poet John Crowe Ransom, who was impressed by Andre's early poetry and who may have influenced Andre's later work by advocating a careful, measured Classicism that became known in literary circles as the New Criticism.

After a short career in the army, Andre settled in New York City, where he briefly shared an apartment with another Phillips Academy alumnus, Frank Stella. Andre was influenced by the simple, minimal black stripes that Stella was painting on large-scale canvases in the late 1950s. Andre also became interested in the ideas of the Romanian Modernist sculptor Constantin Brancusi about the same time, and some of his first sculptures were a response to Brancusi's *Endless Columns* of the 1910s and 1920s. Andre was attracted to the vertical, modular look of Brancusi's late works as well as the way Brancusi cut into the wood at regular intervals. *Last Ladder* is an example of this early phase in Andre's career.

After five years as a freight engineer for the Pennsylvania Railroad and after an epiphany of sorts while canoeing on a New Hampshire lake in the summer of 1965, Andre concluded that his sculptures ought to be as flat and horizontal as the surface of a lake or a road. He shifted from carving wood and instead turned toward the assemblage of prefabricated or industrial materials to create sculpture that was not only modular but structural. In other words, the relationship among modular units rather than the discrete units themselves became the fundamental principle of his constructed work. The earliest example of this new approach was *Lever*, a piece that earned him instant recognition as one of a rising new group of Minimalists, a loose collection of New York City artists who included Donald Judd, Robert Morris, and Dan Flavin.

Lever was a single line of 137 unjoined firebricks that ran across the floor for 10.5 meters, starting at one wall and extending almost out of the room. It was Andre's first site-specific work, set up at the Jewish Museum in New York as part of their *Primary Structures* exhibition in 1966. The work caused a furor in the art press, with some critics denouncing it and others hailing it as a milestone. Andre himself said of the piece, knowing that he would add to the controversy by introducing sexual connotations, "All I'm doing is putting Brancusi's *Endless Column* on the ground instead of in the air. Most sculpture is priapic, with the male organ in the air. In my work, Priapus is down on the floor" (see Bourdon, 1966).

Subsequent to *Lever* Andre constructed several major floor-level pieces. *Equivalent VIII* caused a controversy when it was acquisitioned and displayed by the Tate Gallery of London in 1972. This work, for which the Tate Gallery had paid a fairly high price, appeared to many viewers to be nothing more than a banal arrangement of bricks on the gallery floor, something that any bricklayer could have done in a few minutes. However, this piece articulated Andre's concept of sculpture as place in a complex way. The idea that sculpture was part of a total environment that a viewer experiences, whether the setting be indoors, such as in a gallery space, or outdoors, such as a rock garden between large commercial buildings, expressed the core theories of Minimalism. In *Equivalent VIII*, Andre aimed for the sculpture not only to complement the room in which it was displayed but also to alter the physical space.

Beginning in the 1990s, Andre shifted his focus to sculpture as pure material in order to appreciate the raw materials of sculpture for themselves, rather than as compositional elements in a didactic or symbolic artwork. *Kristall*, for instance, consisted of 144 identical flat squares of lead; here, Andre wanted the viewer to recognize the beauty or aesthetics of lead as much as one appreciates the beauty of diamonds or rare rock crystals. He described his works as "historical" in the sense that the materials used could speak to the viewer of a time well before human history, when the earth was first being formed.

Andre's reputation has experienced many reversals in the last 20 years. In the 1980s critics often accused him of repeating himself and of not developing as an artist. At about the same time, he was charged in the death of his wife, the sculptor and body artist Ana Mendieta, but was acquitted of the crime. The 1990s saw a renewed interest in his work and ideas. Some critics maintained that this heightened interest occurred because of a nostalgia for anything associated with the 1960s, including the Minimalist movement. However, Andre's critical successes probably owe to his unflagging insistence that sculpture be redefined in innovative and radical ways. Besides changing the idea that sculpture must be vertically oriented, he has had a far-reaching effect on all the visual arts, influencing the work not only of sculptors, but also of noted architects such as Caruso St. John and furniture designers such as Pierre Charpin.

MARK SULLIVAN

Equivalent VIII
© Tate Gallery, London / Art Resource, NY and Carl Andre / Licensed by VAGA, New York

See also **Brancusi, Constantin; Contemporary Sculpture; Installation; Judd, Donald; Minimalism; Morris, Robert; Serra, Richard; Smithson, Robert**

Biography

Born in Quincy, Massachusetts, United States, 16 September 1935. Attended Phillips Academy in Andover, Massachusetts, 1951–53, where he studied sculpture with Patrick Morgan; attended Kenyon College, Ohio, where his poetry caught the eye of his teacher, the noted writer John Crowe Ransom; served in the U.S. Army from 1955 to 1956; moved to New York City, 1957, and briefly shared apartment with abstract artist Frank Stella; first exhibited works, 1959; worked from 1960 to 1964 as engineer for the Pennsylvania Railroad, then began to produce his trademark floor pieces. Award from the National Endowment for the Arts in 1968. Lives and works in New York City, United States.

Selected Works

1958	*Last Ladder*; wood; Tate Gallery, London, England
1958	*Untitled (Negative Sculpture)*; acrylic; private collection of Barbara Rose, United States
1966	*Equivalent VIII*; unjoined firebricks (destroyed); remade: 1969, Tate Gallery, London, England
1966	*Lever*; 137 unjoined firebricks; National Gallery of Canada, Ottawa, Canada
1976	*The Tomb of the Golden Engenderers*; western red cedar wood; The Detroit Institute of Arts, Michigan, United States
1977	*Stone Field Sculpture*; glacial boulders; Hartford, Connecticut, United States
1988	*48 Roaring Forties*; weathered cold-rolled steel; Kunstsammlung Nordrhein-Westfalen, Düsseldorf, Germany
1991	*Manet 8 Fathoms*; Quincy granite; artist's collection, United States
1996	*Kristall*; lead; Konrad Fischer Gallery, Düsseldorf, Germany

Further Reading

Batchelor, David, *Minimalism*, Cambridge and New York: Cambridge University Press, 1997

Bourdon, David, "The Razed Sites of Carl Andre," *Artforum* 5/2 (October 1966)

Bourdon, David, *Carl Andre: Sculpture, 1959–1977*, New York: Rietman, 1978

Cole, Ian (editor), *Carl Andre and the Sculptural Imagination*, Oxford: Museum of Modern Art, 1996

Jonge, Piet de (editor), *Carl Andre* (exhib. cat.), The Hague: Gemeentemuseum, 1987

Katz, Robert, *Naked by the Window: The Fatal Marriage of Carl Andre and Ana Mendieta*, New York: Atlantic Monthly Press, 1990

Meyer-Hermann, Eva (editor), *Carl Andre, Sculptor, 1996*, Stuttgart, Germany: Oktagon, 1996

Raussmuller, Urs, and Patricia de Peuter, *Minimal Art*, Brussels: Bank Brussels Lambert, 1998

Rose, Barbara, "ABC Art," *Art in America* (October 1965)

Sculptor 1997: Carl Andre (exhib. cat.), Marseille: Musées de Marseille, 1997

Siegel, Jeanne, *Artwords: Discourse on the 60s and 70s*, Ann Arbor, Michigan: UMI Research Press, 1985

Thorkildsen, Asmund, *Laying Low: Carl Andre, Lynda Benglis, Mel Bochner . . .* , Oslo: Kunstnernes Hus, 1997

Tuchman, Phyllis, "An Interview with Carl Andre," *Artforum* 8/10 (1970)

FRANÇOIS ANGUIER 1604–1669 *French*

Although largely overshadowed by his talented younger brother and fellow sculptor Michel, François Anguier made a substantial contribution to 17th-century French sculpture, particularly in the field of funerary monuments. Born in the town of Eu in Normandy (likely in 1604, although some historians suggest 1613 on the basis of his death notice), Anguier initially apprenticed with the woodcarver Martin Caron before joining Simon Guillain's workshop in Paris. The young sculptor apparently made a name for himself, because according to his earliest biographer (Antoine Nicolas Dezallier d'Argenville), Anguier was "called" to England (his presence there has yet to be verified). Subsequently, he made the requisite voyage to Rome, where he is said to have perfected his talents for two years (*ca.* 1638–40) alongside his French colleagues Nicolas Poussin, Charles-Alphonse DuFresnoy, Pierre Mignard I, and Jacques Stella.

As his later French works reveal, Anguier, like his brother Michel, thoroughly absorbed the influence of antique sculpture, and together the brothers helped transform French sculpture by disseminating this more classicizing mode. The elder Anguier was able to continue his study of the antique upon his return to France; Dezallier d'Argenville states that he was made curator of the royal *cabinet des antiques* and given lodgings in the Musée du Louvre, Paris (see Dezallier d'Argenville, 1781). Confirmation of this role is provided by Anguier's earliest known work, a version of the *Borghese Dancers* relief that he reworked from a rough cast made in Rome, and which may have been intended to accompany Poussin's decoration of the *grande galerie* in the Louvre. Anguier's skill in translating the Classical forms into a more fluid and graceful composition notably attracted the attention of the defender of the *modernes*, Charles Perrault, who praised Anguier's "marvelous elegance" in his *Paralelle des anciens & des modernes* (1692).

During the 1640s Anguier began to establish his reputation as a designer of tomb monuments, beginning with that of the noted historian Jacques-Auguste de Thou in 1647; he then created his most frequently cited work, the tomb of Henri, duc de Montmorency, and his wife, between 1649 and 1652. In both cases the artist successfully synthesized idealized portraits of the deceased with classicizing allegorical elements that serve to identify and immortalize their personal qualities. The more ambitious Montmorency funerary monument, with an overall architectonic design that may have been inspired by Giacomo della Porta's *Aldobrandini Tombs* in the Church of Santa Maria sopra Minerva in Rome Italy, is one of Anguier's few funerary ensembles that is still intact and *in situ*. Commissioned by the wife of Henri de Montmorency, the monument served as a means of reasserting the heroic reputation of the duke, who had been beheaded in 1632 after joining the rebellion of Gaston d'Orléans against the king of France. Anguier was responsible for carving the central figures of the reclining duke, anachronistically garbed in Roman armor, and his wife, who, with hands clasped and eyes raised, symbolizes Sorrow. Although such *gisants* (reclining figures) were typical of French tomb sculpture, the more activated poses and greater psychological presence of these figures were innovations, as was the inclusion of the spouse on this type of warrior tomb monument, as Mary Jackson Harvey has shown (see Harvey, 1989). Allegorical figures representing various virtues of the deceased are found on either side: the powerfully pensive Hercules-type signifying *La Force* (at the lower left) is the work of Michel Anguier, whereas the figure of Liberality to the right and Nobility and Religion above are considered to be workshop productions. The elaborate ensemble became widely known in France through engravings and literary references and influenced later tomb designs by Charles Le Brun and François Girardon.

The dignified poignancy exhibited in these early tomb monuments clearly marked Anguier as a master of the genre and led to additional commissions in the 1650s and 1660s for works that were originally located in Parisian churches. One of the most impressive is the tomb for the ducs de Longueville, the center of which is a towering obelisk inscribed with various attributes of the family expressed via hieroglyphics. The obelisk surmounts a base, on the corners of which four life-size female figures signifying various virtues lean in meditative poses. The unique monument serves not only as a striking tribute to the Longueville ancestors, but also to Anguier's elegant brand of French classicism. It is no wonder that Gianlorenzo Bernini, upon seeing this work in its original location in the Church of the Celestines, remarked to the artist (as Paul Fréart de Chantelou, French art collector, later recorded), "You did well here."

Anguier did not limit himself to funerary monuments, however. In terms of state commissions, he designed two bronze vases for the gardens of Versailles and contributed statues of *La Sureté Publique* (Public Security) and *L'Espérance* (Hope) for the decoration of the Porte Saint-Antoine in commemoration of the royal entry of Louis XIV and his new queen in 1660. He also assisted his brother Michel in the extensive program of sculptural decoration for the Church of Val-de-Grâce in Paris, including two reliefs that adorned the main altar and the statues of *St.-Benoît* and *Ste.-Scholastique* for the exterior facade. Unlike Michel, Anguier never joined the Académie Royale de Peinture et de Sculpture; however, his influence lived on through his students, among whom were such notable sculptors as François Girardon, Thomas Regnaudin, and Balthazard and Gaspard Marsy.

JULIA DABBS

See also **Anguier, Michel; Girardon, François**

Biography

Born in Eu, France, 1604. Father (Honoré) a woodcarver; younger brother Michel also a sculptor. Early training with Martin Caron, then with Simon Guillain in Paris; worked briefly in England in 1630s, then spent time in Rome, ca. 1638–40; upon returning to Paris was employed at the Palais du Louvre, and by late 1640s was documented as a sculptor in ordinary to the king. Died in Paris, France, 8 August 1669.

Selected Works

ca. 1642   *Borghese Dancers*; bronze; Wallace Collection, London, England

1647   Tomb of Jacques-Auguste de Thou and his wives (Gasparde de la Châtre and Marie de Brabançon-Cani); marble and bronze; Musée du Louvre, Paris, France

1649–52   Tomb of Henri, duc de Montmorency, and his wife; marble; chapel, *lycée* Banville, Moulins, France

ca. 1650   *La Maladie*; marble; Musée du Château, Versailles, France

1655   Tomb of Henri Chabot, duc de Rohan; marble; Musée du Château, Versailles, France

1656–59   Tomb for the Cardinal de Bérulle; marble; Church of St. Eustache, Paris, France (only bust extant)

1660   *La Sureté Publique* and *L'Espérance*, for the Porte Saint-Antoine; stone; Musée Carnavalet, Paris, France

1663–69 Tomb for the ducs de Longueville; marble and gilded bronze; Musée du Louvre, Paris, France

1664–66 Sculptures for the Church of Val-de-Grâce (with Michel Anguier), Paris, France, including *Deposition from the Cross*; gilt bronze; Church of St. Pierre-St. Paul, Rueil, France; *St.-Benoît* and *Ste.-Scholastique*; marble (no longer extant)

ca. 1667 Tomb of Jacques de Souvré; marble; fragments: Musée du Château, Versailles, France; Musée du Louvre, Paris, France; Church of St. Gervais, St. Protais, Paris, France

Further Reading

Berckenhagen, Ekhart, "François Anguier als Zeichner," *Berliner Museen* 20 (1970)

Dezallier d'Argenville, Antoine-Nicolas, "François et Michel Anguier," in *Vies des fameux architectes depuis la renaissance des arts*, vol. 2, Paris: Debure, 1781; reprint, Geneva: Minkoff Reprint, 1972

Harvey, Mary Jackson, "The Tomb of Montmorency as Récompense du Martyre," *Gazette des Beaux-Arts* 114 (September 1989)

Monicat, Jacques, "Le tombeau du duc et de la duchesse de Montmorency dans la chapelle du lycée de Moulins," *Gazette des Beaux-Arts* 62 (October 1963)

Stein, Henri, *Les frères Anguier: Notice sur leur vie et leurs oeuvres, d'après des documents inédits*, Paris: Plon Nourrit, 1889

MICHEL ANGUIER *ca.* 1612–1686 *French*

Michel Anguier's stylistic versatility has often perplexed art historians and connoisseurs; his significant contributions to 17th-century French art and theory, however, are incontrovertible. After receiving a Jesuit education, Anguier followed in the footsteps of his father, Honoré, and elder brother, François, by becoming a sculptor. He left his native Normandy in 1627 to work as an apprentice to Simon Guillain in Paris, possibly for as long as ten years. Yet Anguier's mature oeuvre shows few traces of Guillain's influence; instead, his penchant for a profoundly classicizing style has more in common with another great French sculptor of the period, Jacques Sarazin, with whom he may have also trained.

As in the case of Sarazin, the greatest impact on Anguier's formation was during his ten-year sojourn in Rome (1641–51). There he came into direct contact with the three masters of Baroque sculpture: François du Quesnoy, Gianlorenzo Bernini, and Alessandro Algardi. Anguier was among a team of sculptors that assisted Bernini with the pilaster relief decoration for the nave of St. Peter's Basilica, Rome (1648); subsequently, he was documented as working in the workshop of Algardi in about 1650. Anguier also found independent work in Rome, most significantly carving three large reliefs for the nave of the Basilica of San Giovanni in Laterano, which reveal his penchant for anatomical articulation as well as for the dramatic expression of emotion. In these respects the artist was clearly influenced by his prolonged study of ancient sculpture such as the *Laocoön*, which he studied alongside his colleague Nicolas Poussin. Anguier's early biographers indicate that he brought back a model of this masterpiece to France, as well as casts of the Farnese *Flora* and the Farnese *Hercules*, and later donated them all to the Académie Royale de Peinture et de Sculpture.

The influence of the antique is further apparent in the sculptor's first major work after his return to France in 1651: the figure of *Hercules* (representing *La Force*) for the Montmorency funerary monument. The powerfully expressed musculature, a hallmark of Anguier's oeuvre, is here coupled with an emotional pensiveness that immediately distinguishes this figure from the other elements of the monument, which was designed by his brother François. These traits are also manifested in the suite of bronze statuettes of gods and goddesses created by Michel in the following year. Here Anguier's stylistic diversity is fully displayed, ranging from the grand classicism of the *Jupiter* and *Juno* to the more energetically "Baroque" figures of *Neptune* and *Ceres*. As he later described in a lecture to the Académie Royale titled "On the Manner of Representing the Divinities according to Their Temperaments," his intention was to express the character of each god and goddess through physiognomic appearance, as determined by their specific humoral nature. Thus style varied according to the subject being represented, rather than being the result of an aesthetic eclecticism.

The bronze divinities undoubtedly enhanced Anguier's growing reputation, for they were widely reproduced (in varying sizes) and could be found in such notable 17th-century collections as those of Louis XIV and François Girardon. The coyly elegant *Amphitrite* was extraordinarily popular and continued to be cast into the 19th century. Anguier was also asked to make a large-scale version (1654–58) of this charming figure, along with other life-size divinities, for the finance minister Nicolas Fouquet's gallery at Saint-Mandé; yet another copy of the *Amphitrite* was requested for the gardens at Versailles (carved by his assistant Nicolas Massé, *ca.* 1680; Musée du Louvre, Paris). The lively classicism of the artist's works seems to have particularly appealed to the Franco-Italianate taste of his patrons, most notably Fouquet and Anne of Austria. In addition to his works for Saint-Mandé, Anguier created sculptures to adorn the finance minister's château of Vaux-le-Vicomte, some of which are still *in situ*. Perhaps the artist's most significant and loyal patron, however, was the French regent Anne of Austria. From 1653 to 1657 Anguier collaborated with the Italian painter Giovanni Francesco Romanelli in adorning the ceilings of the queen's new apartment in the Louvre (now Denon Wing); perhaps most remarkable are his writhing Apollonian and Dionysian term figures, which exhibit an exuberance rarely before seen in French sculpture. A few years later the queen called on Anguier again, this time to decorate virtually the entire interior of the Church of Val-de-Grâce (Paris) with relief sculpture. The centerpiece of this herculean effort was the main altarpiece group of the *Nativity*, later moved to the Church of St. Roch (Paris) in the 19th century (a copy is at Val-de-Grâce). This masterpiece epitomizes Anguier's interest in juxtaposing antithetical stylistic forms for rhetorical affect, as the amazement openly expressed by the "Baroque" figure of Joseph effectively contrasts with Mary's more introspective demeanor, exquisitely embodied in her contained, classicized form.

Shortly after he completed the decoration of Val-de-Grâce, Anguier joined the Académie Royale de Peinture et de Sculpture. He was immediately named an adjunct professor and in later years was voted to the esteemed position of rector. During his tenure Anguier delivered some 14 lectures, more than any other academician of his day, surpassing even the academy's director, Charles Le Brun. The sculptor emphasized the decorous portrayal of temperament through variations in the proportion, contour, and overall physiognomic form of the body, often referring to casts of ancient

sculptures throughout his lectures. Anguier's ideas provided a crucial corporal complement to Le Brun's emphasis on the facial display of emotions and were adopted or shared by other French 17th-century writers on art such as André Félibien, Henri Testelin, and Roger de Piles.

At this later stage in his career, Anguier did more teaching than sculpting, with his last major project being reliefs for the Porte Saint-Denis (Paris) from 1671 to 1675. Although some historians have downplayed his importance because there are few extant works at Versailles, contemporary documents reveal that Anguier in fact obtained substantive commissions there until age diminished his activity. Through his versatile works and voluminous words, Michel Anguier clearly impacted later generations of French sculptors, including François Girardon, Gaspard Marsy, René Fremin, and Augustin Pajou; the full extent of his influence, however, awaits further study.

JULIA DABBS

See also **du Quesnoy, François; Pajou, Augustin; Sarazin, Jacques**

Biography

Born in Eu, France, 28 September 1612 (or 1614). Son of Honoré a woodcarver; elder brother François also a sculptor; younger brother Guillaume a painter. Attended College of Jesuits in Eu until age 15; as of 1627, in Paris workshop of Simon Guillain; in Rome, 1641–51; worked under Gianlorenzo Bernini's direction at St. Peter's Basilica, Rome (1648), and in Alessandro Algardi's workshop, 1648–50; returned to Paris, 1651; became member of the Académie de Saint-Luc, 1663; accepted into Académie Royale de Peinture et de Sculpture, 1668, and made adjunct professor same day; subsequently elected to the positions of adjunct rector (1669) and rector (1671–86). Died in Paris, France, 11 July 1686.

The Nativity
The Conway Library, Courtauld Institute of Art

Selected Works

1648–49   *The Flood, The Crucifixion*, and *Moses Leading His People Out of Egypt*; stucco; nave of the Basilica of San Giovanni in Laterano, Rome, Italy

1651   *Hercules* (or *La Force*), for the tomb of Henri, duc de Montmorency, and his wife); marble; chapel, *lycée* Banville, Moulins, France

1652   Series of gods and goddesses; bronze: *Jupiter*, J. Paul Getty Museum, Los Angeles, California, United States; National Gallery of Art, Washington, D.C.,

United States; *Neptune*, Metropolitan Museum of Art, New York City, United States; *Amphitrite*, Metropolitan Museum of Art, New York City, United States; *Pluto*, Grünes Gewolbe, Dresden, Germany; *Ceres*, Victoria and Albert Museum, London, England

1654–58 *Amphitrite*; limestone; Toledo Museum of Art, Ohio, United States

1654–58 *Leda and the Swan*; limestone; Metropolitan Museum of Art, New York City, United States

ca. Sculptural decoration for *appartements* of
1655–57 Anne of Austria; stucco and bronze; Musée du Louvre, Paris, France

1658–61 Sculptural decoration, château of Vaux-le-Vicomte (near Melun), France

1662–67 Sculptural decoration (including *The Nativity*); Church of St. Roch, Paris, France; copy: Church of Val-de-Grâce, Paris, France

ca. 1668 *Hercules and Atlas*; terracotta; Musée du Louvre, Paris, France

ca. Reliefs; limestone; Porte Saint-Denis,
1671–75 Paris, France

ca. 1684 *Christ on the Cross*; marble; Church of St. Roch, Paris, France

Further Reading

Black, Bernard, and Hugues-W. Nadeau, *Michel Anguier's Pluto: The Marble of 1669: New Light on the French Sculptor's Career*, London and Atlantic Highlands, New Jersey: Athlone Press, 1990

Charageat, Marguerite, "La statue d'Amphitrite et la suite des dieux et des déesses de Michel Anguier," *Archives de l'art français* 23 (1968)

Dabbs, Julia Kathleen, "Embodying Ethos: Anguier, Poussin, and the Concept of Corporal Expression in the French Academy," (dissertation), University of Maryland, College Park, 1999

Guillet De Saint-Georges, "Mémoires historiques sur les ouvrages de M. Anguier," in *Mémoires inédits sur la vie et les ouvrages des membres de l'Académie royale de peinture et de sculpture*, edited by Louis Dussieux et al., vol. 1, Paris: Dumoulin, 1854; reprint, Paris: De Nobele, 1968

Helsdingen, H.W. van, "Michel Anguier's voordracht over de Hercules Farnese, Parijs 1669," *Nederlands kunsthistorisch Jaarboek* 33 (1982)

La Moureyre, Françoise de, "L'*Hiver* au jardin du Luxembourg: Une statue de Michel Anguier?" *Gazette des Beaux-Arts* 123 (April 1994)

Raggio, Olga, "Sculpture in the Grand Manner: Two Groups by Anguier and Monnot," *Apollo* 106 (November 1977)

Stein, Henri, *Les frères Anguier: Notice sur leur vie et leurs oeuvres, d'après des documents inédits*, Paris: Plon Nourrit, 1889

Wardropper, Ian, "Michel Anguier's Series of Bronze Gods and Goddesses: A Re-Examination," *Marsyas* 18 (1975–76)

BENEDETTO ANTELAMI (*fl. ca. 1170–1220*) *Italian*

Benedetto Antelami was active about 1170–1220, predominantly in the city of Parma. Stylistically, his work draws from the schools of Piacenza and Modena, although he probably spent his formative years in France. His sculpture is stylistically distinguished from that of his Emilian predecessors in the combination of emotive serenity and playful drapery characteristic of the emerging French Gothic, with the solid, plastic forms adapted from ancient Roman works. Antelami was a master of surface texture and narrative; his figures display minutely carved pupils, delicately embroidered garments, compelling gestures, and thoughtful facial expressions. Incorporating iconographic details from Byzantine and French sources, Antelami also adopted a complex symbolic vocabulary previously unknown in Italy.

Antelami's name is known today through two signed and dated works, both executed in Parma. No other documentary evidence has yet been unearthed. Comparing these works with other unsigned works has allowed modern scholars to reconstruct Antelami's oeuvre hypothetically. This stylistic evidence suggests that he may have begun his career in Genoa, where his hand has been detected in the figures of two lions (perhaps originally forming part of a now-dismantled pulpit for the Cathedral of San Lorenzo), or in the Provençal city of Arles, where he might have aided in the execution of the cloister of St. Trophime. After establishing himself, he was given important commissions in Parma. He also worked in Borgo S. Donnino (Fidenza) after completing his first project in Parma.

Antelami's earlier inscription occurs on his relief the *Deposition of Christ*: "In 1178, the sculptor Benedetto called Antelami finished the work." Besides identifying the sculptor, this inscription indicates that he was called "Antelami," which has been interpreted to mean that he belonged to the Magistri Antelami, or architect's guild. This guild was active in Genoa but probably originated near Lake Como. Antelami's membership in the Magistri Antelami is in accord with the stylistic evidence presented by his San Lorenzo lions.

Problems relating to the style, iconography, and original function of the *Deposition* encapsulate the scholarly disputes surrounding Antelami's entire oeuvre. The relief might have belonged to an altar, a pulpit, a choir screen, or a combination of a pulpit and choir screen (as in an analogous example still extant in Modena). Similar problems of original placement exist for his later *Labors of the Months*. The cycle may have formed the Parma Baptistery's sculptural program, but it has also been reasonably hypothesized that it was commissioned for the Parma Cathedral's main portal.

Second, classicizing motifs used in the *Deposition* and other works (e.g., the heads surrounded by circular garlands representing the sun and moon) as well as his high degree of relief have raised the question of how he acquired his knowledge of ancient sculpture. Most scholars conclude that he visited Provence (specifically, the Church of Saint Trophime, Arles, the Abbey of Saint Gilles, and the ancient sites of Orange, Narbonne, and Nimes), where nearby ancient monuments influenced local sculptors. Others look to the Romanesque art of Genoa and the local ancient ruins of Luni, Verona, and Milan. Antelami's association with the Magistri Antelami would place him near Luni and Milan, whereas the close political and commercial relations between Genoa and Provence in this period offer support for his having visited Provençal cities.

The possibility that Antelami sojourned in France is further suggested by iconographic and stylistic considerations. The badly damaged companion relief of the *Deposition* depicts Christ in Majesty, a subject popular on tympana all over France (e.g., Moissac and Chartres) but rare in Italy. On the basis of similarities of drapery handling, facial modeling, and composition, in addition to iconographic affinities, some scholars have proposed that Antelami traveled as far as the Isle de France. In French art, the Christ in Majesty has been connected to contemporary assertions of Christ's divinity. Antelami's use of it has been associated with the same antiheretical motives. Other echoes of French influence occur in Antelami's later works, notably in his *Last Judgment* above the Parma Baptistery's west portal, which relates to Isle de France examples from the 1180s, and the Fidenza Cathedral facade, which replicates certain features of Saint Gilles, leading some historians to hypothesize a second French trip between 1178 and 1196. It cannot be discounted that Antelami learned of these new symbolic configurations from French model books.

Antelami's second inscription, located on the architrave of the Parma Baptistery's main portal, declares

that he began this work in 1196. As the Baptistery was in use by 1216 (both dates, 1196 and 1216, are confirmed by the chronicler Fra Salimbene da Adam), its sculptures were probably mostly completed by this date. The sculptural program is one of the most iconographically and philosophically complex ensembles of Italian medieval sculpture; its complexity recalls the grand French programs. Compared with the 1178 *Deposition*, the Baptistery reliefs illustrate Antelami's progress toward a more realistic narrative style, possibly due to even greater attention to antique models or to new exposure to French Gothic style. He probably began with the *Presentation in the Temple*, which retains a certain rigidity and figural isolation, although it introduces greater spatial complexity. Space further opens up in the expressive and fluid movements of his masterpiece, *Flight into Egypt*. The *Labors of the Months* (a late work whose execution is not uniformly given to the master himself) continue the process of the liberation of space and increased articulation of the body. His *Baarlam and Josaphat* and his *Last Judgment* are the first depictions of these themes in northern Italian monumental sculpture. Although the former contains visual passages recalling an early Aratus manuscript, the latter subtly attends to both religious symbolism (Christ's cross is emphatically made of the tree of life) and narrative detail, as in the inclusion of the tiny figure of St. John dreaming.

The problems in describing Antelami's sources and the chronology of his travels stem precisely from his striking formal and conceptual originality. At no stage of his career does a single model dominate. Antelami's originality—both iconographic and stylistic—might also have contributed to his never having established a proper school, although his influence (or workshop) may be detected in Verona, Milan, Vercelli, Ferrara, Forli, Arezzo, and the Dalmatian city of Trogir. His closest follower was his assistant, the "Master of Abdon and Sennen," who executed sculptures in the Parma Baptistery. Another gifted follower was the "Master of the Ferrara Months," whose reliefs have been used to help reconstruct the original placement of some of Antelami's own.

MAIA WELLINGTON GAHTAN

Biography

There is virtually no known definitive information on the artist's life. All that is known for certain about Benedetto Antelami is that he signed and dated two works in Parma, Italy, in 1178 and 1196. Other claims about Antelami's life are hypothetical and based upon stylistic analysis.

Deposition of Christ
The Conway Library, Courtauld Institute of Art

Selected Works

before 1178?	Historiated capital; marble; Church of Saint Trophime, Arles, France
before 1178?	Two lions; marble; Cathedral of San Lorenzo, Genoa, Italy
1178	*Christ in Majesty*; marble; Galleria Nazionale, Parma, Italy
1178	*Deposition of Christ*; marble; Parma Cathedral, Italy
1178?	Three historiated capitals and other fragments; marble; Galleria Nazionale, Parma, Italy
1178?	Four lions from the bases of columns; marble; Parma Cathedral, Italy
between 1178 and 1196?	Facade sculptures, including *Life of S. Donnino* and the prophets *David* and *Ezechiel*, and facade; marble; Fidenza Cathedral, Italy
between 1178 and 1196?	*Madonna and Child*; marble; Fidenza Cathedral, Italy
between 1178 and 1196?	*Madonna and Child*; marble; Abbey of St. Benedict, Fontevivo, Italy
1196– ca. 1216	*Solomon, Queen of Saba, Last Judgment, Baarlam and Josaphat, Adoration of the Magi, David Playing the Harp, Presentation in the Temple*, and *Flight into Egypt*; marble; Baptistery, Parma, Italy
after 1196?	Bishop's throne; marble; Parma Cathedral, Italy
after 1210?	*Christ in Majesty*; marble; Baptistery, Parma, Italy
after 1210?	*Labors of the Months*; marble; Baptistery, Parma, Italy
1219–25	Facade; marble; Abbey of San Andrea, Vercelli, Italy (Antelami workshop?)

Further Reading

De Francovich, Géza, *Benedetto Antelami, architetto e scultore e l'arte del suo tempo*, 2 vols., Milan: Electa, 1952

Gnudi, Cesare, "Il Maestro dei Mesi di Ferrara e la lunetta di San Mercuriale a Forlì," in *The Year 1200: A Symposium* by François Avril, New York: The Metropolitan Museum of Art, 1975

Parker, Elizabeth, "The Descent from the Cross: Its Relation to the Extra-Liturgical (Dispositio) Drama," (dissertation), New York University, 1975

Porter, Arthur Kingsley, *Lombard Architecture*, 4 vols., New Haven: Yale University Press, 1915–17

Quintavalle, Arturo Carlo, Arturo Calzona, and Giuseppa Z. Zanichelli, *Benedetto Antelami*, Milan: Electa, 1990

Sauerländer, Willibald, "La cultura figurativa emiliana in età romanica" in *Nicholaus e l'arte del suo tempo*, edited by Cesare Gnudi and Angiola Maria Romanini, vol. 1, Ferrara: Corbo, 1985

Stocchi, Sergio, *L'Emilia-Romagna*, Milan: Jaca Book, 1984

Toesca, Pietro, *Il battistero di Parma: Architetture e sculture di Benedetto Antelami e seguaci, affreschi dei secoli XIII e XIV*, Milan: Silvana, 1960

Woelk, Moritz, *Benedetto Antelami: Die Werke in Parma und Fidenza*, Münster, Germany: Rhema, 1995

ANTEPENDIUM

An antependium is any decorated object that is placed in front of an altar. It could be made of many materials, but the most common were wood, metal, mosaic, woven cloth, and painted panel. Unfortunately, constructing an accurate picture of the medieval antependium is impeded by the lack of surviving examples: woven wool, silk, and cotton often deteriorated, and precious metals were both attractive to plunderers and susceptible to being melted down for new works. Nevertheless, enough is known to suggest a general history.

As early as the 4th century, antependiums were made of cloth and were hung on the altar front (hence the term: *ante* [before] + *pendere* [to hang]). By the 7th century altar fronts were decorated with stone, and during the 9th century painted panels, hammered metalwork, and sculpted wood found common use. Metal antependiums were made of metal sheets that were pounded into high relief over a wooden formwork, or hammered out from the reverse using the repoussé technique. The material was usually silver or gold (or gilt on copper) that could be decorated with semiprecious stones, jewels, and elaborate enamel work. Relief sculpture from wooden and stone antependiums was colorfully painted, as was sculpture in general during the Middle Ages, although surviving polychromy is rare. Tempera paint was the most common medium for painted antependium panels until the advent of oil paint during the 15th century.

The subjects and iconographic themes of antependiums remained relatively consistent. Christological scenes (Christ in Majesty, the Crucifixion, the Ascension, etc.) predominated, while apostles, saints, angels, and the Virgin Mary were also popular. Marian depictions increased during the High Gothic period, a direction that parallels the increased veneration of the Virgin Mary during the 13th century. Scenes from the life of the Virgin and her mysteries became as popular as those of Christ. It also appears that, in terms of composition and subject matter, antependiums parallel other artistic media. For instance, the depiction of Christ in Majesty surrounded by the Four Evangelists was a common scene in architectural sculpture, especially in portal sculpture, wall painting, and illuminated manuscripts. The examples below provide a brief overview of the subject matter and iconography as well the materials used for medieval antependiums.

An early example of a painted antependium (*ca.* 1170) comes from the Church of St. Walburgis in Soest, Germany. Made of tempera paint and gold leaf on wood, it depicts Christ in Majesty in the center quatrefoil while St. Walburgis, the Virgin, St. Augustine, and John the Baptist surround Christ in a series of arches divided by columns. The St. Walburgis antependium typifies the general arrangement of the rectangular antependium in which squares, rectangles, medallions, quatrefoils, arches, columns, etc., break up the compositional space into sections. Whether the antependium was made of cloth, sculpture, painted panel, or metal, such devices were used consistently to allocate the compositional space to Christ or the Virgin as the main subjects.

Another antependium, the so-called Pala d'Oro located in the Aachen Cathedral treasury, is a fine example of pounded metalwork. The current grid arrangement of the Pala d'Oro was put together in 1951, yet it remains faithful to medieval arrangements of this type. Twelve square panels and four small circles surround a central *mandorla* (almond-shaped form), which itself depicts Christ in Majesty. The four small medallions show the four symbols of the Four Evangelists (Matthew, angel; Mark, lion; Luke, ox; John, eagle), while the Passion of Christ is illustrated in the 12 panels using a continuous narrative format. The continuous narrative arrangement and the composition of the 12 panels parallel the imagery in contemporary manuscripts. Dating to 1000–1020, the Pala d'Oro is an excellent example of Romanesque metalwork with the delicate *repoussé* (the method of producing relief metal by hammering and punching chiefly from behind) technique.

Fine metalwork similar to the Aachen antependium is especially prevalent along the Meuse Valley in Belgium. On a Mosan antependium (*ca.* 1160) now located in the Museé de Cluny in France is a depiction of the Pentecost constructed of copper, gold, and enamel. Located in the hemicycle at the top is Christ, while the apostles flank him on either side. This Christological scene parallels numerous other antependiums in which columns and square panels are instrumental in dividing the work into clearly delineated compositions.

Most surviving antependiums are sculptural works, yet there are also examples of linen woven with precious metal and silk appliqué. An unusually fine example of Spanish work from the middle of the 15th century is found in the Art Institute of Chicago. Made in two parts, the upper section of the work was hung behind the altar, while the lower section was placed on the altar front, much as the first decorative cloths did during the 4th century. Illustrated are the Madonna and Child (above) along with the image of Christ and six of the apostles, each situated in his own arch (below). Compositional and iconographic traditions continue even in this later antependium: a comparison to the Soest tempra antependium almost 500 years older reveals the striking compositional and iconographic similarities between the two works.

Toward the end of the 14th century, the antependium and its ornamentation gave way to the more ambitious altarpieces of the 15th and 16th centuries. The modest, largely two-dimensional decoration of the altar front was now replaced by single-, double- and triple-winged altarpieces with large painted panels and monumental sculpture. One "transitional" work illustrates this change. The high altar from Cologne Cathedral displays on its front and sides the figurative work and architectural forms found in the antependiums discussed above. On the other hand, the small figures of Christ, the apostles, and the arcade and tracery work are carved as independent pieces of marble. Were these to be rearranged into an entirely new composition, they could easily accommodate the composition of a monumental altarpiece.

KEVIN MCMANAMY

See also **Altarpiece: Northern Europe; Altarpiece: Southern Europe**

Further Reading

Berg-Sobré, Judith, *Behind the Altar Table: The Development of the Painted Retable in Spain, 1350–1500*, Columbia: University of Missouri Press, 1989

Braun, Joseph, *Der christliche Altar in seiner geschichtlichen Entwicklung*, 2 vols., Munich: Alte Meister Guenther Koch, 1924

Humfrey, Peter, and Martin Kemp (editors), *The Altarpiece in the Renaissance*, Cambridge and New York: Cambridge University Press, 1990

Reinle, Adolf, *Die Ausstattung deutscher Kirchen im Mittelalter: Eine Einführung*, Darmstadt, Germany: Wissenschaftliche Buchgesellschaft, 1988

ANTICO (PIER JACOPO ALARI BONACOLSI) *ca.* **1460–1528** *Italian*

Pier Jacopo Alari Bonacolsi, called Antico, was a pioneer in Italian Renaissance bronze sculpture. His surviving work includes medallions, reliefs, a vase, statuettes, heads, and busts. Born in Mantua, he served the ruling Gonzaga family for half a century not only as a sculptor but also as a multifaceted court artist. Although today he is known only for his bronzes, documents show that he worked in gold and silver; that he was involved with architectural design, construction, and interior decoration; and that he was considered an expert judge of antiquities and excelled in their restoration. Over the centuries his name was forgotten until in 1888 Umberto Rossi published a substantial number of documents concerning Antico. The evidence of the documents suggested to Wilhelm von Bode that a group of bronzes of similar style could be attributed to Antico, and in 1910, on the basis of an inscription, H.J. Hermann established the definitive link between the artist and his work.

In response to the desires of his Gonzaga family patrons, Antico was the first artist to create the consummate classicizing, small court bronze. The demand for replicas of his bronzes led Antico to develop a sophisticated process that permitted easy duplication and variation of his motifs. He was one of the earliest, if not the first, of the Renaissance artists to possess this expertise. Furthermore, the style and finish of his bronzes are indicative of Gonzaga family taste, and since each bronze, even when based on an obvious antique prototype, had a specific meaning to the patron who commissioned it, his work provides insight into Mantuan court culture of this period.

It was Antico's innate understanding of Classical principles of ideal form and his wide knowledge of Classical motifs that gave his bronzes their classicizing appearance. Few of his bronzes are directly based on one antique prototype. Some are pastiches derived from various Classical and modern sources chosen to fulfill the intent of each princely commission. Distinguishing features of his bronzes are their relatively abstract but plastic forms, which have been smoothly polished and, according to the commission, sometimes partially gilded and given silver eyes. Restrained in action and emotion in the Classical sense, his bronzes are nevertheless expressive and never static. Antico was sensitive to oppositions of form, emotion, and color. Contrasting to the broader surfaces of his bronzes, he was able to work in miniature details, suggesting a goldsmith's training. The dark patinas of his bronzes could be opposed to accents of gold and silver.

The artist was referred to as Antico from his first notice of 1487. He regarded his small bronzes as *antichità* (antiquities), signs of his full commitment to the humanist culture and classicizing art sponsored by the Gonzaga family. Antico's first known patrons were Gianfrancesco Gonzaga and his wife, Antonia del Balzo. After the death of Gianfrancesco in 1496, his widow moved to Gazzuolo where she and Gianfrancesco's brother, Bishop Ludovico, established a new court.

Antico's medallions, with one exception, were designed for Gianfrancesco and his wife to celebrate the establishment of their new dynasty. The portraits of Gianfrancesco on these medals show an evolution in style from a more naturalistic image to increasing idealization, the last with Gianfrancesco in Roman costume. The famous *Gonzaga Urn* was created to commemorate the founding of the dynasty. Other reliefs by Antico of this and later periods have one theme— the deeds of Hercules. The neutral surface of Antico's early roundel of the *Infant Hercules and the Serpents* (*ca.* 1485) is covered with elongated figures illustrating the event and describing the emotion it aroused. The details of both the *Gonzaga Urn* and this relief are evidence of Antico's wide knowledge of mythology and Classical motifs early in his career.

The sumptuously gilded *Venus Felix* with silver eyes appears to be the sole statuette surviving from this period. Its iconography suggests that it may have been a gift from Gianfrancesco to Francesco II Gonzaga, marquess of Mantua, after Francesco's famous victory at Fornovo in 1495. Its Roman prototype was a portrait statue, which is now in the Vatican. Antico substituted the forms of the more natural but mediocre Roman sculpture with more abstract, plastic, and sen-

Meleager
© Victoria and Albert Museum, London / Art Resource, New York

suous forms. The pubic region is revealed, and due to the backward-blown curvilinear folds at the legs the figure appears to be stepping forward into the wind as would the figure of an antique victory. The attribute torn from her left hand may have been a symbol of victory cast in gold.

By 1498 Antico was in the service of Bishop Ludovico Gonzaga. The majority of Antico's bronzes with luxurious gilding are datable to his service to the bishop. The evolution to Antico's mature and late style can be illustrated by his series of three partial-gilt statuettes of the celebrated *Apollo Belvedere* (2nd century CE), a marble sculpture now in the Vatican and known by the 1490s. It was unusual for Antico to produce autograph versions of a motif, but this personification of the sun god was of particular interest to the Gonzaga family, as the sun was one of their central emblems. Antico probably produced his first model of the *Apollo* for Gianfrancesco, as a document mentions a similar sculpture that was cast in silver. It is generally agreed that the *Apollo* in the Liebeighaus (Frankfurt am Main, Germany) is the earliest version, dated about 1497–98, due to the conversion of the freely striding antique figure to a stiffer, but strong, four-sided quattrocento pose. The figure's proportions are similar to the prototype. In Antico's second version, the *Apollo* in the Galleria Giorgio Franchetti alla Ca d'Oro, Venice, the body is heavier, the surfaces more sensuous, and the movement more vigorous than that of the ancient prototype. A final version, now in a private collection, was produced about 1520–22. Here both the proportions and stride of the antique sculpture have been fully assimilated and the details of the head have been fluidly modeled in Antico's late style. Significantly, and on overt criticism of the pose of the renowned prototype, the right arm has been changed from a stiff to an outstretched position, thereby adding further grace to the figure as a whole.

In contrast to the descriptive composition and elongated figural style of Antico's early roundel of the *Infant Hercules and the Serpents*, his series of the deeds of Hercules (*ca.* 1500) portray solely the deeds themselves, and the adult Hercules is rendered in normal proportions. In the 1510s the female figure also became more natural as well as ample than those of the *Venus Felix*. Antico's most advanced female figure is the *Atropos*. The London *Atropos* (*ca.* 1508–11), whose right hand holds the handles of a pair of scissors, is not only fully nude, but her body forms are monumental and her pose is a twisting *figura serpentinata*. This pose was Antico's response to a modern masterpiece, Leonardo da Vinci's *Leda* (*ca.* 1503). The identification of the *Atropos* as a Fate is confirmed in Antico's period by an inscribed Roman relief with a clothed figure in a somewhat similar pose.

During Antico's career he served the Gonzaga families both in the new state and in Mantua itself. It is not known what Antico did for Cardinal Sigismondo Gonzaga, his patron about 1511/12, but in the Seminario in Mantua today are four bronze heads by the artist set in terracotta busts.

In 1519, when Isabella d'Este was planning the decoration of her new apartments in the Palazzo Ducale in Mantua, she asked Antico to find which models or molds remained of the bronzes that he had produced for the bishop. Some of these were replicated for her and at the time of her death stood on a cornice in her grotto. These hollow-cast replicas could be easily produced because of Antico's development of an indirect method of bronze casting that preserved the original wax model.

Along with the third *Apollo* and other statuettes of this period, Antico created the *Seated Pan*, originally paired with a figure of Olympos. *Seated Pan* was directly based on an antique prototype, which Antico "improved" in design and rendered appreciably more refined. It was during this last period that Antico produced his most elegant busts. The bust of *Ariadne* in Vienna is exquisitely finished from every point of view and was clearly intended to be appreciated at eye level.

Although Antico did not acquire an international reputation, in Mantua he was remembered long after his death. In 1586 Duke Guglielmo Gonzaga, who, as he was born after Antico's death could not have known the artist personally, ordered his artist at Goito to include figures in the scrolls he was to paint. The duke cited two examples of what he desired, those of the "good Antico" and of Giulio Romano.

ANN HERSEY ALLISON

See also **Apollo Belvedere**

Biography

Born in Mantua, Italy, *ca.* 1460. Presumably trained as a goldsmith; initially worked as a medallist; went on to create models and cast them in bronze and restore antique sculpture; by 1487 acquired the pseudonym "Antico"; gained artistic and social success for exclusive service to Gonzaga courts; main patrons included Gianfrancesco Gonzaga, Bishop Ludovico Gonzaga, Cardinal Sigismondo, Isabella d'Este, and her son, Federico II; recorded trips to Rome by 1494 and in 1497; held position as *camerero* (gentleman of the bedchamber) to Bishop Ludovico, 1501; general adviser on artistic matters for Isabella, from 1506; ennobled and assumed the name Bonacolsi, *ca.* 1516. Died in Gazzuolo, Italy, by 19 July 1528.

Selected Works

ca. 1481–83   *Gonzaga Urn*; bronze; Galleria e Museo Estense, Modena, Italy

ca. 1484–85   Medal of Antonia del Balzo/Spes, no. I 5963; bronze; Museo Nazionale del Bargello, Florence, Italy

ca. 1486–90   Medal of Gianfrancesco Gonzaga/Fortuna; bronze; Galleria Giorgio Franchetti alla Ca d'Oro, Venice, Italy (prime example)

ca. 1496   *Venus Felix*; bronze; Kunsthistorisches Museum, Vienna, Austria

ca. 1497–98   *Apollo*, no. 628; bronze; Liebieghaus, Frankfurt, Germany

ca. 1500   Reliefs of *Hercules and the Lion* and *Hercules and the Hydra*; bronze; Museo Nazionale del Bargello, Florence, Italy

ca. 1500   *Meleager*; bronze; Victoria and Albert Museum, London, England

ca. 1501   *Apollo*, no. 97; bronze; Galleria Giorgio Franchetti alla Ca d'Oro, Venice, Italy

1503?   *Seated Nymph*; bronze; formerly collection of Baron Gustave Rothschild, Paris, France

1506–11   *Hercules and Antaeus*; bronze; Victoria and Albert Museum, London, England

ca. 1519–20   *Seated Pan*; bronze; Kunsthistorisches Museum, Vienna, Austria

ca. 1520–22   *Venus Caritas*; bronze; Walters Art Museum, Baltimore, Maryland, United States

ca. 1522   Bust of Alexander the Great; bronze; collection of the princes of Liechtenstein, Vaduz, Liechtenstein

ca. 1522–28   *Pan with a Pipe*; bronze; Metropolitan Museum of Art, New York City, United States

1524   Bust of Antoninus Pius; bronze; Metropolitan Museum of Art, New York City, United States

ca. 1524–28   *Ariadne*; bronze; Kunsthistorisches Museum, Vienna, Austria

Further Reading

Allison, A.H., "The Bronzes of Antico," *Jahrbuch der Kunsthistorischen Sammlungen in Wien* 89–90 (1993–94)

Allison, A.H., and R.B. Pond, Sr., "On Copying Bronze Statuettes," *Journal of the American Institute of Conservation* 23 (1983)

Bode, Wilhelm von, *Die italienischen Bronzestatuetten der Renaissance*, 3 vols., Berlin: Cassirer, 1907; as *The Italian Bronze Statuettes of the Renaissance*, translated by William Grétor, London: Grevel, 1908; revised edition, edited by James David Draper, New York: M.A.S. de Reinis, 1980

Leithe-Jasper, Manfred, *Renaissance Master Bronzes from the Collection of the Kunsthistorisches Museum, Vienna*, Washington, D.C.: Scala Books, 1986

Planiscig, Leo, *Die Bronzeplastiken, Statuetten, Reliefs, Geräte und Plaketten*, Vienna: Schroll, 1924

Pope-Hennessy, John, *An Introduction to Italian Sculpture*, 3 vols., London: Phaidon, 1963; 4th edition, 1996; see especially vol. 2, *Italian Renaissance Sculpture*

Radcliffe, A., "Antico and the Mantuan Bronze," in *Splendours of the Gonzaga*, edited by David Chambers and Jane Martineau, London: Victoria and Albert Museum, 1981

Stone, R.E., "Antico and the Development of Bronzecasting in Italy at the End of the Quattrocento," *Metropolitan Museum Journal* 16 (1982)

Venturi, Adolfo, *Storia dell'arte italiana*, 11 vols., Milan: U. Hoepli, 1901–40; reprint, Nendeln, Liechtenstein: Kraus, 1967; especially see vol. 10

Weihrauch, Hans R., *Europäische Bronzestatuetten*, Braunschweig, Germany: Klinkhardt and Biermann, 1967

HERCULES AND ANTAEUS

Antico (Pies Jacopo Alari Bonacolsi [ca. 1460–1528])
1506–1511
bronze
h. 39.14 cm (with base, 40.64 cm)
Victoria and Albert Museum, London, England
(ca. 1519 version in Kunsthistorisches Museum, Vienna, Austria)

In 1519 Isabella d'Este, marchesa of Mantua, consulted Antico regarding the decorative schemes of her new rooms in the Corte Vecchia of the Palazzo Ducale and asked him to investigate which models or molds still existed of the bronzes that he had made for Bishop Ludovico Gonzaga (d. 1511). Of the eight molds that remained, Antico considered his finest creation to be *Hercules and Antaeus*. Today this model survives in three versions. Two will be considered here: the *Hercules and Antaeus* in the Victoria and Albert Museum in London and that in the Kunsthistorisches Museum in Vienna. The latter has Isabella's inscription executed in the wax state on its base and can be identified in the posthumous inventory of Isabella's belongings of 1542. Antico's letter to Isabella of April 1519 states that he would give cored and finished wax models that were ready to be cast to maestro Iohan, who had been his assistant when in the service of the bishop. Maestro Iohan would cast and, presumably, execute the time-consuming finishing necessary to obtain the smooth, polished surfaces that Antico's Gonzaga patrons preferred.

The London *Hercules and Antaeus* was modeled and likely cast in bronze by Antico himself and is, in all probability, the one produced for the bishop. Consequently, it can be presumed that Antico executed the final detailed wax models of both the London and Vienna bronzes.

The subject of the Classical hero Hercules ridding the world of the cruel giant Antaeus, the son of the Earth goddess, Gaia, was popular in the humanist climate of the Italian Renaissance. In Classical disguise the general interpretation was the triumph of virtue over vice. A principle reason for the popularity of this deed was that Hercules' great strength alone proved insufficient to conquer Antaeus, and that he succeeded only by using his mind. He reasoned that Antaeus derived renewed strength each time he touched his mother, the Earth. Therefore, by lifting and holding Antaeus away from the Earth, Hercules was able to crush the giant in his embrace.

In Antico's motif Antaeus is not depicted as a giant, but is the same size as Hercules. Hercules has lifted him above the level of his own head and braced him against his right chest and shoulder. His embrace is across the abdomen and imprisons Antaeus's left arm. At first glance Hercules' legs form a substantial triangular base, although this stance is momentary at best. Hercules' right foot is gracefully on tiptoe, and his left leg bears all the weight. The right side of Antaeus' form parallels the diagonal of Hercules' right side. Antaeus's head, sagging to his left, is the apex of the composition. The two bodies are plastic, muscular, and smoothly finished. The broader polished surfaces of the figures contrast with the minute facial features, the small curls of Hercules' hair and beard, the unruly mass of Antaeus' hair, the stressed veins on the arms and hands, the genitalia, and the delicate details of the toes. The eyes of the London group are accented with silver, which, as both the London and Vienna groups have dark patinas, draws attention to the differing facial expressions of the combatants. The face of the London Antaeus depicts suffering in the Classical heroic manner with a noble Grecian brow unsullied by pain, eyes turned up to his right, and mouth open. In contrast, the eyes of the Vienna group are not silvered and those of Antaeus turn in a more natural manner to the left, the direction of his head. Wrinkles have been added below the eyes of both figures. The hair of Antaeus is flatter to the head and disheveled in a liquid manner, its curvilinearity matched by the modeling of the ears. Even the natural veins of the hands of the London group have been given a decorative pattern in the Vienna group.

At the time that Antico was creating the London group, he would have known of the now-restored antique group *Hercules and Antaeus* in the Palazzo Pitti in Florence. The torsos were not restored in Antico's lifetime. Philostratus the Elder, an author who Antico probably knew, indicated that the Palazzo Pitti *Hercules and Antaeus* had swelled veins, that in Hercules' embrace the belly of Antaeus had become flabby, and that the giant was panting and groaning. Antico imposed his own style and principles of design, and his

composition has considerably more grace and elegance. He intensified the expression of the group by imprisoning the left arm of Antaeus in Hercules' deadly embrace, rendering Antaeus palpably more helpless. To form the summit of his composition, Antico adapted the position of the head of *Laocoön* and contrasted the suffering facial expression and wild hair of Antaeus to the facial strain and tidy curls of Hercules' head just below. The allusion to the *Laocoön* group would have been appreciated both by his patron and by the Mantuan courtiers.

Slight but significant changes were made in the Vienna bronze. Contrasted with the London group, the expression of the Vienna group is pathetic, the hair of Antaeus is softer and more gracefully formed, and the veins of the hands are more stylized. These deviations were made possible by Antico's pioneering development of the indirect bronze-casting process. The indirect method allowed the artist not only to replicate his models, but also to vary his original conceptions and differentiate between models produced for different patrons simply by reediting the details of the cored wax model to be cast. The variations in details between Antico's two *Hercules and Antaeus* groups were due to the change in the artistic environment of the Gonzaga courts between about 1506/11 and 1519—between the heritage of Andrea Mantegna and the soft style of Lorenzo Costa—and to the artist's sensitivity to the tastes and personalities of his two patrons, Bishop Ludovico and Isabella d'Este.

ANN HERSEY ALLISON

See also **Laocoön and His Sons**

Further Reading

Bober, Phyllis Pray, and Ruth Rubinstein, *Renaissance Artists and Antique Sculpture*, London: Miller, and Oxford: Oxford University Press, 1986

Leithe-Jasper, Manfred, "Isabella d'Este und Antico," in *Isabella d'Este: Fürstin und Mäzenatin der Renaissance*, edited by Sylvia Ferino-Pagden, Vienna: Kunsthistorisches Museum, 1994

Radcliffe, A., "Hercules and Antaeus," in *Splendours of the Gonzaga*, edited by David Chambers and Jane Martineau, London: Victoria and Albert Museum, 1981

ANTINOUS *Greek*

Antinous was a Greek youth from the city of Bithynium (Claudiopolis) in northwestern Asia Minor. Born perhaps in 110 CE, he later came to the attention of the emperor Hadrian, who formed a homoerotic relationship with him. Antinous accompanied the emperor on his extensive travels through the Eastern Empire and tragically drowned in the Nile in October 130 CE. Ancient sources give varying accounts as to whether his death was an accident, suicide, or even ritual self-sacrifice to avert imminent danger from the emperor.

Hadrian was devastated by the death of his beloved and mourned him excessively. Antinous was deified and a new city, Antinoupolis, was founded close to the spot where he had died. From there, the cult of Antinous spread rapidly over the empire, especially the Greek parts, where festivals in his honor were established.

A great number of his images are preserved and comprise many media. There are paintings, representations on coins, gems, and cameos, and above all sculptured portraits. The latest comprehensive study of the sculptures lists 96 pieces, and new examples continue to be found (an over-life-size torso of a seated statue of Antinous, for instance, was discovered in the late 1990s in the villa of the 2nd-century Greek magnate Herodes Atticus near Luku in the Peloponnese). The preserved number of Antinous' portraits thus exceeds even that of many emperors.

The prototype of the sculptured versions, Antinous' "main type," in a sense was one of the last grand creations of ancient ideal sculpture. Arguably, a court atelier, acting on Hadrian's orders (unless the original impetus came from elsewhere), created an eclectic statue heavily based on early Classical images of youthful gods, such as the so-called *Tiber Apollo* (*ca.* 460 BCE). This Classical body type was combined with a portrait head with a smooth, sensuous face and an unusually voluminous cap of curling hair that covered the ears and neck in carefully arranged disarray. The result was a convincing, if slightly ambiguous, blend of classicizing and contemporary elements. Antinous was represented nude. This original full-figure portrait is preserved in two excellent statue copies of the size of the presumed original (one of which is in the Banca d'Italia, Rome), two statues on a smaller scale, and a number of large busts.

The great majority of the preserved images of Antinous' main type (some 78 replicas) closely follow this model. In addition, there are three much smaller groups that depend more or less closely on the main type: a variant with a characteristic fork motif in the hair above the right eye, the so-called Mondragone type, and "Egyptianizing" versions.

In sculpture, Antinous is often represented in divine guise as Dionysus or Apollo. The famous *Mondragone Head* (Musée du Louvre, Paris) with its long, classicizing hair and remains of a vine or ivy wreath is a particularly good example for these likenesses. A well-known relief from Lanuvium, Italy (Banca Romana, Rome), shows Antinous as Sylvanus, another deity. There are also allegorical depictions likening him to the seasons, as on a beautiful relief from Hadrian's villa (Villa Albani, Rome). A peculiar group is the Egyptianizing images showing him as Antinous-Osiris, reborn from the waters of the Nile, probably all originally set up also in Hadrian's villa near Tivoli, Italy.

The dedication of these images coincided with the Greek Renaissance of the 2nd century CE, a movement that strongly promoted Greek cultural traditions and was warmly supported by the emperor. It is therefore no wonder that the veneration of Antinous was taken up enthusiastically in the East: the deified Greek youth, beloved of the emperor, very much embodied the spirit of the time. Only two months after Antinous's death, the city of Thessaloníki (Greece) asked permission to establish his cult, and many others followed suit. Further shrines for Antinous are attested at Mantinea in Greece, and Bithynium. Although the majority of sculpted portraits come from the West, there the only evidence for a temple of Antinous is at Lanuvium. Just as with images of the emperors, the dedication of statues of Antinous was a welcome way to show loyalty to the imperial house and the state as a whole.

Like the portraits of members of the imperial family, the images of Antinous exercised a notable influence on the private portraiture of the time. Many portraits of young men imitated characteristic features of Antinous, particularly the voluminous coiffure, and as a result in some cases appear very similar to Antinous' own portraits.

Traditionally, the vast majority of the images of Antinous have been dated to the narrow span from his own death in 130 CE to the death of Hadrian in 138 CE. It is unclear whether portraits of him existed already before his death. Similarly, there may be posthumous representations of the living Antinous, as has been suggested for the Hadrianic hunting tondi later reused for the Arch of Constantine (312–15) in Rome.

It is of course true that with the death of Hadrian the main motivation for the dedication of Antinous' images—to please the emperor—may have gone, and there is little evidence for a continuing production of his images in the West. In Greece, however, Antinous had played a different role. He continued to be venerated in many places (in Athens, for example, well into the 3rd century CE), and new likenesses of him may well have been dedicated for a longer period than elsewhere.

The images of Antinous provided a lasting legacy in other respects. Well known to later artists, they inspired great Renaissance masters such as Raphael and many others. To archaeologist and art critic Johann Joachim Winckelmann, the *Mondragone Head*, together with the *Apollo Belvedere*, was an epitome of Greek sculpture par excellence.

THORSTEN OPPER

See also **Apollo Belvedere**; **Greece, Ancient**

Further Reading

Evers, Cecile, "Les portraits d'Antinous," *Journal of Roman Archaeology* 8 (1995)

Meyer, Hugo, *Antinoos: Die archäologischen Denkmäler unter Einbeziehung des numismatischen und epigraphischen Materials sowie der literarischen Nachrichten: Ein Beitrag zur Kunst- und Kulturgeschichte der hadrianisch-frühantoninischen Zeit*, Munich: Fink, 1991

Meyer, Hugo, "Antinous and the Greek Renascence: An Introduction," in *Der Obelisk des Antinoos: Eine kommentierte Edition*, edited by Meyer, Munich: Fink, 1994

Royston, Lambert, *Beloved and God: The Story of Hadrian and Antinous*, London: Weidenfeld and Nicolson, and New York: Viking, 1984

MARK MATVEYEVICH ANTOKOL'SKY 1842–1902 *Russian, also active in France*

Mark Matveyevich Antokol'sky is the most important Russian sculptor of the second half of the 19th century, a master of European renown. After receiving his artistic education in St. Petersburg, Russia, at the Academy of Arts, he was awarded the title of academician in 1871 for his statue *Ivan the Terrible*. This work, which brought him fame and glory, was a milestone in the development of realist art. Here, as in his subsequent works, Antokol'sky aimed to penetrate the essence of a historical phenomenon. Subjects from Russian history inspired the sculptor for his entire career.

After he moved to Rome in 1871, he created *Peter I*, which was later repeatedly cast from bronze and installed as a monument in Peterhof (now Petrodvorets), St. Petersburg, Archangelsk, and Taganrog. In Italy, where he spent seven years of his creative life, he made such famous works as *Christ before the People's Judgment*, the *Death of Socrates*, a tomb monument to Mariya Alekseyevna Obolenskaya (1873–76), and portrait busts of Vladimir Vasil'evich Stasov (1874) and Sergei Petrovich Botkin (1874). His striving for humanism and justice is reflected in the choice of subjects he portrayed: the heroes who were martyrs for an idea and friends of humanity. The sculptor was moved by their personal fate (Christ, Socrates), struggle, and the tragic impossibility of the attainment of their goals. Many of his images are presented in the last moments of the subjects' lives; all of them are permeated by belief in the triumph of reason and truth.

In the fall of 1877, Antokol'sky went to Paris, a city connected with 25 years of his life and creative activity. In 1878 he participated in the construction of the sculpture exhibition of the World's Fair in Paris. For the works he presented there, he was given the highest award and the Order of the Legion of

Christ Before the People
© The State Russian Museum

Honor. During these years, he created numerous works, including the statues *Mephistopheles*, *Baruch (Benedict) Spinoza*, *The Chronicler Nestor*, *Yermak*, *The Emperor Alexander III* (1897–99), and tomb monuments to Tat'yana Mikolayevna Yusupova

(1890s) and Fedor Mikailovich Dmitriev (1893), as well as portrait busts of Empress Marya Fyodorovna (1887), Tsar Nicholas II (1896), and Empress Alexandra Fyodorovna (1896).

In his works, Antokol'sky conveyed the multifacetedness and complexity of the inner world of humanity—its individuality and uniqueness. His portraits represent a significant contribution to the gallery of portraits created by Russian artists. For his entire creative career, he worked on the complex compositional problems of plastic art. In his sculptures in the round, Antokol'sky most often represented figures sitting (*Ivan the Terrible*, *Baruch [Benedict] Spinoza*, *The Chronicler Nestor*, *Mephistopheles*) or standing upright (*Peter I*, *Yermak*, *Christ before the People's Judgment*). His figures were often made larger than life. Antokol'sky assigned important meaning to the position of the figure: its pose, gesture, silhouette, and the arrangement of the statue in its surrounding environment. The depiction of objects and specific details helped him achieve the effect of documentary precision and verisimilitude of the historical epoch.

He attached great significance to the refinement of marble finish, distinctly portraying the subtlest nuances. His design of faces and hands merits special attention. The light, free manner of his refinement of marble testifies to his virtuosity and elevated mastery. The problems of sculptural material deeply concerned Antokol'sky. The majority of his surviving works are made of two materials: marble and bronze, materials characteristic of sculpture of the second half of the 19th century, reaching its highest manifestation in the creative activity of Auguste Rodin.

In creating realistic sculpture, Antokol'sky relied on the powerful tradition of Russian plastic arts inspired by the works of Jean-Antoine Houdon and masters of the early Italian Renaissance. The sculptor's main ideas have not lost their significance; they remain just as relevant and contemporary today.

The triumphal 25th anniversary of Antokol'sky's creative career was celebrated on 28 December 1896 in the hall of the Society for the Encouragement of the Arts in St. Petersburg. At the 1900 Paris World's Fair, he was awarded the highest honors for his artistic activity.

Antokol'sky's best known statues were acquired by the Hermitage during his lifetime, and in 1897 they were transferred to the Russian Museum in St. Petersburg. In his will, Antokol'sky specified that the works in his Paris studio should be moved to St. Petersburg; this request was fulfilled by his family after his death.

OLGA KRIVDINA

See also **Houdon, Jean-Antoine**

Biography

Born in Vilno (now Vilnius), Lithuania, 2 November 1842. Studied in St. Petersburg at the Academy of Arts, 1862–71; received the title of academician, 1871, but left Russia for health reasons; worked in Italy, 1871–77; lived in Paris, 1877–1902; traveled annually to Russia; exhibited his works at the St. Petersburg Academy of Arts, 1880 and 1893; awarded the title of professor in 1880; participated in several world's fairs, including 1900 (Paris), in which he received highest honors for artistic activity; awarded the Order of the Legion of Honor in Paris, 1878; elected a member-correspondent of the Paris Academy of Fine Arts and the Academy of Urbino, Italy. Died in Bad Homburg, Germany, 9 July 1902.

Selected Works

Sixty of Antokol'sky's best works are preserved in the Russian Museum collection in St. Petersburg. Plaster of Paris models of statues and sketches are located in the Scientific Research Museum of the Russian Academy of Arts in St. Petersburg.

1864	*Jewish Tailor*; wood; Russian Museum, St. Petersburg, Russia
1865	*Jewish Miser*; wood, ivory; Russian Museum, St. Petersburg, Russia
1871	*Ivan the Terrible*; bronze; Russian Museum, St. Petersburg, Russia
1872	*Peter I*; plaster of Paris; Scientific Research Museum of the Russian Academy of Arts, St. Petersburg, Russia
1874–78	*Christ before the People's Judgment*; bronze; Russian Museum, St. Petersburg, Russia
1875–78	*Death of Socrates*; marble; Russian Museum, St. Petersburg, Russia
1882–87	*Baruch (Benedict) Spinoza*; marble; Russian Museum, St. Petersburg, Russia
1883	*Mephistopheles*; marble; bronze: 1891, both Russian Museum, St. Petersburg, Russia
1890	*The Chronicler Nestor*; marble; Russian Museum, St. Petersburg, Russia
1891	*Yermak*; bronze; Russian Museum, St. Petersburg, Russia

Further Reading

Androssov, Sergei, "Antokol'sky, Mark (Matveyevich)," in *The Dictionary of Art*, edited by Jane Turner, New York: Grove, and London: Macmillan, 1996

Gosudarstvennyi Russkii Muzei (Russian State Museum), *Skul'ptura, XVIII–nachalo XX veka* (Sculpture of the 18th–Early 20th Centuries; exhib. cat.), Leningrad: Iskusstvo, 1988

Krivdina, O.A., *Mark Antokol'skii: Vystavka proizvedenii k 150-letiiu so dnia rozhdeniia: Katalog* (Mark Antokolsky: Exhibition Catalogue for the 150th Anniversary of His Birth), St. Petersburg: Gosudarstvennyi Russkii Muzei, 1994

Kuznetsova, Era Vasilevna, *M.M. Antokol'skii: Zhizn' i tvorchestvo* (M.M. Antokolsky: His Life and Art), Moscow: Iskusstvo, 1989

Lebedev, Andrei Konstantinovich, and Genrietta Kalovna Burova, *Tvorcheskoe sodruzhestvo: M.M. Antokol'skii i V.V. Stasov* (A Creative Union: M.M. Antokolsky and V.V. Stasov), Leningrad: Khudozhnik RSFSR, 1968

Shalimova, Valentina Pavlovna, *Mark Matveevich Antokol'skii*, Leningrad: Izd-vo Khudozhnik RSFSR, 1970

APOLLO BELVEDERE

Anonymous

2nd century CE

marble

h. 2.24 m

Vatican Museums, Rome, Italy

The *Apollo Belvedere* is an over-life-size marble statue of the Greek god Apollo, named after the Belvedere courtyard in the Vatican, where it has been displayed as an important part of the papal collections since the 16th century. Famous almost from the moment of its discovery, the sculpture for centuries enjoyed wide renown as the quintessential embodiment of Greek art and therefore has had a profound and well-documented influence on writers, poets, and artists that is in stark contrast to the continuing uncertainty among modern archaeologists about its correct art historical context.

The statue shows the epiphany of Apollo. The god appears in a wide, effortless stride. The *contrapposto* (a natural pose with the weight of one leg, the shoulder, and hips counterbalancing one another) of the body, although canonical, is reduced; the muscles show no sign of tension. He is nude except for a chlamys (mantle) draped over his shoulders and left arm and elaborate sandals on his feet. A quiver is strapped to his back, and his left arm is raised in a threatening gesture; the hand (now missing from the wrist) must have held a bow. The head, with the long hair knotted above the forehead, follows this movement with a vigorous turn. The right arm is now missing from the elbow; originally it was held slightly forward and close to the body. A marble tree trunk with a winding serpent supports the statue along the right leg. In its present condition, the appearance of the *Apollo* is different not only from what it looked like in Antiquity but also from the time of its discovery. Restorations and derestorations led to the loss of much of the original right arm, and the characteristic smooth polish of the marble is almost entirely due to modern intervention, probably from the 18th century.

The exact origin of the statue (Antium or Grottaferrata have been suggested) and the date of its discovery are unknown; all that can be said is that the statue must have been found before the end of the 15th century. This, together with the instant fame of the *Apollo*, is evident from a fine series of drawings and reproductions made in the following decades. The two earliest drawings (ascribed to the studio of Domenico Ghirlandaio, in the so-called Codex Escurialensis) date to about 1490–95; they show the unrestored statue, with the original right arm and hand that was broken through the palm, in the garden of San Pietro in Vincoli, the titular church of Cardinal Giuliano della Rovere. After della Rovere became pope in 1503 under the name of Julius II, he took the *Apollo* to the Vatican, where the statue formed an important part of a newly established collection of ancient sculptures symbolizing the new *aurea aetas* (golden age) initiated by the pope. The *Apollo* was thus firmly set up as an exemplary icon of ancient sculpture and the programmatic connotations attached to it.

Already in 1497–98 Pier Jacopo Alari-Bonacolsi, called Antico, produced the first small-scale bronze copy of the statue for Ludovico Gonzaga, and a wealth of drawings attest to the *Apollo*'s influence on many famous cinquecento artists who reproduced the statue (a list is given in Bober and Rubinstein) or were inspired by it (for example, Albrecht Dürer).

Under the new Medici pope, Clement VII, Giovan Angelo Montorsoli, a pupil of Michelangelo, was commissioned to restore the sculpture, as the new vogue for complete figures demanded. Montorsoli in 1532 restored the left hand with a fragmentary bow and replaced the right lower arm, perhaps to add a new attribute or because of recent damage, thus creating a slightly more dramatic pose. All that remains of the original arm is a small *puntello* (support) on the right thigh. Despite their considerable influence on the statue's subsequent reception, Montorsoli's restorations (except for some patches on the body and chlamys) were finally removed in 1924–25.

A bronze copy based on a cast made by Primaticcio in 1540 for the court of Francis I of France at Fontainebleau, the first reproduction to include Montorsoli's alterations, served as visual centerpiece of a propagated new Rome. Similarly, in 1798 the *Apollo* figured prominently among the ancient sculptures triumphantly transferred to the Musée du Louvre, Paris, by Napoléon, where it remained until 1816. On a more modest scale, plaster and marble copies became trophies of the grand tour, fueled by the high esteem the statue enjoyed—despite some dissenting voices—among contemporary critics such as J.J. Winckelmann in his influential *History of Ancient Art* (1764). The powerful artistic reception of the *Apollo* continued well into the 20th century (for example, Giorgio De Chirico's 1914 painting, *The Song of Love*).

Apollo Belvedere © Alinari / Art Resource, NY

If the profound influence of the *Apollo Belvedere* on contemporary conceptions of the antique from the 15th century forward is beyond doubt, its original context is much harder to assess. Traditionally the statue has been interpreted as a Roman marble copy of a bronze original by the Attic sculptor Leochares, made about 330 BCE and sometimes identified with a statue by that artist seen by the travel writer Pausanias on the Athenian Agora in the 2nd century CE. Although the general composition of the *Apollo* and details such as the hairstyle are in keeping with late Classical models, nothing that is certainly Leochares' work survives to support this attribution.

Many modern archaeologists, prompted by the apparent lack of replicas and the heterogeneous character of similar works, consider the Belvedere statue to be a much modified copy, or even an eclectic creation of the late Hellenistic or imperial periods. The attribution of some fragments of ancient plaster casts from Baiae to an advocated Classical bronze original of the *Apollo* has recently been challenged, and the exact relationship of related sculptures such as the Apollo from the great frieze of the Pergamum Altar in Berlin and the Steinhäuser Head, Basel, to the *Apollo Belvedere* is unclear. The debate about his original attributes, dress, and footwear has meanwhile reached a dead end.

On balance, it is still likely that the Belvedere statue ultimately derives from a Classical bronze. The original Roman patron may have wanted to adapt the figure to specific needs and taste, just as the popes did later. The *Apollo Belvedere* thus demonstrates in an exemplary way various approaches to the Classical Greek past from the Roman period up to modern times.

THORSTEN OPPER

See also **Montorsoli, Giovan Angelo**

Further Reading

Ackerman, James S., *The Cortile del Belvedere*, Vatican City: Biblioteca Aspostolica Vaticana, 1954

Bober, Phyllis, and Ruth Rubinstein, *Renaissance Artists and Antique Sculpture: A Handbook of Sources*, London: Miller, and Oxford: Oxford University Press, 1986; New York: Oxford University Press, 1991

Brummer, Hans H., *The Statue Court in the Vatican Belvedere*, Stockholm: Almqvist and Wiksell, 1970

Haskell, Francis, and Nicholas Penny, *Taste and the Antique: The Lure of Classical Sculpture, 1500–1900*, New Haven, Connecticut: Yale University Press, 1981

Helbig, Wolfgang, *Führer durch die öffentlichen Sammlungen klassischer Altertümer in Rom*, 4th edition, edited by H. Speier, vol. 1, Tübingen, Germany: Wasmuth, 1963

Himmelmann, N., "Apoll vom Belvedere," in *Il Cortile delle Statue: Der Statuenhof des Belvedere im Vatikan*, edited by Matthias Winner, Bernard Andreae, and Carlo Pietrangeli, Mainz, Germany: Von Zabern, 1998

Landwehr, Christa, *Die antiken Gipsabgüsse aus Baiae: Griechische Bronzestatuen in Abgüssen römischer Zeit*, Berlin: Mann, 1985

Winner, M., "Zum Apoll vom Belvedere," *Jahrbuch der Berliner Museen* 10 (1968)

APOLLO OF VEII

Anonymous

Late 6th–early 5th century BCE

terracotta

h. 1.81 m

Museo Nazionale di Villa Giulia, Rome, Italy

The ancient Etruscans were masters of architectural terracotta sculptural decoration. One of the best-known surviving Etruscan terracottas is the so-called *Apollo* of Veii from the sanctuary of Portonaccio, near Veii, about 20 kilometers north of Rome. An approximately life-size rendering of the striding god, the work has been dated to the end of the 6th and beginning of the 5th century BCE. The sculpture, part of an Etruscan tradition of architectural terracottas that includes *acroteria* (figural or ornamental decorations placed atop a pediment), antefixes, revetment plaques, friezes, and pedimental groups, illustrates the Etruscan adaptation of the ancient Greek tradition of representing anthropomorphic divinities.

The *Apollo* figure, which has been identified as part of a larger sculptural group, is exceptional on several levels. High-quality workmanship and the technical skill required for sculpting and firing such a large figure distinguish the piece. In addition, although the sculpture has been restored, the survival of this approximately life-size figure is unusual because of the fragility of terracotta. Finally, that this sculpture seems to have been part of a freestanding narrative group is unusual in the context of ancient Mediterranean art. Narrative is generally associated with painting or relief and pedimental sculpture, not freestanding sculpture.

It is believed that the *Apollo* figure originally stood in a line with at least three other figures on the ridge-pole of a three-cella archaic temple in the Portonaccio sanctuary. The original bases of the statues, which were not flat but formed to allow the sculptures to rest on the ridge of a roof, suggest this placement. The lyre-shaped ornament seen between the god's legs, which are set widely apart as if in stride, most likely formed a necessary support. The curvilinear design of the lyre mimics the fold patterns of the garment above it (also seen in the figure considered to be Hercules).

Now fragmentary, the other figures of the *Apollo* group are generally identified as Hercules, Hermes, and a *kourotrophos* (woman holding a child). The hero, recognized as Hercules because of the lion skin wrapped around him, seems to be struggling with a hoofed animal, and the god Hermes is wearing his characteristic hat (only the head of Hermes survives). Although the *kourotrophos* has been considered to be Latona/Leto, the mother of Apollo, this is questionable because the suggested narrative involves her adult son.

The group's narrative subject is generally interpreted as the confrontation between Hercules and Apollo over the Ceryneian hind of Delphi, which Hercules was attempting to abduct. It appears that the two protagonists were shown moving toward each other to form the central pair of the group and that each was followed by a second figure. The narrative group atop the temple would have been impressive when seen from below, especially from the side. The figures would have been clearly delineated against the sky, unlike terracotta reliefs or pedimental sculptures, which were more fully integrated into the temple design and thus less prominent.

Most Etruscan sculpture was executed by anonymous craftsmen; the *Apollo* figure, however, has been traditionally associated with what has been termed the Veian school of Vulca, and even with Vulca himself, the master craftsman. The literary sources for Vulca and other craftsmen from Veii include discussions of Rome's Capitoline temple with reference to both the cult image of Jupiter made by Vulca (Pliny the Elder, *Natural History*, completed in 77 CE) and a terracotta

Apollo of Veii
© Alinari / Art Resource, NY

quadriga at the apex of the roof gable (Plutarch, *Life of Publicola*, from *Parallel Lives*, 1st–2nd century CE). No definitive reason can be identified, however, for connecting the *Apollo* of Veii with Vulca except that he seems to have been a well-known and respected craftsman and that the *Apollo* group is of high quality.

Although the *Apollo* resembles archaic Greek kouros figures in some respects, such as the stylized long hair and so-called archaic smile, several differences distinguish this figure from Greek sculptures. This *Apollo* is most likely not a single figure but part of a freestanding narrative group, and the figure, rather than being nude, is clothed in garments with elegantly formed folds. In addition, he is depicted in the act of striding, not in the static pose characteristic of Greek freestanding figures. The depiction of movement derives in part from the material and technique of clay modeling; unlike stone carving, the malleability of clay and the rapidly executed modeling technique it makes possible are conducive to the production of figures that appear to be in motion. That the *Apollo* figure was originally painted is evident from the surviving color; the painted areas include the skin, hair, pupils of the eyes, and decoration on the borders of the cloak.

73

The *Apollo* was discovered in May 1916 in Portonaccio, just outside the ancient city of Veii, in the precinct of an archaic temple. Like the other figures associated with this group, it has been restored from fragments; the lost portions—one lower and one entire arm and the front part of both feet—have not been reconstructed.

The *Apollo* carries particular significance as a generally well-preserved, large-scale terracotta sculpture that was part of the earliest such sculptural group known in Mediterranean art. This figure is considered by some to be the epitome of Etruscan terracotta sculpture, predominantly because of the *Apollo*'s appealing vitality and the sense of life and purpose achieved by his pose, smile, modeling, and coloration. The figures of this group are currently housed in the Museo Nazionale di Villa Giulia in Rome, Italy.

ANN THOMAS WILKINS

See also **Etruscan Sculpture; Kore and Kouros**

Further Reading

Bonfante, Larissa (editor), *Etruscan Life and Afterlife: A Handbook of Etruscan Studies*, Detroit, Michigan: Wayne State Press, 1986

Brendel, Otto, *Etruscan Art*, London and New York: Penguin Books, 1978; 2nd edition, New Haven, Connecticut: Yale University Press, 1995

Spivey, Nigel Jonathan, *Etruscan Art*, New York and London: Thames and Hudson, 1997

ARA PACIS (Augustae)

Anonymous

13–9 BCE

marble

h. 11.5 m

Campus Martius (Field of Mars), on the Via Flaminia (now the Corso), Rome, Italy

In his *Res Gestae* (The Deeds of Augustus), the Roman emperor Augustus states the following:

> On my return to Rome from Spain and Gaul, in the consulship of Tiberius Nero and Publius Quintilius, after the successful conclusion of affairs in those provinces, the Senate in honor of my return decreed [4 July 13 BCE] that an altar to the Peace of Augustus should be consecrated on the Campus Martius, where it commanded the magistrates and priests and the vestal virgins to perform an annual sacrifice.

The permanent marble altar was completed in time for its inauguration on 30 January 9 BCE (Ovid, *Fasti*), the birthday of Augustus's cherished wife, Livia. Located not in the Roman Forum but on the Campus Martius (Field of Mars), the *Ara Pacis* serves as a perfect example of early Roman imperial political and familial propaganda and at the same time draws on formal Greek precedents in its basic composition and decoration. Its location relative to other structures and the intricate meanings discerned in its imagery also make the *Ara Pacis* one of the most complex Augustan monuments.

Although Augustus refused official senatorial triumphs for his achievements in Spain and Gaul, he granted permission for the placement of an altar dedicated to the grander concept of Augustan peace and material prosperity. Its location along the Via Flaminia in the Campus Martius, near the two temples of Honos and Virtus where the Romans performed military training, strongly connected him with military triumph. This area is also where Augustus focused his dynastic building campaign, which included the original Pantheon, the Baths of Agrippa, and his family mausoleum. As another symbol of his military success, Augustus erected a 20.7 meter tall red granite Egyptian obelisk in the plaza between the mausoleum and the *Ara Pacis*, creating a monumental sundial. The cosmic implications of Augustan rule are reinforced by the shadow created by the obelisk, which falls directly on the *Ara Pacis* on 23 September, the emperor's birthday.

The rectangular, open-air, marble complex consists of a highly decorated enclosure with an altar inside. Elevated and approached by steps, the scroll-top altar shows sacrificial scenes performed by the *pontifex maximus* (high priest) and the vestal virgins. The interior of the enclosing wall reveals marble carved to appear like wooden slats and pillars with Corinthian capitals. Traditional temporary features of religious celebratory decoration, thick swags of garland containing fruit and pines, hang mingled with ox skulls and offering bowls. Holes in the base of the altar and in the enclosing wall permit fluids from the sacrifice to be quickly disposed.

The exterior of the enclosing walls possesses far greater complexity in decoration. The lower register displays lush but symmetrically controlled acanthus plants and tendrils entwined with birds, insects, and small animals. Although this form may be inspired by Etruscan or Hellenistic styles, within the context of Augustan iconography it is consistent with the idea of agricultural abundance cosmically brought about by Augustan rule. The so-called Tellus (Mother Earth) panel on the shorter southeastern wall displays the breadth of Augustan bounty with a large, seated female deity holding two infants and flanked by two partially nude female companions. One figure, representing sea breezes, rides a water beast as waves flow out from beneath her, whereas the other, symbolizing freshwater breezes, pours water from a jug while sitting astride a swan. Not only are three major elements present (earth,

Tellus, goddess of the Earth
© Nimatallah / Art Resource, NY

water, and air), but the swan belongs to Venus, patron goddess of Augustus, and the pose of Tellus recalls the goddess of love. Similar imagery appears on the famous *Augustus of Prima Porta* (after 19 BCE, Vatican Museums, Rome) where close ties exist between Augustus and Venus (with the accompanying dolphin and Cupid), and Tellus appears on Augustus' breastplate holding an overflowing cornucopia. Although most of it is missing today, a panel of the armed-warrior allegory of Rome that contrasted with the earthly image of Tellus appeared on the eastern short wall.

The western face of the enclosing wall presented the two mythical stories of Rome's founding, one Greek and one Latin. On the southwestern corner, a large panel showed the Trojan Aeneas offering sacrifices to the *penates*, ancient agricultural gods brought to Italy from Troy by the fleeing hero. Augustus, who often took on the guise of the new Aeneas in imagery, revived their cult, and the Augustan writer Virgil propagated Aeneas' founding role in his *Aeneid*. The other fragmentary panel displays the war god Mars, whose mating with the virgin Rhea Silvia produced the twin sons Romulus and Remus, the legendary founders of Rome.

On the longitudinal walls above carvings of profuse vegetation are the most debated examples of Julio-Claudian portraiture. A westward parade of family members and Roman officials appears in continuous friezes along the north and south walls of the enclosure. The ideal Panathenaic festival portrayed in the Parthenon frieze is a notable precedent for this processional appearance, yet the *Ara Pacis* renders the specific parade that occurred in 13 BCE. Additionally, in accord with Augustan social policies regarding marriage and legitimacy, the reliefs celebrate the family unit. Children mingle with adults, clinging to drapery or touchingly holding adult hands.

Scholars have attempted to identify many of the figures, yet positive attributions may never be possible. On the southern frieze, most agree the figure wearing the cap of *pontifex maximus*, accompanied by official *lictors* (minor Roman officials who cleared the path in front of magistrates) and *flamines* (priests devoted to individual gods), is Augustus himself, acting as high priest for the exiled Lepidus. His pose and appearance mirrors that of Aeneas on the entrance panel. Another prominent figure is his son-in-law, Marcus Agrippa, whose veiled appearance notes his death in 12 BCE, after the beginning of construction but before the consecration of the altar. Other family members, including a number of children, appear rather tightly packed together but carved in varying depths. Unfortunately, the officials possess mostly modern heads, which were placed during the re-erection of the altar by Benito Mussolini's government in the late 1930s. Not only did the *Ara Pacis* set a precedent for Augustus for furthering dynastic ambitions through sculpture, but its imagery inspired later emperors (and at least one fascist) to evoke a sense of power by association.

VALERIE S. GRASH

Further Reading

Borbein, Adolf Heinrich, "Die Ara Pacis Augustae: Geschichtliche Wirklichkeit und Programm," *Jahrbuch des Deutschen Archäologischen Instituts* 90 (1975)

Castriota, David, *The Ara Pacis Augustae and the Imagery of Abundance in Later Greek and Early Roman Imperial Art*, Princeton, New Jersey: Princeton University Press, 1995

Conlin, Diane Atnally, *The Artists of the Ara Pacis: The Process of Hellenization in Roman Relief Sculpture*, Chapel Hill: University of North Carolina Press, 1997

Galinsky, Karl, *Augustan Culture*, Princeton, New Jersey: Princeton University Press, 1996

Kleiner, Diana, "The Great Friezes of the Ara Pacis Augustae: Greek Sources, Roman Derivatives, and Augustan Social Policy," *Mélanges de L'École Française de Rome* 90 (1978)

Moretti, Giuseppe, *Ara Pacis Augustae*, translated by Veronica Priestley, Rome: Instituto Poligrafico dello Stato, 1975

Simon, Erika, *Ara Pacis Augustae*, Greenwich, Connecticut: New York Graphic Society, 1968

Torelli, Mario, *Typology and Structure of Roman Historical Reliefs*, Ann Arbor: University of Michigan Press, 1982

Toynbee, Jocelyn M.C., *The Ara Pacis Reconsidered and Historical Art in Roman Italy*, Oxford: Oxford University Press, 1953

Zanker, Paul, *Augustus und die Macht der Bilder*, Munich: Beck, 1987; as *The Power of Images in the Age of Augustus*, translated by Alan Shapiro, Ann Arbor: University of Michigan Press, 1990

ALEXANDER PORFIREVICH ARCHIPENKO 1887–1964 *Ukrainian, active in France*

The work of Alexander Archipenko, especially the sculptures he created during his period of greatest innovation, 1908–21 in France, contributed significantly to developments in sculpture during the 20th century. Archipenko's spirit of rebellion against tradition was evident even in his student days, when he was forced to leave art school in his native Kiev for being critical of his professors' conservative academic approach to making art. Among the earliest works Archipenko created after his arrival in Paris about 1908 was *Tristesse* (Sorrow), which recalls the wooden sculptures of Paul Gauguin and forms part of a larger group of early archaizing works by the artist in wood, stone, and marble. Significantly different from this group of works is another early figure by the artist, *Kneeling Woman*, in which the smooth volumes of the anatomy, lack of emotional expression, and emphasis on formal design are a conscious response to the emotionalism and overworked surfaces of Impressionist sculpture.

In approximately 1913, Archipenko began to create sculptures that were constructed rather than modeled or carved in the traditional manner. His first known sculpture of this type, *Médrano I (Juggler)*, was made of ordinary materials that were assembled, with the junctures visible to the viewer. Archipenko used color to articulate further the various parts of the sculpture. *Médrano I* was a vivid departure from traditionally sculpted forms, the surface of whose mass represents what is happening underneath. The viewer was now allowed to look inside the figure. As in Cubist paintings of the period, Archipenko's sculptures were composed of fragments of forms and the space between them, which together represented the whole.

Médrano II (Dancer), a work related to *Médrano I*, caused a sensation when it was exhibited at the Salon des Indépendants in 1914. *Médrano II* was composed of assembled materials affixed to a flat, solid ground, the whole of which had been polychromed. The sculptor used color both to describe certain aspects further and to clarify structure. *Médrano II* is one of Archipenko's early sculpto-paintings, a form he later developed during the war years (1914–18) when he took up residence in the south of France. The spatial ambiguities in the sculpto-paintings have been compared by scholars to those in synthetic Cubist paintings of the same period.

Archipenko's extensive use of polychromy contributed significantly to the revival of the use of color in sculpture, a practice that had been virtually abandoned after its popular use by sculptors working under the influence of the Gothic Revival movement in the 19th century. Throughout his career, Archipenko used color to clarify design or to create a sense of movement, as in *Carrousel Pierrot*, or to enhance the vigor of his forms, their tactility, beauty, and spirit.

Archipenko was also a pioneer in the exploration of transparency and reflectivity in sculpture. The figure of the dancer in *Médrano II* wears a skirt that is partly constructed of clear glass. In *Woman in Front of Mirror*, a woman's torso and head are reflected in a mirror, on which Archipenko painted the woman's left arm and a still life. A shiny foil was used to cover the lower backdrop and the base of the sculpture, as well as the woman's feet and one of the legs of her stool. Archipenko's use of transparent materials in these early works anticipates their use by the sculptors Naum Gabo and Antoine Pevsner, who began working with materials of this type in 1920.

Archipenko's introduction of the use of the void, or hole, is considered to be one of his most important contributions to the development of 20th-century sculpture. This innovative approach to the traditional sculptured monolith first appears in *Geometric Statuette*, in which a void surrounded by sculptural mass is used to suggest, paradoxically, the presence of what is absent, the head of the figure. In a well-known later work, *Woman Combing Her Hair*, the void is used to suggest the woman's bent head. In works such as these, Archipenko anticipates the use of the void in the sculptures of Henry Moore and Jacques Lipchitz.

Archipenko's use of the concave shape to suggest convexity and of the void to suggest presence is highly

Walking Woman
Courtesy of Denver Art Museum Collection, Gift of Charles Bayley, Jr. Fund
© 2002 Denver Art Museum

developed in the complex figures of his late Paris period (1919–20). Two important works from this period are *Walking Woman* and *Seated Woman (Geometric Figure Seated)*, both modeled out of a single material. The outline of the torso of *Walking Woman* circumscribes a void that implies the absent substance. Her concave left leg suggests its volumetric curve and, interchangeably, the umbrella the woman carries as she walks. *Seated Woman* exhibits a complex arrangement of convex and concave forms and voids; the woman's left thigh is represented by a tapering, concave form. In *Archipenko: Fifty Creative Years, 1908–1958*, Archipenko wrote, "In the creative process, as in life itself, the reality of the negative is a conceptual imprint of the absent positive."

Both Archipenko and Constantin Brancusi were among the earliest 20th-century sculptors to conceive of partial figures as complete in themselves. An early example of a partially conceived figure by Archipenko is *Bather (Seated Woman)*, parts of whose arms and legs are not represented, as they are nonessential to its formal design or movement. Sculptures such as *Bather* were conceived differently from Auguste Rodin's partial figures, which were arrived at by a process of elimination. Archipenko's reduced, tapering forms, such as *Flat Torso* and *Vase Woman II*, are thought to have had a parallel development with those by Brancusi. The scholar Katherine Michaelsen has compared works such as *Vase Woman II* with Brancusi's *Yellow Bird* of roughly the same period.

Many of Archipenko's representations of the human form in the 1920s and 1930s have a sleek, elegant, stylized appearance. Nonetheless, during this same period, the artist's ever-present spirit of innovation and experimentation led to the creation of some startlingly original forms that would engage his imagination for the rest of his career. This creative drive led him in 1924 to invent *Archipentura*, an apparatus for displaying changeable pictures, which was patented in 1927. It is Archipenko's work, however, that truly defines his original contributions of this period. The rigid outer form of *Standing Vertical*, for example, surrounds and envelops a tapering curvilinear inner form, which implies movement, and terminates in a depression that indicates the head of the figure. Archipenko created a number of inventive variations of this form, which presaged the carved plastic figures, illuminated from within, that he began to make in the 1940s, an important example of which is *Ascension*.

Archipenko's career had a second efflorescence during his late period, from about 1950 until 1963, a year before his death. The boldly formed and colored sculptures from this period are among his most impressive productions. During his late period, Archipenko continued his explorations with light and continued to experiment with new materials such as Bakelite (molded plastic), which, for example, he incorporated in his complex sculpto-painting *Cleopatra (Repose)*. His hierarchical figure *Queen*, the back of which reveals an intense inner core that contrasts with its quiet, rigid exterior, and *King Solomon*, Archipenko's last sculpture, highlight the culmination of the career of a sculptor whose sense of organic forms, their tactility, and their spirit inspired him to create some of the most impressive works in 20th-century sculpture.

GINA ALEXANDER GRANGER

See also **Brancusi, Constantin; Gabo, Naum; Laurens, Henri; Lipchitz, Jacques; Moore, Henry; Pevsner, Antoine**

Biography

Born in Kiev, Ukraine, 30 May 1887. Studied painting and sculpture at Kiev School of Art, 1903–05; moved to Moscow, 1906, and participated in various group shows; moved to Paris, 1908; briefly studied at the École des Beaux-Arts, Paris; exhibited with the Cubists in the Salon des Indépendants, Paris, 1910–14 and 1920; member of the Puteaux Group, which met to discuss issues relating to Cubism; exhibited with the Cubists at the Salon d'Automne, 1911–13 and 1919; opened a school of sculpture in Paris, 1912; solo show at Der Sturm Gallery, Berlin, and in the Armory Show, New York, 1913; co-founder of Section d'Or, 1919–20; moved to Berlin and opened an art school, 1921; emigrated to United States, 1923; started summer art school in Woodstock, New York, 1924; exhibited gilded and silvered bronzes in the new gallery at Saks and Company, New York, and became an American citizen, 1929; six sculptures included in the *Cubism and Abstract Art* exhibition, Museum of Modern Art, New York, 1936; joined faculty of the New Bauhaus, Chicago, as head of modeling workshop, 1937; large retrospective exhibition at Associated American Artists Galleries, New York, 1954; elected associate member of International Institute of Arts and Letters, 1953; awarded gold medal, XIII Biennale d'Arte Triveneta, III Concorso Internazionale del Bronzetto, Padua, Italy, 1959; elected to the Department of Art of the National Institute of Arts and Letters, 1962. Died in New York City, United States, 25 February 1964.

Selected Works

1909   *Tristesse* (Sorrow); painted wood; Hirshhorn Museum and Sculpture Garden, Washington, D.C., United States

1910   *Kneeling Woman*; bronze; Tel Aviv Museum, Israel

1912   *Bather (Seated Woman)*; terracotta; Tel Aviv Museum, Israel

1912   *Walking Woman*; bronze; Denver Art Museum, Colorado, United States

1913   *Carrousel Pierrot*; painted plaster; Guggenheim Museum of Art, New York, United States

1913–14 *Médrano I (Juggler)*; painted wood, glass, sheet metal, wire; location unknown

1914   *Boxing Match (Boxers* or *Boxers Struggle)*; plaster painted black; Guggenheim Museum of Art, New York, United States

1914   *Geometric Statuette*; plaster; private collection

1914   *Médrano II (Dancer)*; painted tin, wood, glass, painted oilcloth; Guggenheim Museum of Art, New York, United States

1914   *Woman in Front of Mirror*; wood, glass, metal, mirror, foil (destroyed)

1915   *Before the Mirror (In the Boudoir)*; oil and pencil on wood, paper, and metal, with photograph of the artist; Philadelphia Museum of Art, Pennsylvania, United States

1915   *Flat Torso*; marble on alabaster base; Hirshhorn Museum and Sculpture Garden, Washington, D.C., United States

1915   *Woman Combing Her Hair*; bronze; Museum of Modern Art, New York, United States

1918–19 *Walking Woman*; terracotta (location unknown)

1919   *Vase Woman II*; bronze; Tel Aviv Museum, Israel

1920   *Seated Woman (Geometric Figure Seated)*; painted plaster; Tel Aviv Museum, Israel

1935   *Standing Vertical*; painted wood; private collection

1950   *Ascension*; carved plastic illuminated from within; private collection

1950   *Iron Figures*; iron; University of Missouri at Kansas City, Missouri, United States

1954   *Queen*; painted wood; private collection

1957   *Cleopatra (Repose)*; painted wood, Bakelite, found objects; private collection

1963   *King Solomon*; painted Hydrocal; private collection

Further Reading

Archipenko, Alexander, et al., *Archipenko: Fifty Creative Years, 1908–1958*, New York: TEKHNE, 1960

Karshan, Donald H. (editor), *Archipenko; International Visionary*, Washington, D.C.: Smithsonian Institution Press, 1969

Karshan, Donald H., *Archipenko: The Sculpture and Graphic Art: Including a Print Catalogue Raisonné*, Tübingen, Germany: Verlag Ernst Wasmuth, 1974; Boulder, Colorado: Westview Press, 1975

Karshan, Donald H., *Sculpture, Drawing, Prints, 1908–1964*, Bloomington: Indiana University Press, 1985

Marter, Joan M., and Nicholas J. Capasso, *Archipenko: Drawings, Reliefs, and Constructions*, Annandale-on-Hudson, New York: Bard College, 1985

Michaelsen, Katherine Jánszky, "Early Mixed Media Constructions," *Arts Magazine* 50/5 (January 1976)

Michaelsen, Katherine Jánszky, *Archipenko: A Study of the Early Works, 1908–1920*, New York: Garland, 1977

Michaelsen, Katherine Jánszky, and Nehama Guralnik, *Alexander Archipenko: A Centennial Tribute*, Washington, D.C.: National Gallery of Art, 1986

ARCHITECTURAL SCULPTURE IN EUROPE: MIDDLE AGES–19TH CENTURY

The nature of architectural sculpture, in contrast to freestanding sculpture, is in its relation to the architecture to which it is integrated. From the earliest examples architects have used architectural sculpture to articulate different building parts, often to indicate important places or zones. Interior architectural sculpture may designate particular ritual spaces. It may also distinguish structural components in a formal way. Typically, the facade carries the greatest share of architectural sculpture. In Europe from the Middle Ages through the 19th century, architectural sculpture is found mainly on religious buildings, primarily churches, as well as other public buildings. Consistently significant has been the influence of ancient architectural sculpture, particularly Roman. While much architectural sculpture is figurative, often conveying detailed iconographic programs, designers have also treated nonfigurative decoration, particularly architectural elements such as engaged arcades, tracery patterns, and rib vaulting, as sculpture.

Particularly in the later Middle Ages and subsequent periods, sculpture decorated domestic buildings, such as town houses, castles, and palaces. Architectural sculpture has always adorned civic monuments such as town halls, theaters, commemorative monuments, triumphal arches, and gates. While most architectural sculpture is in stone, examples of stucco, wood, and ceramic also exist.

Middle Ages: 4th–16th Centuries

The concept of *spolia*—reusing architectural sculpture from earlier monuments—has a long tradition and was a common practice in medieval architecture. Perhaps the most famous example is the Arch of Constantine (312–15), which includes early 4th-century carved

Reims Cathedral, The Visitation, West front, Central portal, South Side
The Conway Library, Courtauld Institute of Art

friezes alongside tondi from a monument of Hadrian and reliefs from a monument of Trajan, as well as other sculptural elements from a monument of Marcus Aurelius. Nonetheless, the notion of earlier monuments as a readily available quarry is oversimplified. *Spolia* are almost always incorporated as part of a larger statement, as on the Arch of Constantine, where it was used partly as political propaganda to proclaim the legitimate authority of the emperor. The portraits of Trajan, for example, were recarved with the features of Constantine. *Spolia* must be seen as products of at least two artistic moments, and of two different artistic intentions, and thereby have a multivalent nature.

Little architectural sculpture dates from the Carolingian period (late 8th to early 10th centuries). The Lorsch Monastery gatehouse (*ca.* 800) is articulated by engaged columns with antique-style capitals on the lower level and fluted pilasters with volute capitals above. Polychrome architecture, different patterns on each level, continued a northern tradition, as seen in the 7th-century baptistery of Saint-Jean, Poitiers.

Romanesque architectural sculpture consists primarily of capitals (interior, facade, or cloister), often historiated with biblical themes and cycles of patron saints. An example of interior historiated capital sculpture includes that from the abbey Church of St.-Germain-des-Près (now in the Musée National du Moyen Age, Paris), mid 11th century. Ambulatory capitals include those from the Abbey of Cluny (*ca.* 1115; now in the Musée Lapidaire, Cluny), and examples of crypt capitals are found in the former Abbey of Saint-Denis (12th century), north of Paris.

The earliest architectural sculpture in medieval Europe is in the form of carved stone slabs used to decorate the sanctuaries of churches. Their focus is on Christ, typically in a posture of blessing and holding the gospel book, such as the chancel screen from the Church of St.-Pierre-aux-Nonnains, Metz (mid 8th century; now in Musée d'Art et d'Histoire, Metz). This tradition of relief carving continued in late 11th-century slabs, such as the reliefs now reemployed in the ambulatory of the Church of St.-Sernin, Toulouse.

In order to mark entrances and focus attention on liminal zones, sculptural decoration appeared around portals and windows in the 11th century. The decorative motifs, emphasis on two-dimensional pattern, and technique of low-relief carving derived from liturgical vessels in metalwork and stone-carved sanctuary decoration.

The Romanesque style of sculpture created in the 11th century was virtually a new language. Symbolic and narrative sculpture on church exteriors from the 11th to 13th centuries (the Romanesque and Gothic styles) directly addressed the faithful. In addition, inscriptions frequently enhanced the symbolism of the sculpture. Whether using a simple symbolic image of a cross or an elaborate sculptural program, designers over the course of the Middle Ages paid increasing attention to sculptural decoration in order to prepare those entering for their transition from the mundane world outside to the sacred space inside.

Romanesque churches sometimes resemble the public monuments of ancient Rome, evoking its triumphal arches, city gates, and palaces. On the west portal of the Church of St.-Pierre at Aulnay, sculptural decoration is limited to the richly carved stepped archivolts, characteristic of this region of western France. This format effectively displays the symbolism of images in a hierarchic order, with a relief of the *Lamb of God* immediately above the doorway.

Romanesque sculpture was typically carved in a precise, detailed manner in the workshop and then assembled at the site. Originating in a period of technical economic progress, this architectural sculpture demanded a new organization of labor between the developer of the program, the architectural designer, the mason, and the sculptor.

Around 1100, many Romanesque portals replaced more symbolic carving with the image of the Enthroned Christ in a *mandorla* surrounded by angels. To emphasize the symbolism of the portal, Romanesque art moved the sacred images from the interior to the exterior. Frequently, facade sculpture combined Christ in a *mandorla* with other images to create a narrative. Romanesque sculpture played an important part in the rise of narrative, one of the great innovations of 11th and 12th-century art and literature.

A dramatic illustration of both symbolism and narrative is the west portal of the Church of St.-Lazare, Autun. The enormous tympanum contrasts a dominating *Enthroned Christ* in *mandorla* with dense narrative compositions of more than 80 figures, many in violent movement. An inscription admonishes viewers that the torments of hell are just as horrible as indicated in the sculpture. On the pier supporting the lintel (*trumeau*), Lazarus (a 19th-century replacement of the 12th-century *trumeau* destroyed during the French Revolution) represents hope to the faithful to be resurrected.

The tension between the flow of a narrative and the form of an architectural element gives Romanesque narrative sculpture its expressive character. The ideal compositional device to avoid fragmentation is the arrangement of narrative in a frieze, an arrangement that remained relatively exceptional in 12th-century sculpture. It occurs extensively at Lincoln Cathedral (England) and the Church of St.-Gilles-du-Gard (France), one of the greatest pilgrimage centers in the 12th century. A particularly rich series of reliefs depicting scenes from Genesis adorns the facade of Modena Cathedral (carved by Master Wiligelmo, *ca.* 1110). Italian churches are often characterized by porches protruding from the facade featuring columns supported on the backs of lions.

Builders also often treated architectural elements such as engaged arcades, archivolts, and tracery as sculpture, such as on the facades of Romanesque churches in western France (the Church of St.-Jouin-des-Marnes), Italy (Pisa Cathedral), and Gothic cathedrals in England (Lincoln and Wells Cathedrals). Interior examples of this treatment are the vaults of Gloucester Cathedral choir and south cloister gallery.

The medieval cloister, comprised of a four-sided arcaded walkway, was the hub of the monastic complex. Up to the mid 11th century, cloisters were generally made of wood and probably had painted decoration, although stone was increasingly used. Toward the end of the 11th century and especially in the 12th century, stone piers and capitals become principal places of sculptural decoration. The regions of what are now southern France and northern Spain, particularly Cata-

lonia, are rich in carved cloister decoration. Among the most extensive historiated cloisters still *in situ* are Moissac, France (*ca.* 1100), S. Domingo, Silos, Spain (12th century), and St.-Trophime, Arles (12th–14th century). All three sites display capitals carved with figures, animals, and foliate decoration and pier reliefs representing single figures or scenes. The various subjects represented include biblical figures, Gospel narratives, apostles, and miracles and martyrdoms of saints. Medieval cloisters also often included carving that had particular relevance to the site, such as the pier relief of Abbot Durandus at Moissac.

Evidence for the decoration of secular buildings in medieval Europe includes the Granolhet House, Saint-Antonin, and the House of Adelaide, Burlats (both France, mid 12th century), with pillars and capitals depicting Adam and Eve among other figurative decoration. Recent discoveries of a synagogue within the Palais de Justice, Rouen, revealed architecture similar to late 11th- or early 12th-century Christian monuments in Normandy, confirming that the same group of masons and sculptors was employed for Jewish and Christian buildings, a situation that also existed in other areas, including England. Another type of decoration is particular to Venetian secular facades: reliefs carved in medallions or lancet-shaped marble plaques. Bilaterally symmetrical compositions include such motifs as animals and birds, as well as foliate designs, most likely derived from textiles and metalwork. The later Middle Ages produced some examples of secular wooden architectural sculpture, such as the Maison Saumon, Chartres, with a salmon carved on one of wood posts, and the Annunciation on another. Angels bearing heraldic shields by Hugh Herland adorn the wooden beams of the Great Hall, Westminster Palace (1397–99).

Medieval city gates combining sculptural decoration and inscriptions were most prevalent in Italy, clearly influenced by the tradition of Roman gates and triumphal arches. Significant examples were built between 1280 and 1340. Polychrome stone and sculptural decoration that included portrait statuary of rulers embellished the gates as a way to impress the approaching wayfarer. Statues on gates could signify many nuances of dominion, protection, intimidation, or defiance. The sacred aspect of thresholds is important; the figure of the archangel Michael long remained a powerful presence at gateways. Both the Virgin and St. Michael appear on the grandiose Arco de Santa Maria at Burgos erected in the mid 1530s to honor Charles V.

The most celebrated gate in medieval Italy, the Capua gate, marked the entrance to the Kingdom of the Two Sicilies. Raised by Frederick II in 1234, the gate's main facade presented the crowned emperor enthroned, accompanied by inscriptions and three enigmatic busts. Frederick certainly knew Classical arches; he is recorded as having looted the statues from the Porta Aurea at Ravenna. Torn down in the late 16th century, the Ravenna gate possessed large tondi comparable in type to those later carved at Capua and may once have contained busts. The setting of the statuary at Capua, however, is without Classical precedents. The contamination of gate iconography with that of the triumphal arch shows how the functional differences between the two had become indistinct by the 13th century.

A communal city gate iconography may be said to begin with the rebuilding and embellishment of cities in the 12th century. At Milan fragmentary reliefs on the Porta Romana of 1171 document the rebuilding of the city after its destruction by Barbarossa. These reliefs are of exceptional importance in that they show, in a continuous narrative, a historical event. As with the earlier and more sophisticated reliefs on the interior of the Arch of Titus (ca. 81), they were meant to be read by the observer passing through, as civic iconography.

The cathedrals built from the second half of the 12th century in northern France, and then throughout Europe over the course of the 13th century and later, witnessed an unprecedented explosion of sculptural decoration. A notable standard feature was the statue column (seen first in mid 12th century cloister decoration). Typically, designers incorporated jambs lined with biblical figures into elaborate iconographic programs. The increasing importance of the Virgin Mary assured her a privileged place in the sculpture of the cathedrals; the coronation of the Virgin was clearly the most prevalent image, as demonstrated at the Reims Cathedral west facade gable and elsewhere. Hundreds of other sculptures animate the main facade, transepts, buttresses, and interior west wall of Reims Cathedral. A particularly English variant is the screen facade, as seen at Lincoln, Salisbury, and Wells Cathedrals. Here, the figurative sculptures (full figures in niches) are contained within a system of arcades whose tracery designs are as important a sculptural element as the figures.

The interiors of Gothic cathedrals displayed a variety of carved decoration, such as foliate capitals, tracery at the clerestory and triforium level, and sometimes fully carved figures of apostles or other holy figures placed against the piers such as at the Sainte-Chapelle, Paris (1246) and Cologne Cathedral (begun 1331). A highly original example of interior architectural sculpture is the series of busts representing Emperor Charles IV and his family, the first archbishops of Prague, as well as the cathedral's master masons Matthew of Arras and Peter Parler, carved at the triforium level of St. Vitus's Cathedral, Prague (ca. 1370).

The choir screen was another important feature of interior architectural sculpture. Especially popular in Gothic cathedrals, a rare early example is seen in the poignant scenes of Lazarus, fragments from the screen of Chichester Cathedral (ca. 1140). Fragments also survive from the mid 13th century rood screen at Bourges Cathedral and the choir screen of the Cathedral of Notre-Dame, Paris (before 1344), that demonstrate the lively narrative of the Infancy and Passion cycles as well as the relationship to private devotional sculpture. The wooden choir screen of the Chapel of St.-Fiacre, Le Faouët in Brittany (1480), maintains its vivid polychrome. Religious and secular themes are carved in bold relief amid delicate flamboyant tracery.

The building of Milan Cathedral spans the Gothic to Gothic Revival styles. Begun in 1387 by Simone da Orsenigo, work continued by Nicolas de Bonaventure and Johann von Freiburg. Workers completed the foundations and began the walls by 1391 but did not complete the piers until 1399. By 1500 the inside of the dome and its octagonal exterior were completed. The facade was not constructed until 1806–13 under architect Carlo Amati. With a length of more than 150 meters and its greatest height over 106 meters, Milan Cathedral is surpassed only by St. Peter's Basilica, Rome. Despite the architectural decoration dating from various periods, the effect of the cathedral is probably close to that envisaged by original builders.

Less detail appears on the interior than the exterior; its vast proportions provide the main impression, as sculptured figures in enormous capitals carry a sense of the smallness of the human scale up into the space overhead. The piers are seemingly innumerable, and the rippling contours encourage a sense of movement. Approximately 3000 statues are embedded within the fabric of the cathedral, about 2000 of which are on the exterior. Not until 1762 was the plan for concave buttresses and the spire by Francesco Croce approved and then built. A statue of the Virgin was placed over the spire in 1774.

Planning for the facade did not begin seriously until about 1540, when Vincenzo Seregni submitted a plan. Little was accomplished during his tenure as cathedral architect. In 1564 Cardinal Carlo Borromeo, newly appointed archbishop of Milan, replaced Seregni with Pellegrino Tibaldi, who subsequently supervised a considerable building program. That work did not include the facade, the matter of which by then had become a test of the relationship between the Gothic style of most of the building and the newer schemes of Renaissance proportion and details. Disputes followed, and a range of other projects were put forward; finally, Napoléon Bonaparte gave orders that the cathedral should be completed. The cathedral architect, Carlo

Amati, carried out most of the work between 1806 and 1813.

Renaissance and Mannerism: 15th–16th Centuries

Renaissance architectural sculpture tends to be restrained, for example, Luca and Andrea della Robbia's interior and exterior terracotta decoration for Brunelleschi's Foundling Hospital in Florence (1419). The Loggetta, Piazza San Marco, Venice, begun in 1536 by Jacopo Sansovino, is embellished with richly carved architectural sculpture that alludes to classicizing motifs: capitals imitating antique models, masks, nude figures at spandrels, and putti holding garland swags decorating the entablature.

Characteristics of the School of Fontainebleau (created in the 1530s by Italian artists working for King Francis I in France) include the incorporation of mythological subjects, antique motifs such as nymphs, satyrs, and putti, and the predilection for nudes of elongated proportions. These features are seen in Francesco Primaticcio's stucco sculpture framing paintings in the Chamber of the Duchess d'Etampes, Château de Fontainebleau (1541–44), Rosso Fiorentino's Galerie of Francis I (ca. 1533–40) features muscular nudes, putti and other classical motifs amid the characteristic strapwork, a form of decoration in which the stucco seems to imitate rolled leather cut into fantastic shapes.

Domestic architecture remains austere on the exterior, a carved coat of arms often the sole sculptural element (e.g., Michelozzo's Palazzo Medici, Florence, 1444), while interior sculpture includes uniform Corinthian-style columns and some decorative medallions above the courtyard arcade depicting coats of arms, as well as some figurative scenes.

For Andrea Palladio's Villa Rotonda in the 1560s, Ionic columns support a pediment crowned by nude figures at apex and ends (as *acroteria*).

In Germany, the facade of the Otto Heinrich Wing of Heidelberg Castle (1557–66) is animated by monumental caryatid and allegorical figures, carved nearly in the round.

Baroque: 17th–18th Centuries

Baroque architectural decoration became increasingly ornate, with elaborate sculptural programs decorating both secular and religious buildings. As Palladio had done, Carlo Maderno also used fully carved figures as ornament across the facade of St. Peter's Basilica, Rome (although here we have Christ and the apostles), when completing Bramante, Michelangelo, and Sangallo's design (1606–12). Bernini continued this decorative scheme with voluminously draped saints standing above his colonnade completing St. Peter's Square (1667).

In the Baroque churches, such as the Church of the Gesù, Rome, designed by Giacomo Barozzi da Vignola (1568–84; redecorated 1669–83), figurative sculpture occupies the level of the clerestory windows and interacts with the painted and stucco decoration in the vaults, pendentives, and dome. Facade sculpture continued to be important, as in Borromini's Church of S. Carlo alle Quattro Fontane, Rome (1665–67, completed after Borromini's death in 1682), where full figures in niches on sides and above doorways convey an iconographic message, with angels carrying an oval frame containing a painted image of the patron saint at the top of the facade.

In transforming the columns of the dome in the Church of S. Andrea delle Fratte into winged cherubs with varying expressions, Borromini participated in the Baroque predilection for metamorphosis. A similar aesthetic appears on the doorway of the town hall at Toulon (1656–57) by Pierre Puget. France saw precedents in Jean Goujon's caryatids (1550; Musée du Louvre, Paris) and Jacques Sarazin's caryatids for the Louvre (1641). Puget created a much more dramatic and tormented expression for his *Atlantes* figures, reminiscent of Michelangelo's slaves. The work of Antonio Gherardi demonstrates the theatrical quality that pervades all media of Baroque art. His ceiling for the Avila Chapel in the Church of S. Maria in Trastavere, Rome, is sculptural as well as pictorial. Four flying angels hold a lantern turret that appears illuminated both from without and within. The carved and transparent angels create an ethereal and dynamic transformation.

The architect Matthäus Daniel Pöppelmann, collaborating with sculptor Balthasar Permoser, created the theatrical fantasy of sculpture for the Zwinger Palace (1711–23) in Dresden, the residence of Frederick Augustus. Faithfully reconstructed after the bombing of World War II, the pavilions and fountains are lavishly carved with classically inspired satyrs, pans, and nymphs, naturalistically carved fauna and flora and sea motifs.

Johann Lukas von Hildebrandt's Hall of Atlantes (1721–22), at the Upper Belvedere Palace, Vienna, transforms architecture into sculpture. Robust, seminude atlantes, backs bent by the strain of their burden, stand on carved pedestals as they support several orders of abaci crowned by carved helmets, weapons, and banners from which spring the vault decorated in low relief with ornamental motifs and putti.

A dramatic transition from architecture to sculpture characterizes Nicola Salvi's design (completed 1762) for the Trevi fountain, Rome. Some figures are con-

Nicola Salvi, Illuminated Trevi fountain in front of Palazzo Poli, 1762, Rome
© Erich Lessing / Art Resource, NY

tained in niches of a Baroque facade that terminates an ancient Roman aqueduct, while others, including a figure of *Neptune* flanked by two tritons, spill out into the basin.

Neoclassical: 18th and 19th Centuries

With the Neoclassical style, figurative architectural sculpture became subsumed under increasingly more important architectural elements, including pediments, cornices, and entablatures. Robert Adam's Osterley Park House (Middlesex), begun in 1761, contains Ionic columns with volute capitals. The delicate relief carving on the pediment of the east portico recalls such Classical themes as luscious vine scrolls and griffins.

The Arc du Carrousel (1806–08) in Paris, by Charles Percier and Pierre-François-Léonard Fontaine, includes reliefs in spandrels of all three arches, relief panels above lower side arches, figures standing on columns, a frieze on the attic level, and a quadriga at top.

Symbol of the reign of Napoléon III, the Paris Opéra (1861–75) immediately became the prestige monument of Baron Georges-Eugène Haussmann's Paris. The grand facade, created by Charles Garnier in 1880, is characteristically French in conception, consisting of a central corps with two slightly projecting end pavilions with arched pediments breaking the horizontality of the cornice. The Opéra's polychromy and the insertion of smaller columns within the colonnade make the structure lighter and more decorative than the 17th-century Louvre. Although Garnier employed steel for the frame of the Paris Opéra, he encased it in richly ornamented masonry and sculpture. The facade

also includes *The Genius of the Dance* (1869) by Jean-Baptiste Carpeaux. Mythological symbols and deities, zodiac signs, flora, and fauna repeat throughout the mosaic, sculpture, and painted decoration. In the interior monumental sculptures recalling those of the facade highlight the vestibule.

Gothic Revival: 18th and 19th Centuries

The Gothic Revival paid less attention to exterior than to interior architectural sculpture, although architects incorporated hood moldings, crenellations, pierced quatrefoils, pinnacles, tracery patterns, and occasionally carved figures in niches, illustrated most elaborately on the Houses of Parliament in London (Charles Barry, ca. 1835–65). These features were already used at Horace Walpole's Strawberry Hill (1749), whose interiors display the full fantasy of this style. Mainly inspired from examples of English Gothic tombs and choir screens (as ecclesiastical decoration is adapted to the domestic setting), the intricate tracery patterns, heraldic shields, and some figurative sculpture cover walls and ceiling alike. The latter was constructed of plaster to give the illusion of stone vaulting. A.W.N. Pugin and J.G. Crace's interior decoration for the Houses of Parliament features intricately carved, painted, and gilded timbered ceilings, engaged columns and tracery on the walls, heraldic motifs and fully carved figures flanking doorways and windows.

Churches that were most consciously imitating the Gothic (and in some cases completing a medieval building) are often replete with all the elements of the Gothic facades: jamb statues, carved tympana, archivolts, dadoes, capitals, and so on. Examples include Milan Cathedral (discussed above), Cologne Cathedral (begun 1331, completed 1880), and the Church of St. Finbars, Cork (rebuilt by William Burges, 1861–70).

LESLIE BUSSIS TAIT

See also **Carpeaux, Jean-Baptiste; Chartres Cathedral; Gothic Sculpture; Goujon, Jean; Michelangelo (Buonarroti); Permoser, Balthasar; Puget, Pierre; Robbia, Della, Family; Sansovino, Jacopo; Sarazin, Jacques; Triumphal Arch; Wiligelmo**

Further Reading

Blunt, Anthony, *Art and Architecture in France, 1500–1700*, London and Baltimore, Maryland: Penguin, 1953; 5th edition, revised by Richard Beresford, New Haven, Connecticut: Yale University Press, 1999

Braunfels, Wolfgang, *Abendländische klosterbaukunst*, Cologne, Germany: DuMont Schauberg, 1969; 3rd edition, as *Monasteries of Western Europe: The Architecture of the Orders*, translated by Alastair Laing, London: Thames and Hudson, 1972; Princeton, New Jersey: Princeton University Press, 1973

Brenk, Beat, "Spolia from Constantine to Charlemagne: Aesthetics versus Ideology," *Dumbarton Oaks Papers* 41 (1987)

Ceysson, Bernard, et al., *La sculpture: La grande tradition de la sculpture du XVe au XVIIIe siècle*, Geneva: Skira, 1987; as *Sculpture: The Great Tradition of Sculpture from the Fifteenth Century to the Eighteenth Century*, New York: Skira/Rizzoli, 1987

Duby, Georges, Xavier Barral i Altet, and Sophie Guillot de Suduiraut, *La sculpture: Le grand art du Moyen Âge du Ve au XVe siècle*, Geneva: Skira, 1989; as *Sculpture: The Great Art of the Middle Ages from the Fifth to the Fifteenth Century*, translated by Michael Hero, New York: Skira/Rizzoli, 1990

Gardner, Julian, "An Introduction to the Iconography of the Medieval Italian City Gate," *Dumbarton Oaks Papers* 41 (1987)

Janson, Horst Woldemar, *Nineteenth-Century Sculpture*, edited by Phyllis Freeman, New York: Abrams, and London: Thames and Hudson, 1985

Kinney, Dale, "Rape or Restitution of the Past? Interpreting Spolia," in *The Art of Interpreting*, edited by Susan C. Scott, University Park: Department of Art History, Pennsylvania State University, 1995

Le Normand-Romain, Antoinette, et al., *La sculpture: L'aventure de la sculpture moderne, XIXe et XXe siècles*, Geneva: Skira, 1986; as *Sculpture: The Adventure of Modern Sculpture in the Nineteenth and Twentieth Centuries*, New York: Skira/Rizzoli, 1986; Geneva: Skira, and London: Weidenfeld and Nicholson, 1987

Pressouyre, Léon, "St. Bernard to St. Francis: Monastic Ideals and Iconographic Programs in the Cloister," *Gesta* 12 (1973)

Sauerländer, Willibald, "Romanesque Sculpture in Its Architectural Context," in *The Romanesque Frieze and Its Spectator: The Lincoln Symposium Papers*, edited by Deborah Kahn, London: Miller, and New York: Oxford University Press, 1992

Seidel, Linda, *Songs of Glory: The Romanesque Façades of Aquitaine*, Chicago: University of Chicago Press, 1981

Welch, Evelyn S., *Art and Authority in Renaissance Milan*, New Haven, Connecticut: Yale University Press, 1995

Wittkower, Rudolf, *Art and Architecture in Italy, 1600–1750*, London and Baltimore, Maryland: Penguin, 1958; 6th edition, 3 vols., revised by Joseph Connors and Jennifer Montagu, New Haven, Connecticut: Yale University Press, 1999

ARMAN (FERNANDEZ) 1928– *French*

In reaction to the informal and abstract tendencies that dominated the world art scene between 1940 and 1950, Arman Fernandez, known as Arman, decided to abandon traditional painting and sculpture in order to adhere to a new phase of research, which can be seen in various modalities in both Europe and the United States in the early 1960s. American Pop artists (such as Robert Rauschenberg and Jasper Johns) and the French Nouveaux Réalistes (Yves Klein, Arman, Daniel Spoerri, and César) felt the need to concretely return to reality, which they captured directly in the objects of everyday life. The basis of this new production was the readymade concept invented by Marcel Duchamp in the 1920s, which destroyed every traditional notion of sculpture. The principal target of this return to the spirit of Dada was the triumph of consumerism.

Fundamental to Arman's participation in the collective shows of Nouveau Réalisme between 1960 and 1963 was his friendship (begun in 1947) with the founder and protagonist of the group, Yves Klein. Kurt Schwitters's show at the Galerie Berggruen in Paris in 1954 was also very important in Arman's artistic formation. Beginning in 1959, Arman abandoned painting to become, with his readymade works, an original and acute witness to the pseudobiological cycle of consumer production and to the destruction of modern society. In his first *Accumulations* series of assemblage multiples, which he produced into the 1990s, Arman heaped identical objects ranging from toys and coffee pots to aluminum pastry cases in transparent containers, altering their meaning with ironic repetition and redundancy. Preferring objects of use, often manufactured and with moving parts, Arman viewed the collectibles as extensions of the human body. In a more sinister variation on this theme entitled *Home Sweet Home*, he collected gas masks in a wooden box, sardonically alluding to his Jewish origins.

Arman followed his aesthetic investigation of refuse with his *Poubelle* (Dustbin) series, in which he formed very particular portraits out of garbage or discarded objects belonging to his friends and placed them in transparent boxes. In *The Mail Affaire*, Arman gathered three months' worth of the official critic of Nouveau Réalisme Paul Restany's mail in a wooden box. In a consumer society, the garbage one accumulates suggests one's portrait. Arman's work resembles that of his contemporary Spoerri, who in his *Tableaux Pièges* exhibited leftovers from lunches and dinners as works of art.

In 1960, in response to Klein's infamous 1957 installation *Le Vide* (The Void) at Galerie Iris Clert in Paris, Arman presented *Le Plein* (Fullness), a gigantic accumulation of rubbish that filled the Clert gallery space from the floor to the ceiling. *Le Plein* existed as a material and conceptual counterpart to *Le Void*, Klein's metaphysical meditation on space, in which he left the gallery completely empty, that is, voided of physical substance and yet full of meaning. Arman's refuse heap filled the space as if to exclude the viewer from the sacred space, simultaneously celebrating a junk aesthetic and satirizing the commodity value of art objects. These two vital installations are considered the first examples of Environmental as well as Performance art. Compared to Klein's work, Arman's is perhaps less philosophical and more concerned with the concreteness of things. In his next cycle, *Rages* (1961–63), Arman revealed the internal structure of objects in the tradition of Cubism by violently breaking them and then gluing their various pieces to wooden panels. The effect obtained was that of a controlled explosion. He generally chose familiar, even banal objects that included beer mugs and coffeepots. Arman's great passion for music and chess often led him to utilize musical instruments and chess pieces in these works as well.

In 1963 Arman commenced with his *Combustions* series. It consisted of burnt objects such as violins that were rearranged on panels or enclosed in transparent boxes. From this moment, Arman seemed more interested in obtaining pleasing aesthetic effects, as in the work *Groupe de Recherches Visuelles (Group of Visual Research)*. As a variant of his *Accumulations*, in the *Inclusions* series (1964–1990s), Arman embedded objects—toy cars, dollar bills, clock parts, telephones, metallic balls—in polyester resin within transparent containers. In this period he resumed the *Poubelle* series, replacing the original glass used for the transparent boxes with Plexiglas.

Clock Tower
© ART on FILE / CORBIS and Artists Rights Society (ARS), NY / ADAGP, Paris (2003)

Beginning in the mid 1960s, Arman traveled frequently to New York. Some of his *Accumulations* from this time included dripping paint brushes, tubes of paint, and ribbons of dripping pigment encased in resin blocks intended as amusing parody of American Abstract Expressionist painting, an aesthetic that espoused painterly gesture and emotional content as primary vehicles for expressing the metaphysical. He began experimenting with rubber stamps around this time, in which he used the repeated stamped image as yet another evocation of accumulation and gesture, albeit without the overt emotionalism of American painter Jackson Pollock's dripped paintings.

During this phase, Arman produced symbolic and ambitious outdoor sculptures of his various collected objects. He shifted from personal portraits to generalized portraits of society in which he attempted to exorcise collective consumer anxiety by means of depicting consumed objects. This marriage of art and industry reached its culmination in the 1967–68 series dedicated to the automobile, *Renault Accumulations*, in which he amassed embedded and often mangled pieces of cars in gigantic towers, as well as exposed pieces of car bodies and motors in the usual transparent boxes. César also used industrial and automotive materials for his *Compressions*, but unlike Arman, who in this period tended to spread his materials out in free forms and large scales, César compressed his in closed, heavy cubes. Arman's largest outdoor sculpture, measuring 100 feet in height and sited in Beirut, Lebanon—*Espoir de Paix* (1995)—comprised 6000 tons of military tanks and weapons buried within a pillar of concrete.

In the 1970s and 1980s Arman cast in bronze some of the *Rages* and *Combustions*. He also used bronze as support in the *Armed Objects* series, in which he created high towers of guns. In this period, Arman also used tools and other instruments used for labor with the usual goal of symbolizing the excesses of a materialist society. In the 1990s Arman contrasted his work with Classical statuary, taking icons from the ancient tradition and rearranging them with the addition of modern objects drawn from everyday life. His *Clock Venus*, of which numerous copies in various formats exist, is renowned. The Classical statuary is cut longitudinally and then summarily rearranged with pocket watches arbitrarily inserted. In place of Classical white marble, Arman utilized gilded bronze with the goal of annulling the elegant tradition of the Classical form.

Arman has always borne out his obsessive preoccupation with consumer society with his feverish activity as a collector. He spared the various objects he has collected, such as radios, cars, Italian pistols, Japanese armor, and African masks, from rapid destruction or obsolescence. From the beginning of his career, Arman has earned public and critical success for his ability to

85

create visual metaphors for, through intensely symbolic works, postwar anxiety. In addition, Arman's work inspired many artists of his generation who were also reacting to the proliferation of European and American consumerism.

Retrospectives in Minneapolis and Amsterdam in 1964 and in Brussels in 1966 consecrated Arman as a protagonist in the international art scene. In the second half of the 1960s, the worldwide success of Pop art, which shifted the axis of the contemporary art world to New York, also brought the European phenomenon of Nouveau Réalisme to the fore. Likewise, Arman has served as a bridge between European culture and American expressiveness since moving to New York in 1972, where he continues to create new works with visual impact.

CATERINA BAY

See also **César (Baldachini); Duchamp, Marcel; Klein, Yves; Schwitters, Kurt; Spoerri, Daniel**

Biography

Born in Nice, France, 17 November 1928. Given name Armand Pierre Fernandez. Began painting under tutelage of father, 1938; enrolled at École National d'Art Décoratif de Nice, France, 1946–49; moved to Paris to attend École du Louvre, 1949–51; first exhibition at Galerie du Haut-Pavé, Paris, 1956; changed name to Arman, 1958; exhibited at Cordier-Warren Gallery, New York City, 1961; first solo exhibitions at Walker Art Center, Minneapolis, Minnesota, and Stedelijkmuseum, Amsterdam, 1964; participated in Venice Biennale, 1968 and 1976; moved to New York City and became U.S. citizen, 1972; first touring retrospective in United States, 1974. Major retrospectives and solo exhibitions: Musée d'Art Moderne de la Ville de Paris, France, 1975; Kunstmuseum, Hannover, Germany, and Tel Aviv, Israel, 1982; Seibu Museum of Art, Tokyo, Japan, 1985; Detroit Institute of Arts, Michigan, 1994; Jeu de Paume, Paris, France, 1998; Museo de Monterrey, Mexico, 2000. Lives and works in New York City, United States.

Selected Works

1960   *Le Plein* (Fullness); refuse filling a space from floor to ceiling; exhibition at Galerie Iris Clert, Paris, France

1960   *Home Sweet Home*; gas masks, wooden box; Centre Georges Pompidou, Paris, France

1961   *Poubelle*; trash in a glass box; Kaiser-Wilhelm Museum, Krefeld, Germany

1961   *The Mail Affaire*; wooden box, letters of Paul Restany; collection of the artist

1963   *Nail Fetish*; accumulation of revolvers; collection of the artist

1967   *Almost Neon*; accumulation of tubes and ribbons of paint in polyester; collection of Mr. and Mrs. Edward Kienholz, Los Angeles, California, United States

1967–68 *Renault Accumulations* series; Renault automobile parts; Fine Arts Museum of San Francisco, California, United States

1969   *Tortured Violin* (*Combustions* series); burned and smashed violin in polyester; private collection, Paris, France

1969   *Venus of the Shaving Brushes* (originally titled *Bluebeard's Wife*, from the *Inclusions* series); shaving brushes embedded in polyester resin, in mannequin form; Tate Gallery, London, England

1970   *Venu$* (*Inclusions* series); one-dollar bills embedded in polyester resin, in mannequin form; collection of the artist

1990   *Clock Venus* series; pocket watches, bronze; collection of the artist

1995   *Espoir de Paix* (*In Hope of Peace*); 6000 tons of military tanks, armored vehicles, and cannons embedded in concrete; Beirut, Lebanon

Further Reading

1960: Les nouveaux réalistes (exhib. cat.), Paris: Musée d'Art Moderne de la Ville de Paris, 1986

Restany, Pierre, *Les nouveaux réalistes*, Paris: Éditions Planète, 1968

ARMATURE

See **Metal Casting**

ARNOLFO DI CAMBIO *ca.* 1245–1302
Italian

Judging from his work with Nicola Pisano on the Siena Cathedral pulpit, it is possible that Arnolfo di Cambio may have collaborated with Pisano on the Arca di San Domenico in the Church of S. Domenico, Bologna, 1265–67. Arnolfo's early style is difficult to distinguish from that of his master in these projects.

Arnolfo's marble carving of *Charles I d'Anjou* depicts the king as a rigid figure holding a baton in his right hand, symbolic of his authority; his seated position indicates his regal status. The throne is supported on the backs of lions, alluding to the throne of Solomon and thus Charles's implied wisdom. Despite Arnolfo's hard carving style, attempts at individualization are evident in his careful record of facial topography. The marble may have been carved to commemorate the renewed appointment of Charles I as a Roman senator in 1281 and may have been installed in Charles's newly constructed chapel at the Franciscan Church of the Aracoeli in Rome.

Recent scholarship has questioned the association of Arnolfo with the monument of Pope Adrian V (*d.* 1276) in San Francesco, Viterbo. More impressive and clearly documented is Arnolfo's tomb of Cardinal de Braye (*d.* 1282). The de Braye tomb was dismantled in 1680 and reassembled in 1934 with some damage and losses. It became an exemplary statement of Italian tomb architecture early in the Italian Gothic period, with a format for wall tombs that was followed well into the Renaissance. This style was characterized by vertical stacking of elements and symbolic allusions to family, church, and civic affiliations. Also in the 1280s Arnolfo created a *presepe* or crib for the Basilica of S. Maria Maggiore, Rome, and in 1287 he designed the tomb of Pope Honorius IV. The latter was moved from Old St. Peter's Basilica to the Church of S. Maria in Aracoeli in 1545, but only the sarcophagus and reclining effigy survive.

Arnolfo's ciborium for the high altar of the Church of S. Paolo Fuori le Mura is signed and dated 1285. He placed relief carvings of Adam and Eve and of the sacrifice of Abel in the spandrels. Another ciborium in the Church of S. Cecilia in Trastevere, Rome, is also signed, "Hoc opus fecit Arnulfus anni dni MCCLXXXXIII M Noveber D XX" (the date is 20 November 1293). Evangelists and prophets appear in relief in the spandrels, and figures of St. Urbano, St. Cecilia, and St. Valeriano at the corners join the striking carving of St. Tiburzio on horseback. Arnolfo adds a naturalistic touch by placing the pointing index finger of Tiburzio's extended right arm above the animal's ear.

Arnolfo's tomb of Cardinal Annibaldi della Molara, which survives only in fragments, commemorates the notary and subdeacon Riccardo Annibaldi (*d.* 1289), who lies in state, his hands crossed over his stomach. The surviving carving of a procession of censing and grieving clerics with their charming naturalism would have added a note of sympathy to the tomb. In the 1290s Arnolfo carved a marble bust of Pope Boniface VIII in relief and cast the venerable bronze figure of *Saint Peter*. The controversial figure was based on an ancient philosopher statue still preserved in the Vatican collection. The attribution and dating of Arnolfo's bronze have been the cause of debate in recent decades, but technical studies have placed it in the 13th century.

Arnolfo's tomb of Pope Boniface VIII was completed in the late 1290s. The original angels flanking the effigy and holding a curtain are missing, and this makes the tomb appear more modest in design than it was originally. The effigy exists as a relief cut off at the waist, with the pope holding a key in his left hand while blessing with his right. Originally installed in a rectangular niche in the Old Basilica of St. Peter, the tomb surmounted the altar of Boniface IV with a mosaic by Jacopo Torriti situated above. It became a model for several other memorials of prominent prelates. A second statue of Boniface VIII with a similarly attenuated tiara is a seated figure in the round (Museo dell'Opera del Duomo, Florence, Italy) and is now thought to be a shop piece. The carving is in the tradition of the Gothic *Ehrenstatuen*, or statues of popes commissioned by cities to commemorate papal visits.

Arnolfo's voluminous *Virgin and Child Enthroned*, originally made for a niche above the central portal of the facade of the Florence Cathedral, is an imposing presence. Both mother and child are remote and inaccessible despite Mary's direct presentation of the Christ Child and the infant's gesture of blessing. He holds a scroll in his left hand, symbolic of Christ as John the Evangelist's *logos* (word made flesh). Early descriptions of the work indicate that the grouping once had glass eyes, a curious concession to naturalism in this highly ceremonial, iconic, stylized carving.

Although Giorgio Vasari associated Arnolfo with a variety of architectural projects in Florence at the end of the century, only the sculptor's work in the Badia, in the Church of S. Croce, and the Florence Cathedral can be documented. His design for the latter challenged Florentine architects for the next 150 years. Arnolfo's tomb designs left his impact on later generations of sculptors such as Tino di Camaino and Andrea Pisano.

EDWARD J. OLSZEWSKI

Biography

Born in Colle di Val d'Elsa, Italy, *ca.* 1245. Name first appears in contract for Nicola Pisano's Siena pulpit of 1265; may have trained with Pisano, from whom he acquired a virile style of stiff figures and rigid drapery; worked in Rome, 1272–76, in service of Charles I d'Anjou, king of Naples and Sicily, summoned to Perugia, Italy, 1277, where employed on fountain near that of Nicola Pisano; resided in Rome through 1280s and 1290s; worked on papal projects where he developed a naturalistic representation of human figures; advised on construction of the Florence Cathedral in late 1290s; appointed *capomaestro* (chief architect) in Florence, 1300. Died in Florence, Italy, 8? March 1302.

Selected Works

1277	Fountain; marble; Perugia, Italy
1277–81	*Charles I d'Anjou*; marble; Musei Capitolini, Rome, Italy
1280s	Crib; marble; Basilica of S. Maria Maggiore, Rome, Italy
1282	Tomb of Cardinal de Braye; marble; Church of S. Domenico, Orvieto, Italy
1285	Ciborium; marble; Church of S. Paolo Fuori le Mura, Rome, Italy
1287	Tomb of Pope Honorius IV, for St. Peter's Basilica, Rome, Italy; marble; Church of S. Maria in Aracoeli, Rome, Italy
1289	Tomb of Cardinal Annibaldi della Molara; marble; Basilica of San Giovanni in Laterano, Rome, Italy
1290s	*Saint Peter*; bronze; St. Peter's Basilica, Rome, Italy
1293	Ciborium; marble; Church of S. Cecilia in Trastevere, Rome, Italy
ca. 1296–30	Tomb of Pope Boniface VIII; marble, Vatican Museums, Rome, Italy
1296– 1302	*Virgin and Child Enthroned*; marble; Museo dell'Opera del Duomo, Florence, Italy

Further Reading

Carli, Enzo, *Arnolfo*, Florence: Casa editrice EDAM, 1993

Cuccini, Gustavo, *Arnolfo di Cambio e la fontana di Perugia "Pedis Platee,"* Perugia: 1989

Gardner, Julian, "The Tomb of Cardinal Annibaldi by Arnolfo di Cambio," *Burlington Magazine* 114 (1972)

Gardner, Julian, "Arnolfo di Cambio and Roman Tomb Design," *Burlington Magazine* 115 (1973)

Maccarrone, Michele, "Il seppolcro di Bonifacio VIII nella Basilica Vaticana," in *Roma anno 1300: atti della IV settimana di studi di storia dell'arte medievale dell'Università di Roma "La Sapienza" (19–24 maggio 1980)*, edited by A. Romanini, Rome: L'Erma di Bretschneider, 1983

Martellotti, Giovanna, "Il Carlo d'Angio Capitolino: Reflessioni dopo il Restauro," *Arte Medievale*, 2nd series, 5/2 (1991)

Moskowitz, Anita, "Arnolf di Cambio," in *Italian Gothic Sculpture, c.1250–c.1400*, New York: Cambridge University Press, 2001

Poeschke, Joachim, "Arnolfos Madonna mit dem Kind in der Florentiner Domopera," in *Argo: Festschrift für Kurt Badt zu seinem 80. Geburtstag am 3. März 1970*, edited by Martin Gosebruch and Lorenz Dittmann, Cologne: DuMont Schauberg, 1970

Romanini, Angiola, *Arnolfo di Cambio e lo 'stil nuovo' del gotico italiano*, Milan: Ceschina, 1969; 2nd edition, Florence: Sansoni, 1980

Romanini, Angiola, "Nuove ipotesi su Arnolfo di Cambio," *Arte Medievale* 5/1 (1983)

Romanini, Angiola, "Nuovi dati sulla statua bronzea di San Pietro in Vaticano," *Arte Medievale*, 2nd series, 4/2 (1990)

Romanini, Angiola, "L'indice tra le pagine: nuovi dati sul monumento Annibaldi di Arnolfo di Cambio," *Weiner Jahrbuch für Kunstgeschichte* 46–47 (1993–94)

Romanini, Angiola, "Gli occhi dipinti degli accoliti De Braye," in *Napoli, l'Europa: Ricerche di storia dell'arte in onore di Ferdinando Bologna*, edited by Francesco Abbate and Fiorella Sricchia Santoro, Catanzaro, Italy: Meridiana, 1995

TOMB OF CARDINAL DE BRAYE

Arnolfo di Cambio (ca. 1245–1302)
1282
marble
h. 6.5 m; w. 3.3 m
Church of S. Domenico, Orvieto, Italy

Arnolfo's tomb of Cardinal Guillaume de Braye (*d.* 1282) established an exemplary format for the Gothic tomb and dictated the appearance of wall tombs well into the Renaissance. Arnolfo's vertical stacking of elements begins with a base decorated with four geometric designs in *cosmati* work (mosaic inlay of stone and/or glass). In other words, the extremities are a pair of horizontal, lozenge-shaped mosaics tangential on their faces to a quartet of smaller circles, and at the center is a pair of circular mosaics interlocked with four smaller circles. These recall the popular quincunx of five *rotuli* or circles in porphyry, with four surrounding a fifth larger *rotulus* at the center, famous in Byzantine Ravenna as marking the place where the Emperor Justinian was to stand during the liturgy. The sarcophagus above is articulated as a blind arcade of six bays flanked by chevroned and Solomonic columns, the spaces filled with coats of arms. An effigy of the deceased with accompanying acolytes rests on top of the sarcophagus. The cover is damaged and partially lost.

In the next register, a central plaque with a Latin inscription is flanked by niches containing a kneeling effigy of Cardinal de Braye at the upper left on whose behalf St. Mark intercedes with a figure of St. Dominic at the right. The Latin inscription mentions the artist, the date, the cardinal, and the intercession of St. Mark, as well as how learning, poetry, reason, and justice mourn the cardinal's passing. The apex of the tomb contains a Virgin and Child seated in a massive throne under a pointed arch supported by Solomonic columns. This is the throne of wisdom, and the Virgin is a stylized figure preserving Arnolfo's hieratic concept for the monument. She wears an elaborate crown in the manner of a Roman matron, and the Christ Child holds a book in his left hand.

In the recumbent effigy, the flaccid flesh along the chin of Cardinal de Braye demonstrates that Arnolfo depended on a death mask for the strong portrait resemblance in this figure. It is in this register of the tomb that the sculptor presents the viewer with the highest degree of naturalism, incorporating a sensitive

Tomb of Guglielmo de Braye
© Scala / Art Resource, NY

handling in the acolytes who draw back the curtains, simultaneously offering the spectator an epiphany and final view of the deceased. The motif of the parted curtain can ultimately be traced back to the Roman emperor Diocletian, who appeared to his people once each year at the center of an imperial window from behind parted curtains in the royal purple.

That the acolytes are parting the drapery is evident from the curtain rings gathered at the opening, although Arnolfo is more equivocal in the movements of his acolytes. These are treated masterfully in terms of design and the human form. Arnolfo gives them normative proportions and demonstrates a feeling for bodily structure in the pressure of the right figure's garment against the shoulders and buttocks, with the fabric relaxing in the small of the back. Arnolfo delights in the interplay of plane and solid in the left-hand figure, outlining a cavity in the folds of the curtain from which the palpable volume of the acolyte emerges.

The tomb was moved from its original location in 1680 with subsequent damage, including loss of its Gothic canopy and architectural frame, as well as part

of the sarcophagus cover. Some of its original polychrome has disappeared, although traces of color are visible in the figures. Nonetheless, it remains a coloristic tour de force with its varied marbles and mosaic inlay, the latter the highly popular and technically superb inlay associated with the *cosmati* workshop in Rome.

Two headless censing angels that were originally part of the tomb are preserved today in the Museo dell'Opera del Duomo, Orvieto, but were not included in the tomb's 1934 reconstruction. Arnolfo marked the tomb with his signature, "Hoc opus fecit Arnolfus," boldly proclaiming that "Arnolfo made this work."

EDWARD J. OLSZEWSKI

See also **Cosmati**

Further Reading

Gardener, Julian, "Arnolfo di Cambio and Roman Tomb Design," *Burlington Magazine* 115 (1973)

Gardener, Julian, *The Tomb and the Tiara: Curial Tomb Sculpture in Rome and Avignon in the Later Middle Ages*, Oxford: Clarendon Press, and New York: Oxford University Press, 1992

Pace, Valentino, "Arnolfo a Orvieto: Una nota sul sepolcro de Braye e sulla recezione dell'antico nella scultura del Duecento," in *Saggi in onore di Renato Bonelli*, edited by Corrado Bozzoni and Giovanni Carbonara, vol. 1, Rome: Multigrafica Editrice, 1992

Romanini, Angiola, *Arnolfo di Cambio e lo stil nuovo del gotico italiano*, Milan: Ceschina, 1969

Romanini, Angiola, "Ipotesi ricostruttive per i monumenti sepolcrali di Arnolfo di Cambio," in *Skulptur und Grabmal des Spätmittelalters in Rom und Italien: Akten des Kongresses "Scultura e monumento sepolcrale del tardo medioevo a Roma e in Italia" (Rom, 4.–6. Juli 1985)*, edited by Jörg Garms and Angiola Maria Romanini, Vienna: Verlag der Österreichischen Akademie der Wissenschaften, 1990

Romanini, Angiola, "Une statue romaine dans la Vierge de Braye," *Revue de l'art* 105 (1994)

Romanini, Angiola, "Gli occhi dipinti degli accoliti De Braye," in *Napoli, l'Europa: ricerche di storia dell'arte in onore di Ferdinando Bologna*, edited by Francesco Abbate and Fiorella Sricchia Santoro, Cantanzaro: Meridiana, 1995

JEAN (HANS) ARP 1886–1966 *German*

Jean Arp, one of the founders of Dada in Zurich in 1916 and an important protagonist of Surrealism and Constructivism, is universally considered one of the pioneers of abstract art. His initial investigation of anthropomorphism, based on a technique found inadvertently, had a great influence on the artistic generation at the end of the 20th century.

In about 1903 Arp completed his first plaster, *Head*, in which references to the sculpture of Medardo Rosso and Auguste Rodin are evident. In 1905 Aristide Maillol's plastic and volumetric sculpture at his retrospective in Paris made an impression on Arp. Meeting Wassily Kandinsky in Monaco in 1911 was also important both for Arp's formation and for his approach to primitivism and German romanticism. In 1915 in Zurich, Arp met Sophie Taeuber, an abstract painter and his future wife, with whom he established a lifelong artistic and spiritual connection.

Arp's intense experience with the Dada movement from 1916 to 1920 was decisive in the development of his characteristic sculptural style. According to Arp, Dada, which destroyed every traditional notion of sculptural technique while exalting the irrational and unconscious in artistic creation, represented the reconciliation of man with nature and the integration of art with life. During this period, Arp, with a technique totally entrusted to chance, created irregularly contoured reliefs inspired by natural forms that were the basis for his rounded sculptures 13 years later.

In 1916's *Forest*, Arp paid homage to Kandinsky's work with an abstract composition inspired by organic forms. He extracted anthropomorphic forms from a thin wood panel painted with bright colors. Every illusionistic appearance is abolished, suggesting the idea of a forest through rounded symbolic figures that evoke the continual metamorphosis of nature.

In 1924 Arp participated in Surrealism, which he interpreted as a prolongation of the spirit of Dada, accentuating the intuitive and paradoxical sides of his works. Certain common objects particularly attracted Arp's attention such as shirts, clocks, masks, teapots, amphoras, bottles, stars, flowers, and leaves. These objects were often used together with animals such as frogs and birds or with fragments of the human body such as torsos, hands, heads, and mustaches. The fundamental goal was to establish an unceasing relationship between the organic and the inorganic, between the vegetable and animal worlds, and between the human body and inanimate objects. The resulting ambiguity is underlined by the titles of these works, which always suggest the idea of a continuous evolution between different forms: in art, as in nature, forms evolve without predetermined names. Arp was fascinated above all by the evocative and surrealistic possibilities of the navel. Its amoebic shape becomes, in brief, the symbol of the various metamorphoses of the human body and the ideal model of a primitive world in a perennial state of flux and transformation. In fact, the amoebic form is able to evoke both microscopic and cellular life as well as universal and cosmic life.

In 1926's relief *Navel-Bottle* (of which various versions exist), Arp transformed the human body into an object, yet at the same time he humanized the object. This process of transfiguration is based on a philosophy of nature oriented to discover basic forms that

Pagoda Fruit
© 2001 Artists Rights Society (ARS), NY / VG Bild-Kunst, Bonn

undergo infinite variations and modifications. In 1930, owing to his progressive involvement in Surrealism, Arp decided to participate in the Constructivist group, with the intention of actively obligating himself to change society. His passage from sculptural reliefs to sculpture in the round is represented by *Fruit of a Hand* from 1929, in which he mounted his typical painted wood relief on a pedestal. This transitional phase ended in 1930 with the beginning of the *Concretions* series in plaster, wood, bronze, and cement. The word "concretions" indicates a willingness to create a new reality against the principle of mimetic reproduction without, however, sliding into pure abstraction. Arp preferred to present his works without pedestals in order to give the impression of forms that exist directly in nature.

Torso (1931), in white marble, is considered the prototype of Arp's sculpture. The torso, one of Arp's preferred themes, was undertaken in numerous versions in various materials such as plaster, marble, and bronze. Arp individualized the basic form of the female body, which is subject to infinite modifications and variations. The strong, sensual, yet at the same time ideal charge of this important sculpture is amazing. In fact, the plastic volumes of Arp's sculptures always remind one of the curves of the female body, but at the same time the purity of their forms transcend their earthly concreteness.

In *Human Concretions on Oval Bowl*, which is part of the *Human Concretions* series completed between 1934 and 1935, Arp sought to condense a physical presence that would provoke a strong impact on the spectator. In 1935 he began the series *Metamorphoses*, orienting his artistic pursuit toward the continuous flux of natural forms. The cast *Giant Seed* is a process of broadening transfiguration: the seed is exaggerated to the point of becoming an enormous reserve of vital energy. *The Growth of Buds* depicts proliferation in transformation: the vital energy pushes outward through protuberances similar to breasts. In the white marble *Growth*, Arp introduced a variation in his attempt to embody energy, no longer imprisoned as in previous works, but pushed upward in light and rhythmic curves.

Elastic curves that alternate with geometric and linear forms characterize *Conjugal Sculpture*, part of a work in wood that Arp realized in collaboration with his wife. Following her death in 1943, Arp accentuated his tendency toward mysticism, concentrating all of his zeal on a few chosen themes. In *Torso-Amphora* (1962), he added a strong, intensely spiritual, religious charge to his usual attempt to establish a relationship between nature and the human form. Arp is often compared to Constantin Brancusi for the simplicity and organic vitality of his forms, but unlike Brancusi, he maintained a tight connection to concrete reality without ever losing himself in an idealized mysticism.

In addition to Arp's attempts to re-elaborate organic forms in figurative or abstract forms, he exercised a great influence on the British sculptors Henry Moore and Barbara Hepworth. Arp's post–World War II trip to the United States was rich in suggestions for the American artistic generation of the 1960s, above all for Junk art and Fluxus, which sought to establish a fluid rapport between art and life.

In 1958 the Museum of Modern Art in New York City dedicated a large retrospective to Arp, which consecrated him as a protagonist on the international art scene for his ability to individuate universal forms by joining the ideal and the real in a continual and unstoppable vital flow.

CATERINA BAY

See also **Constructivism; Maillol, Aristide; Rodin, Auguste; Rosso, Medardo; Surrealist Sculpture; Taeuber-Arp, Sophie**

Biography

Born in Strassburg, Germany (now Strasbourg, France), 16 September 1886. Entered the Kunstge- werbeschule in Strassburg, 1900–1901; studied drawing with painter Georges Ritleng, 1901; visited Paris and enrolled in the Kunstschule in Weimar, Germany, 1904–07; first exhibit at Bernheim Jeune Gallery, Paris, 1907; enrolled at Académie Julian, Paris, 1908–09; moved to Weggis, Switzerland, 1909; a founder/member of Moderner Bund group in Lucerne, Switzerland, 1911–13; started working with collage, 1914; fled to Zurich during World War I, 1915; same year had an exhibition at Galerie Tanner, Zurich; active member of Dada from 1916; involved in the Surrealist movement, sustained close contacts with the artistic groups de Stijl, Abstraction-Création, Cercle et Carré; married Sophie Taeuber, 1922; first trips to United States, 1949–50; traveled to Greece, 1952 and 1955; won First International Prize for Sculpture at Venice Biennale, Italy, 1954; a retrospective at the Museum of Modern Art, New York City, 1958; worldwide exhibits followed; large retrospective at Musée Nationale d'Art Moderne, Centre Georges Pompidou, Paris, 1962; won Carnegie Prize and Nordrhein Grand Prix for Sculpture, 1964. Died in Lucerne, Switzerland, 7 June 1966.

Selected Works

ca. 1903 *Head*; plaster; private collection
1916 *Forest*; painted wood; Fondation Arp, Clamart, France
1926 *Navel-Bottle*; painted wood; Museum of Modern Art, New York City, United States
1929 *Fruit of a Hand*; painted wood; Kunsthaus, Zurich, Switzerland
1931 *Torso*; marble; R. Petzold collection, Basel, Switzerland
1935 *Human Concretions on Oval Bowl*; bronze; Fondation Arp, Clamart, France
1936 *Giant Seed*; limestone on revolving base; private collection, Switzerland
1936 *The Growth of Buds*; bronze; Fondation Arp, Clamart, France
1937 *Conjugal Sculpture*; wood; Fondation Arp, Clamart, France
1938 *Growth*; marble; Guggenheim Museum of Art, New York City, United States
1949 *Pagoda Fruit (Fruit de pagode)*; bronze; Tate Gallery, London, England
1962 *Amphora-Woman*; granite; Pace Gallery, New York City, United States

Further Reading

Arp, Jean, *On My Way: Poetry and Essays, 1912–1947*, New York: Wittenborn and Schultz, 1948
Arp, Jean, *Dreams and Projects*, New York: Valentin, 1951
Arp, Jean, Carola Geidion-Welcker, and Marguerite Hagenbach, *Hans Arp*, Stuttgart, Germany: Hatje, 1957

Bleikasten, Aimée, *Arp: Bibliographie*, 2 vols., London: Grant and Cutler, 1981–83

Buffet-Picabia, Gabrielle, *Jean Arp*, Paris: Les Presses Littéraires de France, 1952

Carmean, E.A., Jr., *Arp: The Dada Reliefs* (exhib. cat.), Washington, D.C.: National Gallery of Art, 1983

Fauchereau, Serge, *Arp*, Paris: Michel, 1988; as *Arp*, translated by Kenneth Lyons, New York: Rizzoli, 1988

Jianu, Ionel, *Jean Arp*, Paris: Arted, 1973

Last, Rex William, *Hans Arp: The Poet of Dadaism*, London: Wolff, and Chester Springs, Pennsylvania: Dufour Editions, 1969

Read, Herbert Edward, *The Art of Jean Arp*, New York: Abrams, 1968

Seuphor, Michel, and Will Grohmann, *Arp*, Paris: Collection Prisme, 1957; as *Arp: Sculptures*, translated by Bettina Wadia, London: Methuen, 1964

Soby, James Thrall (editor), *Arp*, Garden City, New York: Museum of Modern Art, 1958

ART DECO

Art Deco was the dominant style in European and American decorative arts during the 1920s and 1930s. Defining Art Deco poses problems, as it was extraordinarily eclectic. It was a modern style that celebrated the zeitgeist; its sources included archaic Greek, Egyptian, and Aztec art as well as Neoclassicism. Primarily a decorative style, it also profoundly influenced sculpture and architecture. Art Deco had neither manifesto nor ideology and yet, unlike Modernism, it was immediately and immensely popular. Since the late 1960s, when the term was coined by Bevis Hillier, there has been a phenomenal revival of interest in Art Deco, reflected both in literature and in the salesroom. Yet art historians have long underrated its contributions. Two leading Art Deco sculptors, Demêtre Chiparus and Ferdinand Preiss, fail to rate entries in recent art dictionaries. Such omission is partly due to art historical neglect of the decorative arts, and also because Art Deco was denounced for its "modish trivialities" by Modernists such as Walter Gropius.

Art Deco emanated from Paris and first became known to the public with the *Exposition Internationale des Arts Décoratifs et Industriels Modernes* (1925), which inspired its name. The Parisian epicenter of Art Deco has prompted some scholars, such as Suzanne Tise, to define the style narrowly in terms of French works dating from 1920 to 1925, but this limitation overlooks its rapid international popularity. One of the exposition's exhibits, *Nymph and Faun* (1924) by Pierre le Faguays, epitomizes the style and established its immediate appeal. A lovely nymph, naturalistically modeled apart from her zigzagged hair, is chased by a lecherous faun with a Cubist torso. Sleek, stylized, and streamlined, le Faguays's statuette wittily rejects past historical styles and embraces modernity.

In sculpture, a trend toward the dynamic, geometrical, and stylized forms of Art Deco predated the exposition by several years and is seen, for example, in Jacob Epstein's tomb of Oscar Wilde (1912; Père-Lachaise Cemetery, Paris). François Pompon incorporated Egyptian and Oriental influences into his animal sculpture; simple yet sophisticated, this work was acclaimed at the exposition. The sculpture of Paul Manship represented a more sustained move toward a new aesthetic. Although Harry Rand (1989) claimed that "Manship found himself beatified as a patron saint of Art Deco," this designation should be treated cautiously. Manship's training in New York and Rome was academic; his work was formally influenced by archaic Greek and Indian sculpture and his iconography, seen in the Prometheus fountain (1933–38; Rockefeller Center Plaza, New York), was classically based and showed no concern for modernity. Yet Manship anticipated Art Deco in his fine craftsmanship and use of repetitive, symmetrical, and geometric forms.

Manship spent several of the crucial years of Art Deco (1922–26) in Paris. Another expatriate sculptor based there was the Romanian Chiparus, who is now considered one of the style's major figures. Whereas Manship asserted the "fine art" status of his work, Chiparus executed overtly commercial statuettes. They were produced in limited editions and were marketed by jewelers and department stores rather than by dealer galleries. Their commercial context did little to enhance their art historical status. Chiparus is best known for his use of the *chryselephantine* (sculptures of wood, ivory, and gold that suggest drapery over flesh) medium, which combines ivory and painted bronze. His meticulously detailed figures of dancing girls glamorously conveyed contemporary fashions. Chiparus's themes include Ballet Russe figures, Rudolph Valentino and his partner dancing the tango, and a cabaret chorus line in *Les Girls* (ca. 1928; private collection). The stepped marble bases often used for his statuettes are an Art Deco hallmark. Although Chiparus preferred handling bronze to ivory, the reverse applied to the German *chryselephantine* sculptor Preiss. Preiss's figures are more individualized and realistic than Chiparus's and are more erotically charged. Statuettes like *Breasting the Tape* (ca. 1925–30; Virginia Museum of Fine Arts, Richmond) depict scantily clad sportswomen, whereas his *Butterfly Dancers* is a masterpiece of sensuous, abstract form.

Preiss's work was popular in Britain in the early 1930s, but no major British sculptor of the time addressed such risqué themes. Fashionable concerns with elegance and movement are seen in works by the academic sculptors Gilbert Ledward and Charles Wheeler. *The Lure of the Pipes of Pan* (1932; Birmingham City

Paul Manship, *Prometheus fountain* (1933–38); Rockefeller Center Plaza, New York
© Jean-Pierre Lescourret / CORBIS

Art Gallery, England) by Gilbert Bayes marks a convincing transition from his earlier New Sculpture work to Art Deco simplification. The greatest British sculptor in the genre was Rayner Hoff, who immigrated to Australia in 1923. Like many Art Deco sculptors, Hoff collaborated closely with architects; his *Sacrifice*, the focal point of the Anzac Memorial (1931–34; Hyde Park, Sydney), tellingly echoes Bruce Dellit's stripped Classical architecture.

The Art Deco sculptors discussed above were essentially realistic in approach, even if their work involved simplification, stylization, and, with Chiparus and Preiss, fantasy. Several major figures associated with the movement were more adventurously abstract in approach. The work of the Paris-based Gustave Miklos, Jean Lambert-Rucki, and the twin brothers Jan and Joël Martel forms a stylistic crossover with the mainstream Modernism of sculptors such as Jacques Lipchitz and Henri Laurens. Further scholarship in this area may

well reveal that Constantin Brancusi, Ossip Zadkine, and other Modernists have closer affinities with Art Deco than is traditionally assumed; in turn, the more radical Art Deco sculptors clearly had Modernist sympathies.

Although Parisian artists dominated Art Deco in its formative years, by the late 1920s the stylistic lead had passed to the United States. The German-born Paul Jennewein was sometimes compared with Manship; although his work lacked Manship's consistent charm, he convincingly blended Classicism with Art Deco, such as in his statuette *Greek Dance* (1926; San Diego Museum of Art, California). Manship's sometime-assistant, the French-born Gaston Lachaise, did not consistently follow the Art Deco aesthetic, but his Dolphin fountain (1924; Whitney Museum of American Art, New York City) is a classic of the style, deftly conveying the dolphins' playfulness and elegance. Harriet Frishmuth moved from Beaux-Arts Classicism to Art Deco; her design for a radiator cap, *Speed* (ca. 1925), is a typical period artifact, resembling le Faguays's *Nymph and Faun*. John Storrs incorporated Art Deco elegance with Modernism in his Cubist-influenced metal structures such as *Forms in Space* (ca. 1924; Whitney Museum of American Art, New York City), which were inspired by skyscrapers. Architectural decoration was an important aspect of American Art Deco sculpture and is seen in the works of Leo Friedlander, Lee Lawrie, and Sidney Biehler Waugh.

The outbreak of World War II and the triumph of modern abstraction signaled the decline of Art Deco sculpture by the early 1940s, and sculptors such as Chiparus and Manship witnessed their eclipse. Erté (Romain de Tertoff), the French Art Deco designer, was more fortunate: in 1979, at age 87, he capitalized on the style's spectacular revival and produced a hugely popular series of bronze statuettes based on his fashion illustrations of the 1920s. At the salesroom, Victor Arwas (1992) observed that Art Deco *chryselephantine* statuettes have now "reached the somewhat grotesque eminence of frequently being more expensive than a sculpture by Rodin. Or Henry Moore." Although several lavish books on the subject have been published in recent years, there is still a dearth of scholarly literature available on Art Deco sculpture.

MARK STOCKER

See also **Brancusi, Constantin; Chryselephantine Sculpture; Epstein, Jacob; Lachaise, Gaston; Manship, Paul; Zadkine, Ossip**

Further Reading

Arwas, Victor, *Art Deco Sculpture*, London and New York: Academy Editions, 1992

Brunhammer, Yvonne, and Suzanne Tise, *French Decorative Art, 1900–1942: The Société des artistes décorateurs*, London: Flammariion, 1990

Conner, Janis, Joel Rosenkranz, and David Finn, *Rediscoveries in American Sculpture: Studio Works, 1893–1939*, Austin: University of Texas Press, 1989

Curtis, Penelope, *Sculpture, 1900–1945: After Rodin*, Oxford and New York: Oxford University Press, 1999

Duncan, Alastair, *Art Deco*, London and New York: Thames and Hudson, 1988

Duncan, Alastair (editor), *Encyclopedia of Art Deco*, London: Headline, and New York: Dutton, 1988

Hillier, Bevis, *Art Deco of the 20s and 30s*, London: Studio Vista, 1968; revised edition, 1985

Hillier, Bevis, and Stephen Escritt, *Art Deco Style*, London: Phaidon, 1997

Klein, Dan, Nancy A. McClelland, and Malcolm Haslam, *In the Deco Style*, New York: Rizzoli, 1986

Read, Benedict, and Peyton Skipwith, *Sculpture in Britain between the Wars* (exhib. cat.), London: Fine Art Society, 1986

Tise, Suzanne, "Art Deco," in *The Dictionary of Art*, edited by Jane Turner, vol. 2, New York: Grove, and London: Macmillan, 1996

Troy, Nancy J., *Modernism and the Decorative Arts in France: Art Nouveau to Le Corbusier*, New Haven, Connecticut: Yale University Press, 1991

ARTEMISION ZEUS (POSEIDON)

Anonymous (ca. 470–ca. 440 BCE)

ca. 460 BCE

bronze

h. 2.09 m

Provenance: Cape Artemision in northern Euboea, Greece. Current site: National Archaeological Museum, Athens, Greece

The Artemision Zeus (Poseidon) is an original Greek bronze statue of the early Classical period. Together with the Delphi *Charioteer from the Sanctuary of Apollo* and the Riace bronzes, it is one of the very few statues of this kind to survive and therefore is frequently discussed in studies of Greek sculpture. It probably represents Zeus, although an identification as Poseidon cannot be entirely excluded.

In 1926 fishermen discovered the figure's left arm off Cape Artemision in northern Euboea. Two years later, in 1928, sponge divers hired by the Greek archaeological service salvaged the rest of the statue, together with other bronze fragments (the frontal part of a horse and the figure of a young jockey), apparently the cargo of a lost ship. They also recovered fragments of the crew's crockery, anchors, and wooden parts of the vessel. The mission had to be aborted owing to bad weather and was never resumed; more may still be on the bottom of the sea. In 1937 fishermen brought up the hind part of a bronze horse at the same site. This piece has now been reconstructed together with the front part and the jockey as part of one statue (National Archaeological Museum, Athens) and dated to the Hellenistic period.

The port of origin and the ship's destination remain unknown. The cargo's mixed composition suggests that the vessel carried spoils of war rather than works produced for the art market. Unfortunately, the smaller finds have never been properly published, and opinions on their date range widely. A scholar allowed access to the pottery has dated it to the end of the second or early 1st century BCE and proposed that it was made in Pergamon (Pergamum; see Wünsche, 1979). The date of the shipwreck has important consequences for the identification of the statue and possible connections with works known from literary sources.

The Artemision bronze depicts a mature bearded man with powerful physique, striding forward and about to hurl a weapon. His legs are spread, his arms extended, the left one forward and horizontal as he takes his aim, the right one drawn back and poised for the attack. The head is turned to the left to fix his target. The weapon once held in the right hand is now missing.

The statue is best appreciated with a frontal view of the torso, when all limbs appear in their full extension (the arms are imperceptibly elongated, so that their span equals the figure's height). It was cast in several pieces (torso and legs, head, arms, hands, genitals, front part of feet) in the indirect lost-wax technique. Analysis of the clay core seems to point to an Attic provenance, which could indicate that the statue was produced there. Its eyes were once inlaid in different material and are now lost. Grooves in the bronze suggest that the brows were originally encrusted with silver or copper foil. The mouth and nipples were cast separately in a copper-rich alloy producing a lifelike reddish color.

The statue's size, larger than life, and the lack of any other specific attribute leave no doubt that the imposing figure with its highly realistic anatomy represents a god, not an athlete as has occasionally been proposed. The heavily muscled body, long hair, and beard are characteristic of Zeus, the senior Olympian, and his brother Poseidon, both of whom were frequently shown in this particular pose beginning in the Archaic period. Scholarly interest in the statue has focused chiefly on its stylistic attribution and the problem of identification, which rests solely on the missing attribute in the right hand, a thunderbolt for Zeus or a trident for Poseidon. Ample iconographic parallels exist for both.

Coins from Poseidonia (Paestum) in southern Italy and from some other places show Poseidon hurling his trident in the same pose, although he is usually seen from the back, or the shaft of the trident is (anatomically incorrectly) held behind the head so as not to obscure the face. A terracotta relief from the Roman period, depicting a head with similar beard and coiffure as the Artemision statue is characterized as Poseidon/Neptune by a small trident next to the head, but the similarities are too generic and the date may be too late to assume that it was in any sense based on the Artemision god.

Zeus can be represented in an identical position brandishing his thunderbolt; vases and coins frequently depict him in this manner, as do many statuettes. The best-known example is a small early Classical bronze figure from Dodona (Staatliche Museen, Berlin), showing Zeus in virtually the same attitude as the Artemision bronze, except for a stronger forward thrust of the right leg. With the iconographic parallels equally balanced, the main arguments against the reconstruction of a trident for the Artemision god remain that it would obstruct a clear view of his face and that the long shaft extending far beyond the right arm would unbalance the statue's composition.

Scholars have ascribed the Artemision bronze, considered a masterpiece of the early Classical period, to the leading sculptors of that time, namely, Kalamis, Onatas, Hageladas, and Myron, although no solid evidence exists for any such attribution. Stylistically, the Artemision bronze can be firmly dated to the second quarter of the 5th century BCE. Its pose closely resembles that of Aristogeiton from the group of the Tyrant Slayers in Athens, securely dated to 477/476 BCE. The treatment of the musculature and details of the coiffure are close to the so-called Omphalos Apollo, usually assigned to the period 470–450 BCE, and it has been suggested that both statues were made by the same sculptor. Their distinct hairstyle, however, may be more generally a characteristic of the severe style (also comparable in this respect is a similar head of a bearded man from the Athenian Acropolis currently in the Acropolis Museum, Athens).

The high appreciation the statue has enjoyed ever since its discovery (somewhat put in perspective by the Riace bronzes) has encouraged attempts to identify it with famous monuments known from literary sources. Most scholars agree that it was a votive, as the Artemision god's action pose would seem highly unusual for 5th-century BCE cult images. No theory connecting the statue to famous votives of the time (for example, statues of Poseidon dedicated by the Greeks at Cape Artemision and on the Isthmus of Corinth after important victories over the Persians) has so far proved conclusive. The proposed date of the shipwreck would also rule out any identification with works described by writers of the Roman period. A

future reexamination of the wreck site may provide further evidence.

THORSTEN OPPER

See also *Charioteer from the Sanctuary of Apollo at Delphi*; *Greece, Ancient*; *Riace Bronzes*

Further Reading

Houser, Carolyn, *Greek Monumental Bronze Sculpture of the Fifth and Fourth Centuries B.C.*, New York: Garland, 1987

Karousos, Christos, "Ho Poseidon tou Artemisiou," *Archaiologikon Deltion* 13 (1930–31)

Mylonas, G., "The Bronze Statue from Artemision," *American Journal of Archaeology* 48 (1944)

Tzachou-Alexandri, O., "Some Remarks on the Bronze God from Artemision," in *From the Parts to the Whole: 13th International Bronze Conference*, edited by Carol C. Mattusch, Amy Brauer, and Sandra E. Knudsen, *Journal of Roman Archeology* 1/39 (2000)

Wünsche, R., "Der 'Gott aus dem Meer,'" *Jahrbuch des deutschen archäologischen Instituts* 94 (1979)

TIZIANO ASPETTI 1557/58–1606 *Italian*

Tiziano Aspetti is primarily known as a producer of small bronzes, although he worked only occasionally in that field. He should actually be considered, together with his contemporary and rival Girolamo Campagna, the leading sculptor in Venice around 1600, after, beginning in the late 1580s, Alessandro Vittoria's output began diminishing considerably owing to his age. One of the last representatives of the school of Jacopo Sansovino, Aspetti worked successfully in marble and bronze as well as in monumental scale. His position as house sculptor for the patriarch Giovanni Grimani was almost comparable to that of a court artist and is thus entirely atypical for Venice, which may explain some of the oddities of the sculptor's life and the limited size of his oeuvre. Nothing is known about the formation that produced this young artist, who was interesting enough for the erudite collector Grimani to take into his house as restorer of his famous antiques. The only place in his native Padua where Aspetti could have received the necessary education was the circle of the scholar, patron, and collector Marco Mantova Benavides. It was probably there that Aspetti was introduced to Campagna, who most likely served as his teacher.

After Aspetti's arrival in Venice and entry into the service of Grimani in about 1577, another decade passed about which we know little regarding the sculptor's life or activities. Several documents confirm Aspetti's presence in the Grimani palace during this period; he may have also traveled to Florence or even Rome during this time—his fascination with central Italian art strongly suggests early and direct contact.

Aspetti's first extant work is the small marble relief *Forge of Vulcan*, decorating a fireplace in the ducal palace in Venice for which Campagna delivered the two telamones. The relief, although small and in a place where it could be overlooked easily, gives a perfect demonstration of Aspetti's artistic profile: he had a special talent for relief sculpture and was interested mainly in the rendering of the heroic male nude in action. How much he owed this interest to Michelangelo becomes clear when looking at Aspetti's *Hercules* for the balustrade of the Marciana Library, Venice, and his *Gigante* (Giant) for the entrance to the Zecca, the Venetian mint (today the entrance to the Marciana Library's reading room). *Gigante*, one of Aspetti's most important works, impresses not only with its powerful physique, but also with its animated composition, in which the sculptor formulated his own interpretation of the *figura serpentinata*: the pose that becomes almost a leitmotiv in Aspetti's oeuvre is characterized by the sharp turn of the head in order to gaze over one shoulder, which is bent forward because of the energetic movement of the arm reaching across the chest to the other shoulder.

Aspetti's source of inspiration changed according to the material he was using. When working in marble, he tried to emulate Michelangelo, and this adoration even led to his traveling personally to Carrara for choosing the blocks, whereas his works in bronze show the influence of Alessandro Vittoria and Giambologna. Aspetti's monumental bronze statues for the Grimani Chapel in the Church of San Francesco della Vigna in Venice, *Justice and Peace*, demonstrate that these influences were experienced as a stimulating artistic conflict: the personification of Justice owes much to the Classical, polished style of Giambologna, whereas the portrayal of Peace follows the more powerful and less elegant style of Vittoria, as if the artist were deliberately contrasting two different stylistic ideals.

While working on these life-size statues, Aspetti received the important commission to execute two bronze reliefs depicting *St. Daniel Dragged by a Horse* and the *Martyrdom of St. Daniel* for the Padua Cathedral, in which he proved again his masterly skill for this medium. Concentrating on a clear structure in the narrative, he put only a handful of figures on an actual stage formed by the protruding lower edge of the relief, which allowed him to model some of the protagonists almost three-dimensionally. Because the backdrop consists of an impenetrable architectural screen, the figures seem to move toward the spectator instead of producing an illusion of spatial depth. The elegance of the poses and decorative details owe much to the painters Paolo Veronese and Palma Giovane. The figure type of the Classically armored soldier with plumed helmet and a mustache that appears on both reliefs was often used to attribute mediocre bronze statuettes with similar features to Aspetti, but in fact only a few such examples, such as *Mars* (date unknown) in the Frick Collection, New York City, and *Male Nude* (date unknown) in the J. Paul Getty Museum, Los Angeles, may be considered autograph.

The success of these reliefs led to the prestigious commission for the marble Altar of St. Anthony in the Basilica of Sant'Antonio in Padua. In the 11 bronze statues created for this altar, one can observe again the stylistic oscillation between Vittoria and Giambologna, as well as a conception of the figures as compositionally interrelated pairs. In particular, the four female Virtues (today on the balustrade in front of the high altar) are creations of great beauty and elegance. Together with the Zecca giant and the statues in the Grimani Chapel, they give an idea of Aspetti's true artistic qualities, which are often underestimated because of the many small bronzes that have been attributed to him with much generosity but insufficient grasp of his style. His monumental bronze statues for the facade of the Church of San Francesco della Vigna in Venice, especially the powerful *Moses*, demonstrate once again his creative energy.

Aspetti's oeuvre is not extensive because his protected position in the Grimani household seems to have had a negative effect on his productivity. After the patriarch's death, Aspetti sought immediately another secure position and applied, albeit unsuccessfully, for that of curator of the Statuario Pubblico (the public museum that was to be created for the collection that Grimani had donated to the Venetian republic). Aspetti finally tried to compete seriously with Campagna, but hardly any of the ambitious projects he then planned in an outburst of activity could be realized. In 1604 he left Venice for Tuscany, most probably with the intention to procure marble but ending up in the house of the nobleman Camillo Berzighelli in Pisa. Of the many works he executed in Tuscany, according to Florentine art historian Filippo Baldinucci, only a relief depicting the *Martyrdom of St. Lawrence* survived. He died prematurely in 1606, leaving the leading role in Venetian sculpture of that period once and for all to his former rival Campagna. Aspetti's portrait bust, done by his only pupil, Felice Palma, adorns his funerary monument in the cloister of the Carmelite church in Pisa.

CLAUDIA KRYZA-GERSCH

See also **Campagna, Girolamo; Sansovino, Jacopo; Vittoria, Alessandro**

Biography

Born probably in Padua, Italy, between 1557 and 1558. Family were bronze founders; uncle, Tiziano Minio (with whom Aspetti is sometimes confused), was a stuccoist and sculptor; likely apprenticed with Girolamo Campagna and in the circle of Paduan scholar and collector Marco Mantova Benavides; settled in Venice, *ca.* 1577, where he served as house sculptor and antique restorer to the famous collector Giovanni Grimani, until his patron's death, 1593; executed public and ecclesiastical commissions in Venice and Padua; traveled to Carrara, 1599, to Verona, 1602/03, and to Tuscany, 1604. Died in Pisa, Italy, between 27 July and 23 September 1606.

Selected Works

ca. 1587–88	*Forge of Vulcan*; marble; Sala dell'Anticollegio, Doge's Palace, Venice, Italy
ca. 1587–88	*Hercules* and *Atlas*; marble; Scala d'Oro, Doge's Palace, Venice, Italy
ca. 1588–89	*Hercules*; Istrian stone; Marciana Library, Venice, Italy
1590	*St. Theodore* and *St. Marc*; marble; Rialto Bridge, Venice, Italy
1590–91	*Gigante*; marble; Mint (Zecca), Venice, Italy
1592–93	*St. Daniel Dragged by a Horse* and *Martyrdom of St. Daniel*; bronze; Museo Diocesano, Padua, Italy
ca. 1592–94	*Justice and Peace*; bronze; Grimani Chapel, Church of San Francesco della Vigna, Venice, Italy
1593–94	Altar of St. Anthony with 11 statues in bronze; marble; Basilica of Sant'Antonio, Padua, Italy
ca. 1595	*Sebastiano Venier*; bronze; Doge's Palace, Venice, Italy
ca. 1595–99	*Moses* and *St. Paul*; bronze; Church of San Francesco della Vigna, Venice, Italy
ca. 1598–99	Christ on holy water stoup; marble; Basilica of Sant'Antonio, Padua, Italy
ca. 1604–6	*Martyrdom of St. Lawrence*; bronze; Usimbardi Chapel, Church of Santa Trinità, Florence, Italy

Further Reading

Boucher, Bruce, "Tiziano Aspetti," in *The Genius of Venice, 1500–1600* (exhib. cat.), edited by Jane Martineau and Charles Hope, London: Royal Academy of Art, 1983

Cessi, Francesco, "Tiziano Aspetti scultore padovano," *Padova e la sua provincia* 4 (1966)

Kryza-Gersch, Claudia, "A Portrait of Tiziano Aspetti by Leandro Bassano," *The Burlington Magazine* 140 (1998)

Kryza-Gersch, Claudia, "Tiziano Aspetti," in *La Bellissima Maniera: Alessandro Vittoria e la scultura veneta del Cinquecento* (exhib. cat.), edited by Andrea Bacchi, Lia Camerlengo, and Manfred Leithe-Jasper, Trento, Italy: Castello del Buonconsiglio, Monumenti e Collezioni Provinciali, 1999

Kryza-Gersch, Claudia, "Original Ideas and Their Reproductions in Late Sixteenth- and Early Seventeenth-Century Venetian Foundries: Tiziano Aspetti's *Mars* in the Frick Collection—A Case Study," in *Small Bronzes in the Renaissance*, edited by Debra Pincus, Washington, D.C.: National Gallery of Art, 2001

Pope-Hennessy, John, *An Introduction to Italian Sculpture*, 3 vols., London: Phaidon, 1963; 4th edition, 1996, see especially vol. 3, *Italian High Renaissance and Baroque Sculpture*

ASSOCIATIONS

See **Academies and Associations**

AURELIAN COLUMN

See **Column of Marcus Aurelius**

ASSEMBLAGE

The term *assemblage* refers to a technique in which an assortment of things, usually found objects and other discarded materials, are combined together to create a three-dimensional artwork. The resulting sculpture, or assemblage, might be made up of manufactured materials, industrial junk, or objects found in the natural world. Assemblage has associations with other techniques that involve the composition of fragments into a new whole, such as montage, a process generally used in photography and film. It is closely linked to collage, which often employs found objects alongside cloth, paper, and other materials in order to create a surface relief. In the later 20th century, the technique of assemblage expanded into the making of Environments, and it was an important element in Happenings and performance art.

The idiom has a host of connections with other media. Poetry, with its reliance on metaphor and the juxtaposition of words to create layers of meaning, is particularly analogous to assemblage: the Futurist poet Filippo Tommaso Marinetti freely collaged words to produce visual and phonic images that combined vulgarity and nobility, and Dadaists assembled sounds for their humorous nonsensical effect. In cinema, the Soviet film director Sergei Eisenstein used the technique of crosscutting images to convey complex ideas; postwar Beat writers, such as William S. Burroughs in the United States, used assemblage techniques to produce literary "cut-ups." Words and images have been transposed by objects, and the technique of assemblage has been effectively appropriated by every aspect of contemporary culture, embraced by a Postmodern inclination for plurality, multiplicity, and bricolage.

Assemblage, and the closely related technique of collage, has greatly expanded the language of sculpture in the 20th century. By plundering the detritus of consumer society, assemblage brought everyday life into art, asserting that sculpture could be made of anything. The raw materials for assemblage have included ephemera and items normally considered of scant value, such as household trash and industrial waste. Consequently, with its implicit, and sometimes explicit, critique of the revered art object and its repudiation of conventional materials and techniques in sculpture, assemblage has provided an important countercultural trend within sculptural practice and has invited an art historical alternative reading to Modernism. The incorporation of kitsch and the amalgamation of "high" and "low" culture inherent in assemblage have contributed significantly to the breaking down of traditional hierarchies in art and to the disintegration of barriers between art forms such as painting and sculpture. The elevation of trash to art status implies a critique of the commodification of art. It also offers an incisive comment on the economic and environmental waste in contemporary society.

Jean Dubuffet coined the term assemblage in 1953 in order to distinguish his butterfly-wing reliefs from collage, particularly from earlier Cubist *papiers collés* (glued papers). Dubuffet pioneered the making of art from ignoble materials in his *Petites Statues de la Vie précaire*, a series of figurines made in 1954 that were fashioned from newspaper, coal, clinker, soil, sponges, charred wood, rusty nails, volcanic lava, and broken glass held together with cement and glue. However, the term gained common currency after the influential 1961 exhibition *The Art of Assemblage* at the Museum of Modern Art in New York City. The show included work by British artists Eduardo Paolozzi and John Latham and American contemporaries Bruce Conner and Robert Rauschenberg alongside that of artists who had played key roles in the earlier development of the idiom: Kurt Schwitters, Jean Dubuffet, Pablo Picasso, and Marcel Duchamp.

Although assemblage is generally associated with 20th-century art, the collecting, sorting, and arranging of objects has a long history in popular and folk culture: the pasting of cuttings into scrapbooks, the hoarding of souvenirs, and the custom of placing precious objects near images and statues of deities all presage and predate the purposeful incorporation of real objects into sculpture. Outside Western circles, ethnic groups from other cultures have included real objects in cultural and religious artifacts, sometimes investing them with talismanic properties.

One of the earliest precedents for assemblage in Western art is the *Little Dancer, Fourteen Years Old* of 1879–81 by Edgar Degas. In the original wax version,

Louise Nevelson, *An American Tribute to the British People*
© ARS, NY, Tate Gallery, London / Art Resource, NY

the figure had a hair wig, a real tutu with a muslin skirt, a satin hair ribbon, and ballet shoes. Few examples of early 20th-century assemblage are extant, but there is photographic evidence of Umberto Boccioni's *Fusion of a Head and a Window* of 1912 in which he incorporated a real window frame into a sculpture made of plaster and wood. Around 1912, Georges Braques and Picasso developed their Cubist *papiers collés*, in which pieces of decorative and printed papers and cardboard were pasted onto a two-dimensional ground. This introduction of real items into the picture surface, exploited even further by Picasso's *Still Life* of 1914, featuring painted offcuts of ornate wood and real upholstery fringe, laid the foundations for assemblage. A further seminal piece was Picasso's *Guitar* of 1912, which was initially constructed from cardboard and later transposed into sheet metal with string and wire.

Whether independently or through direct influence, other contemporary artists working in Paris arrived at similar artistic solutions in the early 20th century. In 1913 Alexander Archipenko was one of the first artists to experiment with montage with his series of *Médranos*, comic puppetlike figures constructed from wood, glass, metal, and wire. In *Symphonie Number 1* of 1913, Vladimir Baranoff-Rossiné displayed a similarly playful approach to sculpture.

In 1914 Picasso produced his first freestanding sculpture assembled with real objects. The six painted bronze versions of *Verre d'Absinthe* (Musée Nationale d'Art Moderne, Centre Georges Pompidou, Paris, France) were all equipped with real silver spoons. Picasso continued to pioneer and develop new processes involving assemblage. *La Chèvre* of 1950 (Musée Picasso, Paris, France) is a prime example of a sculpture in which he assembled a variety of found objects—toys, domestic utensils, baskets, old metal tools, and pots—

and then cast the whole into bronze; this technique was also used extensively by Paolozzi in the 1950s.

Although largely associated with collage, Schwitters is one of the most influential figures in the development of assemblage. His most important contribution is the three *Merzbau* he constructed in Hannover, Germany (destroyed by wartime bombs in 1943), Oslo, Norway (destroyed by fire in 1951), and Ambleside, England (salvaged and reconstructed in the Hatton Gallery, University of Newcastle on Tyne, England). Schwitters employed all kinds of ephemeral materials and found objects in these chaotic grottoes.

The idea of assembling environments from junk was not solely the legacy of Schwitters. Beginning in the 1930s, Clarence Schmidt spent his life constructing and inhabiting his trash grotto in woodland near New York City. Another extraordinary, long-term architectural assemblage project was Simon Rodia's Watts Towers in Los Angeles, California, a conglomeration of structures pieced together from disposable refuse over the course of 30 years.

Artists associated with Dada, the international anti-art movement that flourished during and just after World War I, adopted techniques that demonstrated an anarchic irreverence for traditional materials. This surfaced in Max Ernst's collages and in the three-dimensional work of Raoul Hausmann, such as *Mechanical Head* of 1919–20, an assemblage of wood, metal, leather, and cardboard.

In the 1930s Surrealist artists made extensive use of collage, montage, and frottage techniques, and their work was overwhelmingly concerned with the juxtaposition of unexpected images and objects. The movement's most important contribution to assemblage was with the "Surrealist Object," which presented "functional" items that were material realizations of fantasies and fetishes but were of no practical use whatsoever.

A new wave of assemblage, referred to as neo-Dada, emerged simultaneously across Europe and in the United States toward the end of the 1950s. In France many of the artists associated with the Paris-based group Nouveau Réalisme, founded in 1960, used assemblage techniques. Seminal artists Yves Klein and Piero Manzoni used it extensively in their work. Other participants of neo-Dada included Niki de Saint Phalle; Daniel Spoerri with his tableaux of inverted paraphernalia; César, an inveterate collector and assembler of bits of machinery; and Arman, the arch collator of rubbish who filled vessels ranging from small glass vitrines to entire rooms, as in *Le Plein*, an exhibition staged in 1960 at the Iris Clert Gallery in Paris, in which the artist crammed refuse into the entire gallery space. Jean Tinguely combined assemblage with mechanical movement most spectacularly in his *Homage à New York* of 1960, which famously self-destructed

in the garden of the Museum of Modern Art, thereby introducing the concept of disposable art and heralding the "dematerialization of the object" of the next generation of artists.

Elsewhere in Europe, other groups of artists were simultaneously exploring alternatives to traditional painting and sculpture techniques and turning to assemblage: for example, in Antwerp, Vic Gentils, an assembler in wood, founded Groupe '58 (i.e., 1958), a collective of artists united in their repudiation of painting. At the same time in England, George Fullard constructed figures from timber offcuts and bits of worn furniture.

Paolozzi was probably the British artist who contributed most to the assemblage aesthetic. Beginning in the 1940s, he collated scrapbooks of printed ephemera from science fiction magazines and pulp fiction novels and went on to adopt a collage approach to much of his work in film, writing, and sculpture. In particular, the series of bronzes he made in the 1950s, such as *Cyclops* of 1957, were cast from assemblages of the detritus of industrial production.

The introduction of real, everyday objects into art was underlined in the United States by Rauschenberg with his much-quoted comment about working in the "gap" between art and life. His "combines," such as *Bed* of 1955, were paintings that appropriated real objects.

The creation of Environments, however, expanded assemblage into real space and time. Pioneering works included Jim Dine's *The House* and Claes Oldenburg's *The Street*, which were both created at the Judson Gallery, New York City, in 1960. One of the most influential figures in these developments was Allan Kaprow who, inspired by John Cage's activities at Black Mountain College, moved from assembling murals and environmental structures to create Happenings. These multimedia performances invited spectators not only to look but to participate and contribute as well. Performance artists physically engaged with objects to comment powerfully on issues related to politics, gender, and sexual liberation. Such events included Carolee Schneeman's 1964 *Meat Joy*, in which naked bodies writhed around the floor with animal guts and blood, or the shamanistic artworks and performances created by Joseph Beuys in which specific objects and materials acquired mythic status.

In 1961 art critic Lawrence Alloway coined the term "Junk art" for works by artists such as Richard Stankiewicz, who utilized scrap metal and industrial debris. This was followed by "Funk art," which related to the work of a collection of West Coast artists including Joan Brown, Bruce Conner, and Edward and Nancy Reddin Kienholz, who again largely assembled found objects to produce sculpture and tableaux preoccupied with dirt, eroticism, and scatological themes. All of these various strands of assemblage laid the foundation for Pop art, which drew heavily on images and objects from mass culture.

Although some artists working in assemblage have concentrated on the significance and meanings generated by the juxtaposition of particular objects, others have demonstrated an aesthetic appreciation and formalist approach. Louise Nevelson, who showed in the seminal exhibition of assemblage at the Museum of Modern Art in New York City in 1961, continued to display an unerring eye for the elegance of wood off-cuts, balusters, and finials, often unifying her constructions with paint and gilding, creating edifying cathedral-like structures that mask their humble origins.

The legacy of assemblage for the art of sculpture has been phenomenal. The "new wave" of assemblage that William Seitz wrote of in 1961 has repeatedly renewed itself. Artists have incorporated the conceptualism of the 1960s and 1970s and have invented new ways with objects. Global concerns for the natural environment and the emergence of recycling movements in the latter part of the 20th century have brought new meaning to the use of throwaway objects in sculpture. Tony Cragg's use of plastic litter and other waste materials in the 1980s was part of a return to the use of objects in sculpture, but it also came within a new social and economic context for art. In the late 1980s and 1990s, the technique of assemblage became the staple mode of producing three-dimensional work for British artists of international renown such as Sarah Lucas and Damien Hirst.

All in all, through the use of valueless objects and fragments, assemblage has undermined the striving for permanency in traditional sculptural practices and techniques and has shifted the emphasis away from sculpture that is viewed as an aesthetic object. Perversely, however, the assemblage of trash can rubble has produced beautiful objects. Equally paradoxical is the way in which the appropriation of the real into sculpture paved the way for an art form that involved literally no things at all. In the late 20th century, however, objects and materiality have been reintegrated into sculptural practice. Assemblage is now fully incorporated into the art of sculpture to the extent that it has become more common in contemporary work than previously traditional techniques such as carving and modeling.

GILLIAN WHITELEY

See also Archipenko, Alexander Porfirevich; Arman (Fernandez); Boccioni, Umberto; Brancusi, Constantin; César (Baldachini); Cragg, Tony; Degas, Edgar; Dine, Jim; Dubuffet, Jean; Duchamp, Marcel; Ernst, Max; Fullard, George; Kienholz, Edward and Nancy Reddin; Klein, Yves; Manzoni, Piero; Nevelson, Louise; Oldenburg, Claes; Paolozzi, Eduardo; Performance Art; Picasso, Pablo; Postmodernism; Saint Phalle, Niki de; Schwitters, Kurt; Surrealist Sculpture; Tinguely, Jean

Further Reading

Forty Years of California Assemblage: UCLA Art Council Annual Exhibition, Los Angeles: Wight Art Gallery, University of California, Los Angeles, 1989

Hapgood, Susan, Maurice Berger, and Jill Johnston, *Neo-Dada: Redefining Art, 1958–1962*, New York: Universe, 1994

Henri, Adrian, *Environments and Happenings*, London: Thames and Hudson, 1974

Janis, Harriet Grossman, and Rudi Blesh, *Collage: Personalities, Concepts, Techniques*, Philadelphia, Pennsylvania: Chilton, 1962; revised edition, 1967

Kaprow, Allan, *Assemblage: Environments and Happenings*, New York: Abrams, 1966

Phillips, Lisa, *Beat Culture and the New America, 1950–1965*, New York: Whitney Museum of American Art, 1995

Seitz, William Chapin, *The Art of Assemblage*, New York: Museum of Modern Art, 1961

Starr, Sandra Leonard, *Lost and Found in California: Four Decades of Assemblage Art, July 16 to September 7, 1988: An Exhibition*, Santa Monica, California: James Corcoran Gallery, 1988

Vergine, Lea, *Trash: From Junk to Art*, Milan: Electa, and Corte Madera, California: Gingko Press, 1997

Waldman, Diane, *Collage, Assemblage, and the Found Object*, London: Phaidon, and New York: Abrams, 1992

AUSTRALIA

In a country not yet 250 years old in its settler population and possibly more than 70,000 years old in living Aboriginal and Torres Strait Island culture, the traditions of Australian sculpture are radically disparate and until recently have been perceived to form a largely unbridgeable gulf. Sculptural production for white Australians has been closely tied to European traditions, particularly those of England, with an intrinsic attachment to notions of permanence and posterity and to commemorative functions and the embodiment of civic ideals. Scholars have frequently argued that such sculpture remained, until recently, underdeveloped in Australia in terms of its resources and patronage, a contributing factor in a history marked by individual, rather than group, production and by a tendency to measure local production in regionalist relation to international art centers. Lying outside the framework of European sculptural tradition, three-dimensional works of the country's Aboriginal and Torres Strait Islander populations form part of a larger repertoire of painting, performance, and installation. This repertoire has been connected from its beginnings to impermanence, to the ephemeral, and to the secret-sacred, as well as the more public rituals and performances of traditionally mobile Aboriginal populations. Aboriginal sculpture, seen in its most durable form in a vast network of rock engravings or carvings covering the continent, was produced in its various aspects for generations before the advent of a receptive art market and continues to play a vital role in the perpetuation of the journeys from which it originates.

The history of Aboriginal art since settlement (1788) has been one of profound disruption to traditional life and religion, yet also of ongoing adaptation to European conceptions of art. For white Australians sculptural production largely proceeded with little reference to, and minimal influence from, indigenous traditions, a situation that appears extraordinary in the hindsight of recent re-perceptions. Traditionally recycled, destroyed, hidden away, left to weather, or later relegated to the stores and exhibition areas of white Australia's museums of natural and ethnographic history, objects of Australia's indigenous past and present have only been liberated into the public-private spaces of art beginning in the second half of the 20th century.

As the centuries-old image of a vast imaginary *Terra Australis* dissolved with the great 18th-century Pacific voyages into the reality of British penal-military settlements, the civilizing apparatus of European art was also transported and transformed. Australian art historian Bernard Smith has maintained that the development of the colony's distinctive genre of landscape painting can trace its origins to James Cook's voyages, with their Enlightenment interest in the careful investigation of topography, natural phenomena, and flora and fauna. However, a similar cohesive vision cannot be said to underlie the development of local sculpture, which proceeded in the first decades of settlement in undirected ways born of spasmodic individual production. Within this context the tenets of Neoclassicism, at their apogee at the time of Australian settlement, proved the most consistently successful stylistic transplant for the young colony.

The first sculpture associated with Australia, a Neoclassicist medallion, *Hope Encouraging Art and Labour, under the Influence of Peace on the Shores of Sydney Cove* (1789), designed in England by Henry Webber in Australian clay sent back by Governor Arthur Phillip, described desires rather than realities of the time. This less transportable, more laborious art appears to have suffered a delayed growth, and little significant work, if produced, has survived from the fledging settlements before the 1830s. Indeed, as Australian sculpture historian Graeme Sturgeon noted, the early years of Australian colonization seemed inimical to sculpture except of a particular kind, that of portrait busts or medallions.

The fortunes of art closely mirrored the developments in prosperity, in population, and in national con-

sciousness of colonial settlement. Early activity centered on the convict towns of Sydney and Hobart (Tasmania). From the small wax portraits of Adelaide-based Theresa Walker—the first woman sculptor to work in Australia—in the 1830s to the fashionable Neoclassicist busts of Rome-trained Achille Simonetti in the 1880s, domestically scaled images of the colony's most successful businessmen, politicians, and explorers, rendered in increasingly codified forms, prescribed the shape and industry of Australian sculpture. The first large monument erected in the colony, English sculptor Edward Hodges Baily's *Sir Richard Bourke* (1841), commemorated a previous governor; so too, similarly prominent men of colonial affairs became the predominant subject in Australia's first exhibition of sculpture (1845).

Hobart's first sculptures may be convicted highway robber Daniel Herbert's carved stone heads (1831–36), but a number of artists there are now renowned for portraits of another order; namely, portraits of Tasmania's (considered doomed) Aboriginal race. Benjamin Duterreau and Benjamin Law produced compelling images of this new order of portraits. The latter is the creator of Australia's earliest major sculptures—powerful plaster busts of *Woureddy, an Aboriginal Chief of Van Diemen's Land* (1835), depicted as "a Greek hero in kangaroo skin," and *Trucanini, Wife of Woureddy* (1836)—which were modeled in Hobart as the last of Tasmania's Aborigines were forcibly removed to Flinders Island.

In the wake of the discovery of gold in 1851, sculptural activity increased, and in the burgeoning city of Melbourne two of the most important colonial sculptors established their Australian careers. Thomas Woolner, Pre-Raphaelite painter-sculptor and disappointed gold seeker, achieved great success in Melbourne and Sydney in the early 1850s with extremely accomplished small portrait medallions of society notables as well as a major public commission for Sydney, the monumental *Captain Cook* (1874–79), executed after the artist's return to England. Charles Summers, who arrived in 1853, subsequently modeled and cast (for the first time in Australia) an exceptional memorial commemorating the famous and tragic explorers who became national heroes, *Burke and Wills* (1865), on a scale and with a sophistication that had until that time been the prerogative of sculptors working at "home."

Although local production was arguably slow to develop, colonial leaders well understood the traditional importance of encapsulating civic ideals in statuary, and the concept of exporting from England proved again a successful model for the colony. Until the 1860s the presence of sculpture relied heavily on visiting artists and on the works of English academicians sent to the colony where they provided a model of sculptural success for aspiring locals. New South Wales Premier Sir Henry Parkes, who understood the value of sculpture as a measure of cultural progression, realized his vision of sculpturally beautifying the colony in the 1880s with imported Victorian statuary and Classical copies. Local facilities for sculpture instruction and for marble carving and bronze casting remained rudimentary until the late 19th century, the latter certainly contributing to significant numbers of early sculptures remaining in temporary materials. Government and private patronage remained limited for local artists, and church commissions were few.

Enormous population growth and an economic boom catalyzed by gold transformed Australian society by the 1880s into one with a new and wealthy urban bourgeoisie willing to support the arts. The domestic market expanded, and colonial building projects achieved a civic importance that allowed for the extensive use of sculptural embellishment, providing artists with long-term, if restricted, work. The work of immigrant sculptors from Italy, France, and Germany ameliorated models of the Royal Academy. Australian sculpture could for the first time be examined with a sense of artists working consistently in the country. These years were also ones of unprecedented activity for women, with artists such as Margaret Baskerville, Theo Cowan, and Dora Ohlfsen producing significant work.

Nonetheless, a perception of the inadequacy of Australian conditions propelled many of a generation of Australian-born sculptors to Europe in the 1890s, where the midcentury shift from Rome to Paris as the center of art had a marked impact on their work. On the eve of the national Federation of States (1901), when cultural debate centered on the possibility of an "Australian" form of art, Charles Douglas Richardson, Harold Parker, Charles Web Gilbert, and Bertram Mackennal—who, it was said, "stood forward in Europe as sons of the Great South Land"—were less interested in an identifiable Australian content than aligning themselves to European tradition. Mackennal established an international reputation as a virtuoso modeler of elegant mythological and allegorical nudes and as a leading civic sculptor under royal patronage. A superb synthesizer rather than an innovator, he produced exceptional works that revealed a response to contemporary French Symbolist and Art Nouveau tendencies and English New Sculpture, particularly the work of Alfred Gilbert, as motivating principles of creation. A cultural hero for artists locally, Mackennal created profound change for sculpture over decades: his move away from the archaic formality of Symbolist masterworks such as *Circe* (1893) toward broadly executed figures in the 20th century revealed something of Auguste Rodin's profound impact.

Although World War I quickened the shifts of perception at the heart of European Modernism, Modernist work did not constitute the primary voice for postwar Australian sculpture. In an era organized socially and culturally around the development of modernity, Brisbane-based Daphne Mayo, the most renowned woman sculptor of her generation, and English immigrant Rayner Hoff created a modernized classicist idiom that dominated interwar sculptural production. Linked in its essentials to postwar reconstruction ideals, the sculpture of Hoff and his academy sought forms appropriate to modern life through a classical canon reformulated by a commitment to vitalism, to contemporary eroticism, and to the stylized devices of Art Deco. As such, these works may be viewed as a regional manifestation, in all its differentiations, of the so-called return to order that accompanied the rhetoric of progress and characterized the sculpture of both the European establishment and the avant-garde of the period.

In the 1930s, as Australians aggressively pursued the idea of progress and protection, artists increasingly shaped European eclecticism and Classical idealism to sculptural images concerning national identity, particularly in large civic projects such as war memorials (as sculptor Web Gilbert noted, "a godsend to Australian sculptors"). These impulses achieved spectacular form in Hoff's massive Anzac Memorial in Sydney (1934), an Art Deco masterwork and one of the most resolved statements of architectural and sculptural unity in the country.

The late 1930s proved watershed years. Contemporary art societies formed to advocate Modernism in reaction to a conservative establishment that constituted the progressive as the (unwanted) "international." Major traveling exhibitions from England and France exposed local artists initially to the work of Henry Moore, Jacob Epstein, Ossip Zadkine, and Henri Gaudier-Brzeska, whose effects were immediately felt. A new architecture emerged and with it demands for sculpture of a different order. Sculptors including Ola Cohn, Margel Hinder, and European immigrants Eleanore Lange and Danila Vassilief returned from Europe with firsthand experience of Modernist aims. Sydney's progressive painters and sculptors worked with Constructivist principles, which were the product of modern European tendencies and local conditions. From within this milieu came the earliest examples of nonfigurative sculpture. Margel Hinder developed and disseminated Constructivist and dynamic symmetry principles initiated in the United States, combined with a growing interest in Cubism. The result was an organic yet geometrical abstraction of textured surfaces and rigorous structures ultimately referenced to natural systems, which found form in major public commissions of the 1950s.

Moore's truth-to-materials dictum had enormous impact, which was reinforced in the 1940s by prominent civic sculptor Lyndon Dadswell and expatriate Oliffe Richmond, for whom Moore's sculptural innovations remained central until later links with the Romantic-humanist output of England's postwar generation. A preoccupation with organicism and biomorphism, which can be attributed ultimately to Moore, marked Australian sculpture for a number of decades. In the 1940s Robert Klippel, Australia's leading sculptor, left Sydney for London and Paris, where the works of High Modernism and postwar intellectual thought initiated a period of intense self-directed study—of nature's forms and systems, of machinery and sculpture. From this Klippel's lexicon or language of forms emerged, itself a catalyst for the artist's move away from figurative carving to the found objects and junk assemblages of his mature years.

Although various artists did much to promote an interest in sculpture, signs of struggle for Australia's progressives remained clear in the 1950s. German immigrant Inge King, who would become one of the country's most rigorously pure abstractionists, creating fabricated steel sculptures of a monumental scale, spent her first ten years in Australia unable to work as a sculptor. If assemblage and collage became the era's new creative means, their immediate effects appeared only in the masterly early sculptures of Klippel. For most sculptors in the 1950s, abstracted figurative sculpture remained the dominant mode.

Although white artists had traveled inland to Australia's deserts beginning in the 1930s, and although much of Sydney's harborside development is built on rock carvings, European knowledge of the extensive traditions of carved sculpture among Aboriginal societies remained minimal. In 1959, 17 magnificent *pukumani tutini* (burial poles) commissioned from Tiwi artists—Big Jack Yarunga, Laurie Nelson Tukialila, Don Burakmadjua, Bob One Galadingwama, Charlie Quiet Kwangdini, and one unknown—from Melville and Bathurst Islands were placed in the Art Gallery of New South Wales in Sydney, Australia, as one of the first public proclamations of such work as living contemporary art. This commission marked the first time that awareness was raised and significant numbers of Australian artists began to feel the impact of indigenous culture.

The spectacular carved and decorated mortuary poles of the Tiwi, characterized by a marked geometry and symbolizing the transition from life to death, became perhaps the most famous of Aboriginal sculptural objects. Like the molded earthen figures of eastern Australia associated with ritual initiation acts, and the

Aboriginal *Mimi* spirit carvings, Arnhem Land, Australia
© Penny Tweedie / CORBIS

funerary sand sculptures of Arnhem Land, these poles have been traditionally ephemeral. Boldly painted figurative sculpture emerged from Aurukun (Cape York), most notably in the work of Arthur Koo'ekka Pambegan. In addition, figure carvings by major Yirrkala (Gulf of Carpentaria) artists Mawalan Marika, Mathaman Marika, and Munggurawuy Yunupingu were publicly collected and exhibited. Like the totemic bearded figures of Mani Luki by Harry Carpenter, these works display the influence of the Macassan traders from Sulawesi who visited the northern shores of Arnhem Land for many years. Paperbark sculptures of totemic emblems in the form of birds and symbolic abstracted shapes from artists in Milingimbi and Maningrida (Central Arnhem Land) also emerged: the latter would be echoed in Lena Yarinkura's installations of paperbark figures and in Brian Nyinawanga's modernized carvings.

Among the art of Maningrida, the *Mimi*—towering wooden figures representing the great supernatural beings who are the makers and eternal presences of the country and that had been created for generations as rock carvings and drawings—also became visible beginning in the 1960s in exceptional carved figures by artists such as England Banggala, Willy Djolpa, Mick Kubarkku, Crusoe Kurddal, and Crusoe Kuningbal. Kuningbal was one of the most prolific early carvers of *Mimis*.

Although Europe had remained a focus for white Australians in the 1950s, the subsequent decade witnessed a political and cultural shift that saw a development away from a Sydney-based abstraction sourced in English and French traditions to abstract modes heavily influenced by the New York school. Some sculptors continued to travel to London (Anthony Caro's radicalism exerted a strong appeal in the mid 1960s), and the textured architectonic work of Melbourne's influential "Centre Five" group spoke ultimately of European concerns. Others, including expatriate Clement Meadmore, moved to New York, responding to Abstract Expressionism or later American moves toward purely mechanical surfaces and non-referential units. Beginning in 1963 Meadmore's New York art developed from small-scale textured planar sculptures to the monumental and dynamic Minimalist forms for which he is renowned.

In the wake of the first comprehensive exhibition of contemporary sculpture, the unprecedented growth of interest and activity in the 1960s formed a background to escalating debates between object sculptors and those keen to dismantle traditional definitions. Artists actively embraced the new materials, including plastics, light alloys, junk, fiberglass, resin, and synthetics. Sculptural orthodoxy eroded into a pluralism of concerns—what Rosalind Krauss has described as the "expanded field" of sculpture. From this field the classic formalism of Ron Robertson-Swann and the energized Minimalist works of Wendy Paramor, Bert Flugelman, and Nigel Lendon emerged as central, together with the work of George Baldessin, western Australian Howard Taylor, and the radically transformative installations and performance works of Ken Unsworth, Mike Parr, and Stelarc. Klippel assumed prominence with an exceptional body of metal, machine-part, and, later, wooden assemblages, forged at the nexus of rationality and mysticism and nature and technology, under his preoccupation to synthesize mechanical and organic energies.

The impact of kinetic, conceptual, and post-object art revealed itself in various ways, as did the influence of feminism. The principles of *arte povera* (an Italian movement often characterized by the use of ephemeral materials) had a dramatic effect on a number of Australian artists in the 1970s, as did Christo and Jean-Claude's *Wrapped Coast* (1969) at Little Bay, Sydney—although white sculptors in Australia have produced relatively few large-scale earth or environmental pieces. Australia's foremost Aboriginal ceramist, Thancoupie, set up her studio, and Declan Apuatimi,

a major Tiwi carver of mythological figures, came to prominence with distinctive works, which have recently been reprised in the art of Pedro Wonaeamirri.

Of immense significance since the 1970s has been the growth, visibility, and influence of contemporary indigenous art, both nationally and internationally. White stereotypes began to give way to the concept of a multicultural society and what Aboriginal curator Hetti Perkins has described as a "revolutionary shift in Indigenous arts ... spanning the continent from Melbourne to Maningrida, from suburban Brisbane to the Western Desert" (see Perkins, 1999). This shift fostered the maturing capabilities of white society regarding the conceptual placement of Aboriginal art. The years covering Aboriginal moves back to traditional lands following the implementation of land rights in the Northern Territory saw a virtual explosion of cultural activity. A diverse range of artists, in both country and cities, adopted more permanent Western materials and techniques and effected a critical transformation to one of the most vibrant art movements globally, which continues to reverberate and gather momentum in Australia today. Until this time the perceived boundaries between traditional and nontraditional art, between the art of the Australian deserts and tropics and the practices of urban Aboriginal artists, had remained largely intact.

As Australia's white sculptors have extensively investigated the crossover potentialities of painting, performance, installation, collaborative production, and ritual function, always central to indigenous creation, they have established closer parallels, in this sense, with traditional and contemporary Aboriginal art practice. It is in this context that one can adequately assess Yvonne Koolmatrie's spectacular recent interpretations of traditional Ngarrindjeri weaving (in the form of enormous eel traps), *Palawa* (Tasmanian), Audrey Frost's coil basket fish traps, and Torres Strait Islander Ken Thaiday's quasi-functional Tiwi dance masks.

In the late 20th century, the era of hybridized forms fostered by the centrality of installation art to recent Australian production, the diversity of sculpture (both black and white) crossing into design, advertising, furniture, architecture, film, dance, music, and theater confounds categorization. If a tighter redefinition of the sculptural object emerged in England in the 1980s with artists of the "New British Sculpture," categories have remained more fluid in Australia, where a new process of cultural reorientation, directed to the Asia-Pacific region, is underway.

The meditative Minimalism of Hilary Mais and Conceptualist investigations of Ari Purhonen, for example, continue in the wake of the ongoing impact of the magic action of Joseph Beuys and other political-creative activists whose marked reliance on metaphor, symbol, and metamorphosis has contributed to a contemporary sculpture that is read largely as referential and metaphorical. Rosalie Gascoigne's austere responses to the specifics of place and the constructions of Kathy Temin have reinforced a strong tradition of junk assemblage, heralded in the early 1960s by the energized constructions of the Annandale imitation Realists. An impulse to figuration as a renewed source of meaning and a return to traditional methods such as carving are evident. The poetic investigations of a generation of major installation artists including Joan Brassil, Robert Owen, Robyn Backen, Hossein Valamanesh, Simone Mangos, and Janet Laurence continue to substantially shape contemporary practice.

These works, along with the diverse explorations of leading contemporary sculptors Fiona Hall, Bronwyn Oliver, and younger artists James Angus and Ricky Swallow, form a complex landscape of production. This comes at a time of renewed patronage for sculpture in Australia, manifested primarily in drives by various government agencies to reinvigorate Australia's urban environments with a diverse range of contemporary work. In this context major collaborative sand sculptures by central Australian Aboriginal artists have been installed in a variety of national and international spaces over the past decade, including the massive *Yam Dreaming* relief by Yuendumu artists at the Centre Georges Pompidou, Paris, in 1989.

In the context of a Postmodern politics of recovery, of notions of the body and the land as redemptive qualities for modern society, contemporary Aboriginal art occupies a seminal place, connected inextricably to land, body, and the past. Its religious and cultural significance and its performative aspects continue to compel its practitioners. Practitioners include artists who produce functional objects in natural materials (ochre, feathers, string, bark) in ways that reflect traditional relationships to country and kin and urban artists who create in reference to both tradition and contemporary practice. Examples include Fiona Foley's *Annihilation of the Blacks* (1986), a potent allegorical sculpture that references classical Aurukun work, or Lin Onus's quirky installation *Fruit Bats* (1991), which synthesizes suburban experience with traditional symbolism. More recent artists working in this vein include Judy Watson, Destiny Deacon, and Julie Gough.

Elaborately decorated *Morning Star* poles by Galiwinku (Elcho Island) artists and major figure carvings animating creation stories by Maningrida artists demonstrate a similar reference to the traditional and the contemporary, as do works of David Malangi, a senior custodian from Ramingining (Central Arnhem Land), women carvers such as those of Ngkwarlerlaneme, Utopia (who have been active since 1980s), and Galuma Maymuru. Their spirit sculptures, coalescences of the supernatural and the everyday and traditionally associated with particular areas of land, now float both free and anchored in the spaces and international exhibition venues of contemporary art. At the same time a whole range of sculptural works and carvings that do not exist in the realm of public art continues to be made by Aboriginal artists, such as rare and compelling *Jigalong* figures from the Gibson Desert.

Among outstanding Australian sculptures of recent decades, *The Aboriginal Memorial* created in 1988 (in reference both to traditional forms of European sculpture and to the 1959 *Pukumani* poles) straddles both the past and present and in so doing particularizes the place of both Aboriginal worlds in contemporary society. An installation of 200 hollow log bone coffins by 43 artists from Ramingining commemorates all Aboriginal people since 1788 who have lost their lives defending their land; at the same time it structurally echoes the living present as a map of clans along the Clyde River. In a neat circle this memorial and the work of both white and indigenous contemporary artists have broken with historical models of importation and segregation and are increasingly exported to the world.

DEBORAH EDWARDS

See also **Abstract Expressionism; Art Deco; Assemblage; Caro, Anthony; Christo and Jeanne-Claude; Epstein, Jacob; Gaudier-Brzeska, Henri; Moore, Henry; Postmodernism; Zadkine, Ossip**

Further Reading

Australian Sculpture Triennial (1981–)

Caruana, Wally, *Aboriginal Art*, New York: Thames and Hudson, 1993

Gleeson, James, *Robert Klippel*, Sydney: Bay Books, 1983

Mundine, Djon, Bernice Murphy, and John Rudder, *The Native Born: Objects and Representations from Ramingining, Arnhem Land*, Sydney: Museum of Contemporary Art, 1999

Perkins, Hetti, *A Material Thing: Objects from the Collection, Aboriginal, and Torres Strait Islander Collection Series* (exhib. cat.), Sydney: Art Gallery of New South Wales, 1999

Scarlett, Ken, *Australian Sculptors*, West Melbourne, Victoria: Nelson, 1980

Sturgeon, Graeme, *The Development of Australian Sculpture, 1788–1975*, London: Thames and Hudson, 1978

Sturgeon, Graeme, *Contemporary Australian Sculpture*, Roseville, New South Wales: Craftsman House, 1991

Sutton, Peter (editor), *Dreamings: The Art of Aboriginal Australia*, New York: Braziller, 1988

AUSTRIA

See **Central Europe**

AVERLINO, ANTONIO DI PIETRO

See **Filarete**

B

JOHN BACON 1740–1799 *British*

John Bacon, royal academician, was one of the most prestigious and prolific British sculptors practicing during the latter part of the 18th century. His early training in modeling came under the tutelage of Nicholas Crispe, who encouraged the young Bacon to exhibit with the Society of Arts. In 1759 Bacon's figure *Peace* won him a premium, and over the next 20 years he was awarded 10 more premiums from the Society of Arts, plus a gold medal. Bacon worked for Crispe until 1764, at which time he began to design for the ceramic and metalwork industries. His clients included Daniel Pincot in Patternoster Row, Spitalfields; Josiah Wedgwood; William Duesbury at the Chelsea-Derby Porcelain Works; Sir William Chambers; Benjamin Vulliamy, royal clock maker in Pall Mall; Matthew Boulton at Soho, Birmingham; and James Tassie of Neal and Company in Hanley. Indeed, Bacon is considered to be the most important designer for British industry before John Flaxman.

Bacon entered the Royal Academy Schools in 1769, where he won the first gold medal ever awarded in sculpture for his relief *Aeneas Carrying His Father from Burning Troy*. In 1770 he was elected an associate of the Royal Academy. The following year proved to be a crucial one for Bacon. He opened a studio at 17 Newmann Street, where he employed numerous assistants, including Henry Webber and Charles Peart, and in the same year he became chief designer and manager of Eleanor Coade's Artificial Stone Manufactory, a position he held until his death.

The turning point in Bacon's career as a sculptor came with the exhibition of his life-size terracotta fig-

ure *Mars*. The statue caught the attention of the archbishop of York, who commissioned a bust of George III. The sittings with the king proved to be highly advantageous to the sculptor. In 1778 Bacon was made a full academician of the Royal Academy. His diploma piece, *Head of Sickness*, served as the model for the sick man on the *Thomas Guy* monument. The 20th-century art historian Margaret Whinney considers the Thomas Guy monument to be "the finest English monument of its time." In 1778, when the competition for the national monument to the first Earl of Chatham was announced, the astute Bacon chose to show his model to the king, usurping the normal competition procedures of the Royal Academy. The sense of favoritism shown to Bacon with the awarding of the Chatham commission was the first of a series of accusations and jealousies brought upon the sculptor. The memorial group to Chatham—*William Pitt the Elder, Earl of Chatham*—some 9.14 meters high, established the scale for all future monuments in Westminster Abbey. The figure of Chatham stands above five allegorical figures: Britannia, Prudence, Fortitude, Earth, and Ocean. The arrangement pleased the king and Sir Joshua Reynolds, president of the Royal Academy, whereas others declared it nothing more than a "clump of marble."

Bacon was praised by the king for not traveling to Rome to study. Many, however, saw this as the primary reason that he seemed ill at ease in his attempts at the new Antique style. His lack of Classical training did not, however, appear to diminish the popularity of his work. In 1784 he won the competition held by the Royal Academy for the figure of Admiral George

Brydges Rodney for Spanish Town, Jamaica. In *Admiral Rodney*, the admiral, clad in Classical garb, stands on a pedestal supporting four relief panels depicting his naval victories over the French near Dominica. The prestige of the Rodney sculpture with its elegant relief panels led to 15 more commissions for funerary monuments for the island, including the work *Earl and Countess of Effingham*. In 1788 Bacon was selected to execute the marble statue *Dr. Samuel Johnson* as well as the work of *John Howard* for St. Paul's Cathedral in London. His initial designs included numerous allegorical figures. The tiredness of the two figures may be a direct result of the problems with supervising sculptural committees that tended, at the time, to be constantly asking for modifications to the designs. When left to his own inclinations, Bacon could, indeed, produce fine monuments. The monument *Sir William Blackstone* of 1784 is just such an example. Bacon's other principal undertaking during this period was his sculptural groups for the new Somerset House, in London, executed between 1778 and 1789. These include the colossal figures *Fame* and *Genius of England*, as well as *George III and the River Thames*, each executed in bronze. The commission underlined the versatility of the sculptor, and his efforts in bronze caused him to be recognized as "exceptional amongst British sculptors of the time." Bacon's success within the public domain caused the directors of the honorable East India Company to commission him to sculpt a series of works beginning in 1793. The first of these was a marble portrait statue of Governor General Charles Cornwallis (*Marquess Cornwallis*) for their general court room. The second was the Pediment Group, pediment decorations for East India House on Leadenhall Street. In addition to the public and corporate commissions, the Bacon studio produced an array of funerary monuments, mantles, garden sculpture, and portrait busts.

The productivity of Bacon's workshop was based on his perfecting the use of a pointing machine, which enabled his assistants to translate his models into full-scale works of sculpture. The second was the development of a pattern book for clients to select a specific design for a monument. Although these brought an extraordinary amount of work and prosperity to the Bacon studios, his entire career came under the speculative eye of the fine art establishment. He had never studied in Rome and lacked a firsthand knowledge of the antique necessary for success in a sphere that leaned more and more toward Neoclassicism and less to Bacon's natural inclination toward sentimentality. Even so, his work was much admired by his clients, the list of which reads like a who's who of the powerful and influential, both within Britain and abroad. John Bacon died in London on 7 August 1799.

MARY ANN STEGGLES

See also **England and Wales: 19th Century–Contemporary; Flaxman, John; Neoclassicism and Romanticism Portrait: Other than Ancient Rome**

Monument to Thomas Guy
The Conway Library, Courtauld Institute of Art

Biography

Born in London, England, 24 November 1740. Apprenticed to Nicholas Crispe, 1755–64; exhibited with Society of Arts, 1759–79, won 11 premiums and a gold medal; began designing for manufacturers, 1764; entered Royal Academy, 24 June 1769; awarded first gold medal in sculpture, 1769; made an associate of the Royal Academy, 1770; chief designer and manager for Eleanor Coade's Artificial Stone Manufactory at Lambeth, 1771–99; established studio at 17 Newmann Street, Marylebone, 1771; made royal academician, 1778; workshop responsible for majority of prestigious public commissions in London, 1771–99, as well as for hundreds of private busts, funerary monuments, and corporate contracts. Died in London, England, 7 August 1799.

Selected Works

1769   *Aeneas Carrying His Father from Burning Troy*; clay; Royal Society of Medicine, London, England

1771   *Earl of Halifax*; marble; Westminster Abbey, London, England

1775   Bust of George III; marble; Windsor Castle, Berkshire, England

1778   *Fame* and *Genius of England*; bronze; Somerset House, London, England

1778   *Head of Sickness*; marble; Royal Academy, London, England

1778   *Mrs. Draper*; marble; Bristol Cathedral, England

1779   *Thomas Guy*; marble; Guy's Hospital Chapel, London, England

1779–83   *William Pitt the Elder, Earl of Chatham*; marble; Westminster Abbey, London, England

1780–86   *George III and the River Thames*; bronze; Somerset House, London, England

1784   *Sir William Blackstone*; marble; All Soul's College, Oxford, England

1784–89   *Atlas* and *Hercules*, for Radcliffe Observatory, Oxford, England; bronze; Nuffield Institute for Medical Research, Oxford, England

1786   *Admiral Rodney*; Portland stone; Government Square, Spanish Town, Jamaica

1788–96   *Dr. Samuel Johnson*; marble; St. Paul's Cathedral, London, England

1791   *Sir Richard and Lady Cust*; marble; Church of St. George, Stamford, Lincolnshire, England

1792   *Samuel Egerton*; marble; Rostherne, Cheshire, England

1793   *Marquess Cornwallis*, for East India Company, London, England; marble; Commonwealth Relations Office, London, England

1796   *Earl and Countess of Effingham*; marble; Cathedral of Spanish Town, Jamaica

1796   *John Howard*; marble; St. Paul's Cathedral, London, England

1796   *Sir George Pocock*; marble; Westminster Abbey, London, England

1796   *Sir William Jones*; marble; St. Paul's Cathedral, Calcutta, India

1796–99   Pediment Group, for East India House, London, England; marble (destroyed)

1796–99   *Samuel Whitbread* (completed by Thomas Bacon and John Bacon the Younger); marble; Cardington, Bedfordshire, England

1799   *Sir William Jones*; marble; St. Paul's Cathedral, London, England

Further Reading

Clifford, Timothy, "John Bacon and the Manufacturers," *Apollo* 122 (1985)

Cox-Johnson, Ann, "Gentlemen's Agreement," *The Burlington Magazine* (1959)

Cox-Johnson, Ann, "Patrons to a Sculptor: The Society and John Bacon, R.A.," *Journal of the Royal Society of Arts* (1962)

Cundall, F., "Sculpture in Jamaica," *Art Journal* (March 1905)

Esdaile, K.A.M., "Bacon's George III, the River Thames at His Feet, at Somerset House," *The Burlington Magazine* (1975)

Gunnis, Rupert, *Dictionary of British Sculptors, 1660–1851*, London: Odhams Press, 1953; Cambridge, Massachusetts: Harvard University Press, 1954; revised edition, London: Abbey Library, 1968

Lewis, Lesley, "Commemorative Sculpture in Jamaica," *Commemorative Art* (November 1965)

Physick, John, *Designs for English Sculpture, 1680–1860*, London: HMSO, 1970

Saunders, Ann, *John Bacon, R.A., 1740–1799*, London: St. Marylebone Society Publications, 1961

Whinney, Margaret, *Sculpture in Britain, 1530–1830*, London and Baltimore, Maryland: Penguin, 1964; 2nd edition, revised by John Physick, London and New York: Penguin, 1988

STEPHAN BALKENHOL 1957–   *German*

At a time when artists were analyzing the language and cynicism of contemporary media culture, Stephan Balkenhol pursued what seemed to be an entirely unrelated path. During the 1980s he rose to prominence with his evocative and neoprimitive figurative sculpture. Balkenhol's early carved heads, such as *Male and Female Heads* of 1982, investigated the power of elemental forms to shape the viewer's consciousness; they also set a precedent for his mature work. In American and European art of the 1980s, the figure reemerged in artistic practice primarily in video and photography, and often through irony and appropriation, as in the work of Katharina Fritsch, Bruce Nauman, and Jeff Koons. Balkenhol instead produced sculpture that both eschewed Expressionism and avoided irony in its straightforward representation of the human and animal form. His sculptures retained the amateur quality of folk or outsider art and can be interpreted as a continuation and development of the German tradition of figurative sculpture in wood.

In 20th-century Western Europe, figurative sculpture came to be associated with that used for propaganda purposes by totalitarian regimes. Balkenhol questioned the idealized representations of the human forms of social realism, producing potent sculptural depictions of the ordinary, everyday man or woman in a manner that appeared to present a universal zeitgeist. However, the over-life-size scale of his works undermined their verisimilitude and asserted their status as art rather than life. Balkenhol's early carved figures, such as *Woman* (1983), were unclothed. However, the artist increasingly clothed his figures in an effort to avoid the allegorical and narrative history of the (female) nude. He further developed this concept of anonymity in works such as *Twelve Friends*, which depicted 12 square reliefs of male and female busts. Unusual for Balkenhol, he modeled the works from life, although their lack of individualization evoked the blankness of the passport photograph or the deadpan social documentary of the photographic portraits of August Sander or Thomas Ruff.

Despite having been trained under the German Minimalist sculptor Ulrich Rückreim, Balkenhol chose to use the base or pedestal in a traditional fashion, undermining the way in which his artistic mentor had rejected such forms. Balkenhol employed bases in order to distance his sculptures from the space of the viewer. In addition, his choice of unseasoned wood (which ages to produce large cracks in the sculptures) contradicted the preciousness and permanence of usual commemorative statuary. In the mid 1980s Balkenhol produced his first outdoor sculptures, which presented a challenge because he worked almost exclusively in wood, a material ill suited to unstable weather conditions. For this reason, he made *Man with Green Shirt and White Pants* in concrete. Although the unassuming location of this work, above a tobacconist's shop in the German town of Münster, proved masterly, the material did not lend itself to Balkenhol's tools and techniques. His roughly carved wooden figures bore the marks of their making; the process of casting removed this direct link to the hand of the artist.

In around 1990 Balkenhol made a series of small-scale works that depicted men with animals. The first of these was *Small Man with Giraffe*. These enigmatic works continue to resist easy interpretation. The way in which the human figures interact with the animals in these sculptures was interpreted as intimate, suggesting interdependency and support. In 1991 Balkenhol created one of his best-known and perhaps most popular sculptures in just ten days, *57 Penguins*. Each of the eponymous penguins crowns its own pedestal, ruffling its wings, hurrying about, or lost in quiet contemplation. This endlessly engaging work has remained one of Balkenhol's most enigmatic works.

Although sculptures such as *57 Penguins* have become immensely popular, perhaps because of their apparently refreshing naïveté, these same qualities have made Balkenhol the subject of criticism. His work is out of step with current artistic practices that draw on the legacies of Minimalist and Conceptual art, and critics frequently accuse his work of lacking intellectual rigor. His sculpture appears to rely on everything that Postmodernism rejects: originality, craft, virtue, and a belief in the transparency of representation. However, subjecting Balkenhol's work to the rigors of critical theory risks closing off its potential meanings. As the artist has remarked: "If I make a work it's like making a proposal to start a conversation. Certainly my sculpture has a particular identity, look or expression, but I want to leave it open" (see *Possible Worlds*, 1990).

JONATHAN JONES

See also **Fritsch, Katharina; Germany: 20th Century– Contemporary; Minimalism; Postmodernism; Wood**

Biography

Born in Fritzlar, West Germany, 10 February 1957. Moved to Kassel, 1968; carved first wooden sculptures of human heads, 1972–76; moved to Hamburg, 1976; took a studio and began study under Ulrich Rückreim at the Hochschule für Bildende Künste; received scholarship from Karl-Schmidt-Rottluff Förderungsstiftung, 1983; first solo traveling exhibition (which toured to Frankfurt and Nuremberg) organized by Kunsthalle Basel in Switzerland, 1988; taught at Hochschule für Bildende Künste in Hamburg, 1988; held teaching posts at the Hochschule für Bildende Künste in Frankfurt and the Akademie für Bildende Künste in Karlsruhe, 1990–91, where he was promoted to professor, 1992; built studio in Meisenthal, France, 1994; first solo show in New York City at the Barbara Gladstone Gallery, 1995; solo show at Hirshhorn Museum and Sculpture Garden, Smithsonian Institution, Washington, D.C., 1995. Lives and works in Karlsruhe, Germany, and Meisenthal, France.

Selected Works

1982   *Male and Female Heads*; painted poplar; Museum Ludwig, Cologne, Germany

1983   *Relief*; painted beech; Ludwig Forum für Internationale Kunst, Aachen, Germany

1985   *Three Figures*; painted beech; private collection, Düsseldorf, Germany

1987   *Man with Green Shirt and White Pants*; colored concrete; artist's collection (installed in Skulptor Projekte in Münster, Germany, 1987)

1988   *Twelve Friends*; painted pine; collection of Emanuel Hoffmann-Stiftung, Depositum Öffentlich Kunstsammlung Basel, Museum für Gegenwartskunst, Basel, Switzerland

1990   *Small Man with Giraffe*; painted conifer; Galerie von Braunbehrens, Munich, Germany

1991   *57 Penguins*; painted wood; Museum für
        Moderne Kunst, Frankfurt, Germany
1995   *Three Hybrids*; painted cedar; Barbara
        Gladstone Gallery, New York City, United
        States

Further Reading

Ammann, Jean-Christophe, and Jeff Wall, *Stephan Balkenhol*, Basel, Switzerland: Kunsthalle Basel, 1988
Balkenhol, Stephan, *Stephan Balkenhol: Über Menschen und Skulpturen*, Stuttgart, Germany: Cantz, 1992
Benezra, Neal, *Stephan Balkenhol: Sculptures and Drawings*, Washington, D.C.: Smithsonian, 1995
Kent, Sarah, *Stephan Balkenhol: Sculptures, 1988–1996 in the Saatchi Collection*, London: Saatchi Gallery, 1996
Possible Worlds: Sculpture from Europe (exhib. cat.), London: Institute of Contemporary Arts and Serpentine Gallery, 1990

BACCIO BANDINELLI 1493–1560 *Italian*

Baccio Bandinelli was long underrated because critical readings of his works were limited by a dogmatic pro-Michelangelo bias. This misfortune was compounded by interpretations that accepted Giorgio Vasari's negative view and by the popularity, from the 18th century on, of Benvenuto Cellini's autobiography, which is venomous toward Bandinelli and reveals the same pro-Michelangelo bias. The reductive judgment of Bandinelli became a critical canon. Even recent reassessments have focused mainly on his drawings and small bronzes, judging them less restrained than the statues. The differences between the drawings or models and the finished sculptures—doubtless more controlled in their expression—have thus been taken as a check on Bandinelli's creativity. In reality, the preparatory drawing—exalted by Bandinelli as the cornerstone of sculpture—was a necessary step toward a solution capable of communicating the princely tone his wealthy patrons desired. Such a goal explains Bandinelli's exhaustive revision of each of his projects, an enterprise that slowly led to a language inspired by his admiration for the Roman Empire, which is visible in his statues in their ultimately proud and austere reference.

Bandinelli's intellectual style was rooted in Classical art, the 15th-century Tuscan tradition, and the innovations of Michelangelo and Leonardo da Vinci. As a boy, Bandinelli trained himself by making wax copies of sculptures by Donatello and Andrea del Verrocchio and studying the works of painters such as Filippino Lippi. Bandinelli was a friend of the painter Andrea del Sarto, who taught him to paint, and from 1518 to 1519 he worked with Andrea Sansovino at the Holy House in Loreto. This is the background against which one should judge Bandinelli's Classical references and his affinities with the painter Rosso Fiorentino and Cel-

lini. One sees these affinities in the engraved prints of Bandinelli's drawings—from the *Cleopatra* (ca. 1515) to the *Massacre of the Innocents* (ca. 1520) and the *Martyrdom of Saint Lawrence* (ca. 1525). These prints were studied throughout Europe for the expressiveness of the nudes and set Bandinelli firmly in the context of Florentine culture, whose strong native tradition proved capable of absorbing the modern taste of Raphael, Polidoro da Caravaggio, and Perino del Vaga, producing peculiar effects of severe refinement.

Bandinelli infused the same refined tone in his sculptures, regardless of their size or technique: in colossal sculpture, bas-reliefs, and small bronzes. Moreover, the unusual solutions Bandinelli tried out in his statues were grounded in the study of ancient art. For instance, in *Orpheus* he made an updated version of the *Apollo Belvedere*, adding a bronze lyre (now lost) that betokened a shameless neo-Hellenism. His grandiloquent tone gained the favor of many monarchs (including Henry VIII and the emperor Charles V, who bestowed upon Bandinelli the prestigious title of Knight of the Order of Santiago de Compostela), who perceived in his works a decorous elegance comparable with what they appreciated in Classical sculpture. Bandinelli's copy of the *Laocoön* so pleased Pope Clement VII that it was not sent to the king of France as planned but was kept as part of the Medici collections in Florence.

Bandinelli's good relations with the Medici family enabled him to survive competition from Michelangelo and to ignore the irritation his proverbial arrogance and eccentricity provoked on the part of the public. It brought him major commissions, such as the *Saint Peter*, in which the saint has been transformed into a sort of athlete straight out of Lysippus; the *Hercules and Cacus*; the unfinished *Neptune* (1529–37; Carrara) intended for the Genoese admiral Andrea Doria; and the imposing tombs of the Medici popes Leo X and Clement VII.

The artist's special relationship with the Medici family reached its peak with Cosimo I and his wife, Eleonora of Toledo. Bandinelli served as court sculptor from 1540 until his death in 1560, and for the young Grand Duke and Duchess he was an intelligent though troublesome arbitrator of artistic creation. In this role, precisely in view of modernizing the local tradition, he would lay the foundations of a national art with a princely and essential Medicean character. In those 20 years Bandinelli first worked on creating the monument to Giovanni dalle Bande Nere, of which he completed only the huge base, adorned with fine architectural decor and an antique-style relief. He then won two major architecture and sculpture commissions that, not by chance, altered the traditional aspect of the Palazzo Vecchio and the cathedral: the *Audience* in the Hall of the Five Hundred (ca. 1540–55; Salone dei Cinquecento) and the enormous chancel in the Florence Cathedral. The latter project in particular engaged Bandinelli's full attention because of its iconographic complexity, which anticipated Counter Reformation dictates, the huge volume within the octagonal paleo-Christian-style architecture of the 88 marble reliefs of *Prophets* (*in situ*), and the gigantic statues portraying *Adam and Eve*, *God the Father*, and the *Dead Christ*. The work required a whole battalion of craftsmen. They included Clemente Bandinelli (Baccio's illegitimate son), Battista Lorenzi, Francesco del Tadda Ferrucci, Giovanni Bandini, called Giovanni dell' Opera (who, starting in 1552, completed the *Prophets*), and Giuliano di Baccio d'Agnolo, who made the presentation model and designed a temporary wooden structure for the cathedral, identical in its lines to the architecture under construction. The *Prophets* are particularly successful works. The figures, all different, are confined in narrow spaces by the chancel architecture, and the resulting relief is highly pictorial, recalling solutions invented by Raphael and Andrea del Sarto as well as ideas that Bandinelli had tried out successfully in the prints previously mentioned.

Bandinelli also did pioneering work in official portraiture for Cosimo I. He produced several bronze and marble portraits of the Duke; the most successful version is the *Cosimo I* now in the Bargello. This bust is especially forceful because of its asymmetrical shape, which infuses vitality, and because of the Duke's gaze, seemingly detached but in reality vigilant and haughty.

Bandinelli's small bronzes are also significant. The best of them are *Jason, Hercules and the Apples of the Hesperides* and *Leda*; they are distinct from other contemporary works for their quasi-antique aspect and their typically Mannerist sense of motion.

The sculptor's last work was the Bandinelli tomb, adorned by a rendition of *Nicodemus Supporting the Dead Christ* in which the artist portrayed himself in the figure of Nicodemus. Admission to this prestigious location was a sign of Bandinelli's artistic triumph and of the noble rank he had acquired upon becoming a knight of the Order of Santiago.

Bandinelli had an enormous influence on many other sculptors (including Giovanni Bandini, Vincenzo de' Rossi, and Battista Lorenzi) who entered his "Academy"—the modern term he used for his workshop to indicate the intellectual side of art instruction—and to whom he passed on the cult of drawing, anatomy, and Classical art. This school was fundamental for the development of Tuscan art in the second half of the 16th century.

The figure of Bandinelli thus offers material for study from multiple standpoints, including that of the history of art criticism, where his work was crushed by comparisons first with Michelangelo and then with other artists such as Cellini.

FRANCESCO VOSSILLA

See also **Apollo Belvedere**; **Bandini, Giovanni**; **Cellini, Benvenuto**; **Donatello (Donato di Betto Bardi)**; *Laocoön and His Sons*; **Portrait: Introduction**; **Rossi, Vincenzo de'**; **Verrocchio, Andrea del**

Biography

Born in Florence, Italy, 12 November 1493. Original name Bartolomeo Brandini; learned the rudiments of art from his father, Michelangelo di Viviano, Lorenzo de' Medici's great goldsmith, curator of the Medici collections, and teacher to Cellini and Raffaello da Montelupo; apprenticed to Giovan Francesco Rustici before 1508, where noticed by Leonardo da Vinci; in Rome in early 1520s; frequented Raphael and his circle; became famous as a draftsman of drawings after Michelangelo's *Battle of Cascina*; learned painting with Andrea del Sarto; entered circle of Pope Leo X and his brother Clement VII; close relations with successive Medici rulers marked entire career; practiced architecture as well as sculpture; among the first to realize potential of engravings as a vehicle for popularizing modern style; claiming connection with the princely Bandinelli family of Siena, assumed their name in order to be named a knight of the Order of Santiago de Compostela by Emperor Charles V, who admired his sculpture. Died in Florence, Italy, 1560.

Selected Works

1515–17 *Saint Peter*; marble; Florence Cathedral, Italy

1519 *Orpheus*; marble; Palazzo Medici Riccardi, Florence, Italy

ca. 1525 *Laocoön*; marble; Galleria degli Uffizi, Florence, Italy

1525–34 *Hercules and Cacus*; marble; Piazza della Signoria, Florence, Italy

ca. 1530 *Hercules and the Apples of the Hesperides*; bronze; Museo Nazionale del Bargello, Florence, Italy

ca. 1530 *Jason*; bronze; Museo Nazionale del Bargello, Florence, Italy

ca. 1530 *Leda*; bronze; Museo Nazionale del Bargello, Florence, Italy

1536–41 Tombs of the Medici Popes Leo X and Clement VII; marble; Church of Santa Maria sopra Minerva, Rome, Italy

1540– Monument to Giovanni dalle Bande Nere;
ca. 1560 marble; Piazza San Lorenzo, Florence, Italy

ca. 1545   *Cosimo I*; marble; Museo Nazionale del
            Bargello, Florence, Italy
1545–60   Florence Cathedral chancel (continued and
            completed in 1572 by Giovanni Bandini
            under supervision of Bartolomeo
            Ammannati and Francesco Sangallo);
            marble; *Adam and Eve*, Museo Nazionale
            del Bargello, Florence, Italy; *God the
            Father*, Opera di Santa Croce, Florence,
            Italy; *Dead Christ*, crypt of Church of
            Santa Croce, Florence, Italy; *Prophets*,
            Florence Cathedral, Italy
1559–   Bandinelli Tomb (*Nicodemus Supporting
ca. 1560   the Dead Christ*); Church of Santissima
            Annunziata, Florence, Italy

Further Reading

Vossilla, Francesco, "L'altar maggiore di Santa Maria del Fiore di Baccio Bandinelli," in *Altari e committenza: Episodi a Firenze nell'età della controriforma*, edited by Cristina De Benedictis, Florence: Pontecorboli, 1996

Vossilla, Francesco, "Da scalpellino a cavaliere: L'altare-sepolcro di Baccio Bandinelli all'Annunziata," in *Altari e committenza: Episodi a Firenze nell'età della controriforma*, edited by Cristina De Benedictis, Florence: Pontecorboli, 1996

Vossilla, Francesco, "Baccio Bandinelli e Benvenuto Cellini tra il 1540 e il 1560," *Mitteilungen des Kunsthistorischen Institutes in Florenz* 41 (1997)

Vossilla, Francesco, "Baccio Bandinelli e Giovanni Bandini nel Coro del Duomo," in *Sotto il cielo della cupola: Il coro di Santa Maria del fiore dal Rinascimento al 2000*, edited by Timothy Verdon, Milan: Electa, 1997

Ward, Roger, *Baccio Bandinelli, 1493–1560: Drawings from British Collections*, Kansas City: Ashcraft, and Cambridge: Fitzwilliam Museum, 1988

Weil-Garris Brandt, Kathleen, "Bandinelli and Michelangelo: A Problem of Artistic Identity," in *Art the Ape of Nature: Studies in Honour of H.W. Janson*, edited by Moshe Barash and Lucy Freeman Sandlers, New York: Abrams, and Upper Saddle River, New Jersey: Prentice-Hall, 1981

Weil-Garris Brandt, Kathleen, "The Self-Created Bandinelli," in *World of Art: Themes of Unity in Diversity*, edited by Irving Lavin, vol. 2, University Park: Pennsylvania State University Press, 1989

HERCULES AND CACUS
Baccio Bandinelli (1493–1560)
1525–1534
marble
h. 4.96 m
Piazza della Signoria, Florence, Italy

In the Middle Ages, when Florence was fighting to extend its power in Tuscany, the city fathers chose an image of Hercules for the emblem on the official seal, together with the motto "Herculea Clava Domat Flore-ncia Prava" (With Hercules' club Florence overcomes all evil). Thus, Hercules embodied the power of Florence and was frequently depicted together with David, a figure often taken to symbolize the city's strength. The controversial installation of Michelangelo's gigantic *David* in the medieval Piazza della Signoria in 1504 disturbed the visual balance of the square. To partially remedy the problem, Michelangelo was commissioned to create a statue of Hercules for the other side of the palace entrance. Michelangelo never completed the colossal Hercules because Pope Julius II kept him working at the Vatican in Rome. In 1525, when the ruling Medici party was at odds with the advocates of an oligarchic republic, the Medici pope Clement VII took up the Hercules idea and commissioned Bandinelli to erect a statue of Hercules at the entrance of the Palazzo Vecchio. Inevitably, a colossal statue of the legendary hero would express the power Florence had gained through the Medici family, which had won the papacy for a second time. The commission thus had princely implications: for the supporters of oligarchy it suggested the identification of the Medici as sole rulers of Florence. In the larger context this was the critical time when the papacy was deciding to side with the French against the Holy Roman Empire, while Niccolò Machiavelli and Francesco Guicciardini were urging Clement VII to free Italy from foreign interference. Accordingly, favor for so monumental a work as the Hercules was compromised by the origin of the commission and by the political and military implications likely to be overlaid on the traditional iconography. Moreover, its assignment to the Medici favorite Bandinelli was a blow to Michelangelo and to the conservatives; they would have preferred the artist who had already interpreted the republican spirit in the *Battle of Cascina*.

Bandinelli was known for sculptures that exemplified modern Classicism, and he was gaining fame through prints engraved from his drawings. He himself suggested the subject of Hercules killing the marauder Cacus (as told by Virgil in the *Aeneid*) because it was rarely depicted in sculpture and could be rendered in a dramatic intertwining of bodies of the sort that had made Bandinelli's drawings famous. In fact, Giorgio Vasari described the wax model of the sculpture as a "pictorial" rendition; the hero was shown wrestling with his enemy in a claustrophobic jumble that would prove an enormous challenge to carve, for it required unaesthetic elements to support the centrifugal movements of the figures. Realizing that the dimensions of the block of marble (brought to Florence in 1525) would not allow him to copy the model, Bandinelli chose a more symbolic solution, in which the hero has already defeated evil. In the marble group Hercules has beaten Cacus and holds him up by the hair, displaying the now-harmless body before administering the final blow. Cacus is unconscious or perhaps already dead, as we understand from his lifeless, rolled-back eyes. The whole group is rich in emblematic elements: Hercules' proud gaze, Cacus's brutish face, the gilded club (now replaced), and the combatants' hypertrophic muscles, intended to evoke an epic struggle and Hercules' superhuman strength.

In 1527, when the imperial forces attacked Rome and the Medici were chased out of Florence, the republicans turned the commission over to Michelangelo, although Bandinelli had already prepared a real-size clay model of the group and started to block out the marble. However, Michelangelo was occupied with a new three-figure composition (*Samson against the Philistines*) that never got past the design phase. In 1530 the oligarchic party was defeated and Clement VII regained control over Florence; thus Alessandro de' Medici became Duke of the republic in order to deprive the republican institutions of power. The block of marble was turned back over to Bandinelli, and, working from his real-size model, he finished the

Hercules and Cacus
The Conway Library, Courtauld Institute of Art

group. In May 1534 it was installed next to the *David* in front of the entrance to the Palazzo Vecchio.

The fundamental difference between the *Hercules and Cacus* and the *David* lies in Bandinelli's desire to clarify the subject through explanatory details, addressing the public purpose of the commission so far as to counteract the ideal character created by Michelangelo. Bandinelli used different models: archaeological repertory, Donatello's *Judith Slaying Holofernes* (*ca.* 1459) and *St. George* (1416–17), Luca Signorelli's hypertrophies, Andrea Sansovino's Expressionism and, for Hercules' pose, Jacopo Sansovino's *St. James of Compostela* (1520). To give the sense of a victorious pause after the action, Bandinelli pulled the hero's left foot back and twisted his shoulders as Sansovino had done in his *St. James*; with his left shoulder forward, Hercules seems to be dominating the piazza. The composition is a triangular arrangement that leads the eye up to Hercules' head; the front view is the most important because that is where the triangular construction is most forceful. Nonetheless, the sculptor created an innovative visual continuity around the statue through its movement and details; he clearly took account of many other points of view, proceeding in upward spirals. The elegant base is adorned with allusions to other labors of Hercules: the Erymanthian boar, one of Hydra's nine heads, the Nemean lion, and one of Cerberus' three heads. The structure of the base was inspired by Leon Battista Alberti's formulas for commemorative architecture and, significantly, includes four half-figures of the god Terminus—an echo of Raphael's solutions in the lower frieze of the Vatican Stanza della Segnatura—as well as the sculptor's signature: "Baccius Bandinell. Flor. Faciebat MDXXXIIII."

Anti-Medici discontent found in Bandinelli's *Hercules and Cacus* a last opportunity for expression, and the work was attacked by many satirists. Apart from criticism of the sculptor as a representative of the government, the loathing that greeted the monument sprang from the defeated but deep-rooted culture of the oligarchic faction, which invoked a return to the virtues of republican government and took an ironic view of the pomp and splendor of Medici Rome. For many of his countrymen, Bandinelli's art was too princely and overly influenced by the new artistic fashions in Rome, compared with the Florentine quattrocento or even with Michelangelo's *David*.

The installation of a pair of colossi in the Piazza della Signoria was justified by the city's Classical heritage, yet *Hercules and Cacus* represented a cultural break with its post-Savonarola moralistic rigor. Bandinelli and the Medici were accused of disseminating an excessive avant-garde Classicism that was considered a sign of the new absolutism in government. This judgment, although biased, was fated to be lazily repeated by later critics.

FRANCESCO VOSSILLA

Further Reading

Bush, Virginia L., "Bandinelli's *Hercules and Cacus* and Florentine Traditions," in *Studies in Italian Art and Architecture, 15th through 18th Centuries,* edited by Henry A. Millon, Rome: American Academy in Rome, 1980

Donato, M.M., "Hercules and David in the Early Decoration of the Palazzo Vecchio: Manuscript Evidence," *Journal of the Warburg and Courtauld Institutes* 54 (1991)

Francini, Carlo, and Francesco Vossilla, *Baccio Bandinelli's Hercules and Cacus,* Florence: Alinea, 1999

Weil-Garris Brand, Kathleen, "On Pedestals: Michelangelo's *David,* Bandinelli's *Hercules and Cacus,* and the Sculpture of the Piazza Della Signoria," *Römisches Jahrbuch für Kunstgeschichte* 20 (1983)

Wright, Allison, "The Myth of Hercules," in *Lorenzo il Magnifico e il suo mondo,* edited by Gian Carlo Garfagnini, Florence: Olshki, 1994

GIOVANNI BANDINI (GIOVANNI DELL'OPERA) ca. 1540–1599 Italian

Described as "the best and most valuable sculptor in Tuscany after Giambologna" in a letter of recommendation to the Duke of Urbino in 1582, Giovanni Bandini attained numerous prestigious commissions from the early stages of his career until its conclusion, proving that this statement cannot be dismissed as simply an exaggerated eulogy. In fact, after the death of his master, Baccio Bandinelli, in 1560, it was Bandini who received the commission to finish the series of 88 reliefs for the choir screen of Florence Cathedral, a task completed in 1572. Immediately after, he was awarded the commission for two apostle statues—*Saint James the Lesser* and *Saint Philip,* both finished about 1577—for the same location; these were later praised by Leopoldo Cicognara as the best within the entire 16th-century series of statues of apostles in the choir of the Florentine Cathedral. For his long-standing activity in the workshop of the cathedral (Opera del Duomo), Bandini was called "dell'Opera." But parallel to his work for the cathedral, he accepted commissions from the Florentine nobility, and particularly from the ruling Medici family. Moreover, according to his contemporary, Rafaello Borghini, he created several statues to be sent outside Tuscany and even into France. So it is no wonder that when Giambologna proved not to be available, Bandini was called to be court sculptor to the Duke of Urbino at Pesaro (in the Marches region). It is also not surprising that when ducal commissions in the Marches became fewer around 1590—at a time when many sculptors left Florence seeking commissions elsewhere—Bandini returned to Florence and

was even assigned the monumental statue titled *Ferdinando I de' Medici* for Leghorn (Livorno) harbor.

Already during his first Florentine period, the sculptor made a name for himself as a sculptural portraitist, creating the canonical images of the Grand Dukes Cosimo I and Francesco I de' Medici in 1572 and 1577, respectively. Not incidentally, in 1582 the first work he was asked to create in Pesaro was a portrait bust, titled *Francesco Maria I della Rovere,* an image of the ruling duke's grandfather, the legendary military leader of the league against the Turks; in the following year, he also carved his patron's portrait bust, *Francesco Maria II della Rovere,* which was later transformed into a companion piece of the former work by Giovanni Battista Foggini. In a precocious parallel to the avant-garde tendency in contemporary Florentine painting, Bandini's naturalistic rendering of the face took the place of a mannered stylization. This naturalism was extended to the draperies *all'antica* (after the antique) employed by the sculptor in place of the complex allegorical armor, which was fashionable around the middle of the century. Bandini created many variations on the above-mentioned busts for the city palaces of Florence, restoring also ancient busts for the courtyards of these buildings.

Both in the genre of large marble sculptures as well as in small bronzes, Bandini was a pioneer in the creation of the Baroque group. His *Hunt of Meleager* shows the ancient hero mounted on a horse raised on its hindquarters at the sight of the vicious boar. This narrative and multifigural bronze group of a decidedly proto-Baroque character (or other similar ones) must have made a deep impression on Bandini's pupil Francesco Fanelli, who with particular fondness dedicated his artistic energies to creating equestrian small bronzes. In marble sculpture, Bandini laid the ground for the Baroque sculptural group with his life-size *Pietà* in Urbino, perhaps originally made for a lavish tomb for Francesco Maria I, then intended by the ruling duke to decorate his own sepulchre, but in the end used for the tomb of his son and heir, Federico Ubaldo della Rovere, whose early death sealed the extinction of the duchy of the della Rovere. For the general composition of the *Pietà,* and also for the postures of its two figures, Bandini's model of inspiration was a painting, Sebastiano del Piombo's *Pietà* carried out after a cartoon by Michelangelo (*ca.* 1513–16; Viterbo, Italy). Similarly, the sculptor based his large statue of Francesco Maria I della Rovere (1585–87)—which his grandson gave as a gift to the republic of Venice after the death of his heir—upon Titian's famous portrait of the ruler (1536–38; Galleria degli Uffizi, Florence), which at that time was in the della Rovere collection.

Bandini's style was not only inspired by his teacher Bandinelli; in the draperies of his figures, the results of studying quattrocento statuary and Andrea Sansovino's works can be noticed as well. Bandini was also a draftsman. Whereas the careers of some of his pupils remain obscure (as with Piermaria, his assistant in the Marches) and others directed their steps into different directions (as with Gherardo Silvani, later a famous architect), it was mainly Fanelli who continued Bandini's artistic legacy.

EIKE D. SCHMIDT

See also **Bandinelli, Baccio; Fanelli, Francesco; Giambologna; Pietà**

Biography

Born in Castello, near Florence, Italy, *ca.* 1540. Apprenticed to Baccio Bandinelli, *ca.* 1552; completed reliefs for choir screen of Florence Cathedral after Bandinelli's death, *ca.* 1552–60; directed Bandinelli's workshop, 1560–72; recognized as key portrait sculptor in Florence, 1560–82; became known as Giovanni dell'Opera; gained membership to Accademia del Disegno, Florence, 1563; then appointed court sculptor to Francesco Maria II della Rovere, Duke of Urbino, in Pesaro, 1582; traveled repeatedly to Florence in early 1590s; returned to Tuscany in 1595 to create statue of Ferdinand I de' Medici, Grand Duke of Tuscany, for the harbor of Leghorn. Died in Leghorn, Italy, 16 or 17 April 1599.

Selected Works

1552–72 *Prophets* and *Ancient Men* (with Baccio Bandinelli); marble; choir screen, Florence Cathedral, Italy

1568–74 *Architecture*, for tomb of Michelangelo; marble; Church of Santa Croce, Florence, Italy

1572 *Cosimo I de' Medici*; marble; Museo dell'Opera del Duomo, Florence, Italy

1572–73 *Juno*; bronze; Studiolo of Francesco I, Palazzo Vecchio, Florence, Italy

ca. 1572– *ca.* 1577 *Saint James the Lesser* and *Saint Philip*; marble; choir, Florence Cathedral, Italy

1576–77 *Presentation of the Virgin in the Temple* and *Marriage of the Virgin*; marble; Gaddi Chapel, Church of Santa Maria Novella, Florence, Italy

1577 *Francesco I*; marble; Portal of Petitions ("delle Suppliche"), Galleria degli Uffizi, Florence, Italy

1577–78 *Hercules and the Hydra*; marble; Camugliano, Niccolini collection

1582 *Francesco Maria I della Rovere*; marble; Villa del Poggio Imperiale, Florence, Italy

1583 *Francesco Maria II della Rovere*; marble; Villa del Poggio Imperiale, Florence, Italy

1583 *Hunt of Meleager*; bronze; Museo del Prado, Madrid, Spain

1585–87 *Francesco Maria I della Rovere*; marble; Doge's Palace, Venice, Italy

1585–88 *Pietà*; marble; Oratorio della Grotta, Urbino Cathedral, Italy

1587 *Francesco Maria I della Rovere* and *Coat of Arms*; marble; Church of Santa Chiara, Urbino, Italy

1595–99 *Ferdinand I de' Medici*; marble; Piazza Micheli, Leghorn, Italy

Further Reading

Avery, Charles, "Giovanni Bandini (1540–1599) Reconsidered," *Antologia di belle arti* 48–51 (1994)

Forlani Tempesti, Anna, "Disegni di 'Apostoli' di Giovanni Bandini," *Prospettiva* 57–60 (1989–90)

Heikamp, Detlef, "Hercules Slaying the Hydra of Lerna: A Forgotten Statue by Giovanni Bandini," in *Essays Presented to Myron P. Gilmore*, edited by Sergio Bertelli and Gloria Ramakus, vol. 2, Florence: La Nuova Italia, 1978

Middeldorf, Ulrich, "Giovanni Bandini detto dell'Opera," *Rivista d'arte* 11 (1929)

Pope-Hennessy, John, *An Introduction to Italian Sculpture*, 3 vols., London: Phaidon, 1963; 4th edition, 1996; see especially vol. 3, *Italian High Renaissance and Baroque Sculpture*

Schmidt, Eike D., "Giovanni Bandini tra Marche e Toscana," *Nuovi Studi* 3/6 (1998)

Schmidt, Eike D., "Scultura sacra nella Toscana del Cinquecento," in *Storia delle arti in Toscana: Il Cinquecento*, edited by Roberto Paolo Ciardi and Antonio Natali, Florence: Edifir, 2000

Weil-Garris Brandt, Kathleen, "Were This Clay but Marble . . . : A Reassessment of Emilian Terracotta Group Sculpture," in *Le arti a Bologna e in Emilia dal XVI al XVII secolo*, edited by Andrea Emiliani, Bologna: CLUEB, 1982

THOMAS BANKS 1735–1805 *British*

Many contemporaries considered Thomas Banks to be the finest Neoclassical sculptor working in England at the end of the 18th century. His marble panel *Death of Germanicus*, for Holkham Hall, Norfolk, is recognized as the first truly Neoclassical work created by a British sculptor. In this high-relief panel, Banks rejected the strict antique tradition by elongating the proportions of the clearly defined figures. In addition, he used a diagonal perspective, which creates a sense of drama around the central figure of the dying hero. These innovative stylistic elements also occur in his marble *Thetis and Her Nymphs Rising from the Sea to Console Achilles for the Loss of Patroclus*, begun in 1778 but left uncompleted at the time of Banks's death.

These marked departures from the antique style received mixed reviews. Many critics saw them as a direct influence of the Swiss-born British painter Henry Fuseli (*b.* Johann Heinrich Füssli), who was a friend of Banks's. John Bacon the Younger suggested that Banks's sculptural relief panels were much finer before his trip to Rome and the influence of Fuseli. Little is known, however, of the works Banks created in Rome; all of them have been lost. One statue that continues to arouse interest is *Cupid Catching a Butterfly on His Wing.* Exhibited at the Royal Academy summer exhibition in 1781, the figure was part of the sculptor's inventory when he left England that same year hoping to find employment at the court of Catherine the Great in Russia. Catherine the Great purchased the statue and placed it at Tsarskoe Selo. Like the work Banks completed in Rome, the statue is now lost.

The sculptor remained in Russia for only one year. On his return to England, the architect George Dance assisted Banks in finding employment with the court of directors of the East India Company. The directors hired him to complete the monument to Sir Eyre Coote for Westminster Abbey. Banks worked on the figure from 1783 to 1789.

Thetis Dipping the Infant Achilles in the River Styx, completed in 1788 for Colonel Johnes, relies on the facial features of Mrs. Johnes for Thetis and on the colonel's daughter for the infant Achilles. The statue is highly original in its treatment of the subject. Banks employed a linear rhythm for both the body and the drapery that is reminiscent of the few works remaining, such as the *Death of Germanicus,* from his studies in Rome under the influence of Fuseli. The figure, however, appears clumsy in its proportions, like many of Banks's later works of sculpture.

In 1792 Banks was the only sculptor to enter the competition held by the Royal Academy for a statue of Governor General Charles Cornwallis, Marquess Cornwallis, for Madras, South India. The statue arrived in Madras in 1800, where it was unveiled on 15 May. The figure shows Cornwallis dressed in his peer's robes standing on a pedestal relief depicting one of the triumphal moments of his term, the surrender of the sons of Tipu Sultan. Inspiration for the subject's depiction came from the paintings being exhibited by Robert Home at the Royal Academy. The relief panel is one of Banks's best attempts at depicting a contemporary event and was no doubt also influenced by painter Benjamin West's *Death of General Wolfe* (early 1770s).

One of Banks's most successful works of sculpture is the monument to Penelope Boothby. In this work, the child lies sleeping on the thick mattress, hands tucked up under her chin. The figure is full of pathos and sentiment. Despite some criticism, the public reacted enthusiastically to the work when it was exhibited at the Royal Academy exhibition. It was said that Queen Charlotte and her children wept, as did Sir

Thetis and Her Nymphs Rising from the Sea to Console Achilles for the Loss of Patroclus
The Conway Library, Courtauld Institute of Art

Brooke Boothby, who had commissioned the memorial from Banks.

Banks completed two heroic groups for St. Paul's Cathedral in London soon before his death, the monuments to Captain Richard Burgess and to Captain George Blagdon Westcott. The two figures, which are the least successful of all the artist's work, display Banks's idea of High Classicism.

MARY ANN STEGGLES

See also **England and Wales: Baroque–Neoclassical**

Biography

Born in London, England, 22 December 1735. Son of gardener and surveyor for Duke of Beaufort at Badminton. Apprenticed to William Barlow, ornamental carver, 1750–57; studied at St. Martin's Lane Academy, 1758; studied at Royal Academy, 1770–72; won gold medal there in sculpture, 1770; awarded Royal Academy traveling scholarship to Rome, 1772; studied in Rome, 1772–79; traveled to Russia, 1781–82; made associate of the Royal Academy, 1784, and royal academician, 1786. Died in London, England, 2 February 1805.

Selected Works

1774   *Death of Germanicus*; marble; Holkham Hall, Norfolk, England

1778   *Thetis and Her Nymphs Rising from the Sea to Console Achilles for the Loss of Patroclus*; marble; Victoria and Albert Museum, London, England

1786   *Falling Titan*; marble; New Place,
        Stratford-upon-Avon, England
1788   *Thetis Dipping the Infant Achilles in the
        River Styx*; marble; Victoria and Albert
        Museum, London, England
1789   Monument to Sir Eyre Coote; marble;
        Westminster Abbey, London, England;
        version: 1784, Commonwealth Relations
        Office, London, England
1793   Monument to Penelope Boothby; marble;
        Ashbourne, Derbyshire, England
1795   *Margaret Petrie*, memorial relief panel;
        marble; parish church, Lewisham, England
1798   *Marquess Cornwallis*, full-length portrait
        statue; marble; Fort Museum, Chennai,
        India
1799   Bust of Warren Hastings; marble;
        Commonwealth Relations Office, London,
        England
1802   Monument to Captain Richard Burgess;
        marble; St. Paul's Cathedral, London,
        England
1805   Monument to Captain Westcott; marble;
        St. Paul's Cathedral, London, England

Further Reading

Bell, Charles Francis, *Annals of Thomas Banks*, Cambridge:
    University Press, 1938
Bryant, Julius, "Mourning Achilles: A Missing Sculpture by
    Thomas Banks," *The Burlington Magazine* 125 (1983)
Bryant, Julius, "The Church Monuments of Thomas Banks,"
    Church Monuments 1 (1985)
Flaxman, John, "Address on the Death of Thomas Banks," in
    Lectures on Sculpture, 2nd edition, by Flaxman, London:
    Bohn, 1838
Whinney, Margaret, *Sculpture in Britain, 1530–1830*, London
    and Baltimore, Maryland: Penguin, 1964; 2nd edition, re-
    vised by John Physick, London and New York: Penguin,
    1988

BAPTISMAL FONT

The sacrament of baptism is a Christian rite administered to a person who is admitted to the faith. The two
methods of baptism are pouring water over the head
of the initiate (affusion) or immersing the body in a
pool of water (immersion). For both methods, a baptismal font is used. A general understanding of the history
of baptism helps illuminate the history and development of the baptismal font itself.

Christ was baptized by St. John the Baptist in the
River Jordan. As one of the two most important sacra-
ments of the Roman Catholic Church (the second being
the Eucharist), depictions of the baptism of Christ are
very common. These usually show St. John pouring
water over the head of Christ, while above Christ's
head a dove, symbolizing the Holy Spirit, is present.

Both the water and the dove suggest the symbolic nature of baptism: before entering the Christian life, a
person is baptized to be cleansed of sin and reborn in
the Holy Spirit. Paraphrasing John 3:5, unless a person
be washed of the water and the spirit, he or she will not
enter the kingdom of God. Without baptism, therefore,
eternal salvation in heaven is not possible.

During the first few centuries of Christianity, baptism likely continued as it is recounted in the Bible:
in rivers and streams. By the first few decades of the
2nd century, special houses or rooms were constructed
to administer the rite of baptism. These are known as
baptisteries. Inside, pools or tubs of water could be
found. Architecturally integrated, they may be sunken
into the floor and entered by one or more steps, or they
may be above ground. The person who was to undergo
baptism would step into the font to be doused with
water or immersed altogether. Total immersion was
probably not possible since most fonts were only a few
feet deep, although some were up to 20 feet in diameter. The shapes of the fixed font varied considerably:
cylindrical, polygonal, cruciform, rectangular, oval,
and other shapes. Ornamentation, too, would have decorated the font and the interior of the baptistery. Mosaics and colorful marbles were not uncommon, and the
interior of a baptistery, with its pool of (sometimes
running) water, must have been a spectacular sight.

Changes in baptismal practices led to changes in
the types of fonts used to perform the sacrament. By
the 6th century, baptisms could take place outside the
baptistery. By the 9th century, the practice of adult
baptism declined as more and more infants were baptized. The emperor Charlemagne declared that all infants should be baptized when they turned one year
old. By the beginning of the 11th century, infants were
baptized much sooner—sometimes a few days after
birth. These series of changes resulted in the manner
in which baptism was administered: now allowed in a
church instead of a baptistery, and with infant baptism
a common practice, smaller, "moveable" (i.e., not architecturally integrated) baptismal fonts inside the
church itself replaced the larger pools of the baptistery.

Precisely when unfixed baptismal fonts were first
created remains unclear, but by the 11th century the
new type was common throughout Europe. The form,
ornamentation, and iconography of baptismal fonts
varied throughout the Middle Ages. Primarily made of
stone and metal, some wood fonts were used as well,
although an accurate history of wooden fonts is frustrated by the fact that wood does not survive as well
as metal or stone. In terms of their vertical composition, early Romanesque examples are comprised of a
simple basin placed directly on the floor. Sometimes

the basin was placed on a plinth or base, in which case the font was made of two separate parts. Toward the end of the Romanesque and beginning with the Gothic period, a varying number of legs were added. In this case, the basin would rest on the legs that themselves stood on the plinth. The five-legged font was the most common, and it resulted in a type in which the basin rested on top of a large column or pedestal centered directly underneath and the remaining four legs or columns surrounded the outside.

In general, the font was made of three essential parts: the plinth or base, the columns or legs, and the basin. The manner in which these were decorated was limitless: the plinth or base itself may take the form of a simple slab in the form of a square, rectangle, octagon, and so on, while the hard edges were carved with decorative molding—similar to the base of a column. The legs or columns themselves also varied considerably. Simple rounded columns were not uncommon, but these may also be decorated with carved patterns, capitals, foliate forms, etc. Five-legged fonts

Relief sculpture with figures on a baptismal font from a church in Loderup, Skåne, Sweden
© Macduff Everton / CORBIS

had the potential for more elaborate decoration. The large central pedestal would provide enough structural support for the basin, and the surrounding four legs could take on a stronger decorative function. In some cases the legs were replaced with figures and even animals.

For the design of the basin itself there were many variations. Extremely large stone basins were not possible since they might break under their own weight. Most basins were designed to accommodate an infant. Infants may have been baptized by full immersion, but affusion—the pouring of water onto the head—became common by the 14th century. Respectively, basin diameters were usually about 60 centimeters, and they had a depth of a little more than 30 centimeters. As with the base, the shape of the basin varied: circular, polygonal, and quatrefoil were all common shapes, and they were often decorated with pure ornament, pure figurative work, or a combination of both.

Baptismal fonts were primarily made of stone and, later, metal. The material used was often dictated by availability. For example, in the region between the Rhine and Meuse Rivers, an apparent absence of suitable stone resulted in a larger number of bronze baptismal fonts. Near the city of Tournai on the Burgundian border, bluish-black marble was in abundance. In fact, some researchers suggest that a large export market of baptismal fonts was established in France due to the wealth of this material. In England, Purbeck marble (a dark purple in color) was used as extensively for baptismal fonts as it was for architecture. Near the city of Münster in Germany, the Baumberg quarry provided large amounts of stone for Westphalia, the Lower Rhine, and the northeast Netherlands. Baumberg limestone was a very fine-grained, warm-colored material used for baptismal fonts, figurative sculpture, and architecture. In Baumberg, as in Tournai, a healthy export operation existed, evidenced by the hundreds of baptismal fonts recorded in the inventories of monuments for Westphalia, the Lower Rhine, and Lower Saxony.

The iconography of medieval baptismal fonts is highly varied. The incarnation, baptism, passion, and resurrection of Christ were all depicted in different combinations. Old Testament prophets, the apostles, saints, and angels were also included, perhaps in combination with one or more Christological scenes. Other themes included the tree of life and the four rivers of Paradise and, surprisingly, images related to demonology (demons, snakes, dragons, and other monsters). Demonic imagery can be explained by the fact that the rite of baptism included prayers of exorcism. These were not to expel demons; rather, they were to ask for protection from evil. Demons and monsters as depicted on a baptismal font, therefore, fulfill an apotropaic function—to ward off evil—much as the prayers when administering the rite itself.

One of the most famous baptismal fonts from the Romanesque period was made by the sculptor/metalworker Rainer of Huy. Originally made for the Church of Nôtre-Dame-des-Fonts in Liège, Belgium, the baptismal font was completed in 1118 and has been in the Church of St. Barthélemy, Liège, since 1804. The font is a simple basin type about 60 centimeters in diameter and slightly less than 90 centimeters deep. The basin itself rests on 12 bronze oxen (two are lost), and a cover, missing since the French Revolution, reportedly contained images of the apostles and Old Testament figures. Divided by very elegant and stylized trees, five figurative scenes related to the rite of baptism decorate the sides. Primary among these is the baptism of Christ in which a half-nude Christ is shown in an abstract depiction of the River Jordan while the Holy Spirit, in the form of a dove, floats above. Cast in one piece, Rainer of Huy's baptismal font is an important example of a growing three-dimensional quality and naturalism in sculpture from the Romanesque period. Although technically relief sculpture, Rainer's figures appear as true figures in the round that are glued to the sides of the basin. This three-dimensional quality is further enhanced by proportional figures that are no longer frontal and hierarchical, but rather twist and turn to reveal all aspects of the body. Drapery, also, is pulled tight to the body to reveal, on the one hand, a rhythmic combination of drapery folds and, on the other, the anatomy of the body underneath. Such elements are hallmarks of Greek and Roman Classical sculpture, and the Rhine-Meuse region of Europe, where Rainer of Huy and Nicholas of Verdun were active, has long been recognized by art historians as an artistic center that favored Classical motifs and styles.

Almost a century later, a baptismal font for Hildesheim Cathedral was cast. Also made of bronze, the Hildesheim baptismal font has strong parallels to the Liège font by Rainer of Huy: a round tublike basin rests atop figural work (in this case four kneeling men representing the Four Rivers of Paradise), and a decorative cover is attached by hinges. Again, the baptism of Christ forms the central iconographic scene on the side of the basin. Stylistically, the Hildesheim font appears to have much in common with Rainer of Huy's font in Liège, even though both examples are separated by more than 100 years. In Germany, the Romanesque style still persisted until around 1230, and the style of the Hildesheim font illustrates Germany's adherence to Romanesque features well after the year 1200.

Contemporary with the Hildesheim baptismal font is a stone example from Limburg Cathedral (Limburg an der Lahn). With a diameter of about a meter, this octagonal font is an ornate example of a nine-legged font. The basin itself rests atop a large central column that is surrounded by eight additional columns, which correspond to the eight corners of the octagonal form of the rim. Different animals/beasts clutch the bases of the eight peripheral columns, while eight figures are depicted on the side of the basin. Elaborately carved vegetative ornament fills the remaining spaces. In size as well as ornamentation, the Limburg baptismal font is one of the most imposing examples from the 13th century.

Octagonal in design, yet of an entirely different form than the preceding examples, the baptismal font from Mainz Cathedral represents the chalice design. Dated to 1328, this baptismal font was originally located in the Liebfrauenkirche in Mainz until it was brought into the cathedral in 1804. Cast of tin by Master Johannes, the eight-sided font depicts the Twelve Apostles, the Virgin, and St. Martin. While both the top and the base are not original, a four-part design remains clear: base, column, basin, top. The diameter of the basin, a bit over a meter, is about almost triple that of the base. Were the Mainz font made of stone, a series of supporting columns would have been required, as they are in the Limburg font. The Mainz example is freed of this extra support requirement, and this allowed the artisan to decorate the large side surfaces of the basin side with delicate tracery designs and figurative works. Having a smaller base and a narrow shaft, the basin widens at the top and closely resembles the shape of a chalice or goblet. This chalice design was one of the most common forms for medieval baptismal fonts, both in metal and stone.

The production of baptismal fonts in areas with abundant materials (marble, limestone, metal, etc.) has been discussed earlier. Westphalia appears to have produced an unusually large number of baptismal fonts due to the resources of the Baumberg quarry. The Church of St. Lüdiger, located in the city of Münster, possessed a baptismal font from about 1500 to about 1525 that is made of Baumberg limestone. A stone version of the chalice design, the eight-sided font in Münster, is richly sculpted with figurative and ornamental decoration indicative of the Late Gothic period. In particular, the series of arcades that surround the figures are made of elegant ogee curves that betray 15th-century origins. Because the chalice design was so common, it is often difficult to distinguish the differences between fonts of different periods. It is only through examination of particular motifs and figure style that chronological differences can be detected.

The examples discussed in the preceding paragraphs illustrate varying degrees of decorative and iconographic complexity. Even more elaborate examples appear in Italy. In the Baptistery of Siena Cathedral, the baptismal font by Lorenzo Ghiberti inaugurated an entirely new type of Renaissance font. Early Italian fonts, such as in Modena or Pisa, were usually made of one large monolithic basin, only occasionally situated on a plinth or base, and placed in a baptistery. In comparison, Ghiberti's design is an exercise in architectural and sculptural complexity. Two flights of steps lead to a six-sided basin. In the center of the basin, a large tabernacle stands atop a series of columns. The tabernacle itself has six sides, five of which are made of marble and depict different apostles, while the sixth side contains a door that opens to the space inside. Here is where the objects and ointments used in the rite of baptism are stored. Atop the tabernacle stands a figure of St. John the Baptist, while at the base of the basin a series of six figures representing the virtues alternates with six bronze panels of relief sculpture depicting the life of St. John the Baptist.

The elaborate design of the baptismal font by Ghiberti is an exception to the thousands of baptismal fonts that are situated in the numerous medieval and later churches throughout Europe. Whether grand examples inside a baptistery, or the modest type inside a small parish church, the importance of the baptismal font is fundamental to the practice of one of the most important rites in the Christian Church.

KEVIN MCMANAMY

See also **Germany: Gothic–Renaissance; Nicholas of Verdun; Rainer of Huy**

Further Reading

Bedard, Walter, *The Symbolism of the Baptismal Font in Early Christian Thought*, Washington, D.C.: Catholic University of America Press, 1951

Davies, J.G., *The Architectural Setting of Baptism*, London: Barrie and Rockliff, 1962

Green, Edmund Tyrrell, *Baptismal Fonts, Classified and Illustrated*, New York: Macmillan, 1928

Noehles, Karl, *Die westfälischen Taufsteine des 12. und 13. Jahrhunderts* (Westphalian Baptismal Fonts of the 12th and 13th Centuries), Münster, Germany: Aschendorff, 1952

Nordström, Folke, *Mediaeval Baptismal Fonts: An Iconographic Study*, Umeå, Sweden: Umeå University, 1984

BARBIERE, DOMENICO DEL

See **Domenico del Barbiere**

ERNST BARLACH 1870–1938 *German*

During the early part of his career, Ernst Barlach was keenly interested in both sculpture and ceramics. He taught ceramics for a brief period, and from 1901 to 1904 he designed small ceramic sculptures for mass production by the Richard Mutz Company. He also explored other artistic media: his woodcuts contributed significantly to the revival of the medium in the 20th century; his writings, some of which he illustrated with his graphic art, include poetry, prose, and drama; and his plays were performed during his lifetime and have been the subject of numerous scholarly studies.

Barlach's early sculpture was heavily influenced by Art Nouveau, which in Germany was known as *Jugendstil*. In these early works the human form, although sometimes decoratively elongated, is naturalistically rendered. An important sculpture from this period, *The Cabbage Picker*, recalls Jean François Millet's peasants bent over their work in his painting *The Gleaners* (1857). Although the proportions of Barlach's figure of a young woman picking cabbages are anatomically correct, the influence of *Jugendstil* is evident in the decorative curvilinear flourish of the cabbages at her feet and in her arm.

The important turning point in Barlach's career as a sculptor was his visit to Russia from 2 August to 27 September 1906, during which he made numerous drawings and also kept a diary, *Russiches Tagebuch*. He was captivated by the sight of the bold figures of the Russian peasants set against the vast space of the steppes and was moved by the suffering that he witnessed among them. As he observed these people moving about in their simple dress, Barlach began to appreciate the expressive potential of the clothed human form. While making drawings of the people who caught his attention, Barlach discovered how to transform and organize what he had observed in nature in order to express his response to the human condition.

After his return from Russia, Barlach created a series of sculptures in various media that were based on the drawings he had made during his journey. These figures, such as *Russian Beggar-Woman II*, show a radical change in Barlach's approach to the human form. In the creation of these monolithic sculptures, he eliminated all naturalistic detail that was not central to the ideas and feelings he wished to express. These poetic figures with their bodies concealed by clothing and only their faces, hands, and feet exposed to view were expressions of both Barlach's compassionate view of the human condition and metaphors of the universal human experience.

Walking Woman (Walking Nun) is one of a group of figures based on his Russian sketches that he designed for production in porcelain. This figure appears to move through space with a lightness of stride that belies the compact bulkiness of her form. The harmony of the folds of her simple garments, the soft white of the porcelain fabric, and the rich glow of the glaze combined with her delicacy of movement give this figure an uplifting and decorative appearance suitable to its intended function as a piece of decorative art. The

The Avenger
Gift of Mrs. George Kamperman in memory of her husband
Dr. George Kamperman
© 1989 The Detroit Institute of Arts

woman's heavy, unsmiling features and her large hands, however, allude to the hardships and grimness of life in the Russian countryside.

The year 1907 marked another important turning point in Barlach's career. He became a member of the Berlin Secession, a group that promoted artistic reform, and he met the publisher and art dealer Paul Cassirer, with whom he contracted to turn over all of his works for a fixed annual salary. This arrangement gave Barlach complete artistic freedom and enabled him to work unfettered by financial concerns. Also in 1907 Barlach began to carve figures in wood, which some scholars cite as his favorite medium. No other modern master has equaled Barlach's artistic output in wood, which forms the core of his sculptural production. Paul Gauguin is credited with the revival of wood sculpture in the 19th century, but Barlach, who was inspired by late medieval German sculpture, carried this revival into the 20th century. In Germany, the last significant sculptor to work in wood before Barlach was the Rococo artist (Franz) Ignaz Günther.

In creating his wood sculptures, Barlach chipped away at his medium in a uniform manner and allowed the tool marks to remain evident in the finished piece. These marks were essential to his artistic expression, and they give texture and animation to his wood figures.

Around 1930 Barlach had become one of Germany's most famous artists, and his work was admired by both critics and the general public. These circumstances led to a significant number of commissions for German war memorials following World War I. One such monument is *Hovering Angel*, which Barlach cre-

ated for Güstrow Cathedral. The face of the vertically suspended, wingless angel was inspired by the face of Barlach's friend, the artist Käthe Kollwitz, who herself had lost her only son to the war. A bronze *Self-Portrait* (Berlin) made by Kollwitz in 1926 expresses both personal strength and sorrow, and a comparison of this work with the face of *Hovering Angel*, which expresses both sorrow and consolation, demonstrates the degree to which Barlach abstracted from nature in order to create a work of art that would have universal significance. In 1937 *Hovering Angel* was removed from the cathedral and melted down for munitions, and the war memorials at Kiel and Hamburg were removed from view. In 1942 a bronze cast of *Hovering Angel* was made in secret from the plaster model, which had been carefully hidden. This cast now hangs in the Antonite Church in Cologne, where it was installed in 1956. In 1953 a duplicate cast was made for the original site in Güstrow Cathedral, where it still hangs.

Barlach's sculptures are either compact and bulky or slender and attenuated. The slender form, which appears to have been favored by Barlach in his late career, was given to the figures in his *Frieze of Listeners*, the major work of his maturity. Barlach also used this form for sculptures that he designed for niches on the facade of St. Catherine's Church at Lübeck in 1930. The artist was able to complete only three figures before the National Socialists put an end to the project. Barlach, who did not believe he would survive the National Socialist regime, chose the artist Gerhard Marcks to complete the project. After the end of World War II, Marcks executed six additional figures according to Barlach's designs, and these, along with the original three, were installed on the church facade.

Barlach's work was condemned by the National Socialists because it did not conform to their ideal of the strong, positive, Teutonic type. In 1936 Barlach's works, along with those by Kollwitz and Wilhelm Lehmbruck, were removed from an anniversary exhibition at the Prussian Academy of Art. The following year Barlach was forbidden to exhibit and threatened with a work ban, and 381 of his sculptures and works on paper were confiscated from public collections in Germany. During the same year, an exhibition of the artist's work in a private gallery in Berlin was closed, and Barlach was advised to resign "voluntarily" from the Prussian Academy of Art. Also in 1937, which was referred to by the artist as *Das schlimme Jahr* (the terrible year), works by Barlach were included in the National Socialist–sponsored *Entartete Kunst* (Degenerate Art) exhibition in Munich in 1937.

After World War II, Barlach's international reputation as one of the most important German artists of the 20th century was once again acknowledged in his native land, and his works in German public collections were returned to view. In 1950 Barlach's sculptures and drawings were amply represented at the Venice Biennale. In 1961 Ernst Barlach Haus, a spacious, modern museum that houses Hermann Reemtsma's large collection of works by Barlach, was constructed in the outskirts of Hamburg. The majority of Barlach's works remains in German collections.

GINA ALEXANDER GRANGER

See also **Gauguin, Paul; Germany: 20th Century–Contemporary; Günther, Franz Ignaz; Kollwitz, Käthe; Lehmbruck, Wilhelm; Marcks, Gerhard; Memorial: War**

Biography

Born in Wedel, near Hamburg, Germany, 2 January 1870. Studied at Hamburg School of Arts and Crafts, 1888–91, and the Dresden Art Academy, 1891–95; won academy's silver medal for *The Cabbage Picker*, 1894; worked with sculptor Carl Garbers, 1887–99, on commissions for public monuments in Hamburg and Altona; exhibited bronze plaques at International Exhibition of Applied Arts in Turin, 1902; taught at Höhr School of Ceramics in Westerwald, 1904–05; awarded the Villa Romana prize, and spent ten months on fellowship at Villa Romana, Florence, 1909; settled permanently in Güstrow, 1910; became member of the Prussian Academy of Art, Berlin, 1919; appointed honorary member of Munich Academy of Fine Arts, 1925; "Barlach Room" a feature of the International Exhibition in Dresden, 1926; Magdeburg War Memorial erected, 1929, but became immediate target of a defamation campaign by right-wing groups; major retrospective exhibition by the Prussian Academy of Arts, 1930; represented at Biennale Exhibition, Venice, 1930; five bronzes included in Modern German Painting and Sculpture exhibition at the Museum of Modern Art, New York City, 1931; commissioned to complete *Frieze of Listeners*, already in progress, 1934. Received Prussian Order of Merit for science and art, 1933; appointed honorary member of the Vienna Secession's Fine Arts Association and its Artists Association of Austrian Sculptors, 1936. Died in Rostock, Germany, 24 October 1938.

Selected Works

1894   *The Cabbage Picker*; tinted plaster; private collection

1907   *Russian Beggar-Woman II*; bronze; Ernst Barlach Haus, Hamburg, Germany; Seattle

Art Museum, Washington, United States (two casts)

1909   *Walking Woman (Walking Nun)*; porcelain; several locations, including Ernst Barlach Haus, Hamburg, Germany; The Detroit Institute of Arts, Michigan, United States

1912   *The Vision*; wood; Neue Nationalgalerie, Staatliche Museen, Berlin, Germany

1914   *The Avenger*; bronze; several locations, including Busch-Reisinger Museum, Cambridge, Massachusetts, United States; Albright-Knox Gallery, Buffalo, New York, United States; The Detroit Institute of Arts, Michigan, United States; private collections

1927   Head of the Güstrow Memorial; bronze; Museum of Modern Art, New York City, United States

1927   *Hovering Angel*, for war memorial at Güstrow Cathedral, Germany; bronze (destroyed); bronze casts from original plaster: Antonite Church, Cologne, Germany; Güstrow Cathedral, Germany

1928   *Warrior of the Spirit*; bronze; Church of St. Nicholas, Kiel, Germany

1929   *The Magdeburg Memorial*; wood; Magdeburg Cathedral, Germany

1930   *Woman in the Wind, Crippled Beggar*, and *The Singer*; vitrified clay; facade of St. Catherine's Church, Lübeck, Germany

1931   *Hamburg War Memorial*; shell limestone; Rathausmarkt, Hamburg, Germany

1931–35   *Frieze of Listeners*; wood; Ernst Barlach Haus, Hamburg, Germany

Further Reading

Barlach, Ernst, *Ein selbsterzähltes Leben*, Berlin: Cassirer Verlag, 1928

Barlach, Ernst, *Die Briefe, 1888–1938*, edited by Friedrich Dross, 2 vols., Munich: Piper, 1968–69

Carls, Carl Dietrich, *Ernst Barlach: Das plastiche, graphische und dichterishe Werk*, Berlin: Rembrandt Verlag, 1931; 7th edition, 1958; as *Ernst Barlach*, New York: Praeger, and London: Pall Mall, 1969.

Groves, Naomi Jackson, *Ernst Barlach: Leben im Werk: Plastiken, Zeichnungen und Graphiken, Dramen, Prosawerke und Briefe*, Königstein im Taunus, Germany: Langewiesche, 1972; as *Ernst Barlach: Life in Work: Sculpture, Drawings, and Graphics, Dramas, Prose Works and Letters in Translation*

Jansen, Elmar, editor, *Ernst Barlach: Werke und Werkentwürfe aus fünf Jahrzehnten* (exhib. cat.), 3 vols., Berlin: Akademie der Kunste der DDR, 1981

Lauden, Ilona, and Volker Probst, editors, *Ernst Barlach: Das Güstrower Ehrenmal* (exhib. cat.), Leipzig: Seemann, 1998

Schult, Friedrich, *Ernst Barlach Werkverzeichnis*, 3 vols., Hamburg, Germany: Hauswedell, 1958 (catalogue raisonné)
Werner, Alfred, *Ernst Barlach*, New York: McGraw Hill, 1966

BAROQUE AND ROCOCO

The Baroque style gained sway in Italy in the first half of the 17th century and spread throughout Europe and Latin America, with local variations, until the mid 18th century. The term was first applied to artworks suggesting the bizarre, asymmetrical, or irregular, beginning about 1730. The etymology has been much debated, but the word "Baroque" probably comes from the Portuguese adjective *barrueca*, which describes an irregularly formed pearl.

As has happened with other art styles, by the time the characteristics of Baroque were described, during the Neoclassical era in the second half of the 18th century, its aesthetic ideals were already outdated. Accordingly, the term was used in a pejorative sense to designate a capricious art, a bad taste that did not respect the Classical rules and was thus antithetical to the ideals of Neoclassicism. Today, Baroque has been reappraised on the basis of thorough scholarly studies and is seen in its proper historical and artistic context.

Baroque art was born in Rome in the early 17th century when the Roman Catholic Church was past its Counter-Reformation phase. The papal state, reaffirming its authority as a political and religious power, had decided that art was to be a principal means of persuading and involving believers. The result was a new, prestigious recognition of the artist's role and a notion of art as a rhetorical instrument. In fact, Baroque art, like 17th-century poetry, was a rhetorical art par excellence. It used metaphors, allegories, and technical and stylistic devices to captivate and convince the viewer. It no longer sought to edify and instruct the faithful, but to involve them by appealing to the senses, rather than the intellect. This does not mean that Baroque artists were not educated and erudite. To the contrary, underlying the great fascination of their works were careful, scientific studies of which the viewer was not supposed to be aware. Gianlorenzo Bernini's Baldacchino (1623–34) and colonnade (1656–67) at St. Peter's Basilica in Rome were the outcome of long, in-depth technical, architectonic, and scenographic studies intended to make them seem perfectly natural and harmonious in their settings despite their enormous dimensions. In fact, optical illusion, which requires scientific study by the artist and gives the observer immediate enjoyment, was one of Baroque's favored means of expression.

Furthering this aspiration to involve the faithful emotionally and in parallel with the fledgling discipline of Christian archaeology—which sought to recover the history, artistic documents, relics, and monuments of early Christianity—Baroque iconography gave preference to the glories of saints and martyrs and their divine ecstasies and mystical visions. It was also a response to Protestant criticism, in that it reaffirmed the legitimacy of the Roman Catholic Church's use of images and her continuity with the early Christian Church. In her aspiration to represent the divine and the supernatural, the Church opened the way to the imagination and eventually arrived at a sumptuous and magniloquent self-celebration that accurately reflected the image of *Ecclesia Triumphans* (Church Triumphant) that the papacy wished to hand down.

Baroque art was thus born in Rome in the context just described, but spread fast and wide across Europe and Latin America, often following the routes taken by the Jesuit order. In France and many other countries, the style was related to the monarchy, rather than the papacy, but some of its basic guidelines remained unaltered. In addition, in this case Baroque reaffirmed art's rhetorical power and its power of persuasion even when it served different ideals.

The new role of art as a rhetorical instrument stimulated sculptors to reach a very high level of technical skill and master a variety of materials and working methods. Many Baroque sculptors knew how to work marble, bronze, stucco, and papier mâché, and they worked simultaneously on widely differing commissions: restoring ancient works and designing and executing procession floats, monuments, bronzes, and table decorations.

Baroque sculpture had an undisputed protagonist: Gianlorenzo Bernini. In his *Apollo and Daphne* (1622–24) and *David* (1623) in the Galleria Borghese in Rome, and in the Throne of St. Peter (1656–66) in St. Peter's Basilica, Bernini established Baroque's most successful and typical themes. Because the figures' movements were perceived as natural and they seemed to have been captured in a fleeting moment, his sculptures established a new relationship with the viewer.

Bernini drew on a variety of models ranging from contemporary and Renaissance painting to Roman and Hellenistic sculpture, and he had the extraordinary technical skill needed to put in practice his new way of conceiving sculpture in pictorial terms. Together with his familiarity with different techniques and materials, he was able to create works in which painting, sculpture in the round, bas-relief, and decoration were joined in a *mirabile composto*, a wondrous compound.

A few sculptors working in Rome in the early 17th century offered cues to the new Baroque generation. Among them were Nicolas Cordier, from Lorraine, and the Venetian Camillo Mariani. Cordier's virtuosity and his fine capacity for penetration in portraits were

Gianlorenzo Bernini, *Apollo and Daphne*
© Bettmann / CORBIS

suggestive for Baroque artists like Giuliano Finelli and Domenico Fancelli. Mariani contributed to the success of a Venetian taste that began to interest sculptors and painters working in Rome around 1620. In sculpture, this meant opening to pictorial rhythms and seeking to create light effects on the forms—suggestions that were taken up by the Tuscans Pietro Bernini and Francesco Mochi.

Pietro Bernini's culture, his acceptance of Mariani's luminist novelties, and his study of Hellenistic and Roman models were starting points for his son Gianlorenzo. Mochi was a different, more complex figure. His first masterpiece was the Orvieto *Annunciation* (1603–09), a group of two freestanding statues linked together by a studied light effect. Mariani's influence is evident in the transparent flesh and in the search for soft light effects, whereas his Mannerist culture is expressed in stylistic and technical refinements already understood in a new way, although perhaps not yet truly Baroque.

The *St. Veronica* (1629–40) Mochi carved for one of the four piers in St. Peter's Basilica is closer to the new style. The will to challenge the solidity of marble and draw from it light, thin drapery suspended in the air reveals Mariani's influence, but the windswept drapery is an altogether new motif: *St. Veronica* is the only one among the four statues of the crossing who seems about to invade the viewer's space. Precisely because of her unrestrained movement and windswept drapery, Bernini seems not to have liked the *St. Veronica*, which goes to show how artistic enterprises based on similar research but different aesthetic ideals and senses of decorum could coexist in what we generically call Baroque.

Within the vast Baroque movement, it is possible to identify different trends, such as the Baroque Classicism that saw particular success in France but had its two most celebrated practitioners, François du Quesnoy and Alessandro Algardi, in Rome. Both worked with or alongside Bernini but did not let themselves be much influenced by him. Like Andrea Sacchi and Nicolas Poussin, they were interested in a different—more lyrical, meditated, and calm—way of telling stories. Among other contributions, Algardi was the first to investigate the potential of relief (such as *Pope Leo Driving Attila from Rome* [1646–53] in St. Peter's Basilica), a genre that may not have satisfied Bernini because of "his desire for spatial interpenetration between sculpture and reality" (see Wittkower, 1958). After Algardi set an example, relief enjoyed great success and was often preferred to painting. In general, during the Baroque age sculpture was held in very high consideration, often higher than paintings and even higher than in Michelangelo's day.

One of Bernini's most talented pupils was Finelli, who soon moved to Naples and, together with Cosimo Fanzago, inaugurated the Baroque season in that city. After the first generation, the principal sculptors working in Rome during the 1650s were Ercole Ferrata, his pupil Melchiorre Caffà, Antonio Raggi, and Domenico Guidi. Raggi quickly assimilated Bernini's teachings, especially his late, more fervent and spiritual style, whereas Ferrata preferred the lyrical Classicism of Algardi.

Caffà and Guidi showed, in different ways, the first signs of the slow decline of the most genuine Baroque ideals. In the works of Guidi, the academic manner undermined the rhetorical force of the first Baroque artists. Caffà opened the way to a sweeter, more sentimental sculpture, one capable of new subtleties destined to find full expression in the 18th century. These and other Baroque sculptors and painters went to work outside Rome, but only toward the end of the 17th century could Bologna, Genoa, Florence, and Venice vaunt their own schools of Baroque sculpture.

Rome's artistic supremacy waned toward the end of the century when the papal state began losing authority in the new balance of European political power, and France affirmed its cultural power. The French Academy was established in Rome in 1666, and French sculptors flocked to it. Many participated in major Roman enterprises. Pierre Legros and Pierre-Étienne Monnot collaborated with Camillo Rusconi on the *Apostles* for the Basilica of San Giovanni in Laterano, Rome, and with Jean-Baptiste Théodon, Legros, and others on the altar of St. Ignatius at the Church of the Gesù, Rome. Their style, like that of the Italians working in the early 18th century, is generally called Late Baroque: the sense of dramatic unity was supplanted by a more verbose and redundant language where the dynamism of Bernini and his most faithful followers was cooled by a graceful Classicism. French gracefulness filtered into the work of Filippo della Valle, one of the last representatives of Italian Baroque, which was already evolving into the new Rococo ideas. Della Valle, who had trained with Giovanni Battista Foggini in Florence and Rusconi in Rome, developed an elegant, sophisticated language that was partial to the sentimental and extremely graceful. If one wishes to speak of what was no more than a bland Rococo trend within Roman sculpture, Della Valle, Pietro Bracci, and a few others would have to be mentioned. The last important collective enterprise was the Trevi Fountain (mid 18th century), where late Baroque and a timid Rococo merge in the huge rocaille shell and in Bracci's graceful *Neptune* (1722).

To see more complete expressions of Rococo, one must leave Italy for other countries. France had a florid Baroque season that was perhaps best defined by the work of François Girardon, Antoine Coysevox, and Pierre Puget. Their work depended closely on the royal court's choices. Girardon, who produced a sophisticated, Classicist Baroque, was preferred over Coysevox for nearly the entire 17th century. Protected by important people at court, he received the most prestigious commissions in Paris and at Versailles. Coysevox, who worked in a more dynamic and daring sculptural style, managed to gain sway only toward the end of the century. His decorations, like the plaster relief of *The Triumph of Louis XIV* (1681–83) in the Château de Versailles, and his busts, which owed much to the "speaking" portraiture conceived by Bernini, are among the most daring specimens of French Baroque. At the same time that Coysevox's inventiveness was beginning to be appreciated, Puget managed to get himself called to court. Puget, more than any of the other French sculptors, had assimilated the Italian style. He had trained in Rome and Florence with the painter Pietro da Cortona, with whom he collaborated at Palazzo Pitti (1643), and in 1666 he opened a shop in Genoa. There he met Filippo Parodi, a talented pupil of Bernini's, and left what was perhaps his most fascinating work, a *Saint Sebastian* (1664–68, which was inspired by Bernini's *Daniel* of 1655–60) in the Church of Santa Maria di Carignano. Even his late works, such as *Milo of Croton* (ca. 1671–82) and *Alexander and Diogenes* (1670–89), show frequent borrowings from Bernini and Algardi transfigured in an incisive style rich in dynamism and pathos.

Knowledge of the great Roman and French Baroque artists also underlies the art of the first Baroque German sculptors, such as Matthias Rauchmiller, but outstanding artists such as the Germans Balthasar Permoser and Andreas Schlüter and the Austrian Johann Bernhard Fischer von Erlach did not appear until the 1680s and 1690s. Permoser had been in Rome, Florence, and Venice, and his sculptures for the altar in the old Dresden court show how he had assimilated Bernini's teachings.

Fischer von Erlach studied for 15 years in Rome, where he came in contact with important figures such as Bernini, Carlo Fontana, and the critic Bellori. He served as court architect in Vienna and wrote a history of architecture. The *Plague* (or *Trinity*) *Column* (1682–94; Vienna) reveals his profound culture and his bent for a sumptuous and sophisticated Baroque style close to Rococo. Schlüter, the court sculptor in Berlin, had likewise studied in Italy. His art combined his studies of the Italian sculptors (Mochi, Bernini, and Algardi) and the French (Coysevox) with a great capacity for synthesis, as can be seen in the equestrian monument to Frederick Wilhelm (1697–98; Berlin), where the realism and the sentimental tone proper to the German tradition are skillfully harmonized with the foreign models.

In England the new style was heralded by Nicholas Stone, who rose to become the leading mason-sculptor about 1625. Initially intrigued by the style of the Fontainebleau school, then studying the ancient works present after 1630 in Charles I's collection, Stone gradually succeeded in renewing the models of local tradition and opened the way to new artistic endeavors. His son John followed in his footsteps, and one of the assistants in John's shop was the Danish sculptor Caius Gabriel Cibber, who moved to England before 1660. In his youth Cibber had traveled in Italy, and his knowledge of Italian Mannerist and Baroque sculpture shows up in his most important English works, such as the allegorical bas-relief on the 1673–75 Monument to the Great Fire of London (also known as *Charles II Coming to the Assistance of the City*) and the free-standing tomb of Thomas Sackville (1677). In the latter, the life-size figures of the parents mourning the deceased direct the viewer's eye toward the center of the monument with a device that was typically Baroque but exactly the opposite of the Bernini school's tendency to make sculptures explode into space. The Dutch part of Cibber's background and his appreciation of Mannerist sculpture prevented him from adhering to the triumphant rhetoric of Bernini-style Baroque, but his English contemporary John Bushnell flaunted it by adopting the most striking but superficial aspects of Bernini's teaching. The Mocenigo monument (*ca.* 1660–63) testifies to Bushnell's sojourn in Italy, but almost certainly he also traveled to Rome, because his style—as exemplified in the monument to John, Viscount Mordaunt of Avalon (1675), and the monument to William Ashburnham and his wife (1675)—reveals a good knowledge of Roman Baroque art. However one may judge Bushnell's artistic results, his importance in the history of English sculpture was fundamental, for "he was the first English artist to show any knowledge of Baroque sculpture" (see Whinney 1988).

The Spanish Baroque expressed a more popular and genuine religious devotion. In Spain, the new style was independent enough of Italian art to create some of its own characteristics: *pasos*, which are statues devoted to stories from the Passion and designed to be carried in procession; the *retablo*, which is a large, architectural panel divided into compartments; and the *transparente*, which is a tabernacle containing the host.

The new style appeared in the first half of the 17th century in painted wooden sculptures carved by Gregorio Fernández in Castille, Juan Martínez Montañes in Seville, and Alonso Cano in Granada. Starting from the Italian Mannerist tradition known in Spain from the works of Pompeo Leoni and Pietro Torrigiani, Fernández and Montañes opted in the second decade for a more passionate and complex modeling of volumes and a more marked chromatism that augmented the expressive force of their works. Fernández developed a high-level style that was extremely incisive and expressive, rich in pathos and overflowing with emotion, as in his *Pietà* (1616; Museo Nacional de Escultura, Valladolid). Montañes's style was more sober and elegant, and his emotion less flaunted, although he managed equally high dramatic effects, as in the Santiponce retable (1609; Monastery of Sant'Isidoro del Campo, Seville). Although Montañes had been in contact with Velázquez and Pacheco, Alonso Cano had been the latter's pupil and was a painter and architect as well as a sculptor. His retable in the Lebrija Church (1629–31; Seville) displayed an original style characterized by delicate idealization, as far from Fernández's realism as from Montañes's dramatic effects. His wooden figures are painted in refined and precious colors and often appear composed and lost in thought. These features are accentuated in his last, very sweet creations, the *Virgin of the Immaculate Conception* (1655–56; Granada Cathedral) and the *St. Diego de Alcalá* (*ca.* 1653–57; Palace of Charles V, Granada). Cano's elegant example was to be developed in the second half of the century by his pupils Pedro de Mena and José de Mora.

Starting in the mid 17th century with the arrival of the Bourbons, the artistic and cultural multicentrism characteristic of early Spanish Baroque was put to a difficult test. The foundation of the Academia de Bellas Artes de San Fernando in Madrid encouraged the formation of a new generation of artists but had repercussions on workshops in the provinces. Two schools thus developed: one continued the tradition of polychrome wooden sculpture, and the other engendered an official art that preferred marble.

At around this time the celebrated Churriguera family of sculptors and architects came to the fore. Working in Salamanca and Madrid, they created a style of their own in which decorative elements covered all the surfaces. The wooden altar of St. Eustace (1693–96; Jesuit Church, Salamanca) is one of the masterpieces that reveal a knowledge of Bernini motifs, which the Churriguera family interpreted in the exuberant platteresque style of decoration. So great was their fame that it gave rise to a new word, *churriguerismo*, designating the decoratively rich work typical of the Spanish Baroque.

Narciso Tom was the artist who reached the peak of Spanish ornamental exuberance in the *Transparente* of the Cathedral of Toledo (1732). The work was designed to enable the congregation to see inside the tabernacle of the host by surreal lighting obtained by cutting a hole in the ceiling of the deambulatory so that the sun's rays could penetrate from above. The host was framed by a cohort of angels flanked by decorated columns and surmounted by a sculptural group of the *Last Supper* and the *Ascension of the Virgin*. The perfect harmony and blending of architecture, sculpture, and painting in an ensemble of curved and wavy lines, polychromy, and the use of different materials heightened the scenographic effect of this extraordinary work, which owes much to Bernini's devices but also reveals new ideas that came to be prized in the Rococo style.

In Spain in the late 17th and early 18th century, the influence of the Italian tradition was joined by the new Francophile taste imported by the Bourbons. Many French sculptors, including Rene Frémin (a pupil of Girardon), Jean Thierry (a pupil of Coysevox), and Jacques Bousseau, were brought in to work on the royal residence of Sant'Ildefonso, known as the Granja. The relationship between garden and palace, sculpture and architecture, was patterned closely on the Versailles model; the interior is sumptuously decorated and the garden is dotted with mythological statues and fountains, giving rise to a complex in which Baroque and Rococo were already cohabiting.

In the meantime, Versailles, which had subscribed to Girardon's elegant Classicism and then to Coysevox's lively Baroque, gave birth to the new Rococo style. Just as Baroque was the style of the Roman Catholic Church in the 17th century, Rococo was the style of the French court in the 18th century. Restorations and new projects at Versailles came at the dawn of this new climate, which found its first expression in Pierre Lepautre's interior decorations.

Like Baroque, the term Rococo was coined in a pejorative sense during the Neoclassical era. It derives from the French *rocaille*, a type of garden and grotto decoration featuring a shell motif. Rococo was considered a late degeneration of Baroque, but it was a style in its own right with its own identifiable characteristics. Many Late Baroque motifs flowed into Rococo, but they were reinterpreted in a different way. Often the two styles coexisted in a single architectural complex, as in the Spanish example of Granja, or contaminated each other, especially in places where the Baroque was assimilated more slowly.

The new Rococo sensibility materialized first in French architecture (palaces and private residences) but found its most felicitous expression in internal decoration and gave new importance to the "minor" arts (porcelain, silver, furniture, and mirrors). It retained the Baroque rhetorical aspect of enjoyment and illusion, accentuating the importance of ornament, gracefulness, and elegance. Sculpture acquired a special role. Except for examples such as Guillaume I Coustou's *Horses Restrained by Grooms* (1739–45; Musée du Louvre, Paris) and Robert Le Lorrain's great relief for the Hôtel de Rohan (1740), large dimensions were either banned or reserved for parks and fountains.

Rococo preferred different materials for different uses: lead for fountain sculptures (because with water its delicate shine creates precious light effects); porcelain, Chinese lacquer, and precious materials for small sculptures (because they are glossy, fragile, and rich in light); and stucco for interior decoration (because its softness and ductility could well express the gracefulness dear to Rococo). Porcelain was used for small objects that formed a separate genre of knickknacks with no meaning other than the sentimental.

The best examples of Rococo were created during the 1730s in France: the Adam Brothers' decoration of the Hôtel Soubise in Paris, the decoration of the anteroom in the Hôtel de Matignon, and the red drawing room in the Hôtel de Roquelaure. All evince the new absolute importance given to the decorative element, which acquired a life of its own no longer subordinated to the architecture.

Nicolas-Sébastien Adam (Adam Family), *Prometheus*, 1762 Collection Musée du Louvre © Scala / Art Resource, NY

The new French taste quickly spread to foreign lands. The first and most original response came from the southern German-speaking countries. The external and internal parts of the castle of Nymphenburg (Munich) show this earliest assimilation starting in the 1730s. Later but equally significant is the palace of Würzburg decorated by Antonio Bossi. Bossi transposed his clear debt to Bernini into a light and graceful style and played with the ductility of stucco to express the amiable gaiety, surprise, and delicate irony that characterize Rococo.

Among the monumental sculptures, one must note Joseph Anton Feuchtmayer and Johan Georg Ublhör's *Gnadenaltar* at the center of the church in Vierzehnheiligen, Bavaria. This is a sort of votive altar on which 11 statues of saints are arranged around a canopy. Made entirely of stucco and following curved lines and inclined planes, the monument flaunts its precarious equilibrium as if it had won a challenge to copy a refined product of the goldsmith's art on the monumental scale.

In garden sculpture, the transition to Rococo can be seen in the works of Ferdinand Tietz for the park at Veitshöchheim. Here monumental Baroque statues appear disguised as playful stage actors who cross the garden dancing and winking at the visitor. From Bavaria the new Rococo style spread to Austria and throughout Germany, thanks in part to traveling artists and books of etchings that circulated the ornamental motifs.

Conversely, Italy participated in the new movement with works of good quality, although episodic or individual. One practitioner was the virtuoso stucco craftsman Giacomo Serpotta, who worked in Sicily in the early 18th century and was famous for his inventive genius and the rich ornamental exuberance of his decorations (1609–1707; Oratory of St. Lawrence). On the whole, however, the Late Baroque style was still vital enough in Italy to slow the progress of the new style.

In England, too, the Rococo gained ground slowly. John Michael Rysbrack, for one, occasionally used figurative solutions close to the Rococo aesthetic ideals, as in his statues of Peter Paul Rubens (1743) and *Hercules* (1744; Stourhead, Wiltshire), but most of his works were characterized by a solemn and magniloquent Classical language.

It was a French artist, Louis François Roubiliac, who opened England's Rococo season. Starting with his earliest works—the statue of George Frideric Handel (1738; Victoria and Albert Museum, London), the busts of William Hogarth (1740; National Portrait Gallery, London) and Alexander Pope (1741; private collection)—Roubiliac fine-tuned the fundamental features of a new conception, intimate and penetrating, of portraiture. He captures his subjects in a fleeting moment—lost in their thoughts, their poses informal and perfectly natural—and that is how he offers them to the public eye. The same unaffected narrative vein reappears in Roubiliac's principal funerary monuments, to the Second Duke of Argyll (1745–49; Westminster Abbey; London), the Duchess of Montagu (1754?; Warkton, Northamptonshire), and Mr. and Mrs. Nightingale (1758–61; Westminster Abbey, London). These works show that Roubiliac had an extensive knowledge of Bernini and the Roman Baroque (he had visited Rome in 1752), but also that his real interest lay in a more graceful and elegant language that could mitigate the force and the rhetorical emphasis of the Italian models. Roubiliac's garland-bearing putti and female figures, in their sweet, languid poses, are his personal, charming responses to the new Rococo style. Among the pupils who further developed Roubiliac's Rococo line, Nicholas Read deserves special mention. His monument to Nicholas Magens shows that the Rococo style was still vibrant in 1779.

While Rococo continued to spread through other European countries, where it would prevail for some years, France was the first to decree its end. In the 1770s and 1780s, the new Neoclassical taste was already making many of the most exquisite Rococo creations seem outdated.

MADDALENA SPAGNOLO

See also **Algardi, Alessandro; Bernini, Gianlorenzo; Bracci, Pietro; Caffà, Melchiorre; Cano, Alonso; Cibber, Caius Gabriel; Coustou Family; Coysevox, Antoine; Fancelli, Domenico; Fanzago, Cosimo; Fernández, Gregorio; Feuchtmayer, Joseph Anton; Finelli, Giuliano; Girardon, François; Guidi, Domenico; Legros II, Pierre; Leoni Family; Mena, Pedro de; Mochi, Francesco; Monnot, Pierre-Étienne; Montañés, Juan Martínez; Parodi, Filippo; Puget, Pierre; Rusconi, Camillo; Schlüter, Andreas; Serpotta, Giacomo; Stone, Nicholas; Torrigiani, Pietro; Valle, Filippo della**

Further Reading

Bauer, Hermann, and Hans Sedlmayr, *Rokoko: Struktur und Wesen einer europäischen Epoche*, Cologne, Germany: DuMont, 1992

Blunt, Anthony, editor, *Baroque and Rococo Architecture and Decoration*, London: Elek, and New York: Harper and Row, 1978

Bottineau, Yves, *L'art baroque*, Paris: Mazenod, 1986

Boucher, Bruce, *Italian Baroque Sculpture*, New York: Thames and Hudson, 1998

Briganti, Giuliano, and Antonia Nava Cellini, "Barocco," in *Enciclopedia universale dell'arte*, Rome: Istituto per la Collaborazione Culturale, 1958

Lavin, Irving, *Bernini and the Unity of the Visual Arts*, 2 vols., New York: Oxford University Press, 1980

Martin, John Rupert, *Baroque*, New York: Harper and Row, 1977

Montagu, Jennifer, *Roman Baroque Sculpture: The Industry of Art*, New Haven, Connecticut: Yale University Press, 1989

Scott, Katie, *The Rococo Interior: Decoration and Social Spaces in Early Eighteenth-Century Paris*, New Haven, Connecticut: Yale University Press, 1995

Souchal, François, *French Sculptors of the 17th and 18th Centuries: The Reign of Louis XIV*, vols. 1–3, Oxford: Cassirer, 1977–87, and vol. 4, London: Faber and Faber, 1993

Whinney, Margaret, *Sculpture in Britain, 1530–1830*, London and Baltimore, Maryland: Penguin, 1964; 2nd edition, revised by John Physick, London and New York: Penguin, 1988

Wittkower, Rudolf, *Art and Architecture in Italy, 1600–1750*, London and Baltimore, Maryland: Penguin, 1958; 6th edition, 3 vols., revised by Joseph Connors and Jennifer Montagu, New Haven, Connecticut: Yale University Press, 1999

Wittkower, Rudolf, and Irma B. Jaffe, editors, *Baroque Art: The Jesuit Contribution*, New York: Fordham University Press, 1972

FRÉDÉRIC-AUGUSTE BARTHOLDI
1834–1904 *French*

The extraordinary fame of the Statue of Liberty (*Liberty Enlightening the World*) has eclipsed the memory of its maker, a sculptor whose civic allegories, statues of heroes, and funerary monuments express profound moral and political convictions. Born into a cultivated and prosperous land-owning family in Alsace, Frédéric-Auguste Bartholdi was encouraged to study art and could freely choose his own subjects. His connections to influential circles in Colmar and Paris helped him attain public commissions, and his determination, diplomacy, and Protestant work ethic enabled his successful completion of many complex long-term projects.

Bartholdi's first success at age 21, with *General Jean Rapp*, already hints at his taste for grand-scale art: the approximately 3.5-meter-high statue of a Napoleonic hero looms up on a 3-meter base. A trip to Egypt in 1856 with Jean-Léon Gérôme and two other painters confirmed Bartholdi's passion for monuments. Awed by the "imperturbable majesty" of the great Nile ruins, he came back with the ambition to create colossal sculpture on dramatic sites. Although he continued to execute conventionally scaled commissions (for example, *Admiral Bruat* and *Funerary Genius*), he returned to Egypt in 1869 to propose an idea worthy of the pharaohs: a gigantic sculpture of a fellah to serve as a lighthouse at the entrance of the new Suez Canal. From this failed project, Bartholdi recycled the concept of a huge torch-bearing female figure for *Liberty* a year later. Indeed, by 1870 Bartholdi was designing not one but three gargantuan public sculptures: *Liberty*, which a group of French republicans had conceived as a gift for the United States; *Vercingétorix*, a 17.5-meter-high monument (much reduced when it was finally installed in 1901) for the city of Clermont-Ferrand; and the *Lion of Belfort*, an over–21-meter-long snarling beast of red sandstone. As with *Liberty*, his Belfort patrons had originally requested a modest memorial; Bartholdi thought big and swept his backers along with him.

After 1871 Bartholdi's art voiced the anguish of France's defeat in the Franco-Prussian War, in which he served as an officer, and his grief over the loss of Alsace to Germany. Patriotic feeling inspired, for example, the snarling *Lion of Belfort*, trapped but terrible in its fury, a symbol of the city's 1871 siege; *Vercingétorix*, which casts the ancient Gallic leader as the hero of the first national defense of France; *Switzerland Aiding Strasbourg*, which commemorates deeds of 1870–71; *Alsace and Lorraine*, part of his monument to Gambetta (1888–91); the tomb of the Garde Nationale; the monument to Sergeant Ignace Hoff, a hero of the siege of Paris; *Three Sieges of Belfort*, which celebrates three valorous historical events; and the *Aeronauts of the Seige of Paris, 1870–71*, which memorializes the vital wartime contribution of balloonists, carrier-pigeon trainers, and other transportation and communication workers.

A republican and Americanophile, Bartholdi also explored themes of Franco-American friendship, notably in *Liberty* but also in an 1871 commission from the French government for *Lafayette Arriving in America*, for New York. Nominally a simple gesture of gratitude for New York's aid after the siege of Paris, the gift, which alludes to Lafayette's critical assistance to the American Revolution, was also intended to strengthen France's ideological, strategic, and commercial relationship with its fellow republic across the Atlantic.

Bartholdi produced his share of conventional 19th-century statues of great men (*Maréchal Vauban*, 1870; *Rouget de l'Îsle*, 1882; *Diderot*, 1884; and *Gambetta*, 1891) that populate the town squares (Avallon, Lons le-Saunier, Langres, and Ville d'Avray, respectively) of provincial France. But he was passionate about their value and their heroism: "To put my name at the feet of great men and to the service of great ideas, this is my ambition," he asserted in 1886.

Some of Bartholdi's monuments, such as *Admiral Bruat*, a fountain with allegorical figures of four continents, incorporate stock symbols in predictable ways. He created his most original work, however, when he jettisoned this cumbersome baggage. In *Funerary Genius*, which recalls the tomb sculptures of Antonio Canova, a single figure expresses mourning through her despondent posture and slowly cadenced drapery alone. (Bartholdi's figures are virtually always clothed; he had little training in the École des Beaux-Arts' pedagogy of studies from the nude.) In the tomb of the Garde Nationale, a tense bronze arm reaches out from a displaced stone slab in a desperate effort to seize a sword, lying just out of reach. It honors the sacrifice of three young soldiers who fell to German guns while defending Colmar in 1870. This surprising, economic image powerfully communicates resistance.

Stylistically, Bartholdi's range reflects that of his century, for he varied his style to suit the needs of each project: *Liberty*'s Grecian draperies and calm, self-contained contours embody Neoclassicism; the *Lion of Belfort* is frankly Egyptian in its hewn stone and hieratic, blocky simplification; *Vercingétorix*, galloping over a fallen Roman soldier, sword stabbing the sky, is all impassioned action, employing a neo-Baroque idiom; and the lost *Aeronauts* monument, which realistically simulated a rising balloon and featured a soldier dangling in midair from one side, explored naturalism.

Bartholdi had wanted the *Aeronauts*'s balloon of glass to be illuminated at night, reflecting his interest in incorporating new technologies of electricity and engineering in his sculptures. Indeed, although largely conventional in his process, generally working in clay for subsequent casting in bronze, Bartholdi sometimes experimented in his choice of final materials: repoussé copper for *Liberty*, carved stone blocks for the *Lion*, and lead for *The Sâone and Its Tributaries*.

Another distinguishing feature of Bartholdi's work is the degree to which he brought his architectural training to bear on sculpture. For each of his monuments, he related sculptural masses and proportions to the configuration of the specific site and thoughtfully designed bases, socles, and columns. His dialogue with Richard Morris Hunt, via letters and drawings, about *Liberty*'s pedestal demonstrate that he contributed creatively and intelligently to its design. In both *Liberty* and the *Lion of Belfort*, whose unforgettable placement against a massive cliff expresses the protective function of the city's fortress atop it, he demonstrated a brilliant scenographic sensibility. His monument to Gambetta, if completed in its intended site, would have been as much architecture as sculpture, playing off the facade of the National Assembly in Paris.

In one important respect, Bartholdi stands apart from contemporaries such as Alexandre Falguière and Auguste Rodin, whose small-scale multiples continue even now to circulate through the auction-dealer system. He concentrated on monuments and did not exhibit in galleries or create small-scale editions for collectors; consequently, few museums own pieces by Bartholdi, except for the Musée Bartholdi, which preserves the contents of his Parisian studio in the family's ancestral home in Colmar.

LYNNE D. AMBROSINI

See also **Canova, Antonio; Falguière, Jean-Alexandre-Joseph; Memorial: Other than War; Public Sculpture; Rodin, Auguste**

Biography

Born in Colmar, Alsace, France, 2 August 1834. Lived in Colmar and in Paris, from 1836; studied art with Antoine Etex and Ary Scheffer, late 1840s; studied architecture with Eugène Viollet-le-Duc and Henri Labrouste, sculpture with Jean-François Soitoux, early 1850s; made debut at Paris Salon of 1853 with *The Good Samaritan*; built house and studio on rue Vavin, Paris, 1854; traveled to Egypt, 1856 and 1869; served as officer in Franco-Prussian War, 1870–71; created approximately 50 monuments, fountains, and tombs, and about 20 portrait busts; inducted into the Freemasons, in the lodge of Alsace Lorraine, Paris, 1875; sojourned in the United States to build support for *Liberty* project, 1871, and again in 1876; visited New York for the inauguration of *Liberty*, 1886; exhibited sculptures at the Chicago World's Fair, 1893; exhibited at 40 Paris Salons, 1853–1904 (honorable mentions at Salons of 1859, 1861, and 1863). Named Knight of the Legion of Honor, 1864, Officer, 1882, and Commander, 1886; received French medal of honor, 1895, for *Switzerland Aiding Strasbourg*; member of the board of the Société des Artistes Français (vice president, 1900–03). Died in Paris, France, 3 October 1904.

Selected Works

1855   *General Jean Rapp*; bronze; Place Rapp, Colmar, France

1864   *Admiral Bruat*; bronze, sandstone; Champs-de-Mars, Colmar, France

1866   *Funerary Genius* (or *Allegorical Statue of Sorrow*), for tomb of Georges Nefftzer; bronze; Montmartre Cemetery, Paris, France

1870   *Vercingétorix*; plaster; Musée Bargoin, Clermont-Ferrand, France

1870–86 Statue of Liberty (*Liberty Enlightening the World*); copper, iron; Liberty Island, New York Harbor, New York, United States

1872   Tomb of the Garde Nationale; stone, bronze; Municipal Cemetery, Colmar, France

1872–80 *Lion of Belfort*; sandstone; Belfort, France

1873   *Lafayette Arriving in America*; bronze; Union Square, New York, United States

1875   *Champollion*; marble; Collège de France, Paris, France

1878   *General de Gribeauval*; bronze; Hôtel des Invalides, Paris, France

1895   *Switzerland Aiding Strasbourg*; marble, bronze; Centralbahnplatz, Basel, Switzerland

1898   *The Sâone and Its Tributaries*; lead; Place des Terreaux, Lyon, France

1904   Monument to Sergeant Ignace Hoff; bronze; Père-Lachaise Cemetery, Paris, France

1906   *Aeronauts of the Seige of Paris, 1870–71*, in Place de la Porte des Ternes, Paris; bronze (destroyed)

1912   *Three Sieges of Belfort* (finished posthumously by Hubert Louis-Noël and Jules Dechin, following Bartholdi's 1903 model); bronze; Place de la République, Belfort, France

Further Reading

Annuaire de la Société d'histoire et d'archéologie de Colmar 28 (1979) (issue devoted to Bartholdi)

Betz, Jacques, *Bartholdi*, Paris: Éditions de Minuit, 1954

Butler, Ruth, and Jane van Nimmen, *Nineteenth-Century French Sculpture: Monuments for the Middle Class*, Louisville, Kentucky: J.B. Speed Art Museum, 1971

Fusco, Peter, and Horst Waldemar Janson, *The Romantics to Rodin: French Nineteenth-Century Sculpture from North American Collections*, Los Angeles: Los Angeles County Museum of Art, and New York: Braziller, 1980

Lami, Stanislas, *Dictionnaire des sculpteurs de l'École fran-çaise au dix-neuvième siècle,* 4 vols., Paris: Champion, 1914–21; reprint, Nendeln, Liechtenstein: Kraus, 1970; see especially vol. 1

Rilliot, M.T., Y. Pagnot, et al., *Le Lion de Belfort et Bartholdi,* Belfort, France: Schraag, 1980

Schmitt, Jean-Marie, *Bartholdi: Une certaine idée de la liberté,* Strasbourg, France: Editions de la Nuée-Bleue, 1985

Schmitt, Jean-Marie, editor, *Cent ans d'études bartholdiennes,* Colmar, France: Archives Municipales, 1985

Vidal, Pierre, *Frédéric-Auguste Bartholdi, 1834–1904, par la main, par l'ésprit,* Paris: Créations du Pélican, 1994

STATUE OF LIBERTY (*LIBERTY ENLIGHTENING THE WORLD*)

Frédéric-Auguste Bartholdi; (1834–1904)

1870–1886

copper (hammered), iron (interior pylons), masonry pedestal

h. 46.4 m (with pedestal, 93.5 m)

Liberty Island, New York Harbor, New York, United States

The Statue of Liberty (*Liberty Enlightening the World*) originated in the internal politics of France. In 1865 Edouard de Laboulaye, a French legal scholar, states-man, and admirer of the U.S. Constitution, conceived the notion of giving a monument to the United States for its 1876 Centennial. He and his moderate republican circle, which included Auguste Bartholdi, hoped to strengthen Franco-American relations and gain support for their pacific libertarian struggle against Napoléon III's repressive Second Empire. For Bartholdi and other Alsatians, moreover, the statue would come to privately incarnate the dream of regaining freedom for Alsace, lost to Germany in 1871.

The statue's immense scale was Bartholdi's idea. He wished to rival antique colossi: the pharaonic sculptures of Egypt, Pheidias's lost *Athena* and *Zeus*, and the Colossus of Rhodes. He had also studied outsized figures by Giovanni da Bologna (*Appennino*, 1580–81) and Cerano (*Saint Carlo Borromeo*, 1598), and a dozen other grandiose 19th-century projects, including Ludwig Schwanthaler's *Bavaria* and Ernst von Bandel's *Arminius. Liberty* would surpass all of these in height.

Bartholdi chose a site off the New York coast, where the statue could appear emblematically before the United States, offering its illumination "across the Atlantic." Like the classical *Pharos* at Alexandria, his monument would function as a lighthouse, albeit one powered by modern electricity.

For *Liberty*'s iconography, conceived between 1870 and 1875, Bartholdi mined allegorical tradition: Lib-erty had been personified as a robed woman as early as the 3rd century BCE, in the Roman goddess of *Liberty* on the Aventine Hill. In Bartholdi's syncretistic image, broken shackles at *Liberty*'s feet celebrate the triumph of freedom over slavery, while her tablet, bearing the date of the Declaration of Independence, alludes to Mosaic tradition and the primacy of law. Her diadem with seven rays of light, conventionally an attribute of Helios (the sun god) or of Faith, likens liberty to the sun's radiance while also evoking Free-masonry and Bartholdi's family emblem (the sun). Rather than Eugène Delacroix's incendiary torch (*Liberty Guiding the People*, 1830), the symbol of revolution, Bartholdi's *Liberty* holds aloft an enlightening beacon. Bartholdi's revisions in the iconography of Liberty proved influential, replacing former standard elements such as the Phrygian cap, which had associations with Communard violence.

In form, *Liberty* exemplifies 19th-century Beaux-Arts Classicism. The artfully arranged folds of an antique Greek chiton and peplum enliven the self-contained figure and draw attention to the expressive arm and idealized Greco-Roman head. The sculpture's simplified planes and unbroken lines bespeak Bartholdi's decades of reflection on the desiderata of colossal art. Considered in the round, the piece offers two distinct aspects: approaching from the Atlantic, the stance suggests a dynamic forward motion, whereas from the statue's front, the pose appears static, iconic. Bartholdi adroitly manipulated site, scale, and composition to amplify *Liberty*'s grandeur and sculptural interest.

The statue's great size, which dictated a hollow structure, posed numerous technical challenges. A final 1.2-meter-high original clay model, completed in 1875, served as guide for a sequence of three progressive enlargements, culminating in a full-scale plaster model. Each labor-intensive enlargement required more than 9,000 measurements. On the basis of the final plaster version, technicians fabricated both wood and more precise molded lead forms. Artisans from the metalwork firm of Gaget, Gauthier et Cie hammered thin (2.5 millimeter) sheets of copper against first the wood and then the lead templates, forming 300 segments that were later riveted together to create the sculpture's final surface. This thin repoussé shell required substantial internal support.

Liberty's more conventional exterior contrasts strikingly with its technologically advanced interior structure, a pioneering feat of engineering. The architect E.E. Viollet-le-Duc initiated the armature's design; after his death in 1879, Bartholdi turned to the engineer Gustave Eiffel, then famous for his bridges. Eiffel produced a rigidly trussed, cross-braced iron tower that attached to the sculpture with flexible lightweight iron bars, forming in essence an elastic suspension system,

Statue of Liberty (*Liberty Enlightening the World*), New York City
The Conway Library, Courtauld Institute of Art

statue could be disassembled and shipped to the United States. Richard Morris Hunt, a French-trained American architect, created the pedestal, a complex and sensitive architectural gem, in 1881–86.

A spectacular dedication ceremony, complete with parade, fireworks, and the presence of President Grover Cleveland, accompanied the unveiling of the sculpture on 28 October 1886 and heralded its future renown. The public for this sculpture is broader than that of almost any other artwork: more than 1 million people visit it every year, and it enjoys instantaneous international recognition. Its fame owes less to its aesthetic qualities than to its colossal scale, interior viewing platform, and symbolic malleability. Indeed, it has undergone several distinct reinterpretations. Inaugurated as a symbol of Franco-American friendship, it quickly took on a second meaning as a welcoming host to immigrants, as in Emma Lazarus's well-known poem "The New Colossus": "Give me your tired, your poor, / Your huddled masses yearning to breathe free." During World Wars I and II, *Liberty* communicated a patriotic message. By the 1960s, when the statue often served as the site for political protests, it had become an icon of the United States itself, displacing Columbia and Uncle Sam. The Statue of Liberty has been used to sell products and to satirize political factions; and it has served as a motif for countless artistic variations. Its flexibility as an image, its bold scale, its testimony to 19th-century progressive ideals, and the technical genius of its construction set it apart from all other sculptures.

Lynne D. Ambrosini

See also **Pheidias:** *Athena Parthenos;* **Public Sculpture**

Further Reading

Agulhon, Maurice, *Marianne au pouvoir: L'imagerie et la symbolique républicaines de 1880 à 1914*, Paris: Flammarion, 1989

Bartholdi, Frédéric Auguste, *The Statue of Liberty Enlightening the World*, New York: North American Review, 1885; reprint, New York: New York Bound, 1984

Blanchet, Christian, and Bertrand Dard, *Statue de la Liberté: Le livre du centenaire*, Paris: Édition Comet's, 1984; as *Statue of Liberty: The First Hundred Years*, translated by Bernard A. Weisberger, New York: American Heritage, 1985

Dillon, Wilton S., and Neil G. Kotler, editors, *The Statue of Liberty Revisited: Making a Universal Symbol*, Washington, D.C.: Smithsonian Institution Press, 1994

Gschaedler, André, *True Light on the Statue of Liberty and Its Creator*, Narberth, Pennsylvania: Livingston, 1966

Hayden, Richard Seth, et al., *Restoring the Statue of Liberty: Sculpture, Structure, Symbol*, New York: McGraw Hill, 1986

Lemoine, Bertrand, *La Statue de la Liberté; The Statue of Liberty* (bilingual French-English edition), Brussels: Mardaga, 1986

the ancestor of modern curtain-wall architecture. Engineer General Charles P. Stone constructed a massive foundation—the largest single concrete mass of its time, weighing 27,000 tons—in which to anchor Eiffel's iron pylon. (The monument, restored in 1982–86, is still remarkably sturdy.)

Liberty was costly. Inspired by the birth of the Third Republic and the sight of the sculpture itself—first the head, which was exhibited at the 1878 Paris Exposition, and then the whole figure, which was erected initially in Paris (1881–84)—the French raised the required 600,000 francs (about $400,000) in five years (1875–80). The United States had to pay for the pedestal.

To help arouse enthusiasm in the United States, Bartholdi had exhibited *Liberty*'s colossal torch-bearing arm at the Philadelphia Centennial Exhibition in 1876. President Ulysses S. Grant formally accepted the gift in 1877, but the campaign to raise $300,000 for the pedestal proved unexpectedly arduous. A dramatic crusade by Joseph Pulitzer, owner of the *New York World*, elicited the last $100,000 in 1885. Finally, the

Provoyeur, Pierre, and June Ellen Hargrove, *Liberty: The French-American Statue in Art and History*, New York: Perennial Library, 1986

Trachtenberg, Marvin, *The Statue of Liberty*, London: Allen Lane, and New York, Penguin, 1976; revised edition, New York: Penguin, 1986

LORENZO BARTOLINI 1777–1850 *Italian*

Lorenzo Bartolini was born near Florence in 1777 and came of age as a sculptor during the Neoclassical period. He was influenced by a variety of artists of his day, including Jacques-Louis David and François Lemot, who employed Bartolini in their shops. Although he is known as an Italian sculptor, Bartolini's reputation took shape initially in Paris, where he landed after joining the French army in 1799. Shortly after receiving several notable public commissions, he was appointed professor of sculpture at the Carrara Academy of Fine Arts. He would eventually become the sculpture chair at the Florence Academy. Bartolini's style is difficult to totalize, as it developed from Neoclassicism to Romanticism to Purism. His work, however, is a notable example of the varied Florentine aesthetic of the time.

Soon after the death of Princess Sofia Zamoyska Czartoryski in Florence on 27 February 1837, Bartolini received the commission for her tomb from her widower, Prince Stanislaw Zamoyski, and their sons. By July 1837 the sculptor had already finished a clay model of the recumbent figure of the deceased, but the tomb was not completed and placed in the Salviati Chapel in the Church of Santa Croce in Florence until 1844. A drawing in a United States private collection (black pencil on paper, 297 centimeters by 368 centimeters) is evidently related to the first design; the figure of the princess is identical to the final version, but the position is reversed. Fortunately, the original plaster model survives and at present is on view at the Galleria dell'Accademia, Florence.

Some doubt exists as to the amount of work actually done by Bartolini. In a handwritten note (1846) he lists the tomb among the works done by his own hand, but his chief assistant, Eliso Schianta, notes in an inventory of Bartolini's works that only the princess's head had been sculpted by the master. Even if true, this is not particularly significant due to the way sculpture workshops were organized during this period. Regardless, the monument as a whole effectively expresses the positions and convictions that made up Bartolini's brand of Purism, which he was defining with increasing specificity in the late 1830s and the early 1840s.

Bartolini preached a faithful imitation of reality, free of idealistic systems or prejudices, and—as a man of his time, permeated with Romantic culture—the teachings of the Tuscan quattrocento masters. To these he attributed the values of naturalness that in his view had lost ground after the 15th century, when academic styles came into vogue. Bartolini hoped thus to restore a "natural beauty" ennobled by Christian concepts, as opposed to the pagan "ideal beauty" produced by Neoclassical aesthetics. His references in the Zamoyska tomb to Florentine sculpture of the second half of the 15th century are almost explicit quotations. For example, the arch-and-plinth composition and the chromatic effects he obtained by juxtaposing differently colored marble (white as the dominant color, blue-gray, and ash-gray) with gilding echo reinterpret those same features in the 15th-century Bruni and Marsuppini tombs in the same church, the first by Antonio Rossellino and the second by Desiderio da Settignano. Likewise, some of the decorative details Bartolini used on the bier—the lion paws and the swirls of acanthus flower clusters and foliage—derive directly from Desiderio and Andrea del Verrocchio. The tondo depicting the *Virgin Adoring the Christ Child* (set in the back, about two meters above the statue of the deceased) could well

Tomb of Princess Sophia Zamoyska Czartoryski, Salviati Chapel, Church of Santa Croce, Florence
The Conway Library, Courtauld Institute of Art

have been sculpted by Rossellino or Benedetto da Maiano, so dependent is it on 15th-century models. Bartolini's attention to the reality of the event is equally tangible in the rumpled folds of the drapery and in his fine rendering of the pallor of death in the glossy skin.

Nonetheless, he subsumed all these passages and observations into a unity of vision that rearranges the whole and ennobles it with references to illustrious forebears. In this way he transcended the post-Romantic particularism that led to unharmonious results in other contemporary art and combined stylization and naturalism in a cohesive whole, explained in this case by a reading that presupposes iconological as well as stylistic choices. While the creased coverlet and the rumpled pillow attest to the dying woman's pain and suffering, her facial expression—not shown pitilessly in rigor mortis but relaxed in renunciation—is meant to convey the certainty reached by a Christian through faith that death is merely the beginning of a new life.

This tomb met with favor in his own day. For instance, not long after its erection Odoardo Fantacchiotti copied the layout for the tomb of Raffaello Morghen (1844–54), also in Santa Croce.

CARLO CINELLI

See also **Benedetto da Maiano; Desiderio da Settignano: Tomb of Carlo Marsuppini; Neoclassicism and Romanticism**

Biography

Born in Savignano di Vaiano, near Prato, Italy, 7 January 1777. After apprenticing with an alabaster craftsman in Florence, had sporadic jobs with sculptors in Florence, then apprenticed with sculptor Giovanni Insom and, in Volterra, with French alabaster craftsman Barthélemy Corneille; joined French army, 1799, as a draftsman, and eventually reached Paris; entered Jacques-Louis David's studio on recommendation of Napoléon's sister, Élisa Bonaparte, and immediately became close friends with Jean-Auguste-Dominique Ingres; received several prestigious public commissions in Paris, 1805–07; appointed professor of sculpture by Élisa Bonaparte at Accademia di Carrara, Carrara, Italy, 1807; fell into disgrace upon downfall of Bonaparte family, but returned to favor toward late 1810s; settled in Florence after 1815; style gradually shifted from Neoclassicism toward naturalistic Romanticism, 1820s, then reached Purism, around 1840; after death of Stefano Ricci, appointed to the sculpture chair at the Florence Academy, 1839; did busts of famous contemporaries such as Gioacchino Rossini, Luigi Cherubini, Adolphe Thiers, and Franz Liszt. Died in Florence, Italy, 20 January 1850.

Selected Works

1818   Tomb of Henrietta Stratford Canning; marble; Lausanne Cathedral, Switzerland

1819   *Grape Presser*; marble (untraced); marble replica: 1842–44, Pinacoteca Tosio-Martinengo, Brescia, Italy

1823–43 Monument to Maria Luisa Bourbon; marble; Piazza Napoleone, Lucca, Italy

1824   *Charity Educating Children*; marble; Palazzo Pitti, Florence, Italy

1830–70 Monument to Count Nikolay Nikitich Demidov (completed in 1870 by Bartolini's pupil Pasquale Romanelli); marble; Piazza Demidov, Florence, Italy

1836   *Trust in God*; marble; Museo Poldi Pezzoli, Milan, Italy

1837–44 Tomb of Princess Sophia Zamoyska Czartoryski; plaster model: 1837, Galleria dell'Accademia, Florence, Italy; marble version: Salviati Chapel, Church of Santa Croce, Florence, Italy

Further Reading

Belli Barsali, Isa, "Bartolini, Lorenzo," in *Dizionario biografico degli italiani*, vol. 6, Rome: Istituto della Enciclopedia Italiana, 1964

Del Bravo, Carlo, *Il genio di Lorenzo Bartolini*, Florence: S.P.E.S., 1977

Del Bravo, Carlo, "Bartolini interpretato con Jean Jacques," *Artibus et historiae* 27 (1993)

L'opera di Lorenzo Bartolini, 1777–1850: Sculture, disegni, cimeli (exhib. cat.), Prato, Italy: Associazione Turistica Pratese, 1956

Lorenzo Bartolini (exhib. cat.), Florence: Centro Di, 1978

Panzetta, Alfonso, *Dizionario degli scultori italiani dell'Ottocentoe del primo Novecento*, 2 vols., Milan: Allemandi, 1994

Tinti, Mario, *Lorenzo Bartolini*, 2 vols., Rome: Reale Accademia d'Italia, 1936

ANTOINE-LOUIS BARYE 1795–1875
French

Critics coined the pejorative term *animalier* to refer to Antoine-Louis Barye, the sculptor responsible for popularizing the genre of animal imagery among the middle classes in the second quarter of the 19th century and for pushing the emotional content of such images to extremes. Certainly, animal subjects existed before the 19th century, but Barye eschewed the idealized and sentimental portrayals characteristic of his 18th-century predecessors. Instead, he created a menagerie of wild, exotic animals usually engaged in violent combat depicted with such realism that his audience cringed. Quintessentially Romantic, Barye's work is a prime example of the sublime in art.

Barye was trained as a metalsmith, and it was perhaps his artisanal background that earned him the contempt of academic critics. He attempted the transition from artisan to artist in the studios of the Neoclassical sculptor François-Joseph Bosio and the Romantic painter Baron Gros and entered the École des Beaux-Arts in 1818. But Barye never succeeded in winning the coveted Prix de Rome that would have assured a lucrative career in the fine arts. During this period he worked for the jeweler Fauconnier, making small bronzes of animals, and he showed his work at the annual salons.

Barye sent *Tiger Devouring a Gavial Crocodile of the Ganges* to the Salon of 1831, where it enjoyed resounding success. With this piece he made the first steps toward elevating a subject long deemed insignificant within an academic hierarchy that had placed images of the human figure at the top and animals at the bottom of the scale. Barye's achievement was to make viewers address their own primordial instincts of aggression and survival.

The Duke of Orléans especially liked Barye's work and commissioned from him in 1834 a magnificent *surtout de table*, or centerpiece. Composed of five hunting groups and four smaller scenes of fighting animals, the entire suite would have covered approximately 6.5 meters and required the construction of a special table that could support its weight. At the center of the cruciform plan was the *Tiger Hunt*. Astride an elephant, Indian hunters clad in turbans thrust long spears into two attacking tigers, one of which claws its way up the side of the unfortunate mount. The other tiger falls beneath the hind legs of the beast and is trampled. The broad gestures dictated by this violence contrast sharply with the minute details that Barye provided. The ferocity of the action inspires morbid curiosity in spectators, who are rewarded with the jewellike precision of bells and other trappings set in motion by the panicked elephant. The other four hunting scenes were similarly handled and included a *Lion Hunt*, *Bull Hunt*, *Elk Hunt*, and *Bear Hunt*. Barye submitted all nine of the pieces to the Salon of 1837, and they were rejected. He did not participate in the annual exhibition again until 1850.

Several years after this setback, Barye established his own company. With the financial backing of Émile Martin, the sculptor started Barye and Company and offered casts of his bronzes directly to a middle-class clientele, a venture that lasted only a few years. He found work as a curator of casts at the Musée du Louvre, Paris, and later as a drawing professor of natural history and zoology, continuing to study his subjects at close hand, often in the company of a fellow Romantic, Eugène Delacroix. *Jaguar Devouring a Hare* is a variation on the theme established with *Tiger Devouring a Gavial Crocodile of the Ganges*. Rather than focusing on the battle, Barye turned almost sadistic

attention to the satisfaction of desire. The vertebrae and ribs of the jaguar, which protrude through its sleek coat, and the taut muscles stretched over a lean frame suggest the length of time since the animal last ate. The cat's ears flat against its head and the folds of skin drawn over its muzzle as it tears into the loins of the limp hare are no doubt behavioral details that Barye had observed in his studies at the Jardin des Plantes, the Paris zoo. He entered the work at the Universal Exposition of 1855 and was awarded a Grand Medal of Honor for his efforts.

Barye benefited from several state commissions, notably the allegories of *War*, *Peace*, *Strength*, and *Order* made for the facade of the Cour du Carrousel at the Louvre, but his fame rested with fashionable private collectors, whose well-appointed salons would have been incomplete without an example of his work. He struck a chord with Americans, whose devotion to the artist had a significant impact on his critical reception in the 20th century. William Walters, an entrepreneur from Baltimore, Maryland, and George Lucas, an art broker who took up residence in Paris in 1857, amassed a huge cache of the artist's work. Walters commissioned 120 casts from Barye in 1873 for the Corcoran Gallery in Washington, D.C. The collector purchased casts of the four allegories from the Cour du Carrousel, which can still be seen at Mount Vernon Place in Baltimore. After Barye's death in 1875, the two men collected his sculpture, oil paintings, and a good stock of watercolors, as well as a sketchbook and even one of the artist's palettes. They commissioned lithographic copies of his portrait, which were published and distributed to his admirers. Walters and Lucas tirelessly promoted a project to erect a monument to the artist (a main part of which was destroyed during World War II) on the Ile St.-Louis in Paris and held exhibitions of his work in Paris in 1889 and again in New York the following year in order to finance it. They published a catalogue of Barye's oeuvre and organized the competition for the design of the monument. Lucas owned a drawing recording the room where Barye died and took a plaster cast of the artist's hand to the painter Léon Bonnat so that it could be painted onto the sculptor's palette. Among American patrons, Barye achieved cult status. The sculptor generated a following of *animaliers*, chief among them Eugène Frémiet, who was known by his contemporaries for his precious depictions of cats more than for his monument to Joan of Arc. Auguste Rodin studied anatomy with Barye in 1863 and credited his elder with having taught him how to conceive of a figure from the inside out. Henri Matisse converted Barye's *Jaguar Devouring a Hare* into a Modernist essay in abstraction.

Although Barye treated classical subjects, such as *Theseus Combating the Minotaur*, he excelled at the predator and prey themes, the physicality of which provoked an empathic response in his audience, prompting the critic Théophile Gautier to dub him the "Michelangelo of the Menagerie."

CHERYL K. SNAY

See also **France: Mid–Late 19th Century; Neoclassicism and Romanticism**

Biography

Born in Paris, France, 24 September 1795. Trained as goldsmith by his father; worked for the engraver Fourier; worked in the shop of a goldsmith to Napoléon; entered the studio of the sculptor François-Joseph Bosio, 1816; entered the painting studio of Baron Gros, 1817; enrolled at École des Beaux-Arts, 1818, where he studied until 1823; worked for the goldsmith Fauconnier, 1820–28; made debut at the Salon of 1827, after which the Duke of Orléans commissioned from him the *surtout de table* (centerpiece); named chevalier of the Legion of Honor, 1836; *surtout de table* rejected by the Salon jury, 1837; in 1843, submitted more work to the Salon, but was rejected; Barye and Company established 1845 to produce and sell his work, but business later failed; given a position at the Musée du Louvre, Paris, 1848, and elected member of Salon jury; appointed professor of drawing of natural history at École d'Agronomie de Versailles, 1850, and showed at the Salon; named professor of zoological drawing at Museum of Natural History, Paris, 1854. Won gold medal at Universal Exposition, 1867; elected to Academy of Fine Arts, 1868; William Walters commissioned 120 of his works in 1873 for the Corcoran Gallery in Washington, D.C. Died in Paris, France, 25 June 1875.

Selected Works

1832 *Lion Crushing a Serpent;* bronze; Musée du Louvre, Paris, France

1832 *Tiger Devouring a Gavial Crocodile of the Ganges*; bronze; Musée du Louvre, Paris, France; plaster model; Detroit Institute of Arts

1833 Equestrian statue of Charles VII; bronze; Walters Art Museum, Baltimore, Maryland, United States

1834 Equestrian statue of the Duke of Orléans; bronze; Walters Art Museum, Baltimore, Maryland, United States

1834–36 Surtout de table, for the Duke of Orléans; bronze; Walters Art Museum, Baltimore, Maryland, United States

1835–40 Lion, for the Bastille Column; bronze; Paris, France

1840–43 *St. Clotilde*; marble; Church of Sainte-Madeleine, Paris, France

1843 *Theseus Combating the Minotaur*; bronze; Walters Art Museum, Baltimore, Maryland, United States

1847 *Seated Lion*; bronze; Musée du Louvre, Paris, France

1850 *Jaguar Devouring a Hare*; bronze; Walters Art Museum, Baltimore, Maryland, United States

1850 *Theseus Combating the Centaur Bienor*; bronze; Corcoran Gallery of Art, Washington, D.C., United States

1854–56 *War*, *Peace*, *Strength*, and *Order*; plaster; Musée d'Orsay, Paris, France

1860–65 Equestrian monument of Napoléon I as a Roman emperor; bronze; Ajaccio, Corsica, France

Further Reading

Ballu, Roger, *L'oeuvre de Barye*, Paris: Maison Quantin, 1890

Benge, Glenn, *Antoine-Louis Barye: Sculptor of Romantic Realism*, University Park: Pennsylvania State University Press, 1984

DeKay, Charles, *Barye: Life and Works of Antoine Louis Barye, Sculptor*, New York: Barye Monument Association, 1889; reprint, New York: AMS Press, 1974

Hamilton, G.H., "The Origin of Barye's *Tiger Hunt*," *Art Bulletin* 18 (1956)

Hubert, Gerard, and Maurice Serallaz, editors, *Barye: Sculptures et peintures, aquarelles des collections publiques françaises*, Paris: Éditions des Musées Nationaux, 1956

Johnston, William R., "The Barye Collection," *Apollo* 100/153 (November 1974)

Lemaistre, Isabelle Leroy-Jay, *La griffe et la dent: Antoine Louis Barye (1795–1875): Sculpteur animalier*, Paris: Réunion des Musées Nationaux, 1996

Millard, Charles, "Sculpture and Theory in Nineteenth-Century France," *Journal of Aesthetics and Art Criticism* 34/1 (fall 1975)

Pivar, Stuart, *The Barye Bronzes: A Catalogue Raisonné*, Woodbridge, Suffolk: Antique Collectors' Club, 1974

Poletti, Michel, and Alain Richarme, *Barye: Catalogue raisonné des sculptures*, Paris: Gallimard, 2000

Wasserman, Jeanne, *Sculpture by Antoine-Louis Barye in the Collection of the Fogg Art Museum*, Cambridge, Massachusetts: Fogg Art Museum, Harvard University, 1982

Zieseniss, Charles Otto, *Les aquarelles de Barye: Étude critique et catalogue raisonné*, Paris: Massin, 1954

TIGER DEVOURING A GAVIAL CROCODILE OF THE GANGES

Antoine-Louis Barye (1795–1875)

1831

bronze

h. 39.7 cm; w. 105 cm

Musée du Louvre, Paris, France

Barye began submitting work to the Salons of Paris in 1827, but it was not until 1831, when he entered a patinated plaster model of *Tiger Devouring a Gavial Crocodile of the Ganges* (plaster model, Detroit Institute of Arts, Michigan) that he finally caught the attention of the critics. Declared by Étienne Delécluze to be "the strongest and most significant work of sculpture of the entire Salon," the savagery of the pair of exotic animals engaged in combat astounded visitors to the exhibition. Théophile Gautier enthused, "What energy, what ferocity, what a thrill of satisfied lust for killing."

The tiger's teeth and extended claws dig into the flesh of the reptile, a species native to India and characterized by its unusual snout. The cat's ears lie flat against its head; the taut musculature of its hindquarters brace against the death throes of the writhing crocodile. The monster's gaping jaws expose an array of razor-sharp teeth that are useless against its tormentor's death grip on its groin. The violent action compressed into a tight composition augments the tension. Barye's ability to translate into mimetic form bone, muscle, and variations of texture—from the striped fur of the predator to the leathery skin of its prey—impressed some critics. The jury awarded him a second medal for his entry. A year later the sculpture was cast in bronze by use of the lost-wax method by Honoré Gonon et Fils. In 1848 the state purchased the piece, and during the Second Empire it was installed in the ministry of the interior. After the artist's death, it was transferred to the Musée du Louvre, Paris.

Animal combat scenes were not uncommon at the Salons, but Barye's treatment elevated the subject to a new level. Not only was his work larger than convention allowed; it also resisted the idealized and humanized animals typical of his predecessors. Barye relied instead on his own studies of his subjects made at the Jardin des Plantes (Paris zoo) and from books on natural history. He probably never witnessed a tiger killing a gavial, and it is possible that he never saw a gavial firsthand. Pages from a sketchbook in the George A. Lucas Collection at the Baltimore Museum of Art do show measured studies of the animal with references to published sources for the information. Faced with the unbridled realism of fang, claw, scales, and fur, the spectator needs to be reminded that the pair is wholly imaginary.

Tiger Devouring a Gavial Crocodile of the Ganges defies traditional iconographical interpretations. It does not lend itself to a political reading, as does the sculptor's *Lion Crushing a Serpent*, a sculpture understood as a metaphor for the July Monarchy, with the noble lion symbolizing the forces of good (that is, King Louis-Philippe) defeating the evil snake (the king's enemies) (see Benge, 1984). Nor does it communicate a moral lesson, as one might expect from an antique example of animal conflict. The work operates on a

Tiger Devouring a Gavial Crocodile of the Ganges© R.G. Ojeda / Neri, Réunion des Musées Nationaux / Art Resource, NY

purely visceral level and embraces 18th-century theories of the sublime that became common parlance by the early 19th century.

With this scene, Barye confronts the viewer with the instinct for self-preservation, which, according to the 18th-century British theorist and politician Edmund Burke, is the source of all pleasure and pain and extends to the beautiful and the sublime. Both pain and pleasure are positive passions that are organs of the mind, the equal exercise of which leads to a transcendent state. The sublime is characterized by terror, especially terror induced by the threat of death. By subjecting oneself to the sublime—vicariously through art or physically by interacting with nature—one can become enlightened. Nonetheless, Burke and his contemporaries accepted the hierarchy of subjects promoted by the academies and referred specifically to artistic representations of tragic history and the demise of ancient heroes as a means of arousing one's sympathies for the characters and experiencing the sublime.

Barye's innovation was to relocate the focus of the viewer's sympathy outside of human experience and place it squarely in the animal kingdom. Spectators probably did not identify with either of the exotic beasts. The tiger's ferocity is repulsive rather than ad-

ANTONIO BEGARELLI ca. 1490s–1565

mirable, and the location of its grip is undignified. Nor is the gavial, despite its compromised position, a sympathetic creature, with its strange nose and awkward body. By depicting animals with which few people were familiar, Barye provided no prospect of sentimentalizing the scene. With no opportunity for narrative, the audience focused on the struggle for survival and the nearness of death.

Barye's success at the Salon of 1831 was tempered by mild criticism of his sculpture's excessive detail. Nevertheless, the piece brought him the patronage of the Duke of Orléans and King Louis-Philippe, which occupied the sculptor for the next decade. More important, it afforded him the wherewithal to establish himself as a commodity in a burgeoning art market. He produced two smaller versions of this sculpture, and over the next 30 years he listed them in catalogues of his work available for purchase. Examples of these can be found in museums and private collections throughout Europe and the United States. There are several variations between the original, full-scale model and the later reductions, such as the position of the crocodile's head, the degree to which the mouth is open, and the overall silhouette of the pair. The popularity throughout the second half of the 19th century of *Tiger Devouring a Gavial Crocodile of the Ganges* attests to Barye's success at creating a new genre of art and the warm reception by the bourgeoisie of the Romantic theory of the sublime.

CHERYL K. SNAY

See also **Neoclassicism and Romanticism**

Further Reading

"Acquisitions—Detroit Institute of Arts," *The Burlington Magazine* 103 (June 1988)

Benge, Glenn, *Antoine-Louis Barye, Sculptor of Romantic Realism*, University Park: Pennsylvania State University Press, 1984

Hubert, Gérard, "Barye et la critique de son temps," *Revue des Arts* 6/4 (December 1956)

Lemaistre, Isabelle Leroy-Jay, *La griffe et la dent: Antoine Louis Barye (1795–1875): Sculpteur animalier*, Paris: Réunion des Musées Nationaux, 1996

Mannoni, Edith, *Barye*, Paris: Les Éditions de l'Amateur, 1996

ANTONIO BEGARELLI *ca.* 1490s–1565

Italian

Antonio Begarelli was a major terracotta sculptor in 16th-century Emilia, although he was fated to remain essentially isolated. Unlike the dramatic expressionism of Niccolò dell'Arca, who worked in Bologna, or the absolutely objective realism of Guido Mazzoni, who was older than Begarelli and also from Modena, Begarelli's work expressed a Classical sense of measure similar to that of Alfonso Lombardi, whose sculpture has

not yet been adequately studied. Even in Begarelli's *Deposition of Christ* and crucifixion groups, where a sense of drama is understandably present, the overall psychological climate is that of a transposition of emotions to a scenario of universality, as opposed to a strong sense of realism. His style thus reflected one of the principal ways of thinking and being in the 16th century, one that can be widely seen in the other arts as well, from music to poetry. The broad gestures Begarelli favored in his sculptures have led some historians to see him as a forerunner of the Baroque, but to the extent that this is true, the particular type of Baroque he heralded was Alessandro Algardi's Classical, measured style. Likewise, Begarelli seems to have been essentially immune to the anxieties of Mannerism, at least in the more explicit forms that it took in the work of Parmigianino, although the quiverings that animate the surfaces of Begarelli's figures justify comparisons with the painter Correggio that have been repeatedly proposed since his own day.

Begarelli's typical works are grandiose stagings of scenes in which he took the more limited and inward-looking compositions of his predecessors to extremes. The best example is the *Deposition of Christ* in the Church of St. Francis in Modena, where the relationships between the individual figures and the groups—distributed as they are in every direction in space, rather than composed on a single plane—is extremely complex. This work is outstanding from a technical standpoint as well. It seems to overcome the natural rigidity of terracotta: the artist bent the material to favor and accompany each movement of the bodies. To fully understand these artistic phenomena, it is useful to look at the contemporary theater and at the sculptures of the Sacro Monte in northern Italy (Varallo, Varese, and Orta). Begarelli's groups can thus be seen as something akin to *tableaux vivants*.

Fundamental to Begarelli's style was his choice to forgo any realistic coloring of his statues; instead, his predilection was for delicately transparent whites that bordered on ivory. To obtain this hue, he probably increased the percentage of kaolin in the raw clay; the fired piece was then finished in tempera, of which only traces remain. Some kind of glaze was, of course, indispensable to overlay the rawness and the chromatic variations in the terracotta and to hide the connections among the parts. The life-size statues were fired in at least three or four pieces and then assembled. The kilns were not large enough to contain a whole statue because they would have been unable to reach the necessary temperatures of 900 or 1,100 degrees Celsius. Begarelli's sole concession to color was the gold applied on the edges of the clothing and in some other decorative details. He may have made limited and occasional use of other colors to bring out the figures' features, but he never used color to cover whole surfaces. Significantly, one of the most important groups in Modena, the *Deposition of Christ* in the Church of St. Francis, was entirely repainted in vivid, realistic colors just after Begarelli's death. In other cases, efforts were made to recapture the white hues by adding layer upon layer of paint, so that today the surfaces are opaque and mute. These refinishings were also intended to hide breakage, which is frequent in terracotta sculpture and inevitable in the case of large ensembles and heavy figures that are moved from place to place—not to mention the fact that respect for the integrity of a work of art was certainly not as great in the past as it is today. In other words, people took no special pains to avoid breakage because they knew that it would eventually be repaired.

This outlook explains the plaster coatings that weigh Begarelli's sculptures down with pounds and pounds of spurious matter and fanciful additions, such as incongruous drapery folds. These ought to be removed; they make it impossible to recognize the artist's hand and assess his work correctly. A restoration project that began in 1975 has freed most of Begarelli's sculptures from these travesties, but other works—especially the funerary monument at the Abbey Church of St. Peter in Modena and the statues at the Abbey Church of St. John in Parma and in San Benedetto Po—remain to be restored.

The impossibility of reading Begarelli's work correctly is largely responsible for the meager consideration in which he has been held. There has been clamorous misapprehension of Begarelli's work—for example, by Adolfo Venturi. Only recently have historians begun to study and appreciate Begarelli's extremely high artistic value (see Lightbown, 1964; Bonsanti, 1992). Giorgio Vasari, in his 16th-century *Lives of the Painters, Sculptors, and Architects*, held Begarelli in high esteem and quoted Michelangelo as saying, "Were this clay marble, the ancient statues would be in trouble." Michelangelo, who does not appear to have been in places where Begarelli's sculptures were on view, probably never said any such thing, but it is significant that Vasari, living in the 16th century, could attribute the judgment to him without fearing contradiction from other authors and/or critics, most of whom spoke quite favorably of Begarelli.

Part of the difficulty art historians have found in reaching a correct assessment of Begarelli's work is due to its uniformity over his whole career. Variations do appear, but they are subtle and limited, making it difficult to date the undocumented works. Moreover, Begarelli lived his whole life in Modena (although there is mention of a "Modona" in London in 1554, it is not certain that it refers to him). He left his hometown only for short journeys to other cities in Emilia

St. Bonaventure
© Arte & Immagini srl / CORBIS

to oversee the installation of his sculptures. His works, mostly intended for large Benedictine abbeys, are still at their original locations in Modena (although some are now in the Galleria Estense) and its province, in Parma and in San Benedetto Po, near Mantua (the work he did for Aversa, near Naples, is lost). He never married and took the vows of a Benedictine lay brother. Only a few pieces ever left Emilia—they now reside in London and Berlin—which helps explain why Begarelli is so little known.

A balanced evaluation of Begarelli, to the extent that one can be expressed today, must surely see in his activity an episode of great importance in 16th-century Italian culture and recognize in works such as the *Deposition of Christ* in the Church of St. Francis, the tomb of Gian Galeazzo Boschetti in San Cesario sul Panaro, the extraordinary *Virgin Mary and Child with Cherubs* in Monteorsello di Guiglia, and the funerary monument at the Abbey Church of St. Peter, Modena, some of the most intense expressions of 16th-century Classicism. In all probability, the original comparison with Correggio is still the most valid key to interpreting and assessing his work.

GIORGIO BONSANTI

See also **Algardi, Alessandro; Lamentation and Deposition Groups**

Biography

Born in Modena, Italy, *ca.* 1490s. Son of a kiln owner; nothing known of education and training; early works similar to those of Alfonso Lombardo, who worked in Bologna; first known work, *Virgin and Child* (1522, also known as *Madonna di Piazza*), established reputation; received regular salary from city government and produced steady stream of works, all in terracotta, from 1528; also received commissions from Ferrara; took vows of a Benedictine lay brother and never married; assisted in later life by his nephew Ludovico. Died in Modena, Italy, 28 December 1565.

Selected Works

1522   *Virgin and Child* (also known as *Madonna di Piazza*); terracotta; Museo Civico, Modena, Italy

1524–26 *Pietà*; terracotta; Church of St. Augustine, Modena, Italy

1525–27 Tomb of Gian Galeazzo Boschetti; terracotta; parish church, San Cesario sul Panaro, Modena, Italy

1525–27 *Crib*; terracotta; Modena Cathedral, Italy

1530–31 *Deposition of Christ*; terracotta; Church of St. Francis, Modena; model: Victoria and Albert Museum, London, England

1532–36 *Virgin Mary and Child, St. Justina, St. Peter,* and *St. Benedict*; terracotta; Abbey Church of St. Peter, Modena, Italy

after   *Virgin and Child with the Infant St. John*
1534   *the Baptist, Baptism* (of Christ), and *Christ with Angels*, for Church of S. Salvatore, Italy; terracotta; Galleria e Museo Estense, Modena, Italy

1535–40 *Christ on the Cross between Four Angels*, for Malavasi Altar; terracotta; Staatliche Museen, Berlin, Germany

after   *Christ in Martha's and Magdalen's Home*;
1540   terracotta; Church of St. Dominic, Modena, Italy

after   31 statues of saints and Old Testament
1541–   personages; terracotta; Abbey Church of
after   St. Benedict, San Benedetto Po, Mantua,
1559   Italy

before *Virgin and Child, Felicity, Benedict,* and

1543   *St. John the Evangelist*; terracotta; Abbey Church of St. John, Parma, Italy

1544–46 *Dead Christ with Joseph of Arimathea, St. Mary, St. John,* and two angels; terracotta; Abbey Church of St. Peter, Modena, Italy

1545   *Virgin Mary and Child with Cherubs*; terracotta; Monteorsello di Guiglia, Modena, Italy

ca. 1545 Bust of Christ; terracotta; Staatliche Museen, Berlin, Germany

after   Funerary monument with statues of *God*
1553   *the Father, Virgin Mary and Child,* and *Saints Geminiano, Peter, Paul,* and *Benedict*; terracotta; Abbey Church of St. Peter, Modena, Italy

Further Reading

Bonsanti, Giorgio, *Antonio Begarelli*, Modena, Italy: Panini, 1992

Draper, James, [review of Bonsanti's *Antonio Begarelli*], *The Burlington Magazine* 136 (1994)

Ferretti, Massimo, "In piazza e in museo: Intorno alla Madonna del Begarelli," in *Le raccolte d'arte del Museo Civico di Modena*, edited by Enrica Pagella, Modena, Italy: Panini, 1992

Lightbown, Ronald W., "Correggio and Begarelli: A Study in Correggio Criticism," *Art Bulletin* 46 (1964)

Weil-Garris Brandt, Kathleen, "Were This Clay but Marble . . .: A Reassessment of Emilian Terracotta Group Sculpture," in *Le arti a Bologna e in Emilia dal XVI al XVII secolo*, edited by Andrea Emiliani, Bologna: CLUEB, 1982

BELGIUM

See **Netherlands and Belgium**

RUDOLF BELLING 1886–1972 *German*

Raised in a bourgeois family, Rudolf Belling began various apprenticeships before he had his first contact with applied art as a modeler and molder in a decoration workshop. During this time Belling learned many techniques that he would find useful in his later work as a sculptor. Owing to this training, the borders between art and handicrafts were fluid for Belling, lending his work its unusual breadth. It also opened him to collaborations with artists from other genres and led him to play a decisive role in the Expressionists' movement toward *Gesamtkunstwerk* (total work of art).

In 1908 Belling established his independence with his own workshop and produced, among other works, decorative pieces for the director Max Reinhardt's theatrical productions. There, he enjoyed a fruitful collaboration with the set designer and painter Ernst Stern.

Belling first took part in an exhibition in 1914, displaying stage figurines molded by Belling and painted by Stern in the Great Berlin Art Exhibition (Grosser Berliner Kunstausstellung). Among Belling's first figures, which are only documented in photographs, was a figurine for one of the early films of Paul Wegener, *Der Golem*, from 1915. That same year Belling was called up for military duty, although he spent the following years in Berlin in the modeling department of an air force squadron. He was also able to continue his artistic work in his studio in the College for the Visual Arts, where he had been a student of Peter Breuer since 1911/12. Belling produced several figural groups around 1916, most notably the dancing figures representing his confrontation with the works of Aleksander Porfirevich Archipenko and Umberto Boccioni. Belling had become acquainted with the artistic movements of his day exclusively through the exhibitions in the Berlin gallery Sturm. He met the Ukrainian Archipenko only in 1921, when the latter moved to Berlin.

Belling, along with Oswald Herzog and William Wauer, began in 1915 to move sculpture in Germany toward greater and greater abstraction, to the point of being nonrepresentational. He became preoccupied, both in theory and in practice, with the problems of sculpture being viewed in the round and the balanced treatment of spatial and physical volumes. His best-known work from this time under the influence of Expressionism is the *Dreiklang* (Triad) from 1919, a work executed in plaster that was presented for the first time in 1920 in the Grosser Berliner Kunstausstellung. Belling executed the sculpture in wood for exhibition in the National Gallery, Berlin, in 1924. In the same year the museum purchased this sculpture.

Along with various, in part decorative, commissioned works for the publisher Wolfgang Gurlitt, Belling and the architect Walter Würzbach came together for an extensive collaboration that could be called a *Gesamtkunstwerk*. The two designed a new interior for a place of entertainment in Berlin, the Scala. Belling designed the prismlike ceiling motif, as well as an elegant abstract fountain made of cement with brass spirals. He also developed an abstract mobile based on this work in concrete and bronze, which became a four-meter-high fountain for the Villa Goldstein in Berlin-Westend.

After his expressive and political works created immediately after World War I, such as the *Entwurf für ein Denkmal für die gefallenen der Berliner Universität* (1920; Monument Design for Those Fallen in War from Berlin University) and the sculpture *Geste Freiheit* (1920; Gesture of Faith), Belling entered a more Constructivist phase with the large fountain for the Villa Goldstein in 1922. *Sculpture 23*, created the

following year, is one of the artist's major works from this time, also indicating his stronger involvement with figural art.

Along with his artistic confrontation with abstraction, Belling took part in the exciting spirit of the 1920s through a great number of projects. He designed window mannequins, a radiator mascot for the automobile company, "Horch," and a gas station designed as sculptural architecture.

In the latter part of the 1920s, Belling collaborated extensively with the architects Bruno and Max Taut, for whose constructions he executed numerous sculptures and relief works for the printers' union and the Gesamtverband der Gewerkschaften (League of Unions). These works resonate stylistically with the Neue Sachlichkeit, although without denying their technoid character. While the double mask *Summation of the Character of the Architect Poelzig* from 1920 had remained his sole expressive work, Belling's work as a portraitist resumed with the image of *Richard Haertel* for the printers' union. The almost caricaturish image of the gallery owner Alfred Flechtheim from 1927 is an impressive study.

Appointed to the Academy of the Arts in 1931, Belling participated beginning in 1934 as a juror in its exhibition commission, but he refused to participate in exhibitions himself since the National Socialists, who took power in 1933, were defaming his art. The artist took the occasion of an individual exhibition in the Galerie Weyhe to travel to New York in 1935, but he did not immigrate and returned to Berlin. Through the mediation of the architect Hans Poelzig, he received an appointment to the art academy in Istanbul in 1936, finally leaving his homeland in 1937 under pressure from National Socialist politicians. That same year the National Socialists exhibited his *Triad* and *Head in Brass* from 1925 in their show of *Entartete Kunst* (Degenerate Art). Absurdly enough, Belling at the same time received an official invitation to participate in the state-sponsored Grosse Deutsche Kunstausstellung. From Turkey Belling selected the portrait statuette of Max Schmelling to be his contribution to the exhibition.

Belling remained in Turkey until 1966, where he carried out Classical figural works for public commissions. In his own works he continued his efforts to create balanced proportions between spatial and physical volumes. His partly figural, partly abstract works correspond in character to the mostly prettified art of the 1950s and 1960s. Belling also received public commissions for these works in Germany. His being awarded the *Bundesverdienstorden* (a federal medal of honor) and reinstatement into the Academy of Arts should be understood as conciliatory gestures to make up for the defamations from the National Socialist period. Belling made his essential contribution to German sculpture in the 1920s, as he tested the possibilities of abstraction in an expressive and technoid language of forms.

JOSEPHINE GABLER

See also **Archipenko, Alexander Porfirevich; Constructivism; Germany: 20th Century–Contemporary**

Biography

Born in Berlin, Germany, 26 August 1886. Studied modeling and forming; worked in a workshop for handicraft decoration; directed his own workshop from 1908; commissioned for stage and film sets; attended the Hochschule für Bildende Künste (College for the Visual Arts) in Berlin-Charlottenburg, under Peter Breuer, around 1911/12; first collaboration in an art exhibition, 1914; cofounder of the art association Novembergruppe (November Group), 1918; became a member of the Prussian Akademie der Künste (Academy of Arts), Berlin, 1931; traveled to New York, 1935; offered appointment at the Academy of Art, Istanbul, 1936, and moved there, 1937; forced to leave the Academy of Arts, Berlin; awarded the Bundesverdienstordens (a federal medal of honor) of the German Federal Republic, 1955; reinstated as member of the Academy of Arts, Berlin, 1956; returned to Germany from Turkey, 1966. Died in Krailling, Germany, 6 June 1972.

Selected Works

1919   *Dreiklang* (Triad); plaster (destroyed); wooden version: 1924; Nationalgalerie, Staatliche Museen zu Berlin Preußischer Kulturbesitz, Berlin, Germany
1921   *Organische Formen (Schreitender Mann)* (Organic forms [Man Stepping Forward]); silver-plated bronze; City Art Museum of St. Louis, Missouri, United States
1922   Fountain for the Villa Goldstein; concrete, bronze (destroyed)
1923   *Skulptur 23*; brass; Museum of Modern Art, New York City, United States
1927   Portrait of Alfred Flechtheim; bronze; Museum of Modern Art, New York City, United States
1929   Portrait statuette of Max Schmelling; bronze; Museum of Modern Art, New York City, United States
1930   *Miner*; cast iron (destroyed)

Further Reading

Heusinger von Waldegg, Joachim, "Rudolf Belling," in *German Expressionist Sculpture* (exhib. cat.), edited by Stephanie Barron, Chicago: University of Chicago Press, 1983

Hofmann, Helga Dorothea, *Rudolf Belling* (exhib. cat.), Munich: Galerie Wolfgang Ketterer, 1967
Nerdinger, Winfried, *Rudolf Belling und die Kunstströmungen in Berlin, 1918–1923*, Berlin: Deutscher Verlag für Kunstwissenschaft, 1981
Schmoll gen. Eisenwerth, J. Adolf, *Rudolf Belling*, St. Gallen, Switzerland: Erker-Verlag, 1971

HANS BELLMER 1902–1975 *German*

Hans Bellmer's work was closely associated with the Paris Surrealist group during the interwar period leading up to World War II. His Modernist-inflected photography, drawings, prints, and essays appeared in Surrealist journals and exhibitions, and his sexually explicit, even perverse, illustrations for the erotic literature penned by prominent members of the movement, such as Georges Bataille, Louis Aragon, and René Crevel, reflected the Surrealists' fascination with fantasy, absurdity, and what Sigmund Freud would describe in his analyses of infant sexuality as the "polymorphously perverse." Bellmer achieved his greatest notoriety with his so-called doll constructions of wood, metal, plaster, and papier mâché (*Die Puppe* or *La Poupée*). He sometimes decorated these mannequins—invariably coded as female—with seductive accoutrements such as veils, ribbons, lace socks, shoes, glass eyes, flowers, and even working light bulbs. Some dolls were disassembled and displayed in a pile of dismembered limbs, whereas others boasted impossible, and indeed dreadful, mutant physiognomies of multiple legs and pelvises that revolved around wooden spherical ball joints. Although Bellmer's dolls have been read as misogynistic expressions of sadistic and vaguely pedophiliac male fantasies, recently historians have begun to investigate his sculpture as a psychosocial attempt to critique authoritarianism.

Bellmer met George Grosz, John Heartfield, and their fellow Dadaists while studying mechanical drawing in Berlin in the 1920s. While employed as a book illustrator in the advertising business, Bellmer became increasingly drawn to the satirical and sometimes grotesque photomontage creations of the Dadaists. Many of the German Dadaists, with whom Bellmer was sympathetic, were attracted to the formal and conceptual relationships between photomontage and the dialectical critiques of modern life found in the writings of Karl Marx and V.I. Lenin and demonstrated in the jarring collages and photomontages of Hannah Höch, many of which featured playful critiques of advertising, gender, and industry.

Bellmer's aggressive three-dimensional experiments in photomontage fragmentation began in earnest with his building, manipulating, and photographing of somewhat realistic mannequins following the Nazi seizure of power in 1933. He claimed in interviews that

143

The Doll
© 2001 Artists Rights Society (ARS), New York, ADAGP, Paris

his constructions were derived from childhood memories of long hours spent playing with dolls in order to escape a tortured family life: his hated father, an avid member of the Nazi Party, brutally dominated his mother. Bellmer's dolls represented efforts to exorcise his childhood traumas; his imagination found "joy, exaltation, and fear" in the doll, he explained, despite the doll's "accommodating and limitless docility." He fantasized the body as a nearly unlimited constellation of erogenous zones, subject to the forces of psychic repression in what he termed "the physical unconscious" (see Taylor, 1996). Moreover, the dolls as objects also served a broader social function: by exploring the articulation of unspoken, often hidden, desire, the artist claimed to help "people come to terms with their instincts." The Surrealists' celebration, even veneration, of the vicissitudes of unconscious fantasies was tinged with the belief, however inaccurate, that the freeing of culturally prohibited desires and their representation (through erotic and pornographic literature, for instance) was socially revolutionary.

Bellmer staged and photographed his dolls in a way that described the visual conflicts between the dummies' animate and inanimate qualities, as well as the tension between the dolls' monstrous bodies and the mental associations and fantasies of the viewers. Ten of these photographs appeared with a brief text in a self-published portfolio called *Die Puppe* (The Doll, 1934) that Bellmer mailed to Surrealists André Breton and Paul Éluard in Paris. His timing was fortuitous, because although the Surrealists had been interested in mannequins—specifically the *femme-enfant*, the sexually provocative girl-woman who functioned as the primary Surrealist muse—since the 1920s, they had recently entered a phase of intense fascination with found and often anti-sculptural objects. The unresolved conflicts between subject/object and lust/dread in Bellmer's pictures engrossed the Surrealists, who immediately printed 18 of Bellmer's doll photographs in the December 1934 issue of *Minotaure* under the title "*Poupée, variations sur le montage*

d'une mineure articulée" (Doll, Variations on the Montage of an Articulated Minor).

Bellmer visited Paris and was energized by discussions he had while attending the daily Surrealist café meetings; by 1936 a translated version of Bellmer's book was available in France. Bellmer eventually moved to Paris in 1938, after years of being harassed by the Nazi party's reform of culture designed to target avant-garde artists who made what was considered *Entartete Kunst* (Degenerate Art). Throughout those years before the outbreak of World War II, Bellmer showed his doll sculptures—Breton called them "golems"—in Surrealist exhibitions in Tenerife, Paris, London, Tokyo, and Amsterdam.

After the war, Bellmer's dolls were featured in a number of solo exhibitions. He had an artistic and romantic relationship at the end of the 1940s with the important postwar Surrealist writer, feminist, philosopher, and Trotskyite Nora Mitrani, a Romanian Jew whose mother died in Auschwitz during the Nazi occupation of Paris. In addition to the lingering specters of fascist violence, Bellmer's assemblages, photographs, and drawings with Mitrani strongly reacted against not only the Nazi preference for Classical bodies, but also the commercialized images of ideal feminine beauty being circulated in Paris at that time.

From 1957 to 1970 Bellmer lived and worked with the German Surrealist poet Unica Zürn, who had been diagnosed as a schizophrenic. Bellmer shared the Surrealist absorption with mental illness, primarily hysteria, schizophrenia, and the studies and photographs of the French neurophysiologist Jean-Martin Charcot. The artist's relationship with Zürn thus revealed a macabre quality in that creativity was romantically aligned with mental suffering, even pathology. One of their first collaborations was a series of sadomasochistic black-and-white photographs titled *Unica ligotée* (Unica Bound). Zürn was posed tightly bound with a tangle of twine, cord, and wire crisscrossing her naked body in such a way that she ceased to resemble a human being. Only after careful inspection of the amorphous and abstracted

144

image, which appeared on the cover of the journal *Le Surréalisme même* in the fall of 1958, did the viewer recognize the trussed back and buttocks of an animalistic Zürn huddled on a mattress. Bellmer's morphological "sculpting" of Zürn's flesh into a bleakly inhuman mass in this photograph read like an apotheosis of the frighteningly cruel deconstruction of the female form that began with his life-size wood and plaster dolls in Berlin in the mid 1930s.

In their own time, the Surrealists perceived Bellmer's work as a marvelous exploration of female love and eroticism, a view that was reexamined by postwar critics as a complex, unstable, and provocative sign for unconscious mental processes including dream and fantasy images. Whether Bellmer's art allures, disturbs, or outrages, it has had a clear impact on a psychoanalytic understanding of the human mind.

DON LACOSS

See also **Surrealist Sculpture**

Biography

Born in Kattowitz, Germany (now Katowice, Poland), 13 March 1902. Attended Technische Hochschule, Berlin, 1923, but joined Dada circles and was influenced by George Grosz; worked in advertising and book illustration; began experiments in photomontage after Nazis seized power in 1933; included in Surrealist circles, 1935; published *La Poupée*, 1936; contributed to Surrealist exhibitions, late 1930s; exhibited at *Exposition Internationale du Surréalisme* at Galerie Beaux-Arts, Paris, 1938; moved to Paris after being labeled degenerate artist by Nazis, 1938; produced variations of his *Doll* throughout his career. Died in Paris, France, 24 February 1975.

Selected Works

1933   *Poupée*; wood, metal, plaster (destroyed)
1935   *Poupée*; wood, hair, cloth, leather; Musée Nationale d'Art Moderne, Centre Georges Pompidou, Paris, France
1936   *Poupée*; aluminum; Tate Gallery, London, England

Further Reading

Bellmer, Hans, "*Poupée, variations sur le montage d'une mineure articulée* (Doll, Variations on the Montage of an Articulated Minor)," *Minotaure* 6 (winter, 1934–35) 30–31
Bellmer, Hans, *Hans Bellmer: Photographe*, Paris: Centre Georges Pompidou, 1983
Burns, Thom, "The Double-Bladed Pelvis," *Arsenal: Surrealist Subversion* 3 (spring 1976)

Les dessins de Hans Bellmer, Paris: Denoel, 1966; as *Hans Bellmer*, edited by Alex Grall, London: Academy Editions, 1972
Foster, Hal, *Compulsive Beauty*, Cambridge, Massachusetts: MIT Press, 1993
Krauss, Rosalind E., *The Optical Unconscious*, Cambridge, Massachusetts: MIT Press, 1993
Lichtenstein, Therese, *Behind Closed Doors: The Art of Hans Bellmer*, Berkeley: University of California Press, and New York: International Center of Photography, 2001
Livingston, Jane, Dawn Ades, and Rosalind Krauss, *L'Amour fou: Photography and Surrealism*, New York: Abbeville Press, 2002
Suleiman, Susan Rubin, *Subversive Intent: Gender, Politics, and the Avant-Garde*, Cambridge, Massachusetts: Harvard University Press, 1990
Taylor, Sue, *Hans Bellmer: The Anatomy of Anxiety*, Cambridge, Massachusetts: MIT Press, 2000
Taylor, Sue, "Hans Bellmer in The Art Institute of Chicago: The Wandering Libido and the Hysterical Body," *Museum Studies*, vol. 22, Chicago, Illinois: The Art Institute of Chicago, 1996
Webb, Peter, and Robert Short, *Hans Bellmer*, London and New York: Quartet, 1985

BELVEDERE TORSO
Apollonios of Athens (1st century)
middle of 1st century BCE
Parian marble
h. 1.59 m
Vatican Museums, Rome, Italy

The *Belvedere Torso* represents an over-life-size, exceptionally muscular man seated on a rock covered by a panther skin. The sculpture is missing its head, upper chest, arms, lower half of each leg, and buttocks; the rock is restored on the lower rear section, but the animal skin is well preserved, retaining paws, tail, and head. The legs, buttocks, and possibly the arms of the torso were attached in antiquity separately, as evidenced by the dowel holes and several unaltered joining surfaces (see Säflund, 1976).

The *Belvedere Torso* is signed by the Athenian artist Apollonios, son of Nestor, on the base between the figure's legs. Signatures are found on some sculptures created by copyists who were looking back to Greek masters during the Roman imperial period. Other examples of signatures appear on the Farnese *Hercules* from the Baths of Caracalla in Rome and the Scylla Group found in Emperor Tiberius's Villa at Sperlonga, Italy (see Robertson, 1975). In light of the inscription, Apollonios was erroneously identified as the artist of the bronze *Terme Boxer* in Rome on the basis of a comparable but barely legible inscription on the boxer's fist-thong (a kind of fingerless glove). The association between the two works has been based on the differences, rather than the similarities. The *Terme*

Boxer displays the physique of a well-trained athlete, and in contrast, the *Belvedere Torso* is the embodiment of a powerful and moving heroic nude with superhuman muscular development. The *Belvedere Torso* is stylistically associated with the Laocoön and the sculptural frieze from the Altar of Zeus from Pergamon, which places the *Belvedere Torso* stylistically in the Hellenistic Baroque period.

No known source from Antiquity directly mentions the *Belvedere Torso* or the artist. Instead, the *Belvedere Torso* became a famed icon through its reincarnation during the Renaissance in Rome. The sculpture was first documented about 1432–35 as part of the collection of Cardinal Prospero Colonna. In 1496–1503 the sculpture was documented as part of the collection of the sculptor Andrea Bregno. Documents placed the *Belvedere Torso* in the Vatican in 1532, where it was installed in the sculpture court of the Belvedere, from which the torso takes its name. The work was moved to a gallery adjoining the sculpture court in the early 18th century and was placed in the newly built Pio-Clementino Museum in the 1770s. In 1797 the *Belvedere Torso* was removed to Paris under the Treaty of Tolentino and was displayed with other revered works of ancient art, including the Laocoön and the *Apollo Belvedere*, until their return to the Vatican in 1816.

Myths have circulated about the original location of the *Belvedere Torso;* the Campo di Fiori and the Baths of Caracalla in Rome have been cited as possible original locations (see Andrén, 1952). Other theories propose that it stood in the Baths of Constantine or that it came from Monte Cavallo (Quirinal Hill) in Rome (see Bober and Rubinstein, 1986).

Ancient sculptures found during the Renaissance often accumulated meaning linked closely to the people who took an interest in it. Appreciation for the *Belvedere Torso* came primarily from academics and artists, including Michelangelo Buonarroti. Michelangelo's interest in the *Belvedere Torso* was expressed in the male nudes found on the Sistine Chapel ceiling, as well as in the figure of *Day* in the Medici Chapel in the Church of San Lorenzo, Florence (see Säflund, 1976). Drawings were made of the *Belvedere Torso* from the Renaissance forward. The drawings provide information regarding the sculpture's location before and after entering the Vatican collection (see Bober and Rubinstein, 1986). In addition to drawings, plaster casts were made of the *Belvedere Torso*, but these casts were mainly for students' use at art academies rather than for display in private collections; this was no doubt attributable to the fragmentary condition of the sculpture, which did not appeal to the taste of most collectors. In subsequent centuries, the *Belvedere Torso* was appropriated by artists as the allegory of the art of sculpture and drawing and can be seen

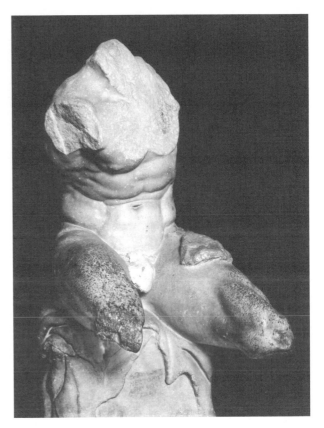

Belvedere Torso
© Alinari / Art Resource, NY

in various media (see Haskell and Penny, 1981; Wünsche, 1998).

A significant feature of the *Belvedere Torso* is that it remained in a fragmentary state. It was common practice during the Renaissance to restore fragments of ancient art to their "original" wholeness, such as the Laocoön. It is believed that the *Belvedere Torso* remained unrestored because of the sentiments of Michelangelo, who was quoted as saying that he was unqualified to restore the ancient fragment by Apollonios (see Fiorio, 1992). Michelangelo's opinion on restoring ancient art seemed to have been on a case-by-case basis, taking into consideration the amount of restoration necessary. Thus leaving a fragment such as the *Belvedere Torso* untouched was a show of respect for the beauty of the authentic, although fragmentary, object and no doubt lent importance to Michelangelo's own "unfinished" works (see Fiorio, 1992).

Since the Renaissance, theoretical reconstructions have been made to restore the fragment. Early designs identified the figure as Hercules Epitrapezios holding a club in one hand and a wine cup in the other. The *Belvedere Torso* was often identified as a Hercules because of the animal skin on which he sits, initially identified as a lion skin, rather than panther. Recent interpretations of the *Belvedere Torso* based on comparisons with images preserved in vase painting, gems, and silver include Philoctetes on the island of Lemnos (see Andrén, 1952); the satyr Marsyas with his arms bound behind him (see Säflund, 1976); Marsyas playing the pipes, possibly opposite a lyre-playing Apollo (see Robertson, 1975); Marsyas teaching Olympos to play the flute (see Smith, 1991; Wünsche, 1998); and a pensive Ajax with his right elbow poised on his right leg (see Wünsche, 1998).

LINDA ANN NOLAN

See also **Apollo Belvedere; Artemision Zeus (Poseidon); Canova, Antonio; Greece, Ancient;** *Laocoön and His Sons;* **Michelangelo (Buonarroti); Pergamon Altar**

Further Reading

Andrén, Arvid, "Il torso del Belvedere," *Opuscula Archaeologica* 7 (1952)

Bober, Phyllis Pray, and Ruth Rubinstein, *Renaissance Artists and Antique Sculpture: A Handbook of Sources*, London: Miller, and Oxford: Oxford University Press, 1986

Brummer, Hans Henrik, *The Statue Court in the Vatican Belvedere*, Stockholm: Almqvist and Wiksell, 1970

Daltrop, Georg, "The Belvedere Torso," in *The Vatican Collection: The Papacy and Art*, New York: The Metropolitan Museum of Art, 1982

Fiorio, Maria Teresa, "Broken Sculpture: Michelangelo and the Aesthetic of the Fragment," in *The Genius of the Sculptor in Michelangelo's Work* (exhib. cat.), Montreal, Quebec: Montreal Museum of Fine Arts, 1992

Haskell, Francis, and Nicholas Penny, *Taste and the Antique: The Lure of Classical Sculpture, 1500–1900*, New Haven, Connecticut: Yale University Press, 1981

Robertson, Martin, *A History of Greek Art*, 2 vols., London: Cambridge University Press, 1975

Säflund, Gösta, "The Belvedere Torso," *Opuscula Romana* 11/6 (1976)

Smith, R.R.R., *Hellenistic Sculpture*, New York: Thames and Hudson, 1991

Stewart, Andrew, *Greek Sculpture: An Exploration*, 2 vols., New Haven, Connecticut: Yale University Press, 1990

Weis, Anne, "Marsyas I," in *Lexicon Iconographicum Mythologiae Classicae*, vol. 6, Zurich: Artemis, 1992

Winner, Matthias, Bernard Andreae, and Carlo Pietrangeli, editors, *Il Cortile delle Statue; Der Statuenhof des Belvedere im Vatikan*, Mainz, Germany: Von Zabern, 1998

Wünsche, Raimund, *Il torso del Belvedere: Da Aiace a Rodin* (exhib. cat.), Vatican City: Direzione Generale Monumenti Musei e Gallerie Pontificie, 1998

BENEDETTO DA MAIANO 1441–1497

Italian

Benedetto di Lionardo di Antonio, known as Benedetto da Maiano after the parish near Florence where his family had once lived, was among the outstanding Florentine woodworkers and stone sculptors in the last decades of the quattrocento, active in decorative and figural commissions for discerning clients in Florence and elsewhere.

Documents indicate that Benedetto was born in 1441. When he died at age 56, his studio contained numerous preliminary models and unfinished commissions, some of which provide important documentation of contemporary studio practice. The renown that he enjoyed for his innate talent and technical virtuosity has been kept alive both by the accessibility of noteworthy creations such as the historiated marble pulpit in the Church of Santa Croce, Florence, and by frequent references to his work in treatises and guidebooks. Nevertheless, as in the case of some of his important peers, interest in his career gradually languished. Benedetto's achievements have recently won renewed recognition due to conferences commemorating the da Maiano family on the occasion of the 500th anniversary (1990) of the death of his eldest brother, Giuliano (a prominent woodworker and architect); close studies of his preliminary models; important reattributions, such as the *Madonna of the Snow* and *Saint Catherine of Alexandria* (probably parts of a larger altarpiece) [presently in the parochial church of Santa Maria Assunta e Sant'Elia,] Terranova Sappo Minulio; and reconsideration of the possibility that the young Michelangelo participated in his workshop.

Benedetto came from a family of artisans who lived in the sparsely populated parish of San Martino a Maiano, very near Florence, in the 1420s and early 1430s. Giovanni, Benedetto's uncle and the eldest of three brothers, worked in Florence as a stoneworker by the early 1420s. From 1432 he and his brothers Attaviano and Lionardo (Benedetto's father) supplied most of the dressed and carved stone for ambitious building campaigns at the Badia and its dependency at Campora (south of Florence). Attaviano, the second brother, established a stonecutting workshop at Piazza San Giovanni in Florence by 1438. Lionardo (Nardo) was matriculated in the Florentine carpenters' guild in 1439 and became a woodworker specializing in the manufacture of secular and ecclesiastical furniture. In 1454 or 1455 he opened a woodworking shop in Via de' Servi in Florence, and by 1459 his eldest son, Giuliano, ran this profitable business.

Benedetto, Lionardo's youngest son, first assisted his brother Giuliano as a woodworker and then worked at this trade independently, first named as such in payments dated January 1469 for the carved wooden frame (lost) for the processional standard of the Florentine Boys' Confraternity of the Purification of the Virgin and of Saint Zenobius. He had earned a reputation for the high quality of his work by 1473, when he displayed a costly, highly praised *lettuccio* (a chest combined with a tall backrest and entablature, used as a daybed) commissioned by the Florentine merchant-banker Filippo di Matteo Strozzi as a gift for the king of Naples, Ferrante I. This lost settle may have been decorated with the [instarsia (lost) after the] *Tavola Strozzi*, attributed to Franceso Rosselli (Museo della Certosa di San Martino, Naples).

Details of Benedetto's early education and artistic training are unknown. He probably learned woodworking from his father or his brother Giuliano, whom he helped complete the complex, figurated intarsias for the Florentine cathedral's north sacristy (commissioned 1463 and 1465). Benedetto's early training in stone carving may have been under his uncle Attaviano. On the basis of stylistic affinities, scholars suggest an apprenticeship with Antonio Rossellino. Vasari's claim that Benedetto first worked in marble at the Hungarian court of Matthias Corvinus remains unsubstantiated.

In 1473 Benedetto traveled briefly to Rome and Naples, matriculated as a *scarpellatore* (stonecutter) in the Florentine Guild of Masters of Stone and of Wood, and opened a stonecarving shop near Giuliano's in Via de' Servi. In 1474 he completed his earliest signed and dated work, the marble bust of Pietro Mellini. This displays the same rigorous physiognomic detail of his later portraits, recalling the verism of Roman republican portraits. It may reflect Benedetto's documented trip to Rome of the previous year. Around this time he carved the narrative reliefs for the altar tomb of the Blessed Fina in the Collegiate Church at San Gimignano. In their apparent simplicity they correspond to the frescoes painted in the same chapel by Domenico del Ghirlandaio, Benedetto's next-door neighbor from 1457 to 1465. Shortly thereafter Benedetto may have begun the Santa Croce pulpit, which is among his masterpieces.

Although he declared his preference for carving marble in 1473, Benedetto continued working in wood, in his last years creating the large, somber crucifix now on the high altar of the Florentine cathedral. Contrary to Vasari's report, he did not complete the wooden *Magdalen* begun by Desiderio da Settignano. Benedetto also worked in clay and plaster, designed a never-realized facade of the Florentine cathedral in 1490 or early 1491, and made a model (lost) for the Talducci Chapel (Church of Santa Trinità, Prato) by 1496. Documents do not support Vasari's contention that he created a model of Palazzo Strozzi in Florence, only receiving payments (1490–95) for wooden models (lost) of iron fittings and for small stone corbels.

Benedetto's figural style evolved from the static forms of his early works (Blessed Fina monument), to the dynamism and rhythmical coherence of the Annunciation Altar at Naples and the heightened elegance of the San Bartolo monument at San Gimignano. He

evidently received many commissions through his well-traveled brother Giuliano. Like comparable masters in Florence, he probably maintained only a small permanent staff, collaborating with other artisans as work demanded. Upon his death, his young associate, the stone-carver Lionardo del Tasso (1465–1500), was consigned his workshop. A number of Benedetto's compositions, including the beautiful Naples *Annunciation*, were copied and disseminated in various media by artists such as the Florentine sculptor Benedetto Buglioni. Although Benedetto's son Giovanni probably did not apprentice with him, he did practice the same profession in England, where he died in 1543. Many of Benedetto's possessions, including part of a *Coronation*, a *Saint Sebastian*, and a *Madonna and Child*, eventually went by bequest to the Confraternity of Santa Maria del Bigallo in Florence.

VIRGINIA BUDNY

See also **Desiderio da Settignano; Pulpit**

Biography

Born probably in the parish of San Piero Maggiore outside the walls of Florence, Italy, 1441. Youngest son of a carpenter; nephew and cousin of stoneworkers. Early education and training unknown; may have learned fundamentals of wood and stone carving from family; assisted in fraternal woodworking shop by 1467; documented as independent woodworker and submitted joint tax return as Florentine citizen with brothers Giuliano and Giovanni (both woodworkers), 1469; traveled for business to Rome and Naples, matriculated in Florentine Guild of the Masters of Stone and of Wood, and opened stone-carving workshop in Florence, 1473; married sister-in-law of Florentine painter Cosimo Rosselli, 1484; made last will and testament and traveled again to Naples, 1492. Died in Florence, Italy, 24 May 1497.

Selected Works

1472–77 Blessed Fina monument; gilt marble; Collegiate Church, San Gimignano, Italy

1474 Bust of Pietro Mellini; marble; Museo Nazionale del Bargello, Florence, Italy

1475 Bust of Filippo Strozzi; terracotta model (formerly polychromed); Skulpturensammlung, Staatliche Museen, Berlin, Preußischer Kulturbesitz, Germany; marble; Musée du Louvre, Paris, France

1476–81 Doorframes with *Justice*, *St. John the Baptist*, and putti with candelabra and garlands for portal between the *Sala* dell'Udienza (audience chamber of the priors) and the *Sala dei Gigli* (antechamber); marble (originally gilt), porphyry; Palazzo Vecchio, Florence, Italy

ca. late 1470s– 1487 Pulpit; white and red marble, stone, glass tesserae, gilding, traces of polychromy; Church of Santa Croce, Florence, Italy

ca. 1489–91 Annunciation Altar; marble; Correale di Terranova Chapel, Church of Sant'Anna dei Lombardi (formerly Santa Maria di Monteoliveto), Naples, Italy; detached *Angel*; marble, Johnson Collection, Philadelphia Museum of Art, Pennsylvania, United States

ca. 1489–91 *Madonna of the Snow* and *Saint Catherine of Alexandria*, for former nunnery of Santa Caterina, Terranova, Italy; marble; Parochial church of Santa Maria Assunta e Sant'Elia; Terranova Sappo Minulio (Reggio Calabria), Italy

1490s Crucifix; wood; Florence Cathedral, Italy

1490s *Saint Sebastian*; marble; Misericordia, Florence, Italy

1490s *Madonna and Child* (completed by Battista Lorenzi, 1575); marble; Misericordia, Florence, Italy

1492–94 San Bartolo monument; marble, gilding; Monastery Church of Sant'Agostino, San Gimignano, Italy

1494–95 King, bishop, and musicians, for (unfinished) *Coronation* for the king of Naples; marble; Museo Nazionale del Bargello, Florence, Italy

Further Reading

Brunetti, Giulia, "Benedetto di Leonardo, detto Benedetto da Maiano," in *Dizionario biografico degli italiani*, vol. 8, Rome: Istituto della Enciclopedia Italiana, 1966

Caglioti, Francesco, "Benedetto da Maiano e Bernardo Cennini nel dossale argenteo del Battistero fiorentino," in *Opere e giorni: Studi su mille anni di arte europea dedicati a Max Seidel*, edited by Klaus Bergdolt and Giorgio Bonsanti, Venice: Marsilio, 2001

Caglioti, Francesco, "Benedetto da Maiano," in *Italian Sculpture from the Gothic to the Baroque*, edited by Andrew Butterfield and Anthony Radcliffe, New York: Salander-O'Reilly and Florence: Galleria il Cartiglio, 2002

Caglioti, Francesco, "La scultura del Quattrocento e dei primi decenni del Cinquecento," in *Storia della Callabria nel Rinascinento: Le arti nella storia*, edited by Simonetta Valtieri, Rome: Gangemi, 2002

Caglioti, Francesco, and Giancarlo Gentilini, "Il quinto centenario di Benedetto da Maiano e alcuni marmi dell'artista in Calabria," *Bulletin de l'association des historiens de l'art italien* 3 (1996–97)

Carl, Doris, "Benedetto da Maiano," "Benedetto da Maiano (bottega di)," and "Benedetto da Maiano e bottega," in *Gio-*

vinezza di Michelangelo, edited by Kathleen Weil-Garris Brandt et al., Florence: Artificio Skira, 1999

Carl, Doris, "Die Madonna von Nicotera und ihre Kopien: Vier unerkannte Madonnenstatuen des Benedetto da Maiano in Kalabrien und Sizilien," *Mitteilungen des Kunsthistorischen Institutes in Florenz* 41/1–2 (1997)

Haines, Margaret, "Giuliano da Maiano capofamiglia e imprenditore," in *Giuliano e la bottega dei da Maiano*, edited by Daniela Lamberini, Marcello Lotti, and Roberto Lunardi, Florence: Octavo, 1994

Pope-Hennessy, John, *An Introduction to Italian Sculpture*, 4th edition, vol. 2, *Italian Renaissance Sculpture*, London: Phaidon 1996

Quinterio, Francesco, *Giuliano da Maiano*: "*Grandissimo domestico*," Rome: Officina, 1996

Radke, Gary M., "Maiano [Majano], da: Benedetto da Maiano [Benedetto di Leonardo]," in *The Dictionary of Art*, edited by Jane Turner, New York: Grove, and London: Macmillan, 1996

Santoro, Fiorella Sricchia, "Tra Napoli e Firenze: Diomede Carafa, gli Strozzi e un celebre lettuccio," *Prospettiva* 100 (October 2000)

Vasari, Giorgio, *Le vite de' più eccellenti architetti, pittori, e scultori italiani*, 3 vols., Florence: Torrentino, 1550; 2nd edition, Florence: Appresso i Giunti, 1568; as *Lives of the Painters, Sculptors, and Architects*, 2 vols., translated by Gaston du C. de Vere (1912), edited by David Ekserdjian, New York: Knopf, and London: Campbell, 1996

PULPIT, CHURCH OF SANTA CROCE
Benedetto da Maiano (1441–1497)
ca. late 1470s–1487
white and red marble, glass tesserae, gilding, traces of polychromy
h. 3.3 m
Church of Santa Croce, Florence, Italy

Benedetto da Maiano's elaborate, restored pulpit remains in its original location in the Franciscan Church of Santa Croce, the family church of its 15th-century patron, Pietro di Francesco Mellini (1411–85). A banker and public official, as well as one of Benedetto's first major patrons, Mellini commissioned this impressive pulpit as a memorial above his tomb and essential church furnishing. It has long been praised as one of the notable Florentine ecclesiastical monuments. Francesco Albertini (*Memoriale* [1510]) cites it for its beauty, and both Giorgio Vasari (*Le vite* [1550, della città 1568]) and Francesco Bocchi (*Le Bellezze di Firenze* [1591]) describe it at length.

The contours of the pulpit and its wooden canopy cleverly mirror the geometric design in the church floor around the tomb cover. Whether the ensemble was originally envisaged as such or evolved in stages remains unknown. The only extant document directly related to the commission for the pulpit was recently discovered by Doris Carl (1994); it refers to an arbitration agreement of 1487 between Domenico Mellini,

Pietro's son and heir, and the men who made, transported, and erected the pulpit for Pietro—Benedetto, his brother Giuliano, and others ("et alios")—and concerns the final payment. The precise dates and circumstances of the inception and execution of the ensemble have not been established.

Church documents indicate that Mellini acquired the gravesite below the pulpit after 1439 (see Pines, 1985). Furthermore, a series of wills shows that by about 1470 he wished to be buried in his new tomb ("selpotura [sic] nuova") in Santa Croce. By 1471 the tomb was built, and in 1476 (last will) he reiterated his wish to be buried there (see Morselli, 1979). A codicil of 1485 mentions burial in his own completed tomb in Santa Croce. Nevertheless, Carl (1994) has questioned whether this tomb in fact is the one mentioned in Mellini's final will. According to her, Mellini only acquired the site after 1480, the year in which he planned to be buried in a new family tomb at the foot of his altar in the Church of San Pietro a Ripoli, near his country villa. Mellini, however, probably intended the much less prestigious tomb at Ripoli for relatives, not for himself, and had probably already initiated the pulpit for his own impressive tomb in Santa Croce.

Mellini's pulpit, supported by brackets, is attached to one of the octagonal piers of the nave arcade. Unique for this period, a stairway was hollowed out of the pier to give access to the pulpit. That seemingly hazardous enterprise was facilitated by Mellini's important connections with Santa Croce (he was a works administrator in 1472). On each of the pulpit's five sides, enframed reliefs depict four canonical scenes from the life of Saint Francis, illustrating the legitimacy of his rule, his order's mission, his perfect imitation of the Crucified Christ, and his sanctity, as well as an unusual scene of a Franciscan martyrdom in which the saint figures as intercessor. These reliefs appear to follow a chronological sequence from left to right: the first scene, thought by Bocchi to represent the confirmation of the rule by Pope Honorius III (1223), probably represents the sanction of the rule by Pope Innocent III (1209/1210). In that case, the next three episodes proceed chronologically, from the trial by fire (1219/1220) to the stigmatization (1224) to a scene combining three closely related episodes: the funeral of St. Francis, the ascent of his soul to heaven, and the confirmation of the stigmata by the learned knight Jerome (1226). The fifth relief, said by Bocchi to depict the beheading of five Franciscan protomartyrs (1220), may show St. Anthony of Padua witnessing the martyrdom of seven Franciscans, while in the background he receives the habit. Yet St. Anthony only became a Franciscan after seeing the remains of five protomartyrs killed in 1220, and not those of seven martyrs of 1227. This disparity

occurs in a 13th-century account of the seven Franciscans who had traveled from Tuscany to Ceuta (a codex from Santa Croce, Biblioteca Medicea Laurenziana, Florence); it is also found in the prototype for Benedetto's relief, a trecento panel by Taddeo Gaddi from the wardrobe of the sacristy of Santa Croce (now Galleria dell'Accademia, Florence). Carl follows Bocchi (see Carl, 1994 and 1995). Her date of 1481 for the commencement of the pulpit depends on Mellini's acquisition of the tomb at Ripoli in 1480 and the canonization of the five protomartyrs by Pope Sixtus IV in the following year. Stylistic analysis of the reliefs, however, suggests a date closer to the time of the Blessed Fina Monument of 1472–77.

Benedetto's role in the design, execution, and installation of the ensemble must be reconstructed. Presumably, his brother Giuliano, architect-in-chief of the Florentine cathedral, oversaw the tunneling of the pier (a task credited by Vasari to Benedetto) and helped design the pulpit's structure. Its five sides may symbolize the five wounds of the stigmata received by St. Francis, founder of the preaching order that built Santa Croce and name saint of Mellini's father. Benedetto was doubtless responsible for designing the decoration

Bust of Pietro di Francesco Mellini, from the Pulpit, Church of Santa Croce, Florence
© Scala / Art Resource, NY

of the pulpit according to a program including its ornament and historiated reliefs. The first is based on an antique vocabulary transformed by Donatello and invested with Christian meaning. The historiated reliefs echo the narrative clarity of the compositions of the same episodes in two abbreviated trecento cycles of St. Francis's life in Santa Croce: Giotto's frescoes in its Bardi Chapel (the first chapel to the right of the choir) and Taddeo Gaddi's panel paintings, now dispersed, for its sacristy.

Although the terracotta model of the pulpit listed in a posthumous inventory of Benedetto's studio is lost, four of the six recorded models for the figural reliefs survive (three in the Victoria and Albert Museum, London, one in the Staatliche Museen, Berlin. The subject of the Berlin relief, omitted from the pulpit, includes three related episodes: Pope Innocent III's rejection of Francis and his two dreams about the young saint. Benedetto made the extant models by constructing scenes inside molded borders, shaping individual figures and setting them into the scenes, and freely incising details into the wet clay. The abundant compositions and the elegant freedom of his modeling are Ghibertian. Benedetto designed the deeply undercut figures from the point of view of the spectator who circumnavigates the pulpit at pavement level. He initiated subtle changes when translating the compositions into marble, projecting the reliefs beyond their frames into the viewer's world, revising the turn of a head or limb to enhance overall movement, and introducing small details, carved with the same great care and precision as in the portrait bust of his patron dated 1474. The style of these reliefs leads to the Naples *Annunciation*, where the broad forms of the figures and the suave rhythms of the drapery announce the High Renaissance.

VIRGINIA BUDNY

See also **Pulpit**

Further Reading

Bocchi, Francesco, *Le bellezze della città di Fiorenza*, Florence, 1591; reprint edition, Farnborough: Gregg, 1971

Boucher, Bruce, editor, *Earth and Fire: Italian Terracotta Sculpture from Donatello to Canova*, New Haven and London: Yale University Press, 2001

Caglioti, Francesco, and Carlo Lalli, "Pulpito," *OPD restauro* 12 (2000)

Carl, Doris, "Il pergamo di Benedetto da Maiano in Santa Croce a Firenze," in *Giuliano e la bottega dei da Maiano*, edited by Daniela Lamberini, Marcello Lotti, and Roberto Lunardi, Florence: Octavo, 1994

Carl, Doris, "Franziskanischer Märtyrerkult als Kreuzzugspropaganda an der Kanzel von Benedeto da Maiano in Santa Croce in Florenz," *Mitteilungen des Kunsthistorischen Institutes in Florenz* 39/1 (1995)

Morselli, Piero, "Corpus of Tuscan Pulpits, 1400–1550," Ph.D. diss., University of Pittsburgh, 1979

Pines, Doralynn Schlossman, "The Tomb Slabs of Santa Croce: A New 'Sepoltuario,'" Ph.D. diss., Columbia University, 1985

Radke, Gary M., "Benedetto da Maiano and the Use of Full Scale Preparatory Models in the Quattrocento," in *Verrocchio and Late Quattrocento Italian Sculpture*, edited by Stephen Bule et al., Florence: Casa Editrice le Lettere, 1992

Radke, Gary M., "Geometria e misura nel pulpito di Santa Croce," in *Giuliano e la bottega dei da Maiano*, edited by Daniela Lamberini, Marcello Lotti, and Roberto Lunardi, Florence: Octavo, 1994

BENZI, MASSIMILIANO SOLDANI

See **Soldani Benzi, Massimiliano**

SARAH BERNHARDT 1844–1923 *French*

The great actress Sarah Bernhardt was also an accomplished sculptor whose work received considerable notice during her lifetime. From an early age, Bernhardt exhibited a keen ability in drawing and painting, and at one point, she debated whether she would make a career as an actress or as a painter. In 1860, when she was only 16 years old, she entered a painting, *The Champs Elysées in Winter*, in an exhibition at the Académie Colombier. The painting won first prize and praise in the *Mercure de Paris*.

Bernhardt did not attempt sculpture until the early 1870s, when she felt underemployed by the Comédie Française and needed more outlets for her considerable creative energy. She studied with Roland Mathieu Meusnier, a popular academic sculptor who specialized in narrative and public monument-type works, and she followed classes in anatomy at the École Pratique de Médecine. Bernhardt established a studio at 11 boulevard de Clichy in Montmartre, which she densely and eclectically filled with furniture, wall hangings, and objets d'art, and where she received visitors for tea each day at 5:00 P.M. This artistically decorated environment became a meeting place for friends, among them some of the leading intellectuals, artists, and politicians of the day. The studio, in its decor and function as a place for artistic production as well as a social meeting ground, was similar to the famous studio of the American Aesthetic-Movement of the painter William Merritt Chase. Chase established his studio in the Tenth Street Studio Building in New York City in 1878, shortly after his return from a sojourn as an art student in Germany.

Bernhardt's first success as a sculptor came when she won an honorable mention for *Après la tempête* (After the Storm, 1876) at the Salon of 1876. This dramatically rendered group, which shows a grief-stricken grandmother holding her dead grandson, recalls Michelangelo's earliest *Pietà* (1498–1500; St. Peter's Basilica, Rome). Bernhardt's sculpture is based on an event she had learned about while vacationing in Brittany. The highly dramatic expression of sorrow and disbelief on the grandmother's face, the limp corpse of the boy who had drowned at sea, and the skillful rendering of textures place this piece comfortably in the 19th-century academic tradition, which highly prized the ability of the artist to render textures and human emotions. The plaster model of *Après la tempête* that was submitted to the Salon was later cast in bronze. The artist also carved two smaller versions of the piece in marble.

Bernhardt was highly skilled in both modeling and carving. Her marble relief bust, *Ophelia*, was exhibited at the Columbian Exposition in Chicago in 1893. In this carving of William Shakespeare's dead heroine, only Ophelia's head and right breast are above the water in which she has drowned. Her left arm and breast are barely covered by the water that swirls around her head and carries with it loose strands of hair. Textures are skillfully rendered, and the effect is masterful.

Bernhardt's sculpture of Ophelia reflects the preoccupation with sickness and death as an aesthetic attribute in women during the second half of the 19th century. Bernhardt, who herself was thin, frail, and sickly, especially in her youth, was famous for her death scenes on stage, and one of her most famous portrayals was the dying Marguerite Gautier in Alexandre Dumas's *La Dame aux camélias*, on which a popular opera of the period, Giuseppe Verdi's *La Traviata* (1853), was based. Ophelia's beautiful corpse is also the subject of Pre-Raphaelite John Everett Millais's painting of 1852 (Tate Gallery, London), and Bernhardt's *Ophelia* recalls this earlier rendition.

Bernhardt was highly skilled at capturing human likeness and mood, and she produced numerous portraits, many of which were special commissions. Her portrait in bronze of the playwright Victorien Sardou shows the author deep in thought and his upper torso emerging from an amorphous area that includes a quill pen and two dramatically rendered female heads. A portrait bust of Bernhardt, which Jean-Léon Gérôme executed in polychromed marble around 1896 (Musée d'Orsay, Paris), shares similarities with Bernhardt's bust of Sardou. In his portrait of Bernhardt, Gérôme incorporated the figure of the muse of tragedy and a group of genii; however, these assisting figures are not as successfully integrated with the whole as those in Bernhardt's bust of Sardou. This may indicate that the idea for the assisting figures in Gérôme's portrait of Bernhardt did not originate with him, but rather was

a suggestion of Bernhardt's that the sculptor halfheartedly implemented.

Some scholars consider Bernhardt's most important sculpture to be *Encrier fantastique* (Fantastic Inkwell), which is in the form of a sphinx whose head is a self-portrait of the artist. The sphinx has the wings of a bat and the tail of a fish, and her paws hold the well from which emerges a horned skull. Ram's horns decorate the sides of the well, and the masks of tragedy and comedy serve as epaulets on the actress's shoulders. A place for the quill pen is reserved in Bernhardt's coiffure at the back of her head.

This enigmatic self-portrait recalls the sphinxes in the paintings of Gustave Moreau (for example, his *Oedipus and the Sphinx*, 1864; Metropolitan Museum of Art, New York City), with whose work Bernhardt would have been familiar. The suggestive character of the various elements making up the design of the inkwell evokes the mysterious works of the Symbolist movement, which came to the fore in the mid 1880s. Most intriguingly, the inkwell recalls the small-scale functional objects with esoteric figural decoration, such as inkstands and lamps, by the Italian Renaissance sculptor Andrea Riccio. The sphinx with a mask forms part of the decorative scheme in both Riccio's Paschal candelabrum (1507–15) in the Basilica of Sant'-Antonio in Padua, Italy, and his oil lamp known as the *Cadogan Lamp* (1507–10), now in the collection of the Victoria and Albert Museum, London. Possibly Bernhardt knew Riccio's work. Finally, the inkwell shares similarities with jewelry designs in the form of insects, plants, or animals with female heads by the Art Nouveau artist René Lalique, who opened a workshop in Paris in 1885 and from whom Bernhardt commissioned works.

Bernhardt's keen understanding of the aesthetic impulses of the period in which she lived was unerring. She was famous for the serpentine line of her posture and movement while acting on the stage and in everyday life. This attribute both presaged and embodied the undulating line of the Art Nouveau aesthetic at the end of the 19th century. Bernhardt's association with Art Nouveau is further reinforced with some small, decorative figures of plants and animals that she made in the 1890s. These objects were cast in metal for exhibition at the Exposition Universelle in Paris in 1900.

Bernhardt continued to model in clay or plaster until the end of her life. About 50 of her sculptures have been documented, and approximately 25 of these have been located. She was a highly skilled, dedicated, and creative sculptor, whose body of work has yet to be documented fully or studied in depth.

GINA ALEXANDER GRANGER

See also **Riccio (Andrea Briosco)**

Biography

Born in Paris, France, 22/23 October 1844. Began acting studies in 1860 at Conservatory of the Comédie Française; graduated from Conservatory, 1862, and embarked on an acting career; began to sculpt, 1872; exhibited works at annual Paris Salon, 1874–76, 1878–81, 1885–86; received silver medal for *Aprés la tempête*, Paris Salon, 1876; exhibited paintings and sculpture at Exposition Universelle, Paris, 1878; while on acting tour in London, exhibited 10 sculptures and 16 paintings at William Russell Galleries, Piccadilly Circus, 1879; during tour of United States and Canada, presented exhibitions of paintings and sculptures at Union League, New York City, and in Philadelphia, 1880–81; exhibited sculpture *Ophelia* at Columbian Exposition, Chicago, 1893; exhibited group of sculptures at the Exposition Universelle in Paris, 1900. Awarded title of Chevalier of the Legion of Honor in recognition of achievements as an actress, 1914. Died in Paris, France, 26 March 1923.

Selected Works

1875	*Le chant*; marble; facade of Casino, Monte Carlo, France
1876	*Après la tempête* (After the Storm); bronze with brown patina; private collection
ca. 1876	Bust of Victorien Sardou; bronze; Musée du Petit Palais, Paris, France
1877	*Jester*; marble; private collection
1878	Bust of Louise Abbéma; marble; Musée d'Orsay, Paris, France
1880	*Encrier fantastique* (Fantastic Inkwell); bronze; multiple casts, including Museum of Fine Arts, Boston, Massachusetts, United States; private collection, Paris, France
1881	*Ophelia*; marble; Royal Theater, Copenhagen, Denmark
1890s	*Sea Plants with Strange Incrustations* (two from a larger group); bronze; private collection, Paris, France

Further Reading

Bernhardt, Sarah, *Ma double vie: Mémoires de Sarah Bernhardt*, Paris: Charpentier et Fasquelle, 1907; as *My Double Life: The Memoirs of Sarah Bernhardt*, translated by Victoria Tietze Larson, Albany: State University of New York, 1999

Brandon, Ruth, *Being Divine: A Biography of Sarah Bernhardt*, London: Secker and Warburg, 1991

Gaze, Delia, editor, *Dictionary of Women Artists*, 2 vols., London and Chicago: Fitzroy Dearborn Publishers, 1996; see especially vol. 1

Hahn, Reynaldo, *La grande Sarah, Souvenirs*, Paris: Hachette, 1930; as *Sarah Bernhardt, Impressions*, translated by Ethel Thompson, London: Elkin Mathews and Marrot, 1932

Richardson, Joanna, *Sarah Bernhardt and Her World*, London: Weidenfeld and Nicolson, 1977

The Romantics to Rodin: French Nineteenth-Century Sculpture from North American Collections (exhib. cat.), Los Angeles: Los Angeles County Museum of Art, and New York: Braziller, 1980

Rueff, Suze, *I Knew Sarah Bernhardt*, London: Muller, 1951

Sarah Bernhardt, 1844–1923 (exhib. cat.), London: Ferrers Gallery, 1973

Skinner, Cornelia Otis, *Madame Sarah*, Boston: Houghton Mifflin, 1966

Taranow, Gerda, *Sarah Bernhardt, the Art within the Legend*, Princeton, New Jersey: Princeton University Press, 1972

GIANLORENZO BERNINI 1598–1680
Italian

The son of distinguished Florentine marble sculptor Pietro Bernini—who moved to Rome in 1604/05—Gianlorenzo Bernini was treated as an infant prodigy, helping his father and beginning to carve creditable portrait busts (Santoni; *ca.* 1610) and groups with putti (e.g., *Goat Amalthea with the Infant Jupiter and a Faun; ca.* 1609). He carved, probably with the help of his father, *Aeneas, Anchises, and Ascanius Leaving Troy*, and then on his own he carved a series of magnificent mythological groups (*Neptune and Triton, Pluto and Proserpina*, and *Apollo and Daphne*) and *David*. His precocious talent for drawing and sculpting rapidly came to the attention of the pope, Paul V Borghese. The pope's patronage and that of his nephew, Cardinal Scipione, enabled Bernini by the age of 23—with his decidedly brilliant series of mythological groups and psychologically penetrating portrait busts in marble—to establish himself as the master sculptor of his generation.

The papacy of Urban VIII Barberini (1623–44) permitted Bernini fame and fortune, with lucrative public posts and commissions for great Christian projects (e.g., the church and statue of Santa Bibiana in Rome [1624–26], the baldacchino [Baldaquin], *St. Longinus*, and other works, including the tomb of Urban VIII). Bernini's friendship with Urban VIII brought him important technical posts in the Vatican; henceforth his oeuvre—apart from portraiture and fountains—was directed exclusively to the promulgation of the Roman Catholic faith. The interior decoration within the then-recently completed St. Peter's Basilica is almost entirely of his designs, notably the eye-catching structures on its central axis: the baldacchino with its spiraling bronze columns (marking the tomb of St. Peter); the high altar, with the display of the principal relic; the Throne of St. Peter (Cathedra Petri); and the *Gloria*. The latter consists of a host of gilded angels amid artificial clouds and rays of light that surround the oval west window, centered with a rendering of the dove of the Holy Spirit in stained glass. These works took many years and successive papacies to complete. They were the result of trial and error concerning the precise theological functions and the huge scale of the statues that proved to be necessary to harmonize with the enormous spaces of the building and Michelangelo's order of colossal pilasters that articulate the walls.

The tombs of Bernini's two best papal patrons, Urban VIII and Alexander VII, vie for attention in the basilica's chancel and transept, and his later Chapel of the Blessed Sacrament (1673–75) off the right aisle is a triumphant and richly colored combination of the three fine arts: architecture, painting (altarpiece by Pietro da Cortona), and sculpture. Bernini's principal office eventually was as chief architect of St. Peter's Basilica. He contributed fine statues, *St. Longinus* and *Countess Matilda of Tuscany*, and also designed the reliquary niches around the crossing and supervised the cladding of the nave with rich marbles and airy ornamentation.

Bernini ruthlessly tried to monopolize the production of sculpture in Rome and was head of a busy workshop of competent carvers, modelers, and bronze specialists (at the Vatican artillery foundry of which Urban had made him head). He was a tremendously gifted draftsman, using the whole range of techniques from pen and ink—for critical exploratory sketches and caricatures—to black chalk for more detailed compositional studies and to three colors of chalk (*à trois crayons*) for academic studies of the nude figure and for portraits. He used some drawings—normally of devotional subjects—as presents for patrons and friends, for example, at Christmas. His graphic oeuvre is enormous and presents a challenge to connoisseurs who attempt to attribute them either to the hands of the master or to his followers, for his strong personality often permeated their efforts. He also painted, although not as successfully, and made a practice of self-portraiture.

Bernini wrote and directed plays, as well as designed ingenious and surprising stage sets with controlled lighting and other special effects. This skill aided him when it came to creating his most impressive *Gesamtkunstwerk* (total work of art), the Cornaro Chapel in the Church of Santa Maria della Vittoria in Rome (1647–52). It occupies the whole of the shallow left transept of the church, to which attention is drawn by a group of life-size figures in animated discussion in a raised gallery visible down the nave from the entrance. One figure is the patron, Federico Cornaro, a Venetian prelate; the others, including some in a similar gallery on the opposite wall, are the patron's most distinguished relatives of several different generations. All are witnesses of an extraordinary spectacle above

Fountain of the Four Rivers, Piazza Navona, Rome
© Scala / Art Resource, NY

the side altar, which Bernini framed in a proscenium structure and illuminated by sunlight falling from a hidden source. The focus of attention is a group of two over-life-size statues in marble depicting the *Ecstasy of St. Teresa*, a mystical experience of levitation that engendered the impression of an angel repeatedly piercing St. Teresa's heart with an arrow—certainly a challenging subject for a sculptor. Every surface of the chapel is clad with colorful decoration to extend, enhance, and celebrate the miracle. Apart from the ghostly spectators on the walls, the heavenly host is shown above in fresco amid stucco clouds that seem to float inside the architecture, all lit by a large window. The floor is inlaid with skeletal reminders of mortality on the entrance covers to the Cornaro burial vaults below, and the altar rail and altar furniture are constructed with rare colored stones and gilt bronze.

This is the epitome of Bernini's promotion of Roman Catholic belief, of which he himself was an ardent adherent.

Beginning in the second half of the 20th century, partly owing to the advent of mass tourism and photography, the highly imaginative designs that Bernini provided for fountains around Rome attracted more attention than previously, when they were suspected of being not quite "high art." Most famous, and a symbol of Rome, is the *Fountain of the Four Rivers* that animates the Piazza Navona, an ancient Roman running stadium that until later served as a marketplace and parade ground for civilians. Commissioned by Pope Innocent X to enhance the outlook from and approach to the Pamphili Palace, the fountain is a bizarre amalgam of ideas that succeeds in enthralling even today. An Egyptian rose granite obelisk is mounted on a rocky eminence (constructed out of travertine stone), which consists of four pylons of rock joined above, with a cavern that passes in four directions penetrating below, all rising from the waters of ocean within a circular pool at ground level. Each scalloped pylon is decorated with a gigantic figure in marble of a seated river god, symbolizing the four continents then known, with appropriate specimens of flora and fauna. These were carved by four other sculptors from Bernini's drawings and clay models. The river gods recall not only ancient Roman examples, such as had formerly inhabited the outer angles of pediments or presided over fountains and still survive in Rome, but also Michelangelo's recumbent statues (1524–34) in the Medici chapel in the New Sacristy of the Church of San Lorenzo in Florence and his *Slaves* (*ca.* 1516) for the tomb of Pope Julius II. They may have been inspired by the more recent four huge *Moors* (1617–27) in bronze made for Livorno by Pietro Tacca, an older contemporary of Bernini, whom he had recently consulted over the technical aspect of casting the columns for the baldacchino. The above-mentioned works are only some of the influences from Tuscany, in addition to the impact of the work of Giambologna in Florence, that permeate Bernini's work, owing not only to their merit and international prestige, but also in part to his father's Tuscan parentage.

The accession of Alexander VII in 1655 provided new opportunities for statues in the context of Chigi family chapels in the Church of Santa Maria del Popolo in Rome and Siena Cathedral, as well as in their palace and churches at or near Ariccia. At St. Peter's Basilica, the oval colonnade forming the piazza was built and the Throne of St. Peter constructed over the high altar. The tomb of Pope Alexander VII in the transept and the equestrian statue of Constantine (1654) in the narthex were also both erected.

In 1665 Bernini spent six months in Paris, proposing a new facade for the Palais du Louvre (not commissioned) and carving his most extraordinary bust, that of King Louis XIV. Under Pope Clement IX he designed all—and carved three—of the statues of angels (1668–69) for the Ponte Sant'Angelo, and under Clement X he carved *Blessed Ludovica Albertoni in Ecstasy* (1671–74; Church of San Francesco a Ripa, Rome).

That Bernini saw himself as a Classicist may come as a surprise to modern eyes conditioned to view him retrospectively as the creator of the exuberant style that has come to be called Baroque. Indeed, rivals such as Alessandro Algardi and François du Quesnoy, as well as the painter Nicolas Poussin (whom Bernini admired), are habitually distinguished from him as being of a more Classical bent. However, Bernini felt that he was at the apex of the tradition that had come down to him from antiquity, frequently in fragmentary form, and which he could meaningfully reinterpret—often to rather different ends—in the light of the styles of his prestigious predecessors, Michelangelo and Giambologna (although his debt to the latter went unacknowledged). Later he realized that his style of exaggerated emotion and extreme, almost contorted, poses would provoke a reaction after his demise; this indeed came to pass with the advent of Neoclassicism, when Grecian purity and clarity were preferred to his passionate, religious romanticism. Nonetheless, his repertory of imagery has informed much of the sculpture produced internationally for the Roman Catholic Church ever since, and this may be his greatest claim to fame. His only statue that survived the almost universal disfavor into which his oeuvre fell for two and a half centuries was the group *Apollo and Daphne*, largely because of its debt to the admired Classical prototype, the *Apollo Belvedere*.

CHARLES AVERY

See also **Algardi, Alessandro;** *Apollo Belvedere;* **Baroque and Rococo; du Quesnoy, François; Fountain Sculpture; Giambologna; Michelangelo (Buonarroti); Tacca Family**

Biography

Born in Naples, Italy, 7 December 1598. Son of the distinguished Florentine marble sculptor Pietro Bernini; moved to Rome, 1604/05; considered a child prodigy; assisted father with carvings of portrait busts and putti; carved *Aeneas, Anchises, and Ascanius Leaving Troy*, 1618–19; then independently carved a series of magnificent mythological groups and *David*, 1620–24; knighted by Pope Gregory XV, 1621; carved many portraits of popes, cardinals, prelates, nobles, and his mistress Costanza Bonarelli; appointed architect for St. Peter's Basilica, 1629; produced fountains; created the Cornaro Chapel in the Church of Santa Maria della Vittoria in Rome, 1647–52; designed the Chapel of the Blessed Sacrament in St. Peter's Basilica, Rome, 1673. Died in Rome, Italy, 18 November 1680.

Selected Works

ca. 1610 Putto and dragon; marble; J. Paul Getty Museum, Los Angeles, California, United States

ca. 1618 Bust of Pope Paul V; marble; Galleria Borghese, Villa Borghese, Rome, Italy

1618–19 *Aeneas, Anchises, and Ascanius Leaving Troy*; marble; Galleria Borghese, Villa Borghese, Rome, Italy

1620 *Neptune and Triton*; marble; Victoria and Albert Museum, London, England

1621–22 *Pluto and Proserpina*; marble; Galleria Borghese, Villa Borghese, Rome, Italy

1622–24 *Apollo and Daphne*; marble; Galleria Borghese, Villa Borghese, Rome, Italy

1623 *David*; marble; Galleria Borghese, Villa Borghese, Rome, Italy

1623–34 Baldacchino; gilt-bronze and marble; St. Peter's Basilica, Rome, Italy

1627–47 Tomb of Urban VIII; marble and bronze; St. Peter's Basilica, Rome, Italy

1632 *Scipione Borghese*; marble; Galleria Borghese, Villa Borghese, Rome, Italy

1638 Bust of Mr. Baker; marble; Victoria and Albert Museum, London, England

ca. 1638 Bust of Pope Urban VIII; marble; National Gallery of Canada, Ottawa, Canada; another example: Galleria Nazionale, Palazzo Barberini, Rome, Italy

1640 Bust of Cardinal Richelieu; marble; Musée du Louvre, Paris, France

1642–43 Triton fountain; travertine stone and marble; Piazza Barberini, Rome, Italy

1647–52 *Ecstasy of St. Teresa*; marble; Cornaro Chapel, Church of Santa Maria della Vittoria, Rome, Italy

1648–51 *Fountain of the Four Rivers*; marble and travertine stone; Piazza Navona, Rome, Italy

1653–55 *Fountain of the Moor*; marble; Piazza Navona, Rome, Italy

ca. *Daniel* and *Habbakuk*; marble; Chigi
1655–60 Chapel, Church of Santa Maria del Popolo, Rome, Italy

1662 *St. Jerome* and *St. Mary Magdalene*; marble; Chigi Chapel, Siena Cathedral, Italy

1665 Bust of King Louis XIV; marble; National Museum, Palace of Versailles, France

1668–69 *Angel with Crown of Thorns* and *Angel with Superscription*; marble; Church of S. Andrea delle Fratte, Rome, Italy

1671–78 Tomb of Pope Alexander VII; marble; St. Peter's Basilica, Rome, Italy

Further Reading

Avery, Charles, *Bernini, Genius of the Baroque*, Boston: Little Brown, and London: Thames and Hudson, 1997

Baldinucci, Filippo, *Vita del cavaliere Gio. Lorenzo Bernino: Scultore, architetto e pittore*, Florence: Stamperia di Vangelisti, 1682; as *The Life of Bernini*, translated by Catherine Enggass and Robert Enggass, University Park: Pennsylvania State University Press, 1966

Borsi, Franco, *Bernini: Architetto*, Milan: Electa, 1980; as *Bernini*, translated by Robert Erich Wolf, New York: Rizzoli, 1984

Gaskell, Ivan, and Henry Lie, editors, "Sketches in Clay for Projects by Gian Lorenzo Bernini," *Harvard University Art Museums Bulletin* 6/3 (spring 1999)

Gould, Cecil, *Bernini in France: An Episode in Seventeenth-Century History*, London: Weidenfeld and Nicolson, 1981; Princeton, New Jersey: Princeton University Press, 1982

Hibbard, Howard, *Bernini*, London and New York: Pelican Books, 1965

Kirwin, William Chandler, *Powers Matchless: The Pontificate of Urban VIII, the Baldachin, and Gian Lorenzo Bernini*, New York: Peter Lang, 1997

Lavin, Irving, *Bernini and the Unity of the Visual Arts*, Oxford: Oxford University Press, 1980

Lavin, Irving, editor, *Gianlorenzo Bernini: New Aspects of His Art and Thought*, University Park: Pennsylvania State University Press, 1985

Lavin, Irving, et al., *Drawings by Gianlorenzo Bernini from the Museum der Bildenden Künste, Leipzig, German Democratic Republic* (exhib. cat.), Princeton, New Jersey: Princeton University Press, 1981

Marder, Tod A., *Bernini's Scala Regia at the Vatican Palace*, Cambridge and New York: Cambridge University Press, 1997

Perlove, Shelley Karen, *Bernini and the Idealization of Death: The Blessed Ludovica Albertoni and the Altieri Chapel*, University Park: Pennsylvania State University Press, 1990

Scribner, Charles, III, *Gianlorenzo Bernini*, New York: Abrams, 1991

Wardropper, Ian, editor, *From the Sculptor's Hand: Italian Baroque Terracottas from the State Hermitage Museum*, Chicago: The Art Institute of Chicago, 1998

Weston-Lewis, Aidan, editor, *Effigies and Ecstasies: Roman Baroque Sculpture and Design in the Age of Bernini*, Edinburgh: National Gallery of Scotland, 1998

Wittkower, Rudolf, *Gian Lorenzo Bernini: The Sculptor of the Roman Baroque*, London: Phaidon Press, 1955; 4th edition, as *Bernini: The Sculptor of the Roman Baroque*, 1997

TOMB OF URBAN VIII

Gianlorenzo Bernini (1598–1680)

1627–1647

marble and bronze

h. 5.6 m

St. Peter's Basilica, Rome, Italy

Gianlorenzo Bernini's tomb of Pope Urban VIII represents a new type of funerary monument in which the emphasis lies on death itself more than on commemorating the deceased. The center of the composition is dominated by a gilt bronze sarcophagus surmounted by a personification of Death depicted as a skeletal figure with wings. Before Death lies an open book in which he inscribes the name of Urban VIII. He is accompanied by two allegorical figures representing Charity and Justice, which stand on either side of the sarcophagus. In the background, Pope Urban sits on a throne elevated high above the viewer on a pedestal, his right hand raised in benediction. The entire monument rests within a niche located on the right side of the apse of St. Peter's Basilica in Rome.

Around 1625 Urban VIII charged Bernini with the task of executing his tomb. The project was placed under the supervision of Monsignor Angelo Giori and was carried out in two main stages: from 1628 to 1631 and from 1639 to 1647. After receiving official approval for his design in May 1628, Bernini proceeded to model and cast the statue of the pope and began work on the sarcophagus. His efforts were temporarily suspended until 1639, when he resumed work on the sarcophagus and began the figure of Death; both were completed in 1644. Charity and Justice, both entirely by Bernini's own hand, were not finished until 1646. Three years after Urban's death, the tomb was unveiled on 9 February 1647 in the presence of his successor, Pope Innocent X.

The tomb's composition was partially determined by structural changes being made to the crossing in St. Peter's Basilica. The project required that Guglielmo della Porta's tomb of Paul III (1549–75) be relocated from the crossing to the apse. This led Pope Urban to select the apse as the location for his own tomb. Taking the close proximity of the monuments into consideration, Bernini adopted Guglielmo's pyramidal composition, which was inspired by Michelangelo's Medici tombs (1520–34; Medici Chapel, Church of San Lorenzo, Florence). Guglielmo's use of both bronze and marble also influenced Bernini: the tomb of Urban VIII is the first sculptural work by his hand composed of more than one type of material. Guglielmo, however, included neither the figure of Death nor a sarcophagus in his design. As sarcophagi rarely appeared in contemporary papal tombs and personified Death was a relatively new concept in funerary art, their presence distinguishes Urban's tomb both in its appearance and its meaning.

A series of preparatory sketches dating from 1627 to 1643 show how the figure of Death evolved as work on the tomb progressed. In the earliest extant drawing of the tomb (1627), Death appears as a winged skeleton leaning across a sarcophagus. This is unusual because Death is rarely depicted with wings. Bernini acquired the motif from the representations of Time to show that Death, like Time, brings about destruction. In a drawing from the early 1630s, Death is represented as sitting on top of the sarcophagus writing on a tablet. Such commemorative tablets were traditionally held by angels or Fame and served to immortalize the name of the deceased. By connecting the tablet with Death, Bernini suggests that Death is the agent of man's immortality, as in his memorials to *Ippolito Merenda* (1640–41; S. Giacomo alla Lungarna, Rome) and *Alessandro Valtrini* (1639; S. Lorenzo in Damaso, Rome). A drawing from 1643 that transforms the tablet into a book reinforces this interpretation. Symbolizing both the Book of Death and the Book of Life, Death inscribes the name of Pope Urban on the open leaf, whereas the name of Gregory XV, his immediate predecessor, is partially visible on the previous page.

Death also recalls the figure Poetry, who is traditionally represented as writing in a book. By depicting Death in the guise of Poetry, Bernini paid homage to Urban's own poetical works in which the immortality of the spirit was a common theme. The two allegorical figures of Charity and Justice bear witness to this idea, because according to Panofsky, they celebrate Urban as the vicar of Christ, who, through divine mercy and justice, brings salvation to mankind (see Panofsky, 1964). Thus Urban, by virtue of his role as the earthly representative of Christ, is a guarantor of man's salvation, hence his gesture of benediction. Although the

Tomb of Urban VIII
© Alinari / Art Resource, NY

pope had always held this role, previous papal monuments did not often represent him in this capacity. Guglielmo's Tomb of Paul III, for example, shows Pope Paul accompanied by Prudence and Justice, which identify him as the ruler of men. However, the attacks at that time on the Catholic doctrine of salvation by the Jansenism movement brought the issue to the fore during Urban's pontificate. Despite his numerous efforts to eradicate Jansenism, the movement prevailed.

A succession of similar failures and problems made Urban VIII extremely unpopular by the time of his death in 1644. As a result, the tomb received some criticism when it was unveiled. One critic supposedly declared that the bees scattered across the tomb refer to the Barberini family, who were dispersed in exile. Bernini's skill, however, could not be denied; even Innocent X approved of it, and Innocent X seldom held Bernini's work in high regard. As a result, the tomb was highly influential, serving as the general model for papal tombs until the end of the Baroque period. Examples of monuments inspired by Urban's tomb include Alessandro Algardi's tomb of Pope Leo XI (1634–44; St. Peter's Basilica, Rome) and Jean-Ange Maucord's tomb of Jean-Baptiste de Sade de Mazan (*ca.* 1709; Cavaillon Cathedral, France). The arrangement of Algardi's tomb and the manner in which he portrays the pope is very similar to those of Bernini, whereas Maucord draws directly on Bernini's idea of Death, showing him writing in a book, although Death lacks wings. Such monuments attest to the vitality and strength of Bernini's design and his ability to translate intangible concepts such as death into stone.

DAVID L. BERSHAD AND GABRIELLA SZALAY

See also **Michelangelo (Buonarroti): Medici Chapel; Tomb Sculpture**

Further Reading

Baldinucci, Filippo, *Vita del cavaliere Gio. Lorenzo Bernino*, Florence: Stamperia di V. Vangelisti, 1682; as *The Life of Bernini*, translated by Catherine Enggass, University Park: Pennsylvania State University Press, 1966

Brauer, Heinrich, and Rudolf Wittkower, *Die Zeichnungen des Gianlorenzo Bernini*, 2 vols., New York: Collectors Editions, 1931

Davis, Howard McP., "Bees on the Tomb of Urban VIII," *Source* 8/9 (1989)

Dreyer, Ilana, "Tomb of Urban VIII," in *Drawings by Gianlorenzo Bernini from the Museum der Bildenden Künste, Leipzig, German Democratic Republic*, Princeton, New Jersey: Art Museum, Princeton University, 1981

Fehl, Philipp, "L'umilta cristiana e il monumento sontuoso: La tomba di Urban VIII del Bernini," in *Gian Lorenzo Bernini e le arti visive*, edited by Marcello Fagiolo, Rome: Istituto della Enciclopedia Italiana, 1987

Hibbard, Howard, *Bernini*, Baltimore, Maryland: Penguin, 1965

Kauffmann, Hans, *Giovanni Lorenzo Bernini: Die figürlichen Kompositionen*, Berlin: Mann Verlag, 1970

Kirwin, Chandler W., *Powers Matchless: The Pontificate of Urban VIII, the Baldachin, and Gian Lorenzo Bernini*, New York: Lang, 1997

Panofsky, Erwin, "Mors Vitae Testimonium: The Positive Aspects of Death in Renaissance and Baroque Iconography," in *Studien zur toskanischen Kunst*, edited by Wolfgang Lotz and Lisa Lotte Mölloer, Munich: Prestel-Verlag, 1964

Pastor, Ludwig von, *The History of the Popes*, 40 vols., translated by Ernest Graf, London: Routledge and Kegan Paul, 1923–53; see especially vol. 29, 1938

Wilkinson, C., "The Iconography of Bernini's Tomb of Urban VIII," *L'arte* 9 (1971)

Wittkower, Rudolf, *Gian Lorenzo Bernini: The Sculptor of the Roman Baroque*, Oxford: Phaidon Press, 1955; 3rd edition, 1981

ECSTASY OF ST. TERESA
Gianlorenzo Bernini (1598–1680)
1647–1652
marble
h. 3.5 m
Cornaro Chapel, Church of Santa Maria della Vittoria, Rome, Italy

Bernini's *Ecstasy of St. Teresa*, his exquisite altarpiece of St. Teresa and the angel set within the Church of Santa Maria della Vittoria's Cornaro Chapel, also designed by the artist, is perhaps the most famous sculpture of the Italian baroque. This carefully orchestrated ensemble of painting, sculpture, and architecture transforms the chapel into a type of theater in which St. Teresa's mystical experience is dramatized and made accessible to the viewer. Every element of the unified design contributes to the expressive and iconographic richness of the whole.

The marble altarpiece and the chapel itself were commissioned of Bernini about 1647 by the wealthy Venetian Cardinal Federico Cornaro, who spared no expense on this mortuary chapel intended for his own burial. The cardinal dedicated the chapel in the Carmelite church to the 16th-century Spanish mystic St. Teresa, the founder of the Reformed Order of Discalced Carmelites. The subject of the marble grouping—St. Teresa's vision in which an angel appeared to her and pierced her with a golden arrow—was the focus of her canonization ceremony at St. Peter's Basilica, Rome, in 1622.

In her *Vida* Teresa recounted how a short, beautiful angel appeared "all afire" and pierced her heart several times with a flaming spear, so that it penetrated her entrails, which he seemed to draw out with the golden spear, leaving her "afire with a great love for God." She moaned in pain but felt such sweetness that she wished "never to lose it." It was "not bodily pain," she explained, "but spiritual, though the body has a share in it as well, indeed a great share." These visions were, as she described them, the "colloquies of love" passing between the soul and God.

Bernini brilliantly translated the saint's famous mystical experience into stone. Carved out of a single block of white marble, the sculpted grouping is installed over the altar and set within an oval niche framed by two pairs of Corinthian columns supporting a large jutting pediment. The dark, richly grained marble panels flanking the recess activate the walls with their varied patterns and contrast with the whiteness of the sculpted grouping, contributing to the illusion that St. Teresa and the angel are floating on a cloud within the altar niche. The illumination of the recess also imparts a visionary quality to the sculpture. The light from an exterior light well, situated behind the pediment, passes through an oculus, originally glazed with golden glass, and is reflected downward along the gilded rods to fall upon the white marble altarpiece. The golden rods, evoking a divine emanation, thus transmit natural light, merging the fictive and the real in an eminently Baroque conception.

More than any other artist before him, Bernini captured the sensuality of Teresa's account of her mystical experience. The beautiful cherub of the sculpted altarpiece is poised in action before the ecstatic saint, the wind rushing through the diaphanous draperies clinging to his body. His smoothly polished face, framed

Ecstasy of St. Teresa
© Alinari / Art Resource, NY

by ringlets of soft hair, is aglow with light. He smiles with the playful tenderness of a lover as he delicately elevates a fold of Teresa's garment, exposing her breast to the repeated thrust of the golden arrow. Bernini focused upon the moment described by the saint when the cherub has just withdrawn the arrow from her heart, leaving her "enflamed with love." The Spanish mystic wholly surrenders to the rapturous experience; her body is disposed in a passive, semirecumbent posture invented by Bernini (other artists had depicted her falling from an upright position). Her hands are limp; her head is thrust backward with her mouth open and eyes rolled back within the lids. The heavy draperies collapsing over her make visible the intense pain and sweet pleasure of her experience. The polish and angle of the folds of her nun's habit cause the light to flicker gently back and forth over her body, like the flame ignited within her.

The sensuality of this sculpture definitely was noticed by critics. An anonymous contemporary of Bernini claimed that the sculptor "made this pure virgin into a Venus, not only prostrate, but prostituted." Moreover, French 19th-century admirers of Bernini such as Stendhal and Hippolyte Taine did not fail to dwell on the "voluptuousness" of the work. Taine went so far as to refer to the sculpture as a "seductive romance." Bernini does make it clear, however, that the saint's physical ecstasy was a spiritual experience that reaped its reward in heaven. The inscription on a banderole of the chapel's entrance arch proclaims, as if spoken by God to St. Teresa, "If I had not created heaven I would create it for you alone." To underscore this point, Bernini had a glory of angels painted in the chapel vault. This fresco, by Guidobaldo Abbatini, creates the illusion that a heavenly cloud fills the upper spaces of the chapel, flowing over and obscuring parts of the architecture, but not entirely concealing the gilded, stucco reliefs recording Teresa's penitential devotions and betrothal to Christ.

On the side walls of the chapel, eight marble portraits of Federico and his ancestors appear behind balconies resembling theater boxes. These men, all cardinals except for Federico's father, seem to react to the saint's vision, which they cannot see. They converse, consult texts, or stare in devotion toward the altar in order to come to terms with St. Teresa's miraculous vision. Undoubtedly they understand that the intercessory powers earned through the saint's mystical union can open the gates of heaven for them. Moreover, the Spanish mystic's ability to liberate souls from purgatory is asserted in the chapel by the marble intarsia pavement, which creates the illusion that two skeletons are rising from the graves beneath the floor. Thus, the Cornaro Chapel, dramatizing Teresa's rapture, also demonstrates her role in the process of salvation.

Bernini's brilliant merging of the arts in the Cornaro Chapel exerted great influence in the history of art; it is ancestor not only to the Bavarian churches of the 18th century but also to the multimedia installations of the 20th century. Bernini was surely indulging in understatement when he called this masterpiece "the least bad" of his works.

SHELLEY KAREN PERLOVE

See also **Altarpiece: Southern Europe**

Further Reading

Avery, Charles, *Bernini: Genius of the Baroque*, Boston: Little Brown, and London: Thames and Hudson, 1997

Baldinucci, Filippo, *The Life of Bernini*, translated by Catherine Enggass, University Park: Pennsylvania State University Press, 1966

Barcham, W., "Some New Documents on Federico Cornaro's Two Chapels in Rome," *The Burlington Magazine* 135 (1993)

Lavin, Irving, *Bernini and the Unity of the Visual Arts*, New York: Oxford University Press, 1980

Lavin, Irving, *Drawings by Gianlorenzo Bernini, from the Museum der Bildenden Künste Leipzig, German Democratic Republic*, Princeton, New Jersey: Art Museum, Princeton University, 1981

Perlove, Shelley Karen, *Bernini and the Idealization of Death: The Blessed Ludovica Albertoni and the Altieri Chapel*, University Park: Pennsylvania State University Press, 1990

Previtali, G., "Il Costantino messo alla berlina or bernina su la porta di San Pietro," *Paregone* 145 (1962)

Weibel, Walther, "The Representation of Ecstasy," in *Bernini in Perspective*, edited by George C. Bauer, Englewood Cliffs, New Jersey: Prentice Hall, 1976

Wittkower, Rudolf, *Bernini: The Sculptor of the Roman Baroque*, London: Phaidon Press, 1977

PIETRO BERNINI 1562–1629 *Italian*

Pietro Bernini was a remarkably skilled sculptor who played a crucial role in the artistic scene of Naples and Rome between the 1590s and 1610s. These decades were a transitional but fruitful artistic period that sowed the seeds of Baroque art both in painting and sculpture. Only recently has the significance of Pietro's output at this threshold of proto-Baroque and Baroque sculpture been fully understood. By the end of the 17th century, the identity and art of Pietro Bernini had become overshadowed by his son Gianlorenzo Bernini's major biographers (Baldinucci and Bernini) in order to highlight Gianlorenzo's genius; the reevaluation of this momentous time occurred only at the beginning of the 20th century.

Pietro was apprenticed to the experienced and learned sculptor Rodolfo Sirigatti, a leading figure in the Florentine milieu. Nonetheless, it was through his probable collaboration as a painter at the Villa Farnese in Caprarola and, above all, the practice of restoring ancient statues in Rome that Bernini acquired his outstanding technical skills. The painter and biographer Giovanni Baglione noted Pietro's unusual speed and mastery in marble carving, having observed him working in Naples, where both artists were documented by the end of the 1580s. In his first known works—two statues of *St. Lucy* and *St. Catherine* carved for Calabrese patrons—Bernini exploited his technical ability and demonstrated his constant fascination with painting in the search for chiaroscuro effects in the deeply undercut drapery. The brief collaboration with the leading Florentine sculptor Giovanni Caccini did not have as much impact on his original style as did Bernini's activity in the major redecoration of the Carthusian Monastery of San Martino. The elongated and elegant figures carved by Bernini during that time show striking affinities with Late Mannerist painting, especially with the work of the Cavalier d'Arpino, who frescoed the choir and sacristy of the Carthusian church. Especially typical are the statues of *St. Peter* and *St. Paul*, whose rigidly voluminous and edged mantles are deeply hollowed out in the interest of reproducing pictorial effects.

By 1600 Bernini had become one of the leading sculptors in Naples, together with the Florentine Michelangelo Nacherino. When juxtaposed, however, the two artists' works prove to be quite different. Although Bernini had to compromise in order to harmonize with the more restrained style of Nacherino, as in the *St. Lawrence* and *St. Stephen* carved for the Amalfi Crypt—where Nacherino was given a more prominent role—he mastered a virtuoso rendering of texture treatment, differentiating the softness of the dalmatic from its unpolished iconographic attributes. The apex of Bernini's Neapolitan period is the marble group of the *Virgin and Child with the Infant St. John*, from the Monastery of San Martino. Although the date of execution of this group is still debated, the work was an important precedent for Gianlorenzo Bernini's first mythological works, especially in the intertwining of the figures, the smooth handling of the surfaces, and the drapery emphasizing the anatomy of the figures.

Pietro Bernini was in Rome by 1606, having received a papal commission to carve the impressively large high relief representing the *Assumption of the Virgin* for the Basilica of Santa Maria Maggiore. Faced with a pictorial subject, Bernini introduced a new painterly approach to marble altarpieces through his tremendous use of chisel and drill in a gradated sequence from high to very low relief. As Lavin points out, Pietro performed in this work "an extraordinary bravura technique with daring perforations which emphasize the fragility of the stone" (see Lavin, 1968). Bernini once again accomplished this "bravura technique" in the relief medium when he sculpted the trompe l'oeil of noblemen in the foreground of the relief representing the coronation of Clement VIII and mastered the inventive cross-legged poses of the four caryatids, which flank the relief itself.

The statue of *St. John the Baptist*, begun by the Flemish sculptor Nicolas Cordier, who died in 1612, confirms Bernini's command of carving figures from rough-hewn marble blocks. The half-seated figure appears to emerge from the niche in an accentuated *contrapposto* (a natural pose with the weight of one leg, the shoulder, and hips counterbalancing one another) so as to break the confinement of the niche. The original pose and treatment of the pelt clothing the nearly nude figure were extremely influential upon Pietro's son Gianlorenzo.

In the mid 1610s Pietro and Gianlorenzo worked in partnership to produce a series of works; the most incredible of these are the *Four Seasons*, a marble tour de force of collaboration between father and son. The four statues, carved out of ancient blocks of marble,

The Virgin Mary from The Annunciation.
The Conway Library, Courtauld Institute of Art

Gabriel from The Annunciation.
The Conway Library, Courtauld Institute of Art

although still indebted to Mannerism, seem to invade the space with their abundance of flowers and fruits.

In the last years of his life, Pietro continued to collaborate with Gianlorenzo, who was by then the most talented and influential sculptor in Rome. The last known works by Pietro are the two exquisite statues of Gabriel and the Virgin for the *Annunciation* in the Church of St. Bruno in Bordeaux. The ensemble was commissioned in Rome of the father and son by the French Cardinal de Sourdis. While Gianlorenzo carved the cardinal's portrait bust, the statues were entrusted with Pietro and the Bernini workshop. The *Annunciation* is a remarkable statement of Pietro's last achievements. The posed hands of the angel and Mary, their mellowed faces, and their floating massed draperies powerfully convey the solemnity of the miraculous greeting.

Debate over Pietro Bernini's position within sculptural production between the late 16th and early 17th centuries has often been confined to the "facile" quality of his technical ability and his lack of a truly great artistic imagination. Yet he more than compensated for these criticisms through his concern for looking at contemporary pictorial and sculptural sources, which enabled him to respond promptly to the key artistic changes that were taking place during his lifetime. Beyond that, he fostered Gianlorenzo's talents, providing him with the essential tools for the germination of Baroque sculpture.

PAOLA D'AGOSTINO

See also **Baroque and Rococo; Bernini, Gianlorenzo; Cordier, Nicolas**

Biography

Born in Sesto Fiorentino, Tuscany, Italy, 5 May 1562. Apprenticed to sculptor Rodolfo Sirigatti in Florence; worked as painter at the Villa Farnese in Caprarola, *ca.* 1582, and spent time in Rome restoring ancient statues; moved to Naples, *ca.* 1584, and carved first statues for Calabrese churches, 1591; went briefly back to Florence, 1594 or 1595, where he worked with Giovanni Caccini; returned to Naples, *ca.* 1595, becoming a leading sculptor together with Michelangelo Naccherino; moved to Rome, 1606; continued to work in Rome on several prestigious commissions for Pope Paul V and Scipione Borghese; by 1616 had started working in partnership with son Gianlorenzo Bernini; appointed architect of the Acqua Vergine, 1623. Died in Rome, Italy, 29 August 1629.

Selected Works

1591	*St. Catherine* and *St. Lucy*; marble; Church of SS. Pietro e Paolo, Morano Calabro, Cosenza province, Italy
1598	*St. Martin and the Beggar*; marble; Museo di San Martino, Naples, Italy
1598–1600	*St. Peter* and *St. Paul*; marble; Naples Cathedral, Italy
1598–1601	*Charity* and *Security*; marble; Church of Monte di Pietà, Naples, Italy
1601	*St. Matthew and the Angel*; marble; Church of the Gesù Nuovo, Naples, Italy
1602	*St. Stephen* and *St. Lawrence*; marble; Cathedral of Amalfi, Campania, Italy
1602–06	Six statues; marble; Ruffo Chapel, Church of Girolamini, Naples, Italy
ca. 1606	*Virgin and Child with the Infant St. John*; marble; Museo di San Martino, Naples, Italy
1606–11	*Assumption of the Virgin*; marble; Basilica of Santa Maria Maggiore, Rome, Italy
1610–11	Caryatids for tomb of Pope Clement VIII; marble; Cappella Paolina, Basilica of Santa Maria Maggiore, Rome, Italy
1612–14	Relief of the coronation of Pope Clement VIII for tomb of Pope Clement VIII; marble; Cappella Paolina, Basilica of Santa Maria Maggiore, Rome, Italy
1615	*Flora and Priapus*; marble; Metropolitan Museum of Art, New York City, United States
1615	*St. John the Baptist*; marble; Barberini Chapel, Church of Sant'Andrea della Valle, Rome, Italy
1616	*Four Seasons* (with son Gianlorenzo Bernini); marble; private collection
ca. 1622	*Annunciation*; marble; Church of St. Bruno, Bordeaux, France

Further Reading

Avery, Charles, *Bernini: Genius of the Roman Baroque*, Boston: Little Brown, and London: Thames and Hudson, 1997

Bacchi, Andrea, "Figlio d'arte: Pietro e Gian Lorenzo," in *Gian Lorenzo Bernini: Regista del barocco*, edited by Maria Grazia Bernardini and Maurizio Fagiolo Dell'Arco, Milan: Skira, 1999

Baglione, Giovanni, *Le vite de' pittori, scultori et architetti dal pontificato di Gregorio XIII, del 1572 fino a' tempi di papa Urbano Ottavo nel 1642*, Rome: Nella Stamperia d'Andrea Fei, 1642; reprint, Vatican City: Biblioteca Apostolica Vaticana, 1995

D'Agostino, Paola, "Un contributo al catalogo di Pietro Bernini," *Dialoghi di storia dell'arte* 2 (1996)

Fruhan, Catherine Elna, "Trends in Roman Sculpture circa 1600," Ph.D. diss., University of Michigan, 1986

Kessler, Hans Ulrich, "Pietro Bernini (1562–1629): Seine Werke in der Certosa di San Martino in Neapel," *Mitteilungen des Kunsthistorisches Institutes in Florenz* 28 (1994)

Kessler, Hans Ulrich, "Pietro Bernini's Statues for the Cappella Ruffo in the Church of the Gerolamini in Naples," *Sculpture Journal* 6 (2001)

Lavin, Irving, "Five Youthful Sculptures by Gianlorenzo Bernini and a Revised Chronology of His Early Works," *The Art Bulletin* 3 (1968)

Martinelli, Valentino, "Contributi alla scultura del Seicento: Pietro Bernini e figli," *Commentari* 4/2 (1953)

Pope-Hennessy, John, *An Introduction to Italian Sculpture*, 3 vols., London: Phaidon, 1963; 4th edition, 1996; see especially vol. 2, *Italian Renaissance Sculpture*, and vol. 3, *Italian High Renaissance and Baroque Sculpture*

Tozzi, S., *Pietro Bernini: Un preludio al Barocco* (exhib. cat.), Florence: Scramasax, 1989

Wittkower, Rudolf, *Art and Architecture in Italy, 1600–1750*, London and Baltimore, Maryland: Penguin, 1958; 6th edition, 3 vols., New Haven, Connecticut: Yale University Press, 1999

ALONSO BERRUGUETE *ca.* 1489–1561
Spanish

Alonso Berruguete's work occupies a prominent place in Spanish 16th-century sculpture because of his adaptation of Italian Renaissance and Mannerist art into a Spanish context. In particular, his elongated, writhing figures have been compared with those of Michelangelo and Donatello, but Berruguete so accentuated their poses that he distorted the figures in a way the Italian artists never did. Nonetheless, he developed an innovative style and designed compositions that influenced a generation of artists in Castile. Among Spanish artists, he is also remarkable for his equal proficiency in sculpture and painting, as well as his ability to design monumental projects and then oversee an atelier that executed them at a consistently high level. Draftsmanship was crucial in this regard, and several drawings assigned to Berruguete throw light on this aspect of his work; even though not all of these attributes are certain, the existence of such a corpus further distinguishes him from most Spanish sculptors whose drawings do not survive.

Born in Paredes de Nava (Palencia), about 1489, Berruguete was the eldest son of Pedro Berruguete, a notable painter whom most scholars believe traveled to Italy. Pedro doubtlessly provided his son his first training as a painter and perhaps an appreciation for Italian art. Alonso's initial instruction in sculpture, however, remains unknown, and for much of his early career he worked as a painter. Sometime after his father's death in 1503, he went to Italy, where he stayed in Rome and Florence. Although his activity is difficult to reconstruct, sources suggest some details: he copied the recently discovered *Laocoön* and met Michelangelo and studied his cartoon of *The Battle of Cascina*. Study of both the *Laocoön* and Michelangelo's work significantly shaped his own appreciation of the human figure.

After returning to Spain (perhaps in 1517), Berruguete attached himself to the court of Charles V, where he was appointed a painter to the king. His first major commission, the tomb of the king's chancellor, Jean Sauvage, came on 20 December 1518. Within a month (17 January 1519), the young artist entered a four-year partnership with the established sculptor Felipe Vigarny. Sauvage's tomb was completed by 13 March 1520, but was extensively damaged in the Peninsular War of 1808–14, and it is difficult to distinguish the artists' contributions from the remaining fragments. The two continued on to Granada, where they worked in the Royal Chapel: Vigarny was entrusted with the high altar and Berruguete undertook an ambitious series of mural paintings that were never completed.

Berruguete subsequently left Granada as he continued to follow the court of Charles V, who in 1523 named him an interrogating magistrate in Valladolid. Although he was granted a royal dispensation and never exercised the post, he nevertheless moved to Valladolid. In that year he received the commission

for the altar of the Hieronymite monastery of La Mejorada in Olmedo with another sculptor, Vasco de la Zarza. When Zarza died the following year, Berruguete continued the project and finished it in 1526. Notwithstanding subsequent remodeling during the 17th century, the altar (moved to what is now the Museo Nacional de Escultura, Valladolid, by the early 20th century) represents the first sculpture in Spain that can be securely attributed to his hand. It also reveals a fully formed sculptor, which may be surprising given the lack of reference to any training or previous works. The life-size reliefs and tondi exhibit the elegant *figura serpentinata* that he would use so effectively throughout his career, whereas the architectural decoration is filled with Italianate classicizing motifs.

In 1526 Berruguete received an even more important commission: the monumental high altar of the Monastery of St. Benedict in Valladolid, a three-story construction involving reliefs, figures, tondi, paintings, and a crucifix at the top. After Berruguete installed the ensemble in 1533, a disagreement arose concerning the work's merits. Vigarny was offered a list of the work's defects, but Berruguete insisted on his satisfaction with it and ultimately the abbot accepted the piece as it was. The controversy may have stemmed from the personal envy of other sculptors as well as the work's novel compositions in which Berruguete de-

Altarpiece of San Benito el Real, Adoration of the Magi
© Archivo Iconografico, S.A. / CORBIS

picted figures moving with an exaggerated motion that enhances their impact.

During the 1530s, Berruguete consolidated his position as a sculptor of retables in Castile, carving an altar with polychromed sculpture and paintings for the Colegio de Fonseca (contracted 1529) and the high altar for the Church of Santiago, Valladolid. In 1539, Berruguete moved to Toledo, where he undertook reliefs of prophets and saints to decorate one side of the upper choir stalls for the cathedral. (His former partner, Vigarny, had previously agreed to carve the others). Before he finished the project in 1548, Berruguete would produce more than 30 wooden reliefs, 30 alabaster reliefs, and, following Vigarny's death in 1543, the reliefs over the archbishop's seat and the figural tableaux of the *Transfiguration* above it. In striking contrast to Vigarny's style and other contemporary Spanish work, Berruguete carved the relief figures with a daring foreshortening and *contrapposto* (a natural pose with the weight of one leg, the shoulder, and hips counterbalancing one another) so that they threaten to break free from the architectural frames. He employed a comparable sensitivity to motion in the *Transfiguration*. One of the few freestanding ensembles of the period, the *Transfiguration* is impressive for its dramatic composition, which vividly evokes the event and is legible from a distance.

While in Toledo, Berruguete undertook other major works. The altar of St. Ursula includes a relief of the *Visitation* that ranks among his best sculpture. His final project was the marble tomb of Cardinal Tavera, begun in 1554 and completed in 1561 just prior to his death. Although its design style is drawn from tombs by Bartolomé Ordóñez and Diego de Siloé, the reliefs again reflect Berruguete's inimitable style. It is difficult, however, to determine how much of this monument the 60-year-old artist may have carved himself.

At the end of Berruguete's life, two further altars were issued from his workshop, and although his own intervention was doubtlessly limited, the designs reflect his unflagging inspiration. The first, the *Transfiguration* (Church of San Salvador, Ubeda) reprises the Toledo choir sculpture. Berruguete signed a contract for the second sculpture, the high altar for the Church of Santiago in Cáceres in 1557, but the pieces were only brought to the church in 1563, two years after the sculptor's death.

PATRICK LENAGHAN

See also **Donatello (Donato di Betto Bardi);** *Laocoön and His Sons;* **Michelangelo (Buonarroti); Ordóñez, Bartolomé; Siloé Family; Spain: Renaissance and Baroque; Vigarny, Felipe**

Biography

Born in Paredes de Nava (Palencia), Spain, *ca.* 1489. Son of the Spanish painter Pedro Berruguete, who trained his son in painting. Traveled in Italy, 1508–17, where he stayed in Rome and Florence and met Michelangelo; on return to Spain, named painter to King Charles V, 1518; entered four-year partnership with Felipe Vigarny, 1519; traveled to Granada; settled in Valladolid when given a post there as interrogating magistrate; set up workshop, 1523; moved to Toledo to work on reliefs for Cathedral of Toledo and high altarpiece, *ca.* 1539. Died in Toledo, Spain, 1561.

Selected Works

1523–26	Altar of la Mejorada; polychromed wood; Museo Nacional de Escultura, Valladolid, Spain
1526–33	Altar of St. Benedict; paintings and polychromed wood; Museo Nacional de Escultura, Valladolid, Spain
1529–31?	Altar; paintings and polychromed wood; Colegio de Fonseca, Salamanca, Spain
1537 (contracted)	Altar; wood; Church of Santiago, Valladolid, Spain
1539–48	Choirstalls and relief of *Transfiguration*; wood; Cathedral of Toledo, Spain
ca. 1545	Altar of St. Ursula; polychromed wood; Museo de Sta. Cruz, Toledo, Spain
1554–61	Tomb of Cardinal Tavera; marble; Hospedal de San Juan Bautista, Toledo, Spain
Completed by 1559	Altar of the *Transfiguration*; wood; Church of San Salvador, Ubeda, Spain
1557–63	Altar; polychromed wood; Church of Santiago, Cáceres, Spain

Further Reading

Azcárate, José María de, *Escultura del siglo XVI*, Madrid: Editorial Plus Ultra, 1958

Azcárate, José María de, *Alonso Berruguete: Cuatro ensayos*, Valladolid, Spain: Dirección General de Bellas Artes, 1963

Camón Aznar, José, *Alonso Berruguete*, Madrid: Espasa-Calpe, 1980

Gómez-Moreno, Manuel, *La escultura del renacimiento en España*, Florence: Pantheon Casa Editrice, 1931; as *Renaissance Sculpture in Spain*, translated by Bernard Bevan, Florence: Pantheon, 1931; reprint, New York: Hacker Art Books, 1971

Gómez-Moreno, Manuel, *Las águilas del renacimiento español: Bartolomé Ordóñez, Diego Siloé, Pedro Machuco, Alonso*

Berruguete, 1517–1558, Madrid: Consejo Superior de Investigaciones Científicas Instituto Diego Velázquez, 1941; reprint, Xarait Ediciones, 1983

Marías, Fernando, *El largo siglo XVI: Los usos artísticos del Renacimiento español*, Madrid: Taurus, 1989

Martín González, Juan José, "Consideraciones sobre la vida y la obra de Alonso Berruguete," *Boletín del Seminario de arte y arqueología de la Universidad de Valladolid* 27 (1961)

Morte García, Carmen, "Carlos I y los artistas de corte en Zaragoza: Fancelli, Berruguete, y Bigarny," *Archivo español de arte* 255 (1991)

MADAME LÉON BERTAUX 1825–1909

French

In addition to being one of the most successful sculptors in France during the second half of the 19th century, Madame Léon Bertaux was also the most important activist for women's right to a free art education during the period. Born into an artistic but humble family, she was the stepdaughter of Pierre Hébert and the sister of Émile Hébert, both sculptors and frequent Salon exhibitors. Her career and importance overshadowed theirs significantly, however, as her contributions to promoting the education of women artists changed the course of French history.

She began working in her stepfather's studio at the age of 12, and she studied privately with Augustin-Alexandre Dumont. By the time she was 24, Bertaux was exhibiting in the Paris salon exhibition under the name of her first husband, Allétit. Although two of her early sculptures, *Love Martyred* and *Love Vanquished* (both *ca.* 1855), were refused admission to the Exposition Universelle of 1855, such failings were a rarity during her mature career. She frequently exhibited at the Paris Salons, winning numerous medals and awards, including an honorable mention in 1863 (for her *Assumption of the Virgin*) and medals in 1864 (for a plaster version of *Young Gallic Prisoner*), 1867 (for a full-scale marble version of *Young Gallic Prisoner*), and 1873 (for the plaster *Young Girl Bathing*). She also exhibited at the Royal Academy, London, in 1874, winning a bronze medal; at the Exposition des Arts Décoratifs, Paris, in 1877, winning a first-class medal (for *The Burial of Christ*); and twice at the Exposition Universelle, Paris, in 1889, when she won a gold medal, and again in 1900. Her works were also exhibited in the Women's Building at the 1893 World's Columbian Exposition in Chicago. After 1857 she exhibited under the name of her second husband (and former student), Léon Bertaux.

Bertaux was an ardent promoter of her own works, and many of her sculptures were acquired by the state through her calculated appeals to the French arts administration. She often labeled herself a religious sculptor, and in fact many of her works were placed in churches throughout France. Of these, the best known are her two works of 1863 for the small church at Saint Gratien, *Three Theological Virtues* and *For the Poor*, the latter a collection box flanked by cherubs. Her *Assumption of the Virgin* was acquired by the state in 1868. She also sculpted representations of St. Philippe and St. Matthieu for the Church of St. Laurent, Paris, in 1865; *L'Agneau Pascal* for St. Francis Xavier, Paris, in 1868; and *The Burial of Christ* for the Church of Augustine de Cambrai, Cambrai, in 1877.

Bertaux also received commissions for public sculptures, beginning with *La Navigation*, commissioned as a pediment on the Tuileries palace in 1867. Other commissions for public buildings included her personification of sculpture for the facade of the Musée du Grenoble in 1872; her *Jean-Baptiste-Siméon Chardin*, produced in 1881 for the Hôtel de Ville, Paris; and two busts for the Opéra in Paris, *Sophie Arnould* and *François Boucher*.

Despite her numerous achievements, Bertaux was mindful of the fact that young women sculptors, especially those from poor backgrounds, had few educational opportunities. Hence she opened her first of several private ateliers in 1873, later called the *ateliers d'études*, which provided training in sculpture and technique. Quite successful, the private ateliers led to her opening a sculpture school for women in 1879, the first of its kind in France. To promote the work of women artists, Bertaux founded the Union des Femmes Peintres et Sculpteurs (UFPS) in 1881 and became its first president, an office she held until 1894, when Virginie Demont-Breton, a naturalist painter, succeeded her. Beginning in 1882, the UFPS began to hold annual exhibitions of the works of its members, called the Salon des Femmes, and through Bertaux's tireless promotion, it managed to have the Salon des Femmes included as one of the annual exhibitions from which the state would select works for purchase.

Bertaux was well aware that many talented women artists could not afford private training and the tuition of a private atelier. Thus in 1889 she addressed the Congrès International des Oeuvres et Institutions Féminines, a government committee on which she served, to propose that a special class be created for women at the École des Beaux-Arts, where they would receive the same level of tuition-free instruction as the male students. She also suggested that women be admitted to all of the competitions held at the school, including those that determined the winner of the Prix de Rome. The Congrès accepted Bertaux's proposal, but it took eight years for the government to fully concede and admit ten women to the École des Beaux-Arts in 1897. Protecting women's "genteel nature" and finding the budget to build a separate school and pay salaries and expenses were often at issue. Although many Modernists could not understand why women would want to gain admission into an institution that so many felt created stagnant artists and boring, traditional works, the point for Bertaux and her supporters was that women should have all of the same opportunities as men.

Bertaux became the first woman elected to the Salon jury in 1898, on which she served until her death. There had never been a woman Salon jury member while the annual exhibition was under governmental command; consequently, after control shifted to the Société des Artistes Français in 1881, the Congrès International campaigned for a woman juror for many years. Although Bertaux applied for membership in the Académie des Beaux-Arts in 1891 and 1892, she was not accepted; however, she was told that in principle her application was admissible. Thus most critics maintained that it was simply because of her gender that she was denied membership.

Although she remained active with the UFPS, after 1900 her artistic production slowed. By the turn of the century, she had promoted the works of literally thousands of women artists through the UFPS and the Salon des Femmes. She died at the age of 84 at her home and studio at the Château de Lassay in 1909.

CATERINA Y. PIERRE

See also **Academies and Associations; Women Sculptors**

Biography

Born in Paris, France, 4 July 1825. Given name Hélène Pilate. Studied sculpture under stepfather Pierre Hébert and privately under Augustin-Alexandre Dumont; married Charles Allétit, *ca.* 1847; exhibited under the name Allétit in 1849 but separated from husband before his death; married painter Léon Bertaux, her student; exhibited under the name Mme Léon Bertaux from 1857; opened private atelier for women sculptors, 1873, followed by a more official Académie, 1879; founder of the Union des Femmes Peintres et Sculpteurs (UFPS), Paris, 1881, and first president, 1881–94; elected officer de l'instruction publique, 1888. Died at Château de Lassay, Saint-Michel-de-Chavaignes, Sarthe, France, 20 April 1909.

Selected Works

1861   *Assumption of the Virgin*; bronze; Musée de Vannes, France

1863   *For the Poor*; marble; Église de Saint-Gratien, Seine-et-Oise, France

1863   *Three Theological Virtues*; marble; Église de Saint-Gratien, Seine-et-Oise, France

1867   *Young Gallic Prisoner*; marble; Musée des Beaux-Arts, Nantes, France

1873   *Young Girl Bathing*; marble; Palais du Sénat, Paris, France

1881   *Jean-Baptiste-Siméon Chardin*; marble; Hôtel de Ville, Paris, France

1881   *Sophie Arnould*; marble; Opéra Garnier, Paris, France

1882   *Psyche under the Empire of Mystery*; bronze; Petit Palais, Paris, France

1885   *François Boucher*; marble; Opéra Garnier, Paris, France

1900   *The Virgin and the Infant Christ (Rest on the Flight into Egypt)*; marble; Chapelle-Sainte-Colombe, Sens Cathedral, France

Further Reading

Easterday, Anastasia Louise, "Charting a Course in an Intractable Profession: Women Sculptors in 19th-Century France," Ph.D. diss., University of California, Los Angeles, 1996

Easterday, Anastasia Louise, "Working the System: Hélène Bertaux and Second Empire Patronage," *Part: The On-Line Journal of Art History* 6 (2000) <dsc.gc.cuny.edu/part/part6/articles/aeaste.html>

Garb, Tamar, "*L'art féminin*: The Formation of a Critical Category in Late Nineteenth-Century France," *Art History* 12 (1989)

Garb, Tamar, *Sisters of the Brush: Women's Artistic Culture in Late Nineteenth-Century Paris*, New Haven, Connecticut: Yale University Press, 1994

Waller, Susan, *Women Artists in the Modern Era: A Documentary History*, Metuchen, New Jersey: Scarecrow Press, 1991

Weisberg, Gabriel P., and Jane R. Becker, editors, *Overcoming All Obstacles: The Women of the Académie Julian* (exhib. cat.), New York: Dahesh Museum, and New Brunswick, New Jersey: Rutgers University Press, 1999

Yeldham, Charlotte, *Women Artists in Nineteenth-Century France and England*, 2 vols., New York: Garland Publishing, 1984

BERTOLDO DI GIOVANNI *ca.* 1430/40?– 1491 *Italian*

Bertoldo di Giovanni referred to himself as "the disciple" of Donatello but never reached a similar commanding level of prominence. With few significant commissions to his credit, much of the work that he did create is either lost or destroyed. Unlike his master Donatello, he did not gain recognition for public- or church-sponsored projects. Bertoldo instead concentrated on producing bronze medals, reliefs, and statuary. In addition, he devoted himself to one of the most influential personages of the early Italian Renaissance, Lorenzo de' Medici (Lorenzo the Magnificent). The unique combination of Bertoldo's intimate work and artistic influences gave him a special position in late-15th-century Florence.

Bertoldo's earliest known work is a medal of Emperor Frederick III, shown at a knighting in Rome. Dated 1469, he created it shortly after his chasing of Donatello's Church of San Lorenzo pulpits following Donatello's death. Bertoldo's support for the Medici family is evident in a medal commemorating the Pazzi conspiracy of 1478. The medal uniquely records the event, including a violent detail of Giuliano de' Medici's murder and Lorenzo de' Medici's narrow escape.

The most sublime example of Bertoldo's relief work is *Crucifixion with SS. Jerome and Francis*. It recalls the influence of Donatello and the technique of *relievo schiacciato* (relief sculpture emphasizing light and shadow through carving methods). Except for some awkward foreshortening, the work demonstrates his mastery over the craft of casting and chasing. The use of diaphanous clothing provides a clear reference to antiquity, yet without overpowering the relief's tragic theme.

Considered his most significant work, Bertoldo's *Battle Relief* displays not only his mastery of relief, but also his influence as a Classical revivalist. Although the work is assumed to be directly inspired by a battle sarcophagus from the Camposanto in Pisa (2nd century CE), Bertoldo's version makes many changes. It borrows from what is evident in the Pisan sculpture and develops upon areas that were destroyed. Bertoldo framed the composition with two Victory figures that calmly watch over the mass of twisted, angular nude figures. Amid the scene Bertoldo inserted a horseman with the attributes of Hercules, considered by some to represent the Florentine republic. Identification of the subject, however, remains uncertain since not all of the figures can be ascertained.

Although the poet Poliziano suggested the theme of Michelangelo's relief *Battle of the Centaurs* (1491–92), Bertoldo's battle relief on the mantel in Lorenzo de' Medici's salon may have provided Michelangelo

with insight into the nature of accomplishing such a complex composition. It is quite possible that Michelangelo viewed it while a student with Bertoldo. Dynamic and forceful in its execution, Bertoldo's bronze battle relief had a profound impact on Giorgio Vasari, as he records in his *Lives of the Painters, Sculptors, and Architects:* "Of the numerous other casts which he made in bronze of battles and of some other things, in the mastery of which there was not then to be found in Florence anyone who could surpass him" (see Vasari, 1550).

When Bertoldo became formally associated with Lorenzo de' Medici, the latter's collection of contemporary sculpture included the formidable work of Antonio Pollaiuolo and Donatello. Unlike Cosimo de' Medici, known as Cosimo the Elder, Lorenzo did not add substantially to his collection but sought out artists he felt showed a strong yet novel interest in antiquity. Although Lorenzo's monumental canvases of the labors of Hercules (date unknown) by Pollaiuolo may have inspired Bertoldo toward the popular hero, Bertoldo's statuette *Hercules on Horseback* seems derivative of sources from the court in Ferrara. The statuette is representative of his seminal efforts at a revived art form. Bertoldo is known to have made only six such works—more than any other Italian Renaissance artist. At times unfinished, the statuettes show Bertoldo's keen interest in exploring new approaches and often with secular themes. *St. John the Baptist* employs much of the spiraling motion first found in Donatello's work. This animated style also appears in Bertoldo's *Shieldbearer*, *Supplicant*, and *Apollo on the Lyre*. Later referred to as *figura serpentina*, these early attempts at a spiraling composition gained prominence during the Mannerist and Baroque periods.

Although small in scale, Bertoldo's innovative *Bellerophon and Pegasus*, on which he was assisted by Adriano Fiorentino, could be easily imagined monumentally. As an open composition, this work—which features the raised limbs of both figure and horse—challenges an important presumption of sculpture, where contours are defined by an idealized mass. Although not as finished as his other works, the rearing horse and figure is a progressive invention.

After an unsuccessful commission and period of time in Padua in 1483–84, Bertoldo returned his interest and attention to Florence under Lorenzo de' Medici's patronage. A project to create a trumpeting pair of angels (*Angels with Trumpets*) for Florence Cathedral in 1485 has not survived. He executed his largest commissions in stucco and terracotta. For the Medici villa at Poggio a Caiano, he designed a glazed terracotta frieze for the facade. An earlier work, the *Apologues*, for Bartolomeo Scala, the Florentine chancellor, includes a series of 12 stucco reliefs for the

Battle Relief
© Alinari / Art Resource, NY

chancellor's palace in Florence. In about 1489 Bertoldo became Lorenzo's official curator of his collection of antiquities and master teacher for his "academy" in the gardens at San Marco in Florence. The academy was the invention of Cosimo the Elder in 1462, when he allowed Florentine philosophers to use his villa at Careggio. Under Lorenzo it evolved into a place for discussion by leading thinkers and poets and for providing training for artists. It was here that Bertoldo, at an advanced age, met Michelangelo, although only for a brief period of two years before his death.

Bertoldo absorbed Donatello's attentiveness to a well-conceived composition and a mastery over the media, rather than the extremes of personal and universal emotion. He directed this approach toward his own work, and with the interest and advent of small bronze statuary, he secured an influential role in Renaissance sculpture.

BARRON NAEGEL

See also **Donatello (Donato di Betto Bardi); Michelangelo (Buonarroti); Pollaiuolo, Antonio**

Biography

Born perhaps in Florence, Italy, *ca.* 1430–40? Worked under Donatello; assisted in chasing Church of San Lorenzo bronze pulpit reliefs after Donatello's death in 1466; produced commemorative medals and bronze reliefs; created several bronze statuettes, a genre for which he is considered instrumental; became member of Lorenzo de' Medici's household and was associated with literati of Lorenzo's "academy"; became curator of Lorenzo's collection of antiquities, marbles, bronzes, and gems, *ca.* 1489; taught young artists, including Michelangelo, modeling and sculpture; worked in bronze, wood, terracotta, and stucco. Died at Poggio a Caiano, near Florence, Italy, 28 December 1491.

Selected Works

1469	Portrait medal of Emperor Frederick III; bronze; private collection
1470–80	*Supplicant*; bronze; Bodemuseum, Berlin, Germany
ca. 1475	*Battle Relief*; bronze; Museo Nazionale del Bargello, Florence, Italy
1478	Medal commemorating the Pazzi conspiracy; bronze; private collection
ca. 1478	*Crucifixion with SS. Jerome and Francis*; bronze; Museo Nazionale del Bargello, Florence, Italy
1479	*Apologues*; stucco; Palazzo di Bartolomeo Scala, Florence, Italy
1470s	*St. John the Baptist*; bronze; Musée du Louvre, Paris, France
1480–90	Models for a frieze (executed by Andrea della Robbia); terracotta; facade, Villa Medici, Poggio a Caiano, Italy
ca. 1480	*Apollo on the Lyre*; bronze; Museo Nazionale del Bargello, Florence, Italy
ca. 1480	*Hercules on Horseback*; bronze; Modena Gallery and Museum, Estense, Italy
ca. 1480	*Shieldbearer*; bronze; versions: Collection of the Princes of Liechtenstein, Vaduz, Liechtenstein; The Frick Collection, New York City, United States
early 1480s	*Bellerophon and Pegasus*; bronze; Kunsthistorisches Museum, Vienna, Austria
1485	*Angels with Trumpets*; for Florence Cathedral of Italy; gilded wood (lost)

Further Reading

Condivi, Ascanio, *Vita di Michelangelo Buonarroti*, edited by Emma Spina Barelli, Milan: Rizzoli, 1964; as *The Life of Michelangelo*, translated by Alice Sedgwick Wohl, edited by Hellmut Wohl, Baton Rouge: Louisiana State University Press, 1976; 2nd edition, University Park: Pennsylvania State University Press, 1999

Draper, James David, *Bertoldo di Giovanni, Sculptor of the Medici Household: Critical Reappraisal and Catalogue Raisoneé*, Columbia: University of Missouri Press, 1992

Gombrich, E.H., "The Early Medici as Patrons of Art," in *Italian Renaissance Studies*, edited by Ernest Fraser Jacobs, London: Faber, 1960

Kent, F.W., "Bertoldo *scultore* and Lorenzo de' Medici," *The Burlington Magazine* 134 (April 1992)

Kristeller, Paul Oskar, "The Platonic Academy of Florence," in *Renaissance Thought II: Papers on Humanism and the Arts*, by Kristeller, New York: Harper, 1965

Pollard, John Graham, *Medaglie italiane del rinascimento nel Museo Nazionale del Bargello; Italian Renaissance Medals in the Museo Nationale del Bargello* (bilingual Italian-English edition), 3 vols., Florence, Italy: Studio per Edizioni Scelte, 1984

Pope-Hennessy, John, *An Introduction to Italian Sculpture*, 3 vols., London: Phaidon, 1963; 4th edition, 1996; see especially vol. 2, *Italian Renaissance Sculpture*

Seymour, Charles, *Sculpture in Italy, 1400–1500*, London: Penguin, 1966

Vasari, Giorgio, *Le vite de' più eccellenti architetti, pittori, e scultori italiani*, 3 vols., Florence: Torrentino, 1550; 2nd edition, Florence: Apresso i Giunti, 1568; as *Lives of the Painters, Sculptors, and Architects*, 2 vols., translated by Gaston du C. de Vere (1912), edited by David Ekserdjian, New York: Knopf, and London: Campbell, 1996

Vermeule, Cornelius Clarkson, III, "Graeco-Roman Asia Minor to Renaissance Italy: Medallic and Related Arts," *Studies in the History of Art* 21 (1987)

FRANCESCO BERTOS *fl.* 1693–1739
Italian

Although Francesco Bertos is today considered one of the most mysterious and singular early 18th-century

Venetian sculptors, to his contemporaries he was indubitably among the most renowned, as is indicated by the presence of his works in some of the most prestigious collections of the time. His bizarre and dynamic sculptural groups—some in marble, most in bronze, with their numerous figures acrobatically entwined and often organized in pyramidal structures—adorned the homes of aristocrats in Venice, such as the Pisani, Sagredo, and Manin families, and enhanced the celebrated collections of Field Marshal Johann Matthias von der Schulenburg, the Savoy court in Turin, and Peter the Great in St. Petersburg. Bertos's production of small statues was unlike anything else in contemporary Venetian sculpture, and he may well have developed it in order to delight refined art patrons who, in keeping with current tastes, were attracted above all by clever conceptions and virtuoso execution, the very qualities embodied in Bertos's sculptures. He devised complicated compositions to expound complicated subjects (usually allegorical and often hard to interpret) and executed them with a technical skill that aroused the greatest admiration among his contemporaries. In some it also aroused such suspicion that Bertos was once summoned before an Inquisition court to defend himself against charges of sorcery.

Little biographical information is known about Bertos, and nearly all of it is based on papers documenting the payment of works commissioned from the artist, many of which are now lost. Concerning his training and cultural background one can only guess, and it is thus difficult to establish a chronology of his vast output. He was probably born in the Veneto region; several 18th-century documents refer to him as a Paduan sculptor. The earliest information places him in Rome in 1693, working as a stone carver.

The genre created by Bertos seems indebted on the one hand to the copious production of bronze sculpture in Padua, for instance the virtuoso groups by 17th-century sculptor Nicolò Roccatagliata, and on the other to ancient statuary, such as the much-admired Farnese *Bull* (3rd century BCE), which was in Rome when Bertos was working there. A bronze version (80.5 centimeters) of this celebrated sculpture, quite faithful to the original and solidly attributed to Bertos, recently appeared on the art market together with a pendant depicting Marcus Curtius. This suggests that the Farnese *Bull* was fundamental in the formation of Bertos's language. At the same time Bertos was undoubtedly fascinated by Giambologna's spiraling groups and emulated this master in a small marble version after Giambologna's *Rape of a Sabine* (1582). Bertos's sculpture is part of a set of eight marble groups by the artist now in Palazzo Reale in Turin, which some historians believe to be the same set known to have been in the Pisani collection in Venice before it was broken up in

the early 19th century. The other seven groups depict *The Four Seasons*, the *Rape of Helen*, and two *Allegories*. All provide eloquent evidence of Bertos's ideal of sculpture intended to be seen from all sides, which draws the viewer to walk around the pyramidal composition, following its spiral movement, partly to observe the way the slender figures twist around their own axes, their elongated bodies and tapered limbs crossing and overlapping in daring balancing acts, and partly to admire the artist's technique and meticulous definition of every detail; the chiseling recalls goldsmith's work.

Bertos alternated between stone and bronze, probably from the beginning of his activity and, as appears from the signed bronze *Allegory* in the J. Paul Getty Museum (Los Angeles), was equally skilled in both. Significantly, in the past Bertos's bronzes have been mistakenly classified as Renaissance works, which links the artist to the great Italian bronze tradition and thereby reveals his possible models. Nonetheless, it is the spirit of the 18th century that informs the elegance, gracefulness, and accurate anatomy of the figures in a pair of bronzes (both signed on their marble bases) depicting *Stupidity Sustaining Fortune* and *Industry Uplifting Virtue*.

Besides the elaborate allegories, Bertos produced a number of sculptures depicting mythological subjects, for the most part dramatic episodes freely drawn from Ovid's *Metamorphoses*. One example is the *Centauress Fighting the Lapiths*, a piece formerly attributed to Agostino Fasolato but now firmly ascribed to Bertos and stylistically more mature than the similar subject in the Victoria and Albert Museum (London). Another example is the *Battle of the Lapiths and the Centaur*, known to have entered Peter the Great's collection in 1722 and thus among the three Bertos works to have a documented *ante quem* date; the other two are the bronze *Allegories* in Turin, for which the sculptor was paid on 9 January 1739.

Fewer religious works figure among Bertos's known sculptures, but some of them are among his greatest accomplishments. The marble *Expulsion from the Garden of Eden* and the dramatic bronze *Crucifixion* capture all the spirituality and pathos inherent in the subject. This short list also includes a set of bronze reliefs of Old and New Testament scenes, two Jesuit saints, and a *Saint Jerome Repentant*. In the *Saint Jerome* the religious subject appears to be almost a pretext for presenting a refined male nude. Despite the static pose, the tension in the figure's muscles gives an impression of leashed motion.

As recent studies have demonstrated, Bertos also worked in larger dimensions, creating interior and exterior statuary for the country houses of the nobility. A signed life-size marble statue identified as *Flora* is especially interesting. This piece enables us to measure the persistence of distinctive stylistic features (such as facial types and drapery arrangements) and to identify, in the pairs *Venus and Adonis* (or *Zephyrus and Flora*) (1730) and *Apollo and Marsyas* (1730), two of the eight large stone groups that, according to documentary evidence, Bertos created in 1730 for the garden at the Villa Manin in Passariano, a town in the Friuli region. However, large dimensions diluted the originality of Bertos's language. In these pieces it appears to attune itself to the manner of the Bonazza family, sculptors who worked in Padua for many years and were deeply involved in the Passariano project.

MONICA DE VINCENTI

See also **Giambologna; Roccatagliata, Nicolò**

Biography

Born perhaps in Veneto, Italy, date unknown. Cited in documents as a Paduan sculptor; first recorded as a stone carver in Rome, 1693; 19th-century sources indicate work in Venice, 1710; worked in Padua and nearby Dolo, from 1715, for the Manin family, executing numerous works for their palace in Venice and villa at Passariano, Friuli, 1715–30; made two candlesticks and bronze cross for Basilica of Sant'Antonio, Padua, 1733–34; listed in accounting ledgers of Field Marshal von der Schulenburg, 1732–39, for whom he made 12 works; made two groups and two bronze bas-reliefs for the Savoy court in Turin, 1738–39. Place and date of death unknown.

Selected Works

1710–39 *Allegory*; bronze; two versions: Art Institute of Chicago, Illinois, United States; J. Paul Getty Museum, Los Angeles, California, United States

1710–39 *Crucifixion*; bronze; Victoria and Albert Museum, London, England

1710–39 *Expulsion from the Garden of Eden*; marble; Victoria and Albert Museum, London, England

1710–39 *Industry Uplifting Virtue*; bronze; J. Paul Getty Museum, Los Angeles, California, United States

1710–39 *Massacre of the Innocents*; bronze; Art Institute of Chicago, Illinois, United States

1710–39 *Stupidity Sustaining Fortune*; bronze; J. Paul Getty Museum, Los Angeles, California, United States

1710–39 *Triumph of Chastity*; bronze; Victoria and Albert Museum, London, England

before *Battle of the Lapiths and the Centaur*;

1722 marble; Hermitage, St. Petersburg, Russia

1729–39 *Centauress Fighting the Lapiths*; marble; Musei Civici, Padua, Italy

1730–39 *The Four Seasons*; marble; Palazzo Reale, Turin, Italy

1738–39 Allegory of the grape harvest; bronze; Palazzo Reale, Turin, Italy

Further Reading

Androssov, Sergei, *Pietro il Grande: Collezionista d'arte veneta*, Venice: Canal, 1999

Banzato, Davide, Franca Pellegrini, and Monica De Vincenti, editors, *Dal Medioevo a Canova: Sculture dei Musei civici di Padova dal Trecento all'Ottocento* (exhib. cat.), Venice: Marsilio, 2000

Binion, Alice, *La galleria scomparsa del maresciallo von der Schulenburg: Un mecenate nella Venezia del Settecento*, Milan: Electa, 1990

Frank, Martina, *Virtù e Fortuna: Il mecenatismo e le committenze artistiche della famiglia Manin tra Friuli e Venezia nel XVII e XVIII secolo*, Venice: Istituto Veneto di Scienze, Lettere ed Arti, 1996

Viancini, Ettore, "Per Francesco Bertos," *Soggi e memorie de storie dell'arte* 19 (1994)

JOSEPH BEUYS 1921–1986 *German*

Joseph Beuys remains among the most controversial artists of the 20th century, merging sculpture, drawing, and performance ideas in his enigmatic works and teachings. Beuys expanded the notion of sculpture to encompass all physical and spiritual human activity, both individual and societal. Beuys refused to separate art from life by means of his theory of art as "social sculpture," the principle underlying all of his art. In his sometimes Christological and often shamanistic self-presentation, and in his brief pursuit of a political career, Beuys refused to conform to the accepted image of the silent, or deliberately obfuscating, artist. Through his development of assemblage and the multiple, and in his powerful late installations, Beuys introduced new materials into the realm of sculpture and posited an explicitly political and activist function for art after 1945.

In interviews, Beuys described different stages in his life as key experiences, particularly his Luftwaffe plane crash in the Crimea during World War II and his subsequent rescue by nomadic Tatars, who allegedly nursed him back to health in part by coating his ravaged and frostbitten body with lard and wrapping him in insulating felt. For Beuys, these recollections were so visceral that they determined his programmatic redefinition of sculpture as social sculpture, with its attendant notion of the "warmth principle" and the assumption that individual creativity is the key to realizing freedom and agency. Beuys's warmth principle traces a line of movement of material, sound, language, and even thought, within and *as* sculpture from an unformed "warm" state to a cold, "crystalline," and ordered one. The thermodynamic shifts between the poles of heat and cold (or vice versa)—from chaos to form, from theoretical concept to praxis—were key elements of his social sculpture. Even earlier then American and European Process artists of the late 1960s and early 1970s, Beuys investigated the principles of insulation, infiltration, and conduction in his investigation of organic materials.

The dynamism of temperature and energy is implied in the objects *Fat Chair I* and *Fond III*. Beuys claimed that he first used fat or margarine as a sculptural material in 1963 at the Galerie Zwirner in Cologne. As an assemblage, *Fat Chair I* presented fat in its crystalline, or ordered, state and in the geometrical form of the triangle or wedge. As material, it infiltrates other materials by staining them; as an insulator, it also protects the human and animal body in severe climates. The inner workings and warmth of the body are also implied in that the fat corner is fitted into a chair where the human torso would be. Beuys also examined electrical conduction and the storage of energy through works such as *Fond III*. In this piece Beuys placed a plate of copper on top of each of nine 110-centimeter-high piles of felt, which evoked the primitive technology of a battery and the principles of heat insulation, storage, and conduction. In a synesthetic fashion, *Fond III* altered the acoustic dynamics of the room in which it was installed, demonstrating how materials might transform a space by altering sound perception.

Beuys also worked with the multiple as a means or vehicle for the dissemination of his art and art theory. Beuys knew Daniel Spoerri's first *MAT (Multiplication d'Art Transformable)* edition of 1959; the multiple was based on the idea of serial multiplication, which allows for a series of originals, not copies made from a single original. Beuys described his populist multiples as conduits for communication between the artist and viewers. *Intuition*, the largest multiple edition Beuys produced (approximately 12,000 were made), circulated Beuys's notion of the primacy of intuitive intelligence and creativity over rationalism. A simple, empty wooden box, *Intuition* was "to be filled with thoughts." Unlike the purposive ironist Marcel Duchamp, who delighted the European avant-garde in the 1920s with his readymades (urinals, bottleracks, wooden boxes, and other utilitarian objects), Beuys was essentially a romantic who believed in the healing and transformative power of the arts through communication.

In the late 1960s, Beuys produced sculptures, objects, multiples, installations, and performances while establishing a number of counterinstitutional frame-

Joseph Beuys, *Felt Suit* (1970)
© Tate Gallery, London / Art Resource, NY and Artists Rights Society, NY

works for the public debate of social and political issues. He turned to the format of the chalkboard, which he often used to illustrate points in his own lectures at the Düsseldorf Kunstakademie, to record, map, and engage discussions held within the Organization for Direct Democracy and the Free International University, activist organizations Beuys helped to found in 1971 and 1974, respectively. Beuys also incorporated chalkboards he had used in dialogues with visitors to the London exhibition *Art into Society Society into Art* in his installation *Richtskräfte* (Directional Forces). The boards integrated the ideas of the social reformer Rudolf Steiner into the theory of social sculpture. In *Richtskräfte*, Beuys arranged the boards on the floor of the gallery, with several propped on easels, thereby incorporating text and the surface upon which text is written, which some historians have interpreted as drawing, into the medium of sculpture (see Temkin).

After suffering a heart attack in 1975, Beuys worked more extensively with objects and installation. Of the works he created during the last decade of his life, the installations *Tram Stop* and *Plight* are among his most resonant. Both of these works return to the theme of the interconnection between Beuys's personal memories and the future of social sculpture. In *Plight*, his last large-scale installation, Beuys outfitted the walls of two rooms in the Galerie Anthony d'Offay in London with 284 double-stacked felt columns, each 150 centimeters tall and 50 centimeters wide; in the center of these, he placed a closed grand piano. The felt-covered walls absorbed all sound and the temperature was raised as soon as a number of visitors entered it, creating a muffled, cocoon-like environment. This final warmth sculpture underscored the tension between silence and the potential for musical and creative sound as it highlighted the sense of physical and spiritual transformation of the human subject. While *Plight* certainly seems to metaphorically represent an isolation chamber, womb, or tomb, its meanings are interminable and determined by the viewer.

Beuys's stature has only increased over the years with his manifest influence on younger American and European sculptors, primarily in the area of Earth art, Body, and performance art. Inheritors of his ideas are wide-ranging and include artists such as Eva Hesse, Ann Hamilton, Anish Kapoor, and Wolfgang Laib. Beuys received the Lehmbruck Prize from the city of Duisburg shortly after this exhibition. His acceptance speech eulogized a predecessor, the German figurative sculptor Wilhelm Lehmbruck, and also himself. Beuys died on January 23, 1986, just days after delivering this speech.

CLAUDIA MESCH

See also **Assemblage; Contemporary Sculpture; Germany: 20th Century–Contemporary; Hamilton, Ann; Hesse, Eva; Kapoor, Anish; Kounellis, Jannis; Modernism; Performance Art; Postmodernism; Spoerri, Daniel**

Biography

Born in Krefeld, Germany, 12 May 1921. Drafted 1941, served in the German air force, 1941–45; crashed in the Crimea and rescued by nomadic Tatars; British prisoner of war, 1945; studied at Düsseldorf Kunstakademie, Düsseldorf, with Joseph Enseling and Ewald Mataré, 1947–54; appointed to teach sculpture at Düsseldorf Kunstakademie, 1961; received contract, 1969; summarily dismissed from position without pay by Johannes Rau, minister of science and research, State of North Rhine-Westphalia, 1972; federal labor board in Kassel deemed dismissal illegal, 1978; allowed to retain title of professor and studio in Düsseldorf; visiting professor, School of the Applied Arts, Vienna, beginning 1978; represented Germany at the Venice Biennale, 1976; retrospective exhibition, Guggenheim Museum, New York City, 1979. Honorary doctorate, Nova Scotia College of Art and Design, 1976; member of Berlin Academy of Arts, 1978; member, Royal Academy of the Fine Arts, Stockholm, 1980; Wilhelm-Lehmbruck Prize, city of Duisburg, 1986. Died in Düsseldorf, Germany, 23 January 1986.

Selected Works

1964   *Fat Chair I*; chair and fat; Ströher Collection, Beuys Block, Hessisches Landesmuseum, Darmstadt, Germany (another version produced in 1985)

1968   *Fond III*; felt, copper; Ströher Collection, Beuys Block, Hessisches Landesmuseum, Darmstadt, Germany

1968   *Intuition*; wooden box, pencil drawing (unlimited edition, approximately 12,000 made)

1974–77 *Richtskräfte* (Directional Forces); blackboards, chalk, painted chalkboard stands, painted walking stick, wood box; Staatliche Museen, Berlin, Germany

1976   *Tram Stop*; iron, debris; Marx Collection, Staatliche Museen, Berlin, Germany

1985   *Plight*; temporary installation for Galerie Anthony d'Offay, London, England; grand piano, 284 felt rolls, chalkboard, thermometer; Centre Georges Pompidou, Paris, France

Further Reading

Beuys, Eva, Wenzel Beuys, and Jessyka Beuys, *Joseph Beuys, Block Beuys*, Munich: Schirmer/Mosel, 1990

Borer, Alain, *The Essential Joseph Beuys*, edited by Lothar Schirmer, London: Thames and Hudson, 1996; Cambridge, Massachusetts: MIT Press, 1997

Schellmann, Jörg, editor, *Joseph Beuys, the Multiples: Catalogue Raisonné of Multiples and Prints*, 2nd edition, Munich: Schellmann, 1972; 8th edition, Cambridge, Massachusetts: Harvard University Art Museums, and Munich: Schirmer/Mosel, 1997

Stachelhaus, Heiner, *Joseph Beuys*, Düsseldorf, Germany: Claassen, 1987; 2nd edition, 1988; as *Joseph Beuys*, translated by David Britt, New York: Abbeville Press, 1991

Szeemann, Harald, editor, *Joseph Beuys*, Zurich: Pro Litteris, 1993

Temkin, Ann, *Thinking Is Form: The Drawings of Joseph Beuys*, New York and London: Thames and Hudson, 1993

Thistlewood, David, editor, *Joseph Beuys: Diverging Critiques*, Liverpool: Liverpool University Press and Tate Gallery, 1995

Tisdall, Caroline, *Joseph Beuys*, New York and London: Thames and Hudson, 1979

Von Graevenitz, Antje, "The Old and New Initiation Rites: Joseph Beuys and Epiphany," in *Robert Lehman Lectures on*

Contemporary Art, edited by Lynne Cooke and Karen Kelly, New York: Dia Center for the Arts, 1996

TRAM STOP
Joseph Beuys (1921–1986)
1976
iron, debris
central column h. 3.68 m; rail w. 8 m; drilled hole
d. 21 m; large rubble pile
Neue Nationalgalerie, Staatliche Museen
Preußischer Kulturbesitz, Berlin, Germany;
Kröller-Müller Museum, Otterlo, Holland

Beuys first realized the installation *Tram Stop*, his contribution to the Venice Biennale in 1976, in the German Pavilion. The installation consisted of four primary elements, three composed of iron: a columnar vertical monument, a drilled hole, a length of rail, and a heap of excavated debris. Although *Tram Stop* was anchored in the muck of the Venetian lagoon, it also served as Beuys's reconstruction of the spaces of his own childhood in Germany and of his discovery of the form and material of sculpture. On a thematic level, the work examines the connection of the realm of private memory to that of historical memory by referencing the militarism, violence, and death that also characterize the German past. The work also returns to central formal and material concerns of Beuys's theory of art as social sculpture. *Tram Stop* was dismantled at the conclusion of the Biennale, and it is currently displayed in a horizontal, disassembled state.

The central element of *Tram Stop* is a cast-iron replica of a 17th-century monument in Beuys's childhood town, Kleve, in Germany. In a 1976 interview, the sculptor explained that as a schoolboy he would take the tram each day and change over at the stop named "To the Iron Man." Beuys was fascinated by the arrangement of iron parts next to the tram tracks, which commemorated something, although no one knew who or what. According to Klaus Gallwitz, old accounts of the city of Kleve refer to a monument or marker erected by the regent Johann Mortiz von Nassau, dating to the year 1654. In that year the marker consisted of an upended field cannon barrel, the mouth of which featured a snake's head, crowned by a sphere and a figure of Cupid; four mortar bombs were arranged around the base. The figure of Cupid had been removed around 1672 during the French war against the Netherlands, but the snake column and the mortars remained. In 1976 Beuys had the entire extant monument, the canon barrel and the four mortars, recast in iron with some proportional changes. He replaced the earlier Cupid figure at the top of the cannon barrel with the form of a human head, which has been variously attributed to either Beuys himself (see Tisdall, 1976, and Gallwitz, 1981) and to an unnamed female student (see Luckow, 1998). In *Tram Stop* Beuys erected this recast arrangement vertically in the German Pavilion. This columnar structure was further framed by the entrance and was visible to viewers upon their approach to the building.

To the left of this group, Beuys installed a train rail, acquired from the Düsseldorf tram system, horizontally into the ground of the pavilion, sinking it into the ground at each end to give it the appearance of rising out of the ground and returning to it in a gradual arc. In contrast to the dark, matte iron of the copy of the "Iron Man" monument, the length of rail was polished to reflect light and to add the appearance of movement in a fashion reminiscent of Constantin Brancusi's highly polished sculptural forms. Between the rear wall of the gallery and the "Iron Man," Beuys arranged two further elements. First, a pile of dirt, stones, and other debris that had been excavated from the drilling into the foundation and the canal was heaped at the foot of the vertical column. To the right of this pile was a small round opening into the ground in which the viewer could see the reflections of the canal water below the building. A thin, rounded iron handle or crank bent at two 90-degree angles projected from this hole.

Beuys spoke of the Iron Man monument as his earliest recognition of the possibilities of sculptural form. On one level, as a "reconstruction" of a space of childhood and of the German landscape by means of horizontal and vertical axes, *Tram Stop* resonates with the autobiographical content that marks much of Beuys's art, from his earlier performances to the installations that came to dominate his artistic production after 1971. *Tram Stop* realizes the 17th-century cannon as sculpture in that Beuys casts these objects found in Kleve. He made use of the drill hole to connect his installation to the Venetian landscape outside the German Pavilion and to invoke an archeological descent into the past in a manner similar to Walter de Maria's 1970–72 proposal for a deep shaft on the grounds of the Munich Olympic Games (de Maria realized his proposal as *Vertical Earth Kilometer* in Kassel in 1977). Beuys's repeated use of the modern material of iron in recasting military weaponry and including a segment of iron track in *Tram Stop* resonated with the fascist architecture of the German Pavilion, which was built during the Nazi period. The "Iron Man" of Kleve, which marked Beuys's first encounter with three-dimensional form, was also the ruins of weaponry; the rails of the tram that brought the boy Beuys to these forms simultaneously reference the most nefarious gashes of rail in the German landscape that delivered

Jews and others to death camps. A 20th-century German childhood cannot be separated from this historical memory, and in *Tram Stop* Beuys struggles with the tensions inherent in the material of iron itself for a postwar German sculptor.

In *Tram Stop*, Beuys returned to formal motifs he had explored in earlier works and to his theory of social sculpture as a universal notion of human creativity and social change. In various drawings and performances, he had emphasized the head as the site of the cognitive process and of creativity, of intuition as well as rationality. The tormented head of *Tram Stop* further sets the viewer's intuitive creativity and thought, the only means whereby change and social sculpture can be realized upon the ruins of the past.

CLAUDIA MESCH

Further Reading

Gallwitz, Klaus, "Stationen der Erinnerung: Joseph Beuys und seine 'Strassenbahnhaltestelle,'" in *Festschrift für Eduard Trier zum 60. Geburtstag*, edited by Müller Hofstede and Werner Spies, Berlin: Mann, 1981

Luckow, Dirk, *Joseph Beuys und die amerikanische Anti Form-Kunst*, Berlin: Mann, 1998

Tisdall, Caroline, "*Tram Stop:* Joseph Beuys' Terminal Memory," *Beuys, Ger, Ruthenbeck: Biennale 76, Venedig, Deutscher Pavillon*, S.l.: Kommissar der Bundesrepublik Deutschland, 1976; reprint, *Flash Art* 26/169 (1993)

LUIGI BIENAIMÉ 1795–1878 *Italian*

The son of the Flemish sculptor Francesco Giuseppe from Rance and Maria Cateriana Iori, Luigi Bienaimé received his early training in his father's house under the direction of his half-brother Pietro Antonio Bienaimé. In 1811, at the age of 16, Bienaimé won accolades for his copy of contemporary Antonio Canova's seated figure *Letizia Ramolino*, which was acquired by Maria Beatrice d'Este, daughter of Grand Duchess Maria Teresa Cybo d'Este, the founder of the Carrara Academy. The academy had gained new life in 1805 with the arrival of Elisa Bonaparte-Baciocchi and introduced in 1810 a stipend for artists to stay in Rome. Bienaimé studied at the Carrara Academy with Lorenzo Bartolini, who had a great influence upon him. Bienaimé took part in the legacy of Neoclassical aesthetics that propagated the beauty ideals of Roman and Greek antiquity.

In 1817 Bienaimé won the first prize in a competition for the Rome stipend with the theme *Giasone alla conquista del vello d'Oro* (Jason Wins the Golden Fleece). Maria Beatrice d'Este preferred his competitor, Bernardo Tacca, and annulled the competition. The competition was then announced again the following year with the theme of *Mitras, Son of Anobazan Slay-ing Datmus*. Bienaimé once again received the first prize but had to share the Rome stipend with Tacca for three years.

Arriving in Rome early in 1818, Bienaimé took part in the instruction at the Accademia di San Luca and was admitted into Bertel Thorvaldsen's workshop. His sculpting studio was next to Thorvaldsen's workshop on the Piazza Barberini, where the Hôtel Bristol stands today.

In 1819 Bienaimé submitted his trial relief to the Carrara Academy with the theme *David*; it was judged to be very good with the exception of the proportions, described in the records as being flawed. He worked in Thorvaldsen's workshop with other students from Carrara (Bernardo Tacca, Niccolò Bernardo Raggi, Giuseppe Livi, and Giovanni Bogazzi) on a Venus and the *Portrait of Graf von Holstein* (ca. 1820–25) under the direction of Pietro Tenerani. Bienaimé was counted among the most important of Thorvaldsen's students, along with Pietro Galli and Tenerani.

In 1820 Bienaimé created the figure *San Giovanni predicatore* (Saint John at Prayer), which received great praise both in Carrara and from Maria Beatrice d'Este in Vienna. She extended his stipend, which he still had to share with Tacca. His third trial piece was the figure *Amore che abbevera le colombe di Venere* (Cupid with the Doves of Venus), which he executed in 1821/22 in marble for Count Giovanni Battista Sommariva, and later on in 1848 it was copied for Czar Nicholas I.

In most cases Thorvaldsen first designed a clay *bozzetto* (a small-scale preparatory study or model) for his works, which his assistants then carried out in stone. In addition, after Canova's death in 1822, Thorvaldsen held a monopoly on the production of Classical sculpture in Rome. Bienaimé was one of Thorvaldsen's most skilled modelers and built many of the latter's large-scale works in clay models, including the Lion Monument in Lucerne, the *Apostle Matthew* and *Saint Peter*, and tympanum figures for *Saint John's Sermon* for the Church of Our Lady in Copenhagen. Evidence suggests that he also worked on Thorvaldsen's monumental tomb of Pope Pius VII for St. Peter's Basilica in Rome. In 1827 Bienaimé took over as Thorvaldsen's master student from Pietro Tenerani, who had fallen out with Thorvaldsen during the execution of the tomb of Eugène de Beauharnais in the St. Michael Church, Munich.

The patron setting the tone in Rome at the time was Prince Alessandro Torlonia, whose palazzo exhibited a decidedly iconographic program, consisting of unambiguous references to the heroes of Classical art—Hercules and Lichias, Alexander the Great—as well as to Anacreontic motives from bucolic art: Theseus and Bacchus, Cupid and Psyche, and Apollo and the Parnassus of the Muses. Torlonia employed many sculptors, including Rinaldo Rinaldi, Antonio Solà, Camillo Pistrucci, Ercole Dante, Pietro Galli, and Bienaimé. Bienaimé carried out the statues *Venus* (1838–40, begun by Giuseppe Chialli) and *Mercury* (1844), as well as a copy of Canova's *Female Dancer* (1838–44).

The Milan politician and art collector Giovanni Battista Sommariva, who already owned sculptures by Luigi Acquisti, Canova, Massimiliano Laboureur, Thorvaldsen, Adamo Tadolini, and others, completed his collection in the Villa Carlotta in Cadenabbia on Lake Como with Bienaimé's *Cupid Gives Water to the Doves* (1821/22) and *Innocence* (1821/22).

Bienaimé sent a good portion of his work to Russia, assisted by his patron, the Russian Count Teodor Galitzin, who arranged for many of the Russian czars' commissions to be given to him. Grand Duke Michael of Russia acquired Bienaimé's *Bacchante* (1836) and *Zephyr* (1837) when he went to Italy in 1838. One year later Prince Alexander of Russia visited Rome and ordered a number of the sculptor's works for his collection, including *Telemach*, *Diana*, *Andromache*, *San Giovannino*, and *Cupid Gives Water to the Doves*, which today are located in the Winter Palace in St. Petersburg, together with the sculptures owned by Grand Duke Michael. The Russian ambassador in Rome, Count Dimitrievich Gur'ev, an admirer of Canova, also owned a number of his works, including the *Hebe* (1816), *Female Dancer with Index Finger on Chin* (1814), and *Cupid Sharps the Arrow* (ordered 1833).

The poet Angelo Maria Ricci, schooled in Naples, combined antique Arcadian motives and themes with Christian contents, admired Thorvaldsen, and left behind numerous odes to the beauty of the work of the Danish Pheidias (Thorvaldsen). This friendship also extended to Bienaimé; Ricci published the first monograph on Bienaimé in Rome in 1838 and provided engraving captions and verses for it.

Little is known about Bienaimé's works and activities during the two decades before his death in 1878. The *Guardian Angel* group (1831) adorns his family grave in the Campo Verano in Rome.

TAMARA HUFSCHMIDT

See also **Bartolini, Lorenzo; Canova, Antonio; Pheidias; Schadow, Johann Gottfried; Thorvaldsen, Bertel**

Biography

Born in Carrara, Italy, 2 March 1795. Son of the Flemish sculptor Francesco Giuseppe. Trained at home under his half-brother Pietro Antonio Bienaimé; studied at the Carrara Academy with Lorenzo Bartolini; twice won the Rome Prize at the Accademia di Belle Arti e Licea Artistico, Carrara, for a scholarship to study in Rome, 1817 and 1818; studied in Rome at the Accademia di San Luca, from 1818; worked in Bertel Thorvaldsen's studio, Rome, from 1818; took Pietro Tenerani's place as Thorvaldsen's master student, 1827; produced many works for Russian clients, 1820s to *ca.* 1846. Died in Rome, Italy, 17 April 1878.

Selected Works

1817   *Giasone alla conquista del vello d'Oro* (Jason Wins the Golden Fleece); plaster; Gipsoteca, Carrara, Italy

1819   *David*; plaster; Gipsoteca, Carrara, Italy

1820   *San Giovanni predicatore* (St. John at Prayer); plaster; Gipsoteca, Carrara, Italy

1821   *Amore che abbevera le colombe di Venere* (Cupid with the Doves of Venus); plaster; Gipsoteca, Carrara, Italy; marble; Villa Carlotta, Cadenábbia, Como, Italy

1821/22 *Innocence*; marble; Villa Carlotta, Cadenábbia, Como, Italy

1835   *Andromache*; marble; Hermitage, St. Petersburg, Russia

1835   *Diana*; marble; Hermitage, St. Petersburg, Russia

1836   *San Giovannino*; marble; Metropolitan Museum of Art, New York City, United States

1837   *Zephyr*; marble; Hermitage, St. Petersburg, Russia

1838   *Venus* (with Giuseppe Chialli); marble; Galleria Corsini, Rome, Italy; another version in marble (1842), Galleria Civico d'Arte Moderna, Turin, Italy

ca. 1843 Bust of Napoléon (based on model by Bertel Thorvaldsen); marble; Protomoteca Capitoline, Rome, Italy

Further Reading

Bertel Thorvaldsen: Skulpturen, Modelle, Bozzetti, Handzeichnungen: Gemälde aus Thorvaldsens Sammlungen (exhib. cat.), Cologne, Germany: Bachem, 1977

Bertozzi, Massimo, editor, *I Marmi degli Zar: Gli scultori Carraresi all'Ermitage e a Petergof* (exhib. cat.), Milan: Charta, 1996

Campori, Giuseppe, editor, *Memorie biografiche degli scultori, architetti, pittori, ec. nativi di Carrara e di altri luoghi della provincia di Massa*, Modena, Italy: Vincenzi, 1873; reprint, Bologne, Italy: Forni, 1969

De Micheli, Mario, Gian Lorenzo Mellini, and Massimo Bertozzi, *Scultura a Carrara: Ottocento*, Bergamo, Italy: Bolis, 1993

Hartmann, Jörgen Birkedal, *Antike Motive bei Thorvaldsen: Studien zur Antikenrezeption des Klassizismus*, edited by Klaus Parlasca, Tübingen, Germany: Wasmuth, 1979

Le Grice, Hawks, *Walks through the Studii of Sculptors at Rome with a Brief Historical and Critical Sketch of Sculpture*, 2 vols., Rome: Puccinelli, 1844; see especially vol. 1

Panzetta, Alfonso, *Dizionario degli scultori italiani dell'ottocento e del primo novecento*, 3 vols., Milan: Allemandi, 1994

Ricci, Angelo Maria, Sculture di Luigi Bienaimé da Carrara descritte dal cavaliere Angelo Maria Ricci, Rome: Tipografia delle Belle Arti, 1838

Russo, Severina, editor, La gipsoteca dell'Accademia di Belle Arti di Carrara, Carrara, Italy: Internazionale Marmi e Macchine, 1992

Saletti, B. Asor Rosa, "Bienaimé," in *Dizionario biografico degli Italiani*, vol. 10., Rome: Istituto della Enciclopedia Italiana, 1968

Tesan, Harald, "Bienaimé," in *Allgemeines Künstlerlexikon: Die bildenden Künstler aller Zeiten und Völker*, vol. 1, Munich: Saur, 1992

BIGARNY, FELIPE

See **Vigarny, Felipe**

BISSEN, HERMANN WILHELM

See **Scandinavia**

LEONARDO BISTOLFI 1859–1933 *Italian*

Leonardo Bistolfi, known to many as the "poet of death," was the major Symbolist sculptor of funerary monuments, groups, and figures in Italy at the beginning of the 20th century. A major figure during the Art Nouveau period, Bistolfi was the son of a woodcarver (who was a specialist in intarsia, or wood inlay). Although his mother struggled financially following the death of her husband two years after Bistolfi's birth, Bistolfi showed a talent for art in his youth and obtained a scholarship to the Academia di Brera in Milan, which he entered at the age of 15, about 1875. At Brera, Bistolfi studied under Giosuè Argenti, Giovanni Strazza, and Giulio Monteverde. Also during this time, Bistolfi was inspired by and involved with the anti-academic cultural movement known as *La Scapigliatura* (literally, "disheveledness" or "the disheveled ones"), and he admired the work of the movement's major founder, Giuseppe Grandi, and followers such as Medardo Rosso and Giorgio Belloni. In 1880 Bistolfi moved to Turin and briefly attended the Accademia Albertina, where he took up more advanced studies under the sculptor Odoardo Tabacchi, who was the academy's chairman at that time.

During these early years, Bistolfi's works were distinctly naturalist in their subject, which is especially evident in pieces such as *Evening* (1883), *Lovers, Pastoral* (1884), and *Twilight (Il Crepuscolo)*. Much of his oeuvre from the 1880s consists of small bronze figures and groups, for which there was a large market. His involvement with Symbolism began with his first tomb sculptures, but he was also interested in exploring aspects of humanitarian socialism. In addition, he produced paintings and small sculptures depicting genre scenes and naturalist subjects and occasionally wrote poetry. After 1896 he traveled widely throughout Italy, Germany, and Switzerland.

Bistolfi primarily sculpted funerary monuments, which are by their very nature a bridge from the material to the spiritual worlds; further, the mysterious and the sublime were the essence of Symbolist ideals. His first major tomb commission, which included a figure entitled *Angel of Death*, came from the Braida family in 1881. The commission allowed him to open his own studio in Turin that year and to begin his major activity. He also received commissions for numerous portraits and memorial sculptures. His other major tombs included *Sphinx* (1889–92), a marble tomb for the Panza family; the marble relief *Brides of Death* for the Vochieri family; the bronze relief *Grief Comforted by Memories* for the Durio family; *Recollection* for the Erminia Cairati Vogt family; *The Bed of Roses* for the Fanny Lecroix tomb; and a 1906 monument to the painter Segantini. Many of Bistolfi's sculptures also included portrait busts and monuments to poets and writers, such as Giuseppe Giacosa and Gerolamo Rovetta.

Bistolfi was recognized as Italy's leading sculptor in 1905 when he became the first Italian artist to receive a one-man show at the Venice Biennale. He was inspired by the work of Auguste Rodin, which he first encountered at a previous Venice Biennale (Bistolfi may have met Rodin in the fall of 1902), and also with the work of Renaissance sculptors such as Michelangelo, in whom there was renewed interest during the second half of the 19th century.

By 1908 Bistolfi was at the height of his fame, and in that year received a commission to produce a monument to the poet and critic Giosuè Carducci (*d.* 1907) for the Piazza Carducci in Bologna. The monument would occupy Bistolfi for the next two decades. The sculptural group contains various elements, including a portrait of the poet, seated and facing the piazza. Two other groups depict allegories of Liberty and Nature and include a triptych relief behind the poet representing Generosity, Love, and Strength. Liberty, astride a rearing horse, is shown flanked on either side by personifications of Rhythm and Rhyme, in reference to the poet's craft. The highly dynamic *bozzetto* (a small-scale preparatory study or model) for this group is extant in a private collection; the finished product is characteristic of the *stile liberty*, the Italian

Monument to Giosuè Carducci
© Massimo Listri / CORBIS

equivalent to Art Nouveau. Bistolfi worked on models for the monument between 1910 and 1914, but he was forced to halt work on the project because of the advent of World War I. The marble version of the monument was not completed until 1927. In the 1920s Bistolfi made many other monuments commemorating the fallen Italian heroes of the war.

Bistolfi's influence was not limited to his students and collaborators in Piedmont and Lombardy but spread throughout the Italian peninsula and lasted for more than 20 years. Writers of the period called his influence "bistolfismo" and noted that he had many imitators. By the 1920s the then up-and-coming Italian Futurists (such as Umberto Boccioni, who by many accounts had admired Bistolfi's work) began to work against the Symbolists' ideals, seeing the earlier movement as too sentimental and decorative. At that point, Bistolfi's influence began to wane.

At the end of his life, Bistolfi turned again to painting and poetry. He died in Turin of a cerebral hemorrhage at the age of 74. The Museo Civico at Casale Monferrato holds a large collection of his works, including models for his major projects, bronzes, and bas-reliefs.

CATERINA Y. PIERRE

See also **Boccioni, Umberto; Rodin, Auguste; Rosso, Medardo**

Biography

Born in Casale Monferrato, Piedmont, Italy, 15 March 1859. Son of the woodcarver Giovanni Bistolfi. Studied at the Accademia di Brera, Milan, under Giosuè Argenti, *ca.* 1875–79, and at the Accademia Albertina, Turin, under Odoardo Tabacchi, 1880–81; opened his own studio in Turin, 1881; completed major tomb sculptures, 1889–1911; helped to organize the exhibition *Mostra Internazionale di Arte Decorativa Moderna*, Turin, 1902; cofounder of the periodical *L'arte decorativa moderna*; honored with the first solo exhibition devoted to an Italian sculptor at the Venice Biennale, 1905; completed major war monuments, 1922–26; turned to painting at the end of his life. Died in Turin, Italy, 2 September 1933.

Selected Works

1881   *Angel of Death*, for tomb of the Braida family; marble; Turin Cemetery, Italy
1884   *Lovers*; marble; Museo Civico, Casale Monferrato, Piedmont, Italy
1887–88 Monument to Giuseppe Garibaldi; bronze; Castello Sforzesco, Milan, Italy
1892   *Twilight* (*Il Crepuscolo*); marble; Galleria Civico d'Arte Moderna, Turin, Italy
1893   *Twilight* (*Il Crepuscolo*); bronze; private collection, United States
1895   *Brides of Death*, for tomb of the Vochieri family; marble; Frascarolo Lomellina Cemetery, Turin, Italy
1895   Toscanini tomb relief; terracotta; private collection, United States
1898   *Grief Comforted by Memories*, for tomb of the Durio family; Cemetery of Madonna di Campagna, Turin, Italy
1902–04 *The Resurrection*, for monument to Hermann Bauer; marble; Staglieno Cemetery, Genova, Italy
1905–08 Monument to Giuseppe Garibaldi; bronze, marble; Giardini dell'Imperatrice, Sanremo, Italy
1906   Monument to Segantini; marble; Galleria Nazionale d'Arte Moderna, Rome, Italy
1908–27 *Sauro Destrier della Canzone* (monument to Giosuè Carducci); marble; Piazza Carducci, Bologna, Italy
1909–11 Bauer-Toscanini tomb; marble; Cimitero Monumentale, Milan, Italy

1928   *To The Fallen*; marble; Casale Monferrato, Piedmont, Italy

Further Reading

Anzani, Giovanni, and Luciano Caramel, *Scultura moderna in Lombardia, 1900–1950*, Milan: Cassa di Risparmio delle Provincie Lombarde, 1981

Bistolfi, Leonardo, *Bistolfi, 1859–1933: Il percorso di uno scultore simbolista*, Casale Monferrato, Italy: Piemme, 1984

Bossaglia, Rossana, *Arte e socialità in Italia: Dal realismo al simbolismo, 1865–1915*, Milan: La Società per le Belle Arti ed Esposizione Permamente, 1979

Caramel, Luciano, "Tra Ottocento e Novecento: Medardo Rossa e Leonardo Bistolfi," in *Scultura Moderna in Lombardia, 1900–1950*, Milan: Cassa di Risparmio delle Provincie Lombarde, 1981

De Micheli, Mario, *La scultura del Novecento*, Turin, Italy: UTET, 1981

Lavagnino, Emilio, *L'arte moderna dai neoclassici ai contemporanei*, 2 vols., Turin, Italy: Unione Tipografico-Editrice Torinese, 1956

Migliorini, Maurizia, *Strofe di bronzo: Lettere da uno scultore a un poeta simbolista: Il carteggio Bistolfi-Pascoli*, Nuoro, Italy: Ilisso, 1992

Wardropper, Ian, and Fred Licht, *Chiseled with a Brush: Italian Sculpture, 1860–1925, from the Gilgore Collections* (exhib. cat.), Chicago, Illinois: Art Institute of Chicago, 1994

UMBERTO BOCCIONI 1882–1916 *Italian*

Umberto Boccioni's approach to art emerged through a continuous, parallel process of theoretical codification and concrete experimentation. With the *Manifesto of Futurist Painters* (11 February 1910) and the *Technical Manifesto of Futurist Painting* (11 April 1910), both signed by Boccioni, Carlo Carrà, Luigi Russolo, Gino Severini, and Giacomo Balla, Boccioni established himself as one of the main voices of the modern trend in painting. In 1911–12 a series of exhibitions helped to position his painting in the context of the most advanced conventions.

At the beginning of 1912 Boccioni participated in an international touring exhibition of Futurist painting in Europe that traveled to Paris, Berlin, and London. It is at this point that his writings first mention his increasing interest in sculpture. "I am obsessed these days by sculpture!" he wrote to his friend Vico Baer on 15 March, "I think I can perceive a complete renewal of this mummified art" (see Coen, 1988). This obsession led Boccioni to a reconsideration of the medium, determined through an analysis of its historical and critical implications as well as through attempts to produce innovative models of sculpture.

The *Manifesto Tecnico della Scultura Futurista* (Technical Manifesto of Futurist Sculpture), signed by Boccioni alone, bears the same month and day as the *Technical Manifesto of Futurist Painting* (11 April 1910), but it seems not to have been made public until the end of the summer of 1912. The text opens with a harsh indictment of contemporary European sculpture: "Such a pitiable spectacle of barbarism, stupid clumsiness, and monotonous imitation."

According to Boccioni, the solution was the complete renewal of the essence of sculpture itself, that is, "the vision and conception of the line and of the masses" forming its structural frame. This could be realized by following the Futurist principle of interpenetration of planes, already proposed in the *Technical Manifesto of Futurist Painting*. Applied to sculpture, it would consist in rendering, through the use of several possible materials, the atmospheric planes that link and intersect things, as Boccioni explains in the 1912 manifesto: "Sculpture must make objects come to life by rendering their prolongation into space perceivable, systematic, and three-dimensional. Because . . . there is nothing surrounding our body—bottle, automobile, house, tree, street—that is not also cutting through it and slicing it into cross-sections with an arabesque of curves and straight lines." Boccioni's conception of space as a continuity of matter is deeply indebted to his reading of Henri Bergson. Thus, in prospecting the absolute and total abolition of the finite line and of the statue complete in itself, Boccioni proclaims in the manifesto: "The entire visible world must come sweeping down on us, become one with us, and thereby create a harmony whose only guiding principle will be creative intuition." Modern sculpture should then render the continuity of the environment, abolishing the artificial concept of figures isolated from their surroundings.

Such a view explains Boccioni's strong rejection of the Cubists' adoption of elements derived from primitive sculpture. In a letter written in July 1913 to Vico Baer, he stresses their fall "into archaism and the barbaric": "Our 'primitivism' should be entirely free of analogy with the ancients' one. Ours is the farthest point of complexity, the ancient is a mere babbling of simplicity."

Briefly summarizing previous attempts to modernize sculptural language, Boccioni focused his attention on Medardo Rosso, whose texts on Impressionism in sculpture had been published in Italy some years before by the critic and eventual Futurist Ardengo Soffici. For Rosso the authenticity of things can be known only through perception, in particular, "in that short moment when the vision breaks upon us, as it were, as a surprise—that is to say, before our intellect, our knowledge of the material form of time to come into play and to counteract and destroy their first impression" (see Rosso, 1907).

However, despite Impressionism's primary concern with rendering the exact moment of visual impression,

Unique Forms of Continuity in Space, 1913, bronze (cast 1931) 43 7/8″ × 34 7/8″ × 15 3/4″, Museum of Modern Art, New York. Acquired through the Lillie P. Bliss Bequest Photo © 2000 The Museum of Modern Art, New York

Boccioni focused on "rendering systematic and definitive—thus, synthesizing—what Impressionism offered as fragmentary, accidental, and consequently analytical." This process of systematization and, in Boccioni's own words, "solidification" of Impressionism led him to search for the definitive form, the unifying visualization of the diverse interactions between the object and its surroundings. These continuous interactions define the "dynamism" of the objects, which he also called "form-force." Boccioni employed the Cubist analytical style in a large series of drawings in order to determine each of the possible "form-forces" of the objects he decided to represent in his sculptures. He later exhibited the drawings together with the sculptures, dividing them in small groups and naming each group according to his formal intentions, such as "I want to fix human forms in movement" (22 drawings), "I want to model light and atmosphere" (5 drawings), or "I want to present the fusion of a head with its surrounding" (9 drawings).

Of the 11 plastic ensembles created by Boccioni during the years 1911–13, only three examples survive; most were accidentally destroyed after a retrospective exhibition in 1917. None of his works was cast in bronze during the artist's life. Nearly half of them were actually assembled from various materials. Works such as *Head + House + Light* and *Fusion of a Head and a Window* consist of assemblages of plaster casts intersected by real objects, while *Unique Forms of Continuity in Space* is modeled in a single plaster cast. With this latter work Boccioni believed he had reached his goal. In the preface to the catalogue of the *First Exhibition of Futurist Sculpture*, which opened in Paris at the La Boétie Gallery on 20 June 1913, he explained his effort to fix not the trajectory of a body in motion but the synthetic form that expresses its continuity through space. This form is determined through a new closed line of contour, which contains and suggests to the viewer the variety of all the other outlines of movements, past and future.

In his review of the exposition, written for *L'Intransigeant*, Apollinaire, remarking on the varied materials, the sculptural simultaneity, and the violent movement of the works, called it the "first exhibition of modern sculpture."

MARIA ELENA VERSARI

See also **Modernism; Rosso, Medardo**

Biography

Born in Reggio di Calabria, Italy, 19 October 1882. Began studies in Padua, and continued them in Catania; moved to Rome, 1899; met Gino Severini and Giacomo Balla; made first trip to Paris and Russia, 1906; returned to Italy, lived in Padua and Venice, then settled in Milan, where he met Gaetano Previati; studied masterworks of the past and the Divisionists; signed first *Manifesto of Futurist Painters*, 1910, and the *Technical Manifesto of Futurist Painting* (both with Carrà, Russolo, Severini, and Balla); participated in several group exhibitions, often writing the prefaces; published articles in *Lacerba* on Futurism and Cubism; became interested in sculpture, 1912; his works constituted first exhibition of Futurist sculpture, Galerie La Boétie, Paris, 1913; published first book, *Futurist Painting Sculpture: Plastic Dynamism*. Died in Verona, Italy, 17 August 1916.

Selected Works

1912 *Development of a Bottle in Space*; plaster; Museo de Arte Moderna, São Paolo, Brazil; bronze, Museum of Modern Art, New York City, United States

1912 *Fusion of a Head and a Window*; plaster, other materials (destroyed)

1912 *Head + House + Light*; plaster, other materials (destroyed)

179

ca. 1912 *Abstracted Hollows and Fulls of a Head*;
plaster (destroyed)

ca. *Anti-graceful*; plaster; Galleria Nazionale
1912–13 d'Arte Moderna, Rome, Italy

1913 *Unique Forms of Continuity in Space*;
plaster; Museo de Arte Moderna, São
Paolo, Brazil; bronze, Museum of Modern
Art, New York City, United States

ca. 1913 *Forms-Forces of a Bottle*; plaster
(destroyed)

ca. 1913 *Muscles in Quick Motion*; plaster
(destroyed)

ca. 1913 *Spiral Expansion of Muscles in Movement*;
plaster (destroyed)

ca. 1913 *Synthesis of Human Dynamism*; plaster
(destroyed)

ca. 1913 *Horse + Houses* (or *Dynamic Construction
of a Gallop*); wood, cardboard, metal;
Peggy Guggenheim Collection, Venice,
Italy

Further Reading

Ballo, Guido, *Boccioni: La vita e l'opera*, Milan: Il Saggiatore,
1964

Birolli, Zeno, *Umberto Boccioni: Racconto critico*, Turin, Italy:
Einaudi, 1983

Boccioni, Umberto, *Gli scritti editi e inediti*, edited by Zeno
Birolli, Milan: Feltrinelli, 1971

Boccioni, Umberto, *Altri inedit e apparati critici*, edited by
Zeno Birolli, Milan: Feltrinelli, 1971

Calvesi, Maurizio, and Ester Coen, editors, *Boccioni*, Milan:
Electa, 1983

Coen, Ester, *Umberto Boccioni* (exhib. cat.), New York: Metropolitan Museum of Modern Art, 1988

Golding, John, *Boccioni: Unique Forms of Continuity in Space*,
London: Tate Gallery, 1985

Mattioli Rossi, Laura, editor, *Boccioni 1912 materia*, Milan:
Mazzotta, 1991

Rosso, Medardo, "Impressionism in Sculpture: An Explanation," *Daily Mail* (17 October 1907)

Rylands, Philip, editor, *Umberto Boccioni: Dinamismo di un
cavallo in corsa e case* (exhib. cat.), Venice: Peggy Guggenheim collection, 1996

BOHEMIA

See **Central Europe**

BON FAMILY

See **Buon Family**

ANTONIO BONAZZA 1698–1763 *Italian*

Antonio Bonazza, who worked mostly in Padua and
Venice, was certainly one of the most representative
and interesting Italian artists of the 18th century. His
language, with its variegated wealth of stimuli and nuances, was not only the outcome of his interest in the
naturalistic portrayal of common folk and his attention
to Classical composure in the attitudes and drapery of
his figures, but also of the Rococo taste that typified
his century. His vast output consisted, for the most
part, of altars and sculptures made for parish and monastic churches in Padua and the surrounding region,
but he also produced numerous sets of statuary with
mythological and other secular themes for the gardens
of the Venice nobility's country houses.

Bonazza trained and did his first works in his father's shop. Giovanni Bonazza had moved to Padua in
1695, and because of the originality of his language he
became one of the leading figures in Venetian Baroque
sculpture in the late 17th and early 18th centuries. His
son Antonio's first known works, done in collaboration
with his father and his brother Tommaso, are two large
marble panels in high relief—one depicting *The Nativity*, and the other the *Adoration of the Magi*—for the
famous series dedicated to the Virgin Mary in the Rosary Chapel of the Venetian church of Santi Giovanni
e Paolo. Art historians have identified Antonio's hand
in the strongly and spontaneously naturalistic figures
of shepherds and peasants flanking the main scenes.
The same naturalistic intent is plain in two other important early works, *St. Zeno* and *St. John the Baptist*,
which Bonazza probably did only a few years later for
the high altar of the parish church in Borso del Grappa.
(The clay model of the *St. John* is preserved in Padua's
Museo Civico.) These unrhetorical figures are distinguished by the simplicity of their attitudes and their
restrained shapes. By contrast, the statues of *St. Bartholomew* and *St. Andrew* in the Church of Santa Lucia
in Padua, although similar to an early phase of Bonazza's activity, show a strong dependence on Venetian
Baroque examples. The *St. Bartholomew*, whose
flayed body is depicted with crude and macabre realism, was inspired partly by Giovanni Bonazza's earlier
rendition of the same subject, but still more by the one
made by Bernardo Falcone in 1681 for Santa Giustina
in Padua. On the other hand, the *St. Andrew* appears
to have been copied from the one Enrico Merengo
sculpted in 1701 for Sant'Andrea della Zirada in Venice, itself inspired by François du Quesnoy's *St. Andrew* (1629–40) in St. Peter's Basilica, Rome. However, Bonazza's *St. Andrew* differs in its meeker and
more human expression and attitude from both the intense pathos of Merengo's and the heroic tone of du
Quesnoy's.

Bonazza's major works also include eight large statues of the *Virtues* installed in niches along the walls
of the church of Santa Maria del Torresino in Padua.
In keeping with the Baroque taste for theatrics, the
figures were conceived with a scenographic intent. The

figures seem to be conversing with one another and are to be viewed as a whole and in their harmonious relationship with the clear-cut lines of this particular church (which was designed by the Paduan Girolamo Frigimelica). These majestic figures, with their broad and solemn gestures, are individually characterized by a full and varied range of expressions. With the frankness of common people, each of them reveals a sincere and deep-felt sentiment and a spontaneous piety. Here, more than in other works by Bonazza, one can appreciate the play of the light flowing in varied nuances over the broad surfaces, which seems to lighten the weighty figures.

The group of stone statues Bonazza sculpted around 1742, by this time in his full maturity, for Villa Widmann in Bagnoli di Sopra in the Veneto is the 18th century's most extraordinary and original set of garden sculpture. Characters and themes from contemporary life share the stage with the Olympic deities depicted in conventional garden themes. Noblemen and gentlewomen, peasants and soldiers, hunters, horsemen, and many other figures are paired off face to face, giving the impression that they are talking to each other. The amusing scenes thus created seem akin to intermezzi in the theater. The character and the uniqueness of this set of sculptures cannot be fully grasped unless one bears in mind the proprietor's passion for the theater. Ludovico Widmann had a theater built inside his country house, and his summer guests included the Venetian playwright Carlo Goldoni. The witty realism and the satirical intent of Bonazza's figures are reminiscent of, and indeed anticipate, the subtle irony and the modern characters of Goldoni's "new comedy."

A few years later, Bonazza sculpted *St. Peter* and *St. Paul* for the parish church in Bagnoli. These monumental figures, which were depicted in solemn poses and with their drapery studiously arranged in rhythmic cadences, reveal a balanced composition and a Classical composure that seem to derive from an attentive study of late 16th-century Venetian sculpture, in particular of Alessandro Vittoria's works.

Bonazza's propensity for a naturalistic component coexisting or alternating with a Classical component did not prevent him from giving expression to a vein of Rococo decorativeness in other works of his maturity. In *St. Agnes* in the Cathedral of Chioggia, for example, and in the two *Worshipping Angels* on the high altar of the Church of San Tommaso Martire in Padua, the tresses, clothing, and even the clouds at the figures' feet are blown and faceted into myriad segments that reflect the light and give an impression of sumptuousness, generating painterly effects that call to mind the paintings of Sebastiano Ricci or Giambattista Tiepolo.

Figure from the Garden of Villa Widmann, Bagnoli di Sopra, Padova Province, Italy
The Conway Library, Courtauld Institute of Art

Among the religious works of Bonazza's last period is the *Pietà* group originally installed in the Paduan Church of San Giovanni in Verdara but now in the Museo Civico in Padua. This masterpiece deserves mention for its strong dramatic impact, imparted not only by the pained expressions but also through the studied composition, the agitated folds of the rich drapery, and the strong chiaroscuro effects.

Bonazza was also a fine portraitist, as is evident, for example, in his bust of the scholar Alessandro Knips Macoppe (*ca.* 1744; Padua University). This piece clearly exhibits the sculptor's interest in psychological exploration and naturalistic treatment. Other examples are the busts of Pope Benedict XIV and Bishop Carlo Rezzonico (later Pope Clement XIII) commissioned in 1745 by the Padua Cathedral chapter. In his portraits of these two prelates, Bonazza's bold realism verged on the irreverent. In the end, the cathedral authorities disliked Bonazza's pieces so much that they replaced them with a pair by Giovanni Maria Morlaiter and relegated Bonazza's to the outside of the building. Morlaiter's sculptures combined a solemn, magniloquent tone and a frivolous decorativeness that was totally absent from Bonazza's portraits, indifferent as they were to passing fashions and skin-deep elegance. Belonging to the later activity of the master and still connected with the tradition of Venetian garden statuary are the mythological couples of Zephyr and Flora, and of Vertumnus and Pomona, sculpted by Bonazza in 1757. These works were originally placed at Oranienbaum but later situated in the upper part of the park of Peterhof, near St. Petersburg, Russia.

SIMONE GUERRIERO

See also **du Quesnoy, François; Morlaiter, Giovanni Maria**

Biography

Born in Padua, Italy, 23 December 1698. Son of the sculptor Giovanni Bonazza and Maddalena da Treviso (known as Tartaglia), and brother of the sculptors Tommaso and Francesco Bonazza. Trained and completed earliest works in his father's workshop in Padua; enrolled for the first time in the Padua stonecutters' guild (which included sculptors), 1735; according to documents from the Padua guild, served in various positions: as *massaro*, 1743–44, *sindaco* in 1745, and *secondo gastaldo* in 1749. Died in Padua, Italy, 12 January 1763.

Selected Works

1730–32 Reliefs of *The Nativity* and *Adoration of the Magi* (with brother Tommaso and father Giovanni); Carrara marble; Cappella del Rosario, Church of Santi Giovanni e Paolo, Venice, Italy

ca. *St. Zeno* and *St. John the Baptist*; Carrara
1730–35 marble; parish church, Borso del Grappa, Italy

1732–40 *St. Bartholomew* and *St. Andrew*; stone; Church of Santa Lucia, Padua, Italy

1737 *Blessed Immaculate Virgin*; painted wood; parish church, Terradura, Italy

ca. 1741 Eight statues of the *Virtues*; stone; Church of Santa Maria del Torresino, Padua, Italy

1742 Statues of Olympic deities and other figures; stone; garden of Villa Widmann, Bagnoli di Sopra, Padova province, Italy

1742–50 Two statues of *Worshipping Angels*; Carrara marble; Church of San Tommaso Martire, Padua, Italy

ca. 1744 *Alessandro Knips Macoppe*; Carrara marble; Palazzo del Bò, University of Padua, Italy

ca. 1745 *St. Agnes*; Carrara marble; Cathedral of Chioggia, Chioggia, Italy

1745–46 *Pope Benedict XIV* and *Bishop Carlo Rezzonico*; stone; Padua Cathedral, Italy

1746 *St. Peter* and *St. Paul*; Carrara marble; parish church, Bagnoli di Sopra, Padova province, Italy

ca. 1750 Various subjects; stone; garden of Torosay Castle, Isle of Mull, Scotland

1753–55 Reliefs of *Sacrifice of Isaac, Elijah and the Angel*, and *The Last Supper*; Carrara marble; Church of Santa Maria Montagnana, Padova province, Italy

1755–60 *Pietà*, for Church of San Giovanni in Verdara, Padua, Italy; Carrara marble; Museo Civico, Padua, Italy

1757 *Flora, Zephyr, Vertumnus*, and *Pomona*; Carrara marble; Peterhof Garden, St. Petersburg, Russia

1758 *St. Anne*; painted wood; parish church, Carrara San Giorgio, Italy

Further Reading

Banzato, Davide, Franca Pellegrini, and Monica De Vincenti, editors, *Dal Medioevo a Canova: Sculture dei Musei civici di Padova dal Trecento all'Ottocento* (exhib. cat.), Venice: Marsilio, 2000

Goi, Paolo, "Giunte al catalogo dei Bonazza," in *Per sovrana risoluzione: Studi in ricordo di Amelio Tagliaferri*, edited by Giuseppe Maria Pilo and Bruno Polese, Monfalcone, Italy: Edizioni della Laguna, 1998

Gould, Cecil, "A Note on F.A. Bustelli and Antonio Bonazza," *The Burlington Magazine* 103 (1961)

Guerriero, Simone, "Antonio e Francesco Bonazza: Tre sculture e un dipinto," *Venezia arti* 11 (1997)

Pavanello, Giuseppe, "La scultura," in *Storia di Venezia—Temi: L'arte*, edited by Rodolfo Pallucchini, vol. 2, Rome: Istituto dell'Enciclopedia Italiana, 1995

Rossi, Sergio, "Giovanni ed Antonio Bonazza e la componente naturalistica nella scultura veneta del Settecento," *Quaderni sul Neoclassico* 3 (1975)

Semenzato, Camillo, *Antonio Bonazza*, Venice: Neri Pozza, 1957

Semenzato, Camillo, *La scultura veneta del Seicento e del Settecento*, Venice: Alfieri, 1966

PIERRE BONTEMPS *ca.* 1512–*ca.* 1568 (before 1572) *French*

Pierre Bontemps, with Jean Goujon, is one of the two sculptors most closely identified with the classicizing period of French art during the reign of Henri II. He carved the seated effigy of Charles de Maigny, many of the figural elements of the tomb of Francis I, and the funerary urn of the heart of the same king. The effigies of Jean III d'Humières and Philippe Chabot, the bronze relief commonly called *Crossing of the Granicus*, and the tomb of Guillaume du Bellay are attributed to Bontemps on the basis of style, but the attribution of the relief is most uncertain.

Bontemps's birthplace remains unidentified. His first known artistic activity (1536) was in the second rank of artists working at Fontainebleau for the stuccoes in the *chambre de la reine* (bedroom of the queen); Maurice Roy has suggested that he must have been born around 1505–10 (see Roy, 1929). Bontemps was one of the sculptors employed by Francesco Primaticcio to retouch molds of antiquities to be cast for Francis I in 1541, and for Benvenuto Cellini, he chased parts of the bronze relief *Nymph of Fontainebleau* (1543; Musée du Louvre, Paris). Payment records show that over a period of about ten years, he advanced to a better position at Fontainebleau before moving to Paris, where he prospered as a sculptor preferred by Henri II's architect Philibert de L'Orme, notably for the tomb of Francis I. Bontemps, a Protestant, had to flee from the city in December 1561, early in the Wars of Religion, but he returned by 1563, when the Edict of Pacification took effect. In 1572 he was mentioned as deceased in a document about his son Apelles; his wife was described as a widow the same year.

In addition to Roy, Jean-Pierre Babelon also summarized the complex history of the tomb of Francis I (Roy, 1929, and Babelon, 1975). This elegant monument, with exquisitely chiseled architectural members, is a paragon of pure French Renaissance architecture. It was commissioned in late 1547 or early 1548 by Henri II from de L'Orme, who assigned the tomb's sculptures to François Carmoy. (Carmoy came from a family of successful artists in Orléans and had also worked on the stuccoes of the *chambre de la reine* at Fontainebleau.) The tomb, designed by de L'Orme on the plan of a Greek cross, is like a triumphal arch, articulated by Ionic columns and pilasters that shelters the *gisants* (reclining figures) of Francis I and Claude de France. (These rest on sarcophagi that are substitutions provided by Viollet-le-Duc to replace originals lost in the French Revolution.) The monument is crowned on its upper level by *priants* (praying figures) of the king, queen, and three of their children. In April 1548, the two *gisants* and the *priants* of the king, queen, Louise de Savoie (the king's mother; it is believed lost), the dauphin François, and his brother Charles, the Duke of Orléans, were commissioned. In one month, the *priants* were sufficiently advanced to be transported from Orléans (where the blocks of marble had been roughed out) to Paris for completion, but the *gisants* remained in Orléans with Carmoy, who died that same year. De L'Orme then transferred the

commission to Bontemps and François Marchand, another sculptor from Orléans.

In 1551 a *priant* of the king's daughter, Charlotte, was commissioned from Bontemps, as well as a figure of the king's infant daughter, Louise, from Marchand, which is believed lost. Marchand, however, died around that time. The *gisants* were transported from Orléans in August 1551. It is likely that the relatively stiff *priants* of the king and queen were finished by Marchand. The figure of Charles, with its somewhat richer drapery, would show the intervention of Bontemps, as would the *priant* of the dauphin, although Bontemps temporarily ceded its work to Pierre and François Lheureux. The queen's realistic, tragic *gisant* is a traditional representation of a cadaver not far removed from the *gisants* of the earlier tomb of Louis XII (Basilica of Saint-Denis, Saint-Denis), but the king's *gisant* is remarkably robust, with a subtle torsion that would seem to belong only to a living body. The turn of the king's head and the diagonal twists in the patterns of folds in the drapery on which the body rests imbue the composition with remarkable dynamism. The skill of the sculptor of this figure should not be underestimated.

In 1551 and 1552 Bontemps was awarded the commissions for reliefs depicting the battles of Marignan and Cérisoles, respectively, which wrap the stylobate of the tomb. These individual panels, which Babelon described as "a narrative which presses the whole length of the stylobate, wed, by use of small vertical elements, [to] all facets of the bases of the columns," are of varying quality (see Babelon, 1975). The most accomplished reliefs are characterized by soft transitions in the depth of the marble and surprisingly economical treatments of perspective, particularly in figures seen from the back. In some reliefs, various details, such as the tail of a rearing horse or the branches of a tree, break over the border of the panel with whimsical inventiveness.

Bontemps's most significant surviving sculpture is the funerary urn for the heart of Francis I, commissioned in 1550 through de L'Orme. Its style refers directly to the art commissioned by the king it memorializes: the ornamental strap work, elongated and flattened Mannerist nudes, and the layering of perspectives are among the last uncorrupted vestiges of the true School of Fontainebleau (the first one), invented by Rosso Fiorentino under the aegis of Francis I. The funerary urn, from which all religious symbols are banished, pays homage to the king's humanist patronage. Death is evoked only by the tiny skulls and bones near the bottom of the base; the subjects of the reliefs on the urn (architecture, geometry, sculpture, and painting) and the base (astronomy, music, singing, and lyric poetry) make no reference to the monument's traditional purpose; only a small heart, now lost, that once topped the ensemble alluded to the urn's function.

The reclining effigy of Philippe Chabot is attributed to Bontemps by comparison to the seated effigy of Charles de Maigny. Paul Vitry called them "dramatized effigies," in contrast to traditional, recumbent figures; this new type was likely due to the Italian influence in French sculpture at the time. Chabot died in 1543, but his effigy was not installed until 1565. A late 16th-century account attributed Chabot's tomb to Jean Cousin the Elder (*ca.* 1490–*ca.* 1560), famed as a draftsman and painter. The unusual appearance of the tomb, destroyed in the revolution, was recorded in a drawing in the Gaignières collection (Bibliothèque Nationale de France, Paris): the effigy was on a sarcophagus above a contorted, prone figure; these were set in an ornate, circular black-and-white marble frame and flanked by two small standing figures of funerary genii. (These and the prone figure are in the Musée du Louvre.) The frame's strikingly graphic character makes it resemble an ornamental print more than a tomb. This supports the attribution of the design to Jean Cousin, but the identity of the sculptor who carved the effigy remains uncertain. Given Chabot's elevated rank in the French court, it is reasonable to believe that his majestic effigy would have been carved by a very skilled artist—quite possibly, and logically, Bontemps.

MARY L. LEVKOFF

See also **Cellini, Benvenuto; Primaticcio, Francesco ("il Bologna")**

Biography

Probably born in Sens, France, *ca.* 1512. First documented in 1536 working on stuccoes in *chambre de la reine* (bedroom of the queen) at Fontainebleau; repaired molds for casts of Roman antiquities commissioned by Francis I from Primaticcio, 1540–*ca.* 1543; active sculptor in France throughout subsequent decades, with works completed for Francis I, Henry II, and others; because he was a Protestant, fled Paris during sectarian strife, 1561; returned 1563; resided at Verneuil-sur-Oise (home to a significant Protestant community). Died presumably in France by 1572.

Selected Works

ca. 1540–45	*Crossing of the Granicus*; bronze; Musée du Louvre, Paris, France (uncertain attribution)
1548/ 49–*ca.* 1557/58	Elements for the tomb of Francis I; marble; Basilica of Saint-Denis, Saint-Denis, France
1550–56	Funerary urn for the heart of Francis I; marble; Basilica of Saint-Denis, Saint-Denis, France
ca. 1550–53	Effigy of Jean III d'Humières; marble; Musée du Louvre, Paris, France (attributed)
1555	(commissioned) *Four Seasons* relief, for chimney of Henri II's bedroom at Fontainebleau; marble (presumed destroyed)
1556	(commissioned) *Francis I* for the Palais de Justice, Paris, France; painted and gilded stone (destroyed by fire 1618)
1557	Seated effigy of Charles de Maigny, *Capitaine des Gardes de la Porte du Roi*; stone; Musée du Louvre, Paris, France
ca. 1557	Tomb of Guillaume du Bellay; marble; Cathedral of Le Mans, France (attributed)
1561	(commissioned) Twenty allegorical figures for triumphal arch of Charles IX; plaster and other materials (destroyed)
ca. 1565?	Reclining effigy of Admiral Philippe Chabot (designed by Jean Cousin); marble; Musée du Louvre, Paris, France (attributed)
mid 16th century	Fragment of a horseman seen from the back; terracotta; Musée du Louvre, Paris, France (uncertain attribution)

Further Reading

Babelon, J.-P., A. Erlande-Brandenburg, Fr. Jenn, and J.-M. Jenn, *Le Roi est mort: Gisants et Tombeaux de la Basilique de Saint-Denis* (exhib. cat.), Saint-Denis: Archives départementales de la Seine-Saint-Denis, 1975

Beaulieu, Michèle, "Nouvelles attributions à Pierre Bontemps," *La Revue des Arts* 3/2 (1953)

Beaulieu, Michèle, *Description raisonnée des sculptures du Musée du Louvre*, 2 vols., Paris: Éditions de la Réunion des Musées Nationaux, 1978; see especially vol. 2, *Renaissance française*

Bresc-Bautier, G., "Relief Fragment with Horseman," in *Nouvelles acquisitions du Département des sculptures: 1988–91*, Paris: Éditions de la Réunion des Musées Nationaux, 1992

L'École de Fontainebleau (exhib. cat.), Paris: Éditions des Musées Nationaux, 1972

Grodecki, C., "Le Séjour de Benvenuto Cellini à l'hôtel de Nesle . . . ," *Bulletin de la Société de l'Histoire de Paris et de l'Île-de-France* 98 (1971)

Roy, Maurice, *Artistes et Monuments de la Renaissance en France*, vol. 1, Paris: Champion, 1929

Roy, Maurice, "Pierre Bontemps, un grand artiste de la Renaissance française," *Mémoires de la Société des Antiquaires de France* 70 (1910)

Vitry, Paul, "Le tombeau de Jean d'Humières et l'oeuvre de Pierre Bontemps," *Monuments et mémoires publiés par l'Académie des Inscriptions et belles-Lettres. Fondation Eugène Piot* 38 (1941)

Wingert, P., "The Funerary Urn of Francis I," *Art Bulletin* 21 (1939)

Zerner, Henri, *L'art de la Renaissance en France*, Paris: Flammarion, 1996

BORGOÑA, FELIPE DE

See **Vigarny, Felipe**

BOROBUDUR

Anonymous

Central Java, Indonesia, ca. 824 CE

Borobudur, the largest Buddhist monument in the world, is situated in Central Java, north of the modern-day city of Yogyakarta. It was constructed on the Kedu Plain at the confluence of two rivers, the Progo and the Elo, and has a unique setting flanked by four volcanoes. Built on an artificial hill, this pyramidical structure comprises a square base that supports four square terraces. Surmounting these are three circular terraces. These levels are connected by a series of staircases and archways that bifurcate each of the four sides of the monument. At Borobudur's summit, 31.5 meters above its ground line, is a central stupa (a domelike or rounded structure that usually holds a relic of the Buddha, a great teacher, or an honored devotee, and which may be architectural or constructed in miniature). Borobudur measures approximately 123 meters from north to south and 117 meters east to west, and it has been estimated that more than 1 million blocks were used for its construction, representing 55,000 square meters of andesite stone. Although it is traditionally dated to 824 CE on the basis of an indirect epigraphic source, it is more probable that the monument was constructed sometime during the early Central Javanese period, roughly between 780 and 830 CE.

Borobudur is associated with the patronage of the Buddhist Sailendra royal family, a short-lived ruling lineage that encouraged an efflorescence of Buddhist monuments and sculpture during their approximately 50-year overlordship in the area of Central Java. Borobudur then abruptly disappears from Javanese history. In the early years of the 20th century, Dutch colonial scholars and archaeologists led a modest restoration of the then-deteriorating monument. This was succeeded by a more extensive ten-year restoration project—which was completed in 1983—under the auspices of the Indonesian government and the United Nations Educational, Scientific, and Cultural Organization (UNESCO).

Borobudur may be regarded as a monumental sculpture. It also represents a masterwork of sculptural relief and three-dimensional sculptural imagery. There are 1,460 panels of narrative reliefs that line the base and four square terraces of the monument. Practically all have been identified and their sources may be found in various sutras (teachings of the Buddha) and Buddhist texts; however, no extant recensions of this literature correspond to Borobudur's interpretation of these stories. The base of the monument is sculpted with 160 reliefs illustrating the *Mahākarmavibhanga*, or "The Great Classification of Cause and Effect," which describes the rewards for those who perform specific meritorious deeds, as well as the Buddhist hells prescribed for those guilty of a Buddhist sin. This area is also known as the Hidden Foot, as a series of large undecorated stone blocks completely covers these narratives. It was previously theorized that this was intended for theological reasons, to shield devout Buddhist pilgrims from their contents. Current belief is that this outer structure represents a change in building plans, as Borobudur may have demonstrated engineering flaws during its construction and the inclusion of the blocks was an attempt to buttress the monument. The narrative program of the balustrade and the lower section of the main wall of the first gallery includes a series of selected episodes from the *Jātakas* (stories of the Buddha in his earlier incarnations) and *Avadānas* (stories of virtuous or heroic behavior). This was complemented on the upper register of the first gallery wall by 120 reliefs from the *Lalitavistara*, a version of Buddha's biography. These episodes detail the Buddha's life through his first sermon in the Deer Park at Benares, India. The balustrade of the second gallery continues the visual narration of the *Jātakas* and *Avadānas*, whereas the corresponding wall commences an extended series of 460 reliefs illustrating the *Gandhavyūha*. This text relates the story of the Indian prince

Borobudur Buddhist temple complex
© Bettmann / CORBIS

Sudhana, a Buddhist pilgrim who seeks enlightenment. He received spiritual instructions from 53 different *kalyanāmitra*s (spiritual teachers); subsequently, he was taught directly by the bodhisattvas Maitreya and Samantabhadra. This story continues on the balustrade and wall of the third gallery, as well as the balustrade of the fourth gallery. The fourth gallery wall concludes the program with an addendum to the *Gandhavyūha*, the *Bhadracarī* (a vow to follow the example of Samantabhadra). The space allotted this sutra suggests the heightened significance that it held for the Javanese of this era.

In addition to the narrative program, the terraces of Borobudur are embellished with more than 1,200 ornamental panels. The monument's large decorative vocabulary includes a myriad of foliate patterns, drainage spouts in the form of three-dimensional *makaras* (mythological crocodile-like creatures associated with water and the primordial source of life), and ornate carvings of *kālamakara* (a composite motif of animal and vegetal imagery containing a monster head flanked by two *makara*s) on the edifice's gateways. Conversely, the three-dimensional sculptural repertory at Borobudur is limited to images of seated Buddhas. Seventy-two of these sculptures are found on the upper three circular terraces; each is placed within a trellised stupa. Another 432 examples are situated in open niches on the main walls of the four square terraces below.

The exact meaning of Borobudur is still widely debated, and it is indeed possible that the monument is simultaneously emblematic of a multitude of beliefs or religious systems. Borobudur has often been called a "cosmic mountain." This element held significance in ancient Javanese beliefs as well as among the Indian religions that influenced Java. It has also been referred to as a stupa; however, as no relic has been discovered in its interior, it cannot be ascertained whether Borobudur had any mortuary associations. Borobudur is also traditionally perceived as a tripartite three-dimensional diagram of the Buddhist world. The subject matter of the Hidden Foot relates this area with Kāmadhātu (Realm of Desire), whereas that of the four square terraces above, relating themes of Buddhist virtue and stories of those searching for a release from materialistic pleasures and worldly existence, may epitomize the Rūpadhātu (World of Form). The three circular terraces, which are devoid of any decorative or narrative program and comprise only the imagery of stupas and Buddhas, are considered Arūpadhātu (World of Formlessness). The most widely debated hypothesis is that Borobudur was intended as a mandala (a diagram of the cosmos in either a two-dimensional or three-dimensional format that was employed in Indian religions as a guide for meditation or visualization). The

Buddhas at Borobudur, which have been identified on the basis of their mudras (hand gestures), are arranged hierarchically to suggest that they represent the Five Tathāgatas: the transcendental Buddha Vairocana, who has the power to transform himself into innumerable Buddhas, and the four cosmic Buddhas of the cardinal directions. Furthermore, Borobudur's four gateways are a common feature of a mandala. However, too many iconographic inconsistencies exist to substantiate this theory further, and the religious imagery of Borobudur defies any mandala system that may have been known by the Javanese of this era. It is more probable that the resolution to Borobudur's enigma may be found in its narrative program that parallels the spiritual goals of Buddhist devotees.

CECELIA LEVIN

Further Reading

Bernet Kempers, A.J., *Borobudur: Mysteriegebeuren in steen, verval en restauratie, Oudjavaans volksleven*, Wassenaar, The Netherlands: Servire, 1974; revised edition, as *Ageless Borobudur: Buddhist Mystery in Stone, Decay and Restoration, Mendut and Pawon Folklife in Ancient Java*, Wassenaar: Servire, 1976

Boeles, Jan J., *The Secret of Borobudur*, Bangkok: Boeles, 1985

Fontein, Jan, *The Pilgrimage of Sudhana: A Study of Gandavyuha Illustrations in China, Japan, and Java*, The Hague: Mouton, 1967

Fontein, Jan, *The Law of Cause and Effect in Ancient Java*, Amsterdam and New York: North Holland, 1989

Gomez, Luis O., and Hiram W. Woodward Jr., editors, *Barabudur: History and Significance of a Buddhist Monument*, Berkeley: University of California, 1981

Klokke, Marijke J., "Borobudur: A Mandala?" *IIAS Yearbook* (1996)

Krom, Nicolaas Johannes, *The Life of the Buddha on the Stupa of Barabudur, according to the Lalitavistara Text*, The Hague: Nijhoff, 1926; reprint, Varanasi, India: Bhartiya, 1974

Krom, Nicolaas Johannes, *Borobudur, Archaeological Description*, 2 vols., The Hague: Nijhoff, 1927; reprint, New York: AMS Press, 1986

Miksic, John, *Borobudur: Golden Tales of the Buddhas*, Boston: Shambhala, and London: Bamboo, 1990

Nou, Jean-Louis, and Louis Frédéric, *Borobudur*, Paris: Impr. Nationale, 1994; as *Borobudur*, New York: Abbeville Press, 1996

Snodgrass, Adrian, *The Symbolism of the Stupa*, Ithaca, New York: Southeast Asia Program, Cornell University, 1985

FRANCIS VAN BOSSUIT ca. 1635–1692
Dutch, active in Italy

Born in Brussels and trained in Antwerp, Francis van Bossuit settled in Rome about 1655. He worked predominantly as a carver in ivory and wood, as well as a modeler in clay and wax. About his artistic origins nothing is known. He remained in Italy for about 25 years. In Rome he was a member of the Bentvogels, a company of Dutch artists in the city known under the nickname "Waernemer" (observer). In Rome, Bossuit seems to have worked alongside the young German sculptor Balthasar Permoser, as is evidenced by their similarities in style. His works also exhibit stylistic links with the Florentine Academy in Rome. About 1680 he moved to Amsterdam, where he stayed for the rest of his life. Here, his Italian Baroque style began to mix with influences of the local classical Baroque style of Artus Quellinus and Rombout Verhulst.

Critics in Holland immediately praised his works in ivory, which remained sought after throughout the 18th century. His first and most important Dutch patrons during these years were apparently the wealthy Amsterdam merchant Adam Oortmans and his wife Petronella Oortmans-De la Court. The couple owned a famous art cabinet, which included ten works by Bossuit. Moreover, Petronella also possessed a large and famous dollhouse, which contained some works by and after Bossuit. Adam was an amateur ivory carver himself, instructed by Bossuit. He may have been one of several dilettante artists who worked under the guidance of Bossuit. This would explain the relatively large number of copies of different quality of some of Bossuit's inventions, notably the *Judith with the Head of Holofernes*. This work is known through many versions and copies. Around 1730 it was cast in Meissen in so-called Böttger stoneware; moreover, several German sculptors copied the composition, among them Paul Heermann and Christian Rauschner.

Through Petronella, the work of Bossuit was much in demand among her relatives in Leiden. The collection of her distant cousin Allard de la Court contained no fewer than 12 bronzes after Bossuit's ivories, possibly cast by the Leiden founder Philip van der Mij. The link with Leiden also provided an interesting artistic connection: the local painter Willem van Mieris included several of Bossuit's compositions in his paintings and made a considerable number of drawings after Bossuit's ivories, many of them in the collection of the De la Court family. The composition of Bossuit's small *Venus and Adonis* relief reappears in a slightly adapted form in van Mieris's large *Rinaldo and Armida* (1709).

Only a handful of works are attributable to Bossuit's Italian period, including pendant reliefs of *Eliezer and Rebecca* and *Judith and Holofernes*. Among his major works can also be reckoned a large relief of *Bathsheba* and a figure of a *Dead Christ*. These works demonstrate Bossuit's extraordinary skill at convincingly rendering several figures in a limited space. Moreover, they also show his mastery at rendering textures in ivory, especially the hair and flesh of the figures. Often the background of his reliefs is flecked.

David with the Head of Goliath
© Arte & Immagini srl / CORBIS

Of his later works made in Amsterdam and documented by Matthys Pool, only one freestanding statuette has been preserved, a 48-centimeter-high ivory figure of *Mars*. Van Mieris used this monumental figure for the figure of Odysseus in one of his paintings. Possibly the painter was competing with Bossuit, seeking to emulate the ivories in a more colorful way.

Although Bossuit's oeuvre after 1680 is well documented through a publication in Dutch, French, and English by Pool, the *Beeld-snyders Kunst-kabinet* (1727), the chronology of his earlier works remains entirely speculative. Pool's publication, an early example of a monograph art book, contains a portrait and biography of Bossuit, followed by a series of engravings after his later ivories.

FRITS SCHOLTEN

See also **Permoser, Balthasar; Quellinus (Quellin) Family; Verhulst, Rombout**

Biography

Born in Brussels, Belgium, *ca.* 1635. Trained in Antwerp; traveled to Rome, studied antique art, *ca.* 1655–*ca.* 1680; associated with Schildersbent (Flemish artists in Rome); worked predominantly as ivory- and woodcarver, and modeled in clay and wax; member of Bentvogels (Dutch artists in Rome), an organization known by nickname Waernemer (observer); moved permanently to Amsterdam, 1680; received commissions from Dutch patrons Adam Oortmans and wife Petronella Oortmans-De la Court, who promoted his career; complete works documented in publication by Matthys Pool, *Beeld-snyders Kunst-kabinet* (1727). Died in Amsterdam, the Netherlands, 22 September 1692.

Selected Works

ca. 1660–80	*Eliezer and Rebecca* and *Judith and Holofernes*; ivory; Museo Civico, Bologna, Italy
ca. 1660–80	*Dead Christ*; ivory; Palazzo Pitti, Florence, Italy
ca. 1670–80	*Mercury, Io, and Argus*; ivory; private collection of Reiner Winkler, Wiesbaden, Germany
ca. 1670–80	*Apollo and Marsyas*; ivory; private collection of Kenneth Thomson, Toronto, Canada
ca. 1680–92	*Bathsheba*; ivory; Wallace Collection, London, England
ca. 1680–92	*David with the Head of Goliath*; ivory; Victoria and Albert Museum, London, England
ca. 1680–92	*Judith with the Head of Holofernes*; ivory; two versions: Bayerisches Nationalmuseum, Munich, Germany; National Museums of Scotland, Edinburgh, Scotland
ca. 1680–92	*Mars*; ivory; Rijksmuseum, Amsterdam, the Netherlands
ca. 1680–92	*Venus and Adonis*; ivory; Rijksmuseum, Amsterdam, the Netherlands

Further Reading

Baker, Malcolm, "Francis van Bossuit: Böttger Stoneware and the 'Judith' Reliefs," in *Skulptur in Süddeutschland, 1400–1770: Festschrift für Alfred Schädler*, edited by Rainer Kashnitz and P. Volk, Munich: Deutscher Kunstverlag, 1998

Scholten, Fritz, "'Een ijvore Mars van Francis,' de beeldsnijder Van Bossuit en de familie De la Court," *Bulletin van het Rijksmuseum* 47 (1999)

Theuerkauff, Christian, "Zu Francis van Bossuit (1635–1692), 'Beeldsnyder in yvoor,'" *Wallraf-Richartz-Jahrbuch* 37 (1975)

Theuerkauff, Christian, *Elfenbein: Sammlung Reiner Winkler Band II, mit Addenda und Corrigenda zu Teil I, 1984*, S.l.: Wolf und Sohn, 1994

FERNANDO BOTERO 1932– *Colombian*

Fernando Botero, with his typical sculptures of exaggeratedly abundant and sensual forms, has received extraordinary public success throughout the world. The reasons for this are found in his simple, immediate, and easily understood figurative language. It is necessary, however, to underline that the singular communicative power of his work is owing, in fact, not to spontaneity or ingenuity, but, on the contrary, to his cultivated and refined study of the entire history of sculpture. Botero has compared himself to all of those artists who have centered their work on the pursuit of the problem of volume and form, attempting to build universal archetypes and refuting the mimetic reproduction of reality.

His first trip to Europe in 1952 was decisive in the formation of his style. Botero had the opportunity to directly study the plastic and volumetric forms of the Renaissance masters, especially Italians of the 15th century, such as Donatello, Jacopo della Quercia, and the Pisano family, and of the 16th century, such as Michelangelo. To this fundamental experience Botero added his intense attraction to the colonial Baroque and the pre-Columbian sculptural tradition. He has always been fascinated with the exceptional communicative capacity and the particular magical power that inspired old colonial Baroque multicolored statuettes.

The importance of these influences is evident in his first attempts at sculpture in 1963 and 1966. These sculptures are small and painted with human hair attached, as in an ancient talisman. Botero seemed to be inspired by the use of color as a means of giving the ancient idols a real concreteness and a life of their own. Thereafter, he only sporadically created polychromatic sculptures, substituting the effect of color with a patina to complete the work in bronze.

In the middle of the 1970s, Botero's typical monumental and obese sculpture was born from the original mixture of the Italian Renaissance tradition and a Latin American spirit. In that period, he was already famous for his paintings based on a clamorous plasticism. With sculpture he had the opportunity to carry out all of his tension toward volume and the third dimension, which had always distinguished his work, in a real object. In addition, sculpture allowed the figure to be isolated from the narrative context, enormously emphasizing its universal force. Botero's imposing figures, with their totally inexpressive eyes, appear anonymous and impassive, far from everyday occurrences. The numerous human fragments separated from the rest of the body, such as torsos, hands, and heads, are emblematic of Botero's work. In his most monumental work, *Large Torso*, the typical sculptural theme of the torso becomes an expressive archetype for itself, rather than for the particulars of an individual body. The round curves always tend to model the harmonious perfection of the sphere. The effect is enriched by the use of a green patina that contributes in alienating the work from the world of pure ideas.

Botero seems to have brought back to the 20th century the Neoplatonic Renaissance idea in which the universal form is obtained only through overcoming all that is accidental and strange. That which differentiates his style, however, is the strength of the point of equilibrium between figure and soul typical of Renaissance philosophy. In Botero, the individual soul becomes an obstacle for the body that tends to gain weight and grow excessively until gaining a life of its own in communion with nature, an untiring creature of luxuriant and exuberant shape. All of Botero's sculptures are joyful, expansive, full of irony, and inviting to the touch with their round forms. In an amusing polemic with the modern culture of anorexia, Botero creates feminine bodies that are the quintessence of maternity. His women, with their exaggerated Renaissance proportions, seem to be talismans of fertility.

In addition to his enormous interest in the human body, Botero is also very attracted to the representation of domestic and wild animals. His numerous dogs, cats, birds, tigers, and parrots inspire a sacredness that recalls archaic Babylonian sculpture. The small *Polycrome Snake*, in which he recovers the polychromy of his first works, is very interesting. The plump and winding serpent seems to move with its own vitality, creating a magical effect of intense suggestion.

To be able to fully appreciate Botero's monumental works, it is necessary to exhibit them outside in order to allow the public to interact directly with them and to allow the natural light to shape and emphasize the surfaces of the bronze patina or marble. In fact, the exhibition on the Champs-Élysées in Paris in 1992 confirmed his worldwide success, inaugurating a long series of exhibitions in the world's principal squares and streets. All of Botero's works from the 1970s were completed in his studio in Paris, whereas from the beginning of the 1980s, he has lived and worked in Pietrasanta, Italy. Following the traditional Renaissance conception of sculpture, Botero always hires expert artisans to produce his works. Next to his monumental works in marble and bronze, he receives commissions to work in other mediums such as terracotta, plaster cast, resin, and polyester. His craftsman's attention to technique, his preference for noble mediums such as marble and bronze, and his exultation of volumetric and plastic forms result in his isolated position among contemporary artists who tend to reject Classical forms.

With *Guitar*, Botero exhibited his need to confront Pablo Picasso's celebrated 1912 guitar, which opened the door to everyday objects in sculpture. Botero accused Picasso of having separated the public from the object, and he proposed the creation of a sensual and curvilinear guitar. He created many monumental works in plaster and bronze that bring to mind Pop art subjects, although he did not intend an anticonsumer society message.

In *Coffee Pot*, Botero reinterpreted the typical Pop theme of the monumentalization of the everyday. He did not insert the actual common object in his work; rather, with the mentality of an ancient sculptor, he modeled his coffeepot in bronze. By applying Renaissance rules of harmony to a banal theme such as a coffeepot, Botero emptied them of all of their moral and social meanings, thereby obtaining an ironic and irreverent effect that is characteristic of his work. The Pop artist Claes Oldenburg also created a similar effect with his enormous and surreal plaster hamburgers.

Botero is often linked to other contemporary sculptors interested in volume and form, such as Henry Moore and Aristide Maillol. He is a great admirer of Auguste Rodin and Henri Matisse. In general, however, his work, although popular with the public, appears solitary and unusual in the art world. In spite of the reservations and accusations of academicism by

Roman Soldier
The Conway Library, Courtauld Institute of Art

some critics and many contemporary sculptors, Botero nevertheless offers an interesting possibility for the revitalization of the figurative tradition by giving it his own entirely personal interpretation.

CATERINA BAY

See also **Donatello; Maillol, Aristide; Michelangelo; Moore, Henry; Oldenburg, Claes; Jacopo della Quercia; Rodin, Auguste**

Biography

Born in Medellín, Colombia, 19 April 1932. Attended Jesuit schools; enrolled in the San José de Marinilla high school in Medellín, 1949; moved to Bogotá and had his first solo-exhibition, 1951; traveled to Paris and Madrid; studied at the Academia de San Fernando, Madrid, 1952–53, and at the Accademia San Marco in Florence, 1953; departed Europe for Mexico, 1956; professor of painting at the Académie d'Art in Bogotá, 1958; first U.S. exhibition at Gres Gallery in Washington, D.C., United States; received first prize at the ninth Colombian Salon, 1958, and the Guggenheim award, 1959; lived in New York, 1959–65; visited Italy and Germany, 1966; lived in Paris, 1973–74, and in Pietrasanta, Italy, 1975–83. Major retrospectives in Marlborough Gallery, New York City, 1993; Grant Park, Chicago, 1994; Museo Nacional de Belles Artes, Madrid, 1997; Museu de Arte de São Paulo, Brazil, 1998. Lives and works in Paris, France; Pietrasanta, Italy; and New York City, United States.

Selected Works

1963   *Little Head*; acrylic and sawdust with hair; private collection, artist's estate
1966   *Horse*; acrylic and sawdust with hair; private collection, artist's estate
1977   *Adam and Eve*; bronze; Museo de Antioquia, Medellín, Colombia
1981   *Coffee Pot*; bronze; private collection
1981   *Guitar*; clay; private collection
1981   *Polycrome Snake*; painted epoxy; private collection
1983   *Large Torso*; bronze; private collection
1984   *Chat*; bronze; Marlborough Gallery, New York City, United States
1985   *Roman Soldier*; bronze; Pietrasanta, Italy
1988   *Venus allongée*; bronze; Fondation Pierre Gianadda, Martigny, Switzerland
1992   *Hand*; bronze; Museu de Arte de São Paulo, Brazil

Further Reading

Arciniegas, Germán, *Fernando Botero*, New York: Abrams, and Madrid: Edilerner, 1977
Botero (exhib. cat.), Munich: Galerie Buchholz, 1970
Botero in Chicago (exhib. cat.), Chicago: Chicago Department of Cultural Affairs, 1994
Durozoi, Gérard, *Botero*, Paris: Hazan, 1992
Ratcliff, Carter, *Botero*, New York: Abbeville Press, 1980
Restany, Pierre, *Botero*, Geneva: SJS, 1984; as *Botero*, New York: Abrams, 1984
Serra, Silvestro, Giorgio Van Straten, and Massimo Pacifico, *Botero al Forte Belvedere di Firenze*, Florence: Fos, 1990
Soavi, Giorgio, *Fernando Botero*, Milan: Fabbri, 1988
Spies, Werner, editor, *Fernando Botero: Paintings and Drawings*, Munich: Prestel-Verlag, 1992
Sullivan, Edward J., *Botero Sculpture*, New York: Abbeville Press, 1986
Virmaitre, Charles, Pierre Daix, and Jean Cau, *Botero aux Champs-Élysées*, Paris: Didier Imbert, 1992

EDMÉ BOUCHARDON 1698–1762 *French*

Displaying an extremely disciplined and highly intellectual, reserved attitude, Edmé Bouchardon's art aligns itself with a recurrent tendency, often labeled Classicism, in French art. This stylistic choice coexists in his work with an uncompromising realism of structure, surface, and detail. His oeuvre is resultantly precise, correct, and somewhat cold; his perfectionism also resulted in a relative sparseness. His numerous drawings, which include sketches after ancient sculpture and paintings by Raphael and other admired artists, studies for his sculpture, and designs for engraving, also demonstrate the clarity and accuracy of his forms and his admirable technical skill.

In Rome, like all students maintained at the French Academy, Bouchardon was required to copy an ancient statue for the royal collection; he fulfilled this obligation by producing a version of the Barberini *Faun*. He lost the competition for the Trevi Fountain to Lambert-Sigisbert Adam, his rival and fellow Prix de Rome winner, and also failed to realize his other major projects. Despite these disappointments, he won fame and a sizable clientele in Rome as a result of his skill in portraiture.

The first such work, his bust of Philip, Baron von Stosch, is a startling turn away from the elaboration, spatial dynamics, and temporality of his Baroque predecessors. Wigless and bare-chested, with only a drapery gathered over one shoulder, the image of the antiquarian Stosch is reminiscent of the antique busts restored or copied by 17th-century sculptors. On the other hand, his bust of the newly elected Pope Clement XII adopts an extreme realism of detail and surface texture as well as physiognomic specificity. These qualities suggest not so much the ebullient Baroque portraiture of Gianlorenzo Bernini as the more restrained but also virtuoso works of Alessandro Algardi. The combination of realism and Classicism that characterizes Bouchardon's production is evident in his

Christ Leaning on the Cross, his reception piece for the Royal Academy of Painting and Sculpture. The anatomy of the figure, its drapery, and the surface of the cross display a careful realism, but the gracefully posed Christ projects a mood of quiet resignation.

In 1739 Bouchardon received the commission for the fountain in the rue de Grenelle from the city of Paris. As with the Trevi Fountain in Rome, this work sets the water and figures before an architectural facade, but the effect is totally different. Instead of Baroque active figures, spouting water, and a density of elements, Bouchardon's ensemble is characteristically calm and quiet. In keeping with its civic purpose, the white marble figures of the central block include the seated city of Paris, in the form of a Classical *tyche* (city goddess), with the somewhat lower reclining side figures of the rivers Seine and Marne. The triangular arrangement is reminiscent of those of the Medici tombs by Michelangelo, even to the inclusion of a male and a female figure for the rivers. Niches on both sides contain figures of the Four Seasons; reliefs beneath them feature putti engaged in activities appropriate for each season. The ensemble is located on one side of a narrow street, causing forward extension to be virtually impossible, so that the water—the purpose for the fountain's installation—is emitted only from two small outlets at the bottom of the facade, an arrangement that provoked considerable contemporary criticism.

Bouchardon's *Cupid Cutting a Bow from the Club of Hercules* was a royal commission, intended for placement in the Salon d'Hercule at the Château de Versailles. The sculptor's predilection for realism, however, caused criticism at court, and the sculpture was soon sent out to the smaller Château of Choisy. Instead of a winsome putto, Bouchardon's Cupid has the gangling form of an actual adolescent, a disturbing quality for a mythological figure made all the more troublesome by his contorted pose. Bouchardon based the statue on the Parmigianino painting of the same subject, although it rivals its predecessor by virtue of the much more natural appearance of the figure.

After Cardinal de Fleury, chief minister to Louis XV, died in 1743, Bouchardon won the competition for the cardinal's tomb design over four contestants who included Nicolas-Sébastien Adam and Jean-Baptiste II Lemoyne. For unknown reasons, he never completed the work, and Lemoyne ultimately sculpted it. Two preserved maquettes by Bouchardon display relationships to ministerial tombs of the previous century by François Girardon and Antoine Coysevox but also a progressive simplification.

In 1749 the city of Paris commissioned Bouchardon to make an over-life-size bronze equestrian statue of Louis XV (destroyed 1792) to be placed in the new

Cupid Cutting a Bow from the Club of Hercules
© Giraudon / Art Resource, NY

Place Louis XV (now Place de la Concorde). He made an extraordinarily large number of studies for this major monument, which recalls the equestrian statue of *Marcus Aurelius* in Rome, following in this way a tradition extending back to the statue of Louis XIII by Pierre II Biard and including Girardon's equestrian monument to Louis XIV in the Place Louis-le-Grand (now Place Vendôme). Engravings and a small copy show that Bouchardon's statue portrayed the king in Roman armor. The figure was cast in 1758, but the statue was not inaugurated until 1763, at the end of the Seven Years' War. Earlier royal monuments, such as Giambologna and Pietro Tacca's *Henri IV, King of France* on the Pont Neuf, had displayed four chained captives at their bases, but Bouchardon's equestrian statue instead placed four Classical figures of virtues at the corners of the pedestal, in keeping with the Enlightenment paternalistic image of the monarch. After Bouchardon's death, Jean-Baptiste Pigalle, whom the sculptor had chosen to complete the monument, finished these figures.

191

Bouchardon demanded much of himself and of others and was highly esteemed by the art lovers and connoisseurs of his time. The French author Denis Diderot particularly admired his abilities as a draftsman and claimed that his works all reveal an understanding of nature and antiquity; the highly influential artist-writer Charles-Nicolas Cochin called him "the greatest sculptor and the best draftsman of his century." His reputation has since declined to some extent, no doubt because his works lack broadly or powerfully innovative qualities.

ANNE BETTY WEINSHENKER

See also **Adam Family; Algardi, Alessandro; Equestrian Statue of Marcus Aurelius; Lemoyne Family; Michelangelo (Buonarroti): Medici Chapel; Pigalle, Jean-Baptiste; Tacca Family**

Biography

Born in Chaumont-en-Bassigny, Haute-Marne, France, 29 May 1698. Son of Jean-Baptiste Bouchardon, an important provincial sculptor and architect; brother of Jacques-Philippe Bouchardon, a sculptor and draftsman. Studied with his father and after arriving in Paris in 1721 with Guillaume Coustou the Elder, won Prix de Rome for sculpture, 1722; pensioner at the French Academy in Rome, 1723; returned to Paris, 1733; *agréé* (admitted) at Royal Academy of Painting and Sculpture, 1735; named designer for the Academy of Literature and Inscriptions, 1736; received as member of the Royal Academy, 1745; appointed assistant professor, 1746; made full professor, 1747. Died in Paris, France, 27 July 1762.

Selected Works

1727 Bust of Philip, Baron von Stosch; marble; Staatliche Museen, Berlin, Germany

1730 Bust of Pope Clement XII; marble; Prince Tommaso Corsini private collection, Florence, Italy

1730 Copy of Barberini *Faun*; marble; Musée du Louvre, Paris, France

1737–46 *Cris de Paris*; suite of drawings; British Museum, London, England

1743 First maquette for mausoleum of Cardinal de Fleury; red wax, wood; Musée du Louvre, Paris, France

1745 Second maquette for mausoleum of Cardinal de Fleury: *Cardinal de Fleury Dying in the Arms of Religion*; wax; Musée du Louvre, Paris, France

1745 *Christ Leaning on the Cross*; marble; Musée du Louvre, Paris, France

1745 Fountain; marble, stone; rue de Grenelle, Paris, France

1750 *Cupid Cutting a Bow from the Club of Hercules*; marble; Musée du Louvre, Paris, France

1763 Equestrian monument of Louis XV (completed by Jean-Baptiste Pigalle), for Place Louis XV (now Place de la Concorde), Paris, France; bronze (destroyed 1792)

Further Reading

Bouchardon, Edmé, *Edmé Bouchardon: Sculpteur du roi, 1698–1702* (exhib. cat.), Chaumont, France: s.n., 1962

Diderot, Denis, "Sur la sculpture, Bouchardon, et Caylus," in *Oeuvres complètes*, by Diderot, vol. 5, Paris: Le Club Français du Livre, 1970

Duclaux, Lise, editor, *La statue équestre de Louis XV: Dessins de Bouchardon, sculpteur du roi, dans les collections du Musée du Louvre* (exhib. cat.), Paris: Éditions des Musées Nationaux, 1973

Jordan, Marc, "Edmé Bouchardon: A Sculptor, a Draughtsman, and His Reputation in Eighteenth-Century France," *Apollo* 121 (1985)

Parker, K.T., "Bouchardon's 'Cries of Paris,'" *Old Master Drawings* 19 (1930)

Rombouts, Stephen, "Art as Propaganda in Eighteenth-Century France: The Paradox of Edmé Bouchardon's Louis XV," *Eighteenth-Century Studies* 27 (1993–94)

ÉMILE-ANTOINE BOURDELLE 1861– 1929 *French*

Critics have mythologized Émile-Antoine Bourdelle's southern roots and peasant ancestry, citing them as the origin of the unadorned directness, or "primitivism," of his simplified sculpture. His style was often described as a modern interpretation of archaic Greek art. Auguste Rodin, for example, referred to Bourdelle as a "Greek from the South of France" (see Dufet and Lavrillier, 1979). Bourdelle himself liked to say that he sculpted in the rustic "langue d'oc" (the language of Languedoc, the region of France where he was born).

More likely, Bourdelle's aesthetic of reduction was a reaction against the formative influence of Rodin, in whose studio he worked from 1893 to 1908. Bourdelle's first important public monument revealed the extent of his initial debts to Rodin. Bourdelle's *Monument to the Defenders of 1870–71* was commissioned by Bourdelle's hometown of Montauban. Its expressionistic updating of traditional war allegory recalls Rodin's *Call to Arms* (1879), particularly in the figure of the languishing, tragically contorted nude warrior. Bourdelle ignored traditional rules of unity, however, in the monument's asymmetrical, additive composition. Its four loosely linked figures move separately and outward from the center. Each side has a radically different view. Although its bodily deformations initially outraged the citizens of Montauban, other critics recognized them as innovative attempts to symbolize the brutality of war.

Bourdelle's *Beethoven, Tragic Mask*, outdid even the frenzied modeling of Rodin. The work's pummeled surfaces and exaggerated physiognomic distortions evoke a sense of the musician's inner anguish. Beginning in the 1880s until his death in 1929, Bourdelle made more than 80 images of the German composer. Early on, Bourdelle was struck by his own physical resemblance to Beethoven and strongly identified with him. Beethoven was to Bourdelle as Balzac was to Rodin. *Tragic Mask* can be considered a culmination of the entire series of Beethoven images, in which Bourdelle conveys a romantic attachment to the idea of the tormented genius.

Perhaps because Bourdelle knew Rodin's work so intimately (he would later write a book about it, published posthumously in 1937), he also realized the necessity of developing an entirely different sculptural language. Although not exhibited until 1925, Bourdelle's *Head of Apollo* illustrates how he could break definitively from Rodin. The mixture of styles in this work testifies to that break; one side of the head has a cracked and fissured surface, seemingly scarred by studio accidents, whereas the other is characterized by smooth synthesis. From then on, Bourdelle chose stability of form over spontaneity of expression. He suppressed superfluous detail in favor of an ordered articulation of clearly delineated volumes. He would later refer to himself as the "antidiscipline" of Rodin (see Varenne, 1937). This is especially evident in Bourdelle's more chaste and sober approaches to the female body, such as *Penelope* and *Fruit*.

The manifesto of Bourdelle's sculptural aims, however, is an image of heroic masculine strength. *Hercules the Archer* epitomizes the artist's idea of sculpture as a simplified architecture of human forms. A massive stabilizing rectangle, formed by the extended limbs of the figure, dominates the composition. Hercules' left leg, raised to waist height, steadies his physique against a rock, while his arm holds the ready bow. His muscles, rippling with potential energy, are as taut as his weapon. *Hercules the Archer* achieves a dynamic tension between the precariousness of the pose and its impression of weighty permanence. This work solidified Bourdelle's reputation when exhibited at the Salon de la Société Nationale in 1910.

Bourdelle's devotion to mythological subjects such as Hercules encouraged critics to label his art as archaism. His well-known sculpture for the Théâtre des Champs-Elysées in Paris, *Meditation of Apollo with the Muses*, is one of the few projects that may actually

Hercules the Archer, Musée d'Orsay, Paris, France
© Erich Lessing / Art Resource, NY

deserve the description, because his approach here seems conceived with specific conventions of early Greek temple decoration in mind. The *in situ* central frieze (14 meters long) represents the *Meditation of Apollo with the Muses*, and five low reliefs depict *Tragedy, Comedy, Dance, Music,* and *Architecture and Sculpture*. This last relief, where one figure holds a column while another lowers a winged statue on its capital, is an appropriate emblem for Bourdelle's guiding principle at the theater, which was nothing less than the synthesis of sculpture and architecture.

Apollo lounges at the center of Bourdelle's frieze while muses in two side panels rush headlong toward him. The sinuous abstract patterns of their flowing drapery add to the somewhat static, stylized sense of movement. In each of the lower reliefs, pairs of allegorical figures interact with dramatic gestures. In powerfully compact rhythms, their bodies twist and bend under the limits of their rectangular frames. Although based on a series of life drawings after the dancer Isadora Duncan (the source for the innovative poses here), these figures first and foremost serve the architectural context of the theater. Bourdelle wanted to evoke the impression that his sculpture emerged directly from the wall and was not independent from it. Indeed, the extreme linearity of his carving echoes the facade's

193

geometry, designed by Auguste Perret with Bourdelle's assistance.

Bourdelle focused on public commissions after World War I, which led to his subsequent reputation as a maker of official monuments. He remained deeply committed to public sculpture long after many avant-garde sculptors had abandoned the idea. He continued his search for a legitimate, effective language of commemoration, and his sources were eclectic. *Virgin of the Offertory*, a colossal stone statue overlooking the Alsatian town of Niederbruck, reveals how he was equally drawn to medieval models. According to Bourdelle, the rustic order of French Romanesque architecture was a pervasive influence on his work. In his *Monument to General Carlos Maria Alvear*, Bourdelle attempted to reactivate the equestrian tradition in a modern idiom. A statue of the general, a hero in the Argentine wars for independence, is mounted on a square granite pillar. At each corner of its base are four architectonic and attenuated youths, rising like monumental columns. Each holds a symbolic attribute of the civic virtues they represent: *Force, Eloquence, Victory*, and *Freedom*.

Bourdelle represents a crucial transition in early 20th-century French sculpture, as his oeuvre is both innovative and tradition-bound. As an early attempt to construct primarily with essential masses instead of modeled surfaces, his work anticipates formal abstraction. Yet much of his commissioned work, in its reliance on myth and allegory, remains faithful to inherited ideals of the 19th-century heroic monument. Bourdelle was well aware of the dangers in idealizing the past. About his *Dying Centaur*, he once lamented, "He is dying because no one believes in him" (see Jianu and Dufet, 1965).

ELLEN McBREEN

See also **Rodin, Auguste**

Biography

Born in Montauban, France, 30 October 1861. Son of a cabinetmaker, who taught him how to carve; nephew of a stonecutter. Studied at École des Beaux-Arts in Toulouse, under Maurette, 1876; moved to Paris to study at École des Beaux-Arts under Falguière, 1884; left in rebellion after two years and took studio in the Impasse du Maine (now Musée Bourdelle), where Aimé-Jules Dalou was his neighbor; began exhibiting at Salon of the Société des Artistes Français, 1884; Sociétaire, Société Nationale des Beaux-Arts, 1891; worked as assistant in Rodin's studio, 1893–1908; taught at Académie Rodin on boulevard Montparnasse, beginning 1900, then at the Académie de la Grand Chaumière, 1909–29. Alberto Giacometti and Ger-

maine Richier were students; founded Salon des Tuileries with Albert Besnard and Auguste Perret, 1923. Made commander of the Legion of Honor in 1924. Died in le Vésinet, near Paris, France, 1 October 1929.

Selected Works

1895–1902   *Monument to the Defenders of 1870–71*; bronze and granite; Place Antoine Bourdelle, Montauban, France

1900–09   *Head of Apollo*; bronze; Musée d'Orsay, Musée Bourdelle, Paris, France

1901   *Beethoven, Tragic Mask* (from the *Beethoven* series); bronze; versions in Museum of Modern Art, New York, United States; Hermitage, St. Petersburg, Russia

1906   *Fruit*; bronze; Musée Bourdelle, Paris, France

1905–07   *Penelope*; bronze; versions in Musée d'Orsay, Paris; Musée Bourdelle, Paris, France

1908–29   Monument to Adam Mickiewicz; bronze; Cours de la Reine, Paris, France

1909   *Hercules the Archer*; bronze; versions in Art Institute of Chicago, Illinois, United States; Musée d'Orsay, Paris, France; Ho-Am Art Museum, Seoul, Korea; Metropolitan Museum of Art, New York City, United States

1911   *Dying Centaur*; bronze; Princeton University Art Museum, Princeton, New Jersey, United States

1911–13   *Meditation of Apollo with the Muses*; marble; Théâtre des Champs Elysées, Avenue Montaigne, Paris, France

1912–1925   *Monument to General Carlos Maria Alvear*; bronze and granite; Plaza de la Recoleta, Buenos Aires, Argentina

1919–22   *Virgin of the Offertory*; stone; Haut-Rhin, Niederbrück, France

Further Reading

Barruel, Thérèse, and Claude Loupiac, *1913: Le Théâtre des Champs-Elysées*, Paris: Éditions de la Réunion des Musées Nationaux, 1987

Basdevant, Denise. *Bourdelle et le théâtre des Champs-Elysées*, Paris: Hachette, 1982

Bourdelle, Emile-Antoine, *Écrits sur l'art et sur la vie*, compiled by Gaston Varenne, Paris: Plon, 1955

Bourdelle, Emile-Antoine, *La sculpture et Rodin*, Paris: Éditions Émile-Paul Frères, 1937

Cannon-Brookes, Peter, *Emile Antoine Bourdelle: An Illustrated Commentary*, London: Trefoil Books, 1983

Le catalogue du Musée Bourdelle, Paris: Paris-Musées, 1990

Cogniat, Raymond, *Hommage à Bourdelle*, Paris: Plon, 1961

Dufet, Michel, and Carol-Marc Lavrillier, *Bourdelle et la critique de son temps*, Paris: Musée Bourdelle, 1979

Émile Antoine Bourdelle: Pioneer of the Future (exhib. cat.), West Bretton, Wakefield: Yorkshire Sculpture Park, 1989

Gautherin, Véronique, *L'oeil et la main: Bourdelle et la photographie*, Paris: Musée Bourdelle, 2000

Jianu, Ionel, and Michel Dufet, *Bourdelle*, translated by Kathleen Muston and Bryan Richardson, Paris: Arted, 1965; 2nd edition, 1978 (with catalogue raisonné)

Le Normand-Romain, Antoinette, *Héraklès archèr: Naissance d'une œuvre*, Paris: Paris-Musées, 1992

Varenne, Gaston, *Bourdelle par lui-même: Sa pensée et son art*, Paris: Fasquelle, 1937

LOUISE BOURGEOIS 1911– *French, active in United States*

Louise Bourgeois is arguably one of the principal sculptors of the 20th century. Although her work was rarely seen by mainstream audiences until the 1970s, Bourgeois's artistic influence began in the 1940s, when she emerged as a striking, albeit quiet, voice among the clattering noise of the émigré Surrealists and Abstract Expressionists with whom she exhibited in New York City. Over the decades, her work in both abstract and figurative modes has continued to speak to a variety of physical and psychological experiences that poignantly deal with the personal and the primal, pleasure and pain.

Bourgeois was born in France in 1911 to a family who owned a tapestry restoration studio and business. She began sketching at an early age, and she often helped in the atelier by making drawings for missing sections of tapestries. In 1932 Bourgeois began studying mathematics at the Sorbonne in Paris, but she left to pursue her interest in art, studying with French Modernist painters André Lhote and Fernand Léger. In 1938 she married American Robert Goldwater, who would later build a reputation as the preeminent art historian on modern art and Primitivism. The couple moved to New York that year. The following year Bourgeois enrolled in classes at the Art Students League and began study with the painter Vàclav Vytlacil.

In the 1940s Bourgeois exhibited paintings in group shows with artists such as Willem de Kooning and Jackson Pollock, who would later be associated with the Abstract Expressionist movement. Similar to her peers, Bourgeois was influenced by Surrealism with its emphasis on automatism, and the power and symbolic language of the unconscious. Her early paintings, such as the *Femme maison* (Woman House, ca. 1947–49) series, for example, depict a naked female body with a house in place of the head or face. Such images articulated the troubling relation between femininity and domesticity, with the home replacing or obliterating any sense of self. She conceived of these paintings as

self-portraits—which would later become icons for the 1970s feminist movement—and indeed her oeuvre has always been interwoven with threads of autobiography. Bourgeois reworked the *femme maison* in a 1982 neo-Baroque marble sculpture of the same name, suggesting that the artist drew upon a reservoir of themes or iconographies over long periods of time. While Bourgeois's sculpture shared an approach that related to the Surrealist vocabulary of symbols, her art remained fiercely personal, eschewing the popularized "dream images" of Max Ernst, André Breton, and Salvador Dalí, and instead referenced her own struggles as an artist, wife, and mother with three small children in postwar America.

In 1949 Bourgeois stopped making paintings and began to work with three-dimensional media. That year she had her first solo sculpture exhibition at the Peridot Gallery in New York with 17 wood sculptures that she termed *personages*. Over the next six years Bourgeois produced more than 80 such pieces, which were generally made of wood and painted, and cast in bronze in later years. The sculptures resembled tall, narrow spears, often smoothed and attenuated to emphasize surface nuance. Their simplicity and minimal articulation suggested the influence of Constantin Brancusi and Alberto Giacometti as well as African totems. Still, Bourgeois's installation of the *personages* and the relationship between her artwork and its audience were uniquely her own. Bourgeois described the *personages* as representations for personal friends and family members, or as symbolic of ambiguous personalities, emotions, or mythologies, such as seen in *Spring*. When placed alone, these sculptures evoked isolation, but when grouped together, relationships between the objects emerged. The Peridot Gallery exhibition was truly one of the earliest examples of installation art in America, given that Bourgeois intentionally displayed the sculptures without bases, in clusters, so that viewers could move in and around the space. She even went so far as to describe the relation among the pieces as "dialogical," a conception that reconceived the notion of the Modernist sculpture as wholly autonomous.

In the late 1940s and 1950s Bourgeois shifted from making discrete wood sculptures to more complex assemblages. For example, *The Blind Leading the Blind* featured two rows of thin, fragile leglike stakes held together by a horizontal piece of wood. This sculpture, with its simple post-and-lintel construction and rigid, interconnected forms, explored ideas about the individual and his or her relation to the group or the whole. Its title, which Bourgeois did not choose until 1949, the year she was called to testify before the House Committee on Un-American Activities, might suggest the folly of regimented thinking and the danger of rit-

The Blind Leading the Blind
Founders Society Purchase, Mr. and Mrs. Walter Buhl Ford, II Fund
© Detroit Institute of Arts, and Louise Bourgeois / Licensed by VAGA, New York, NY

ual. While her work was rarely overtly political, Bourgeois was sensitive to her position as an outsider in America during the so-called Red Scare, and her pieces of the time reflected existential and expressionist notions of self and other.

A piece of clustered totems such as *One and Others* clearly exemplified this trend. Bourgeois crowded several similar bulbous, organic wooden forms close together on a very low stand. Many of the wooden "figures" are painted in a variety of patterns such that the viewer's eye is drawn to individual pieces but also perceives the whole.

In the 1960s Bourgeois shifted from wood as her primary material to experiment with plaster and latex, transient and malleable substances associated with the Post-Minimal or Anti-Form movement whose practitioners included Robert Morris, Eva Hesse, Lynda Benglis, and Richard Serra, among others. Her work became increasingly organic and profoundly focused on the body and bodily metaphors. She began to produce plaster sculptures that resembled nests, such as *Lair*. With a rough-hewn plaster exterior, *Lair* resembled an amorphous, enclosed cave or refuge with air holes. These nestlike constructions exuded a deliberate duality: on the one hand, they could be interpreted as nurturing, dark, safe places; on the other hand, they

might be seen as isolating or even as traps. Bourgeois continued to stretch her use of organic shapes, and throughout the 1970s her art became increasingly and overtly sexual. Sculptures such as *Avenza*, *Hanging Janus* and *Cumul I* echoed combinations of male and female sexual organs, strange and exuberant constellations of breast-, penis-, testicle-, finger-, and tongue-like forms marked by inherent inconsistency and ambivalence. Bourgeois also invoked female sexuality, carving small-scale, abstract figures of the female body and sculptures that referred to not only female genitalia but also powerful phallic forms. Bourgeois's embrace of forms both abstract and figurative, masculine and feminine, interior and exterior, and alluring and repulsive has prompted critics and historians to link her work with psychoanalysis, primarily through a shared language of the unconscious, the passions, and fantasy. The artist has welcomed such interpretations while at the same time eschewing literal narratives, preferring metaphors that shed light on her intensely personal oeuvre.

Bourgeois began to receive artistic acclaim in part due to the burgeoning 1970s women's movement. Although some female artists objected to being identified as "women's" artists and attempted to distance themselves from the term *feminist* (because of rampant art world discrimination), Bourgeois embraced the politics of the time. She made herself accessible to feminist journalists and art historians and participated in numerous exhibitions that supported the work of women artists.

The 1980s marked another decade of change for Bourgeois. In 1982 she was the subject of a full-scale retrospective at the Museum of Modern Art in New York City, an honor seldom awarded to living artists. The exhibition was the first time that Bourgeois's work could be seen in its totality, and it commenced a flurry of scholarly research on the artist and her career. Although for many this might mark the twilight of an enduring artistic career, Bourgeois has continued to produce vital art, most recently involving multimedia installations of found and sculpted objects, steel, bronze, marble, glass, and fibers such as tapestries, twine, and fabrics. At the age of 82, she was elected to represent the United States at the Venice Biennale, an exposition of contemporary art from around theworld. In 2000 she was invited to create the inaugural piece for the Tate Modern's Unilever Series in the Turbine Hall of the Tate Gallery, London. Both opportunities serve as signs of her continued vitality as a preeminent contemporary sculptor.

ALEXIS L. BOYLAN

See also **Abstract Expressionism; Brancusi, Constantin; Contemporary Sculpture; Ernst, Max; Giacometti, Alberto; Hesse, Eva; Installation; Modernism;**

Morris, Robert; Oppenheim, Meret; Postmodernism; Surrealist Sculpture; Women Sculptors

Biography

Born in Paris, France, 25 December 1911. Studied mathematics at the Sorbonne, Paris, 1932–35; left to begin formal artistic training at the École des Beaux-Arts, 1936–38; also studied at the École du Louvre (1936–37), Atelier Bissière (1936–37), and Académie de la Grande Chaumière (1937–38); married Robert Goldwater, art historian and critic, 1938, and moved to New York City, where she studied with Vàclav Vytlacil at the Art Students League; first solo show of paintings at the Bertha Schaefer Gallery, New York City, 1945; first solo sculpture show at the Peridot Gallery, New York City, 1949–50. Received artist grant, National Endowment for the Arts, 1973; elected fellow, American Academy of Arts and Sciences, 1981; retrospective exhibition at the Museum of Modern Art, New York City, 1982; elected member, American Academy and Institute of Arts and Letters, 1983; gold medal of honor for excellence in art, National Arts Club, 1987; distinguished artist award for lifetime achievement, College Art Association, 1989; Grand Prix National de Sculpture from the French minister of culture, 1991; chosen to represent the United States at the Venice Biennale, 1993. Presently lives in New York City, United States.

Selected Works

1945–47 *Femme Maison*; oil and ink on linen; John D. Kahlbetzer collection, Santa Barbara, California, United States
1947–53 *Quarantania*; bronze with white patina; Museum of Modern Art, New York City, United States
1949 *The Blind Leading the Blind*; painted wood; The Detroit Institute of Arts, Michigan, United States
1949 *Spring*; balsa wood; National Gallery of Art, Washington, D.C., United States
1955 *One and Others*; painted and stained wood; Whitney Museum of American Art, New York City, United States
1962–63 *Lair*; plaster; Robert Miller Gallery, New York City, United States
1967 *Germinal*; bronze; Galerie Lelong, Zurich, Switzerland
1968 *Hanging Janus*; bronze; Galerie Lelong, Zurich, Switzerland
1968–69 *Avenza*; plaster and latex; cast in 1992; Tate Gallery, London, England
1969 *Cumul I*; marble; Centre Georges Pompidou, Paris, France
1984 *Nature Study*; bronze; Whitney Museum of American Art, New York City, United States
1989–93 *Cell (Eyes and Mirrors)*; marble, mirrors, steel, glass; Tate Gallery, London, England
1996 *Spider*; bronze cast with silver nitrate patina; cast in 1997; National Gallery of Art, Smithsonian Institution, Washington, D.C., United States

Further Reading

Bernadac, Marie-Laure, and Hans-Ulrich Obrist, editors, *Destruction of the Father, Reconstruction of the Father: Writing and Interviews, 1923–1997*, Cambridge, Massachusetts: MIT Press, and London: Violette, 1998
Cole, Ian, editor, *Louise Bourgeois*, Oxford: Museum of Modern Art, 1996
Kotik, Charlotta, Terrie Sultan, and Christian Leigh, editors, *Louise Bourgeois: The Locus of Memory: Works, 1982–1993*, New York: Abrams and The Brooklyn Museum of Art, 1994
Kuspit, Donald, *Interview with Louise Bourgeois*, New York: Vintage, 1988
Lippard, Lucy R., "Louise Bourgeois: From the Inside Out," in *From the Center: Feminist Essays on Women's Art*, New York: Dutton, 1976
Louise Bourgeois: Memory and Architecture (exhib. cat.), Madrid, Spain: Museo Nacional Centro de Arte Reina Sofía, 1999
Storr, Robert, "Louise Bourgeois: Gender and Possession," *Art in America* 71 (April 1983)
Weiermair, Peter, and Cornelia Walter, editors, *Louise Bourgeois*, Frankfurt: Kunstverein, 1989
Wye, Deborah, *Louise Bourgeois*, New York: Museum of Modern Art, 1982

PIETRO BRACCI 1700–1773 *Italian*

Once the most famous sculptor in Rome, Pietro Bracci fell into obscurity during the Neoclassical period and is rarely mentioned in modern texts. Born in Rome, Bracci received his early training in the studio of Giuseppe Bartolomeo Chiari. His biographer, Franceso Maria Niccolò Gaburri, claims that Bracci also studied under Camillo Rusconi, but his connection to the latter is questionable. In 1725 Bracci entered a competition sponsored by the Accademia di San Luca, sharing first prize with Filippo della Valle for his terracotta relief of *Josiah Assigning Money for the Temple*. This victory firmly established his reputation, with Bracci executing portrait busts of Cardinal Fabrizio Paolucci and Pope Innocent XII that same year.

These busts constitute the first two entries in an inventory of works listed in Bracci's diary, which he kept from 1725 to the end of his career. According to this inventory, Bracci's next monument was a memorial to Cardinal Fabrizio Paolucci, in which a winged figure of Fame ascends a pyramid, holding a portrait medallion depicting the deceased. This design was first used by Gianlorenzo Bernini in his memorial to Alessandro Valtrini and became the dominant type of commemorative monument in the early 18th century. Bracci himself returned to this general formula in three of his later tombs, those of Cardinal Innigo Caracciolo in Anversa Cathedral, Cardinal Renato Imperiale in the Church of Sant'Agostino, Rome, and Cardinal Carlo Leopoldo Calcagnini in the Church of Sant'Andrea della Fratte, Rome.

Monuments such as these illustrate Bracci's popularity among papal circles, particularly during the pontificate of Clement XII (r. 1730–40). Under Pope Clement, not only was Bracci involved in the decoration of the Corsini Chapel in the Basilica of San Giovanni in Laterano, the funerary chapel of the papal family, but he was also assigned the important task of restoring the Arch of Constantine. Both works reveal an extensive knowledge of Classical art, with his relief of *St. Andrew Corsini Washing the Feet of the Poor* for the Corsini Chapel recalling those of ancient Rome; his restoration of the Arch of Constantine was aided by a study of Roman coins. As with most sculptors of the period, Bracci attained this knowledge by restoring antique statuary for wealthy patrons such as Cardinal Alessandro Albani, for whom he mended a statue of *Antinous* in 1733 and reconstructed a marble torso into the god *Apollo* a few years later.

Albani also belonged to a committee that commissioned Bracci in 1734 to execute the tomb of Benedict XIII, designed by Carlo Marchionni. Benedict XIII appears atop a raised pedestal at whose base lies a sarcophagus flanked by allegorical figures representing *Religion* and *Humility*. Bracci carved both the pope and the figure of *Religion*, whereas Bartolommeo Pincellotti was responsible for the figure of *Humility*. In a manner typical of Bracci's approach to portraiture, the pope's countenance is highly individualized. Because *Religion* represents a personification, she does not share this characterization but instead has more Classical features. The same is true of the figure of *Charity* for the tomb of Maria Clementina Sobieska Stuart. Once again, Bracci was responsible for the execution, not the design, of the tomb. Nevertheless, the Sobieska monument is one of Bracci's finest works, with *Charity*'s complex drapery and delicate features revealing Bracci's tremendous technical ability.

Throughout the 1740s, Bracci continued to refine his style, culminating with the elegant tomb of Cardinal Carlo Leopoldo Calcagnini in 1748. In a manner reminiscent of Bernini's tomb of Urban VIII (1627–

Tomb of Maria Clementina Sobieski Stuart
© Alinari / Art Resource, NY

47), a winged Fame inscribes the cardinal's epitaph on a pyramid. Also Berninesque is the use of various materials, such as white and black marble, bronze, and paint, in the same monument, a practice that had fallen out of favor with younger artists. This retroactive quality is typical of Bracci's work, visible in his relief of *St. Flavius in the Council of 465*, which belongs to a tradition begun in the 1630s by Alessandro Algardi's *Scenes of Cardinal de' Medici's Legation to France*, part of the tomb of Leo XI (completed in 1644). Despite such conservatism, Bracci continued to receive important commissions, including a relief for the Chigi Chapel in Siena Cathedral illustrating the *Presentation of the Virgin in the Temple*.

In the next decade, Bracci was involved in two of the most important projects in Rome: a series of statues representing founders of religious orders for St. Peter's Basilica and the completion of the Trevi Fountain (mid 18th century) under the patronage of Clement XIII. For the first project, Bracci carved statues of *St. Vincent de Paul*, the *Blessed Girolamo Emiliani*, and *St. Norbert*. Bracci was not particularly innovative in their design, merely reworking his earlier *St. Peter Nolasco* and *St. Felix of Valois*. His work for the Trevi Fountain, for which he carved the central group, is much more impressive. Working from the designs of Giovanni Battista

Maini, Bracci carved an imposing figure of *Oceanus*, noted in his diary as being larger than the *Dioscuri* of the Campidoglio, accompanied by two *Tritons* in a shell-shaped chariot drawn by sea horses. Bracci altered Maini's designs significantly, giving *Oceanus* a much more emphatic gesture, his arm extending beyond his niche, and directing his gaze toward the figures below him, drawing the viewer into the composition.

In 1763, a year after completing his work on the fountain, Bracci began his last great monument, the tomb of Pope Benedict XIV for St. Peter's Basilica. Located above a doorway, the tomb resembles Bernini's tomb of Alexander VII (1671–78), with the pope appearing above while two allegorical figures, representing *Sacred Knowledge* and *Disinterestedness*, are seated to the side. Bracci carved the statue of Pope Benedict and *Sacred Knowledge*, whereas Gaspare Sibilla carved *Disinterestedness*. The tomb is unique in showing the pope standing upright rather than seated or kneeling, his right hand raised in a gesture of benediction. Unlike some of his other funerary monuments, Bracci himself was responsible for this design, which inspired a number of later artists such as Antonio Canova.

Despite this influence, Bracci's impact on the succeeding generation of artists was nominal; his style was a late manifestation of the art of Bernini, Algardi, and other Baroque artists such as Domenico Guidi. With the advent of the Neoclassical period, this style fell into disfavor, and many artists such as Bracci disappeared from guidebooks, remaining relatively unknown to this day.

DAVID L. BERSHAD AND GABRIELLA SZALAY

See also **Algardi, Alessandro; Bernini, Gianlorenzo; Fountain Sculpture; Guidi, Domenico; Rusconi, Camillo**

Biography

Born in Rome, Italy, 16 June 1700. Son of woodcarver Bartolomeo Cesare. Trained as sculptor by Giuseppe Bartolomeo Chiari; established independent studio in Rome, 1724; elected to Accademia d'Arcadia, 1724; received first prize in competition sponsored by Accademia di San Luca, 1725; completed many important commissions for funerary monuments, the Trevi Fountain, and other projects, in Rome, 1726–70; became member of Accademia di San Luca, 1740, and elected *principe* (director) in 1756. Died in Rome, Italy, 13 February 1773.

Selected Works

1725   *Josiah Assigning Money for the Temple*; terracotta; Accademia di San Luca, Rome, Italy

1725   Portrait busts of Cardinal Fabrizio Paolucci and Pope Innocent XII; marble; Church of Santi Giovanni e Paolo, Rome, Italy

1726   Memorial to Cardinal Fabrizio Paolucci; marble; Church of San Marcello al Corso, Rome, Italy

1730   *St. Felix of Valois* and *St. Peter Nolasco*; marble; Basilica of Mafra, Portugal

1732   *St. Andrew Corsini Washing the Feet of the Poor*; marble; Corsini Chapel, Basilica of San Giovanni in Laterano, Rome, Italy

1734   Statues of Pope Benedict XIII and *Religion*, for the tomb of Pope Benedict XIII; marble; Church of Santa Maria sopra Minerva, Rome, Italy

1736–38   Tomb of Cardinal Innigo Caracciolo; marble; Anversa Cathedral, Italy

1739–42   Tomb of Maria Clementina Sobieski Stuart; polychrome marble, alabaster, bronze; St. Peter's Basilica, Rome, Italy

1741   Tomb of Cardinal Renato Imperiale; marble; Church of Sant'Agostino, Rome, Italy

1742   *St. Flavius in the Council of 465*; marble; Basilica of Santa Maria Maggiore, Rome, Italy

1748   Tomb of Cardinal Carlo Leopoldo Calcagnini; marble, bronze, paint; Church of Sant'Andrea della Fratte, Rome, Italy

1749   *Presentation of the Virgin in the Temple*; marble; Siena Cathedral, Italy

1754   *St. Vincent de Paul*; marble; St. Peter's Basilica, Rome, Italy

1756   *Blessed Girolamo Emiliani*; marble; St. Peter's Basilica, Rome, Italy

1758   *St. Norbert*; marble; St. Peter's Basilica, Rome, Italy

1759–62   *Oceanus*; marble; Trevi Fountain, Rome, Italy

1763–70   *Benedict XIV* and *Sacred Knowledge*, for tomb of Pope Benedict XIV; marble; St. Peter's Basilica, Rome, Italy

Further Reading

Domarus, Kurt von, *Pietro Bracci: Beiträge zur Römischen Kunstgeschichte des XVIII. Jahrhunderts*, Strasbourg, France: Heitz, 1915

Gradara, Costanza, *Pietro Bracci: Scultore romano, 1700–1773*, Milan: Alfieri and Lacroix, 1920

Honour, H., "Bracci, Pietro," in *Dizionario biografico degli Italiani*, vol. 13, Rome: Istituto della Enciclopedia Italiani, 1971

Kieven, Elisabeth, and John Pinto, *Architecture and Sculpture in Eighteenth-Century Rome: Drawings by Pietro and Virginio Bracci in the Canadian Centre for Architecture and*

Other Collections, University Park: Pennsylvania State University Press, 2001

Pinto, John A., *The Trevi Fountain*, New Haven, Connecticut: Yale University Press, 1986

Riccoboni, Alberto, *Roma nell'arte: La scultura nell'evo moderno dal Quattrocento ad oggi*, Rome: Casa Editrice Mediterranea, 1942

CONSTANTIN BRANCUSI 1876–1957

Romanian, also active in France

Born in Hobitza, Romania, to a peasant family, Constantin Brancusi became one of the most esteemed, influential, and innovative sculptors of the 20th century. Fiercely independent, he ran away from home several times before leaving finally at age 11. In 1892 he moved to Craiova, where two years later he enrolled in the School of Arts and Crafts. Here, he learned the craftsmanship that would temper his artwork, studying industrial design, mechanical drawing, and mathematics. Graduating with honors in 1898, he moved to Bucharest and entered the Academy of Fine Arts, studying sculpture under Wladimir Hegel and responding positively to the academic training modeled on French Beaux-Arts curriculum; he won one silver and several bronze medals for sculpture based on academic criteria.

Although he initially intended to visit Italy, Brancusi instead traveled to Paris by foot and train, arriving in the French capital in the summer of 1904. In April 1905, at the age of 29, he enrolled in the Académie des Beaux-Arts under the instruction of Antonin Mercié, concentrating primarily on portraiture rather than modeling after the antique. His first exhibited pieces were all portrait heads or character-type busts. Auguste Rodin noticed Brancusi's entries in the 1906 Salone d'Automne and subsequently advised the younger sculptor, even employing him for a short time as a studio assistant.

Brancusi responded to the master's example—Rodin is thought to have had the most discernible influence on Brancusi's art in the truncation of figural forms, series work, and a looser, more interpretative style of modeling—but in essence Rodin served as a tradition for him to push against. He diverged from Rodin most markedly in his development of unified surface, abandonment of modeling for carving, and rejection of a large atelier/assistant system of production. While Brancusi greatly appreciated Rodin's guidance, he found that the ease with which he could mimic Rodin's visual style was leading him to a crisis regarding his own sculptural language and development. He finally left Rodin's studio, remarking, "Nothing can grow in the shadow of the great trees."

Brancusi's breakthrough came with a monument commission for Petre Stanescu in Buzau, Romania, in April 1907. Here, the sculptor made his first great stand against realism, paring a female mourning figure down to essential forms and volumes, truncating limbs and smoothing surfaces until the composition and form manifested only essential elements of the concept. Titled *The Prayer*, the piece was Brancusi's first major statement in his new style. From this point Brancusi derided slavish adherence to academic realism and anatomy as "beefsteak sculpture." His mature work is instantly recognizable, displaying qualities from which he never wavered: simplicity, purity, and unity.

In 1907 Brancusi began developing his method of direct carving, first in stone and then, beginning in 1913, wood. He essentially abandoned modeling and concentrated on reductive processes. *The Kiss*, his first direct carving in stone, was also one of the first mature motifs that he examined periodically throughout his career. He also developed his axiom of "truth to materials," meticulously attempting to match the correct material to his subject through repeated experiments with different types of stone and wood and different colors of marble, and by casting carved works into bronze. By the 1920s and 1930s he was working in a fully developed style characterized by reduced, rounded forms and smooth, highly polished finishes. Conceptually, he consistently examined Platonic ideas regarding the formal essence of his subjects.

Concurrently, Brancusi knew of the Paris avant-garde's interest in primitivism—particularly the folk art of Africa and Oceania. Although most scholars agree that, as with the other Paris artists, African carvings influenced Brancusi, Sidney Geist notes that Romanian scholars reject this theory, insisting that only Brancusi's Romanian background influenced the sculptor (see Geist, 1968). Romanian folklore does inform his work, perhaps most directly with the *Maiastra* series, and visually many native Romanian architectural forms can be seen as antecedents for his carved cups, columns, and tables. However, Brancusi subtly integrated the influences of many cultures and artists into his work, which makes clear attributions difficult. Despite mythologizing himself as a simple peasant-artisan, he was a highly intelligent, aesthetically sophisticated, and fully respected member of the Paris avant-garde; his many friends included Fernand Léger, Georges Braque, Man Ray, Erik Satie, Marcel Duchamp, and James Joyce.

Brancusi often worked in series. Around 1910 he started casting into bronze from his carvings, and from then he executed his series sculptures such as *Mlle. Pogany*, *Sleeping Muse*, and *Bird in Space* in either bronze or stone. Starting about 1915 Brancusi began to experiment with carved modular bases in wood and stone; these base forms shared formal importance with the supported sculpture and gave the pieces context.

He would also move sculptures onto different bases and photograph the results. Some of the base forms later developed into pieces themselves, such as the rhomboid form of the *Endless Column*.

Leveling the status between the "formal" art object and the "functional" object of the base intrigued Brancusi. He displayed handcrafted functional objects or furniture alongside his sculpture, indicating clearly that both types of object were of equal value. While he had a complete disregard for a hierarchical classification of his objects, he obsessively organized and presented his work as a kind of installation in his Paris studio. This environment has been reconstructed and preserved as an addition to the Musée National d'Art Moderne at the Centre du Beaubourg in central Paris.

Brancusi himself considered his masterwork to be the monumental pieces that he created in Tirgu Jiu, Romania, built to commemorate soldiers who died in World War I. He used the opportunity to create something even deeper: an integrated sculptural environment with perfect balance between land, art, and viewer. Completed in 1938, the works present a synthesis of three motifs: *Endless Column*, *The Gate of the Kiss*, and *Table of Silence*. This monumental environment was the only large-scale project that Brancusi ever completed; the balance of his career he spent reworking established themes. He profoundly influenced the sculpture of Amedeo Modigliani, and in the late 1920s he employed Julio Gonzáles and Isamu Noguchi as studio assistants. Brancusi became a French citizen in 1956, a year before his death at the age of 81.

ROCCO LIEUALLEN

See also **Andre, Carl; Gonzáles, Julio; Modernism; Noguchi, Isamu; Rodin, Auguste**

Biography

Born in Hobitza, Romania, either 19 or 21 February 1876. Fifth of seven children, parents rural peasants. Entered School of Arts and Crafts in Craiova, Romania, 1894, specializing in sculpture; studied sculpture under Wladimir Hegel at the Academy of Fine Arts in Bucharest, 1898–1902; arrived in Paris, mid July 1904; entered Académie des Beaux-Arts, April 1905, under instruction of Antonin Mercié; first exhibition, Salon de la Societé Nationale des Beaux-Arts, 1906; work in Salon d'Automne of 1906; noticed by Rodin, and began method of direct carving, 1907; exhibited in United States for first time, Armory Show, 1913; first major solo exhibition, Brummer Gallery, New York City, 1926; Tirgu Jiu project completed, 1938; adopted French citizenship, 1956. Died in Paris, France, 16 March 1957.

Selected Works

1907   *The Kiss*; stone; Muzeul de Arta (Museum of Art), Craiova, Romania
1907   *The Prayer*; stone; Dumbrava Cemetery, Buzau, Romania
1911   *Maiastra*; marble; Museum of Modern Art, New York City, United States
1912   *Mlle. Pogany*; marble; Philadelphia Museum of Art, Pennsylvania, United States
1916   *Princess X*; bronze; Arensberg Collection, Philadelphia Museum of Art, Pennsylvania, United States
1918   *Endless Column*; oak; private collection
1923   *Bird in Space*; white marble; private collection; another version: 1925, private collection, Eugene Meyer, Mt. Kisco, New York, United States; another version: 1926, private collection, New York City, United States
1924   *Bird in Space*; bronze; Arensberg Collection, Philadelphia Museum of Art, Pennsylvania, United States; another version: 1926, private collection, Edward Steichen, Connecticut, United States; another version: 1927, private collection, Taft B. Schreiber, Beverly Hills, California, United States; another version: 1928, Museum of Modern Art, New York City, United States; another version: 1940, Peggy Guggenheim Collection, Venice, Italy; another version: 1941, Museum of Modern Art, New York City, United States; two versions: 1941, Musée Nationale d'Art Moderne, Centre Georges Pompidou, Paris, France
1925   *Bird in Space*; yellow marble; Arensberg Collection, Philadelphia Museum of Art, Pennsylvania, United States
1925   *Bird in Space*; gray marble; Kunsthaus Museum, Zurich, Switzerland
1927   *Bird in Space*; brass; private collection, Philippe di Rothschild, Pauillac, France
1933   *Bird in Space*; black marble; private collection, Maharani Usha Devi, Indore, India
1938   *The Gate of the Kiss*; stone; Tirgu Jiu, Romania
1938   *Table of Silence*; stone; Tirgu Jiu, Romania

Further Reading

Chave, Anna C., *Constantin Brancusi: Shifting the Bases of Art*, New Haven, Connecticut: Yale University Press, 1993

Elsen, Albert Edward, *Modern European Sculpture, 1918–1945: Unknown Beings and Other Realities*, New York: Braziller, 1979

Geist, Sidney, *Brancusi: A Study of the Sculpture*, New York: Grossman, 1968; revised edition, New York: Hacker Art Books, 1983

Geist, Sidney, *Brancusi: The Sculpture and Drawings*, New York: Abrams, 1975 (a catalogue raisonné)

Giedion-Welcker, Carola, editor, *Constantin Brancusi*, New York: Braziller, 1959

Miller, Sanda, *Constantin Brancusi: A Survey of His Work*, Oxford: Clarendon Press, 1995

Spear, Athena T., *Brancusi's Birds*, New York: New York University Press, 1969

Tucker, William, *The Language of Sculpture*, London: Thames and Hudson, 1974

BIRD IN SPACE

Constantin Brancusi (1876–1957)

1928 (unique cast)

bronze

h. 1.37 m

The Museum of Modern Art, New York

Bird in Space is one of the most important and widely known pieces of Romanian sculptor Constantin Brancusi. The *Bird*s developed over 20 years, beginning in 1923, and were executed in plaster, marble, bronze, and brass. While the editions all share similar visual elements and effects, to Brancusi each one was unique; what may appear to be negligible variations of scale, material, and composition were to him major developments. The *Bird*s all share the same general form: a stylized cylindrical body that tapers to truncated points from the center outward toward the top and bottom and that terminates with a conical footing at the base.

Using Roman numerals, Brancusi listed 11 original types of the sculpture in 1936, although he made several examples of each type in different materials. Of the original surviving versions ten exist in polished bronze, four in white marble, and one each in gray, yellow, black marble, and brass. He carved the first *Bird* (1923) in white marble. The second (1923)—also the smallest at 1.16 meters—was yellow marble. He created the third (1924) in polished bronze, and he carved the largest (1931–36; 1.95 meters) out of black marble. He typically made the bases out of three stacked elements in ascending order: wood, stone, and metal.

Brancusi made the *Bird*s by either direct carving or casting into plaster or bronze from a stone or plaster original. He never considered the series truly completed and to the end of his career continued to experiment with the motif. The pieces began as his *Maiastra* series, inspired by Romanian folklore as well as Igor Stravinsky's ballet *Firebird*. The Maiastra is the Romanian version of a mythical supernatural bird, of which the phoenix is the best-known type. Brancusi simplified and reduced the *Maiastra* composition to the intermediate *Golden Bird* form, finally reducing and abstracting it further until he achieved the form of *Bird in Space*.

The *Maiastra* form combined both the phallic and ovoid imagery often used by Brancusi. The earlier pieces were frontal, more recognizable as a bird, and did not feature implied movement. With the completion of the *Golden Bird* series, Brancusi was inspired to show his bird in flight, further simplifying the form, and adjusting proportions until he reached the final composition.

Conceptually, *Bird in Space* expresses Brancusi's vision of sculpture as a way to capture a subject's essential qualities, while serving as a symbol of the ineffable elements of life in concrete form. Above all, the series is a fine example of Brancusi's overall artistic aim, to impart joy and serenity to the viewer through plastic means. With the *Bird*s Brancusi combined his universal themes of harmony and love with animal imagery, all executed in his signature style—reduced, abstracted forms with a highly polished and gleaming finish.

Visually, the *Bird*s display an elegant balance of form, composition, weight, space, and light. Structurally, their attenuated forms posed a great challenge to the sculptor, who pushed his materials—especially the marble versions—to their physical limit. Brancusi did not take advantage of the structural flexibility of bronze but used its tight grain to achieve a brilliant finish. He meticulously polished both stone and bronze works himself; the bronze pieces especially benefit from this attention since one of their primary compositional factors is the play of light on the surface, which serves to "dissolve" the matter inherent in the form. Brancusi's use of finish can also be seen as an effective incorporation of the Modernist machine ethos—a celebration of manufactured, polished, precise elements, yet, ironically, made by hand. In this fashion *Bird in Space* can be particularly understood as an atavistic totem for a new religion; although handcrafted, it still celebrates the machine age through animistic animal imagery.

The finish led to an unintended controversy in 1926, when U.S. Customs officials in New York refused to believe that a bronze *Bird in Space* being imported by Edward Steichen was a work of art. Customs officials classified the piece as a metal utensil and insisted on a payment of $210 duty. Steichen refused to pay, and the case went to litigation, becoming a cause célèbre in the United States as modern art was put on trial, with a U.S. court seemingly asked to determine once and for all what constituted art.

With the *Bird in Space* in court, the avant-garde had a rare tangible opportunity to subvert the status quo. Avant-garde artists and experts testified on Brancusi's behalf, and U.S. newspapers carefully followed the story, characterizing the dispute as a struggle between highbrow snobs on one side and the common citizen and common sense on the other—although Brancusi himself was the subject of sympathetic treatment in the press. In 1928 the court found with Brancusi that *Bird in Space* constituted a work of art, the end results being vindication of modernity and his name becoming even more well known in the United States.

Brancusi's designated heirs, Natalia Dumitresco and Alexandre Istrati, who worked for the sculptor as studio assistants toward the end of his life, have produced posthumous editions of *Bird in Space*. They won the right to reproduce the sculpture in a suit against the Museé Nationale d'Art Moderne and used a plaster original of the Steichen *Bird*. However, the question remains whether the pieces can be considered truly authentic if Brancusi, who always personally saw to the finishing and polishing process and considered it one of the most important stages of the process—in essence, the final carving—had no part in their creation. Seemingly, the art market's voracious appetite for this signature piece has outstripped any ethical concerns manifested by the aesthetic community; both public and private collections have accepted these posthumous casts as true Brancusis, which are still being produced today.

ROCCO LIEUALLEN

Further Reading

Chave, Anna C., *Constantin Brancusi: Shifting the Bases of Art*, New Haven, Connecticut: Yale University Press, 1993

Geist, Sidney, *Brancusi: A Study of the Sculpture*, New York: Grossman, 1968; 2nd edition, New York: Hacker Art Books, 1983

Geist, Sidney, "Brancusi's *Bird in Space*: A Psychological Reading," *Source* (spring 1984)

Hultén, Karl Gunnar Pontus, Natalia Dumitresco, and Alexandre Istrati, *Brancusi*, New York: Abrams, 1987

Miller, Sanda, *Constantin Brancusi: A Survey of His Work*, Oxford: Clarendon Press, and New York: Oxford University Press, 1995

Tacha, Athena, *Brancusi's Birds*, New York: New York University Press, 1969

Tucker, William, *The Language of Sculpture*, London: Thames and Hudson, 1974

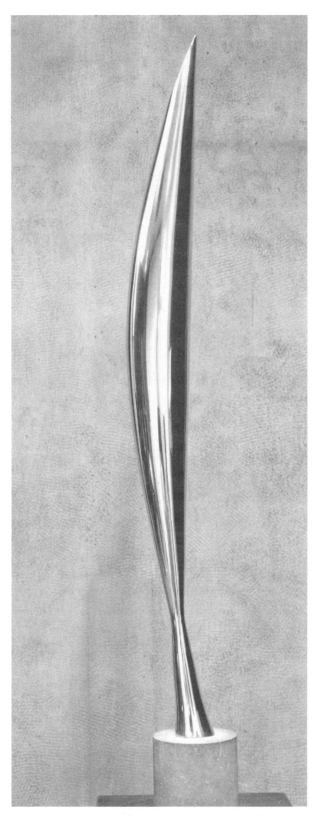

Bird in Space, 1928, bronze (unique cast), 137.2 × 21.6 × 16.5 cm Museum of Modern Art, New York, given anonymously Photograph © 2000 The Museum of Modern Art, New York

VICTOR BRECHERET 1894–1955

Brazilian

The Baroque style dominated the first three centuries of artistic production in Brazil, beginning in the 16th century and continuing until Neoclassicism became prevalent in the 19th century. Only after the abolition of slavery (1888) and the replacement of the empire with a republic in 1889 did a small but resolute Modernist movement emerge in the second decade of the 20th century. The movement was led by poets, novelists, architects, musicians, painters, and sculptors. At the forefront of the latter group of artists was Victor Brecheret.

Brecheret was born and raised in São Paulo, the capital of the state of São Paulo, Brazil. The city and state underwent extraordinary cultural and economic change during the artist's developmental years. Coffee exports, burgeoning commerce, and emerging industrialization made São Paulo the most dynamic state in the new republic. This prosperity attracted waves of immigrants, who came mostly from northern Italy and Portugal but also from Japan and the Middle East, swelling the population, as well as the cultural diversity and consciousness, of the state.

Brecheret began his artistic studies at the local school for arts and crafts. The prosperity and pride of the *paulistas*, residents of São Paulo, encouraged support of the plastic arts as the city elite attempted to give the growing metropolis a culturally refined and progressive character. Graduates of this school formed a generation of artisans who significantly, yet often anonymously, enhanced the homes and public buildings and spaces of the city.

To distinguish himself, Brecheret, who understood the advantage of studying abroad, traveled to Italy. With the Roman sculptor Arturo Dazzi, Brecheret learned anatomy and how to throw clay. The young artist even opened a small studio of his own in Rome in 1915. The following year he participated in the exhibition *Amatori e Cultori* (Amateurs and Professionals, from the arts organization in Rome, Società degli Amatori e Cultori di Belle Arti) and in the international fine arts exhibition in Rome, winning first prize for his work *Despertar* (Awakening; 1916). In 1917 Brecheret traveled to Paris for the funeral of Auguste Rodin, the sculptor who had such influence on Brecheret's generation, particularly in regard to the female form. Before returning to Brazil, Brecheret participated in 1919 in the *Mostra degli stranieri alla Casina del Pincio* (Casina del Pincio Exposition by Foreigners) in Rome.

Brecheret had learned well in Italy a style of modern sculpture that would appeal to *paulista* taste. His work's Art Deco manner was suited to public works in granite that exhibited robustness and force, as well as to small, individual works in bronze or marble that were elegant, elemental, and dynamic. Representative of this latter style is *Eva*, a representation of the creative feminine. The São Paulo city government acquired

Monument to the Pioneers (detail)
© Robert Holmes / CORBIS

the work in 1921, and it now stands in the cultural center of the city.

Brecheret also received from the government a contract to build public monument to the frontiersmen who developed São Paulo, the *Monument to the Pioneers*, his most significant work. Because he spent so much time abroad, he finished the work only shortly before his death.

From 1921 to 1936 Brecheret lived primarily in Paris, periodically returning to Brazil. Although abroad, he nevertheless participated in the groundbreaking *Week of Modern Art* in February 1922 in São Paulo by contributing a dozen sculptures, including *Idol*. For more than a decade he exhibited and won prizes in Paris at the Salon d'Automne, Salon des Artistes Français, Salon des Tuileries, and Salon des Indépendants. The French government acquired his work *Group* for the Musée du Jeu de Paume (later removed during the war) and awarded him the Legion of Honor. He further contributed to the development of Brazilian Modernism in 1932 as one of the founders of the Modern Art Society.

With his return to Brazil in 1936, Brecheret's subject matter also changed, reflecting the interest in native subjects that often defined Brazilian Modernism. Instead of statues of Diana, fauns, or ballerinas, he now produced works of Brazilian Indians, animals, folk characters, and national heroes. His work continued to acquire a character of abstraction found also in European artistic developments. In 1941 he produced a commemorative statue of the Duke of Caxias, a 19th-century Brazilian war hero. After the war, in the last decade of his life, Brecheret came to symbolize the apotheosis of modern Brazilian sculpture. At the first São Paulo arts biennial in 1951, he won the national prize in sculpture.

Two years later, his *Monument to the Pioneers* was inaugurated, 50 meters long and 12 meters high. The work portrays the major races of São Paulo and Brazil forging the Brazilian frontier in a heroic style. The work comprises some 40 figures, the largest six meters high. With his *obra prima* (principal work, or masterpiece) completed, he died in his native city on 17 December 1955.

Brecheret was not an original sculptor, but he was a skilled imitator of the dominant artists of his time, particularly Rodin, Constantin Brancusi, and Henry Moore. Such an accomplishment was significant to distinguish him as a central model for and influence on the development of modern Brazilian sculpture. More important, after returning from France and residing in Brazil for the last two decades of his life, he applied his imitative style with original and singular effect to Brazilian themes and personalities.

EDWARD A. RIEDINGER

See also **Bourdelle, Émile-Antoine; Brancusi, Constantin; Latin America; Moore, Henry; Rodin, Auguste**

Biography

Born in São Paulo, Brazil, 22 February 1894. Student in local school for arts and crafts, 1912–13; went to Rome and studied under Arturo Dazzi, influenced by Ivan Meštrovic and especially Émile-Antoine Bourdelle, 1913–16; won first prize for *Despertar* at the international fine arts exposition of Rome, 1916; returned to Brazil, 1919, and in 1920 won competition to produce *Monument to the Pioneers*; returned to Paris following year with a scholarship, yet contributed to *Week of Modern Art* in São Paulo, 1921; won prize for sculpture at Autumn Salon, 1921; met Constantin Brancusi, 1923; resided in Paris until 1936 but regularly returned to Brazil for individual expositions and to found the Modern Art Society, 1932; awarded membership in Legion of Honor, 1934; returned to São Paulo, 1936;

participated in all three avant-garde artists' May salons, São Paulo, 1937–39; won competition to build monument to the Duke of Caxias, 1941; participated in 25th Venice Biennale, 1950, and First and Third Biennale of São Paulo, 1951 and 1955; received national prize for sculpture at First Biennal of São Paulo, 1951. Died in São Paulo, Brazil, 17 December 1955.

Selected Works

ca. 1919 *Idol*; bronze; collection of Matheus Aprile, São Paulo, Brazil
1921 *Eva*; marble; Cultural Center, São Paulo, Brazil
1923 *The Entombment*; granite; Consolação Cemetery, São Paulo, Brazil
1924 *The Perfume Bearer*; gold, plaster; Pinacoteca do Estado de São Paulo, Brazil
1934 *Group*; granite; public square, La-Roche-sur-Yon, France
1941 Monument to the Duke of Caxias; granite; Princesa Isabel Square, São Paulo, Brazil
1953 *Monument to the Pioneers*; granite; Ibirapuera Park, São Paulo, Brazil

Further Reading

Bardi, Pietro Maria, editor, *Um século de escultura no Brasil; One Century of Sculpture in Brazil* (bilingual Portuguese-English edition), São Paulo: Museu de Arte de São Paulo Assis Chateaubriand, 1982

Batista, Marta Rossetti, *Bandeiras de Brecheret: História de um monumento (1920–1953)*, São Paulo: Departamento do Patrimônio Histórico, 1985

Brazilian Sculpture from 1920 to 1990, Washington, D.C.: Cultural Center, Inter-American Development Bank, 1997

Brecheret: 100 anos (bilingual Portuguese-English edition), Rio de Janeiro: Centro Cultural Banco do Brasil, 1994

Fabris, Annateresa, "O múltiplo de Brecheret," *Panorama* 4 (1995)

Klintowitz, Jacob, editor, *Victor Brecheret (São Paulo, 1884–1955)*, São Paulo: Museu Lasar Segal, 1976

WILLEM VAN DEN BROECKE (PALUDANUS) 1530–1579 *Netherlandish*

Willem van den Broecke is still one of the less well known sculptors of 16th-century Antwerp, his work having been rediscovered only in the early 20th century. Although he had been praised during his lifetime as *princeps . . . inter statuarios* (first among sculptors) for a long time, his name could not be linked with important commissions for church furniture or architecture as could those of Cornelis II Floris and Jacques Du Broeucq. Apparently van den Broecke specialized in smaller cabinet sculpture and bronze medals. Nevertheless, some more important epitaphs, a fragment of a mantelpiece, and part of the sculptural decoration made for the facade of the house of fellow artist Cornelis van Dalem I (or Cornelis I van Dalem) are known. These works show van den Broecke as probably the more intellectual among Antwerp Renaissance sculptors. This was confirmed by Ludovico Guicciardini, who described him as "studioso e diligente," and there are speculations about his membership in the House of Love, a group of humanists and philosophers in the circle of the Plantin Press.

Born in Mechelen, van den Broecke became a member of the Guild of St. Luke in Antwerp in 1557. Before this, he probably made the voyage to Italy, as is suggested by his knowledge of the Italian language.

JAN VAN DAMME

See also **Du Broeucq, Jacques**

Biography

Born in Mechelen, now in Belgium, 1530. Became a member of the Guild of St. Luke, Antwerp, 1557; may have traveled to Italy; specialized in cabinet sculpture and bronze medals; produced sculptures for Antwerp Cathedral, 1560s. Died in Antwerp, now in Belgium, 11 March 1579.

Selected Works

1559   *Venus and Cupid*; marble; Hamal manor
        house, Tongeren, Belgium
1560   *Crucifixion*; alabaster; Maximilianmuseum,
        Augsburg, Germany

Further Reading

Gurock, Elisabeth, "Broeck, van den: Willem (Guillaume) van den Broeck," in *The Dictionary of Art*, edited by Jane Turner, New York: Grove, and London: Macmillan, 1996

Van Damme, J., "Portretbuste van Albrecht Dürer," in *Antwerpen, verhaal van een metropool, 16de–17de eeuw* (exhib. cat.), Ghent, Belgium: Snoeck-Ducaju, 1993

BROEUCQ

See **Du Broeucq, Jacques**

FERDINAND MAXIMILIAN BROKOF
1688–1731 *Bohemian*

The Brokof (Brokoff) family from Central Europe included many gifted sculptors. Johann (Jan) Brokof (1652–1718) was born in Upper Hungary in Szepesszombat (German St. Georgenberg, now Spišská Sobota, Slovakia) and later moved to Prague. He created

his best-known work, the model for the bronze statue of *St. John of Nepomuk*, on the *bozzetto* (a small-scale preparatory study or model) by Matthias Rauchmiller. The life-size bronze statue was erected in 1683 on Charles Bridge in Prague and in turn became a model for numerous other statues with similar themes in central Europe.

Johann's son Ferdinand Maximilian Brokof was a leading figure in Bohemian Baroque sculpture. He was born in Červený Hrádek, Bohemia (German Rothenhaus, now Czech Republic). After finishing his studies in his father's workshop, he studied in Vienna before 1708, possibly at the Fine Arts Academy of Peter and Paul Strudel. He was influenced by such Viennese artists as the Strudel brothers, Giovanni Giuliani, and Johann Bernhard Fischer von Erlach, with whom he later worked. After returning to Prague, he was influenced by the realistic sculpture of Jan Jiří Bendl and the paintings of Karel Škréta. He created his earliest works, those created before 1710, together with his sculptor brother Michael Johann Joseph (Mihal Jan Josef) Brokof (1686–1721) and his father, working on the Charles Bridge in Prague.

Some of the most significant Bohemian Baroque outdoor sculptures still in existence are the signed Bohemian sandstone series of statues Brokof himself carved for the Charles Bridge between 1710 and 1714. Among these is the *St. Francis Borgia between Two Angels* group in 1710. As a commission from the Jesuits in Prague, he created *St. Ignatius of Loyola* and its pendant, the *St. Francis Xavier* group in 1711. The figure of *St. Francis Xavier* is held on the shoulders of men who represent the continents; in front of the saint, the Oriental king kneels. Brokof's self-portrait is represented in one of the servants. The polychromed, wooden *St. Ignatius of Loyola* is thought to have been the model for the group of stone statues. Here, the saint stands on a globe held by female personifications of the continents. Brokof created the *St. Vincent Ferrer and St. Procopius* group for the bridge in 1712, followed by a statue of *St. Vitus* in 1713–14. He carved one of his most important works, the *St. John of Matha, St. Felix of Valois, and St. Ivan* group, in 1714. The narrative composition of this group represents the praying St. Ivan and the Trinitarian saints who brought freedom to the Christians suffering in Turkish captivity. Brokof made use of drawings by Johann Georg Heintsch for the statues of the Charles Bridge.

After finishing the bridge, Brokof received a series of commissions in Prague. He carved the signed sculptural decorations of the Morzin Palace in Prague in 1714 from sandstone, among them the *Moors* and the allegorical figures of the *Continents*, the *Day*, and the *Night*. During the same period, he carved the signed sandstone statue of the *Maltese Knightly Order, the St.*

John the Baptist with Angels group of statues. Between 1714 and 1716, he created the sandstone tomb of Count Wratislav Mitrovic in St. James's Church in Prague, from the design of Fischer von Erlach. The figure of *Glory* holds the count's reclining figure while *Fame* engraves the count's achievements on the obelisk behind them. *Chronos* appears on the right and the allegorical figure of *Contemplation* on the left. This tomb is one of Brokof's major signed works. He designed the sculptural decoration for the Morzin Palace in Kounice (Kaunitz) between 1718 and 1719; his signed sandstone statues *Moors* from this palace are among his most popular works. His major wooden works include *Calvary* and the *Stations of Cross*, made for the St. Castulus's Church in Prague in 1716, and the wooden statues *Calvary* and *Evangelists* created for the chapel of St. Gall's Church in Prague, which were influenced in part by Bendl, in 1719–20.

After his huge success, Brokof received commissions from Breslau in Silesia (now Wrocław, Poland). About 1720–22 he made sculptural decorations for the Chapel of Electors in the Cathedral of Breslau, which was designed by Fischer von Erlach. The huge marble statues for the marble and stucco altar, standing figures of *Moses* and *Aaron*, are among Brokof's major works and show the influence of Nicolas Cordier and Michelangelo. Using marble and stucco, Brokof also created the funerary monument to Johann Georg Wolf in the St. Elisabeth's Church in Breslau. Fischer von Erlach designed the architectural portions. Similar to the tomb of Count Wratislav Mitrovic in Prague, the realistic portrait of Wolf is in front of the obelisk and surrounded by mourning angels.

After his brother's death, Brokof led the family's workshop with his mother from 1721. Especially after the 1720s, his workshop played an important role in the execution of his wooden and stone statues. During this time, he carved a number of statues of St. John Nepomuk on the basis of his father's models. Among the best of these is his sandstone *St. John Nepomuk Giving Alms*, which is found next to the Church of the Holy Ghost in Prague. With his workshop, Brokof created in 1724–26 the *Lady Column* for the Old Town Square in Prague. After this, he worked in Vienna, where he created the marble and stucco funerary monument of Johann Leopold Trautson in the Church of St. Michael. In recognition of his talents, he received the commission to create the high altar of the Church of St. Charles, the models of which were designed in 1728.

Among Brokof's monumental late works are the sandstone statues *Moses* and *St. Gregory* (1729–30) for the facade of the monastery church in Grüssau, Silesia (now Krzeszów, Poland). The weakening of his creative powers can be seen in the wooden statues

St. Francis Xavier
The Conway Library, Courtauld Institute of Art

made about 1730 for the high altar of St. Thomas's Church in Prague. He died from tuberculosis, which was becoming a frequent illness of stone sculptors, at the age of 43, leaving behind a tremendous oeuvre. The influence of his powerful works and his realistic Baroque style for Bohemian sculpture could still be seen in the works of Josef Václav Myslbeck.

KATALIN HÁMORI

See also **Central Europe**

Biography

Born in Červený Hrádek, Bohemia (German Rotenhaus, now Czech Republic), 12 September 1688. Son of Johann (Jan) Brokof, a sculptor. Studied in his father's workshop; studied possibly at Peter and Paul Strudel's Academy of Fine Arts, Vienna, before 1708; earliest works completed with father and elder brother,

Michael Johann Joseph (Mihal Jan Josef) Brokof for Charles Bridge, Prague, before 1710; completed series of sandstone sculptures for Charles Bridge, 1710–14; carried out commissions for monumental works in Prague, 1710–20 and 1730, in Silesia (now Poland), *ca.* 1720–23 and 1729–30, and in Vienna, before 1728; directed the family workshop with his mother, from 1721. Died in Prague, 8 March 1731.

Selected Works

1710   *St. Francis Borgia between Two Angels*; sandstone; Charles Bridge, Prague, Czech Republic

1711   *St. Ignatius of Loyola*; wood; National Gallery, Prague, Czech Republic; sandstone: Lapidarium National Museum, Prague, Czech Republic

1711   *St. Francis Xavier*; sandstone; Lapidarium National Museum, Prague, Czech Republic; sandstone copy: Charles Bridge, Prague, Czech Republic

1712   *St. Vincent Ferrer and St. Procopius*; sandstone; Charles Bridge, Prague, Czech Republic

1713–14 *St. Vitus*; sandstone; Charles Bridge, Prague, Czech Republic

1714   *St. John of Matha, St. Felix of Valois, and St. Ivan*; sandstone; Charles Bridge, Prague, Czech Republic

1714–16 Tomb of Count Wratislav Mitrovic; sandstone; St. James's Church, Prague, Czech Republic

1718–19 *Moors*, from Kounice (Kannitz), sandstone; National Gallery, Prague, Czech Republic

ca.   Statues of *Moses* and *Aaron*, for the altar;
1720–22 marble, stucco; Chapel of Electors, Cathedral of Breslau, Silesia, now Wrocław, Poland

1721–23 Funerary monument to Johann Georg Wolf; marble, stucco; St. Elisabeth Church, Breslau, Silesia, now Wrocław, Poland

ca. 1725 *St. John Nepomuk Giving Alms*; sandstone; Church of the Holy Ghost, Prague, Czech Republic

before   Funerary monument to Johann Leopold
1727   Trautson; marble, stucco; Church of St. Michael, Vienna, Austria

Further Reading

Alsterová, Alena, "Ferdinand Maximilian Brokof," in *Allgemeines Künstlerlexikon: Die bildenden Künstler aller Zeiten und Völker*, vol. 14, Munich: Saur, 1996

Blažíček, Oldrich J., *Ferdinand Brokof*, Prague: Odeon, 1976
Kořán, Ivo, "Ferdinand Maximilián Brokof," in *The Dictionary of Art*, edited by Jane Turner, New York: Grove, and London: Macmillan, 1996
Neumann, Jaromír, *Český barok*, Prague: Odeon, 1969
Swoboda, Karl Maria, editor, *Barock in Böhmen*, Munich: Prestel, 1964

BRONZE AND OTHER COPPER ALLOYS

The first age of metals is called the Chalcolithic, the Copper-Stone Age. It is the transition from Neolithic times to modern times and marks the beginning of modern technology. Copper, gold, and silver were the first metals to be discovered and used in their pure forms; all previous use of metals had been in ground pigment form, such as iron oxide for red ocher.

The most common copper ore is malachite, easily recognized by its blue-green color. Copper ores are abundant in all parts of the world, with some metal and ore deposits spanning thousands of cubic acres. Copper ore is also often found on surface outcroppings, making the detection of veins easy. Early users of copper ore would have found traces of pure unoxidized metal mixed in and perhaps experimented with it, finding it easily hammered and shaped.

The first copper technology developed in Anatolia (present-day Turkey) during the 5th millennium BCE. A few copper objects have been discovered from an earlier date, but scholars have not found a sustained technology to accompany them. Obtaining copper from ore required the development of smelting, in which copper is reduced from its oxidized state into its pure form. Smelting requires temperatures of at least 1,084 degrees Celsius, the melting point of copper, and a "reduced" atmosphere in which the furnace is starved of oxygen while remaining high in atmospheric carbon. When the furnace is starved of free oxygen, the heated atmosphere draws oxygen from all available sources, including the metal ore. With enough time and heat, pure copper is reduced or separated from the ore, which becomes a lighter mixture of elements called slag. Forced draft will increase the temperature of the furnace, and many of the most ancient smelting sites were located on hillsides and at the tops of cliffs in order to take advantage of natural wind flow. Bellows were also likely to have been invented concurrent with the smelting process.

Pottery makers already had much of the needed knowledge to develop smelting technology because they used metal oxides in glazes to color the clays and used reduction atmospheres during firing. However, because the temperatures they could reach for pottery were far lower than that required for reducing copper, the process gave only minor clues toward the smelting of metals. Possibly, some small pebbles, or "prills," of copper were reduced from the pottery kilns, leading to the search for higher heats to make more of the precious metal.

Smelted copper technology seems to have spread from Anatolia through the Sinai Peninsula into Egypt and the Mediterranean, and possibly from there into Europe, reaching Italy by 3000 BCE and England by 2000 BCE. Evidence suggests that smelting began independently in Yugoslavia at Rudna Glava during the 5th millennium BCE, which may have begun the path of information dispersion through Europe. Smelted copper also appeared in Central America, although not until 500–800 CE. The Copper Culture of the Great Lakes in North America began about 3200 BCE but was due to a large amount of native pure copper; smelting technology never developed in this region.

Copper is an attractive metal and was valuable to early people, but it is soft. Craftsmen experimented with adding various elements to molten copper to make it stronger and more functional. The first common additions were arsenic and antimony, which noticeably affect the melting point and viscosity of the molten metal and when cooled and tempered or work-hardened increase its strength. Tin, at a proportion of 10 percent, was found to be the best partner for copper. Melting tin with copper lowers the melting point to 950 degrees Celsius and improves its viscosity while highly increasing the metal's strength even without tempering. Its low melting point meant using less fuel, and its improved viscosity meant the ability to cast intricate objects that were not possible with arsenical copper. Its remarkable strength lent itself to architectural details and to weaponry, and it corroded more slowly than previous alloys. This was the first true bronze, developed during the 4th millennium BCE in Mesopotamia and Anatolia.

Tin is not a common metal. It is rarely found near copper ore, and even today its price can be eight to ten times that of copper. Trade routes that spanned from India to Egypt and southern Europe allowed for the wide distribution of tin and the development of the Bronze Age. Tin oxide or cassiterite can be panned like gold from alluvial streams and rivers, where it resembles heavy black gravel, and it is also found in veins in granite and other hard rock. Cleaned and purified, both tin and its oxide are white. Tin bronze quickly replaced arsenical copper for the manufacturing of various items, including works of art.

Casting methods for bronze became highly developed during the next millennium, especially *ciré perdue*, or lost-wax casting, the oldest known casting method, which dates from the 4th millennium BCE and is still practiced today in some parts of the world as it was in the past. The Tokyo University for the Arts,

for example, still teaches ancient methods of lost-wax casting, although most modern art schools teach advanced methods of bronze casting.

Technology in China evolved independently from the Bronze Age of the Near East. By the 4th millennium BCE the Chinese already had an extensive knowledge of high-temperature firing techniques and craftsmanship in porcelain. In China, copper smelting developed alongside the ceramics technology, and the Bronze Age of China became even more advanced than that of the West. The Shang dynasty (1600–1122 BCE) in particular was extraordinary in its technological and artistic accomplishments. Located in the Henan province in central China, it was a remarkably stable social hierarchy. The artistic developments of its bronze works are directly linked to the aesthetics of its porcelain vessels, and all designs are distinctly Chinese in origin.

The first Chinese Bronze Age metallurgists worked not with lost-wax methods but with clay. They would make a pattern of clay and fire it, then take an impression of the pattern in clay and fire that, then pour molten bronze into the fired impression. They also developed a kind of "permanent mold," a pattern formed of stone, often of small ritual objects or figurines that may have been used in household shrines. Artists cast from the molds until the patterns lost too much detail, after which they were thrown away. Hundreds of identical casting could be made using this method, and a rich archaeological record has been left behind. Shang dynasty foundries were essentially factories and had the capacity to pour huge amounts of metal at a single time. The Shang created the largest single-pour casting in the world from this period, a ritual cauldron called a *ting* that weighs 875 kilograms. They were prolific in their manufacture of utensils, from delicate cups to farm tools.

Though iron and steel have replaced copper as the basic metals for our technology, copper alloys have retained their value for specific applications. Alloys of copper that are widely used today include bronzes, brasses, and yellow, red, and white metals. Brass or "yellow metal" at its most basic is an alloy of copper and zinc, with the zinc at no more than 40 percent. Alloys developed for specialized applications may contain small percentages of antimony, arsenic, aluminum, manganese, cobalt, chromium, silicon, and other elements in a copper base. "Yellow metal" usually refers to brass with a zinc content of 35 to 40 percent zinc, and various trace metals are added for specific applications. Red brass is a widely used alloy containing 85 percent copper and 5 percent each of tin, lead, and zinc. White metals, or "nickel-silvers," are alloys of copper, zinc, nickel, and silver. Bronwite is a patented alloy of 59 percent copper, 20 percent zinc, 20 percent manganese, and 1 percent aluminum. Bronwite is the industry replacement of nickel-silver. Copper is also used in imitation gold leaf and in silver plate.

The type of bronze most commonly found in art foundries today is silicon bronze, or herculoy, which is composed of approximately 91 percent copper, 4 percent zinc, and 5 percent silicon, with some possible trace elements. Silicon bronze is fairly expensive, hard, and quite difficult to work, often needing large amounts of chasing, or finishing work. Silicon bronze cannot be mixed with any other kind of bronze because the resulting metal is stringy and will not flow when poured. However, silicon bronze by itself flows better than any other form of bronze, allowing the casting of patterns that could not otherwise be made. Silicon bronze has excellent corrosion resistance, and it can be remelted repeatedly without changing composition.

Bronze is so valuable to artists in part because of its ability to take a patina, color developed through the application of acids or metal salts to the surface of the metal. Copper can form a wide variety of colors, from dull reds, rich browns, and vivid greens to electric blue, pastel pink, black or white, orange, and yellow. The amount of copper in the bronze allows a patina to take hold. Green-blue patinas develop naturally on a bronze that is exposed to weather or buried in acidic soil, as the copper on the surface is oxidized into its ore, malachite. Many applied patinas are unstable and will break down over time, but several are permanent: they will not wear off with typical weathering or will only occur because of specific weathering. Some patinas actually protect the bronze from severe corrosion because salts and oxygen cannot easily penetrate the oxidized surface layers. Some bronzes are famous for their patinas; the patina of the Shang dynasty bronzes, for instance, cannot be reproduced.

AMBER GENEVA ERKILETIAN

Further Reading

Cunliffe, Barry W., editor, *The Oxford Illustrated Prehistory of Europe*, Oxford and New York: Oxford University Press, 1994; as *Prehistoric Europe: An Illustrated History*, 1998

Mills, John W., *The Encyclopedia of Sculpture Techniques*, New York: Watson-Guptill, 1989; London: Batsford, 1990

Raymond, Robert, *Out of the Fiery Furnace: The Impact of Metals on the History of Mankind*, South Melbourne, Victoria: Macmillan Australia, 1984; University Park: Pennsylvania State University Press, 1986

Yang, Xiaoneng, editor, *The Golden Age of Chinese Archaeology: Celebrated Discoveries from the People's Republic of China*, New Haven, Connecticut: Yale University Press, 1999

HANS BRÜGGEMANN ca. 1480–after 1523 *German*

An important transitional figure between Late Gothic and Renaissance sculptural styles and a key example

of print reception by a sculptor, Hans Brüggemann was likely working in the service of the Duke of Schleswig-Holstein (North Germany), who from 1523 was King Frederick I of Denmark, when he created his magnum opus, the *Bordesholm Altar*. The high artistic quality of this nonpolychrome double-winged retable carved in oak places it among the most significant shrines surviving from the Late Middle Ages. Brüggemann made this altarpiece for a cloister of Augustinian canons in the town of Bordesholm. The inscription at the base, "Opus hoc insigne completum est anno incarnationis dominice 1521 ad Dei honorem," gives its date of completion. A Latin chronicle written by the German humanist Heinrich Rantzau in 1597 is the first document to name Hans Brüggemann as the artist.

The *Bordesholm Altar* served as the high altar of the monastery church, which was also the location of the ducal tomb. Frederick's wife, Anna von Brandenburg, was buried there in 1514. Since the Duke also commissioned the choir stalls in 1509, Frederick was likely the patron of the *Bordesholm Altar* as well. Together with the tomb, it formed a competing project to the Danish royal grave monument in Odense (Denmark), for which Queen Christine ordered a retable from the royal artist Claus Berg after King Hans's death in 1513.

In 1666 the *Bordesholm Altar* was transferred to Schleswig Cathedral. The retable depicts the Passion of Christ and also includes all of salvation history from the Fall to the Last Judgment in the crest. The predella (a painted panel, usually small, belonging to a series of panels at the bottom of an altarpiece) consists of four scenes referring to the Eucharist, which was originally displayed in the middle niche. An iconographical peculiarity is the Supper of the Early Christian Community. Some critics have claimed to recognize Duke Frederick's portrait in this scene.

With its sequence of 20 small compartments, the retable basically follows the structure of southern Netherlandish altarpieces. Although no written sources have been preserved, Brüggemann must have had a wide knowledge of the works from this area (he probably held an apprenticeship close to the workshop of Jan Borman), and he must have also been familiar with the work of Lower Rhinish artists, such as Ludwig Jupan, Arnt van Zwolle, and Henrick Douwerman. Some of his scenes and figures reflect works manufactured in Bremen or nearby in North Germany.

The example set by Albrecht Dürer's series the *Small Woodcut Passion*, which was published as a book in 1511, inspired Brüggemann's pictorial conception. However, Brüggemann did not simply follow Dürer's model but rather entered into a dialogue with the graphic arts and succeeded in creating a Passion cycle in the three-dimensional medium of sculpture that equaled those of Dürer and Dürer's predecessor, Martin Schongauer. Although Dürer's *Small Woodcut Passion* was the main resource, Brüggemann also used figures from Dürer's *Large Woodcut Passion*, as well as prints and engravings from other artists, such as Martin Schongauer, Hans Schäufelein, the Monogrammist W, and—never mentioned before—Lucas van Leyden. The artist also followed the invention of early Netherlandish paintings, such as Jan van Eyck's *Ghent Altarpiece* and Rogier van der Weyden's work.

Brüggemann's adaptations of these sources to the sculptural form, as well as his deep engagement with the most current achievements of the graphic arts—which reached the pinnacle of the visual arts at that time—enabled him to bring the art of woodcarving to a new height. Taking prints and engravings as a starting point, the artist created images that were in effect new formulations of the primary religious themes of Dürer's time.

Little is known about Brüggemann's life. The only surviving contemporary written source is a contract from 1523, which mentions the artist's origin. According to this source, Hans Brüggemann was born in Walsrode, a town in Lower Saxony that was the seat of a cloister of Benedictine nuns. The document indicates that the cloister ordered an altarpiece (lost since the 17th century) depicting the *Assumption of the Virgin Mary*. The recently discovered figure of the *Apostle St. James the Greater* was originally part of a lost altarpiece that depicted either the death or the assumption of the Virgin. This figure may have belonged to the lost *Walsrode Altar*.

Brüggemann's works also include images of the most popular saints, *St. George* and *St. Christopher*, and a figure of the Virgin Mary. The sculpture of the *Virgin and Child*, depicted as the woman of the Apocalypse, was originally incorporated in a lost sacrament house that was created for the Church of St. Mary in Husum and completed in 1520. A preserved inventory from 1763–64 mentions Hans Brüggemann as the creator of this work, which also included an *Angel Playing the Lute*. At a height of 20.2 meters, the work competed with such prominent South German examples as Adam Kraft's sacrament house in Nuremberg, and the suspended *Virgin and Child* competed with Benedikt Dreyer's earlier vision of the Virgin and Child as the woman of the Apocalypse from the lost choir screen of the Church of St. Mary in Lübeck. The inventory also mentions a sculpture of *St. George Defeating the Dragon*, now in the National Museum in Copenhagen, which followed the example set by Bernt Notke's group in Stockholm.

Husum, the original location of the latter works, was a major center for trade with the Netherlands. It was the transfer point for Baltic shipping, and one of the seats of the Dukes of Schleswig-Holstein. Since the preserved inventory calls Hans Brüggemann a resident of the city, it is most likely that the artist's workshop was located there. The chronicle from 1597 tells us that Hans Brüggemann was buried in Husum but does not give the year of his death.

Consisting of more than 400 figures, the *Bordesholm Altar* is the artist's only completely preserved ensemble. Otherwise only single works survive or, in the case of the lost tabernacle, only a figural fragment that originally belonged to a larger complex. Brüggemann's complete preserved oeuvre is thought to have been created within only one decade and is so homogeneous in style that it is difficult to discern any development within it. That no early work of the artist is known and that only two of his works—the tabernacle and the *Bordesholm Altar*—are precisely dated make determining the artist's stylistic development even more difficult. In his few works Brüggemann shows himself to be a mature virtuoso woodcarver. Although other outstanding artists, such as Tilman Riemenschneider, Hans Leinberger, and Master H.W., also used prints in their work, Brüggemann is the one sculptor who advanced furthest into the new world of Dürer's representational thought.

CHRISTINE KITZLINGER

***See also* Germany: Gothic–Renaissance; Kraft, Adam; Leinberger, Hans; Notke, Bernt; Riemenschneider, Tilman**

Biography

Born in Walsrode, Lower Saxony (Germany), *ca.* 1480. No early work is known; complete preserved oeuvre thought to have been created *ca.* 1511–23; sculptures show a wide knowledge of South Netherlandish, Lower Rhenish, and North German works; inspired by prints of Albrecht Dürer. Died in Husum, Schleswig-Holstein (Germany), after 1523.

Selected Works

year unknown	*St. Christopher*; oak; Schleswig Cathedral, Germany
1520	Tabernacle (dismantled): *Virgin and Child*; oak; royal property, Copenhagen, Denmark; *Angel Playing the Lute*; oak; Skulpturensammlung und Museum für Byzantinische Kunst, Staatliche Museen zu Berlin, Germany
1521	*Bordesholm Altar*; oak; Schleswig Cathedral, Germany
1523	*Walsrode Altar*, for the Benedictine Cloister, Walsrode, Germany (lost)

year *Apostle St. James the Greater*, part of lost
unknown retable; oak; private collection, Zurich,
        Switzerland
year *St. George*, oak; National Museum,
unknown Copenhagen, Denmark
year *Goschhof Altar*, depicting the Holy
unknown Family; oak; Schleswig-Holsteinisches
        Landesmuseum, Schleswig, Germany
        (workshop?)

Further Reading

Albrecht, Uwe, et al., editors, *Der Bordesholmer Altar des Hans Brüggemann: Werk und Wirkung*, Berlin: Reimer, 1996

Appuhn, Horst, "Der Bordersholmer Altar: Studien zum Werk Meister Hans Brüggemanns," Ph.D. diss., Christian-Albrechts-Universität, Kiel, 1952

Appuhn, Horst, *Hans Brüggemann aus Walsrode*, Walsrode, Germany: Gundlach, 1966

Appuhn, Horst, *Der Bordesholmer Altar und die anderen Werke von Hans Brüggemann*, Königstein im Taunus, Germany: Langewiesche, 1987

Buczynski, Bodo, "Der lautenspielende Engel vom ehemaligen Sakramentshaus in Husum von Hans Brüggemann," in *Flügelaltäre des Späten Mittelalters*, edited by Hartmut Krohm and Eike Oellermann, Berlin: Reimer, 1992

Ellger, Dietrich, et al., *Die Kunstdenkmäler der Stadt Schleswig II: Der Dom und der ehemalige Dombezirk*, Munich and Berlin: Deutscher Kunstverlag, 1966 (with bibliography)

Fuglsang, Fritz, *Der Bordesholmer Altar des Hans Brüggemann*, Schleswig, Germany: Bernaerts, 1959

Kähler, Ingeborg, *Der Bordesholmer Altar—Zeichen in einer Krise*, Neumünster, Germany: Wachholtz, 1981

Kitzlinger, Christine, "Eine unbekannte Apostelfigur von Hans Brüggemann," *Zeitschrift des Deutschen Vereins für Kunstwissenschaft Berlin* 54 (2000)

Osten, Gert von der, "Über Brüggemanns St. Jürgengruppe aus Husum in Kopenhagen," *Wallraf-Richartz-Jahrbuch* 37 (1975)

BUON FAMILY *Italian*

Giovanni Buon *ca. 1360–1442*

Bartolomeo Buon *ca. 1400/05–1464/67*

There are only a few documents pertaining to the life and work of sculptor and stonemason Giovanni Buon, son of Ser Bertuccio Buon. The first time he is documented with certainty is as a witness in a testament on 20 June 1382. Further documents give information on stone deliveries and payments (1385–88, 1423) but do not name any works.

The activities of his son Bartolomeo, on the contrary, are much easier to follow. Bartolomeo probably received his training in his father's workshop. The two worked together until Giovanni's death. In the following years, Bartolomeo was to become the most significant sculptor-architect in Venice before the emergence of architect Mauro Codussi and sculptor Antonio Rizzo.

In a contract between Giovanni and Marin Contarini for the Ca' d'Oro in Venice, Bartolomeo's name is listed for the first time on 18 January 1422 for nonspecified work. Through 1431, he and his father produced architectural sculpture and windows for the Ca' d'Oro, the most magnificent palatial structure of its time. Bartolomeo himself created the figures of *Spes* (Hope), *Fides* (Faith), and *Caritas* (Charity)—which, at times, are strongly reminiscent of the work of Lorenzo Ghiberti but also reveal the influence of the master of the Mascoli altar in San Marco—on the fountain in the courtyard of the Ca' d'Oro. Probably by Bartolomeo as well, and from the same time period, is the fountain formerly situated in the Corte Bressana of SS. Giovanni e Paolo.

Architectural work stood in the foreground of the Buons' careers between 1431 (Ca' d'Oro) and 1438 (commission for the Porta della Carta of the Doge's Palace), as is evident at the Palazzo Bernardo, on houses near Ca' Foscari, and at the Corte Nuova. The extent of the work done on the Scuola Grande di S. Marco (1437) is a matter of contention. From its portal, which was destroyed in 1485, only the figure of *Caritas* reused by Mauro Codussi still exists.

In terms of sculpture, both the *Annunciation* (or *Maria Annunziata*), which still bears echoes of the aforementioned Mascoli altar in the figure of St. Peter, and the group of sculptures featuring the *Judgment of Solomon* from the northwest corner of the Doge's Palace were probably created during this period. The portal of Santa Maria Gloriosa dei Frari (1430–35) is stylistically similar, and thus could likewise have been produced by Bartolomeo. All of the works show a true affinity with contemporary Florentine sculpture, particularly with the works of Nanni di Banco, to whom some attribute the above-mentioned Solomon group. Its iconography of justice, at any rate, is closely connected with the theme of the adjacent entrance to the Doge's Palace, the Porta della Carta, the construction of which was entrusted to Bartolomeo shortly thereafter. The signature on the stipe of the portal, "Opus Bartolomei," in a modern Renaissance capital, refers proudly to his authorship. Although the four *Virtues* in the niches of the flanking pinnacles and the bust of St. Mark are probably the work of other members of the workshop, only the crowning *Justice*, as well as the group of figures featuring the Doge Francesco Foscari in front of the lion of St. Mark, are works by Bartolomeo himself. Of these, only the impressive head of the doge, influenced perhaps by the portraits of Gentile Bellini, escaped the vandalism of the revolution in 1797, whereas the rest of the group were later reproduced. Giovanni died in 1442 at more than 80 years of age while work was still being done on the Porta.

Afterward, Bartolomeo was the sole director of the workshop, which had primarily been occupied in the 1440s with work for the Church of S. Maria della Carità. Here he assumed the position of a manager who designed the works, but he delegated the actual production to others both in and outside of his workshop. The tracery windows (now destroyed), which formed a central element of the Porta della Carta as they had done on the Ca' d'Oro, were already added to the churches of S. Gregorio and S. Zaccaria by 1450. Of the portal (for which Bartolomeo was paid during 1442–44 and 1449), only the tympanum relief in the sacristy of the Church of S. Maria della Salute, featuring the crowning of Mary flanked by two angels playing musical instruments, has remained. This was probably the work of the entire workshop. Its design is based largely on the images of the painter Antonio Vivarini, who also created the main altar of the Church of S. Maria della Carità. An *Annunciation* in the Victoria and Albert Museum could be attributed to the same sculptor, whose style is comparable to that of Agostino di Duccio. Bartolomeo probably also passed the commission for the Madonna statue for the Loggia Comunale in Udine on to another sculptor, although sources often give him credit for it. Unfortunately, no trace can be found of the tomb of Bartolomeo Morosini, which had been under construction since 1444 and was not completed until 1468 after Bartolomeo's death. It would have been an important piece for assessing Bartolomeo as a sculptor.

Both the dating and attribution of the lunette on the portal of the Scuola Grande di S. Marco, which depicted the members of the confraternity kneeling on either side of the enthroned saint, pose difficulties. Particularly striking is its strongly individualized physiognomy, which does not, however, extend to the portrait of the Doge Foscari on the Porta della Carta. That the lunette is not one of Bartolomeo's early works is indicated by the door measurements given in the first contract with Giovanni in 1437. In 1443, the confraternity decided to finish the work started six years earlier. Whether or not this included the lunette cannot be proved because the building burned down in 1485. Although Wolters sees the author as an anonymous sculptor (see Wolters, 1976), Schulz sees the work of a young Bartolomeo from the 1430s in the lunette (see Schulz, 1978).

The lunette featuring the *Madonna della Misericordia* (Madonna of Mercy) was probably begun at the end of the 1440s. In 1451 the statue was completed and placed above the portal of the Scuola Vecchia della Misericordia. Bartolomeo is documented once again in 1453 when he, in collaboration with others, prepared a report on Donatello's equestrian monument to Gattamelata in Padua.

The end of the 1450s was characterized by intense activity. In 1457, Bartolomeo began working on the Palazzo Corner on the Grand Canal (later the Palazzo Sforza), for which he probably provided the designs as well. The project, which was abandoned in 1461, and from which only meager remains have been recovered, distinguishes Bartolomeo as one of the founders of the Renaissance in Venice. Almost contemporaneously, he produced the portal of the Church of SS. Giovanni e Paolo, followed by the portal of the Church of S. Maria dell'Orto.

On 8 August 1464, Bartolomeo drafted his will and must have died shortly thereafter, as his wife Maria, mother of their two daughters, is referred to as a widow in a document from 28 April 1467.

NICOLAS BOCK

See also **Ghiberti, Lorenzo; Nanni di Banco**

Giovanni Buon

Biography

Born in Venice, Italy, *ca.* 1360. Documented as a witness on a testament dated 10 June 1382; maintained an architectural and sculptural workshop in Venice until death; mentioned in documents relating to stone deliveries and payments for 1385–88 and 1423; not identified as the sculptor of any known work; succeeded by son, Bartolomeo Buon. Died in Venice, Italy, 1442.

Bartolomeo Buon

Biography

Born in Venice, Italy, *ca.* 1400/05. Probably trained in the workshop of his father, the sculptor and stone mason Giovanni Buon; documented for the first time on a contract for an unspecified work for the Ca' d'Oro, Venice, 14 January 1422; worked with his father on sculptural decorations for the Ca' d'Oro, until 1431; worked primarily as an architect, 1431–38; managed family workshop after father's death in 1442; designed and created many sculptural decorations for churches and palaces in Venice, 1440s to mid 1460s. Died in Venice, Italy, between 1464 and 1467.

Selected Works

1427   Statues of *Spes* (Truth), *Fides* (Faith), and *Caritas* (Charity); marble; fountain, Ca' d'Oro, Venice, Italy

ca. 1427 Fountain from Church of SS. Giovanni e Paolo, Venice, Italy; marble; Victoria and Albert Museum, London, England

1430–35 *St. Francis*; marble; Church of Santa Maria Gloriosa dei Frari, Venice, Italy

mid 1430s	*Annunciation* (or *Maria Annunziata*); marble; Liebieghaus, Frankfurt, Germany
mid 1430s	*Judgment of Solomon*; marble; Doge's Palace, Venice, Italy (attributed)
1438–41	Head of Doge Francesco Foscari, for the Porta della Carta, Doge's Palace, Venice; marble; Museo dell'Opera, Palazzo Ducale, Venice, Italy
1438–41	*Justice*; marble; Porta della Carta, Doge's Palace, Venice, Italy
1444–68	Tomb of Bartolomeo Morosini; probably marble (destroyed)
1448–51	*Madonna della Misericordia* (Madonna of Mercy) for portal of Scuola Vecchia della Misericordia, Venice, Italy; marble; Victoria and Albert Museum, London, England (attributed or from his workshop)
1458	Portal; marble; Church of SS. Giovanni e Paolo, Venice, Italy
after 1460	Portal; marble; Church of Santa Maria dell'Orto, Venice, Italy

Further Reading

Arslan, Edoardo, *Venezia gotica*, Milan: Electar, 1970; as *Gothic in Venice*, translated by Anne Engel, London: Phaidon, 1971

Connell, Susan, "The Employment of Sculptors and Stonemasons in Venice in the Fifteenth Century," Ph.D. diss., Warburg Institute, 1976

Goy, Richard John, *The House of Gold: Building a Palace in Medieval Venice*, Cambridge and New York: Cambridge University Press, 1992

Howard, Deborah, *The Architectural History of Venice*, London: Batsford, 1980; New York: Holmes and Meier, 1981

Lewis, Douglas, "Bon, Giovanni/Bon, Bartolomeo," in *Macmillan Encyclopedia of Architects*, edited by Adolf K. Plazcek, London: Collier Macmillan, and New York: Free Press, 1982

McAndrew, John, *Venetian Architecture of the Early Renaissance*, Cambridge, Massachusetts: MIT Press, 1980

Paoletti, P., "Bono, Bartolomeo di Giovanni," and "Bono, Giovanni di Bertuccio," in *Allgemeines Lexikon der bildenden Künstler von der Antike bis zur Gegenwart*, edited by Ulrich Thieme, Felix Becker, and Hans Vollmer, vol. 4, Leipzig: Engelmann, 1910; reprint, Leipzig: Seemann, 1978

Pincus, Debra, "The Arco Foscari: The Building of a Triumphal Gateway in Fifteenth-Century Venice," Ph.D. diss., New York University, 1976

Pope-Hennessy, John, *An Introduction to Italian Sculpture*, 3 vols., London: Phaidon, 1963; 4th edition, 1996; see especially vol. 1, *Italian Gothic Sculpture*

Romano, Serena, *La Porta della Carta: I restauri* (exhib. cat.), Venice: Palazzo Ducale, 1979

Schulz, Anne Markham, *The Sculpture of Giovanni and Bartolomeo Bon and Their Workshop*, Philadelphia, Pennsylvania: American Philosophical Society, 1978

Wolters, Wolfgang, *La scultura veneziana gotica (1300–1460)*, Venice: Alfieri, 1976

Wolters, Wolfgang, "Buon," in *The Dictionary of Art*, edited by Jane Turner, New York: Grove, and London: Macmillan, 1996

MADONNA DELLA MISERICORDIA
Buon Family
1448–1451
marble
h. 2.51 m
Victoria and Albert Museum, London, England

The relief referred to as the *Madonna della Misericordia* in the Victoria and Albert Museum, attributed to the Buon family workshop, originally belonged together with the statues of two angels and the three theological virtues as part of the ornamentation on the portal of the Scuola Vecchia della Misericordia, the palace of a Venetian confraternity. The work depicts the Virgin Mary standing and, with the assistance of the two angels, spreading her cloak protectively over nine kneeling members of the confraternity who are clad in their habits. Drawing on the Byzantine Madonna type of the *playtera* (Mary Orans with a *clipcus* [mandorla/shield] in front of her breast), as was typical for artists in Venice, the Christ child appears in the mandorla making the sign of the cross. The long, smooth folds of Mary's cloak and her clear, simple face are in distinct contrast to the individualized faces of the members of the confraternity and to the turbulent background of the Root of Jesse behind her, in the tendrils of which the half-figures of four prophets and, higher up, two kings can be seen.

The portal and its decoration are not explicitly mentioned in the documents of the guild, but they are probably connected with the guild's decision on 6 August 1441 "to redo the facade of the *scuola* [house of the confraternity for assemblies and veneration] on account of its poor condition." Ten years later, on 15 August 1451, another document reports the intention "to place the figure of Mary above the portal of the Corte Nuova." This decision to transfer the old *Madonna della Misericordia* of the 14th century—a Mary Orans relief in half-figure—from the portal of the Scuola Vecchia to the portal of the Corte Nuova probably indicates that the new *Madonna della Misericordia* had been completed. According to an annotation to an engraving by Giovanni Grevembroch (1754), the portal relief was then transferred to its spot above Jacobo Sansovino's portal of the Scuola Grande (Nuova) della Misericordia, where it remained until the beginning of the 19th century. Shortly after 1828, the entire ensemble was placed in the interior of the church. The relief with the Madonna was finally sold to the Victoria and Albert Museum; the statues are now missing.

The authorship of the facade remains unaccounted for. Its opulent tracery windows are similar to those of the Church of Santa Maria dell'Orto in Venice. The design of the portal and windows was first attributed to Bartolomeo Buon by Francesco Sansovino (1581). This suggestion was long accepted in scholarship because Bartolomeo was a member of the confraternity of the Misericordia and also acted as a patron. More recent critical work, however, does not attribute the relief to Bartolomeo because of its poor technical quality and its lack of expression on the faces of the members of the confraternity, which are reminiscent of works from the 14th century. For this reason, Anne Markham Schulz attributed the design of the portal to Bartolomeo's father, Giovanni. Schulz saw Bartolomeo's style in the two angels that are still situated on the lintels of the portal and suggested a dating of about *ca.* 1423/24 on the basis of a period when the Buon workshop was not working on the Ca' d'Oro. The already outmoded style, which was based on models from the turn of the 15th century, led her to view the relief as the personal work of Giovanni himself (see Schulz, 1978).

According to Wolfgang Wolters, on the other hand, Bartolomeo was assigned the job and probably did indeed design the portal and the facade, but he left the production to his less modern and less well trained assistants (see Wolters, 1976). This hypothesis explains the combination of progressive elements of the architecture on the facade, which anticipate the Renaissance (for instance, the Arco Foscari of 1437 and the Ca' del Duca of 1457), with the dry, somewhat antiquated style of the sculptures in the lunette. The type of head given to Mary, which does not correspond to that which Bartolomeo normally used for his Madonnas, but rather that which he developed for allegories (Justice on the Porta della Carta), would also indicate that the work had been done by members of his workshop. Thus in connection with the documents mentioned above, Wolters placed the development of the relief in the 1440s.

The portal's former relief, a half-figure Maria Orans with the *episkepsis*, probably reflects the religious symbol (cult image) of the confraternity. This sort of Byzantine religious symbol was widespread in Venice, particularly after the fall of Constantinople in 1204. For the new portal relief, the old tradition was revisited and modernized: the iconography was expanded through the motif of the protective cloak, the virtues, and the Root of Jesse. The combination of the Madonna and her protective cloak with a tree or a Root of Jesse frequently can be found in Venice and also appears on the guild's processional banner, the *Mariegola* (*ca.* 1392). The theme of the Madonna with the protective cloak was particularly favored by confraternities, although it was initially believed that the theme was grounded in the Marian mysticism of the Cistercians (see Pedrizet, 1908). In his *Dialogus miraculorum* (1205), Caesarius of Heisterbach related a vision

in which Mary in heaven took the members of the Cistercian order protectively under her cloak (*pallium*). The motif already appears, however, in the calls for help that Bernhard of Clairveaux addresses to Mary, even if it is not the *pallium* but rather the *ala* and *sinus*, with which Mary should shelter the faithful. Finally, Gregor of Tours was the first to mention Mary's protective cloak specifically. The image of a protective cover can be found in Islamic, Anglo-Saxon, and Greek sources, as well as in the Old Testament. The motif is already anticipated in the iconography of Roman coins.

The launching point for this tradition was Constantinople, where Mary's cloak (*maphorion*) was worshiped as a relic in the Blachernen Church. More recently, the crusaders had disseminated throughout Europe the belief in the protection of Mary's cloak with a piece of the relic. Particularly under the influence of the Franciscans, the Madonna with the protective cloak became a symbol for mercy (*Mater Misericordiae*), for which reason the charitable confraternities, which established themselves in Italian municipalities during the 11th and 12th centuries, chose it as a symbol of their activities. The Madonnas with the protective cloaks therefore appear as altars and as devotional pictures; they also frequently decorate the entrances of hospitals and the banners of the confraternities, which were carried through the cities during processionals.

NICOLAS BOCK

Further Reading

Belting-Ihm, Christa, *Sub matris tutela: Untersuchungen zur Vorgeschichte der Schutzmantelmadonna*, Heidelberg: Winter, 1976

Pedrizet, Paul, *La Vièrge de Miséricorde: Étude d'un thème iconographique*, Paris: Fontemoing, 1908

Schulz, Anne Markham, *The Sculpture of Giovanni and Bartolomeo Bon and Their Workshop*, Philadelphia, Pennsylvania: American Philosophical Society, 1978

Wolters, Wolfgang, *La scultura veneziana gotica (1300–1460)*, Venice: Alfieri, 1976

BURY ST. EDMUNDS CROSS

See **Cloisters Cross (Bury St. Edmunds)**

JOHN BUSHNELL 1635/36–1701 *British*

John Bushnell brought Italian Baroque sculpture styles, techniques, and modeling practices to England in the late 1660s. An eccentric and vain man, Bushnell expected universal recognition in England, but he had competent rivals, and his many overambitious schemes led to disappointment, poverty, and legal problems toward the end of his life. He died bankrupt and deranged. George Vertue, the 18th-century antiquarian, collected some details of his life.

The son of a plumber, Bushnell was apprenticed to the mason Thomas Burman. Bushnell was apparently accused by his master of seducing a servant girl and escaped to the Continent, taking some of Burman's money. Bushnell spent 11 years overseas improving his skills and working on the Mocenigo screen monument originally designed by Guiseppe Sardi and begun by Josse de Corte in the Church of San Lazzaro, Venice. Bushnell contributed two vast reliefs representing the *Siege of Martinengo* (a crowded land battle with dozens of tangled figures and horses) and the *Battle of Paros* (a sea battle); both were victories for the Venetians led by Alvise II Mocenigo over the Turks. For this work, Bushnell received the handsome sum of 2,500 ducats. De Corte's dramatic and highly emotional style influenced Bushnell's subsequent work.

Traveling via Rome, Vienna, Hamburg, and Flanders, Bushnell returned to England in 1667–68. In April 1670, for the sum of 35 pounds, he made a wax and stucco effigy of the Duke of Albemarle for the Westminster Abbey funeral. Bushnell's first major public commission was to carve four royal figures for Temple Bar, the triumphal gateway between the city of London and Westminster, and for which he was paid 480 pounds between May 1670 and April 1671. James I wears Jacobean clothes, but Elizabeth I is unrecognizable (without her ruff and farthingale) as a Roman matron; in addition, Bushnell portrayed Charles I and Charles II as Roman generals. Although Elizabeth I and Charles II wear crowns, Charles I and Charles II have sandals and bare legs, with the Garter uselessly under the left knee. This sort of anachronism was misconstrued in Protestant England, where anything Romish was controversial.

London's international trading center, the Royal Exchange, with its famous sequence of royal statues, was destroyed in 1666 during the Great Fire. Christopher Wren's spirit stood behind the new Baroque development of 1669–71. Bushnell was commissioned to carve a statue of the founder, Sir Thomas Gresham, in Elizabethan dress, and a pair of 2-meter statues of Charles I and Charles II in Roman dress (1671–73; Old Bailey, London), which were to stand on the triumphal entranceway on Cornhill. Bushnell's compositions were often maladroit, but the kings' twisting, expansive gestures indicate that the sculptor had seen Gianlorenzo Bernini's work in Rome. Bushnell also adopted Bernini's clawing of the surface finish, which helps distinguish different textures when viewing at a distance. Again, these statues did not receive universal acclaim

because of their Roman clothing and anachronistic detail.

Bushnell began six more "Caesars," hoping to begin replacing the line of kings for the Exchange, but they were not accepted, and a stalemate ensued that lasted a dozen years. He also became involved in litigation over an order for garden sculpture for Sir Robert Gayer. Bushnell speculated in the emerging coal industry and developed a machine for breaking iron bars, but his mental health had begun to deteriorate. He became increasingly litigious in relation to the various properties that he bought and inherited. Before he died, he began building a cavernous house, without stairs or floors, on a large plot near the present-day Hyde Park Corner. Visiting Bushnell's sons there in 1725, Vertue saw the six statues for the Exchange, a model of an equestrian Charles II never cast, a giant Trojan horse designed internally for use as a tavern, a bust of William Talman, and a statue of Alexander the Great that Bushnell had carved to prove he could represent nude anatomy. Bushnell made other royal statues, including an Italian marble bust converted to represent Charles II, a standing Roman figure of Charles II, a life-size (1686; now lost) for Southwark Town Hall, and a standing Roman figure of James II. However, a terracotta model of Charles II at the Fitzwilliam Museum, Cambridge, and the related marble bust have recently been reattributed to Caius Gabriel Cibber. James II commissioned Bushnell to carve figures of St. Peter and St. Paul (presumably 1685–88) for Somerset House Chapel, for which the artist was still owed money in 1689.

Church monuments provided Bushnell with a continuous income throughout his time in England. He carved the bust of Elizabeth Pepys after her death, but it is a real speaking likeness, with her mouth open and head turned sharply to one side. The monument to John, Viscount Mordaunt of Avalon, consists of five sections. A strutting figure, wearing timeless garments and making a rhetorical gesture with a baton, the viscount stands on a central black podium. Behind are inscriptions rising from two pedestals; in front, two more pedestals bear his gauntlets and coronet. Another complex monument, to Sir William Ashburnham and his wife, Jane, in Ashburnham Church, Sussex, was damaged in transit to its destination. Jane predeceased William, and she is shown recumbent while he kneels grieving at her feet. Behind, cupids hold aside the curtains of a baldachin, and the four pedestals again occur. The monument to Lady Mary May, carved during her lifetime, shows another recumbent figure within a lightweight, almost Rococo framework. The portrait of Elizabeth, Lady Myddleton, was sent to Bushnell in London so that he could make a posthumous monument; it shows her reclining and nursing an infant. The baldachin, putti, gadrooned sarcophagus, and inverted pear-shaped urns are common features in many of Bushnell's monuments, which often comprise separate parts and use strong contrasts of white marble on black backgrounds. The drapery frequently seems unnecessarily complicated, but the lettering of his inscriptions is distinctive. There are numerous monuments in his increasingly quirky style; the monument to Henry Thomond and family may be his last. The ten figures have large, chubby heads and diminutive bodies.

As Bushnell's dementia grew his skills deteriorated, and he was probably assisted by his sons, who continued in business after his death.

KATHARINE GIBSON

See also **Bernini, Gianlorenzo; Cibber, Caius Gabriel; Corte, Josse de; England and Wales: Baroque–Neoclassical**

Biography

Born in London, England, *ca.* 1635/36. Apprenticed to Thomas Burman, 1650s; traveled in Europe, *ca.* 1656–1667/68; carved two reliefs for the monument to Alvise II Mocenigo in Venice, Italy, *ca.* 1660–63; returned to England via Rome, 1667/68; given public commissions for royal statues for Temple Bar and the Royal Exchange in London in early 1670s; private commissions for church monuments occupied him throughout his time in England, but he considered schemes other than sculpture for making money, 1690s. Died in Paddington, England, 15 May 1701.

Selected Works

ca. 1660–63	Reliefs for monument to Alvise II Mocenigo; marble; Church of San Lazzaro dei Mendicanti, Venice, Italy
ca. 1668	Bust of Charles II; marble; Cliveden, Buckinghamshire, England
ca. 1670	Bust of Elizabeth Pepys; marble; St. Olave's Church, Hart Street, London
1670–71	*Elizabeth I, James I, Charles I,* and *Charles II,* for Temple Bar; Portland stone; in storage with English Heritage
1671–73	*Thomas Gresham, Charles I,* and *Charles II,* for the Royal Exchange Building; Portland stone; Antechamber to the Central Criminal Court, Old Bailey, London, England
1674	Monument to Abraham Cowley; marble; Westminster Abbey, London, England
1675	Monument to John, Viscount Mordaunt of Avalon; marble; All Saints Church, Fulham, London, England
1675	Monument to Sir William Ashburnham and his wife; marble; Ashburnham, East Sussex, England
1676–81	Monument to Lady Mary May; marble; Mid Lavant, West Sussex, England
1677	Monument to Elizabeth, Lady Myddleton, and monument with busts of Sir Thomas and Lady Myddleton; marble; Chirk Parish Church, Clwyd, Wales
ca. 1680	*Charles II*; bronze; private collection
1685–88	*James II*; stone; Cork Art Gallery, Cork, Ireland
1700	Monument to Henry Thomond; marble; Church of St. Andrew, Great Billing, Northamptonshire, England

Further Reading

Borean, Linda, "John Bushnell in Venice," *Church Monuments* 14 (1999)

Esdaile, Katharine, "John Bushnell, Sculptor," *The Walpole Society* 15 (1926–27)

Esdaile, Katharine, "Additional Notes to John Bushnell," *The Walpole Society* 21 (1932–33)

Gibson, Katharine, "The Kingdom's Marble Chronicle: The Embellishment of the First and Second Buildings, 1600–1690," in *The Royal Exchange*, edited by Ann Saunders, London: London Topographical Society, 1997

Gunnis, Rupert, *Dictionary of British Sculptors, 1660–1851*, London: Odhams Press, 1953; Cambridge, Massachusetts: Harvard University Press, 1954; revised edition, London: Abbey Library, 1968

Vertue, George, *Vertue Note Books*, 7 vols., Oxford: University Press, 1930–55; see especially vols. 1, 2, and 4

Whinney, Margaret, *Sculpture in Britain, 1530–1830*, London and Baltimore, Maryland: Penguin, 1964; 2nd edition, John Physick, London and New York: Penguin, 1988

BUST

See **Portrait**

AGOSTINO BUSTI (BAMBAIA) *ca.* 1483–1548 *Italian*

Agostino Busti—better known by his nickname, Bambaia—was born in Milan at a time when the dukedom's culture was passionately engaged in a fanciful and bizarre recovery of ancient art and just touched by Leonardo da Vinci's new style.

Bambaia is generally thought to have trained with Benedetto Briosco, who was working at the Certosa di Pavia in the 1490s. It is not certain that Bambaia was also there, although Giorgio Vasari wrote that some very beautiful works of his were at the Certosa. At any rate, Briosco's teachings—his quest for a softer style echoing the Classical, capable of unusual elegance, and leaning toward a delicate descriptivism—must have been of primary importance to the young artist.

In 1512 Bambaia was hired to work at Milan Cathedral. His name has been recently suggested (although necessarily only as a hypothesis) for the attribution of a series of reliefs depicting stories of the Virgin Mary on Giovanni Antonio Amadeo's Pinnacle (1509–13; Milan Cathedral).

It is nearly certain that on 24 September 1513, Bambaia departed for Rome with da Vinci and his followers. Evidence of this extremely important experience appears in a group of drawings (Kupferstichkabinett, Berlin) that show how the young sculptor took time almost exclusively to copy a few pieces of ancient sculpture and architecture.

On his return to Milan, Bambaia began to work in the Church of San Marco on the tomb of the celebrated poet Lancino Curzio. This was a prestigious commission, and Bambaia (assisted by Cristoforo Lombardo) executed it brilliantly as a wall tomb. The figure of the deceased is shown recumbent as a *gisant* (reclining figure) facing the viewer, guarded in his last sleep by a Classical group of the Three Graces and by three winged figures. Two of the latter are sitting beside a decorated altar; the third—nude and about to wind a ribbon around his legs—terminates the top end of the monument.

In Milan during this time, no other funerary monument had ever dispensed so successfully with religious symbolism. Here sweet feminine allegories replace the Christian Virtues, and the monument is crowned not by the Resurrected Christ, but by a figure—perhaps Fame—who flaunts the sensuality of her nude body. Although the Curzio tomb is damaged (at least three of the figures have been decapitated) and cannot be read easily, it retains all of its allure: unparalleled ele-

gance and refined execution in a composition that appears gently animated and substantially different from the traditional style of Lombard wall tombs in which Amadeo worked.

Judging by the undulant drapery, the fluttering torch flames, and the way Fame's silk ribbon wafts in the air around her, one would think that an actual breeze had made its way into Bambaia's marble. This effect of delicate motion reached its peak in later sculptures: the apostles on the tomb of Gaston de Foix; the Virtues in London (Victoria and Albert Museum) and Fort Worth, Texas (Kimbell Art Museum); and a delightful figure in Florence (Palazzo Pitti) on whose identification and attribution to Bambaia not all scholars agree.

After the Curzio tomb, Bambaia worked with Bernardino Daverio on the tomb of Francesco Orsini in the Church of Santa Maria della Scala in Milan. Here Bambaia tried out a new, naturalistic rendition of the deceased's portrait and flaunted his skill in carving the two small pillars—decorated with escutcheons, medallions, putti in the role of guardian angels, fluttering ribbons, and cartouches—with a refined and minutely detailed treatment that recalls ancient cameo work.

Bambaia's balanced and delicate Classicism in the Curzio tomb and his variegated decoration of the Orsini pillars found new expression in the tomb of Gaston de Foix, the governor of Milan. The history of this prestigious commission is closely tied to that of the French regime in northern Italy. In 1512 de Foix died at the age of 23 on a battlefield in Ravenna. Three years later, when the French reconquered Milan, they decided to honor his memory with a monument in the Church of Santa Marta. Bambaia received the commission and worked on it with Cristoforo Lombardo and others. When the French were forced out of Milan in 1522, the work had not been finished but came to an abrupt end.

The monument, in which suggestions from French sculpture have been noted, was probably designed to stand alone in the center of a chapel, visible from all sides. This arrangement, rather than the traditional wall tomb, reflected a change of taste that began in Milan in the late 15th century. A drawing by Bambaia (Victoria and Albert Museum) gives an idea of his plan.

The surviving elements are the recumbent statue of the soldier, 12 seated apostles (and perhaps prophets), a series of rectangular reliefs depicting scenes from de Foix's life, several Virtues, and a series of small decorated columns and pilasters hung with trophies. Bambaia's intelligence can also be seen working in the way he diversified his language according to the type of element. In the apostles and the Virtues, he shows

Tomb of Gaston de Foix
© Alinari / Art Resource, NY

that he had absorbed Leonardo's teachings, particularly his portrayals of states of mind. By contrast, Bambaia's narrative reliefs, bustling with people moving against backgrounds of trees, mills, and turreted cities, recall Briosco's descriptive style.

The statue of the deceased Gaston de Foix reflects a more composed Classicism owing in part to Bambaia's reluctance to display his technical virtuosity. This he reserved for the decoration of the columns, where he concentrated weapons, grotesques, Satyrs, chariots, torches, and lion heads—almost a representational transcription of the long, redundant lists of the *Antiquarie Prospetiche Romane* (1496–98). The de Foix sculptures manifest Bambaia's great skill in treating marble as a ductile and malleable material to render the texture of fabrics and flesh with mimetic and light effects that defy the very essence of sculpture. Unfortunately, the work was never finished. As early as 1568, Vasari decried its state of abandon, affirming that some of the figures had been "stolen and then sold and placed elsewhere."

In 1522 the now-celebrated and appreciated Bambaia had no trouble finding a new commission right away: the tomb of Gian Marko and Zenone Birago in the Church of San Francesco Grande, Milan. This work was soon dismantled, but some elements survive: a funeral arch, several figures (including those of St. John the Baptist and St. Jerome), and a series of reliefs depicting scenes from the Passion, where the narrative is infused with new ideals of clarity and conciseness in composition that were absent in the de Foix tomb.

From 1535 on, Bambaia worked on a regular basis at Milan Cathedral, where he executed the Altar of the Presentation (1543). In the last 15 years of his career, he produced, among other works, the tomb of a jurist in the Church of Santo Stefano Maggiore, to which some reliefs now at the Castello Sforzesco (Sforza Castle) were recently related; the Melchiorre Langhi tomb in Novara Cathedral, commissioned in 1538; the Martino Carracciolo tomb (1540) in Milan Cathedral; and the Altar of St. Evasius in the Cathedral of Casale Monferrato. In this late phase, Bambaia seemed to have been seeking solemnity and essentiality, whereas his earlier style leaned more toward ornamental values.

Nearly all of Bambaia's monuments have come down to us dismembered, many are still hard to reconstruct even on paper, and many are in such poor condition that it is still hard to interpret them. Nonetheless, this original and refined artist—lauded by Vasari and Cesare Cesariano, appreciated by Antonio Canova and Leopoldo Cicognara—is recognized today as one of the most significant figures in Lombard Classicism.

MADDALENA SPAGNOLO

See also **Certosa di Pavia**

Biography

Born in Milan, Italy, *ca.* 1483. Worked on Milan Cathedral with brother Polidoro, January 1512; perhaps traveled to Rome with Leonardo da Vinci and others, 1513; began work on tomb of Gaston de Foix, 1517; noted and praised in Cesare Cesariano's *Vitruvius* (1521); acted as the agent of Traiano Alicorno, 1525–30; regularly mentioned in records of Milan Cathedral as sculptor in the workshop from 1535. Died in Milan, Italy, 11 June 1548.

Selected Works

1513–15 Tomb of Lancino Curzio, for Church of San Marco, Milan, Italy; marble; Museo d'Arte Antica del Castello Sforzesco, Milan, Italy

1516 Tomb of Francesco Orsini, for Church of Santa Maria della Scala, Milan, Italy; marble (dismantled): fragments: Galleria San Fedele, Milan, Italy; Museo d'Arte Antica del Castello Sforzesco, Milan, Italy

1517–22 Tomb of Gaston de Foix, for Church of Santa Marta, Milan, Italy; marble (dismantled): fragments: Museo d'Arte Antica del Castello Sforzesco and Pinacoteca Ambrosiana, Milan, Italy; Museo Civico d'Arte Antica, Turin, Italy; Victoria and Albert Museum, London, England

1522 Tomb of Gian Marko and Zenone Birago, for Church of San Francesco Grande, Milan, Italy; marble (dismantled): fragments: Museo Borromeo, Isola Bella, Italy

1525–30 Jurist's tomb; marble, sandstone (dismantled); fragments: Church of Santo Stefano Maggiore, Milan, Italy; Museo d'Arte Antica del Castello Sforzesco, Milan, Italy

1539 Tomb of Melchiorre Langhi; marble, sandstone; Novara Cathedral, Italy

Further Reading

Agosti, Giovanni, *Bambaia e il classicismo lombardo*, Turin, Italy: Einaudi, 1990

Agostino Busti, detto il Bambaia, 1483–1548, Milan: Longanesi, 1990

Bober, Phyllis Pray, and Ruth Rubinstein, *Renaissance Artists and Antique Sculpture: A Handbook of Sources*, Oxford: Oxford University Press, 1986

Bossaglia, Rossana, "Scultura," in *Il Duomo di Milano*, edited by Carlo Ferrari da Passano, Angiola Maria Romanini, and Ernesto Briuio, vol. 2, Milan: Fabbrica del Duomo, 1973

Fiorio, Maria Teresa, *Bambaia: Catalogo completo delle opere*, Florence: Cantini, 1990

Fiorio, Maria Teresa, "Bambaia [Busti, Agostino]," in *The Dictionary of Art*, edited by Jane Turner, vol. 3, New York: Grove, and London: Macmillan, 1996

Fiorio, Maria Teresa, "La 'buona maniera moderna' del Bambaia e lo 'sperperato avello' del Birago," in *Scultura Lombarda del Rinascimento: I monumenti Borromeo*, edited by Natale Mauro, Turin, Italy: Allemandi, 1997

Longsworth, Ellen, "The Renaissance Tomb in Milan," Ph.D. diss., Boston University, 1987

Pope-Hennessy, John, *Catalogue of Italian Sculpture in the Victoria and Albert Museum*, 3 vols., London: HMSO, 1964

Vasari, Giorgio, *Le vite de' più eccellenti architetti, pittori, e scultori italiani*, 3 vols., Florence: Torrentino, 1550; 2nd edition, Florence: Apresso i Giunti, 1568; as *Lives of the Painters, Sculptors, and Architects*, 2 vols., translated by Gaston du C. de Vere (1912), edited by David Ekserdjian, New York: Knopf, and London: Campbell, 1996

REG BUTLER 1913–1981 *British*

Reg Butler, the English sculptor, was born in Hertfordshire in 1913. After studying architecture from 1933 to 1936, he taught for several years in London at the Architectural Association and, under the name of Cotterell Butler, practiced as an architect, designing two smaller houses in Hertfordshire and the clock tower on the town hall in Slough, Buckinghamshire. From 1941 to 1945, as a conscientious objector to World War II, he lived in Iping, West Sussex, where he worked as a blacksmith and became an expert welder, especially with the oxyacetylene torch, a technique that would be important for him later in his sculpture. From 1946 to about 1950 he continued to work as a consultant to various architectural firms, most notably Ove Arup and Partners. In the meantime he had begun to study sculpture, attending life-drawing classes at the Chelsea School of Art. In 1949 he held his first solo exhibition at the Hannover Gallery, London, exhibiting pieces that exploited the possibilities both of hand-forging metal, in the manner of the Spanish sculptor Eduardo Chillida, and the formal constructions seen in the work of Julio González. Butler's forms were more sinuous than those of González, because he made preliminary models always shaped in wire.

From 1950 to 1953, while teaching at the Slade School of Fine Arts in London, Butler was also Gregory Fellow in sculpture at Leeds University. During these years, he had his greatest success, taking part in several international exhibitions, most notably the Venice Biennale of 1952, where he was one of a group of British sculptors, including Lynn Chadwick, Ken-

neth Armitage, and William Turnbull, whose work made a great international impression; it was then that Alfred Barr bought one of Butler's works for the Museum of Modern Art in New York City. Many of these artists, like Butler, had come to sculpture through ironwork or architecture. They stood against the ideas of Henry Moore and Barbara Hepworth and their concern with natural materials and monumentality and what they called organic form. The younger sculptors, more interested in the process than in creating images in deliberately and consciously realized forms, produced pieces, with surrealism and the images of science behind them, that seem fragmented and almost convulsive, full of anthropomorphic suggestions of teeth and claws.

Butler is especially remembered, however, for the controversy surrounding his winning project for the competition for the *Monument to the Unknown Political Prisoner*, the first model for which was made in 1953. Butler designed the monument, a vast project some 15 meters tall, to stand on the Humboldt Höhe in Wedding, a suburb of Berlin, near the border of East Germany. A deeply haunting construction of skeletal forms, in three parts, raised high and enclosed in a boxed grid, the work suggested the isolation of prisons, while in its delicacy it recalled the forms of Alberto Giacometti, a sculptor whom Butler admired deeply. Butler had made a number of projects of this kind for colossal monuments. Nothing came of the *Monument to the Unknown Political Prisoner* project, however, which had been sponsored by the Institute of Contemporary Art in London and quietly funded by the American John Hay Whitney. Criticism came from both left and right in 1953; socialist writers saw the piece as defeatist, whereas conservatives objected to its style. A Hungarian refugee artist, protesting against the abstraction of modern art, destroyed the original maquette while it was on display at the Tate Gallery in London. Public disagreement reached even the House of Commons, orchestrated in part by Sir Winston Churchill, who urged Sir Alfred Munnings of the Royal Academy to criticize all modern art. The artist Wyndham Lewis also attacked Butler in his essay "The Demon of Progress in Modern Art" (1954), repeating a purposely misleading claim of Churchill that the sculpture was intended to stand about 152 meters high on the cliffs of Dover, a site venerated by all people in England.

By this time, however, under the influence of the French artist Germaine Richier, Butler had begun to change his concerns with sculpture, and in the later 1950s he turned to figures, producing studies of the female form, made with welded bronze sheets on steel and often encased in frames or shown twisting around metal bars, as he put it, like kites on a string. Also at this time, in some lectures to students, Butler criticized what he saw as the exclusively formal preoccupations of modern art and declared that Modernism would be followed quickly by a "postmodernism", here invoking a term used first in literature of the 1950s. During this time he worked slowly, producing only three or four pieces a year, basing the designs on exquisitely rendered drawings that set the figures in often contorted poses, while representing others reclining on striped cushions of bronze, with gestures that mimic what he referred to as the disarray of sexual activity. He subsequently moved away from steel to work with figures cast in bronze: "naked ladies", as he called them, shown with a realism that seems paradoxically to emphasize their unreality. They are painted or given details of real hair wigs or resin eyes, so that they appear physically close, yet distant like dolls or mannequins, with their parts always seemingly separable. Here the influence came from the painters Francis Bacon or Lucien Freud, with whom Butler had worked at the Slade. It was also at the Slade that in 1980 Butler gave a lecture explaining his new working methods in detail. But these arresting figures did not find an audience; four of them were exhibited at the Pierre Matisse Gallery in New York City in 1974, to be put away until 1998, when they appeared in a show at the Kent Gallery to more critical acclaim and interest.

Butler's influence can be seen in the work of the Chapman brothers and, in painting, in the work of Lisa Yuskavage. In 1983, two years after his death, the Tate Gallery held a memorial exhibition of his work.

DAVID CAST

See also **England and Wales: 19th Century–Contemporary; Gonzálezs, Julio; Hepworth, Dame Barbara; Modernism; Moore, Henry; Postmodernism**

Biography

Born in Buntingford, Hertfordshire, England, 28 April 1913. Educated privately and at Hertford Grammar School; trained as an architect, 1933–36; lecturer at Architectural Association, School of Architecture, London, 1937–39; began sculpting in 1944 without prior formal training; first solo exhibition at Hannover Gallery, London, 1949; Gregory Fellow in sculpture, Leeds University, 1950–53; also teacher at Slade School of Fine Arts, London; showed at Venice Bien-

nale, 1952, 1954. Won first prize, international competition for *Monument to the Unknown Political Prisoner*, 1953; major exhibitions at Curt Valentin Gallery, New York City, 1953, 1955; Pierre Matisse Gallery, New York City, 1974. Died in Berkhamsted, Hertfordshire, England, 23 October 1981.

Selected Works

1949   *Woman*; iron; Tate Gallery, London, England
1950–51 *Girl and Boy*; iron; Art Council Collection, London, England
1951   *The Birdcage*; iron; Festival of Britain, London, England
1952   *The Oracle*; iron; University of Hertfordshire, England
1955   *Doll*; bronze; private collection, United States
1955–56 *Monument to the Unknown Political Prisoner* (destroyed); working model: Tate Gallery, London, England
1956–57 *Girl*; bronze; City Art Gallery, Leeds, England
1968–71 *Girl Bending*; bronze; private collection, United States
1975–81 *Girl on Back*; bronze, hair, foam base, velvet; private collection, London, England

Further Reading

Burstow, R., "Butler's Competition Project for a Monument to 'The Unknown Political Prisoner': Abstraction and Cold War Politics," *Art History* 12 (1989)
Butler, Reg, *Creative Development: Five Lectures to Art Students*, London: Routledge and Kegan Paul, 1962
Nairne, Sandy, and Nicholas Serota, *British Sculpture in the Twentieth Century* (exhib. cat.), London: Whitechapel Art Gallery, 1981
Reg Butler (exhib. cat.), London: Tate Gallery, 1983
Schwartz, Paul Waldo, *The Hand and Eye of the Sculptor*, New York: Praeger, 1969
Strachan, W.J., "The Sculptor and His Drawing: 1. Reg Butler," *Connoisseur* (March 1974)
Taplin, R., "Reg Butler at Kent," *Art in America* 86 (1998)

BYZANTINE

See **Early Christian and Byzantine Sculpture (4th–15th Century)**

C

MELCHIORRE CAFFÀ 1638–1667

Maltese, active in Italy

In a drawing, at one time located in the Pio Collection and now held by the National Museum in Stockholm, Sweden, Melchiorre Caffà looks lost in thought, his face tinged with melancholy. The mood of this portrait was later confirmed by Caffà's contemporary, Lione Pascoli, who described Caffà as being reserved, with a tendency toward sadness. Pascoli did not try to conceal his disappointment and sorrow following Caffà's premature death, which occurred in 1667 when one of his statues fell on him while he was working in the foundry of St. Peter's Basilica. Although Caffà's career, expected from the beginning to be outstanding, ended with his untimely death, this is precisely why an analysis of his works is so captivating. The controversy in distinguishing what was Caffà's work and what was finished by his teacher, Ercole Ferrata, and his pupil, Giuseppe Mazzuoli, is replete with uncertainty and is often considered by scholars to be limited in its final analysis.

Although sources indicate that Caffà was born in 1631, Daniela Jemma, on the basis of documents found in the archives of the parish of Medina, the sculptor's native town, has suggested 1638 as a more precise date. Caffà was also a qualified architect and illustrator. We know of projects for altars from sketches, such as that of the chancel of the Church of S. Nicola in Valletta, and another for St. John in the same city; and the Roman altar of St. Mary in Campitelli, which Jennifer Montagu has connected to autographed drawings preserved in Paris, Darmstadt, and Leipzig (see Montagu, 1984).

Except for a brief stay in his native Malta from 1665 to April 1666, Caffà continued sculpting in Rome until his death. After Gianlorenzo Bernini and Alessandro Algardi, Caffà is considered to be among the most important sculptors of his generation. He possessed a refined and aesthetic sense that approached virtuosity. Indeed, looking at past sculptural examples such as those by Bernini and Algardi, Caffà, especially in his renderings of the figures, leaves a message of personal intensity at once significant and emotional.

In his portrait of Alexander VII, now in the Kunsthistoriches Museum in Vienna, Austria, Caffà endows the aged pope—already a patron and benefactor of Caffà during his young apprenticeship in Malta—with a significant, psychological wisdom and knowledge. Caffà's art reached its height with his sketches, which were characterized by his originality of using quick and fluid strokes, and by his clay models, which did not always find an equivalent in the marble productions completed or executed by other artists.

After a brief apprenticeship in Ferrata's Roman workshop, Caffà received his first private commission in December 1660 after the death of Algardi. Caffà's *Martyrdom of St. Eustace with His Sons Agapius and Theopistus*, for the Church of Sant' Agnese in Agone, Rome, provokes an analogy to Algardi's *Pope Leo the Great Driving Attila from Rome* (1646–1653) in St. Peter's Basilica; it is possible that Caffà used one of Algardi's sketches for this work. His transfer to marble of St. Eustace took a long time, and when Caffà died, only the figure of the saint was finished, whereas the figures of Agapius and Theopistus were barely hewed. A bas-relief sketch of this terracotta figure resides in

Ecstasy of St. Catherine of Siena
The Conway Library, Courtauld Institute of Art

the Museo di Palazzo Venezia in Rome, and another terracotta with a lion is in the Hermitage in St. Petersburg, Russia. The saint's characteristic lankiness and liveliness depicted in the sketch resisted accurate rendering in marble. One can see in this sculpture Bernini's influence, that is, the method of sculpting figures to be viewed from bottom to top.

Among Caffà's first works is *Charity of St. Thomas of Villanova* in the Pamphili Church of St. Augustine in Rome. At Caffà's death, the saint was completed, but the figure of Charity was merely sketched and was later finished by Ferrata. Caffà's sketch of Charity, now in Berlin, has a sweet and smiling expression that not only reveals the intimate and maternal feelings of his subject but also indicates the artist had studied and captured the true nature of Charity.

The figure of St. Catherine in the *Ecstasy of St. Catherine of Siena*, in the Church of St. Catherine in Magnanapoli in Rome, is attributed to Caffà. Although no documented proof has surfaced, Filippo Titi has attributed the entire project of the apse of St. Catherine to Caffà (see Titi, 1987). White figures stand out on a background of colored marble. The saint, enveloped in drapery, crosses her arms over her breast in a gesture typical of the hagiographical Baroque representations related to external space. Analogies between this relief and Bernini's *Ecstasy of St. Teresa* (1647–52) can be based on a similar expressive intensity, but in Caffà's work, the originality of a colored background demonstrates how the artist wanted to render the idea that

not only sculpture but also painting could be three-dimensional.

The sculpture of the *St. Rosa of Lima (St. Rosa's Death)*, now in the Church of S. Domenico in Lima, Perù, is inscribed with the date 1669 and was probably finished after Caffà's death. Here there is a theme of Holy Death, which was frequent in Baroque paintings, and it is presumed that Bernini had this work in mind when he finished his *Blessed Ludovica Albertoni in Ecstasy* (1671–74). Pascoli defined *St. Rosa's Death* as "the principal and most esteemed work by Caffà"; Caffà received the commission before the canonization of St. Rose in 1668. The marble group was not placed in Lima until 1670.

The *Baptism of Christ*, which consists of the two figures of Christ and St. John the Baptist, was executed for the altar of the Church of St. John, Valletta, Malta. Caffà was working on these figures just before his death, and the group saw completion by Caffà's pupil Mazzuoli about 1700.

Although no definitive proof points to Caffà's activity as a painter, he was accepted as such on the basis of the anonymous inscription "pictor, sculptor, et architectus" in his portrait drawing. Caffà's influence on Genoese painters and sculptors has been noted. The friendship between Caffà and the painter Baciccio (Giovan Battista Gaulli) is remembered by Pascoli, and Caffà's work is closely related to the graphic activity of Domenico Piola.

Caffà developed a strong link between sculpture and architecture, which is evident in the altar and tabernacle relief projects and is considered to be a true and characteristic representation of theatrical scenes. The integration of sculpture, painting, and theatrical design surfaces in the *Immaculate Virgin* by Pierre Puget in the Genoese Albergo dei Poveri, and again in the *Glory of St. Martha*, a work by Filippo Parodi. The latter captures Caffà's teachings of transferring to marble the vivacity of the clay model. In this case, both the motif of the clouds—which was already manifest in the *Ecstasy of St. Catherine of Siena*—and a virtuosity in the draping, characteristic of *St. Eustace*, find amplification. Finally, the intense gestures remain the most significant and encompassing aspect of the Maltese sculptor's output.

SILVIA HUOBER

See also **Ferrata, Ercole; Mazzuoli, Giuseppe**

Biography

Born in Vittoriosa near Medina, Malta, 1638. Before 1660 joined sculptor Ercole Ferrata's workshop in Rome; remained affiliated with Ferrata even after becoming an independent artist; first commission, by Prince Camillo Pamphili, was for Church of Sant' Agnese in Agone in Rome, December 1660; became member of Accademia di San Luca, 27 August 1662; later nominated for position of Prince of the Academy; renounced position and forced to pay a penalty; back in Malta, 1665–66; started project for high altar at Cathedral of Valletta, 1666; cathedral finished posthumously by his student, Giuseppe Mazzuoli, and his brother, Lorenzo Caffà, an architect. Died in Rome, Italy, before 10 September 1667.

Selected Works

1659   High altar; Church of St. Mary in Campitelli, Rome, Italy; clay; Hermitage, St. Petersburg, Russia

1659   *Portico Madonna*; stucco; high altar, St. Mary in Campitelli, Rome, Italy

1659   Portrait of Alexander VII; bronze; Kunsthistorisches Museum, Vienna, Austria

1660   *Martyrdom of St. Eustace with His Sons Agapius and Theopistus*, for Church of Sant' Agnese in Agone, Rome, Italy; terracotta model: Museo di Palazzo Venezia, Rome, Italy; marble version: Church of Sant' Agnese in Agone, Rome, Italy

1663   *Charity of St. Thomas of Villanova*; terracotta; copy: National Museum, Valletta, Malta; marble version: Church of St. Augustine, Pamphilii Chapel, Rome, Italy

1665   Choir; clay; Church of San Nicola di Bari, Valletta, Malta

1666   *Baptism of Christ*; bronze; Metropolitan Museum of Art, New York, United States; marble version: Church of St. John, Valletta, Malta

ca. 1666 *St. John the Baptist*; terracotta; Museo di Palazzo Venezia, Rome, Italy

1667   *Alexander VII*; terracotta; Palazzo Chigi, Ariccia, Italy

1667   *Alexander III*; marble; Opera of Duomo, Siena, Italy

1667   *Ecstasy of St. Catherine of Siena*; marble; Church of St. Catherine in Magnanapoli, Rome, Italy

ca. 1668 *St. Rosa of Lima (St. Rosa's Death)*; terracotta; Museo di Palazzo Venezia, Rome, Italy; bronze: Museo di Palazzo Venezia, Rome, Italy; marble: Church of S. Domenico, Lima, Peru

Further Reading

Fleming, J., "A Note on Melchiorre Caffà," *The Burlington Magazine* (1947)

Montagu, Jennifer, "The Graphic Work of Melchior Caffà," *Paragone* 35/413 (1984)

Montagu, Jennifer, "Bernini and Others," *Sculpture Journal* 3 (1999)

Pascoli, Lione, *Vite de' pittori, scultori, ed architetti moderni*, 2 vols., Rome: de' Rossi, 1730–36; reprint, 1 vol., edited by Valentino Martinelli, Perugia, Italy: Electa Editori Umbri, 1992

Preimesberger, R., "Caffà, Melchiorre," in *The Dictionary of Art*, edited by Jane Turner, vol. 5, New York: Grove, and London: Macmillan, 1996

Sammut, E., "Melchior Caffà, Maltese Sculptor of the Baroque: Further Biographical Notes," *Scientia* 23 (1957)

Sant' Angelo, Antonino, *Il Museo di Palazzo Venezia: Catalogo delle sculture*, edited by Carlo Colombo, Rome: Colombo, 1954

Titi, Filippo, *Studio di pittura, scoltura et architettura*, Rome: Mancini, 1674; reprint, 2 vols., edited by Bruno Contardi and Serena Romano, Florence: Centro Di, 1987

Wittkower, Rudolf, "Melchior Caffà's Bust of Alexander VII," *Metropolitan Museum of Art Bulletin* 17 (1959)

CAFFIÉRI FAMILY   *Italian, French*

It is not surprising that Jules Guiffrey's 1877 monograph on the Caffiéri family reserves for these artists of Neapolitan descent a seminal place in France's artistic canon, alongside sculptors such as François Girardon, Antoine Coysevox, Edme Bouchardon, Jean-Baptiste Pigalle, and Jean-Antoine Houdon. From Philippe Caffiéri's decoration of the palace of Versailles to Jean-Jacques Caffiéri's portrait busts for the foyer of the Comédie-Française, here was a dynasty of furniture designers, master bronze sculptors, and academic artists that left its mark on nearly every aspect of sculptural practice and production in the late 17th and 18th centuries. Moreover, the various paths their individual careers took serve as a unique lens through which to view how official institutions—the Gobelins workshops, the Royal Academy of Fine Arts, and the Direction of Royal Buildings—coalesced to control a newly centralized conception of culture produced under the auspices of France's absolutist regime. The same regime in turn yielded a remarkably diverse (and historically inscribed) set of responses by three generations of Caffiéris to the very centralization on which it was based: first, the triumphal ostentation of the Louis XIV style; second, the studied refinement of Rococo and early Neoclassical sensibilities; and third, the didactic impact and deeply philosophical character of late Enlightenment sculpture.

Philippe Caffiéri 1634–1716

The story of the Caffiéris' influence on French art begins with Philippe Caffiéri, a woodcarver, decorative

sculptor, and master bronze worker. His migration north in 1660 from the papal court in Rome to the Gobelins workshops in Paris was a continuation of a long-standing tradition of artists—initiated by Italian Mannerists making their way after the Sack of Rome in 1527 to Fontainebleau to work at the court of Francis I—who switched allegiances to find new avenues of creative expression through royal as opposed to papal patronage. France's Sun King, Louis XIV, had recruited Philippe through Cardinal Mazarin, whose representatives at the court of Pope Alexander VII in Rome negotiated the young artist's release from the latter's services. What Philippe then encountered at the Gobelins workshops, which came under the direction of the king's *premier peintre* Charles Le Brun in 1664, was the center of production for the decorative arts and furniture design under Louis XIV. The goal was to create, down to the minutest aspect of decor, the illusion of the sovereign's inviolability. In order to accomplish the task, Le Brun called on the talents of Italian artist Domenico de Cucci to establish an environment of collective labor in which cabinetmakers well acquainted with the art of marquetry were joined by a talented assembly of stone carvers, stucco workers, bronze workers, weavers, and gilders.

Philippe thus soon found himself collaborating on projects at the Louvre, the Tuileries Palace, Versailles, Saint-Germain-en-Laye, and Marly, devoting his time to both exterior and interior decorative elements of royal residences (including architectural sculpture, polychrome marble work, and elaborate frames for mirrors and paintings, as well as monumental mantelpieces, staircases, and doors). He contributed to the furnishing of remodeled royal apartments, producing exquisitely worked pieces such as the sumptuously gilt round table whose striking red porphyry top had once belonged to Louis XIV's ill-fated superintendent of finance, Nicolas Fouquet. The ornate support that Philippe designed sets four cherubic caryatids as periphery to a central column adorned by acanthus leaves. He also contributed to the ceremonial setting of public spaces such as Versailles's Hall of Mirrors, where his gilt-bronze pilaster capitals staged an extravagant metamorphosis of the Ionic order's spiraling volutes into French cocks with splayed wings. Such innovative examples of fine craftsmanship manifest the lavish flair of the significant detail in the late Baroque *Gesamtkunstwerk* (total work of art) on which Louis XIV capitalized in order to elaborate a personalized visual mythology of despotism.

Jacques Caffiéri 1678–1755

If Philippe helped to determine the direction the decorative arts took in late 17th-century France, the works of his son Jacques and grandson Philippe bear witness to the eclecticism of 18th-century tastes. Jacques's childhood was necessarily marked by the artisanal world to which his father belonged, and this seems to have sealed his fate to become a master bronze worker. By 1714 he was a highly respected member of the Parisian guild of bronze founders; his status as much as his skill explains why he was chosen to design the pall adorning the coffin of deceased guild members. Archival records document his activities beginning in 1736 at royal palaces such as Versailles, Choisy, and Fontainebleau. He created major pieces such as the chest of drawers on which he collaborated with Antoine-Robert Gaudreaus for the king's new bedroom at Versailles. Other pieces such as the nine- and twelve-light chandeliers in the Wallace Collection in London are among the finest remaining examples of Louis XV gilt bronze. Here, separately cast pieces soldered onto a central iron cage offered Jacques a unique framework for formal inventiveness; the smaller chandelier displays assorted foliage motifs with upturned flower heads for drip pans and leaf sprays bolted onto arms, whereas the larger chandelier juxtaposes C-scroll–shaped plates with kidney-shaped apertures. Purely decorative abstraction of the latter sort gives way to representational passages in objects such as gilt-bronze firedogs, in which lion and boar heads are framed by a scroll paired with a single vase-shaped finial.

Philippe Caffiéri 1714–1774

The versatility of Jacques's son Philippe, detected, for instance, in the intricately choreographed circuit of laurel garlands and urn of the gilt-bronze wall lights in the J. Paul Getty Museum in Los Angeles, has its origins in the decorative conceits to be found in his father's work. Furthermore, the transitional character that Philippe's works exhibit—he seemed equally at home with the precious magnificence of the Louis XV style as with the elegant restraint of a more classicized approach—was likely due as much to his training under and collaboration with his father as to his inheritance of the latter's collection of bronze casts, which he frequently used in imaginative combination with his own designs.

Philippe's career differed from his father's in the way that it registered subtle yet important shifts in patronage that occurred over the course of the 18th century. Particularly in the wake of the Seven Years' War (1756–63), Louis XV's artistic administration under the direction of the Marquis de Marigny found itself increasingly incapable of honoring the financial terms of the decorative commissions it handed out—a fact that had unfortunate implications for the economic stability of the craftsman's milieu to which Philippe be-

Jean-Jacques Caffiéri, *Pierre Corneille*© Giraudon / Art Resource, NY

longed. His solution was to turn to the Catholic Church for more lucrative opportunities. He made in this context an assortment of cult objects—candlesticks, candelabra, and monumental crosses—as altar elements for the cathedrals of Notre Dame (Paris) and Bayeux.

Jean-Jacques Caffiéri 1725–1792

Philippe's artistic identity centered in the artisanal realm, as did that of his forbears. By contrast, his younger brother Jean-Jacques emerged as one of the more successful products of the Royal Academy of Fine Arts by mastering the brand of official high art that it codified and promulgated. His apprenticeship with Jean-Baptiste II Lemoyne (1704–1778) proved to be the key to future success, which began with a victorious bid for the Rome prize in 1748. Jean-Jacques had a brilliant academic career, and the attention he received from art critics such as Denis Diderot attests to a well-deserved reputation for artistic competence punctuated by moments, such as the Salon of 1771, of truly extraordinary success.

While Jean-Jacques's early works exhibit an extreme facility paired with an uncurbed willingness to explore all sculptural genres, he ultimately emerged as a portraitist of first rank, whose particular merit lay in the sensitive translation of male physiognomies. Some contemporaries claimed that he rivaled the great Jean-Antoine Houdon in this genre, and to contemplate seminal works such as his bust of Jean-Philippe Rameau or the statue of Pierre Corneille is to recognize an undoubtedly impressive psychological immediacy. With portraiture as his specialty, Jean-Jacques contributed to what could be construed as Enlightenment sculpture's *raison d'être:* the image of the illustrious man—military hero, political leader, social philosopher, or literary genius—and the exemplary morality that, according to the Encyclopedists, his likeness was meant to inspire in the viewer. Nonetheless, highlighting this aspect of Jean-Jacques's oeuvre runs the risk of devaluing what art historians have seen as a notable stylistic flexibility. The influence of Gianlorenzo Bernini is tangible in the energetically conveyed spiritual ecstasy of stigmatization in the *Saint Francis* group, for example. However, Jean-Jacques could easily exchange the bombastic depiction of passionate states for the severe purity of form discerned in neoantique works such as *Friendship Mourning at the Tomb.* One can thus celebrate his achievement in terms of—but not limit it to— the secular didacticism and rationalist philosophical messages underpinning ambitious portraiture during the Enlightenment.

ERIKA NAGINSKI

See also **Bernini, Gianlorenzo; Bouchardon, Edme; Coysevox, Antoine; Girardon, François; Houdon, Jean-Antoine; Pigalle, Jean-Baptiste**

Philippe Caffiéri

Biography

Born in Rome, Italy, 1634. Served under Pope Alexander VII, until 1660; left for employment at the Gobelins factory, Paris; became French citizen, June 1665, and was granted title of sculptor of royal furniture; married a cousin of painter Charles Le Brun, 1665; collaborated with Mathieu Lespagnandelle on the decoration of the Louvre, Paris, late 1660s and 1670s, then with Antoine Coysevox, Jean-Baptiste Tuby, and others, at Versailles; named master sculptor of the royal fleet, Le Havre, France, 1687, then Dunkirk; resigned position, 14 April 1714, and returned to Paris. Died in Paris, France, 7 September 1716.

Selected Works

1669   Round table; wood, red porphyry, gilded bronze; Musée du Louvre, Paris, France
1670   Portal and peristyle capitals (with Mathieu Lespagnandelle); stone; Musée du Louvre, Paris, France

1674 Ionic capitals for the Escalier des Ambassadeurs; bronze; Château, Versailles, Yvelines, France (destroyed 1750)

1680 Pilaster capitals for the Hall of Mirrors; gilded bronze; Château, Versailles, Yvelines, France

Jacques Caffiéri

Biography

Born in Paris, France, 25 August 1678. He was the son of Philippe Caffiéri. Trained from a young age at the Gobelins workshops; joined the Parisian guild of bronze-founders, by 1714; was involved in the interior decoration of the château of Versailles, from 1736, as well as of royal residences such as Bellevue, Choisy, Compiègne, Fontainebleau, and Marly; joined by his son Philippe Caffiéri as an associate in the family workshop, 1747; later succeeded by him. Died in Paris, France, 23 November 1755.

Selected Works

1739 Chest of drawers (with Antoine-Robert Gaudreaus); oak, kingwood veneer, gilded bronze; Wallace Collection, London, England

1751 Nine-light chandelier; gilded bronze, iron; Wallace Collection, London, England

1751 Twelve-light chandelier; gilded bronze, iron; Wallace Collection, London, England

1752 Pair of firedogs; gilded bronze; Cleveland Museum of Art, Ohio, United States

Philippe Caffiéri

Biography

Born in Paris, France, 19 February 1714. He was the son of Jacques Caffiéri. Trained with father, then collaborated with him, establishing a partnership in 1747; granted title of master founder by the guild of bronze-founders, 1756; gradually stopped relying on royal commissions and sought employment that was more remunerative from ecclesiastical institutions in the 1760s and 1770s; respected member of the Academy of Saint Luke. Died in Paris, France, 8 October 1774.

Selected Works

ca. 1756 Mounts for writing desk; gilded bronze; Musée Condé, Château de Chantilly, France

1760 Chandeliers, candelabra, and monumental cross, for the Cathedral of Notre Dame, Paris; gilded bronze (destroyed during the French Revolution)

1765 Pair of wall lights; gilded bronze; Getty Museum, Los Angeles, California, United States

Jean-Jacques Caffiéri

Biography

Born in Paris, France, 30 April 1725. He was the son of Jacques Caffiéri. Studied with Jean-Baptiste II Lemoyne; won the Prix de Rome at the Académie Royale de Peinture et de Sculpture, Paris, with his bas-relief *Cain Killing Abel*, 1748; studied in Rome from 1749; left Italy, 1753; pursued a distinguished official career; *agréé* (admitted) by the Académie Royale, Paris, 1757, and the marble version of his celebrated *River God* was accepted as a reception piece, 1759; named professor at the Académie Royale, 1773; exhibited regularly at the Paris Salon, 1757–89; benefited from state commissions such as the statues of *Molière* and *Corneille* for Comte d'Angiviller's *Illustrious Frenchmen* sculpture series. Died in Paris, France, 21 June 1792.

Selected Works

1752 *Trinity*; stucco; Church of San Luigi dei Francesi, Rome, Italy

1755 *River God*; terracotta; Fitzwilliam Museum, University of Cambridge, England

1757 *Saint Francis*; plaster; Musée du Louvre, Paris, France

1760 Bust of Jean-Philippe Rameau; terracotta; Musée de Dijon, France

1767 *Friendship Mourning at the Tomb*; plaster; Musée du Louvre, Paris

1771 Bust of Jean-Baptiste Lully; marble (destroyed 1873)

1774–88 Statues of *St. Sylvia*, *St. Satyrus*, and *St. Alipius*; marble (destroyed during the French Revolution)

1777 Bust of Benjamin Franklin; terracotta; Bibliothèque Mazarine, Paris, France

1779 *Pierre Corneille*; marble; Musée du Louvre, Paris, France

1783 Bust of Jean de Rotrou; marble; Comédie-Française, Paris, France

1787 *Molière*; marble; Institut de France, Paris

1788 Bust of the astronomer Pingré; terracotta; Musée du Louvre, Paris, France

Further Reading

Dowley, Francis F., "D'Angiviller's *Grands Hommes* and the Significant Moment," *Art Bulletin* 39 (December 1957)

Eriksen, Svend, *Early Neo-Classicism in France: The Creation of the Louis Seize Style in Architectural Decoration, Furniture and Ormolu, Gold and Silver, and Sèvres Porcelain in the Mid-Eighteenth Century*, translated and edited by Peter Thornton, London: Faber, 1974

Guiffrey, Jules, *Les Caffiéri, sculpteurs et fondeurs ciseleurs: Étude sur la statuaire et sur l'art de bronze en France au XVIIᵉ et XVIIIᵉ siècle*, Paris: Morgand et Fatout, 1877; reprint, Paris: Laget, 1993

Honour, Hugh, *Cabinet Makers and Furniture Designers*, London: Weidenfeld and Nicolson, and New York: Putnam, 1969

Hughes, Peter, "Gilt Bronze by Caffiéri in the Wallace Collection," *Magazine Antiques* 153 (January 1998)

Jervis, Simon, "A River-God by Caffieri: An Eighteenth-Century Terracotta on a Classical Theme," *National Art-Collections Fund Annual Review* (1992)

Jouin, Henri Auguste, *Jean-Jacques Caffiéri: Sculpteur du roi (1725–1792)*, Paris: L'Artiste, 1891

Lavalle, Denis, "Le choeur de Saint Louis des Français" in *Les fondations nationales dans la Rome pontificale*, Rome: Académie de France, École Française de Rome, 1981

Louis XV: Un moment de perfection de l'art français (exhib. cat.), Paris: Hôtel de la Monnaie, 1974

Quarre, Pierre, *Bustes de Caffiéri offerts à l'Académie de Dijon*, Dijon, France: Bernigaud, 1947

Souchal, François, *French Sculptors of the 17th and 18th Centuries: The Reign of Louis XIV*, vols. 1–3, Oxford: Cassirer, 1977–87, and vol. 4, London: Faber and Faber, 1993

Verlet, Pierre, *Le mobilier royal français*, Paris: Éditions d'Art et d'Histoire, 1945; as *French Royal Furniture*, translated by Michael Bullock, New York: Potter, and London: Barrie and Rockliff, 1963

Wilson, Gillian, et al., "Acquisitions Made by the Department of Decorative Arts in 1982," *J. Paul Getty Museum Journal* 2 (1983)

ALEXANDER CALDER 1898–1976 *United States, active in France*

Alexander Calder was born in Philadelphia in 1898 to an artistic family of Scottish descent; his father and grandfather were well-known sculptors, and his mother was a painter. After earning an engineering degree in 1919, he also became interested in art. Nonetheless, his technical training turned out to be essential to his artistic career. The ceaselessly changing equilibria of his "mobiles"—the most original of his inventions—owe much to his study of mechanics and kinetics while attending college.

In 1923 Calder enrolled in the Art Students League in New York. His inclination for continuous-line drawing was already apparent in cartoons he published at the time in a local satirical newspaper. His adroit use of wire in subsequent sculptural works seems to transpose the same thin but resolute line from paper to space.

From 1926 on, Calder divided his time between Europe and the United States. In his first studio in Paris, he created the tiny performers of his *Circus* out of such disparate materials as cloth, string, tin, and wire. Animated with strings and the artist's hands, these wire acrobats, animals, and dancers performed to the delight of the avant-garde artists in Paris at the time, from Jean (Hans) Arp and Fernand Léger to Piet Mondrian and Joan Miro. Together with the *Circus* performers, Calder created a series of small wire figures of artists (*Josephine Baker I*) and animals (*Horse*, 1928; Whitney Museum of American Art, New York). Two sets of bronze and wood sculptures depicting jugglers, swimmers, and animals—such as *Horse* (1928; Museum of Modern Art, New York)—exhibited the stylistic influence of the Spanish-American Modernist José de Creeft (1884–1982).

These were Calder's last figurative works. After visiting Mondrian's studio in the summer of 1930, he turned definitively to abstract art. In 1931 he joined the Abstraction-Création group and exhibited his new abstract sculptures: circular and spherical wire constructions resting on bases that radiated wooden hoops, disks, and spheres. Sensitive as they are to the slightest vibration, these sculptures personify the idea of motion. The next year Calder (still in Paris) showed his first mobile works, some powered by motors or manual devices, others oscillating naturally. *Calderberry Bush*, a sort of metal shrub with odd artificial fruits waving to and fro, was the first of Calder's mobiles and initiated the most successful part of his career. *Cône d'ébène*, his first suspended mobile, consists of three geometric solids attached to steel wires and produces a slow, unstable swinging motion. The term "mobile" was suggested by Marcel Duchamp to define this type of sculpture, where different structures and elements suspended on wires are free to move according to the whim of air motion and chance. The unpredictably changing states of equilibrium create an elegant play of lines and surfaces in space. Calder's mobiles, set in motion by every draft or tiny change in the air, were a totally novel invention in the history of sculpture. Although the Dadaists, the Constructivists, and other avant-garde artists were interested in moving sculpture, only Calder's mobiles were capable of unpreordained motion and interaction with surrounding space.

In the same period, Calder produced another series of interesting works, which began with *Chick-Lett* and that Arp dubbed "stabiles" in ironic contrast with the term "mobiles." These curious assemblages of sheet metal cut into various shapes and bolted together constituted an altogether unusual form of sculpture. Mobiles and stabiles, midway between geometric regions and zoological fantasy, are both emblematic of Calder's creativity. Combining the two techniques, Calder came up with what he called "stabiles-mobiles": stand-

229

ing structures, sometimes majestic, topped by delicate and elegant mobiles, such as *Reims Croix du Sud.*

After buying an old house in Roxbury, Connecticut, Calder could rely on an extraordinary creative space— a real foundry—although he continued to travel to Europe. Using a great variety of materials, he began to make fanciful jewelry—sculptures designed to be worn. These objects, inspired by Native American art, fit in perfectly with his poetic conception and are by no means a minor part of his oeuvre. Indeed, Native American art, with its wealth of simple shapes and brilliant colors, was one of Calder's chief sources of inspiration, as is evident in such works as *Indian Feathers.*

Paris became a significant backdrop for Calder's work. Introduced to Paris by Miró, with whom he had become close friends, Calder was invited to exhibit his works in the Spanish Pavilion at the World's Fair in 1937. For the occasion he invented a truly unique work called *Mercury Fountain*—an iron structure in which a device triggered by liquid mercury moves an ingenious mobile.

In the 1940s Calder was forced to relinquish his usual materials because of the wartime scarcity of aluminum and other metals. Instead, he did a series of *Constellations* and another of *Towers* (structures made up of variously shaped and colored wooden objects interconnected by steel wire), and several plaster sculptures inspired by Surrealism. At the end of the war he returned to mobiles, creating some of his finest masterpieces, such as *Seascape* and *Triple Gong.* By this time he had achieved extraordinary worldwide recognition and was awarded the grand prize for sculpture at the Venice Biennale in 1950. He bought a home at Saché in the French countryside and his sojourns in Europe lengthened.

At the invitation of the Venezuelan architect Carlos Raúl Villanueva, Calder created a suspended ceiling for the great hall of the University of Caracas. The structure is punctuated by colored shapes hanging from metal wires of different lengths, which act as sound absorbers. This was the beginning of Calder's important activity in architecture and urban decor. With *Teodelapio*, a large sculpture executed with the help of industrial workers, Calder's stabiles reached monumental proportions. His sheet-steel giants fit unaggressively into the urban fabric and become an integral part of the local landscape. Calder's huge stabiles, executed at metal plants under the artist's close supervision, have been disseminated in cities around the world.

After a long and fortunate career, Alexander Calder died in New York City in 1976. Closely related to the avant-garde and its kinetic experiments—and to Alexander Rodchenko's Constructivism and Mondrian's Neo-Plasticism—and influenced by Miró's colors and Arp's organic forms, Calder was one of many American artists deeply involved in European experimentation. He was a leading player on the Parisian scene, to which he brought the wealth of his own roots. Through Calder, American representational art—especially the lively primitivism of Native American art— merged with the most advanced positions of European art, engendering a new, joyous, and suggestive form of sculpture.

Lucia Cardone

See also **Arp, Jean (Hans); Constructivism; Duchamp, Marcel; Gabo, Naum; Miró, Jean; Pevsner, Antoine; Tinguely, Jean**

Biography

Born in Philadelphia, Pennsylvania, United States, 22 July 1898. Father and grandfather well-known sculptors; mother a painter. Earned degree in mechanical engineering, 1919; enrolled at Art Students League, New York, 1923; moved continually between United States and Europe, from 1926; in Paris, met and kept company with European avant-garde artists Joan Miró, Jean (Hans) Arp, Antoine Pevsner, Jean Cocteau, Theo Van Doesburg, Le Corbusier, Fernand Léger, and Piet Mondrian; became friendly with Marcel Duchamp, Alberto Magnelli, Francis Picabia, and American art historian James Johnson Sweeney; joined avant-garde group Abstraction-Création, 1931; starting in the 1930s, created "mobiles" and "stabiles"; received Grand Prize for Sculpture at 25th Venice Biennale, 1950; began to create monumental sculptures for cities around the world, 1960s. Died in New York City, United States, 11 November 1976.

Selected Works

1926   *Josephine Baker I*; wire; Musée Nationale d'Art Moderne, Centre Georges Pompidou, Paris, France

1926–32 *Circus*; wood, wire; Whitney Museum of American Art, New York City, United States

1928   *Horse*; wood; Museum of Modern Art, New York City, United States

1928   *Horse*; wire; Whitney Museum of American Art, New York City, United States

1932   *Calderberry Bush*; metal, wood, wire; Whitney Museum of American Art, New York City, United States

1933   *Cône d'ébène*; ebony, metal, wire; Knoedler Gallery, New York City, United States

1934   *Chick-Lett*; sheet metal; Walker Art Center, Minneapolis, Minnesota, United States

1937   *Mercury Fountain*; iron, mercury; Miró
        Foundation, Barcelona, Spain
1939   *Lobster Trap and Fish Tail*; sheet metal,
        wire, paint; Museum of Modern Art, New
        York City, United States
1943   *Constellation with Mobile*; steel wire,
        wood; Leo and Nora Lionni Collection,
        New York City, United States
1943   *Tower*; steel wire, wood; Jan Krugier
        Gallery, Geneva, Switzerland
1947   *Seascape*; wood, metal, string;
        Guggenheim Museum of Art, New York
        City, United States
1951   *Triple Gong*; aluminum, brass, steel, wire;
        Metropolitan Museum of Art, New York
        City, United States
1962   *Teodelapio*; steel; Spoleto, Italy
1969   *Indian Feathers*; Whitney Museum of
        American Art, New York City, United
        States
1970   *Reims Croix du Sud*; sheet steel; École
        National des Impôts, Paris, France

Further Reading

Baal-Teshuva, Jacob, *Calder, 1898–1976*, Cologne, Germany,
    and London: Taschen, 1998
Burnham, Jack, *Beyond Modern Sculpture: The Effects of Sci-
    ence and Technology on the Sculpture of This Century*, New
    York: Braziller, and London: Allen Lane, 1968
Calder, Alexander, "What Abstract Art Means to Me," *Museum
    of Modern Art Bulletin* 28/3 (1951)
Calder, Alexander, *Calder: An Autobiography with Pictures*,
    New York: Pantheon, 1966
Carandente, Giovanni, *Calder: Mobiles and Stabiles*, London:
    Collins, and New York: New American Library, 1968
Marcadé, Jean-Claude, *Calder*, Paris: Flammarion, 1996
Marchesseau, Daniel, *The Intimate World of Alexander Calder*,
    Paris: Thierry, and New York: Abrams, 1989
Marter, Joan, *Alexander Calder*, Cambridge and New York:
    Cambridge University Press, 1991
Prather, Marla, *Alexander Calder: 1898–1976*, Washington,
    D.C.: National Gallery of Art, and New Haven, Connecticut:
    Yale University Press, 1998
Sartre, Jean Paul, *Les mobiles de Calder*, Paris: Carré, 1946
Wilmerding, John, *American Art*, London, and New York: Pen-
    guin, 1976

LOBSTER TRAP AND FISH TAIL
Alexander Calder (1898–1976)
1939
sheet metal, wire, paint
h. 2.6 m; w. 2.9 m
Museum of Modern Art, New York City, United States

Alexander Calder's *Lobster Trap and Fish Tail* is a
typical example of the mobile sculptures that the artist

created consistently throughout his career. The conceptual artist Marcel Duchamp in 1932 dubbed these
flat, brightly colored shapes, suspended from the ceiling with wires and rods and that move with the aid of
motors or currents of air, "mobiles." Although other
artists, such as the Italian Futurists, Russian Constructivists, and Naum Gabo, with his kinetic sculpture, had
already experimented with dynamism, Calder's mobiles transformed the changing relations of form in
space, creating new effects through material, color, and
outdoor scale. Through his sculptures, one could observe the dynamism and unity of three-dimensional
objects and open forms in space.

Calder's initial forays with mobiles, such as *Gold-
fish Bowl* (1929) and *Black Frame* (1934), began with
observations of natural forms and movements, which
he distilled into basic geometric elements. His early
interest in cosmic themes eventually gave way to organic shapes and images derived from plant and animal
life. Made of painted metal, Calder's characteristic material, *Lobster Trap and Fish Tail* comprises a series
of bent wires of unequal length that are liberally connected together with curvilinear plates. The delicate

Lobster Trap and Fish Tail, 1939, hanging mobile, painted
steel wire and sheet aluminum, about *h.* 2.6 m; *w.* 2.9 m,
Museum of Modern Art, New York. Commissioned by the
Advisory Committee for the stairwell of the Museum
© The Museum of Modern Art, New York

231

elements hanging from the wires at the extremities of the sculpture recall the shapes of bones, feathers, leaves, or tails. In this case, the metal loses its typically industrial associations, evoking a poetry found in nature. The shadow play of the moving work and the rhythmic pattern of the colored panes, which revolve above the staircase at the Museum of Modern Art in New York City, create a sense of unpredictability and an awareness of movement and life.

Originally trained as an engineer, Calder used his knowledge of kinetics and mechanics to construct and develop his mobiles. Among other inspirations were his close friendships with the artists Piet Mondrian and Joan Miró. From his association with Mondrian, Calder learned to introduce primary color into his sculptures and to experiment with movement and form. His friendship with Miró deeply affected the Surrealist sense of fantasy and the natural flow of forms that appeared in Calder's sculpture throughout his career. Although he did not adopt the doctrines of Surrealism—which accentuated the role of dreams, the imagination, and the unconscious in creation—Calder's organic and whimsical vocabulary shares certain affinities with the Surrealists.

LUCIA CARDONE

Further Reading

Gibson, Michael, *Calder*, London: Art Data, Paris: Hazan, and New York: Universe Books, 1988

Guerrero, Pedro E., *Calder at Home: The Joyous Environment of Alexander Calder*, New York: Stewart Tabori and Chang, 1998

Zafran, Eric M., Elizabeth Mankin Kornhauser, and Cynthia E. Roman, *Calder in Connecticut*, New York: Wadsworth Atheneum Museum of Art, and London: Troika, 2000

CAMBIO, ARNOLFO DI

See **Arnolfo di Cambio**

CAMBODIA

The artistic culture of Cambodia, remarkable for its ancient architectural and sculptural monuments, is one of the most brilliant pages in the history of Southeast Asian civilization. Like the other states in this expansive region, Cambodia was caught up in the general process of "Hinduization"—the assimilation and reworking of Indian cultural influences—that swept the area at the beginning of the first millennium CE. Information on the first states existing in this territory comes mostly from Chinese written sources. Another important source of information is epigraphy, inscriptions cut into stone in ancient Khmer and Sanskrit. Sanskrit was brought to Cambodia from India by means of the sea trade, which also brought India's great religions, classical literature, and elements of social organization.

The history of ancient Cambodia can be divided into two major periods. The pre-Angkor period started in the beginning of the Common Era and extended to the end of the 8th century. The Angkor period can be further divided into the following stages: 9th to 10th century, consolidation of land under a single central royal power; 11th to the beginning of the 13th century, a period of flourishing empire and expansion of borders to include nearly the entire Indo-Chinese peninsula; 13th century to 1431, a period that saw the gradual weakening of centralized power and economic might in the country and which ended with the desertion of the capital and its transfer to the southeast.

According to Chinese sources, two government bodies existed in the territory of contemporary Cambodia until the beginning of the 7th century. The first, Funan, was connected with the sea trade and occupied the southern regions of contemporary Vietnam, including the Mekong Delta, the lower basin of the Menam (Chao Phraya), and the south of contemporary Cambodia. The second, Chenla, was located in the interior of the Indo-Chinese peninsula and included northern Cambodia, a piece of Laos, and a piece of the Khorat Plateau (in northeastern Thailand). Information about these kingdoms is so scarce that even their names are unknown, entering history only by means of Chinese transcriptions. Only in the 1940s, after the excavations of the French archaeologist Louis Malleret in the Mekong Delta, did it become clear that Funan had conducted large-scale maritime trade. Digs in the major port city of Oc Eo produced not only objects of Chinese and Indian origin but also Roman and Parthian coins and Roman applied arts. These objects speak of Funan's ties to the Hellenistic states of Asia and to the Mediterranean basin.

In the middle of the 6th century, Funan began to decline, slowly becoming subordinate to its neighbor and rival, Chenla. Chenla absorbed Funan at the beginning of the 8th century. The founding of Iśānapuri, the capital of Chenla, in the first half of the 8th century signaled the appearance of the first fixed artistic style of ancient Cambodia, the style of Phnom Da. The earliest inscriptions in stone also date from about the 8th century. A subsequent period of fragmentation and civil strife, as well as subordination of part of Funan to governments in Java and Sumatra, continued until the beginning of the 9th century.

In 802 Jayavarman II, having united the various separate princedoms under his power, announced the creation of an independent state. From that moment, the Angkor period proper began in the history of Cam-

Lokeśvara Bodhisattva, *ca.* 1181–13th century
© Luca I. Tettoni / CORBIS

bodia. In the center of the territory, which had become the cradle of Khmer culture and government, on Mount Kulen, Jayavarman II established the cult of *devarāja*, "the king-god." The king was considered the incarnation of divinity and, after death, fused with it. Ceremonial dedications were conducted under the supervision of the supreme Brahman priest. From that time, the role of Brahmans in the Khmer court remained extremely important. In art the concept of *devarāja* found embodiment in the linga, a symbol of the creative energy of Śiva, the emblem of fertility and prosperity. The linga was located in temples devoted to Śiva, and it is primarily these temples that have been preserved. The concept of *devarāja* provided the Khmer monarchy with the powerful religio-ideological

basis needed for the kingdom's foundation over the course of nearly 500 years.

The kingdom's economic foundations were laid later, however, during the reign of one of Jayavarman II's earliest successors. Indravarman I began intensive irrigation of the numerous fertile valleys in the Angkor region. This transformed them into rich granaries of rice, the basic product of the Khmer. During this period, the first examples of types of religious architecture that in the future would be developed brilliantly began to appear: enormous water reservoirs; sanctuary towers built of brick; and five-tiered temple pyramids, "mountains," which were the symbol of the cosmic Mount Meru, believed to be the center of the universe.

The first Angkor (a distortion of *nokor*, from the Sanskrit *nagara*, meaning city or walled fortress) was built by Yaśovarman I, who gave the new capital his own name, Yaśodharapura, "abode of glory." The capital of the empire was known by this very name until the 13th century. In the center of the city, on the natural hill Phnom Bakheng, an enormous five-tiered temple-mountain was erected during the reign of Yaśovarman I and dedicated to the cult of the royal lingam.

The capital was briefly transferred from Angkor under the successor to Yaśovarman I, but all Khmer kings after him, beginning with Rajendravarman II, kept the Angkor region as the center of political and religious rule. The 11th and 12th centuries were a period of the greatest flourishing and might of the Angkor empire. Its boundaries spread wide to include, along with its own lands, significant portions of what is now Laos, Thailand, and Vietnam. The country's economic power permitted the erection of more and more temple-mountains, the construction of roads, and the installation of elaborate reservoirs. Construction was especially intensive in the area of Angkor, for which the entire state and culture were named. Here, on a comparatively small parcel of land (13 by 18 kilometers), can be found an enormous number of architectural monuments from antiquity. This area holds a complex web of city-temples interconnected by roads, reservoirs, bridges, and canals. Each city was a precisely planned ensemble. The successive king-builders were primarily Hindu, but among them one finds adherents of Mahāyāna Buddhism. This fact is not reflected in the principles of construction or ornamentation of religious architecture, however.

Around the 11th century, Khmer architecture achieved developmental perfection. The classical structural types had already taken shape. Concentric walls enclosed a tall, tiered pyramid surrounded by covered galleries around the perimeter. Five towers rose on the expansive upper terrace of the pyramid, four on the sides and a central sanctuary accessible from each side by a wide staircase. The walls of all structures were richly ornamented with reliefs and decorative carvings. Three-dimensional sculpture representing different personages of the Hindu and, more rarely, Buddhist pantheon adorned the stairwells and flanked approaches to the city walls and bridges. The sanctuary towers were decorated with statues of the gods to whom those structures were devoted. The following are among the most remarkable ensembles of the time: the colossal Baphuon (mid 11th century), raised on an artificial earthen mound, and the world-renowned Angkor Wat, built during the reign of king and Viṣṇu follower Sūryavarman II (1113–ca. 1150). He was one of the mightiest of Cambodia's kings and significantly expanded the state's boundaries.

After the death of Sūryavarman II, the country experienced a series of military conflicts. In 1177, after the invasion by neighboring longtime enemy Champa, the country found itself on the verge of catastrophe. The last great ruler of the empire, Jayavarman VII, drove out the Cham and restored the might of the country, expanding its borders to previously unseen limits. Jayavarman VII, unlike almost all of his predecessors, was a Buddhist of the Mahāyāna school. He established the cult of *buddharāja*, the royal apotheosis, in which the king was equated with the absolute. *Buddharāja* became the state cult of his rule and for a time pushed out the cult of *devarāja*. The bodhisattva (saints who help people on the path to liberation) of compassion and mercy, Avalokiteśvara, or, in its Khmer form, bodhisattva Lokeśvara, was the central personage in art of the late 12th and early 13th centuries. Under Jayavarman VII, a vast number of structures were raised, transforming the face of the country. The change occurred because many hospitals, court inns, and other buildings were erected along with temples. More important, the fundamental architectural element in all structures became a tower bearing four faces of the bodhisattva Lokeśvara, each looking at one of the four cardinal points. These bodhisattvas were given the portrait features of Jayavarman VII. The most concentrated version of this style occurred in the last Angkor ensemble, Angkor Thom, Jayavarman VII's majestic 900-square-hectare capital. The Bayon, the central temple, is decorated with 52 towers, each with four faces of Lokeśvara.

The 13th century proved pivotal for Cambodian history. The fever for construction that had gripped the country under Jayavarman VII undermined the economy. The water resources and soil of the capital region were exhausted. Breaching of irrigation systems in the area caused agriculture to decline. A short-lived Hindu reaction following the death of Jayavarman VII was unable to counter the ever more powerful spread of Buddhism among the population. Moreover, Theravada Buddhism, with its more democratic tendencies, rejection (at least in principle) of luxurious construction, and other principles more accessible to the peasantry was making inroads. One after another, the outlying domains, once unified, fell away. And although the 13th-century Chinese ambassador Chou Ta Kuan still spoke ecstatically of the land of the Khmer and could find no particular traces of destruction after recent wars, the country was gradually weakened and the central region fell into decline.

The fall of the empire continued until about the mid 15th century, when, in 1431, Angkor was captured and pillaged by Thai warriors. The ruling dynasty abandoned the capital and relocated in the south. The new capital, Phnom Penh, was founded where the Mekong, Tonle Sap, and Bassak Rivers converge and stands there to this day.

The transfer of the political and cultural center of the state to a new location provoked a gradual desertion of the old cultural hearths. This abandonment was accelerated by the tropical climate and lush vegetation of the region. The French naturalist Henri Mouhot, who penetrated the jungles to "the dead city" in 1861, left the first enthusiastic description of the sights of Angkor. Following the establishment of a French protectorate in 1863, scholars began a gradual study of the monuments, which were discovered one after another. The development of aviation made aerial surveys of the Angkor region possible in the 1920s. This revealed all of Angkor's squares and the precise location of all of the monuments. The French École Française de l'Extrême Orient began a decades-long clearing and restoration of architectural monuments using the method of *anastilos*, in which a monument is cleaned, disassembled, and then reassembled. In 1927 the French archaeologist and art historian Philippe Stern proposed the first chronology of Angkor architecture based on analysis of its most important architectural components and details of decor (see Stern, 1927). His work was continued by Gilberte de Coral-Rémusat and Jean Boisselier (see Coral-Rémusat, 1940; Boisselier, 1955). The styles of Khmer sculpture are named for the temples for which each particular statue or relief was created.

The art of the ancient Khmer was sacred and reflected the religious ideas of two great Indian religions, Hinduism and Buddhism. As the evidence of the epigraphy demonstrates, both religions were widespread in Funan by the 4th or 5th century.

Hinduism considers the entire apparent world to be a manifestation of Highest Absolute, the world spirit without qualities, which is personified in Trimurti, the triad of divinities. These are Brahmā, creator of the world; Śiva, the world's destroyer; and Viṣṇu, the preserver and defender. The cult of Brahmā receded very early even in India, so Hinduism involves two main tendencies, Śivaism and Viṣnuism, each with its own theology, mythology, and rituals. In ancient Cambodia, Śivaism played a significantly greater role, although Viṣnuism had its own staunch devotees.

Hinduism possesses an extensive pantheon of personages, each with its own defined physical features, individual attributes, and animal mount (*vāhana*). The multiple limbs of divinities are one of the characteristic elements of the iconography. This element is connected with the conception of the possibility for increasing the divinity's power. In Cambodia the iconography of Hindu personages had a series of specific characteristics.

For Saivas, Śiva is not only destroyer but also creator and preserver of the created world. He is usually represented with one head and two arms, although five-headed, ten-armed images do occur. Śiva has a third, vertical eye in his forehead. His hair, put up in a high, complexly piled hairstyle called a *jatāmukuta*, is usually decorated with the crescent moon. His characteristic attributes are a fly whip and rosary. Śiva is often portrayed symbolically as a linga, a stylized phallus symbolizing his creative energy.

The female aspect of the higher divinities' creative energy, the Śakti, is often personified as the wife of a divinity. Śiva's Śakti, depending on her hypostasis as merciful or threatening, preserving or destroying, is represented either as a typical human face (Umā, Pārvati) or as an armed, multilimbed goddess (Kali, Durgā). The sons of Śiva and Pārvati are the elephant-headed Ganesa, god of wisdom and knowledge, and the six-armed Skanda, god of war.

Viṣnu, the defender and savior, is usually represented with four arms but only one head. His attributes are a baton, a conch shell, the wheel-shaped *cakra* and a globe that symbolizes the earth (the globe replaced the Indian lotus). He usually sleeps reclined on the Serpent of Eternity in the Ocean of Tranquility. However, when the world is threatened with periodic catastrophes, he takes on one or another form and descends to earth. Having performed glorious deeds, he again sinks into sleep. These earthly incarnations of Viṣnu are called *avatārās*. Of these the most significant are Rāma, hero of the epic poem *Rāmāyana*, and the shepherd Krsna, who performed a multitude of glorious deeds.

Of the different divinities, Sūrya the sun god and Indra, master of thunder and the heavens, are the most frequently represented. Śiva's *vāhana* is Nandi the bull, Viṣnu's is Garuda the eagle, Indra's is Airavata the elephant, Skanda's is a peacock, and Sūrya's is the chariot.

In Cambodia the cult of Harihara was widely disseminated, much more so than in India. Harihara is a combined representation of Viṣnu (Hari) and Śiva (Hara), with the characteristic traits of both. Besides these images, the middle- and lower-level personages were very popular. Innumerable nameless deities (*deva*), nature spirits (*yakṣa*), demons (*asura*), celestial dancers (*apsara*), and other creatures played an enormous role in the decor of architectural monuments.

Buddhism, in the figure of the Buddha and his teachings, brought to the world the doctrine of liberation from rebirth. Very early Buddhism distinguished two major tendencies: Hinayāna, "the Small Vehicle," later known as Theravāda, "the School of the Elders"; and Mahāyāna, "the Great Vehicle." Theravāda is widespread today in Sri Lanka and Indochina, whereas Mahāyāna is practiced in Nepal, Tibet, China, Japan, and Korea. The canonical literature of Theravāda is written in Pāli; that of Mahāyāna is in Sanskrit. Theravāda is devoted to the propositions of early Buddhism, which established the individual efforts of a given person as the condition for liberation. At the center of its dogmatics is the figure of the Buddha Shakyamuni himself. Mahāyāna places special emphasis on magical and ritual practice, on the role of the bodhisattvas, and Dhyanī-Buddhas (transcendental Buddhas). Therefore, its pantheon is extensive and complex. In Cambodia in the 1st century CE, both Hinduism and Hinayāna Buddhism were known. The establishment of *devarāja* elevated Śivaism to prominence and relegated Buddhism to the shadows. Viṣnuism always retained a significant position and achieved its heyday during the reign of Sūryavarman II, the builder of Angkor Wat. Mahāyāna Buddhism, appearing in Cambodia only in the 7th century, was twice the state religion of the ancient Khmer under Sūryavarman I and Jayavarman VII, when it experienced a short but extraordinarily brilliant triumph. Following the stormy Sivaite reaction of the mid 13th century, the Pāli Theravāda began to be disseminated. This event is connected with the general penetration of this form of Buddhist teachings into many Indo-Chinese countries as a result of their contact with Sri Lanka during the 13th century.

In Buddhist iconography, the Buddha is represented either in monastic garb or with adornments, including a crown or diadem (Crowned Buddha). One of the most popular episodes in the Buddha's life for Cambodian art shows him seated in meditation atop the glittering coils of Mucalinda, king of the Nagas. The king and his family protect the Buddha with their hooded heads.

Among the Mahāyāna personages, the most popular in Cambodia was Lokeśvara, the bodhisattva of compassion, and his female hypostases Prajñāpāramitā, "perfection of wisdom," and Tārā, "savior." Externally, only the presence of the figure of a seated, meditating Buddha in the deity's headress distinguishes these images from Hindu deities. Lokeśvara is often portrayed with four arms; his attributes are a bowl of water, a book, a rosary, and a lotus bud.

Despite the unity of architecture and sculpture in the art of ancient Cambodia, on the whole sculpture played an undoubtedly lesser role in comparison with architecture. But in different periods this correlation changed slightly. In early, pre-Angkor art, it is sculpture, and not architecture, that proves more interesting and abundant. Freestanding stone sculpture appeared comparatively late, at the very end of Funan's existence, and no earlier than the mid 6th century. Before that time, sculpture was made primarily of wood. The statue of the eight-armed Viṣṇu is an example of the earliest style of Phnom Da (first half of 7th century). The frontal and hieratic placement of the figure emphasizes the power of the supreme deity. Although the cylindrical miter and the method of piling the braids of hair speaks of its Indian sources, the short garb around the thighs, with its fanlike stylized pleats, betrays local provenance. On the whole, one does not sense a connection with Indian prototypes in the piece already. An arch supporting the hands and attributes (an especially fragile part of the sculpture) is one of the most characteristic aspects of all early Khmer sculpture until the early 9th century.

Early Buddhist sculpture, to a greater degree than Hindu sculpture, reveals its ties to Indian art of the Gupta and post-Gupta periods (4th to mid 7th century). Nevertheless, even these works are quite original. Although the arms of the standing Buddha at Wat Romlok (6th to 7th century) have been broken off, they most likely gave the gesture of mercy. This gesture, as well as the form of the *ushnisha* (a protuberance on the top of the head) and the large curls of hair, recall the Indian tradition. However, the character of the Buddha's monastic garb, as well as the entire placement of his figure, testifies to a divergence from that tradition.

The most significant monuments of early artwork are the representations of Harihara, a deity uniting within himself the essence of Viṣṇu and Śiva. Thus the remarkable statue of Harihara from the National Museum, Phnom Penh (Prasat Andet style, 7th to 8th century) is easily identified despite the lack of arms and attributes, for the right side of his headdress is a chignon, the sign of Śiva, whereas the left side shows Viṣṇu's miter. By the same token, the forehead displays half of Śiva's third, vertical eye. The anatomic precision is irreproachable. The superior modeling of the well-proportioned, light figure with its rounded hips completes the perfect image of the deity. Slight alterations in his costume are evident. The end of the drapery, arrayed in folds, is tucked at the belly inside, forming a so-called pocket-fold. A thin metal chain (a precursor to a future belt) lies across the hips. The hair

on the lower part of the head is adorned with a narrow metal headband, which would soon become a diadem, the favorite type of ornamentation in a later period.

The 9th century was one of the great epochs in Khmer sculpture. The Phnom Kulen style (marking the reign of Jayavarman II) signified a transition from the old forms to a new aesthetic canon. This canon retained much in common with the sculpture of previous times—such is the Viṣṇu from a sanctuary at Prasat Thma Dap (first half of the 9th century). Although the modeling still preserves its superior qualities, the massive, rather heavy head, mustaches, and single, uninterrupted line of the brow are far from previous aesthetic ideals. This is the final instance in the history of ancient sculpture when the head of a deity is decorated with a miter. From this point one encounters only diadems or crowns. Continuing the evolutional line in costume already taking shape in the Prasat Andet style, the "pocket-fold" began to occupy the place on the belly where it would on future works. For the first time, folds appear on the *sampot* (men's apparel worn on the hips), as well as on women's clothing. From this point, the arch supporting the arms and attributes disappears, and figures stand alone. Although Jayavarman II was a Sivaite, only representations of Viṣṇu are known from this period. Śiva apparently was portrayed chiefly in the form of the linga.

One of the most hieratic styles in Khmer art is that of Preah Ko, with its slightly stout, heavy figures. In the second quarter of the 10th century (Koh Ker style), the iconography became more varied, and a previously unseen effort toward gigantism made itself known (for example, the colossal statue of Śiva from the temple at Prasat Thom, Jayavarman IV's state temple). The art of this brief period shows different, and at times opposing, tendencies. Hieratic stiffness and monumentality stand beside works executed with unusual power and dynamism, the likes of which will not be seen in later years (*Wrestlers*, 10th century CE).

In the art of the second half of the 10th century, one must note the Banteai Srei style, which offers its own kind of pivotal moment in the history of ancient Khmer sculpture. Two aesthetic tendencies are combined in this style. The old, traditional tendencies appear in cult images (the image of Viṣṇu or that of the seated Śiva and Umā, called Umāmaheśvara). The other, innovative tendency is reflected in narrative reliefs and architectural decor. Masterfully executed figures of characters from the *Rāmayāna* and *Mahābhārata* are full of vivacity, softness, and charm (*Scenes from the* Mahābhārata [pediment from Banteai Srei]; Musée National des Arts Asiatique-Guimet, Paris, France). The rich, endlessly varied vegetal decor, spreading freely over the walls, transformed the hard rock into delicate lace. Of the two tendencies, this second exerted strong influence on the Khmer art of the 12th and 13th centuries.

The art of the 10th century concluded with the Khleang style (last quarter of the 10th century), which foreshadowed the rise of developed classical art during the first half of the following century. Toward the end of the 10th century, modeling became more plastic. Facial expressions softened, although they retained the previous strict frontal posture. The lower part of the body became heavier. Male figures acquired great mass in response to the necessity of giving the sculpture stability following the disappearance of the supporting arch (*Śiva*, late 10th or early 11th century CE).

The Baphuon style encompasses nearly the entire 11th century. It began with the prolonged reign of Sūryavarman I; achieved maturity under Udayādityavarman II, who built the temple for which the style is named; and extended to the reign of Harṣavarman III. Naturally, such a vast stretch of time cannot but provoke a certain evolution within the style itself. Above all, this evolution appears in the sculptural reflection of alterations in courtly fashion—types of ornament and means of wearing clothes. Regarding aesthetic and plastic characteristics, these changed little.

The Baphuon style possesses a series of clear, distinguishing features. Although the figures themselves decreased in size, their proportions were extended. The bodies became more delicate and well proportioned. This change applied to both male and especially female images. Faces were illuminated by barely noticeable smiles and became more youthful. The eyes were often encrusted with stones. The contours of eyes, lips, mustaches, and beards were emphasized with engraved lines. Both male and female dress was often layered with tiny folds and held by a belt with pendants. The contour of the clothing fell sharply downward in a semicircle from the hips or waist, leaving bare the belly and navel and emphasizing the harmony of the figure (*Female Divinity*, 11th century CE). The narrow waist contrasted with the broad shoulders.

At this time, the first representations of the Buddha so characteristic of later art began to appear. These works involved the Buddha in meditation, seated on the glittering coils of the serpent Naga (*Buddha Protected by the Naga*, 11th century CE). The presence of the Naga can be explained not only by the importance of this episode in the life of the Buddha, but also by the important role of snakes in Khmer beliefs.

Bas-reliefs of this style are distinguished by their generous vegetal decor, done in rather high relief. Narrative scenes of plots from the *Rāmāyana* were accurately and vividly done, while at the same time showing touching naïveté (*Lintel: Scenes from Krishna's Life, ca.* mid 11th century CE).

This same period is notable for the creation of one of the most grandiose sculptures of ancient Cambodia, the *Viṣnu Anantaśāyin*, or *Viṣnu Reclining on the Serpent Ananta*. This work was no less than six meters long, given that the preserved fragment of the head and upper torso measures more than two meters. Cast in bronze, this piece speaks to the high level of mastery achieved by the ancient craftsmen. The sculpture was cast in parts. Apparently there was a removable diadem (not preserved) on the head. The eyes, brows, and beard were ornamented with precious stones, as can be seen from the empty settings. This statue was found in 1936 at the bottom of an enormous reservoir on the western Mebon. This reservoir was excavated under King Udayadityavarman II in the mid 11th century and was probably meant to symbolize the Ocean of Tranquility, the waters on which Viṣnu sleeps his cosmic sleep. The luxury and wealth of ornament on this sculpture anticipated one of the typical traits of art in the first half of the 12th century.

With Sūryavarman II's rise to power and the founding of the temple at Angkor Wat, classical architecture reached its developmental apogee, whereas freestanding sculpture seems to have regressed to the aesthetic canons of the past. Frontal posture and hieratic poses returned, as did the simplicity in treatment of the volumes. The animated, lively faces were replaced by dry, faceless expressions. This archaizing tendency was combined with great thoroughness in the treatment of the stone surface, jewelry, and decorative details of costume. Thus are the innumerable representations of the four-armed Viṣnu wearing a conical *mukuta* and diadem (*Viṣnu*, 12th century CE). More interesting and various in iconography are the Buddhist images of the time: the Buddha was presented standing (*Crowned Buddha*, 12th century CE), or seated on a serpent, or the frequently met crowned Buddha (*Crowned Buddha Protected by the Naga*, 12th century CE). Buddhist sculpture was significantly more often cast in bronze than was Hindu sculpture. These statues are distinguished for their comparatively small size, the high quality of the casting, and the delicate work on the tiniest details.

The rule of Jayavarman VII brought with it new and radical changes. The new religious ideals of Mahāyāna Buddhism, of which the king was a devout follower, had repercussions not only in the iconography of sculpture (now almost exclusively Buddhist), but also in aesthetic ideals. The modeling was simplified, far from perfect, and proportionality was often violated. Craftsmen, it seems, were interested only in the personage's facial expression and hand gestures. Stressing the idea of compassion, the sculpture and reliefs of this time emanated a certain mysterious inner light. They were deeply contemplative, worldly, and human. Their faces were lit by a hardly perceptible, soft smile, which has won them world fame.

Lokeśvara, the bodhisattva of compassion and mercy, is the most common personage in this period's art, known as the Bayon style. The towers of this temple were decorated with his faces to symbolize the power of the new teaching as it spread to all four cardinal faiths. In statuary, he was often represented with four arms, his simple attire deprived of all ornament. Gone are the tiny folds that most leap to the eye in feminine clothing. Stone statues were often composed of component parts joined together with the help of original T-shaped stone tangs. This was a purely architectural method of fastening individual parts in Khmer structures. Its transfer to sculpture was brought about by the lack of solid stone block of great size (*Lokeśvara*, late 12th to early 13th century CE).

In 1191, as an inscription on the temple at Preakh Khan makes clear, Jayavarman VII issued a decree requiring the distribution of 23 representations of Jayabuddhamahānātha, "Buddha, sovereign of victory," to all ends of his vast empire. According to the latest research, these may be identified with a large group of representations (more than a dozen), which were named "Radiating Lokesvara" or "Radiating Avalokiteśvara" by Louis Finot (*Lokeśvara [Jayabuddhamahānātha]*, late 12th century CE). The torso and hair of these four- or eight-armed Lokeśvaras are completely covered with a multitude of minute images of the Buddha. These minute images create the impression that the statue is covered with a shirt of mail or net. By the same means, these bodhisattvas seem to radiate from the pores of their bodies these innumerable emanations of divine substance for the people's salvation. Such sculptural embodiment of the macrocosmic aspect of Avalokiteśvara was created only during the reign of Jayavarman VII.

The art of Jayavarman VII's rule is distinct for yet another trait, which was completely uncharacteristic of ancient Khmer art in general. This was the aspiration to portraiture in sculpture. The members of the royal family were presented in the form of personified Buddhist or Hindu characters, with appropriate physical and personal characteristics. Such is the sculpture of Lakṣmī, portraying, in all likelihood, the king's first wife, who died young. Another example is the statue of Tārā in the form of a baby (a princess by birth? the daughter of Jayavarman? *Tārā*, late 12th or early 13th century CE). And finally, there are the two remarkable statues of seated men with such expressive, individual, portraitlike features (hairstyle, facial features, treatment of the body and legs) that they are unanimously considered (along with several similar heads) "portraits" of King Jayavarman VII himself (*Jayavarman VII*, late 12th or early 13th century CE). These faces

look out on the world from the towers at the temple of Bayon, reflecting the religious conception of *buddharāja* and speaking of Jayavarman VII's aspiration to identify himself with the Buddha.

Very little is known about the art of the 13th century after Jayavarman VII. The gradual replacement of Hinduism and Mahāyāna Buddhism with Hinayāna Buddhism was hastened thanks to increasingly powerful influences from the western and northwestern provinces of the empire (modern Thailand). Various schools and styles of pre-Thai (the Khmerized school of Lop Buri) and Thai art (the school of U Tong, the art of the Sukhothai, and the early Ayutthaya styles) exerted influence over Khmer art from the 13th to the mid 15th century. This influence is most apparent in the treatment of facial features, braids in the hair, and ornamentation. But on the whole, Khmer Buddhist art after Bayon and Thai art from the mid 13th to the mid 15th century developed rather independently of one another. However, Thai art of the U Tong A and B, as well as the Ayutthaya style up until the 16th century, shows definite Khmer influences. In Khmer art itself, a new type of Buddha portraiture was established, one decked in the ideals of Theravāda Buddhism. The portraits are more dry, undifferentiated, and at times even monotone (*Standing Buddha*, 14th century CE). A small number of Hindu images from this period also survive.

OLGA DESHPANDE

Further Reading

Boisselier, Jean, *La statuaire khmère et son évolution*, 2 vols., Saigon: École Française de l'Extrême Orient, 1955

Coral-Rémusat, Gilberte de, *L'art khmer: Les grandes étapes de son évolution*, Paris: Les Éditions d'Art et d'Histoire, 1940; 2nd edition, 1951

Giteau, Madeleine, *Histoire du Cambodge*, Paris: Didier, 1957

Giteau, Madeleine, *Khmer Sculpture and the Angkor Civilization*, New York: Abrams, 1965

Jessup, Helen Ibbitson, and Thierry Zephir (editors), *Sculpture of Angkor and Ancient Cambodia: Millennium of Glory*, Washington, D.C.: National Gallery of Art, 1997

Stern, Philippe, *Le Bayon d'Angkor et l'évolution de l'art khmer*, Paris: Geuthner, 1927

CAMEO

See **Engraved Gems (Intaglios and Cameos)**

GIROLAMO CAMPAGNA 1549–1621
Italian

Girolamo Campagna was trained by Danese Cattaneo, Jacopo Sansovino's favorite pupil, and was fortunate enough at the start of his career to inherit all his master's models and drawings, which included those that Cattaneo had inherited from Sansovino. Campagna may therefore be regarded as Sansovino's spiritual heir, and his early work is clearly indebted to the Tuscan. For example, Campagna's relief *St. Anthony Raising the Youth in Lisbon* shares stylistic affinities with Sansovino's *Miracle of the Maiden Carilla* (commissioned 1536; installed 1563) in the same cycle. Campagna had fought stiff competition from Francesco Segala and Antonio Gallini to win the commission to complete this relief, which Cattaneo had started just before he died, and he used it as a reception piece to show off his abilities, signing it prominently.

Campagna went to similar pains in his first independent work in Venice, the small pathos-filled relief of the *Dead Christ Supported by Two Angels*, changing the composition significantly between the preliminary sketch (private collection) and the final work to make Christ's idealized body more slumped and the angels' expressions more imploring. Eclectic in its sources, it reveals the influence of not only Cattaneo but also of antique sculpture, with Christ's body recalling that of the *Laocoön* in anatomy and pose. The relief also betrays Campagna's debt to contemporary Venetian painting, above all to the work of Paolo Veronese, although his later sculptures are more indebted to paintings by Jacopo Tintoretto and Jacopo Palma il Giovane.

Campagna's efforts paid off; in 1578 he was awarded the prestigious state commission to carve a colossal statue of *Santa Giustina* for the Arsenal in Venice, which recalls Michelangelo's *Rachel* (1542–45) in her *contrapposto* (a natural pose with the weight of one leg, the shoulder, and hips counterbalancing one another). Moreover, the following year Campagna beat Francesco Segala, Francesco Franco, and Alessandro Vittoria to win the extremely important commission to redesign the high altar of the Santo in Padua.

Campagna's forte lay in the field of religious statuary, for which there was huge demand in Counter Reformation Venice, and this accounts for the majority of his output. His secure grasp of anatomy, combined with his skill in portraying credible emotion and expressive gestures, allowed him to create weighty, monumental figures capable of inspiring religious devotion. He did occasionally fashion portrait busts and statues of mythological subjects, but these were generally commissioned from his more versatile rival Alessandro Vittoria, being areas in which the older sculptor excelled. Most of Campagna's works are life-size and in marble, but works such as his intimate *Dead Christ Supported by Two Angels* and the colossal *Gigante* prove that he was capable of carving on all scales. In addition to being a proficient carver, he was also a superb modeler. Although he made comparatively few

works in stucco—for example, the Annunciation group (Church of S. Sebastiano, Venice; 1582)—he produced numerous models in wax, which were cast into bronze by professionals. These too range in size from small statuettes, such as the *St. Agnes* and *St. Anthony of Padua* (Church of S. Maria dei Frari, Venice), to the monumental, such as the *St. Anthony Abbot*.

By the early 1580s Campagna had established himself as second only to Vittoria, and indeed preferable when it came to large-scale religious sculpture. This is clearly shown by the fact that in 1582 it was he, rather than Vittoria, who was commissioned by Marc'Antonio Barbaro to carve six *Virtues* for the funerary monument of Doge Nicolò da Ponte (whereas Vittoria modeled only the doge's portrait bust). A run of high-profile state commissions followed, and Barbaro may have been influential in obtaining these for Campagna. In addition to three female statues for the Sala delle Quattro Porte, Doge's Palace, Venice, *War*, *Peace*, and *Minerva* (1585–86), he carved a pair of nude *Telamones* (ca. 1587) for a chimneypiece in the Sala dell'Anticollegio, which display his skill in portraying the male nude, and (with his brother's help) seven statues of antique deities for the crowning balustrade of the Marciana Library, Venice. He also carved a colossus—known as the *Gigante*—for the entrance of the Mint (now the entrance of the Marciana Library) in direct competition with Tiziano Aspetti, a younger sculptor from Padua, who had been commissioned to carve an equally gargantuan companion. Had Aspetti lived longer, he may well have proved quite a threat to Campagna, but he spent much of his brief career in Tuscany, and died prematurely in Pisa, in 1606.

Campagna's *Gigante* was carved in between his two most important sculptural complexes, the high altars of the churches of Il Redentore and S. Giorgio Maggiore, both in Venice. The presence of monumental bronze figures in Venetian altarpieces was rare, and Campagna seems to have been keen to rival the precedents, namely the figures in the Zen Chapel (St. Mark's Basilica) by Antonio Lombardo and Paolo Savin (1504–21) and those of the *Virgin* and *St. John the Evangelist* by Vittoria for the Scuola di S. Fantin (ca. 1582–83). The altarpiece at the church of Il Redentore, which Campagna later described as "famosissimo," combines beauty with pathos, the sensuous *Crucified Christ* recalling that by Donatello in the Santo in Padua. The S. Giorgio altar complex is no less compelling in its authority, and both works served to reinforce Campagna's preeminent position.

Many significant commissions resulted, such as the *Virgin and Child with Angels* group (Church of S. Giorgio Maggiore, Venice; ca. 1595–96), which created a new compositional type that was adopted by younger sculptors such as Nicolò Roccatagliata. Campagna was also involved in tombs for three doges, Pasquale Cicogna, Marino Grimani, and Leonardo Loredan; in each, the deceased is differently presented. Although the semirecumbent pose of Cicogna, which derived from mid 16th-century tombs by Andrea Palladio, did not prove influential, perhaps because it was insufficiently dignified, the seated position of Loredan (probably from a design by Cattaneo) did and introduced a new iconographic type into the Venetian tomb. In 1604 Campagna was commissioned by the Duke of Urbino, Francesco Maria II della Rovere, to carve a statue of *Federico da Montefeltro*. This was his only work that was poorly received, and to counter negative criticism, Campagna wrote the Duke an apologia, extolling his own abilities by recounting his previous achievements. After this commission, Campagna produced several more works in bronze, including his proto-Baroque *St. Anthony Abbot* and the statuettes *St. Agnes* and *St. Anthony of Padua* (ca.1610). His last major commissions, the high altars of the Scuola Grande di S. Rocco and the Church of S. Lorenzo, were in marble, and although more restrained, they still exhibit technical accomplishment.

VICTORIA AVERY

See also **Aspetti, Tiziano; Sansovino, Jacopo; Vittoria, Alessandro**

Biography

Born in Verona, Italy, between 11 January and 26 March 1549. Brother Giuseppe a sculptor with whom he occasionally collaborated. Apprenticed to Danese Cattaneo, probably when older master in Verona executing Fregoso Monument in S. Anastasia, 1562–65; had graduated to master-mason status by 1571 and was living and working with former teacher in Venice; followed Cattaneo to Padua, 1572, and assisted with relief of *St. Anthony Raising the Youth in Lisbon*; inherited all Cattaneo's models, plaster casts, and drawings upon his death in 1572; went briefly to Augsburg, Germany, May 1574, to restore antiquities for Hans Fugger; returned to Padua, July 1574, and completed Cattaneo's Santo relief; returned to Venice, ca. 1577, where he established himself as Alessandro Vittoria's chief rival; by the early 1590s, superseded elderly Vittoria as most important sculptor active in Venice and the Veneto and, although temporarily threatened by younger sculptor Tiziano Aspetti from Padua, retained this preeminence until death. Died in Venice, Italy, 27 October 1621.

Selected Works

1574–77 *St. Anthony Raising the Youth in Lisbon*;
marble; Tomb chapel of St. Anthony, Basilica of S. Antonio (Il Santo), Padua, Italy

1577–78 *Dead Christ Supported by Two Angels*; marble; Chapel of the Most Holy Sacrament, Church of S. Giuliano, Venice, Italy

1578 *Santa Giustina*; marble; Arsenal, Venice, Italy

1579–84 High altar for Basilica of S. Antonio, Padua, Italy (destroyed 1895): reliefs of prophets and angels; marble; statuettes of the Evangelists and Church Fathers; bronze; Museo Antoniano, Basilica of S. Antonio, Padua, Italy

ca. Six *Virtues*, for funerary monument of
1582–83 doge Nicolò da Ponte; marble (lost)

1588–91 *Mars, Venus, Jupiter, Juno, Pomona, Pluto,* and (lost) *Prometheus*; marble; Marciana Library, Venice, Italy

1589–90 *Crucified Christ, St. Mark,* and *St. Francis*; bronze; Church of Il Redentore, Venice, Italy

1590–91 *Gigante*; marble; Marciana Library, Venice, Italy

1592– Altarpiece of the *Holy Trinity and*
93/94 *Evangelists*; bronze, gilded copper; Church of S. Giorgio Maggiore, Venice, Italy

1600–04 Funerary monument of doge Pasquale Cicogna; marble; Church of S. Maria Assunta (Il Gesuiti), Venice, Italy

1604–06 *Federico da Montefeltro*; marble; Palazzo Ducale, Urbino, Italy

1605 *St. Anthony Abbot*; bronze; Altar of Goldsmiths' Guild (Scuola degli Orefici), Church of S. Giacomo di Rialto, Venice, Italy

ca. 1605 Seated effigy for funerary monument of doge Leonardo Loredan; marble; Church of SS. Giovanni e Paolo, Venice, Italy

1607–14 Statues of saints and prophets (*St. Sebastian* completed before 3 April 1613; *St. Roch* and *St. John the Baptist*, before 18 August 1614); marble; Scuola Grande di S. Rocco, Venice, Italy

1615–17 *St. Lawrence* and *St. Sebastian*; marble; Church of S. Lorenzo, Venice, Italy

Further Reading

Bacchi, Andrea, "Girolamo Campagna," in *"La bellissima maniera": Alessandro Vittoria e la scultura veneta del Cinquecento* (exhib. cat.), edited by Bacchi, Lia Camerlengo, and Manfred Leithe-Jasper, Trent, Italy: Castello del Buonconsiglio, Monumenti e Collezioni Provinciali, 1999

Boucher, Bruce, *The Sculpture of Jacopo Sansovino*, 2 vols., New Haven, Connecticut: Yale University Press, 1991

Boucher, Bruce, "La scultura nell'età del Sansovino," in *Storia di Venezia—Temi: L'arte*, edited by Rodolfo Pallucchini, vol. 1, Rome: Istituto della Enciclopedia Italiana, 1994

Boucher, Bruce, "Campagna, Girolamo," in *The Dictionary of Art*, edited by Jane Turner, vol. 5, New York: Grove, and London: Macmillan, 1996

Frosien-Leinz, H., "Campagna, Girolamo (Gerolamo)," in *Allgemeines Künstlerlexikon: Die bildenden Künstler aller Zeiten und Völker*, vol. 15, Munich: Saur, 1997

Martin, Susanne, *Venezianische Bildhaueraltäre und ihre Auftraggeber, 1530–1620*, Marburg, Germany: Tectum Verlag, 1998

Rossi, Paola, *Girolamo Campagna*, Verona, Italy: Vita Veronese, 1968

Timofiewitsch, Wladimir, *Girolamo Campagna: Studien zur venezianischen Plastik um das Jahr 1600*, Munich: Fink, 1972

Timofiewitsch, Wladimir, "Campagna, Girolamo," in *Dizionario Biografico degli Italiani*, vol. 17, Rome: Istituto della Enciclopedia italiana, 1974

ALTARPIECE OF THE *HOLY TRINITY AND EVANGELISTS*

Girolamo Campagna (1549–1621)

1591 (design), 1592–93/94 (execution), 1595 (erection)

bronze (figures), gilded copper (globe), and marble (socle)

h. (whole group) ca. 3.5 m; diameter (globe) ca. 1.2 m; God the Father, h. ca. 1.4 m; St. Mark, h. ca. 1.4 m; St. John, h. ca. 1.3 m; St. Luke, h. ca. 1.3 m; St. Matthew, h. ca. 1.3 m; angel of Matthew, h. ca. 0.6 m; dove, h. ca. 0.4 m

Church of S. Giorgio Maggiore, Venice, Italy

Campagna's highly unusual bronze group, the *Holy Trinity and Evangelists*, for the high altar of S. Giorgio Maggiore, was arguably the most important sculptural commission of late 16th-century Venice. Its innovative form and iconography resulted from its novel function as both an altarpiece and a grandiose sacramental tabernacle, as well as its novel location, on a freestanding altar situated between the nave and the choir and thus equally visible to both congregation and clerics. Four vigorous, life-size *Evangelists* (identified by their symbols) half kneel on a substantial socle and support on their shoulders and necks a great globe on which stands a triumphant, life-size *God the Father*—the First Person of the Trinity—with a dove symbolizing the Holy Spirit—the Third Person of the Trinity—affixed below. Originally, Christ was not portrayed in sculptural form but had a more mystical presence, in the form of the reserved Blessed Sacrament kept in a tabernacle inserted into the middle of the marble socle. It must have been decided, however, that Christ, as the Second Person of the Trinity, needed greater visibility in order to clarify the Trinitarian subject—unusual for a high altar—because a bronze crucifix was added in the early 17th century. This crucifix was replaced by a larger one in the 18th century. The pair of flanking life-size bronze angels are also later additions, modeled by Sebastian Nicolini in 1636 and cast by Pietro Bosello in 1644, apparently to replace a pair in gilt wood made in 1597.

The unprecedented altarpiece-cum-tabernacle was the result of collaboration, as the contract of 20 January 1592 reveals. In return for 1,650 ducats, Campagna, together with his brother Giuseppe and the bronze founder Francesco Mazzoleni, agreed to execute the five bronze figures "as per the drawing which has been given them by the Reverend Father," the abbot, Michele Alabardi. This proves that Campagna was not responsible for the design. According to Carlo Ridolfi, writing shortly after the event, the work was conceived by his teacher, the painter Antonio Vassilacchi, called Aliense, at the specific request of the Benedictine fathers, who were uncertain about the numerous, rather conventional designs, composed solely of "columns and the usual sort of ornaments," submitted to them for their high altar. Considering that Aliense was one of the signatories of the 1592 contract, it is likely that it was he who produced the drawing that Campagna and his colleagues were obliged to follow. However, two drawings by different hands (one in the Art Gallery of Ontario, Toronto, the other in the Staatliche Graphische Sammlung, Munich), appear to contradict Ridolfi's assertion that Aliense was responsible for the actual invention. Both are clearly projects for the commission, because both portray a kneeling *St. John* and *St. Mark* who support a globe on which *God the Father* stands, and both include a prominent tabernacle, although differently located in each case. Because neither folio relates convincingly to known drawings by either Aliense or Campagna, they are probably entries presented by two unsuccessful contestants. If so, their identical iconography and formal correspondence indicate that the design of the group was firmly established before the competition and that the artists were obliged to follow strict precepts in their designs, which allowed for limited creativity. This would mean that it was Abbot Alabardi, rather than Aliense, who invented the novel design. The source may have been a woodcut in Achille Bocchi's *Symbolicarum quaestionum* (Bologna, 1555), in which Socrates is shown supporting a globe on his shoulders with the Trinity above.

Certainly, the sheer complexity of the altar's iconography argues in favor of a theologian, rather than

Altarpiece of the *Holy Trinity and Evangelists*, S. Giorgio
Maggiore, Venice
The Conway Library, Courtauld Institute of Art

an artist, as the designer. The reverent yet rather obscure and mysterious manner in which the Sacrament is presented, for example, speaks of a Benedictine mind and stands in contrast to the much bolder presentation at the nearby Capuchin church of Il Redentore, where a life-size *Crucified Christ* dominates the high altar and is adored by life-size figures of *St. Mark* and *St. Francis*—all three bronze statues by Campagna. Moreover, the *Evangelists* do not conform to the traditional physiognomic types but are unusually characterized so as to each represent a different humor: *St. John* represents melancholy, *St. Mark* choler, *St. Luke* sanguine, and *St. Matthew* phlegm. The difference in movement between the pair that faces the nave and the pair that faces the choir also seems deliberate: *St. John* and *St. Mark* (seen by the lay community) strain to support the globe and could thus personify the active Christian life, whereas *St. Matthew* and *St. Luke* (seen by the monks) struggle less visibly and are calmer, perhaps personifying the contemplative Christian life. The two pillars of the Benedictine rule are meditation and study, and it seems that the thoughtful *Luke* represents the former and studious *Matthew* the latter. After all, *Matthew* not only kneels on one gospel book (like his companions); he also self-consciously holds a second, whose cover is proudly signed "Opvs Hieronimi. Campaneae Veronensis" (The Work of Girolamo Campagna of Verona). Thus, the altar speaks of the Benedictine mission—that is, to spread the Catholic

faith worldwide through the divinely inspired gospel texts.

The choice of Campagna to execute the design was no doubt a direct result of the fame accruing from the monumental bronze Crucifixion tableau that he had recently executed for the high altar of the nearby Redentore church. The even greater challenge of the S. Giorgio commission, with its multiple viewpoints, spurred Campagna to produce a masterpiece of compelling authority, which reinforced his position as the preeminent sculptor of the city. In their powerful torsion, the heroic *Evangelists* of the altarpiece recall Michelangelo's *Slaves* (*ca.* 1519).

The 1592 contract obliged Campagna to finish the statues by Easter 1593 or forfeit 100 ducats of the total sum agreed of 1,650 ducats. According to Emmanuele Cicogna, Campagna received 1,550 ducats in 1593, which means that the statues must have been consigned late, that is, at some point after Easter 1593 and before 28 February 1594 (the last day of the year according to the Venetian calendar). However, because the copper globe still had to be made (commissioned from Bartolomeo Salvioni on 6 June 1594) and the altar built (commissioned from Bortolo di Domenico, *proto*, or foreman, of the project, on 25 June 1594), the figures were not installed until spring 1595. They evidently met with Alabardi's approval, because in August 1595 he commissioned Campagna to carve a marble group of the *Virgin and Child with Angels* for another altar in the same church.

VICTORIA AVERY

Further Reading

Cicogna, Emmanuele Antonio, *Delle iscrizioni veneziane*, vol. 4, Venice, 1834

Cooper, Tracy Elizabeth, "The History and Decoration of the Church of San Giorgio Maggiore in Venice," Ph.D. diss., Princeton University, 1990

McTavish, David, "A Drawing by Girolamo Campagna for the High Altar of San Giorgio Maggiore," *Arte Veneta* 34 (1980)

Pope-Hennessy, John, *An Introduction to Italian Sculpture*, 3 vols., London: Phaidon, 1963; 4th edition, 1996; see especially vol. 3, *Italian High Renaissance and Baroque Sculpture*

Ridolfi, Carlo, *Le maraviglie dell'arte*, Venice, 1648; edited by Detlev Freiherrn von Hadeln, 2 vols., Berlin: Grote, 1914–24

Zorzi, Giangiorgio, *Le chiese e i ponti di Andrea Palladio*, Venice: Pozza, 1967

CANADA

A diversity of cultures and traditions marks the history of Canadian sculpture. Indigenous peoples in the precontact period produced modeled and carved artifacts (e.g., Iroquoian clay and stone effigy pipes [900–1600

CE]) and masks, as well as Dorset culture ivory harpoon heads (1st–5th century CE) that are both functional objects and sculpture. The Northwest Coast communities encountered by Captain Cook had a long tradition of carving masks, housefronts, and totem poles from the monumental Douglas fir, a tradition that saw a revival in the 1960s and 1970s.

Euro-Canadian sculpture began in 17th-century Quebec City, the center of French imperial influence in the New World that united church and state in a cultural and religious enterprise focused on religious sculpture and church architecture. In the years following 1659 (the date of arrival of François de Laval, who was instrumental in strengthening the Catholic Church in New France), imported paintings, sculpture, and sacred vessels adorned even the smallest parish churches. The arrival of the Jesuits in New France in 1666 stimulated construction of new churches and more elaborate ornamentation of chapels and church interiors. European-trained sculptors, such as Jacquiès dit Leblond de Latour, came to the colony and quickly adapted Old World designs to suit local materials. Artists gilded and polychromed tabernacles, pulpits, and other essential church furnishings carved and built from wood to simulate the richness of French metal and stone. Sculptors such as Latour established an apprenticeship system modeled on the guild system to train apprentices such as Noël Levasseur and his cousin Pierre-Noël Levasseur, who went on to establish one of the leading sculptural dynasties in New France. Pierre-Noel Levasseur, the principal sculptor for the Levasseur workshop, designed their first major commission, the altar screen for the Ursuline Chapel in Quebec City (1730–37), one of the key sculptural achievements in New France. The Levasseurs dominated sculptural production in both religious and secular spheres well into the late 18th century. The Ursuline nuns collaborated with their workshop on religious commissions for over a hundred years (1671–1799). Mother Saint Ursula, Mother Saint Monica, and Sister Marie-Joseph Hallé, a niece of Noël Levasseur, gained renown at home and abroad for their carving and gilding of statues, ornamental designs, chandeliers, and sacred vessels.

Louis-Aimable Quévillon introduced a new collective and standardized model of sculptural production. Based on a well-structured hierarchical system of apprentices and journeyman, his workshop undertook numerous contracts over a broad geographical area. One of the best preserved of the Quevillon workshop productions is the Church of St. Mathias, a small parish church near Chambly, Quebec.

The reconstruction of Quebec City after the British conquest in 1759 provided the conditions for the establishment of a second dynastic sculptural workshop started by the architect Jean Baillairgé. His son, François Baillairgé, the first Canadian-born sculptor to be trained in France, incorporated traditional academic practices such as drawing and watercolor designs and life-size maquettes sketched from live models. The complex interplay of figure and architecture transforms his sculptural production beyond mere craftsmanship. The culmination of his style occurs in the interior decoration of the Church of Saint-Joachim (begun 1816) in Saint-Joachim de Montmorency, a collaboration with his son Thomas. By 1832 control of the workshop had been handed over to Thomas's former students, collectively known as the Thomas Baillairgé School, allowing him to focus on his architectural and sculptural design projects.

The introduction of industrial techniques of plaster casting by immigrant Italian craftsmen made the large woodcarving workshops obsolete. Carvers such as Jean-Baptiste Côté and Louis Jobin carried on individual woodcarving practices.

On the Atlantic coast, sculptural production focused on gravestones with either imported slate from New England or local sandstone as the preferred material.

Jacobine Jones, *Electricity,* detail from *The Trades of Canada,* facade of the Bank of Canada, Ottawa. Commissioned by the Government of Canada for the Canadian Pavilion, New York World's Fair, 1939
Photo courtesy Jacobine Jones Papers, Queen's University Archives

The practice of the Seaman family of Horton and Cumberland, including Abraham Seaman, son of a New York Loyalist, and brothers Thomas Lewis Seaman and Abraham Seaman, is exemplary. The iconography of Nova Scotian gravestones shares affinities with New England designs such as winged angel and death heads. Full three-dimensional figures are rarely found; exceptions include James King's carving of Margaret Sutherland (*ca.* 1893) in Pictou County and the Margaret Webster white-stone memorial (1864, carver unknown) in Yarmouth County.

Throughout the early 19th century, English and French artisans produced ornamental shields, coats of arms, and over 10,000 figureheads for British Navy vessels. After 1850 woodcarving continued as folk and popular tourist art that even today remains a key signifier of maritime and Quebecois cultural identities.

The turn of the 20th century saw an interest in civic and commemorative memorials, with particular attention paid to specific individuals who had forged the early political and cultural life of Canada. Public sculpture became an essential component in the establishment of civic, national, and local identities across the nation. As more Canadian-born sculptors gained professional training abroad, the focus on imported expertise lessened.

In Quebec City, Edward Taché, the architect responsible for the new parliament buildings, commissioned Louis-Philippe Hébert to produce a series of bronze statues celebrating national heroes. Hébert produced more than 50 monuments, including the Maisonneuve and King Edward VII monuments (Montreal), the South African war memorial (Calgary), the Queen Victoria monument (Hamilton), statues of *Queen Victoria, Sir George Cartier*, and *Sir John A. MacDonald* (Ottawa), and numerous smaller bronzes that often featured Aboriginal and Acadian subjects. His successor, Parisian-trained Alfred Laliberté, continued the practice of producing bronze statuettes of rural genre subjects, as well as monumental public art commissions commemorating national heroes (e.g., *Dollard des Ormeaux*, 1920; Montreal), political figures (e.g., tomb of Sir Wilfred Laurier, 1919; Ottawa), and historical subjects (e.g., La fermière [The Farmer's Wife], 1914; Fountain, Maisonneuve).

In 1918, during World War I, the Canadian government commissioned nine bronze statuettes celebrating the home front and Canadian munitions workers from the American-born sculptors Frances Loring and Florence Wyle. Two years later a special government committee established the Canadian War Memorials Commission to direct the erection of memorials in France and Belgium, with sculptors to be selected by juried competition. The largest and most significant of these was the Vimy memorial, designed by Walter Allward.

Allward had completed his first important commission, the Northwest Rebellion monument in Toronto, when only 19 years old. Influenced by the styles of Auguste Rodin and Augustus Saint-Gaudens, Allward won acclaim for his dramatic renditions in a modern Classical style of historical individuals and events such as the South African War memorial (Toronto), the Baldwin and Lafontaine memorial (Ottawa), the Alexander Graham Bell memorial (Brantford), and the William Lyon Mackenzie memorial (Toronto).

Allward's most significant work, the Vimy memorial, was located in France. Towering above the Douai Plain, the memorial was original in concept and heroic in scale, with a base measuring approximately 69 meters in length and dual pylons rising 38 meters high. Contemporaries acknowledged Allward's fusion of Classical symbolism and modern Expressionist concepts, epitomized in the sorrowful figure of *Canada Bereft* overlooking a laurel-crowned sarcophagus, as one of the major commemorative designs of its time.

The federal government erected four national memorials, two in Ottawa and one each in Halifax and Victoria. In smaller communities memorials could be as simple as a cairn of stones or decorated archways. Emanuel Hahn's designs for a solitary soldier in mourning or in action (e.g., *Going over the Top*) had widespread appeal and can be found across Canada in bronze and stone renditions. Women sculptors proved more than equal to the task of producing war memorials. Elizabeth Wyn Wood's innovative design for the Welland-Crowland War memorial uses a dynamic wedge-shaped base to support the symbolic figures of *Man the Defender* and *Woman the Giver*. Florence Wyle's memorial to English nurse Edith Cavell (Toronto) and the *Nurses Memorial* (Ottawa) recognize women's contribution to the war effort. During the same period, Wyn Wood's series of small novel island sculptures either carved in stone (*Passing Rain*) or cast in metal (*Reef and Rainbow*) experimented with Modernist form.

The formation of the Sculptors Society of Canada (SSC) in 1928 marked a defining moment in the development of Canadian sculpture. With the goal of promoting closer cooperation between Canadian sculptors and encouraging, improving, and cultivating the art of sculpture, the six charter members worked to engage a wider audience. They advised on public art projects, organized the first large-scale national exhibitions of sculpture and smaller traveling shows across Canada, presented lectures and workshops, and made use of the national radio network to broadcast a lecture series on great sculpture (1939), which was delivered by Frances Loring. SSC members held the most important teaching positions in art schools across Canada.

Although the Great Depression and the war years produced many hardships, including rationing of materials, collaborative projects with architects and town planners provided opportunities for a number of sculptors, such as the 1935 project to beautify the Niagara Parkways in Ontario and the construction of the Rainbow Bridge (1938). In Toronto and Vancouver, public building projects also employed artists. Painter-designer Charles Comfort designed a carved frieze for the new Toronto Stock Exchange; Emanuel Hahn won competitions for the *Sir Adam Beck* monument (Toronto) and Canadian coinage designs for the silver dollar (1935) and quarter (1937); Jacobine Jones took on her first national commission, *The Trades of Canada*, on the facade of the Bank of Canada (Ottawa); Loring and Wyle designed the impressive entrance to the new Queen Elizabeth Highway; and Wyn Wood worked on public memorials such as her monumental plaster figure *Linda* to honor western pioneer women. In British Columbia Beatrice Lennie produced a number of sculptural reliefs (e.g., Shaughnessy Hospital, Vancouver), including those for the lobby of the Hotel Vancouver. Recently arrived Italian Charles Marega designed and carved the sculptural program for the library extension to the British Columbia provincial parliament buildings, as well as the popular lions guarding the Lion's Gate Bridge.

In the postwar years, architectural sculpture became increasingly popular as a way of enhancing corporate headquarters. One of the largest projects, the Bank of Montreal headquarters in Toronto, engaged a team of six sculptors to design and carve Classical and Canadian subjects for the bank's exterior and interior. At the same time sculptors tried to develop a broader clientele. In 1946 the SSC, with support from the T. Eaton Company Fine Art Galleries, mounted a unique exhibition, *Sculpture in the Home*, displaying affordable, small sculptures designed for domestic spaces. Despite its critical success, the exhibition did not result in many sales.

By the late 1940s many Canadian sculptors and sculpture went international. Sibyl Kennedy moved to New York to study with Russian sculptor Alexander Archipenko; Jacobine Jones and others sought out Swedish sculptor Carl Milles at the Cranbook Academy of Art (Bloomfield Hills, Michigan) and Ivan Meštrovic, who was then teaching in upper New York State. Wyn Wood's participation in the first General Assembly of the United Nations Educational, Scientific, and Cultural Organization in Paris (UNESCO)(1946) led to exhibitions of Canadian sculpture touring Europe. The establishment of the Canada Council for the Arts in 1957 provided opportunities for sculptors to travel to Europe and resulted in more diverse approaches to sculptural form that could also be seen in exhibitions of work by leading European sculptors in public galleries in Toronto, Montreal, and Vancouver.

By the late 1940s some, such as E.B. Cox began to experiment with organic abstraction. However, the majority of Canadian sculptors continued to produce figurative work, albeit with a Modernist accent, a move particularly evident in Quebec, where Les Automatistes attracted younger sculptors such as Charles Daudelin, Louis Archambault, John Ivor Smith, William McElcheran, and Anne Kahane who sought to transform the conservative sculptural legacy into a more contemporary form. Kahane's honorable mention in the 1953 International Sculpture Competition for the *Monument to the Unknown Political Prisoner* projected a new image of Canadian sculpture both at home and abroad. Five years later the Canadian Ministry of Transport commissioned Kahane and several other artists as part of the first public art program of its kind in North America. Louis Archambault, a younger and more radical sculptor, gained international exposure and acclaim by showing at the International Sculpture Exhibition at Battersea Park, London, alongside well-known international sculptors, and collaborating on a critically acclaimed sculpture wall for the Canadian Pavilion (Brussels's World's Fair, 1958). Support for exhibitions and travel through the Canada Council for the Arts, formed in 1957, gave the public at home opportunities to see work and encouraged sculptors. The staging of large-scale outdoor sculpture exhibitions such as that held in Montreal (Ile de Ste. Hélène, 1956) also did much to increase public awareness of Canadian sculptors.

In the Canadian Arctic, artist James Houston encouraged Inuit to carve small sculptures as a way to generate a cash income. The establishment of Inuit art cooperatives in Cape Dorset and other locations across the north beginning in the late 1950s introduced a new direction in Canadian sculpture. For many foreign tourists, Inuit carvings became the quintessential Canadian sculpture.

By the 1960s and 1970s, an adventurous generation of Canadian sculptors emerged eager to explore new materials and new sculptural practices. Summer workshops at Emma Lake, Saskatchewan, with Barnett Newman and Anthony Caro, introduced Canadian sculptors such as Robert Murray and Douglas Bentham (Caro's workshop assistant) to the high Modernist, self-referential Minimalist aesthetic so prevalent in the United States and United Kingdom. A seminal figure in Canadian Minimalist sculpture, Murray went on to create inventive colored steel pieces that gained national notoriety and international acclaim. Others such as Roland Poulin and André Fauteux extended this aesthetic using steel and wood, while twin brothers David and Royden Rabinovitch exploited the weight and mass of rolled steel. Michael Snow reintroduced figurative content in silhouettes for the *Walking Woman* series that incorporated references to popular as well as high culture. Walter Redinger's exploration of isolated organic fiberglass body forms introduced an erotic undercurrent into the dominant Minimalist aesthetic. Joyce Wieland's innovative use of materials (quilts, embroideries, gardens, and cake making) traditionally associated with women's work predated her American contemporary Judy Chicago.

The federal government's One Percent Program (1964) promoted the commissioning or buying of works of art to embellish public-access government buildings. This program not only provided contemporary sculptors with much-needed opportunities but also sought to engage a broader public in discussions about contemporary sculptural practice. The results were often mixed, with citizens and politicians requesting removal of controversial works such as Robert Murray's painted steel abstractions (e.g., *Tundra, for Barnett Newman*, Ottawa) and Gathie Falk's ceramic murals (e.g., *Veneration of the White and Blue Collar Workers*, Ottawa). In 1964 art dealer Dorothy Cameron collaborated with galleries in Toronto to present a large outdoor exhibition entitled *Canadian Sculpture Today*; it was followed three years later by *Sculpture 67*, marking Canada's centennial year. In the 1970s public sculpture projects for the Toronto subway, corporate headquarters, and government buildings spawned many successful and innovative projects, such as Michael Hayden's sound and light sculpture *Arc-en-Ciel* in Toronto, and established the foundation for public art programs that flourish today in Vancouver, Toronto, and Ottawa.

Like their counterparts in the United States and United Kingdom, some Canadian sculptors began to work directly with the landscape, using natural materials that decomposed with time. Marlene Creates traveled to Baffin Island and other remote areas in Canada, gathering stones and photographing her projects, Bill Vazan incorporated performance into his stone environmental works, and Liz Magor used found natural objects in new works that addressed issues of history and processes of the natural world.

Individual and regional responses to materials and subject matter became more pronounced in the late 1970s and 1980s. West coast sculptors more than others in Canada engaged in a wide range of styles, including Pop Art, Minimalism, Earthworks, and Performance Art. Their work was equally individualistic, ranging from the poetic transformation of everyday objects in Gathie Falk's ceramic sculpture to the social satire and conceptual conundrums of the N.E. Thing Company (Iain and Ingrid Baxter). At the same time,

Montreal sculptors and art activists, including Melvin Charney and Françoise Sullivan, mounted a temporary and contested outdoor collaborative project, *Corridart* (1976), which addressed collective social and cultural impact of the tension between heritage architecture and modern urban development.

In the decades that followed, sculptors such as Mowry Baden, George Trakis, and Roland Brener designed site-specific experiential sculptures that focused on relationships between body, space, and sculpture. For Kim Adams, Robin Collyer, Murray Favro, and Gerry Pethick, issues of technology, urban living, and vernacular culture provided the impetus for imaginative constructions. The elegant, high Modernist installations created by Jocelyn Alloucherie, winner of the first Governor General's Award for Visual Arts, integrate elements of theatricality, desire, and memory.

For many contemporary Canadian sculptors the human body remains a central theme, with sculptors incorporating body casting in plaster and polyester resin. The results are diverse, encompassing Evan Penny's pairing of Classical with contemporary nudes, Mark Prent's fantastic creatures, Joe Fafard's miniature vernacular ceramic portraits of local and national personalities, Colette Whiten's preoccupation with plaster molds showing the absence rather than presence of the body (e.g., *September*, 1975), Jana Sterbak's questioning of contemporary issues surrounding the body, fashion, and technology (e.g., *Vanitas: Flesh Dress for an Albino Anorectic* and *Remote Control*, 1987), and Aganetha Dyck's collaboration with honey bees in her extraordinary wax sculptures (e.g., *The Glass Dress: Lady in Waiting*, 1998).

The sculpture of contemporary Aboriginal and Inuit artists also demonstrates diversity of materials, strategies, and content. The decriminalization of the Potlach in 1952 encouraged the reemergence of traditional Northwest Coast practices. The British Columbia Provincial Museum and the Museum of Anthropology, University of British Columbia, employed Mungo Martin and others to carve totem poles. First Nations artists Bill Reid, Robert Davidson, and Susan Point draw inspiration from traditional Northwest Coast carving practices to fashion new images from precious metals, wood, and stone. Others such as Edward Poitras, Theresa Marshall, Joane Cardinal-Schubert, and Ron Noganosh use provocative mixed-media installations to address issues of traditional culture and contemporary political realities. Inuit sculpture ranges from the carving of traditional shamanic images from local stone and whalebone to the work of younger sculptors such as David Ruben Piqtoukun whose work reflects his exposure to Western abstraction, and Ovilu Tunnillie, whose subject matter includes personal narratives of contact (e.g., *This Has Touched My Life*, 1991–92).

Canadian sculpture today reflects a variety of responses toward local, regional, and global issues and styles. Ecological/environmental sculpture, mixed media and Installation art, and new genre public art coexist alongside traditionalist representational forms and media. Most important, awareness and support from private, corporate, and governmental sectors for public sculpture as a means to humanize urban centers and enhance national identity has increased. The vital and energetic response from Canadian sculptors continues to expand the boundaries of sculptural practice in works that ultimately engage both nature and culture.

NATALIE LUCKYJ

Further Reading

Anderson Dolcini, Catherine, "One Percent for Whom? Canada's Public Works Fine Art Programme, 1964–1978," Master's thesis, Carleton University, 2000

Baker, Victoria A., *Emanuel Hahn and Elizabeth Wyn Wood: Tradition and Innovation in Canadian Sculpture* (exhib. cat.), Ottawa, Ontario: National Gallery of Canada, 1997

Barbeau, Charles Marius, *Saintes artisanes*, 2 vols., Montreal, Quebec: Fides, 1944–46

Blodgett, Jean, *Grasp Tight the Old Ways: Selections from the Klamer Family Collection of Inuit Art* (exhib. cat.), Toronto: Art Gallery of Ontario, 1983

Boyanoski, Christine, *Loring and Wyle: Sculptors' Legacy* (exhib. cat.), Toronto: Art Gallery of Ontario, 1987

Dompierre, Louise, *Walking Woman Works: Michael Snow, 1961–67: New Representational Art and Its Uses* (exhib. cat.), Kingston, Ontario: Agnes Etherington Art Centre, 1983

Lambton, Gunda, *Stealing the Show: Seven Women Artists in Canadian Public Art*, Montreal and Buffalo, New York: McGill-Queens University Press, 1994

Leroux, Odette, Marion E. Jackson, and Minnie Aodla Freeman (editors), *Inuit Women Artists: Voices from Cape Dorset*, Vancouver, British Columbia: Douglas and McIntyre, Hull, Quebec: Canadian Museum of Civilization, and Seattle: University of Washington Press, 1994

Lippard, Lucy R., Marie Fleming, and Lauren Rabinovitz, *Joyce Wieland* (exhib. cat.), Toronto: Art Gallery of Ontario, 1987

Luckyj, Natalie, *Visions and Victories: 10 Canadian Women Artists, 1914–1945* (exhib. cat.), London, Ontario: London Regional Art Gallery, 1983

Luckyj, Natalie, *Put on Her Mettle: The Life and Art of Jacobine Jones*, Manotick, Ontario: Penumbra Press, 1999

Noppen, Luc, and René Villeneuve, *Le Trésor du Grand Siècle: L'art et l'architecture du XVIIᵉ siècle à Québec*, Quebec City: Musée du Québec, 1984

Swinton, George, *Sculpture of the Eskimo*, Toronto, Ontario: McClelland and Stewart, Greenwich, Connecticut: New York Graphic Society, and London: Hurst, 1972

Trask, Deborah E., *Life How Short, Eternity How Long: Gravestone Carving and Carvers in Nova Scotia*, Halifax: Nova Scotia Museum, 1978

Villeneuve, René, *Baroque to Neo-Classical: Sculpture in Quebec* (exhib. cat.), Ottawa, Ontario: National Gallery of Canada, 1997

ALONSO CANO 1601–1667 *Spanish*

Alonso Cano was one of the most influential Baroque sculptors in Spain. His style initially developed under the influence of the Sevillan master Juan Martínez Montañés, and he worked for ecclesiastical patrons as well as the court in Madrid. His ecclesiastical commissions usually involved executing paintings and sculptures, as well as constructing retables. Cano carved mainly in wood and contracted other artists to polychrome or paint the sculptures. He executed many of the same themes in both painting and sculpture, creating them in accordance with the theology of the Counter Reformation.

Cano sculpted two images of the Immaculate Conception, a popular subject in Spanish art, in his early career. The theological concept that holds that Mary was born without original sin had developed as a theme in art over several centuries. Although Cano sometimes varied the conventional symbols, he tended to use a minimal amount of details in his sculptures for the sake of clarity. His earliest known sculpture, the *Immaculate Conception* (ca. 1615–20), carved in stone for the niche portal over the Church of the Concepción in Seville, lacks the quality of his other works. He sculpted another *Immaculate Conception* (1620–25) for the high altar of the Church of San Andrés, Seville. Both sculptures depict Mary holding her hands in prayer, with drapery arranged over her arm, as Montañés had done for Nuestra Señora de las Consolación, El Pedroso, Seville, in 1606–08.

On 3 August 1629 Cano received the commission of the architecture and sculpture for the high altar for the Church of Santa María de Oliva, Lebrija, from his father, Miguel Cano. Pablo Legote was responsible for the paintings. In the center of the retable Cano sculpted a life-size *Madonna and Child* that recalls Italian Renaissance conventions, with the nude Christ Child and covered head of Mary. She wears a deep blue cope with gilded arabesques and broad gilded border, a white-and-gold tunic, and a tan headdress with red ornament. Cano used sgraffito for the drapery, a technique that involves laying down a ground surface of gold leaf, covering it with another color, and scratching it away. Cano also produced life-size bearded sculptures of *St. Peter* and *St. Paul* for the top sides of the retable. He derived inspiration for these figures, shown in stationary and walking positions, respectively, from Montañés's sculptures in the retable of the Church of San Miguel in Jerez de la Frontera. Cano, however, imparted a sense of melancholy that is different from exaggerated and dramatic intensity of Montañés and others. Felipe de Ribas completed the *Crucifixion of Christ*, located in the summit, after a model by Cano. The contract also called for statuettes of the evangelists; Cano portrayed *St. Mark* and *St. Luke* sitting and writing their Gospels, while *St. Matthew* and *St. John* are standing and preaching.

Cano produced several other retables and single figures in Seville that illustrate his interest in beauty and spirituality. He originally carved the figure of *St. Theresa*, a Carmelite nun and mystic, for the central niche of an altar in the Church of San Alberto. She wears a black, brown, and gold leaf brocade cope over her habit, decorated with a faint design in black, rather that her usual dull monastic garb, and looks somberly upward for divine inspiration as she writes. Similarly, *St. John the Evangelist*, which Cano sculpted for the center of the retable in the Church of Santa Paula, Seville, holds a pen as he looks toward heaven for inspiration. A figure of *St. John the Baptist* sculpted for the central niche of the high altar of the Church of San Juan de la Palma, Seville, shows the young saint in a melancholic mood.

From 1653 to 1657 Cano worked as an architect, painter, and sculptor for the nuns of the Convento del Angel Custodio in Granada. Cano and his workshop produced a *Guardian Angel* in white marble with detachable wooden wings for the niche over the portal of the church. He depicted the angel holding its hand on its heart and protecting the plump infant. In this sculpture Cano's style has softened as a result of his study of the Venetian Renaissance paintings at the Madrid court. Cano's student Pedro de Mena assisted him in carving over-life-size sculptures of *St. Joseph with the Christ Child, St. Anthony of Padua with the Christ Child, St. Diego de Alcalá,* and *St. Pedro de Alcántara* for the transept of the convent. In these sculptures Cano used a more simplified drapery instead of the dramatic dark and light contrasting drapery used by Montañés. *St. Pedro de Alcántara* is standing, not walking like the others, and is also more realistic. The figures of *St. Joseph with the Christ Child* are similar to his painting of the *Holy Family* (1653–57) for the same church. He depicted Saint Joseph here as a young man and a caring father to the Christ Child, a new type replacing the depictions of the saint as an old man. The figure of *St. Diego de Alcalá*, a Franciscan lay brother, looks downward as his tense hands clutch his monastic habit. *St. Anthony of Padua with the Christ Child* inspired a later model and statuette of the saint for the Church of San Nicolàs, Murcia.

Cano also completed a few other sculptures in Granada, including a polychromed wood sculpture of *St. John the Evangelist* for the Church of Loja and a lectern for Granada Cathedral with a statuette of the *Virgin of the Immaculate Conception*. In this work Cano used the tapering silhouette that he had been experimenting with for years. The statuette was so well received that it was transferred to a small case in the sacristy so it could be seen.

From 1657 to 1660 Cano was in Madrid to protest his discharge from his prebendary by the canons of Granada Cathedral. They reinstated him as a prebendary, and he received his holy orders in April 1658. In Madrid he produced only one sculpture—a large wooden crucifix for the Benedictine Church of Nuestra Señora de Montserrat. It is now missing.

Cano returned to Granada and worked there until the end of his life. His *Madonna of Bethlehem* for the tabernacle at the top of the choir lectern at Granada Cathedral is one of his masterpieces. She wears a white mantle, blue gown, and copper veil and bends her head forward so that she can be seen from below. The *Madonna of Bethlehem* and *Virgin of the Immaculate Conception* from the sacristy of Granada Cathedral represent Cano's mature style with their delicacy, sweet demeanor, tapering rippling outline, and flowing drapery. Cano also sculpted colossal polychromed wood busts of Adam and Eve for niches in the triumphal arch of the sanctuary of the cathedral. He depicted Eve as the beautiful adolescent female type that he favored in his late career and depicted Adam with tousled hair and a moustache. The large size of these unprecedented works creates an imposing sentiment.

Many other artists tried to emulate Cano's style, which was quite popular. His style lived on for many years in the work of his students José de Mora and Pedro de Mena; Cano left his unused drawings and models to the latter, which also aided in continuing his work. The 19th century saw a renewed interest in Spanish Baroque masters by many artists, including Théodule Ribot, who painted *The Torture of Alonso Cano* in 1867.

JENNIFER OLSON-RUDENKO

See also **Mena, Pedro de; Montañés, Juan Martínez; Polychromy**

Biography

Born in Granada, Spain, 19 March 1601. Family moved to Seville; learned to build retables from father, 1614; apprenticeship with Francesco Pacheco, father-in-law of Diego Velázquez, 1616–*ca.* 1621; obtained license from painters' guild to practice his trade, 12 April 1626; called to Madrid by the Count Duke of Olivares, prime minister of Philip IV; there produced paintings and restored canvases damaged in fire of Buen Retiro palace, 1638; left for Valencia, 1644; returned to Madrid after 15 months to work for ecclesiastical patrons; held office of *mayordomo* in Hermandad de Nuestra Señora de los Siete Dolores, a religious confraternity of artists, in Madrid, 1647; moved to Granada and worked primarily for religious institutions, 1652–57; after spending three years in Madrid, returned to Granada to work for the remainder of his life. Died in Granada, Spain, 3 September 1667.

Selected Works

ca. 1615–20	*Immaculate Conception*, for Church of the Concepción, Seville, Spain; painted stone; Church of Nervión, Seville, Spain
1620–25	*Immaculate Conception*; polychromed wood; Church of San Andrés, Seville, Spain
1629	*St. Theresa*; polychromed wood; Church of Santa María del Buen Suceso, Seville, Spain
ca. 1629–31	High altar (statues of *Madonna and Child, St. Peter, St. Paul, St. Matthew, St. Mark, St. Luke*, and *St. John*); polychromed wood; Church of Santa María de Oliva, Lebrija, Spain
1634	*St. John the Baptist*, for Church of San Juan de la Palma, Seville, Spain; polychromed wood; Collection Conde de Ruiseñada, Barcelona, Spain
ca. 1653–57	*St. John the Evangelist*, for Church of Loja, Spain; polychromed wood; Church of Santa Paula, Seville, Spain
ca. 1653–57	Statues, for the Convento del Angel Custodio; polychromed wood: *St. Diego de Alcalá, St. Joseph with the Christ Child, St. Anthony of Padua with the Christ Child*, and *St. Pedro de Alcántara* (all with Pedro de Mena); Museum, Palace of Charles V, Granada; marble: *Guardian Angel* (with workshop); Convento del Angel Custodio, Granada, Spain
1655–56	*Virgin of the Immaculate Conception*; polychromed wood; sacristy, Granada Cathedral, Spain
1664	*Madonna of Bethlehem*; polychromed wood; Granada Cathedral, Spain
ca. 1666–67	Bust of Adam and Bust of Eve; polychromed wood; sanctuary, Granada Cathedral, Spain
ca. 1666–67	*St. Anthony of Padua and the Infant Christ; polychromed wood; Church of San Nicolás, Murcia, Spain*

Further Reading

Alonso Cano (1601–1667) y la escultura andaluza hacia 1600 (exhib. cat.), Cordoba, Spain: Obra Social y Cultural de CajaSur, 2000

Alonso Cano dibujos (exhib. cat.), Madrid: Museo del Prado, 2001

Bernales Ballesteros, Jorge, *Alonso Cano en Sevilla*, Seville: Excema. Diputación Provincial de Sevilla, 1976; 2nd edition, 1996

Enggass, Robert, and Jonathan Brown, *Italy and Spain, 1600–1750: Sources and Documents*, Englewood Cliffs, New Jersey: Prentice-Hall, 1970

Figuras e imágenes del Barroco: Estudios sobre el barroco español y sobre la obra de Alonso Cano, Madrid: Fundación Argentaria, 1999

Palomino de Castro y Velasco, Antonio, *Las vidas de los pintores y estatuarios eminentes españoles*, London: Woodfall, 1744; as *Lives of the Eminent Spanish Painters and Sculptors*, translated by Nina Ayala Mallory, Cambridge and New York: Cambridge University Press, 1987

Stratton, Suzanne L., *The Immaculate Conception in Spanish Art*, Cambridge and New York: Cambridge University Press, 1994

Wethey, Harold, "Alonso Cano's Drawings," *Art Bulletin* 34 (1952)

Wethey, Harold, *Alonso Cano: Painter, Sculptor, Architect*, Princeton, New Jersey: Princeton University Press, 1955

ANTONIO CANOVA 1757–1822 *Italian*

Antonio Canova, the greatest Neoclassical sculptor from the 1790s until his death in 1822, was the most famous artist of his time. His Roman studio drew visitors from all over Europe and America, and the international scope of his commissions solidified his reputation abroad. In an age convinced of the supremacy of Antiquity, Canova was unique in refusing to copy ancient statuary, but he assimilated its stylistic values to form his own original concept of aesthetic perfection. In his quest to achieve a modern synthesis of ancient art and naturalistic observation, Canova established new canons of heroic male and ideal female beauty and developed variant genres of sculpture in which to express these innovations. Despite the condemnation by 19th-century Romantic critics of Neoclassicism in general and Canova in particular for what they considered unspontaneous, cold academicism— a view that prevailed until the late 1950s—Canova's experimentations were progressive in their implications and, when stripped of their antiquarian syntax, pivotal to the evolution of modern sculpture.

Born in Possagno, Italy, Canova was in Venice from the early 1770s, studying at the Academy and at the Farsetti palace, which contained replicas of ancient and modern masterpieces, as well as original Baroque terracottas. Canova's earliest works exhibited a late Baroque or Rococo sensibility, emphasizing twisting movements, dramatic facial expressions, fleshy anatomy, and picturesque details, as evident in his first major independent sculptures, the statues of *Orpheus* and *Eurydice* and a marble group of *Daedalus and Icarus*.

The turning point in Canova's career occurred during his visits to Rome in 1779 and again in 1780/1, when he took up permanent residence there. He studied famous antiquities and came under the influence of the British Neoclassicist Gavin Hamilton. His first Roman marble, a statuette of *Apollo Crowning Himself*, was intended to demonstrate the young artist's assimilation of ancient models. A Classical nude devoid of extreme passion, *Apollo Crowning Himself* heralded the predominantly calm sentiment of Canova's mature work. His next commission, a life-size *Theseus and the Minotaur*, represented the hero resting after slaying his foe. Similarly, Canova later depicted *Cupid and Psyche Standing* pondering a butterfly and *Venus and Adonis* (1789–94) sharing an affectionate gaze without a hint of the violent tragedy that would end their affair.

Among his most famous mythological groups, *Cupid Awakening Psyche* depicted two semirecumbent, embracing lovers, their almost-touching lips framed by the circle of Psyche's arms. This gentle eroticism, heightened by the glossy finish of the surface (criticized by those who preferred the uniform, matte appearance typifying marbles of that period), further distinguished Canova from other sculptors. The unique, suspended sensuousness of Canova's group moved Gustave Flaubert to kiss Psyche's armpit—one can hardly imagine a similar anecdote in connection with stricter Neoclassicists such as Bertel Thorvaldsen.

Canova's ability to wed Classical reference and lifelikeness attracted the attention of Napoléon and his entourage, who flooded Canova's studio with portrait commissions after 1802. His full-length representation of *Paolina Borghese Bonaparte as Venus Victorious*, with its nude torso and luminous, velvety surface, was one of the most risqué productions in the history of official portraiture. Beginning in 1811, Canova's exploration of female beauty led to the development of a new genre that he called "ideal heads," loosely depicting mythological, allegorical, or historical subjects such as Helen, Beatrice, Sappho, or Philosophy. Rather than presenting specific individuals, the sculptures conveyed a concept of ideal beauty, removed from the irregularities of nature but informed by its principles, to strike a perfect balance between real and abstract. Frequently executed as gifts or tributes for Canova's friends, these busts were personal, revealing embodiments of his aesthetic aspirations.

After his first public triumph with the 1783–87 monument to Clement XIV, which distilled and simplified conventional Baroque formulas, Canova also achieved major innovations in the design of funeral monuments. Canova's greatest tomb began in 1790 as a never-realized monument to Titian for the Church of the Frari in Venice. Canova resurrected the design about a decade later for the monument to Maria Christina of Austria, in which a procession of draped figures move toward the open door of a pyramid decorated with a portrait medallion of the deceased, the traditional elements of sarcophagus and effigy no longer needed to convey funereal themes. The powerful, stark geometry of the composition and the sheer beauty of the figures, who turn away from the viewer toward the tomb as if leading the inevitable march of death, make this the most sublime memorial of its time.

Less than a decade after moving to Rome, Canova's studio was one of the busiest in Europe. Initially working alongside his assistants on all stages of his marbles, his methods began to change, by necessity, with the execution of large-scale and numerous commissions. By around 1791 Canova left the roughing out of the marble largely to others, reserving work on the final layer, or "skin," of the stone for himself. Although he often produced several versions of a composition from the same model, he strove to improve and vary it in this final stage. Canova was extremely generous toward other sculptors, sometimes allowing them to produce copies of his works, leading to the proliferation of replicas made outside his studio, both during and after his lifetime. His death in 1822 provoked widespread mourning and a spate of eulogistic verses and essays. Canova's heir built the Gipsoteca Canoviana in Possagno, 1834–36, to house the original models, marbles, and paintings remaining in the sculptor's Roman studio.

Not since Raphael was an artist so intimately and knowledgeably associated with the study of antiquities in Rome. Canova supposedly listened to readings of Classical texts while working in his studio. When Napoléon removed the *Apollo Belvedere* and *Medici Venus* to Paris, Canova's sculptures took their places, a tribute not only to his stature but to his profound understanding of the ancient masterpieces. In 1802 Canova was named inspector general of antiquities and the fine arts in Rome, and he used his position to acquire works for the Vatican and restrict the export of ancient sculptures. After the fall of Napoléon, Canova negotiated the return to Italy of antiquities confiscated by the French, and the same year, 1815, he went to London to verify the authenticity of the Parthenon marbles. "A modern Praxiteles," "a truly divine man," and "the supreme minister of beauty" were among the accolades showered on Canova by poets and critics who saw him as the true rival to the ancient Greeks, and their praise hardly seems excessive in light of his achievements.

PEGGY FOGELMAN

Biography

Born in Possagno, Italy, 1 November 1757. He was the son of Pietro Canova, a stonecutter. Raised by paternal grandfather, Pasino, a sculptor of late Baroque-style altars; apprenticed to sculptor Giuseppe Bernardi in Pagnano di Asolo, 1770–71, and moved with him to Venice; after 1774, briefly worked in studio of sculptor Giovanni Ferrari; first independent works, two marble *Baskets of Fruit*, executed 1774; set up own studio in cloister of Santo Stefano, Venice, 1775; nominated as member of Venetian Academy, 1779; traveled to Rome as guest of Venetian ambassador Girolamo Zulian, 1779; patronized by Abbondio Rezzonico, nephew of Pope Clement XIII; returned to Rome, settling permanently; set up workshop in Vicola delle Colonette di S. Giacomo degli Incurabili, 1783; awarded commission for monument to Clement XIV, 1784, unveiled 1787, which led to major commissions in Italy and throughout Europe; named inspector general of antiquities and the fine arts, and Knight of the Golden Spur, by Pope Pius VII, 1802; traveled to Paris to model bust of Napoléon, 1802, and again in 1810, when Napoléon offered him government appointment, which Canova refused; elected president of Academy of St. Luke, 1810, and perpetual president, 1814; appointed delegate to Paris and secured return of looted Italian art treasures, 1815; went to London to authenticate Parthenon marbles, 1815; began construction of Temple of Possagno, 1819, which later became his burial site; health declined beginning 1820. Died in Venice, Italy, 13 October 1822.

Selected Works

1774   Two *Baskets of Fruit*; marble; Museo Correr, Venice, Italy

1775   *Eurydice*; vincentine stone; Museo Correr, Venice, Italy

1775–76 *Orpheus*; vincentine stone; Museo Correr, Venice; marble version: 1777, Hermitage, St. Petersburg, Russia

1778–79 *Daedalus and Icarus*; marble; Museo Correr, Venice, Italy

1781–82 *Apollo Crowning Himself*; marble; Getty Museum, Los Angeles, California, United States

1781–83 *Theseus and the Minotaur*; marble; Victoria and Albert Museum, London, England

1783–87 Monument to Clement XIV; marble; Church of SS. Apostoli, Rome, Italy

1787–93 *Cupid Awakening Psyche*; marble; Musée du Louvre, Paris; marble (with variations): 1794–96, Hermitage, St. Petersburg, Russia

1796–   *Cupid and Psyche Standing*; marble;
1800   Musée du Louvre, Paris, France; 1800–03: marble; Hermitage, St. Petersburg, Russia

1797–   *Perseus Triumphant*; marble; Vatican
1801   Museums, Rome, Italy; 1804–06: marble; Metropolitan Museum of Art, New York City, United States

1798–   Monument to Maria Christina of Austria;
1805   marble; Augustinian Church, Vienna, Austria

1804–08 *Paolina Borghese Bonaparte as Venus Victorious*; marble; Galleria Borghese, Villa Borghese, Rome, Italy

1804–12 *Venus Italica*; marble; Palazzo Pitti, Florence, Italy; 1807–10: marble; Residenzmuseum, Munich, Germany

1812–16 *The Three Graces*; marble; Hermitage, St. Petersburg, Russia; 1815–17: marble; Victoria and Albert Museum, London, England; National Gallery of Scotland, Edinburgh, Scotland (jointly owned)

1816–17 *Ideal Head*; marble; Kimbell Art Museum, Fort Worth, Texas, United States

Further Reading

Bassi, Elena, *La Gipsoteca di Possagno: Sculture e dipinti di Antonio Canova*, Venice: Neri Pozza, 1957

Eustace, Katharine, *Canova: Ideal Heads*, Oxford: Ashmolean Museum, 1997

Finn, David, and Fred Licht, *Canova*, New York: Abbeville Press, 1983

Honour, Hugh, "Canova's Studio Practice—I: The Early Years," and "Canova's Studio Practice—II: 1792–1822," *The Burlington Magazine* 114 (1972)

Johns, Christopher M.S., *Antonio Canova and the Politics of Patronage in Revolutionary and Napoleonic Europe*, Berkeley: University of California Press, 1998

Pavanello, Giuseppe, and Mario Praz, *L'opera completa del Canova*, Milan: Rizzoli, 1976; 2nd edition, 1981

Pavanello, Giuseppe, and Giandomenico Romanelli (editors), *Canova* (exhib. cat.), Venice: Marsilio Publishers, 1992

Stefani, Ottorino, and Giuseppe Mazzariol, *La poetica e l'arte del Canova: Tra arcadia neoclassicismo e romanticismo*, Treviso: Edizioni Canova, 1980; 2nd edition, 1984

Teotochi Albrizzi, Isabella, and Leopoldo Cicognara, *Opere di scultura e di plastica di Antonio Canova*, 4 vols., Pisa: Capurro, 1821–24; as *The Works of Antonio Canova, in Sculpture and Modelling*, 2 vols., London: Septimus Prowett, 1824

THE THREE GRACES

Antonio Canova (1757–1822)
First version: 1812–1816
marble
h. 1.82 m
Hermitage Museum, St. Petersburg, Russia
Second version: 1815–1817
marble
h. 1.73 m

National Gallery of Scotland, Edinburgh, Scotland; and Victoria and Albert Museum, London, England (jointly owned)

Throughout his career, Antonio Canova sought the perfect balance between naturalism and idealization on the basis of the principles of ancient art. *The Three Graces* represents the most sophisticated and most famous embodiment of this aesthetic exploration. Occasionally, a fortuitous coincidence between the subject and the artist's stylistic aim occurred in Canova's work. For instance, his *Herm of a Vestal Virgin* (1821–22; J. Paul Getty Museum, Los Angeles, California) was the optimum vehicle by which to render ideal beauty, because in ancient society, young women who served the goddess Vesta had to be perfect in body and mind, without blemish or defect. Likewise, the subject of the Graces presented Canova with multivalent challenges, including rendering the abstract concept of Grace with all its ancient, Renaissance, and contemporary nuances in tangible human form.

The Graces were of divine origin; the Latin *Gratiae* or Greek *Charites*—Aglaia (the Radiant), Thalia (the Flowering), and Euphrosyne (Joy)—were associated with Venus and imbued with allegorical meaning. For ancient authors, the Graces represented benevolence and the three aspects of generosity—giving, receiving, and returning gifts. Renaissance theorists saw them as Beauty, Desire, and Fulfillment—the three stages of love—or Chastity, Beauty, and Love. Their interpretation as symbols of generosity or friendship dictated the conventional arrangement of the three nude figures in ancient and later art: two sisters were presented frontally and one was shown from the back to signify the reciprocity of beneficence. Such representations of the Graces were known to Canova in several antique examples, including a damaged group in the Piccolomini Library of the Siena Cathedral and two groups in the Casino Borghese and the Palazzo Ruspoli in Rome. In the Neoclassical period, Grace was an aesthetic category—according to some, Grace was the aspect of beauty that pleases the senses; according to others, Grace delights the mind through reason. For Canova, Grace was that quality capable of translating into real, human terms the divine, abstract nature of beauty, and his own marble group had to convey that concept as well as the legacy of interpretation inherited from antiquity.

Canova experimented with the subject of the Graces as early as about 1795, when he executed a plaster low relief of *Venus and the Graces Dancing before Mars* and several paintings of the same or similar themes. Canova's 1799 half-length painting of the Graces in a compact, frontal grouping unified by the interplay of tilted heads and entwined hands foreshadowed his marble composition, suggesting that Canova had envisioned a sculptural group before its commission in June 1812 from Josephine de Beauharnais, the divorced wife of Napoléon. Despite Canova's concern that the idea was "difficult and thorny" (indicating his awareness of its iconographical and formal complexity), he immediately undertook its development in drawings and clay models. He experimented with several arrangements in which one sister was seen from the back, or in which all three were completely frontal. Common to his preparatory sketches was the use of arm and head positions to unite the figures while varying their expressions. The clay model for the final composition (Museum of Fine Arts, Lyon, France) showed each figure oriented differently, with a frontal, central sister flanked by one in three-quarter view and one in profile. Their total absorption in their own intimate exchange rendered them oblivious to the viewer's presence and as a result heightened the voyeuristic potential of the nude group.

Canova made subtle changes between the clay and the full-scale plaster model, which was completed in the summer of 1813. Most importantly, he altered the arm gestures of the right-hand sister to weave her, vis-

The Three Graces© Victoria and Albert Museum / Art Resource, NY

ually and emotionally, more tightly into the primary action, because she had seemed somewhat self-contained. He also replaced the fluted column, necessary as a support in the final marble, with a rectangular altar. Although the marble had been roughed out by the spring of 1814, Josephine's death in May, the uncertain fortunes of the Bonaparte family after Napoléon's abdication, and the lack of payment to Canova, put the commission in jeopardy. In 1815 John Russell, sixth Duke of Bedford, saw the Beauharnais *Graces* in Canova's studio and, unable to obtain it, commissioned a second version for his Woburn estate. By the summer, having received partial payment from Josephine's son Eugène, Canova worked on the two versions simultaneously. Both were completed by 1817. Eugène's sculpture was shipped to Munich; the Duke of Bedford's marble arrived in 1819 and was installed in the Temple of the Graces, which was built to house the group. Typical of Canova's practice, he made slight modifications between the first and second versions, although they were derived from the same plaster model: the altar was changed back to a round column, the width of the base was reduced, and greater volume was added to the back of the central figure. Canova typically issued engravings of his sculptures to secure his international reputation through their circulation. His alteration of the engraving of the *Graces* to reflect the second marble demonstrated his preference for it over the first version.

The Three Graces became famous even before it left Canova's studio. Most critics applauded Canova for capturing the essence of Grace as a concept, for elevating truth over verism, and for creating an unrivaled vehicle for the appreciation of divine beauty. However, the obvious erotic appeal of the figures led others to construct a more human context for them. Henry Stendhal (1866) provided a narrative explanation for their gestures, in which the youngest goddess, with the help of her sibling, demands a kiss from her stubborn elder. The Bavarian sculptor J.M. Wagner supposedly remarked that Canova's *Graces* recalled the type of women who nightly frequented the Palais Royal in Paris. Such divergent views were echoed in the 1990s during a campaign to buy the Duke of Bedford's *Graces* for the British nation when the marble received more public attention than it had since its creation. The dichotomy between sensuous humanity and frigid abstraction alternately attributed to *The Three Graces* stems from the inherent dialectic of nature and the ideal in Canova's work. That *The Three Graces* so forcefully conveys this tension and inspires such debate underscores the work's overwhelming success as a statement of the sculptor's aesthetic aims.

PEGGY FOGELMAN

Further Reading

Borghese, Leonardo, "Antonio Canova e l'estetica classica morale," in *Arte Neoclassica*, Venice: Istituto per la Collaborazione Culturale, 1964

Clifford, Timothy, et al., *The Three Graces, Antonio Canova* (exhib. cat.), Edinburgh: The National Galleries of Scotland, 1995

Finn, David, and Fred Licht, *Canova*, New York: Abbeville Press, 1983

Malamani, Vittorio, *Canova*, Milan: Hoepli, 1911

Venturi, Gianni, "Grace and the Graces," in *Antonio Canova* (exhib. cat.), edited by Giuseppe Pavanello and Giandomenico Romanelli, Venice and New York: Marsilio, 1992

CANTURBURY CATHEDRAL

See **England and Wales: Romanesque**

CAPITAL

One of the most flexible fields for architectural sculpture is the capital, the uppermost member of a column, pilaster, or pier. Its name is derived from the Latin *caput* (head). Crowning the shaft, the capital receives the weight of an entablature or arch above but is not tectonically necessary. The transition may be visualized by means of an abacus, a flattened area at the top of the capital. In this way, the capital articulates the load-bearing function of the column, and its decoration marks the meeting of support and structure.

The variety of form for capitals is infinite, and the form characterizes particular styles. Because architecture recreates natural spaces such as those formed by forests, treelike columns evolved in many cultures. In ancient Egypt, where bundles of papyrus supported mud walls, stone columns were based on plant forms, resulting in capitals resembling papyrus buds and blossoms over fluted, angled shafts. In addition, capitals may be shaped like animals, persons, or deities, as in Persia, India, and medieval Europe. They can assume abstract shapes with sharply angled moldings or rounded forms that express or deny the weight of the building. In Minoan architecture, for example, the pillar widens from a narrow base to the cushion capital, ballooning outward to meet the ceiling.

The predominant capitals in the Western tradition derived from the Classical orders, and they are "bearers of meaning," as John Onians has characterized them (see Onians, 1988). The Greek Doric capital consists of a rounded echinus and squared abacus. The Ionic capital has a thin abacus atop volutes hanging over two sides of the echinus, which is decorated with molding. The third major order, Corinthian, has a bell capital covered by acanthus leaves, a squared crown with volutes at the corners, and a boss, or projecting ornament, at the center of each side. The Romans combined elements from different orders into composite capitals. Long before the Roman theorist Vitruvius described the orders, writers identified Doric simplicity as masculine and Ionic ornament as feminine. Classical caryatids, or columns formed as women, and later the Gothic statue column made visible the personification of architecture, frequent in literature. The transition from exterior to interior of a building, or zones of differing importance, may be marked by a change from one type of capital to another.

Corinthian capitals lend themselves to tremendous variation. Beginning in the 4th century CE, Byzantine and then Islamic capitals flattened high-relief Corinthian forms into lacy patterns. Christian authors saw capitals as "teachers of the faithful"—hence, the rich development of the Romanesque and early Gothic capital, which could be ornamental, foliate, figured, or historiated. In Renaissance Florence, architects such as Filippo Brunelleschi, Leon Battista Alberti, and Filarete melded medieval and ancient capital types to produce an Italian, moralized form. Such was their impact that the classicizing orders, throughout Europe and the colonies, endowed buildings with nobility and authority. The government buildings in Washington, D.C., exemplify the wit with which a capital may perform its expressive or ideological function; there, native plants such as corn substitute for traditional acanthus. Capitals remained an essential part of Western art until the 20th century, when modern sensibility stripped architecture of its ornament.

ELIZABETH VALDEZ DEL ALAMO

Further Reading

Onians, John, *Bearers of Meaning: The Classical Orders in Antiquity, the Middle Ages, and the Renaissance*, Princeton, New Jersey: Princeton University Press, 1988

Pollitt, J.J., *Art and Experience in Classical Greece*, Cambridge: Cambridge University Press, 1972

Sauerländer, Willibald, "Die gestörte Ordnung oder le châpiteau historié," in *Studien zur Geschichte der europäischen Skulptur im 12./13. Jahrhundert*, edited by Herbert Beck and Kersten Hengevoss-Dürkop, Frankfurt: Heinrich, 1994

Stokstad, Marilyn, "Column and Colonnade," and "The Greek Architectural Orders," in *Art History*, by Stokstad et al., revised edition, vol. 1, New York: Abrams, 1999

CAPITOLINE WOLF (LUPA) Anonymous

500–480 BCE

bronze

h. 75 cm

Musei Capitolini, Rome, Italy

The vigilant ancient bronze she-wolf that has long been associated with the legendary founding of Rome is usually dated *ca.* 500–480 BCE, some 250 years after the city's establishment. Since the Renaissance, the wolf has been displayed with figures of Romulus and Remus, but the infants are not antique and are often attributed to the 15th-century sculptor Antonio Pollaiuolo.

The sculpture is well preserved with the exception of the restored tail, other minor repairs, and the damaged hind legs. Stylistically, this work combines naturalistic observation with stylization. Most likely produced in Rome, the wolf may be an amalgam of Etruscan, Greek, and Roman traditions, craftsmanship, themes, and materials. Johann J. Winckelmann in 1764 considered the she-wolf to be Etruscan in origin but produced under the influence of a Greek sculptor. It was not unusual for patrons of ancient Rome to commission works from Etruscan artisans or from Greek craftsmen who incorporated Etruscan style and casting techniques. The identity of the sculptor or workshop remains unknown, but the treatment of the rib cage has been likened to that of a torso from the Portonaccio group from Veii (Villa Giulia, Rome), which would link the work to the school of Vulca. That this work is one of the earliest surviving examples of large hollow-cast bronze sculpture is indicative of its significance for our comprehension of the development of Etrusco-Roman art.

The wolf is alert and defiant, her ears pricked up, her teeth bared, and her body tense. Her head turns at a right angle, which suggests an air of vigilance, and her muscles and rib cage are sharply delineated. Her eyes, unlike those of contemporary Greek bronze sculptures, are cast in bronze and thus integrated into the surface of the sculpture.

Her anatomic form, particularly the canine shape of her head and her pointed nose, clearly depicts a she-wolf, but the manelike fur rendered in a decorative pattern around her face and neck does not. The surface treatment of the fur, with its repeated patterns, seems more ornamental than realistic and suggests the mixed appearance of lion and wolf. Perhaps the animal's leonine aspect was meant to render her more ferocious.

Ancient literary sources confirm the existence of a sculptural group that represented Romulus, Remus, and the wolf, and republican coins exist that depict the wolf and the twins. The *Capitoline Wolf*, correctly or incorrectly, has been associated with these versions.

Stories abound pertaining to this sculpted wolf: it was struck by lightning on the day that Julius Caesar was assassinated, for instance, and it was used as a prop for a performance of Voltaire's *La Mort de César*. A 10th-century source locates this sculpture outside the Lateran palace, where executions were held. By the late 12th or early 13th century, the wolf was noted as part of a group in which she stalked a bronze ram

Capitoline Wolf (suckling Romulus and Remus), 6th–5th centuries BCE; Musei Capitolini, Rome, Italy
© Scala / Art Resource, NY

(now lost) in the portico at the palace's entrance. It is also reported that both animals spouted water (the wolf from her teats), apparently for hand washing. In 1471 Pope Sixtus IV gave the wolf to the conservators of Rome, and by 1509 the addition of the twin brothers had been made. Nearly 30 years later (*ca.* 1536), the sculpture was seen above the entrance to the Palazzo dei Conservatori, and by 1544 it had been placed inside. Eventually the fact that the figures of Romulus and Remus were Renaissance additions seems to have been overlooked or simply forgotten, and the group was firmly established as an ancient complex representing the founding of Rome. During the 19th and 20th centuries, the she-wolf nursing the infants was co-opted for the cause of nationalism and what is known as *Romanità* (a revival of the ideals and spirit of ancient Rome).

Antique bronze statues were most likely of religious or commemorative significance. Although it is generally thought that the *Capitoline Wolf* served as a public monument in ancient Rome, she may or may not represent the wolf of Rome's foundation. If this she-wolf is associated with the maternal figure of Romulus and Remus fame, perhaps the young republic wished to encourage the memory of the pre-Tarquin monarchy and to equate this particular wolf with the legend that the twins were nourished on the banks of the Tiber.

On the other hand, this sculpture may have been created without reference to the legend. The wolf's obvious function as the provider of nourishment in conjunction with her alert and ready appearance render her both nurturer and protector in a general sense. Furthermore, as nurturer, she may also represent fertility.

As Winckelmann proposed, this sculpture may originally have had a funereal function. There is evidence that wolves symbolized death among the Etruscans,

perhaps because of the real threat they posed in central Italy at this time. The Etruscans equated wolves with death and underworld deities, as seen in ritual and art. Several reliefs on cinerary urns and tomb paintings stress the underworld association of the wolf. In the Tomba dell'Orco in Tarquinia, for example, the underworld's ruler is depicted wearing a wolf head and pelt, thus associating this animal with the god of the underworld.

If the *Capitoline Wolf* was not originally produced as a symbol of Rome's origins but was intended as a public monument to serve a funereal or fertility purpose, perhaps she was later co-opted by the Romans to serve as a reminder of the origins of Rome. The Renaissance additions of the Romulus and Remus figures clearly established the identity of the she-wolf as the nurturer of Rome's first king; it is this interpretation that has since become firmly established.

The she-wolf remains a compelling and imposing animal who steadfastly is ready to nourish and to protect. At the beginning of the 21st century, she endures as a well-established symbol of the city of Rome.

ANN THOMAS WILKINS

Further Reading

Brendel, Otto, *Etruscan Art*, London and New York: Penguin, 1978; 2nd edition, New Haven, Connecticut: Yale University Press, 1995

Elliot, John, "The Etruscan Wolfman in Myth and Ritual," *Etruscan Studies* 2 (1995)

Haskell, Francis, and Nicholas Penny, *Taste and the Antique: The Lure of Classical Sculpture, 1500–1900*, New Haven, Connecticut: Yale University Press, 1981

Jacks, Philip, *The Antiquarian and the Myth of Antiquity: The Origins of Rome in Renaissance Thought*, Cambridge and New York: Cambridge University Press, 1993

Kleiner, Diana E.E., *Roman Sculpture*, New Haven, Connecticut: Yale University Press, 1992

Winckelmann, Johann Joachim, *Geschichte der Kunst des Altertums*, 2 vols., Dresden: Waltherischen Hof-Buchhandlung, 1764; as *The History of Ancient Art*, 4 vols., Boston: Osgood, 1849–73; reprint, New York: Ungar, 1969

CARICATURE

The term "caricature" comes from the Italian *caricare*, in the sense of overloading or exaggerating, and refers to a sculptural genre that originated in northern Italy in the 17th century.

Caricatures depict humans and reality; as Filippo Baldinucci, the Italian artists' biographer, observed, they always bear a close resemblance to their subjects, so that a sculptor who creates caricatures must be skilled in portraiture. Caricature involves accentuating facial features and casting ridicule on physical defects to make them seem grotesque. Exaggerated expressions degenerate into smirks and grimaces, and gestures are emphasized to seem clumsy and stilted.

Caricature is much rarer in sculpture than in drawing and etching because sculpture requires elaborate, time-consuming techniques that prevent spontaneity. The sculptural mediums used most often are terracotta, bronze, wood, and papier mâché. Their fragility, especially that of terracotta, makes caricatural sculptures rare and more vulnerable to damage. If "ugliness" is caricature's paramount feature, it came to be so in the modern age, although there were forerunners in ancient times. In Phoenician culture a series of terracotta statuettes (7th–6th century BCE) depicted the god Bes, whose image, with its clumsy build, was often used on amulets. In ancient Egypt, it was the god Typhon, with his broad face and hanging tongue, who was portrayed with caricatural expressions. Typhon was the forerunner of the gorgons affixed on Greek and Etruscan temples, and of the figures of Lewdness carved on the capitals of medieval church columns. In Hellenistic times, the sculptors of Alexandria in the 1st century BCE created bronze Mahdià, statuettes with stumpy limbs and fat, obscenely writhing bodies. The taste for the deformed took a particular shape in Alexandria at the same time that the study of physical features was encountering favorable terrain in Hellenistic science and art, where the human body, investigated in detail,

became an object of wonder. The intentional exaggeration of the nose and chin in the portrait of Ptolemy Soter on a coin from the 1st century BCE is an early example of caricature in the plastic arts.

Ancient Roman art borrowed the masks used by the Greeks and Phoenicians in their farces and comedies. These grotesque faces, with their huge, wide-open, grimacing mouths became fashionable ornaments in the form of sculptures affixed on lamps and monstrous figures hung on house walls. Some art historians see them as the ancestors of modern caricatures.

In central Asia the Khotan terracottas—folk art depicting camels, horses, felines, and monkeys with human expressions, playing musical instruments, or grouped in sensuous embraces—were produced. The artists' knowledge of these animals can be traced to the remote times when the Khotan were in contact with the ancient cultures of northwestern India and eastern Persia. Next came the Ming ch'i statuettes (1368–1644 CE), made in China for funerary use. Here the effort to caricature the physical features of various ethnic types bespeaks pride in the superiority of the Chinese over the "barbarians."

In the Middle Ages obscene good-luck figures spread across Europe. In many medieval English churches, Vices such as Duplicity and Intrigue were satirized by the figure of a fox in clerical dress. The grimace motif returned in the choir stalls of a church in Stratford-upon-Avon, England.

Grotesque facial deformation and zoomorphic masks with human expressions characterized Italian Mannerism in the second half of the 16th century and spread from Florence to Rome and throughout Europe until the 18th century. Sculptors seeking to amaze could give full vent to their imagination in garden statuary, where grotesque figures proliferated. In Florence zoomorphic creatures appeared in the cartouches ornamenting escutcheons on palace facades and on fountains, such as the *Mascherone della Fontana dello Sprone* (Mask of the Spur Fountain). All this vanished in late 16th-century Italy with the Counter Reformation's theoretical dictates, leaving more room in the following centuries for greater realism in caricature. Caricaturing a face presupposes an accurate analysis of the living model, which must be perfectly recognizable despite the deformation. Thus the study of emotions and facial expressions entered the art academies' curriculum, and as in the commedia dell'arte, improvisation in caricature became a source of inspiration. Gianlorenzo Bernini delighted in drawing caricatures, but his only sculpture of this kind was a marble bust, now missing of Don Paolo Orsini (*ca.* 1635), a personage with a long mustache who took part in the entertainments Bernini organized around caricature.

Statuette of a Man (caricature), bronze, 300–100 BCE
© The Metropolitan Museum of Art, New York, Rogers Fund

In the 18th century, the two traditional lines—fanciful masks and caricatures of real people—came to influence each other. The German sculptor Franz Xaver Messerschmidt portrayed himself in a long series of character studies—heads with different facial contortions—beginning in 1770. In a psychoanalytic study of Messerschmidt's heads, Ernst Kris acknowledged the artist's great talent as a portraitist and his skill in capturing features and expressions but saw in these heads all the symptoms of schizophrenia (see Kris, 1952). It is interesting to note that Messerschmidt, like Francisco de Goya, had an "official" line of production, consisting of conventional portraits, and a private, extravagant one devoted to caricature. It would seem that at least until the end of the 18th century, caricature for sculptors was also what Jean Le Rond D'Alembert called an "espèce de libertinage de l'imagination" (kind of freedom of the imagination) for the artist, who gave full expression to his inventiveness only in the freedom of his private life.

In Italy, the sculptor Giovanni Bendazzuoli based his artistic style on Giambattista Tiepolo's and Jacques Callot's sketches. The 18 dwarfs (after 1774) Bendazzuoli carved in soft stone for Villa Valmarana in Vicenza were true caricatures. The marble figures of sailors and Chinese figures (early 18th century) carved by Giovanni Bonazza were based on ivory caricatures from China that influenced garden sculpture in Italy and the ceramics industry in Meissen and Nymphenburg.

With Honoré Daumier, caricature left the private sphere and became a public language. Daumier aimed his satiric shafts at the vices of French bourgeois society. During the Second Empire, he attacked obscurantists and reactionaries, and the personages he portrayed became symbolic. In the 36 surviving bronze portraits (1830) of members of parliament under the July Monarchy (1830–48), conceived out of political necessity, Daumier combined facial characterization and acute psychological insight. His caricatures were influenced by Johan Kaspar Lavater, who maintained that people's moral and intellectual qualities can be inferred from their facial features; by the German phrenologist Franz Josef Gall; and by Charles Darwin's study of the expression of emotions. Daumier's *Ratapoil*, a bronze statuette from 1850, caricatures a retired military officer who was among the Bonapartist leaders. Unfortunately, many other Daumier caricatures were destroyed.

The person regarded as the real father of caricature sculpture was Jean-Pierre Dantan. He is credited with more than 300 caricature portraits of politicians and other famous people of the day. These terracotta and bronze works earned Dantan great success, especially in England, and he is known to have drawn inspiration from his travels. His best-known work is a caricature bust of the architect Hippolyte Lebas (*ca.* 1850; Fabius Frères Collection, Paris).

Both Daumier and Dantan were impelled to describe and to be exact, and sculpture readily lends itself to these aims. These two French examples were influential throughout Europe, especially in Italy. Among the most significant Italian caricature sculptors were Adriano Cecioni, famous for his *Yorick* (1871), and Umberto Tirelli, whose *Wooden Heads*, created for the puppet theater, portrayed the most famous political and cultural figures in Italian culture and politics during the 1920s. Tirelli was a highly skilled deformer of bodies and vices. He modeled his heads in clay, cast them in plaster, then finished the plaster in paper and glue. His characters include the poet Gabriele D'Annunzio, the politician Giovanni Giolitti, and the actor Ettore Petrolini. Caricature lends itself well to the theater, which reveals the world's vices, virtues, passions, and visions more clearly than anywhere else, and where we can best understand the people around us and, perhaps with a laugh, forgive human weaknesses.

In modern art, deformation is taken to be a stylistic process that is no longer opposed to that of form; hence, the purpose and usefulness of caricature, in sculpture as in drawing, loses meaning and relevance.

SILVIA HUOBER

See also **Dantan, Jean-Pierre; Daumier, Honoré; Messerschmidt, Franz Xaver**

Further Reading

Barilli, Renato, *Dalla caricatura al burattino: I grandi personaggi delle teste di legno di Umberto Tirelli* (exhib. cat.), Florence: Artificio, 1989

Battisti, Eugenio, et al., "Carattere," in *Enciclopedia universale dell'arte*, vol. 3, Rome: Istituto per la Collaborazion Culturalle, 1958

Campbell, Douglas, and Usher Caplan (editors), *Daumier, 1808–1879*, Ottawa, Ontario: National Gallery of Canada, 1999

Durbè, Dario, *Daumier scultore* (exhib. cat.), Milan: Ed. Poldi Pezzoli, 1961

Gianeri, Enrico, *Storia della caricatura*, Milan: Omnia, 1959

Gombrich, Ernst H., and E. Kris, "The Principles of Caricature," *British Journal of Medical Psychology* 17 (1938)

Honoré Daumier: Sculture, disegni, litografie, Florence: Vallecchi, 1980

Kjellberg, Pierre, *Les bronzes du XIXᵉ siècle: Dictionnaire des sculpteurs*, Paris: Ed. de l'Amateur, 1987; as *Bronzes of the 19th Century: Dictionary of Sculptors*, translated by Kate D. Loftus, Alison Levie, and Leslie Bockol, Atglen, Pennsylvania: Schiffer, 1994

Kris, Ernst, "The Psychology of Caricature," in *Psychoanalytic Explorations in Art*, London: Allen and Unwin, 1952

Lavin, Irving, "Bernini and the Art of Social Satire," in *Drawings by Gianlorenzo Bernini, from the Museum der Bildenden Künste, Leipzig, German Democratic Republic* (exhib.

cat.), Princeton, New Jersey: Art Museum, Princeton University, 1981

Ward-Jackson, Philip, "Dantan," in *The Dictionary of Art*, edited by Jane Turner, vol. 8, New York: Grove, and London: Macmillan, 1996

Wechsler, Judith, "Caricature," in *The Dictionary of Art*, edited by Jane Turner, vol. 5, New York: Grove, and London: Macmillan, 1996

Wright, Thomas, *History of Caricature and Grotesque in Literature and Art*, London: Virtue Brothers, 1865; reprint, New York: Ungar, 1968

CARLO DI CESARE DEL PALAGIO
1538–ca. 1598 *Italian*

The Munich court artist Carlo Pallago and Carlo di Cesare, an artist active in Saxony, were considered in earlier scholarship to be two separate people, until Herbert Keutner in 1992 established their identity as one person (see Keutner, 1992). Carlo di Cesare del Palagio was born in Florence, the son of a certain Cesare di Bartolomeo di Domenico (Caesar de Palatiis). The family's surname, del Palazzo (or del Palagio), probably derived from Cesare's position as a *donzello*, or guard at the Palazzo Vecchio in Florence.

For the greater part of his professional life, Carlo di Cesare worked at German princely courts. Possible works by him preserved in Italy require more research. Several accounts shed light on his early years as an assistant to Giorgio Vasari and Giambologna at the court of the Medici family in Florence. In 1560 he worked as a *garzone* (apprentice/assistant) for Giambologna, who was still young at the time and had not yet become court artist, on the latter's monumental model for the contest over the Neptune Fountain in Florence. Carlo di Cesare may have trained more as a plasterer or terracotta sculptor than as a stone or bronze sculptor, which would have qualified him for this sort of stucco sculpture. He appears as an independent sculptor (*scultore*) for the first time in 1565 with his preparatory work on the decorations for the famous Florentine royal wedding of Francesco I de' Medici to Joanna of Austria. He was entrusted by Vasari with ten papier-mâché herm figures for the Sala de' Cinquecento for these decorations. In the same year he was accepted, along with the other artists involved in the decorations, to the Florentine Accademia del Disegno and paid his membership dues through 1568.

Carlo di Cesare seems to have made a good name for himself through this and other works of decorative room design, because the German banker Hans Fugger took him into his service in Augsburg (Swabia) between 1569 and 1573 in the retinue of Friedrich Sustris. For Fugger's house, the artist created sculptural decorations in stucco and terracotta, which, like all the interior decorations designed by Sustris, closely emulate Vasari's taste for the grotesque. Twelve pairs of somewhat under-life-size satyrs in terracotta by Carlo di Cesare have been preserved in the library, one of the earliest and finest ensembles in the Florentine Mannerist style in Germany.

After completing his work in Augsburg, Carlo di Cesare moved in 1573 to the imperial court in Vienna. But the prospects for work there were poor, and he soon allowed himself to be recruited by the Bavarian crown prince William, who wanted to have his residence in Burg Trausnitz above Landshut decorated by Sustris after the fashion of Hans Fugger. Beginning in 1574, he worked in Munich on marble busts for the Antiquarium of the Residenz, in Landshut on the stucco decoration of Burg Trausnitz, and on bronze figures for a fountain that the crown prince had ordered for the gardens in Landshut. After considerable difficulties with the cast, to which Carlo di Cesare attended personally, the figures were displayed in 1578. Two explicitly Florentine satyr figures and several putti from this fountain have been preserved in the Munich Residenz. Thus, he may be considered the initiator of figural bronze casting at the Bavarian ducal court. Whether a fountain figure of Venus in the National Gallery in Washington, D.C., belongs to the ensemble, as Keutner has suggested, is still debated (see Keutner, 1992).

Carlo di Cesare resided in Florence between 1579 and 1581. In 1581 he began working for the Fuggers again; from this point on he produced almost all of his works in Augsburg and Munich in collaboration with the sculptor Hubert Gerhard. In 1582–84 they created 12 over-life-size figures of famous men and women for the hall of Hans Fugger's castle in Kirchheim (Mindel). The terracotta figures of the apostles on the gate of the Fugger Chapel in the Church of Ss. Ulrich and Afra in Augsburg can also be attributed to these same artists. After completing his work for the Fuggers, Carlo di Cesare returned to the service of Duke William V of Bavaria, who had a tremendous need for sculptors for his architectural projects: the Church of St. Michael (Michaelskirche) in Munich and his new Residenz, designed by Sustris. From 1585 until 1588 Carlo di Cesare received large sums of money from the Munich court, probably for interior decorations in the buildings of the Residenz all around the Grottenhof (grotto courtyard) and in the Antiquarium. The Antiquarium, which was damaged in World War II, has been restored. Because the other constructions by Sustris are completely lost, one should look at the Fugger house in Augsburg to obtain a better idea of this phase in Carlo di Cesare's career.

In 1588 Carlo di Cesare returned to Florence and in the same year was recruited by Prince-Elector Christian I of Saxony (*r.* 1586–91) through Giambologna's mediation. Between 1590 and 1593 Carlo worked on the sculptural decoration of the Wettiner Memorial Chapel (Wettiner Begräbniskapelle), renovated from the old choir in Freiberg Cathedral (Saxony) by Giovanni Maria Nosseni. This was to be his greatest independent work. He decorated Nosseni's architecture from top to bottom with life-size figures. On the bottom are the electoral princes and princesses, five kneeling portrait figures in bronze. On the altar are the figures of the Crucified Christ with St. John the Baptist and St. Paul (bronze), and above is the *Resurrection*, in stucco. *Day of Judgment*, a painted panorama with stucco figures, is on the ceiling. To the upper wall decoration, Carlo di Cesare added eight prophets and putti (in stucco) with musical instruments. Carlo di Cesare drew strongly on the example of Giambologna, most pronouncedly in the adoption of the hard, rigid features of his forms. The faces are severe, almost torpidly stylized, which lends a particular dignity to the portrait figures of the princes. The casting and chasing were quite painstaking.

While Carlo di Cesare was still working on the projects in Saxony, Emperor Rudolf II attempted to obtain leave for the sculptor to come to Prague for a short time. For what purpose he intended to use Carlo di Cesare remains unclear, as Adriaen De Vries was already in Prague at that time. In 1592 the Bavarian Duke William V inquired after Carlo, probably with an eye to the large project he had planned for a tomb for himself and his wife, Renata von Lothringen (Renata of Lorraine), in the Church of St. Michael in Munich, which the Duke had founded. Carlo di Cesare immediately pursued this offer at the end of his commitment in Freiberg (Saxony) in 1593. He worked in collaboration with Gerhard on the tomb monument for Duke William and his wife. Although almost all of the figures were cast, the monument was never erected, owing to the duke's abdication. Of the remaining bronze figures, the following have been assigned to Carlo di Cesare: two knights (later relocated to tomb of Louis IV the Bavarian at the Cathedral Church of Our Lady [Frauenkirche], Munich), two lions (west facade of the Munich Residenz), and four richly decorated candelabras (Church of St. Michael, Munich). Also attributed to him is the ornamental heraldic cartouche under the St. Michael on the facade.

In 1597 the sculptor returned to Italy. He drew up his final will on 22 August 1598 and may have died shortly thereafter, certainly before September 1600. Carlo di Cesare's remaining oeuvre stands as one of the most prolific among those sculptors trained in Florence in the entourage of Giambologna and Vasari. His work consists almost exclusively of large figures in bronze and terracotta. The few surviving works of interior decorations in stucco and terracotta demonstrate

his superior abilities in this genre as well. In terms of small bronzes, as yet only one has been attributed to him, although he must have made many of them, as Nosseni's inventory in Dresden indicates. Carlo di Cesare's monumental figures reveal his knowledge of the repertory of Florentine late Mannerism, yet he never strove to create a complicated, multiview figural construction in the fashion of Giambologna. In his collaboration with Gerhard, he proved his stylistic flexibility.

DOROTHEA DIEMER

Biography

Born in Florence, Italy, 1538. Worked as assistant to Giambologna, 1560; worked under Giorgio Vasari on decorations for Florentine royal wedding, 1565; completed stucco and terracotta decorations in the house of Hans Fugger in Augsburg, Germany, 1569–73; worked under Crown Prince William of Bavaria in Landshut and Munich, 1573–79; resided in Florence, 1579–81; called back to Augsburg by the Fugger family, 1581; in the service of Duke William V of Bavaria, 1584–88; worked on a large commission from Prince-Elector Christian I of Saxony for bronze and stucco figures for Wettiner tomb in Freiberg Cathedral, Saxony, Germany, 1590–93; collaborated on tomb in Church of St. Michael, Munich, for its founder, Duke William V of Bavaria, 1593–97; returned to Italy, 1597. Died in Mantua, Italy, *ca.* 1598.

Selected Works

1569–73 Figurative decorations; terracotta, stucco; Fugger House, Augsburg, Swabia, Germany

1573–78 Two satyrs and several putti; bronze; Residenz, Munich, Germany

1582–84 Twelve statues of famous men and women (with Hubert Gerhard); terracotta; Palace (Schloss), Kirchheim an der Mindel, Swabia, Germany

1590–93 Statues of *Crucifixion, Resurrection*, and electoral princes and princesses; bronze, terracotta, stucco; Wettiner Memorial Chapel, Freiberg Cathedral, Germany

1593–97 Coat of arms of Bavarian dukedom; bronze; facade of Church of St. Michael, Munich, Germany

1593–97 Four candelabra; bronze; Church of St. Michael, Munich, Germany

1593–97 Two knights carrying banners with coats of arms, for the tomb of Duke William V of Bavaria; bronze; Cathedral Church of Our Lady, Munich, Germany

1593–97 Two lions bearing emblems; bronze; Residenz, Munich, Germany

Further Reading

Baxandall, Michael, "A Masterpiece by Hubert Gerhard," *Victoria and Albert Museum Bulletin* 1/2 (April 1965)

Diemer, Dorothea, "Quellen und Untersuchungen zum Stiftergrab Herzog Wilhelms V. von Bayern und der Renate von Lothringen in der Münchner Michaelskirche," in *Quellen und Studien zur Kunstpolitik der Wittelsbacher*, edited by Hubert Glaser, Munich: Hirmer, 1980

Diemer, Dorothea, "Carlo di Cesari del Palagio," in *The Dictionary of Art*, edited by Jane Turner, vol. 5, New York: Grove, and London: Macmillan, 1996

Diemer, Dorothea, "Small Bronzes by Hubert Gerhard," *Studies in the History of Art* 62 (2001)

Feuchtmayr, Karl, "Pallago, Carlo," in *Allgemeines Lexikon der bildenden Künstler von der Antike bis zur Gegenwart*, edited by Ulrich Thieme, Felix Becker, and Hans Vollmer, vol. 26, Leipzig: Engelmann, 1932; reprint, Leipzig: Seemann, 1978

Keutner, Herbert, "Carlo di Cesare del Palagio (1540–1598): Eine Bronzevenus aus dem Garten der Burg Trausnitz?" *Münchner Jahrbuch der bildenden Kunst* 3rd series, 42 (1992)

Meine-Schawe, Monika, and Giovanni Maria Nosseni, *Die Grablege der Wettiner im Dom zu Freiberg: Die Umgestaltung des Domchores durch Giovanni Maria Nosseni 1585–1594*, Munich: Tudov, 1992

Sigismund, E., "Carlo de Cesare," in *Allgemeines Lexikon der bildenden Künstler von der Antike bis zur Gegenwart*, edited by Ulrich Thieme, Felix Becker, and Hans Vollmer, vol. 6, Leipzig: Engelmann, 1912; reprint, Leipzig: Seemann, 1978

CARMONA, LUIS SALVADOR

See **Salvador Carmona, Luis**

ANTHONY CARO 1924– *British*

Anthony Caro studied engineering at Cambridge, an interest that would emerge in his sculpture, and spent his vacations studying at Farnham School of Art in Surrey, England. After serving in the Royal Navy for two years, he continued to study sculpture in London and worked as an assistant to the sculptor Henry Moore for three years until 1953. Moore's influence can be seen in Caro's earliest works. Modeled in clay and cast in bronze, they deal with representations of the human body. However, Caro was less interested in rendering the external form of the body than in expressing the feeling of an action. *Woman Waking Up* and *Man Taking Off His Shirt* express the inner effort of the action and its effect on the body, the "livedness" of the body, as Michael Fried, the author of the most important analyses of Caro's earlier work, has called it (see Caro exhibition catalogues, 1963, 1969). Although these examples seem far removed from the steel constructions for which Caro was to become better known, their at-

tempt to create a connection between the object and the viewer foreshadows the later sculptures. These early attempts revealed to Caro the limitation of modeling and casting, as well as the shortcomings of what was still a rather literal, and hence artificial, form of expression. The necessity of using a pedestal to present the sculptures further served to accentuate the isolation of the object.

Caro's visit to the United States in 1959 was a turning point for him. Among the artists he met were Kenneth Noland and David Smith, who had a profound influence on his work. Clement Greenberg wrote of Caro that "he is the only sculptor whose sustained quality can bear comparison with Smith's. With him it has become possible at long last to talk of a generation in sculpture that really comes after Smith's" (see Greenberg, 1967). Noland's geometric abstraction and Smith's metal constructions are both visible in Caro's first abstract sculpture, *Twenty-Four Hours*, which he executed immediately after returning from the United States. A planar composition of cut steel, bolted and welded together, *Twenty-Four Hours* marked the beginning of Caro's lifelong preoccupation with metal assemblages. By placing the sculpture on the floor rather than on a pedestal and leaving welding seams undisguised, Caro indicated his rejection of what he called the "precious-object, precious-material convention." *Midday*, a larger metal construction made in the same year, demonstrates that although Caro borrowed from Smith's method of sculpture making, his work is configured in an entirely different manner. Unlike Smith's sculptures, which, despite their abstraction, can still be read as a coherent, often figurelike, form, Caro removed any resemblance to a tangible image.

Early One Morning
© Tate Gallery, London / Art Resource, NY

Early One Morning, a steel and aluminum construction painted red, dismembers the sculptural image into a series of parts. The longest element measures over six meters. It dominates the side view of the whole work and seems to determine the relationship of the other parts. From the front, however, the sculpture appears to lose its horizontal emphasis by compressing itself into a nearly unified plane, which Rosalind Krauss has identified as a "pictorial" tendency in Caro's work of that period (see Krauss, 1977). Depending on where the viewer stands, the sculpture yields two opposite experiences, one emphasizing its construction, the other presenting a pictorial image. The absence of a single fixed focus continues in subsequent works, such as *Red Splash* and *Prairie*. By using the ground, rather than a pedestal, as a base, the works directly share the space of the viewer. They attempt to describe a space and the viewer's relationship to it rather than an object or image.

In an interview in 1961, Caro stated that "America was the catalyst for a change in my work—there's a fine art quality about European art even when it's made from junk." Caro's rejection of a "fine art" aesthetic played an important part in the development of European sculpture. During a second, longer trip to the United States in 1963, Caro's affinity with American sculpture became further entrenched. He held a teaching post at Bennington College, Bennington, Vermont, and kept in contact with Noland and Smith. His sculptures from this period are simpler, more linear, mostly very low to the ground, and suggest the influence of American Minimalist sculpture. Although Caro cannot be described as a Minimalist, his work can be seen in the context of the "floor sculpture" that originated in the United States with artists such as Donald Judd, Carl Andre, and Robert Morris.

During his long career, Caro's work continued to undergo a series of transitions, beginning in 1966, with a series of tabletop sculptures. The use of a table could be read as a resurrection of the pedestal that Caro had previously abolished from his work, but it was also a solution for the presentation of works too small to be placed on the floor. Caro's inventory of materials opened up with the introduction of lead, wood, and paper. He continued to make smaller pieces, such as the calligraphic "writing pieces" that began in 1978 and paper reliefs in 1981, but he also moved toward larger, monumental structures. The correlation to architecture, already suggested in works from the early 1960s by the use of steel girders, I-beams, and other materials associated with the construction industry, became increasingly visible from the 1970s. A visit to the Ripamonti Steel Works in Italy inspired Caro to work with enormous sheets of rolled steel. The resulting *Verduggio Sound* series was highly architectonic in tone, its tall, open structures suggesting walls, arches, and portals. Caro was able to continue similar sculptures in 1974 at the steel works in Toronto, where the facilities again allowed him to work with large pieces of steel. In 1984 he exhibited his first architectural piece, *Child's Tower Room*, a structure large enough for children to climb into, for which Caro coined the term "*sculpitecture*."

Caro continues to make and exhibit sculptures and takes an active interest in architecture. A knighthood in 1987 recognized his contribution to both sculpture and architecture. More recently, he collaborated with the British architect Norman Foster on the Millennium Bridge Project to build the first pedestrian bridge over the river Thames in London since 1894.

MARTINA DROTH

Biography

Born in New Malden, Surrey, England, 28 March 1924. Worked in studio of Charles Wheeler until 1942; studied engineering at Cambridge and art at Farnham School of Art, 1942–44; studied sculpture at Royal Academy Schools, London, 1947–52, then at Regent Street Polytechnic, London, 1956–57; worked as part-time assistant to Henry Moore, 1951–53; taught at St. Martin's School of Art, London, 1953–79; first solo exhibition, Milan, Italy, 1956, then London, 1957; showed at Venice Biennale, 1958; traveled to United States, 1959; met Kenneth Noland and David Smith; returned to Britain and made first abstract sculpture, *Twenty-Four Hours*, 1960; in the United States again, 1963; taught at Bennington College, Bennington, Vermont, and had first solo exhibition in New York City; made a series of steel sculptures in Italy, 1972, and in Canada, 1974; began making "table sculptures," 1977; appointed Trustee of the Tate Gallery, London, 1982; won international design competition for pedestrian bridge over the river Thames, London, in collaboration with architect Norman Foster and engineer Ove Arup. Retrospective exhibitions include Hayward Gallery, London, England, 1969; Museum of Modern Art, New York City, United States, 1975; Musée des Beaux-Arts, Calais, France, 1990; Trajan Markets, Rome, Italy, 1992; Annely Juda Fine Art, London, England, 1994. Presently living in London, England.

Selected Works

1955   *Woman Waking Up*; bronze; Tate Gallery, London, England

1955–56 *Man Taking Off His Shirt*; bronze; collection of Philip King, London, England

1960 *Midday*; steel painted yellow; Museum of Modern Art, New York City, United States

1960 *Twenty-Four Hours*; painted steel; Tate Gallery, London, England

1962 *Early One Morning*; steel and aluminium painted red; Tate Gallery, London, England

1964 *Bennington*; painted steel; Jules Olitski collection, Bennington, Vermont, United States

1966 *Red Splash*; steel painted red; David Mirvish Gallery, Toronto, Ontario,Canada

1967 *Prairie*; steel painted ochre; private collection, Princeton, New Jersey, United States

1972–73 *Verduggio Sound* series; steel, rusted and varnished; Kunsthaus, Zurich, Switzerland

1983–84 *Child's Tower Room*; Japanese oak, varnished; private collection, London, England

1991 *Tower of Discovery*; painted steel; Annely Juda Fine Art, London, England

Further Reading

Anthony Caro: Sculpture, 1960–1963 (exhib. cat.), London: Whitechapel Gallery, 1963

Anthony Caro (exhib. cat.), London: Arts Council of Great Britain, 1969

Anthony Caro, Table Top Sculptures, 1973–1974 (exhib. cat.), London: Greater London Council, 1974

Aspects of Anthony Caro: Recent Sculpture, 1981–89 (exhib. cat.), London: Annely Juda Fine Art, 1989

Blume, Dieter, *The Sculpture of Anthony Caro*, 9 vols., London: Lund Humphries, 1992

Fenton, Terry, *Anthony Caro*, London: Thames and Hudson, and New York: Rizzoli, 1986

Greenberg, Clement, "Anthony Caro," *Studio International* (September 1967)

Krauss, Rosalind, *Passages in Modern Sculpture*, London: Thames and Hudson, and New York: Viking, 1977

CAROLINGIAN SCULPTURE

The terms "Carolingian sculpture" and "Carolingian art" generally refer to the body of works promoted by the court of Charlemagne and his successors, chiefly his son Louis the Pious and his grandsons Lothair I and Charles the Bald. More exactly, the time frame extends from the mid 8th century (the beginning of the reign of Pepin the Short) to the early 9th century when the Frankish empire was breaking down.

Charlemagne, Pepin's eldest son, was elected king of the Franks in 751 and crowned at the abbey of Saint-Denis by Pope Stephen II. He extended his dominions to the north by conquering Saxony and to the south by destroying the Lombard kingdom. He proclaimed himself king of the Franks and the Lombards and placed the Papal States under his protection. On Christmas Eve in the year 800, at St. Peter's Basilica in Rome, Pope Leo II crowned Charlemagne emperor with the title of *Romanum gubernans imperium*—a new Constantine. The date marks the birth of the Carolingian empire—a new political and cultural unit with close ties to the Catholic Church—which consolidated the hegemony of the Germanic people over the whole of central Europe.

Among the many initiatives of the Carolingian court (some planned by Pepin but actually carried out by Charlemagne) were the reinstatement of written Latin as the universal language, reform of the cathedrals, and the establishment of capitular schools and a Palatine School, for which Charlemagne summoned the Irish monk Alcuin to direct. The political and religious underpinnings of this resurrected unity engendered throughout the empire a revival of learning and the arts, which is now known as the Carolingian Renaissance. In the arts, this development began in the court's cultural centers—Aachen, Ingelheim, and Paderborn—and the great monasteries patronized by the royal family (first and foremost the Abbey of Saint-Denis, but also Reims, Metz, Tours, Mainz, Lyons, Fulda, and Lorsch). From the very outset, it was propagated through the monastic network to Switzerland (St. Gallen and St. John's at Münster) and northern Italy (Bobbio and S. Benedetto at Malles Venosta). After Charlemagne's death in 814, the revival faded. In 817, Louis the Pious divided the empire among his three surviving sons, Louis the German, Lothair, and Charles the Bald. Thereafter, the lack of a central government and internecine struggles among the three successor kings caused the activities of the great work-

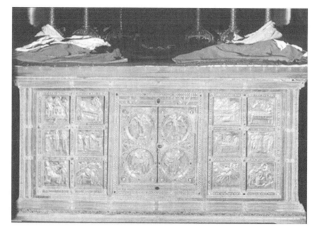

Master Wolvinus: *Paliotto* (Golden Altar) of S. Ambrogio, early 9th century, Milan, Italy
© Scala / Art Resource, NY

Detail of medallion with animal from Basilica of Aquileia, *ca.* 820–30
© Elio Ciol / CORBIS

shops of Gaul to cease. By the end of Charles the Bald's reign, patronage of the arts had virtually ceased.

Sculpture, like the other arts practiced in the Carolingian era, was characterized by an intentional return to the formal values of Late Antiquity in accordance with Charlemagne's project of *Renovatio romani imperii*, restoring the Roman Empire. Despite the scarcity of surviving works and scholarly studies, today art historians recognize in Carolingian sculpture, as well as architecture, a language that was in common use throughout the empire, although with regional differences. In an overall evaluation of early medieval art, this common language and its rereading of antiquity represents the acme of artistic development between late Roman times and the Romanesque era.

From this standpoint, perhaps the best example is the small 9th-century bronze equestrian statue from Metz (now in the Musée du Louvre, Paris). The rider, with his sword, crown, and orb—the symbols of power—is probably Charlemagne himself. The piece is clearly modeled on ancient examples. Moreover, it is one of the few examples of Carolingian sculpture in the round, as relief was the dominant form of sculpture in that day.

According to tradition, Charlemagne was also portrayed in a stucco statue on the eastern end of St. John's Church in Münster, where an important abbey was founded at the emperor's behest. Here he is represented standing, crowned, and bearing his orb and scepter. A

great deal of decorative work in stucco, combined with frescos, survives in Carolingian churches, such as S. Salvatore in Brescia, Italy, and S. Benedetto in Málles Venosta, Italy. Sculpture in stucco, as well as bronze and stone, is known to have been widely used during the period in the restoration and decoration of old and new religious buildings. Many cathedrals and monastic churches were reoriented to the west following the Roman models of St. Peter's Basilica and the Basilica of S. Giovanni in Laterno, and stone panels were installed to separate the worshippers from the altar. Like the ciborium (canopy over the altar) and the pulpit (facing the worshipers in the nave), these panels lent themselves to sculptural decoration. Many of these 8th- and 9th-century examples, carved in geometric or wickerwork patterns, survive in far-flung locations. Throughout the empire, the patterns were strikingly similar. The region with the highest density of these carved partitions is around the present-day borders of Italy, Switzerland, and Austria, where the old stone quarries are still operating. When the Aquitaine stoneworkers were unable to keep up with the needs of the architectural renaissance, the workshops of this region began to export their output, and knot-work decoration spread far and wide. The abstract motifs of the panels made for S. Benedetto in Málles Venosta (now in Bolzano), Schänis (Switzerland), and Aix-en-Provence, to name only a few of the best-known examples, were not an original creation of Carolingian art, but an original reworking of familiar Nordic and oriental patterns. Similar motifs appeared, for example, in the illumination of contemporary manuscripts. Likewise, the decorative elements adorning the stone ciborium at the Church of Sant'Apollinare in Classe in Ravenna, carved with knot work and stylized animals, and the cross at Budrio, near Bologna—both dating from the early 9th century—call to mind a Merovingian taste that typified the artistic output of the regions dominated by the Merovingians from the 5th to the 8th centuries. The only decoration that can be considered a true creation of the Carolingian Renaissance appears on the partition at Saint-Pierre-en-Citadelle, in Metz, and it is marked by its explicit reference to Classical art. This work dates to the latter part of the 8th century, but, not surprisingly, it was long thought to be from the early Christian era.

Political motivations fueled Charlemagne's emulation of Antiquity. From this standpoint, Theodoric, in Ravenna, was Charlemagne's prototype, Aachen was the ideal center of his ideological program, and the Palatine Chapel in Aachen, consecrated in 805, was its symbol. Its architecture imitated that of Church of S. Vitale in Ravenna, the Eastern Roman Empire's last seat in the West. Columns, capitals, and other architectural elements came to Aachen directly from Ravenna, together with an equestrian statue of Theodoric. A stucco capital from the Carolingian era, still preserved in the Palatine Chapel next to its stone model, attests to this project for imitating the ancients. Many other examples in carved partitions, columns, arches, and capitals installed throughout the empire's territory—in the Fulda Abbey church (today in Marburg), in Lorsch, in the museum complex of S. Giulia in Brescia, and so forth—display the great skill with which the Carolingian sculptors read and faithfully imitated Classical language.

The Carolingians' evocation of ancient art appears most clearly in carved ivories and metalwork, such as the eight bronze gates of the Palatine Chapel's tribune parapet. Because their structure is quite similar to that of the stone balustrades at Sant'Apollinare Nuovo in Ravenna, they were long thought to have been taken from Theodoric's mausoleum in that city. However, the discovery of a foundry on the palace grounds suggests their local construction at a sort of court workshop that would also have produced the chapel's whole-cast portals and side doors. The compositions are simple, and the details—acanthus leaves wreathing a lion's head—are clearly derived from late Roman models.

The Carolingians used ivory almost exclusively for religious purposes—diptychs and book covers—hence ivory objects were often carved at the same centers that produced illuminated manuscripts, in particular at the school at Aachen. High-quality ivories appeared even before Charlemagne's time, but their production increased considerably during his reign in order to meet the needs of the scriptoria and libraries involved in the great cultural revival. Today we know that the royal treasury contained a huge number of early Christian ivories, most of them produced by the schools of Milan and Ravenna and acquired as war spoils in northern and southern Italy. Since these works served as models for the Carolingian ivories, it is particularly difficult to date the latter. Splendid examples can be seen in the covers of Dagulf's Psalter (783–95; Louvre) and the following works from the early 9th century: the Oxford Psalter (Bodleian Library, Oxford), the Genoels-Elderen diptych (Musées Royaux d'Art et d'Histoire, Brussels), and the diptych of the Lorsch Gospels (covers of the Codex Aureus, Victoria and Albert Museum, London; Biblioteca Apostolica Vaticana, Museo Sacro, Rome). The iconography appearing in these works corresponds faithfully to their respective models, but the style is new; the figures attach to one another and their anatomy is increasingly blurred. The Leipzig *St. Michael* (Museum für Kunsthandwerk), the Darmstadt *Ascension* (Hessisches Landesmuseum), and the Narbonne *Crucifixion* (in the Cathedral Treasury), all from the early 9th century, further verify this development, and are perhaps its apotheosis.

After Charlemagne's death, the court humanists continued to hold to the Antiquity-oriented ideas of the Aachen school, but as the central government disintegrated, its artistic style was dispersed to peripheral centers controlled by bishoprics and monasteries. The ivories produced in this period at the schools of Tours, Reims, and above all, Metz—for instance, the covers of Bishop Drogo's Sacramentary (mid 9th century, Bibliothèque Nationale, Paris)—resemble the last works of the Aachen school in their quasi-pictorial style, despite a more limited sense of space, freer iconography, and more animated composition.

The great personage who rebuilt the unity of the empire after its tripartite division was Charles the Bald, a lover of ancient art and a protector of the various artistic schools. The ivory objects he commissioned from the workshops of Corbie, Reims, and especially Saint-Denis confirm that, following Charlemagne's example, he also used the arts to augment his own imperial majesty. The ivories crafted early in his reign recall those of Charlemagne's school, whereas the later ones, such as the covers of Charles the Bald's Psalter (Bibliothèque Nationale, Paris), tend to depart from the prototypes.

It is in the ivories and the goldsmiths' work produced by these schools that their output seems most unified. The goldsmiths' works display a sure mastery of the various techniques—filigrain, granulation, intaglio, embossing, embedding, and enamel chasing (the latter entered the repertory at that very time)—and reflect the Carolingian artists' particular taste for precious materials. This type of production was related to liturgical developments and to the growing demand for articles such as chalices, holy-water fonts, crosses, and reliquaries. The combination of knot work and stylized animals in the ornamentation of the earlier works—for instance, the first binding of the Lindau Gospels (early 9th century, Pierpont Morgan Library, New York) or Duke Tassilo III's chalice (*ca.* 777, Kremsmünster Abbey)—leads one to think that they must have been derived from works made in the British Isles. Indeed, it has been suggested that an Irish or Anglo-Saxon school was operating on German soil. Conversely, the style in later works is distinguished by highly plastic effects. Especially during Charles the Bald's reign, the goldsmiths of Saint-Denis and Reims, in particular, produced excellent works. One of the most impressive for quality and style is the altar made by Vuolvinius for S. Ambrogio in Milan (*ca.* 840). Originally designed as a sarcophagus-reliquary, it is faced with embossed gold and silver leaf, and the panel frames are studded with gems and inlaid with enamel. On the front, a Christ Triumphant is flanked by 12 panels depicting scenes from his life; on the back are another 12 panels embossed with scenes from the life of St. Ambrose and two unique scenes that, together with an inscription in capital letters, enable us to identify the people responsible for the work. One of these two silver panels shows Archbishop Angilberto II of Milan, who commissioned the reliquary, offering it symbolically to St. Ambrose, who places a crown on the prelate's head. In the second, the craftsman shows himself being crowned by St. Ambrose and signs himself *Vuolvinius Magister Phaber* (Vuolvinius the Smith). The appearance of the artist's name, not to mention a self-portrait, can be taken as another symbol of the revival of the arts in the Carolingian era.

LORENZO CARLETTI

Further Reading

Braunfels, Wolfgang (editor), *Karl der Grosse: Werk und Wirkung* (exhib. cat.), Aachen, Germany, and Düsseldorf, Germany: Schwann, 1965

Braunfels, Wolfgang, *Die Welt der Karolinger und ihre Kunst*, Munich: Callway, 1968

Bullough, Donald A., *Carolingian Renewal: Sources and Heritage*, Manchester: Manchester University Press, 1991

Goldschmidt, Adolf, Paul Gustav Heuloner, and Otto Homburger, *Die Elfenbeinskulpturen aus der Zeit der karolingischen und sächsischen Kaiser*, Berlin: Deutscher Verlag für Kunstwissenschaft, 1969

Hegemann, Hans Werner, "Elfenbeinkunst in der Karolingerzeit," in *Das Elfenbein in Kunst und Kultur Europas: Ein Überblick von der Antike bis zur Gegenwart*, Mainz, Germany: Von Zabern, 1988

Hinks, Roger Packman, *Carolingian Art*, London: Sidgwick and Jackson, 1935

Hubert, Jean, Jean Porcher, and Friedrich Wolfgang Volbach, *L'émpire carolingien*, Paris: Gallimard, 1968; as *The Carolingian Renaissance*, translated by James Emmons, Stuart Gilbert, and Robert Allen, New York: Braziller, 1970

Lasko, Peter, *Ars Sacra, 800–1200*, London and Baltimore, Maryland: Penguin, 1972; 2nd edition, New Haven, Connecticut: Yale University Press, 1994

Volbach, Fritz Wolfgang, *Elfenbeinarbeiten der Spätantike und des frühen Mittelalters*, Mainz, Germany: Von Zabern, 1976

JEAN-BAPTISTE CARPEAUX 1827–1875
French

As the leading French sculptor of the Second Empire, Jean-Baptiste Carpeaux challenged contemporary French academic sculpture by expressing a new sense of naturalism and rhythm in his works. He received his initial artistic instruction in his native town of Valenciennes before studying at the Petite École in Paris, the state school for training in the applied arts. In 1844 he entered the École des Beaux-Arts as a student of François Rude. Winning the Prix de Rome in 1854 enabled Carpeaux to study, as a pensioner at the Villa Medici, the works of the Italian Renaissance sculptors (Michelangelo, Donatello, and Andrea del Verrocchio). While in Rome, Carpeaux often questioned the rules of academia, frequently disagreeing with Jean-Victor Schnetz, the director of the Académie de France, over his student works' subject matter and composition.

Although critics denounced Carpeaux's two major works sent to Paris from Rome, the realistic *Fisherboy Listening to a Seashell* and the monumental *Count Ugolino and His Sons*, these works introduced his name in Paris and helped him begin his career as an official sculptor. Michelangelo's principles strongly influenced *Count Ugolino and His Sons*, commissioned by the French state, but its Dantesque inspiration and agonized realism offended the French tradition of the ideal. Carpeaux took several years to complete the final pyramidal five-figured composition. Despite the criticism, the French government nevertheless placed this work, cast in bronze, in the Tuileries Gardens. The Salon of 1863 established Carpeaux's name; he exhibited finished versions there of *Fisherboy Listening to a Seashell* and *Count Ugolino and His Sons*, as well as a portrait bust of *Princess Mathilde*, the emperor's authoritative cousin, which gained him a first-class medal. That same year brought him major monumental commissions, such as the architectural decoration of the Pavillon de Flore at the Palais du Louvre (*Imperial France Enlightening the Word and Protecting Science and Agriculture and Flora*), the group of *Temperance* on the facade of the Paris Church of La Trinité, and *The Dance* for the facade of the Paris Opéra, which was officially commissioned in 1865 and unveiled in 1869.

As early as 1864 Carpeaux entered the imperial circle as artistic tutor to the prince imperial and executed *The Prince Imperial and His Dog*. This work introduced informality in 19th-century portraiture, and Carpeaux's success with the imperial family combined with increasing public recognition.

In 1866 Carpeaux established a studio to reproduce his works for sale. Most were reductions of his Salon sculptures, public monuments, or portraits, which appealed to the bourgeois market, commercialized in a variety of materials (terracottas, bronzes, plasters, and even in Sèvres porcelain), dimensions, and mounts under the direction of his father, Joseph. Carpeaux's younger brother, Emile, played the role of a sales manager and organized auctions of his brother's works in Paris, London, Amsterdam, and Brussels. Extremely attracted to technical procedures, Carpeaux took an active interest in studio matters and developed a new method for the fabrication of terracottas.

Carpeaux received a commission in 1867 for the monumental Statues of the Four Cardinal Points, to be the crowning element of the Fontaine de l'Observatoire in the Jardin du Luxembourg in Paris. In 1869 the completion of the group *The Dance* for the Paris Opéra provoked outrage; it was vandalized and threatened with removal. Its unbalanced composition received hostile criticism, and the sensuality of the naked figures shocked public morals.

A tireless modeler, Carpeaux would start from an initial clay sketch with rough surface treatment in order to produce a smoother final version. He then expanded the original small-scale model to the size of the full-length final composition. Drawing was essential to those first stages of his sculptural production, as he could examine new ideas and experiment with variations in composition, gesture, and movement. His working method for portrait busts was slightly different; for these he first executed a life-size model in clay, which he then cast in plaster using the waste-mold process. His early education had given him a solid background in reproductive techniques and had introduced him to the principles of plaster casts.

After the events of the Commune and the Franco-Prussian War, Carpeaux lived for a time in London, where he found a market for his portrait busts and decorative sculptures. His last years were unhappy; he was estranged from his wife, Amélie de Montfort, and he fought cancer, which eventually killed him. His widow gained control of the Auteuil studio and managed it until her death, when their daughter, Louise Clément-Carpeaux, undertook those duties.

Carpeaux's work provided an alternative to academic norms, and his portraits were more naturalistic and expressive than those by his contemporary Albert-Ernest Carrier-Belleuse; the rich vocabulary Carpeaux used in his compositions contributed to the pictorial character of his sculpture. His influence is evident in the works of a whole generation of sculptors and especially prefigures Auguste Rodin, his student at the Petite École and admirer. In addition, Carpeaux's serial commercialization of sculptures throughout his career helped sculptors of his own generation realize the commercial importance of diffusing their works.

ANNA TAHINCI

Biography

Born in Valenciennes, France, 11 May 1827. Moved to Paris with family, 1838; enrolled at Petite École, Paris, by 1842, and at École des Beaux-Arts, 1844; won Prix de Rome, 1854; arrived in Rome, January 1856, for a five-year fellowship; executed two envois; back in Paris, 1861; received major official commissions and established own atelier in 1866; after the Commune and Franco-Prussian War, exiled in London. Died in Courbevoie, France, 11 October 1875.

Selected Works

An important collection of Carpeaux's sculptures is at the Musée des Beaux-Arts in Valenciennes, France.

1857   *Fisherboy Listening to a Seashell*; plaster; Musée du Louvre, Paris, France; Musée des Beaux-Arts, Valenciennes, France

1857–61 *Count Ugolino and His Sons*; plaster; Musée d'Orsay, Paris; bronze version: 1860, Musée d'Orsay, Paris; marble version, Metropolitan Museum of Art, New York City, United States

1863   *Princesse Mathilde*; marble; Musée des Beaux-Arts, Valenciennes, France

1863–66 *Flora*; stone; Pavillon de Flore, Musée du Louvre, Paris, France

1863–66 *Imperial France Enlightening the Word and Protecting Science and Agriculture*; stone; Pavillon de Flore, Musée du Louvre, Paris, France

1863–66 *Temperance*, for Church of La Trinité, Paris, France (destroyed, copy *in situ*)

1866   *The Dance*, for facade of Paris Opéra (1964 copy *in situ*); stone; Musée d'Orsay, Paris, France

1867   *The Prince Imperial and His Dog*; marble; Musée d'Orsay, Paris, France

1867   Statues of the Four Cardinal Points; bronze; Fontaine de l'Observatoire, Jardin du Luxembourg, Paris, France

Further Reading

Fusco, Peter, and H.W. Janson (editors), *The Romantics to Rodin: French Nineteenth-Century Sculpture from North American Collections* (exhib. cat.), Los Angeles: Los Angeles County Museum of Art, and New York: Braziller, 1980

Jeancolas, Claude, *Carpeaux: La farouche volonté d'être*, Lausanne, Switzerland: Edita, 1987

Margerie, Laure de, *Carpeaux: La fièvre créatrice*, Paris: Gallimard, 1989

Wagner, Anne Middleton, *Jean-Baptiste Carpeaux: Sculptor of the Second Empire*, New Haven, Connecticut: Yale University Press, 1986

THE DANCE (LE GÉNIE DE LA DANSE)

Jean-Baptiste Carpeaux (1827–1875)
1866
stone
h. 4.2 m
Musée d'Orsay, Paris, France; 1964 copy at the original site on the facade of the Paris Opéra, France

Sculptural ornament on architecture assumed an importance in the second half of the 19th century, and with Baron Georges Eugène Haussmann's rebuilding of Paris, sculptors benefited enormously. Carpeaux contributed to the sculptural decoration of major edifices: the Musée du Louvre and the new Paris Opéra. A group of dancing children depicting the *Triumph of Flora* for the Louvre indicated Carpeaux's quest for movement in sculpture and portended the furor that *The Dance* would create. He used the same circular format in the arrangement of the figures in the fountain representing the *Four Parts of the World* in the National Observatory in the Jardin du Luxembourg in Paris.

In September 1860, Napoléon III ordered the construction of a new opera house to replace that in rue Le Peletier. The young architect Charles Garnier won the contest. For 14 years he devoted himself to the prestigious building site. Although the facade was unveiled in August 1867, the opera house only officially opened in 1875, after the fall of the empire.

By the end of 1863, Garnier commissioned his friend Carpeaux to execute a monumental sculpture group for the principal facade of the new opera. The official commission, dated 16 August 1865, stipulated only the size, material, and placement of the group, making no mention of the subject. After many months of work Carpeaux executed several preparatory studies for *The Dance*. Instead of representing the allegory of the Dance, he decided to represent a circle of naked women whirling around the Genius. He later added the figures of a faun and putto. After Garnier had approved the plaster sketch in 1868, Carpeaux translated the group into stone. Aided by a group of *praticiens* (practitioners), Carpeaux began to carve the group *in situ*.

Unveiled to the Parisian public in 1869, the sculpture group provoked an enormous scandal. Among the series of sculptures that surround the doorways of the building on the ground floor, *La Musique* by Eugène Guillaume, *La Poésie lyrique* by François Jouffroy, and *La Drame lyrique* by Jean-Joseph Perraud appear today particularly academic compared with Carpeaux's *Dance*. Nevertheless, the public was shocked at the figures' wild, unclothed abandon, which violated contemporary standards of decent public statuary. Although the sculpture expressed joyful abandon with its intertwined figures, graceful draperies, and energetic facial expressions, the press published a series of critical articles and caricatures. Critics wrote about the group's realism and modernity, using those terms in both veneration and reproach. The sculpture even endured an act of vandalism: someone threw a bottle of ink at it during the night of 27 August 1869. Claiming he was protecting his right to diffuse pictures of his own work, Carpeaux persecuted a photographer who documented the damage and sold pictures. Public ani-

mosity nearly resulted in the sculpture's removal from the building, and Garnier was obliged to commission a new group from Charles Gumery. This group was made but was never erected because of the Franco-Prussian War of 1870 and Carpeaux's death in 1875. Carpeaux's death put an end to the controversy.

Due to the financial loss that Carpeaux endured, he decided to cast separate works inspired by his controversial group. This idea gave birth to nine separate sculptures connected to *The Dance*. The figure of the *Genius* proved extremely popular, and Carpeaux cast it in several different editions, dimensions, and materials (bronze, terracotta, plaster, and marble). The *Amour à la folie* was produced in bronze, terracotta, and plaster, and the *Three Graces* in bronze, terracotta, and marble. He cast the *Bacchante aux yeux baissés* (Bacchante with the eyes dropped), the *Bacchante criant* (Bacchante shouting), and the *Faune* in separate bronze editions, and Carpeaux's workshop produced the *Bacchante aux laurriers*, *Bacchante aux roses*, and *Bacchante aux vignes* in terracotta and marble. Carpeaux's

La Danse (Le Génie de la Danse)
© Erich Lessing / Art Resource, NY

workshop also produced terracottas of the *Genius* in three different dimensions and sold them until 1873.

The plaster preparatory model of the group is in the Detroit Institute of Arts, Michigan. In 1873 Carpeaux started executing a group of the monument in terracotta, inspired by the monumental plaster in his workshop. Carl Jacobsen, founder of the Ny Carlsberg Glyptotek in Copenhagen, bought the terracotta group. Plaster casts were inventoried in the Carpeaux studio after his death, and the Susse bronze foundry made posthumous editions of the *Genius* under the terms of a contract between the foundry and the artist's heirs in 1909.

After several petitions, *The Dance* was transported by the committee of the Monuments Historiques to the Musée du Louvre in 1964 and replaced at the Opéra by a copy carved by the sculptor Paul Belmondo. In July 1986 the group joined the sculpture collections of the newly opened Musée d'Orsay.

Ironically, although the scandal that the group caused was among the biggest in 19th-century world of sculpture, it was largely forgotten, and *The Dance* soon came to be hailed as Carpeaux's masterpiece. The vivaciousness of the figures and the lively effect of chiaroscuro created by the modeling of their surfaces have a strong affinity with Rococo art and confirm Carpeaux as Auguste Rodin's principal precursor.

ANNA TAHINCI

Further Reading

Margerie, Laure de, *La "Danse" de Carpeaux*, Paris: Éditions de la Réunion des Musées Nationaux, 1989

ALBERT-ERNEST CARRIER-BELLEUSE 1824–1887 *French*

From his earliest artistic training, a short apprenticeship to the chiseler Beauchery, then in the workshop of the goldsmith Jacques-Henri Fauconnier, Albert-Ernest Carrier-Belleuse's interests lay in the decorative arts. His family's friendship with David d'Angers opened doors for the young Carrier-Belleuse, enabling him to attend occasional classes at the École des Beaux-Arts and compete at the Paris Salon. He did not, however, enroll officially at the École des Beaux-Arts, preferring instead to study at the École Royale Gratuite de Dessin, or the Petite École, as it was also known, which offered commercially oriented design courses. He began to make his mark as a decorative artist by freelancing for well-known French manufacturers, including Barbedienne and Charpentier. Having taken part in the June revolution of 1849, Carrier-Belleuse fled to England, where he was invited to work as a modeler at Minton China Works in Stoke-on-Trent, the beginning of his lifelong involvement in porcelain design for Minton, Wedgwood, and Sèvres.

During his stay in England he taught regularly at local schools, exerting considerable influence on a generation of young designers in the region. He continued to build on his French contacts by sending designs to Parisian manufacturers. In 1855 Carrier-Belleuse returned to Paris and moved into a studio on the Rue de la Tour d'Auvergne, where he established himself as a decorative sculptor and portrait artist. His work quickly became regarded as highly fashionable and sought after in France and abroad, particularly in London and Brussels. With the rapid expansion of his atelier beginning in the late 1850s, Carrier-Belleuse employed many assistants. Several key figures in French 19th-century sculpture, including Alexandre Falguière, Aimé-Jules Dalou, Joseph Chéret, and most famously Auguste Rodin, began their artistic careers as apprentices in the Carrier-Belleuse atelier.

Carrier-Belleuse's productivity was as extraordinary for its scale as for its diversity. He applied sculpture to a great variety of forms, including statuettes and small figure groups, portrait busts, chinaware, metalwork, and various objets d'art, as well as to architectural and monumental sculpture. His work combined a decorative neo-Rococo and Mannerist style with a predilection for rich, luxurious colors and materials, qualities that especially came to the fore in his statuettes and vases designed for Sèvres, where he worked as artistic director from 1875 until his death. He was a particularly consummate modeler of clay, with a crisp, fresh, animated style strongly reminiscent of the 18th-century terracotta tradition embodied in Clodion and Jean-Antoine Houdon. Carrier-Belleuse's terracotta portrait busts were of contemporary individuals, such as Honoré Daumier, and historic figures, including John Milton, as well as fantasy busts of female figures, such as *Printemps* and *Bacchante*. The lively realism and flamboyancy of his busts, achieved by a careful surface finish with deep undercutting and decorative detail, departed radically from the staid Neoclassical ideals that were still standard practice at that time. For his statuette groups, he often chose subject matter that could be exploited for innuendo, including bacchantes and satyrs, Venuses and Cupids, and various other mythological nymphs and goddesses. The playful eroticism, coupled with a free, lighthearted tone, had immense popular appeal in his day.

Carrier-Belleuse also excelled in decorative metalwork, most famously his torchères, a stylistic convention prevalent in the 17th and 18th centuries, which enjoyed a revival during the Second Empire. His best-known torchères are the two magnificent figure groups that flank the grand staircase of Charles Garnier's Paris

Opera building. The Paris Opera torchères epitomize Carrier-Belleuse's mature style: ambitious and grandiose in conception, sumptuously decorative in execution, these eclectic figures look back unashamedly to the excesses of the 18th century while invoking a modern aesthetic for naturalistic forms. Their fine finish is characteristic of the artist, and it is this polished execution that endeared his work to the taste of the period. That he was able to uphold such high standards despite the large scale of his output suggests that he retained a significant degree of control over his workshop and remained personally involved in his productions. Indeed, it would be difficult to doubt his personal engagement with his work, considering that his distinctive style remained largely unmodified despite the presence of such exceptional artists as Rodin and Falguière in his workshop.

Disparaged by some for his trivial, even gaudy, subject matter, his disregard for stylistic convention, and his factory-scale output (the Goncourt brothers referred to him as "this shoddy trader in 18th-century style"), Carrier-Belleuse nevertheless won popular support for his commitment to raising the profile of the decorative arts. His disinclination to uphold divisions between fine and applied art was generally applauded, winning him the Diploma of Honor from the Union Centrale in 1884 and promotion to officer in the Legion of Honor for "services rendered to the Decorative Arts." Carrier-Belleuse occupied an unusual position in the art world. His ability to balance commercial productions with serious Salon sculptures ensured that he maintained his reputation as a skilled fine artist while simultaneously spreading his name and fame through a multiplicity of decorative objects in France and abroad. Despite his populist appeal, he stood outside the rules of convention, his animated, antiacademic realism winning him as much favor as it did controversy. Napoléon III, who bought the sculptor's nude *Bacchante* for the Tuileries at the Salon of 1863, affectionately referred to him as "our Clodion," a compliment turned into reproach by the Goncourts, who denounced Carrier-Belleuse as "that copier of Clodion," illustrating the artist's enigmatic position between acceptance and rejection.

Ironically, Carrier-Belleuse's versatility as sculptor and decorative artist—the key to his success in the mid 1800s—contributed to his neglect in modern art criticism. The strong decorative tendency that runs throughout his work diminished his standing as a serious sculptor in the history of art, and as a result, his artistic achievements and his influence on the 19th-century plastic arts has been largely overlooked. Ironically, the connection with his former pupil Rodin served to further damage his reputation. Rodin's rebellion against Carrier-Belleuse and the ultimate rejection

Torchères, Opera House, Paris, France
The Conway Library, Courtauld Institute of Art

of everything the elder stood for signified to modern sensibility the end of the eclectic, decorative commercialism in French sculpture and the birth of Modernism.

MARTINA DROTH

Biography

Born in Anizy-le-Château, France, 12 June 1824. Moved to Paris, *ca.* 1835; entered workshop of Beauchery, *ca.* 1837, then worked for Fauconnier until 1839; attended classes at École des Beaux-Arts, then enrolled at Petite École in early 1840s; made Salon debut, 1850; went to Britain to work at the Minton Factory, 1850; returned to Paris, 1855, to establish atelier; showed regularly at Paris Salon from 1857 on and began to take commissions mainly for decorative works and portraits; among notable studio assistants were Auguste Rodin, Aimé-Jules Dalou, and Alexandre Falguière; cofounded Paris Union Centrales des Arts Decoratifs, 1863; taught design at Académie Julian, 1860s; began work on Hotel Païva, 1865, assisted by Rodin; moved operations to Belgium at outbreak of Franco-Prussian War in 1870; worked with Rodin on new Bourse in Brussels; returned to Paris, 1871; appointed artistic director of Sèvres, 1875. Died at Sèvres, France, 3 June 1887.

Selected Works

1855   *Diana Jug*; Minton majolica; Victoria and Albert Museum, London, England

1863   *Bacchante*; marble; Tuileries gardens, Paris, France

1865–70 *Honoré Daumier*; plaster, patinated; Musée du Château, Versailles, France

ca. 1865 *Printemps*; biscuit; Musée Adrien-Dubouché, Paris, France

1866   *Angelica Chained to the Rock*; terracotta; private collection

1874   *Torchères*; bronze; Opéra, Paris, France

late   *Vase des Titans* (with Auguste Rodin);

1870s   ceramic; Maryhill Museum of Art, Goldendale, Washington, United States

1880s   *Portrait of John Milton*; bronze; Fine Arts Museums of San Francisco, California, United States

1883   *Reading Woman*; bronze, ivory; Lotherton Hall, Leeds Museums and Galleries, England

1885   *Diana Victorious*; terracotta; private collection

Further Reading

French Sculpture: An Anthology of French Sculpture, with Drawings and Related Material, 1775–1945 (exhib. cat.), Bruton, Somerset: Bruton Antiques and Gallery, 1979

Fusco, Peter, and H.W. Janson (editors), *The Romantics to Rodin: French Nineteenth-Century Sculpture from North American Collections*, Los Angeles: Los Angeles County Museum of Art, and New York: Braziller, 1980

Hargrove, June, "Carrier-Belleuse, Clésinger, and Dalou: French Nineteenth-Century Sculptors," *Minneapolis Institute of Arts Bulletin* 61 (1974)

Hargrove, June, *The Life and Work of Albert Ernest Carrier-Belleuse*, New York: Garland, 1977

Hargrove, June, *French Sculpture, 1780–1940* (exhib. cat.), Bruton, Somerset, and New York: Bruton Gallery, 1981

Nineteenth-Century French Sculpture: Monuments for the Middle Class (exhib. cat.), Louisville, Kentucky: J.B. Speed Art Museum, 1971

Ségard, Achille, *Albert Carrier-Belleuse, 1824–1887*, Paris: Champion, 1928

CARYATID

The word *caryatid* is used to denote four types of statue of female subjects that originated in the ancient city of Caryae, near Sparta in the inner Peloponnese (Greece).

The first type represents Artemis, the main goddess of Caryae, who was called Caryatid. The second type, the nymphs and Spartan girls dancing in honor of Artemis Caryatid, were called caryatids. They were also associated with Dionysus. In 401 BCE the Spartan Klearchos made a present of a ring, the intaglio of which bore a group of dancing caryatids, to a friend. A sculptural group of caryatids was made by Praxiteles around 350 BCE.

The third type of caryatid relates to the city of Caryae, which sympathized with the Persians during the Second Persian War (480–479 BCE). The Spartans, after the Greek victory against the Persians, are said to have destroyed Caryae and taken the married women of that town into captivity. The architects of those times designed marble statues of these robed women for use in place of conventional columns on buildings of the Doric order, with the women holding up the upper load of these structures as a symbol of their enslavement. These caryatids probably supported the entablature with one hand, as suggested by a remark of Eucrates in the 4th century. Diogenes of Athens made statues of such caryatids around 25 BCE (perhaps copies of the one from the 5th century BCE) for the Augustan phase of the Pantheon of Rome.

The portrayals of long-robed women in Early Classical severe style found on a 2nd-century CE relief at Naples (National Museum) were probably copies of the 5th-century BCE caryatids. They support the entablature with one hand, and an inscription states that the relief represents a trophy set up for Greece. This peculiar iconography is related to the series of long-robed female figures holding with one or both hands an object upon their heads. This iconography was widely diffused in the Near East, in ancient Greece (especially on mirror handles), and in Hellenistic and Roman monuments, which were probably influenced by the 5th-century BCE caryatids.

The fourth type of caryatids are the statues of maidens with lowered arms used in place of columns in buildings of the Ionic order, known in Greece from the 6th century BCE (e.g., the treasuries of the Cnidians and of the Siphnians at Delphi). The most important and famous examples of this type are the caryatids of the Erechtheum on the Acropolis of Athens (late 5th century BCE). In Antiquity, these figures were simply called "girls" and were probably meant to represent libation bearers. In modern times, however, they have come to be known as caryatids, a label introduced by the 18th-century travelers James Stuart and Nicholas Revett.

These Ionian caryatids inspired many variants throughout the Late Classical, Hellenistic, and Roman periods. In particular, the caryatids of the Erechtheum were copied in many important Roman monuments and are one of the most influential creations of Classical Antiquity. Their legacy has also been highly relevant for modern monuments, especially for early 19th-century Neoclassical architecture, such as the caryatids in the Church of St. Pancras in London.

ANTONIO CORSO

Further Reading

Congdon, Lenore O. Keene, *Caryatid Mirrors of Ancient Greece: Technical, Stylistic, and Historical Considerations of an Archaic and Early Classical Bronze Series*, Mainz, Germany: Von Zabern, 1981

Huxley, George, "The Medism of Caryae," *Greek Roman and Byzantine Studies* 8 (1967)

King, Dorothy, "Figured Supports: Vitruvius' Caryatids and Atlantes," *Numismatica e Antichità Classiche, Quaderni Ticinesi* 27 (1998)

Lauter, Hans, "Die Koren des Erechtheion," in *Antike Plastik*, edited by Felix Eckstein, vol. 16, Berlin: Mann, 1976

Lloyd-Morgan, Geoffrey, "Caryatids and Other Supporters," in *Architecture and Architectural Sculpture in the Roman Empire*, edited by Martin Henig, Oxford: Oxford University Committee for Archaeology, 1990

Plommer, Hugh, "Vitruvius and the Origin of Caryatids," *The Journal of Hellenic Studies* 99 (1979)

Schmidt, Erika, "Die Kopien der Erechtheionkoren," in *Antike Plastik*, edited by Felix Eckstein, vol. 13, Berlin: Mann, 1973

Schmidt, Evamaria, *Geschichte der Karyatide: Funktion und Bedeutung der menschlichen Träger- und Stützfigur in der Baukunst*, Würzburg, Germany: Trillsch, 1982

Schmidt-Colinet, Andreas, *Antike Stützfiguren: Untersuchungen zu Typus und Bedeutung der menschengestaltigen Architekturstütze in der griechischen und römischen Kunst*, Frankfurt: Deutschen Archaeologischen Instituts, 1977

Scholl, Andreas, *Die Korenhalle des Erechtheion auf der Akropolis: Frauen für den Staat*, Frankfurt: Fischer Taschenbuch, 1998

Shear, I. Mylonas, "Maidens in Greek Architecture: The Origin of the 'Caryatids,' " *Bulletin de correspondance hellénique* 123 (1999)

Vickers, Michael, "Persepolis, Vitruvius, and the Erechtheum Caryatids," *Revue Archéologique* 1 (1985)

BENVENUTO CELLINI 1500–71 *Italian,*
also active in France

Benvenuto Cellini, admired by Goethe and by Burckhardt as one of the *uomini universali* (universal men) of his age, worked as a goldsmith, bronze caster, marble carver, and architect. Known not only for his art but also for the volumes of garrulous, self-aggrandizing texts he penned and dictated at the end of his life, Cellini's oeuvre offers an incomparably informative perspective on the sculptural profession in 16th-century Italy.

Cellini was born in Florence in 1500 and spent his early years passing through the workshops of goldsmiths and miniaturists in Florence, Siena, Bologna, Pisa, and Rome. In 1528 he was in Mantua, where he designed a seal for Cardinal Ercole Gonzaga. From 1529 to 1534 he served as the die cutter for Pope Clement VII's mint. Beginning in this period, the earliest one for which there are surviving metal works by Cellini, the artist became known for his coins and medals, executing examples for Clement VII, Duke Alessandro de' Medici of Florence, Cardinal Pietro Bembo, and King Francis I of France.

In 1540 Cellini moved to France, having been invited to make a series of 12 life-size silver candleholders in the forms of Roman deities for the king's dining room. Of these, only a few seem to have progressed to the design stage and only one, no longer extant, was carried out. Cellini, rather than seeing to his charge, used the security of his new court position to tackle more varied and ambitious projects. His Vienna saltcellar, based on a design he had made several years earlier for Cardinal Ippolito d'Este in Rome, must count among the wittiest pieces of tableware ever conceived. Its depicted conjunction of Earth and Sea evokes contemporary ideas about the etiology and composition of salt, and the work exemplifies the interests that both contemporary artists and their patrons had in natural history. The saltcellar's users would have taken the salt from a miniature boat formed in part as a self-portrait of Cellini, suggesting that they feed themselves, so to speak, on the artist's own smarts. While working on the saltcellar, Cellini also began to redesign Fontainebleau's Porte Dorée, complementing frescoes by Francesco Primaticcio with his own overdoor of a bronze *Nymph of Fontainebleau*, a pair of Victories, and two satyrlike figures as bearers. In addition, he tried, and failed, to convince King Francis I to let him build a 16-meter-high fountain featuring the king himself in the guise of Mars as its centerpiece, surrounded by personifications of Letters, Philosophy, Design, and Music.

After Cellini returned to Florence in 1545, now to work for Alessandro's successor, Duke Cosimo I de' Medici, he pursued similarly monumental assignments. For nine years, while at work on the *Perseus and Medusa* for the Piazza della Signoria, Cellini oversaw a large workshop through which numerous talented founders, sculptors, and goldsmiths passed. As a result, works associated with Cellini from this period continue to raise attribution problems: Willem de Tetrode, for example, has good claim to be the maker of the marble *Ganymede* that often goes under Cellini's name; Francesco Ferrucci del Tadda, Stoldo Lorenzi, Cesare da Bagna, and Pier Pagolo Romano were all paid to execute parts of *Perseus and Medusa*, and Cellini records paying the bell founder Zanobi di Pagno "for his services in founding, forming and cleaning the metal" of the more-than-life-size bronze portrait of Cosimo now in the Museo Nazionale del Bargello,

Florence. However collaborative, the products that came out of the shop in these years threw Cellini himself into a new position of public prominence. The colossal *Perseus and Medusa*, which contributed to the revival of bronze as a popular medium, was emulated in other Italian and European centers. Both this and other works, meanwhile, were championed in Florence itself by the circle of intellectuals around the writer Benedetto Varchi, who took Cellini's depictions of young male beauty to represent an alternative to the massive strongmen featured in the work of the dominant sculptor of the period, Baccio Bandinelli.

After 1554 Cellini's efforts were shadowed by compromises and disappointments. Planning his own tomb, Cellini responded to the wooden crucifixes made by Florentine predecessors from Filippo Brunelleschi to Raffaelo da Montelupo with a *Christ* of white and black marble. After negotiations with two different churches failed, Cellini gave up on finding a public site for the work and gave it, a fragment of larger plans, to Cosimo. Similarly frustrated was Cellini's pursuit of the commission for the largest public project that became available in those years, the Neptune Fountain Cosimo envisioned as the next major addition to the Piazza della Signoria. Having convinced the Duke to allow a competition for the assignment, Cellini spent months preparing first a small wax design, then a full-scale gesso mock-up of his idea, only to lose the commission to Bartolomeo Ammanati. Assigned to make a series of bronze reliefs for the pulpits of Florence Cathedral, Cellini's work on these was interrupted when he was sent twice to prison, for assault in 1556 and for sodomy in 1557. Cellini returned to the reliefs with a revised scheme in the early 1560s but completed none of them. Both the seal designs he proposed for the newly formed Florentine Accademia del Disegno in 1563 and the catafalque design he proposed for the obsequies of Michelangelo in 1564 were rejected. When the city's artists collaborated on far more extravagant decorations for the marriage of Grand Duke Francesco I de' Medici to Joanna of Austria, Cellini did not participate. In his final years, the artist who had earlier boasted about his triumphal advancement from goldsmith to monumental sculptor opened a new goldsmith's shop. By the time of his death in 1571, designs for the objects this shop produced seem to have been his only artistic possibilities.

It is no accident that it was in the late 1550s and in the 1560s that Cellini first turned seriously to writing about himself, filling books with comments on his earlier practice, verbally defending the honor that these works had done him. Cellini's two treatises on goldsmithing and sculpture, a discourse, a letter, and several poems were published in his lifetime. A number of his other texts must have been in circulation, and

Cellini came to be known as one of the most outspoken critics of the new Florentine cultural regime of the 1560s, led by Giorgio Vasari. What is now his best-known piece of writing, the autobiography he began dictating to an amanuensis in 1558, was not published until the 18th century.

MICHAEl COLE

Biography

Born in Florence, Italy, 3 November 1500. Entered a succession of different goldsmiths' and painters' workshops in Florence, Siena, Bologna, Pisa, and Rome, 1513–21; started independent studio, Rome, 1524; die cutter for Pope Clement VII's mint, 1529–34; in Florence, 1535, making coins for Alessandro de' Medici, Duke of Florence; in Padua, 1537; created medal for Cardinal Pietro Bembo; in France, 1537, where he made medal for King Francis I; back in Rome, 1538; imprisoned for theft; released 1539, joined entourage of Cardinal Ippolito d'Este, of Ferrara, for whom he made a seal and the first design for the Vienna saltcellar; at the court of King Francis I, 1540–45; began series of 12 silver candleholders in form of Roman deities for the king; made *Nymph of Fontainebleau* and designed caryatids for the Porte Dorée; completed saltcellar for Francis I; in Florence, 1545–54, where he entered the service of Cosimo I de' Medici and completed *Perseus and Medusa* and several independent works in marble and bronze; at work on marble *Crucifix*, originally for his tomb, 1558–62; started writing his autobiography, 1558, and also wrote *Two Treatises on Goldsmithing and Sculpture*, 1565–67; set up new goldsmith business, 1568. Died in Florence, Italy, 13 February 1571.

Selected Works

ca. 1533   Portrait medal of Pope Clement VII; bronze; Museo Nazionale del Bargello, Florence, Italy

1542–43   Saltcellar of Francis I; gold, enamel, ebony; Kunsthistorisches Museum, Vienna, Austria

1542–43   *Nymph of Fontainebleau*; bronze; Musée du Louvre, Paris, France

1545–48   Bust of Cosimo I; bronze (originally gilded); Museo Nazionale del Bargello, Florence, Italy

1545–54   *Perseus and Medusa*; marble, bronze, gold, iron; Piazza della Signoria, Florence, Italy

ca. 1548   *Apollo and Hyacinth*; marble; Museo Nazionale del Bargello, Florence, Italy *ca.* 1548 *Narcissus*; marble; Museo Nazionale del Bargello, Florence, Italy

1556–62 *Christ*; marble; Monastery of S. Lorenzo el Real, Escorial, Madrid, Spain

Further Reading

Calamandrei, Piero, *Scritti e inediti celliniani*, edited by Carlo Cordiè, Florence: La nuova Italia, 1971

Cellini, Benvenuto, *The Treatises of Benvenuto Cellini on Goldsmithing and Sculpture*, translated by C.R. Ashbee, London: Arnold, 1898; reprint, New York: Dover, 1967

Cellini, Benvenuto, *The Autobiography of Benvenuto Cellini*, translated by Robert H. Hobart Cust, London: Bell, 1956

Cellini, Benvenuto, *L'opera completa del Cellini*, Milan: Rizzoli, 1981

Cervigni, Dino S., *The Vita of Benvenuto Cellini: Literary Tradition and Genre*, Ravenna, Italy: Longo, 1979

Cole, Michael, "Benvenuto Cellini's Designs for His Tomb," *The Burlington Magazine* 140 (1998)

Cole, Michael, *Cellini and the Principles of Sculpture*, New York: Cambridge University Press, 2002

Davis, Charles, "Benvenuto Cellini and the Scuola Fiorentina," *North Carolina Museum of Art Bulletin* 13 (1976)

Galucci, Margaret Ann, "Cellini's Trial for Sodomy: Power and Patronage at the Court of Cosimo I," in *The Cultural Politics of Duke Cosimo I de' Medici*, edited by Konrad Eisenbichler, Aldershot, England, and Burlington, Vermont: Ashgate, 2001

Jacobs, Fredrika H., "An Assessment of Contour Line: Vasari, Cellini, and the Paragone," *Artibus et Historiae* 18 (1988)

Lavin, Irving, "The Sculptor's 'Last Will and Testament,' " *Allen Memorial Art Museum Bulletin* 35 (1977–78)

Meller, Peter, "Geroglifici e ornamenti 'parlanti' nell'opera del Cellini," *Arte Lombarda* 3/4 (1994)

Pope-Hennessy, John, *Cellini*, New York: Abbeville Press, and London: Macmillan, 1985

Rossi, Paolo, "The Writer and the Man: Real Crimes and Mitigating Circumstances: *Il caso Cellini*," in *Crime, Society, and the Law in Renaissance Italy*, edited by Trevor Dean and K.J.P. Lowe, Cambridge: Cambridge University Press, 1994

Rossi, Paolo, "*Sprezzatura*, Patronage, and Fate: Benvenuto Cellini and the World of Words," in *Vasari's Florence: Artists and Literati at the Medicean Court*, edited by Philip Jacks, Cambridge: Cambridge University Press, 1998

Vickers, Nancy J., "The Mistress in the Masterpiece," in *The Poetics of Gender*, edited by Nancy K. Miller, New York: Columbia University Press, 1986

PERSEUS AND MEDUSA

Benvenuto Cellini (1500–71)

1545–53

bronze (partially gilded), marble, gold, and iron (Perseus's sword)

h. 3.2 m

Loggia dei Lanzi, Piazza della Signoria, Florence, Italy

Cellini's *Perseus and Medusa* is among the best-documented artworks of the Late Renaissance. Detailed account books cover the daily activities of Cellini's workshop for the entire period during which the work was being made. The artist himself left narrations of the inception and making of the work, as well as other compositions reflecting on its significance. Numerous people involved in its production, as well as visitors to Cellini's studio, wrote letters concerning the statue. Contemporaries responded to the work in dozens of poems, some writing at the work's unveiling, others writing even before the bronze was poured.

Work on the *Perseus and Medusa* was initiated in 1545, when Cosimo I de' Medici asked Cellini, who

Perseus and Medusa (with Bandinelli's *Hercules* in background, Loggia dell' Orcagna, Florence)
The Conway Library, Courtauld Institute of Art
© M. Hirst

had just returned from France, to design a figure of the ancient hero with the head of the Gorgon in hand. The Duke was seeking a pendant for Donatello's *Judith Slaying Holofernes* (*ca.* 1459), which was at that time the only bronze work in the Piazza della Signoria and which had recently been moved to the westernmost archway of the Loggia dei Lanzi. Cosimo likely chose the subject, familiar from the imagery of his predecessor, Alessandro I, because he required an absolutist image to neutralize the traditionally republican sense of Donatello's piece, and because the context invited for this a beheaded victim. According to Cellini, the artist himself subsequently convinced the Duke to let him undertake a larger and more complex work than originally envisioned: he would make Perseus five *braccia* tall rather than three, add the body of Medusa at Perseus's feet, and set the pair on a great marble base, with extensive further ornamentation.

These amplifications set the original political connotations of the work into a considerably more sophisticated literary framework. By changing the composition to include not only Perseus's petrifying display of Medusa's head but also the beheading itself, Cellini could allude to the birth of Pegasus, the creator of the Castalian fount, from Medusa's blood. On the base itself, Cellini could incorporate figures of Mercury and Minerva, noted in the myths as the gods who armed Perseus but more generally known as the sources of eloquence and wisdom, the twin pillars of the humanistic education and of the academy. It is telling that the base of the Perseus includes an emblem in the form of Diana of Epheseus, of what Cellini's account books identify as the "iddea della Natura" (idea/goddess of nature). This is the same emblem that Cellini would later propose for the seal of the Accademia del Disegno; its presence here indicates that Cellini wanted the *Perseus and Medusa* to read as a work about the poetics of art and about the nature of sculptural creation.

Situated as it was in the piazza, the *Perseus and Medusa* suggested a dialogue with the victory imagery that surrounded it. Cellini and others who wrote about the monument drew attention to the statue's antithesis between a self-contained conqueror, guided to virtue by an inner spirit (Minerva's gift), and an undone victim, losing her own spirits with the blood that fell into the square. This secured the work's conceptual proximity to its neighbor, the *Judith Slaying Holofernes*, which Vasari described in 1550 in very similar terms. It also underscored the difference between the new statue from the major addition to the piazza from the 1530s, the *Hercules and Cacus* carved by Cellini's despised rival, Baccio Bandinelli. The scowling Hercules seemed to the fans of the *Perseus and Medusa* to be ludicrously envious of the latter's surety and composure. The *Perseus and Medusa* countered the *Hercules and Cacus*'s seeming promotion of brutish force with an icon of grace and beauty (Perseus's mother, Danäe, also included in Cellini's base, could be mistaken for Venus). Cellini thus translated what had become a conventional victory conceit into a new model of autocratic sculptural propaganda. When Cellini's rival Leone Leoni set a tranquil Emperor Charles V atop a Furor (Museo del Prado, Madrid) "in a most contorted attitude" and when the Giambologna shop produced for Cosimo I's successors, Francesco I de' Medici and Ferdinand I de' Medici, a series of variations on similar victor/victim antitheses, it was in part to Cellini's idea that they were responding.

In making the *Perseus and Medusa*, Cellini also hoped to impress viewers with his technical achievements as a sculptor. The base of the sculpture was Cellini's first (and last) commissioned work of marble; with the help of such assistants as Willem de Tetrode and Francesco del Tadda, he sought to demonstrate the range of his professional capabilities. More important, though, were the monumental figures above, with which Cellini aimed to prove his ingenuity as a bronze caster. Although in fact helped by professional founders, Cellini claimed to have engineered the pouring of the *Perseus and Medusa* himself, jointly mastering the domains of the modeler and the caster. Whether or not his stories are true, the success of the sculpture did spearhead a revival of Donatello's medium at a moment when most sculptors and patrons were enthralled by Michelangelo's unwavering devotion to Carrara marble. Part of the wit poets noticed in the sculpture's placement in the Piazza della Signoria was its ostensible gorgonization of its predecessors: Michelangelo's *David* (1501–04) and especially Bandinelli's *Hercules and Cacus* (1525–34), looking on the Medusa head, could seem to have become, as Ovid put it, "stone without blood." That the *Perseus and Medusa* was not marble, that it was in fact made in a coppery material that (especially before its oxidation) could seem infused with blood, was part of its aesthetic power. In his later writings, Cellini presented the casting of the sculpture, the pouring of molten spirits into a human-shaped earthen mold, as a divine act. He satirized sculptors who failed to cast so well. Guglielmo della Porta, who used the *Perseus and Medusa* as a touchstone when accounting for his own colossal bronze figure of Paul III (1544), Hubert Gerhard, who made his own large *Perseus and Medusa* for the *Grottenhof* of Duke Wilhelm V in Munich, and Adriaen de Vries, who like Cellini attempted monumental one-piece casts, would surely have appreciated Cellini's pride.

MICHAEL COLE

Further Reading

Braunfels, Wolfgang, *Benvenuto Cellini: Perseus und Medusa*, Berlin: Mann, 1948

Cole, Michael, "Cellini's Blood," *Art Bulletin* 81 (1999)

Even, Yael, "The Loggia dei Lanzi: A Showcase of Female Subjugation," *Woman's Art Journal* 12 (1991)

Hirthe, Thomas, "Die Perseus-und-Medusa-Gruppe des Benvenuto Cellini in Florenz," *Jahrbuch der Berliner Museen* 29 (1987/88)

Pope-Hennessy, John, *Cellini*, New York: Abbeville Press, and London: Macmillan, 1985

Shearman, John, *Only Connect: Art and the Spectator in the Italian Renaissance*, Princeton, New Jersey: Princeton University Press, 1992

Weil-Garris, Kathleen, "On Pedestals: Michelangelo's *David*, Bandinelli's *Hercules and Cacus*, and the Sculpture of the Piazza della Signoria," *Römisches Jahrbuch für Kunstgeschichte* 20 (1983)

CENTRAL EUROPE: HUNGARY, AUSTRIA, THE CZECH REPUBLIC, AND SLOVAKIA

The sculpture of Central Europe, also referred to as Eastern Central Europe, primarily includes sculptural remains known from Austria, Hungary, the Czech Republic, Slovakia, and their adjoining areas. Because of the blend of Western and Eastern influences, the sculpture of this region is extremely diverse.

Hungary

Árpád Era (1000–1301)

The earliest sculpture in Hungary is from the Árpád era (1000–1301). The so-called *St. Stephen's Sarcophagus* (Garden of Ruins, Székesfehérvár), most probably the stone tomb of Stephen I, king of Hungary (r. 997–1038), is a recarved ancient Roman sarcophagus from the first half of the 11th century decorated with low-modeled Romanesque ornamental interlaces, rosettes, cherubs, and an angel carrying the soul of the deceased; the symbolism followed the motifs of Byzantine reliefs. Hungarian reliefs known from the end of the 11th century also manifest the Byzantine style, for example, the fragment of a tombstone from Aracs (National Gallery of Hungary, Budapest) and the tympanum relief *Christ in Majesty* above the south portal of the Cathedral of Gyulafehérvár (Alba Iulia, Romania). Surviving from the middle of the 12th century are mostly relief fragments on rood screens, such as those from St. Peter's Priory in Óbuda, now northwest Budapest (National Gallery of Hungary, Budapest), and the Abbey of Somogyvár (Museum Rippl-Rónai, Kaposvár). One of the most significant centers of Romanesque Hungarian sculpture was in the cathedral in Pécs, where a local workshop about 1170 produced the Holy Cross Altar, the screen, and the series of reliefs covering the walls of the two staircases leading into the crypt, including scenes from the *Life of Christ* and *Life of Samson*. The sculptors, mostly of French and Italian training, emerged from the so-called Pécs workshop, and their work can be evidenced in the whole of western Hungary. The late 12th-century sculptural decoration of the royal palace and the Cathedral of St. Adalbert in Esztergom shows mainly French influence. The most significant remains of Late Romanesque sculpture surviving in relatively good condition include the sculptural decoration (*ca.* 1230) of the west facade and chancel of the Benedictine Abbey in Ják in western Hungary, which are related to the 13th-century statues of Bamberg Cathedral.

Gothic Period

Early Gothic sculpture in Hungary appeared in the second half of the 13th century on sculptural decorations following the French trend, such as the plant-ornamental fragments of the Church of Our Lady (now Matthias Church) in Buda (now west Budapest). During the first half of the 14th century, French influences also prevailed, and the most significant imported works arrived from France, such as the silver Altar of Queen Elisabeth made about 1340 in Paris and decorated with statues (Metropolitan Museum of Art, New York City). Lindenwood sculpture with polychromy also followed French models, such as one of the earliest remains, a small-size winged altar from Krig (Vojňany, Slovakia, *ca.* 1320, in Slovenská Národná Galéria, Bratislava), and the *Virgin with Child* (*ca.* 1340–50, in National Gallery of Hungary, Budapest) from Toporc (Toporec, Slovakia). South German and Austrian influence appeared in sculpture during the second half of the 14th century, evident in the sculpture on the north portal of the Cathedral of St. Martin in Pozsony (Bratislava, Slovakia), the chancel statues of the Parish Church in Szászsebes (Sebeş, Romania), and the south portal of the Church of Our Lady in Buda. The south German and Austrian influence can also be seen in the red marble fragments of the tomb monument to Louis I of Anjou (r. 1342–82) in Székesfehérvár (Garden of Ruins, Székesfehérvár) and on the red marble tomb monument fragments in Buda. One of Tino di Camaino's Neapolitan followers must have carved the tomb monument of Princess Margaret Árpád from white marble (fragments are in the National Gallery of Hungary and Budapesti Történeti Múzeum, Budapest). The sculptor brothers Martin and George of Klasenburg (Márton and György of Kolozsvár, Cluj-Napoca, Romania), working in Nagyvárad (Oradea, Romania) between 1360 and 1390, belonged to the front ranks of European sculpture; their only surviving authentic and signed work is the bronze statue *St. George and the Dragon* (1373; National Gallery, Prague), a nearly life-size equestrian statue belonging to the masterpieces of International Gothic style.

In the late 14th and early 15th centuries, Hungarian sculpture followed the forms and subjects of the Bohemian, Silesian, and Austrian *Schöner Stil* (Beautiful Style), witnessed in the wood statues *Virgin and Child* (*ca.* 1370–80) from Szlatvin (Slatvin, Slovakia; National Gallery of Hungary, Budapest), *Man of Sorrows* (*ca.* 1410–20; Ecclesiastical Museum, Veszprém), and *Virgin with Child*, from Toporc (Toporec, Slovakia; *ca.* 1420, in National Gallery of Hungary, Budapest), the stone *Pietà* (*ca.* 1420) from the St. Giles Church of Bártfa (Bardejov, Slovakia), and the sandstone *Calvary* group of statues signed by the Austrian Petrus Lantregen from the Holy Cross Chapel in Nagyszeben (1417; Sibiu, Romania). Among the most striking lindenwood statues of the Beautiful Style are *St. Dorothy* and its pendant, *St. Catherine*, from Barka (Borka, Slovakia; National Gallery of Hungary, Budapest) that must have been pieces of a large-size altar dating from 1410–20. The most important surviving works of stone sculpture reflecting the influence of Peter Parler's workshop in Prague are the limestone statues of Buda from the 1420s (Budapesti Történeti Múzeum, Budapest), which decorated the royal palace in Buda during the reign of the Holy Roman Emperor and king of Hungary and Bohemia, Sigismund of Luxembourg (*r.* 1387–1437).

In the Late Gothic period, from about 1470 until the mid 16th century, winged altars following south German and Austrian models flourished in Hungary. Most of them are known from northern Hungary (now Slovakia), such as in the churches of Kassa (Košice), Löcse (Levoča), Bárfa (Bardejov), Eperjes (Prešov), Kisszeben (Sabinov), and Szepeshely (Spišská Kapitula), as well as from churches of Erdély (Transylvania, now Romania), such as Szászsebes (Sebes) and Csíkménaság (Armaşeni) of Erdély. Most often artists assembled winged altars after engravings and model books from large-size statues, reliefs, panel paintings, and ornamental decorations. They generally carved the sculpture parts from lindenwood, which were then polychromed and gilded. On the majority of Late Gothic wood statues from Hungary, the influence of Hans Multscher and Veit Stoss may be detected. The statues of the St. Elisabeth main altar, erected in 1474–77 in the Cathedral of St. Elisabeth in Kassa (Košice, Slovakia), followed Multscher's style. Master Pavel of Levoča (Pál of Löcse, Levoca, Slovakia) studied in Stoss's workshop in Krakow and, after establishing his style, worked in northern Hungary. His masterpiece is the main altar (1508–17) of the Church of St. James in Levoča, one of the most beautiful Hungarian winged

Franz Anton Zauner, *Monument to Emperor Joseph II*, 1795–1806, Vienna, Austria
The Conway Library, Courtauld Institute of Art

altars preserved in its original site and state. The sculpture decoration of the *Easter Catafalque* (*ca.* 1470–80) from the Benedictine Abbey of Garamszentbenedek (Hornský Beňadik, Slovakia) also followed south German models (now in Christian Museum, Esztergom). In the second half of the 15th century and the first half of the 16th century, Italian Renaissance sculpture flourished alongside south German- and Austrian-style Late Gothic art in Hungary.

Renaissance Period

During the reign of Matthias Corvinus (*r.* 1458–90), king of Hungary and Bohemia, the Renaissance sculptural decorations of the royal palaces in Buda and Visegrád represented the most significant centers of the Central European Renaissance. In the palace of Buda, mainly Florentine sculptors followed the influence of Benedetto da Maiano and Desiderio da Settignano, including Chimenti Camicia and the "Master of the Marble Madonnas," who is usually identified as Tommaso Fiamberti, a pupil of Desiderio da Settignano. Giovanni Dalmata, of Dalmatian origin, was employed in the palace of Buda beginning in 1481 and is mentioned in the documents by the name of Johannes Ducnovich

Otto Gutfreund, *Anxiety*, 1911
The Conway Library, Courtauld Institute of Art

de Tragurio. He carved his most significant work, the *Madonna from Diósgyőr* relief (National Gallery of Hungary, Budapest), from white marble before 1490, and after the death of King Matthias he returned to Dalmatia. After 1473 King Matthias replaced the Anjou-era fountains of his summer palace in Visegrád with Late Gothic, and later with Renaissance, fountains. The most beautiful red marble fountain (1484) is either wholly or partially the work of Dalmata, for the formal courtyard, and the *Hercules Riding the Hydra of Lerna* group was placed on top of the fountain basin (King Matthias Museum, Visegrád). The "Master of the Marble Madonnas" is said to have produced the red marble relief known as *Madonna from Visegrád* (ca. 1484–85; Christian Museum, Esztergom), which must have been originally placed above the portal of the palace chapel in Visegrád.

The rich Tuscan-style sculptural fragments surviving from the palaces of Buda and Visegrád indicate that large stonecarver workshops operated during this period. One of the most beautiful, and relatively intact, architectural and sculptural ensembles is the Bakócz Chapel in the main Cathedral of Esztergom. Tamás Bakócz, archbishop of Esztergom, commissioned this

tomb chapel between 1506 and 1519; plant ornamentation decorated its red marble walls, and Andrea Ferrucci carved a white marble altar into its eastern niche in 1519.

After defeat at the battle at Mohács in 1526, the middle part of Hungary was subdued under Ottoman Turk occupation, which led to the regression of sculptural production. In the first half of the 16th century, Tuscan influence continued in Late Renaissance Hungarian sculpture, such as in Márévár, Kolozsvár, Lőcse. Among the local sculptors' works, the most outstanding is the *Madonna of András Báthory* (1526; National Gallery of Hungary, Budapest), a relief carved from white marble following Tuscan models in a provincial manner. During the same period, the influence of the Renaissance style of the Lower Austrian Danube school could be sensed in western Hungary. The sandstone *St. George Main Altar* (ca. 1527) of the parish church in Pozsonyszentgyörgy (Jur pri Bratislave, Slovakia) is an example. A rare example of Late Renaissance secular sculpture is Andreas Lutringer's *Roland Fountain* (1573) in front of the town hall in Pozsony (Bratislava, Slovakia). From the late 16th and early 17th centuries, mainly tomb memorials survive; the tomb monument to István Dobó (1575; István Dobó Castle Museum, Eger), the tomb monument to Imre Thurzó (1614; St. James's Church, Levoca), and the tomb monument to Szaniszló Thurzó (1625; St. James's Church, Levoča) depict the deceased in armor.

The Ottoman Turk wars divided Hungary into three parts. Provincial Turkish art thrived in the middle area occupied by the Ottoman Turks, whereas Tuscan and southern German Late Renaissance styles remained in the northern and western parts of the Hungarian kingdom. In the eastern part, in Transylvania, Late Renaissance styles retaining Hungarian peculiarities flourished. During the Counter Reformation, large-scale constructions contracted by the Catholic clergy and the nobility provided new opportunities for sculpture, especially altars and sculptural decorations of buildings.

Baroque Period

In the first half of the 17th century, along with the emerging Early Baroque style, two new sculptural forms became established in Hungary. Italian artists such as architect Philiberto Luchese popularized interior stucco decoration; he designed stuccos for the castles at Rohonc (1640–42; Reichnitz, Austria) and Borostyánkő (1648; Bernstein, Austria). The other new form, the garden sculpture, also developed at this time, as exemplified in works at the Esterházy Castle in Frakno (Forchtenstein, Austria). Monumental altars, such as the main altar of the Jesuit St. John the Baptist Church in Nagyszombat (Trnava, Slovakia) by Balthasar Knillinger and Veit Stadler, were carved mostly by Austrian and local Hungarian sculptors. Knillinger and Stadler created the main altar in 1637–40 with dark-brown architecture, gilded and painted wood statues, columns with abundant ornamentation, and a large-size painting placed in the center, similar to Austrian Baroque altars. Often medieval wood statues were embedded into the new altar ensembles, such as in the main altar of the parish church in Eperjes (1696; Prešov, Slovakia). In the 17th century, gilded and painted epitaphs carved from wood also became established, such as the 1659 epitaph of the Hain family in St. James Church in Löcse. The dynamic sculptures of the Apostles standing on the main and side facades of the Jesuit Church in Nagyszombat are a significant and curious stone remnant of 17th-century Hungarian sculpture.

After 1686, following the reoccupation of Buda (the western region of Budapest) from the Ottoman Turks, Hungarian Baroque sculpture experienced rapid development. Pietro Antonio Conti, a Lombard stuccoist, created the stuccos of the main nave of the Church of St. John the Baptist in Nagyszombat in 1686–89. During the Rákóczi War of Independence, the Swedish medalist Daniel Warou produced seals, coins, and memorial medals in the early 18th century. Several votive victory columns were erected in memory of the defeat of the Ottoman Turks, such as the *Maria Column* (1686) in Györ, as were columns in memory of warding off the plague, such as the *Holy Trinity Column* (1715–17) in Buda. The triumphal arch of Charles VI (1724) in Gyulafehérvár with statues by Johann König, commissioned and erected by Prince Eugene of Savoy, was a significant sculptural monument. Another important surviving sculptural work is the *Ark of the Covenant* from Györ, executed in 1731 after a design by Joseph Emmanuel Fischer von Erlach. Georg Raphael Donner's Hungarian workshop helped to establish the Late Baroque style widely. His followers included, for example, Ludwig Gode from Pozsony, Jakob Christoph Schletterer from Kismarton (Eisenstadt, Austria), and Jakob Gabriel Mollinarolo (Müller) from Györ.

The Bavarian Philipp Jakob Straub, who was an outstanding representative of Hungarian Rococo sculpture, created painted and gilded wood statues, such as those of *St. Roch* and *St. Sebastian* (ca. 1757) from the Church of Egervár (National Gallery of Hungary, Budapest). Johann Anton Kraus, probably of Moravian origin, produced monumental statues for the Premonstratensian Abbey in Jászó (Jasov, Slovakia) in 1767–70 and for the Jesuit Church in Eger in1769–70.

19th Century

István Ferenczy, the most significant Hungarian sculptor of the first half of the 19th century, acquired marble-carving experience in Rome in Bertel Thorvaldsen's workshop, where he was also exposed to Antonio Canova's sculpture. After returning to Hungary in 1824, Ferenczy produced portraits, tombs, and monuments. His masterpieces are the white marble *Shepherdess* (1820–22), the portrait of Ferenc Kazinczy (1828), and the monument to Ferenc Kölcsey (1846; all in National Gallery of Hungary, Budapest). Other representatives of Hungarian Classicism include Lörinc Dunaiszky, József Huber, and Rudolf Czélkúti Züllich. The most gifted Hungarian Romantic sculptor was Miklós Izsó, who studied in Munich. His best-known and most successful work, the white marble *Melancholic Shepherd* (1861–62; National Gallery of Hungary, Budapest), is also the first significant example of Hungarian folk genre sculpture. Along with several monuments and portraits, Izsó sculpted statues depicting peasants, such as his terracotta *Dancing Peasant* (ca. 1870; National Gallery of Hungary, Budapest). János Fadrusz, a prominent sculptor of the Academic Historicist style, produced his bronze monument to Matthias Corvinus on the square outside St. Michael's Cathedral in Kolozsvár (Cluj-Napoca, Romania) in 1895–1902. Another Hungarian Academic Historicist, Alajos Stróbl, executed the monument to King St. Stephen on the Fishermen's Bastion in Buda (1906), and György Zala created the *Millenary Monument* (1891–98) on the Heroes' Square in Pest, Hungary. Both works became emblems of Budapest.

20th Century

At the beginning of the 20th century, which belonged to the second generation of Historicism, József Róna, György Vasthag, and Miklós Ligeti produced public statues in Budapest; Ede Telcs and Ödön Moiret were already working in the framework of Secession; and "The Eight," a group of artists that included sculptors Márk Vedres, Fülöp Ö. Beck, and Vilmos Fémes Beck, birthed Modernism. At the same time, János Máttis Teutsch was producing organic nonfigurative statues. Zsigmond Kisfaludi Stróbl was striving for idealized naturalism, following Auguste Rodin's style. Béla Ohmann, Pál Pázay, and the classicizing Béni Ferenczy followed Italian trends. Ferenc Medgyessy depicted scenes of everyday life. Sándor Mikus and László Mészáros both belonged to the so-called School of Rome. Dezsö Bokros Birmann and György Goldmann depicted the life of the working classes. Members of the European School, among them Lajos Barta in geometric nonfigurative style, Jósef Jakovits in organic nonfigurative style, and Erzsébet Forgách Hahn, worked within the framework of Expressionist style. After 1948 the Communist regime commissioned representative large-scale monuments and friezes that were executed by sculptors belonging to the Socialist Artist's Group and the School of Rome according to the requirements of socialist realism. In large part, József Somogyi, Jenö Kerényi, Tamás Vigh, and Imre Varga carried out these state commissions. The gigantic, public Communist statues were exhibited in an outdoor sculptural museum unique to Central Europe, the Statue Park (District 22 of Budapest). Anthropomorphic abstraction can be detected in the works of Tibor Vilt, Erzsébet Schaár, and Miklós Borsos. The avant-garde emerged in Hungary in the 1960s. Leading artists of contemporary sculpture include Miklós Erdély, István Haraszty, Miklós Melocco, György Jovánovics, and András Böröcz, who carved the *Hanged People* (Museum of Fine Arts, Budapest) wood statue group in 1989–90.

Austria

Romanesque Period
Austrian Romanesque wood and stone sculpture had strong connections to German traditions. One of the earliest surviving wood sculptures, a small *Crucifixion* relief (Oberösterreichisches Landesmuseum, Linz), comes from the region of Kremsmünster Abbey. On the west portal (*ca.* 1170) of the Benedictine Monastery of Millstatt in Carinthia, the Lombard influence was already obvious. Around 1220 stone masks, animals, and biblical reliefs on the apse of the parish church in Schöngraben (Lower Austria), including scenes from the *Fall* to the *Life of Christ*, and the *Last Judgment*, followed southern German models. The *Riesentor*, or *Giant's Gate* (*ca.* 1230), which is the west portal of St. Stephen's Cathedral (Stephansdom) in Vienna, is one of the most important Late Romanesque decorative stone works.

Gothic Period
In the second half of the 13th century and early 14th century, the tympanum relief showing the representation of the *Virgin and Child* became a frequent subject of early Austrian Gothic art, including the sandstone relief on the portal of the abbey in Seckau (*ca.* 1260). The *Virgin and Child* statues modeled in elegant court style, such as the wood statue from Admont (*ca.* 1310; Alte Galerie, Graz). A current subject was the Y-shaped crucifix, such as the wood *Crucifix* in the Dominican Church in Freisach (*ca.* 1300). The dramatic naturalism of the sculptural decorations of Stephanskirche, now Stephansdom (St. Stephen's Cathedral) in Vienna, created during the reign of Rudolf

IV (*r.* 1358–65), followed the trends of Germany and Prague. During the second half of the 14th century, the most common scene of representation was the *Schöne Madonna* (Beautiful Madonna) modeled after Silesian and Bohemian models, such the *Virgin with Child* (*ca.* 1410–15) in the Franciscan Monastery of Salzburg. The pietà was also a common subject, such as the limestone *Pietà* from Admont (*ca.* 1400; Alte Galerie, Graz). The sculptor known as the Master of Grosslobming and his workshop in Styria represented the elegant and vivid court style, the *Schöner Stil* (Beautiful Style).

Austrian Late Gothic sculpture flourished from 1400 to about 1500, the most important form being the retable. Sculptors were already known by name by this time, the most outstanding among them being Hans von Judenburg, Jakob Kaschauer, Hans Klocker, and Hans Multscher, whose works were characterized by realism. Michael Pacher, a sculptor and painter from Tyrol and one of the most significant artists of the era, created finely carved sculptural works. His masterpieces are the statues in the altar shrine of the Church of St. Wolfgang (1471–81). One of the finest examples of Austrian winged altar art, it shows the influence of the Italian Renaissance as well as the traditional realist attitude of the late 15th century. At the same time, in St. Stephen's Cathedral in Vienna, Nicolaus Gerhaert von Leyden created the lid of the tomb monument to Frederick III (*d.* 1493), which marked the beginning of the representative *Reichsstil* (Imperial Style).

Renaissance Period
Gregor Erhart, the imperial sculptor of Emperor Maximilian I (*r.* 1493–1519), mediated the influence of the Renaissance sculpture of Augsburg toward the Austrian regions. Erhart and Alexander Colin, together with several other artists, designed the models for one of the masterpieces of 16th-century Austrian sculpture, the monument to Maximilian I in the Hofkirche (Court Church) in Innsbruck. The figures were cast in bronze by Gilg Sesselschreiber, Stefan Godl, and the members of the Vischer workshop in Nuremberg. At the same time, the Danube school also produced remarkable sculpture, as witnessed in the altar of the Heiligblutkirche (Pulkau, Lower Austria) and the Irrsdorf reliefs (*ca.* 1520; Museo Carolino Augusteum, Salzburg). Hubert Gerhard and his pupil Caspar Gras were leading artists of Late Renaissance and Mannerist Austrian bronze sculpture, and together, they created the bronze tomb monument to Archduke Maximilian III in Innsbruck Cathedral. Italian stuccoists primarily executed the stucco decorations that became popular in Austria in the later 16th century.

Baroque Period

The Alpine region around Salzburg and Vienna produced the most significant sculptures of the Austrian Baroque, influenced primarily by southern German and Italian art. The 17th-century sculptors Hans Waldburger, Thomas Schwanthaler, the Zürn family, and the Swiss woodcarver Johann Meinrad Guggenbichler with his workshop created abundantly decorated, painted, and gilded altars and wood statues. Guggenbichler produced several altars in the 1670s and 1680s in Mondsee and the surrounding area, such as the Holy Ghost Altar (Monastery Church, Mondsee). In stone sculpture, Bernhard Mändl's works from Salzburg were outstanding, evidenced by the monumental marble statues of *St. Peter* and *St. Paul* in Salzburg Cathedral (1697). The leading artist of Styrian high Baroque, Josef Stammel, worked primarily in the Abbey of Admont. After the withdrawal of the Turks in 1683, Baroque sculpture thrived, and large-scale constructions and renovations provided abundant opportunities for sculptural works. The marble statues and reliefs of the *Trinity Column* (or *Plague Column*) on the Graben were produced at this time in Vienna. The column was completed in 1692 on the basis of the designs of Matthias Rauchmiller, Johann Bernhard Fischer von Erlach, Lodovico Ottavio Burnacini, Paul Strudel, and others. The outstanding 17th-century portrait sculptors Peter and Paul Strudel carved a series of imperial portrait busts and statues from marble. The Venetian Giovanni Giuliani worked for the Viennese aristocracy and the Monastery of Heiligenkreuz and trained Georg Raphael Donner, one of the superb artists of Austrian sculpture. Around 1700 Matthias Steinl produced delicately carved ivory statues in Vienna, such as the equestrian statue of Emperor Leopold I (*ca.* 1690; Kunsthistorisches Museum, Vienna). Lorenzo Mattielli, one of the most popular Viennese sculptors during the reign of Emperor Charles VI (*r.* 1711–40), created the statues on the front facade of the Karlskirche (Church of St. Charles).

Donner, the most gifted artist in Late Baroque sculpture, carved marble statues in the staircase of the Mirabell Castle in Salzburg (1725–27) and also worked for Count Imre Esterházy, prince archbishop of Hungary, and the archbishop of Esztergom in Bratislava (Hungarian Pozsony, German Pressburg, now Bratislava in Slovakia), producing sculptural decoration for the St. John the Almsgiver's Chapel in St. Martin's Cathedral (1729–32) and the main altar of St. Martin's Cathedral (1733–35), of which the middle sculptural group, *St. Martin and the Beggar*, is one of the most significant remains of Central European lead sculpture. Donner's other major work for the Viennese city council (*magistrat*), the lead *Fountain of Providence* (Österreichische Galerie, Vienna), was unveiled

Georg Raphael Donner, *Fountain of Andromeda*, 1740–41, Old Town Hall, Vienna, Austria
© Erich Lessing / Art Resource, NY

in 1739 on the Mehlmarkt (Neuer Markt) in Vienna. Johann Nikolaus Moll, one of Donner's followers, produced the lead sarcophagus of Emperor Charles VI in the crypt of the Viennese Capuchin Church; his brother, Balthasar Ferdinand Moll, made further sarcophagi at the commission of Empress Maria Theresa (Kapuzinerkirche, Vienna). In the 1760s Franz Xaver Messerschmidt produced Late Baroque and Rococo portraits of the imperial family and the Viennese aristocracy, such as the zinc-copper *Empress Maria Theresa as Hungarian Queen* (1764–66; Österreichische Galerie, Vienna), as well as Neoclassicist portraits of the followers of the Enlightenment. Messerschmidt was intensively absorbed in making a series of busts called the *Character Heads* (*ca.* 770–83) from a lead-zinc alloy or alabaster; these were probably sculpted as physiognomical and proportion studies.

Neoclassicism

The first representatives of Austrian Neoclassicist sculpture were followers of Donner and Messerschmidt. The most influential early Neoclassicist sculptor in Vienna was the German Christian Friedrich Wilhelm Beyer, who was in charge of making the park statues of the Schönnbrunn Palace in 1773–80. Franz Anton Zauner created the most significant bronze equestrian statue of Viennese Classicism, the Emperor Joseph II monument (1807) on the Josefsplatz. Zauner became director of the Viennese Academy of Fine Arts, where he further established the Classical style in the circle of his students. The Austrian Neoclassicist sculptors were mostly influenced by the Italian Antonio Canova, as shown in the works of Josef Klieber, the teacher of the Hungarian Neoclassicist sculptor István Ferenczy at the Academy of Fine Arts, Vienna.

Romanticism and Historicism

Southern German influence was amplified again in Austrian sculpture in the second half of the 19th century. The leading sculptor of the Munich school, Ludwig von Schwanthaler, received several commissions in Austria. The most significant Austrian Romantic Historicist sculptors, such as Hans Gasser and Anton Dominik Fernkorn, who studied in Munich, followed Schwanthaler's trend. Fernkorn founded the K.K. Kunst-Erzgiesserei (Imperial Bronze Foundry), where along with several other commissions, his monument to Archduke Charles (1859; Heldenplatz, Vienna) was executed. Kaspar Clemens Zumbusch's bronze monument to Ludwig van Beethoven (1873–80; Beethovenplatz, Vienna) signaled the beginning of the Historicist style. One of the masterpieces of Historicism is the marble monument to Wolfgang Amadeus Mozart (1896; Burggarten, Vienna), carved by Victor Tilgner in Vienna. This naturalistic, academic style prevailed in Vienna until the end of the 19th century.

20th Century

The naturalistic and academic styles continued in Austrian sculpture at the beginning of the 20th century, while the Viennese *Jugendstil* and *Secession* emerged and produced monumental decorative statues, such as Arthur Strasser's *Marcus Aurelius* (1899–1900; Sezession, Vienna) and Josef Müllner's monument to Lueger (1926; Luegerplatz, Vienna). Anton Hanak, one of the most significant Austrian sculptors, following the styles of ancient Egyptian and Greek art as well as the styles of Michelangelo and Auguste Rodin, created stirring bronze sculptures such as *Burning Man* (1922) and *Margaret Stonborough-Wittgenstein* (1930), both at the Anton Hanak Freilichtmuseum, Langenzersdorf. His contemporary, the popular Austrian sculptor Fritz Wortruba, produced under the influence of Aristide Maillol and Wilhelm Lehmbruck human figures made up of simple cubic and cylinder

forms, such as the limestone *Seated Figure* (1949; Österreichische Galerie, Vienna). In the 1950s Cubist formal language developed under Wortruba's influence. Another significant artist of modern Austrian sculpture, Rudolf Hoflehner, represented the Abstract trend after 1950. In the second half of the 20th century, several trends, schools, and styles existed concurrently in Austrian sculpture. Oswald Oberhuber followed Abstractionism, the members of Aktionismus were influenced by experimental art, Franz West produced fetishlike statues, and Franz Rosei and Christian Frank created expressive stone statues.

Czech Republic and Slovakia

Romanesque Period

One of the earliest Romanesque examples of Bohemian sculpture is known from the end of the 11th century in the Benedictine Monastery of Božetěch. The relief of *Christ Enthroned with St. Peter and St. Paul* (ca. 1150; Lapidarium, Historical Museum, Prague) from the tympanum of St. John the Baptist in the castle of Oldřís shows primarily Byzantine influence similar to Hungarian Romanesque sculpture. Eastern and Western influences mingled in late 12th- and early 13th-century Bohemian sculpture, as seen on the relief of *Christ with Bohemian Saints* (ca. 1165) on the south facade of St. James's Church in Kutná Hora, the portal decoration of St. Procopius's Church in Zábori (ca. 1200), and the *Virgin Enthroned with Abbesses and King Ottokar Přemsyl I* in the tympanum of St. George's Church in Hradčany, Prague (after 1220). One of the most significant remains of Bohemian Romanesque sculpture is the stone relief from the quarter tower of Charles Bridge in Prague, which represents a donor kneeling in front of the sovereign (ca. 1170–1250; Museum of the City, Prague). The Cistercian Church portals (ca. 1250), for example, Třebič and Trišnov, show the influence of the Late Romanesque sculpture of Vienna and Ják.

Gothic Period

Bohemian early Gothic sculpture formed in the second half of the 13th century mainly under French influence and advanced rapidly during the reign of the Holy Roman Emperor Charles IV of Luxembourg (r. 1346–78), who resided in Prague. Peter Parler, an architect and sculptor of Prague from the middle of the 14th century, continued the works of the Cathedral of St. Vitus from 1353 after the death of Matthieu d'Arras. Parler strove for realism in his sculpture while following French traditions and applying simple forms. On a series of portrait busts on the triforium in the Cathedral of Prague, he presented the members of the imperial family, the higher clergy, d'Arras, and himself. Parler's workshop produced six tomb monuments with reclining figures of the Přemyslids and St. Wenceslas's standing statue in the St. Wenceslas Chapel for the cathedral. Parler was the most significant sculptor of Central European Gothic style, and his influence can be seen on Gothic works of art from Bohemia, Vienna, and Buda, now west Budapest.

Artists formulated two basic scenes during the second half of the 14th century in High Bohemian Gothic with the *Schöner Stil* (Beautiful Style). One scene, the Virgin and child, or *Schöne Madonna* (Beautiful Madonna), represented the interior and exterior beauty of the Gothic Madonna ideal in an elegant and decorative style, such as the sculpture of the Madonna from Krumlov (after 1390; Kunsthistorisches Museum, Vienna). The second most common scene was the *pietà*, a depiction of the lifeless body of Christ reclining nearly horizontally in his mother's lap, such as the painted and gilded wood statue of St. Ignatius's Church in Jihlava (*ca.* 1400). The Hussite Iconoclasm blocked the development of Bohemian sculpture in the 15th century.

Renaissance Period

Independent sculptors reappeared after the Hussite iconoclasm (*ca.* 1500). These artists primarily followed the sculptural tendencies of the Danube school and those of southern Germany—for instance, in the wood relief *Lamentation* by the Master of Žebrák (after 1500; National Gallery, Prague). The architect and sculptor Anton Pilgram, an outstanding talent of Bohemian and Moravian Late Gothic and Early Renaissance styles, followed Parler's realistic traditions. Pilgram worked mainly in his hometown of Brno for St. James's Church and the town hall; from 1513 he worked in St. Stephen's Cathedral in Vienna, where he influenced Austrian sculpture. Italian Renaissance styles emerged in Bohemian sculpture beginning in the 16th century. Ferdinand I (*r.* 1556–64), the Holy Roman Emperor, king of Bohemia and Hungary, mostly employed Italian sculptors, and under the directions of Paolo Stella, he commissioned in 1538–52 sandstone reliefs that were based on contemporary and mythological scenes for the Belvedere, the summer palace in Prague. Under Emperor Maximilian II (*r.* 1564–76) in 1562, Francesco Terzio designed for the garden at Belvedere the *Singing Fountain*, which was modeled by Hans Peisser from Nuremberg, then cast in bronze by Tomáš Jaroš in 1568. The Flemish Alexander Colin sculpted the tomb of Ferdinand I and Anne of Jagiellon under the commission of Maximilian II for the Cathedral of St. Vitus in 1566, which was completed in 1573 in the Mannerist style.

Bohemian Mannerism reached its zenith during the reign of Emperor Rudolf II (*r.* 1576–1612). Adriaen de Vries, one of Giambologna's followers who was working in Prague during this time, depicted Emperor Rudolph II several times in life-size busts and reliefs. After the emperor's death, de Vries created fountains and garden statues for the palace of Count Albrecht von Wallenstein (Valdštejn) in 1623–26.

Baroque Period

The Counter Reformation and the relative peace following the Thirty Years' War provided a favorable environment for the development of Bohemian Baroque sculpture. In the first half of the 17th century, southern German, Munich, and Augsburg influences largely affected altar sculpture. The leading sculptor of Prague during this period was Jan Jirí Bendl, who carved the stone equestrian statue of *St. Wenceslas* (before 1680; Municipal Gallery, Prague). In the late 17th century, Italian stuccoists created Bohemian stucco decorations. Johann Georg Heermann from Dresden mediated the Italian and southern German Baroque styles with the monumental series of statues made in the staircase of the archbishop of Prague's castle in Trója, a village outside of Prague. The most significant representative of Bohemian outdoor stone sculpture was Ferdinand Maximilian Brokof, whose Bohemian sandstone masterpieces stand among the monumental statues of Charles Bridge in Prague. Bernard Barun represented the dramatic Berninesque Baroque style in Bohemian sculpture with his masterpieces at the estate of Count Franz Anton Sporok at Kuks. The main representatives of Bohemian Rococo at the beginning of the 18th century included Karl Josef Hiernle, Jan Antonín Quitainer, František Ignác Weis, and Josef Klein. From the middle of the 18th century and in the wake of the works of Johann Platzer and Gottfried Fritsch, the influence of Georg Raphael Donner's classicizing Late Baroque style appeared in Bohemian and Moravian sculpture.

19th Century

Bohemian sculpture improved after the Napoleonic wars in the early 19th century. Josef Malínský was the representative of folk realism, and František Xaver Lederer produced Empire-style tomb monuments, but the most significant Bohemian sculptor of this time was Václav Prachner, who created the iron monument to Bishop Lev Thun-Hohenstein (1830) in the Košíře Cemetery, Prague. Josef Václav Myslbek, a professor at the Academy of Fine Arts in Prague, intertwined realist and academic elements in his monumental works for the National Theater in Prague (1871–74), the statue groups of the Palancký Bridge (1887–97), and the equestrian statue *St. Wenceslas* (1900–13) in Wenceslas Square, Prague. His students paved the way for modern sculpture. Stanislav Sucharda established French Symbolism, Ladislav Šaloun instituted Art Nouveau, and Josef Mařatka and Bohumil Kafka mediated the influence of Auguste Rodin into Bohemian sculpture.

20th Century

In the early 20th century, Otto Gutfreund established Czech Cubism and then later worked in realism. The leading artist of the interwar period was the avant-garde movement's Vincent Makovský. After 1948 socialist realism prevailed in state commissions. Contemporary Czech sculpture attempted to adjust itself to Western European trends. After 1918 the national style of Slovak sculpture developed, making use of the abundant folk art. The Slovak sculptor Jan Koniarek produced primarily Impressionist portraits. Slovak sculpture in the 20th century had strong connections to Czech art. The Slovak artist Miroslav Motoška was a student of Jan Štrusa and Ladislav Šaloun in Prague, and he created the equestrian monument to Prince Svatopluk. The portraits and monuments of Jozef Kostka, a leader modernist Slovak sculpture, follow Ivan Meštrovic's style. The most significant sculptor of the Slovak avant-garde was Rudolph Uher. Jozef Jankovič created a statue for the Olympic Village Sculpture Garden in Seoul, South Korea.

KATALIN HÁMORI

See also **Brokof, Ferdinand Maximilian; Donner, Georg Raphael; Erhart, Gregor; Gerhard, Hubert; Gras, Caspar; Guggenbichler, Johann Meinrad; Messerschmidt, Franz Xaver; Meštrovic, Ivan; Multscher, Hans; Pacher, Michael; Parler Family; Zürn Family**

Further Reading

Białostocki, Jan, *The Art of the Renaissance in Eastern Europe: Hungary, Bohemia, Poland*, Ithaca, New York: Cornell University Press, and Oxford: Phaidon, 1976

Biedermann, Gottfried, and Wim van der Kallen, *Romanik in Österreich*, Würzburg, Germany: Stürtz, 1990

Brusatin, Manlio, and Gilberto Pizzamiglio (editors), *The Baroque in Central Europe: Places, Architecture, and Art*, Venice: Marsilio, 1992

Galavics, Géza (editor), *Barokk művészet Közép-Európában: Utak és találkozások* (Baroque Art in Central Europe: Crossroads) (exhib. cat.), Budapest: Budapesti Történeti Múzeum, 1993

Galavics, Géza, et al., "Hungary, Republic of: III. Sculpture," in *The Dictionary of Art*, edited by Jane Turner, vol. 14, New York: Grove, and London: Macmillan, 1996

Korán, Ivo, "Czech Republic: III. Sculpture," in *The Dictionary of Art*, edited by Jane Turner, vol. 8, New York: Grove, and London, Macmillan, 1996

Korán, Ivo, "Slovakia: IV. Sculpture," in *The Dictionary of Art*, edited by Jane Turner, vol. 28, New York: Grove, and London: Macmillan, 1996

Larsson, Lars Olof, "Bildhauerkunst und Plastik am Hofe Rudolfs II.," in *Prag um 1600: Kunst und Kultur am Hofe Kaiser Rudolfs II.* (exhib. cat.), vol. 1, Freren, Germany: Luca Verlag, 1988

Stadlober, Margit, et al., "Austria: IV. Sculpture," in *The Dictionary of Art*, edited by Jane Turner, vol. 2, New York: Grove, and London: Macmillan, 1996

Stangler, Gottfried, et al. (editors), *Matthias Corvinus und die Renaissance in Ungarn, 1458–1541* (exhib. cat.), Vienna: Niederösterreichische Landesregierung, 1982

Tóth, Melinda, and Ernőo Marosi (editors), *Árpád-kori kőfaragványok* (Stone-carving of the Árpád Era) (exhibition cat.), Székesfehérvár, Hungary: MTA Mőuvészettörténeti Kutatócsoport, 1978

CERTOSA DI PAVIA   *Pavia, Italy, 1396*

The Certosa is a Carthusian monastery founded in 1396 by Giangaleazzo Visconti, who so generously endowed it that it became the most elaborately decorated monastery in Europe and the second greatest center of Lombard Renaissance sculpture after the Cathedral of Milan. The exuberant sculptural encrustation of the church facade, which combines courtly sumptuousness with Classical magnificence, continues throughout the church and cloisters and includes masterpieces by the finest Milanese Renaissance sculptors. The iconography of the monastery is Carthusian as well as courtly, and it focuses on Giangaleazzo's pious donation. Augustine's *City of God* and the doctrine of salvation by grace are the inspiration for many of the iconographs.

The high standard for sculptural quality was set with the purchase, shortly after 1396, of a marble altar by Campionese sculptors and, between 1400 and 1409, of an ivory and bone triptych and two coffers covered with carved bone plaques from Baldassare degli Embriachi and his workshop. Most of the finest sculpture produced for the Certosa was made during the reign of the Sforza Dukes, between 1462 and 1523, although significant sculpture continued to be made into the Baroque period. The Certosa was an artistic satellite of the Cathedral of Milan, built largely by architects, stonecutters, sculptors, and stone vendors who worked for the cathedral. Many of the stone elements and sculptures were made in Milan and transported to the monastery. The high quality of the sculpture makes it possible to attribute individual pieces to particular sculptors.

The sculpture made between 1462 and 1499 was largely by associates of the architects Giovanni and Guiniforte Solari and their pupil, Giovanni Antonio Amadeo. Francesco Solari produced terracotta sculptures for the two cloisters from 1463 to 1469. Amadeo made sculptures for the cloisters, the church, and its facade. He also directed the facade work in 1492–99, coordinating the efforts of the best sculptors of the Milanese Renaissance. The brothers Cristoforo and Antonio Mantegazza made many sculptures for the cloisters, the church, and its facade.

Other Milanese Renaissance sculptors who worked on the Certosa include Cristoforo Solari (old sacristy portal and facade medallions), Benedetto Briosco (collaborator on the tomb of Giangaleazzo Visconti, parts of the portals of the twin sacristies, facade medallions, main portal socle reliefs, later reliefs on the main portal, and other facade reliefs and statues), Tommaso Cazzaniga (south sacristy portal and parts of the facade windows), Antonio della Porta, called Tamagnino (facade with New Testament reliefs and medallions, parts of facade windows, piscina right of the main altar, and later statues), Giovanni di Stefano and Giovanni Battista da Sesto (assistants to Briosco on the main portal, pilaster panel left of the main portal, parts of facade windows, and facade statues), and Biagio Vairone (pilaster panel right of main portal, assistant to Briosco

on the main portal, and the tabernacle left of the main altar). Non-Milanese sculptors who worked on the Certosa include Alberto Maffiolo da Carrara (parts of the south sacristy lavabo), Gian Cristoforo Romano (tomb of Giangaleazzo and roundels for the south sacristy portal), Pace Gaggini (assistant to della Porta on the facade and the piscina right of the main altar), and Angelo Marini (statues for the facade in the 1550s).

CHARLES MORSCHECK

Further Reading

Albertini, Ottolenghi, et al., *La Certosa di Pavia*, Milan: Cassa di Risparmio, 1968
Bernstein, JoAnne Gitlin, "The Architectural Sculpture of the Cloisters of the Certosa di Pavia," Ph.D. diss., New York University, 1972
Morscheck, Charles R., *Relief Sculpture for the Facade of the Certosa di Pavia, 1473–1499*, New York: Garland, 1978
Morscheck, Charles R., "Augustinian Influences in the Iconography of the Certosa di Pavia," in *Augustine in Iconography*, edited by Joseph C. Schnaubelt and Frederick Van Fleteren, New York: Peter Lang, 1999

Antonio Mantegazza, *St. Augustine*
© Charles Morscheck

CÉSAR (BALDACCINI) 1921–1998 *French*

César Baldaccini's earliest three-dimensional works date from the years 1947 and 1948 and consist of strictly naturalistic figures executed using unconventional industrial materials (iron scrap metal and wood bound together with wire and plaster). He also fashioned a series of figures out of wire and lead in a frenzied, graphic style resembling some of the works of Alberto Giacometti, whose sculpture was an admitted influence. Over the next decade César became interested in the work of Germaine Richier, Pablo Gargallo, and Constantin Brancusi. In 1952, using oxyacetylene and arc welding techniques, he expanded the range of found materials in his figures, favoring in particular the detritus of heavy industry—screws, nuts, bolts, pipes, and recycled pot metal—with which he constructed naturalistic or seminaturalistic human and animal figures that at once affirm the artist's commitment to the appearances of the physical world and express his disdain for traditional artistic contexts and methods.

In 1954, taking the professional name César, he held his first solo show at the Galerie Lucien Durand in Paris. In it a series of animal figures of bewildering variety revealed their shape and identity through a jumble of industrial discards and spelter. He created his large-scale works from the later 1950s and early 1960s out of slabs of metal welded into high-relief compositions, combining figurative and nonobjective elements. *The Devil* (1956) is representative of this style. The

The Devil
© Giraudon / Art Resource, NY

was seen with increasing frequency in the company of Marie-Laure de Noialles, the Rothschilds, and a host of celebrated Paris entertainers, prompting members of the critical community to question his seriousness as an artist. In the mid 1960s his large-scale naturalistic works, *Thumb* and *Breast*, caused a stir within the mainstream press and extended his fame beyond Europe to the United States. With the aid of a pantograph, he created a group of enlarged castings of his thumb, the best known of which is in polished bronze; and he was commissioned by the French film industry to create a figure for their use as an award (now known simply as the "César").

Perhaps César's most innovative technical achievement came in 1967 with the creation of a series of so-called expansions out of molded polyurethane foam. *Expansion No. 14* is typical of these works, often executed on a monumental scale, which resemble, sometimes explicitly, the extrusions of paste from a tube. He coated many of these works in vinyl or resin and painted them in a variety of brilliantly pigmented industrial paints. The scale and subject matter of these pieces are not unrelated to the large-scale projects undertaken by Claes Oldenburg during the same period and share some of the characteristics of "process art."

After 1970 César's technical and formal innovations became fewer, and he spent more than 20 years revisiting the themes of his early career.

ANDREW MARVICK

Biography

Born in Marseille, France, 1 January 1921. Studied art and sculpture at École des Beaux-Arts, Marseille, 1935–43, under Cornu, who had worked as a studio assistant and stonecutter for Rodin; received scholarship and moved to Paris, 1943; gained admission to École des Beaux-Arts, Paris, completing training in 1950; assumed professional name César, and held first solo exhibition, 1954; exhibited compressed automobiles at Salon de Mai, 1960; major retrospectives of work mounted during the 1970s and 1980s. Died in Paris, France, 6 December 1998.

Selected Works

1954   *Seated Nude ("Pompeii")*; scrap metal; Musée Nationale d'Art Moderne, Centre Georges Pompidou, Paris, France
1958   *Flat Sculpture*; iron, bronze; Tate Gallery, London, England
1962   *Ricard*; directed automobile compression; Musée Nationale d'Art Moderne, Centre Georges Pompidou, Paris, France

works of these years occasionally suggest the solidity and gravity of Classical Greek relief and freestanding sculpture, as for example *The Other One's Sister* (1962) and *Seated Nude ("Pompeii")*.

César's reputation grew after 1960 with the exhibition of his first "compressions." These sculptures essentially consist of artfully crushed cars and car parts, such as *Ricard*, similar in appearance to a series of roughly contemporary works fashioned out of compressed car wreckage by John Chamberlain. It was also during this decade that César's sculpture became associated with the art of the Nouveaux Réalistes, a group that included Yves Klein, Arman, Jean Tinguely, and Christo, and whose work was linked, according to the movement's primary champion and critic Pierre Restany, by "the fundamental characteristic of European New Realism—the appropriation of the real by means of its parts" (see Restany, 1975).

César's social standing rose as well at this time; he

1965   *Thumb*; bronze; Centre Georges Pompidou, Paris, France
1970   *Expansion No. 14*; polyurethane, vinyl lacquer; Musée Nationale d'Art Moderne, Centre Georges Pompidou, Paris, France

Further Reading

Baldaccini, César, *César par César*, Paris: Denoël, 1971
Baldaccini, César, *César: Rétrospective des sculptures* (exhib. cat.), edited by R.M. Mason, Geneva: Musée de l'Art et de l'Histoire, 1976
César: 1955–1985 (exhib. cat.), Dunkirk: Musée de l'Art Contemporain, 1985
Cooper, Douglas, *César*, Amriswil, Switzerland: Bodensee-Verlag, 1960
Hagen, Yvonne, "Sculptured Scrap," *The New York Herald Tribune* (20 May 1959)
Mathey, François, and Douglas Cooper, *César* (exhib. cat.), Marseille: Musée Cantini, 1960
Mathey, François, and Pierre Restany, *César* (exhib. cat.), Paris: Centre Nationale Art Contemporain, Archives de l'Art Contemporain, 1970
Restany, Pierre, *César*, Monte Carlo: Éditions Andreé Sauret, 1975; as *Cesar*, New York: Abrams, 1975
Restany, Pierre, *Les nouveaux réalistes*, Paris: Éditions Planète, 1968

SIR FRANCIS (LEGATT) CHANTREY
1781–1841 *British*

Sir Francis Chantrey is one of the most accomplished sculptors of 19th-century British art. His achievement lay in his ability to endow his likenesses, be they portrait busts or full-scale statues, with an esteemed public image enlivened with a deep sense of character and life. His supple handling of marble enabled him to convey the quality of flesh and bone with enhanced naturalism, and his clever manipulation of light helped further to reveal the subtleties of the sitter's character.

A man of considerable innate ability, Chantrey had no formal training as a sculptor, and unlike many of his contemporaries, he largely rejected the Neoclassical tradition. His work does, however, possess something of the simplicity of form associated with that style, especially in his treatment of the female form. The indelible influence came from an admiration for and careful study of the work of Louis-François Roubiliac and the Parthenon marbles.

Chantrey's contemporaries particularly acclaimed him for his portrait busts. Perhaps his most sensitive characterization is that of the radical reformer John Horne-Tooke, exhibited at the Royal Academy in 1811. This highly successful work secured Chantrey's considerable reputation as a master of the rendered mind, which developed from Chantrey's studied obser-

vations of his subjects in movement and animated conversation and his unusual practice of finishing many of his portraits from life.

Chantrey executed busts of many of the notable men and women of his time, channeling his energy and inventive powers into images of those people he respected personally and who possessed the qualities of the "thinking mind." His deepest respect was for the practical aspects of creativity rather than the abstract or emotional.

Chantrey's delayed appointment as a Royal Academician, which eventually came in 1818, was due at least in part to the opinion that until then, he had only proved himself as a carver of busts. Indeed, his early statues display relative awkwardness in their treatment of surface decoration. The success of his later statues is attributable to their simplicity, which was directly enabled by the choice of contemporary dress over Classical drapery. By 1824 Chantrey was producing stoic grandeur and dignity with the utmost simplicity in works such as his monument to Robert Dundas of Arniston and his brilliant monument to James Watts, an exercise in balanced informality. The pose of the seated hero adopted here by Chantrey recalls Michelangelo's figures of *Lorenzo de' Medici* and *Giuliano de' Medici* in the Medici Chapel in Florence (*ca.* 1520–34).

Monument to David Pike Watts
The Conway Library, Courtauld Institute of Art

Chantrey's adoption of a more informal rendering of the subject set him apart from his contemporaries. He displayed further innovation in rejecting the traditional reclining pose for his monuments to bishops, choosing instead to present his subjects kneeling as if in prayer, as in the monument to Bishop Heber.

One of Chantrey's most significant stands was against the use of allegory to convey meaning. This radical advance can be seen clearly in his moving funerary groups, which present death as a purely secular event, with the focus firmly centered on articulate human emotions. The heightened Romantic sentiment exploited here by Chantrey was particularly suited to a society whose imagination was fired by passion and self-expression. The monument to Marianne Johnes of Hafod, for example, is a family group of considerable energy. The grave and deeply moving emotion carved onto the face of the father in this deathbed scene was highly acclaimed by Chantrey's contemporaries and by those fortunate enough to see the monument before it was destroyed by fire in 1932. This pyramidal grouping, which recalls the intensity of Thomas Banks's monument to Mrs. Hand (1785), possessed a degree of reality that inspired onlookers to reflect on their own mortality.

A better-known monument of this type is Chantrey's monument to David Pike Watts, the largest funerary group executed by the sculptor. Again a deathbed scene, here, the dying philanthropist and patron of the arts is shown supporting himself so that he may comfort his mourning daughter, who kneels at his bedside with her three young children. The parental gesture of the father is echoed by the young mother who comforts her youngest child. The dignity of this parting scene sets it apart from Chantrey's earlier Hafod group, with the inevitability of death softened by the allusion to life shown in the inquisitive infants who witness the scene. Chantrey used this more palatable treatment of loss in other monuments as well—for example, the monument to the Robinson daughters, the *Sleeping Children*, and the monument to Lady Frederica Stanhope, who are all represented as if in sleep; the latter is a remarkable study of the mothering experience.

Chantrey returned to the theme of the mother to great effect in his monument to Mrs. Dorothea Jordon, the actress and longtime mistress of the Duke of Clarence, later King William IV. The monument betrays nothing of the sitter's private character and circumstances and therefore conforms with the proscribed ideologies associated with the representation of women at this time. Yet Chantrey successfully portrays a moment that embodies and communicates the significance of the relationship depicted.

The enduring influence of Chantrey's mastery of skill and the radical departures made by him in the realms of sculpture can be seen in the work of the generation of sculptors who followed him. Not only Chantrey's assistants but also those sculptors who were inspired and motivated by the realism of the Pre-Raphaelites, Thomas Woolner and Alexander Munro among them, perpetuated his ideals of expression and character. When he died in 1841, he left a fortune of 150,000 pounds, which was ultimately left to the Royal Academy for the purchase of works by British artists, to encourage the progress of art in Britain. This became known as the Chantrey Bequest. A growing interest in phrenology, which found a flowering in the work of sculptors such as Samuel Joseph, may also have benefited from Chantrey's success (despite the criticism in 1862 of the critic Francis Turner Palgrave, who spoke of the "corrupt school of Chantrey"). That the realist tradition survived and enjoyed something of a revival at the end of the century with the New Sculpture movement is perhaps a testament to Chantrey's foresight and confidence in the potential of British sculpture.

FIONA DARLING-GLINSKI

Biography

Born in Norton (near Sheffield, South Yorkshire), England, 7 April 1781. Apprenticed in 1797 to Robert Ramsay, decorative carver and gilder of Sheffield, who also dealt in prints and plaster models; paid to cancel his own indentures at 21; set up as portrait painter under encouragement of John Raphael Smith and William Paulet Carey; visited London, Scotland, Ireland, 1802; forced to return home due to serious illness; moved to London permanently, 1807; studied evenings at Royal Academy schools; received first sculptural commission, 1805; married and set up studio in Belgrave Place with wife's considerable dowry; by 1814 he had several assistants; visited Paris, 1814, 1815; elected associate of the Royal Academy, 1816; full member, 1818; visited Italy, 1819; established bronze foundry at Eccleston Place, London, 1827; appointed Sculptor-in-Ordinary to King William IV, 1830; health began to decline in 1838 but continued to work until his death. Died in London, England, 25 November 1841.

Selected Works

1805 Monument to the Reverend James Wilkinson; marble; Sheffield Cathedral, England

1811–18 Portrait bust of John Horne-Tooke; marble; Fitzwilliam Museum, Cambridge, England

1812   Monument to Marianne Johnes, Hafod,
        Wales; marble (destroyed 1932)
1814–15 *George III*; marble (destroyed 1940);
        London, England
1817   *Sleeping Children* (monument to the
        Robinson children); marble; Cathedral
        Lichfield, England
1817–26 Monument to David Pike Watts; marble;
        Church of the Holy Cross, Ilam, England
1820   *Benjamin West*; marble; National Portrait
        Gallery, London, England
1820   *Sir Walter Scott*; marble; Abbotsford
        House, Borders, Scotland
1820–24 Monument to James Watts; marble;
        Church of St. Mary Handsworth,
        Birmingham, England
1823   Monument to Lady Frederica Stanhope;
        marble, Chevening Church, Kent, England
1824   Monument to Robert Dundas of Arniston;
        marble; Parliament House, Edinburgh,
        Scotland
1826–35 Monument to Bishop Heber; marble; St.
        Paul's Cathedral, London, England
1829–30 *George IV*; bronze; Trafalgar Square,
        London, England
1831–34 Monument to Mrs. Dorothea Jordon;
        marble; Royal Collection, Buckingham
        Palace, London, England
1833–34 *Lady Mary Sommerville*; marble; Royal
        Society, London, England

Further Reading

Binfield, Clyde, *Sir Francis Chantrey: Sculptor to an Age, 1781–1841*, Sheffield: University of Sheffield, 1981

Penny, Nicholas, *Catalogue of European Sculpture in the Ashmolean Museum, 1540 to the Present Day*, 3 vols., Oxford: Clarendon Press, and New York: Oxford University Press, 1992; see especially vol. 3

Potts, Alex, *Sir Francis Chantrey, 1781–1841: Sculptor of the Great* (exhib. cat.), London: National Portrait Gallery and Mappin Art Gallery, 1980

Whinney, Margaret, *Sculpture in Britain, 1530–1830*, London and Baltimore, Maryland: Penguin, 1964; 2nd edition, revised by John Physick, London and New York: Penguin, 1988

Yarrington, Alison, et al., *An Edition of the Ledger of Sir Francis Chantrey, R.A., at the Royal Academy, 1809–1841*, Oxford: The Walpole Society, 1994

CHARIOTEER FROM THE SANCTUARY OF APOLLO AT DELPHI *Anonymous*

ca. 478–474 BCE

bronze

h. 1.8 m

Archaeological Museum, Delphi, Greece

Of the few surviving Greek bronze statues of the Classical period, the Delphi *Charioteer* is the one whose original context can be established more precisely because it has survived with a part of its inscribed base. It therefore provides an important point of reference in any history of Greek sculpture.

The statue was discovered in 1896 in the sanctuary in Delphi between the Temple of Apollo and the Theater. Broken in three pieces (lower body and feet, upper body and head, right arm with reins), it formed part of the fill of a large terrace behind the so-called Ischegaon Wall, erected after a devastating landslide had caused widespread damage in the sanctuary in 373 BCE. The *Charioteer* was likely among the many monuments then destroyed. Bronze fragments of a horse team (two rear legs, a front hoof, and a tail) and a chariot (a pole and yoke) and the left arm of a second, smaller statue were found with the statue, together with an inscribed base block of marble. These fragments all seem to have belonged to a single monument.

The *Charioteer* is extraordinarily well preserved, with only the left arm missing. A young man, he wears a *xystis*, a long, short-sleeved tunic belted high above the waist typical for his profession. A band worn over shoulders and armpits and crossing over the back would prevent the garment from catching the wind during a race. He stands erect, his feet close together and the weight evenly distributed. The entire body turns to the right in an unusual, gradual spiral movement along its vertical axis, leading from the feet upward to the head. This pose, together with the slight asymmetries in the face, strongly suggests that the charioteer was originally intended to be seen in a three-quarter view from the statue's right. The preserved right arm bends at the elbow and extends forward with a set of reins still in the hand. The missing left arm was doubtlessly in the same position. A broad band holds the charioteer's short hair; the curls are engraved above the band and plastically rendered below. His smooth, beardless face, with a heavy chin, is severe and expressionless. The long, almost fluted vertical folds of the garment, only part of which would have been hidden by the chariot case, further highlight the statue's plain, columnlike character.

The statue was cast in seven main pieces (head, upper body down to belt, lower body, arms, feet), possibly in the direct lost-wax technique. Smaller details were added separately. The eyes were made of glass paste with pupils of black stone and irises of brown onyx. Eyelashes and lips were made of copper, the teeth of silver, and the inlaid *meander* pattern of the hair band both of copper and silver.

The exact reconstruction of the complete monument

The *Charioteer* of Delphi
© Nimatallah / Art Resource, NY

rious Apollo). Polyzalos, a member of the powerful Deinomenid family, ruled as tyrant over Sicilian Gela from about 478 to 467/466 BCE, while his brothers Gelon and Hieron were lords of Syracuse. The Delphi monument was in all likelihood created for Polyzalos's victory in the chariot race at the Pythian Games. The victors' lists for these games are preserved except for the years 478 and 474 BCE, and either one must be the date after which the monument was commissioned. (According to an alternative, not unproblematic, theory, it may have been set up posthumously by Polyzalos in the 460s BCE to commemorate a Pythian victory of his late brother Hieron in 470 BCE [see Rolley, 1990]). These dates conform well to the style of the charioteer (a professional driver, rather than the owner, Polyzalos himself), whose facial structure and general composition can be linked to other early Classical sculptures such as the Harmodios from the Tyrannicide group (477/476 BCE) and the Kritios Boy and Blond Boy from the Athenian Acropolis (*ca.* 480–470 BCE).

Scholars have considered a number of well-known sculptors in connection with the *Charioteer*, both from the Greek mainland and the Greek colonies in southern Italy and Sicily. On purely stylistic grounds and with the limited number of preserved originals, the identity of the sculptor cannot be resolved. A reexamination of the *Charioteer* base has reportedly uncovered traces of a previously overlooked signature by Pythagoras of Rhegion, a renowned artist from southern Italy (see Vatin, 1991–92). According to the Roman writer Pliny the Elder in his *Natural History* (1st century CE), this Pythagoras had been "the first sculptor to show the sinews and veins and to represent the hair more carefully," and indeed, the *Charioteer*'s feet have always been noted for the strong naturalistic detail that contrasts with other parts of the statue. Until this reading of the signature is independently confirmed, however, the authorship of the Delphi monument remains open. The new reading of the main inscription also maintains that the text remained unchanged from the beginning, whereas previously scholars thought that the first line had at one point been erased and reinscribed differently in order to omit any reference to Polyzalos as the lord of Gela after his downfall in the 460s BCE. Nonetheless, it seems that the inscription was renewed several times and moved to a different position; equally, secondary cuttings suggest that the base was reassembled at least once after the initial dedication. Altogether, these circumstances indicate that the Delphi *Charioteer* belonged to an important monument and that great care was taken to adjust or repair it during the time it stood in the sanctuary.

THORSTEN OPPER

remains to some extent controversial. The remaining base block has on its top surface three sockets for the fastening of hooves, none of which can be definitively linked to one of the preserved bronze fragments. In relation to the inscribed face of the base, it is therefore possible to reconstruct the chariot group frontally or in profile, the latter perhaps more likely because of the pronounced turn of the charioteer. The arm of the second figure, if indeed it is part of the same monument, would belong to a groom leading the horses or even mounted on a further horse, as Pausanias describes for a similar monument dedicated for the Sicilian tyrant Hieron at Olympia. The base inscription itself is essential in providing a date and historical context for the monument. It originally consisted of two lines of one hexameter (possibly originally followed by a pentameter) each, about half of which are extant. The following text is preserved: "[. . . P]oluzalos m' anethek[e . . .] / [. . . t]on aex' euonym' Apoll[on . . .]" (Polyzalos set me up/prosper him glo-

Further Reading

Chamoux, François, *L'Aurige des Delphes*, Paris: De Boccard, 1955

Hampe, Roland, *Der Wagenlenker von Delphi*, Munich: Bruckmann, 1941

Houser, Caroline, *Greek Monumental Bronze Sculpture of the Fifth and Fourth Centuries B.C.*, New York: Garland, 1987

Jacquemin, Anne, *Offrandes monumentales à Delphes*, Athens: École Française d'Athènes, 1999

Rolley, Claude, "En regardant l'Aurige," *Bulletin du Correspondence Hellenique* 114 (1990)

Stucchi, Sandro, "Il monumento per la vittoria del Gelas anasson Polizalo," *Archeologia Classica* 42 (1990)

Vatin, Claude, "Das Viergespann des Polyzalos in Delphi. Weihinschrift und Künstlersignatur," *Boreas* 14–15 (1991–92)

CHARTRES CATHEDRAL *Chartres,*

France, 12th–13th century

Following a fire at Chartres Cathedral in 1134, a new, twin-towered west front was attached to the 11th-century nave. Its centerpiece was the royal portal, the installation of which can be deduced from contemporary chronicle evidence to have been under way by 1145.

This triple entrance featured all three doorways opening into the central vessel of the existing nave, and this permitted a design remarkable for its integration. Originally, 24 life-size column figures representing Old Testament figures, including kings and queens, none of which can be identified with certainty, formed a horizontal band running across the composition, ten on the jambs of the central portal and seven on each flanking portal. Over their heads are canopies, and above these the capitals of the colonnettes are carved in a unifying narrative frieze illustrating the life of the Virgin and the life and Passion of Christ. This composition allowed two orders of figural archivolts on each flanking portal and three in the center, with relatively small, slightly pointed tympana.

The central tympanum shows an apocalyptic Christ in majesty surrounded by evangelist symbols above a lintel with standing apostles under arcading, a design rooted in the Romanesque sculpture of Burgundy. Tangentially carved angels and elders of the Apocalypse occupy the archivolts. The two flanking portals illustrate the beginning and end of Christ's life on earth. Above the right-hand doorway, the tympanum shows a frontal Virgin and Child with angels, and the two lintels below form a narrative frieze of incarnation scenes from the Annunciation to the Presentation in the Temple. These are carefully composed so that Christ appears three times, and the Virgin twice, on the central vertical axis; the lower lintel shows signs of adjustment to achieve precisely this result. Chartres Cathedral was dedicated to the Virgin, the sculptural representation of whom held an important relic in her girdle; her prominence on the royal portal marks a new phase in the cult of the Virgin. In the archivolts of the right-hand portal are personifications of the Liberal Arts, which serve as reminders of the importance of the School of Chartres. The left portal shows Christ ascending into heaven, borne by angels. On the upper lintel, four angels announce the event to the apostles, seated under arcading on the lower lintel. Carved signs of the zodiac and labors of the months decorate the archivolts.

Additional sculptures of small figures and angels appear on the doorjambs and the pilasters between the doorways. One of only two inscriptions on the portal identifies a seated figure as Jeremiah. The second inscription, the single word *Rogerus*, has been the subject of a good deal of controversy, but it is probably simply a sculptor's signature.

The unprecedented volume of sculpture on the royal portal necessitated the employment of at least four sculptural workshops, two of which must be mentioned here. The left portal outer column figures show the distinctive ridged folds and concentric patterns of the workshop responsible for the south portal of the

Chartres Cathedral, South Transept, West Portal
The Conway Library, Courtauld Institute of Art

Church of Notre-Dame at Étampes. Other Étampes features, such as the capital frieze and the fluted plinths, indicate that the head of this workshop had an important role in the overall design of the royal portal. Important sculpture at the center of the composition, including the center portal tympanum and column figures, are by a workshop associated with the name of the headmaster, traditionally assumed to be the overall head of the combined workshop. The distinctive style of these attenuated figures clad in drapery with narrow parallel folds betrays a workshop background at Souvigny and La-Charité-sur-Loire.

In 1194 the cathedral was again damaged by fire, and the decision was adopted to replace everything to the east of the facade block. Each transept of the new work was given a porched triple portal of the type recently used for the west front of Laon Cathedral. The iconography of the three major portals followed the most popular schemes then current: Christ in majesty, following Cluny, remained on the royal portal; the Last Judgment, as at Saint-Denis and Autun, formed the centerpiece of the south transept portal; and the Coronation of the Virgin, following Senlis and Laon, occupied the north transept central tympanum. On the south, the Last Judgement occupies the tympanum, lintel, and archivolts, as at Saint-Denis, and the column figures below depict the apostles holding the instruments of their martyrdom. The two flanking tympana show the martyrdom of St. Stephen on the left and the confessor saints Martin and Nicholas on the right. The column figures of these two portals continue the theme of martyr and confessor saints.

Around the coronation of the Virgin in the central tympanum of the north portal, the archivolt contains a Tree of Jesse, as at Senlis, showing the genealogy of the Virgin, and the column figures of this portal depict the prophets who foretold her destiny. The left portal column figures form narrative groups of the Annunciation and Visitation—the earliest example of the narrative use of column figure groups—and the Incarnation cycle continues in the tympanum with the Nativity, annunciation to the shepherds, and adoration of the Magi. The embrasures of the right-hand portal are occupied by Old Testament figures whose actions in some way prefigured those of Christ or the Virgin, such as Joseph and Judith, and similar prefigurations also appear in the little narratives in the archivolts. Finally, Christ's wisdom and suffering are exemplified in the tympanum scenes of the sufferings of Job and the wisdom of Solomon, which form Old Testament echoes of the examples of the martyrs and confessors that form the subject of the south transept portals.

In addition to the portal sculpture, the porches themselves are rich with column figures and relief panels, including a series of Virtues and Vices in which the figure of Pride falling from his horse was one of many Chartrain motifs copied by Villard de Honnecourt.

This enormous sculptural undertaking occupied several workshops with distinctive styles. The most prominent is a restrained Classicism characterized by voluminous draperies falling in soft, fine folds, but a few of the latest figures (for example, St. Modeste in the north porch and St. Theodore and St. George on the south transept, left portal) are carved in a crisp *muldenstil* (trough-shaped fold style) with angular intersecting trough folds with rounded ends. Finally, the figures of St. Avit and St. Laumer on the south transept, right portal, are carved in a heavy Classical style, with folds falling in bold loops.

After the completion of the transept portals, a *jubé*, or choirscreen, was built for the new choir, which was dismantled and used as building material in 1763, and partially reexcavated in 1848. The surviving panels show scenes of Christ's infancy and Passion, and animal and hunting subjects, and their style indicates production between about 1230 and 1240 by sculptors from Chartres and Paris.

RON BAXTER

Further Reading

Armi, C. Edson, *The "Headmaster" of Chartres and the Origins of "Gothic" Sculpture*, University Park: Pennsylvania State University Press, 1994

Branner, Robert (editor), *Chartres Cathedral*, New York: Norton, and London: Thames and Hudson, 1969

James, John, *Chartres, les constructeurs*, 3 vols., Chartres: Société archéologique d'Eure-et-loir, 1977–82; as *The Contractors of Chartres*, Dooralong, New South Wales: Mandorla, 1978; London: Croom Helm, 1979; 2nd edition, 2 vols., Wyong, New South Wales: Mandorla, and London: Croom Helm, 1981

Katzenellenbogen, Adolf, *The Sculptural Programs of Chartres Cathedral: Christ, Mary, Ecclesia*, Baltimore, Maryland: Johns Hopkins University Press, 1959

Kidson, Peter, and Ursula Pariser, *Sculpture at Chartres*, London: Tiranti, 1958; New York: St. Martin's Press, 1974

Lapeyre, André, *Des Façades occidentales de Saint-Denis et de Chartres aux portails de Laon*, Mâcon, France: Protat, 1960

Meulen, Jan van der, "Sculpture and Its Architectural Context at Chartres around 1200," in *The Year 1200: A Symposium*, by François Avril et al., New York: Metropolitan Museum of Art, 1975

Sauerländer, Willibald, and Max Hirmer, *Gothic Sculpture in France, 1140–1270*, New York: Abrams, 1972

Stoddard, Whitney S., *Sculptors of the West Portals of Chartres Cathedral: Their Origins in Romanesque and Their Role in Chartrain Sculpture: Including the West Portals of Saint-Denis and Chartres, Harvard 1952*, New York: Norton, 1987

CHASING AND JOINING CAST-METAL SCULPTURE

Sculptors frequently make cast-metal sculpture in sections according to the capacity of the foundry or the complexity of the sculpture. It is sometimes easier to take molds from a complex form if the original master is cut into sections and the sections cast separately. With modern technology, it is easy to join the sections together consistently, accurately, and strongly by welding.

The term "welding" is a generic name for a variety of methods by which metal components are melted locally at the joint and the sections fused together. An intense heat source is essential in order to build up enough heat at the precise site of the joint and melt the metal in a controlled way before the heat dissipates throughout the components. In each case the joint area is heated to melting point to create a weld pool. To allow fusion to occur through the full depth of the joint, a small gap is left between the components or the joint is ground to a V cross section. One can achieve welding temperatures by using a mixture of gases, commonly oxygen and acetylene (oxyacetylene welding), forced under pressure through a nozzle and ignited, or by using an electric arc as the heat source, whereby the weld pool is created by an arc jumping between an electrode and the work piece. Arc welding is the most basic form of electric welding; the filler rod is the electrode and progressively melts into the weld pool until it becomes a stub and is replaced by the welder. Metal Inert Gas (MIG) welding is a semiautomated version of arc welding using a continuous wire feed. Tungsten Inert Gas (TIG) welding uses a nonconsumable tungsten electrode and separate filler rods. These techniques are the processes primarily associated with sculpture because they are quite accommodating in the hands of a skilled welder. Other means of providing a heat source for welding are more applicable to engineering production.

In all cases, atmospheric oxygen must not be allowed access to the weld pool or the oxygen will combine with the metal and create a flawed weld. The mantle of burned gas is the shield in oxyacetylene welding. In arc welding, filler rods are coated in a "flux" that burns away to form an inert fume that envelops the weld pool; shields of carbon dioxide and argon gases are blown over the weld pool in the case of MIG and TIG welding, respectively.

Each technique has some advantages in different circumstances: oxyacetylene or other gases for lead and its alloys, arc or MIG for ferrous metals, and TIG for copper and its alloys, aluminum, and stainless steel. Each technique works at temperatures that are considerably higher than the melting point of the metals: the electric arc, for instance, produces a temperature about double that of the melting point of bronze. Localized heating of metal creates stressing as the heated metal expands and the cooler adjacent area does not, but although the electric arc is more than a thousand degrees

centigrade hotter than the oxyacetylene flame, it causes less stressing and resultant distortion because the weld is completed and the heat dissipates rapidly.

Other joining techniques that employ heat include hard soldering and soft soldering. Both exploit the characteristics of the lower melting points of a different alloy to the metal(s) to be joined. Hard soldering temperatures are close to those needed to achieve welding, whereas soft soldering uses alloys with a very low melting point. Both techniques form a bond at the joint, as opposed to fusing the joint together. Hard-soldered joints will take significantly more stress than a soft-soldered joint, but both techniques are useful for joining dissimilar metals or delicate forms.

Before welding became the most convenient means of joining together sections of a sculpture, sculptors made joints by forming a "Roman joint," a variation on the mortise-and-tenon joint commonplace in woodworking. One section to be joined is provided with an internal socket and the other with a precisely fitting tongue. Screw-threaded studs that pass through the enveloping socket and into the tongue hold the two sections together. The head of the stud is riveted over to blend with the external surface of the sculpture, and the whole process demands considerable skill and absolute accuracy to make the joint visually unobtrusive.

Although the principle of the Roman joint is simple, it is a relatively recent introduction. Cast sculptures of the 18th century and before were joined by assembling the sections with a mold around the joint area into which was poured additional molten metal. Either side of the joint was usually slightly tapered so that the additional metal could be made flush with the surface. As the metal froze, it shrank to create a tight mechanical joint.

Whatever method is used for joining the sections together, some dressing back or "fettling" at the joints is needed, and the runners and risers have to be cut off. At that stage, most of the surface will be dark with an "as-cast" texture with patches of bright smooth metal where the joints, runners, and risers have been fettled. Some of these areas may be more smooth and even than the sculptor wants, so they are chased, or worked over with small punches with a variety of shaped points.

Some of the best examples of the chaser's skills can be seen on 18th-century English lead sculptures, which were entirely worked after casting; the chaser cut the detail in hair with a variety of gouges, used punches to provide background texture of minutely raised dots (each one applied individually and smaller than a pinhead), and created patterns on fabrics with punches, reproducing stitching, tiny flower repeats, and, in one example (John Cheere's portrait statue of King George II, erected in 1751 in Royal Square, St. Helier, Jersey,

Channel Islands, United Kingdom), even the texture of fine linen. In this instance chasing has been used to add and refine detail to a fine figurative portrait statue, but it can be used on all types of cast sculpture to vary or harmonize surface texture. In addition to the traditional punches and points, sculptors of today have a range of industrial equipment available to them, including mechanical grinders and polishers, and shot blasting equipment with shot materials ranging from large, hard, and abrasive to fine, soft powder. All of these processes are used to change and enhance the surface and, as such, they all constitute a form of chasing.

ANDREW NAYLOR

Further Reading

Kowal, Dennis, and Dona Z. Meilach, *Sculpture Casting: Mold Techniques and Materials, Metals, Plastics, Concrete*, London: Allen and Unwin, and New York: Crown Publishers, 1972

Mills, John, *The Encyclopedia of Sculpture Techniques*, London: Batsford, 1990

Vasari, Giorgio, *Vasari on Technique*, translated by Louisa S. Maclehose, edited by Gerard Baldwin Brown, New York: Dutton, and London: Dent, 1907; reprint, New York: Dover, 1960

ANTOINE-DENIS CHAUDET 1763–1810
French

Antoine-Denis Chaudet was one of the leading French sculptors during the period of the Revolution, the Consulate, and the Napoleonic empire. He has been described as the most important French interpreter in sculpture of Neoclassicism, a style more often associated with artists who worked in Italy, notably Antonio Canova and Bertel Thorvaldsen. Chaudet worked more or less simultaneously in two manners: a sober style, ultimately derived from Roman imperial art, for state commissions, and a more elegant, sensual style derived from Hellenistic Greek examples for his uncommissioned private works.

A winner of the Grand Prix de Rome for sculpture in 1784, Chaudet spent four years at the French Academy in Rome, where he was influenced by antique sculpture and the work of Canova. The works he showed at the Paris Salon, beginning in 1789, carried into the years of the Revolution a taste for eroticism and sentiment more characteristic of the ancien régime (*La Sensibilité*, 1789; *Nest of Cupids*, 1791, private collection, Paris, France). In addition, he provided drawings for engravings such as a *Kneeling Youth Embracing a Girl* (ca. 1790s). Chaudet, whose wife, Jeanne-Elizabeth Gabiou, was a successful painter of sentimental genre scenes, also was active as a history

painter; in 1793 he exhibited *Archimedes Killed by a Barbarian Soldier During the Siege of Syracuse* (current location unknown).

Perhaps finding it more discreet to produce a work demonstrating revolutionary fervor, Chaudet executed a large stone relief in 1792–93 for the Panthéon in Paris, which was transformed from the Church of St. Geneviève to a revolutionary national monument under the direction of the archaeologist and critic Antoine Quatremère de Quincy. Chaudet's *Devotion to the Motherland* depicts a heroic, seminude dying warrior supported by nude and draped female figures derived from antique prototypes. The sculptor also designed temporary decorations for Maximilien de Robespierre's Festival of the Supreme Being in 1794.

During the late 1790s, Chaudet began a series of more personal compositions of life-size nude figures in mythological subjects, including *Cyparissus Mourning for a Stag that He Loved, Oedipus as a Child Restored to Life by the Shepherd Phorbas*, and the well-known *Cupid Playing with a Butterfly*. Executed with refined, Alexandrian elegance and restrained sensuality, these works demonstrate a poetic quality that is at the heart of Chaudet's sensibility. The choice of nude ephebe as the subjects of several of these sculptures is in harmony

Cupid Playing with a Butterfly (Amour au papillon)
© Giraudon / Art Resource, NY

with the taste of this period of war and violence, as is best seen in paintings by Jacques-Louis David, Anne-Louis Girodet, Jean Broc, and others. Curiously, the marble versions of these sculptures, today Chaudet's most familiar works, were completed only belatedly (the *Cyparissus*) or posthumously by other sculptors. It is possible that either poor health or the press of state commissions in Chaudet's later career hindered him in completing these uncommissioned works.

The complex history of Chaudet's Napoleonic state commissions, subsequently confused by the vicissitudes of war and physical destruction of works, has been elucidated by Gérard Hubert and his collaborator Guy Ledoux-Lebard (see Hubert, 1999). Eventually the leading, and indeed the official, portraitist of Napoléon, Chaudet seems to have begun around 1802 with an uncommissioned bust of *Napoléon Bonaparte as First Consul*, combining elements of ancient Roman portraiture with modern costume. In 1804–05 Chaudet produced a life-size *Napoléon as Legislator* for the hemicycle of the Corps Législatif, Paris (subsequently displaced to Berlin, then to the Hermitage in St. Petersburg, Russia). Napoléon is shown in the guise of a standing Roman emperor wrapped in a voluminous cloak (ambiguously antique or modern) and holding a scroll representing the *Code Napoléon*. The head was modified into a bust in herm format that became the Emperor's official portrait, which was reproduced in hundreds of examples in bronze, marble, and Sèvres porcelain.

A life-size, seated allegorical figure of *Peace* in gilded silver, commemorating the short-lived Peace of Amiens, was not complete until 1806. One of Chaudet's finest public works, *Peace* combines the impassive facial features of the Napoleonic portraits with a superb handling of the classicizing draperies, which elaborated on that of the much earlier *Devotion to the Motherland*. Chaudet then went on to complete his most ambitious commission, a colossal bronze *Napoléon*, ten feet in height, surmounting the Vendôme Column in Paris (1808–10; lost). Also destroyed was a stone relief of 1810 for the exterior of the Palace of the Corps Législatif, *The Emperor Presenting the Colors Conquered at the Battle of Austerlitz*. At the end of his career, Chaudet also executed in a Mannerist-derived linear style decorative reliefs in stone and plaster for the exterior and interior of the Musée du Louvre, Paris.

Besides his Napoleonic images, Chaudet produced a number of fine portraits, both full-length (*General Jacques-François Dugommier*) and in bust format (*ca.* 1810; *The Empress Marie-Louise*; Musée du Louvre). Some of his most striking busts, such as the bust of Chrétien-Guillaume de Malesherbes, combine a classicizing herm format with a vital realism of detail. A prolific draftsman, Chaudet also made designs for bronze decorations on furniture and for goldsmith work.

Contemporary critical appraisals of Chaudet's Salon submissions were generally favorable, and in the 19th century, the Musée du Louvre boasted a Salle Chaudet. There is, nevertheless, no monograph on this artist, and the disappearance of some of his works has limited his subsequent reputation. Chaudet's public career, although brief, was highly successful; his is one of the most individual talents of the turbulent period of the Revolution and Napoleonic empire.

DONALD A. ROSENTHAL

Biography

Born in Paris, France, 3 March 1763. Married the painter Jeanne-Elizabeth Gabiou, 1793. Studied in Paris with Jean-Baptiste Stouf and Etienne-Pierre-Adrien Gois; received second prize for sculpture in Prix de Rome competition, 1781; first prize in 1784 for *Joseph Sold into Slavery by His Brothers*; in Rome, 1784–88; came under the influence of Antonio Canova; *agréé* (admitted) as an associate of the Royal Academy of Painting and Sculpture in Paris, 1789, but never became a full member; member of the Institut de France, 1805; member of the Legion of Honor; professor at École des Beaux-Arts, Paris, 1810. Died in Paris, France, 19 April 1810.

Selected Works

1784   *Joseph Sold into Slavery by His Brothers*; painted plaster; Museé de Louvre, Paris, France

1792–93 *Devotion to the Motherland*; stone; Panthéon, Paris, France

1798   *Cyparissus Mourning for a Stag that He Loved*; plaster (lost); 1810, marble; Hermitage, St. Petersburg, Russia

1799–   *Oedipus as a Child Restored to Life by the*
1801   *Shepherd Phorbas*; plaster (lost); 1815–18, marble (posthumously completed by Pierre Cartellier and Louis-Marie Dupaty); Musée du Louvre, Paris, France

1801   Bust of Chrétien-Guillaume de Malesherbes; marble; Musée du Louvre, Paris, France

1802   *Cupid Playing with a Butterfly*; plaster (untraced); 1817, marble (posthumously completed by Pierre Cartellier): Musée du Louvre, Paris, France

1802   *Napoléon Bonaparte as First Consul*; plaster; Musée David d'Angers, Angers, France

1803–05 *Peace*; gilded silver (cast 1806); Musée du Louvre, Paris, France

1804–05 *Napoléon as Legislator*; Hermitage, St. Petersburg, Russia; another version in Musée Nationale du Château, Compiègne, France

ca. 1808–10 *General Jacques-François Dugommier*; marble; Musée National du Château, Versailles, France

1810 *Emperor Holding a Winged Victory*; bronze (destroyed 1814); surviving figure of *Victory*, Musée National du Château, Rueil-Malmaison, France

1810 *The Emperor Presenting the Colors Conquered at the Battle of Austerlitz*; stone (destroyed after 1814)

1810 *Heroic Poetry, Homer*, and *Virgil*; stone; Musée du Louvre, Paris, France

Further Reading

Hubert, Gérard, "Chaudet, Antoine-Denis," in *The Dictionary of Art*, edited by Jane Turner, vol. 6, New York: Grove, and London: Macmillan, 1996

Hubert, Gérard, "Notes sur deux oeuvres retrouvées du sculpteur Chaudet," *Archives de l'art français* 22 (1959)

Hubert, Gérard, and Guy Ledoux-Lebard, *Napoléon: Portraits contemporains, bustes et statues*, Paris: Arthena, 1999

Lemaistre, Isabelle Leroy-Jay, "Chaudet," in *Allgemeines Künstlerlexikon: Die bildenden Künstler aller Zeiten und Völker*, vol. 18, Munich: Saur, 1998

Levey, Michael, *Painting and Sculpture in France, 1700–1789*, New Haven, Connecticut: Yale University Press, 1993

Sculptures françaises néo-classiques, 1760–1830 (exhib. cat.), Paris: Association Française d'Action Artistique, 1989

Skulptur aus dem Louvre: 89 Werke des französischen Klassizismus, 1770–1830 (exhib. cat.), Duisburg, Germany: Stadt Duisburg, 1989

West, Alison, *From Pigalle to Préault: Neoclassicism and the Sublime in French Sculpture, 1760–1840*, Cambridge and New York: Cambridge University Press, 1998

CHIMERA

Anonymous

375–350 BCE

bronze

h. 65 cm

Museo Archeologico, Florence, Italy

The Etruscan civilization flourished between the 9th and 1st centuries BCE across a section of Italy corresponding to the present regions of Tuscany, Umbria, and upper Latium. Many artifacts survive from this still partly mysterious civilization. Etruscan sculpture stands out for its votive figures, funerary monuments, and architectural embellishments. Artists used bronze and terracotta in all these genres but preferred stone for funerary sculpture. The masterpieces of bronze sculpture are from the period coinciding with the so-called Classical style. Among the most important pieces in this style are two extraordinary statues: the Todi *Mars*, from the late 5th century BCE (Gregorian Etruscan Museum, Rome), and the Arezzo *Chimera*.

The *Chimera* was discovered in the Tuscan town of Arezzo, near the San Lorenzo gate, on 15 November 1553, during excavations preceding the construction of a new bastion. The excavations also uncovered a votive offering comprising numerous bronze sculptures that eventually disappeared. According to a document in the Aretine archives, they included small figures of men and birds, as well as a horse's hoof. These works may have ended up in the hands of Tuscany's Grand Duke Cosimo I de' Medici. The magnificent hollow-cast statue shows the three-headed mythological monster responding to an attack. The animal seems contracted in a moment of terrible stress: anger and pain mix in a tragic representation. The body rests firmly on the front paws, with the neck twisted to the right and the goat head turning in dialectic tension to the left. The beast's terrible jaws are wide open, and a thick mane crowns its head in sharp relief. The mane consists of six rows of geometrically arranged flamelike locks tapering off into a double row of similar locks running down the animal's back. The paws, all equipped with powerful claws, each have a distinctive feature. The right forepaw presents an inscription ("tinscvil," a dedication to the divinity Tinia) cast in the bronze, the left forepaw has a deep blood-spouting wound. The left rear paw is a reconstruction generally

Chimera of Arezzo, late 5th century
© Gianni Dagli Orti / CORBIS

thought to have been made in the 16th century (probably by the famous sculptor Benvenuto Cellini). The statue is impressive for the strong naturalism that underlines each anatomical detail, although naturalism seems almost a contradiction for this mythological subject.

Although the *Chimera* was discovered in a town known to have been founded by the Etruscans, much uncertainty surrounds its attribution. Some scholars have suggested that it belongs to the Greek or Magna Graecia tradition. In early 20th-century archeological literature, it was thought a Corinthian, Ionian, Sicilian-Greek, or Italic work. Only in the second half of the 20th century were numerous studies published that left no doubt as to its Etruscan origin, a conclusion confirmed by a meticulous stylistic examination. Despite some archaic elements—present mainly in the face, which recalls the Gorgon or certain terracotta gargoylelike figures on Magna Graecia temples, and in the geometric arrangement of the furry parts—it exhibits strong analogies with other prestigious Etruscan sculptures. For instance a small bronze discovered near Ancona recalls the *Chimera*'s attitude and the bases of numerous candlesticks made at Volsinii between the 5th and 4th century are similar to the *Chimera*'s claws. Moreover, its goat head resembles the head of the goat found in the Bibbona votive offering in both the modeling of the fleece and the facial features. In addition, it seems clear that the bronze *Chimera* relates closely to the isolated images of Chimeras on 5th- and 4th-century Etruscan scarabs.

To date the Arezzo *Chimera* and understand its function, one must refer to the story of Bellerophon and the Chimera, which was frequently depicted on 4th-century Faliscan and Vulcian mirrors and pottery. However, the statue's admittedly strong similarity to contemporary Greek works can be misleading. The Arezzo *Chimera* represents a mythological subject in monumental terms; its resemblance to the great tufa lions guarding the entrances to so many tombs in the necropolises of southern Etruria points to the existence of a line of expression that started with the lion of Val Vidone, near Tuscania, and proceeded to the forms seen in the Arezzo bronze. Likewise, many small bronzes testify to the development of the Chimera iconography. Based on these parallels, scholars have determined that the bronze *Chimera* was probably made sometime between 375 and 350 BCE. The inscription "tinscvil" indicates that the statue must have been a votive offering. Given its high value, the bronze likely was offered by the community or a rich benefactor.

Many scholars have thought it odd that only the monumental freestanding *Chimera* was found at the site. Some have suggested that it was part of a still more monumental group that would have included Bellerophon mounted on Pegasus. Indeed, many contemporary ceramic iconographies show all three figures. Even the *Chimera*'s dynamic pose, braced for the attack, presupposes the presence of the opponent who has already wounded it. The story of Bellerophon's combat with the Chimera took shape at the end of the 6th century BCE and became one of the fundamental elements in Greek mythology. It spread especially in the northeastern Peloponnesus, where three cities—Argos, Sicyon, and Corinth—were dedicated to Bellerophon, the semidivine hero who rid the Lycian kingdom of the Chimera. No one could have resisted the monster's fiery breath, but Athena gave Bellerophon the winged horse Pegasus, enabling the hero to attack and kill the Chimera from above.

Cosimo I considered the discovery of the Arezzo *Chimera* a good omen; the Medici saw the defeated monster as a symbol of their own vanquished enemies. Not by chance has the beautiful marble statue of Pegasus (Aristodemo Costoli, 1865) that still dominates the Boboli Gardens in Florence become the emblem of modern-day Tuscany.

GIOVANNA CHECCHI

Further Reading

Cherici, Armando, *La chimera di Arezzo*, Arezzo, Italy: Comune, 1992

Cristofani, Mauro, *I bronzi degli Etruschi*, Novara, Italy: Istituto Geografico de Agostini, 1985

D'Hancarvilles, Pierre, "Antiquités étrusques," in *1768: Europa à la greque: Vasen machen mode*, edited by Martin Flashar, Munich: Biering und Brinkmann, 1999

Grassi, Paola Zamarchi, "Introduzione all'iconografia della chimera," in *La chimera e il suo mito*, by Mario Cygielman et al., Arezzo, Italy: Arti Grafiche il Torchio, 1990

Paturzo, Franco, *Arezzo antica: La città dalla preistoria alla fine del mondo romano*, Cortona, Italy: Calosci, 1997

Sebregondi, Ludovica, Raffaella Maria Zaccaria, and Paolo Viti, editors, *Arezzo antichissima*, Rome: Editalia, 1998

Simon, Erika, *Schriften zur etruskischen und italischen Kunst und Religion*, Stuttgart, Germany: Steiner, 1996

Tafi, Angelo, *La chimera e gli aretini*, Cortona, Italy: Calosci, 1986

CHINA: NEOLITHIC, BRONZE AGE, AND THREE KINGDOMS

Sculpture and religious practice were inextricably bound together in ancient China. Funerary sculpture and statuary, either above ground or buried in tombs, characterize the strongest and most persistent art tradition in Chinese history. When Buddhism was introduced to China in the 1st century CE, sculpture received the greatest attention among all the arts, and Buddhist sculpture flourished in the centuries that followed. However, because funerary sculpture was not the subject of traditional antiquarianism, the collecting and studying of early Chinese sculpture did not fully develop until the late 19th and the early 20th centuries, when Westerners began to explore China. At that time, the digging for the railway system in central China, especially in Henan and Shaanxi provinces, brought to light a large number of bronze vessels, jade ornaments, mortuary ceramics, and tomb figures. These discoveries attracted the attention of Chinese as well as Western and Japanese collectors and scholars. Stimulated by lucrative foreign and local art markets, tomb robbery became rampant. When Western archaeologists entered China in the 1920s, the discovery and study of Chinese sculpture dramatically accelerated. Since then, continuous archaeological discoveries have augmented our knowledge of early Chinese sculpture, and ancient sculpture has become an important basis for studying Chinese culture and society.

Neolithic (*ca.* 6500–1600 BCE)

Pottery and jade objects are the two main types of sculpture that are excavated from Neolithic sites in China. Like most early art in other parts of the world, designs related to human forms, animal figures, and mythic creatures were the main subject matter in Neolithic sculpture. Although their specific meanings are still in dispute, most come from a mortuary context and allow some understanding of prehistoric life from a religious perspective. Since Swedish geologist J.G. Andersson discovered the first prehistoric site at Yangshao in Henan Province in 1921, archaeologists have excavated thousands of Neolithic sites all over the country and have identified several regional pottery traditions and jade-working centers.

The painted pottery of the Yangshao culture (*ca.* 5000–3000 BCE) flourished in central China. Made of loess clay, Yangshao sculpture and vessels characteristically have a red body. Most were shaped by hand, and the vessels were usually built up by coiling long strips of clay. Cord, mat, or basket impressions and painted, stylized flower and fish motifs, as well as animal and human faces, decorate the vessels. Human forms are rare, but when they occur, they are often incorporated onto the body of the vessel, for example, in a painted pottery jar excavated from Luonan in Shaanxi Province and a flask from Dadiwan, Qin'an, Gansu Province. In both cases, the human head was shaped from the short neck of the vessel, and facial features are accurately modeled. Examples of animal-shaped designs also exist. The eagle-shaped tripod vessel unearthed at Taipingzhuang, Hua County, Henan Province, is a realistic portrayal of a strong, robust bird with a sharp, powerful beak and protruding eyes. Other famous examples of Yangshao sculpture include repre-

sentations of the dragon and tiger, both delineated by mollusk shells and accompanied a human skeleton, discovered in Xishuipo, Puyang, Henan Province.

In northwest China, the Majiayao culture (*ca.* 3100–2000 BCE) is closely related to that of central China. Simple designs and complicated geometric decoration characterize Majiayao pottery. A common vessel type is the funerary urn, hundreds of which might be buried in a tomb. The urn is typically a narrow-necked, short, stout vessel that is painted with red, black, or brown spiral or geometric patterns. Some of the lids are in the shape of a human head painted with geometric patterns. During the 1930s, a large number of funerary urns was excavated, many of which entered European and American museums and private collections. An unusual funerary urn discovered at Liuwan, Ledu, in Qinghai Province is adorned with an androgynous nude figure in relief.

Along the east coast of China grew jade-working centers and a third ceramic tradition, the black pottery cultures: the Dawenkou (*ca.* 4300–2500 BCE), the Longshan (*ca.* 2500–2000 BCE), and the Liangzhu (*ca.* 3300–2200 BCE). The great technological achievement of the Dawenkou culture was the invention of the fast potter's wheel. The skillful use of advanced wheel-throwing techniques and careful control of the kiln enabled Dawenkou and Longshan potters to create eggshell-thin ceremonial vessels. They also molded vessels in the shape of pigs, dogs, and turtles. Excavations of Dawenkou and Longshan tombs have also revealed ritual implements and luxurious ornaments carved from animal bones, ivory, and jade.

A distinctive monsterlike decoration adorned Longshan jades, such as a ceremonial blade (*ca.* 2000

Horse trampling a barbarian, tomb of Huo Qubing (d. 117 BCE), stone, Maoling, Shaanxi
Courtesy Ann Paludan

297

BCE) discovered at Liangchengzhen, Rizhao, in Shandong Province. On both sides of the blade are incised monster faces, depicted through elaborate curved lines symmetrically arranged around a dominant eye motif. Another elegant jade object from the Longshan culture is a turquoise-inlaid hair ornament, discovered at Zhufeng, Linqu, Shandong Province. It is a thin jade plaque with delicate openwork of a symmetrical design connected to a round, exquisitely crafted pin.

Southward was found the Majiabang culture (*ca.* 4300–3200 BCE) in southern Jiangsu Province and the Hemudu culture (*ca.* 5000–3300 BCE) in northern Zhejiang Province. Carving on bone and wood is a characteristic of Neolithic sculpture in this area. One exquisite bone dagger excavated from a Majiabang site is in the shape of a slim fish, the handle decorated with a geometric pattern. At the Hemudu site a red lacquered wooden bowl was discovered, the earliest specimen of lacquer craft.

The jade carving of the Liangzhu culture (*ca.* 3300–2200 BCE), also located in this area, was one of the high points of this art in Neolithic China. A characteristic object of the Liangzhu culture is the *cong*, a cylindrical tube enclosed by a square prism from top to bottom. Animal masks with pronounced, round eyes and sometimes fanged mouths are usually carved in the corners. Another jade type is the *bi*, a large, perforated disk. Some are incised with pictographic emblems of birds standing on top of stepped platform. These jades were often used in sacrifices and interred with the dead.

The Hongshan culture (*ca.* 4500–3000 BCE) of northeast China is named after a site in Chifeng, Inner Mongolia. In 1979 Chinese archaeologists excavated a complex stone structure, consisting of circular altars and square platforms, at Dongshanzui in Kazuo, Liaoning Province. Constructed of piled rocks and slabs, this monument presumably had a religious function. Among 20 fragments of clay human figures discovered, two small "Venus figurines," naked and pregnant, suggest that this place may have related to some fertility cult. In 1983 archaeologists excavated another, similar structure at Niuheliang, Jianping, Liaoning Province, and discovered the head of a painted statue. The head, ears, nose, and lips, all well proportioned, are shaped out of unbaked clay, while the eyes are inlaid with turquoise to represent the pupils. Judging from its size (22.5 centimeters high) and the associated fragments of body parts, it was originally from a life-size image of a goddess. The technique for sculpting these images was quite sophisticated. In the core of the statue was a wooden skeleton, enclosed by coarse clay mixed with grass. On top of this coarse clay was another layer of fine clay, out of which the image was created. The

Hongshan sculptures represent the finest and highest level of artistic creation in Neolithic China.

Another achievement of the Hongshan culture is jade sculpture. The most impressive jades of the Hongshan culture are coiled dragons in small or large C shapes, plaques with abstract animal designs, and ornaments in the shapes of owls, fish, turtles, cicadas, and birds. These jade works were buried exclusively in large tombs, suggesting that they were symbols of social status. The Lower Xiajiadian culture (*ca.* 2000–1500 BCE), which succeeded the Hongshan culture in the same region, was characterized by its elaborately painted, brightly colored ceramics. Unlike painted pottery in other traditions, the Lower Xiajiadian vessels were decorated after firing.

One characteristic of sculptural art in the region south of the Yangzi River is the large number of small-scale clay human and animal figures. Discoveries from Qujialing culture (*ca.* 3000–2500 BCE) sites include small clay sculptures of domesticated animals such as chickens, sheep, and dogs, wild animals such as birds, fish, and turtles, and human heads. Archaeologists have also found spectacular jade disks, pendants, tubes, cicadas, and ceramic sculpture of various animals from the Shijiahe culture (*ca.* 2500–1900 BCE). Archaeologists have not yet fully investigated south and southeast China. A unique type of cord-marked pottery was widely distributed in south China. The Shixia culture (*ca.* 3000–2000 BCE) sites have produced examples of stone and jade sculpture, and Beinan culture (*ca.* 3300–300 BCE) sites, located in eastern Taiwan, have yielded a strange jade ornament—two parallel jade anthropomorphic fugues connected by a fishlike creature on the top of the heads.

Bronze Age: Shang (*ca.* 1600–*ca.* 1050 BCE) and Zhou (*ca.* 1050–221 BCE) Dynasties

The Shang and Zhou dynasties encompass the Bronze Age in China. Ancient Chinese used bronzes mainly in casting ritual vessels for offering wine and food to the spirits of the ancestors. Although the plastic qualities and the ways in which the materials were worked differed, craftsmen treated bronze, pottery, jade, and stone in almost the same manner artistically, applying similar designs, decoration, and styles to all these media. Since the excavation of the last Shang capital at Anyang, Henan Province, in 1928, archaeological materials have drastically deepened modern understanding of artistic output during the Shang and Zhou dynasties.

Casting techniques, which dominated Chinese bronze technology, helped determine the evolution of style and motif in Shang and Zhou bronze vessels and sculptures. In Erlitou and Erligang (two early phases of Shang culture), craftsmen used the section-mold technique to cast bronzes. A clay model was first made and then packed with fine clay. Then the outer layer of clay was removed in sections to produce a negative. The model was then transformed into a core by paring down a thick layer to make the hollow space for pouring the bronze. Finally, the mold sections were fitted back together around the core, and molten bronze was poured into through the inlet. Sometimes small chips of metal supported the mold assembly, especially when several cores were used in casting objects of complicated form. During this process, the artisan carved the decoration directly on the mold, thus producing the simple thread relief of Style I in Loehr's five-style classification of Anyang bronzes.

For bronzes in Loehr's Styles II and III, the artisan first carved the decoration on the model and then transferred the decoration to the mold in the process of forming the mold sections. This technique enabled the creation of a variety of complex forms of decoration. The motifs in Style II were mirror images of Style I. Technically, no difference exists between Styles I and II. Style III was an elaboration of Style II, in which the decor spread to cover more of the vessel surface. Style IV saw the emergence of the distinction between images and background patterns. Finally, Style V is characterized by the appearance of images in high relief, which enabled the Shang casters to create elaborate animal and human figures and incorporate them into a vessel's design. Craftsmen created some of the complicated designs of the Shang and Western Zhou bronzes using casting-on and precast techniques.

During the Eastern Zhou period, craftsmen adopted new decorative techniques, such as pattern etching, metal inlay, and pattern blocks. The lost-wax casting method also developed during this time. Many bronze weapons from the southern states of Chu and Yue received special surface treatments through which geometric patterns were etched using chemicals. In the metal-inlay technique, craftsmen first precast or cut the decoration from sheet metal, then embedded it in the mold, thus incorporating the inlays onto the finished vessels. This method developed further in the Warring States period (475–221): bronze vessels were cast with depressions to hold the inlay materials, after which the inlay was added; the most common inlay materials included silver, copper, glass, rock crystal, malachite, turquoise, and jade. The bronzes of the so-called Jincun style, named after an Eastern Zhou royal cemetery site near Loyang, Henan Province, were cast using this technique.

The most spectacular technological achievement of the Eastern Zhou period was the pattern-block technique. Through analyzing the bronzes unearthed at Liyu and Hunyuan and clay molds and models unearthed at a foundry site at Houman, both in Shanxi Province, scholars discovered that decorative models were reused in the process of making the mold. A model of a unit of the decoration was first carved in relief on a block, and then the block was used to produce multiple, identical clay negatives to be embedded in the mold. Pattern blocks made possible the mass production of decoration.

The first lost-wax cast bronzes were two 5th-century BCE ritual vessels, a set of *zun* (a wine vessel) and *pan* (a water vessel), discovered in the tomb of the Marquis Yi of the state of Zeng at Leigudun in Suizhou, Hubei. The complicated ornament of interlaced dragons was first made in a wax model and then cast in bronze, attached to the main vessel with solder. Chinese archaeologists found another spectacular example of lost-wax casting in the Chu tombs at Xiasi, Xichuan, Henan. The same technique was used for 6th-century BCE vessels. Later artisans also used the lost-wax technique in casting group sculpture in the Dian culture in southwest China during the pre-Han and early Han period (206 BCE–220 CE).

Animals were prominent subjects in Shang sculpture. Many bronzes include decorations of real or imagined animal motifs; in addition, many ritual vessels were cast in the shape of an animal. Artisans also created animal sculpture in other media, such as white marble, jade, stone, bone, and clay. From the royal consort Fu Hao's tomb at Anyang, over 750 pieces of jade sculpture, 60 pieces of stone sculpture, and 560 pieces of bone carvings were unearthed. Among the real animals depicted were the tiger, bear, elephant, horse, ox, water buffalo, sheep, monkey, hare, crane, owl, eagle, pigeon, swallow, goose, fish, frog, mantis, cicada, and turtle; imagined creatures include the monster mask, dragon, phoenix, and fantastic birds of different forms. Scholars have debated whether the animal motifs in Shang art have meaning or are purely decorative. Although most consider bronze decoration to have symbolic meanings, no consensus has been reached.

The human figure rarely occurred in Shang and early Western Zhou art. When it did, it usually occupied a minor and subsidiary position incorporated into animal forms. For example, on a bronze wine vessel (late Shang dynasty; Musée Cernuschi, Paris), a voracious tigerlike animal embraces a human figure. A small number of pottery figurines of prisoners of war have also been unearthed at Anyang, whereas large bronze anthropomorphic statues have been discovered in peripheral regions such as Sanxingdui, Guanghan, Sichuan. Two "sacrificial" pits were filled with ivory tusks, eccentric bronze vessels, life-size bronze heads, a standing human figure, bronze human masks, gold leaf masks, and other unusual precious objects. The most impressive is a large bronze mask with a hooked-cloud ornament, two protruding cylindrical eyes, and two large ears. The Sanxingdui bronze culture, contemporary with the late Shang period, was probably extraneous to the Shang-Zhou sequence of cultural development, and the meaning of these bronze human figures is still an enigma.

A shifting in the representation of the human figure from peripheral, subordinate decoration to independent decorative motif began in the late Western Zhou, a period of transition not only in bronze decoration but also in the social and cultural milieus. The sculpture of the early Spring and Autumn period (770–475 BCE) continued the general trends developed in the late Western Zhou period. According to one theory, however, in the late Spring and Autumn and early Warring States (475–221 BCE) periods, human figurines (*yong*) emerged with the appearance in tombs of clay and wooden substitutes for real human sacrifice. These figures were skillfully carved and painted with bright colors or dressed with real clothes and wigs.

During the Warring States period, depictions of both animal and human figures in sculpture advanced. New techniques and new materials were introduced, and ritual vessels made of lacquer and clay began to replace those made of bronze. The creation of *mingqi* (spirit artifacts), substitutions for real objects meant to demarcate the distinction between this world and the other world, came into practice during this period. Inlaid bronze sculptures excavated from tombs of the Zhongshan kingdom (late 4th century BCE) at Sanji, Pingshan, Hebei, reveal the influence of northern nomadic art. The motifs of winged beasts and a tiger capturing a hapless deer are two such examples. The human figure holding snakes in a lamp from the same tomb is another excellent specimen of Warring States human sculpture; it is well proportioned, skillfully modeled, and elegantly dressed. His expressive face, cast in silver, and the widely opened eyes with black jewel pupils convey a sense of humor, which is rare in the ritual art of the earlier periods.

Lacquer craft also flourished in the southern state of Chu during this period. The tomb of the Marquis Yi of Zeng, for example, contained a duck-shaped painted lacquer box, a ritual lacquer vessel, and lacquer deer. These lacquerwares were all painted with black or red geometric patterns. Another magnificent lacquer sculpture is a screen found in a Chu tomb at Wangshan, Jiangling, Hubei Province. It is a rectangular frame with two sets of animal sculptures in the round, including deer, frogs, birds, and intertwined snakes, arranged symmetrically. Many southern tombs contained tomb guardian figures, such as the monstrous creature with real deer horns, bulging eyes, and long tongue de-

vouring a snake found at Changtaiguan in Xinyang, Henan Province.

Qin Dynasty (221–207 BCE)

The state of Qin defeated its six rival states, unified China, and founded the first empire in Chinese history in 221 BCE. The first emperor used art and architecture to display his wealth and power. According to historical records, he issued orders to collect all the weapons from the other six states and have them melted down to make 12 colossal bronze statues of giants. After relocating the rich and the nobles of the other six states to the capital Xianyang (near present-day Xi'an in Shaanxi Province), he copied the architectural styles of the conquered states and built splendid palaces in the capital. The varieties of building materials such as eave tiles, carved bricks, and painted walls scattered in the ruins testify to the glory of the once-magnificent imperial palaces. The exquisite eave tiles decorated in relief with real and mythical animal motifs are splendid examples of Qin architectural sculpture. The first emperor also ordered his own mausoleum to be constructed in the Lishan Mountain at Lintong in Shaanxi Province, the interior of which was modeled as a microcosm of the universe: above were depicted celestial constellations and below the terrestrial topography, with rivers and oceans made of mercury. Robbed soon after the fall of the Qin dynasty, this mausoleum has not yet been excavated, though early records detail its interior.

The sculpture of the Qin dynasty reached an unprecedented scale in artistic creation, both in quantity and quality, because political unification provided the Qin with enormous economic resources, manpower, and artistic inspiration. Its extraordinary artistic realism was revealed when, in the midst of the Cultural Revolution in 1974, an underground terracotta army was accidentally unearthed in a pit located to the east of the first emperor's mausoleum. Four large pits have been excavated since then. The largest is pit 1, which contains a military formation of approximately 6,000 life-size terracotta soldiers of various types, several chariots, and life-size horses. Pit 2 includes a smaller, complementary force of 1,400 terracotta figures of cavalrymen, infantry, and horses, and 90 wooden chariots. Pit 3 contains 68 soldiers, one chariot, and four horses, likely representing an elite command unit. The last pit is empty, probably left unfinished. All pits were looted to varying extents and the wooden structures burned, presumably by the rebel army led by Xiang Yu (232–202 BCE) at the end of the Qin dynasty.

In addition to the array of terracotta figures, two well-preserved bronze chariots were discovered in a pit to the west of the first emperor's mausoleum. A standing charioteer shaded by an umbrella drove the first chariot, while the second chariot contained a kneeling figure in front of a compartment with ventilated shutter windows and a 36-ribbed umbrella roof. The second chariot, 3.28 meters long, 1.04 meters high, and weighing 1,200 kilograms, has been successfully restored. The bronze chariots were originally elaborately painted with bright colors on a white ground. The fingers and nails of the charioteer were naturalistically depicted.

Although isolated examples of stone sculpture occurred in the Shang and Zhou dynasties, the systematic use of stone sculpture in a funerary context probably came to China from Central Asia through the state of Qin, which was originally located on the northwest border of China proper and which had close contact with the northern steppe tribes. The practice of using large stone slabs to construct monumental Kurgan tombs and placing anthropomorphic stone sculptures either inside or in front of the tomb flourished in the northern and northwest steppes, which predated the Chinese practice of stone sculpture by several centuries. Two Spring– and Autumn–period stone figures 22 centimeters in height were discovered in the funerary park of the Qin state in Xicun, Fengxiang, Shaanxi Province. Historical records also report that a few stone animals were carved for the mausoleum of the first emperor. After the Qin unification of China, the use of funerary stone sculpture and stone inscriptions spread to a wider area.

Han Dynasty (206 BCE–220 CE)

The lavish military, cultural, and artistic projects of the first emperor of Qin and his successor exhausted the country's revenues. After only 17 years, rebel armies overturned the Qin dynasty. Another ruling house reunified China in 206 BCE and established the capital in Chang'an (present-day Xi'an in Shaanxi Province), instituting the Western Han dynasty (206 BCE–8 CE). After the interregnum period of the Xin dynasty (8–23 CE), the Han capital moved to the city of Luoyang (present-day Luoyang in Henan Province), which lies to the east of Chang'an; this period was subsequently called the Eastern Han dynasty (25–220 CE). The sculpture that developed during this period can be classified into four groups based on medium: terracotta sculpture, wooden sculpture, stone sculpture, and jade and bronze sculpture.

As during the Qin period, terracotta figures were buried in imperial mausoleums and the tombs of high-ranking officials, but their size and number were much reduced. For example, naked male and female clay figurines 60 centimeters in height were excavated near the mausoleum of Emperor Jing Di's mausoleum at Zhangjiawan, Xianyang, Shaanxi Province. The 2,500 figures in the army in an early Western Han tomb at Yangjiawan, Xianyang, Shaanxi Province, measure 50 centimeters in height. Another example is the terracotta army excavated from the tomb of a local prince at Shizishan, Xuzhou, Jiangsu Province. Most of the figures in Han tombs are soldiers, but servants, farmers, artisans, and entertainers are also represented. During the Eastern Han dynasty, the common subjects changed to genre scenes of everyday life, such as banquets, gambling, performances, or hunting and clay models such as multistory watchtowers, castles, water wells, granaries, rice fields, carts, ships, and figures of domestic animals. Figures of musicians and dancers were often the most dynamically depicted, some in flowing movement and others with humorous expressions. A well-known example is the storyteller excavated at Tianjiongshan, Chengdu, in Sichuan Province (National Museum of Chinese History, Beijing).

Wood had been the major medium for sculpture in the south since the Warring States period. Wooden sculpture experienced a trend of development during the Western Han similar to that of clay figures. Wooden human figures, animals, carts, and house models from the late Western Han and the Eastern Han periods in northwest China were discovered in tombs at Wuwei in Gansu Province. Among them are two unique examples worthy of special mention due to their simple form yet vivid depiction. A small wooden monkey (11.5 centimeters high), kneeling with one upper limb supporting the body and the other placed at the chin, strikes a sad, meditative pose. A raging unicorn is ready to attack any offender with its horizontal, sharp horn and vertical tail, which seems to have been a popular motif in the Wuwei region; another sculptured unicorn in bronze strikes the same pose.

The earliest extant large-scale stone sculpture dates from the Han dynasty. Monumental stone carvings of animals and officials were often placed along the so-called spirit road (shendao) that led to the burial mound, a tradition that persisted continuously into the 19th century. The best-known and likely earliest of such figures is a group of 16 animal sculptures in front of the 2nd-century BCE tumulus of General Huo Qubing in Xingping, Shaanxi Province. According to historical records, the mound was built to resemble the Qilian Mountain (also known as Tianshan; literally "Heavenly Mountain") on the northwest border where General Huo won many battles against the Xiongnu nomads. Some of the sculptures depict imaginary or mythical animals, and others portray real animals. The best known is a horse standing over a trampled barbarian. The figures of both the horse and the man are static and crudely carved, yet the total effect is powerful and impressive.

Stone became the preferred material for sculpture during the Eastern Han period. Funerary sculptures, stelae, and memorial gates were carved from stone, as were shrines, tomb chambers, and coffins. Relief carving on the walls of shrines and memorial gateways also flourished. The spirit road developed in the centuries that followed. A popular motif in stone sculpture of this period was the winged beast, sometimes called chimera, which was related to the fantastic bronze winged, horned, and bearded animals of the Warring States period. A stone sculpture of a winged beast from Sunqitun, Luoyang, Henan Province, exemplifies this development. This bearded and winged beast strides forward with the two right legs advanced and the two left legs planted firmly on the ground. Its long beard hangs from the chin to the chest, as the powerful animal raises its head in an upright position and roars. The tradition of using winged beasts in stone as tomb guardians reached its final development at the imperial tombs of the southern dynasties in the region of Nanjing and Danyang in Jiangsu Province.

Jade and bronze sculpture still flourished, especially in the imperial house and local kingdoms, although it lost its dominant position in the major arts of the Han dynasty. A superb example of Han imperial jade work is a 7-centimeter-high winged figure on horseback, carved in pure white jade, unearthed at the site of a Han mausoleum near Xianyang in Shaanxi. Archaeologists have also discovered exquisite jade carvings of dancing girls, twined dragons, and geometric decorations from the tombs of the king of Nanyue in Guangzhou, Liu Sheng, the prince of Zhongshan and his consort Dou Wan, at Mancheng in Hepei, and the princely tombs at Dabaotai near Beijing. The Han also used jade for preserving the corpse. Because of the popular belief that preserving the vital energy (*qi*) inside the human body enabled one to obtain immortality, many members of the Han royal family were buried clothed in jade suits, holding jade objects in the hand and mouth, and with the nine apertures on the head and body covered with jade plugs to keep the *qi* in their bodies. The suits consisted of over 2,000 small jade plaques sewn together using gold, silver, and copper threads according to the rank of the deceased. To date, over 40 complete or fragmented jade suits have been discovered in Han royal tombs.

In the early Western Han dynasty, the use of bronze in funerary art was greatly reduced. The two Mawangdui tombs yielded just a few bronze weapons and mirrors. Only a few royal tombs contained buried bronze objects. The tombs of Liu Sheng and Dou Wan contained several bronze vessels and utensils, but most were small, simple, and undecorated utilitarian objects such as a gilt-bronze lamp held aloft by a kneeling figure, two censers in the shape of a magic mountain, and two lamps in the shapes of a kneeling ram and a fantastic bird. Most representative of the high artistic achievements of Han bronze sculpture are the bronze horses discovered at Wuwei County in Gansu Province, the most famous of which is a flying horse with one foot poised on a swallow.

Three Kingdoms (220–280 CE), the Jin Dynasties (265–420 CE), and the Northern and Southern Dynasties (420–581 CE)

After the fall of the Eastern Han, China divided into the three kingdoms of Wu, Wei, and Shu. In 280 a general of the Wei kingdom subsequently unified China, usurped the throne, and established the Jin dynasty. In 311 the Xiongnu sacked the Jin capital; the Jin court fled to the south. The waves of invasions of non-Han tribes from the north pushed the Chinese southward and triggered one of the most spectacular mass immigrations in Chinese history. The southern Chinese dynasties eventually established their political center in the Yangzi delta region around present-day Nanjing in Jiangsu Province, while in northern China several non-Chinese dynasties fought each other for territory until the ruler of the Sui dynasty reunified China in 581. This turbulent period nonetheless saw the maturation of the production of funerary stone sculpture and the introduction and flourishing of Buddhist sculpture in China.

Although Buddhism was influential in the southern dynasties, their imperial burials remained unchanged and still followed the age-old tradition of constructing spirit roads. In the vicinity of Nanjing, 31 such sites have been identified. The most fabulous example of spirit-road sculpture is the stone winged beast placed along the processional way to the tomb of the Emperor Jing Di of the Qi dynasty (479–502) in Danyang County in Jiangsu. The graceful, gigantic animal has a colossal lifted head with large eyes and wide-open mouth, a strong and flexible body in a horizontal S shape, and four powerful limbs.

Other funerary sculptures of this period included gray stoneware of male and female servants, armed soldiers, cavalries, carts, tomb guardians, domestic animals, and everyday utensils such as lamps, vases, urns, and pots. In the southern Jiangsu and northern Zhejiang regions, a unique type of porcelain urn, sometimes called the "soul urn," has been found in burials. On the top of the lid are depicted multistory pavilions, the fronts of which are often crowded with dancers, musicians, acrobats, fantastic beasts, birds, tortoises, rams, dogs, monkeys, and so on. The custom of burying this type of urn lasted less than a century in this region, and scholars still debate their function.

Winged feline, tomb of Qi Jingdi (494 CE), stone, Danyang, Jiangsu
Courtesy Ann Paludan

Buddhist sculpture became the major sculptural form during this period. The traditional account of the introduction of Buddhism from India to China, which probably occurred at the end of the Eastern Han dynasty in the 1st century CE, is that it occurred via a land route stretching from Central Asia through Xinjiang in northwest China and finally reaching the Chinese heartland. Both textual and archaeological materials attest to the validity of this theory, which is also supported by the stylistic evolution of Buddhist sculpture from the Gandharan style to more sinicized styles. Recent scholarship, however, suggests that a sea route possibly connected India and southern China. Indeed, the earliest Buddhist images discovered in southern China predate those found in northwest China.

When Buddhist art first arrived in China, it apparently fused with indigenous religious practices. Engravings on boulders depicting the image and stories of the Buddha have been discovered at Kongwangshan, Lianyungang, Jiangsu Province. Not only are figures from Chinese mythology included in the engravings, but the style also resembles Eastern Han tomb paintings and relief carvings. The Buddha images also appeared among the wall reliefs in cave tombs, on the bases of clay and bronze money trees (symbols of good fortune), and among the decorations on the soul urn. All the sites at which these objects were discovered are located in southern China.

The earliest purely Buddhist images did not appear until the northern and southern dynasties. Buddhist sculptures were created for worship and for transferring merit to one's ancestors, parents, living relatives, kings, and people from all walks of life. Buddhist sculptural forms were related to the availability of local materials. In northern China, various kinds of stone suitable for sculpture are found in abundance; thus, sculptors created many cave temples and gigantic stone sculptures. In southern China, however, with a few exceptions such as the cave temples at Qixiashan near Nanjing and at Xinchang in Zhejiang Province, most of the extant examples are small-scale bronze, wood, or clay images made for worship in temples, palaces, and family shrines.

Most of the Buddhist cave temples were located in the territories of the northern dynasties, where Buddhism was adopted as the state religion. Under imperial patronage, Buddhist art prospered. The most important cave temples include the Yungang Caves and the Tianlongshan Caves in Shanxi, the Longmen Caves and the Gongxian Caves in Henan, the Mogao Caves at Dunhuang, the Maijishan Caves and the Binglingsi Caves in Gansu, and the Xiangtangshan Caves in Hebei. The Yungang Caves, constructed during the northern Wei dynasty (384–534) near the royal capital in present-day Datong, contain the most impressive stone Buddhist sculpture of the period: the seated Buddha of Cave 20, one of the five major caves constructed under the supervision of monk Tanyao in the early 460s. Originally protected by a multistory wooden facade, this colossal Buddha (13.7 meters high) in meditation and the standing Buddha that flanks it on the left were carved out of living sandstone. The well-proportioned bodies of both Buddhas are clothed with an Indian monk's robe. The facial features have a stiff and angular quality. These stylistic traits demonstrate a Chinese interpretation of the Gandharan style, itself a fusion of Indian, Hellenistic, and Central Asian elements.

After the northern Wei moved its capital to Luoyang in Henan Province in 494, the construction of cave temples at Yungang gradually diminished, and attention transferred to the Longmen Caves located near the new capital. Following Yungang, members of the northern Wei royal family sponsored most of the earliest cave temples. The famous stone relief titled *Empress and Court* (Nelson-Atkins Gallery of Art, Kansas City, Missouri) was found in the Binyang cave. Later sculptures in the Longmen caves tend to have more slender bodies and delicate limbs, and the Buddha figures often wear Chinese robes with multiple layers of draping and outwardly sweeping folds.

Where stone was not available as a material for sculpture, sculptors often made Buddhist images in cave temples out of clay. The most famous are the Mogao caves at Dunhuang, where the earliest construction began about 366. The earliest surviving Buddhist images, dating from the northern Liang dynasty (396–439), are located in cave 275. The central figure on the west wall is a sculpture of the Buddha (3.34 meters high) in meditation. Made in clay over wood and straw and then painted, this image bears stylistic similarities to the colossal Buddha in Cave 20 at Yungang. The images of two seated Buddha figures on the west wall in Cave 259 represent the highest achievements in painted clay sculpture of the northern Wei period. In later sculpture of the northern and western Wei (535–557) periods, the Chinese characteristics are even more pronounced.

Many clay Buddhist sculptures in temples have been destroyed over the centuries. In 1979 Chinese archaeologists excavated the once-glorious Yongning Temple of the northern Wei dynasty near Luoyang, which yielded hundreds of clay fragments of Buddhist images. Buddhist sculpture in other media followed the same stylistic development as stone or clay sculpture located in cave temples. The earliest dated gilt-bronze sculpture is a seated Buddha in meditation (338; Asian Art Museum, San Francisco). The Buddha, in a strictly frontal pose, wears a stylized Buddhist monk robe with the folds falling in a U shape. Similar examples include a bronze Buddha in the Nelson-Atkins Museum of Art and a gilt-bronze Buddha discovered in Mancheng, Hebei. All display strong Gandhara influences in the facial features and style of robes. A 522 Buddhist triad (Fujii Yûrinkan, Kyoto, Japan) and a 524 Buddhist triad (Metropolitan Museum of Art, New York) elegantly depict the characteristic Chinese-style garment. Both probably originate from the Dingzhou region in Hebei Province.

Few Buddhist sculptures from the southern dynasties have survived. According to historical records, however, tens of thousands of Buddhist temples were built in the south. In fact, the earliest Chinese sculptors recorded in history came from the eastern Jin period in the 4th century: Dai Kui and his son Dai Yong, who were renowned for their technical innovations in sculpture. Archaeological discoveries at the site of the Wanfo Temple in Chengdu, Sichuan Province, have supplied further valuable information about Buddhist sculptural art in the southern dynasties.

GUOLONG LAI

Further Reading

Bagley, Robert W., *Shang Ritual Bronzes in the Arthur M. Sackler Collections*, Cambridge, Massachusetts: Harvard University Press, 1987

Chang, Kwang-chih, *The Archaeology of Ancient China*, New Haven, Connecticut: Yale University Press, 1963; 4th edition, 1986

Kuwayama, George (editor), *Ancient Mortuary Traditions of China: Papers on Chinese Ceramic Funerary Sculptures*, Los Angeles: Los Angeles County Museum of Art, 1991

Paludan, Ann, *The Chinese Spirit Road*, New Haven, Connecticut: Yale University Press, 1991

Rawson, Jessica, *Western Zhou Ritual Bronzes from the Arthur M. Sackler Collections*, 2 vols., Cambridge: Harvard University Press, 1990

Rawson, Jessica, *Chinese Jade from the Neolithic to the Qing*, London: British Museum, 1995

Rawson, Jessica (editor), *Mysteries of Ancient China: New Discoveries from the Early Dynasties*, London: British Museum Press; and New York: Braziller, 1996

Rhie, Marylin M., *Early Buddhist Art of China and Central Asia*, Leiden and Boston: Brill, 1999

So, Jenny F., *Eastern Zhou Ritual Bronzes from the Arthur M. Sackler Collections*, Washington, D.C.: Arthur M. Sackler Foundation, 1995

Yang, Xiaoneng (editor), *The Golden Age of Chinese Archaeology: Celebrated Discoveries from the People's Republic of China*, New Haven, Connecticut: Yale University Press, 1999

CHINA: SUI AND TANG DYNASTIES

The period of the Sui (581–618) and Tang (618–906) dynasties saw the reunification of China and the reestablishment of centralized political control over the north and south after three and a half centuries of disunion. Broad-based social, political, and cultural change characterized the previous period—population movements, foreign incursion, and regional autonomy. Buddhism had become firmly established and was a major source of inspiration in the production of art. Measures to reunify China extended from political administration and the construction of major transportation routes to the cultural and religious spheres. The use of Buddhist art as an expression of the authority of rulers contributed to the establishment of various kinds of images as authoritative and representative of various periods and regimes.

As part of the Sui consolidation of power, the rulers undertook grand construction projects. After declaring himself ruler of the new dynasty, the first emperor, Yang Jian, Emperor Wen, began to build a new capital at Chang'an on an enormous site southeast of the old capital. He and his empress, both devout Buddhists, established numerous Buddhist temples and monasteries and commissioned artists to create sculpted images and paintings as part of the capital's construction. He lifted the restrictions on Buddhism and Daoism initiated in 574 by Emperor Wu of the Northern Zhou dynasty (557–81) that had destroyed many Buddhist establishments and had forced monks to return to lay life. Under Emperor Wen's reign and that of his successor Emperor Yang, thousands of monasteries were rebuilt or established, hundreds of thousands of monks and nuns ordained, and countless images produced across the new empire.

The making of new images in the Sui drew heavily on traditions of the northern and southern dynasties that had preceded it. Features from northern Qi (550–77) and northern Zhou (557–81) sculpture are particularly apparent. The carving of freestanding figures in stone with columnar forms, on the surface of which details were subtly defined and flattened close to the surface of the body, emerged in the northeastern region controlled by the northern Qi during the second half of the 6th century. This type continued in the new dynasty in stiffly upright and symmetrical images, sometimes of colossal size. Such a colossal marble image (5.78 meters high), a standing Buddha, identified in its dedicatory inscription as Amitabha, is in the British Museum, London. The inscription records that a group of 80 donors commissioned the image in 585 for the Chongguang Temple in Hancui village, along with statues of two attendant bodhisattvas. An over-life-size standing bodhisattva in the Tokyo National Museum from the same temple and made in the same year is likely one of the original attendant bodhisattvas.

To the west, in the area of the capital Chang'an, which had been under northern Zhou control, the new Sui sculptures continued to show regional characteristics of bolder modeling of the figure and ornamental details. A large and impressive bodhisattva (Boston Museum of Fine Arts, Massachusetts) is of this type, finely carved with fluid lines in the gracefully draping garments, rounded surfaces of the body, and detailed rendering of jewelry. The deity sways forward and slightly to one side with the weight on one foot.

These impressive images appear today mostly in isolation and out of context in museums. However, the survival of smaller bronze altar groups and of stone images and painted murals in caves offers a clue to the original placement and arrangements of the larger freestanding images. A bronze altar group with a central Amitabha seated under a flowering tree hung with jeweled pendants on a lotus throne surrounded by attendants and guardians (Boston Museum of Fine Arts, Massachusetts) shows the development of paradise imagery during this period. In the Sui period the tradition of carving of Buddhist images in stone grottoes and on stelae also continued. At some of the important cave sites such as Dunhuang and Tianlongshan, new caves and configurations of images augmented an already existing complex. New groups of caves appeared at other sites, such as Tuoshan and Yunmenshan in Shandong Province. The Simenta, a constructed stupa at the former Shentong monastery in Licheng county, Shandong province, has a Buddha on each of four sides of a central square pillar, as seen in caves of this period as well.

With the consolidation of Tang power under Emperor Taizong, the empire began to look outward. While the central government extended its power over all parts of the empire and expanded its territory, the empire's stability and growing prosperity also attracted a larger volume of foreign contact through official embassies, merchants, and religious figures. Such contact stimulated interest in foreign products, assimilation of new ideas, and new modes of sculptural representation.

In many areas of artistic endeavor, including sculpture, the Tang dynasty is considered a "golden age" in Chinese history. Buddhism continued to be the chief inspiration for major sculptural projects, evidence of which is found throughout the empire. Buddhism in the Tang did not enjoy the degree of official promotion it did in the Sui, as official policy vacillated from one reign to the next. Religious Daoism enjoyed official support during the Tang, and its followers produced images for veneration, adopting many of the same conventions seen in representations of Buddhist deities. In the early part of the Tang period, the ruling house favored Daoism over Buddhism and sought to reduce the size and influence of the Buddhist establishment. In order to conciliate the masses of devout Buddhists, however, the court also adopted a policy of constructing monasteries at key sites and sponsoring Buddhist services for the welfare of the people and of the state. The Binyang South Cave at Longmen, begun in the northern Wei, was completed in 641 and dedicated by the prince of Wei, Li Tai, to the memory of his deceased mother, the Wende empress. The production of Buddhist sculpture also continued on the local level without official sponsorship. These and other dated early Tang images display a variety of appearances distinct from Sui Buddhist sculpture—such as a stur-

Vairocana Buddha (675), Tang dynasty, Fengxian Cave, Longmen, near Luoyang
Courtesy Ann Paludan

dier, more broad-shouldered physique—but not a consistent, well-defined style.

The return of the monk Xuanzang in 645 with scriptures and images after more than 15 years of study at Buddhist monasteries in India stimulated renewed interest in support of Buddhism at the official level. Emperor Gaozong wished to learn of the foreign lands the monk visited and treated him with deference. He invited Xuanzang to live at the Da Cien monastery and made it the center of a large-scale project to translate Buddhist texts under the monk's direction. After Xuanzang's death in 664, Daoism received increased imperial support and remained the state religion until the end of Gaozong's reign. However, Xuanzang's influence was indelible in the introduction of new teachings and, quite likely, new imagery from India. Projects supported by Gaozong's empress, the Lady Wu Zhao or Wu Zetian, demonstrate such new tendencies. A Buddhist devotee who became the power behind the throne with the emperor's deteriorating health in the last decades of his reign, Wu Zetian sponsored the creation of the colossal Vairocana image of the Fengxiansi at Longmen Cave site in 676 near Luoyang, which she established as the eastern capital. After Emperor Gaozong's death, she declared herself emperor of her own dynasty, the Zhou, with herself as emperor. She used Buddhism to further her formidable political ambitions and actively promoted Buddhist activity—translation projects, image making, and the construction of a network of Buddhist temples across the empire. She commissioned a large group of images for the Qibaotai (Seven Treasures Platform) at the Guangzhai Temple in the capital (*ca.* 700) toward the end of her reign that shows a more Indian-inspired, sensual treatment of the body in the definition of swelling forms of the torso and the more supple and dynamic poses of the bodhisattvas.

From the late 7th through the 8th century, Buddhist sculpture is in general characterized by greater sensitivity to the modeling of the body and patterns of clothing and scarves draped over it. This is apparent at various cave sites across the empire, including Longmen, Tianlongshan, and Dunhuang, as in the Buddha from Tianlongshan (Sackler Museum, Harvard University, Cambridge, Massachusetts). The idealized physical beauty and sense of worldly well being of these images came to represent the attainment of spiritual perfection, salvation, and the rewards of rebirth in paradise. New types of religious concepts and their visualization also became apparent in the images, such as multiarmed and multiheaded bodhisattvas and Buddhas wearing crowns and jewels.

The 8th century saw the emergence of esoteric Buddhism in China. Emperor Xuanzong, who in the first part of his reign reinstated Daoism as the official religion and promoted its activities while curtailing the wealth and influence of the Buddhist establishment, took an interest in esoteric Buddhism during the latter part of his reign. Tantric masters from India, Subhakarasimha and Vajrabodhi, and Chinese experts Yixing and Bukong became known at the capital for their ritual incantations and magic. The esoteric monks conducted consecration ceremonies and other rituals, as well as recitations of sutras for the protection of the state and victory in battle. They were instrumental as well in the introduction and translation of esoteric texts such as the *Dari jing*, or *Mahavairocana sutra*. The Mahavairocana Buddha was the central and supreme Buddha of this belief system and the focus of royal cults. Bukong profoundly influenced Emperor Daizong (*r.* 762–79), providing spiritual intercession for the imperial family and presiding over state rituals at specially constructed altars in imperially sponsored temples.

Painting and sculpture are known to have played an important role in these Tantric rituals; however, few examples survive. A group of ten magnificently carved marble sculptures—including Buddhas, bodhisattvas, and fierce guardians of the faith—unearthed from a burial pit at the site of the Tang temple Da Anguo Si in 1959 and now in the Forest of Steles Museum, Xi'an, provides a rare view of the art of Tantric Buddhism at the Tang capital. The group displays a highly developed skill in representing the human figure fully in the round without the abrupt transitions from one part to the next found in sculpture of the earlier Tang period. In addition, the figures contain richly realized three-dimensional floral elements and animal forms. The Anguo temple appears to have enjoyed particular favor during Daizong's reign. The images there may have been made during his reign and were likely arranged as a kind of three-dimensional mandala, playing a role in the performance of esoteric rituals. The Tantric images of fearsome guardians and sublimely beautiful bodhisattvas and female divinities, while suggesting the innate and mysterious power of Buddhist transcendent wisdom, also have a physical presence of unprecedented force, at times violent. These compelling images of esoteric Buddhism encompassed a large pantheon of deities of various aspects—benevolent, wrathful, or transcendent—who were placed in hierarchical arrangements in ritual spaces or represented in cosmic diagrams known as mandala. The imagery of this form of Buddhism was introduced from Indian esoteric Buddhism and Hinduism.

Regional developments and the growth of sectarian Buddhism added to the range of artistic production. Cave temples cut into rock cliffs and mountainsides near urban centers and along transport routes, such as Longmen near Luoyang, Tianlongshan near Taiyuan,

Yaowangshan and Dafosi in the Chang'an region, and Maijishan and Dunhuang in Gansu Province, preserve a sense of the tremendous richness of early Chinese Buddhist art in architectural settings that have been lost. The Mogao Grottoes at Dunhuang, hundreds of cave shrines containing mural paintings in combination with sculpture, are particularly valuable for this purpose. Outside the northern metropolitan areas, sculptural activity in the northwestern and southwestern parts of the empire often show regional characteristics and foreign elements introduced through contact with or domination of other cultural groups, including the Khotanese, Uighur, Tibetan, and Nanzhao. In the vast region of Sichuan Province, sites in Guanyuan, Bazhong, Jiajiang, Leshan, and Anyue preserve rich complexes of images in caves and niches of the Tang and later periods, many of which are only beginning to be studied. The groups of images at cave complexes reflect an intermingling of doctrine and popular beliefs, representing various deities to which people appealed for assistance in this life and Buddhist paradises in which they aspired to be reborn after death. Small personal shrines and large colossal images of the death of the Buddha, or *Mahaparinirvana*, and of the future Buddha Maitreya were placed side by side at these sites of community worship. With the decline of central authority in the second half of the 8th century, powerful local patrons increasingly supported activity at temples and monasteries in all parts of the empire.

Buddhism experienced another period of rapid growth in the latter part of the 8th and early 9th centuries. Although officially the government did not support unbridled expansion and even sought to curb the power of the Buddhism, bureaucratic controls were lacking or ineffective. By the 9th century the tax-exempt Buddhist temples and clergy had become a great economic burden on the declining empire, and critics succeeded in turning official policy against Buddhism by pointing to its abuses and foreign character. A policy of suppression began during the reign of Emperor Wuzong (*r.* 840–46), an ardent Daoist, who ordered the return of hundreds of thousands of monks and nuns to lay life, as well as the confiscation of vast quantities of temple treasures and lands, destroying tens of thousands of temples and monasteries and their contents. This catastrophic proscription was finally reversed after Wuzong's death, but later in the 9th century a widespread rebellion lasting almost a decade caused further irreparable damage to the Buddhist establishment, with the result that Chinese Buddhist art surviving from the Tang and earlier periods is but a tiny fraction of what once existed.

Sculpture made for secular and funerary purposes also flourished in the Sui-Tang period. Large stone images placed along the approaches to the tombs of prominent officials and royalty included officials and animals, the number and variety depending on the rank of the deceased. Images of officials, foreign emissaries, fine steeds, and exotic animals such as the rhinoceros, ostrich, elephant, lion, and fantastic winged beasts lined the roads to imperial tombs. The figures demonstrated the ruler's dominion over the world in his lifetime and served as a center for state ritual after his death. Artists produced the bulk of funerary sculpture to accompany the dead in burial. Archaeologists have excavated some fine examples in stone from tombs of the Sui and Tang periods, probably made by the same artisans that carved Buddhist images. Wooden figures are also known, but for the most part funerary sculpture was the work of potters.

Advancements in ceramic technology in the Sui period included the application of a clear glaze and white slip to a clay body, providing a base for the application of painted ornament. In the Tang dynasty the manufacture of pottery funerary sculpture burgeoned into a distinctive art form. From the early part of the 7th century, with the use of clear glaze and painting on the surface, potters explored increasingly lifelike forms and bolder colors and used techniques of mass production. The boldness of design, size of figures, and sheer volume of production reached a peak in the late 7th and early 8th centuries with the tremendously popular *sancai* or three-color wares. The term refers to the lead glaze with its lively spots and streaks of green, amber yellow, and blue. Artists skillfully sculpted and molded a great variety of vessels and figures—fearsome tomb guardians, household officials and servants, beautiful women, equestrian figures, musicians, and fine horses and camels accompanied by foreign grooms—in response to huge demands by the urban elite around the capitals at Chang'an and Luoyang. The resulting tremendous extravagance in tomb furnishing led to an official ban on the production of three-color glazed wares for burial, so that the later part of the dynasty saw a return to the manufacture of unglazed, painted pottery. These later Tang figures of guardians, musicians, court ladies, and so on continued to be of great vitality and charm, although less exuberantly decorative.

KATHERINE R. TSIANG MINO

Further Reading

Duhuang wenwu yanjiusuo (Dunhuang Research Institute), *Zhongguo Shiku: Dunhuang Mogaoku (The Grotto Art of China: The Mogao Grottoes of Dunhuang)*, 5 vols., Beijing: Wenwu chubanshe/Heibonsha, 1982–87
Howard, Angela Falco, "Tang Buddhist Sculpture of Sichuan: Unknown and Forgotten," *Bulletin of the Museum of Far Eastern Antiquities* 60 (1988)

Karetzky, Patricia, "New Archaeological Evidence of Tang Esoteric Art," *Tang Studies* 12 (1994)

Longmen wenwu baoguansuo and Beijing daxue kaoguxi (Depository of Cultural Relics of Longmen and Department of Archaeology of Peking University), *Zhongguo Shiku: Longmen Shiku (The Grotto Art of China: The Longmen Grottoes)*, Beijing: Wensu chubanche/Heibonsha, 1991

Sirén, Osvald, *Chinese Sculpture from the Fifth to the Fourteenth Century: Over 900 Specimens in Stone, Bronze, Lacquer, and Wood, Principally from Northern China*, 4 vols., London: Benn, and New York: Scribner, 1925; reprint, New York: Hacker Art Books, 1970

Vanderstappen, Harrie, and Marylin Rhie, "The Sculpture of T'ien Lung Shan: Reconstruction and Dating," *Artibus Asiae* 27 (1964–65)

Weinstein, Stanley, *Buddhism under the T'ang*, Cambridge and New York: Cambridge University Press, 1987

Wright, Arthur, *The Sui Dynasty*, New York: Knopf, 1978

Yen, Chuanying, "The Significance of the Tower of Seven Jewels and Empress Wu," *Yishu Xue* 1 (1987)

CHINA: FIVE DYNASTIES, LIAO, SONG, AND JIN

Sculpture in China from the 10th through the 13th centuries is highly diverse, using a wide variety of media and displaying new modes of representation. Many more examples in perishable or fragile materials survive—clay, wood, ceramic, and lacquer—than from earlier periods. The great variety of sculpture can be attributed in part to changes in government and society and the division of the Chinese Empire. Following the decline of central authority in Tang China in the 9th century, eastern Asia as a whole entered a period of tremendous political instability. Large nations collapsed, and independent local regimes inside China and in the border regions vied with one another for control. The Chinese Empire was divided into a number of kingdoms and a succession of ruling houses known in the north as the Five Dynasties and in the south as the Ten Kingdoms. In the border regions the Uighur, Tibetan, and Nanzhao kingdoms went into a period of disintegration at the end of the Tang period, and other leaders of ethnic groups and multiethnic alliances arose. China reunified for a century and a half under the Song dynasty (960–1279) but was then once again divided when the court lost control of the north. During this time non-Chinese peoples, most notably the Khitan, Jurchen, and Tangut, continued to hold the northern and western frontier areas and encroached on Chinese territory to varying degrees. The Jurchen established a dominant position, declared their own dynasty, the Jin (1115–1234), and in 1127 drove the Song court from its seat in Kaifeng south of the Yangzi River to Hangzhou.

One of the regimes established with the downfall of the Tang empire was Wuyue, at first a principality in the late Tang and then the independent kingdom of Wuyue (923–78) in present-day Zhejiang Province on the eastern coast of China. During the half-century of its sovereignty, it was relatively stable. Famous across much of Asia for its porcelaneous, green-glazed celadon ware, the kingdom grew in wealth during the reign of the Qian family rulers, who promoted celadon ware's manufacture for trade and diplomatic tribute. Buddhist devotees, the rulers appear to have sponsored Buddhist image making, including stone sculpture in caves and the casting of bronze images of the bodhisattva Guanyin. A distinctive type of image, carved in the entrance of the Yanxia Cave near the Wuyue capital at Hangzhou, is the standing Guanyin with a shawl draped over its head, partially hiding its high crown. The king of Wuyue, Qian Hongchu, was a particularly devout Buddhist who took as his example the legendary 3rd-century BCE King Ashoka of the Maurya period. In 955 Qian Hongchu made a vow to make 84,000 stupas, as Ashoka had done, to distribute the Buddha's relics all over the world. The Wuyue stupa reliquaries were cast in bronze or iron with scenes from the life or past lives of the Buddha represented in relief on the sides.

In the northeast, the Khitan-ruled Liao dynasty (907–1125) arose at the beginning of the 10th century and by mid century had extended its power from Manchuria and Mongolia down to Kaifeng, south of the Yellow River, before being beaten back by Chinese forces. The Liao established their southern capital at Beijing and throughout the Northern Song period (960–1127) held parts of northern Hebei and Shanxi Provinces. Buddhism was the official religion of the Liao. During this period artists produced many large-scale Buddhist constructions, temples with tall pagodas built of brick or wood, and sculptures made of stone, clay, bronze, and ceramic. Due to the large number of pieces that survive, art of the Liao period has received substantial scholarly attention. Among the impressive architectural structures with surviving sculptures are the Guanyin Hall (984) of the Dule Temple in Jixian, Hebei Province, the Lower Hall of the Huayan Temple in Datong (1038), and the wooden pagoda of the Fogong Temple in Yingxian (1056), the latter two both in Shanxi Province. The wooden pagoda of the Fogong Temple, the tallest and oldest surviving wooden pagoda in China (over 66 meters high), has five main stories with sculpted images of clay. It is iconographically of great interest; although it is known as the Shakyamuni (the historical Buddha) pagoda, groups of images on each level appear to be arranged hierarchically in a kind of vertical mandala, with Mahavairocana Buddha and eight bodhisattvas on the uppermost level.

A tall, freestanding Guanyin carved of stone stands at the site of the former supreme capital of the Liao,

Shangjing, in Inner Mongolia. Interestingly, it appears to be quite similar to one in the Yanxia Cave near Hangzhou. A fine gilt-bronze bodhisattva of this type with a shawl covering the head and crown is in the University of Pennsylvania Museum, Philadelphia. Seated images of Guanyin wearing a shawl over the head also appear in painting of the Song period and have come to be known as the "White-Robed Guanyin." Another form of the bodhisattva Guanyin, which continues the tradition of Tang sculpture, is the 11-headed image made around 984 at the Dule Temple, in Jixian, Hebei, not far from Beijing. A colossal figure made of clay on a wooden armature, it is housed in a three-story structure hollowed out in the middle to accommodate the towering height of the image, almost 16 meters. A third type of Guanyin, seated on a rock in the position of "royal ease," or *maharaja lalitasana*, was a new type of image in the Liao period and became especially common in the Song and Jin periods. A group of eight impressive *sancai* (three-color glazed) ceramic *luohan* (arhats) of the Liao period are known in collections in the West. Believed to have been from a cave in Yixian, Hebei, they are life-size figures seated on rocklike bases, skillfully modeled, heroic in their proportions

Monumental guardian, Yuling, tomb of Song emperor Shenzong (*d.* 1085), stone, Gongxian, Henan
Courtesy Ann Paludan

and expressions, and covered with yellow and green lead glaze.

Buddhist sculpture of the Song period shows parallel developments and the production of images with similar iconography. Cave 1 at the Ten Thousand Buddha Caves at Yan'an, Shaanxi Province, contains Northern Song dedicatory inscriptions recording the carving of 16 *luohan* and a Guanyin seated in the *maharaja lalitasana* pose (1078), as well as a standing 11-headed Guanyin image. Although large-scale Buddhist projects also occurred in the Song period, the more centrally located temples have largely been lost in the wake of wars and the changeover of political power. In 971 a colossal bronze image of a multiarmed Guanyin, 22 meters high, was cast in seven sections from the lotus pedestal to the top of the head at the Longxing Temple in Zhengding, Hebei. The image and its stone base, finely carved with musicians, dancers, and atlantes-like figures, still survive. Song emperor Taizu personally inspected this major project. Guanyin continued to be a principal cult deity in the Song and Jin periods, and numerous images exist, especially of the bodhisattva seated in the pose of royal ease on a rocky throne, one leg raised and the other resting flat or with the lower leg pendant. Made of many materials (stone, bronze, and clay), they are best known in the West from wooden examples that have been removed from their original placement in temples and are now in museum collections. Gesso, paint, or gilding originally covered these wooden images, which are usually life-size or larger. One early and beautifully preserved example of this type is in the Nelson-Atkins Museum, Kansas City. Stone images of this type frequently appear in caves and niches of the Song period in the Yan'an area and in Shaanxi and in Sichuan province, and smaller gilt-bronze versions are known from the Liao and early Song. Their princely demeanor, relaxed pose, and sense of worldly accessibility had great popular appeal, which lasted throughout the Song and Jin dynasties into the succeeding Yuan period (1279–1368).

The depictions of groups of arhats or enlightened monks (*luohan*) also became popular in the Song period. They vary widely in number, usually from 16 or 18 up to 500. Groups of *luohan* images became associated with the bodhisattva Guanyin and with Chan Buddhism in the Song period. Forty clay figures of *luohan*, believed to be from the middle of the 11th century, are seated around the walls of the Thousand Buddha Hall at the Lingyan Temple in Changqing, Shandong. The figures are vivid and portraitlike, with dynamic gestures. Other groups of *luohan* cast in bronze, carved in wood and stone, or modeled of clay and lacquer continued to be made through the Song period. A group of 500 was carved in wood in Guangzhou in the 11th century, of which 360 are preserved at the Nanhua Temple, near Shaoguan, Guangdong Province. These are rendered in a rather rough-hewn summary manner. Nanhua Temple is an important Chan Buddhist center, where the body of the Sixth Patriarch Honing is enshrined. The delicate and realistic representation of the 31 life-size clay figures of female attendants in the Daoist Shengmu Hall (dated 1087), at Jinci, near Taiyuan, Shanxi Province, and sculpted portraits of the deceased found in tombs of the Five Dynasties and Song period also demonstrate interest in portraitlike sculptures.

Cave sculptures in various parts of the Song dynasty, including Fuxian, Yan'an, and Zizhang in Shaanxi Province and Anyue and Dazu in Sichuan Province, provide additional evidence of the vitality and enormous variety of Song sculpture. They are characteristically complex, with many deities in a single cave or niche in a single composition with multiple themes. The carving is frequently highly detailed, with great attention given to costumes and ornament, and less to the modeling of the forms of the body, as compared to Tang sculpture. Large numbers of cave shrines and cliffside images were produced in Sichuan, many of monumental size. The complex iconography of the Sichuan material includes imagery of esoteric Buddhist and Daoist teachings that were popular in the region. Developments in Buddhist art in the western border areas reflect the introduction of new religious concepts and imagery. The Tangut Xi Xia, who promoted Buddhism and became followers of Tibetan esoteric Buddhism in the 12th century, seized the northwestern part of Gansu, which included the Dunhuang Caves, in 1035. The Tangut Xi Xia kingdom (ca. 982–1227), which promoted Buddhism, seized the northwestern part of Gansu, which included the Dunhuang Caves, in 1035. The Yulin Caves in Anxi and the Mogao Caves in Dunhuang, as well as finds from present-day Ningxia and Inner Mongolia, reveal elements of the Tibetan esoteric Buddhism that the Xi Xia adopted in the 12th century. Features of esoteric Buddhism are also clearly apparent in sculpture of the Dali kingdom (937–1253), based in Kunming, Yunnan Province.

Funerary sculpture for burial in tombs continued to be made in the Song and Jin dynasties, although generally not on as grandiose a scale as in the Tang. Those made of ceramic show a great deal of variety in types of wares, and techniques of firing, glazing, and painting reflect advances in technology at local kilns. For example, the Cizhou kilns in the north produced sculptures with underglaze and overglaze painted decoration on a white slip ground, while the Longquan kilns in Zhejiang province made pieces with their characteristics celadon glaze, and kilns in Jiangxi province produced those with quingbai (bluish white)

glaze. Stone figures outside of the imperial tombs of the Northern Song continued traditions from the Tang and earlier periods. With the court's move to the south, which was considered a temporary situation, imperial burials were greatly reduced in scale, and the large stone figures lining the spirit road, symbols of dynastic permanence, were discontinued.

KATHERINE TSIANG MINO

Further Reading

Franke, Herbert, and Denis Twitchett (editors), *The Cambridge History of China*, vol. 6, *Alien Regimes and Border States, 907–1368*, Cambridge: Cambridge University Press, 1994

Gridley, Marilyn Leidig, *Chinese Buddhist Sculpture under the Liao: Free Standing Works in Situ and Selected Examples from Private Collections*, New Delhi: International Academy of Indian Culture and Aditya Prakashan, 1993

Howard, Angela Falco, "Buddhist Sculptures of the Liao Dynasty," *Bulletin, Museum of Far Eastern Antiquities* 56 (1984)

Paludan, Ann, *The Chinese Spirit Road: The Classical Tradition of Stone Tomb Statuary*, New Haven, Connecticut: Yale University Press, 1991

Sirén, Osvald, *Chinese Sculpture from the Fifth to the Fourteenth Century: Over 900 Specimens in Stone, Bronze, Lacquer, and Wood, Principally from Northern China*, 4 vols., London: Benn, and New York: Scribner, 1925; reprint, New York: Hacker Art Books, 1970

CHINA: YUAN–CONTEMPORARY

As the expression of religious ideals in China, sculpture reached its high point during the Tang dynasty. The sculpture of later periods tends to be repetitive and mechanical, reproducing well-established iconographical conventions. Yet while neglected by art historians, the sculpture of China from the Yuan period onward is surprisingly varied.

Monumental sculpture in the Yuan period (1260–1368), nonetheless, did go into a considerable decline. The new non-Chinese Mongol rulers, not initially adherents to Buddhism, were slow to adopt traditions of tomb sculpture and memorial stelae. Interest in Buddhism in general was waning, and relatively few temples were founded during this period. Probably the most intriguing sculptural monuments of the Yuan dynasty are the rock-cut grottoes at Hao Tien Guan, in Shanshi Province. The images in the grottoes are not Buddhist but rather Daoist. Apparently, one Pi Yun Su established the site as a Daoist temple; in 1295 he retired to the site, engaging in practices aimed at the acquisition of immortality. Standard throughout the caves are rows of images of Daoist immortals. Their postures are stiff and motionless, and the overall execution is formulaic. Pi Yun Su is himself probably the main subject in at least two of the grottoes. In cave 1 a Daoist sage, possibly Pi, is seated cross-legged within a niche on a broad platform. Above him are two flying celestials amid cloud patterns, while a pair of standing male figures, their feet also covered with clouds, attend him. Cave 3 shows a sagelike figure lying on a bench, guarded by two attendants, possibly representing Pi passing into immortality. Interestingly, while the other caves tend toward abundant (yet summarily rendered) decorative patterns and sharply incised linear drapery forms, the artist treated this recumbent figure in a naturalistic, almost impressionistic manner.

The Buddhist rock-cut site of Lung Dung Su, in Shantung Province, exhibits a similarly blunt, hard-edged style. A grotto with a sculpture datable to 1318 shows the Buddha flanked by figures of monks and bodhisattvas. Carved from friable stone, the sculptures are poorly preserved, but even so, the modeling is hard and planar, the facial expressions masklike. More attractive Buddhist sculpture survives on a smaller scale. Notable examples are two bodhisattva Guanyin figures in private collections. One is a standing figure of about 91 centimeters. Rather columnlike, its disproportionately small arms and hands are in a praying gesture. The rectangular face has a fleshiness that hearkens back to Tang or Song prototypes.

The second example is a small stela, about one meter high, with a Guanyin seated cross-legged on a pedestal. Nearly in the round, the figure sits against a flat slab upon which are scenes in low relief of Guanyin rescuing her devotees. A highly poetic small-scale figure in the University of Pennsylvania Museum of Archaeology and Anthropology, Philadelphia, shows the Buddha seated casually in dreamy meditation with his chin resting on his hands, supported in turn by his upraised knee. This gilded, dry lacquer figure (81 cm) is almost expressionistic, with its rounded bodily contours, flowing (not stiffly incised) drapery, and large expressive eyes.

Architectural sculpture survives on the Long Huda Pagoda at Shen Dong Su (30 miles southwest of Tsinan-fu). Guardians flank doorways on all four sides, with various celestials, other mythological figures, and Buddha images above the lintels. The carving is rich and exuberant, with the motifs moving upward in steady curvilinear rhythms. A similar dynamism occurs in carvings on the gateway of Chu Yung Kuan, near Nankou. Four regal figures carved in shallow relief represent the guardians of the directions; each formulaic image, showing the guardians trampling on enemies, is flanked by equally fierce attendants.

Esoteric (tantric) forms of Buddhism arrived from Tibet during the Yuan dynasty, with various Tibetan monks becoming prominent in the court of the Mongol rulers. Sculptures now designated Sino-Tibetan show a mix of Chinese and Tibetan (also Nepalese) elements in both style and iconography. Usually associated with small bronze sculptures used as votive images and in the elaborate rituals of Tibetan Buddhism, monumental examples exist as well. About a hundred stone sculptures came from Feilai Peak in Hanzhou, Zhejiang Province, carved between 1285 and 1291. Like other large-scale Yuan sculptures, the forms are stiff

Horse and groom, tomb of Zhu Yuanzhang's parents, late 14th century, Zuling, Lake Hongzi, Jiangsu
Courtesy Ann Paludan

Qing Buddhist relief carving on the Wu Ta temple, Beijing
Courtesy Ann Paludan

and heavy, combining but not synthesizing Tibetan characteristics (formalized poses and gestures, elements of iconography) with Chinese characteristics (flowing drapery forms, plump physiognomies).

The artist Anige, who served at the Mongol court for over 40 years and established numerous workshops, introduced Nepalese elements here. A small bronze bodhisattva in the Beijing Palace Museum datable to 1305 possibly came from his workshop. With its insets of coral and turquoise, it foreshadows Sino-Tibetan traditions of the Ming period.

Sino-Tibetan sculpture reached its apogee during the Ming dynasty (1368–1644). Little Buddhist sculpture in stone remains from this time. Rather, bronze and brass were the preferred media, and scale tends to be small. Objects were used in rituals and often as presentation pieces given by royalty to Tibetan clerics. The presence of Tibetan Buddhism at the Ming court reached its height during the Yongle (1403–24) and Zuande (1426–35) eras. Artists made hundreds of images, many now found in Western museums, in the imperial workshops, bearing imperial inscriptions.

Uniformity in style and iconography marks Yongle bronzes, suggesting that artists modeled images after textual descriptions. The close contact between the early Ming emperors and various Tibetan lamas probably contributed to an attitude of close correlation between text and image. A characteristic image represents the *mahasiddha* ("great adept") Virupa (Cleveland Museum of Art, Ohio). With an imperial inscription of the Yongle era, the image bears several characteristics of Yongle bronzes, including a distinctive facial type, with broad forehead, lengthened eyes, squarish jaw, and distinctive treatment of ornamentation (a beaded necklace arranged in loops with a central three-part element of pendant bead chains) and costume (a tightly wrapped Nepalese-style skirt). As a *mahasiddha*, Virupa has a solid, powerful physique, powerful limbs, and a full round belly.

An image of the bodhisattva Manjushri (British Museum, London) is more delicate in proportions, with a slender curving waist (showing Nepalese influence) and four slender arms carrying various attributes. Jewelry is similar to that of the Virupa image, but the bodhisattva also wears an elaborate crown that frames a substantial topknot. The face is square-jawed with a delicately smiling mouth. This facial type, along with the flowing scarves hanging from the shoulders, gives the piece a strongly Chinese character.

Images from the subsequent Xuande era are less numerous and also less fine. They closely follow Yongle models but are rather hardened in both pose and formal expression. A Buddha image in the Berti Aschmann Collection, Zurich, illustrates this type well. As in Yongle sculpture, it has a basically Chinese facial type, with a lithe body recalling Nepalese art, and the abundant iconographical detail of Tibetan Buddhism.

By the mid 15th century a definite trend had set in regarding Chinese norms of representation. Poses are stiff, frontal, and symmetrical, with little curve to the waists, while faces are square-jawed. The period also saw a relaxation in the adherence to the set iconography of Tibetan texts.

Various increases and decreases in the production of Buddhist sculpture occurred during the remainder of the Ming period, this activity corresponding to Buddhism coming in and out of favor at court. A drop in the production of Buddhist images in the late 15th century preceded an acceleration under the Wanli emperor in the late 16th and early 17th centuries. These images tend to be hybrid and lower in quality than the "classic" examples of the Yongle and Xuande eras.

During the Qing dynasty (1644–1911) Sino-Tibetan art had a final, if somewhat decadent, flowering. The new Manchurian rulers were adherents to Buddhism, and Tibetan influence was strongest in the 18th century under the Yong Zheng and Qianlong emperors. The latter, especially, was noted for his close relationship with the lama Rolpay Dorje, who served the emperor as mentor, religious counselor, artistic adviser, and friend. Qing Buddhist art tends toward elaborate decoration and somewhat effeminate forms, clearly illustrated in two images in the Asian Art Museum of San Francisco—an Amitayus and a Vajradhara. The wood and lacquer images (the Vajradhara is inlaid with precious stones) are slender in physique and stiffly posed. The lines of the eyes and mouths are particularly hard. Minimal modeling produces flat harsh surfaces to the limbs, torsos, and faces. The overall effect is one of psychological distance, with an emphasis on polished decorative surfaces.

While little monumental Buddhist sculpture was made during the Yuan and later periods, large-scale work does exist from these times, found on the "Spirit Roads," avenues of stone figures and monuments lining the approach to the tombs of royalty and prominent persons. A major funerary tradition from earlier periods, few Spirit Roads were constructed during the Yuan dynasty, as this foreign Mongol dynasty retained its own burial customs. The Ming dynasty (a native Chinese dynasty) revived the custom, the earliest Spirit Road sculptures being from the tombs of the ancestors of the first Ming emperor, Honwu, at Fengyang (Anhui Province), and at Lake Hongze (Jiangsu Province), and Hongwu's own tomb at Nanjing, (Jiangsu Province), which was finished about 1415.

New symbolic concepts emerged for the Spirit Road in the early 15th century, where it came to represent the empire itself. Carvings of animals (horses, camels, elephants) symbolized regions of the empire, while images of officials were abstract symbols of office, at the service of the emperor. Early Ming figures recall the slenderness of Song dynasty prototypes. By the early 15th century the forms became heavier and more full. Surface decoration, linear in conception, however, remained intense, with intricate patterns carved on robes and armor.

The Spirit Road sculptures of the Qing dynasty are in a way a postscript to the tradition. While the non-Chinese Manchurian rulers adopted Chinese burial customs, in part to demonstrate their legitimacy as China's rulers, the Manchu approach to sculpture was primarily surface oriented, even with monumental figurative images. The sculptures tend to be flat and angular. The most successful Qing stone sculpture relates to architecture, as in the decorated architectural members at the Forbidden City and Summer Palace in Beijing. These carvings show virtuosity and a plethora of detail, the same aesthetic that dominates small-scale sculpture of the Qing as well.

Sculptures on a miniature scale served primarily as accoutrements for the scholar's desk, household decoration, or objects for export. Artists used a variety of materials, the most prominent being jade, soapstone, bamboo, and ivory, creating brush pots, wrist rests, and other accessories for calligraphy, although figurative images were popular as well. Frequently represented are various Daoist deities and immortals, as well as characters from folk and fairy tales. While in earlier times jade had various symbolic meanings, mostly in relation to immortality, these associations seem to have receded into the background by the Ming period. No longer used for ritual or official functions, jade work became purely decorative. Jade work from the Ming period tends toward simplicity and solid robust forms, although works of great delicacy appeared as well. In the Qing dynasty jade came into a period of splendor, as political stability and economic prosperity led to a great proliferation in the arts in general. Objects tend toward lavish effects and intensive detail, for example, a miniature jade mountain in the Palace Museum, Beijing.

Bamboo retained its associations with the scholarly virtues of steadfastness, resilience, and adaptability. While cylindrical brush pots are the most frequent examples of bamboo carving from the Ming and Qing dynasties, artists also made sculptural carvings of animals, Daoist immortals, and mountain landscapes. These landscapes, which include pavilions, scholar recluses, and the like, are three-dimensional renderings of traditional landscape painting. During the Qing period artists could work bamboo with the same elaborate virtuosity as jade or ivory. Emerging in the 18th century, this style is called *xiandi shenke* (sunken-ground

deep carving). A mountain landscape in the Asian Art Museum of San Francisco exemplifies this style.

Unlike jade, ivory had no real symbolic or magical associations, being essentially a rare material from which beautiful objects could be made. Some ivory work survives from the Yuan period, but ivory production flourished mainly in the Ming and especially the Qing periods.

From the late 16th to the mid 17th century, a body of work appeared that is now referred to as Sino-Spanish: ivory figures of Christian religious subjects that were produced, strictly for export and profit, in the area of Zhanzhou for the use of Jesuit missionaries in the Philippines. The subject matter is completely Western, although stylistically, something of Chinese linearity does come through. These images, particularly of the Virgin and Child, inspired certain Chinese images, particularly representations of Guanyin holding a child and carrying a rosary, arranged in the same manner as in Sino-Spanish Virgin and Child images.

Far more numerous were ivory works made for domestic Chinese use, including images of various Daoist figures such as stellar gods, immortals, and their attendants. Chinese documents state that these images were made "for pleasure," as ornamentation and "conversation pieces" in the home. The Chinese, then, did not view ivory as particularly appropriate for religious, that is, Buddhist images. By the Ming period Daoist deities had become figures of popular legend and myth and exerted little real power on the Chinese religious imagination. Hundreds of these lively figures survive, notably in the collections of the Victoria and Albert Museum in London and the Sir Victor Sassoon Chinese Ivories Trust.

The Qing dynasty saw trends toward ostentation and deliberate display. The Chinese concept of *ya* (elegance), traditionally associated with such materials as bamboo, began to be vulgarized, losing its sense of austerity, with ivory objects being displayed in homes alongside those of bamboo and porcelain. Highly elaborate ivory work came to the fore, with such intricate details as to make these works curiosities. Primary among these were the so-called devil-work balls, concentric ivory balls, each inner ball carved one within the other. A 19th-century example is in the Victoria and Albert Museum. Other intricate works included landscape and architectural scenes, such as the *Model of a Monastery* (late 19th or early 20th century) in the Sir Victor Sassoon Chinese Ivories Trust. Work in ivory, jade, and other materials continues to be made of various traditional subjects, much of it for export, in China today.

The status of sculpture as a fine art in China has never equaled that of painting or calligraphy, the latter two being strongly associated with the intellectual and literary classes. Sculpture tended to be considered the work of artisans or craftsmen, who worked primarily on the dictates of established religious or political iconography. In other words, sculpture was never the vehicle of self-expression, as were painting and calligraphy. Thus, in the early 20th century, when modern Western ideas of art were introduced into China, sculpture took on a minor role, and even today sculpture is much less prominent than painting. In the 20th century large-scale sculpture retained the role it had always had, as a vehicle of political (but no longer religious) expression.

During the Republic period (1912–49) monumental statues of political leaders appeared, although made by foreign artists. With the founding of the People's Republic (1949–present), the style of socialist realism emerged. Engendered by a close relationship with the Soviet Union, and occurring during a period of isolation from the West, Chinese socialist realism owes little to Western Modernism. Its best examples, however, bear a poetic romanticism not found in the Soviet version. A striking example in sculpture is *The Rent Collection Courtyard* (1965). A powerful propaganda piece, over one hundred life-size clay figures depict, with a touching although often theatrical realism, the oppression of tenant farmers before the Revolution. Created during the Cultural Revolution by anonymous artists in Sichuan Province, it illustrates a shift in artistic activity from the cities and art academies to rural locations.

Not all modern Chinese sculpture is anonymous. Liu Huanzhang works in wood and stone, depicting a variety of figural and animal subjects. At age 15 he was apprenticed to a master seal carver in Beijing, and he graduated from Beijing's Central Institute of Fine Arts in 1954. His work from the 1960s through the 1980s shows awareness of 20th-century artists such as Henry Moore and Constantin Brancusi, demonstrating a conservative Modernism. Liu had a one-person exhibition in 1981 at Beijing's National Art Gallery, the first ever given to a sculptor.

An avant-garde began to emerge in the late 1970s. Most prominent was a group of artists calling itself The Stars. A dissident exhibition they held in 1979 at the China Art Gallery, Beijing, was notable for the work of sculptor Wang Keping. Claiming the influence of Samuel Beckett and Eugene Ionesco, his work is strongly political and often satirical. *Gun*, for example, is a parody of Jiang Qing, the wife of Mao Zedong and leader of the Cultural Revolution. Wang immigrated to France in 1984.

While Modernist in style, Wang Keping's work is recognizably figural. Another of The Stars, Chen Yanshen, uses abstraction in his work; his *Out of the Sky* is a collage sculpture of miscellaneous everyday objects.

Chinese critics did not react positively to this experimental mode, showing the prevalent conservatism of China's official art circle.

Public sculpture made from 1990 onward provides both a summary of past trends and an indication of future developments. Traditional figurative sculpture, such as portrait statues or busts of political figures and cultural heroes, continue to be made as they were in the 1940s and 1950s—highly realistic but uninspired. Socialist realist works cast in the same mold as *The Rent Collection Courtyard* continue to be made as well. But abstract public sculpture is becoming more and more common. The majority of works are derivative of Modernist styles of the 1960s and 1970s. A small group of progressive artists are breaking new ground, however, such as Fu Zhong Wang, whose unique stone and wood pieces exhibit the natural characteristics of their materials. Beyond the realm of public sculpture, installation and performance art is taking hold in China. The performance/installation works of Zhan Wang take on an environmental scale and are highly poetic in their ephemeral nature. The installations and performances of Xiao Lu recall those of Chris Burden (one included a telephone booth and firearms). This small cadre of progressive sculptors promises to grow as China opens up more and more to the West, enabling artists slowly to gain more of a footing in the international art scene. Chinese officialdom, however, remains by and large suspicious of most progressive tendencies in the arts in general.

WALTER SMITH

Further Reading

Bartholomew, Terese Tse, "Sino-Tibetan Art of the Qianlong Period from the Asian Art Museum of San Francisco," *Orientations* 22/6 (June 1991)

Bills, Sheila C., "A Chronological Study of Sino-Tibetan Metal Sculpture (1260–1450)," Ph.D. diss., Case Western Reserve University, 1983

Bills, Sheila C., "Tibet in China—China in Tibet: Bronze Sculpture of the Early Ming (1403–1450)," *Arts of Asia* 25 (September/October 1994)

Bills, Sheila C., "Sino-Tibetan Sculpture: The Tibetan Legacy," *Marg* 47/4 (1996)

Chinese Ivories: From the Shang to the Qing (exhib. cat.), London: Oriental Ceramic Society, 1984

Clark, John (editor), *Modernity in Asian Art*, Broadway, New South Wales: Wild Peony, 1993

Galikowski, Maria, *Art and Politics in China, 1949–1984*, Hong Kong: Chinese University Press, 1998

Paludan, Ann, *The Chinese Spirit Road: The Classical Tradition of Stone Tomb Statuary*, New Haven, Connecticut: Yale University Press, 1991

Paludan, Ann, "China: Funerary and Secular Sculpture," in *The Dictionary of Art*, edited by Jane Turner, vol. 6, New York: Grove, and London: Macmillan, 1996

Pearce, Nicholas, "China: Bamboo Carving," in *The Dictionary of Art*, edited by Jane Turner, vol. 7, New York: Grove, and London: Macmillan, 1996

Rawson, Jessica, and Carol Michaelson, *Chinese Jade: From the Neolithic to the Qing*, London: British Museum Press, 1995

Sculpture by Liu Huanzhang: Contemporary Chinese Art, Beijing: Foreign Language Press, 1984

Sirén, Osvald, *Chinese Sculpture from the Fifth to the Fourteenth Centuries*, 4 vols., London: Benn, and New York: Scribner, 1925; reprint, New York: Hacker Art Books, 1970

Sorensen, Henrik, "China: Buddhist Sculpture," in *The Dictionary of Art*, edited by Jane Turner, vol. 6, New York: Grove, and London: Macmillan, 1996

Sullivan, Michael, *A Short History of Chinese Art*, Berkeley: University of California Press, and London: Faber, 1967; revised edition, as *The Arts of China*, Berkeley: University of California Press, and London: Thames and Hudson, 1973; 4th edition, Berkeley: University of California Press, 1999

Till, Barry, and Paula Swart, "China: Jade Carving," in *The Dictionary of Art*, edited by Jane Turner, vol. 7, New York: Grove, and London: Macmillan, 1996

Young, John T., "Public Art in China," *Sculpture* 15 (July/August 1996)

JOSEPH CHINARD 1756–1813 *French*

French sculptor Joseph Chinard is best known for his remarkable portrait busts, although his oeuvre also consists of official monuments, intimate terracottas, and medallions of revolutionary and, later, imperial figures. His work exemplifies the dual influences of the Rococo and the nascent Neoclassical style of the later 18th century. Neoclassicism reflected the high-minded idealism of the Enlightenment, as espoused by contemporary philosophers such as Jean-Jacques Rousseau. For the proponents of the Neoclassical style, Classical art and architecture symbolized the philosophical and political virtues of the ancient world. Unlike some of his contemporaries, Chinard was able to unify Rococo beauty and the noble simplicity of Neoclassical style without undue rigidity or overwhelming academicism.

Chinard became a master at the age of 24 and initially focused his efforts on sculptures and reliefs for churches in and around his native Lyon, where he was well received by his contemporaries. He executed a great deal of his artistic production there, although he also completed work in Marseille, Clermont-Ferrand, Bordeaux, and beyond in Rome and Lucca. An educational trip to Rome in 1784, taken with the support of a private patron, was instrumental in shaping Chinard's career. While in Rome he completed numerous works that freely interpreted antique sources, such as his 1789 marble based on the *Centaur Borghese* (*Centaur Borghese*, Musée des Beaux-Arts, Lyon, France). In 1786 he competed in the sculpture competition held at the Academy of St. Luke in Rome and won first prize for his terracotta rendition of *Perseus Delivering Androm-

eda*; this represented the first time a Frenchman won first prize at the prestigious academy in Rome. This delicately modeled terracotta shows the influence of Chinard's interest in the antique as well as the work of his contemporaries, such as Antonio Canova. The original group remains at the Academy of St. Luke. Chinard completed another terracotta version, as well as a marble version, upon his return to Lyon.

On a later visit to Rome in 1791, Chinard received a commission from the Lyonnais, van Risamburgh to model a pair of candelabra bases depicting *Liberty in the Guise of Jupiter Smashing the Aristocracy* and *Reason in the Guise of Apollo Trampling Superstition Underfoot*. The figure of *Superstition* on one of the bases had recognizable attributes of religion, which led papal officials to investigate Chinard's seemingly subversive intentions. They determined that Chinard's work revealed anticlerical sentiments, and he was incarcerated in the Castel Sant' Angelo. Intervention by a prominent official led to his release only two months later.

Upon his return to Lyon, Chinard received a commission for a public work depicting *Liberty and Equality* for the facade of the Hôtel de Ville in 1793. Authorities felt that the figure of *Liberty* did not exhibit the necessary propagandistic vigor and strength worthy of the revolutionary figure, and Chinard was incarcerated again, this time on the grounds of being counterrevolutionary. After this incident his work became increasingly Neoclassical.

Despite such notable examples of opposition, Chinard achieved acclaim both regionally and nationally. By the turn of the 19th century, he became one of Napoléon's favorite sculptors, possibly second only to Canova. He completed numerous portrait busts and medallions of the emperor and the Bonaparte family. Around this time Chinard also received many private commissions for portraits. With these busts he earned his reputation as a brilliant portraitist whose style varied according to his patron. His official portrait style as seen in his works for the Napoleonic effort is decidedly more formal and restrained, such as his bust of Napoléon. In comparison, his portrait busts of Madame Récamier demonstrate a more personable and private nature. They are carefully composed yet exhibit a pervasive lyricism. Chinard's sculptural talents are perhaps most recognizable in these female busts; they are remarkable for their realistic and masterful modeling and in their innovative treatment of the problem of truncation. The fashionable drapery and costumes that adorn Chinard's figures also serve to unify the bust and its socle or pedestal. His father, who was a silk merchant in Lyon, possibly influenced Chinard's interest in and understanding of fashion.

Although the personalities and fashions of his time influenced Chinard, the religious and political atmosphere of 18th-century France pervades many of his works. Revolutionary events, for example, shaped his career not only by determining the sources of his commissions but also by dictating the style of his works. Through the eyes of his contemporaries, Chinard's work commonly inspired fervor, either religious or political. Today, they are appreciated more for their inherent beauty, masterful modeling, and innovative arrangements.

MARIA L. SANTANGELO

See also **Canova, Antonio**

Biography

Born in Lyon, France, 12 February 1756. Admitted to École Royale de Dessin in Lyon and trained under painter Donat Nonotte, 1770; later worked with sculptor Barthélemy Blaise; independent by 1780; moved to Rome, 1784; won first prize at the Academy of St. Luke, 1786; returned to Lyon, 1787; back briefly in Rome, 1791; incarcerated for two months (by papal authorities), 1792; returned to Lyon end of 1792; incarcerated again, 1793, and released, 1794; visited Paris, 1795; worked in Carrara, 1804–08; returned to Lyon, 1808; taught at École Impériale de Dessin; exhibited at the Paris Salons, 1798, 1802, 1806, 1808, 1810, and 1812. Died in Lyon, France, 20 June 1813.

Selected Works

1780   Statues of *St. Paul, St. Sacerdos*, and the *Four Evangelists*; chalk (destroyed)
1786   *Perseus Delivering Andromeda*; terracotta; Detroit Institute of Arts, Michigan, United States; marble version: 1787, Musée des Beaux-Arts, Lyon, France
1790   Allegorical portrait of the van Risamburgh (van Risembourg?) family; marble; J. Paul Getty Museum, Los Angeles, California, United States
1791/2 *Venus and Aeneas* (?); terracotta; Los Angeles County Museum of Art, California, United States
1794   *The Republic*; terracotta; Musée du Louvre, Paris, France
1801/02 Bust of Madame Récamier; terracotta; J. Paul Getty Museum, Los Angeles, California, United States; another terracotta version, private collection
1801   Bust of Madame Récamier; marble; Musée des Beaux-Arts, Lyon, France
1802   Bust of Napoleon Bonaparte; plaster; Musée National de Malmaison, France

1804   Bust of Empress Joséphine; marble; Musée National de Malmaison, France
1804/8 *Honor and Country* for the Arc de Triomphe, Bordeaux, France; terracotta model; Musée des Beaux-Arts, Lyon, France
1805   *Peace*; marble; Château Borély, Marseille, France
1807   *Vase*; terracotta; Musée des Beaux-Arts, France
1808   *Carabineer*; stone; Arc de Triomphe du Carrousel, Paris, France
1808   *The Family of General Philippe-Guillaume Duhesme*; terracotta; J. Paul Getty Museum, Los Angeles, California, United States

Further Reading

L'oeuvre de Joseph Chinard, 1755–1813, au Musée des Beaux-Arts de Lyon, Lyon: Musée des Beaux-Arts, 1978
Musée des Beaux-Arts de Lyon, *Le muses de Messidor: Peintres et sculpteurs lyonnais de la révolution à l'empire* (exhib. cat.), Lyon: Musée des Beaux-Arts, 1989
Rocher-Janeau, M., "Chinard and the Empire Style," *Apollo* 80 (1964)
Rocher-Janeau, M., "Chinard," in *The Dictionary of Art*, edited by Jane Turner, vol. 6, and New York: Grove, London: Macmillan, 1996,
The Age of Neo-Classicism (exhib. cat.), London: Arts Council of Great Britain, 1972
Vitry, Paul, *Exposition d'oeuvres du sculpteur Chinard de Lyon (1756–1813)* (exhib. cat.), Paris: Levy, 1909

BUST OF MADAME RÉCAMIER

Joseph Chinard (1756–1813)
1801
marble
life-size
Musée des Beaux-Arts, Lyon, France

Juliette Récamier was born Jeanne-Françoise-Julie-Adélaïde Bernard. Her father was a Lyonnais notary, eventually employed by Louis XVI as Receveur des Finances. After Louis XVI's execution in 1793, Juliette married the Lyonnais banker-financier Jacques-Rose Récamier; he was 28 years her senior, and it was said that their relationship was of a paternal nature. A noted beauty of her time, she was greatly admired for her charm and sense of fashion. The Récamiers actively participated in the social and artistic scene of late 18th-century Paris. A celebrated compatriot, Juliette became a popular subject for contemporary artists such as Jacques-Louis David, Antonio Canova, and François Gérard.

Joseph Chinard met Juliette Récamier on his first visit to Paris in 1795. The relationship proved very fruitful for Chinard, who completed numerous portrait medallions and busts of her in marble, plaster, and terracotta. It is likely that the Récamiers had other works by Chinard in their collection, and they even invited Chinard in 1805 to live in their fashionable Parisian home. He completed the earliest portrait of Juliette when she was only 17; she did not receive the last, a marble in the Museum of Art in the Rhode Island School of Design, until after Chinard's death in 1813. The portraits vary in material, size, composition, hairstyle, and dress. The marble bust in Rhode Island, for example, lacks arms and bosom. These were removed later at Madame Récamier's request after 1828. The Récamiers received the bust in the Musée des Beaux-Arts, Lyon, in 1801; it is signed "Chinard de Lyon" on the back of the socle. A marble version with arms is in the Minneapolis Institute of Art (Minnesota, United States).

Many consider the bust of Madame Récamier to be an unparalleled example of turn-of-the-century portraiture. Germain Bapst noted in a 1911 exhibition of Chinard's works in Paris that "grâce à ces travaux, l'oeuvre de Chinard est aujourd'hui connu" (Thanks to this piece, Chinard's work is known today). Although the sculptor completed numerous portraits of fashionable women, this one stood apart during his time and even today remains his best-known work. He carved Juliette with a masterful exactness; what immediately distinguishes this work is her exquisite beauty and the graceful manner in which Chinard captures her attitude and nature. In Chinard's hands Juliette became an emblem of her time as well as an eternal beauty. Her dress is in the then fashionable Neoclassical taste, and her head is bound in a Greek turban. A translucent shawl is coquettishly pulled around her partially exposed torso and drapes over the socle. The seemingly haphazard placement of drapery is in fact quite calculated. With this fashionable accessory Chinard innovatively unified the portrait and its support by blurring the line between bust and pedestal. He employed this technique in many of his female portrait busts, including the terracotta of his wife, Madame Chinard. Innovative as it may appear, some of Chinard's contemporaries employed a similar approach, such as Canova's *Venus Italica* (1804–12; Galleria Palatina, Florence) which also dates to the turn of the century; it is uncertain which work preceded the other.

Chinard's success with the bust of Madame Récamier earned him celebrity and possibly brought his works to the attention of a larger social and political circle, including Napoléon and his family.

MARIA L. SANTANGELO

Bust of Madame Récamier, *ca.* 1801–02 life-size
© J. Paul Getty Museum, Los Angeles, California

Further Reading

Madame Récamier (exhib. cat.), Lyon: Musée Historique, 1977

CHRISTO AND JEANNE-CLAUDE

Christo and Jeanne-Claude's combined efforts in environmental art have yielded some of the most awe-inspiring images in recent art. Until February 1994 their artworks were known solely as the product of Christo's inspiration and efforts. At that time, to acknowledge her role as a participant in the creative process, Christo declared that all past and present projects ascribed to him since 1961 should be known as the work of Christo and Jeanne-Claude. Their large-scale projects require the enormous coordination of the work of many people.

Christo Vladimirov Javacheff was born in Gabrovo, Bulgaria, the son of working class parents, and received his first art training in Bulgaria. He studied at the Fine Arts Academy of Sofia from 1953 until 1956. While there he was required to participate in work-study. Christo's assignment proved fortuitous in helping him develop an aesthetic and artistic system based on large-scale, collaborative projects; the academy assigned him and his classmates to "prettify" the Bulgarian landscape, teaching farmers how to stack and place farm implements, products, and equipment in view so that passengers on the luxurious Orient Express would observe the tidy, organized Communist landscape.

Interrupting his Bulgarian art training, Christo went to Prague for six months. It was there that he first chanced upon Russian Constructivism and its colossal imaginative constructions, which would prove important in his later work with Jeanne-Claude. Disenchanted with Communism, Christo fled to Vienna in 1957 and studied for a short time at their Academy of Fine Arts. In 1958 he went to Paris, where he met Jeanne-Claude when he was hired to paint her mother's portrait.

Although their relationship might have caused a scandal since she was the daughter of a French general, Christo and Jeanne-Claude's union instead proved fortuitous; her capabilities as a mediator and manager proved enormously helpful for the kind of art Christo wanted to realize.

In 1958 Christo began converting commonplace items such as bottles or magazine by wrapping, stacking, or draping them. By 1961 he and Jeanne-Claude were collaborating on making larger versions of these modest alterations. They found a group of artists in Paris similarly disenchanted with abstraction who had organized under the name Nouveaux Réalistes. This group included artists Yves Klein and Arman, as well as the critic Pierre Restany, and was somewhat loosely organized although the group did produce a manifesto. Christo participated in some of their activities, but he remained on the periphery, never signing their manifesto or fully acknowledging involvement, even though he probably most represented the group's stated

Valley Curtain, Grand Hogback, Rifle, Colorado © 1972
Christo and Harry Shunk

aesthetic. Like Robert Rauschenberg and Jasper Johns in the United States, this group foreshadowed Pop Art with its interest in the everyday object. Christo's work of this period largely involved disruptions to small-scale objects, such as *Wrapped Chair* of 1961. Also in 1961 he created a manipulated photograph to which drawing and collage have been applied, *Project for a Wrapped Public Building*, which portrays a strange, draped presence in the otherwise ordered urban environment. Christo and Jeanne-Claude soon started working on a larger scale in *Stacked Oil Barrels* and *Dockside Packages*, both in Cologne Harbor, and then by blocking the narrow Rue Visconti in Paris with oil barrels on 27 June 1962, a creation wittily titled *Iron Curtain—Wall of Oil Barrels, 1961–1962*.

By 1964 the artists were searching for new opportunities and decided to move to New York City. There they began expanding their range of images and forms by shielding and draping plate-glass windows in a series of works titled *Store Fronts*, which negate the subjects' utility and rationale. This open-endedness was characteristically antimainstream, at a time when the New York art world was centered on the clarity of Pop art and the initial sparks of Minimalism were becoming evident.

By the late 1960s Christo and Jeanne-Claude were creating large-scale projects on a regular basis, first in Eindhoven in the Netherlands and Minneapolis, Minnesota, and then in larger metropolitan areas. In 1968 they realized several large projects in Kassel, Bern, and Spoleto, but it was the wrapping of a coast in Australia that catapulted them to a new level of size and scale in their work. The project *Wrapped Coast, Little Bay, One Million Square Feet, Sydney, Australia, 1968–69*, which consisted of 1.6 kilometers of coastline, 93,000 square meters of fabric, and 58 meters of rope, involved hundreds of people in the negotiations, realization, and completion of the project. The artists altered the normal look and function of the landscape with unexpected elements. Their gentle intrusions into the landscape helped establish environmental art as a movement, as many artists, uninterested in the overemphasis on the commodity and objectness of art, were seeking an environmental approach to art making. These large-scale projects required the viewer to actively participate, the artists facilitating an experience for a short period of time with temporary installations.

The projects of the 1970s further extended Christo and Jeanne-Claude's reputation and sphere of influence in the art world and beyond. *Valley Curtain, Grand Hogback, Rifle, Colorado, 1970–72* consisted of a bright orange nylon curtain, 381 to 417 meters wide and 56 to 111 meters high, stretched across a valley. The work existed for only 28 hours before wind ripped the curtain in two, forcing the artists to remove it. While the work was installed, a photographer documented the immense scale.

Christo and Jeanne-Claude began *Running Fence, Sonoma and Marin Counties, California*, in 1972, finally realizing it in 1976. The fence extended through the rolling hills of this area, ending in the ocean. Complete permissions to extend the piece into the ocean had not been provided; thus, after the installation of the majority of the 5.5-meter-high and 39-kilometers-long fence, the artists and a few others continued the fence into the waters as though it were emerging or waning. The Maysles brothers filmed this work, as well as *Valley Curtain* and most subsequent projects.

In 1983 the artists encircled 11 landfill islands between Miami and Miami Beach in Florida by floating fabric around each, resulting in *Surrounded Islands, Biscayne Bay, Greater Miami, Florida, 1980–83*. The bold pink color reflected much of the splendid flora and fauna of the region and could be seen from all viewpoints. Equally visually compelling was the dramatic *The Pont Neuf, Wrapped*, begun in 1975 and realized in 1985. In this work the artists shrouded the oldest bridge in Paris in champagne-colored fabric. The spectacular work shimmered in the day and glowed at night, reflecting the water below, as well as being reflected in the water. In 1991 they completed *The Umbrellas, Japan-USA*, in process since 1984. This binational work marked a departure from Christo and Jeanne-Claude's previous artworks: workers installed enormous umbrellas, blue in Japan and yellow in California, simultaneously over the landscape. The next project, *Wrapped Reichstag*, had been in process even longer due to the building's oft-contested role in Germany's past; the project, begun in 1971, was finally brought to fruition in 1995. The 1.2 million small swatches for distribution to visitors became one of the most collected items of the project. Despite all of these realized projects, many of the artists' works remain in the unrealized state while permissions are sought.

The artists acquire the financing for their art, which they provide themselves, through the sale of preparatory drawings, collages, and early works done by Christo. They have their own corporation for financing and managing the financial aspects of each project.

The physicality of the objects, their transitory existence, and the ensuing public dialogue have made the works of Christo and Jeanne-Claude important examples of environmental and Installation art. Their work has often resulted in brief utopian periods of active social engagement through the dialogue each work prompts and fosters. Their work has become synonymous with the drama and grandeur of artists dealing with the rural and urban landscape.

Anne Swartz

See also **Arman (Fernandez); Contemporary Sculptors; Installation; Klein, Yves; Performance Art**

Christo

Biography
Born in Gabrovo, Bulgaria, 13 June 1935. Given name Christo Vladimirov Javacheff. Studied at Fine Arts Academy of Sofia, 1953–56; went to Prague, 1956–57; briefly studied at Academy of Fine Arts, Vienna, 1957; moved to Paris, 1958, where he met future wife and collaborator, Jeanne-Claude, née de Guillebon; married Jeanne-Claude in 1960 (one son, Cyril); began utilizing everyday objects in art, 1958; artworks became larger in scale by 1961; in Paris, encountered Nouveaux Réalistes movement; first major projects made in 1962; moved to New York City, 1964; became American citizen in the 1960s; began to work in monumental environmental scale, 1968–69; produced numerous wrapping projects, some of which still in progress. Most projects self-financed. Lives and works in New York City.

Jeanne-Claude

Biography
Born in Casablanca, Morocco, 13 June 1935. Given name Jeanne-Claude de Guillebon; daughter of a French general; met Bulgarian immigrant Christo in 1958; married him in 1960 (one son, Cyril); Christo assigned her credit as collaborator on all past and present projects solely ascribed to him since 1961. Lives and works in New York City.

Selected Works
1961   *Stacked Oil Barrels*; oil barrels; realized at Cologne Harbor, Germany
1961   *Wrapped Chair*; chair, fabric, rope; private collection of Jeanne-Claude and Christo, New York City, United States
1962   *Iron Curtain—Wall of Oil Barrels, 1961–1962*; fabric and rope; blocking of the Rue Visconti, Paris, France
1969   *Wrapped Coast—One Million Square Feet, Little Bay, Sydney, Australia*; 1.6 kilometers of coastline, fabric, and rope; Sydney, Australia
1970–72 *Valley Curtain, Grand Hogback, Rifle, Colorado, 1970–72*; orange nylon curtain stretched across a valley; Rifle, Colorado, United States
1972–76 *Running Fence, Sonoma and Marin Counties, California, 1972–76*; 39 kilometers long fabric fence; Sonoma and Marin Counties, California, United States

1975–85 *The Pont Neuf Wrapped, Paris, 1975–85*;
a bridge, rope, and fabric; Paris, France
1980–83 *Surrounded Islands, Biscayne Bay,
Greater Miami, Florida, 1980–83*; 11
landfill islands and fabric between Miami
and Miami Beach; Florida, United States
1984–91 *The Umbrellas, Japan–USA*; 3,100
umbrellas (1,340 blue in Japan and 1,760
gold in California); Ibaraki Prefecture,
Japan, and area south of Bakersfield,
California, United States
1971–95 *Wrapped Reichstag, Berlin, 1971–95*; rope,
fabric; Reichstag, Berlin, Germany

Further Reading

*Christo and Jeanne-Claude Projects: Selected from the Lilja
Collection*, with photographs by Wolfgang Volz, London :
Azimuth Editions, 1995
Laporte, Dominique-Gilbert, *Christo*, Paris: Art Press-Flamma-
rion, 1985; as *Christo*, translated by Abby Pollak, New York:
Pantheon, 1986
Schellmann, Jörg, and Joséphine Benecke (editors), *Christo and
Jeanne-Claude, Prints and Objects, 1963–1995: A Cata-
logue Raisonné*, Munich and New York: Edition Schell-
mann, 1995
Swartz, Anne, *Christo and Jeanne-Claude: Two Works in
Progress: Over the River, Project for the Arkansas River,
Colorado, and The Gates, Project for Central Park, New
York City*, Savannah, Georgia: The Savannah College of Art
and Design, 1999
Vaizey, Marina, *Christo*, New York: Rizzoli, 1990

CHRYSELEPHANTINE SCULPTURE

Composite images of gold (*chrysos*) and ivory
(*elephas*) were fashioned in Mesopotamia and the Aegean at least as early as the 2nd millennium BCE, a
thousand years before the Classical Greeks coined the
compound adjective *chryselephantinos*. Bronze Age
statues were small in scale, apparently no larger than
life-size. Technical innovations allowed for larger images in the 1st millennium BCE, but *chryselephantine*
images of all periods also served as components of
functional ensembles, such as luxury furniture, weaponry, and toilet articles.

Although freestanding statues could be fashioned
from single tusks or even tusk sections, many were
nonetheless assembled from individually carved ivory
components that were attached to one another or to
wooden cores by mortises, tenons, dowels, and pins.
Creamy, white ivory was reserved for exposed flesh—
often just hands, face, and feet; clothing and hair were
rendered in gold or polychromy over wood. Thus carvers did not employ precious imported ivory where it
would not be seen, nor did they waste any of the tusk.

The composite technique and the precious materials
of ancient *chryselephantine* statues made them vulnerable to looters as well as to the ravages of time. What
has survived tends to be poorly preserved, but despite
its fragmentary condition, it is of the highest quality,
far outstripping more complete works in other media.
Ivory's dense structure, finer than any wood, allows it
to hold detail better than marble, bronze, or terracotta;
gold is the most attractive and versatile of metals. The
cost of these materials, as well as their aesthetic appeal,
ensured that they would be entrusted to the most accomplished craftsman, and surviving components indicate the character of what has been lost. Indeed, the
most remarkable statues in any medium from the Aegean Bronze Age are composite *chryselephantine* statues from Crete, which exhibit exquisitely carved sub-
cutaneous anatomical details, such as networks of
veins and tendons. The *Youth* from Palaikastro, excavated 1987–90, was fashioned from at least 20 components. Gold clothing, a steatite coiffure, rock crystal
eyes, and inlaid wooden nipples enhanced its hippopotamus ivory body. (Polychromy was an integral element
of ivory sculpture, as of all ancient statuary.) The famous *Leapers* from Knossos, recovered by Arthur
Evans in 1902, inspired a series of "Minoan" forgeries
in the early 20th century, most depicting goddesses,
some of which are still exhibited in North American
museums.

Greek and Latin authors recorded over 200 gold-
and-ivory statues, and the remains of others have been
recovered archaeologically (e.g., at Delphi in central
Greece). Most renowned were the temple statues of
Pheidias, fashioned in the 5th century BCE. Adapting
age-old techniques of furniture makers, carpenters,
shipwrights, and bronze casters, the Athenian sculptor
contrived to construct composite statues on a monumental scale by unscrolling elephant tusks into large,
thin sheets of ivory that could then be chemically softened and molded to a desired shape. These veneers
were attached to wooden armatures along with gold,
glass, and other materials. In this way, Pheidias surpassed any limitation imposed by the size of tusks.
The celebrated *Athena* in Parthenon on the Acropolis,
decked with over a ton of gold, stood over 12 meters
tall. Equally large was the *Zeus* at Olympia, which
came to be considered one of the Seven Wonders of
the Ancient World.

Whether small or large, the cost and splendor of
chryselephantine statues ensured that they served as
status symbols as well as tokens of piety; although
often dedicated to the gods, they nonetheless asserted
the power, or pretensions, of men, whether individual
donors or competing city-states. In the wake of Pheidias, who is also recorded as having produced gold-
and-ivory statues for the citizens of Elis, Megara, and
Pellene, competitive emulation spurred other Greek
states to commission monumental *chryselephantine*

images from the foremost artists (e.g., *Hera* at Argos by Polykleitos, *Asklepios* at Kyllene by Kolotes, *Asklepios* at Epidauros by Thrasymedes, and *Dionysos* at Athens by Alkamenes). This trend continued into the Hellenistic and Roman periods, when kings and emperors commissioned portraits as well as divine images; indeed, in some cases (e.g., Leochares' royal Macedonian family group in the Philippeion at Olympia), there seems to have been little difference.

Ivories continued to be carved, gilded, and painted in late antiquity and the Middle Ages, but the composite *chryselephantine* technique for freestanding statuary seems to have fallen into disfavor until it was revived by Neoclassicists in the 19th century, such as Antoine Quatremère de Quincy. Gold-and-ivory statues were especially popular in the early 20th century, when Art Deco compositions by Dimitri Chiparus and others continued to serve elite patrons, although almost entirely on a small scale and in secular and decorative contexts.

KENNETH D.S. LAPATIN

See also **Pheidias; Polychromy**

Further Reading

Arwas, Victor, *Art Deco Sculpture*, London: Academy Editions, and New York: St Martin's Press, 1992

Barnett, Richard David, *Ancient Ivories in the Middle East*, Jerusalem: Hebrew University of Jerusalem, 1982

Blühm, Andreas, et al., *The Colour of Sculpture, 1840–1910* (exhib. cat.), Zwolle, The Netherlands: Waanders, 1996

Connor, Carolyn Loessel, *The Color of Ivory: Polychromy on Byzantine Ivories*, Princeton, New Jersey: Princeton University Press, 1998

Flynn, Tom, "Amending the Myth of Phidias: Quatremère de Quincy and the Nineteenth-Century Revival of Chryselephantine Statuary," *Apollo* 145 (January 1997)

Lapatin, Kenneth D.S., "Pheidias Elephantourgos," *American Journal of Archaeology* 101 (1997)

Lapatin, Kenneth D.S., *Chryselephantine Statuary in the Ancient Mediterranean World*, New York: Oxford University Press, 2001

Lapatin, Kenneth D.S., *Mysteries of the Snake Goddess: Art, Desire, and the Forging of History*, Boston: Houghton Mifflin, 2002

MacGillivray, J.A., Jan M. Driessen, and L.H. Sackett, *The Palaikastro Kouros: A Minoan Chryselephantine Statuette and Its Aegean Bronze Age Context*, London: British School at Athens, 2000

Shedd, Meredith, "Phidias at the Universal Exposition of 1855: The Duc de Luynes and the 'Athena Parthenos,'" *Gazette des Beaux-Arts* (1986)

St. Aubyn, Fiona (editor), *Ivory: An International History and Illustrated Survey*, London: Thames and Hudson, and New York: Abrams, 1987

CAIUS GABRIEL CIBBER 1630–1700
Danish, active in England

Caius (Kai) Gabriel Cibber was born in Denmark, the son of a royal cabinetmaker. He brought Italian and Dutch styles to England where, in 1667, he was appointed sculptor to Charles II. With Sir Christopher Wren's backing, Cibber was commissioned to make several public sculptures, but he also had an extensive private practice with the nobility. He was the most gifted and versatile sculptor of his generation in England, modeling in terracotta and carving wood, stone, and marble, and he was one of the earliest to popularize the casting of statues and garden ornaments in lead. He was also an architect.

With a grant from the Danish king, Frederik III, in around 1647, Cibber traveled to Italy, where for several years he learned Italian sculpture techniques. Later, in the Netherlands, he probably met Peter de Keyser, who could have given him an introduction to his brother-in-law, John Stone, in London. Cibber arrived in England about 1655 during the Commonwealth and became foreman to Stone who, at the Restoration, was appointed master mason at Windsor. From 1660, when Stone had a seizure, Cibber ran his workshop in Long Acre in London. On 20 June 1667 Cibber was sworn into the royal household. That year he was recommended for replacing the famous line of sculptures of kings at the Royal Exchange, which were destroyed during the Great Fire. He made *modelli* (models, two of which survive), but a long hiatus followed, and other craftsmen eventually executed some of his designs.

Although he was a cultured man, he was impractical with money and was periodically imprisoned for debt. His royal position, however, allowed him to be released daily to continue work. His first major public commission was for the *Monument to the Great Fire of London*.

Cibber's first known carving in England is a chimneypiece at Lamport Hall according to John Webb's design. He expanded his reputation carving church wall monuments, some of which, such as the Essington monuments, bear a distinctive flower motif, which served as a personal signature. He joined the Leathersellers' Company in 1668, but, unable to pay the fee (25 pounds), he presented a fountain: a mermaid with fishtail legs and jetting water from her breasts, which stood in Leathersellers' Yard until 1799. This was inspired by Giambologna's *Fountain of Neptune* (1563–67) in Bologna and Hubert Le Sueur's *Diana Fountain* (mid 1650s) at Hampton Court.

Robert Hooke mentioned that Cibber made the figures of *Gog* and *Magog* for London Guildhall in 1672, and Cibber also supplied ephemeral decorations for the Lord Mayors' Feasts. His *Fountain of Four Rivers of England* in Soho Square, London, was based on Gianlorenzo Bernini's *Fountain of the Four Rivers* (1648–51) in the Piazza Navona, Rome. A statue of Charles II stood at the summit of the fountain; figures of old men representing the Thames, Humber, Tyne, and Severn

Rivers once existed, but today only Charles II remains in Soho Square. Two busts of Charles II, previously attributed to John Bushnell, have been reattributed to Cibber: the life-size terracotta model was made *ad vivum* (from life) around 1677, and the subsequent marble carving was presented to Sir Jacob Astley, the present owner's ancestor, by King Charles himself. In about 1678 Cibber competed with Grinling Gibbons to design a monument to Charles I in a mausoleum at Windsor, which never materialized.

Cibber supplied four allegorical figures for the roofline of Wren's new library at Trinity College in Cambridge. According to Cibber's son, he was responsible for *Raving* and *Melancholy Madness*, the male figures that reclined on broken pediments over the gateposts of London's lunatic asylum, Bedlam Hospital. These are startling creations: both bald and nearly naked, their contorted limbs are strained; one lies chained and shrieking, whereas the other is coiled and catatonic. They are extraordinary reflections of Michelangelo's Medici Tomb figures, and they inspired the painter William Hogarth's *The Rake's Progress* (1735) and works by the poets Alexander Pope and William Wordsworth. The terracotta model for *Raving Madness* is currently in the Staatliche Museen, Berlin.

Another masterpiece is his monument to Richard, Earl of Dorset, and Thomas Sackville. The contract exists for this freestanding tomb, which had to meet the approval of Peter Lely, the king's painter. The mother and the deceased father of the dead boy kneel as if they are still alive on either side of the youth, who lies contemplating death. Life-size and lifelike, the work is also emotionally charged. Cibber is thought to have been responsible for several other church monuments (by 1678 he had five workshop assistants), but documentation has not yet been found. The wall monument to Sir Greville Verney (*d.* 1668), a fine architectural memorial with putti and a bust of the deceased, falls into this category.

Cibber answered the early calls for garden statuary. Inspired by Giambologna's genre bronzes, Cibber produced his *Boy with Bagpipes* (1680–90), who sits with a small dog entranced at his feet. This figure, now in the Victoria and Albert Museum, London, cannot be firmly documented. Cibber was prepared to travel in order to work with locally quarried stone. At Belvoir Castle, Leicestershire, England, he carved seven pastoral figures in Ketton stone. Nearby at Belton, Lincolnshire, is a fine *Father Time Sundial*, although this also is undocumented. He was paid 536 pounds by the Earl of Kingston (*ca.* 1687) for numerous architectural and garden pieces at Thoresby House, Nottinghamshire (now lost). He moved on to Chatsworth, where he produced handsome figures, in fine white marble, of *Apollo* and *Pallas Athene* for the great staircase and

Faith and *Justice* for the magnificent altarpiece, which he designed and executed in the chapel. For the garden in Roche Abbey Stone, he carved two *Sphinxes*, a *Triton Fountain with Four Seahorses* (the Triton figure inspired by Bernini), and other Classical statues. He was paid the sum of 450 pounds for these works, some of which were unfinished when he was summoned to Hampton Court Palace.

For Wren's new garden front, Cibber created the pediment relief showing Hercules (with whom William III particularly identified) triumphing over Superstition, Tyranny, and Fury while Fame leads him toward the Arts of Peace. This was his most linear composition. He also carved two stone crests for Clock Court and cast four metal gods for the roofline. He made a colossal marble urn—with a relief of *Meleager Hunting the Calydonian Boar* (1691–96)—supported on the shoulders of three baby satyrs. Cibber himself, possibly, took casts in lead from another set of four bacchanalian vases that he made (examples can be viewed at Wrest Park, Drayton House, Chatsworth, and Anglesey Abbey). He worked at Kensington Palace, but his final achievements for Wren were at St. Paul's Cathedral. Here he carved, *in situ*, the giant keystones to the eight great arches under the dome, the *Phoenix* in the south pediment, and finials and other details. In 1693 was made Sculptor-in-Ordinary to William III.

Cibber was the surveyor for rebuilding the Steel Yard in London after the Great Fire and was also paid 10 pounds for "contriveing [sic] of the Sessions House" in Northampton (1683). He refused payment as architect of the German Lutheran Church in London, which he probably designed in 1672, and also for the Danish Church in Wellclose Square near the Tower of London (1694–96). The building was later demolished, but John Kip made engravings, naming Cibber as the architect, for Christian V of Denmark. Cibber donated four wooden *Saints* for the altarpiece and three lead statues of *Faith*, *Hope*, and *Charity*, which survive.

KATHARINE GIBSON

Biography

Born in Flensborg, Slesvig Holstein, Denmark, 1630. From 1647 traveled to Italy and the Netherlands; settled in England, ca.1655; from 1660 ran John Stone's workshop as foreman after Stone suffered a seizure; appointed royal sculptor by Charles II, 1667; employed by Christopher Wren to work on rebuilding of London after the Great Fire, 1682; imprisoned for debt on several occasions, but able to continue work on public commissions, private monumental sculptures, and house and garden figures; worked at Hampton Court and St. Paul's Cathedral during latter portion of life. Died in London, England, 1700.

Selected Works

ca. 1656 Chimneypiece; marble and wood; Lamport Hall, Northamptonshire, England

before 1662 Wall monuments to Anna Essington and Thomas Essington; marble; Brightwell, Suffolk, England

ca. 1668 Monument to Sir Grevill Verney; marble; Compton Verney, Warwickshire, England

1673–75 Relief on the *Monument to the Great Fire of London*; Portland stone; London, England

1677 Monument to Richard, Earl of Dorset, and Thomas Sackville; marble; Withyham Church, Sussex, England

1677–78 Busts of Charles II; terracotta; Fitzwilliam Museum, Cambridge, England; marble: private collection, England

1680 *Juno, The Four Seasons*, and two of *The Senses*; Ketton stone; Belvoir Castle, Leicestershire, England

ca. 1680 *Raving* and *Melancholy Madness*, for Bedlam Hospital gate; Portland stone; Museum of London, England

1681 *Divinity, Law, Physics*, and *Mathematics*; stone; Trinity College Library, Cambridge, England

ca. 1681 *Fountain of Four Rivers of England* with *Charles II;* Portland stone; Soho Square, London, England (Charles II still *in situ*)

1687–91 Altarpiece with *Faith* and *Justice* in Chapel: *Apollo* and *Pallas Athene* on Great Staircase; marble; the Triton Fountain; *Diana and Her Nymphs, Flora*, and *Venus:* Roche Abbey stone; Pleasure grounds, Chatsworth, Derbyshire, England

1691–96 *Triumph of Hercules over Envy;* Portland stone; Hampton Court Palace, England

1694–96 *Faith, Hope*, and *Charity*; lead; Ny Carlsberg Glyptotek, Copenhagen, Denmark

1694–96 *Moses, St. Peter, St. John the Baptist*, and *St. Paul*; wood; Danish Church, Regent's Park, London, England

1697– 1700 *Phoenix* and keystones; Portland stone; St. Paul's Cathedral, London, England

Further Reading

Blatchly, J., and G. Fisher, "Thomas Essington at Brightwell and the Identity of His Sculptor," *Proceedings of the Suffolk Institute of Archaeology and History* (2000)

Cibber, Colley, *An Apology for the Life of Mr. Colley Cibber*, London: Watts, 1740; reprint, Mineola, New York: Dover, 2000

Colvin, Howard Montagu, *A Biographical Dictionary of British Architects, 1600–1840*, London: John Murray, 1978; 3rd edition, New Haven, Connecticut: Yale University Press, 1995

Colvin, Howard Montagu, *The History of the King's Works*, 6 vols., London: HMSO, 1963–82; see especially vol. 5, *1660–1782*

Davis, John P.S., *Antique Garden Ornament: 300 Years of Creativity: Artists, Manufacturers, and Materials*, Woodbridge, Suffolk: Antique Collectors' Club, 1991

Faber, Harald, *Caius Gabriel Cibber, 1630–1700: His Life and Work*, Oxford: Clarendon Press, 1926

Gunnis, Rupert, *Dictionary of British Sculptors, 1660–1851*, London: Odhams Press, 1953; Cambridge, Massachusetts: Harvard University Press, 1954; revised edition, London: Abbey Library, 1968

Knoop, Douglas, and G.P. Jones, *The London Mason in the Seventeenth Century*, Manchester: Manchester University Press, 1935

Stewart, J. Douglas, "A Militant, Stoic Monument: The Wren-Cibber-Gibbons Charles I Mausoleum Project," in *The Restoration Mind*, edited by W. Gerald Marshall, Newark: University of Delaware Press, 1997

Whinney, Margaret, *Sculpture in Britain, 1530–1830*, London and Baltimore, Maryland: Penguin, 1964; 2nd edition, revised by John Physick, London and New York: Penguin, 1988

The Wren Society 15 (1938) and 17 (1940)

RELIEF ON THE *MONUMENT TO THE GREAT FIRE OF LONDON*

Caius Gabriel Cibber (1630–1700)

1673–1675

Portland stone

h. 5.79 m; w. 5.79 m

London, England

During the four days between 2 and 6 September 1666, fire consumed a great part of the City of London, which was then, as now, the financial hub of England. Eighty-nine churches—including St. Paul's Cathedral—400 streets, 13,200 houses, and all of the public buildings were destroyed. A catastrophe on such a devastating scale had to be commemorated. The following year, Parliament passed an act ordaining that a monument should be raised near Pudding Lane where the fire originated and that coal duty should be put toward the cost (Acts 19. Charles II.c.3). Sir Christopher Wren, surveyor of the king's works, was appointed as one of six commissioners to oversee the rebuilding of the city. He was in charge of the erection of the monument, together with Robert Hooke, the city's surveyor, and another commissioner who served in the supervisory role. Caius Gabriel Cibber was their chosen sculptor.

Relief on the *Monument to the Great Fire of London*
The Conway Library, Courtauld Institute of Art

In the renewal that followed the Great Fire, the confusion of the City's medieval buildings, which had been largely made of wood, was replaced with uniformity in brick and stone, and public buildings adopted the Classical style. John Evelyn's translation of Freart de Chambray's *Parallel of the Antient Architecture with the Modern* (1664) had illustrated Trajan's column, but Wren proposed that the monument should surpass all such columns from antiquity. The monument adopted the form of a vast Doric column made in Portland stone and topped by a flaming, gilded bronze urn. Wren had wanted a 3.66-meter (12-foot) statue of the king for the summit, but of Cibber's three alternative plans this was the most expensive, and the cheapest option was finally chosen. The column is 61.5 meters high and has 345 steps inside that lead to a public viewing gallery high beneath the urn. The city's griffins (probably subcontracted by Cibber and carved by Edward Pierce) prowl around the pedestal, which has inscriptions on three sides telling the story of the fire and the subsequent reconstruction. Cibber's relief, measuring about 5.8 meters by 5.8 meters, is on the west side. The friezelike quality may have been deliberately intended to recall the reliefs of antiquity.

The allegorical relief showing Charles II coming to the assistance of the City was executed by Cibber while he was imprisoned for debt. The records for several payments amounting to 600 pounds made to him during the years 1673–75 survive. The relief's composition resembles a history painting more than any other English picture of the period; in fact, the format is very close to an illustration from the *Pompa Triumphalis Introitus Ferdinandi Austriaci* (Pomp of the Triumphal Entry of Ferdinand of Austria) by C. Gevartius (1642), which shows Peter Paul Rubens's welcome for the Cardinal-Infante Ferdinand to Antwerp in 1635. Cibber almost certainly owned this book, as well as a copy of Cesare Ripa's collection of allegorical personifications, *Iconologia* (first published in Rome in 1603), upon which his allegories on the Monument are based. Influences from both of these books are visible in Cibber's other sculptural work.

The monument allegories can be read from left to right. The female figure of London languishes in front of her wailing citizens while the fire rages behind. She is tended by a winged Father Time and Industry with her beehive, who points with the scepter of Dexterity toward Peace (with her olive branch) and Plenty (tipping out the wealth of the land) in the sky above. In the center, a figure embodying Ripa's attributes for both Invention and Imagination, which might be termed Ingenuity, bends to help London. A complex character, she wears a winged crown of little children (revealing her inspired thoughts) and carries the small figure of a many-breasted Nature (who succors all). Her dress is inscribed "Non Aliunde," which means "Nowhere else but here." Slightly in front is Ichnografia, or Architecture, with her compass and plans for rebuilding. Behind her, Liberty waves her hat. Liberty and Ingenuity have both been associated with the lifting of the ban on foreign craftsmen working in the city after the fire. To the right, the king directs the rebuilding. He is represented as a Herculean figure dressed as a Roman victor and was identified in contemporary poetry as Caesar. Next to him is Victory or, alternatively, Mars, who has equally been identified as James, Duke of York. The Duke, like the king, had taken part in the fire fighting. Also represented are Reason and Justice, and behind them, in receding perspective, the new city rises. Envy is quelled beneath the king's feet.

Deciphering these "hieroglificks," as they were called at the time, largely defeated the contemporary public. When Ripa's *Iconologia* was first translated into English (published in 1709 but planned before Cibber's death), Cibber himself drew illustrations of the personifications, as evidenced by the signature "C.G.C. delin" (or "drawn by C.G.C."). The frontispiece shows an old man instructing a young man about the underlying meanings of the allegories on the monument.

KATHARINE GIBSON

Further Reading

Batten, M.I., "The Architecture of Dr. Robert Hooke, F.R.S.," *The Walpole Society* 25 (1937)

Moore, J.E., "The Monument; or, Christopher Wren's Roman Accent," *Art Bulletin* 80/3 (September 1998)

Robinson, Henry William (editor), *The Diary of Robert Hooke, 1672–1680*, London: Wykeham, 1938

Vertue, George, *Vertue Note Books*, 7 vols., Oxford: University Press, 1930–55; see especially vols. 1, 4, and 5

Wren, Christopher (compiler), *Parentalia; or, Memoirs of the Family of the Wrens*, London: Osborn, 1750; reprint, Farnborough, Hampshire: Gregg Press, 1965

The Wren Society 5 (1928) and 18 (1941)

CAMILLE CLAUDEL 1864–1943 *French*

In the Paris of the 1890s, Camille Claudel was considered one of the major sculptors in the age of Auguste Rodin. Those who advocated her art valued the dimension of intellectuality she brought to sculpture, thanks to the expressive and narrative technique she had developed to convey emotions and concepts.

The public arena of the Paris Salons, where Claudel first exhibited in 1885, fueled the sculptor's career. *Çacountala*, an ambitious composition contrasting the male and female nude, signaled her intellectual sophistication with its subject inspired by Hindu mythology. Undertaking the portrait bust of an eminent artist defined a sculptor's status: Claudel's *Rodin*, exhibited in 1892, confirmed the high esteem in which she was held in professional circles. Claudel studied under Rodin in the mid 1880s and set up her independent practice in 1893, never to collaborate with him again.

In the 1890s Claudel contributed sculptures on the themes of fate, love, and destiny, of death's omnipresence, and of the importance of mental and private experience. The rendering of the human body in her works is envisaged as a signifying process. In *The Waltz* the illusion of a movement freed from gravity relates thematically to the portrayal of a relationship signified in the sculpture by facial expressions and physical contact, and yet restraint. Thus, Claudel portrayed love as a spiritual as much as a physical union. She represented Fate as a woman rendered skeletal with age in a sculpture titled *Clotho* after Greek mythology. *Maturity* interrelates all these themes. A draped version of *Clotho*, placed to the left of the composition, is shown leading forward an aging man. The figure of a young woman shown kneeling to the right developed from a work Claudel had exhibited as *The Lost God*, a title referring to the myth of Psyche. *Maturity* interweaves connoted meanings and narrative. The base, an integral part of the sculpture, depicts patterns of waves rising or breaking, and the sea imagery combines with the floating drapery to evoke the image of a ghostly ship, a recurrent symbol of fate in Western art. The compositional structure itself has symbolic meaning, with the movement from right to left indicating the passage of time, while the oblique line described in space by the gaze of the young woman toward the departing group signifies the cycle of life. To make clear that the scene represented conceptual rather than visual reality, Claudel subtitled *Maturity* "*un groupe fantastique.*"

In the mid 1890s Claudel also pioneered a new mode of scenic compositions, in which small-scale figures are placed within a sculptural environment. In *The Gossip* two slabs positioned at right angles define an intimate corner where four naked women sit on opposite benches. *The Wave*, with three of these figures integrated in an environment evoking a huge wave rising vertically, similarly conveys a climate of secrecy and impending threat.

It was Claudel's capacity to transform figurative art into an imaginative experience that won her the admiration of the eminent critics of Rodin's circles such as Gustave Geffroy and Roger Marx, who in 1899 spoke of Claudel's "tragic and fantastic imagination that enthralls us." Critics who advocated her art thought that her sculptures functioned like poetry by leaving open a field of interpretation via associated ideas. Writer Octave Mirbeau saw how Claudel's work interwove Baudelairian images associating sexuality and mental suffering to evoke a state of consciousness that poignantly characterized the modern predicament.

Claudel contributed to a fundamental change in the conception of sculptural practice. Breaking with 19th-century studio practice, she carried out a greater part of the technical processes herself and demanded that originality and authorship be evaluated on the entire production of the sculpture, in particular on the carving technique she deployed.

Maturity
© Erich Lessing / Art Resource, NY

With its time-consuming method, the viability of Claudel's practice depended on her ability to obtain private sponsorship to finance the transfer of her designs into durable material. Most of her famous sculptures were commissioned by her network of clients, such as the banker Peytel and Comtesse de Maigret, or Capitaine Tissier for the 1903 bronze of *Maturity*. In the first decade of the 20th century, the art dealer Eugène Blot undertook the edition of bronze multiples of 12 of her designs.

With the reputation she had acquired as a major contributor to Symbolist art and her extensive exhibition program, which culminated in her retrospective at the gallery Blot in 1908, Claudel's career appeared highly successful. Her position in the art establishment, however, had never been secured. A difficult terrain for Claudel was the sexual dimension of her work in a period when women's claim of access to the public discourse on sexuality was considered problematic and subject to institutionalized oppression. *The Waltz*, for instance, fell under censorship from the state art administration because "the violent accent of reality which comes from it" and "the proximity of the sexes conveyed with a surprising sensuality of expression" made the work unsuitable for public display, unless the figures were covered with drapery. A different issue was her identity as Rodin's student, which made her the target of his opponents, who were anxious to argue that Rodin had failed to establish a school of sculpture. It is noticeably at the time of the dispute over Rodin's *Balzac* (1898) that Claudel fell under adverse criticism. By 1906 some of her supporters felt it urgent to call attention to the precarious situation in which Claudel now found herself. In 1913 Claudel's relatives felt that her mental illness necessitated confinement in a mental asylum. She remained institutionalized for the last 30 years of her life.

A 1951 essay written by Paul Claudel (the sculptor's brother) for the Musée Rodin exhibition catalogue marks a shift in the mode of interpretation of Claudel's work from Symbolist aesthetics to biographical. This was the prelude to the imaginative interpretations of the late 20th century, which have often sought to identify the oeuvre and the woman artist. In 1914 Rodin had agreed to Mathias Morhardt's idea that a room of his projected museum should be dedicated to Camille Claudel, to install the works that were left in her studio. This has become a reality, thanks to donations from the Claudel family and purchases, including *The Wave*, put *in situ* in 1995.

CLAUDINE MITCHELL

Biography

Born in Frère-en-Tardenois, Aisne, France, 8 December 1864. Moved to Paris with family, 1882; studied sculpture at Académie Colarossi and in independent studio shared with Jessie Lipscomb, where Alfred Boucher and Auguste Rodin came to give instruction; assistant in Rodin's workshop; relationship with Rodin broke up by 1898; took first independent Paris studio, 1888, and moved to Quai Bourbon, 1899; exhibited with several artists' associations: Societé des Artistes Français, Paris, 1885–1905; Societé Nationale des Beaux-Arts, Paris, 1892–1902; La Libre Esthétique, Brussels, Belgium, 1894; Salon d'Automne, Paris, 1904–05. Honorable Mention, Paris Salon, 1888; bronze medal, Universal Exhibition, Paris, 1900; sociétaire and juror for sculpture, Societé Nationale des Beaux-Arts, Paris, 1895. Health declined from 1906; confined to mental asylum at Ville-Evrard, 10 March 1913, eight days after her father's death; remained institutionalized for remainder of life. Died in Villeneuve-lès-Avignon, France, 19 October 1943.

Selected Works

1884   *My Brother*; bronze; Musée d'Art, Toulon, France

1888   *Çacountala*; plaster; Musée Bertrand, Châteauroux, France; cast: 1905, bronze, Musée Rodin, Paris, France

1889   *Rodin*; plaster; cast: bronze; 1892; both Musée Rodin, Paris, France

1893   *Clotho*; plaster; Musée Rodin, Paris, France; marble version: 1897 (untraced)

1894   *The Lost God*; plaster; private collection

1894–95 *Maturity*; plaster study; Musée Rodin, Paris, France; definitive plaster model: 1899 (lost); bronze versions: 1903; Musée Rodin, Paris, France; Musée d'Orsay, Paris, France

ca. 1895 *The Waltz* (second version); bronze; Musée Rodin, Paris, France

1896   *Petite Châtelaine*; marble; Musée d'Art et d'Industrie, Roubaix, France

1897   *The Gossip*; onyx, bronze; Musée Rodin, Paris, France

ca. 1898 *The Gossip*; marble; private collection, on loan to the National Museum of Women in the Arts, Washington, D.C., United States

1900   *The Wave*; onyx, bronze; Musée Rodin, Paris, France

1900–05 *Imploration*; bronze; Metropolitan Museum of Art, New York City, United States

1902   *Perseus and the Medusa*; marble; Assurances Générales de France, Paris, France

1905   *Vertumne and Pomone*; marble; Musée Rodin, Paris, France

1907   *Niobide Wounded*; bronze; Musée Sainte-Croix, Poitiers, France

Further Reading

Cassar, Jacques, *Dossier Camille Claudel*, Paris: Séguier/Archimbaud, 1987 (source documents)

Claudel, Paul, *Musée Rodin, Camille Claudel* (exhib. cat.), Paris: Aulard, 1951

Gaudichon, Bruno (editor), *Camille Claudel (1864–1943)* (exhib. cat.), Paris: Musée Rodin, 1984

Mirbeau, Octave, *Combats esthétiques*, 2 vols., edited by P. Michel and J.F. Nivet, Paris: Séguier, 1993

Mitchell, Claudine, "Intellectuality/Sexuality: Camille Claudel, the Fin de Siècle Sculptress," *Art History* 12/4 (1989)

Paris, Reine-Marie, *Camille Claudel, 1864–1943*, Paris: Gallimard, 1984; as *Camille: The Life of Camille Claudel, Rodin's Muse and Mistress*, London: Aurum, and New York: Seaver, 1988

Paris, Reine-Marie (editor), *Camille Claudel* (exhib. cat), Washington, D.C.: National Museum of Women in the Arts, 1988

Paris, Reine-Marie, and Arnaud de la Chapelle, *L'oeuvre sculpté de Camille Claudel*, Paris: Biro, 1990; new edition, 1991 (a catalogue *raisonné* with extensive bibliography) Pingeot, Anne, editor, *"L'age mûr" de Camille Claudel*, Paris: Éditions de la Réunion des Musées Nationaux, 1988

Rivière, Anne, Bruno Gaudichon, and Danielle Ghanassia, *Camille Claudel: Catalogue raisonné*, Paris: Biro, 1996; new edition, revised and augmented, 2000 (with extensive bibliography)

CLAY AND TERRACOTTA

Artists and artisans have used terracotta (hard-baked clay) uninterruptedly in sculpture and architectural decoration since prehistoric times. The continued success of this medium is due to the extreme ease with which the raw material can be modeled, its relative lightness, and, most important, its abundance. For this last reason, artists have found terracotta, like stucco, to be an excellent substitute for marble.

Terracotta is made up primarily of clay, a mixture of minerals derived from sedimentary rocks whose composition varies from place to place. These minerals are classified into four main families: chlorite, smectite, illite, and kaolinite. Two basic characteristics make them unique. First, the clay particles have the capacity to fix water molecules on their surface, so that the particles slide easily on top of each other, increasing the plasticity of the clay and making it easy to model. Second, when fired, clay hardens and becomes irreversibly compact, assuming its characteristic colors: reddish if baked in an oxidizing (oxygen-rich) atmosphere, and grayish if baked in a reducing atmosphere.

Before it reaches this advanced stage of the production process, the raw clay first goes through a long and carefully executed series of operations, starting with the choice of a clay suitable for the type of object and its final destination. During the Italian Renaissance, for instance, technical writers dwelled at length on the importance of using good-quality clay. Cipriano Piccolpasso, author of *Li tre libri del arte del vasaio* (The Three Books of the Potter's Art; 1557–58) distinguished between two different types of clay: the kind found in riverbeds (known as *belletta*) and the kind excavated from the ground at a specific depth, which he advised potters to use for particularly refined works. Likewise, the 17th-century writer Francesco Baldinucci dwelled at some length in his *Vocabolario toscano dell'arte del disegno* (Tuscan Dictionary of the Art of Drawing; 1681) on the best qualities of excavated clay, whose greatest advantage, according to Baldinucci, is that it is made up of "very minute and very uniform particles"; it could be found "in great abundance in the Montespertoli hills, 13 miles from Florence." Whatever its nature, one must adequately prepare clay before modeling and firing it. The first step was to remove leaves, pebbles, and the coarsest part of the clay, mixing the clay with water and settling out the slurry by allowing it to flow through a series of vats (generally four) set up on a slope. Workers put the last watery mixture into small open containers set out in the sun so that the excess water would evaporate. They then beat the resulting blocks of moist clay with a blade to remove air bubbles.

At this point the clay was ready to be modeled. In the 15th century this operation was the subject of a great theoretical debate, especially in Florence. After a decline in the use of terracotta during the Middle Ages, the medium bloomed once again in Florence, due to the efforts of artists such as Donatello and Luca della Robbia and architects such as Filippo Brunelleschi, who was the first to insert terracotta decorative elements in his buildings. Another architect, Leon Battista Alberti, supported and defended the validity of this technique in his treatise *De statua* (1450). In his view the essential characteristic of the terracotta process is that the material is modeled by "adding and removing, as those whom the Greek call πλαστικουζ do with wax and clay," unlike more conventional sculpture, the practitioners of whom (according to the well-known neo-Platonic idea that Michelangelo also espoused) only "remove the excess" and "bring to light the human figure they seek, which is hidden within the block of marble." In the most ancient modeling method, the potter would assemble a number of equally thick strips of clay, then press them together with his fingers. The revolutionary invention of the potter's wheel in the 3rd millennium BCE made it possible to create small objects from a single block of clay. Potters made large jars by turning the components separately on the wheel, then joining them with slip. They used the same technique to add spouts, handles, and other kinds of decoration. Sculptors likewise made statues in separate parts, usually working from the bottom up. They left the legs and arms solid, while carefully scooping out the torso and head in order to lighten the structure. Unlike works in stucco or other cold-modeled plastic mediums, a terracotta statue could not be modeled around an armature; when the piece was fired the internal structure would generate cracks that could go through to the outer surface. To solve the problem the sculptor could build a mock armature out of rags and sand, removing it just before the piece was fired. Another way to prevent the statue from bending under its own weight was to brace it with wooden supports. Sculptors formed anthropomorphic and zoomorphic objects, and other elements that could not be turned on the wheel, with molds from a cast of the marble or bronze original. This process made it possible to manufacture works in series, keeping the same quality throughout but reducing costs. In the case of reliefs sculptors made a mold of each individual section. For statues in the round and jars, the artist made two-part or "shell" molds from casts of the front and back sections. To add the finishing touches, such as the details of faces and hair, the potter would use sticks that, according to Vasari's 16th-century *Lives of the Painters, Sculptors, and Architects*, should be made "of bone, iron, or wood."

The modeled object then needed to dry out. The drying process had to be quite slow and could take as much as two weeks; it also reduced the object's volume to a degree. When the piece was dry, workers fired it in a kiln at up to 1200 degrees Celsius. After the first firing pottery is perfectly solid and quite hard; at this stage it is called "biscuit." A second firing is necessary to fix the glazes and ornamentation that distinguish different types of products. To obtain majolica, for instance, artists first waterproofed the biscuit piece with glaze and then decorated it. To make glaze the artists added potassium ash extracted from tartar deposited in wine casks to a siliceous base composed primarily of sand, next adding a lead-and-tin alloy to the mixture; the tin improved the quality of the glaze and made it more shiny. While this white coating was still wet, the artist decorated the piece with metal-oxide pigments. In the second firing the kiln temperature was around 900 degrees Celsius. The majolica technique spread through Europe as a result of the Arab conquest of Spain and was imitated with great success in the 15th century by manufacturers in Faenza, Italy, and in the 16th century at Delft, Holland.

Artists also used tin-based glaze to finish terracotta sculptures. The first sculptor to use this technique was Luca della Robbia, who worked in Florence in the second half of the 15th century. Vasari relates that della Robbia "found that coating with a glaze made of tin, *terraghetta* (crystalized lead protoxide) antimony, and other minerals and mixtures . . . created this effect extremely well and made clay works almost eternal." This method made della Robbia's works highly resistant to atmospheric agents, allowing them to be widely used as decorative elements in Brunelleschi's and Michelozzo's architecture. Moreover, sculptures and reliefs made in this way enjoyed immense success in interior decoration because the glaze gave the terracotta a dignity equivalent to that of marble. The extremely wide range of colors of della Robbia's glazes, which he obtained (as in the case of majolica) with metal oxides, added to their uniqueness. He used cobalt to produce a blue hue, copper for green, antimony for yellow, tin for white, and manganese for purple (which replaced red, the only color absent from this palette). The artist usually applied the glaze with a paintbrush. The temperature for the second firing was around 900 degrees Celsius, but always slightly lower than for the first firing. The success of this line of production, especially reliefs depicting the Virgin and Child and other works designed for popular devotion, did not end with della Robbia's death in 1482 but continued undimmed for the whole of the 16th century, due above all to Andrea della Robbia, Luca's nephew and assistant, who inherited his shop, and Luca's sons Giovanni and Gerolamo.

In more recent times artists regularly used terracotta in the production of sketches and preparatory models for large sculptural groups. In these studies the sculptor arranged the basic lines of the composition and the positions of the figures, often working with quick gestures and not bothering with the details. The sculptor would refine the details if the model was to be presented to the patron for final approval or was to guide the master's assistants in rough-cutting the block of marble. The latter practice was common in the sculpture workshops of Baroque Rome, in which different projects were often under way simultaneously. Gianlorenzo Bernini's workshop is a case in point. For the tomb of Pope Alexander VII at St. Peter's Basilica, Bernini first set out the final version of the complex structure in a series of drawings and then made terracotta models of the individual figures. Only one of these figures has survived, the beautiful figure of the pope kneeling in prayer (Victoria and Albert Museum, London), which still bears Bernini's fingerprints and the marks left by his tools. After this conceptual and preparatory phase, Bernini did none of the work on the monument himself, instead supervising his assistants who carved the marble.

Such terracotta sketches soon came to be considered true works of art and beginning in the 18th century were desired as collector's items. Some artists, including the Flemish sculptor John Michael Rysbrack and the French sculptor Clodion, chose terracotta as their principal medium. Clodion's reliefs of Greek mythological subjects reveal an extremely delicate and fresh touch, in which the evocation of Classical sculpture merges with a typical 18th-century elegance. Clodion did not use glazes or painted decoration but exploited fully the ductility of terracotta, modeling his surfaces with all the available techniques, from engraving to sculpture in the round, in order to create highly naturalistic effects.

Terracotta has been widely used in every geographic area since Antiquity. In pre-Classical Greece and Italy, builders used it to make roof tiles for temples. Except for the Classical era, when marble came to be the only material used for public buildings, this practice continued in Hellenic times and throughout the Roman age. The oldest terracotta artifacts, however, have been found in Africa: pottery from the sub-Sahara dating to around the 8th millennium BCE. The first African terracotta sculptures—the famous life-size heads created by the Nok tribe in what is now northern Nigeria—date to the 5th century BCE. In China artisans used terracotta as early as the 6th millennium BCE. The first funerary statuettes date from the 5th century BCE. The huge army of 7,000 life-size terracotta warriors, with their horses and carts, discovered in the 1970s near the tomb of the Emperor Ch'in Shih Huang Ti at Lintong, dates from the end of the 3rd century BCE.

A ceramic material made from clay, porcelain was invented in China in the 9th century BCE. Porcelain consists of a mixture of kaolin, feldspar, and a small percentage of quartz. Kaolin, a type of fine clay, takes on a white color and does not melt at even the highest temperatures, but feldspar does melt (binding together all other elements), and quartz makes the porcelain glossy and more cohesive. Porcelain is fired at temperatures from 1400 to 1500 degrees Celsius, and one uses the same metal oxides to color porcelain as for terracotta. Marco Polo (1254–1324) described porcelain in his account of his travels to Cathay, and Jesuit missionaries first brought white porcelain to Europe at the end of the 16th century. The secret of its composition was discovered in the West only at the beginning of the 18th century, by the German alchemist Johann Friedrich Böttger.

CRISTIANO GIOMETTI

See also **Bernini, Gianlorenzo; Clodion (Claude Michel); Donatello; Robbia, della, Family; Michelangelo (Buonarroti); Rysbrack, Michael**

Further Reading

Alberti, Leon Battista, *On Painting, and On Sculpture: The Latin Texts of De Pictura and De Statua* (bilingual Latin-English edition), edited and translated by Cecil Grayson, London: Phaidon, 1972
Baldinucci, Filippo, *Vocabolario toscano dell'arte del disegno*, Florence: Santi Franchi, 1681; reprint, Florence: Studio per Edizioni Scelte, 1975
Gentilini, Giancarlo (editor), *I Della Robbia e l'arte nuova della scultura invetriata* (exhib. cat.), Florence: Giunti, 1999
Maltese, Corrado (compiler), *Le tecniche artistiche*, Milan: U. Mursia, 1973
Penny, Nicholas, *The Materials of Sculpture*, New Haven, Connecticut: Yale University Press, 1993
Piccolpasso, Cipriano, *Li tre libri dell'arte del vasaio* (1557), edited by Giovanni Conti, Florence: All'Insegna del Giglio, 1976; as *The Three Books of the Potter's Art; I tre libri dell'arte del vasaio* (bilingual English-Italian edition), 2 vols., translated by Ronald Lightbown and Alan Caiger-Smith, London: Scolar Press, 1980
Vaccari, Maria Grazia, *La scultura in terracotta: tecniche e conservazione*, Florence: Centro Di, 1996
Vasari, Giorgio, *Le vite de più eccellenti architetti, pittori, e scultori italiani*, 3 vols., Florence: Torrentino, 1550; 2nd edition, Florence: Apresso i Giunti, 1568; as *Lives of the Painters, Sculptors, and Architects*, 2 vols., translated by Gaston du C. de Vere (1912), edited by David Ekserdjian, New York: Knopf, and London: Campbell, 1996

(JEAN-BAPTISTE) AUGUSTE CLÉSINGER 1814–1883 *French*

A prominent French sculptor of the Second Republic (1848–52) and Second Empire (1852–70), Auguste Clésinger made a successful career without following the usual academic paths. Hard working and largely self-taught, Clésinger in his sculpture mined a vein of sensuality that appealed to many patrons during the pleasure-seeking Second Empire. In the long run, however, Clésinger's imaginative limitations and need for money forced him into a pattern of repetition that wearied both the critics and the public.

Clésinger's father, Georges-Philippe Clésinger, was a professor of drawing and sculpture at the local art academy in Besançon; his work habits, reportedly rapid and facile, may have influenced his son's artistic approach. Auguste Clésinger's desultory training included little formal academic education. In 1832 the patronage of Cardinal de Rohan-Chabot, archbishop of Besançon, enabled the 17-year-old Auguste and his father to travel to Rome, where they remained for a year and a half. Auguste worked for a time in the studio of the famous Neoclassical sculptor Bertel Thorwaldsen and studied drawing with the architect Gaspare Salvi; he also greatly admired the work of Michelangelo Buonarroti. Already, however, Clésinger showed a tendency toward lack of discipline, and little of his work survives from this period.

Following his return to Besançon, Clésinger began an extended period wandering Europe, probably occasioned by his mounting debts. Stays in Switzerland alternated with his enlistment in the French army; posted for a time to Paris, he worked briefly in the studio of David d'Angers. From Florence in 1843 Clésinger sent his first exhibition piece, a portrait bust, to the Paris Salon. Established in Paris by 1845, he gradually became friendly with an influential circle of art critics and patrons.

Clésinger created a sensation at the Salon of 1847 with his life-size marble *Woman Bitten by a Snake*, establishing a major reputation virtually overnight. The voluptuous, naturalistic nude figure, writhing in agony or ecstasy, was seen by some as revitalizing the tired conventions of academic sculpture and by others as a descent into vulgarity. The conservative critic Gustave Planche accused Clésinger, with some justice, of having molded the figure from his model, the well-known courtesan Apollonie Sabatier. This figure and a contemporary marble bust of Mme Sabatier in the guise of a Rococo nymph (1847; Musée d'Orsay, Paris) show Clésinger at his best: an artist with a superb natural facility for carving marble. Clésinger's notoriety surpassed for a time that of his principal rival in sculpting the female nude, the older academician James Pradier.

An opportunist who supported all the changing political regimes of his time, Clésinger in 1848 offered the new Republican government a monumental bust of *Liberty* (for the Hôtel de Ville, Paris) and a statue of *Fraternity* that was erected in the Champ de Mars, Paris (both destroyed). Later he had no qualms about executing an equestrian bronze of Napoléon III and, for the birth of the prince imperial, a marble *Infant Hercules Strangling the Snakes of Envy*. Named a chevalier of the Legion of Honor under the Republic, Clésinger was made an officer under Napoléon III in 1864. Clésinger also made an advantageous marriage

to Solange-Gabrielle Dudevant, daughter of the celebrated novelist George Sand, but the couple separated in 1852.

Clésinger's colossal plaster equestrian statue of Francis I for the courtyard of the Musée du Louvre, Paris, was severely criticized and never cast in bronze. The sculptor responded by moving to Rome in 1856, living there in grand style for eight years and making numerous variants on his most successful earlier compositions. At this time and later, with expiring *Cleopatras, Lucretias,* or *Magdalens,* Clésinger sought to trade on the fame of the *Woman Bitten by a Snake*, although the eroticism of the later works was somewhat more restrained. He also produced many bust-length versions of his full-length female figures. In some works he experimented with the then rare technique of polychrome sculpture, including semiprecious stones (e.g., *Cleopatra before Caesar*). The best works emerging from his time in Rome are probably his animal subjects, such as the *Roman Bull*. Clésinger also sent to the Paris Salon landscape paintings of scenes in the Roman Campagna, executed in a rough and naturalistic style.

After his return to Paris, Clésinger continued to work on a limited range of themes, such as that of a nude woman riding a wild animal; his *Triumph of Ariadne* was praised by the critic Théophile Gautier as the outstanding sculptural work of the era. Short of money, Clésinger arranged for the auction sale of the entire contents of his studio in 1868 and 1870; the catalogue of the latter sale was one of the first photo-illustrated auction catalogues. Despite the failure of his Francis I statue, he continued to be flooded with state commissions for bronze equestrian figures, including a *Charlemagne* (destroyed), although his works in this genre seem heavy and unoriginal. At the time of his death, he was working on four equestrian figures of French generals—completing the figures of Marceau and Kléber—and a Marquis de Lafayette (never completed) for the United States.

Critics and the public largely ignored Clésinger's later Salon submissions. Many of his later pieces, although extremely well carved, suffer from a lack of expressive power. His prolific creation of close variants of his compositions has also led to confusion in identifying specific works.

Alexander Estignard, Clésinger's principal biographer, balanced a realistic evaluation of the sculptor's vanity and careerism with an appreciation for the artist's genuine instinct for marble carving. Despite his limited creative range, Clésinger was outstanding in sculpting the nude female figure; many of his early portrait busts, such as the faunlike bust of Charles Weiss, shown at the 1845 Salon, and the impetuous artist-portrait of Thomas Couture, also possess a great

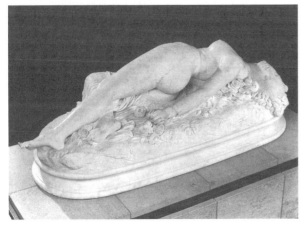

Woman Bitten by a Snake
© Giraudon / Art Resource, NY

vitality. It is inaccurate to find a revival of the Rococo style in Clésinger's work; his sculpture embodies a heavier, less playful 19th-century eroticism. He does, however, anticipate by almost a generation the naturalism and energy associated with the work of Jean-Baptiste Carpeaux.

DONALD A. ROSENTHAL

Biography

Born in Besançon, France, 22 October 1814. Son and pupil of sculptor Georges-Philippe Clésinger. Intermittent studies with Bertel Thorvaldsen and Gaspare Salvi in Rome, Pierre-Jean David d'Angers in Paris; traveled to Paris, 1838; in Switzerland, 1840; in Florence, 1843; back to Paris, 1845; befriended the critic Théophile Gautier and other literary figures; second-class medal at Salon for *Woman Bitten by a Snake*, 1847; first-class medal at Salon, 1848; Chevalier of the Legion of Honor, 1849, and Officier, 1864; lived in Rome, Italy, 1856–64; continued to exhibit at the Paris Salon until 1883. Died in Paris, France, 6 January 1883.

Selected Works

1845   Bust of Charles Weiss; marble; Bibliothèque Municipale, Besançon, France

1847   Bust of Mme Sabatier; marble; Musée d'Orsay, Paris, France

1847   *Woman Bitten by a Snake*; marble; Musée d'Orsay, Paris, France

1848   Bust of Thomas Couture; bronze; Los Angeles County Museum of Art, California, United States; Musée Nationale du Château, Compiègne, France

1848   *Liberty* and *Fraternity* (destroyed)

1853–55 Equestrian statue of Francis I; plaster (destroyed)

1857   *Infant Hercules Strangling the Snakes of Envy*; marble (destroyed)

1858   *Roman Bull*; marble; formerly Palais du Luxembourg, Paris, France

1859–66 Equestrian statue of Napoléon III; bronze; Chislehurst Castle, Chislehurst, France

1866   *Triumph of Ariadne*; marble; Musée de Picardie, Amiens, France

1868   *Cleopatra before Caesar*; polychrome marble; formerly Desfossés collection, Paris, France

1882   Equestrian statue of General Marceau and General Kléber; bronze; École Militaire Saint-Cyr, Coëtquidan, France

Further Reading

Estignard, Alexander, *Clésinger, sa vie, ses oeuvres*, Paris: Floury, 1900

Fusco, Peter, "Jean-Baptiste, called Auguste Clésinger," in *The Romantics to Rodin: French Nineteenth-Century Sculpture from North American Collections* (exhib. cat.), Los Angeles: Los Angeles County Museum of Art, and New York: Braziller, 1980

Lindsay, Susanne G., "Jean-Baptiste Clésinger," in *The Second Empire, 1852–1870: Art in France under Napoleon III* (exhib. cat.), Philadelphia, Pennsylvania: Philadelphia Museum of Art, 1978

Pingeot, Anne, "Clésinger, (Jean-Baptiste) Auguste," in *The Dictionary of Art*, edited by Jane Turner, vol. 7, New York: Grove, and London: Macmillan, 1996

Thomas-Maurin, Frédérique, "Clésinger, Jean-Baptiste (gen. Auguste)," in *Allgemeines Künstlerlexikon: Die bildenden Künstler aller Zeiten und Völker*, vol. 19, Munich: Saur, 1998

CLODION (CLAUDE MICHEL) 1738–1814 *French*

"Le sculpteur des grâces" (the sculptor of grace)—this is how Clodion is described in the "Lettre d'un Italian sur l'exposition de 1779" in the *Mercure de France* (1779), and it perhaps remains the most accurate description of the sculptor's work. In fact, little is known about Clodion. Having worked primarily in terracotta and for private collectors, the trajectory of his career does not appear in the public record. Dates for his works are uncertain, and attributions are frequently problematic. Yet it is the same uncertainties that give rise to Clodion's unique status in the 18th century. Rather than striving for monumental greatness through l'Académie Royale de Peinture et Sculpture (the Royal Academy) and the Salon, Clodion worked to create beauty and pleasure for amateurs, and his works embodied the charm of the Ancien Régime, a quality approvingly noted by the Goncourts.

Claude Michel was born in Nancy, France, in 1738 and was quickly known simply by the diminutive, Clodion. He was the tenth child of Thomas Michel and Anne Adam, sister to sculptors Lambert-Sigisbert, Nicolas-Sébastien, and François-Gaspard Adam. Lambert-Sigisbert trained Clodion and at least three of his brothers, who also became sculptors and made livings imitating their more inventive and skilled sibling. Under his uncle's tutelage, Clodion competed for the Prix de Rome and lost in 1757 and 1758. In 1759 Lambert-Sigisbert Adam died, and Clodion apprenticed briefly to Jean-Baptiste Pigalle before winning the Prix de Rome in the same year.

Before traveling to Rome, Clodion entered the École Royale des Élèves Protégés in Paris. The school, founded by the *directeur des bâtiments du roi* (director of buildings of the king) Charles-François-Paul-Lenormant de Tournehem and the *directeur de l'académie* Charles-Antoine Coypel in 1748, provided young students with further artistic and intellectual training before their time in Rome. The instruction included studies in history and literature, particularly in the classics, which provided the framework for the still-nascent Neoclassical style. The government expected that students then would be able better to assimilate the glories of Rome and produce works for the state.

Clodion's career, however, took a different path. By the time he arrived in Rome in 1762, after three years of study at the École Royale, he had already established an important private clientele, including the famous collector and amateur Pierre-Jean Mariette. While there, rather than working exclusively or even primarily toward the *morceau de réception* (reception piece) that would ensure his admission into the Royal Academy, Clodion cultivated private commissions. His first biographer claimed that during the sculptor's time in Rome "people sought out his charming works, some inspired by the antique. . . . They were purchased even before they were finished." This is not to say that his state education did not shape the sculptor's oeuvre. His vase with five women offering sacrifice (1766) shows Clodion's absorption of the codes of Neoclassicism, particularly the *goût grecque* (Greek taste) in the style of the painter Joseph-Marie Vien. Clodion's terracotta interpretation of *Minerva* demonstrates the influence of ancient sculpture, particularly the *Minerva Giustiniani* in the Vatican collections in Rome. Yet the sculptor also combined attributes of the stern warrior—*Minerva*'s shield and helmet—with the beauty and charm of her face and body. Souvenir copies of ancient sculpture for those making the Grand Tour were common work for the *pensionnaires* of the French Academy in Rome, but in his work Clodion always reinterpreted rather than imitated the glories of the ancient past, suffusing them with his own sense of grace. The *Minerva* notably entered the collection of Jacques-Onésyme Bergeret, one of the most important collectors of the time, who also favored the works of Jean-Honoré Fragonard and François Boucher. By the time that the *directeur des bâtiments du roi*, the Comte Marigny, ordered Clodion to return to Paris in 1771, the sculptor was hardly a typical ward of the state.

When Clodion was made *agréé* (admitted) of the Académie Royale in 1773, Catherine the Great had already tried unsuccessfully to lure him to be her court sculptor. As *agréé* Clodion received the privilege of exhibiting in the state-sponsored Paris Salons, and he showed eight works the same year, including *The River Rhine Separating the Waters*. He also established a successful workshop in the Place Louis XV. Although Clodion would never become a full academician, having never bothered to complete the *morceau de récep-*

tion, (a piece submitted as part of the requirement for membership), he did receive at least one important crown commission, that for the sculpture of *Montesquieu* for the *directeur des bâtiments du roi* marquis d'Angiviller's Great Men of France project. When Clodion exhibited his plaster model, now lost, in 1779, the work was harshly criticized; yet when the marble version of *Montesquieu* appeared at the Salon of 1783, it was a great success. His fine technique in carving was particularly praised, proving that Clodion, despite his preference for the immediacy of terracotta, was more than competent in the use of marble.

Clodion spent most of the revolutionary period away from Paris, in his hometown of Nancy, and after the *Montesquieu* it was not until the 1801 Salon that he displayed in the official sanctioned exhibition again. Upon his return to Paris, Clodion still produced small-scale intricate terracotta works on themes of love, such as his *Zephyrus and Flora* for his private collectors, but he had also developed a more grim and severe style, suitable for public work of the era. When he did exhibit again it was with *Deluge*, a life-size plaster study of four reactions to the biblical flood, which seems closer to Théodore Géricault's interpretation of the same subject than to any of Clodion's previous work. And it was a style that earned Clodion state commissions such as the *Cato*, intended for Napoléon's Gallery of the Consuls in the Palais des Tuileries, and work for Napoléon on the Vendôme Column. Clodion remains better known, however, for his light-hearted works that evoke Fragonard and the Rococo rather than this stoic Neoclassical work. As one critic summed up the essence of Clodion, his nymphs, satyrs, and bacchantes, "His interest in Antiquity is *au fond* liberty of spirit; his religion is the need for love."

DENISE AMY BAXTER

See also **Adam Family**

Biography

Born in Nancy, Meurthe-et-Moselle, France, 20 December 1738. Tenth child born to Thomas Michel and Anne Adam, sister to sculptors Lambert-Sigisbert, Nicolas-Sébastien, and François-Gaspard Adam. At least three brothers also became sculptors and were trained by their uncle Lambert-Sigisbert Adam. Upon his uncle's death, Clodion was apprenticed briefly to Jean-Baptiste Pigalle; won the Prix de Rome, 1759; studied at École Royale des Elèves Protégés, Paris; spent nine years in Rome, 1762–71, befriending Johan Tobias Sergel and sharing studio with Jean-Antoine Houdon; ordered to return to Paris by the marquis de Marigny, *directeur des bâtiments du roi*, 1771; *agréé* in l'Académie Royale de Peinture et Sculpture, 1773; established workshop in the Place Louis XV, but never produced a *morceau de réception*; married Catherine-Flore Pajou, daughter of the sculptor, 1781; left Paris for Nancy, *ca.* 1793–98, but ultimately returned to Paris. Died in Paris, France, 28 March 1814.

Selected Works

1765   *The River Rhine Separating the Waters*; terracotta; Kimbell Art Museum, Fort Worth, Texas, United States

1766   *Minerva*; terracotta; Metropolitan Museum of Art, New York City, United States

1766   Satyr with two bacchantes and baby satyr; terracotta; Frick Collection, New York City, United States

1767   *Penitent Magdalen*; terracotta; Musée du Louvre, Paris, France

1772–73 *Mausoleum for Ninette*; terracotta; Musée Historique Lorrain, Nancy, France

1777   *Saint Cecilia*; marble; Notre-Dame Cathedral, Rouen, France

ca. 1780 *Satyr and Bacchante*; terracotta; Metropolitan Museum of Art, New York City, United States

1782   *Pan and Syrinx; pierre de Tonnerre* (limestone); Musée du Louvre, Paris, France

1783   *Montesquieu*; marble; Musée du Louvre, Paris, France

1784–85 *Montgolfier Balloon Project*; terracotta; Metropolitan Museum of Art, New York City, United States

1799   *Zephyrus and Flora*; terracotta; Frick Collection, New York City, United States

1800   *Deluge*; terracotta; Boston Museum of Fine Arts, Massachusetts, United States

1804   *Cato*; plaster; Sénat, Palais du Luxembourg, Paris, France

Further Reading

Draper, James David, "French Terracottas," *The Metropolitan Museum of Art Bulletin* 49 (1991–92)

Levey, Michael, *Painting and Sculpture in France, 1700–1789*, New Haven, Connecticut: Yale University Press, 1993

Poulet, Anne L., *Clodion Terracottas: In North American Collections*, New York: Frick Collection, 1984

Poulet, Anne L., "Clodion's Sculpture of the Déluge," *Journal of the Museum of Fine Arts, Boston* 3 (1991)

Poulet, Anne L., et al., *Clodion, 1738–1814*, Paris: Réunion des Musées Nationaux, 1992

West, Alison Elizabeth, *From Pigalle to Préault: Neoclassicism and the Sublime in French Sculpture, 1760–1840*, Cambridge and New York: Cambridge University Press, 1998

PAN AND SYRINX RELIEF
1782

pierre de Tonnerre (limestone)
h. 1.04 m
Musée du Louvre, Paris, France

The graceful style of Claude Michel, better known by the diminutive, Clodion, epitomized the spirit of sculpture in the age of Louis XVI. Yet despite winning the Prix de Rome, attending the École Royale des Élèves Protégés, and sojourning for approximately ten years at the French Academy at Rome, Clodion eschewed the traditional state-sponsored career of a sculptor in France, never becoming an *academicien* and focusing instead on private works for educated amateurs, of which his elegant *Pan and Syrinx* relief for Baron Peter-Josef-Victor de Besenval is a supreme example.

The *Pan and Syrinx*, now in the Musée du Louvre, Paris, was commissioned originally as a part of the decorative scheme of the *salle de bains* (bathing room) of the l'hôtel Besenval in the Saint-Germain district of Paris, now the Swiss Embassy. Besenval himself, lieutenant general of the king's armies, was one of the great patrons of the arts of 18th-century France. He was passionate about the arts and became an amateur member of the Académie Royale. A friend of Marie Antoinette and of the comte d'Artois, for whom Clodion would also produce reliefs for the dining room of his château de Maisons, Besenval was known in particular for his collection of eroticized Neoclassical themes by Joseph-Marie Vien and Jean Honoré Fragonard, among others.

Besenval engaged the architect Alexandre-Théodore Brongniart to build a *salle de bains* complex in the basement of his hotel, which would be completed in 1782. Surprisingly, the architect's preparatory drawings for the project still exist and indicate that the room was intended as an interpretation of an ancient bath. The design was united by a Tuscan colonnade and had as its focal point a round basin, the spigot for which was decorated with the figure of a sleeping nymph.

Pan and Syrinx relief
© R.G. Ojeda. Réunion des Musées Nationaux / Art Resource, NY

Clodion's subject of Pan and Syrinx is also ancient in origin, coming from Ovid's *Metamorphoses*. In Ovid's account, Syrinx was a virginal nymph devoted to Diana. She fled from the amorous pursuits of Pan and, when the River Ladon blocked her escape, cried out to the gods to preserve her. In response, she was transformed into the reeds that form Pan's flute. Clodion's *Pan and Syrinx*, however, functions within a larger decorative framework. In the first of the two panels, Venus disarms Cupid on the left side of the composition, holding him back by the wings while two of her nymphs grasp his bow. This image is separated by a tree from the right side of the relief, which consists of a scene of Leda trying to fend off the approaches of Jupiter, who is in the guise of a swan. Cupid again looks on; a finger is pressed to his mouth, indicating discretion. Cupid appears again in the *Pan and Syrinx* relief, looking on as the frustrated Pan grasps the reeds into which the beloved nymph has been transformed while the sisters of Syrinx flee.

Indeed, although Pan and Syrinx's history derives from Ovid, Clodion has given the reliefs as a group a larger theme not found in the *Metamorphoses*: the triumphant power of love. In the first scene, although held back by Venus, Cupid appears to aid Jupiter in his pursuit of Leda; in the second, he both raises Pan's desire and vanquishes it. The reign of love and the licentious possibilities of the Neoclassical are then augmented by Clodion's decorative vases with reliefs of nymphs, satyrs, and bacchantes, which flanked each of the reliefs.

The theme of a battle between Pan and Cupid is not of Clodion's own invention and may well be one with which he would have been familiar from his student days. The subject is treated in Bernard de Montfaucon's *Antiquité expliquée et représentée en figures*, a text thought to have been taught at the École Royale des Élèves Protégés during the sculptor's tenure. Furthermore, in addition to works that Clodion might have encountered in person during his years in Rome, an image from Herculaneum of the subject is reproduced in the famous and often-consulted *Le Pitture antiche d'Ercolano*. More generally, the theme of Pan and Syrinx, although not always under the watch of Cupid, was a popular one in 18th-century sculpture. Clodion would have been well aware of other sculptors' interpretations of the subject. He chose, however, to model his figures of Pan and Syrinx fairly closely on Nicolas Poussin's rendition of the subject, with which Clodion would have been familiar from the 1724 publication of Bernard Picart's engraving of the painting. In style and composition, it also fits self-consciously into the history of French decorative sculpture. The influence, in particular, of works such as François Girardon's *Bain des Nymphes* (1668–70) at the Château of Ver-

sailles—with similarities in both figural groupings and general compositional elements—is evident.

Yet despite the range of influences that Clodion amalgamated in his *Pan and Syrinx*, he successfully made the work his own. For instance, in revising Girardon's *Bain des Nymphes*, Clodion included a serious attention to the details of nature not often found in contemporary sculpture. *Pierre de Tonnerre* was a notoriously difficult stone to carve with such detail, and the combination of his eloquent rendering of the *Pan and Syrinx* relief with his marble *Montesquieu*, done within one year of one another, should be seen as Clodion's conscientious attempt to demonstrate his skill in the material typically used in the monumental works of state commissions.

The lithe figures of the nymphs—with their almond-shaped eyes, straight noses, and graceful postures—fleeing Pan epitomize Clodion's style, in which he illuminates the pleasures of the antique. In keeping with the purposes of the room—for bathing—he has created a scene by the river. In keeping with its libertine nature, he has depicted the triumphs of love. The *Pan and Syrinx* stands in opposition to the public strains of stoic Neoclassicism and service to the state best known through the paintings of Jacques-Louis David and instead creates an idyllic scene for the private room of an individual client in one of the last manifestations of the taste of the Ancien Régime.

DENISE AMY BAXTER

Further Reading

Scherf, Guilhem, "Un chef-d'oeuvre de Clodion," *Connaissance des arts* (April 1992)

Scherf, Guilhem (editor), *Clodion et la sculpture française de la fin du XVIIIe siècle*, Paris: La Documentation Française, 1993

CLOISTERS CROSS (BURY ST. EDMUNDS CROSS)

Anonymous

mid 12th century

walrus ivory

h. 57.5 cm; w. 36.2 cm

Metropolitan Museum of Art, The Cloisters Collection, New York City, United States

The Cloisters Cross, a Latin cross form, is composed of five pieces of *morse* (walrus) ivory carved with nearly 100 figures and more than 60 inscriptions. Some traces of polychromy remain. The corpus (body of the crucified Christ) and the base plaque are missing. Carved on the front, back, and edges, the cross was intended to be viewed, at least occasionally, in the round. It is one of three medieval ivory crosses to survive, and it probably functioned as a processional cross that could be detached from its holder and set into a base on an altar.

The front, carved as a *Tree of Life*, displays angels holding a central medallion with *Moses and the Brazen Serpent* raised up before the Israelites, saints, and prophets. The hand of God extends from the *titulus* (inscription above Christ on the cross), and the high priest Caiaphas and Pontius Pilate debate above. Nearly square plaques at the terminals represent scenes from Holy Week and Easter, including the *Deposition/ Lamentation*, the *Holy Women at the Tomb/Resurrection*, and later the *Ascension*. The *Nativity* was possibly depicted on the now-missing lower plaque. Scrolls held by the figures bear quotations from the Scriptures, identifying the individuals and presenting commentary on the scenes. Adam and Eve cling to the foot of the cross.

On the back in the central medallion supported by angels the personification of Synagogue is about to pierce the Lamb of God with a spear as St. John the Evangelist mourns and Jeremiah, an angel, and a monk hold inscribed scrolls. The terminal plaques display the winged beasts symbolizing the four Evangelists. (The Winged Man of Matthew is missing.) Prophets, identified by inscriptions and holding scrolls with biblical quotations, populate the shaft (as busts) and the crossbar. The sides of the shaft and the edges are engraved with Latin couplets: "The earth trembles, Death defeated groans with the buried one rising. / Life has been called, Synagogue has collapsed with great foolish effort," and "Cham laughs when he sees the naked private parts of his parent. / The Jews laughed at the pain of God dying." The Greek and Latin of the *titulus* read "Jesus of Nazareth, King of the Confessors," whereas the pseudo-Hebrew is undeciphered.

The Cloisters Cross, generally considered a product of 12th-century England and possibly made at Bury St. Edwards Abbey in East Anglia, has engendered much controversy over its provenance, date, and iconographic program. In spite of an abundance of scholarship, divergent opinions persist. The cross has been dated from the mid 11th century to around 1200. In 1989 a carbon 14 test of the ivory was performed. The result placed the walrus tusk in the last quarter of the 7th century, thereby leaving scholars to rely on other methods to date the carving.

Before its acquisition by the Metropolitan Museum of Art, New York City, in 1963, the cross was attributed to England on iconographic and stylistic grounds. Thomas Hoving proposed the localization to Bury St. Edmunds, finding stylistic parallels between the cross and illuminations of the Bury Bible by Master Hugo (Corpus Christi College, Cambridge, *ca.* 1135) and in later works of Bury provenance. In studies of the in-

The Metropolitan Museum of Art, The Cloisters Collection, New York City, United States

scriptions, Sabrina Longland found the Bury St. Edmunds connections inconclusive (see Longland, 1969). Several other scholars have refuted the Bury attribution, including Ursula Nilgen, Willibald Sauerländer, and T.A. Heslop (see Nilgen, 1985; Sauerländer, 1971; and Heslop, 1994). Although the localization to Bury St. Edmunds cannot be proved unequivocally, Parker and Little present arguments for this attribution in the mid 12th century based on iconographic and stylistic analysis as well as the liturgical and intellectual context likely to produce the cross (see Parker and Little, 1994).

The complexity of the cross's iconographic program and its dramatic narrative style find closer parallels to monumental works than small-scale liturgical objects. The plaques and medallions are crammed with figures creating composite scenes with unusual iconographic features. The Passion narrative of St. John's Gospel dominates the obverse of the Cloisters Cross, whereas the apocalyptic vision informs the reverse. The iconographic program emphasizes the sacramental meaning of the True Cross within a typological framework. Parker and Little consider the person responsible for the program to have been a Benedictine monk. More specifically, they identify two monastic scholars as probable sources of inspiration: St. Anselm of Bec, archbishop of Canterbury, and Hugh of St.-Victor. The carvings of the cross, texts, and images are thoroughly integrated, displaying liturgical and typological associations that would have been familiar to a monastic audience.

Parker and Little suggest that perhaps the corpus was detached on Good Friday, as was the practice with life-size wood corpora used in the later medieval *Depositio Crucis* rite (an optional rite that represents the removal of Christ's body from the cross and its burial). The fully carved central medallion indicates that the missing corpus might not have been attached permanently, allowing occasions for unobstructed views of the medallion and the front inscription. Evidence of repeated mountings of a corpus supports this hypothesis; several holes indicate original points of attachment of hands to the crossbar, and the shaft is damaged where a *suppedaneum* (footrest) for the feet was attached. Although the Oslo corpus (late 12 century, Kunstindustrimuseet, Oslo, Norway) was displayed affixed to the Cloisters Cross during two exhibitions in the 1970s, it is now considered to be from a later period. (Similarly, the plaque of Christ before Caiaphas, also in the Cloisters Collection and once thought to be the missing base plaque, is no longer affiliated with the cross.)

Several features have led many authors to view the Cloisters Cross as anti-Semitic or even as an object created to persuade the local Jewish population to convert to Christianity. Such features include the prominent inscriptions, Synagogue's spear at the Lamb's breast, and some figures wearing conical hats typically seen in medieval derogatory images of Jews. Parker and Little argue that consideration of the broader social context, particularly intellectual disputes between Christians and Jews, refutes the opinion that the cross was conceived as a polemic against contemporary Jews. A sophisticated liturgical object, the cross was not likely designed for the additional purpose of either castigating or converting the small Jewish population in England in the mid 12th century. To the contrary, part of its message for its monastic audience may have included a spiritual identification within the liturgy with the Jews present at the Crucifixion.

LESLIE BUSSIS TAIT

Further Reading

Heslop, T.A., [book review of Parker and Little's *The Cloisters Cross*], *The Burlington Magazine* 136 (1994)

Hoving, Thomas P.F., "The Bury St. Edmunds Cross," *Metropolitan Museum of Art Bulletin* 22 (1964)

Lasko, Peter, "Altar Cross," and "Christ before Pilate," in *English Romanesque Art, 1066–1200* (exhib. cat.), edited by George Zarnecki, Janet Holt, and Tristram Holland, London: Weidenfeld and Nicolson, 1984

Longland, Sabrina, "A Literary Aspect of the Bury St. Edmunds Cross," *Metropolitan Museum of Art Journal* 2 (1969)

Nilgen, Ursula, "Das grosse Walrossbeinkreuz in den 'Cloisters,'" *Zeitschrift für Kunstgeschichte* 48 (1985)

Parker, Elizabeth C., and Charles T. Little, *The Cloisters Cross: Its Art and Meaning*, London: Miller, and New York: Metropolitan Museum of Art, 1994

Sauerländer, Willibald, "Exhibition Review of 'The Year 1200,'" *Art Bulletin* 53 (1971)

ALEXANDER COLIN ca. 1526–1612
Flemish, active in Austria

Alexander Colin belongs to the group of itinerant artists who spread the Renaissance style throughout Europe beginning in the middle of the 16th century. It is not known whether he spent his apprentice years in Italy, as did the Dutch sculptors of the next generation—Hubert Gerhard and Adriaen de Vries—and as did his contemporary Johann Gregor van der Schardt. Colin's knowledge of Renaissance forms may well have instead come from graphic sources.

The first work that can be positively attributed to Colin is the Ottheinrich building of Heidelberg Castle. According to his contract he was to make its mullions, doorframes, fireplaces, and 14 figures, for which he followed a *Visierung*, that is, designs sketched by another artist. He executed the decorative stonework in a modern manner, in line with the so-called Floris style (featuring ornate or fantastic features that signaled a break from the prevailing Gothic style); the cartouche appeared here for the first time in Germany. Despite the somewhat rigid demeanor of the figures of the deities, they acquire a special significance within the facade's ensemble of forms since they go beyond pure architectural decoration. The Ottheinrich building, whose special magnificence stems from its sculptural decorations, is one of the most important pieces of Renaissance architecture in Germany. Although the palace was largely destroyed in the 17th century, its facade remains a much-admired architectural and sculptural masterpiece.

After Ottheinrich's death Colin returned to his hometown of Mecheln. In 1562 he entered the services of the Holy Roman emperor, Ferdinand I, and moved to Innsbruck. There, as a stone sculpture specialist, he participated in one of the greatest projects of the northern Renaissance: the tomb of Emperor Maximilian I (d. 1519), which had been planned since the start of the 16th century. By 1562 the 28 bronze over-life-size ancestral figures had been completed, five of which were made according to Albrecht Dürer's designs. By the time Colin joined the project, artists were working on the 24 alabaster reliefs for the tomb. The sculptor

Arnold Abel, who had recruited Colin in Mecheln, had begun this work with his brother Bernhard according to the designs of their other brother, Florian. The three Abel brothers, however, only partially completed three reliefs. After their deaths in 1563 and 1564, Colin took over responsibility for all of the sculptural work on the monument.

By 1564 Colin and several assistants completed the relief cycle with episodes from the life of Maximilian I, carved according to drawings by Florian Abel. The multifigured pictorial panels exhibit fine and detailed work. Their rich pictorial effect and depth of perspective are astonishing, and they are considered to be Colin's major work.

Colin was not only a specialist in stone sculpture but also created the models for bronze casts for the Maximilian monument. The first to be realized was the trophy frieze, for which Colin clarified Abel's richly detailed designs. Hans Christoph Löffler made the bronze cast in Innsbruck in 1565. From 1564 to 1570 Colin created the bronze figures of the four cardinal virtues—*Temperance*, *Justice*, *Fortitude*, and *Prudence*—referring to the emperor's virtues as a ruler. These female figures, which crown the four corners of the tomb, deviate from Florian Abel's design of caryatids. The calm seated figures, wrapped in richly folded robes, show the influence of Italian High Renaissance models (e.g., Andrea Sansovino) and of figures from the French royal tombs in the Abbey of Saint-Denis. Colin may have studied these during one of his journeys back home. In 1569 Colin received the commission for the crowning figure of the kneeling emperor. He served as model himself along with his son Abraham. A caster for the statue was not found until ten years later. The Sicilian Ludovico del Duca realized the bronze, which was erected on the tomb in 1584. This brought to completion Emperor Maximilian I's monument 60 years after it was begun.

During the work on the Maximilian tomb, work on the tomb of Emperor Ferdinand I, his wife Anna, and Emperor Maximilian II also took place; it was erected in the Cathedral of St. Vitus in Prague. Its construction resembles the Innsbruck monument, although for this Colin was responsible for the overall design. The tomb, on which the three deceased are depicted reclining, is elevated on a two-stepped pedestal. On the front side is the figure of the *Resurrected Christ*. Angels supporting coats of arms sit at the corners.

Through these imperial monuments Alexander Colin became one of the most successful sculptors of his time. On his own gravestone (Volkskunstmuseum in Innsbruck) he is lauded as the builder of three imperial tombs. He also created the monuments for Archduke Ferdinand, his wife Philippine Welser, and her aunt Katharina Loxan. He constructed these monuments in a similar manner: he depicted the deceased as recumbent figures and included reliefs as well as wall figures in the design, as in Ferdinand's more elaborate tomb. Colin also produced several marble fountains for the Habsburg family from 1570 to 1583 for the garden of the Neugebäudes (New Building) in Vienna, although these have not been preserved.

Colin also received other commissions, particularly as a designer of tombs. For example, he created the epitaphs for the bronze caster Gregor Löffler and for Hans Dreyling. The latter also involved the craft of bronze casting; as the inscription plaque on the Dreyling epitaph states, Dreyling was "Berg- und Schmelzherr" (patron of miners and casters), and indeed, the epitaph depicts a miner and a caster. This bronze panel gives a clearer indication of the origins of Colin's style; in his ornamentation he remained bound to the Floris style, but in his figures he was a successor to the Italian Renaissance (particularly Jacopo Sansovino), and the figural relief derives from a woodcut by Albrecht Dürer. Although Colin carried out mostly stone sculptures during his long career, these small-scale bronze epitaphs display his talent for multiple narrative reliefs. His plaque commemorating the opening of the emperor's gallery in the salt mine in Halle also shows his talent, with scenes depicted in careful detail.

Between 1580 and 1587 Colin executed the tomb of Hans Fugger (transferred to the Church of Saints. Ulrich and Afra, Augsburg) based on a model by sculptor Hubert Gerhard. That artist moved to Innsbruck in 1602, when Colin's own career was already coming to an end. Relieved of his duties at court in 1595, he remained in Innsbruck but was hardly active. A younger generation with Italian influences had already left his work behind.

URSEL BERGER

Biography

Born in Mecheln, Brabant, Belgium, *ca.* 1526. Trained presumably with his uncle, Symon Colyns; worked on the Ottheinrich building in the Heidelberg Castle, 1558/59; returned to Mecheln after Ottheinrich's death; became master, 1560; summoned to Innsbruck into emperor's services, 1562; worked on relief cycle for monument to Emperor Maximilian I in Court Church until 1570; crowning bronze figure of the kneeling Emperor, 1569–84; parallel imperial monuments for Ferdinand I, Anna, and Maximilian II in Cathedral of St. Vitus, Prague; trips to Mecheln, 1566, 1576, and 1599; relieved of court duties after Archduke Ferdinand's death, 1595. Died in Innsbruck, Austria, 17 August 1612.

Selected Works

1558/59 Mullions, door-frames, fireplaces, and figures; sandstone (mostly destroyed, facade remaining); Ottheinrich building, Heidelberg Castle, Germany

1562–83 Tomb of Emperor Maximilian I, including 24 marble reliefs of the Emperor's life (1562–1566), bronze statues of the Emperor (1583) and the four Cardinal Virtues (1570), and bronze trophy friezes and other decorations; bronze, marble; Court Church, Innsbruck, Austria

1566–89 Tomb of Ferdinand I, Queen Anna, and Maximilian II; marble; Cathedral of St. Vitus, Prague, Czech Republic

1567 Epitaph of Gregor Löffler; bronze; Tiroler Landesmuseum Ferdinandeum, Innsbruck, Austria

1568 Plaque commemorating the opening of the Emperor's gallery in the salt-mines in Halle; bronze; Tiroler Landesmuseum Ferdinandeum, Innsbruck, Austria

1570–83 Fountains, for Neue Berg, Vienna, Austria; marble (destroyed)

1578 Epitaph of Hans Dreyling; bronze; parish church, Schwaz, Austria

1580–81 Monument to Katharina von Loxan; marble; Court Church, Innsbruck, Austria

1580–81 Monument to Philippine Welser; marble; Court Church, Innsbruck, Austria

1584–87 Tomb of Hans Fugger, for Palace Church, Kirchheim bei Mindelheim, Germany; marble; Church of Saints Ulrich and Afra, Augsburg, Germany

1588–97 Monument to Archduke Ferdinand; marble; Court Church, Innsbruck, Austria

Further Reading

Dressler, Helga, "Alexander Colin," Ph.D. diss., Karlsruhe University, 1973

Egg, Erich, *Die Hofkirche in Innsbruck: Das Grabdenkmal Kaiser Maximilians I. u. die Silberne Kapelle*, Innsbruck, Vienna, and Munich: Tyrolia Verlag, 1974

Krapf, Michael, "Alexander Colin," in *Ruhm und Sinnlichkeit: Innsbrucker Bronzeguss, 1500–1650* (exhib. cat.), Innsbruck: Athesia-Tyrolia Druck, 1996

Oberhammer, Vinzenz, *Die Bronzestandbilder des Maximiliangrabmales in der Hofkirche zu Innsbruck* (The Bronze Figures of the Tomb of Maximilian I in the Court Chapel in Innsbruck), Innsbruck: Tyrolia, 1935

COLLECTING AND PATRONAGE

Both collecting, which is the acquisition of existing works, and patronage—the support of contemporary artists—are integral elements in the history of sculpture. Although a collection is generally assembled by an individual, it frequently has a broader purpose; the display of the collection promotes the owner's prestige or authority while also inspiring and instructing the community that views it. The level of a patron's influence on the outcome of a sculptural commission has varied significantly throughout history, but the impact of the patron's individual taste and ultimate goal for the work is an important aspect in the discussion of patronage in any period.

Collecting sculpture dates to ancient times. Inventories of Egyptian and Mesopotamian temples and palaces indicate that statues were among the numerous votive offerings recorded there, displayed as evidence of the owner's power, wealth, and status. Similarly, a ruler could reinforce his reputation for military prowess by displaying the spoils of war, as in the Egyptian sculptures and obelisks Ashurbanipal exhibited in his palace at Nineveh in the 7th century BCE. In another vein, Attalos I (3rd century BCE) collected statues for the acropolis of Pergamon to be displayed for their aesthetic and historical value.

In addition to collecting sculpture, Greek patrons also commissioned original works. For example, Pericles' master plan for the Acropolis in Athens in the 5th century BCE produced sculptural masterpieces such as the Parthenon pediment sculptures and the caryatids—female figures serving as columns—on the south porch of the Erechtheion. Sculptures from the Parthenon are significant not only for their subsequent artistic influence but also for their continued importance in questions related to the ethics of collecting. Lord Elgin, the British ambassador, removed numerous Parthenon sculptures and sent them to England in the beginning of the 19th century, receiving permission to do so from the Turkish government ruling Greece. Elgin eventually sold the sculpture to the British government at a personal financial loss, and the works have since been displayed in the British Museum in London. The debate over their return continues today as Greece struggles to regain possession of these cultural objects while England maintains its right of ownership by purchase.

Personal commissions by Greek citizens were also common; for example, Alexander the Great in the 4th century BCE selected the sculptor Lysippos of Sikyon to create his official portrait because of the sensitivity of this artist's work. In the later Hellenistic period, Dionysios of Berytos (Beirut) commissioned an unknown sculptor to create a marble group of *Aphrodite, Eros, and Pan* for display in a private club.

As the Roman Empire expanded to encompass Athens, Roman culture absorbed Greek artistic influences. Like others before them, Romans collected and displayed antique sculpture as symbols of military prowess and cultural prestige. Marcus Claudius Marcellus displayed sculpture taken from the conquered Syracuse in 211 BCE, and Hadrian's villa at Tivoli in the 2nd century CE exhibited antique sculpture and contemporary reproductions of Greek masterpieces, including exact scale replicas of the caryatids from the Erechtheion, as evidence of his cultured taste.

Romans also commissioned works for propagandistic purposes. In particular, in the 1st century CE Augustus, Rome's first emperor, originated the connection of art and ideology in Roman culture by using portrait and relief sculpture as a tool to communicate policies and propaganda. A prime example is his military portrait, *Augustus of Primaporta*. The pose is from Classical Greek sculpture, the idealized face and body connect the emperor to his deified father, and motifs on his cuirass refer to contemporary military conquests. Marcus Aurelius continued the tradition in the 2nd century with works such as a bronze equestrian portrait, which shows him controlling his steed while extending his arm in a gesture that combines greeting, blessing, and clemency—a figure at once powerful and compassionate. A century and a half later, Constantine's portrait images clearly illustrate the patron's intent as they metamorphose from a geometrically inspired, bearded tetrarch into a Trajan-inspired, smooth-faced leader with a Classical cap of hair, as in the colossal sculpture portrait from the Basilica Nova, Rome.

Beyond the emperors' use of sculpture as propaganda, however, was its role as a tool for social control; by law only certain classes of citizens could display ancestral portraits in their homes. Even so, sculpture was an integral part of everyday life in Rome. Freedmen who were financially able frequently commissioned sculpture, generally tomb monuments decorated with sculptural funerary portraits and scenes of their profession. The nobility displayed ancestral portrait sculpture in their homes and decorated villa gardens with a variety of sculptural works such as those displayed in public spaces, including baths, temples, and theaters. The Romans set aside special buildings for the display of art, such as the Porticus Metelli that contained Roman replicas of Greek masterpieces and contemporary Roman interpretations of favored Greek prototypes. These early museums and Roman patronage practices established patterns that would significantly influence Western approaches to collecting and patronage.

Sculpture was also an important element of life in the Middle Ages, as the Catholic Church joined political rulers as a major patron. In the 9th century court artisans created small carved ivory book covers and other small-scale works, while craftsmen carved decorative but edifying capitals for medieval churches. One significant incident of documented large-scale sculptural patronage was the commissioning of the bronze doors for the Abbey Church of St. Michael by Bishop Bernward of Hildesheim in 1015 (now at the Hildesheim Cathedral). Although probably inspired by early Christian wooden doors decorated with biblical scenes and based on contemporary doors with bronze plaques attached to a wooden core, Bernward's commission specified a significant innovation—each of the two five-meter-high doors would be cast as a single piece. The finished doors revealed another innovation: the sculptors manipulated the modeling of the figures on each panel to create the illusion that the figures are free of their background and not merely raised elements of a shallow relief.

New developments in ecclesiastical uses of sculpture continued in the 12th century, when the construction of Gothic cathedrals was accompanied by their adornment with elaborate sculptural elements. Among the most innovative and influential was Abbot Suger's design for the Basilica of Saint-Denis. The central portal of the west facade included full-length sculptures of Old Testament figures, attached at their back to portal columns. Although these figures are now known only through drawings, later Gothic churches widely emulated the use of large-scale figures in doorways. The Basilica of Saint-Denis is notable for another example of patronage in Jeanne d'Evreux's endowment of the Chapel of Notre-Dame-la-Blanche in 1343. The sculptural elements installed in the chapel included column figures of Jeanne d'Evreux and her deceased husband, King Charles IV, a small silver statue of the Virgin Mary, and another in alabaster, from which the chapel derived its name. Jeanne d'Evreux's patronage was typical of women's increasing involvement in the arts in early modern Europe.

Economic growth in 15th-century Europe resulted in a newly rich middle class and a rise in art patronage. The members of the Medici family in Florence exemplify Renaissance patronage in Italy, and their patronage served much the same purpose as the propagandistic portrait sculpture of the Roman era: it promoted the family's popularity in the community and increased this political family's notoriety outside Florence. Their patronage of sculpture typifies this ongoing pattern of support for the arts.

Cosimo de' Medici is considered the greatest private patron of his time. Under his patronage Donatello produced bronze doors and other sculptural elements for the Old Sacristy of S. Lorenzo, as well as two large-scale bronzes, *Judith Slaying Holofernes* and *David*, for the Palazzo Medici in the Via Larga, Florence. The works produced for Cosimo and under his generous patronage were both influential in the further development of sculpture and patronage in Italy.

In the second half of the 15th century, Lorenzo de' Medici, known as Lorenzo the Magnificent, expressed his interest in Classical antiquity through an extensive collection of antique sculpture and his involvement in a humanist circle of poets, artists, and philosophers that included Michelangelo. Lorenzo continued the family tradition of patronage through commissions to Michelangelo, Verrocchio, and others and promoted artists to foreign courts through letters of introduction and gifts of artwork, such as the two marble reliefs by Verrocchio sent to the king of Hungary. Lorenzo also established a sculpture garden at the Piazza San Marco, where artists studied from the antique and where Michelangelo created his *Virgin of the Steps* and the *Battle of the Centaurs*. Lorenzo's treatment of artists—he took Michelangelo into his household—was unprecedented in Florence and set the tone for a new type of patronage and an elevated status for artists in Italy.

Pope Leo X (Giovanni de' Medici) was also both collector and patron. He appointed Raphael supervisor of all archaeological excavations in and near Rome and conservator of any discovered antiquities. Among the most notable discoveries was the excavation of the monumental statue of the river god *Nile*. Michelangelo's involvement with Pope Leo, however, typifies the potential difficulties of Medici patronage. Pope Leo commissioned Michelangelo to design a facade for the Church of S. Lorenzo in Florence but canceled the commission in favor of another project even after Michelangelo had spent three years developing the facade plans and quarrying marble for the sculptures. Despite Michelangelo's protests of wasted time and money, Leo transferred the funds to a new project, a tomb chapel for two Medici Dukes. The statues of *Lorenzo* (Duke of Urbino) and *Giuliano* (Duke of Nemours) for the tomb exemplify the propagandistic nature of Medici patronage. Rather than recognizable portraits, Michelangelo created stylized images of masculine greatness, dignity, introspection, and power.

Cosimo I de' Medici expanded the tradition of Medici patronage as grand Duke of Tuscany (r. 1569–74). Perhaps more than any previous Medici, Cosimo I utilized art and architecture to promote the family name and his personal dynasty. Among his most notable contributions are the creation of the Accademia del Designio for the instruction of artists, the redesign of the garden at the Villa di Castello to include allegorical sculptures honoring the Medici, and the addition of the bronze *Perseus and Medusa* (1545–53) by Benvenuto Cellini, commissioned for the Piazza della Signoria, Florence. Cosimo I also focused on commissioning ancient sculpture, augmenting the collection begun by Lorenzo the Magnificent in the 15th century with Cosimo's own extensive collection of bronze and marble statuettes. Even before Cosimo's reign as the next

Grand Duke of Tuscany, Francesco I de' Medici was paying a monthly salary to the Flemish sculptor Giambologna for works such as *Samson Slaying a Philistine* (1560–62) and the marble group *Florence Triumphant over Pisa* (ca. 1567–72), created to celebrate Francesco's marriage in 1565. Another commission of stylistic importance was the romanticized portrait bust of Francesco (ca. 1564) created by Domenico Poggini and considered a forerunner of idealized Baroque ruler portraits. Ferdinando I de' Medici continued the tradition of sculpture patronage while serving as Grand Duke of Tuscany from 1587 to 1609. Ferdinando began acquiring antique sculpture during the first of his many extensive periods in Rome, and his sculptural commissions promoted the Medici dynasty in forms inspired by Roman monuments and the Grand Duke's love of the antique. Giovanni Bandini's over life-size marble statue of Ferdinando for the Piazza Micheli (1595–99) dominates the port of Livorno and was the first of many monumental public portraits of Ferdinando (ca. 1590) and his predecessors.

Ferdinando II de' Medici continued the tradition of sculpture patronage as part of a public works project to counteract an economic depression in the early 1630s. These projects involved both new sculptural commissions and the reuse of existing and antique pieces. Several sculptors were commissioned to create new works for the courtyard of the Palazzo Pitti, while two of Giambologna's monumental sculptures were recut and/or relocated in the palazzo garden. Public sculptures included numerous fountains that featured new and antique sculptures. Other notable Medici sculpture patrons in the 17th century include Cardinal Leopoldo de' Medici, son of Cosimo II and collector of classical antiquities including the Ludovisi *Hermaphrodite*, and Cosimo III de' Medici who established the Accademia Fiorentina in Rome where Florentine painters and sculptors could train and which was an essential element in the development of the Baroque in Florence. Cosimo III also continued Cardinal Leopoldo's program to organize the Medici collections and, in 1677, Cosimo moved three Classical masterpieces including the *Venus de' Medici* from the Villa Medici in Rome to the Galleria degli Uffizi in Florence.

The Medici were not the only Renaissance patrons, of course. In 15th-century Florence the guilds commissioned statuary as part of their responsibility for the care and upkeep of various public buildings in the city. Some of the works resulting from these commissions are now considered landmarks of Italian art. For example, the wool guild commissioned a statue of the prophet Jeremiah from Donatello and Michelangelo's *David* (1501–04), while the cloth guild commissioned Lorenzo Ghiberti to create the *Gates of Paradise*

(1425–52), the gilded-bronze doors depicting Old Testament stories, for the Florence Baptistery.

Royal patronage remained prevalent throughout Europe in the 16th century, as typified by the Habsburg emperors. Holy Roman Emperor Charles V, for example, employed Leone Leoni to create the bronze over-life-size *Charles V and Fury Restrained* (1549–55), commemorating a recent war victory. Leoni's work for Charles V widened his circle of patrons to other European nobility, but his crowning work was a bronze *Crucifixion*, created with his son, Pompeo Leoni, for another Habsburg emperor, King Philip II.

Royalty and religious leaders continued to dominate patronage in the 17th century, as seen in the career of Gianlorenzo Bernini. Among his more notable works are the funerary monument for Pope Urban VIII (1627–47), a multifigured composition of bronze, gilt bronze, and white and colored marbles, and a dynamic marble bust of Louis XIV of France (1665), so convincing in its image of authority that it would influence European art for the next century.

Louis XIV was also the primary patron of François Girardon, sculptor and collector. Examples of his royal commissions include the marble *Apollo and the Nymphs of Thetis* (1666–1675), one element of the sculptural plan for Versailles, and the colossal bronze equestrian statue of Louis XIV. The tomb of Cardinal Richelieu (1675–94) is Girardon's masterpiece of tomb monuments and evidence of his extensive work for nonroyal patrons. Girardon's collection of approximately 800 sculptures was second only to that of his patron, Louis XIV, and contained examples of plaster and wax models, contemporary work in bronze and marble, and 66 antique pieces.

In the 18th century women took an increasing role in patronage and collecting. For example, Madame de Pompadour, mistress to Louis XV, was a prominent collector of many media, including the marble sculptures *Nymph Leaving the Bath* and *Menacing Cupid* (1757) by Étienne-Maurice Falconet. In England, Sarah Churchill commissioned three monuments for Blenheim Palace to commemorate her late husband, the Duke of Marlborough. In the 1730s Churchill was actively involved in every aspect of the three monuments, from selecting artists and determining the sites to the selection and ordering of marble.

The English continued to be active collectors and patrons beyond the 18th century as well. For example, the architect Sir John Soane built his home/museum in London in the 1820s to inspire the imagination of his community, incorporating his diverse collection into the building's design to illustrate the unity of the arts. Soane's sculpture collection included architectural fragments and casts, as well as antique marbles and fragments, including one from the Erechtheion

frieze, along with works by contemporary sculptors John Flaxman, Thomas Banks, Sir Richard Westmacott, and Francis Chantrey. Shortly before his death Soane obtained a special act of Parliament that allowed him to leave his house to the British nation as a museum.

The grand tour, an educational excursion through France and Italy taken by wealthy young European men, particularly influenced English patterns of patronage and collecting. Frequently, the tourist would purchase fragments or replicas of ancient sculpture to be shipped home. Several major British sculpture collections began this way, such as that of Charles Townley, who formed the most important collection of Classical antiquities in England in the 18th century (now held at the British Museum). By the mid 19th century the concept of the Grand Tour had spread to the United States and with it the opportunity for artistic patronage. Visits to artists' studios were a prerequisite of the tour, and sculpture purchases were common. American artists working in Rome who benefited from this type of patronage included Thomas Crawford, whose marble bust of Charles Sumner commemorates this young man's Grand Tour, and Harriet Hosmer, who sold copies of her marble conceit of *Puck* (1856) to Americans and European nobility.

In addition to increased private patronage, the 19th century also saw the formation of museum collections. In the 1820s the Boston Atheneum began its sculpture collection with plaster casts of famous works, but the collection soon included works by every major contemporary American sculptor. The donation of a private collection frequently aided museum collections, as in the case of J.P. Morgan, whose encyclopedic sculptural holdings were eventually donated to the Metropolitan Museum of Art in New York.

Similar trends continued in the United States in the 20th century with the work of Anna Hyatt Huntington, who was both sculptor and patron. Huntington had a successful career in bronze sculpture (e.g., the equestrian *Joan of Arc*), and in 1930 she and her husband created Brookgreen Gardens, an outdoor sculpture museum in South Carolina featuring 300 works. Another collection that became available to the public was that of Joseph Hirshhorn, who focused on modern sculpture. He collected works by Henri Matisse, Henry Moore, Alberto Giacometti, and David Smith, along with a cast of Auguste Rodin's *Burghers of Calais* (original, 1884)—the only cast of this work in private hands. This exemplary collection eventually became part of Washington, D.C.,'s Smithsonian Institution as the Hirshhorn Museum and Sculpture Garden.

Newspaper tycoon, politician, and millionaire William Randolph Hearst accumulated artwork as voraciously as he did newspapers, amassing an immense and diverse collection of art and artifacts from around the world. As eccentric in his manner of display as in his collecting, Hearst's home in San Simeon, California, known as the Hearst Castle, features a Roman pool with eight marble statues carved in Italy as copies of famous Classical sculptures. Another Californian, Norton Simon began collecting art in 1954, eventually forming three separate collections: the private collection was kept in Simon's California home, while the Norton Simon Foundation and the Norton Simon, Inc. Museum of Art (now the Norton Simon Art Foundation) were collections primarily existing on loan to American museums. All three collections featured European and East Asian sculpture as well as European paintings. Since 1974 the Simon collections have been housed at the Norton Simon Museum, formerly the Pasadena Art Museum, California.

Sculptors continued to enjoy active patronage in Europe in the 20th century as evidenced by the collection amassed by Helene Kröller-Müller and now exhibited at the Kröller-Müller Museum, Otterlo, the Netherlands. The sculpture park features works by major 19th and 20th century sculptors including Rodin, Moore, Claes Oldenburg, Jean Dubuffet, and Barbara Hepworth. English collector Charles Saatchi continues to collect multiple works by contemporary artists, particularly new emerging artists such as Britain's Damien Hirst, known for his work utilizing sections of animals preserved and sealed in glass containers.

Sculpture patronage and collecting continue today in private, museum, and even corporate collections such as PepsiCo's Sculpture Garden, Blind Brook, New York, which since 1970 has served as one of the largest corporate sculpture collections in the world. The General Mills Sculpture Garden at the corporation's Minneapolis headquarters is also exemplary for its encouragement of contemporary sculptors. Of the numerous works installed on the 34 hectares site, only Richard Serra's *Core* (1987) was purchased by General Mills and then sited by the artist. All other sculptors, including Richard Artschwager, Jonathan Borofsky, Jackie Ferrara, and Scott Burton, among others, received commissions to create a work specific to the site the artist had selected. In 1998 the Altoids company formed a collection to support emerging visual artists working in America. The works are selected by a panel of contemporary art experts and the resulting collection represents some of the major American artist of today, such as E.V. Day, whose work was part of the 2000 Whitney Biennial. The Altoids company donated its collection to the New Museum of Contemporary Art, New York.

Corporate patronage in Europe is equally supportive of sculptors, even if for less altruistic reasons than those of private patrons. Cartier International, Paris, maintains a 37-acre site in the suburb of Jouy-en-Josas near Versailles that includes living spaces and studios for artists-in-residence, exhibition spaces, and a library. The venue also features sculpture installations— such as Terre de Granade by Richard Tuttle—in the exhibition halls and in the landscape. The Foundation Cartier was formed as a response to a survey conducted by the company tha revealed that 75 percent of young people in five European countries expressed an interest in contemporary art, leading the firm to promote contemporary art as a means of promoting the company. These collections serve many of the same purposes as when collecting began in ancient times: to advertise status, taste, or wealth and to inform, enlighten, and inspire the viewer.

JULIE A. DUNN-MORTON

Further Reading

Constable, W.G., *Art Collecting in the United States of America: An Outline of a History*, London and New York: Nelson, 1963

Craven, Wayne, *Sculpture in America*, New York: Crowell, 1968; revised edition, Newark, Delaware: University of Delaware Press, and New York: Cornwall Books, 1984

Foss, Michael, *The Age of Patronage: The Arts in England, 1660–1750*, London: Hamilton, 1971; Ithaca, New York: Cornell University Press, 1972

Herrmann, Frank (editor), *The English As Collectors*, New York: Norton, and London: Chatto and Windus, 1972

Hollingsworth, Mary, *Patronage in Renaissance Italy: From 1400 to the Early Sixteenth Century*, Baltimore, Maryland: Johns Hopkins University Press, and London: John Murray, 1994

King, Catherine E., *Renaissance Women Patrons: Wives and Widows in Italy, c. 1300–c. 1550*, Manchester and New York: Manchester University Press, 1998

Kleiner, Diana E.E., *Roman Sculpture*, New Haven, Connecticut: Yale University Press, 1992

Lawrence, Cynthia (editor), *Women and Art in Early Modern Europe: Patrons, Collectors, and Connoisseurs*, University Park: Pennsylvania State University Press, 1997

Lipman, Jean (editor), *The Collector in America*, New York: Viking Press, 1970; London: Weidenfeld and Nicolson, 1971

Miller, Lillian B., *Patrons and Patriotism: The Encouragement of the Fine Arts in the United States, 1790–1860*, Chicago: University of Chicago Press, 1966

Saarinen, Aline B., *The Proud Possessors: The Lives, Times, and Tastes of Some Adventurous American Art Collectors*, New York: Random House, 1958

Stewart, Andrew F., *Greek Sculpture: An Exploration*, 2 vols., New Haven, Connecticut: Yale University Press, 1990

Trevor-Roper, Hugh R., *Princes and Artists: Patronage and Ideology at Four Habsburg Courts, 1517–1633*, London: Thames and Hudson, and New York: Harper and Row, 1976

Zarnecki, George, *Art of the Medieval World: Architecture, Sculpture, Painting, the Sacred Arts*, Englewood Cliffs, New Jersey: Prentice-Hall, 1975

MICHEL COLOMBE *ca.* 1430–*ca.* 1514

French

Michel Colombe was celebrated in his own day, referred to as "the leading sculptor in the kingdom of France." While he was highly influential and much imitated, few works can now be solidly attributed to him. Documentation indicates that he received numerous commissions, but most of these works have been destroyed or are untraced. The works that do survive are from relatively late in his career, making it impossible to outline his stylistic development. What does survive demonstrates why Colombe's work was highly favored; it embodies a grave solemnity and monumental dignity combined with a strong sense of naturalism. This overall serenity places Colombe well within the tradition of the Loire Valley.

Although not definitely attributable to Colombe, the *Entombment of Christ* in the Abbey Church at Solesmes (1496) combines all these traits. Placed within a magnificent stagelike architectural setting, seven figures gather around the dead Christ as he is being laid in the tomb. Details of costume reflect contemporary styles, and faces are strongly idealized. While the poses of the figures are varied, they all demonstrate a grave and dignified resignation. The solidity of the figures and the simple, rather heavy folds of drapery further convey a sense of somber stillness. It has been suggested that the figure of Mary Magdalene, seated in the foreground of the group while all others are standing behind the tomb, is a later addition, but compositionally it is in harmony with the whole ensemble.

To commemorate a visit of King Louis XII to Tours in 1500, Colombe designed a commemorative gold medallion. The front side bears a portrait of the king in profile, his hat extending over the edge of the beaded frame and onto the field of the encircling inscription. His genial but lined face is unidealized, almost homely. The back of the medallion portrays a porcupine, quills bristling, with a crown floating above it.

The Tomb of François II, Duke of Brittany, and Marguerite de Foix, his wife, is considered to be Colombe's masterpiece. Jean Perréal designed the tomb, commissioned by their daughter, Anne of Brittany, queen of France, in 1499, but Colombe carved the ensemble. Originally placed in the Carmelite Abbey Church at Nantes, the tomb was dismantled during the French Revolution and reassembled in Nantes Cathedral in 1817. Made of various white, red, and black marbles purchased by Queen Anne, the sarcophagus is two tiered. Its lowest level has a continuous row of roundels bearing seated mourners (*pleurants*, "weepers"), while the upper tier bears statues of saints standing in an arcade, which is decorated with pilasters

bearing classicizing Italianate designs. This decoration is the extent of Italian influence here, for the saints' images, as well as the remaining figures, are fully within the French late Gothic manner.

At each corner of the sarcophagus stands an allegorical figure, representing the four Cardinal Virtues of *Justice, Temperance, Fortitude,* and *Prudence.* Atop the sarcophagus lie two *gisants* (reclining effigy figures) representing the Duke and Duchess, with angels tending to cushions placed beneath their heads. The *gisants* are affecting in their frozen stillness, the faces bearing no trace of animation. As is common in Gothic *gisants*, although the drapery of the figures is realistic, it defies gravity (as do the figures' praying hands). Folds adhere to the figures rather than falling to the surface on which they lie; the *gisants* are essentially standing figures placed on their backs. The detailing on Marguerite's headdress, imitating jewel and beadwork, is particularly fine.

The Virtues are certainly the most remarkable components of the whole tomb ensemble. These allegorical female figures embody a classical harmony that yet has no parallel in contemporary Italian sculpture. The sober calmness of their individualized faces complements the simple, sweeping folds of voluminous drapery. This overall compositional harmony is seen especially in the figure of *Prudence*, which ingeniously balances the unusual iconography of a Janus-like head, the front face being that of a young woman, the back one an aged bearded man.

A work in which Italian influence seems at first more prominent is the marble relief of *Saint George and the Dragon,* carved in 1509 for the chapel of the château of Gaillon (destroyed) and now in the Musée du Louvre, Paris. The frame, carved by Jérôme Pach-

Tomb of François II, Duke of Brittany and Marguerite de Foix
The Conway Library, Courtauld Institute of Art

erot, a Genoese sculptor, is completely Italianate, and Colombe probably knew of Genoese versions of the Saint George theme. A comparison of Colombe's relief with Donatello's relief on the same subject from Orsanmichele in Florence is instructive. While Donatello's landscape setting is sketchy and schematic, Colombe's is highly detailed, although stagelike. Colombe's relief replaces Donatello's classically carved princess with a young woman in contemporary French garb, and Colombe's dragon is a whimsical Gothic creation. Most illustrative of Colombe's Gothic spirit, however, is his equestrian group of Saint George. Rearing up on its hind legs, Colombe's horse, while solid, naturalistic, and highly detailed, is stiff and frozen compared with Donatello's.

Colombe's influence was considerable. Various disciples from his workshop, Jean de Chartres and Colombe's nephew Guillaume Regnault among the most prominent, carried the style into the early 16th century. Works from minor workshops as late as 1518 (for example, an *Entombment of Christ* now at Joigny in Burgundy) show Colombe's influence both in their broad use of Gothic spirit and in their use of particularized motifs and details.

WALTER SMITH

See also **Donatello**

Biography

Born probably in Bourges, France, *ca.* 1430. Possibly trained with his father, Philippe Colombe, a sculptor of Bourges; received commissions from Jean de Bar, the royal Chamberlain, 1462; collaborated with Jean Fouquet on various projects from 1470; moved to Tours by 1478; worked in Moulins, 1484; back in Tours by 1496, where he spent the rest of his career, established a workshop, and produced his most significant work. Died in Tours, France, *ca.* 1514.

Selected Works

1496	*Entombment of Christ*; stone; Abbey Church of St. Pierre, Solesmes, France
1499–1500	Commemorative medallion of Louis XII; gold; Bibliothèque Nationale, Paris, France
1499–1507	Tomb of François II, Duke of Brittany, and Marguerite de Foix; marble, Cathedral of Nantes, Nantes, France
1502–07	*St. George and the Dragon*, marble, Musée du Louvre, Paris, France

Further Reading

Blunt, Anthony, *Art and Architecture in France 1500 to 1700*, London and Baltimore, Maryland: Penguin, 1970; 5th edition, revised by Richard Beresford, New Haven, Connecticut: Yale University Press, 1999

Forsyth, William H., *The Entombment of Christ: French Sculptures of the Fifteenth and Sixteenth Centuries*, Cambridge, Massachusetts: Harvard University Press, 1970

Pradel, Pierre, *Michel Colombe: Le dernier imagier gothique*, Paris: Plon, 1953

Rouillard, Philippe, "Michel Colombe," in *The Dictionary of Art*, edited by Jane Turner, vol. 7, New York: Grove, and London: Macmillan, 1996

Vitry, Paul, *Michel Colombe et la sculpture française de son temps*, Paris: Librairie Centrale des Beaux-Arts, 1901

COLOSSAL SCULPTURE

Colossal sculptures are statues of remarkable proportions, usually several times larger than human proportions. Originally the notion of *kolossos* was a pre-Grecian, west Asian designation for a statue or statuette, and in this meaning it was adopted by the Dorian Greeks who had settled in Dodekans and in southwest Asia Minor around 1000 BCE. It was with this meaning that the term was first applied to the *Colossus of Rhodes*. After the statue was erected (293 BCE) and listed among of the Seven Wonders of the World, however, the use of the term became more and more limited to designating statues of gigantic size. In this way, the *Colossus of Rhodes* provided the name for a certain sculptural format. Since then, *colossus* has become a technical term for statues with sizes ranging from 3 to 30 meters and higher. Colossal sculptures are defined as over life-size sculptures, usually including the entire figure in a standing or seated position; colossal group sculptures, equestrian statues, and colossal heads also developed as particular forms. The term is also used for colossal seated and recumbent figures—for example, those seen in Egyptian and Buddhist art.

Among the most significant colossal figures from antiquity in Egypt are the monolithic seated figures of Ramses II in the facade of the cliff-temple of Abu Simbel (19th dynasty, first half, 13 BCE) and the two approximately 20-meter-high seated figures of Amenophis III, the so-called *Memnoncolossi* (15 BCE). Over life-size kouroi are known from early Greek art. Although they no longer exist today, other colossal statues are indicated in the descriptions of Pliny and Pausanius, as for example the gold-and-ivory figures of *Athena Parthenos* in Athens and the *Zeus* in Olympia. The most famous colossal figure from Greek Antiquity, also not preserved, was the above-mentioned *Colossus of Rhodes*, which was probably created by Chares of Lindos (*ca.* 290 BCE), a student of Lysippus. The over 29-meter-tall figure depicted the sun god Helios and was made of bronze. Examples of the colossal groups from Roman antiquity are the *Dioscures* (5.6 meters) on Monte Cavallo in Rome. The *Colossal*

Head of Constantine is based on a lost seated figure (2.4 meters; Palazzo dei Conservatori, Rome).

Renaissance artists also took up the idea of colossal statues. They were erected in prominent locations on public squares, such as Michelangelo Buonarroti's *David* (1501–04), which is 4.36 meters, and Baccio Bandinelli's colossal marble group *Hercules and Cacus* in front of the Palazzo Vecchio in Florence (presented 1534), which is 4.96 meters, as well as the two giants *Mars* and *Neptune* (1553) by Jacopo Sansovino on the Scala dei Giganti in Venice (height 4.40 meters). Young artists experimented with ephemeral materials such as plaster in order to demonstrate their abilities in proportioning and optics for the public before they were allowed to try their hand with expensive materials such as marble or bronze. The equestrian statue of *Marcus Aurelius*, the only preserved equestrian statue from antiquity, as well as the equestrian statues *Gattamelata* by Donatello (1446/47) and *Colleoni* by Andrea del Verrocchio (1479–88), had a formative influence on large-scale sculpture until the end of the 19th century. From the 17th century, there exist only sporadic colossal sculptures such as the *Carlone of Arona* (1697; S. Carlo Borromeo) by Giovanni Battista Crespi or the *Hercules* by Johann Jakob Anthoni near Kassel (1713/15), which was based on the model of *Hercules Farnese*.

Colossal sculpture found general acceptance in the 19th and 20th centuries in the form of public monuments, where it was the expression of collective feelings. The statue of Napoleon I (1811; destroyed) by Domenico Banti and sited on the Palazzo Ducale in Venice was meant to honor the emperor. Some colossal sculpture could be entered and climbed, such as the *Bavaria* in Munich (1838–45) by Georg Schwanthaler and Ferdinand von Miller and the *Statue of Liberty* by Frédéric Bartholdi in New York (1871–84).

Outside of Europe and North America, colossi arose in the cultures of Central America and Near and Far East Asia. Heads of colossal proportions, so-called baby-faces (around 300 BCE in the Olmec empire), were found during excavations in La Venta in Mexico. Buddhist art in India and China produced many standing, seated, and recumbent figures, often carved from live cliffs.

The triumph of the colossus began in the 20th century through the prevalence of colossal sculptures in totalitarian states—socialist and fascist—and through the enthusiasm for everything "big" in the United States. Pop art artists and the so-called Minimalists distanced themselves explicitly from representations of sublime and heroic motives, although not without occasionally flirting with greater physical proportions and monumental formats. The nonrepresentational co-

Olmec colossal sculpture head
© Danny Lehman / CORBIS

lossus has increasingly developed between sculpture and architecture, calling for a new definition of colossal sculpture.

In defining the concept of the colossal, one must refer to quantitative values—to absolute and measurable proportions such as height, volume, and weight—and to the colossal as a basic aesthetic category considered primarily within the aesthetics of effect. The latter reference also corresponds to idiomatic speech, where the term is roughly synonymous with the words *great*, *solemn*, and *overbearing*. In early modernity, Pomponius Gauricus related these two aspects to one another in his treatise *De sculptura* (1504). He divided large-scale sculpture into four categories: the *pariles* (those that are exactly life-size); the *magnae* (those that reach a size one and a half times that of natural size); the *maiores* (double life-size); and the *maximae* or *colossi*, a term synonymous with the image of a deity (at least three times normal body size). According to the ancient etymology of the work, he derived *koloss* from the Greek *kolouein ta ossa*, which he believed to mean "to ruin eyes." This is explained as the viewer's fear that he or she might lose vision when looking up at the great height of the statue, as well as being blinded by its gilding.

Colossal sculpture appears not only in the guise of a formal or technical problem, but also as a vision won from antique literary sources. In colossal sculpture, the astonishment over its incomprehensible size is heightened into a horror with regard to its power, which is equal to that of nature. This applies in an exemplary manner to the no longer preserved colossi of Phidias (*Zeus in Olympia*, *Athena Parthenos*, *Athena Promachos*). Phidias was criticized for having transgressed against proper proportioning, despite the great size of the temple, because the artist depicted Zeus seated and yet with his head almost touching the ceiling, thereby occasioning the viewer to imagine that if Zeus stood up straight, he would break through the ceiling. This criticism demonstrates that the size of an artifact, in relation to the human viewer or user and to his or her artificial or natural environment, can be increased to the point of exploding all dimensions. The colossal does not refer to an absolute size, but rather to its proportional relationship to the ensemble and to its effect on the viewer, whose standard of measure is unsettled in his or her encounter with the colossus. A colossal object is formed not through a progressive series of enlargements but through a leap into a different scale, the sudden transition into a larger standard of measure. Gestures of humility and rituals shortening the body serve to increase the distance symbolically. From such a perspective, the colossus seems without measure or form, criteria that connect the figure back to elemental nature.

Vitruvius was the source of the most extreme manifestations of the colossal (and the engineering achievements connected with it) ever dreamed up in Antiquity. He reported that the architect Deinokrates acquired the favor of Alexander the Great through a project in which he lent the mountain of Athos the shape of a human statue. A great city was to be depicted in one hand, whereas in the other, a bowl would be setting the water from all the rivers of this mountain into the sea. Someone of Alexander's stature apparently could be content only by a synthesis of colossal sculpture, architecture, and landscape.

A continuous tradition runs from Deinokrates himself up to the monumental spectacles at the beginning of the 20th century, especially the presidential portraits carved directly into the cliffs of Mount Rushmore (1927–41) by Gutzon Borglum. This tradition visualizes nature's creation in concert with the man-made artifact. The artist's dream of creating a sculpture like a mountain—and of transforming figures into mountains, as shown by the ancient poet Ovid in his *Metamorphoses*—was partly realized in modernity: Michel-angelo, according to Ascanio Condivi's account, was overcome during his stay in the marble quarries in Carrara by the desire to form a colossus from a mountain that overlooked the sea, a colossus that would be a sign to the sailors from far away. Giambologna also created a crouching mountain giant around 1580 as the embodiment of the *Apennines*. It is located north of Florence in the grounds of the former Medici Villa at Pratolino. Earlier travel literature reports that the *Apennine* would reach a height of almost 30 meters if it stood up straight. The colossus crouches in front of an artificial rock face surrounded by woods. Neither people nor architecture serve as a measure of comparison for the sculptural work, but only the natural creation that formed mountains and lakes.

The conflict as to whether nature is to be understood to be the proper, natural power producing order, or rather as the purely disordered, chaotic, monstrous, and barbaric power to be overcome and against which man should set his artificial order, is the theme of the Karlsberg near Kassel in Germany, called Wilhelmshöhe since 1798. *Hercules* stands above an architectonic pedestal construction with pyramids reaching a height of 60 meters and stands as a symbol casting its presence everywhere from on top of the mountain. He looks down on his defeated enemy, the earth-born giant *Enkelados*, as well as the area underneath him, which he subjugates and unifies. The colossal is distinguished from the gigantic in that it does not embody the intention of appearing enormous, but rather appears to be of a natural size when viewed from the right distance. The gigantic, however, has an overly large and ungainly, and therefore flawed, appearance. As with Deinokrates' theme, *Hercules* collects the water from the various streams in front of him and draws it into a huge cascade as the city spreads out at the foot of the mountain. As with the *Apennine*, *Hercules* and the pyramids could be entered and traversed. The visitor's view is that of the colossus over the broad countryside. What was still a courtly game in the *Apennine* becomes here an absolutist allegory of the state. Here the regal virtue of *providentia*, which connotes both a concern for as well as control over the state, receives its monumental expression.

Climbing the *San Carlone* (23.4 meters), a colossal sculpture of St. Charles Borromeo (*ca.* 1690), produces a religious sense of affirmation. For a short time, the viewer can slip into the giant's frame on the mountain near Arona on Lago Maggiore, which has been partly relandscaped into a sacred setting, and so gather an intimation of the immeasurable greatness of the saint and the overwhelming power of the Catholic Church. The Christian colossus is echoed in modern times by *Christ the Redeemer* (1931; 38 meters), which rises above the ocean and the city on the highest top (709 meters) in Rio de Janeiro.

The question remains whether someone in front of a colossus "regresses" temporarily, conjuring fantasies of helplessness or omnipotence when entered and climbed. The second half of the 18th century provided answers to this question as a new interest in aesthetic, anthropological, and psychological questions led to a subjective comprehension of the sublime. Older art was understood to be an art of limitation, whereas modern art was an art of the sublime that aspired to represent the unrepresentable and unspeakable. Before, the colossus was condemned as a transgression because it threatened to destroy every "reasonable" limit from the perspectives developed within the aesthetics of production, reception, and the work character of art. Alternatively, when it was deemed successful, it was admired as a bold but dangerous effort on the part of its producer. An artwork has a sublime effect when it invokes a mixed feeling in which admiration and astonishment are connected with the experience of a threatening, horrifying, and infinite presence. The human being feels small and inferior in the face of the highest terrestrial or extraterrestrial power. The feeling of the sublime can be awakened not only through works of art, but also in the face of untamed nature. Colossi were able to evoke the sublime by connecting elements of nature and of art.

Much can be learned about this from the collections that Eugène Lesbazeilles (1881) and Bartholdi compiled to promote the construction of the *Statue of Liberty*. According to Lesbazeilles, in monumental art "it is appropriate to depict power, majesty, and infinity, and it is entitled to awaken effects similar to that of the wind blowing, the waves of a vast sea, or the rolling of thunder" (*Les colosses anciens et modernes*, 1876). In its proportions, the copper-clad *Statue of Liberty* is one of few statues in modernity that was modeled on the *Colossus of Rhodes*. And just as the complicated inner construction of the *Colossus of Rhodes* drew admiration, the technical accomplishment of Gustave Eiffel, the engineer/architect of the Eiffel Tower, was impressive for the human skill exhibited in employing technology and machines to realize such an enormous project, a skill that only becomes apparent when one studies the construction.

The first historical and critical reflections concerning the essence of the colossal arose on the threshold of the 19th century. Quatremère de Quincy wrote in his work on Phidias's *Olympian Jupiter* (1814) that the colossus belonged to the early religions of humanity and was a predecessor of sculptural creativity. The Greeks had adopted these ungainly idols and course signs from primitive peoples and then refined them through their best sculptors into a metaphor of the sub-lime. The irrational power of the colossal can be explained from its archaic provenance, which cannot be grasped by reason. De Quincy saw an approximation of the natural principle of creation in the ability to augment a given measure arbitrarily. This is the only appropriate means of depicting the divine. Such ideas made it possible to employ the colossal as the propagation of devotion and subjugation. This attitude was tied to an increasing appreciation for hard materials (such as granite) that seemed to bespeak inviolability, indestructibility, and immortality. Along with this appreciation came the idea of the monolith, where one could appeal to Michelangelo, or rather turn directly to Herodotus, Diodorus, and Strabo, who characterized the Egyptian colossus as a work carved from a single stone.

In the Soviet Union, the kurgan, originally a traditional burial construction, became common as a monument of the modern political cult of the dead. Although the kurgan already encouraged the practice of the climbing procession on a smaller scale, this idea was more fully developed in the memorial complexes after 1965. The most imposing example is the ensemble in Stalingrad (now Volgograd) by Jevgenij Vutschetitsch (1963–67). Such places, where a synthesis of nature, sculpture, and architecture is created, became the setting for ritual acts of self-assurance on memorial days and days commemorating victories. In Wolgograd, the colossal statue *Mother Russia* serves as the visual background for the hero: he seems to be protecting her with his body from an unrepresented attacker, although she is following him at the same time. This constellation of figures conveys the official interpretation of the defense of Stalingrad in a double sense: the soldier's sense of duty is depicted (they are called into the war from their homelands), and the soldier's reckless willingness to sacrifice himself is shown.

This manner of drawing a monumental defensive posture into a martial attitude can also be seen in *Readiness* (1939), a work by the national-socialist sculptor Arno Breker. Here a naked male figure is depicted with a half-drawn sword. As the 11-meter-high crowning figure of the 45-meter-high middle section of the Mussolini monument, it was supposed to serve as the counterpart to the victory column (*Siegessäule*) on the east-west axis of Berlin. Also planned for this area was *The Torchbearer* (1942), also by Breker, a 30-meter-high allegory of the party conceived as an answer to the *Statue of Liberty* and the *Palace of the Soviets*. Breker sought to outdo Michelangelo's *David* by isolating its warlike aspect and heightening it to colossal proportions; the muscular *Readiness* was intended to be a model for the male youths marching off to war. What was new here was the extreme departure from nature in the attempt to present the colossus in its smooth and hard metallic quality.

In opposition to the quest for the greatest possible proportions, artists in the 1960s found a possibility of representing the unrepresentable and unspeakable by negating or reversing the colossal. Claes Oldenburg's *Proposed Underground Memorial and Tomb for President John F. Kennedy* (1965) projected a gigantic statue of the assassinated president, which was marked as a hollow space in the earth. It was supposed to have the same proportions as the *Statue of Liberty*. This set in motion the questioning of visual and perceptual experience of the colossal, which stretches back over 2,500 years. Key conceptions in the present, appearing in the most varied artistic projects, work with invisible and negative forms that often have colossal dimensions. One example is the 1995 plan of Basque artist Eduardo Chillida to excavate a large regular hole in the holy mountain of Tindaya (Fuerteventura).

KRISTINE PATZ

See also **Bandinelli, Baccio; Bartholdi, Frédéric-Auguste; Donatello; Giambologna; Michelangelo (Buonarroti); Oldenburg, Claes; Pheidias; Sansovino, Jacopo; Verrocchio, Andrea del**

Further Reading

Allen, Leslie, *Liberty: The Statue and the American Dream*, New York: Statue of Liberty–Ellis Island Foundation, 1985

Bush, Virginia, *The Colossal Sculpture of the Cinquecento*, New York: Garland, 1976

Clayton, Peter A., and Martin I. Price, *The Seven Wonders of the Ancient World*, London and New York: Routledge, 1988

Daidalos 61 (1996)

Derrida, Jacques, *La vérité en peinture*, Paris: Flammarion, 1978; as *The Truth in Painting*, Chicago: University of Chicago Press, 1987

Golomshtok, Igor, *Totalitarian Art: In the Soviet Union, the Third Reich, Fascist Italy and the People's Republic of China*, translated by Robert Chandler, London: Collins Harvill, and New York: IconEditions, 1990

Harbison, Robert, *The Built, the Unbuilt, and the Unbuildable*, London: Thames and Hudson, and Cambridge, Massachusetts: MIT Press, 1991

Michalski, Sergiusz, *Public Monuments: Art in Political Bondage, 1870–1997*, London: Reaktion Books, 1998

MAXIMILIAN COLT late 16th CENTURY–ca. 1647/50 *British*

Maximilian Colt is remembered chiefly for his creation of the monument to Queen Elizabeth I in Westminster Abbey, London, a work for which he was chosen from relative obscurity to create. His swift rise to artistic eminence may be credited in part to the sensitive historical situation surrounding the creation of a tomb for Mary Queen of Scots and to a fortuitous marriage and family connections. Nonetheless, his resourceful integration of Classical elements with the Elizabethan style and his focus on ornamental detail garnered him regular commissions and the position of master sculptor to the crown. Along with his Flemish and German contemporaries, Colt ushered the Jacobean style into England.

Colt has traditionally been classed among the refugee artists who brought to England at the close of Elizabeth's reign a rich and variegated cache of aesthetic archetypes. A Huguenot, he left France to escape the volatile relations between Protestants and Catholics that resulted in frequent civil clashes in the years before the Edict of Nantes in 1598. After a short sojourn in Utrecht, the Netherlands, he arrived in England and by 1596 had settled with his elder brother John, also a sculptor, outside London in the parish of Saint Bartholomew, Smithfield.

With his marriage in 1604 to Susanna Gheeraerts, niece to then deputy (and later sergeant) painter John de Critz, Colt embarked on what promised to be a distinguished career. De Critz likely introduced Colt to Sir Robert Cecil, First Earl of Salisbury and influential minister to King James I. In 1604, when James wished to make a monument to his mother, Mary Queen of Scots, Salisbury counseled the king on the political expedience of also creating a memorial to her immensely popular cousin, Elizabeth I. The king's master mason, the renowned Cornelius Cure, completed the tomb for James's mother, while the relatively unknown Colt received the commission from Salisbury to produce Elizabeth's tomb.

Elizabeth's monument adheres to the traditional sepulchral formula of an effigy recumbent on a tomb chest. Elizabeth is in full regalia. Both she and the bier on which she lies are made of marble, an imported material uncommon for monuments at that time. With the coffered arch supported by ten columns, Colt drew a symbolic parallel between Elizabeth's reign, the Tudor dynasty, and the Roman Empire. From the outside, the viewer can read the canopy as a tripartite Roman triumphal arch, which finds its source in the arch of Septimius Severus (203) in the Roman Forum. In contrast to Cure's idealized representation of Mary, Elizabeth's face clearly suggests a portrait and may have been modeled after her death mask. Upon the monument's completion, de Critz gilded and polychromed the marble in an ostentatious display of color that complied with prevailing fashion.

Contemporaries widely regarded Elizabeth's tomb as a success in its elegant use of the Classical style, although artists did not ultimately duplicate the tomb's elements in their own works. In 1607, after the death of James's infant daughter Sophia, Salisbury commissioned Colt to create another royal memorial. Stationed

Monument to Sir Robert Cecil, Earl of Salisbury
The Conway Library, Courtauld Institute of Art

at the foot of Elizabeth's tomb, Sophia is depicted not as deceased, but rather asleep in a cradle. Never before had a child not in direct line to the throne been depicted on such a scale or with such tender attention to detail. The sepulchre inspired many reproductions throughout England.

Colt petitioned Lord Salisbury and Lord Chamberlain for a permanent royal position and was subsequently named master sculptor in 1608, in recognition of his talent and service to the crown. In the following year, he was granted a gift of broadcloth and fur to be renewed annually as confirmation of his position. While he completed the occasional royal monument, his daily work involved the design and production of more mundane decorative items such as sculpted coats of arms, friezes, garden ornaments, and chimney-pieces.

With Salisbury's tomb of around 1614–18, Colt reached the apex of his creative energies. He worked closely on the monument's design with Salisbury himself, who had the sculptor create models for the project as early as 1609. Regarded as unique in an age still dominated by the Elizabethan style, the work appears to be a composite of elements Colt possibly encountered in France or while en route to England via the Netherlands. Scholars have likened Colt's Virtue figures, stationed at each corner of the black limestone bier, to those found on the tomb of Louis XII (1517–31) and those around the sepulchre of Francis II (1502–17) of Brittany at Nantes, France, ascribed to Michel Colombe. Salisbury's tomb also shows similarities to the 16th-century monument to Englebert II (*ca.* 1535) of Nassau, a work located in Breda, the Netherlands, and attributed to the sculptor Jean Mone. The entire

design of Salisbury's tomb may have originated with an engraving published in Jacques Androuet du Cerceau's *Second Livre d'Architecture* (1561). Depicting the Earl on a simple black bier with his skeleton just underneath, Colt's work also makes strong reference to medieval memento mori, whereas his allegorical figures of the Virtues are a certain deference to Renaissance iconography. The monument also diverges from Elizabethan stylistic dictates and moves closer to the Italian Renaissance aesthetic through its conspicuous lack of gilding and polychromy.

Colt returned to more provincial Elizabethan artistic precedents with his monument to David, Lord Scone, in 1619 and in his tomb commission for Sir George Savile. His reluctance to embrace more progressive and refined European styles did not find favor with James's successor, Charles I, who cast himself as a grand arts patron and wished to spur on greater creativity and innovation. Colt consequently received fewer commissions and fell into obscurity. He was ultimately sent to Fleet debtors' prison, but was released in 1641, when a petition for inquiry into the prison warden's legal practices was sent to the House of Lords. Colt died in London sometime between 1647 and 1650.

SAVANNAH SCHROLL

Biography

Born in Arras, France, exact date of birth unknown. Originally Maximilian Poultrain. Immigrated to England via Utrecht, the Netherlands, mid 1590s; anglicized surname to Colt; also in official documents as Coult; settled with elder brother John outside London, *ca.* 1596; developed relationship with native London Anglo-Dutch population; signed agreement with Robert Cecil, First Earl of Salisbury, to carve tomb monument for Queen Elizabeth I, 4 March 1604; made master sculptor to James I, London, 28 July 1608; granted suit of broadcloth and fur to be conferred yearly confirming position, 3 March 1609; imprisoned in the Fleet prison for debt, date unknown; released from the Fleet prison, 1641. Died in London, England, *ca.* 1647–50.

Selected Works

1604–06 Monument to Queen Elizabeth I; marble; Westminster Abbey, London, England
1607–09 Monument to Princess Mary; marble; Westminster Abbey, London, England
1607–09 Monument to Princess Sophia; marble; Westminster Abbey, London, England
ca. Chimneypiece in the King James Drawing
1609–11 Room; marble; Hatfield House, Hertfordshire, England

ca. 1611   Monument to Sir George Home, Earl of
              Dunbar; alabaster, marble; Dunbar parish
              church, East Lothian, Scotland
ca.   Monument to Sir Robert Cecil, Earl of
1614–18   Salisbury; marble, limestone, alabaster; St.
              Etheldreda Church, Hatfield, Hertfordshire,
              England
1619   Monument to David, Lord Scone; alabaster
              and marble; Scone Palace, Perth, Scotland
1627–28   Monument to Sir George Savile; alabaster
              and marble; St. Michael's Church,
              Thornhill, West Yorkshire, England

Further Reading

Esdaile, Katharine, "The Part Played by Refugee Sculptors, 1600–1750," *Proceedings of the Huguenot Society of Great Britain and Ireland* 18 (1949)

Mann, J.G., "English Church Monuments," *Walpole Society Proceedings* 21 (1932)

Taylor, K., "The Monument to George Home, 1st Earl of Dunbar, by Maximilian Colt, c. 1611, in Dunbar Parish Church," in *Sculpture Conservation: Preservation or Interference?* Brookfield, Vermont: Scolar Press, 1997

Whinney, Margaret, *Sculpture in Britain, 1530–1830*, London and Baltimore, Maryland: Penguin, 1964; 2nd edition, revised by John Physick, London and New York: Penguin, 1988

White, Adam, "Maximilian Colt: Master Sculptor to King James I," *Proceedings of the Huguenot Society of Great Britain and Ireland* 27 (Summer 1988)

White, Adam, "Westminster Abbey in the Early Seventeenth Century: A Powerhouse of Ideas," *Church Monuments* 4 (1989)

White, Adam, "The Booke of Monuments Reconsidered: Maximilian Colt and William Wright," *Church Monuments* 9 (1994)

COLUMN OF MARCUS AURELIUS

Anonymous

ca. 180–193 CE

marble

h. 42 m

Piazza Colonna, Rome, Italy

The Column of Marcus Aurelius was originally about 52 meters high and consisted of three parts: a rectangular base with an inner chamber; a Doric column with an internal spiral staircase of 203 steps, 21 bands of a continuous exterior relief, and 56 windows; and a bronze statue of Marcus Aurelius that stood on top of the column. Although the statue is lost and the base altered, the column shaft preserves its original aspect.

In the topography of ancient Rome, the Column of Marcus Aurelius was located in the Campus Martius in an area designated for imperial funerary monuments. It stood in the center of an open space between the Temple of the Deified Marcus Aurelius (dedicated after that emperor's death) and a road, the Via Flaminia, toward which it faced. Currently positioned in much the same way, the column stands in the Piazza Colonna in front of a columnar facade, that of Palazzo Wedekind, still facing the ancient Via Flaminia (now called Via del Corso).

The precise date of the column's creation remains unknown. One literary source notes a column, generally assumed to be this column, among the honors voted to Marcus Aurelius at his death in 180 and thus provides a plausible commencement date. An inscription found near the column records letters concerning the construction of a house in the neighborhood for the Column's caretaker. These letters, dating between August and September of 193, indicate that the column of Marcus Aurelius was finished by 193.

The structural and thematic model for the Column of Marcus Aurelius was the Column of Trajan, dedicated in 113. Trajan's column, consisting of the same three fundamental elements, recounts on its shaft the events of Trajan's two Dacian wars in 22 bands of continuous narrative relief. The two wars are separated by a figure of a Victory. Similarly, the spiraling narrative on the Column of Marcus Aurelius recounts two wars, and between the wars, in the middle of the column shaft on the tenth band facing the street, is the figure of a Victory. The scenes on Marcus Aurelius's column feature neither Lucius Verus—his adopted brother and brief coruler—nor Commodus, Marcus's son. The wars depicted, therefore, should date between 169 (the death of Lucius Verus) and 175 (when Commodus joined his father on campaign) and they should be the wars against the Quadi and Marcomanni (172–173) and the Sarmatians (174–175).

A 4th-century catalogue of the monuments of Rome describes the monument as a spiral column next to the Temple of Antoninus Pius; it makes no reference to Marcus Aurelius. Subsequently, the column became known as the Column of Antoninus, presumably because of its vicinity to the Temple of Antoninus Pius. In fact, at the end of the 16th century, when the Column was restored, a new inscription placed on the base erroneously proclaimed that Marcus Aurelius had erected the column in honor of Antoninus Pius. The misconception persisted until 1704, when the base for the Column of Antoninus was discovered.

A major restoration of the Column of Marcus Aurelius was commissioned by Pope Sixtus V in 1589 and supervised by Domenico Fontana. It involved erecting a bronze statue of St. Paul on the top of the column and filling its numerous lacunae with marble taken from ancient monuments. The new fillers were carved *in situ* in a manner that copied the original relief both iconographically and stylistically. The chief sculptor

Column of Marcus Aurelius, Rome, Italy
© Carmen Redondo / CORBIS

and erection of a statue of St. Paul (on its front side); and the sacredness and triumph of the column that resulted from this representation of Paul, the "disciple" of Christ. The statue of St. Paul formed a pendant to the statue of St. Peter erected on the Column of Trajan.

In the 20th century scholars have focused on the differences between the reliefs of the Column of Trajan and those of the Column of Marcus Aurelius. The reliefs of the Column of Marcus Aurelius feature fewer scenes, deeper carving, and more animated actions. There is less interest in background scenery, space is less clearly defined, and the figures tend to be ill proportioned. It has more violent war scenes and fewer scenes of the army involved in feats of structural engineering. It also depicts two miracle scenes, one of which (the rain miracle) ancient authors variously described as a response to prayers: of Christian soldiers to the Lord, of Marcus Aurelius or Julian the Apostate to pagan gods, or of an Egyptian magician to Hermes of the air. Finally, Marcus Aurelius often appears frontally, whereas Trajan never does. The reliefs on the Column of Marcus Aurelius have therefore been used as evidence for the decline of Classical art in the later empire, the rise of the "plebeian" (crude populist) style, growing interest in the supernatural and spiritual, and an increasingly iconic representation of the role of the emperor, all of which have been related to the end of the high Roman Empire.

These ideas have been mostly refuted by recent scholarship. At the end of the 2nd century, artists in the imperial service could work to the highest formal standards. Elegant portraits of the family of Marcus Aurelius as well as the fine historical relief panels of the period attest to this notion. Furthermore, it has been demonstrated that the style of carving on the column, often compared with sarcophagi, was in part because of its role on the monument: narrative friezes in Roman architecture traditionally used a more expressive plebeian style. The small frieze of the Ara Pacis and the victory processions of the Arch of Titus or the Arch of Trajan at Benevento are obvious examples.

The idea that the Column of Marcus Aurelius presents iconic representations of the emperor is exaggerated. The frequent frontal views are part of its design for greater legibility; the position of the emperor was no more exalted in the period of Antoninus Pius than in the period of Trajan. Furthermore, frontality and symmetric arrangement of individuals to illustrate hierarchy appears in Roman coins, medallions, and small objects already in the early 1st century.

The great attention given to the human figures and their expression may also be explained as a deliberate attempt to create greater legibility and to correct the mistakes made by the sculptors of the Column of Trajan. Fewer figures and figures with more pronounced

was Silla Longhi da Viggiù, best known for his work in the Sistine Chapel and the Cappella Paolina in the Basilica of Santa Maria Maggiore, Rome. The column's base also underwent significant alterations. The damaged relief decoration on the base's fourth course—which featured Victories with garlands on three sides and, on the fourth (the front side), a scene of Marcus Aurelius with defeated barbarians—was scraped away, and the portion of the base that stood above ground was encased with new marble slabs. Notwithstanding this intervention, four meters of the base, visible in Antiquity, and a further three meters of support, never visible, still remain untouched today below the modern city level.

On each side of the restored base, a different inscription was engraved. Reflecting papal ideology, these note: the column's ancient glory (including the error that it originally honored Antoninus Pius); the column's state of decrepitude prior to restoration; the cleansing of the column's pagan character by Sixtus expressions are easier for a spectator looking up at a tall relief column to understand. The artistic capabilities and the concepts of the emperor and Roman military glory had not undergone significant changes between the erection of the Column of Trajan in 113 and the erection of the Column of Marcus Aurelius in the 180s. Rather, the visual expression of those concepts had been improved and standardized for greatest clarity. The Column of Marcus Aurelius thus represents less a rupture, and more a continuation and development of a Roman tradition of detailed historical narratives in marble relief.

JULIA LENAGHAN

Further Reading

Brilliant, Richard, *Visual Narratives: Storytelling in Etruscan and Roman Art*, Ithaca, New York: Cornell University Press, 1984

Caprino, G., et al., *La colonna di Marco Aurelio*, Rome: Bretschneider, 1955

Claridge, Amanda, *Rome: An Oxford Archaeological Guide*, Oxford and New York: Oxford University Press, 1998

Kleiner, Diana, *Roman Sculpture*, New Haven, Connecticut: Yale University Press, 1992

Maffei, Stefania, "Columna Marci Aurelii Antonini," in *Lexicon Topographicum Urbis Romae*, Rome: Edizioni Quasar, 1993

Petersen, Eugen, A. von Domaszewski, and G. Calderini, *Die Marcus Säule auf Piazza Colonna in Rom*, Munich: Bruckmann, 1896

Pirson, Felix, "Style and Message on the Column of Marcus Aurelius," *Papers of the British School at Rome* 64 (1996)

Wegner, Max, "Die kunstgeschichtliche Stellung der Marcussäule" *Jahrbuch des deutschen Archäologisches Instituts* 46 (1931)

Zwikker, W., *Studien zur Marcussäule*, Amsterdam: Niu. Noord-Hollandsche Uitgevers mij., 1941

CONSERVATION: STONE AND MARBLE

There are three main sources of decay in stone and marble: physical, chemical, and organic growth.

Physical decay is generally the result of vandalism, damage in transit, and abrasion from a variety of sources, such as windblown dirt and dust, inappropriate cleaning with brushes or dirty cloths, and, ironically, chafing from protective covers. The effects of extreme temperatures on stone and the variable latent effect of sculptors' tools and carving techniques are also sources of physical decay.

Stone, particularly marble, will undergo dimensional change in contrasting weather conditions of hot, sunlit days and rapidly cooling evenings and cold nights. In such conditions the stone structure of bonded marble crystals will deteriorate as crystals loosen and break away, causing a characteristic "sugaring" at extremities such as fingertips and drapery edges. Another

more obvious form of decay caused by temperature change is the freeze-thaw action of frost on damp and wet stone.

Temperature changes will also affect metals in stone statuary. The expansion of metal repair and fixing dowels will cause cracks to emanate from them, often at the expense of repaired limbs and other extremities of figural sculpture.

Opportunities to minutely survey the surface of sculptures with laser and ultrasound have developed a new interest in the effect of carving tools and techniques on the resistance of stone to weathering. One sculpture can include a variety of surface strengths caused by an inconsistency in porosity across its surface. A stone surface stunned and bruised by carving tools held at right angles to the stone block, such as the point and claw chisel used to provide a rough texture for the hair, will be more prone to staining by atmospheric dirt and suffer the consequences of weathering than a highly polished area of the statue, such as the face or bare shoulder.

Staining (the chemical reaction of stone to strongly acidic and alkaline cleaning agents) and atmospheric pollutants are both well-known sources of chemical decay. Staining is an unwanted surface coloration or shading. Natural pigments in the minerals of stone rising to the surface or absorption of atmospheric deposits will cause stone to darken. If the coloration is welcome, then it is considered patination; if it is unwanted, then it is a stain.

The chemical reaction of pollutants and cleaning agents is caused by salt activity on the stone surface. All stone has a degree of porosity, which exposes it to harmful soluble salts from a number of sources; these chemical pollutants are in the ground (nitrates and chlorides) and the atmosphere (sulfates and nitrates) and arise from inappropriate coatings (such as gypsum). If salt content on the surface of the stone is in high enough concentrations and the sculpture is exposed to damp conditions, degradation of the stone can be rapid. The decay of the Romanesque frieze sculptures of the Cathedral of Lincoln in England (*ca.* 1123–1248) carved in dolomitic limestone is a dramatic example. Dry and wet acidic deposits (commonly known as acid rain) combined with the stone surface to form soluble sulfate compounds. The repetitive process of the salts passing in and out of this solution over the course of centuries led to a dramatic loss of surface detail. The process was made worse by the tendency of the polluted stone surface to harden and fall away because of additional salt crystallization beneath it.

Organic growths are not easily discernible, as the action is mainly microscopic. The presence of lichen algae and mosses on stone will be detrimental. As well as encouraging dirt deposits with the eventual risk of staining, such growths will harbor dampness, and in some cases produce harmful chelating deposits of, among others, oxalic acid.

As with all artifact conservation, preparation is of the utmost importance. Before any work takes place there must be a comprehensive analysis of decay, a thorough understanding of the methods of production of the sculpture, and a clear understanding of the effect that the treatment will have. The choice of materials for conservation is important. Conservators should aim to repair "like with like" so that the treatment ensures the option of future reversibility.

Diagnosis of the decay is essential before any treatment is started. Diagnosis is not limited to the sculpture: environmental monitoring is increasingly playing a part in the conservation of sculpture. Humidity and temperature monitoring at the surface of the stone and in the surrounding atmosphere over long periods of time can prevent costly and unnecessary treatment programs.

Consider the example of the eroding marble tomb of Speaker Chaloner Chute carved by John Cheere's workshop in 1776. Erosion of the marble in a damp tomb chamber at the Vyne in Hampshire, England, called for intervention. Rather than merely carry out repairs to the sculpture effigy, the environmental conditions of the tomb chamber were monitored for several seasons with surface temperature and internal and external dampness readings before specifying a course of treatment for the marble. As the causes of the erosion were a damp atmosphere, identification of the sources of dampness, together with their control, treated the tomb without (as yet) major interference to the structure.

Other nondestructive analysis methods include the use of radiography to uncover the interior materials and structure of a sculpture. A relatively thin stone relief or larger, less dense plaster statuary can be accurately surveyed with high-resolution X-rays, and more powerful, but less clear, gamma radiography can also be employed. Illuminated thin sections taken for microscopy will reveal mineralogical content, and X-ray diffraction will assist identification of other compounds.

Contentious issues accompany the removal of unwanted dirt, paint, overpaint, discolored varnishes, and waxes, and it is argued that the removal of such coverings is detrimental to the appearance of the sculpture since dirt is often important evidence of a sculpture's former time and place. The original protective lime coating documented on Ghandaran sculpture would never be cleaned away today, but the disfiguring red clay accretions—windblown deposits from the sculpture's time—has at times been removed. Similarly, vestiges of organic growths of moss and lichen algae

on garden statuary have been removed prior to their resetting in the interiors of museums and houses.

The call to clean unwanted dirt and coverings on sculpture, in order to show the sculpture as the artist intended, has risks. Only from the account of members of his workshop do we learn of Antonio Canova's tinting "in the antique" of his marble statuary with a light ocherish wash of the marble with iron oxide water. The coloring could be mistaken at times for atmospheric discoloration. Antique statuary may have acquired both naturally deposited burial dirt and applied restorer's patination from the years of the European cognoscenti. The guiding rule for cleaning sculpture should be that only dirt that is proven to be damaging to the sculpture is removed and that a full visual and documentary analysis is made prior to any cleaning.

Repair and prevention conservation is a process that circumvents decay before it takes hold in order to greatly minimize the risk of damage. If stone statuary is maintained in a generally stable environment without extremes of dampness and temperature, then there should be little cause for dramatic change in the condition of the sculpture. Garden statuary can be protected by insulating, waterproof covers. Regular dusting and swabbing with water and nonionic detergent will keep the sculpture generally dirt free. Further precautions against disfiguring stains and dirt lie in the use of colorless protective waxes applied and removed regularly (to prevent the waxes themselves from becoming a source of staining). For reversibility, synthetic waxes such as cosmolloid and Regalrez are preferred to the more traditional coverings of beeswax and damar, which have a low boiling point and tend to soften in normal temperatures and attract dirt. By monitoring a sculpture and acting on early signs of deterioration, costly repair programs can be avoided.

Simple but effective preventative work includes ensuring that plinths and pedestals are stable and that joints in the sculpture remain closed and sound. Garden statuary should be washed regularly to prevent buildup of harmful atmospheric deposits, and organic growths should be inhibited from growing too thickly by applying biocides. Historic paint should not be allowed to deteriorate: surface coatings not only decorate, but often also protect. It could be argued that statuary in the ancient world was painted partly for conservation reasons. Trajan's column (ca. 2nd century CE) was painted in an ochre lime wash and thereby effectively sheltered. The painted statues on the western front of the Cathedral of Wells in England (ca. 1310) were protected from strong winds.

In broken statuary, harmful, corroded, and expanding ferrous fixings can be removed, provided that there is no doubt as to their location. This is a measure that will inevitably require a great deal of individual skill and manual dexterity on the part of the conservator whose use of levers, chisels, and small tools should leave no trace. At times it may be preferable to treat the fixings *in situ* with rust inhibitors, rather than wholly remove them, some of which may be of historical value in themselves. Roman sculpture at Aphrodisias in western Turkey exhibits ancient repairs with iron dowels set in lead to fix broken limbs.

Loose elements, which are often loosened restorations, should be readhered with reversible adhesives, the choice of which depends on the strength of bond required and the type of sculptural material. A plaster bust will require the lightest metal support with resin adhesive compared with the amount of reinforcement needed to hold two pieces of stone together. The dislocated hand of Michelangelo Buonarroti's *Pietà* (St. Peter's Basilica, Rome), vandalized in 1982, was repaired with both long, shaped, stainless steel dowels and acrylic adhesive to hold the hand and wrist in place and relocate the many broken marble shards caused by the numerous hammer blows of the vandal. Acrylic resin tailored to act as a repair medium by holding colored minerals and pigments in the correct refractive index mirrored that of the marble of the *Pietà* in order to be undetectable.

Stone that has become so weakened by decay that it no longer supports itself, losing surface detail and possibly material at depth, can be strengthened with irreversible stone strengtheners. Application of synthetic polymers that are absorbed by the porosity of the stone harden at depth, and in so doing—provided that they do not entirely saturate and prevent normal transfer of water vapors throughout the stone—give enough strength to prevent the stone from decaying further.

For plaster in a similar decayed condition, conservation is less complex than in stone, requiring simpler, and generally weaker, treatments.

Plaster sculpture is rarely encountered in a raw state. Almost certainly it is painted or "stopped" with a surface treatment to prevent discoloration from atmospheric dirt and grime. As plaster repair often involves replacement of decay, losses are made good beneath the surface and the painted surface repaired. It is this replacement approach that sets plaster conservation apart from stone and other material conservation. In marked contrast to the conservation procedure of the marble and stone conservator, the plaster conservator frequently makes use of a restorer's skill.

TREVOR PROUDFOOT

See also **Canova, Antonio**

Further Reading

Ashurst, John, and Frances G. Dimes (editors), *Conservation of Building and Decorative Stone*, 2 vols., London and Boston: Butterworths, 1990

Cennini, Cennino, *The Craftsman's Handbook (Il libro dell'arte* [1437]), translated by Daniel V. Thompson, Jr., New York: Dover, 1933

Horie, C.V., *Materials for Conservation: Organic Consolidants, Adhesives, and Coatings*, London and Boston: Butterworths, 1987

Lindley, Philip (editor), *Sculpture Conservation: Preservation or Interference?* Brookfield, Vermont: Scolar Press, 1997

Naudé, Virginia Norton (editor), *Sculptural Monuments in an Outdoor Environment: A Conference Held at the Pennsylvania Academy of Fine Arts, Philadelphia, November 2, 1983*, Philadelphia: Pennsylvania Academy of Fine Arts, 1985

Sandwith, Hermione, and Sheila Staunton, *National Trust Manual of Housekeeping*, London: Allen Lane, 1984

Schaffer, Robert John, *The Weathering of Natural Building Stones*, London: HMSO, 1932

Simpson and Brown, Architects (compilers and editors), *Conservation of Plasterwork: A Guide to the Principles of Conserving and Repairing Historic Plasterwork*, Edinburgh: Crambeth Allen, 1994

CONSERVATION: OTHER THAN STONE AND MARBLE

The conservation of sculpture has received less attention—theoretical, methodological, and technical—than that of painting, mainly because painting has been traditionally and historically held in higher esteem than the other fine arts. For a long time (essentially from the 15th to the 18th century), conservators considered the conservation of sculpture to consist solely of adding missing pieces to statues; they took no account of interventions related uniquely to consolidation of existing parts or of further complications related to surface coloring. In the 19th and 20th centuries, the theoretical debate on conservation dealt mainly with painting. The small attention paid to sculpture focused largely on marble, the "noblest material." A vast bibliography exists on conserving marble sculpture, with far fewer studies concerning other materials.

Certain principles that some conservation traditions consider generally valid for paintings are also considered appropriate for sculpture. The Western tradition recognizes the need to cultivate a deep respect for the original object and to consider its value as testimony, as well as its aesthetic value. Consequently, conserving a work does not mean giving it artificial and fictitious values imagined by the modern conservator but putting the work in the physical condition that will best ensure its endurance and its ability to transmit its own values. It is nonetheless true in the Western tradition that the particular quality an object assumes by the very fact of being recognized as a work of art implies that its aesthetic characteristics must be taken into account and that conservation work must also enhance the capacity of the original to transmit its original aesthetic values. However, the attention to the aesthetic aspect implies that modern conservation work must not falsify the original on the pretext of reconstructing artistic values that historical events or the passage of time have diminished or erased. Support provided to a work's aesthetic values should be limited, easily recognizable, and easily reversible to enable any future adjustments required for technical reasons or by changes in taste. Latin countries, following the conservation theory formulated by the 20th-century Italian art historian Cesare Brandi, respond to the needs of recognizability and reversibility more strongly than do Anglo-Saxon countries. By the same token, in Latin countries the advice of historians of art, architecture, and Antiquity influence more the results of conservation work, while scientific approaches more widely influence conservation in Anglo-Saxon countries. Nonetheless, while conservators are the only people authorized to work physically on art objects, collaboration with both historians and scientists is fundamental for conservation purposes.

Thus, one should always plan conservation work with full respect for the original. Conservators should save as much as possible of the surviving components and pay attention to both the structural and the aesthetic aspects of the piece. They should fill in missing elements with moderation, finding ways to show the viewer that they are not original and making sure that they can be removed as easily as possible, if appropriate. In many cases a vital issue is whether to redisplay a sculpture outdoors or indoors, possibly placing a copy outdoors (the development of laser-based three-dimensional copying systems will increase the availability of high-quality copies).

Whether a sculpture was originally indoors or outdoors, its surface will certainly have changed. Over time deposits, ranging from grayish films to black incrustations several inches thick, will have built up on the surface. They should be removed not only for aesthetic reasons but because cleaning the surface is the essential and preliminary action without which one cannot proceed to stabilize, consolidate, and protect the sculpture. However, freeing the surface of deposits should never entirely destroy the traces left by time; the "time component" is fundamental for and inseparable from a work of art from the past and constitutes a positive value as historical evidence.

Cleaning is often made more difficult when the underlying work is in poor condition. Here lies a paradox: a work must be cleaned before it can be consolidated, but before being cleaned it should be consolidated.

The substances used in consolidation fall into two basic categories: natural and artificial (obtained by synthesis). The latter are usually organic chemicals and may pose problems of compatibility, which is generally not the case with the former. As regards cleaning, the means used may be mechanical (e.g., lancets and blades, abrasive sprays, various types of brushes and hammers, ultrasound emitters), chemical (various sol-

vents applied in different ways), or physical (e.g., laser beams, whose use is spreading rapidly).

Conservators must always adapt to compromises, using the materials and application techniques that offer the greatest advantages and the smallest drawbacks under the particular circumstances. Good conservators also know that, while they are doing their utmost to make a work as durable as possible, it will certainly not be the last intervention on the piece in question; hence, they must do their best not to prevent but rather to facilitate future conservation work.

Regarding diagnostic techniques, it is worth emphasizing the importance of physical analyses aimed at ascertaining the internal conditions of the structure and identifying any fractures. X-rays are valuable, as are gamma rays, which penetrate deeper because of their shorter wavelength. Ultraviolet rays are useful for revealing the status of any surface coloring and whether it is original.

The basic conservation procedure consists of a series of successive steps (in practice, some are occasionally skipped). First, the conservator marks an object for conservation according to criteria that take account of its urgency, which may depend on the object's state of preservation, its historical, artistic, and anthropological importance, or other reasons, such as the desire to display a piece long relegated to a museum's storerooms. Next is a careful survey of the object's state of preservation; this process involves visual analysis and a series of scientific analyses. Third, the conservator must prepare a conservation project specifically for the object in question. Such projects are differentiated according to different criteria, for instance, whether the object will be eventually displayed indoors or outdoors. Fourth, a skilled conservator will begin the work in an orderly and well-equipped shop, aided by specialists (historians and scientists, depending on the object) and precise photographic and descriptive documentation. Based on tests made at this point, the conservator will determine the techniques, methodologies, and materials appropriate for the specific object. These parameters may later change in accordance with further information gained during the work. Fifth, the conservation work will take into account solely conservation needs and not have a restoration intervention hurried on because of the opening of an exhibition, for example. Sixth, the conservator will have to deal with any problems raised by the future location of the work so that corrections required for long-term conservation can be made promptly.

Terracotta Sculpture

Artists have used terracotta for both small and life-size statues, firing the modeled clay piece at a temperature preferably between around 900 and 1200 degrees Celsius. It was essential to let the clay dry out as much as possible before firing to avoid the unevenness that would result if the kiln dried it out too fast. To this end, some large pieces were hollowed out to reduce their mass, while others were modeled around an armature; if made of wood, the armature would burn up around 300 degrees Celsius. Before firing a large piece, the artisan cut it into several parts, using a wire to keep the edges sharp. Sometimes the artist first roughly blocked out the figure and added the details later, but this procedure could cause problems with adhesion between the two layers. The artist used slip (liquid clay) to join the parts of a figure after firing.

In restoring a terracotta statue, the conservator must pay special attention to the structure, which is often fragile and may have numerous cracks due to firing defects (commonly repaired in the past with stucco, plaster, or mortar) or breakage during relocation (which always leaves traces). In general, the conservator should carefully dismantle the sculpture, separating the pieces resulting from the original technique and any breakage. Pins applied in past conservation work are usually made of iron and can easily rust; in some cases they were secured with molten lead. These pins should be removed and replaced with steel, light metal, or fiberglass. The conservator should demolish additions, replacements, or resurfacing applied in the past that are aesthetically unacceptable today or, more importantly, dangerous from the standpoint of conservation (e.g., parts in cement or plaster absorb water, which always creates problems), although it is sometimes impossible to do so. It may be necessary to devise elastic junctions. In principle, the conservator should eliminate excessive rigidity, striking a balance between the need to support the structure firmly and the need to provide some elasticity in order to avoid cracks and breakage.

In colored works, the conservator should stabilize the glaze or paint with an adhesive. Acrylic adhesives such as the widely used Paraloid B72 are usually a better choice than natural adhesives such as casein because they generally spread more easily. Sometimes the original colors were repainted or simply laid over with plaster (for example, tinted a bronze color), so that the work would seem to be made of a more expensive material. In these cases the conservator will have to use stratigraphy and careful examinations to establish how many coats of paint were applied, how extensively and exactly where (a sample taken for analysis is meaningful only for the exact spot from which it was removed). If the original color is too fragmentary, the conservator may decide not to recover it but, as in the case of a 15th-century sculpture, leave the 17th- or 18th-century overpainting. In general, the cleaning process will alternate between the use of a lancet and

of solvents or gels (such as ammonium carbonate), applied with a paintbrush or a compress, usually consisting of some form of cellulose. To avoid direct contact, the conservator often places Japan paper between the compress and the paint. The conservator also needs to repair any damage due to biological agents or soluble salts (sulfates, nitrates, etc.), if possible, transforming the salts chemically or extracting them with compresses.

When the parts are ready to be reassembled, an epoxy resin will provide strong adhesion where appropriate. The conservator can make additions with various types of natural or synthetic stucco. Polyfilla resins are widely used for this purpose because they are easy to shape and can be tinted during the mixing phase. Additions are usually highly susceptible to breakage when struck. If it is decided to touch up the original paint, various types of binders can be used with the pigments, which can be protected with a substance such as a 3 percent solution of Paraloid in xylene. A thin coat of microcrystalline synthetic wax can provide further protection but will make the surface oilier and thus more likely to retain atmospheric deposits.

One can often date terracotta pieces fairly accurately with thermoluminescence. In general, the techniques described for terracotta conservation also apply to sculptures in plaster, stucco, and unfired clay.

Bronze Sculpture

Sculptures can be cast in any metal, but the vast majority of metal sculptures are in bronze. Casting techniques are often complex and are not described here. The artist must clean and polish the surface of the casting before it can receive the final patina. (Traditionally, each shop had its own highly guarded secret recipe, and cleaning sometimes took more time than the modeling and casting operations together.) Bronze sculptures may have been originally painted or gilded; upon careful observation, one may sometimes see traces of gold (applied to emphasize the edges of a garment, for instance) and other colors.

Bronze sculptures were coated with substances derived from plants, which gave them a yellowish, reddish, brownish, or blackish hue. These original patinas, which usually cannot be detected today, should not be confused with the patina formed over time through corrosion and the formation of salts. Today, a bronze statue that has been displayed outdoors may have taken on a black or greenish color in the parts exposed to rain, while the unexposed parts are covered with black incrustations formed by atmospheric deposits and the degeneration of the original metal. It has been said, almost philosophically, that the elements that make up bronze tend naturally and inexorably to separate and return to their natural state. In fact, open-air bronzes are subject to highly corrosive electrochemical oxidation processes characterized by the presence of copper sulfates and—most damaging—copper chlorides. The conservator must therefore distinguish between "noble" patinas—essentially the often extraordinarily beautiful green ones, which must be preserved—and those that should be removed as far as possible. The process requires repeated washing: surface cleaning with chemicals or tools such as revolving iron brushes, soft-iron percussion-drill bits, lancets, and ultrasound emitters (tools are preferable because they enable continuous visual control). At present conservators widely promote lasers for this work, which are more safely used on recent statues (beginning in the mid 19th century) than on ancient ones.

The conservator must eliminate the earth from the original model remaining inside the artifact after casting because it gathers moisture and can start new corrosion processes. After these operations, the conservator can apply a corrosion inhibitor such as benzotriazol. Corrosion inhibitors have limited adhesive properties and have to be coated with other protective substances, but these often alter the sculpture's optical conditions. It is not possible to achieve an ideal result without compromises; the most effective substances are often contraindicated for aesthetic reasons.

Sculptures in other metals, including gold and silver, present similar problems and call for similar techniques.

Polychrome Wooden Sculpture

Because wood is relatively easy to carve, artists in every age have used it for sculpture, but its relatively low durability has not helped the survival of wooden sculptures. As with other materials, artists applied paint to wood for protection, for aesthetic reasons, and as a way to imitate reality. Because of the relative effortlessness of transporting them (due to their limited weight), and their liturgical purpose (if we consider how many statues there are of Christ on the cross in the Western Christian tradition), wooden statues more than others were thought of as merely functional. They were finished with dresses, wigs, and crowns of thorn, and they were repainted continuously, as soon as usage damaged the existing polychromies. It is not uncommon to discover a dozen layers of color on these sculptures, identified by means of cross sections. In addition, moisture causes the plaster and glue beneath the paint to swell, and insects attack the wood without mercy.

The conservator must therefore deal with the problems of the structure as well as the visible surfaces of a wooden sculpture. The wood may be badly worm eaten and cracked and must be consolidated with traditional glues or acrylic resins. The original paint may be in very bad shape, and often the conservator will decide to restore a later but coherent polychromy. Some schools of conservation believe that all nonoriginal paint should be removed, even if none of the original is left. This position, although widely held, should be judged negatively because the result is that, contrary to the sculptor's intention, the bare wood is displayed with all the marks left by hatchet and chisel. From a practical standpoint, the paint is like that of an easel painting, so the same methods are used for cleaning it: lancet and microscope, or solvents. More and more frequently, conservators are using alternative methods based on resin soaps, solvent gels, or enzymes (biocleaning), which have the advantage of being highly selective—they act only on the substances to be removed and do not affect the others—and totally harmless for the conservator. For the treatment of woodworms, impregnation with an aqueous medium such as Permetar, which is minimally toxic to humans, is replacing impregnation with poisonous substances such as Xylamon, which are harmful to humans, and fumigation with methyl bromide, which is difficult to apply and volatilizes quickly. Wooden sculptures are highly sensitive to humidity.

Other Materials and Contemporary Art

Sculptors have used many other materials in addition to the materials already discussed. Ivory, for instance, was widely used in the Gothic era and again in the Baroque, especially for small pieces. Ivory has problems with adhesion between layers and hence consolidation problems; humidity is an important factor and must be kept under strict control. For contemporary works, conservators must consider the very concept of sculpture and the materials used in a totally new way. In a contemporary sculpture one may encounter an object from everyday life (e.g., a sink or bicycle handlebar), as well as synthetic materials such as fiberglass, foam rubber, and artificial foam. In any case, it is essential to follow a principle enunciated by the Italian conservation theorist Cesare Brandi: restore only the materials of a work, not its image (although restoring the materials inevitably affects the image as well). A conservator who follows this principle will be ready to deal with any unusual problem or material by relying on that mixture of tradition and innovation, experience and research, that characterizes conservation and makes it such a fascinating discipline.

GIORGIO BONSANTI

Further Reading

Baracchini, Clara (editor), *Scultura lignea: Lucca, 1200–1425* (exhib. cat.), 2 vols., Florence: Studio per Edizioni Scelte, 1995

Baxandall, Michael, *The Limewood Sculptors of Renaissance Germany*, New Haven, Connecticut: Yale University Press, 1980

Burresi, Mariagiulia (editor), *Sacre passioni: Scultura lignea a Pisa dal XII al XV secolo* (exhib. cat.), Milan: Motta, 2000

Chapuis, Julien, *Tilman Riemenschneider: Master Sculptor of the Late Middle Ages*, Washington, D.C.: National Gallery of Art, 1999

Dolcini, Loretta (editor), *Verrocchio's Christ and St. Thomas: A Masterpiece of Sculpture from Renaissance Florence* (exhib. cat.), New York: Metropolitan Museum of Art, 1992

Formigli, Edilberto (editor), *I grandi bronzi antichi: Le fonderie e le tecniche di lavorazione dall'età arcaica al Rinascimento*, Siena, Italy: Nuova Immagine, 1999

Scultura dipinta: Maestri di legname e pittori a Siena, 1250–1450 (exhib. cat.), Florence: Centro Di, 1987

Vaccari, Maria Grazia (editor), *La scultura in terracotta: Tecniche e conservazione*, Florence: Centro Di, 1996

CONSTRUCTIVISM

Constructivist sculpture encompasses the work of a wide range of artists and geographic regions. Although constructed sculpture first gained recognition in the work of Pablo Picasso and Georges Braque, the genre as a whole has come to be associated with the geometric abstractions of the Constructivist movement. During the first half of the 20th century, the Constructivist sensibility moved throughout Europe in work by artists as diverse as Ben Nicholson and László Moholy-Nagy. In postrevolutionary Russia, however, artists created Constructivist sculpture with a utopian mindset, visualizing their work as representative of larger societal changes.

Although the term *constructivist* did not emerge until after the Russian Revolution of 1917, the constructed aesthetic began in Russian sculpture as early as 1914. Vladimir Yevgrafovich Tatlin, considered the main founder of Russian Constructivism, was influenced by the sculpture of the Cubists, whose works were constructed from separate elements rather than carved or modeled. After seeing Picasso's work in person, Tatlin made a series of "painterly" relief constructions in cardboard, wood, and metal. Like the Cubists, Tatlin used found objects and scrap materials, attempting to break down distinctions between high art and low culture. His *Counter-Relief* (1915) may have been a direct response to Braque's now-destroyed constructions that hung in corners. Braque had attempted in this way to expand the boundaries of art by extending the work into its environment. Tatlin took this integration of art and life one step further, hanging his constructions on wires suspended across a corner instead of attached to the wall in any way.

In the postrevolutionary period, Russian Constructivism became an organized movement. Konstantin Medunetsky, Alexander Rodchenko, and Varvara Stepanova, among others, founded the First Working Group of Constructivists in 1921 within Inkhuk, the Institute of Artistic Culture in Moscow. They defined the idea of construction in terms of new technology and engineering: constructions were made of industrial materials and were to be practical rather than decorative. Although some still experimented with painting, the assertion of the practical over the decorative lent itself mainly to three-dimensional work.

The definitions set forth by the Constructivists also implied a utopian aspect to the movement. Following the Revolution, Constructivists saw little place for an art without a social purpose. Rather than creating for personal expression, Constructivists aimed to aid in the creation of a new society. To this end, they consciously distanced themselves from the perceived classism of such terms as *art* and *artist*. They labeled themselves constructors and engineers, using their skills for the benefit of society rather than for their own pleasure, and some took employment in factories. Their use of industrial materials further indicated their intentions. Because machines and industry were seen as symbolic of the working class, and hence of the new classless society, Constructivists most often used industrial metals in their works. Although the constructions were abstract in nature, the Constructivists hoped that their materials would be intuitively comprehensible to the working masses.

Whereas most Constructivist sculpture was utopian in theory, Tatlin created a model for a literally utilitarian work. He conceived his *Monument to the Third International* (1919–20) as a working building in the

Antoine Pevsner, *For the Facade of a Museum*, 1943–44
© ARS, NY, Tate Gallery, London / Art Resource, NY

form of a large-scale Constructivist sculpture. Although the monument was never built, it would have stood more than 395 meters high; the model alone reached more than 6 meters. The iron spiral frame would have enclosed a glass cylinder, cube, and cone, which were to house the administrative, executive, and propaganda offices of the Comintern (Third International). The inner components would have revolved, once a day, once a month, and once a year, respectively. This realization of kinetic sculpture spoke to a new, modern machine age, while the ascending spiral form symbolized the aspirations of Communism, on both local and global levels.

The tenure of Russian Constructivist sculpture was short-lived. Because the artist-constructors aimed in large part for utilitarian ends, they soon branched out into more concrete design projects. The geometric Constructivist aesthetic found its way into graphic, theater, and textile design. The shift from theoretical to practical may also have been necessary for the movement's survival; even so, the Soviet leader Joseph Stalin eventually replaced it with socialist realism.

On the international front, however, the Constructivist aesthetic continued in a variety of forms. International Constructivism officially began at the Düsseldorf Congress of International Progressive Artists in May 1922. El Lissitzky, Theo van Doesburg, and others issued a declaration emphasizing their view of art as a method of systematic organization and as a tool of universal progress. Although they did not adhere to the socialist agenda set forth by the Russian Constructivists, artists in Germany, Poland, Czechoslovakia, and the Netherlands continued their methods of working with industrial materials in constructed geometric formations.

Of the international Constructivists working primarily in sculpture, Naum Gabo and Antoine Pevsner were the best known. Russian by birth, the brothers spent much of their lives in Western Europe, disseminating Constructivist ideas. Both worked with geometric forms and industrial materials, but unlike the Russian Constructivists, Gabo and Pevsner did not believe that art must necessarily serve a social function. Their *Realistic Manifesto* (1920) affirmed the possibility of an independent art and also suggested specific characteristics for the new sculpture, ranging from an integration of sculpture and its surrounding space to new kinetic and temporal aspects.

With his move to England in the 1930s, Gabo encouraged and loosely directed Constructivist ideas within a wider circle. Sculptures by Ben Nicholson and Barbara Hepworth both incorporated some Constructivist elements. The most definitive example of English Constructivism, however, is found in *Circle: International Survey of Constructive Art*, 1971, a compilation

of writings by artists and architects, edited by Gabo, Nicholson, and the architect Leslie Martin. Although the aesthetic of constructed and Constructivist sculpture later found periodic renewal in the post–World War II period, it was never as coherent or as idealistic as its more organized precedents.

RACHEL EPP BULLER

See also **Gabo, Naum; Moholy-Nagy, László; Pevsner, Antoine; Rodchenko, Alexander; Tatlin, Vladimir**

Further Reading

Andel, Jaroslav, et al., *Art into Life: Russian Constructivism, 1914–1932*, Seattle: Henry Art Gallery, University of Washington, and New York: Rizzoli, 1990

Bann, Stephen (editor), *The Tradition of Constructivism*, New York: Viking Press, 1974

Bowlt, John (editor), *Russian Art of the Avant-Garde: Theory and Criticism, 1902–1934*, New York: Viking Press, 1976; revised edition, London: Thames and Hudson, 1988

Lodder, Christina, *Russian Constructivism*, New Haven, Connecticut: Yale University Press, 1983; 3rd edition, 1987

Martin, J.L., Ben Nicholson, and Naum Gabo (editors), *Circle: International Survey of Constructive Art*, New York: Praeger, 1971

Rickey, George, *Constructivism: Origins and Evolution*, New York: Braziller, 1967; revised edition, 1995

CONTEMPORARY SCULPTURE: 1965–PRESENT

In the contemporary period, a number of approaches (all in some fashion three-dimensional) have been called sculpture, from single objects to elaborate multimedia installations. A trend toward diversity in sculpture was already underway by the beginning of the contemporary period in 1965, but after that time one finds increasing variety as well as a disparate treatment of materials. Among the various approaches and media already well established by the mid 1960s were assemblage and Junk, motion and light, Pop and Pop-related Environments, and Happenings.

By 1965, however, the dominant sculptural movement—at least in the United States and primarily New York—was Minimalism. Minimalists such as Donald Judd, Robert Morris, Sol LeWitt, Dan Flavin, Tony Smith, and Carl Andre created simple, often symmetrical forms with a machine-made or industrial look. The artist's touch was eliminated, as were any traditional notions of composition, any hint of subject matter, or any reference to the world of representation. Form became the sole focus. Minimalist sculptures were attached directly to the wall or placed on the floor without a base, giving them a physical presence not found in traditional sculpture and placing emphasis on the relationships among the object, the environment, and the observer. Although Minimalism was largely an American phenomenon, in the mid 1960s a group of British artists known as the New Generation, including William Tucker and Phillip King among others, produced reductive forms with a similar machine-made look, although they were more likely to use color and their sculptures often resembled product design.

In the last half of the 1960s, various challenges to the limitations of Minimalism emerged, and a set of practices that were described as Post-Minimalist emerged. One early reaction to Minimalism's formal restrictions, Process art, emphasized the process of making, and artists associated with the movement often used malleable, perishable, or impermanent materials—such as latex rubber—that change over time. Among the artists important to Process (also called Anti-Form) art were Eva Hesse, Louise Bourgeois, Lynda Benglis, Hans Haacke, Bruce Nauman, Richard Serra, and Robert Morris (the former Minimalist who by this time was making felt pieces that responded to gravity and changed when moved, draped, or hung). An early proponent of this type of work was the New York critic Lucy Lippard, whose groundbreaking exhibition "Eccentric Abstraction" at the Fishbach Gallery in October 1966 gave rise to an aesthetic of the organic, the absurd, the abject, and the bodily. Work similar to Process art was produced in Europe, where Minimalism never took hold as it did in the United States. Innovative German artist Joseph Beuys, for one, was creating process-related works using unorthodox materials such as felt, fat, gold, and live animals by the mid 1960s, and soon thereafter a movement known as *arte povera* (literally "poor art"), which shared many traits with American Process art, developed in Italy. *Arte povera* artists such as Jannis Kounellis, Mario Merz, and Michelangelo Pistoletto rejected the Minimalist aesthetic, which they saw as too limiting because of its formal constraints and perceived lack of content. The imperfection and messiness of everyday life, rather than the pure reductive form of Minimalism, appealed to them. As with American process artists, they used perishable or changeable materials such as rags, smoke, dirt, excrement, lettuce, or live animals. One might also find fragments of Classical sculpture, as in Pistoletto's *Venus of Rags* (1967), which combines an idealized Classical statue with a pile of rags.

Another challenge to Minimalism was Conceptual art, which sought to "dematerialize" the art object by placing prime importance on the idea behind the work of art. Although Conceptualists commonly used two-dimensional formats (often with photographs and language), some either used actual sculptural forms or suggested them in a conceptual manner. One artist who produced Conceptual sculpture was Bruce Nauman, who used words and neon signage to convey his ideas

but created sculptural forms out of those words, as in his *Waxing Hot* (1966–67). Another was Lawrence Weiner, who used text in a two-dimensional format (usually in cryptic or decontextualized sentences and printed on a wall) to describe a certain arrangement of objects, thereby creating a "sculpture" solely in the mind of the viewer.

Performance art—perhaps the dominant art form in the 1970s—went beyond Conceptualism and did away with the art object altogether, putting the focus instead on onetime performances staged by the artist. Although often enigmatic and absurdist, performance art allowed the artist to communicate directly with an audience. Minimalism, by contrast, had tried to shift the focus away from the artist to the object. Significant performance artists included, among many others, Joseph Beuys (who was early on perhaps the most influential artist in the movement), Nam June Paik (who was also a pioneer in video art), and Laurie Anderson (whose work has combined acting with music and electronic sounds in multimedia presentations). Related to performance art was Body art, so-called because artists—such as Nauman, Vito Acconci, Marina Abramovic, Gina Pane, and Chris Burden—made their bodies the visceral and often painful heart of the performance. For these artists the body itself and the limits of its physicality usurped the aura of the sculptural object. In highly ritualized ways, these artists cut, pinched, bound, gagged, and bled their own bodies as a means of speaking about the metaphysical and the psychological self.

Earth or Land art also emerged in the Post-Minimalist period and became—along with other kinds of site-specific artworks—prominent in the 1970s. Believing in the superiority of nature to man-made art,

Louise Bourgeois, *Untitled With Foot*
© The Corcoran Gallery of Art / CORBIS and Louise Bourgeois / Licensed by VAGA, New York, NY

Earth artists rejected the museum setting and the history of Western art in order to make large-scale works outdoors, usually in remote locations, but sometimes in urban settings. Among the key artists associated with Earth and Land art are Robert Smithson, Michael Heizer, Walter De Maria, James Turrell, Richard Long, Christo and Jeanne-Claude, Nancy Holt, and Alice Aycock. Smithson's *Spiral Jetty* (1970), located in the Great Salt Lake in Utah, was a significant early example. Christo and Jeanne-Claude modified the existing landscape or architectural structures in a dramatic and monumental way, often marking vast areas of land such as their *Surrounded Islands of Biscayne Bay* (1980–83) project in which they enveloped the 11-mile island with swaths of pink fabric. In contradistinction, Long, an English artist tended to make more subtle modifications of a natural site, often by walking or marking a path through beaches or woods. For Long, the walk was the work of art, and like Christo and Jeanne-Claude, this art form relied upon photographic and textual documentation even though traditional forms of museum or gallery exhibition were intentionally nullified. Beginning in the mid 1970s, several sculptors began creating site-specific works in urban settings. A significant early work among these public monuments was Claes Oldenburg's large-scale *Clothespin* (1976) in Philadelphia. The prominent locations of such urban monuments made them especially vulnerable to public scrutiny, and a few have caused controversy. The most well-known example was Richard Serra's *Tilted Arc* (1979–81), installed in New York City's Federal Plaza and later dismantled because of opposition from those who considered it an eyesore and inconvenient to pedestrian traffic. Other public monuments, however, such as *Clothespin* and Maya Lin's Vietnam Veterans' Memorial (1981–83) in Washington, D.C., have been largely well received.

Figurative art began to make a resurgence in the 1970s, most notably with Superrealist sculpture, where artists such as Duane Hanson and John De Andrea produced uncannily lifelike figures. By the latter part of the 1970s, and continuing into the 1980s, the figure became much more prominent, appearing in sculptural works by Barry Flanagan, Joel Shapiro, John Ahearn, Stephan Balkenhol, and many others. Also becoming prevalent in the 1970s were installations, room-size works that often included a variety of media and materials. This medium continued to grow in reputation in the 1980s, when it became a principal Postmodernist art form. Among the key Installation artists in the 1970s and '80s were Jonathan Borofsky, Jenny Holzer, Judy Pfaff, Christian Boltanski, and Ilya Kapakov.

During the Post-Minimalist period, many artists produced sculpture with strong social and political content. Feminism, in particular, became a vital force in the 1970s, as many artists confronted the sexism and exclusivity of art establishments including universities, museums, and canonical written histories. Feminist artists tended to dismiss Minimalism as cold and remote, admiring instead Process art that focused on personal experience, metaphor and the body such as that by Louise Bourgeois and Eva Hesse. Significant to feminism in 1970s art was the critique of patriarchal ideas, conventions, and formalist values that manifest in western philosophical thought, including Modernist theory and Minimalism. Although some female sculptors used conventional methods to convey political and personal issues important to women, many (Carolee Schneemann and Hannah Wilke, for example) chose to forego traditional art media—which they viewed as too historically male dominated—in favor of radical and more contemporary approaches such as Body and performance art. Others incorporated craft media as a way of valorizing its traditional "feminine" associations (as in Judy Chicago's *The Dinner Party: A Symbol of Our Heritage*, 1974–79). Feminist themes have remained a focus of much contemporary sculpture, as have other identity-related issues such as race. One byproduct of feminism (and subsequently multiculturalism) was the elevation of the status of traditional craft media, which in turn resulted in increased application of those media to sculpture, not only in gender-related works, but in others as well (for instance, Magdalena Abakanowicz's expressive figurative sculptures, in which she incorporated fiber materials such as burlap; Mike Kelley's tableaux incorporating stuffed animals, crocheting, and knitting; and Dale Chilhuly's fantastical blown glass creations).

By the 1980s a number of artists were becoming increasingly immersed in Postmodern ideas, such as the claim that Modernist notions of progress and originality (the "grand narratives") are but an illusion. As the writings of French philosophers Jean Baudrillard and Jean-François Lyotard among others became widely translated and studied, artists and critics began weaving these ideas in and through their work and writings. Many of these artists have been termed Neo-Conceptualists because of their preoccupation with ideas and theory. Jeff Koons, Haim Steinbach, Robert Gober, and Katharina Fritsch are among the key Neo-Conceptualists, many of whom used appropriation (a common Postmodernist approach). The choice to appropriate images—that is, to borrow or pilfer already existing images from culture and the media rather than create "original" artistic images—rests on the Postmodern assumption that art is essentially self-referential and lacks any underlying truth, an idea that Modernist theory espoused. Americans Koons and Steinbach—whose work was known as Neo-Geo or commodity sculpture—took appropriation to the extreme in the tradition of Andy Warhol by exhibiting consumer items as art. Koons, for instance, displayed objects such as vacuum cleaners and basketballs in pristine Plexiglas vitrines, like trophies to be admired by the viewer. The underlying irony of Koons' work is an essential part of its self-consciousness.

The sculpture produced in the 1980s was highly diverse in terms of media, modes of expression, and content. Social and political concerns remained pertinent, but a number of artists were primarily interested in abstract form. Although many artists in the 1980s continued to work in multimedia, performance art, and installation, others produced formalist sculptural objects that seemed to suggest a return to Modernism in their treatment of materials and universal themes. Among the latter are abstract sculptures such as the finely crafted, open forms of Martin Puryear, the minimal stone sculptures of Scott Burton, the architectural sculptures of Siah Armajani, and the mystical sculptures of German artist and Buddhist monk Wolfgang Laib that he made from pollen and beeswax harvested by hand. Becoming increasingly acclaimed in the 1980s was Louise Bourgeois, whose career had already spanned several decades. In the 1980s she continued to produce a wide variety of innovative sculpture and installation, much of it melding figuration and metaphorical abstraction in bronze, granite, marble, textiles, and found objects. Since 1990 her work has included evocative and psychological mixed-media pieces and installations that explore notions of selfhood, fantasy, dreams, and sexuality in an expressionistic fashion.

One source of vital work in the 1980s was a group of British artists who studied at the Royal College of Art in London. These artists tended to use found objects and fragments in their works. One key member, Tony Cragg, arranged discarded objects in geometric layouts reminiscent of Long's museum pieces, then painted them a gradation of rainbow colors. Other significant artists in the group were Bill Woodrow (who also used discarded materials), Antony Gormley (who made figures in lead, cast from his own body), and Anish Kapoor (who covered strangely-shaped organic forms with extremely fine, jewel-colored pigments found in his native India).

In the 1990s issues such as the critique of the museum, multiculturalism, the environment, and identity politics—especially those related to race, gender, and sexual orientation—became quite common and more mainstream, with major museums staging exhibitions examining such artists, most notably the Whitney Biennial of 1993. Many artists in the 1990s, such as Kiki Smith (whose works concentrate on the corporeal body as the key aspect of identity), Adrian Piper (whose multimedia installations focus on her mixed-race heritage), and Barbara Kruger (whose photo-

graphic and text-based installations analyze how language constructs femininity and masculinity) produced sculptural and installation work related to gender and race.

A vast variety of sculpture was produced in the 1990s, including public sculpture, performance art, installations, mixed media and assemblage, and more traditional figurative and abstract objects. A number of artists (Tony Oursler and Bill Viola, for example) used video or computer technology in their work, and various approaches in the 1990s can be termed Conceptual, particularly those of Guy Limone, Gabriel Orozco, and Felix Gonzales-Torres. The most prevalent art form of the 1990s, however—particularly in the first half of the decade—was installation. Often Installation artists (most notably at the 1993 Whitney Biennial) were more concerned with making radical and satirical social statements than they were with formal aspects, although this was not always the case. (That biennial's inclusion of George Holliday's videotape of the Rodney King beating of 1991 is a prime example of how the boundaries between art and visual culture began to blur, even within the venerated museum.) Artists in the 1990s who used installation as a medium through which to communicate emotions and ideas included Jessica Stockholder, Mona Hatoum, Ann Hamilton, Mike Kelley, Yukinori Yanagi, Fred Wilson, and David Hammons. Although this work is conceptually different, it all exploits the flexible nature of the installation. Ann Hamilton's redolent installations ranged from works consisting of vast amounts of one particular item (such as sumptuous swaths of fabric, rooms covered in feathers, carpets of pennies or horse hair meticulously laid or sewn by hand) to her elaborate entry at the 1999 Venice Biennale, which comprised a 27.4 meter glass and steel wall outside the pavilion and a multiroom, mixed-media installation inside.

In the 1990s innovative sculpture was produced by a group of artists in England who became known collectively as Young British Artists (also known as YBAs or the "Brit Pack"). Two key YBAs who made sculpture were Rachel Whiteread and Damien Hirst. Whiteread's best-known work, for which she won the prestigious Turner Prize in 1993, *House* (1993, destroyed 1994), was a site work formed by making a cast of the interior of a low-rent house. Conceived as a commentary on London's lack of housing for the poor, *House*'s eerily white, ghostly presence called attention to what is usually "absent" to the eye, that is, space. Its abstract form referenced Minimalist geometry as well as more subjective iconographic associations with domestic space and architecture. Hirst's notorious works are of animal cadavers—often sliced and exhibited as cross sections—preserved within tanks of formaldehyde. Artworks by the YBAs and others in the 1990s exemplify the provocative often challenging nature of contemporary sculpture, which has continually expanded the limits of what sculpture can be.

JOHN ALFORD

See also **Andre, Carl; Assemblage; Balkenhol, Stephan; Beuys, Joseph; Bourgeois, Louise; Christo and Jeanne-Claude; Cragg, Tony; Flanagan, Barry; Fritsch, Katharina; Gormley, Antony; Hanson, Duane; Hesse, Eva; Installation; Judd, Donald; Kapoor, Anish; Koons, Jeff; Kounellis, Jannis; LeWitt, Sol; Lin, Maya; Long, Richard; Merz, Mario; Morris, Robert; Oldenburg, Claes; Performance Art; Postmodernism; Serra, Richard; Smith, Kiki; Smithson, Robert**

Further Reading

Archer, Michael, *Art since 1960*, London and New York: Thames and Hudson, 1997

Barrie, Brooke, *Contemporary Outdoor Sculpture*, Gloucester, Massachusetts: Rockport, 1999

Causey, Andrew, *Sculpture since 1945*, Oxford and New York: Oxford University Press, 1998

Fineberg, Jonathan David, *Art since 1940: Strategies of Being*, New York: Abrams, 1995

Gravity and Grace: The Changing Condition of Sculpture, 1965–1975 (exhib. cat.), London: South Bank Centre, 1993

Hoffman, Katherine, *Explorations: The Visual Arts since 1945*, New York: HarperCollins, 1991

The Human Factor: Figurative Sculpture Reconsidered (exhib. cat.), Albuquerque, New Mexico: Albuquerque Museum, 1993

Hunter, Sam, and John Jacobus, *Modern Art from Post-Impressionism to the Present: Painting, Sculpture, Architecture*, New York: Abrams, 1976; 3rd revised edition, as *Modern Art: Painting, Sculpture, Architecture*, by Hunter, Jacobus, and Daniel Wheeler, 2000

In Three Dimensions: Women Sculptors of the '90's (exhib. cat.), Staten Island, New York: Newhouse Center for Contemporary Art, 1995

Individuals: A Selected History of Contemporary Art (exhib. cat.), edited by Howard Singerman, New York and Los Angeles: The Museum of Contemporary Art and Abbeville Press, 1986

Lippard, Lucy, "Eccentric Abstraction," *Changing: Essays in Art Criticism*, New York: Dutton, 1971

Lucie-Smith, Edward, *Sculpture since 1945*, New York: Universe, 1987

McEvilley, Thomas, *Sculpture in the Age of Doubt*, New York: Allworth Press and School of Visual Arts, 1999

Possible Worlds: Sculpture from Europe (exhib. cat.), London: ICA and Serpentine Gallery, 1990

COPTIC SCULPTURE

The term *Coptic* is here construed broadly to describe cultural groups of historic and contemporary Egypt, from the pagans and earliest Christians of Late Antiquity to the few immigrant and dwindling indigenous populations of medieval Christians to today's resurgent Coptic Christian communities. The sculpture of these different groups thus spans nearly two millennia, and the range of influences affecting their sculptural production varies enormously depending on distinct historical circumstances. The earliest works called Coptic—stelae from Terenouthis (Kom Abou Billou) thought to date from the Roman period—juxtapose Greek inscriptions and Greco-Roman motifs with Egyptian styles and iconographic motifs; similarly heterogeneous artistic mixtures were produced during later periods of Byzantine and Islamic rule. This inclusive aesthetic sensibility underlies Coptic sculpture as it is currently produced in Egypt and in diaspora communities.

The earliest scholarship concerning Coptic sculpture, which was largely inspired by limestone tomb reliefs from Late Antique Heracleopolis Magna and Oxyrhynchus, set the stage for continued explorations (especially in the 1960s during the period of the greatest popularity of these works on the art market, in museum exhibitions, and in scholarly publications) of the cultural expressions of these works, attempting to discern particularly Coptic (meaning Egyptian) stylistic and iconographic repertories in contradistinction to an expected Hellenistic tradition in an Alexandrian style. Stylistic studies were furthered in the 1980s as the identification and study of works of doubtful authenticity, aided by close physical analysis of both carving and polychromy, became a focus of scholarship. More recent productive avenues of research investigate the tremendously rich textual heritage of late antique Egypt for commentary on the production and use of these sculptures and integrate Coptic works into the study of Late Antique, Early Christian and Byzantine, and Islamic sculpture.

Late Antique Coptic sculpture has received the most attention in archaeological exploration and art historical research, as well as museum collecting and exhibitions. Late Antiquity comprises the politically defined periods of the later Roman Empire (3rd to 4th centuries) and early Byzantine Empire (4th to 6th centuries) and extends into the early Islamic Empire (from the mid 17th century), when Egypt was part of larger, pan-Mediterranean political entities. The first examples of Late Antique Coptic sculpture came to light at the turn of the 20th century in a small number of city cemeteries; best known are Oxyrhynchus, also known by the Arabic name Behnasa, in Upper Egypt and Heracleopolis Magna or Ahnas in the Fayum. Funerary sculptures of the 4th and 5th centuries from these city cemeteries and later stelae from numerous other burial sites comprise the most closely analyzed categories of Late Antique Egyptian sculpture. Among the 4th- and 5th-century works are pagan and Christian scenes, apparently carved by the same sculptors. These compositions are of special interest for their seamless merging of local practices with later Roman and early Byzantine conventions. Commonly cited as a salient feature of these works is a dramatic play of light and shadow in emphatically carved relief. Whereas regional (or local) styles are exhibited by these works and by the large group of 6th- and 7th-century stelae from the Delta monastery of Esna, the paucity of excavated remains from Alexandria has severely limited informed discussion of a distinctively Hellenistic Alexandrian style, for which the principal examples are undocumented ivories and other small-scale, portable works.

Continued archaeological explorations throughout the Nile Valley have established important Late Antique sites with architectural sculptures *in situ* at the monasteries of Apa Jeremias at Sakkara in the Delta, Apa Apollo Bawit in Upper Egypt, and the Red and White Monasteries of Apa Shenute at Sohag, for example, and from locales as far south as Nubia in Upper Egypt and northern present-day Sudan. A large group of pieces of doubtful authenticity attributed to the Upper Egyptian site of Antinoe, also known as Sheik Ibada, appeared in time to be included in the initial major exhibitions of Coptic art that traveled around Europe in the 1960s and thus entered the first definitive assembly of Coptic sculpture. The corpus of Late Antique Coptic sculpture, including documented artifacts from known excavations and isolated pieces introduced on the art market, has continued to grow and is now extensive, comprising several thousand known works, usually stone fragments of architectural decoration, in museums and private collections worldwide. Chief among the museum collections based on works of known origin are those at the Coptic Museum in Cairo, the Graeco-Roman Museum in Alexandria, the Metropolitan Museum of Art in New York City, and the Musée du Louvre in Paris.

With the advent of the Umayyad dynasty (mid 7th to mid 8th century), Coptic artisans were employed in the crafting of an Arab Islamic style at caliphal monuments in Jordan and in Jerusalem, and so Egypt's sculptural expertise became an integral part of a new artistic tradition. In Egypt medieval Christian artisans and patrons came to embrace this developing repertory of styles. One such example is the 10th-century Church of al'-Adhra, where the emphatically textural relief of the beveled-edge "Samarra" style is visible in the architectural decoration. Another example, also dating to the 10th century, can be seen in the inlaid wood and ivory screens of intricately interlaced flowing vegetal forms—"arabesques"—in the churches of al'-Adhra and Sitt Maryam. These churches are in a monastery, in the Wadi Natrun in the Delta, that was bought by Syrians from Egyptian Christians in the 8th or 9th century and came to be known by the ethnicity of its monks as Dayr al'-Suryan. The monastery is still in operation today.

From the Medieval period onward, Coptic sculpture is found almost exclusively in the relief decoration of church architecture and furnishings. Old Cairo preserves a concentration of relief sculptures from Coptic churches, some of which have been in use more or less continuously since Late Antiquity. The Church of Sitt Miriam, or al'-Mu'allaqah, in Old Cairo offers one telling example of continued stylistic variation of Coptic sculptural forms. The church contained the well-known wooden lintel dating probably from the 5th century commemorating clerics in its Greek inscription and representing the Entry into Jerusalem and the Ascension. It includes a pan-Mediterranean figure type—exaggeratedly lively, swaying bodies of stocky physique, with proportionally large heads—and dramatic chiaroscuro. This lintel (now in the Coptic Museum) came to be part of an accumulative decorative scheme that included a set of wooden door panels (now in the British Museum, London, England), dating perhaps from the 13th century, carved with scenes from the life of Christ. The scenes are framed by pearl borders and executed in a low relief of overlapping tiers of shallow stages indicating spatial recession characteristic of contemporary sculpture of the Mamelukes (1250–1517). Almost emblematic of the geometric mode associated with medieval Islamic ornament up to the present day are the many inlaid screens of wood and ivory crafted into intricate geometric patterns, including examples based on obviously cross-shaped motifs still *in situ* in al'-Mu'allaqah. Such works are distinguishable from Islamic works by function and context as well as symbolism. Contemporary Coptic church decoration in Egypt and in diaspora communities elsewhere draws upon the full range of this venerable legacy of sculptural forms.

THELMA K. THOMAS

Further Reading

Beckwith, John, *Coptic Sculpture, 300–1300*, London: Tiranti, 1963

Boyd, Susan, and Gary Vikan, *Questions of Authenticity among the Arts of Byzantium* (exhib. cat.), Washington, D.C.: Dumbarton Oaks, 1981

Cody, A., "Dayr al-Suryan," in *The Coptic Encyclopedia*, edited by Aziz Suryal Atiya, vol. 3, New York: Macmillan, and Toronto, Ontario: Collier Macmillan Canada, 1991

Coquin, Charalambia, "Church of Al-Mu'allaqah,"in *The Coptic Encyclopedia*, edited by Aziz Suryal Atiya, vol. 3, New York: Macmillan, and Toronto, Ontario: Collier Macmillan Canada, 1991

Hooper, Finley, *Funerary Stelae from Kom Abou Billou*, Ann Arbor, Michigan: Kelsey Museum of Archaeology, 1961

Kitzinger, Ernst, "Notes on Early Coptic Sculpture," *Archaeologia* 87 (1938)

Koptische Kunst: Christentum am Nil (exhib. cat.), Essen, Germany: Villa Hügel, 1963

Thomas, Thelma K., "Christians in the Islamic East," in *The Glory of Byzantium: Art and Culture of the Middle Byzantine Era, A.D. 843–1261*, edited by Helen C. Evans and William D. Wixom, New York: Metropolitan Museum of Art, 1997

Thomas, Thelma K., *Late Antique Egyptian Funerary Sculpture: Images for This World and the Next*, Princeton, New Jersey: Princeton University Press, 2000

CORAL

Coral is the calcium carbonate material produced by the coral polyp (a marine invertebrate of the Anthozoa class) to form an external or internal skeleton. It occurs in a variety of colors, textures, and ocean habitats, but the species most used by artisans is red or precious coral (*Corallium rubrum*), found in the Mediterranean Sea off the coasts of Algeria and Tunisia, fished by divers or fishermen. Workers separate the branchlike pieces of each stem of the coral, which is then ground, cleaned, and polished, drilled, or carved.

Coral has been used for decorative, apotropaic, and medicinal purposes throughout history. In Antiquity its color and oceanic derivation associated coral with life-giving forces and protective qualities: it was thought to prevent or treat ailments such as the plague and leprosy, to be an aphrodisiac, and to soothe teething children and strengthen mother's milk.

It is unclear when coral began to be used in crafts. Archaeologists have found roughly shaped coral beads in prehistoric burial sites in France, Germany, and Hungary. In the ancient Near East artists used it with precious stones to decorate religious and secular objects; the Phoenicians and Egyptians used coral regularly for jewelry and as talismanic amulets. The Romans fashioned amulets and figural works from coral, and the ancient Celtic peoples used it to decorate their weapons and bronze objects and as jewelry.

During the Middle Ages coral continued to be used in jewelry and luxury items: artists commonly made paternosters, buttons, and jewelry in coral. By the 12th century coral workshops had been established in Genoa, Sicily, Barcelona, Naples, Paris, and Lyon to supply markets in western Europe and India.

In the late 15th century coral emerged as a medium in the figurative arts. Large amounts of coral were shipped to northern court workshops for carving, but the majority of production remained primarily in Naples, Genoa, and Trapani, Sicily. In addition to the use of coral for objects such as jewelry and silverware handles, or as decorative accents in *pietra dura* (hard stone) cabinets, during the Renaissance wealthy Europeans included coral pieces as rare and beautiful works of nature in their art collections.

The 17th and 18th centuries saw increased technical innovation and appreciation of coral in art. Its color, form, and texture complemented the vegetal curving motifs of the Baroque and Rococo styles, and artists used coral to decorate a host of luxury items, embroidery and textiles, and ecclesiastical objects. By the 19th century the use of coral pervaded the decorative arts, and the industry became concentrated in Naples and Torre del Greco, where factories produced large quantities of objects.

KATHERINE BENTZ

Further Reading

Ascione, Gina Carla, *Storia del corallo a Napoli dal XVI al XIX secolo*, Naples: Electa Napoli, 1991

Daneu, Antonio, *L'arte Trapanese del corallo*, Palermo, Italy: Banco di Sicilia, 1964

Liverino, Basilio, *Red Coral, Jewel of the Sea*, Bologna: Analisi, 1989

Liverino, Basilio, *Il corallo dalle origini ai nostri giorni*, 4th edition, Naples: Arte Tipografica, 1998

Maltese, Corrado, et al., *Coralli: Talismani sacri e profani*, Palermo, Italy: Novecento, 1986

Tescione, Giovanni, *Il corallo nella storia e nell'arte*, Naples: Montanino, 1965

Tescione, Giovanni, *Il corallo celle arti figurative*, Naples: Fiorentino, 1972

CHARLES-HENRI-JOSEPH CORDIER
1827–1905 *French*

Charles Cordier's reputation as an artist suffered a decline in the years following his self-imposed exile in 1880. The very qualities that earned him the admiration of sovereigns across Europe at mid century led to the critical neglect of his oeuvre well into the 20th century. The decorative nature of his work and his willingness to put art in the service of science and politics constitute the artist's major contributions to sculpture. Familiarity with his work as an artist, ethnographer, and technician is helpful in understanding the various functions that sculpture served in 19th-century France.

After he apprenticed as a jeweler, Cordier trained at the Petite École, where many sculptors, including Jules-Aimé Dalou and Auguste Rodin, had their start. As an art school the Petite École differed from the École des Beaux-Arts in its purpose, pedagogy, and models. Organized to teach craftsmanship, its curriculum emphasized the mastery of practical techniques, and its models tended toward those of the Rococo rather than the Classical. Cordier next moved into the studio of François Rude, the sculptor most closely associated with the Romantic movement. The impact of these formative experiences is evident in the wealth of details and precise execution characteristic of Cordier's animated compositions.

The portrait bust of *Saïd Abdullah of the Mayac, Kingdom of Darfur* marked Cordier's debut at the Salon of 1848, the same year that a constitutional amendment was passed freeing slaves in France. The broad, flat nose, full lips, and sloping forehead were often regarded by Europeans as evidence of an inferior intellect, a justification of the French government's "civilizing mission" in Africa. The nobility and dignity Cordier bestowed on his model can be read not as recognition of the validity of an alien society but as the attempt of Europeans to impose a classical ideal on cultures other than their own. Two years later he provided a pendant, a female portrait bust dubbed the *African Venus* by the critic Théophile Gautier. Queen Victoria acquired both sculptures after she saw them displayed at the Great Exhibition of 1851 in London. Casts of the pair were subsequently ordered by the French state for the Museum of Natural History in Paris, where a gallery devoted to ethnography was formed. Visitors to the museum found Cordier's sculptures in a room amid a glass case that held mummies, skeletons, and casts of various "exotic" races. Cordier secured a position as an ethnographic sculptor at the museum and provided variations of the African subjects as well as examples of a Chinese couple and Arabs. The series of racial types, listed in a catalogue by Marc Trapadoux in 1860, was conceived not only as works of art appreciated for their aesthetic value but as scientific models objectively rendered in order to facilitate racial comparisons and, implicitly, to support foreign policies on the African and Asian continents.

Although he did not initiate the trend toward polychromed sculpture in the 19th century, Cordier certainly helped to advance it. Scientific investigations into spectral light and archaeological discoveries led to new theories of color and treatises on the use of painted architectural ornament and sculpture in Classical Antiquity, such as *The Principles of Harmony and Contrast of Colours* (1839) by Eugène Chevreul and *Lectures on Architecture* by Viollet-le-Duc (1863). Once Classical examples of polychromed sculpture had been found, artists could justify indulging their penchant for rich, sensual color. *Jewess from Algiers*, first shown in the London International Exhibition of 1862 and a later version at the 1867 Exposition Universelle in Paris, demonstrated the new embrace of color by artists and audiences long conditioned to accept Neoclassical austerity.

It should be remembered that these international exhibitions were organized to promote industry and commerce, and Cordier's sculpture was as much an advertisement for French technological ingenuity as it was an argument for aesthetic superiority. Improved methods of electroplating allowed Cordier to produce a life-

Negro in Algerian Costume
© Scala / Art Resource, NY

size, half-length female portrait made of silvered bronze, porphyry, gilt, onyx, and enamel. Similarly, he used bronze and various types of marbles to render the exotic coat and headdress of *Negro in Algerian Costume*, another tour de force of mixed-media sculpture.

Cordier succeeded in popularizing polychromed sculpture by making it operate on two levels simultaneously. His works were luxury items that appealed to wealthy patrons whose conspicuous consumption could be thinly disguised as erudition and liberality. Despite his trips to the region financed by the government, Cordier ignored the larger reality of living in Africa—the disease, poverty, and colonial oppression—and chose, instead, to create the illusion of a society parallel to that of his own, one in which his upper-class audiences recognized their exotic counterparts. His subjects are dignified and sumptuously dressed; they were presented to the public in a context of purported scientific objectivity (a museum) and international camaraderie and political neutrality (the universal expositions). The pseudo-scientific approach of his ethnographic studies and the claim that they were based on the direct observation of nature made the opulence of the works even more acceptable to his patrons during the Second Empire.

The late 19th century witnessed a veritable explosion of the genre that culminated in Ernest Barrias's *Nature Revealing Herself to Science*, a gilt bronze and ivory sculpture displayed at the Exposition Universelle of 1900. A host of other sculptors, Jean-Léon Gérôme and Emmanuel Frémiet among them, benefited from Cordier's success in creating a market for polychromed sculpture.

CHERYL K. SNAY

See also **Hoffman, Malvina**

Biography

Born in Cambrai, France, 1 November 1827. Trained at Petite École in Paris; worked in studio of François Rude; made debut at Salon of 1848, Paris; awarded position at Museum of Natural History as ethnographic sculptor, 1851; traveled to Algeria, 1856; Greece, 1858–59; and Egypt, 1865, at the expense of the state; maintained own studio producing portrait busts and public commissions; left France for financial reasons, 1880. Died in Algiers, Algeria, 30 April 1905.

Selected Works

1848   *Saïd Abdullah of the Mayac, Kingdom of Darfur*; plaster; private collection, France; casts: 1852, bronze, Walters Art Museum, Baltimore, Maryland, United States; Royal Collection, Osborne House, Isle of Wight, England

1851   *African Venus*; plaster; private collection, France; initial bronze: Royal Collection, Osborne House, Isle of Wight, England; bronze reduction: 1852, Walters Art Museum, Baltimore, Maryland, United States

1856–57 *Negro in Algerian Costume (Negro of the Sudan)*; marble, onyx, bronze; versions: Musée d'Orsay, Paris, France; Musée Nationale du Château, Compiègne, France; Minneapolis Institute of Art, Minnesota, United States

1858   *Chinese Couple*; enamel, copper; private collection

ca. 1862 *Arab Sheik*; onyx, partially gilt bronze; Van Gogh Museum, Amsterdam, the Netherlands

ca. 1862 *Jewess from Algiers*; onyx, partially gilt bronze, silvered bronze enamel, semiprecious stones; Van Gogh Museum,

Amsterdam, the Netherlands; cast: Musée des Beaux-Arts, Troyes, France

1868–72 *Ibrahim Pasha*; bronze; Opéra Place, Cairo, Egypt

1872–75 *Christopher Columbus*; marble, bronze; Paseo de la Reforma, Mexico City, Mexico

Further Reading

Blühm, Andreas, *The Colour of Sculpture, 1840–1910*, Zwolle, The Netherlands: Waanders, 1996

Durand-Revillon, Jeannine, "Charles-Henri-Joseph Cordier," Ph.D. diss., École du Louvre, Paris, 1980

Durand-Revillon, Jeannine, "Un promoteur de la sculpture polychrome sous le Second Émpire: Charles-Henri-Joseph Cordier," *Bulletin de la Société de l'histoire de l'art française* (1982)

Honour, Hugh, *From the American Revolution to World War I*, 2 vols., Houston: Menil Foundation, and Cambridge, Massachusetts: Harvard University Press, 1989

NICOLAS CORDIER *ca.* 1567–1612
French, active in Italy

Nicolas Cordier, nicknamed "il Franciosino," was a successful marble sculptor working in Rome in the first decade of the 17th century. He briefly enjoyed great contemporary success until it vanished completely after the second half of the 17th century.

Initially trained as a wood sculptor in Lorraine, Cordier worked primarily in marble statuary while in Rome, but he also furnished wax models for bronzes and for decorative fountain sculpture. He was active as a restorer of antique sculpture, and his most famous restoration work is the marble group the *Three Graces*, which was commissioned by Cardinal Scipione Borghese.

Another aspect of Cordier's artistic activity, which can be considered a combination of restoration and creative work, is the reemployment and reinterpretation of ancient sculpture in new work. This work is characterized primarily by a predilection for rare and precious materials and for the polychromatic relationships between them. The most extraordinary work of this kind is the statue of *Saint Agnes*, which was executed by Cordier at the commission of Cardinal Alessandro de' Medici for the high altar of the Basilica of Sant' Agnese fuori le Mura (Rome). But the artist's research of a striking correspondence between the chosen materials and the represented subjects is evident principally in the famous *Zingarella* (Galleria Borghese, Rome) and in *The Moor*, where the brown, lucid skin of the young and charming figures is rendered with black marble and bronze.

This part of Cordier's activity is probably the one that elicits the most interest within current criticism, but the chief activity of the sculptor lay in making monumental marble sculpture for public destinations. Cordier always worked for the highest curial patronage, principally for popes, but also for cardinals, particularly Cardinal Cesare Baronio. The most important work done by Cordier for Pope Clement VIII (Aldobrandini) was the major part of the sculpture decoration for the Aldobrandini family chapel in the Church of Santa Maria sopra Minerva in Rome, where Cordier worked together with Camillo Mariani and Stefano Maderno. Here he realized the pendant funerary statue portraits of the pope's parents, recumbent on their respective tombs. Particularly remarkable is the portrait of *Lesa Deti Aldobrandini.* Another high-level commission for the important collective workshop, the sculptural decoration of the Cappella Paolina in the Basilica of Santa Maria Maggiore, Rome, prompted Cordier to work together with Francesco Mochi, Maderno, and Pietro Bernini at the commission of Pope Paul V. His work on *Saint Gregory the Great* for the Church of S. Gregorio al Celio in Rome was believed to have been carved from a block abandoned by Michelangelo.

The most colossal and public work on which Cordier's celebrity depends is the monument to Henry IV, which was commissioned by the *canonici lateranensi* (regular canons of the Basilica of San Giovanni in Laterano) to express their gratitude to the newly converted French king for the benefits received from him. The enormous bronze statue stands on a high pedestal formed by a granite column richly decorated with an inscribed plaque of precious materials. The statue presented relevant problems in casting because of its co-lossal size. The monument is placed at the entrance of the Basilica of San Giovanni in Laterano in the portico of the Loggia della Benedizione. The king is represented as a commander with trophies at his feet. The figure wears ancient armor decorated with great virtuosity in relief goldsmith's work, and the face—a portrait—bears a remarkable likeness to the king. The monument was immediately reproduced in engravings by Jacques Lemercier (1608) and later by Robert Picou and Jerome David, and it always retained its importance in ancient guide books as well as in historical literature and unspecialized literature on art. The constant dissociation of this work from the name of its creator characterizes the critical success of this work largely because of the political importance of its subject.

The dissociation between works and their creator distinguishes almost the entirety of Cordier's critical tradition. The sculptor has been largely ignored by art historians following Giovanni Baglione, the only Cordier biographer. The biography furnishes a fundamentally trustworthy and positive catalogue of Cordier's works. The theme most emphasized is the professional success of the Lorraine sculptor, as well as topical anecdotes on the privileged relations he had, primarily with the reigning popes.

Apart from art historical literature, Cordier's work saw emphasis in two other sources: guide books and poetry. In the guides books to Rome, Cordier's monumental works always appear, but almost always without the name of the artist. Panegyric poetry celebrates the French sculptor with traditional clichés within the description and praise of other works of art.

The recurrent problems of attribution in the reconstruction of the artist's catalogue depend largely on this peculiar critical tradition that has forgotten the artist's name and ignores a stylistic definition of his work and yet records a good number of his works, sometimes with erroneous attributions.

FRANCESCA PELLEGRINO

Tomb of Lesa Deti Aldobrandini, funerary figure, Aldobrandini Chapel
The Conway Library, Courtauld Institute of Art

Biography

Born in Saint-Mihiel, Meuse, Lorraine, France, *ca.* 1567. Trained at Saint-Mihiel, in the successful Lorraine wood- and stone-sculpture workshop of the Richier family; first employed in Nancy in service of Charles III, Duke of Lorraine; moved to Rome, *ca.* 1592 (documented from 1593); worked in Rome as an independent master; member of the Accademia di San Luca, and of the Accademia dei Virtuosi del Pantheon, 1604; son was sculptor Giovanni Pietro (1608–43). Died in Rome, Italy, 24 November 1612.

Selected Works

1602–04 *Saint Gregory the Great*; marble, polychrome encrustations in details; Oratory of the Triclinium (or of Santa Barbara), Church of S. Gregorio al Celio, Rome, Italy

1602–04 *Santa Silvia*; marble; Oratory of Santa Silvia, Church of S. Gregorio al Celio, Rome, Italy

ca. *Saint Agnes*; alabaster, gilt bronze, silver,
1604–05 with reemployment of ancient pieces; Church of Sant' Agnese fuori le Mura, Rome, Italy

1604–05 *Saint Sebastian*, *Silvestro Aldobrandini*, and *Lesa Deti Aldobrandini*, and group *Charity* (all with Camillo Mariani, Stefano Maderno, Ambrogio Bonvicino, and Ippolito Buzio); marble; Aldobrandini Chapel, Church of Santa Maria sopra Minerva, Rome, Italy

1606–09 Monument to Henry IV (casting by Gregorio de' Rossi from Cordier's wax model); bronze, granite, marble, encrustations of polychrome marbles; portico of the Loggia della Benedizione, Basilica of San Giovanni in Laterano, Rome, Italy

ca. *The Moor*; marble, polychrome marbles,
1607–12 alabaster, onyx, polychrome encrustations of semiprecious stones and of colored pastes, gilt painting in details, with reemployment of ancient pieces; Musée du Château, Versailles, France

ca. *Seneca*; marble, porphyry, with
1607–12 reemployment of ancient pieces; Musée du Louvre, Paris, France (attributed)

ca. *Zingarella*; marble, bronze, polychrome
1607–12 encrustations, gilt painting in details, with reemployment of ancient pieces; Galleria Borghese, Villa Borghese, Rome, Italy

ca. *Zingarella*; marble, bronze, with
1607–12 reemployment of ancient pieces; Musée du Louvre, Paris, France (attributed)

1608 *Saint Peter* and *Saint Paul*; marble; Church of San Sebastiano fuori le Mura, Rome, Italy

1609 Fountain with a putto between two dragons; marble; Ospedale of S. Spirito, Palazzo del Commendatore, Rome, Italy

1609 *Three Graces* (restoration), for Galleria Borghese, Villa Borghese, Rome; marble; Musée du Louvre, Paris, France

1609–12 *David, Aaron, St. Bernard of Clairvaux*, and *Dionysius the Areopagite* (with

Francesco Mochi, Stefano Maderno, Pietro Bernini, et al.); marble; Cappella Paolina, Basilica of Santa Maria Maggiore, Rome, Italy

ca. 1611 *Pope Paul V*; bronze, marble; Piazza Cavour, Rimini, Italy

Further Reading

Brummer, Hans Henrik, "Cesare Baronio and the Convent of Gregory the Great," *Konsthistorisk Tidskrift* 43 (1974)

Freiberg, Jack, "Paul V, Alexander VII, and a Fountain by Nicolò Cordier Rediscovered," *The Burlington Magazine* 133 (1991)

Harwood, Barry Robert, "Nicolo Cordieri: His Activity in Rome, 1592–1612," Ph.D. diss., Princeton University, 1979

Haskell, Francis, and Nicholas Penny, *Taste and the Antique: The Lure of Classical Sculpture, 1500–1900*, New Haven, Connecticut: Yale University Press, 1981

Hess, Jacob, "Michelangelo and Cordier," *The Burlington Magazine* 82 (1943)

Montagu, Jennifer, *Roman Baroque Sculpture: The Industry of Art*, New Haven, Connecticut: Yale University Press, 1989

Pope-Hennessy, John, *An Introduction to Italian Sculpture*, 3 vols., London: Phaidon, 1963; 4th edition, 1996; see especially vol. 3, *Italian High Renaissance and Baroque Sculpture*

Pressouyre, Sylvia, *Nicolas Cordier: Recherches sur la sculpture à Rome autour de 1600*, 2 vols., Rome: École Française de Rome, 1984; see especially vol. 2

Pressouyre, Sylvia, "Cordier, Nicolas," in *The Dictionary of Art*, edited by Jane Turner, vol. 7, New York: Grove, and London: Macmillan, 1996

Zanuso, Susanna, "Nicolas Cordier," in *Scultura del '600 a Roma*, edited by Andrea Bacchi, Milan: Longanesi, 1996

ANTONIO CORRADINI 1688–1752 *Italian*

Antonio Corradini was probably the most celebrated Venetian sculptor of the 18th century before Antonio Canova. Even if he cannot be considered the best among his contemporary colleagues, his own specialty—a veiled female figure sculpted in marble—won him an overall appreciation and recognition of local and foreign patrons, followed by an international career without parallel at the time.

Corradini is believed to have studied under the local sculptor Antonio Tarsia, who later became his father-in-law. Tarsia's style in the first years of the 18th century, during Corradini's apprenticeship, was considerably influenced by Alessandro Algardi and Giuseppe Maria Mazza. Only a few years later, however, along with other contemporary artists, Tarsia discovered famous Venetian predecessors such as Jacopo Sansovino and Alessandro Vittoria; the figurative style that emerged could loosely be labeled *Neocinquecentismo*. Corradini's own stylistic development must have been parallel with Tarsia's, but his early authenticated works already show a sensible reelaboration of the cinquecento figurative models, successfully blended with *settecento*-like technical virtuosity in modeling the surface of marble, the latter possibly under the influence of Filippo Parodi and Giovanni Bonazza. Moreover, Corradini looked with interest on the work of the elder colleague Giuseppe Torretti, who was his collaborator on various projects, including the altar in the Church of Santa Maria del Carmine, Venice, for which the two sculptors provided statues in 1722–23. Corradini's *Virginity* for that altar proved to be a very popular image, and it was soon engraved by Andrea Zucchi after a drawing made by Giambattista Tiepolo. In fact, in the early 1720s Corradini was already one of the leading sculptors in Venice, receiving important commissions from churches, *scuolas* (confraternities), and private patrons. Among the works in Venice, the *Pietà* of 1723 in the Church of San Moisè especially stands out, as does the boldly sculpted *Triumph of the Eucharist* of the Blessed Sacrament altar in the Cathedral of Este in Veneto, Italy.

Corradini's activity for private and ecclesiastical patrons went hand in hand with government commissions. In 1716 he was chosen to carve the statue of the field marshal Johann Matthias von der Schulenburg for a public monument on the island of Corfu (Greece), in 1719 his model for a new state ceremonial ship *Bucintoro* was accepted, and in the mid 1720s he was involved in the restoration of the statuary adorning the doge's palace. Moreover, he is traditionally held responsible for the separation of sculptors from the stonemasons' guild, resulting in the formation of the Collegio dei Scultori in 1724.

Corradini's fame began spreading outside Venice by 1717, when the Veronese painter Antonio Balestra wrote to the Florentine art historian and collector Francesco Gabburri about the young sculptor who astonished the entire city of Venice with a veiled statue of *Faith*. In fact, in 1716 Corradini was the youngest among the Venetian masters asked to supply a large number of statues for the Russian czar Peter the Great, but this was only the first of his international commissions that later impelled him to leave Venice permanently. By 1719, and throughout the early 1720s, Corradini was producing marbles for Augustus the Strong, king of Poland and elector of Saxony, of which at least three virtuoso two-figure groups should be mentioned: *Time Unveiling Truth*, *Apollo Flaying Marsyas*, and *Zephyrus and Flora*.

Corradini's decision to leave Venice probably came with the commission of the statues for the St. Joseph Fountain on Hoher Markt in Vienna. Still in Venice, he sent the group of *The Marriage of the Virgin* to the Austrian capital in November 1728, but some months later, and certainly by 1730, he moved to Vienna. In the following years Corradini collaborated with the court architect Joseph Emanuel Fischer von Erlach, and in 1736 Corradini's most important work of the period was installed in the Cathedral of Prague: the sepulchral monument to St. John of Nepomuk. When in 1732 he was appointed court sculptor to the Emperor Charles VI, Corradini was at the peak of his career. In the late 1730s his position and fame might have been threatened by Georg Raphael Donner; Corradini's title of the court sculptor, however, was confirmed by the empress Maria Theresa in 1742. Still, he left Vienna for Italy later that same year.

Settling down in Rome, Corradini submitted eight models in the spring of 1743 for the colossal statues to be used for the dome of the Basilica of St. Peter according to the restoration project of the architect Luigi Vanvitelli. Because the project was soon altered, however, Corradini's statues were never realized. In the autumn of 1743 he finished another veiled female figure, *Vestal Tuccia*, which was—while still in the studio—admired by the pretender to the British crown, James Stuart, and his sons. Despite the noble admirers (in 1747 even Pope Benedict XIV visited his studio), Corradini's stay in Rome was probably not as successful as were the preceding years.

Corradini's links with the Masonic lodge may have helped him obtain a major commission from Raimondo di Sangro, prince of San Severo and the grand master of the Neapolitan lodge, who entrusted to him the decoration of his private chapel in the palace in Naples. The sculptor left Rome for Naples before Easter 1748, but he died in the summer of 1752, having executed only a small part of the grandiose project of the Cappella Sansevero. Of his works in marble only the tomb monument to Cecilia Caietani, the mother of the patron, with the statue of *Modesty*, is of real significance, and can be regarded as the last display of his technical bravura. Corradini supposedly left models in terracotta that were then used by his followers to complete the decoration: Giuseppe Sanmartino carved a figure of the *Veiled Christ* (depicted in death) in 1753, and the major part of the remaining statues was executed by Francesco Queirolo.

Apart from Neapolitan followers of Corradini, his veiled figures were occasionally emulated by artists such as Antonio Gai in Venice and Innocenzo Spinazzi in Florence. Even in the 19th century, when Corradini's fame was seriously undermined by the writings of Leopoldo Cicognara, his veiled figures still fascinated the public and the sculptors, and the motif of the veil, displaying the sculptor's technical abilities in making marble look transparent, and accentuating nudity by revealing more than concealing, was even taken over in the mid 19th century by sculptors such as Raffaelle Monti.

MATEJ KLEMENČIČ

Biography

Born in Venice, Italy, 19 October 1688. Studied sculpture in Venice under Antonio Tarsia, before 1709; began creating sculptures for royal figures from abroad, 1716; worked in Venice until *ca.* 1729, then moved to Vienna to become court sculptor to Emperor Charles VI (nomination in 1732, confirmed by Empress Maria Theresa, 1742); returned to Italy by 1743, first to Rome and later to Naples, *ca.* 1748. Died in Naples, Italy, 12 August 1752.

Selected Works

1716–18 *Field Marshal Johann Matthias von der Schulenburg*; marble; Corfu, Greece
1719–23 *Apollo Flaying Marsyas* and *Zephyrus and Flora*; marble; Victoria and Albert Museum, London, England
1719–23 *Time Unveiling Truth*; marble; Grosser Garten, Dresden, Germany
ca. 1720 *Faith*; marble; La Granja Palace, San Ildefonso, Spain
1722–23 *Virginity*, for altar of the Scuola del Carmine; marble; Church of Santa Maria dei Carmini, Venice, Italy
1722–25 *Triumph of the Eucharist*, for altar of the Holy Sacrament; marble; Cathedral of Este, Italy
1723 *Pietà*; marble; *Church of San Moisè*, Venice, Italy
1728 *The Marriage of the Virgin*; marble; St. Joseph's Fountain, Hoher Markt, Vienna, Austria
1733–36 Tomb of Saint John of Nepomuk; silver, other materials; Cathedral of Stivitus, Prague, Czech Republic
1743 *Prophets*; terracotta; Museo Petriano, Vatican City, Rome, Italy
1743 *Vestal Tuccia*; marble; Barberini Palace, Rome, Italy
1752 *Modesty*, for tomb of Cecilia Caietani; marble; Cappella Sansevero, Church of Santa Maria della Pietà dei Sangro, Naples, Italy

Further Reading

Androssov, Sergei, *Pietro il Grande: Collezionista d'arte veneta*, Venice: Canal and Stamperia, 1999
Cioffi, Rossana, *La cappella Sansevero: Arte barocca e ideologia masonica*, Salerno, Italy: Edizioni 10/17, 1987
Cogo, Bruno, *Antonio Corradini: Scultore veneziano, 1688–1752*, Este, Italy: Libreria Gregoriana Estense, 1996 (with comprehensive bibliography)
Hodgkinson, Terence, "Two Garden Sculptures by Antonio Corradini," *Victoria and Albert Museum Bulletin* 4 (1968)
Limena, Angelo (editor), *Celebrazioni centenarie in onore dello scultore estense: Antonio Corradini, 1668–1752*, Este, Italy: Euganea, 1968
Matsche, Franz, "Das Grabmal des hl. Johannes von Nepomuk," *Wallraf-Richartz-Jahrbuch* 38 (1976)
Semenzato, Camillo, *La scultura veneta del Seicento e del Settecento*, Venice: Alfieri, 1966

MODESTY (TOMB FOR CECILIA CAIETANI)

Antonio Corradini (1668–1752)
1752
marble
h. over-life size
Cappella Sansevero, Church of Santa Maria della Pietà dei Sangro, Naples, Italy

Cecilia Caietani's tomb was erected in 1752 by her son Raimondo di Sangro, prince of San Severo, in the grand family chapel next door to the Sangro palace in the center of Naples. The commission was awarded to Antonio Corradini, who had supervised the chapel's redecoration. For the small amount of space available for the tomb, the aged sculptor (he died later that year) designed a multilevel structure, evidently with di Sangro's agreement. At the base is a *Noli Me Tangere* in high relief flanked by the branches of a leafy oak tree. In the central section supporting a broken tombstone bearing the funerary inscription is a statue of *Chastity*, the last and doubtlessly the most celebrated of the many veiled figures sculpted by Corradini. Crowning the structure is the traditional pyramid obelisk on which Caetani's profile appears in a *clipeus* (round shield). A tablet crediting the work to the Venetian sculptor was later inserted among the roots of the oak tree. The 18th-century type funerary art was thus contaminated with a Baroque tradition that "was rooted, however, in the emblematic culture of the late 16th century" (see Cioffi, 1987). Thus a Virtue—Chastity, in this case, and an *Allegory of Deception Unmasked* on the facing tomb of Antonio di Sangro, Raimondo's father—was placed at the center of the composition, whereas the image of the deceased was reduced to a simple half-bust *clipeus* and relegated to a secondary position.

Both scholars and the public have focused their attention almost exclusively on the *Chastity*, which is a genuine tour de force, especially in the damp appearance of the drapery, an effect that had made Corradini famous. Before the statue was even completed, Pier Leone Ghezzi remarked on the excellent quality of the execution. A few years later, the Frenchman Abbé Richard recalled the work in his observations on his travels in Italy, as "truly a beautiful thing in its execution and its intelligence; unless you see it for yourself, you cannot imagine how the sculptor, working in marble, was able to bring out all the features of a figure hidden beneath a veil, and in a way that gives the idea of their regularity."

As the cultural climate shifted toward Neoclassicism, the standard used to judge a work so closely reflecting the 18th-century spirit was bound to become stricter. The Marquis de Sade, in his *Voyage d'Italie*, wrote of the chapel as the "peak of folly and bad taste," and remarked, apropos of the *Chastity* and Francesco Queirolo's *Allegory of Deception Unmasked*, "to find any perfection in these two works, one's taste must be totally depraved." Even Antonio Canova, who on several occasions appeared much more kindly disposed toward his countryman, was quite cool to the artificiality of Corradini's Neapolitan enterprise.

The judgment which weighed decisively in tarnishing the monument's reputation during the 19th century was that of Leopoldo Cicognara. In his *Storia della scultura in Italia* (1818), Cicognara stigmatized the sculpture in these words:

> As everyone knows, a chaste and modest woman's way is to keep her limbs as close to her body as possible, and to wrap herself up so as to hide every part of it from any worldly glance. This figure, to the contrary, reveals as much of herself as possible, thrusting out her shoulders and arms; and the sculptor brings out the depths of every hidden fold, where their effect is exactly the opposite of the subject, and the lewdest. Many of the folds either blend into the body or crudely detach themselves from it; nowhere does the clothing appear to be girded, and indeed one sees only a naked body gracelessly wrapped up in a sheet, so that a step or a light breeze would change the figure of *Chastity* into a perfectly nude woman. And these flaws are all the less forgivable because there is nothing noble about the bodily forms or the extremities, so that the eye, passing them over, desires all the more to see the hidden parts.

Selvatico's opinion (1847) was substantially the same, although he thought the statue "does not deserve the scorn Cicognara poured on it." The artful transparency of the veil, seen as the antithesis of the chastity it pretends to represent, was likewise targeted by later critics—including Burckhardt (1855), Callegari (1930), and even Wittkower (1958), who faulted Corradini for excessive and inappropriate virtuosity; yet many of them failed to go any further or deeper in their judgment of the work. Only recently, in the course of a reassessment of the artist begun by Mariacher (1948), have critics reached a more balanced judgment, one that takes due account of the historical context and of Corradini's extraordinary technical skills.

A subtle iconological interpretation was suggested by Cellini (1952). She saw possible Masonic origins

Modesty (Tomb for Cecilia Caietani)
© Scala / Art Resource, New York

in the *Chastity*, which she took to be at once an allegory of the Resurrection and the veiled wisdom to which only Freemasons could accede. More recently and more promisingly, Cogo (1996) has pointed out the semantic ties between the monument to di Sangro's mother and the one to his father on the opposite side of the nave. Cogo sees the pair as a Christian allegory of filial love. He thinks di Sangro was set on using an allegory of this kind to commemorate his parents, especially his mother who died shortly after his birth. This would explain the broken tombstone held by *Chastity* as an allusion not only to Caietani's brief existence, but also to Christ's breaking the seals of his burial vault, the event to which the relief on the base refers.

Corradini's *Chastity*, the last of a long series of veiled figures, shows the artist at the peak of the extraordinary powers he honed over a long career. Preceded by the *Vestal Virgin Tuccia* in Palazzo Barberini (completed in 1743) Rome, Italy, it has the same Classical elegance in the progression of compositional rhythms. In the *Chastity*, Corradini was clearly moving beyond the Rococo features that marked his earlier works, from the *Veiled Figure* in the Musée du Louvre Paris, France—tentatively identified with the one in the Manfrin collection (see Cogo, 1996)—to the less felicitous *Faith* on the altar of St. Emma in the Cathedral of Gurk, Austria, the *Christian Religion* on the Manin monument in the Cathedral of Udine, Italy, and finally the bust of *Chastity* in the Museo del Settecento Veneziano at Ca' Rezzonico in Venice.

MASSIMO DE GRASSI

Further Reading

Cicognara, Leopoldo, *Storia della scultura in India*, 1818

Cioffi, Rosanna, *La Cappella Sansevero: Arte barocca e ideologia massonica*, Salerno, Italy: Edizioni 10/17, 1987

Cogo, Bruno, *Antonio Corradini: Scultore Veneziano, 1688–1752*, Este, Italy: Libreria Gregoriana, 1996

Nava Cellini, Antonia, *La scultura del Settecento*, Torino, Italy: UTET, 1982

Sade, Marquis de, *Voyage d'Italie, précédé des premières oeuvres, suivi de Opuscules sur le théâtre*, Paris: Tchou, 1967

Semenzato, Camillo, *La scultura Veneta del Seicento e del Settecento*, Venice: Alfieri, 1966

Wittkower, Rudolf, *Art and Architecture in Italy, 1600 to 1750*, Baltimore, Maryland, and London: Penguin, 1958

JOSSE DE CORTE (GIUSTO LE COURT) 1627–1679 *Flemish, active in Italy*

The Flemish sculptor Josse de Corte was a true innovator and the leading figure in Venetian sculpture during the second half of the 17th century because of the originality of his sculptural language. Much in demand by both private and public patrons throughout his career, de Corte was a constant participant in the most important decorative projects undertaken in Venice, and he often worked in close collaboration with the famed Venetian architect Baldassare Longhena.

After apprenticing with his father, in all likelihood the sculptor Jean le Court, de Corte trained in Antwerp, (not in Rome, as was long thought) at Cornelis van Mildert's workshop and later in Amsterdam, with Artus Quellinus the Elder. The language of these two artists, which combined the teachings of François du Quesnoy and the representational culture of Peter Paul Rubens, decisively influenced de Corte's style even after his arrival in Venice, in Italy 1655. Under van Mildert's direction, in 1648 de Corte sculpted a marble statue of the *Virgin Mary and Child* for the inner portal on the south side of the Cathedral of Antwerp. According to contemporary sources, his inspiration for this piece was the *St. Susanna* (1629–33) du Quesnoy had done for the Church of Santa Maria di Loreto in Rome. The portal was eventually broken up, but two fragments of the statue are preserved in the cathedral's chapterhouse: the Virgin's head, which significantly resembles the head of du Quesnoy's *St. Susanna*, and the bust of the Christ Child. In the years de Corte spent in Amsterdam before departing for Venice, he most likely worked with Quellinus on the sculptural decoration of the facade and interior of the new city hall (now the royal palace). The statues and reliefs created for this building depicted historical, mythological, and allegorical subjects, and both the themes and the style were largely inspired by ancient Roman art.

The Classical language of de Corte's first works in Venice was thus the outcome of these experiences. Elements that recall du Quesnoy's style and taste—elegant postures, drapery adhering tightly to the body and enhanced by a studied play of folds and knots, and facial types and expressions—characterize the two candle-bearing angels de Corte sculpted for the Labia family chapel in the Church of San Nicolò da Tolentino (1655), the allegorical figures of *Honor* and *Virtue* for the monument to Girolamo Cavazza in the Church of Santa Maria dell'Orto (*ca.* 1657), and the allegorical figures of *Prudence* and *Fortitude* for the monument to Tommaso Alvise Mocenigos in the Church of San Lazzaro dei Mendicanti (1658–64). The four statues of the Virtues contain significant references to Rubens's work (*Honor* is based on a Rubens drawing), but although the classicizing accents remain, one can already see de Corte moving toward the Baroque with a more emphatic tone in the figures, more grandiose shapes, and a stronger interplay of light and shadow.

The two beautiful busts of *Envy* and *Honor*, which de Corte sculpted around 1661 for Archduke Leopold Wilhelm of Habsburg's gallery, are notable examples of the kind of work intended for collectors that must have accounted for a good part of the Flemish sculptor's output.

Envy is especially interesting. In its violent, expressive power and the naturalistic rendition of the haggard face and the wrinkled skin, it anticipates the *Queen of Heaven Expelling the Plague* de Corte sculpted a few years later for the high altar designed by Longhena for the Church of Santa Maria della Salute in Venice. The group of marble statues de Corte sculpted for this altar in the early 1670s shows his language in full bloom and perfectly integrated with the artistic culture of the Venice of his day. *St. Mark* is an excellent example: it displays a new monumentality; a strong plasticism that brings out the muscle structure, the pose, and the restrained movement; and a convoluted arrangement of the drapery animated by strong chiaroscuro contrasts. Like the realistic skeletal figure of the *Queen of Heaven Expelling the Plague*, the powerful *St. Mark* and the other figures adorning the high altar of the Church of Santa Maria della Salute were clearly influenced by the contemporary paintings of the so-called *tenebrosi* (who produced paintings characterized by high contrast between light and shade). Conversely, the charming musician angels depicted in relief on the lower part of the altar are instances of a Classical theme recurring throughout de Corte's work, which were evidently very successful: chubby putti derived from du Quesnoy's work. Other significant examples are the two putti representing *Autumn* and *Winter* on the great stairway of Ca' Rezzonico in Venice, and the relief of the *Young Bacchus* in the Museo Civico, Padua, Italy.

In 1674 de Corte signed a contract in Venice to sculpt two statues of *Adoring Angels* for the altar in the Basilica of Santa Giustina in Padua. In that same period, he sent another masterpiece to Padua: the monument to Caterino Cornaro in the Basilica of Sant'Antonio, where the commanding figure of the Venetian admiral appears against a background of weapons, escutcheons, and war trophies. Equally significant for its originality is the monument to Giorgio Morosini that de Corte made for the Venetian Church of San Clemente in Isola. In one of de Corte's finest portraits, Morosini kneels atop a high base supported by two mighty caryatids, his intensely melancholy gaze turned toward the viewer standing below.

The high altar in the Venetian Church of Sant' Andrea della Zirada was the last work de Corte completed before his premature death. According to the inscription on the back, he was both the sculptor and the "architect" of this piece. In the group of statues depicting the *Transfiguration on Mount Tabor*, the artist had lost none of his Baroque inventiveness and creative power. Here, as in the altar at Santa Maria della Salute, de Corte staged a sort of miracle play with Christ at the summit of Mount Tabor and Moses, Elijah, and the apostles watching from below. The scene is animated by a vehement tone and a dramatic agitation; the skillful orchestration of poses and gestures is underlined by a violent chiaroscuro effect; the figures are rendered with vigorous naturalism, and their facial features are strongly characterized.

For nearly a century, through the early decades of the 18th century or longer, de Corte's example was decisive for the development of Venetian sculpture and for the training of whole groups of sculptors, whether direct disciples such as the German-born Enrico Merengo and the Venetian Paolo Callalo, or artists with far stronger and more original personalities, such as Orazio Marinali and Giovanni Bonazza.

SIMONE GUERRIERO

Biography

Born in Ypres, Flanders, Belgium, 1627. Son of the sculptor Jean le Court. Worked in Antwerp under Cornelis van Mildert, 1648, then in Amsterdam; traveled to Venice, probably arriving early 1655; present in Venice before 29 August 1655, as documented by contract signed with nobleman Giovan Francesco Labia for the candle-bearing angels to be placed in family chapel in San Nicolò da Tolentino, Venice; name appeared on the list of members of the Stonecutters' Guild, 1672, which at the time included sculptors; lived and had shop in the parish of San Felice, Venice; moved late in life to nearby parish of Santa Sofia. Died in Venice, Italy, 4 October 1679.

Selected Works

1648   *Virgin Mary and Child*; marble; fragments: Chapter House, Cathedral of Antwerp, Belgium

1655   Candle-bearing angels; Carrara marble; Labia Chapel, Church of San Nicolò da Tolentino, Venice, Italy

ca. 1657   *Honor* and *Virtue*, for monument to Girolamo Cavazza; Carrara marble; Church of Santa Maria dell'Orto, Venice, Italy

1658–64   *Prudence* and *Fortitude*, for monument to Tommaso Alvise Mocenigo; Carrara marble; Church of San Lazzaro dei Mendicanti, Venice, Italy

ca. 1660   Ten mythological and allegorical busts; Carrara marble; Villa Pisani, Stra (near Venice), Italy

1661   *Honor* and *Envy*; Carrara marble; Kunsthistorisches Museum, Vienna, Austria

1661–72   *Adoring Angels* and *Caryatid Angels*; Carrara marble; high altar, Church of San Nicolò da Tolentino, Venice, Italy

ca. 1663–65   *Autumn* and *Winter*; Carrara marble; Ca' Rezzonico, Venice, Italy

1663–65   *The Blessed Lorenzo Giustiniani* and *St. Paul*, and putti; Carrara marble; Church of San Pietro di Castello, Venice, Italy

ca. 1664–65   *The Young Bacchus*; Carrara marble; Museo Civico, Padua, Italy

ca. 1670–72   *Queen of Heaven Expelling the Plague*; Carrara marble; high altar, Church of Santa Maria della Salute, Venice, Italy

1674   Two statues of *Adoring Angels*; Carrara marble; Basilica of Santa Giustina, Padua, Italy

1674   Monument to Caterino Cornaro; marble; Basilica of Sant'Antonio, Padua, Italy

1677   Monument to Giorgio Morosini; marble; Church of San Clemente in Isola, Venice, Italy

1678   Two statues of *Angels*; Carrara marble;
        Ca' Mocenigo Oratory, Aevisopoli (near
        Venice), Italy

1678   *St. Peter*; Carrara marble; Ca' Memmo
        Oratory, Cendon di Silea (near Treviso),
        Italy

1679   *Transfiguration of Christ*; Carrara marble;
        high altar, Church of Sant'Andrea della
        Zirada, Venice, Italy

Further Reading

Casteels, M., "Cornelis van Mildert," in *La sculpture au siècle de Rubens dans les Pays-Bas méridionaux et la principauté de Liège* (exhib. cat.), Brussels: Musée d'Art Ancien, 1977

Guerriero, Simone, "'Di tua Virtù che infonde spirto ai sassi': Per la prima attività veneziana di Giusto Le Court," *Arte Veneta* 55 (1999)

König, P., "Giusto de Corte (1627–1679): Sein Beitrag zur venezianischen Plastik der zweiten Hälfte des 17. Jahrhunderts," Ph.D. diss., Universität Wien, 1973

Rossi, Paola, "La scultura," in *Storia di Venezia—Temi: L'arte*, edited by Rodolfo Pallucchini, vol. 2, Roma: Istituto dell'Enciclopedia Italiana, 1995

Rossi, Paola, "La scultura a Venezia nel Seicento," in *Venezia: L'arte nei secoli*, edited by Giandomenico Romanelli, Udine, Italy: Magnus, 1997

Semenzato, Camillo, *La scultura veneta del Seicento e del Settecento*, Venice: Alfieri, 1966

COSMATI

Cosmati is the traditional term used since the end of the 18th century to describe Roman marble workers active in the 12th and 13th centuries in the Patrimony of Saint Peter, which closely corresponds to the present-day Latium in Italy. The term was coined in 1791 as the result of a mistaken assumption that one dynasty of artists—the Cosmatus family, active during the second half of the 13th century—produced all Roman marble work in the Middle Ages. Although the expression *marmorarii romani* (Roman marble workers) is preferable, the term *cosmati* is still useful since it conventionally also describes the so-called *cosmatesque* art, the typical style in which mosaic inlay and geometric patterns of contrasting polychrome marble surfaces set against a white background in *opus sectile* ("cut work," a form of inlay in marble and other materials used for flooring and walls) prevail. The unbroken activity of the *cosmati* may be followed through two centuries, roughly unfolding from the Norman plunderings and destructions in Rome in 1084 to the exile of the papal court in Avignon in 1309.

The marble workers' main field of activity was the furnishing of church interiors, which included a pavement whose patterns guided the processions during the liturgy. It also included small-scale liturgical architecture such as the *schola cantorum*, an enclosure that delimited the sacred space along the central axis of the nave and that contained the Gospel ambo on the right, with a paschal candlestick nearby, the Epistle pulpit on the left, the altar surmounted by a ciborium in the center, and a papal throne beneath in the apse. The Church of S. Clemente in Rome offers the best preserved and perhaps the earliest liturgical ensemble of this kind, dating from Pope Paschal II's reign (1099–1118). Further examples in Rome include the Church of S. Maria in Cosmedin (*ca.* 1125) and the Church of S. Lorenzo fuori le Mura (*ca.* 1230). The work of the *marmorarius* included not only marble fittings and ornamental stonework but also tasks appropriate to architects, sculptors, and pictorial mosaicists (see Claussen, 1996).

As parts of the different guilds active in Rome during the Middle Ages, some families handed down a specific privilege through posterity and expanded as true companies in order to exert an absolute monopoly on the use and probably also on the trade of antique marble. Claussen has demonstrated the existence of five to six contemporary workshops that shared the work between them for 200 years (see Claussen, 1987). As evidence of a strict and deliberate market organization, other building activities also demonstrate such a phenomenon of specialization. Preister has been able to show that four brick masons' workshops specialized in the building of bell towers in Rome during the 12th and 13th centuries (see Preister, 1993). In all probability these same craftsmen built the earliest Roman cloisters of the 12th century. But less than a century later, as Preister remarks, marble workers superseded them: for instance, Vassallettus and his father erected in toto the cloister of the Church of San Giovanni in Laterano, Rome, Italy, shortly before 1238 (see Preister, 1993). Indeed, the *cosmati* applied themselves more and more in the course of the 12th century to the carving of architectural elements. Their intervention was at that time limited to the disposition of columns, capitals, and decorative elements carved at the workshop, occasionally exported in pieces to be set up *in situ* with the help of other artists, as in the case of the cloister of the Church of S. Croce at Sassovino near Foligno (1229) or the south side of the cloister of S. Scholastica at Subiaco (*ca.* 1200), where still-decipherable setting signs seem to indicate a prefabrication in Rome for an ultimate setting *in situ*.

At first the *cosmati* established a system to reuse antique *spolia* (plunder) for architectural purposes (representing considerable financial savings), which they then followed by creating new elements consciously imitated from genuine antique items. Abandoning the use of *spolia* eventually led to the creation of a "medieval antique" (see Claussen, 1987). By the end of the 12th century, however, the *marmorarii* also emerged as skillful sculptors. A thematically rather limited repertoire representing sphinxes, atlantes (sculptured male figures serving as supports), lions guarding church entrances, eagles placed at the center of architraves or on the back of ambo lecterns, masks, and small-scale human and animal figures then appeared. One can still see these details on a work of art made in the early years of Innocent III's pontificate (1198–1216), the paschal candlestick of the Church of S. Paolo fuori le Mura, Rome, Italy, carved by Nicolaus de Angelo and Pietro Vassallettus. During the second half of the 13th century, with the introduction of basic Gothic forms, this repertoire was soon to be implemented with the introduction of recumbent effigies on wall tombs, which permitted the development of funerary sculpture (Pietro di Oderisio and Johannes Cosmati are among those who contributed the most in this respect).

The *cosmatesque* workshop would have been somewhat like a warehouse attached to a construction company, in which the commissioners or patrons would have found both the building materials and the necessary craftsmen, managed by a head contractor. Starting in the mid 12th century the *cosmati* took part in most of the Roman architectural projects, thus becoming essential protagonists in the *renovatio Romae* (rebirth of Rome). This status, combined with a strict family organization, consequently strengthened the passing down of a specific knowledge, defined as a repertory of models and formal solutions (see Bassan, 1994). A strong unity of style and forms characterized the *cosmatesque* art, which prevented the formation and development of any alternative style for about 150 years. This characteristic, common to all Roman marble workshops until the 1260s, clearly distinguishes the *cosmati* from other Romanesque artists. In addition, the *cosmati* insistently and systematically signed their works (e.g., Paulus in the Church of S. Ambrogio at Ferentino, around 1100: "Hoc opifex magnus fecit vir nomine Paulus" [a great artist, a man named Paulus, made this]). Although artists' signatures are frequent in the Middle Ages, in Rome and elsewhere, the *cosmati* emphasized their mastery and above all their *romanitas* more than their contemporaries. The signature thus functioned as a clear trademark and certified the work's quality. But it was also a pretext for the sculptor to show his legitimacy and to underline his adherence to a specific, authorized, and perhaps intellectually defined group. It is likely that this legitimacy took root in the deliberate appropriation of the antique and in the fact that the *cosmati* were conscious of actively participating in the *renovatio Romae* begun under Pope Paschal II.

The *cosmati*, especially Jacobus Laurentius and the Vassalletus, produced their most significant works

during Innocent III's and Honorius III's pontificates (1216–27). The *cosmatesque* art developed after the Gregorian Reform and in part as the Catholic Church's response to the investiture controversy. A consequence of Urban II's liturgical reform at the end of the 11th century, the *renovatio Romae*, of which the *cosmati* were important protagonists, was eventually stopped by the reforms led by two 13th-century French popes, Urban IV and Clement IV. A short revival under Nicholas III adopted Gothic forms, but the transfer of the curia to Avignon in 1309 put an end to the commissions; *cosmatesque* art was to survive only in the field of painting.

PIERRE ALAIN MARIAUX

Further Reading

Bassan, Enrico, "Cosmati," in *Enciclopedia dell'arte medievale*, vol. 5, Rome: Istituto della Enciclopedia Italiana, 1994

Claussen, Peter Cornelius, *Magistri doctissimi Romani: Die römischen Marmorkünstler des Mittelalters*, Stuttgart, Germany: Steiner Verlag, 1987 (a standard monograph)

Claussen, Peter Cornelius, "Marmi antichi nel medioevo romano: L'arte dei Cosmati," in *Marmi antichi*, edited by Gabriele Borghini, Rome: Edizioni d'Arte, 1990

Claussen, Peter Cornelius, "Cosmati," in *The Dictionary of Art*, edited by Jane Turner, vol. 7, New York: Grove, and London: Macmillan, 1996 (with bibliography)

Glass, Dorothy F., *Studies on Cosmatesque Pavements*, Oxford: BAR, 1980

Preister, Ann, "Bell Towers and Building Workshops in Medieval Rome," *Journal of the Society of Architectural Historians* 52/2 (1993)

COUSTOU FAMILY
French

Nicolas Coustou, 1658–1733

Nicolas Coustou moved from Lyon to Paris to take advantage of the presence of his uncle, Antoine Coysevox, with whom he studied for six years. After winning first prize at the Académie Royale in 1682, he went to Rome as *pensionnaire* (fellow) at the Académie de France. There, he dutifully carved the requisite student's copy of an antique sculpture, *Commodus as Hercules*, which was employed for the decoration of Versailles. The statue demonstrates his technical mastery in carving as well as his ability to conceive not a servile copy but a noble, less austere statue by changing details from the original and treating it with more naturalism.

In Paris, Nicolas took six years to finish his *morceau de réception* (a piece submitted as part of the requirement for membership) in order to enter the Académie

Guillaume I Coustou, *Horses of Marly*, 1740–45
© Giraudon / Art Resource, NY

Royale, where he rose to the highest grade. The first painter at the time, Charles Le Brun, asked the sculptors to realize allegorical themes in marble relief relating to the glory of the king. Nicolas's relief, *The Recovery of Louis XIV from Illness*, shows that he was not at ease with such a subject, and although he used a few details that show a Baroque influence to give his composition more animation, it does not display the talent his later works demonstrate.

From 1691 to 1699, Nicolas contributed to the interior decoration of the Dôme des Invalides in Paris, where he created rich and varying compositions, perfectly suited to the architecture, and animated the space within his reliefs with graceful figures. He was then employed, like his uncle and later his brother Guillaume I Coustou, to produce a great number of works for the park at the Château of Marly, in order to decorate this favorite residence (more quiet and intimate than Versailles) of the old king, Louis XIV, in a new atmosphere of pleasure and ease. Nicolas displayed his talent by giving life to ancient gods through charming statues and bucolic themes in the park. He carved an *Apollo Running* and two *Meleagers* (1703–06) in a dynamic manner, showing the figures in action. Even seated figures such as the *Nymphs* strike animated, nearly dancing poses, through the spiral movement of their bodies. Without exaggerating the figures' ges-

tures or details such as windblown draperies, Nicolas emphasized the graceful effects of naturalism.

In contrast to his brother, however, Nicolas never excelled in the art of portraiture; he instead possessed a brilliant talent in monumental religious art. In the choir of Cathedral of Notre-Dame, for the ensemble of the *Vow of Louis XIII*, he was responsible for the central group of the *Pietà*. The calm draperies and the pyramidal composition respect the traditional French sense of harmony and equilibrium, whereas the sorrowful expression of the crying Virgin, the large gesture of her arms, and the intervention of the angel belong clearly to the Roman Baroque. His technical prowess and ease with working in a large scale imparts to the group a great nobility.

Nicolas Coustou must be considered one of the best protagonists of the transitional period between the Classical art of Versailles and the softer, more animated style that announced the art of Louis XV's reign.

Guillaume I Coustou 1677–1746

Guillaume I Coustou followed in his brother Nicolas's footsteps and also had a successful academic career. Nevertheless, although he won the first prize at the Académie Royale, he was not nominated *pensionnaire* at the Académie de France. However, not wishing to lack training in Rome, like his uncle Antoine Coysevox, he realized the journey at his own expense. In Rome Guillaume received the opportunity to work in Pierre Legros's workshop, who was then creating his groups for the churches of the Gesù and S. Ignazio and whose style left a notable influence on Guillaume's later production.

Back in France, Guillaume helped his uncle finish the statues of *Fame* and *Mercury* for the park at the château of Marly and carved his *Hercules on the Funeral Pyre* in order to enter the academy. Like his brother, he worked on the main artistic projects of the end of Louis XIV's reign, and his works are often closely connected to Nicolas's: for example, his *Rhône* is symmetrical to his brother's *Saône* for Louis XIV's monument in Lyon; his statue of *Louis XIII* kneels toward Nicolas's *Pietà* in the choir of Notre-Dame; and his *Hippomenes* and *Daphne* belong with his brother's *Apollo* to the group of the *coureurs* (runners) for Marly.

Guillaume I made a substantial contribution to the chapel of Versailles; between 1707 and 1710 he created many reliefs and statues for its interior and exterior decoration. These works, whose Baroque inspiration is evident in, for example, the dynamism of *St. Augustine*'s silhouette and the gesture of *Hope* and *Faith*, introduced a style that is more free and animated than that of the first sculptural decoration of Versailles.

Guillaume I also received many commissions to create busts. For official portraits he paid careful attention to the facial details of his sitter's physiognomy, while giving richness and movement to wigs and clothes in order to promote an effect of dignity and vitality, as in the *Samuel Bernard*. In a far more simple manner and with noticeable naturalism, he demonstrated in the *Nicolas Coustou* his intense link with his brother, whereas the marble bust of *August the Strong of Saxony* displays a strength of character, due to the head's torsion. Even though the Lemoyne family was rising to fame in this medium, Guillaume must still be considered one of the principal and most successful portraitists of his generation.

Guillaume I's most famous works are the Marly *Horses Restrained by Grooms*, commissioned to fill, at the end of the great central perspective of the park at Marly, the former location of those by his uncle that had been removed to the Tuileries. The sculptor paid careful attention to the proportions of the groups according to their position at Marly, making many studies after nature not only for the grooms but also for the horses; he then carved each group from a single Carrara marble block, taking care over every detail. At the end of his career, then, Guillaume could claim the creation of these two masterpieces, which contempor-

aries judged superior to antique groups and which perfectly illustrate the French Baroque style that a new generation of sculptors would then develop during the mid 18th century.

Guillaume II Coustou 1716–1777

Faithful to his family's tradition, Guillaume II Coustou carried out a brilliant official academic career. Trained by his father, Guillaume I Coustou, he won first prize for the Académie Royale in 1735; he was only 19 when he arrived at the end of the year in Rome as *pensionnaire* at the Académie de France. There, he realized first a *Bust of Christ* copied from Michelangelo and a copy of the *St. Susanna* by François du Quesnoy (1629–1633). Although students had previously made copies of Renaissance art at the French academy in Rome, this was the first time that, in place of copying an antique statue, as was the tradition, a student copied a modern masterpiece. In 1740 Guillaume II returned to France and helped his father install the *Horses* at the park at Marly. He executed in one year his sculpture of *Vulcan* (his *morceau de réception* for the Académie Royale), which demonstrates his mastery in carving but lacks originality in its composition; he thus entered the academy at a very young age, where he was regularly promoted.

Guillaume II's first individual commission of importance in France was the marble *Apotheosis of St. Francis Xavier* for the Jesuit church in Bordeaux; its style clearly reveals the influence of Baroque monuments he had seen in Rome but which is not found in his later works. As an official sculptor to the court, he received commissions to create many reliefs or statues for important churches, as well as for Madame de Pompadour's residences in Paris; unfortunately, many of these decorations have disappeared.

Guillaume II acquired esteem and reputation not only in France but also abroad; Frederick the Great of Prussia ordered two marble statues, of *Mars* and *Venus*, from him for the Schloss Sanssouci in Potsdam. Moreover, in 1776, Marigny, director of the *bâtiments du roi*, (buildings of the king), preferred him as the sculptor for the statue of *Louis XV* the king offered to Marigny for his castle at Ménars. Most significant, Guillaume II received the commission for the tomb of Louis de Bourbon and his wife in Sens Cathedral. Conceived by Charles-Nicolas Cochin and first set up in the choir, where it could be seen in the round, the monument consists of two urns as a central point and four allegorical figures. The style of the latter is in marked contrast with that of the *Apotheosis of St. Francis Xavier*. Nothing remains of Guillaume II's earlier Baroque influence, although the statue of *Religion* from this tomb recalls in the draperies and in the head the *St. Susanna* that he copied in Rome. The monument's conception is quite innovative, lacking the dramatic effect seen, for example, in the tomb of Maurice, *maréchal* de Saxe (1753–76) by Jean-Baptiste Pigalle. The figures, with their calm gestures, their bodies nude or covered by simple draperies imitated from the ancients, and their sorrowful expressions, show that this masterpiece of French funerary art belongs to the Neoclassical era.

ANNE-LISE DESMAS

See also **Coysevox, Antoine; Legros II, Pierre**

Nicolas Coustou

Biography

Born in Lyon, France, 8 January 1658. Brother a woodcarver, mother the sister of sculptor Antoine Coysevox, and wife the daughter of painter René-Antoine Houasse. Left Lyon and trained in Paris under Coysevox, 1676; won first prize at Académie Royale de Peinture et de Sculpture, 1682; *pensionnaire* (fellow) of Académie de France, Rome, 1683–86; returned to France, stopping in Lyon for work, and arriving in Paris, April 1687; official career followed as sculptor of the king in Paris, Versailles, and Marly; workshop in the Louvre, from 1700, and lodging, from 1703 to his death; admitted *(agréé)* in Académie Royale de Peinture et de Sculpture, April 1687, received *(reçu)*, August 1693; appointed assistant professor, 1695, professor, 1702, assistant rector, 1715, rector, 1720, and chancellor, 1733. Died in Paris, France, 1 May 1733.

Selected Works

1686   *Commodus as Hercules*; marble; Parterre de Latone, Château, Versailles, France

1691–99 Four pairs of *Prophets*, two pairs of *Angel Musicians*; stone; Dôme des Invalides, Paris, France

1693   *The Recovery of Louis XIV from Illness*; marble; Musée du Louvre, Paris, France

1696– *Julius Caesar*; marble; Musée du Louvre,
1722   Paris, France

1699– *The Seine and the Marne*, for the Château
1712   of Marly; marble; Musée du Louvre, Paris, France

1701–6 *St. Louis*; marble; Dôme des Invalides, Paris, France

1708–10 *Adonis, Nymph with a Quiver*, and *Nymph with a Dove* for the Château of Marly; marble; Musée du Louvre, Paris, France

1711–14 *Apollo Running*, for the Château of Marly; marble; Musée du Louvre, Paris, France

1712–28 *Pietà*; marble; Cathedral of Notre Dame, Paris, France

1714–20 *The Saône*; bronze; (pedestal of the equestrian statue—now destroyed—of Louis XIV by Desjardin), Place Bellecour, Lyon, France

1715–38 *Crossing of the Rhine* (with Guillaume Coustou I); marble; Chapel of the Château, Versailles, France

1726–31 *Louis XV as Jupiter*; marble; Musée du Louvre, Paris, France

Guillame I Coustou

Biography

Born in Paris, France, 25 April 1677. Brother of Nicolas Coustou. Trained by his uncle, with his brother, in Paris; won first prize at Académie Royale de Peinture et de Sculpture, 1697; studied in Rome, 1697–1700; worked in atelier of Pierre Legros; official career followed as sculptor of the king in Paris, Versailles, and Marly; had lodgings and workshop in the Louvre, from 1733 until his death; admitted *(agréé)*, in the Académie Royale de Peinture et de Sculpture, 1703, received *(reçu)*, in 1704; appointed assistant professor, 1706, professor, 1715, assistant rector, 1726, and rector, 1733. Died in Paris, France, 22 February 1746.

Selected Works

1704   *Hercules on the Funeral Pyre*; marble; Musée du Louvre, Paris, France

1707–08 *Hope* and *Faith*; stone; Chapel of the Château, Versailles, France

1708   *St. Jerome* and *St. Augustine*; stone; Chapel of the Château, Versailles, France

1711   *Hippomenes*, for the Château of Marly; marble; Musée du Louvre, Paris, France

1712–15 *Louis XIII*; marble; Cathedral of Notre Dame, Paris, France

1713–14 *Daphne*, for the Château of Marly; marble; Musée du Louvre, Paris, France

1714–20 *The Rhône*; bronze; (pedestal of the equestrian statue—now destroyed—of Louis XIV by Desjardin), Place Bellecour, Lyon, France

1726–31 *Marie Leczinska as Juno*; marble; Musée du Louvre, Paris, France

ca. 1727 *Samuel Bernard*; marble; Metropolitan Museum of Art, New York City, United States

1739–45 *Horses Restrained by Grooms* (also known as the Horses of Marly); marble; Musée du Louvre, Paris, France

year   *Nicolas Coustou*; terracotta; Musée du
unknown Louvre, Paris, France

year   *August the Strong of Saxony*; marble; unknown Kunstsammlung, Dresden, Germany

Guillame II Coustou

Biography

Born in Paris, France, 19 March 1716. Son of sculptor Guillaume I Coustou. Trained by his father; won first prize at Académie Royale de Peinture et de Sculpture, 1735; *pensionnaire* of the Académie de France, Rome, November 1735 to July 1740; had lodgings and workshop in the Louvre, from 1746 until his death; admitted *(agréé)*, in the Académie Royale de Peinture et de Sculpture, April 1741, received *(reçu)*, in July 1742; appointed assistant professor, 1743, professor, 1746, assistant rector, 1765, and rector, 1770. Died in Paris, France, 13 July 1777.

Selected Works

1736–39 *St. Susanna* (copied after François du Quesnoy); marble; Château, Versailles, France

1742 *Vulcan*; marble; Musée du Louvre, Paris, France

1743–48 *Apotheosis of St. Francis Xavier*; marble; Church of Saint-Paul, Bordeaux, France

1746 *Visitation of the Virgin*; bronze; Chapel of the Château, Versailles, France

1751–53 *Apollo*, for château of Bellevue; marble; Chapel of the Château, Versailles, France

1752 *The Cardinal de Tencin*; marble; Musée des Hospices, Lyon, France

1761–69 *Agriculture* and *Felicity*; stone; Gabriel's Palaces, Place de la Concorde, Paris, France

1764–69 *Mars* and *Venus*; marble; Schloss Sanssouci, Potsdam, Germany

1765 *Hélène de Courtenay, Marquise de Listenois*; marble; private collection

1766–77 Tomb of Louis de Bourbon and his wife; marble; Sens Cathedral, France

1774–75 *The Abbé Terray*; marble; Musée Jacquemart-André, Chaalis, France

Further Reading

Dézallier d'Argenville, Antoine-Joseph, *Vies des fameux architectes depuis la Renaissance des arts*, 2 vols., Paris: Debure l'Aîné, 1787; reprint, Geneva: Minkoff Reprint, 1972

Levey, Michael, *Painting and sculpture in France 1700–1789*, New Haven and London: Yale University Press, 1993

Rosasco, Betsy, *The Sculptures of the Château de Marly during the Reign of Louis XIV*, New York and London: Garland, 1986 (on Nicolas and Guillaume I Coustou)

Souchal, François, *French Sculptors of the 17th and 18th Centuries: The Reign of Louis XIV*, vol. 1, Oxford: Cassirer, 1977, and vol. 4, London: Faber and Faber, 1977 (on Nicolas and Guillaume I Coustou)

Souchal, François, *Les frères Coustou: Nicolas (1658–1733), Guillaume (1677–1746), et l'évolution de la sculpture française du Dôme des Invalides aux Chevaux de Marly*, Paris: Boccard, 1980

Souchal, François, "Guillaume II Coustou (1716–1777): Notes biographiques sur un sculpteur de Louis XV," in *Thèmes et figures du siècle des lumières: Mélanges offerts à Roland Mortier*, edited by Raymond Trousson, Geneva: Droz, 1980

ANTOINE COYSEVOX 1640–1720 *French*

The son of a master craftsman originally from Franche-Comté, Antoine Coysevox was born in Lyon, where his mother's family originated. (George Keller-Dorian has corrected a common misconception that Coysevox's father's family originated in Spain [see Keller-Dorian, 1920].) At the age of 17, Coysevox arrived in Paris, where he began art instruction at the Académie Royale de Peinture et de Sculpture. He worked closely with Louis Lerambert, who had spent ten years in Italy, and was likely an assistant under Lerambert at the Tuileries. By 1666 Coysevox had received the title Sculpteur du Roi. Following the death of his wife, Lerambert's niece, Coysevox left for Saverne and entered the service of Cardinal François-Egon de Fürstenberg, prince bishop of Strasbourg, for whom he did much work, unfortunately now lost or destroyed. Unsigned portrait busts of important court notables, including one of Charles Le Brun, the official court painter, may date from after his return to Paris. Subsequently, Coysevox relocated to Lyon, where he was appointed professor at the Lyon Académie. *Virgin and Child*, an energetic ensemble with billowing drapery, was originally intended for a roadside niche. For a time, Coysevox may have considered opening an art school in Lyon that would have been associated with the Lyon Académie. Soon, however, he returned to Paris.

Following his appointment as a professor at the Académie Royale de Peinture et de Sculpture in 1678, Coysevox continued to record the likenesses of France's most powerful individuals, among them Louis XIV and again, in 1679, Charles Le Brun. The latter played an important and ongoing role in Coysevox's career, acting both as mentor and collaborator. Coysevox's best-known single work, indicative of this cooperation, is the stucco bas-relief of Louis XIV on horseback for the Salon de la Guerre at Versailles, which shows Louis XIV astride his mount and dressed in Roman battle gear; the king tramples his enemies, who lie helpless under the prancing horse's hooves. Le Brun's decoration on the domed ceiling, *Victorious France Subduing Her Enemies*, provides a fitting and thematically coherent canopy. Two other equestrian statues, *Mercury and Fame*, originally intended for one on each side of the entrance to Marly, the king's palace, also proclaim the glory of the Sun King. In 1719 they were placed at the entrance to the Tuileries Gardens in Paris (reproductions stand in for the originals, which are now in storage).

At Versailles, Coysevox worked alongside other sculptors, including François Girardon, Jean-Baptiste Tuby, and Étienne Le Hongre, and in association with a host of other less-well-known sculptors who produced works sometimes indistinguishable one from the other. Their art collectively has been described as being of dignified attitude and is characterized by a common gracefulness of movement and noble restraint. Coysevox worked on a variety of projects at Versailles, including vases, garden sculpture, architectural detailing, and a bust of Louis XIV (*ca.* 1681 or earlier), memorable in his powdered wig and elegant lace fall, originally intended for the grand stairway (now destroyed). Coysevox also produced marble copies of antique sculpture for Versailles, such as *Venus Crouching* (1684–86) and other important garden sculpture, including his renowned war vase (*Vase de la Guerre*, 1684), which was paired with Tuby's *Vase de la Paix*.

Coysevox erected a full-length bronze statue of Louis XIV, again dressed in Roman garb, in 1689 in front of the Hôtel de Ville in Paris in recognition of the king's reconciliation with the city fathers. The statue (missing and presumed destroyed during the revolution) included two splendid bas-reliefs illustrating in one the king offering nourishment to the poor and in the other the king fighting heresy through the revocation of the Edict of Nantes. Coysevox's so-called *Vow of Louis XIV* (1713–15) in the Cathedral of Notre Dame in Paris is a later work, portraying the king sumptuously dressed but in a more contemplative mood. Coysevox was one of a group of artists who ably fulfilled the king's intention that his own fame would be fittingly glorified through his patronage of the arts.

Not all Coysevox's portrait busts were of well-known people. One of his most notable commissions was for *Marie Serre*, which portrayed the painter Hyacinth Rigaud's mother. The figure appears not only as an ideal model but also as a real person touched by life and old age. The painter had prepared a sketch of her in full face, profile, and three-quarter view for Coysevox to use as his model.

Although Coysevox's portrait busts far outnumber other kinds of commissions, he also received commissions to do other forms of commemorative work. Especially impressive are his funerary monuments. Upon the death of Ferdinand-Egon de Fürstenberg, he was

Louis XIV© Giraudon / Art Resource, NY

asked in 1698 to produce a tomb (now destroyed). His tomb of Cardinal Mazarin is considered among his finest works. It is a collaborative effort, with some sections attributed to Tuby and Le Hongre, but scholars generally agree that Coysevox was wholly responsible for the marble kneeling statue of the cardinal atop the sarcophagus, a fine portrait image, as well as the statue of Fidelity, a bronze figure that kneels below. Within a somber memorial, Coysevox added a particularly human detail of Fidelity's faithful dog enveloped in her voluminous drapery folds.

Following Louis XIV's death, Coysevox turned his attention to recording likenesses of Louis XV, marking birthdays and subtle changes to the royal physiognomy. Coysevox's Louis XV, portraying the king at age nine, in 1719, is one of his last works as official sculptor to France's royal family. Jean-Baptiste Lemoyne II, the son of one of Coysevox's students, carried on Coysevox's tradition of royal portraiture.

Together with their father, Coysevox trained Nicholas and Guillaume Coustou; Coysevox's continuing reputation at court also aided their careers. François Souchal has called Coysevox "one of the great portraitists in the history of sculpture" (see Souchal, 1996).

MARILYN BAKER

See also **Coustou Family; Lemoyne Family**

Biography

Born in Lyon, France, 29 September 1640. Son of the sculptor Pierre Coyzevox. Went to Paris, 1657, and entered studio of Louis Lerambert; granted title Sculpteur du Roi, 1666; worked in Saverne, 1667–71, in Paris, 1671, and in Lyon, 1675–77, where he taught at the Académie Royale de Peinture et Sculpture; settled in Paris and Versailles, 1677; a professor at the Académie Royale de Peinture et de Sculpture, 1678; lived at the Gobelins factory; had a studio at Versailles and, after 1698, an apartment in the Palais du Louvre; rector of Académie Royale de Peinture et de Sculpture, 1694; director, 1702. Received numerous royal, private, and public commissions. Died in Paris, France, 10 October 1720.

Selected Works

1671   Bust of Charles Le Brun; marble; Musée du Louvre, Paris, France; terracotta version: 1676, Wallace Collection, London, England

1676   *Virgin and Child*; marble; Church of St. Nizier, Lyon, France

1679   *Charles Le Brun* (bust); marble; Musée du Louvre, Paris, France

1681–83 *The Crossing of the Rhine* (bas-relief from *The Triumph of Louis XIV*); stucco; Château, Versailles, Yvelines, France

1686   Equestrian monument to Louis XIV; bronze (destroyed); fragments: *France Triumphing over the Seas* and *Louis XIV Receiving the Ambassadors from Siam*, Musée des Beaux-Arts, Rennes, France

1689   *Louis XIV*; bronze; courtyard, Musée Carnavalet, Paris, France

1689–93 Tomb of Cardinal Mazarin; marble and bronze; Chapel of the Institut de France, Paris, France

1695–   *Charlemagne*; marble; Dôme des
1706   Invalides, Paris, France

1699   Bust of Louis XIV; bronze; Wallace Collection, London, England

1702   *Mercury and Fame*; marble; Musée du Louvre, Paris, France

1706   *Marie Serre*; marble; Musée du Louvre, Paris, France

1719   *Louis XV*; marble; Musée du Château, Versailles, Yvelines, France

Further Reading

Blunt, Anthony, *Art and Architecture in France, 1500–1700*, London and Baltimore, Maryland: Penguin, 1970; 5th edition, revised by Richard Beresford, New Haven, Connecticut: Yale University Press, 1999

Keller-Dorian, Georges, *Antoine Coysevox (1640–1720): Catalogue raisonnée de son oeuvre*, Paris: Keller-Dorian, 1920

Levey, Michael, *Painting and Sculpture in France, 1700–1789*, New Haven, Connecticut: Yale University Press, 1993

Souchal, François, *French Sculptors of the 17th and 18th Centuries: The Reign of Louis XIV*, vols. 1–3, Oxford: Cassirer, 1977–87, and vol. 4, London: Faber and Faber, 1993; see especially vol. 4

Souchal, François, "Coysevox, Antoine," in *The Dictionary of Art*, edited by Jane Turner, vol. 8, New York: Grove, and London: Macmillan, 1996

Tapié, Victor, *Baroque et Classicisme*, Paris: Plon, 1957; as *The Art of Grandeur: Baroque Art and Architecture*, translated by A. Ross Williamson, New York: Praeger, 1960

TONY CRAGG 1949–   *British, active in Germany*

In the early 1970s a generation of British sculptors was looking for a freedom of expression in which conceptual art replaced the formalism of the "New Sculpture." Tony Cragg was among those who translated this freedom by applying it to systems and natural processes in order to create new and provocative possibilities. Cragg's work cannot be classified in or as one single genre, but rather, challenges the bounds of object-based sculpture. His exploration of widely varying materials, techniques, themes, and motifs disregards conventional codes.

Cragg's attraction to science and technology may have come from his father, an engineer in the aeronautics industry. Trained in technology at Hartfield, Cragg worked as laboratory technician at the National Rubber Producers' Research Association. He also attended art school, which enabled him to nurture his scientific curiosity and his fascination with the scientific method. Stone and glass were from the beginning his chosen materials. He was attracted by their ethereal luminosity, by which the objects could seem to cease to be representations and could suggest something more general about light.

During his first years at Royal College of Art, Cragg became interested in nature and landscape. He had much in common with Richard Long, Hamish Fulton, and Roger Ackling (Cragg's professor at the Royal College of Art), whose sculptures had demonstrated in a new manner the relation between humankind and nature.

Three themes consistently reappear in Cragg's works: the body, the object, and the landscape. Cragg could transform waste materials through a Duchampian process of designation, but his projects did not stop with the readymade. Cragg structured his early works on a system for reordering and reconstructing scattered fragments. Using materials such as building debris and plastic fragments, he recycled waste as a strategy for generating value out of nothing (for example, *New Stones, Newton's Tone*). In this conception, he shows kinship with Richard Long and Carl Andre.

One of Cragg's most important works using this method is *Stack*, remade on numerous subsequent occasions but first assembled in 1975. The work consists of myriad kinds of building and organic materials scavenged from the immediate surroundings, as well as the studio, and compressed into strata to form a dense cubic edge. *The Self Portrait with Sack* (1980) is comprised of a figure turned at a three-quarter angle from the viewer toward a bag standing by itself in the ground and is composed principally from four basic hues: red, blue, green, and yellow. These elements were the preferred media in Cragg's art at this time. Applied to the wall, they became for him a mode of drawing; deployed on the floor, they offered a means of making sculpture. *Self Portrait with Sack* is at once representative and unique in Cragg's oeuvre of the 1980s, when he showed that sculpture could occupy the wall and even create a picture without yielding to pictorial aesthetics. The freedom Cragg found by 1984–85 is apparent in the distinctive particularities of *Echo* (1986), and especially *Three Modern Buildings* (1984), which was composed of porous, synthetic thermalite and imitated Manhattan skyscrapers.

Even in his early work *New Stones, Newton's Tone*, one sees already one of the major themes that still preoccupies Cragg today and that he has summarized as follows: "Man's relation to his environment. The relationships between objects, materials and images. The creation of objects that don't exist in the natural or in the functional world which can reflect and transmit information and feelings about the contemporary world and my own existence." Through Cragg's sensibility, the pink, gray, and yellow reflected light of London's riverfront transformed material, as with the towers of *Minster*.

With *Plough*, Cragg began another series. He intended his sculpture to accommodate the tool's function of plowing the earth. After obtaining a plow from a farmer, Cragg reproduced each part in wax. The heat served to soften and distort each section, and Cragg then cast each element to reconstruct the plow.

Cragg also treated the issue of fragmented states of materials or the temporary appearance of wholeness that evolves from their composition into a recognizable representation. Fragmentation involves another theme—infinity—because it contains everything that is beyond definition and distinction. The theme of fragmentation and dissolution led Cragg to yet another theme: change. Losing their integrity, objects could be associated in new forms that sometimes appear like quasi-architectural sculptures, such as *Als es Wieder war wurde* (As it Was it Will Again Be; 1985) and *Città* (City; 1986).

Cragg is deeply committed to an analysis of the relationship of human beings with their material environment, a commitment that has both an ethical and an aesthetic dimension. He saw his first solo exhibition at the Whitechapel Art Gallery in 1981 as an excellent opportunity to evoke political associations, for example, with *Crown Jewels*, *Policeman*, and *Britain Seen from the North*, all from 1981.

The idea of the growth of scientific knowledge is a characteristic feature of Cragg's work, who is said to have studied science and specialized in geology and fossil gathering in order to investigate not only the organic world but its constructed and fabricated counterpart. *Palette* (1982) is an example of a piece comprising a range of natural and synthetic materials in sheet form, the edges of which have been overpainted in white to allow the material to emerge.

Moving to Wuppertal in 1977, Cragg settled in an industrial area, where he recovered different types of materials: plastic, wood, bricks, and bottles. Through a variety of methods, he produced forms and transformed them into new and more complex combinations.

Pieces such as *Branching Form, Bodicea, Unit* (1989), and *Forminifera* (1989) demonstrate the multiple relations between cellular or crystalline models and primitive forms of animal or vegetable life. The group of works called *Early Forms* is another, larger example of a combination of geometric and organic motifs. The group consists of large bronze sculptures based on contorted combinations. Clearly, Cragg's oeuvre is quite varied and extremely rich.

DOÏNA LEMNY

Britain Seen from the North
© Tate Gallery, London / Art Resource, NY

Biography

Born in Liverpool, England, 9 April 1949. Worked as a laboratory technician at the National Rubber Producers' Research Association, 1966–68; studied at Gloucestershire College of Art, Cheltenham, 1969–70, and at the Wimbledon School of Art, 1970–73; studied at the Royal College of Art, London, 1973–77; moved to Wuppertal, Germany, 1977, and showed in group exhibitions. Began teaching at the Kunstakademie in Düsseldorf, 1978; first solo exhibition at the Lisson Gallery, London, 1979; major exhibits in Brussels, 1985, and London, 1987; nominated as the British representative at the 43rd Venice Biennale, 1988; later the same year, major exhibition at the Tate Gallery, London; awarded the Turner Prize; designated professor at the Kunstakademie, Düsseldorf; nominated as Royal Academician, 1994. Lives and works in Wuppertal, Germany.

Selected Works

1979　*New Stones, Newton's Tone*; plastic; The Arts Council of Great Britain, London, England

1979　*Spectrum*; plastic; artist's collection, Wuppertal, Germany

1980　*Stack*; wood, metals, plastic; temporary installation (dismantled)

1981　*More and More and More*; painted wood; private collection, Wuppertal, Germany

1981　*Postcard Union Jack*; plastic; City Art Gallery, Leeds, England

1982　*Five Bottles (Green, Yellow, Red, Orange, and Blue)*; glass; Buchmann Gallery, Saint Gall, Switzerland

1984　*Evensong*; steel; Saatchi Collection, London, England

1984　*George and the Dragon*; plastic, wood, aluminum; The Arts Council of Great Britain, London, England

1984　*Mittelschicht* (Middle layer); wood; private collection

1985　*Birnam Wood*; plastic; private collection, the Netherlands

1987　*Mollusk*; steel; Fundacio Caixa de Pensions, Barcelona, Spain

1988　*Loco*; wood; private collection of Gerald S. Elliott, Chicago, Illinois, United States

1988　*Spill*; glass, wood; Chantal Crousel Gallery, Paris, France

1988　*Three Cast Bottles*; metal; private collection, Paris, France

1988　*Trilobiten*; bronze; private collection of John and Maria Pappajohn, United States

1988　*Untitled (Shell)*; steel; Saatchi Collection, London, England

1989　*Bodicea*; metal, wood; Tucci Russo Gallery, Torino, Italy

1989　*Early Forms*; bronze; New Academy for Art Studies, London, England

1989　*Forminifera*; plaster; private collection

1989–90　*Minster*; metals; private collection, Barcelona, Spain

1990　*Beasts of Burden*; stone; Marian Goodman Gallery, New York City, United States

1990　*Complete Omnivore*; ceramics; private collection

1990　*Early Forms*; glass, bronze; Von der Heydt Museum, Wuppertal, Germany

1990　*Glass Hybrids*; glass; private collection of Christine and Isy Brachot, Brussels, Belgium

1990　*Plough*; metal; Chantal Crousel Gallery, Paris, France

1992　*Terris Novalis*; steel; Lisson Gallery, London, England

1992　*Two Rivers*; painted bronze; Landeszentralbank, Düsseldorf, Germany

1993　*Complete Omnivore*; plaster, wood, steel; Marian Goodman Gallery, New York City, United States

1993　*Early Forms* (large version); bronze; Buchmann Gallery, Cologne, Germany

1993　*In Camera*; ceramic; Stedelijk van Abbemuseum, Eindhoven, the Netherlands

1994　*Taking Place*; paraffin wax; Buchman Gallery, Basel, Switzerland

1995　*Trade Winds*; plaster; Tucci Russo Gallery, Torino, Italy

Further Reading

Cooke, Lynne, "Tony Cragg at the White Chapel," *Artscribe* 28 (1981)

Cooke, Lynne, "Tony Cragg: Thinking Models," in *Tony Cragg: George and the Dragon* (exhib. cat.), London: South Bank Centre, 1993

Cragg, Tony, *Ecrits; Writings; Geschriften: 1981–1992* (trilingual English-Dutch-French edition), Brussels: Éditions Isy Bachot, 1992

Cragg, Tony, *Tony Cragg: Tramway, Centre for Contemporary Arts*, Glasgow: Tramway, Centre for Contemporary Arts, 1992

Davvetas, Démosthène, Interview with Tony Cragg, in *Tony Cragg* (exhib. cat), Brussels: Société des Expositions du Palais des Beaux-Arts de Bruxelles, and Paris: Musée d'Art Moderne de la Ville de Paris, 1985

Delbbaut, Jan, "The Metamorphosis of the Object," in *Tony Cragg* (exhib. cat.), Eindhoven, The Netherlands: Stedelijk Van Abbemuseum, 1991

Francis, Mark, "Full Circle: Tony Cragg's Work, 1977–1981," in *Tony Cragg: Sculpture, 1975–1990* (exhib. cat.), edited by Sue Henger, Newport Beach, California: Newport Harbor Art Museum, 1990

Grenier, Catherine, "Explorer on the Moon," in *Tony Cragg: Musée nationale d'art moderne* (exhib. cat.), edited by Grenier, Paris: Centre Georges Pompidou, 1995

Lampert, Catherine, "Tony Cragg," in *Tony Cragg: XLIII biennale di Venezia, 26 June–25 September 1988*, London: Visual Arts Department, British Council, 1988

Müller, Maria, "Tony Cragg: Neue Bilder," in *Tony Cragg: Kunstsammlung Nordrhein–Westfalen* (exhib. cat.), edited by Müller, Düsseldorf, Germany: Kunstsammlung Nordrhein-Westfalen, 1989

Schimmel, Paul, et al., editors, "Tony Cragg: Interaction of Matter and Thought," in *Tony Cragg: Sculpture, 1975–1990* (exhib. cat.), edited by Sue Henger, Newport Beach, California: Newport Harbor Art Museum, 1990

Schwarz, Michael, editor, *Tony Cragg: Skulpturen* (exhib. cat.), Karlsruhe, Germany: Badischer Kunstverein, 1982

Wildermuth, Armin, editor, *Tony Cragg: Early Forms*, Basel, Switzerland: Galerie Buchman, 1994

THOMAS CRAWFORD *ca.* 1813–1857

United States

Thomas Crawford began his studies as an artist by attending drawing classes at the National Academy of Design, New York City. Around 1827 he began an apprenticeship with a woodcarver that was to last until 1832, when he entered the marble firm operated by John Frazee and Robert E. Launitz. As with many 19th-century marble firms, the bulk of Frazee and Launitz's business was limited to grave markers and ornamental stonework. However, both of the firm's founders were known for their own artistic output, providing Crawford with two artistic exemplars: Launitz tending toward classicizing ideal and mythological subjects and Frazee producing primarily naturalist portraits. During his time with Frazee and Launitz, Crawford produced his own work, which he exhibited at the National Academy of Design before his departure for Rome in 1835.

In Rome, Crawford entered the studio of Danish Neoclassical sculptor Bertel Thorvaldsen with a letter of introduction from Launitz. Thorvaldsen provided his American pupil with studio space and occasional criticism and was also no doubt responsible for Crawford's early severe Neoclassical style. After a year, Crawford moved into his own studio in Rome, where he earned his living initially through portrait commissions. Thorvaldsen had encouraged Crawford to look to Antique models, an influence apparent in portraits such as *Mrs. John Jones Schermerhorn* of 1837, which demonstrates Crawford's knowledge of Roman portraiture. That same year Crawford also copied the Vatican's *Demosthenes* and modeled his first full-length ideal composition, *Paris Presenting the Golden Apple to Venus*, a thoroughly Neoclassical male nude inspired by Antonio Canova's *Paris*.

As the sole American sculptor in Rome, Crawford benefited from the patronage of American tourists. Among his early patrons was future Senator Charles Sumner of Boston, Massachusetts, with whom he developed a friendship in 1839. Crawford modeled a bust of Sumner that summer, during which time he was also at work on a subject for which he had no commission, a life-size plaster sculpture of *Orpheus and Cerberus*. Sumner was instrumental in organizing a subscription for the acquisition of a marble version of the *Orpheus and Cerberus* for the Boston Athenaeum. *Orpheus and Cerberus*, which was based on the Greek myth, continued Crawford's exploration of the Neoclassical male nude, a rare subject in the United States. To avoid any sense of impropriety, Crawford supplied the sculpture with a fig leaf, thereby making it acceptable to a conservative Boston audience. After much fund-raising, *Orpheus and Cerebus* was unveiled in Boston in 1844, where it met with overwhelming approval, establishing Crawford's reputation at home. This sculpture was exhibited in Boston with several other works by Crawford in what is considered the first one-man exhibition by an American sculptor. In the wake of his success, Crawford returned to the United States in late 1844. While in New York, he pursued a wealthy young

The Broken Tambourine
© Smithsonian American Art Museum, Washington, DC / Art Resource, NY

woman named Louisa Ward, sister of Julia Ward Howe, whom he had met in Rome. Crawford and Ward were married in 1844.

The couple returned to Rome late in 1845, where Crawford made his wife the subject of an affectionate portrait bust. With steady support from American patrons, Crawford undertook a number of playful subjects, becoming especially noted for depictions of children—for example, *Boy Playing Marbles*. He also continued to create large-scale allegorical and literary subjects, such as *Christ and the Woman of Samaria* (1846). *Dying Mexican Princess* of 1848 marks a departure from the Classical and biblical themes Crawford so often depicted in favor of a New World subject. This sculpture also highlights a stylistic move away from severe Classicism to greater naturalism and sentimentality in Crawford's work.

Political unrest in Rome forced Crawford to return to the United States in 1849, where he entered the competition for a monument to George Washington to be erected by the state of Virginia in Richmond. In 1850 he received this major public commission. Crawford's design was composed of three parts: a bronze equestrian statue of George Washington, statues of six of Virginia's famous sons, and six republican eagles. Crawford quickly returned to Rome to undertake the commission, preparing for this rare opportunity to treat an equestrian subject by studying other well-known equestrian groups, including the Marcus Aurelius (*ca.* 161–180 BCE). Crawford met the added challenge of depicting the first president and integrating the additional figures into the design of this extremely ambitious project.

In 1854 Crawford received a commission to design the Senate pediment for the United States Capitol. The pediment illustrates the *Progress of Civilization*, a complex, multifigured composition with a classicizing personification of *America* at the center. To the right of the figure of *America*, a settler swings his ax at a tree, a harbinger of civilization. Farther right is a group of classically inspired Native Americans contemplating their fate. The left side shows a civilized *America* with historicizing figures from its past wearing contemporary dress. Additional Capitol commissions followed in 1855, including two figures of *History* and *Justice* for the Senate portico, the bronze doors for both the House of Representatives and the Senate, and the 5.8-meter-high bronze *Armed Freedom* surmounting the dome.

While engaged with his projects for the Capitol, Crawford simultaneously worked on other public commissions, including a statue of *Beethoven* for the New England Conservatory of Music and a 3-meter-high statue of *James Otis* for Mount Auburn Cemetery, Boston. During this period of intense activity, Crawford also continued to produce a number of ideal figures, such as *Flora* and *Peri*, and sentimental genre subjects, such as *The Broken Tambourine* (*ca.* 1853).

Although he had achieved unprecedented success in securing commissions, by the mid 1850s, Crawford's health began to fail. In 1856 he ceased working entirely because of trouble with his eyes. After seeking treatment in Paris and London, he died at the age of 44 as a result of cancer. At the request of his widow, colleagues in Rome completed many of his unfinished commissions.

AKELA REASON

See also **Thorvaldsen, Bertel**

Biography

Born probably in New York, United States, *ca.* 1813. Studied drawing at the National Academy of Design; apprenticed to a woodcarver, *ca.* 1827–32; entered the marble firm of Frazee and Launitz, 1832; went to Rome and studied with Bertel Thorvaldsen, 1835; established own studio in Rome, *ca.* 1836; had first solo exhibition by American sculptor, Boston, 1844; returned to Rome, 1845–49; received several major commissions for sculptural work on U.S. monuments, 1850–55; traveled to Paris, seeking treatment for illness, 1857. Died in London, England, 10 October 1857.

Selected Works

1837	*Mrs. John Jones Schermerhorn*; marble; New-York Historical Society, New York City, United States
1837	*Paris Presenting the Golden Apple to Venus*; marble; Chrysler Museum, Norfolk, Virginia, United States
1839	*Orpheus and Cerebus*; marble; Boston Museum of Fine Arts, Massachusetts, United States
1839	Bust of Charles Sumner; marble; Museum of Fine Arts, Boston, Massachusetts, United States
1842	*Genius of Mirth*; marble; Metropolitan Museum of Art, New York City, United States
1844	*Boy Playing Marbles*; marble; Worcester Art Museum, Massachusetts, United States
1847	*Flora*; marble; Newark Museum, New Jersey, United States
1850	Equestrian statue of George Washington; bronze; Richmond, Virginia, United States
ca. 1853–54	*The Broken Tambourine*; marble; Smithsonian American Museum of Art, Washington, D.C.

1854   *Peri*; marble; versions in Corcoran Gallery of Art, Washington, D.C., United States; Academy of Fine Art, Philadelphia, Pennsylvania, United States

1854   *Progress of Civilization*; marble; pediment of the Capitol, Washington, D.C., United States

1855   *Armed Freedom*; bronze; Capitol dome, Washington, D.C., United States

1855   *Beethoven*; bronze; New England Conservatory of Music, Boston, Massachusetts, United States

1855   *History* and *Justice*; marble; portico of Capitol; Washington, D.C., United States

Further Reading

Clark, Henry Nichols Blake, *A Marble Quarry: The James H. Ricau Collection of Sculpture at the Chrysler Museum of Art*, New York: Hudson Hills Press, 1997

Crane, Sylvia E., *White Silence: Greenough, Powers, and Crawford, American Sculptors in Nineteenth-Century Italy*, Coral Gables, Florida: University of Miami Press, 1972

Dimmick, Lauretta, "A Catalogue of the Portrait Busts and Ideal Works of Thomas Crawford (1813?–1857), American Sculptor in Rome," Ph.D. diss., University of Pittsburgh, 1986

Dimmick, Lauretta, "Thomas Crawford's *Orpheus*: The American *Apollo Belvedere*," *American Art Journal* 19 (1987)

Dimmick, Lauretta, "Veiled Memories; or, Thomas Crawford in Rome," in *The Italian Presence in American Art, 1760–1860*, edited by Irma B. Jaffe, New York: Fordham University Press, and Rome: Istituto della Enciclopedia Italiana, 1989

Dimmick, Lauretta, " 'An Altar to Heroic Virtue Itself': Thomas Crawford and His Virginia Washington Monument," *American Art Journal* 23 (1991)

Gale, Robert L. *Thomas Crawford, American Sculptor*, Pittsburgh, Pennsylvania: University of Pittsburgh Press, 1964

CRETAN SCULPTURE

The height of civilization on the island of Crete (located south of the Greek mainland in the Aegean) was the Minoan culture, named after the legendary King Minos. From approximately 3000 to 1450 BCE, the Minoans led a seemingly ideal lifestyle with few enemies, enjoyable weather, and a bountiful sea. With a flourishing navy the Minoans had both excellent defenses and extensive trade. The sculpture of Minoan Crete reflects this carefree, leisurely lifestyle in its organic form and frivolous subject matter. Detailed knowledge of the island is due largely to the efforts of British antiquarian Sir Arthur Evans. In 1894 Evans traveled to Crete and excavated the palace at Knossos, declaring it to be the legendary palace of King Minos and the link to the origin of the Greeks.

At Crete the palace served as a dwelling for the local ruler and as the economic center of town. The Minoans built and used the palace at Knossos between 1900 and 1450 BCE on the hillside of Kefala, a site admired for its elevated position, water supply, and access to the sea and forest. Knossos's complex layout contributed to theories connecting it to Greek myths of the labyrinth and the Minotaur who lived there surviving on human flesh. Sculpture found at this and other sites provides insight into both the everyday lives and the spiritual world of the Minoans, reinforcing the notion that these people were indeed fairly peaceful, joyous, and spiritual.

The representation of the human form in sculpture at Crete is distinctive. Minoans rendered the human form in a highly stylized manner with elongated graceful limbs, slim waists, long black wavy hair, and feminine facial features. Although the body forms for both males and females are similarly feminine and sometimes hard to distinguish, one can sometimes discern genders in paintings by skin color, a lighter skin tone for women and a darker one for men. In sculpture distinguishing gender may become problematic unless distinctively male or female clothing is shown. Human figures are typically represented in action, taking part in leisurely or spiritual activities.

Serpent goddess of Knossos
© Nimatallah / Art Resource, NY

An intriguing example of sculpture found at Knossos and other Minoan sites is a female figurine called the serpent goddess. Artisans occasionally created these female statuettes out of ivory and gold but more commonly used faience, a type of glazed earthenware similar to porcelain. These sculptures may have been considered luxury items because of the rarity and fragility of the materials. The snake goddess statues from the palace at Knossos wear long layered skirts and bolero-type jackets that leave the chest open, identical to the outfits worn by the women of Crete (as represented in painted and sculpted images). The statues hold a serpent in each raised hand or allow serpents to crawl over their arms. Sitting on the top of their headdresses is often a small docile feline. The women's eyes are wide as if entranced, and they may be partaking in a ritual or a dance. Although it is not certain whether these women represent actual goddesses or merely mortal devotees, the statues are likely of a religious nature. This idea is supported by the location where the sculptures are found; one snake goddess figure (*ca.* 1600 BCE), for example, was found beneath a shrine in a courtroom at Knossos.

The most popular subject at Crete was the bull, generally accepted to be representative of ideas such as male fertility and masculine strength. A variety of sculptures, in ivory, stone, and metal, depict images of the bull. Artisans would carve intricate ritual objects into the shape of a bull's head. From the "Little Palace" at Knossos comes a steatite rhyton, or soapstone libation vessel, (*ca.* 1600–1500 BCE) carved in the shape of a bull's head with inlaid eyes of rock crystal and gilded wooden horns. Scholars assume such objects to be of a ceremonial nature in part because of the wealth of materials employed, the excellent craftsmanship, and the presence of such vessels incorporated into fresco images on the palace walls.

Minoans also used the horns of the bull alone as sculptural decorative symbols, called "Horns of Consecration" by Evans. The south entrance to the palace of Knossos includes a large-scale stylized representation of a set of bull's horns (now reconstructed), which create a silhouette against the Aegean sky. The double horn image may have been meant to mirror the double peaks of Mount Jukus, visible in the distance, where an important shrine or sanctuary was located. Evidence also shows that a second set of these horns was constructed at the palace's north entrance.

It is not unusual to find imagery of a bull jumping game or ceremony in which both men and women took part. From fresco paintings one can reconstruct that this game was carried out by running toward the front of the bull, grabbing hold of his horns, and jumping onto or vaulting over its back, then jumping off and landing on one's feet. Both painted and sculptural depictions of various stages and techniques of this game have been uncovered; one noteworthy ivory sculpture (*ca.* 1600–1500 BCE) includes the bull and a figure in midair.

From Hagia Triada, a site on the southern central coast of Crete, comes the *Harvesters Vase* (*ca.* 1500 BCE), possibly the finest example of Minoan relief sculpture. Only the upper portion of the soapstone vase remains. It is a small-scale work, its greatest diameter approximately 13 centimeters. The relief shows a joyous crowd going to or returning from the fields carrying harvesting implements and perhaps sheaths of grain. A man in a cloak carrying scales and a staff leads the procession. The workers who follow him are individualized; many sing or shout, and one even marks time with a rattle, his mouth wide in song and his lungs shown filled to capacity. The dynamism achieved by the image enhances the emotional quality of the work, unprecedented in ancient art.

CATHERINE BURDICK

Further Reading

Cadogan, Gerald, *Palaces of Minoan Crete*, London: Barrie and Jenkins, 1976

Cotterell, Arthur, *The Minoan World*, New York: Scribner, 1980

Evans, Arthur John, *The Palace of Minos*, 4 vols., London: Macmillan, 1921–35; reprint, London: Hafner, and New York: Biblo and Tannen, 1964

Higgins, Reynold Alleyne, *Minoan and Mycenaean Art*, New York: Praeger, 1967; new revised edition, London and New York: Thames and Hudson, 1997

MacGillivray, J. Alexander, "Labyrinths and Bull-Leapers," *Archaeology* 53/6 (November/December 2000)

Marinatos, Spyridon, and Max Hirmer, *Crete and Mycenae*, New York: Abrams, 1960

Pendlebury, John, *The Archaeology of Crete*, London: Methuen, 1939

CZECHOSLOVAKIA

See **Central Europe**

D

SALVADOR DALÍ 1904–1989 *Spanish*

Primarily known as a Surrealist painter of the early to mid 20th century, Salvador Dalí never limited himself to one art form or medium. During the more than six decades of his artistic career, Dalí experimented with styles, materials, and processes including found-object sculpture, performance, and Installation. As a principal member of the initial Parisian Surrealist community in the 1930s, Dalí concentrated on the use of novel and nontraditional artistic practices. His use of ordinary and recognizable objects distorted in odd combinations and contexts by means of dream symbols personified the core of illusionistic or figurative Surrealism. Even though Dalí formally broke with most of the ideals and individuals of the Surrealist movement (he and the group's leader André Breton disagreed on the movement's fundamental goals), his art continued to exhibit Surrealist characteristics until the end of his career.

Named Salvador after an older brother who died, Dalí was obsessed with the idea of death and destruction from boyhood. Along with images of blood, decay, sex, and religious icons, these two elements became the mainstays of Dalí's paintings, objets d'art, and later, his sculptures. From an early age all types of art intrigued Dalí, and his evolving style was inspired by everything he saw, heard, and touched. Major influences included the Catalonian landscape of his childhood, the emotional conflicts with his father and schoolmates, and the works of artists such as Futurist sculptor and painter Umberto Boccioni and Surrealists Max Ernst and Giorgio de Chirico.

Boccioni strongly advocated the artist's right to use distortion and fragmentation of any figure or object to the fullest, and he firmly believed artists should make use of every material possible, including glass, wood, iron, cement, leather, mirrors, electric lights, and even horsehair. In his creation of pop objects such as *Aphrodisiacal Dinner Jacket*, *The First Thinking Machine*, and *A Tray of Surrealist Objects*, Dalí embraced these ideas. Another aspect of Boccioni's art that appealed to the young Dalí was the anthropomorphic combinations of figures and architecture, evident in works such as *Fusion of a Head and a Window* and *Head and House and Light*. Dalí's relationship with Max Ernst furthered his interest in textures and materials. Dalí admired Ernst's *frottages*, or rubbings, especially for the way the random images created by the rubbings could be interpreted in many different ways. Dalí derived much of his use of space, light, and modeling from the early *pittura metafisica* (metaphysical painting) of De Chirico.

Dalí's marriage to Gala Eluard in 1929 inspired him to a new level of achievement. Gala tempered his madness and encouraged Dalí in the reinvention of himself as a living work of art. Everything from his mustache and clothes to his paintings and sculptures was a part of the Dalí *Gesamtkunstwerk*: the artist's intention was to transform his life and work into a complete and total performance or corpus. Moreover, similar to the Dadaist's merging of art and life, Dali embraced the performative aspects of Modernism. His oeuvre, along with his melodramatic public persona, represented a journey from the two-dimensional to the three-dimensional. It seemed logical for him to make the step from painting and creating trompe l'oeil (extreme realism in art; literally "deception of the eye") replicas of objects and situations to executing objets d'art and sculpture.

Dalí designed sets for the theater and films, created jewelry and Pop objects, and worked with materials ranging from oil paints and watercolors to bronze and cork. He was a writer (*La Femme Visible* [1936] and *The Secret Life of Salvador Dalí* [1948]), a painter (*The Persistence of Memory* [1931] and *Anthropomorphic Echo* [1937]), and a sculptor (*Cosmic Elephant* [1971–81] and *Gala Leaning Out of the Window* [1971–81]).

Dalí conceptualized and planned the creation of many sculptures, but he never executed any of the pieces until late in his career. Even his *Venus de Milo with Drawers* (1935) was the execution of another artist. Dalí took a replica of the *Venus de Milo* and marked where he wanted the drawers to be cut, thus creating the *Venus de Milo with Drawers* and transforming an ordinary replica into an extraordinary Dalínian object. A similar situation occurred in the creation of Dalí's *Bust of Dante*. Peter Moore, Dalí's assistant, commissioned Christine Forani, a Belgian sculptor, to produce the original bust. Once the work was completed, Dalí took the clay sculpture and had a grotesque hole cut in the right cheek and then added a wreath of gold spoons as a finishing touch. Again, the idea was Dalí's, but another artist completed the work.

By 1971 Dalí's health was failing, and his relationship with Moore had disintegrated. He partnered with a new assistant, a fellow Catalan, Enrique Sabater, who turned out to be a keen businessman, reinforcing Dalí's reputation as an artist deeply informed by the possibilities of American capitalism for the visual arts. During his tenure with Dalí, Sabater encouraged the artist to produce almost 50 wax sculptures entirely by his own hand from 1971 until 1981, shortly before Gala's

death. Sabater interested a Spanish businessman, Isidro Clot, in the sculptures. Clot quietly acquired almost all of these original wax sculptures executed by Dalí. The cost of the Clot Collection ran into the millions of dollars.

Dalí's turn to sculpture toward the end of his career can be attributed to many factors. Due to his frail health, Dalí's hands became too unsteady to maintain the level of control over his paintbrush necessary to create works equaling the quality of those created in his younger days. The wax medium was more forgiving of Dalí's physical limitations, namely his shaking hands. The sculptures in the Clot Collection are a seemingly logical end to the evolution of Dalí's art. He was finally able to bring to life some of the dream and fantasy images of his paintings. He molded them with his own hands and made his two-dimensional visions three-dimensional realities.

The sculptures in the Clot Collection range in subject from the simple (*Gala Leaning Out of the Window*) to the abject (*Guts and Head*) to the fantastical (*Cosmic Elephant*). In this collection Dalí dealt with much of the subject matter that dominated his art throughout his life—Gala, Port Lligat, St. George, Don Quixote, and symbols of Christ—but he also included surprises with the addition of new material that he made his own, such as *Guts and Head*.

Eventually, Isidro Clot had the collection cast in bronze; the Salvador Dalí Museum in St. Petersburg, Florida, now houses a set of 44 of these surreal sculptures. Ultimately, even though Dalí will be best remembered for his role as a Surrealist painter, his contributions to the world of sculpture can be noted for bringing his subjective dreamworld to life as objective and often unsettling reality.

JENNIFER OVERHULSE-KING

See also **Assemblage; Boccioni, Umberto; Duchamp, Marcel; Ernst, Max; Modernism; Surrealist Sculpture**

Biography

Born in Figueras, Gerona, Spain, 11 May 1904. Practiced drawing and sketching while convalescing from frequent illness, until deciding to become an artist at the age of ten; enrolled in the San Fernando Royal Academy of Fine Arts, Madrid, 1921, where he met Federico Garcia Lorca and Luis Buñuel; with Buñuel, dabbled in filmmaking and produced two films, *Un chien andalou*, 1929, and *L'âge d'or*, 1930; formally joined Surrealist movement in Paris, France, 1930; became a vital part of the Surrealist movement until supposed sympathies for Hitler and the Nazis and quest

Lobster Telephone

for money led to his expulsion from the group. Married Gala Eluard, former wife of Surrealist poet, Paul Eluard, 1929; Gala instantly became not only inspiration for art but frequent subject of paintings, drawings, objets d'art, and sculptures; mostly noted for paintings, which he called "hand-painted dream photographs"; turned focus to pop objects and sculpture late in life. Died in Figueras, Spain, 23 January 1989.

Selected Works

1928   *Anthropomorphic Beach*; painted cork; Salvador Dalí Museum, St. Petersburg, Florida, United States

1935   *Venus de Milo with Drawers*; bronze; Teatre-Museu Dalí, Figueras, Spain

1936   *Aphrodisiacal Dinner Jacket*; objet d'art: dinner jacket, hanger, shot glasses, liqueur, straws (accidentally destroyed)

1941   *The Eye of Time;* watch decorated with precious stones; collection of the Owen Cheatham Foundation, New York City, United States

1958   *The Ovocipede*; objet d'art: clear plastic sphere with a female figure inside (accidentally destroyed)

1959   *Angelic Crucifixion*; objet d'art: gold, platinum needles with diamonds and motor, lapis lazuli, coral, topaz; collection of the Owen Cheatham Foundation, New York City, United States

1966   *The Slave of Michelangelo*; plaster, old painted tires; collection of M. Berrocal Negrar, Verona, Italy

1971–81   Clot Collection (collection of 44 wax sculptures); wax; titles include: *Nude Woman Descending a Staircase, Cosmic Elephant, The Soul of Don Quixote, Gala Leaning Out of the Window, The Young Trajan,* and *Guts and Head*; complete set of casts: bronze; Salvador Dalí Museum, St. Petersburg, Florida, United States

Further Reading

Alexandrian, Sarane, *L'art surréaliste*, Paris: Fernand Mozan, 1969; as *Surrealist Art*, translated by Gordon Clough, New York: Praeger, 1970

Arnason, H. Harvard, *A History of Modern Art: Painting, Sculpture, Architecture*, New York: Abrams, 1968; London: Thames and Hudson, 1969; 4th edition, revised by Marla F. Prather, New York: Abrams, and London: Thames and Hudson, 1998

Dalí, Salvador, *Esculturas; Sculptures*, Madrid: Diejasa, 1986

Descharnes, Robert, *Salvador Dalí*, translated by Eleanor R. Morse, New York: Abrams, 1976

Faerna, Jose Maria (editor), *Dalí*, translated by Teresa Waldes, New York: Abrams, 1995

Gérard, Max (editor), *Dalí . . . Dalí . . . Dalí*, Paris: Draeger, 1974, and New York: Abrams, 1974

Gibson, Ian, *The Shameful Life of Salvador Dalí*, London: Faber, 1997; New York: Norton, 1998

Hibbard, Howard, *Masterpieces of Western Sculpture from Medieval to Modern*, New York: Harper and Row, 1966; London: Thames and Hudson, 1997

Lubar, Robert S., *The Salvador Dalí Museum Collection*, Boston: Bulfinch Press, 2000

Parinaud, André, *Comment on devient Dalí: Les aveux inavouables de Salvador Dalí*, Paris: Laffon, 1973; as *The Unspeakable Confessions of Salvador Dalí: As Told to André Parinaud*, translated by Harold J. Salemson, New York: Morrow, 1976; London: Quartet Books, 1977

Passoni, Franco, Reynolds Morse, and Albert Field, *Dalí nella terza dimensione* (exhib. cat.), Milan: Master Fine Art Gallery, 1987

Rubin, William Stanley, *Dada and Surrealist Art*, New York: Abrams, 1968

Stratton Foundation, *Dalí*, S.l.: Stratton Foundation for the Cultural Arts, 1989

Wach, Kenneth, *Salvador Dalí: Masterpieces from the Collection of the Salvador Dalí Museum*, New York: Abrams, 1996

AIMÉ-JULES DALOU 1838–1902 *French*

The life and works of Aimé-Jules Dalou have recently regained the attention of scholars after having been neglected throughout most of the 20th century. This revival of interest coincides roughly with trends in Postmodernism, such as a self-conscious aestheticism, a purposeful quotation of historical styles, and the emphasis on the political rather than purely aesthetic content of art. Dalou's contribution to the history of sculpture was his ability to exploit fully the political potential of public art through iconographical innovation, stylistic appropriation, and the modernization of artistic traditions.

Like the Impressionists who were his contemporaries, Dalou rejected an academic career only after he failed to gain recognition through conventional means. He tried four times to win the Prix de Rome. His work was accepted into the Salons of 1861, 1864, 1867, and 1869 but went virtually unnoticed. He secured a position as a decorator during the 1860s, his most notable commission being the Hôtel de la Païva, where he worked with Albert Carrier-Belleuse and the painter Paul Baudry. There he provided figural sculpture for chimneypieces, doors, ceiling and wall panels, and furniture in plaster, bronze, and marble inspired by Baroque models. Finally in 1870 his Salon entry, the *Embroiderer*, won him the critical acclaim he sought. Although the subject of a seated woman in contemporary dress sewing was not particularly new, the life-size scale was. Dalou is credited with translating Baudelaire's "heroism of modern life" into a three-dimensional medium; however, the fall of the Second

Empire in September 1870 and the political chaos that ensued in Paris cut short the celebration of his success at the Salon.

During this period of upheaval the sculptor joined Gustave Courbet's Federation of Artists and assumed a curatorial position at the Musée du Louvre. When the Versailles troops crushed the Commune in May 1871, Dalou escaped with his wife and daughter to England. He stayed there for eight years, teaching at the South Kensington School of Art and filling orders for intimate subjects, such as *Hush-a-bye* and *Woman Reading* (1872–75), and portrait busts of aristocratic and middle-class patrons. His first public commission was for an allegorical sculpture of *Charity* for the Royal Exchange in London in 1877. A year later he was asked to provide a monument commemorating the deceased grandchildren of Queen Victoria for the Royal Chapel at Windsor Castle.

It is difficult to assess Dalou's precise role in the Commune. Police records are inherently conservative; eyewitness accounts of his activities gathered in the reactionary period after the war are likewise suspect. Similarly, the reader should be skeptical of the efforts, undertaken years after the events occurred, of his apologists to rehabilitate the artist by dismissing his behavior as youthful indiscretion. It is fair to say, however, that the experiences of the Franco-Prussian War, Commune, exile, trial, and condemnation had a profound effect on the sculptor and his art.

A turning point in Dalou's career occurred in 1879 when the municipal council in Paris organized a competition to erect a monument to the republic in the Place de la République. He entered the contest but lost to Léopold Morice for technical reasons. The jury was so enthralled with Dalou's *Triumph of the Republic*, however, that they commissioned it as well and decided to install it in the Place de la Nation, the working-class quarter of the city. For this public monument the sculptor designed a complex allegory in a style that deliberately recalled the era of Louis XIV. In response, Auguste Rodin dubbed Dalou "the Lebrun of the Third Republic." To the figures of *Republic*, *Liberty*, *Justice*, and *Abundance* that are expected in such propagandistic pieces, Dalou added an allegory of *Work*. Wearing the sabots, trousers, and apron of a contemporary artisan, an idealized worker takes his place opposite *Justice* to propel the chariot bearing the republic. Never before had the worker been elevated to such heroic status—cast in bronze and over-life-size—or enjoyed official sanction. Thereafter, sculptural projects glorifying the worker proliferated, for example, those by the Belgian sculptor Constantin Meunier. (Dalou secretly worked on his own monument to workers that was found unfinished in his studio after his death.) Flush with the success of *Triumph of the Republic* and con-

Triumph of the Republic
The Conway Library, Courtauld Institute of Art

vinced that public art had an important role to play in the political process, Dalou put aside the private, domestic scenes that characterized his early career. Instead, he devoted himself to securing a democratic society through public art. In 1889 a full-scale plaster model of *Triumph of the Republic* was made the centerpiece of a republican rally ostensibly to celebrate the centenary of the French Revolution but really held to shore up voter support on the eve of an election critical to the survival of the regime. The inauguration of the 40-ton behemoth in 1899 was again the occasion of a socialist demonstration at the height of the Dreyfus affair, the decade-long scandal of a Jewish military officer falsely accused of spying that politicized all segments of French society. Toward the end of the 20th century the monument provided the backdrop for a memorial concert and protest organized when an Algerian folk singer cum political activist was killed in the summer of 1998.

Dalou showed reliefs illustrating major events in the history of the republic, *Mirabeau Responding to Dreux-Brézé* and *Fraternity*, at the Salon of 1883, where he was awarded the Medal of Honor. He designed monuments to republican heroes, including Auguste Blanqui, Jean-Charles Alphand, and Victor Hugo, the latter being a source of contention between himself and Rodin. The most notable among these is the tomb monument to Victor Noir, where the artist successfully modernized the medieval *gisant* (reclining statue) tradition. About 30 years after Noir became a martyr by engaging in a duel with Napoléon III's cousin, the family asked Dalou to memorialize the fallen journalist. The victim is shown immediately after the event lying on his back, his silk top hat rolling to one side. The tomb was the site of annual pilgrimages in the last decade of the century and became the subject of legend. Even today, visitors lay fresh flowers in the hat and on his chest; the feet and hands are worn smooth by a century of reverent stroking.

In the decade prior to his death, Dalou continued to promote a socialist agenda with his art. In addition to completing *Triumph of the Republic* and laboring over his monument to workers, he accepted commissions for sculptures commemorating men who demonstrated their faith in democracy, including the scientist Boussingault, the entrepreneur Jean Leclaire, and the radical republican Charles Floquet. Dalou's late pieces bear the same Neo-Baroque characteristics—handling of the masses, asymmetrical compositions, irregular treatment of the surfaces, dynamic poses, forceful gesture—visible in his early works, although the themes shifted from the personal and private to the communal and public. In the obituary published in *Le Gaulois* (16 April 1902), the artist was quoted: "The task of the future will be to put at the service of democracy all the brilliant pomp of the art from the century of Louis XIV." The deliberate act of appropriating a style associated with the Ancien Régime became a signifier of revolution and should not be misread as a lack of originality. The continuing political relevance of Dalou's monuments is testimony to the sculptor's talent and the significance of figural sculpture in both modern and postmodern art.

CHERYL K. SNAY

See also **Carrier-Belleuse, Albert-Ernest; France: Mid–Late 19th Century**

Biography

Born in Paris, France, 31 December 1838. Trained at the Petite École, Paris, under the guidance of Jean-Baptiste Carpeaux, 1852–54; entered the École des Beaux-Arts, 1854, and worked for three years in the atelier of Francisque Duret; worked as a decorator throughout the 1860s; submitted entries to the Paris Salons of 1861, 1864, 1867, and 1869; established reputation at the Salon of 1870 with *Embroiderer*; during period of Commune in France, joined Gustave Courbet's Federation of Artists and acquired a curatorial position at the Musée du Louvre; went into exile in London, 1871–79; tried in absentia in France and sentenced to life at hard labor, 1874; taught sculpture at South Kensington School of Art, London; completed many private portrait commissions and several public commissions while in London; granted amnesty in 1879 and returned to Paris, where he was awarded many public commissions; founding member of the Société des Artistes Français, 1881; awarded Medal of Honor at the Salon of 1883 and named chevalier of the Legion of Honor; named officer of the Legion of Honor, 1889. Died in Paris, France, 15 April 1902.

Selected Works

1864   Figures for chimneypieces, doors, and ceiling and wall panels; plaster, bronze, marble; Travellers' Club (formerly the Hôtel de la Païva), Paris, France

1870   *Embroiderer*; cast (reduced) in bronze; Musée de la Ville, Mont-de-Marsan, France; plaster cast: Petit Palais, Paris, France

1875   *Hush-a-bye*; marble (untraced); another version: terracotta, Victoria and Albert Museum, London, England

1877–79 *Charity*; marble (untraced); bronze copy after marble original: Royal Exchange, London, England

1879–99 *Triumph of the Republic*; bronze; Place de la Nation, Paris, France

1883   *Mirabeau Responding to Dreux-Brézé*; bronze; Palais Bourbon, Paris, France

1884–90 Monument to Delacroix; bronze; Luxembourg Gardens, Paris, France

1886   Project for the tomb of Victor Hugo; plaster; Petit Palais, Paris, France

1890   Tomb of Victor Noir; bronze; Père-Lachaise Cemetery, Paris, France

1890–   Monument to workers (unfinished);
1902   plaster; Petit Palais, Paris, France

1896   *Jean Leclaire*; bronze; Square des Epinettes, Paris, France

1899   Monument to Jean-Charles Alphand; stone; Avenue Foch, Paris, France

Further Reading

Hargrove, June, "Décor: L'hôtel de la Païva," *Les monuments historiques de la France* 102 (1979)

Hunisak, John, *The Sculptor Jules Dalou: Studies in His Style and Imagery*, New York: Garland, 1977

Hunisak, John, "Jules Dalou: The Private Side," *Bulletin of the Detroit Institute of Arts* 56, no. 2 (1978)

Hunisak, John, "Dalou's *Triumph of the Republic*: A Study of Private and Public Meanings," in *La Scultura nel XIX Secolo; La sculture du XIXᵉ siècle; Nineteenth-Century Sculp-*

ture (multilingual edition), edited by H.W. Janson, Bologna: CLUEB, 1979

Hunisak, John, "Jules Dalou," in *The Romantics to Rodin: French 19th-Century Sculpture from North American Collections*, edited by Peter Fusco and H.W. Janson, Los Angeles: Los Angeles County Museum of Art, and New York: Braziller, 1980

Roos, Jane Mayo, "Rodin's Monument to Victor Hugo: Art and Politics in the Third Republic," *Art Bulletin* 68/4 (December 1986)

ANNE SEYMOUR DAMER 1748–1828
British

Anne Seymour Damer, née Conway, was a woman of varied interests and wide-ranging achievements in 18th-century England. Socially connected in artistic, literary, theatrical, political, and aristocratic circles, she was well educated, an accomplished sculptor, and in politics an ardent Whig. She made for herself a life beyond the traditional expectations of a woman of her station. Allan Cunningham wrote of her:

> Her birth entitled her to a life of ease and luxury, her beauty exposed her to the assiduities of suitors, and the temptations of courts: but it was her pleasure to forego all such advantages, and dedicate the golden hours of her youth to the task of raising a name by working in wet clay, plaster of Paris, stubborn marble, and still more intractable bronze. (Cunningham, 1830)

Damer was born to a wealthy and prominent family. Although she spent her youth with her family in London, during her parents' frequent absences from England on military affairs, she was left in the care of her godfather, the author Horace Walpole. Walpole introduced her to a number of artistic and political figures who became her lifelong friends, such as Mary Berry.

The philosopher David Hume tutored Damer in the classics. Through her education, she developed an interest in ancient Greek civilization that was to later influence her artistic style. Her first attempt at sculpture, according to Cunningham, resulted from a disagreement in artistic taste between herself and Hume. When she criticized his interest in what she considered inferior sculpture, Hume told her that, "with all your attainments, now, you cannot produce such works." She quickly set to work producing his portrait bust in wax. When Hume responded that modeling in wax was much easier than carving in marble, she transferred the wax bust into marble.

Damer subsequently pursued technical instruction, studying modeling with Giuseppe Ceracchi and marble carving with John Bacon. Ceracchi was so taken with her artistic desires, as well as her beauty, that he used her as the model for his *Muse of Sculpture* (ca. 1777). She wanted to continue her pursuit of a career in sculpture but was delayed by her early marriage to John

Damer. Their marriage was not a happy one, and during their nine years together, she produced little art. John Damer was heir to a large fortune but consistently lived beyond their means. Facing insurmountable debt, he committed suicide in 1776, leaving Anne Damer a childless widow. To recover from failing health brought on by the strain, she traveled abroad. While in continental Europe, she renewed her interest in sculpture. Two of her earliest works were the reliefs *Antony and Cleopatra* and *Coriolanus* for Boydell's Shakespeare Gallery, London.

Throughout her life, Damer made several trips abroad to France, Italy, Spain, and Portugal and established sculpture studios to continue her work wherever she went. She studied in the galleries and studios of Italy and France; however, she remained a skilled amateur, to which her status as an honorary exhibitor at the Royal Academy attests. She pursued sculpture primarily for her own enjoyment and satisfaction rather than for the income it could provide. She gave most of her works to friends and family or donated them to public institutions; she received few commissions. Free from the constraints of patrons, Damer was able to choose for herself her subjects and stylistic treatment.

Damer's work consists chiefly of naturalistic animal sculpture, allegorical figures, and classicizing portrait busts of her friends and family in the English Neoclassical style. She worked in a variety of mediums, beginning in wax and terracotta, then stone and marble, and eventually bronze. Her animal sculpture, such as *Two Sleeping Dogs*, received excessive praise from Walpole, who compared her abilities to those of previous great masters. According to Walpole, her "busts from

A Dog
Photographic Survey of Private Collections, Courtauld Institute of Art

the life are not inferior to the antique, and theirs we are sure were not more like. Her shock dog, large as life, and only not alive, has a looseness and softness in the curls that seemed impossible to terra-cotta: it rivals the marble one of [Gianlorenzo] Bernini in the royal collection." Her animal subjects are more animated than her human figures. This can be attributed to her elaborate surface treatment of undulating streams of stylized fur (more decorative than purely naturalistic) rather than to her ability to capture and express the life force of the subject.

Damer's limitations in revealing the soul beneath the surface are more apparent in her portrait busts. Her early portraits of friends depicted in the guise of Classical figures with *all'antica* (after the antique) costume and coiffure (a popular type) reveal her interest in creating a sculptural style emulating the idea of Greek sculpture, as it was interpreted at the time. These portraits, such as *Elizabeth (Farren), Countess of Derby, as Thalia*, possess the quiet, reserved, and balanced qualities and stylized details found in Classical Greek sculpture but lack the introspective countenance this reserve implies. This absence and the smoothed, almost abstract treatment of the features cause Damer's classicized versions to appear stiff, lifeless, and severe. Furthering the Classical connection, the figures usually carry Greek inscriptions providing the sculpture's factual data.

In public sculpture, Damer is best known for her heads of the river gods Thame and Isis for the keystones at Henley Bridge in Oxfordshire and her 2.4-meter-high statue of George III for the Register House in Edinburgh. She received both these commissions through personal contacts rather than open competition. The keystone heads *Thame* and *Isis*, carved in relief, are necessarily architectonic in form. Damer designed flat, broad, stoic faces surrounded by depictions of deep-cut beard and hair. Appropriate to their location on a bridge, the beard and hair seem to actively drip with wetness, providing a satisfying contrast to the passive faces. Damer's *George III* presents a posed, austere figure whose accoutrements, such as the flowing full-length cape, metal crown, and scepter, animate the statue.

Damer also sculpted modern heroes whom she knew personally and believed to possess the virtues of the ancients. Now also using bronze, an unusual choice at the time, she created portrait busts, such as *Admiral Nelson* (1805), depicting sitters not in the guise of allegories or Classical figures but as themselves, in modern costume appropriate to their profession and status and taken from life. Damer once again maintained the spirit of the antique in these works through their balance and reserve in the Neoclassical manner. They also bear Greek inscriptions.

Damer was the foremost woman sculptor of her time. Artists such as Angelica Kauffman and Joshua

Reynolds painted her image, her former teacher Ceracchi portrayed her in sculpture, and her likeness was engraved and reproduced often. However, even her contemporaries often questioned her artistic ability, so overpraised by Walpole as to work to her detriment. Joseph Farington thought her reputation as a "high" sculptor unwarranted. Cunningham saw her as an exceptional amateur but not as a first-rate professional artist. The range of unevenness in her execution that some observed in her oeuvre led her critics to suspect the degree to which her assistants aided her in the creation of her work. Although the use of assistants was an accepted practice for most sculptors, women sculptors were more often accused of not being responsible for their own work or had the best parts of their work attributed to their teachers (for example, American sculptor Harriet Goodhue Hosmer). The variations in sculpting ability noted in Damer's work may not be hers alone but may be owing in part to the varying abilities of her assistants as she moved from her English studios to her continental European ones.

CHARLENE G. GARFINKLE

See also **Bacon, John; England and Wales: Baroque–Neoclassical; Hosmer, Harriet Goodhue; Public Sculpture; Women Sculptors**

Biography

Born at Coomb Bank, Sundridge, Kent, England, 1748. Tutored in classics by David Hume; showed artistic talent at early age; studied clay and wax modeling with Giuseppe Ceracchi, anatomy with surgeon William Cumberland Cruikshank, and marble carving with John Bacon, in whose studio she may have assisted; independent study in France, Italy, Spain, and Portugal; devoted to study of sculpture following husband's suicide, 1776; asked to contribute sculpted self-portrait to Galleria degli Uffizi, Florence, 1778; honorary exhibitor at the Royal Academy, 1784–1818. Known for classicizing portrait busts and naturalistic animal sculptures; encouraged in art by Horace Walpole; inherited Strawberry Hill from Walpole, 1797; lived there until 1811; studios at several residences; invited by acquaintance Joséphine Bonaparte to France, 1802; met Napoléon I and presented him with copies of busts of Admiral Nelson and Charles James Fox. Died in London, England, 28 May 1828.

Selected Works

1777   *Antony and Cleopatra* and *Coriolanus*, for Boydell's Shakespeare Gallery, London, England; terracotta (untraced)

1778   *Self-Portrait*; marble; Galleria degli Uffizi, Florence, Italy

1784   *Two Sleeping Dogs*; terracotta; Chillington Hall, Staffordshire, England; marble version: Goodwood House, West Sussex, England

1785   *Thame* and *Isis*; Portland stone; keystones of the central arch, Henley Bridge, Henley-on-Thames, Oxfordshire, England

1788   *Elizabeth (Farren), Countess of Derby, as Thalia*; marble; National Portrait Gallery, London, England

1789   *Mrs. Freeman as Isis*; marble; Victoria and Albert Museum, London, England

1794   *George III*; marble; Register House, Edinburgh, Scotland

1799   *Admiral Nelson*; marble (untraced); bronze versions: 1805, Guildhall, London, England; 1828, Royal Collection, London, England

1802   *Charles James Fox*; plaster (untraced); marble version: 1812, Musée du Louvre, Paris, France

1813   *Joseph Banks*; bronze; British Museum, London, England

1814   *Caroline, Princess of Wales*; terracotta; Ranger's House, London, England year unknown *Self-Portrait*; marble; British Museum, London, England

Further Reading

Benforado, Susan, "Anne Seymour Damer, 1748–1828: Sculptor," (dissertation), University of New Mexico, 1986

Cunningham, Allan, *The Lives of the Most Eminent British Painters, Sculptors, and Architects*, 6 vols., London: Murray, 1829–33; 3rd edition, London: Tegg, 1830–54; see especially vol. 3

Dawson, Aileen, *Portrait Sculpture: A Catalogue of the British Museum Collection, c.1675–1975*, London: British Museum Press, 1999

Gunnis, Rupert, *Dictionary of British Sculptors, 1660–1851*, London: Odhams Press, 1953; Cambridge, Massachusetts: Harvard University Press, 1954; revised edition, London: Abbey Library, 1968

Jackson-Stops, Gervase (editor), *The Treasure Houses of Britain: Five Hundred Years of Private Patronage and Art Collecting*, Washington, D.C.: National Gallery of Art, and New Haven, Connecticut: Yale University Press, 1985

Noble, Percy, *Anne Seymour Damer: A Woman of Art and Fashion, 1748–1828*, London: Kegan Paul, 1908

Whinney, Margaret, *Sculpture in Britain, 1530–1830*, London and Baltimore, Maryland: Penguin, 1964; 2nd edition, revised by John Physick, London and New York: Penguin, 1988

Yarrington, Alison, "Damer, Anne Seymour," in *Dictionary of Women Artists*, edited by Delia Gaze, London and Chicago: Fitzroy Dearborn, 1997

D'ANGERS

See **David d'Angers**

JEAN-PIERRE-EDOUARD DANTAN
1800–1869 *French*

Jean-Pierre Dantan was born in Paris into a family of sculptors. His brother, Antoine-Laurent, who was two years his senior and thus known as Dantan the Elder, made a name for himself as a serious sculptor and Prix de Rome winner; yet of the two he is the lesser known. Their father, Antoine-Joseph-Laurent Dantan, a military infantryman and later an ornamental woodcarver, provided them with their earliest education in the medium. Jean-Pierre Dantan, often called Dantan the Younger, or Dantan *jeune*, is known to have helped his father in carving church ornaments by age nine; a decade later, he held a position as a restoration sculptor at the Basilica of Saint-Denis. Dantan entered the École des Beaux-Arts in 1823, seven years after his brother entered, and both studied under the accomplished portrait sculptor François-Joseph Bosio. One of Dantan's earliest works, considered by some to be his first caricature, was a portrait of the armless painter *Louis-Cesar-Joseph Ducornet*, an early example of Dantan's Romanticist fascination with odd human characteristics, exaggerations, and deformities. He even added a proto-Surrealistic dimension to his signature, which on at least one early sculpture was cryptically given as a rooted molar tooth (*dent*), the scythe of Father Time (*temps*), and a youthful angel (*jeune*). He began showing his work at the Paris Salon exhibitions as early as 1827 and continued to submit works to the exhibition throughout his life.

In 1828 Antoine-Laurent Dantan won the Prix de Rome, and since it was forbidden for brothers to enter the competition in the same year, Jean-Pierre simply accompanied his brother to the city and remained there with him for three years. Little is known of Jean-Pierre Dantan's production and studies while in Rome, but when he returned to France in 1831, he began almost immediately to market humorous caricatures of famous actors, lawyers, musicians, painters, playwrights, poets, and politicians (the caricatures depict men almost exclusively, as caricaturing women was considered improper). Although Dantan also produced numerous portrait sculptures for public buildings and patrons, including state portraits for Versailles, the huge commercial success of his caricatures, which he called his *portraits chargés* (literally, "loaded portraits"), overshadowed his serious work. He aspired to be a great portraitist and was known to have felt that his caricatures damaged his reputation as a serious sculptor.

According to Dantan scholars, the artist may have been inspired by the science of phrenology (the study of the conformation of the skull on the basis of the belief that it indicates mental facilities and character), which was at the height of its popularity in the 1820s. Even though he was working during the age of France's greatest print caricaturists (J.-J. Grandville, Paul Gavarni, and Honoré Daumier), Dantan's sculptural caricatures were new for the medium, and they influenced later artists such as Daumier to produce caricatures in sculpture as well. Dantan's sculptures brought ancient humorous sculpture and the style of medieval gargoyles to a new, popular, and more journalistic level. It was often noted that if a person was chosen by Dantan as a subject for one of his *portraits chargés*, that person's fame and celebrity was assured. Some of his best-known *portraits chargés* depict musicians such as Niccolò Paganini, Louis-Hector Berlioz, and Gioacchino Antonio Rossini, writers such as Victor Hugo and Honoré de Balzac, painters such as Horace Vernet, and the painter and inventor of photography, Louis-Jacques-Mandé-Daguerre. Although dangerous to do so, Dantan also caricatured political figures, such as his *Louis Phillippe, King of France*, a work sculpted a year before the major censorship laws of 1831 were widely passed in France, protecting leaders and the government from slander and public attacks (a crime for which Daumier, for example, was briefly jailed).

Dantan was at the height of his fame during the 1830s. In these early years he kept a studio at 31 rue Saint-Lazare and paid his first two years' rent with the proceeds from the sale of serious portrait busts. Briefly around the years 1831–33, he drew political caricatures for the journal *Le Charivari*. He spent significant time in London during the decade, living there in 1833–34 and returning in 1842, and he caricatured a number of English subjects, such as *Samuel Rogers*. In 1834 his caricatures were removed from a public exhibition in London, but the reason for the expulsion is unclear; possibly someone in a position of power took offense to the French sculptor's usually humorous, but sometimes scathing, caricatures.

One finds the first mention of Dantan's *Dantanorama* (the exhibition of his caricatures) in 1833. He used the prominent foundry and art publishers Susse Frerès, who acted as his agents (in a time before modern art dealers). The Salon de Susse, in part a stationers, offered a public viewing of Dantan's *portraits chargés*, which was hugely successful and became known as the first *Musée Dantanorama*. The artist also opened his studio to the public, calling it the *Musée Dantan*, and opened a *Musée Secret*, which was devoted to erotic art. At the end of the 1830s, the critic Gustave Planch noted in the journal *L'Artiste* that Dantan had "with every justification, earned for himself the reputation of being the most inexhaustible humorist of this age."

During the 1840s Dantan traveled to Algeria and Egypt, finally settling down at age 44 and marrying Elisa Polycarpe Moutiez, who was 28 years his junior. The marriage was childless, and Moutiez was protective of her husband's work and reputation. Scholars have suggested that she edited his oeuvre after his death, possibly destroying some of his *portraits chargés* that she felt damaged his legacy. Notwithstanding, she was responsible for donating a large collection of over 550 *portraits chargés*, some serious portraits, and archival material to the Musée Carnavalet in 1888, where many of Dantan's works remain on permanent view.

Dantan continued to exhibit in his later years. At the Great Exhibition in 1851 at London's Crystal Palace, he exhibited a now-lost sculpture of Queen Victoria seated, which was cast in zinc. His oeuvre consisted of more than 400 portrait statues, statuettes, medallions, and busts and more than 500 caricatures in sculpture. He died of apoplexy in Baden-Baden and is buried at the Père-Lachaise Cemetery in Paris.

CATERINA Y. PIERRE

See also **Caricature; Daumier, Honoré**

Biography

Born in Paris, France, 18 December 1800. Known as Dantan the Younger; elder brother Antoine-Laurent Dantan, also a sculptor, known as Dantan the Elder. Worked on church ornaments and sculptures, 1819–23; studied at École des Beaux-Arts under François-Joseph Bosio, 1823; exhibited at the Paris Salon exhibitions, 1827–69; traveled to Rome with his brother, 1828–31; began making caricatures, *ca.* 1828; traveled to London, 1833–34, 1842; traveled to Algeria, 1844; traveled to Egypt, 1848; showed work at Crystal Palace exhibition, London, 1851. Died in Baden-Baden, Germany, 6 September 1869.

Selected Works

1826	*Louis-Cesar-Joseph Ducornet*; plaster; Musée Carnavalet, Paris, France
1829	*Horace Vernet*; plaster; Musée Carnavalet, Paris, France
1930	*Louis Phillippe, King of France*; plaster; Musée Carnavalet, Paris, France
1831	*Alexandre Dumas, père (portraits chargés)*; bronze; Musée Carnavalet, Paris, France
1831	*Gioacchino Antonio Rossini*; plaster; Musée Carnavalet, Paris, France
1832	*Victor Hugo (portraits chargés)*; plaster; Musée Carnavalet, Paris, France

1832   *Niccolò Paganini (portraits chargés)*; bronze; Musée Carnavalet, Paris, France

1833   *Louis-Hector Berlioz*; plaster; Musée Carnavalet, Paris, France

1833–34 *The Duke of Gloucester and the Duke of Cumberland (portraits chargés)*; plaster; Royal Collection, Windsor Castle, Berkshire, England

1833–34 *Samuel Rogers*; plaster; National Portrait Gallery, London, England

1835   *Honoré de Balzac*; plaster; Musée Carnavalet, Paris, France

1838   *Louis-Jacques-Mandé-Daguerre*; plaster; Musée Carnavalet, Paris, France

1860   *Amédée de Noë, called Cham, (portraits chargés)*; plaster; Musée Carnavalet, Paris, France

Further Reading

Dantan, Jean-Pierre, *Dantan jeune: Caricatures et portraits de la société romantique* (exhib. cat.), Paris: Paris-Musées, 1989

Fusco, Peter, and Horst Woldemar Janson (editors), *The Romantics to Rodin: French Nineteenth-Century Sculpture from North American Collections* (exhib. cat.), Los Angeles, California: Los Angeles County Museum of Art, and New York: Braziller, 1980

Hale, Richard Walden, *Dantan jeune, 1800–1869 and His Satirical and Other Sculpture, Especially His "Portraits Charges,"* Meriden, Connecticut: Meridan Gravure, 1940

Janson, Horst Woldemar (editor), *La scultura nel XIX Secolo; La sculpture du XIXᵉ siécle; Nineteenth-Century Sculpture* (trilingual Italian-French-English edition), Bologna, Italy: CLUEB, 1984; London, Thames and Hudson, and New York: Abrams, 1985

Kjellberg, Pierre, *Les bronzes du XIXᵉ siècle: Dictionnaire des sculpteurs*, Paris: Éditions de l'Amateur, 1987; as *Bronzes of the Nineteenth Century: Dictionary of Sculptors*, translated by Kate D. Loftus, Alison Levie, and Leslie Bockol, Atglen, Pennsylvania: Schiffer, 1994

Kunsthistorisches Museum Wien, *Die Karikaturen des Dantan, Paris–London, 1831–1839* (exhib. cat.), Vienna: Kunsthistorisches Museum, 1933

Lami, Stanislas, *Dictionnaire des sculpteurs de l'école française au dix-neuvième siècle*, 4 vols., Paris: Champion, 1914–21; reprint, Nendeln, Liechtenstein: Kraus, 1970; see especially vol. 6

Pingeot, Anne (editor), *Sculpture française, XIXᵉ siècle*, Paris: Grand Palais, 1986

Seligman, Janet, *Figures of Fun: The Caricature Statuettes of Jean-Pierre Dantan*, London and New York: Oxford University Press, 1957

VINCENZO DANTI 1530–1576 *Italian*

Vincenzo Danti's artistic personality owes much to his native Perugia in Umbria, where he was born on 17 April 1530. First trained as a goldsmith in the workshop of his father, Giulio, he may also have received a theoretical education with his aunt, Theodora. He went to Rome around 1545 to finish his training and familiarize himself with the latest works in what was then the undisputed center of artistic development. Although it seems unlikely that he met Michelangelo during his stay with the goldsmith Panfilio Marchesi, he clearly studied Michelangelo's works closely.

In 1553 the Perugian Priori (Priors) commissioned Danti and his father for a bronze statue of Pope Julius III. Cast in one piece in 1555, the monumental statue of the seated pope in benediction is an exceptional accomplishment. However, it also shows obvious problems with the organic conjunction of the different finely worked parts, which betray the goldsmith's attention to miniature works.

Danti moved to Florence in 1557. There he entered the circle of artists working for Duke Cosimo I de' Medici and was protected by the courtier Sforza Almeni, a fellow Perugian and friend of Giorgio Vasari. Although his first commission to create a crowning bronze group of *Hercules and Antaeus* for Tribolo's fountain at the Medici villa at Castello ended in disaster, he was already employed again in 1559 to execute a bronze safe door for Duke Cosimo I. Like the giant Hercules group, this work was miscast at least once, which professed his continuous experimentation with the casting technique and is also visible in his huge relief of *Moses and the Brazen Serpent* in the Museo Nazionale del Bargello, Florence. The two contemporary reliefs differ remarkably in style. In *Moses and the Brazen Serpent*, one of the most innovative reliefs of late 16th-century Florence, Danti fused countless dynamically moved figures into a highly complex composition that stretches continuously from high to extraordinarily low relief. The formal inspiration is not to be found in sculpture but in the paintings of the late Michelangelo and Agnolo Bronzino.

Like other young sculptors, in 1560 Danti participated in the contest for the Florentine Neptune fountain, although he did not have a chance of winning. Perhaps in relation to the contest, Danti worked on his masterpiece in marble: *Honor Triumphant over Falsehood*, which was finished in 1561. Perhaps this group, just like Vincenzo de' Rossi's *Theseus Abducting Helen* (1558–1560), was intended to prove to Cosimo I Danti's ability of working marble, one decisive feature in the Neptune contest. He presented the Mannerist masterpiece to his protector Almeni, but it remains unclear if it was done to Almeni's commission, what was intended by the subject matter, and above all where Danti acquired his extraordinary virtuosity in carving. It has been proposed that he worked with Baccio Bandinelli on the reliefs for the choir of Florence Cathedral, but the formal characteristics of the group point more to Benvenuto Cellini's and Bartolomeo

Ammanati's late work. The topic of the psychomachia (conflict of the soul) group and several formal characteristics are clearly derived from Michelangelo's *Victory* (1519–30) but have been meditated into a highly exteriorized essay in monolithic marble sculpture in the round where the figure of *Falsehood* is held artificially upturned to permit an axial confrontation face to face. Danti's profound knowledge of Michelangelo's works is used in a highly personal manner in order to create a sculpture that, although continuously referring to the master, is entirely different in spirit and execution from any of Michelangelo's works. In particular, the accentuated carnosity (fleshiness) of the body has been understood as the direct prefiguration of Danti's later theories in his *Trattato* (1567).

The success of *Honor Triumphant over Falsehood* was contrasted by the weakness of Danti's remaining works in the 1560s. From 1562 to 1564 he executed the *Monument to Carlo de' Medici* in the Cathedral of Prato, basing himself on Michelangelo's *Madonna of Bruges*. A second *Madonna and Child* group, today in the Church of Santa Croce in Florence, is based on

Michelangelo's 16th-century *Madonna* in the Medici Chapel in San Lorenzo, Florence. Both groups are bulky, inexpressive works that suffer from their monumentality.

The commission for the crowning group on Vasari's courtyard facade of the Galleria degli Uffizi (1564) was fraught with difficulties. Vasari's scheme projected an allegorical portrait statue of Cosimo I between the personifications of Rigor and Equity. Although the latter two reclining figures were successfully completed in 1566, the first seated statue of Cosimo I was turned into a Perseus and ended as a garden sculpture for Boboli. The second version (1572–73) also was ill fated. The standing, heavily stylized figure in the Bargello was intended to show Cosimo I as Hercules and Augustus simultaneously. Inspired by Bandinelli's 16th-century figures of the Udienza in Palazzo Vecchio, Florence, the iconographically overloaded sculpture was already outmoded by the time of its installation in 1573 and was replaced by Giambologna's simpler version in 1585.

After his entry into the Accademia del Disegno in 1563, Danti participated in the decorations for the funeral of Michelangelo in 1564, and for the wedding of Francesco I de' Medici in 1565. In 1570–71 he worked on the central statue of *St. Luke* for the Accademia's burial chapel in the Church of Santissima Annunziata. His acceptance to the Florentine Accademia del Disegno inspired him to reflect on the theoretical foundation of his art, culminating in his unfinished *Trattato delle perfette proporzioni* (Treatise on Perfect Proportions) of which the first book was published in 1567.

In 1571 he was called by Vasari for the reconstruction of the tomb of the Blessed Giovanni da Salerno, which had been destroyed during Vasari's remodeling of the Church of Santa Maria Novella. In this case, Danti created a work in the early Renaissance style. Before this, he adapted to the style of Andrea Sansovino, finishing and completing the latter's Baptism group on the Florentine baptistery (1569). For the same location he created the three-figure bronze group of the *Beheading of St. John the Baptist*, which was installed in 1570. Despite its elegance and lightness of movement in the round, this monumental bronze masterpiece betrays the growing influence of Giambologna: the figures nevertheless maintain a statuesque weight and ponderousness. The same holds true for Danti's marble Venus with two *amorini*, the so-called Pitti Venus—long believed to be a work by Michelangelo—and the charming *Leda with the Swan*. His last works in bronze, among them the *Deposition* and the *Venus Anadyomene* for the Studiolo of Francesco I de' Medici, attest to his absolute mastery in this field. The *Deposition* especially is a flawless cast, technically one

Honor Triumphant over Falsehood
The Conway Library, Courtauld Institute of Art

of the most accomplished of the 16th century. Sometimes taken for a work of Ammanati, the *Venus* helps one to understand the common resistance to Giambologna undertaken by Danti and Ammanati, although in the 1570s they both were forced to succumb to the Fleming's artistic style.

Danti only in part followed Ammanati's flight into architecture with his project for the Escorial in 1572, preferring to return to his hometown in 1573, where he lived his last three years as a celebrated man, but without creating further sculptural works.

JOHANNES MYSSOK

See also **Ammanati, Bartolomeo; Bandinelli, Baccio; Cellini, Benvenuto; Giambologna; Michelangelo (Buonarroti); Rossi, Vincenzo de'; Sansovino, Andrea**

Biography

Born in Perugia, Italy, 17 April 1530. First son of Giulio Danti, a well-known goldsmith and architect from a family of scientific and artistic renown. Trained as a goldsmith with his father, then went to Rome, *ca.* 1545–53, and worked with Panfilio Marchesi, a goldsmith from Brescia; in 1553 commissioned with his father to create a statue of Pope Julius III for the Perugian Priori, finished in 1555; went to Florence, 1557, receiving patronage of Duke Cosimo I with help of the Perugian courtier Sforza Almeni; first commission failed after miscasting his model for crowning group of fountain at Castello three times; despite this created further works for the duke, but in 1560 suffered further setback by losing competition for Florentine Neptune fountain; worked on numerous pieces in bronze and marble, in part for his protector Almeni but mainly for the Florentine court, 1560s; started to work as an architect and engineer, also in the 1560s, participating in the planning of the Escorial near Madrid, 1572; returned to his hometown, 1573, where he founded the local academy and received the honorific title of leading architect of the city. Died in Perugia, Italy, 26 May 1576.

Selected Works

1553–55   *Pope Julius III* (with his father, Giulio Danti); bronze; Perugia Cathedral, Italy

1559   *Moses and the Brazen Serpent*; bronze; Museo Nazionale del Bargello, Florence, Italy

1559   *Sportello*; bronze; Museo Nazionale del Bargello, Florence, Italy

1561   *Honor Triumphant over Falsehood*; marble; Museo Nazionale del Bargello, Florence, Italy

1562–64   Monument for Carlo de' Medici; marble; Cathedral of Prato, Italy

1564–66   *Rigour* and *Equity*; marble; Galleria degli Uffizi, Florence, Italy

after 1566   Cosimo I as Perseus; marble; Boboli Gardens, Florence, Italy

ca. 1567–68   *Madonna and Child*; marble; Church of Santa Croce, Florence, Italy

1569   *Christ and the Baptist* (with Andrea Sansovino); marble; Baptistery, Florence, Italy

ca. 1570   *Deposition*; bronze; National Gallery of Art, Washington, D.C., United States

1570–71   *St. Luke*; stucco; Cappella di S. Luca, Church of Santissima Annunziata, Florence, Italy

ca. 1570–72   Venus with two *amorini* (Pitti Venus); marble; Casa Buonarroti, Florence, Italy

1571   *Beheading of St. John the Baptist*; bronze; Baptistery, Florence, Italy

1571   Tomb of the Blessed Giovanni da Salerno; marble; Church of Santa Maria Novella, Florence, Italy

ca. 1572   *Venus Anadyomene*; bronze; *studiolo* of Francesco I, Palazzo Vecchio, Florence, Italy

1572–73   Duke Cosimo as Hercules and Augustus, for the Galleria degli Uffizi, Florence; marble; Museo Nazionale del Bargello, Florence, Italy

ca. 1572–73   *Leda with the Swan*; marble; Victoria and Albert Museum, London, England

Further Reading

Avery, Charles, *Florentine Renaissance Sculpture*, London: John Murray, and New York: Harper and Row, 1970

Davis, Charles, "Working for Vasari: Vincenzo Danti in Palazzo Vecchio," in *Giorgio Vasari*, edited by Gian Carlo Garfagnini, Florence: Olschki, 1985

Fidanza, Giovan Battista, *Vincenzo Danti, 1530–1576*, Florence: Olschki, 1996

Keutner, Herbert, "The Palazzo Pitti 'Venus' and Other Works by Vincenzo Danti," *The Burlington Magazine* 100 (1958)

Poeschke, Joachim, *Die Skulptur der Renaissance in Italien*, vol. 2, *Michelangelo und seine Zeit*, Munich: Hirmer, 1992; as *Michelangelo and His World: Sculpture of the Italian Renaissance*, translated by Russell Stockman, New York: Abrams, 1996

Pope-Hennessy, John, *An Introduction to Italian Sculpture*, 3 vols., London: Phaidon, 1963; 4th edition, 1996; see especially vol. 3, *Italian High Renaissance and Baroque Sculpture*

Santi, Francesco, *Vincenzo Danti: Scultore*, Bologna, Italy: Nuova Alfa, 1989

Summers, John David, "The Sculpture of Vincenzo Danti: A Study in the Influence of Michelangelo and the Ideals of the Maniera," (dissertation), Yale University, 1969

DA RAVENNA

See **Severo da Ravenna**

DAUCHER FAMILY *German*

Adolf Daucher *ca.* 1460–1523/24

After 1500 the southern German commercial metropolis of Augsburg developed into the nucleus of Renaissance art in the German-speaking world. The interest in art was fueled by important patrons, such as Emperor Maximilian I, and successful entrepreneurs, such as the Fugger family. Intensive transalpine business contacts fostered the adoption of Italian Classical style elements. Moreover, in Augsburg patriotic pride prevailed regarding the history of its founding during the ancient Roman era. In sculpture this development manifested itself in new representative forms for funerary monuments, in donations for elaborate altars, and in the emergence of new genres of small sculpture, such as small bronzes or portrait medals. In the work of Augsburg sculptors Adolf Daucher and his son, Hans Daucher, a clear example emerges that represents the changes that took place in the style and vocation of two generations of sculptors in Augsburg during the transition from the Medieval to the Renaissance era.

Adolf emigrated from Ulm about 1490/91. Shortly after acquiring citizenship, he received numerous assignments. Although these works were documented, almost all of them have been lost, destroyed in the iconoclasm of the Protestant Reformation, or replaced by modern works during the Baroque period. Both Adolf's high tax payments and the number of apprentices he employed clearly indicate the prosperity of his enterprise. His workshop was among the leading providers of workers in stone and wood sculpture in Augsburg between 1500 and 1525.

Despite the number of sources documenting his work, isolating Adolf's individual style poses a problem: not one of his known works can be attributed to him with certainty. All attributions, therefore, are highly speculative. In all probability, Adolf acted primarily as a provider and coordinator for large sculptural projects, including the Fugger Chapel in St. Anna's Church in Augsburg. As a businessman, he concentrated more on directing the projects and less on the practical and artistic aspects of the production, which he assigned to his assistants or outside sculptors. Clear evidence of this practice can be found on two stone reliefs depicting the Lamentation of Christ in Saverne (Alsace) and Meissen (Saxony). Although both are recorded as having been commissioned from Adolf between 1519 and 1522 and then delivered by him to the client, they diverge entirely from one another in terms of style. Obviously, although Adolf's name was the one recorded, he entrusted two, now anonymous, subordinate sculptors with the production of the works. In 1504 he was put on trial by the guild for this sort of business practice. Adolf had illegally employed journeymen painters in his joiner's shop, which was prohibited by the *Handwerksrecht* (Craftsman's Law) in Augsburg for reasons of fair competition.

The large-scale high altar at St. Anna's Church in Annaberg (Saxony) stands as the largest complex of works by Adolf's company that remains preserved today. The work was completed in 1521. The patron was the Saxon Duke George the Bearded, who, it seems, especially admired, as Adolf described it, the *hibschen Marbel* (the beautiful pieces of marble) in which Adolf dealt and which, with the surging reception of the Italian Renaissance, became an essential material for architects and sculptors. A retable about 6.5 meters high and made out of a variety of polychromatic limestone was produced in Augsburg. The architecture of the altar and retable incorporates a modern, Italian-inspired design for the columns and pilasters with sharply defined timber work and capitals and spandrels filled with volutes. Efforts to create a polychromatic and varied effect are clearly inspired by the Venetian interior designs of the Lombardo family members. The triaxial structure corresponds to that of Venetian doges' tombs of the era. The sculptures depict the *Wurzel Jesse*, the family tree of Christ, consisting of approximately 30 almost-life-size figures in high relief surrounded by putti. Typical of the struggle for purity of the Augsburg Renaissance artists, their dramatic, rhetorical gestures are less exaggerated than those in the contemporaneous sculpture of the upper Rhine or the Danube School. Even in the folds of the garments there is conflict between Late Gothic virtuosity and Classical decorum.

Hans Daucher *ca.* 1485–1538

Whereas Adolf's individual style is difficult to reconstruct, the work of his son, Hans, has been preserved in many signed pieces. Hans's work also documented a changing generation that manifested itself in a turn to new sculptural media: small sculptures for private enjoyment were the prized collector's object of humanism. The core of Hans's oeuvre consisted of small reliefs carved in minute detail from the finest limestone. They display religious scenes or portraits of contemporaries in a mysterious environment. Thus, German art historians such as Wilhelm Bode placed Hans "at the head of the artists who had brought the High Renaissance to Germany."

The 12 surviving reliefs by Hans distinguish themselves technically through the virtuosity of their production. For the most part, they are signed with Hans's monogram "HD." Flat reliefs displaying the images of then-famous contemporaries performing a representative or allegorical action were carved with scalpel-like tools into small stone tablets, which were usually about the size of a book. In one, Emperor Maximilian is portrayed on a horse in the role of St. George slaying the dragon. In another, Albrecht Dürer appears in fictitious combat with his famous Classical predecessor, Apelles, over whom the "modern" painter Dürer symbolically conquers.

This sort of pictorial theater was produced very elaborately on the *Allegory of Virtues and Vices*. The scene depicts Emperor Charles V along with his royal household and some other lords in the process of crossing a bridge, during which several members of the company fall into the water. The bridge tower bears the title of the depiction: *Virtutum et Viciorum Adumbracio* (Allegory of Virtues and Vices). The scene and the title allude to the divine judgment, which had been depicted in various forms since Antiquity. The virtuous keep their feet on steady ground and the depraved tumble from the bridge. It is the emperor's political opponents, such as willful imperial knights, who encounter the misfortune of falling from the bridge, and thus are characterized as depraved villains.

A typical aspect of Hans's scenic reliefs is that through detailed carving the figures function as portraits and can thus be identified; the relief consequently honors the political establishment of the time. In festive, moralizing, and venerating scenes, the reliefs narrate and critique political current events, relevant biographical information, or scenes glorifying heroes. They reflect tendencies that graphic artists had developed in ruler panegyrics, such as Emperor Maximilian's *Theuerdank* (1517) or the large wood engraving of Maximilian's *Triumphal Arch* (1515–17), designed by Hans's contemporaries Hans Burgkmair, Hans Schäuffelein, and Dürer. Hans Daucher's achievement lies in having translated this sort of pictorial theme into the medium of sculpture. Sculpture was able to confer a greater honor upon the portrait's subject because it was more labor intensive than a woodcut.

There is a lack of information as to the conditions surrounding the commission of any of Hans's pieces. Their production is concentrated in the years around 1520 and 1522. In terms of style and motif, Hans's small reliefs displayed modern accents in that he employed Italian-inspired Renaissance architecture. Both of the early Marian reliefs in Vienna and Augsburg present the Madonna beneath powerful Classical triumphal arches; Classical ornamentation fills the architectural surfaces, complemented by rows of putti

and Roman script. The flatness of the reliefs and their similarity to reproduction graphics suggest that they were also used for making molds in stucco or for casting plaquettes; a few corresponding stucco replicas have been preserved. Given the technical conformity to his stone reliefs, we may safely say for certain that Hans also worked as a medalist.

Hans's limestone reliefs now represent the most significant and the only certain area of work in his oeuvre. A few midsize epitaph reliefs bearing his signature have been preserved in Augsburg and the surrounding area. Regarding his large-scale sculpture in the round, suppositions can be made based on the pieces accredited to him in written sources. In this category are the delightful five putti on the balustrade in the Fugger Chapel in Augsburg and a *John Grieving from a Crucifixion Scene*. His participation in his father's business assignments probably took place in the capacity of an employee, since his name never appears as a partner on business contracts: Hans's large sculptures remain anonymous among the work of the many employees in his father's business.

THOMAS ESER

See also **Erhart, Gregor; Erhart, Michel**

Adolf Daucher

Biography

Born in Ulm, South Germany, or Vienna, Austria, *ca.* 1460. Moved to Augsburg, *ca.* 1490–91; worked with Michel Erhart; worked in Augsburg as a *Kistler* (master carpenter); business emphasized specialty carpentry (altar shrines, furniture for town hall, architectural models) and sculptures in wood and stone, from *ca.* 1495; likely coordinated and directed decoration of Fugger Chapel (*ca.* 1512–18); worked with Erhart and Hans Holbein, 1494–1508; outside assignments for high altars in Kaisheim and Church of St. Anna in Augsburg; worked on tomb and portal reliefs in Meissen, 1519–21, and Saverne, *ca.* 1522. Died in Augsburg, Germany, between October 1523 and October 1524.

Selected Works

1493–97   St. Simpert's altar (lost) and St. Simpert's tombstone, for the Church of Saints Ulrich and Afra, Augsburg, Germany; Bayerisches Nationalmuseum, Munich, Germany

1493–98   Large retable for *Frühmessaltar* (altar for the morning mass); Church of Saints Ulrich and Afra, Augsburg, Germany; probably wood (destroyed)

ca.   High altar for Cistercian Monastery

1498–	Church, Kaisheim near Donauwörth,
1502	Germany; wood (destroyed)
ca. 1515	Architectural model for Luginsland Tower of Augsburg city fortification; wood; Städtische Kunstsammlungen, Augsburg, Germany
before 1519	*Christ with Mary and St. John* (probably with Hans Daucher); limestone; Fugger Chapel, Church of St. Anna, Augsburg, Germany
ca. 1519–22	Two reliefs of the *Lamentation*; limestone; portal of St. George's Chapel, Meissen Cathedral, Germany; parish church in Saverne, Alsace, France
1521	High altar with *Tree of Jesse* group; limestone; Church of St. Anna, Annaberg, Saxony, Germany

Hans Daucher

Biography

Born probably in Ulm, South Germany, *ca.* 1485. Beginning in 1500, apprenticed under Augsburg sculptor Gregor Erhart, his uncle; obtained mastership as sculptor in the city of Augsburg, Germany, 1514; probably shared a workshop with Adolf, his father, 1518–21; presumed decline in creative opportunities, late 1520s, as indicated by decrease in tax payments; in Stuttgart, 1536; documented as "servant" with no specified activity at court of Ulrich VI, Duke of Württemberg; mentioned in 1537 as patient in Stuttgart "sick house." Died probably in Stuttgart, Germany, after November 1538.

Selected Works

ca. 1515–20	Two stone reliefs for the Passion scenes: *Christ on the Mount of Olives* and *The Flagellation of Christ*; limestone; Cleveland Museum of Art, Ohio, United States; Bayerisches Nationalmuseum, Munich, Germany (attributed)
1518	*Holy Family*; limestone; Kunsthistorisches Museum, Vienna, Austria
1520	*Mary with Child*; limestone; Städtische Kunstsammlungen, Augsburg, Germany
1520–23	Monument to Konrad Adelmann; limestone; parish church, Holzheim near Dillingen, Germany
1522	*Albrecht Dürer's Allegorical Combat with Apelles*; limestone; Staatliche Museen, Skulpturensammlung, Berlin, Germany
1522	*Allegory of Virtues and Vices*; limestone, Metropolitan Museum of Art, New York City, United States
1522	*Judgment of Paris*; limestone; Kunsthistorisches Museum, Vienna, Austria
1522	*Maximilian I as St. George*; limestone; Kunsthistorisches Museum, Vienna, Austria
1522	Portrait medals of the Palatinate Counts Philipp and Ottheinrich; limestone; Wittelsbacher Ausgleichsfonds, Munich, Germany
ca. 1522	Monument to Melchior Funk; limestone; Städtische Kunstsammlungen, Augsburg, Germany
ca. 1524	*John Grieving from a Crucifixion Scene*; limestone; Victoria and Albert Museum, London, England (attributed)
1527	*Emperor Charles V and his Brother, King Ferdinand (Meeting of Charles V and Ferdinand I)*; limestone; Pierpont Morgan Library, New York City, United States
ca. 1530	Five balustrade putti; limestone; Fugger Chapel, Church of St. Anna, Augsburg, Germany (attributed)

Further Reading

Baxandall, Michael, *The Limewood Sculptors of Renaissance Germany*, New Haven, Connecticut: Yale University Press, 1980

Eser, Thomas, *Hans Daucher: Augsburger Kleinplastik der Renaissance*, Munich: Deutscher Kunstverlag, 1996

Müller, Hannelore, "Die Künstlerfamilie Daucher," in *Lebensbilder aus dem Bayerischen Schwaben*, vol. 6, edited by Götz Freiherr von Pölnitz, Munich: Hueber, 1958

Scher, Stephen K. (editor), *The Currency of Fame: Portrait Medals of the Renaissance*, New York: Abrams, 1994

Smith, Jeffrey Chipps, *German Sculpture of the Later Renaissance, c. 1520–1580: Art in an Age of Uncertainty*, Princeton, New Jersey: Princeton University Press, 1994

FUGGER CHAPEL, CHURCH OF ST. ANNA

Early 16th century, Augsburg, Germany

In 1506 three brothers of the powerful Fugger merchant and banking family decided to have a chapel built in the Augsburg convent Church of St. Anna. In the following 12 years, a magnificent interior of modern architectural design and decoration was created and eventually added to the nave of the church as a sort of west choir. Even its dimensions, which correspond to the nave, greatly exceed the conventional scale of private chapels. It was intended to serve as a funerary chapel for the male family members, and thus to serve as their spiritual salvation as well as their earthly "memoria" as a representative family monument.

Two of the three founders, the brothers Georg and Ulrich, died during the construction. As head of the business, Jakob Fugger "the Rich" became the sole authority for the Dauchers to consult for the decoration from 1510 until 1518. Jakob has gone down in economic history as the personification of early capitalism. Legend was, for example, that he financed the election of Emperor Charles V in 1519 by bribing the princely electors entitled to vote to do so in favor of the Habsburgs.

The sculptural portions of the Fugger Chapel originally comprised six decorative areas: a *Corpus Christi* group as an altarpiece, three reliefs on the predella (a painted panel at the bottom of an altarpiece) with scenes of the *Passion*, four large epitaph reliefs on the rear wall of the room, and six putti on the balustrade leading toward the nave (today five remain). Carved entirely in stone, these four object groups have remained in the chapel up to this day. The wooden figures and decorations of the former choir stalls as well as an elaborate bronze gate, which set the room apart from the nave of the church, are stored elsewhere or were simply destroyed.

The Fugger Chapel today is dominated by the almost-life-size group of four figures depicting the *Lamentation of Christ* with the Virgin Mary and St. John, which forms the altarpiece. The lifeless body taken down from the cross is held by an angel and mourned by Christ's mother and his favorite disciple. Thus the group uses the angel *pietà* motif. Although the effects of the stone sculpture in the round are oriented around the Late Gothic tradition of a mysticized Passion emphasizing the suffering of Christ, the physiognomies and the dress of the supporting figures are informed by the new figural ideal of Italian-Venetian tomb sculpture (for instance, Pietro Lombardo's *Mocenigo Monument, ca.* 1480–95, SS. Giovanni e Paolo, Venice).

The three reliefs on the predella of *Christ Bearing the Cross, Christ's Descent from the Cross,* and *Christ in Limbo* are done in limestone. Thematically, they complement the altarpiece group—in keeping with the chapel's *patrozinium* (patronage), which was dedicated "in the honor of the dear body of our Lord, Jesus Christ" on 17 January 1518. From both a technical and artistic perspective, the predella reliefs may be considered to be the most outstanding examples of German small sculpture in relief of the Early Renaissance. To a great extent, the depictions correspond to the eponymous woodcarvings from Albrecht Dürer's *Great Passion* series (1511). However, the sculptor translated Dürer's pathos into a more subtle production; the fold of the drapery is more even and the group dynamic is less expressively developed. With the staggering of high-relief figures in the foreground and very flat figures in the background of horizontal landscapes, the sculptor was able to achieve a refined and spacious

Corpus Christ Group, Fugger Chapel
© Erich Lessing / Art Resource, NY

perspectival effect that tested the limits of relief sculpture.

Four reliefs finished by round arches take up the entire back wall of the chapel. Both of the center epitaphs show the *Resurrection of Christ* and *Samson's Battle against the Philistines* in a powerful composition; below them are the prone figure of the dead body of Ulrich Fugger (left-hand side) and Georg Fugger (right-hand side). Dürer designed the center epitaphs. Six of Dürer's sketches from between 1506 and 1510—which trace the artistic process from the first fleeting sketch to the magnificent final draft—have been preserved. In terms of quality, the sculptural interpretations of Dürer's designs fell far short of the drawings. Particularly in the management of the relief surface, the sculptor was not equal to the task and succumbed to a schematic flatness. The symmetrical outer epitaphs display heraldic motifs from the Fugger crest. Compared with the Dürer epitaphs, the motifs are more conventional and emphasize the Fugger family's claim to a position among the nobility of the empire. A clear admiration for Italian perspective emerged; the very similar reliefs on the facade of the Scuola di San Marco in Venice may have been an inspiration.

A carefully thought-out iconographic program is inherent in the chapel's balustrade putti, which are the most engaging group. Five of the cherubs rest in a melancholic gesture with their arms propped up on balls. The three on the left-hand side touch their ear, eye, and mouth with their fingers. The group symbolizes the transitory nature of the earthly senses of hearing, sight, and taste, and, in this way, the watch brigade of children provides a commentary on the *vanitas* (transient) atmosphere of a funerary chapel. In terms of style, they are formed with a great deal of verism and are masterfully carved. Their plump bodies show their physiognomy with unshrinking anatomical precision, which—not without a touch of humor—contrasts with their Classical costumes of togas and laurel wreaths. Here, for the first time in German sculpture, a putto is given a complex thematic autonomy extending far beyond its ornamental function as a sculptural detail.

Originally, the sides of the chapel were marked off by two-part choir stalls. As early as 1517, the chapel was described by an Italian traveler as "*oaken*, very bizarre, with figures of prophets and sibyls in high relief" (see Bushart, 1994). Engravings and drawings document the rich architectural and sculptural construction of the choir stalls, which were removed from the chapel in the 19th century; their 16 life-size busts ended up on the art market. Four of these busts remain: three in the Skulpturensammlung in Berlin and one in the Museum of Fine Arts in Boston, Massachusetts. Their costumes and accessories were based on a proto-humanist understanding of Antiquity, which prompted a sort of fantastical sensibility.

Aside from limestone and wood, bronze was the more elegant and expensive sculptural material used in the chapel. In the beginning stages of planning the chapel, around 1506, the Nuremberg foundry of Peter Vischer the Elder was commissioned with the planning and casting of a large bronze gate, which was to separate the chapel from the nave of the church. Although large portions of the gate were finished and large sums of money were paid in advance, it never made it to Augsburg. In 1529, the Fuggers canceled the delivery. The gate remained in Nuremberg at the town hall, and in the early 19th century it ended up on the art market (remaining parts can be found in the Montrottier Castle, Lovagny, Savoy, France). The gate would have been part of the carefully structured architecture of the chapel facade, where the arms of the chapel donors were placed in the middle of scenes depicting Classical mythological figures engaged in battle and a procession filled with figures. As such, it represents the procession of souls into the underworld: figures from the Classical cult of the dead gain entry into Christian funerary architecture. Perhaps it was precisely this provocative, pagan element that ultimately prevented the erection of the gate.

In contrast to the bronze gate, the question of the identity of the artists working on the other sculptural complexes remains unclear. Neither documents pertaining to the commissions, nor ledgers from the Fugger firm, nor any signatures have been preserved. Critical examinations of the stylistic elements have considered over 12 names, such as Sebastian Loscher, as well as Italian masters. However, sculptors working on the project were not part of the artistic circle in Augsburg. Adolf Daucher, who was the leading supplier of large sculptural complexes in Augsburg, may safely be accredited with coordinating the decoration. What his artistic contribution was, however, remains unclear. Stylistic parallels to the verified work of his son, Hans, suggest that Hans participated in the production of the altar group, particularly the putti on the balustrade. The reliefs on the predella, on the other hand, seem similar to the work of the contemporary Augsburg sculptor Jakob Murmann the Elder (see Baxandall, 1980). The time frame for the completion of the chapel's entire decoration was established by the verified dates of the *Einwoelbung* (vaulting of the chapel) (1512) and the dedication of the chapel (1518), between which the sculptural decoration could have taken shape. Only the putti on the balustrade were completed later, probably around 1530, as a substitute for the bronze gate.

Recent scholarship has attempted to find Dürer as the formative power for the artistic conception of the chapel and its decoration (see Bushart, 1994). The Dürer argument is substantiated by his stay in Italy immediately before the planning of the chapel, his participation as a designer for the epitaph reliefs, and his contact with the Fuggers. Nonetheless, not a single relevant document has been preserved that would lend credence to the accreditation of the "first truly Renaissance-style funerary chapel in Germany" (see Smith, 1994) to Dürer. As an artwork based on the highest expectations and expenditures, the Fugger Chapel represents the struggle of a powerful, private merchant for the same kind of acceptance as the traditional, medieval powers of the nobility and the clergy. The term "Renaissance" is politically charged and signifies the characteristic style of the unconventional, future-oriented drive of the merchant class to establish itself. In terms of its elaborateness, the Fugger Chapel stands on the same plane as the other major funerary chapel projects of its time: the family grave for Maximilian I in Innsbruck, Michelangelo's tomb for Pope Julius II in Rome, and the Medici Chapel in Florence. Although the Fugger Chapel is not equal to the Italian High Renaissance projects in terms of artistic detail, it is very much so in terms of the intentions of the clients.

THOMAS ESER

Further Reading

Baxandall, Michael, *The Limewood Sculptors of Renaissance Germany*, New Haven, Connecticut: Yale University Press, 1980

Bushart, Bruno, *Die Fuggerkapelle bei St. Anna in Augsburg*, Munich: Deutscher Kunstverlag, 1994

Feuchtmayr, Karl, "Die Bildhauer der Fuggerkapelle bei St. Anne's zu Augsburg: Stilkritische Bermerkungen zu Sebastian Loscher und Hans Daucher," in *Die Fugger und die Kunst im Zeitalter der Spätgotik und frühen Renaissance*, by Norbert Lieb, Munich: Schnell and Steiner, 1952

Halm, Phillip Maria, *Adolf Daucher und die Fuggerkapelle bei St. Anna in Augsburg*, Munich: Duncker and Humbolt, 1921

Schindler, Herbert, *Augsburger Renaissance: Hans Daucher und die Bildhauer der Fuggerkapelle bei St. Anna*, Munich: Bayerische Vereinsbank, 1985

Smith, Jeffrey Chipps, *German Sculpture of the Later Renaissance, c. 1520–1580: Art in an Age of Uncertainty*, Princeton, New Jersey: Princeton University Press, 1994

HONORÉ DAUMIER 1808–1879 *French*

Honoré Daumier is best known as a lithographer because of his satirical prints on political and social themes; however, his achievements in sculpture, although less recognized, are extraordinary. None of his sculptures was cast in bronze during his lifetime, and he did not intend for his three-dimensional production to be exhibited in public. The corpus of the widely accepted sculptures that he produced from the 1830s to at least the early 1850s is limited to about 50 clay models, which parodied political abuses (for instance, *Ratapoil*) and caricatured pompous and self-important public figures.

Daumier was one of the first French artists to experiment with caricature sculpture. His predecessor, Jean-Pierre Dantan (called *Dantan jeune*), had created the grotesque-type *Robert Macaire*. Thirty-six of Daumier's sculptures are a set of polychrome unbaked-clay maquettes, grotesque portrait busts of government deputies known as *"Célébrités du juste milieu."* The ensemble was commissioned around 1832 by Charles Philipon, the liberal editor of the satiric and politically motivated journals *La Caricature* and *The Charivari*, where Daumier published his lithographs. Those busts ridiculed the foibles of disreputable politicians. Daumier apparently modeled from memory, relying on his keen observer's eye, his understanding of the body's structure, and his ability to isolate the most eloquent gesture. His subject matter, like in his lithographs, was the everyday, the unheroic, and the ordinary presented with a freshness that made the most ordinary subject seem charged with significance. He succeeded in giving each of these figures individuality and satiric force by flagrant exaggeration of the sitter's most prominent features and typical expression.

Modeled in wet clay, an extremely fragile medium, the busts survived by having changed hands only twice. They remained in the Philipon family until 1927 when they were sold to Maurice Le Garrec and then acquired by the French national museums in 1980; today they are at the Musée d'Orsay in Paris. In 1927–29 the sculptor Pierre-Félix Masseau, known as Fix-Masseau, repaired the busts and had plaster molds made of each. The Barbedienne bronze foundry used the molds between 1929 and 1952 to cast a bronze edition of 30 pieces using the lost-wax method. Three further series of bronzes were cast by the Valsuani foundry between 1953 and 1965. Another set in baked polychrome clay was edited by Sagot Le Garrec in 1937.

Except for this ensemble, the only surely documented statuette by Daumier is *Ratapoil*. Executed around 1851, it is a personification of the reactionary forces of Bonapartism, a portrait of Napoléon III's henchmen. *Ratapoil* is modeled with a ragged top hat and frock coat, whose wide-legged stance is said to have inspired the posture of Edgar Degas's *Little Dancer, Fourteen Years Old* (1879–1881). Although Daumier produced prints inspired by the same subject, his *Ratapoil* sculpture emerges as an independent work produced for the artist and his circle, modeled possibly in the middle of his print series for *Le Charivari*. *Ratapoil* was diffused through posthumous bronze casts by Siot-Decauville, Alexis Rudier, and Valsuani.

Daumier also modeled three low-relief variants titled *Emigrants* (also known as *Fugitifs*) and executed them around the same time, representing a procession of anonymous, unindividualized nude figures. This frieze depicts approximately 20 men, women, and children in their tragic cortege carrying voluminous packages. The relief was posthumously cast in a number of different bronze editions by Siot-Decauville, Georges Rudier, Alexis Rudier, and the Clémenti foundry.

The conclusion that the busts were made by an untrained artist stems from an unclear notion of their purpose. Except for *Ratapoil*, Daumier's documented sculptures were called maquettes or sketches in the artist's lifetime; they were thus defined as private preliminary efforts, not as finished works. None was apparently produced for public exhibition or sale. Most critics and the public only learned of Daumier's three-dimensional production at his retrospective in 1878, the year before he died. The resemblance of the sculpture to the two-dimensional oeuvre has caused scholars to consider the surely attributed examples as study pieces, rather than as attempts to experiment in a different medium.

Although little is known about Daumier's sculptural training, it seems likely that his teacher, the museum director and archaeologist Alexandre Lenoir, and

Charles Guillaume Etienne
© Hervé Lewandowski. Réunion des Musées Nationaux / Art Resource, NY

friends Auguste Préault, Adolphe-Victor Geoffroy-Dechaume, and Jean-Jacques Feuchère encouraged Daumier to practice sculpture. Geoffroy-Dechaume is important for having cast the clay models of the *Emigrants* and the *Ratapoil* into plaster and storing them in his studio.

Daumier was particularly close to sculpture, its makers, and the public. Many of his prints depict sculptor's studios, the process of casting, and amateurs and collectors holding statuettes; they also explore the public's disinterest in Salon sculpture and the symbolic power of public monuments. Those lithographs illustrate Daumier's interpretation of the theme of looking at sculpture in either a public or private sphere and explain the difficulties that 19th-century sculptors had in promoting their works. One of his best examples is the print *Sad Appearance of Sculpture Placed in the Midst of Painting* of 1857.

There is no doubt that Daumier's sculptures were private studies made for the artist and his circle alone, unlike the lithographs—his widely published images—which were consciously intended for the public. The posthumous diffusion of his statuettes made a significant contribution to modern sculpture and influenced Constantin Meunier, Auguste Rodin, and possibly Henri Matisse in their capacity to suggest the epic or monumental quality in modern life.

ANNA TAHINCI

See also **Caricature; Clay and Terracotta; Dantan, Jean-Pierre-Edouard; Meunier, Constantin; Rodin, Auguste; Wax**

Biography

Born in Marseille, France, 26 February 1808. Son of a glazier. Moved to Paris, 1814; started working as lithographer for satiric newspapers and Charles Philipon, 1830; imprisoned for satires against Louis-Philippe for some months in 1832; due to escalating confrontations with authorities over political caricatures, restricted public work mainly to nonpolitical subjects after 1835; sculptural studies remained satirical throughout career, however. Died in Valmondois, France, 10 February 1879.

Selected Works

1832–35 36 busts of parliamentarians; terracotta; Musée d'Orsay, Paris, France; posthumous bronze casts in various private and public collections, including National Gallery of Art, Washington, D.C., United States; Akademie der Künste, Berlin, Germany; Musée des Beaux-Arts, Lyon, France

1850–51 *Ratapoil*; plaster; Albright-Knox Art Gallery, Buffalo, New York, United States; posthumous bronze casts in various private and public collections, including Ashmolean Museum, Oxford, England; Musée des Beaux-Arts, Marseille, France

after   *Emigrants* (also known as *Fugitifs*);
1853   plaster; Musée d'Orsay, Paris, France; patinated plaster; National Gallery of Australia, Canberra, Australia; posthumous bronze casts in various private and public collections, including National Gallery of Art, Washington, D.C., United States; Fogg Art Museum, Harvard University, Cambridge, Massachusetts, United States; Minneapolis Institute of Arts, Minnesota, United States

Further Reading

Campbell, Douglas, and Usher Caplan (editors), *Daumier, 1808–1879* (exhib. cat.), Ottawa, Ontario: National Gallery of Canada, 1999

Wasserman, Jeanne L., *Daumier Sculpture: A Critical and Comparative Study*, Cambridge, Massachusetts: Harvard University, Fogg Art Museum, 1969

DAVID D'ANGERS 1788–1856 *French*

David d'Angers, possibly the greatest Early Romantic sculptor, was a controversial figure in the 19th century, partly because of his art, which was often strongly antiacademic, and partly because of his uncompromising opinions on the moral function of sculpture. He was especially concerned with the sculptural commemoration of great men, a concept with late 18th-century origins that was extremely important during the Romantic period. David made a point of being on personal terms with the celebrity artists and writers of his time, whose portraits he attempted to disperse to a popular audience through the medium of the engraved medal. David executed approximately 500 of these portrait medallions, for which he was not paid, believing in their social utility rather than in their intrinsic artistic value. His medallion depicting the Angevin priest and republican François-Yves Besnard (1752–1842) is typical of David's style in this genre, which utilizes exaggerated, almost caricatured features to create an emblematic image. The notion of cultural diffusion inherent in the relatively cheap, portable medallions is relevant in considering this artist, who aggressively cultivated provincial patronage during the 1830s, when he was on poor terms with the government administration. Despite his opposition to the July Monarchy, David was himself a celebrity artist in the capital, where his provincial works were remarked upon with interest, and both artists and the well-to-do public collected his medallions.

The journalistic criticism that surrounded his death makes clear David's stylistic innovations. In 1853 the critic Gustave Planche, a friend and supporter of David, heralded the sculptor as the leader of *l'école réaliste* (the realist school) and praised his adaptation of Greek art (considered highly naturalistic at the time). Three years later, after the artist's death, the same critic found much to blame in David's oeuvre: a preference for visual impact over beauty, exaggerations of anatomy and pose, and a general tendency toward "painterliness." The range of these remarks reflects the challenges David posed for his contemporaries, as he was criticized simultaneously for being too real and for departing from nature (often the two criticisms were made of a single work). One must therefore carefully consider David's stylistic innovations, especially when dealing with his reception of Classical art. Despite his frequent depiction of modern dress, in principle David unquestioningly adhered to the precept of nudity and the idealized human form. His sculpture, then, constitutes a reaction against a particular form of sculptural classicism: the so-called Neoclassical style associated with the Italian sculptor Antonio Canova, whose influence dominated the Empire and Restoration periods in France.

An examination of *Philopœmen*, commissioned by the French government for the Tuileries Gardens in Paris, demonstrates how David's use of "heroic nudity" could provoke severe criticism in his lifetime. The choice of nudity in this case was beyond discussion because the subject was antique. The emotional intensity and anatomical attention in this work, however, are without precedent. Philopœmen wrenching the spear from his thigh presents us with several overlapping emotional states. The hero is at once in extreme pain and in a state of extreme concentration, fixed simultaneously on the act of removing the spear and on monitoring the battle from afar. Planche, a perceptive critic, lauded the work but criticized the choice of Philopœmen's intensely violent gesture; the critic favored, not surprisingly, the more traditional motif of the dying warrior. Planche also worried about the anatomical realism of David's figure: again, a laudable goal, he maintained, but not entirely suited to the demands of monumental sculpture.

David's literal treatment in *Philopœmen* of this nevertheless heroic body is strongly reminiscent of the central adult warrior in François Rude's famous *Marseillaise* (1833–1836) relief. Rude, however, consistently adhered to what could be called a realist heroic manner, whereas David was equally committed to other, indeed antithetical, styles. His monument to Bichat illustrates his other major sculptural mode well. Instead of *Philopœmen*'s anatomic exactitude, David creates here a series of simplified masses, the proportions of which were radical for the time: a large head, squat body, and rounded pneumatic limbs. The child figure next to Bichat bears a similarly large head, but his youthful body is more realistically rendered: his narrow shoulders and slight belly would not have fit the current Classical canon. The shrouded, partially hidden mass that appears at the base of the group is essential to the work, registering at once as metaphoric evocation of death (consistent with sculpture's traditional allegoric function) and as inert human matter. Disturbingly amorphous, the prone form fails to offset the viewer's initial impression of a corpse. David, in fact, wrote admiringly in his journals of Bichat's extensive use of cadavers, of which the sculptor was aware from contemporary published accounts. David distances himself here from standard commemorations of the man of science by underlining in an extreme and insistent way the link between social good and passionate scientific interest. The tone of this message was radical for David's time, although the sculpture's overall conception was not what came under attack. It was rather David's treatment of the body, which violated canons of male beauty, the privileged sign for moral and civic values in the 19th century.

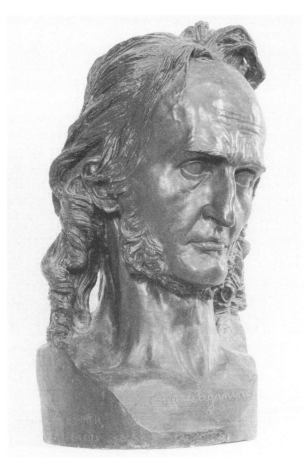

Bust of Paganini
The Conway Library, Courtauld Institute of Art

After his death, David's reputation declined. The situation worsened with Auguste Rodin's extraordinary rise to fame and the popularity of his highly sexual and psychological images of men and women. David, by contrast, was interested in the social and political morality of his subjects. He envisioned an ideally transparent relationship between the human being and his physical form—or, put otherwise, between meaning and sculptural form. David's work is hardly straightforward, however, for the range of his formal experimentation was unprecedented. This artist's contribution may be considered a kind of sculptural sign language, arbitrary and precise, coherent and powerful in the context of any single work. David was to have an enormous influence on following generations of Romantic sculptors, in particular on his student Auguste Préault, who was to push these innovations in an even more radical direction.

LUCIA TRIPODES

See also **Canova, Antonio; France: Mid–Late 19th Century; Neoclassicism and Romanticism; Rodin, Auguste; Rude, François**

Biography

Born in Angers, France, 12 March 1788. Son of an artisan wood sculptor who served in the republican army. Began artistic training at local École Centrale des Beaux-Arts, 1808; left for Paris, 1808, earning meager living assisting in sculptural decoration of *Arc du Carrousel* and Musée du Louvre facade; studied in atelier of sculptor Philippe-Laurent Roland and that of Neoclassical painter Jacques-Louis David; won Prix de Rome in 1811 with relief *Epaminondas after the Battle of Mantinea*; began sending plaster models to Angers; these formed basis of the collection of the Musée David, inaugurated 1839; studied at Villa Medici in Rome, as required for Prix de Rome winners, then returned to Paris, 1816; executed statue *Le Grand Condé*, 1817, a commission given to him upon the death of his teacher Roland; began series of bronze portrait medallions in 1820s; continued for remainder of career; awarded *Croix* of the Legion of Honor, 1825; from 1826, professor at École des Beaux-Arts, Paris, where he established an influential studio; took part in July Revolution of 1830 alongside the republicans; absent from Salon during 1830s, but executed numerous monuments and statues in the provinces, as well as important pediment of the Panthéon in 1837; held political office under the republic in 1848; following 1851 coup d'état, exile in Brussels; returned to France, December 1852. Died in Paris, France, 5 January 1856.

Selected Works

1817   *Le Grand Condé* (The Count); plaster; Musée David d'Angers, Angers, France
1824   Monument to Bonchamps; marble; Church of Saint-Florent-le-Vieil, Saint-Florent-le-Vieil, France
1827   *Young Greek, at the Tomb of Marco Botzaris*; marble; Missolonghi, Greece
1827   Monument to General Foy; marble; Père-Lachaise Cemetery, Paris, France
1834   *Pierre Corneille*; bronze; Rouen, France
1834   *Bust of Nicolá Paganini*; bronze; Courtauld Institute of Art, London, England
1835   *The Motherland Calling Her Children to the Defense of Liberty*; stone; Porte d'Aix, Marseille, France
1835   *Georges Cuvier*; marble; Museum of Natural History, Paris, France
1837   *Philopœmen*; marble; Musée du Louvre, Paris, France
1837   *Aux Grand Hommes La Patrie Reconnaissante* (To Great Men the Fatherland is Grateful); stone; pediment of the Panthéon, Paris, France

1838   *Joseph Barra*; marble; Musée David
        d'Angers, Angers, France

1838   *Pierre-Paul Riquet*; bronze; Béziers,
        France

1839   *Liberty*; bronze; Musée David d'Angers,
        Angers, France

1840   *Jean Gutenberg*; bronze; Place Gutenberg,
        Strasbourg, France

1845   *The Child with Grapes*; marble; Musée du
        Louvre, Paris, France

1843   Monument to Bichat; bronze; Promenade
        du Bastion, Bourg-en-Bresse, France

1846   Monument to Larry; bronze; Val-de-Grâce,
        Paris, France

1847   Tomb of General Gobert; marble; Père-
        Lachaise Cemetery, Paris, France

Further Reading

Aux grands hommes, David d'Angers, Saint-Rémy-lès-Chevreuse, France: Fondation de Coubertin, 1990

De Caso, Jacques, "Le romantisme de David d'Angers," in *La scultura nel XIX secolo*, edited by H.W. Janson, Bologna, Italy: CLUEB, 1984

De Caso, Jacques, *David d'Angers: L'avenir e la mémoire: Étude sur l'art signalétique à l'époque romantique*, Paris: Flammarion, 1988; as *David d'Angers: Sculptural Communication in the Age of Romanticism*, Princeton, New Jersey: Princeton University Press, 1992

Driskel, Michael Paul, " 'Et la lumière fut': The Meanings of David d'Angers's Monument to Gutenberg," *Art Bulletin* 73/3 (September 1991)

Huchard, Viviane (editor), *Galerie David d'Angers*, Angers, France: Musées d'Angers, 1995

Johnson, Dorothy, "David d'Angers and the Signs of Landscape," *Gazette des Beaux-Arts* 115/1455 (April 1990)

Le Neuëne, Patrick, and Catherine Lesseur, *Autour de David d'Angers: Sculptures du XVIIIe siècle et du début du XIXe dans les collections des musées d'Angers*, Angers, France: Musée des Beaux-Arts, 1995

McWilliam, Neil, "David d'Angers and the Pantheon Commission: Politics and Public Works under the July Monarchy," *Art History* 5/4 (December 1982)

West, Alison, "The Sculptor's Self-Image from Falconet to David d'Angers," in *World Art: Themes of Unity in Diversity*, edited by Irving Lavin, University Park: Pennsylvania State University Press, 1989

RICHARD DEACON 1949– *British*

One of the more intriguing aspects of contemporary British sculptor Richard Deacon's work is his interest in creating sculpture that is simultaneously exceptional and ordinary. Responding to the conventions of representation, language, scale, and the process of making, he uses common materials to build sculptures that are highly poetic.

An early turning point in Deacon's artistic maturation came while reading Rainer Maria Rilke's *Sonnets to Orpheus* (1923) during a visit to New York in 1978–79. He was particularly influenced by Rilke's use of abstract schematic types of metaphors that stand in for whole conditions of being. Rilke's writings about Orpheus—whose head continued to sing even after it was severed from his torso—inspired Deacon to begin a body of work based on the image of a head with an opening. First in a series of drawings called *It's Orpheus When There's Singing* and then in sculpture, Deacon used repeated, sometimes overlapping, lines that suggest not only organs of sense but musical instruments and domestic objects with openings, such as bowls and pockets. *Untitled* is an example. Built with strips of laminated wood, the work is a large, geometric, open, circular structure. It could be described as a larger circle with S-shaped ribs perpendicular to the circle leading to a smaller circle—only the smaller of the two is actually a teardrop shape of which the tapering end continues up the side, interrupting the pattern formed by the ribs. Placed at an angle on its side, the structure is reminiscent of a ribbed vessel (an airplane or ship), whereas the opening in the sculpture is a schematic for both a tear and a vagina. With work like this, Deacon has collapsed the divisions between the customary sculptural categories of representation and abstraction. He addresses communication and the difficulties inherent in language by alluding to orifices and parts of the body associated with communication.

Deacon's sculptures refuse to be merely objects to be seen. Reflective and highly detailed surfaces, indefinite spatial boundaries, visual conundrums, and complexities give his sculpture a fluidity not usually associated with static objects. His work has a vitality that makes it seem to respond to the viewer's gaze—an effect that is amplified by the titles. Rather than verbally qualifying each work, a Deacon title functions more like an appendix, an addendum, or a footnote. The titles of his work are explicit but never specifically describe the subject; they both conceal and reveal, thereby heightening the tension between the word and image. Deacon often chooses idiomatic phrases for titles such as *Tell Me No Lies*, *Between the Two of Us*, and *The Eye Has It*, all from the mid 1980s. In the case of *The Heart's in the Right Place*, the sculpture is an open structure built of metal strips with an implied volume. The center of the sculpture is a schematic outline of a valentine heart. Curved cross-members bisect the heart and connect at two small circles, one on either side of the heart, putting the heart in the middle, or interior. Both the title and the sculpture are matter-of-fact and symbolic while managing to comment on one another. Together they convey the initial attraction and eventual inadequacy of all forms of communication. With his sculpture, repeated looking and thinking offer increasing satisfaction but provide no answers, only the possibility of a continuing conversation.

The relationships between the artist, the viewer-audience, and the artwork have always interested Deacon. A seminal work, *Stuff Box Object*, focused on repetitive forming, routine, and event. This work had several different phases beginning as a communal student project, then a performance site with Deacon working inside it in a fetal position, and finally ending up as a process-based sculptural object. Realizing that an object that contained the history of its making could act as a surrogate for the artist, he began creating sculpture. With the artist absent, however, the object exists somewhere between the artist and the audience. A body of work called *Art for Other People* strongly evidences this quality of separateness. As Deacon stated in the November 1999 issue of *Sculpture*, "when you look at it as a viewer you don't think it's for you—and you wonder who the other people are." Beginning in the early 1980s and continuing through the present, this sequentially numbered series of small experimental sculptures has informed his larger work. Paradoxically, Deacon thinks of the smaller works as being more public and accessible than the larger. Because they are more easily viewed and do not require a physical engagement to understand them, the *Art for Other People* series could be thought of as an open forum, whereas the larger sculpture requires bodily interaction that tends to happen on an individual basis. A recent sculpture, *Art for Other People #39*, is a germane example. The sculpture is comprised of two elements: a vertically oriented, translucent pink hollow tube topped by an open earlike appendage wrapped with black thread. The viewer can quickly apprehend the sculpture—it does not seem to require repeated looking. Much like joining a conversation in progress, one understands the smaller sculptures without complete certainty of what has been said.

Typically, Deacon uses materials like linoleum, sheet metal, wood, and plastic. He has distanced himself from more traditional sculptural procedures and materials such as casting bronze, carving stone, and welding steel cutoffs. To this end he has often called himself a fabricator, rather than an artist or sculptor. Although using common materials is typical for his generation of British sculptors (which includes Tony Cragg and Bill Woodrow), Deacon manipulates the materials, leaving the evidence of the building method completely visible. Dripping glue between laminated strips of wood, screw holes, fasteners, and joints are all part of his highly crafted aesthetic. This aesthetic celebrates the ordinary—the way in which furniture, plumbing, boats, planes, and buildings are made and the people who make them. Empowered by his utopian ideals, he articulates the territory between common ob-jects and architecture with sculpture that asserts the importance of art while denying it a privileged status.

JOHN J. RICHARDSON

See also **Assemblage; Contemporary Sculpture; Cragg, Tony; Wood Sculpture**

Biography

Born in Bangor, Wales, 15 August 1949. Attended foundation course at Somerset College of Art, 1968; studied performance-based work at St. Martin's School of Art, London, 1969–72; studied in the M.A. course in Environmental Media at the Royal College of Art, London, 1974–77; traveled to the United States with his wife, Jacqueline Poncelet, 1978–79; started work on the *Art for Other People* series, 1982. Major exhibitions at the Bonnefanten Museum, Maastricht, The Netherlands; Whitechapel Art Gallery, London; Kunstverein, Hanover, Germany; and Museum of Contemporary Art/CT, Los Angeles. Awarded the Turner Prize, 1987, and the Chevalier de l'Ordre des Arts et Lettres, 1996 (by the Ministry of Culture, France). Lives and works in London, England.

Selected Works

1970–71 *Stuff Box Object*; small box of wood and plaster; temporary installation realized at St. Martin's School of Art, London, England (no longer extant)

1980 *Untitled*; laminated timber, steel; Saatchi Collection, London, England

1981 *If the Shoe Fits*; galvanized and corrugated steel; Saatchi Collection, London, England

1983 *The Heart's in the Right Place*; galvanized steel; Saatchi Collection, London, England

1983–84 *The Eye Has It*; wood, stainless and galvanized steel, brass, cloth; The Arts Council of Great Britain, London, England

1986 *Listening to Reason*; laminated wood; private collection

1987–88 *More Light*; plywood, aluminum; The Saint Louis Art Museum, Missouri, United States

1990 *Lock*; laminated hardboard, aluminum, vinyl; Weltkunst Foundation, Zurich, Switzerland

1992 *Keeping the Faith*; beech wood, epoxy; private collection

1993 *What Could Make Me Feel This Way A*; bent wood with glue, screws, cable ties; Sprengel Museum, Hanover, Germany

1994 *Almost Beautiful*; wood, polycarbonate, steel; Kiasma, The Museum of

Contemporary Art, Helsinki, Finland

1996 *Laocoön*; beech wood, aluminum, bolts; private collection

1997 *Art for Other People #39*; nylon net, linen thread, medium density fiberboard; artist's collection

1998 *After*; wood, stainless steel, aluminum; private collection

1999 *Blow*; spun aluminum; artist's collection

Further Reading

Clark, Vicki (editor), *Richard Deacon*, Pittsburgh, Pennsylvania: The Carnegie Museum of Art, 1988

Deacon, Richard, *Stuff Box Object*, Cardiff, Wales: Chapter Arts Centre, 1984

Deacon, Richard, *New World Order*, London: Tate Gallery, 1985

Deacon, Richard, *For Those Who Have Eyes: Richard Deacon Sculpture, 1980–86; Arddangosfa Deithiol a Drefnwyd Gan Ganolfan y Celfyddyddau Aberystwyth* (exhib. cat.; bilingual Welsh-English edition), Aberystwyth, Wales: Aberystwyth Arts Centre, 1986

Deacon, Richard, *Atlas: Gondwanaland and Laurasia*, Oslo: Kunstnernes Hus, 1990

Deacon, Richard, and Bill Woodrow, *Only the Lonely and Other Shared Sculptures*, London: Chisenhale Gallery, 1993

Thompson, Jon, Pier Luggi Tazzi, and Peter Schjedahl, *Richard Deacon*, London: Phaidon Press, 1995

Trump, Ian, "Undetermined Pleasure and Unnecessary Beauty: An Interview with Richard Deacon," *Sculpture* 18/9 (November 1999)

JOHN DEARE 1759–1798 *British, active in Italy*

One of the most accomplished sculptors working in Rome at the end of the 18th century, John Deare distinguished himself from the majority of his Neoclassical contemporaries through his choice of unusual subjects, his inventive and highly sensual compositions, and his exceptional facility as a marble carver. In his lifetime, Deare enjoyed critical acclaim and the patronage of important British collectors, such as Henry Blundell, Edward Poore, Thomas Hope, and Prince Augustus Frederick (Duke of Sussex). However, Deare's work has been little studied by historians of Neoclassical art and has only recently attracted scholarly attention. This neglect is likely due to a variety of factors: he died at a very young age, many of his sculptures were lost and remain untraced because of the confiscation of art during the French occupation of Rome, and few of his compositions are on public display.

After moving to London in 1776, Deare apprenticed with Thomas Carter and enrolled in the Royal Academy, becoming the youngest artist ever to win a Gold Medal competition in 1780. Although receiving his first independent commission in 1783–84, Deare continued to work for Carter, as well as John Cheere, John Bacon the Elder, and the clock maker Benjamin Vulliamy. Clocks based on Deare's models are the only identifiable works of his that survive from this period. Selected to go to Rome as a Royal Academy pensioner in 1785, Deare remained in Italy and produced his most significant sculptures there. Competition for patronage and Deare's general disdain for the antiquities trade, which had by then become a lucrative but often unscrupulous entrepreneurial endeavor, put him in direct conflict with other British artists in Rome, such as Thomas Jenkins, Christopher Hewetson, and John Flaxman.

An indefatigable student of antique sculpture who often incorporated ancient motifs into his work, Deare was unusually open to other sources of inspiration. He seems to have been particularly influenced by Italian Renaissance and Mannerist art. His first major work in marble, a large relief depicting *The Judgment of Jupiter* for Richard Worsley, was based on a plaster that Deare sought to exhibit at the 1787 Royal Academy exhibition but which was rejected because of its large size. The multifigured composition was clearly intended to demonstrate Deare's assimilation of Classical models and his ability to work on a monumental scale. Nevertheless, he rejected the friezelike arrangements of uniform depth known from ancient sarcophagi and organized the main figures into a semicircular arc of high relief in the foreground. Although several of the deities derive from famous antique statues, others—such as Minerva, whose pose is based on the figure of Esau in Ghiberti's early 15th century *Gates of Paradise*—recall Renaissance art. Deare's next relief, *Edward and Eleanor*, depicting Eleanor of Castile sucking venom from the wound of her husband, Prince Edward (later King Edward I), was accepted to the 1788 Royal Academy exhibition and acquired by Henry Blundell. Deare applied his classicizing style to a medieval British subject but again incorporated Renaissance sources, such as a mourning figure inspired by Donatello's *Entombment* from the Tabernacle of the Sacrament in St. Peter's Basilica, Rome. Deare's only other surviving historical relief, *The Landing of Julius Caesar in Britain* for John Penn, was perhaps his most ambitious and successful in terms of integrating numerous figures into a complex, action-filled drama placed within a naturalistic landscape setting.

In the late 1780s and early 1790s, Deare began a series of two-figure mythological compositions that set the smooth, classically conceived torso of a nude figure against the fur of an animal or the drapery of a clothed lover. These included *Marine Venus*, *Cupid and Psyche*, *Bacchus Feeding a Panther*, and *Hebe Feeding the Bird of Jupiter*. Contrasting, for example, the fluid anatomy of the reclining nude with such exquisitely rendered details as the sea goat's shaggy pelt in *Marine Venus*, Deare exploited his extraordinary technical skill to achieve a greater variety of surface depth and texture than is found in any of his previous works. The deep undercutting, the juxtaposition of concave and convex elements, and the sophisticated dialogue between projection and recession make these compositions masterpieces of relief carving. Their gentle eroticism was equaled only, with significant differences, by Antonio Canova. Although based on antique prototypes, these late works of Deare embody stylistic values more often associated with the art of such Italian Mannerists as Benvenuto Cellini, Vincenzo Danti, and Pierino da Vinci.

Deare also produced a number of portrait busts. His bust of John Penn is an early example of a nude portrait combining a Neoclassical, geometric truncation with realistic, sensitively handled facial features. The bust of Marshall Stanislaus Malachowski has a similar pentagonally shaped nude chest and unidealized portrait head. Several of Deare's portrait busts are now lost, such as those depicting Madame Martinville; Prince Augustus Frederick, Duke of Sussex; and Lady Elizabeth Webster. Deare was commissioned to design William Henry Lambton's (*d.* 1797) tomb monument, which may have included a portrait bust or medallion, but it is uncertain whether he ever did so.

Copies of famous antiquities were not a large part of Deare's output. He did, however, execute a copy of the Capitoline Bust of Ariadne (*ca.* 1789–90) for John Latouche, a copy of an antique *Antinous* (date unknown) for Thomas Hope, and a paired *Apollo Belvedere* (at Attingham Hall, Shropshire, until 1827; present location unknown) and Medici Venus (1792–95), the size of the originals, for Lord Berwick. Deare seems to have been contemptuous of restoration work, which provided a secure income for so many other British and Italian sculptors, but he apparently restored

an ancient candelabrum, a statuette of Aesculapius, and a sarcophagus for Lord Berwick.

Deare's oeuvre generally conformed to the mainstays of 18th-century British patronage, which concentrated on ornamental works and chimneypieces with mythological themes, portraiture, and copies of antiquities, with little opportunity for independent, original statuary. Nevertheless, Deare was able to forge a highly individual style that still satisfied the tastes of antiquarian collectors. In his best reliefs, it could be argued that he achieved a level of greatness unrivaled by his British contemporaries.

PEGGY FOGELMAN

See also **Canova, Antonio; Donatello (Donato di Bettos Bardi); Flaxman, John; Ghiberti, Lorenzo; Ghiberti, Lorenzo:** *Gates of Paradise*

Biography

Born in Liverpool, England, 26 October 1759. Moved to London, became apprentice to Thomas Carter, 1776; enrolled in Royal Academy, 1777; won gold medal in sculpture with relief of *The Angels Surprising Satan at the Ear of Eve* from Milton's *Paradise Lost*, 1780; worked for Carter, John Cheere, John Bacon the Elder, and the clock maker Benjamin Vulliamy; began receiving independent commissions in 1783/84; sent to Rome as Royal Academy pensioner and found lodgings on the Corso, 1785; closely associated with amateur painter and art critic George Cumberland and fellow artists Charles Felix Rossi, Charles Grignon, Robert Fagan, and Hugh Robinson; *The Judgment of Jupiter* refused for exhibition by Royal Academy because of its large size, 1787; received commissions for works in marble from British patrons starting in 1787; *Edward and Eleanor*, first work exhibited by Royal Academy, 1788; relocated to lodgings near Piazza Barberini, Rome, by 1788; went to Naples with John Penn, 1791; arrested in Rome "for affairs of the state," possibly because of involvement with a religious sect, 1794; patronized by Prince Augustus Frederick, Duke of Sussex, and his brother, the Prince of Wales, 1795; suffered failing eyesight by January 1798. Died in Rome, Italy, 17 August 1798.

Selected Works

1786   *Edward and Eleanor*; plaster: Ince Blundell Hall, Lancashire, England; Walker Art Gallery, Liverpool, England; Lyons Demesne, County Kildare, Ireland; marble: 1788, private collection

1786–87 *The Judgment of Jupiter*; plaster (destroyed); marble version: 1788–*ca.*

Judgment of Jupiter
Courtesy of Los Angeles County Museum of Art, Gift of Anna Bing Arnold
© 2001 Museum Associates / LACMA

1790; County Museum of Art, Los
Angeles, California, United States

1787   *Marine Venus*; marble; Parham Park, West
Sussex, England; marble version: *ca.* 1788,
Getty Museum, Los Angeles, California,
United States; bronze version: *ca.* 1790,
Musée du Louvre, Paris, France

1789–90 Bust of Madame Martinville; marble (lost)

ca. 1791 *Cupid and Psyche*; plaster; Lyons
Demesne, County Kildare, Ireland

1791–94 *The Landing of Julius Caesar in Britain*;
marble; Stoke Manor, Stoke Poges,
Buckinghamshire, England

1793   Bust of John Penn; marble; College
Library, Eton College, Berkshire, England

1793   Bust of Marshall Stanislaus Malachowski;
marble; National Museum, Warsaw,
Poland

ca. 1795 Bust of Lady Elizabeth Webster;
presumably marble (lost)

ca. 1795 Bust of Prince Augustus Frederick, Duke
of Sussex; presumably marble (lost)

ca. 1795 Chimneypiece with festoons and masks;
marble; Frogmore House, Berkshire,
England

Further Reading

Clifford, Timothy, "John Bacon and the Manufacturers," *Apollo* 122 (1985)

Clifford, Timothy, "Vulliamy Clocks and British Sculpture," *Apollo* 132 (1990)

Fogelman, Peggy, Peter Fusco, and Simon Stock, "John Deare (1759–1798): A British Neo-classical Sculptor in Rome," *Sculpture Journal* 4 (2000)

Gunnis, Rupert, *Dictionary of British Sculptors, 1660–1851*, London: Odhams Press, 1953; Cambridge, Massachusetts: Harvard University Press, 1954; revised edition, London: Abbey Library, 1968

Honour, Hugh, *Neo-classicism*, London: Penguin, 1968; Baltimore, Maryland: Penguin, 1973

Smith, John Thomas, *Nollekens and His Times*, 2 vols., London: Colburn, 1828; reprint, London: Century Hutchinson, 1986

EDGAR DEGAS 1834–1917 *French*

Fascinated by the ephemeral, the incomplete, and the transient, Degas modeled some of the most intriguing sculptures in the history of modern art, devoting a great deal of time, energy, and effort to his idiosyncratic three-dimensional creations. Considering himself a painter, he liberated his three-dimensional work of sculptural conventions and constantly experimented with new materials and techniques. Degas never cast his figures in bronze, preferring the flexibility of wax, clay, plasticine, and plaster. He used complex wire armatures and interior structures for his sculptures including experimental materials, such as corks, nails, and pins. Largely intending these to be private and used as sketches, he exhibited the ones he most esteemed in glass cases in his studio. About 1900 Degas asked the founder Adrien A. Hébrard to make plaster casts of several of his sculptures that he considered finished or worthy of preservation.

As a sculptor, Degas modeled mostly in wax or clay throughout his career. As both a painter and a sculptor, he used the same subjects in two and three dimensions, focusing particularly on ballerinas and horses in motion. He trained himself by drawing Classical sculpture and plaster casts. He recorded the manners and movements of figures to aid his experiments with light, space, and form. His first sculptural attempts consisted of studies of horses standing, walking, balking, trotting, rearing, or galloping, conceived as sketches and models for his paintings. It is not known when Degas began to model the human form; *Little Dancer, Fourteen Years Old*, modeled between 1879 and 1881, is the only sculpture he ever personally titled and exhibited. His passionate investigations of movement inspired his preoccupation with the human figure as well as the emergent medium of photography. His favored compositional motifs included the representation of women caught in poses that captured an arrested movement, such as a dancer at rest, doing arabesques, bowing, or rubbing her knees or a woman arranging her hair, massaging her back, or stretching her neck, most often caught unawares of the artist's gaze.

Degas often reworked his statuettes in order to perfect them and better study their complicated poses. Moreover, sculpture allowed him to explore problems of movement and form that could not be solved in two dimensions. Although scholars have often cited his poor vision as an explanation of why he started modeling, the dating of those works is doubtful, and his initial work in three dimensions clearly predated any serious deterioration of his eyesight.

After Degas's death in 1917, his dealer, Joseph Durand-Ruel, found some 150 items, some complete sculptures and some fragments in the artist's studio. Due to the combination of soft wax and frail armatures, the sculptures were highly unstable, and many needed restoration. The artist's heirs and the foundry owned by Hébrard signed a contract authorizing the reproduction of Degas's sculptures in bronze in a limited run of 20 casts of each figure, lettered "A" to "T," plus a complete set of master casts marked "Modele." In addition to those sets are two complete sets, one for Degas's heirs, marked "HER.D," and one for the foundry, marked "HER." Casts sold by some of the heirs to Hébrard are also marked "HER." The founder also cast 74 pieces in a limited edition using the lost-wax method. The actual casting of the bronzes seems to have been the work of Albino Palazzolo, Hébrard's chief founder.

Degas's work in sculpture has had a strange destiny, from almost total neglect in his lifetime to complete adulation after the posthumous casts were realized. His study of motion, time, and gesture liberated sculpture from its fixed position, and the spiraling of his figures encouraged the viewer to circle the work and view it from different angles. Technically, Degas remains a formidable experimenter and innovator of the medium, incorporating new materials and forming techniques. He played an essential part in the formation of modern sculpture and effected significant influence on his contemporaries and successors.

ANNA TAHINCI

See also **Clay and Terracotta; France: Mid–Late 19th Century; Modeling**

Biography

Born in Paris, France, 19 July 1834. Enrolled at the École des Beaux-Arts, 1855; pupil of Jean-Auguste-Dominique Ingres; stayed in Italy, 1856–59; returned to Paris, 1859; began to make wax sculptures of horses, 1869; visited relations in New Orleans, 1872–73; ceased exhibiting at the Salon, 1870; participated in First Impressionist Exhibition, 1874; exhibited 24 works at Second Impressionist Exhibition, 1876; showed 25 works at Third Impressionist Exhibition, 1877. Interest in women dancers, singers, and laundresses as subject matter grew in 1880s; became major figure in Parisian art world. Died in Paris, France, 27 September 1917.

Selected Works

An important collection of Degas's waxes, from the Paul Mellon collection, is at the National Gallery of Art, Washington, D.C., United States. A set of bronze models is at the Norton Simon Museum, Pasadena, California, United States. A complete set of Degas's bronzes (set numbered "A"), from the collection of Mrs. H. O. Havemeyer, is at the Metropolitan Museum of Art, New York City, United States. Another complete set (numbered "P") is at the Musée d'Orsay, Paris, France. The Ny Carlsberg Glyptotek, Copenhagen, Denmark, owns a third complete set.

1879–81 *Little Dancer, Fourteen Years Old*; wax, hair, ribbon, linen, satin, muslin, wood base; National Gallery of Art, Washington, D.C., United States; posthumous bronze casts: Norton Simon Museum, Pasadena, California, United States (master cast);

Metropolitan Museum of Art, New York City, United States; Fogg Art Museum, Cambridge, Massachusetts, United States

ca. *The Schoolgirl*; wax; National Gallery of
1880/81 Art, Washington, D.C., United States

ca. *Arabesque over the Right Leg, Left Arm in*
1882–95 *Front*; wax with metal frame; National Gallery of Art, Washington, D.C., United States

ca. *Grande Arabesque, First Time*; wax;
1882–95 National Gallery of Art, Washington, D.C., United States

ca. *Grande Arabesque, Second Time*;
1882–95 plasticine, wax, and cork; National Gallery of Art, Washington, D.C., United States

ca. *Grande Arabesque, Third Time*; plasticine;
1882–95 National Gallery of Art, Washington, D.C., United States

ca. 1885 *The Bow*; wax and plasticine; National Gallery of Art, Washington, D.C., United States

1889 *The Tub*; wax, lead, plaster, cloth; National Gallery of Art, Washington, D.C., United States

1889–90 *Horse Galloping on Right Foot*; wax and cork; National Gallery of Art, Washington, D.C., United States

1890 *Picking Apples*; wax, plasticine, wood; National Gallery of Art, Washington, D.C., United States

Further Reading

Campbell, Sara, "A Catalogue of Degas' Bronzes," *Apollo* 142 (August 1995)

Millard, Charles W., *The Sculpture of Edgar Degas*, Princeton, New Jersey: Princeton University Press, 1976

Pingeot, Anne, *Degas: Sculptures*, Paris: Imprimerie Nationale Éditions, 1991

Rewald, John, *Degas's Complete Sculpture: Catalogue Raisonné*, San Francisco: Alan Wofsy Fine Arts, 1990

LITTLE DANCER, FOURTEEN YEARS OLD
Edgar Degas (1834–1917)
1879–1881
yellow wax, hair, ribbon, linen, satin, muslin, wood base
h. 99.1 cm
National Gallery of Art, Washington, D.C., United States

There are 28 casts of this work in existence; notable examples can be found in the Norton Simon Museum, Pasadena, California, United States (master cast); the

Metropolitan Museum of Art, New York City, United States; and the Fogg Art Museum, Cambridge, Massachusetts, United States. Other examples are found in galleries and museums throughout Europe and the Americas as well as in private collections.

Degas's *Little Dancer, Fourteen Years Old* is his best-known sculpture and the only one he ever personally titled and exhibited. Although the original wax, from the collection of Mr. and Mrs. Paul Mellon and at the National Gallery of Art in Washington, D.C., was listed in the catalogue of the Fifth Impressionist Exhibition in 1880 in Paris, Degas showed it only in the 1881 Impressionist Exhibition. This was the only time Degas exhibited the sculpture during his lifetime.

After returning from New Orleans in 1873, Degas started studying ballet's "little rats," the lower-class student dancers who were beginning their careers to become ballerinas at the Paris Opéra. They included his model, Marie Van Goethem. The daughter of a Belgian tailor, she lived in Montmartre, a few blocks from Degas's studio. Degas had started exploring the nude composition in 1878 and developed the dressed figure during 1880 and 1881. At that time France saw a renewed interest in wax sculpture, and it is also likely that Degas had seen polychrome wax at Madame Tussaud's in London.

The sculpture's realism and the audacious pose of the little dancer outraged some art critics and the majority of the public. The dancer appears to be offstage, possibly in a rehearsal room, with her arms behind her back, chin thrust forward, and eyes half-shut. Degas heightened the intense realism of the sculpture by the way in which he dressed the wax model: a wax-covered cloth bodice, a real gauze shirt, real ballet slippers and a green-satin ribbon dangling from a real horsehair wig. The art critic Paul Manz called the *Little Dancer* ugly, perceiving in her face a vicious character: "Mr. Degas dreamed of an ideal of ugliness. The happy man! He has achieved it" (*Le Temps*, April 1881). J.K. Huysmans, who reviewed the exhibition, wrote about Degas's sculpture: "At once refined and barbaric, with her costume and colored skin, palpitating, contoured by the work of the muscles, this statuette is the only true attempt of which I know in modern sculpture." The sculpture remained in Degas's studio; he refused to sell it and resumed work on it about 1903.

The *Little Dancer* marked a turning point in Degas's development as a sculptor. Whereas previously he had concentrated on statuettes of horses, he started focusing in the human figure, modeling a figure two-thirds life size and innovating in his unorthodox use of techniques, materials, and colors. As part of his preparatory work for the sculpture, Degas drew eight sheets of drawings. He also modeled a smaller nude study of

Little Dancer, Fourteen Years Old
© P. Schmidt, Réunion des Musées Nationaux / Art Resource, NY

the body of the dancer, which scholars consider as having been modeled later.

After the artist's death in 1917, his heirs and the foundry owned by Adrien A. Hébrard entered into a contract authorizing the reproduction of Degas's sculptures in bronze, with a limit of 20 casts of each figure (lettered A to T), plus a complete set of master casts marked "Modele." The *Little Dancer*'s cast started around 1922 in a bronze edition of unknown size. The bronze casts do not reproduce the colors of the original wax statuette: the face is not colored, the yellow bodice of the cast was originally white, and the shoes and hair are cast in metal. Whereas the tutu of the original wax statuette was white, Mademoiselle Lefèvre, Degas's niece, had the bronze casts dressed in a grayish-green skirt made of muslin, the same material as the original.

Twenty-eight casts of the *Little Dancer* have been located, although not all may be authentic. Bronze casts of the statue are to be found in the Norton Simon Museum, Pasadena, California (bronze inscribed "modèle"); the Metropolitan Museum of Art, New York City (bronze inscribed "A"); the Fogg Art Museum, Cambridge, Massachusetts (bronze inscribed "C"); the Sterling and Francine Clark Art Institute, Williamstown, Massachusetts (bronze inscribed "D"); the Nathan and Marion Smooke Collection, Los Angeles (bronze inscribed "E"); the Staatliche Kunstsammlungen, Dresden (bronze inscribed "F"); the Philadelphia Museum of Art, Pennsylvania (bronze inscribed "G"); the St. Louis Art Museum, Missouri (bronze inscribed "M"); the Musée d'Orsay, Paris (bronze inscribed "P"); the Ny Carlsberg, Copenhagen (bronze inscribed "S"); the Virginia Museum of Fine Arts, Richmond (bronze inscribed "HER D"); the Baltimore Museum of Art, Maryland (bronze without letter); the Museum of Fine Arts, Boston (bronze without letter); the Museum Boijmans-van Beuningen, Rotterdam (bronze without letter); the Foundation Bührle, Zurich (bronze without letter); Sainsbury Center for Visual Arts, University of East Anglia, Norwich, England (bronze without letter); Museu de Arte de Sao Paulo (bronze without letter); the Tate Gallery, London (bronze without letter); and in various private collections. Two examples in plaster cast by Palazzolo are known, one of which is at the Joslyn Art Museum in Omaha, Nebraska.

Degas's *Little Dancer* inaugurated Modernism in sculpture in three different ways: thematically, in the choice of a sharply unheroic figure from contemporary life; stylistically, by expressing her gesture, costume, characteristic movement, and expression in a naturalistic way; and technically, in the search of new materials and techniques.

ANNA TAHINCI

Further Reading

Kendall, Richard, *Degas and the Little Dancer*, New Haven, Connecticut: Yale University Press, and Omaha, Nebraska: Joslyn Art Museum, 1998

DOROTHY DEHNER 1901–1994 *United States*

Dorothy Dehner began her career as a visual artist in the late 1920s. She did not begin sculpting until the 1950s, but her art training prior to that time significantly impacted her later sculptural style. While attending the Art Students League in New York City, Dehner abandoned her plan to study sculpture due to the conservative nature of the program; she instead studied painting with the abstract art instructors Jan Matulka and John Graham. Over the years Dehner's paintings shifted in style from abstraction to representational works. In the 1940s she created a series of Surrealist-inspired paintings with desolate landscapes and emaciated, disfigured human forms. By the late 1940s she returned to the abstract work she had abandoned earlier in her career. Her ink-and-watercolor *Star Cage* (1948), which served as a model for her husband David Smith's sculpture of the same name, illustrates her return to abstraction.

The scholar Joan Marter maintains that Dehner's representational work was a rebellious act against Smith, who was pressuring her to paint in abstraction. In addition to viewing Dehner's work as a response to the war-torn culture of the mid 20th century, Marter has suggested that it is also autobiographical, relating directly to Dehner's abusive relationship with Smith. Dehner herself expressed the oppressive nature of being the wife of Smith and its impact on her art career: "I defy any woman who is married to David Smith to become a sculptor. I couldn't even be an artist with David. Deep, deep, deep inside I felt that I was an artist. I was painting all the time, and I did some damn good work" (see DeBethune, 1994). Dehner left Smith for six months in 1945, and they divorced in 1952. It was not until her divorce from Smith that Dehner began to work actively as a sculptor.

Beginning in 1952 Dehner shifted her focus to printmaking, studying in New York at Atelier 17 and the Pratt Graphic Art Center, and in Albuquerque, New Mexico, at the Tamarind Institute. Her works on paper have been described as highly sculptural, and, indeed, she returned to sculpture, an ambition she had held since her days at the Art Students League, at the same time she was experimenting in printmaking. In 1955 she attended the Sculpture Center in New York and began to work actively as a sculptor. As she explained, "The minute I started working in sculpture I felt that it was something I had been doing all my life" (see Marter, 1993). Almost immediately Dehner gained recognition for her sculpture, including a solo show at the Jewish Museum in New York (1965) only ten years after she had made a serious commitment to the medium, followed by solo exhibitions at the Jane Voorhees Zimmerli Art Museum, New Brunswick, New Jersey (1984), the Phillips Collection, Washington D.C. (1990), and the Katonah Museum of Art, Katonah, New York (1993).

Dehner's first sculptures were small-scale bronzes, generally less than 1.5 meters in height, cast from wax-slab constructions. She developed a unique technique for casting her sculpture, using wax models to create solid rather than hollow bronze forms. She repeatedly based her sculptures on paintings and drawings from her earlier years. Often architectonic in overall design, they combine geometric and organic shapes into abstract constructions.

In the tradition of Abstract Expressionism, Dehner's sculpture aims to uncover universal principles as spiritual nourishment for a world ravaged by the destructive forces of war. Her search for spiritual origins can be seen in *Rites of Sal Safaeni #1*, inspired by a subterranean ritual chamber from the Neolithic period that she viewed on a trip to Malta in 1936. *Reliquary Kingdom #2* also invokes the sacred, in which a variety of individualized abstract shapes reminiscent of African sculpture are embedded in a bronze stand that connects them. Dehner further explored the interrelationship of abstract objects in *Encounter*, in which six bronze structures similar in shape but of differing heights are arranged in a cluster. Works such as *Queen* and *Egyptian King* invoke the heroism that also characterizes Abstract Expressionism. *Queen* emphasizes solidity of form and is decorated with protruding bronze elements suggesting hieroglyphics, while *Egyptian King* is characterized by more highly organized, open geometric forms that give the sculpture a weightlessness and a direct connection to the surrounding environment. Although their titles reference royalty, there is a contemplative understatement to these sculptures due to their small scale. *Signpost* is an example of Dehner's totemic sculpture; although clearly reminiscent of a human form, its exaggerated flatness gives it an emblematic quality, and the title suggests that the form is symbolic of something beyond a literal reading of the work.

After working in bronze constructions Dehner experimented with wood, steel, and aluminum. The wood sculpture *Window with View* is reminiscent of Louise Nevelson with its boxlike shapes, but it is distinguished by a far more organized, open, and geometric design. When Dehner began working with steel, she enlarged her sculptures to the monumental size characteristic of other Abstract Expressionist works. *Scaffold*, over two meters high, is an example, and is similar to earlier bronze sculptures by Dehner except for its large scale. She constructed the approximately four-meter-high *Sanctum with Window II*, an aluminum wall construction based on an earlier bronze, as an outdoor sculpture. Two large solid aluminum forms embrace a rectangular central element filled with geometric shapes. As in other works, the construction design is open to engage the surrounding environment. Owing to loss of vision beginning in 1986, Dehner's later works required close collaborative efforts with a fabricator.

Throughout her life Dehner experimented in a variety of artistic styles and media. With a career that spanned more than 60 years, she created a large body of work that has yet to be examined thoroughly. As with Abstract Expressionist sculpture in general, more scholarship is needed regarding the historical and cultural roots of Dehner's work and its relationship to postwar culture, as well as the symbolic content of individual sculptures.

CYNTHIA FOWLER

See also **Abstract Expressionism; Smith, David**

Biography

Born in Cleveland, Ohio, 23 December 1901. Traveled in Europe, 1925 and 1935; studied at Art Students League, New York City, 1925–31; married to sculptor David Smith, 1927–52; began artistic career as an abstract painter, 1920s; shifted to representational and then Surrealist work, through the 1930s and 1940s; began to work actively as a sculptor in 1955, making small-scale bronzes; served on art faculty at Barnard College, 1952–56; first solo exhibition of sculpture, at Willard Gallery, New York, 1957; became member of Federation of Modern Sculptors and Sculptors Guild, 1957; sculpture exhibited at Whitney Annual Exhibition, New York, 1960; included in Paris exhibition Aspects of American Sculpture, 1960; ten-year retrospective at Jewish Museum, New York, 1965; changed material for sculpture to wood, 1974; began making monumental steel sculptures, 1981; received award for outstanding achievement in art from Woman's Caucus for Art, 1983; award of distinction at National Sculpture Conference, Cincinnati, Ohio, 1987; solo exhibitions at The Phillips Collection, Washington, D.C., and Twining Fine Art, New York, 1990; retrospective at Katonah Museum of Art, Katonah, New York, 1993; Died in New York City, United States, 22 September 1994.

Selected Works

1956   *Signpost*; bronze; private collection of John and Judith Hannan

1958   *Reliquary Kingdom #2*; bronze; private collection of Wilder Green

1959   *Rites of Sal Safaeni #1*; bronze; Jewett Arts Center, Wellesley College, Massachusetts, United States

1960   *Queen*; bronze; Twining Gallery, New York City, United States

1969   *Encounter*; bronze; Twining Gallery, New York City, United States

1972   *Egyptian King*; bronze; Twining Gallery, New York City, United States

1979   *Window with View*; wood; Jane Voorhees Zimmerli Museum, Rutgers University, New Brunswick, New Jersey, United States

1986   *Scaffold*; corten steel; Twining Gallery, New York City, United States

1990–91 *Sanctum with Window II*; painted aluminum; Andre Emmerich Gallery, New York City, United States

Further Reading

DeBethune, Elizabeth, "Dorothy Dehner," *Art Journal* 53 (Spring 1994)

Gibson, Ann Eden, *Abstract Expressionism: Other Politics*, New Haven, Connecticut: Yale University Press, 1997

Glaubinger, Jane, *Dorothy Dehner: Drawings, Prints, Sculpture*, Cleveland, Ohio: Cleveland Museum of Art, 1995

Jewish Museum, *Dorothy Dehner: Ten Years of Sculpture*, New York: Jewish Museum, 1965

Keane-White, Dorothy, *Dorothy Dehner, Sculpture, and Works on Paper*, New York: Twining Gallery, and Allentown, Pennsylvania: Muhlenberg College, 1988

Marter, Joan M., "Dorothy Dehner," *Woman's Art Journal* 1 (fall 1980/winter 1981)

Marter, Joan M., *Dorothy Dehner: Sixty Years of Art*, Katonah, New York: Katonah Museum of Art, 1993

Marter, Joan M., "Postwar Sculpture Re-viewed," *Art Journal* 53 (Winter 1994)

Marter, Joan M., and Sandra Kraskin, *Dorothy Dehner: A Retrospective of Sculpture, Drawings, and Paintings*, New York: Baruch College Gallery, 1991

Marter, Joan M., and Judith McCandless, *Dorothy Dehner and David Smith: Their Decades of Search and Fulfillment*, New Brunswick, New Jersey: Jane Voorhees Zimmerli Museum, 1984

Phillips, Lisa, *The Third Dimension: Sculpture of the New York School*, New York: Whitney Museum of American Art, 1984

Polcari, Stephen, *Abstract Expressionism, and the Modern Experience*, Washington, D.C: Smithsonian Institute Press, 1990; Cambridge and New York: Cambridge University Press, 1991

JEAN DELCOUR 1631–1707 *Belgian*

Jean Delcour was perhaps the most prolific Baroque sculptor of the *Cité ardente* ("burning city," or Liège), the artistic center of the former Principality of Liège. His catalogue runs to nearly 200 works spread over a variety of forms: rood screens, altars, pulpits, fountains, chimneypieces, funerary monuments, reliefs, ornaments, and, above all, statues. He worked not only in wood (chiefly limewood [lindenwood]), but also in marble and ivory, and he also produced maquettes for statues in bronze and silver.

A number of project drawings by his hand prove that Delcour was also capable of planning decorative schemes in their entirety. In these he was particularly fond of the contrast between black and white marbles, introducing mottled marble only rarely. This preference gave his large decorative pieces, such as the high altar at Herckenrode or the funerary monument of Allamont, a Classical air that contrasts with the animated style of his statues. In addition to his numerous signed works, the recently discovered partial copy of the *livre de raison* (account book) in which Delcour recorded his output has made it possible to attribute a considerable number of sculptures to him with greater certainty.

Delcour's earliest surviving work is the fine bronze crucifixion from the Pont des Arches in Liège, produced in 1663, two years after the artist had returned there from Rome. Nothing else is known from his hand until 1666, when he began work on the Fountain of St. John the Baptist in the rue Hors-Château in Liège. This piece, which possesses a number of weaknesses, was followed by one of his masterpieces, the funerary monument of Eugène Albert d'Allamont at Ghent, for which he signed the contract in 1667. This monument clearly displays the influence of Gianlorenzo Bernini, whose work Delcour studied in Rome. In this and other works of Delcour's first period, the figures are swathed in cloaks whose lines closely follow the contours of the body in a way that recalls François du Quesnoy's *St. Susanna.* By introducing the wind as a full participant in his compositions, Delcour discovered other possibilities for the treatment of drapery. Wind made its first appearance in the d'Allamont *Virgin*, in which the artist created his first known example of "flying" drapery. Bernini's influence is evident. From the outset of Delcour's career until its close, his angels exhibit the most complex poses, and the wind that gives life to their drapery again calls to mind Berniniesque models.

Over the course of Delcour's second stylistic phase, the drapery continued to emphasize the main joints of the body but became more detached from it, to the point of extending autonomously in space. An analysis of the allegorical figure for the Society of Jesus in the Church of St. Loup at Namur, Belgium (*ca.* 1677), which exhibits both approaches simultaneously, allows the differences to be clearly appreciated. The composition of the upper half conformed to the approach of the first period: the drapery of the cloak that clings to the shoulders and arms was structured by ribbed folds with a relatively uniform outline. In the same spirit, the "torch" is made up of more or less regular "links." It is notable that the general volume of this "torch" is starkly detached from the rest of the drapery, as if it had been added on. In the lower part, the flying drapery represents the emergence of the cloth, which frees itself from the structure of the body to acquire its own autonomy and unfold in space. This flying drapery is still distinguished from what followed in the second period, chiefly through the lack of modulation of the relief by means of more or less pronounced variations in thickness that alternately separate the material from the body and bring it closer. It was specifically these modulations in relief that created multiple variations in light value and gave rise to the "vibrato" so prized by Baroque sculptors.

Over the course of his second period, during which Delcour seems to have been most productive, the artist gave further proof of his great skill in bringing drapery to life by splitting up the surfaces to create an extended range of light values. The ribbed folds, which tend to be deeply incised, increase the range of nuances still further. Delcour's flying drapery was more turbulent and more Berniniesque than that of any other Liegois sculptor of the Baroque. Over this second stylistic period, a number of his best works exhibit new possibilities in modeling. The following are especially noteworthy: the high altar of the abbey church at Herckenrode, the series of large statues in the Church of St. James in Liège, and the *Virgin* of the Fountain of Vinâve-d'Ile in Liège, as well as the funerary monument of Walter de Liverlo and his wife, of which only the dead Christ remains (Cathedral of St. Paul, Liège, Belgium)

The works that have survived from the end of the artist's career—that is to say, the beginning of the 18th century—are much less interesting. Analysis of several major works reveals that from 1700, at which time Delcour was 69 years old, their execution was entrusted to his pupil Jean Hans, whereas the master merely produced the clay maquettes and perhaps a few intricate parts, such as the heads and hands.

Delcour may have been the most important representative of the Berniniesque influence in Liège, yet he had no noteworthy followers. Hans, who continued to exploit his master's models, was succeeded by Jacques Vivroux and other even less talented imitators. Delcour's main rival, the sculptor Arnold Hontoire, surrounded himself with skillful collaborators and gifted pupils such as Robert Verburg, Cornelis Vander Veken, and Renier Rendeux. Within his art, Delcour was able to develop a personal synthesis of various stylistic currents popular in Rome during the 17th century. His talents as a contractor and ornamentalist led him, with the help of his collaborators and pupils, to undertake the decoration, in accordance with the taste of the time, of a good many buildings in the territory of the former principality of Liège.

MICHEL LEFFTZ

See also **Bernini, Gianlorenzo; du Quesnoy, François; Netherlands and Belgium**

Biography

Baptized in Hamoir, Belgium, 13 August 1631. Son of cabinetmaker; brother to painter Jean Gilles Delcour. Trained by Robert Arnold Henrard; traveled to Rome, 1648; influenced by style and association with Gianlorenzo Bernini; returned through France, 1657, then settled in Liège, Belgium, *ca.* 1660–63, with commissions from local patrons; stayed briefly in Paris, 1665; became a member of Guild of Stonemasons, Liège, 1668; rented house in Quartier de l'Ile, Liège, 1667; lived with brother Jean-Gilles, along with only pupil, Jean Hans. Died in Liège, Belgium, 4 April 1707.

Selected Works

1663   *Christ on the Cross*, for the Pont des Arches; bronze; Cathedral of St. Paul, Liège, Belgium

1666–68 Fountain of St. John the Baptist; bronze; rue Hors-Château, Liège, Belgium

1667–72 Funerary monument of Eugène Albert d'Allamont; marble; Cathedral of St. Bavo, Ghent, Belgium

1672–94 High altar for former abbey church of Herkenrode; polychrome wood, marble; Church of Our Lady, Hasselt, Belgium

1682–95 Six statues of saints; polychrome wood; Church of St. James, Liège, Belgium

1690–96 Nine statues of saints for Church of St. Anthony; polychrome wood; Musée d'art religieux et d'art Mosan, Liège, Belgium

1692   *St. Catherine*; polychrome wood; Church of St. Catherine, Liège, Belgium

1692   *Immaculate Conception*; polychrome wood; (former abbey church), Floreffe, Belgium

1696   *Dead Christ*; marble; Cathedral of St. Paul, Liège, Belgium

1697–99 Perron fountain; stone, marble; Place du Marché, Liège, Belgium

1704   *St. Roch*; polychrome wood; Church of St. Catherine, Liège, Belgium

1704–07 Fourteen reliefs in Chapel of the Holy Sacrament; marble; Church of St. Martin, Liège, Belgium

Further Reading

Lefftz, Michel, "La sculpture baroque liègeoise," (dissertation), Université Catholique de Louvain, 1998

Lemeunier, Albert, *Jean Del Cour et la sculpture baroque à Liège: Chefs-d'oeuvre du Musée d'art religieux et d'art Mosan* (exhib. cat.), Liège, France: *Musée d'art religieux et d'art Mosan*, 1994

Lesuisse, René, *Le sculpteur Jean Del Cour, sa vie, son oeuvre, son evolution, son style, son influence*, Nivelles, Belgium: s.l., 1953

DE LIÈE, JEAN

See **Jean [Hennequin] de Lièe**

DELLA QUERCIA, JACOPO

See **Quercia, Jacopo della**

DELLA ROBBIA

See **Robbia, Della, Family**

DELLA VALLE, FILIPPO

See **Valle, Filippo della**

DELPHI CHARIOTEER

See **Charioteer from the Sanctuary of Apollo at Delphi**

LAURENT DELVAUX 1696–1778 *Belgian*

Laurent Delvaux is best known for his extravagant pulpits in the great churches of Ghent and Nivelles, towering compositions in marble and oak, encrusted with a profusion of naturalistic ornaments. These virtuoso exercises are but one aspect of a long and diverse career, during which the artist blended Classical and Baroque elements for sculpture in the Counter Reformation churches of Belgium and also satisfied secular patrons, first in Augustan (Neoclassical) England and then as court sculptor to two successive regents of the Austrian Netherlands.

After training in a provincial studio, Delvaux worked under Pierre-Denis Plumier in Brussels and then in London. Plumier was alert to international developments and combined naturalistic elements from his native tradition with Classical allusions, a formula refined by Delvaux during his mature years. Delvaux's first known carving, the allegorical figure of *Time* for a monument designed by Plumier for the Duke of Buckingham in Westminster Abbey, belongs to the Flemish tradition, but thereafter his English monuments carved in tandem with Peter Scheemakers became increasingly Classical in feeling.

Commissions for garden ornaments gave Delvaux the opportunity to carve convincingly realistic figures. The colossal *Hercules* for Lord Castlemaine's gardens at Wanstead (teamed with an *Omphale* by Scheemakers) is a powerful, muscular figure. By contrast, the tender group of *Vertumnus and Pomona*, pendant to Scheemakers's *Apollo and Venus* and for the Duke of Chandos at Cannons, gave Delvaux his first opportunity to explore a favorite theme, the subtle interaction between pairs of figures.

In 1728 Delvaux traveled to Rome with an introduction from Sir Andrew Fountaine to Cardinal Corsini (later Pope Clement XII). Delvaux spent five fruitful years there, making drawings of antique and more recent sculpture and marble copies of excavated works, particularly for the Duke of Bedford. He also carved two delicate angels of colossal size for a major decorative program, the Basilica of the Royal Palace at Mafra, Portugal.

Delvaux returned to Brussels in 1732 with an introduction from Pope Clement to the regent, the Archduchess Marie-Elisabeth, who in 1733 appointed him her court sculptor. During the 1730s he contributed extensively to decorative programs in two great churches in Nivelles, providing an ambitious reredos group of the *Conversion of St. Paul* originally for St. Paul's and in the Collegiate Church of Sainte-Gertrude, roundel portraits of bishops and seated personifications of *Strength* and *Prudence* above the south door. These two commissions made his reputation, and throughout the rest of his career he was in demand for devotional figures in religious foundations throughout the Low Countries.

Work on an elaborate pulpit for the Cathedral of St. Bavo, Ghent, began in 1741. Below the pulpit is an

Detail of the Pulpit at the Cathedral of St. Bavo, Ghent
Photograph courtesy Ingrid Roscoe and © A.C.L. Bruxelles

allegorical group of *Christian Truth Triumphing over Time* (an ideal female figure juxtaposed with a bearded old man), and behind is a tree, stretching up above the preaching platform to a sounding board encrusted with foliage and putti. Delvaux's other pulpits are modest by comparison. In 1743–44 he carved a group of Elias and the Angel for the Carmelite church in Nivelles and later in 1770–72 a last tableau of *Christ and the Samaritan*, which again explores tension between a male and female figure.

Delvaux received only one monumental commission after leaving England in 1728, for General Leonard-Matthias Van der Noot's memorial in the Carmelite church, Brussels. All that remains is a pensive seated figure of *Minerva* and two putti.

After Charles of Lorraine's accession as regent in 1750, Delvaux was employed principally on secular projects. His groups of tussling cherubs representing the *Elements* and *Seasons* for the Royal Park at Tervuren were inspired by the sculpture of François du Quesnoy, a sculptor whose sweetly ideal figures find frequent echoes in Delvaux's work. Less appealing is a series of terms with white marble heads and feet, set in blue consoles.

During the mid 1760s Delvaux was occupied with sculpture for the facades of the Royal Palace in Brussels. He provided juvenile representations of the Cardinal Virtues for the balustrades, relief panels of cherubs playing at Peace and War in panels below, a tympanum scene of the *Triumph of Flora*, and sensuous female figures of Ethical Virtues. His final contribution, perhaps the most prestigious of his career, was a majestic statue of *Hercules* at the foot of the grand palatial staircase.

INGRID ROSCOE

See also **Netherlands and Belgium**

Biography

Born in Ghent, Belgium, 17 January 1696. Trained with Gery Helderenberg in Ghent, and from 1713 to 1714 with Pierre Denis Plumier; worked in Brussels and then London; in partnership with Peter Scheemakers, 1722–28; lived in Rome, 1728–33; returned to Brussels, 1732, where he was appointed court sculptor by Archduchess Marie-Elisabeth; established a large workshop in Nivelles, Belgium; retained his official post until 1777, working for two successive regents. Died in Nivelles, Belgium, 24 February 1778.

Selected Works

1721–22 *Time*, for monument to John Sheffield, First Duke of Buckingham (with Peter Scheemakers); marble; Westminster Abbey, London, England

1722 *Hercules*; marble; Waddesdon Manor, Buckinghamshire, England

1724–25 Monument to First Earl and Countess of Rockingham (with Peter Scheemakers); marble; Rockingham, Northamptonshire, England

before 1728 *Vertumnus and Pomona*; marble; Victoria and Albert Museum, London, England

1730s Roundel portraits of bishops, and *Strength* and *Prudence*; marble; Collegiate Church of Sainte-Gertrude, Nivelles, Belgium

1730–32 Angels; marble; Royal Palace, Mafra, Portugal

1736–38 *Conversion of St. Paul* and other woodwork; oak; Collegiate Church of Sainte-Gertrude, Nivelles, Belgium

1741–45 Pulpit; marble, oak, gilding; Cathedral of St. Bavo, Ghent, Belgium

1743–44 Group of Elias and the Angel for pulpit; oak; Carmelite church, Nivelles, Belgium

1746 Monument to Leonard-Matthias Van der Noot; marble (destroyed); fragments in Rijksmuseum, Amsterdam, the Netherlands

1760 Four groups of *Seasons* and *Elements*; marble; Royal Park, Tervuren, Belgium

1768–70 *Hercules*; marble; Royal Palace, Brussels, Belgium

Further Reading

Avery, C., "Laurent Delvaux's Sculpture at Woburn Abbey," *Apollo* 118 (October 1983)

Delattre, Jean Luc, and Rene Laurent, *Laurent Delvaux, 1696–1778* (exhib. cat.), Nivelles, Belgium: Collegiale Sainte-Gertrude, 1978

Jacobs, A., "L'archange Raphael et l'ange tutélaire du Royaume du Portugal Sculptés a Rome vers 1730–1730 par Laurent Delvaux," *Gazette des Beaux-Arts* (September 1996)

Jacobs, A., *Laurent Delvaux: Gand, 1696–Nivelles, 1778*, Paris: Arthena (1999) (comprehensive and up to date)

Physick, J., and M. Whinney (editors), *Sculpture in Britain, 1530–1830*, Paris: Arthena, 1988

Popelier, F. (compiler), *Laurent Delvaux, les terres cuites dans les collections publiques belges* (exhib. cat.), Nivelles, France: Imprimerie Lavaux, 1975

Vertue, George, *Vertue Note Books*, 7 vols., Oxford: University Press, 1930–55 (an invaluable early source)

WALTER DE MARIA 1935– *United States*

Walter de Maria's career has engaged a broad variety of cultural categories including Fluxus, Minimalism, Land art, Conceptual art, avant-garde music, and film. This diverse practice is anchored in his consistent explorations of and challenges to the medium of sculpture over four decades and into the 21st century. As a result De Maria plays a vital and innovative role in the history of twentieth century art.

De Maria, like many of his contemporaries, began his career as a painter, earning his master of art degree at the University of California, Berkeley in 1959. During the late 1950s, he began sculpting simple boxlike forms that would become one prototype for Minimalist sculpture in the 1960s. At the same time he was performing as a musician and was involved in West Coast Happenings; both activities were often in collaboration with the important composer and innovator of minimal music, LaMonte Young. As a result, de Maria arrived in New York in 1960 with an established interdisciplinary interest that would greatly inform the development of his sculptural work.

Seemingly simple objects and configurations that explore complex experiences for the viewer constitute de Maria's sculptural practice. For example, *Boxes for Meaningless Work* (1961), consists of two small wooden boxes on one wooden base, with an inscription instructing the viewer to transfer things back and forth from one box to another with the accompanying dictum "Be aware that what you are doing is meaningless." His equally conceptualist *High Energy Bar*

(1966), a small, minimal, stainless steel form reminiscent of an elongated gold bar in shape, is accompanied by a certificate of lifetime ownership and responsibility for the owner. Other sculptures evoke more complex associations through symbolic shapes such as the swastika, as in *Museum Piece* (1965), or a cross, such as *Cross* (1965); or they require careful visual consideration of subtle mathematical configurations such as a series of five, six, seven, eight and nine-sided open stainless steel polygons, such as *5 Through 9* (1973), or different manifestations of equal areas, as in the *Equal Area Series* (1977). That the seemingly straightforward or mathematical may be intimately connected with the more mysterious and perhaps even the sublime becomes apparent in de Maria's work as well. His *360° I Ching 64 Sculptures* (1981), presents the sixty-four possible hexagrams associated with the ancient philosophy of the *I-Ching: Book of Changes*. Over many decades, de Maria's work has explored the variant physical and psychological experience that even the most the minimal form may engender.

An early text piece by de Maria, *On the Importance of Natural Disasters, 1960*, indicates the degree to which this experience might extend: "If all of the people who go to museums could just feel an earthquake. Not to mention the sky and the ocean." De Maria explored this extreme desire most explicitly in his site-related work, much of which has been historically and critically associated with Land art or Earthworks. He conceived of massive, remote, site-related pieces in the desert as early as 1961, but it was not until 1968 that he actually reached the desert to produce work, the first of which was two parallel lines hand-drawn in chalk on the floor of the Mojave desert in California, *Mile Long Drawing* (1968). The reference to the body (and the organic) was complete in the fact that de Maria used his own body height—lying on the ground—as the unit of measure that established the distance between the two parallel lines. De Maria's *Mile Long Drawing* shares affinities with other postwar artists, who were also exploring the temporal and spatial possibilities of site as an aspect of sculptural practice, such as Richard Long, whose *A Line Made by Walking England, 1967* is an investigation of both the extended possibilities of sculpture into nontraditional spaces and the integration of sculpture with the process of making; and Richard Serra, whose *Splashing* (1968) and *Casting* (1969) were realized by throwing molten lead against a wall and leaving the lead to embed onto the site. De Maria, Long, Serra, and many others were instrumental in manipulating a variety of materials and activities as a means to reconceive the physical and conceptual boundaries of three-dimensional artwork.

De Maria's most well known and most extensive work is *The Lightning Field* (1971–77), permanently installed outside of Quemado, New Mexico. This work consists of a grid of 400 precisely positioned stainless steel poles, one mile by one kilometer, six meters in size. Each pole is precisely aligned in vertical, horizontal and diagonal rows and is embedded in the ground so as to create a perfectly flat plane across their pinnacles aimed at the sky. The proportions of the perimeter of the grid also embody the golden mean, an ancient mathematic ratio derived from nature. This meticulous array exists against the remote and austere landscape of the high western plateaus of New Mexico. It is to be experienced over the course of twenty-four hours; viewers must make reservations to visit the work and are driven out to the site and dropped off for an overnight stay in the comfortable quarters of a homesteader's cabin positioned there. The work extends then not only into the vast space of the landscape but also into the infinite number of shifts in light, weather, and conversation that occur over the course of a day. While precise in its material and structural components, *The Lightning Field* echoes a wide range of experience that resists interpretive control.

Other works from this period continue to question the limits of sculptural practice, first widely critiqued by de Maria's peers the Minimalists and Conceptualists in New York City. *Buried Kilometer* (1977) consists of a brass rod, one kilometer long, drilled vertically into the earth. In its physical form the rod represents a massive spatial potential and enormous technical undertaking yet is invisible to the viewer, save one simple circular form encased within a red sandstone square serving as a marker. More visible, but equally challenging are the three different manifestations of "Earth Rooms"—entire galleries filled with bare earth in a gesture that intimately links context with sculpture and subtly comments on the place of art in a commodified world. The last of these, *The New York Earth Room* (1977) remains on permanent exhibition at a gallery space on Wooster Street in New York City. De Maria's oeuvre also includes several films, musical compositions, hundreds of drawings, elaborate commissions, and ambitious plans for sculptures that span continents, or test the established boundaries of art in other ways. His career demonstrates an astute and critical understanding both of the growing possibilities for art and the limits of various art world institutions.

De Maria's insistence on the complexity of experience in art has coincided with a careful and considered choice to remain silent in the interpretation of his own work. Thus in a thoroughly complex and postmodern era of disparate artists' voices, multiplying reproductions, and documentations, de Maria's contribution in this realm has been limited to a few textual works from the early 1960s or carefully chosen conceptual photographic pieces contributed to magazines and catalogs in the decades since. As a result de Maria often occupies an ambiguous place in historical accounts of postwar sculpture. However, de Maria's practice serves as a crucial example for understanding the complex ramifications of postwar sculptural practices—in which one finds sculpture pushing the limits of that term itself.

JANE MCFADDEN

See also **Andre, Carl; Contemporary Sculpture; Heizer, Michael; Installation; Long, Richard; Morris, Robert; Performance Art; Postmodernism; Serra, Richard; Smithson, Robert; Turrell, James**

Biography

Born in Albany, California, 1 October 1935. Attended the University of California, Berkeley from 1953 to 1959; earned a B.F.A. in history and a M.F.A. in art; moved to New York in 1960 where he has been a practicing artist for the past four decades. Published essays on art in LaMonte Young's *An Anthology*, collections of critical discussions of avant-garde music and arts in 1963; became active in Happenings in both New York City and San Francisco during the 1960s; performed as a drummer for the avant-garde band The Velvet Underground in 1963. Started making pieces in metal (in addition to wood) in 1965; participated in the seminal *Primary Structures* exhibition of Minimalist art along with Carl Andre, Donald Judd, and Robert Morris at the Jewish Museum, New York City, 1966; emerged as a leader of Earthworks movement in 1968 with *Mile Long Drawing* (Mojave Desert, 1968). Continues to work on large-scale, site-specific sculptural and installation-related work in New York City.

Selected Works

1961   *Boxes for Meaningless Work*; plywood; collection of the artist
1965   *Cage*; stainless steel; Museum für Moderne Kunst, Frankfurt am Main, Germany
1966–96 *High Energy Bar*; stainless steel; unlimited edition, including The Menil Collection, Houston, Texas, United States
1968   *The Munich Earth Room*, 50 cubic meters of dirt covering 72 square meters installed at Galerie Heiner Friedrich, Munich, Germany; no longer exists; moved to 141 Wooster Street, New York City, United States in 1977
1968–69 *Bed of Spikes*; stainless steel; Kunstmuseum Basel, Switzerland
1969   *Hard Core*; 16mm Eastman Color Film, 28 minutes, natural leather, metal plaque; edition of 100, including the Whitney

Museum of American Art, New York City, United States
1971–77 *The Lightning Field*; 400 stainless steel poles permanently installed in Quemado, New Mexico; maintained by the Dia Art Foundation, New York City, United States
1977   *Vertical Earth Kilometer*; solid brass rod, earth, red sandstone; Dia Art Foundation, New York City, United States, commissioned for Documenta VI and the City of Kassel, Germany
1977   *The New York Earth Room*; 250 cubic yards of earth in 335 square meters of gallery space; removed from its original location, Galerie Heiner Friedrich, Munich, Germany; 141 Wooster Street, New York City, New York, United States; Dia Art Foundation, New York City, United States
1979   *Broken Kilometer*; 500 solid brass rods; Dia Art Foundation, New York City, United States
1981   *360° I Ching/64 Sculptures*; 576 lacquered wood rods; commissioned by Dia Art Foundation, New York City, United States

Further Reading

Baker, Kenneth, *Minimalism: Art of Circumstance*, New York: Abbeville Press, Publishers, 1988
Bourdon, David, "Walter de Maria: The Singular Experience," *Art International*, vol. 12 (1968)
Celant, Germano, *Walter de Maria*, Milan: Fondazione Prada, 1999
Kellein, Thomas, *Walter de Maria: Five Continent Sculpture*, Stuttgart: Staatsgalerie Stuttgart, 1987
Meyer, Franz, *Walter de Maria*, Frankfurt am Main: Museum für Moderne Kunst, 1991
Schoon, Talitha, ed., *Walter de Maria*, Rottterdam: Museum Boymans-van Beuningen, 1984
Tiberghien, Gilles, *Land Art*, Princeton: Princeton Architectural Press, 1995

DENMARK
See **Scandinavia**

DE NOLE FAMILY
See **Nole, de, Family**

DEPOSITION GROUP
See **Lamentation and Deposition Group**

DE' ROSSI, PROPERZIA
See **Rossi, Properzia de'**

DE' ROSSI, VINCENZO
See **Rossi, Vincenzo de'**

DESIDERIO DA SETTIGNANO *ca.* 1429–1464 *Italian*

Desiderio da Settignano's career spanned only about a dozen years (*ca.* 1453–64), but his achievements during this time had a profound impact on the course of Italian Renaissance sculpture. For his technique, he must be considered among the foremost stone carvers of his generation, and his mastery of *relievo schiacciato* (relief sculpture emphasizing light and shadow through carving methods) is rivaled only by its inventor, Donatello. A Renaissance contemporary once characterized Desiderio as "sweet and fair" because of the delicacy of his carving and the charming vivacity of his figures. Today he is recognized not only for his technical brilliance but also for his contributions to the design of monuments, pictorial relief, and decorative ornament, and for the sensitive characterization of his figures.

Desiderio's oeuvre revolves around his three most important and best documented works, all in Florentine churches: the tomb monument of Carlo Marsuppini in the Church of Santa Croce, the sacramental tabernacle for the Church of San Lorenzo, and his statue of Mary Magdalene in the Church of Santa Trinità. The tomb monument of Carlo Marsuppini, state chancellor of Florence, is the only work by Desiderio still in its original setting. Located on the left aisle wall of Santa Croce, it complements a similar monument located across the nave and sculpted by Bernardo Rossellino. However, Desiderio's creation is more elaborate, contains more decorative embellishments, and is carved more meticulously. Its influence was enormous and typifies Desiderio's artistic contributions as the most accomplished sculptor working within various genres.

The sacramental tabernacle for San Lorenzo has been called by John Pope-Hennessy the outstanding decorative achievement of the century. With this work, Desiderio displays an advanced combination of pictorial illusionism, mathematical perspective, and decorative ornament unseen in Florentine marble carving until that time. Its influence was so pervasive that practically all Tuscan tabernacles of the second half of the 15th century are variations on Desiderio's. The *Blessing Christ Child* that stands atop the monument became such a popular image that for a time a copy was put in its place so Desiderio's original could be carried in processions and made more visible.

The theme of youth proved to be of particular importance in Desiderio's art, as witnessed in his portrait busts of children, now located in Washington, D.C., and the unique *Laughing Child* in Vienna. The latter is the most animated of all such busts of the period. Desiderio also introduced young putti as shield bearers on his Marsuppini monument, carved youthful candle

bearers on the San Lorenzo tabernacle, and emphasized youth in his two depictions of St. John the Baptist, both in the Museo Nazionale del Bargello, Florence. Perhaps the most delightful and significant image of youth is a relief carving in the Musée du Louvre, Paris, in which young Christ and St. John the Baptist are depicted together with playful and joyous expressions. This and other such images by Desiderio thus satisfied contemporary advisements for child rearing to show the Christ Child and young St. John together as exemplars of youthful virtue.

In addition to his depictions of children, Desiderio was famous for his portrait busts of women. One such bust depicting Marietta Strozzi achieved considerable renown for its beauty, but it is now lost. Though many extant portraits of women have been ascribed to Desiderio (including several fakes), the only generally accepted attribution is the *Portrait Bust of a Woman* in the Museo Nazionale del Bargello, Florence.

In the third quarter of the 15th century, Desiderio had virtually no peer in relief carving. Desiderio achieved this success primarily through his unique ability to carve in *relievo schiacciato*, which offers the sculptor illusionistic and emotive benefits normally reserved for painting or drawing. Desiderio produced many Madonna and Child reliefs by this method. The reliefs were so accomplished that in 1462 Francesco Sforza, the Duke of Milan, craved an example at almost any cost, yet for unknown reasons Desiderio refused his requests. Desiderio's interpretations of the popular theme are distinguished by the nuanced characterizations of the figures and the tender interaction between mother and child. The finest independent example of his style is the Panciatichi Madonna in the Bargello, Florence. Desiderio produced other Madonna and Child reliefs in both marble and stucco, and he often used the services of specialists to help with gilding and painting the reliefs. In 1462 one such specialist, Neri di Bicci, records the sale of a gesso Madonna, and his description closely matches an example in the Victoria and Albert Museum in London that retains its original pigmentation.

Other distinguished reliefs by Desiderio include the bust of Caesar in the Musée du Louvre, the relief bust of St. John the Baptist in the Bargello, and the narrative relief of *St. Jerome in the Wilderness* in the National Gallery, Washington, D.C. This last relief combines technical skill and pictorial innovation to produce an unusual narrative effect in which the calm piety of Jerome is in sharp contrast to the implicit threat of the emerging lions and the fear of a fleeing acolyte.

The statue of *St. Mary Magdalene*, in Santa Trinità, is notable for being Desiderio's lone surviving sculpture in wood and for being well documented. It was commissioned in 1458 by an important female patron,

Annalena Malatesta, and was finished by another sculptor after Desiderio's untimely death. While 16th-century sources claim the Magdalene was finished by Benedetto da Maiano, documents indicate that Giovanni d'Andrea completed the sculpture by 1499 and that it became the property of Malatesta's notary, Pierozzo Cerbini. Malatesta and Pierozzo also commissioned from Desiderio a terracotta bust of Christ, now lost, but at the time considered unusually beautiful. Other significant lost works include the portrait bust of Marietta Strozzi, a bronze and marble base made for Donatello's *David*, and 12 portraits for the personal study of Giovanni de' Medici.

Desiderio spent his brief career almost exclusively in Florence, where his works were owned by the most prominent patrons, including members of the Medici, Rucellai, Strozzi, and Martelli families. He is also mentioned in contemporary sources as far as Milan, Urbino, and Naples. Nonetheless, some aspects of Desiderio's career remain enigmatic because of a lack of documentation. Little is known about his artistic training and workshop composition. Certainly Desiderio was inspired by the monumental achievements of Donatello and may have executed several works normally associated with him. Desiderio was also deeply influenced by the precision and delicacy of Ghiberti. While Desiderio worked closely with his brother Geri, no documented work by the latter is known. When the brother's property was divided in 1461, Geri received the stones of "macigno" and Desiderio the material in marble and clay, which may indicate the two sculptors' relative specialties.

Desiderio enjoyed close working relationships with his peers, a group that included Antonio and Bernardo Rossellino, Mino da Fiesole, Benedetto da Maiano, and Andrea del Verrocchio. The style of Desiderio and these sculptors would dominate sculpture during the latter half of the 15th century until the emergence of Michelangelo.

ARNOLD VICTOR COONIN

See also **Benedetto da Maiano; Italy: Renaissance–Baroque; Verrocchio, Andrea del**

Biography

Born in Prugniano, near Settignano, Italy, *ca.* 1429. Son of Bartolommeo di Francesco; Father and two older brothers, Francesco and Geri, were members of the stonemason's guild in Florence before him; matriculated in 1453; by 1457 shared a studio with Geri on the ground floor of a palace then owned by Antonio Panciatichi next to Santa Trinità; brothers split professionally, *ca.* 1461. Died in Florence, Italy, 16 January 1464.

Selected Works

ca. 1453–59	Tomb of Carlo Marsuppini; marble; Church of Santa Croce, Florence, Italy
ca. 1453–64	Panciatichi Madonna; marble; Museo Nazionale del Bargello, Florence, Italy
ca. 1458–64	*St. Mary Magdalene*; wood; Church of Santa Trinità, Florence, Italy (completed by Giovanni d'Andrea by 1499)
ca. 1453–64	Boni chimneypiece; *pietra serena* (sandstone); Victoria and Albert Museum, London, England
ca. 1453–64	*Laughing Child*; marble; Kunsthistorisches Museum, Vienna, Austria
ca. 1453–64	Martelli Baptist; marble; Museo Nazionale del Bargello, Florence, Italy
ca. 1453–64	*Portrait Bust of a Woman*; marble; Museo Nazionale del Bargello, Florence, Italy
ca. 1453–64	Relief bust of St. John the Baptist; *pietra serena* (sandstone); Museo Nazionale del Bargello, Florence, Italy
ca. 1453–64	*St. Jerome in the Wilderness*; marble; National Gallery of Art, Washington, D.C., United States
ca. 1453–64	*Young Christ* and *St. John the Baptist*; marble; Musée du Louvre, Paris, France
ca. 1460–64	*Bust of a Child* (known as *Vanchetoni Child*); marble; National Gallery of Art, Washington, D.C., United States
ca. 1460–64	Tabernacle; marble; Church of San Lorenzo, Florence, Italy

Further Reading

Butterfield, Andrew, Caroline Elam, and Arnold Victor Coonin, "Desiderio da Settignano's Tabernacle of the Sacrament," *Mitteilungen des Kunsthistorischen Institutes in Florenz* 43 (1999)

Cardellini, Ida, *Desiderio da Settignano*, Milan: Edizioni di Communità, 1962

Coonin, Arnold Victor, "New Documents concerning Desiderio da Settignano and Annalena Malatesta," *The Burlington Magazine* 137 (1995)

Coonin, Arnold Victor, "Portrait Busts of Children in Quattrocento Florence," *Metropolitan Museum Journal* 30 (1995)

Darr, Alan Phipps, and Brenda Preyer, "Donatello, Desiderio da Settignano and His Brothers, and 'Macigno' Sculpture for a Boni Palace in Florence," *The Burlington Magazine* 141 (1999)

Darr, Alan Phipps, and Giorgio Bonsanti (editors), *Italian Renaissance Sculpture in the Time of Donatello*, Detroit, Michigan: Founders Society, The Detroit Institute of Arts, 1985

Kurz, Otto, "A Group of Florentine Drawings for an Altar," *Journal of the Warburg and Courtauld Institutes* 18 (1955)

Pope-Hennessy, John, *An Introduction to Italian Sculpture*, 3 vols., London: Phaidon, 1963; 4th edition, 1996; see especially vol. 2, *Italian Renaissance Sculpture*

Waldman, Louis, "The Mary Magdalene in Santa Trinita by Desiderio da Settignano and Giovanni d'Andrea," *Pantheon* 58 (2000)

Wittkower, Rudolf, "Desiderio da Settignano's 'St. Jerome in the Desert,'" *Studies in the History of Art* 6/37 (1971–72)

Zuraw, Shelley E., "Desiderio da Settignano," in *The Dictionary of Art*, edited by Jane Turner, New York: Grove, and London: Macmillan, 1996

TOMB OF CARLO MARSUPPINI

Desiderio da Settignano (ca. 1429–1464)

ca. 1453–1459

marble

h. 6.13 m

Church of Santa Croce, Florence, Italy

The most celebrated of Desiderio da Settignano's creations is the tomb monument of Carlo Marsuppini, state chancellor of the Florentine Republic from 1444 to 1453. Desiderio must have received the commission shortly after Marsuppini's death in 1453, at which time Desiderio was a relatively young, yet reputable, sculptor. The exact dates of production are not documented; however, the fact that the epitaph was yet to be written in 1459 indicates a prolonged execution extending through the 1450s.

Desiderio's tomb of Carlo Marsuppini was one of the crucial commemorative monuments of the 15th century and helped determine the development of a funerary type generally called the humanist tomb. Predecessors include Bernardo Rossellino's tomb of Leonardo Bruni (*ca.* 1444), which stands directly opposite Desiderio's tomb monument in the Church of Santa Croce in Florence. In these and most later examples, the basic form consists of a Classical triumphal arch that encases an effigy resting on a bier. The bier sits against a background of porphyry stone panels, and a circular Madonna and Child relief fills the lunette, with adoring angels to each side. Additionally, the monuments usually contain full-length figures that support coats of arms or carry iconographical attributes.

Of all such tomb monuments, Desiderio's is among the most elegantly presented and certainly the most beautifully carved. In comparison with Rossellino's prior example, Desiderio accentuates the Marsuppini tomb monument as a work of elaborate sculpture and not simply as decorated architecture. In the 16th century Giorgio Vasari singled out for praise the carving of Marsuppini's sarcophagus; this portion of the monument displays some of the finest virtuoso carving in all of Renaissance sculpture. For example, Vasari declared that the wings attached to a scallop shell seem to be actual feathers and not marble. Other magnificent details of the sarcophagus include realistic leaves, rosettes, shells, and lion's-paw feet. Indeed, one key to Desiderio's fame was his ability to transform stone visually into the substance that it imitates. Through his chisel marble becomes feather, plant, fur, and flesh.

The figurative elements are equally impressive. Desiderio turns the effigy slightly toward the viewer so that one can more easily follow the expressive lines in Marsuppini's face and the unusually realistic hands. In the lunette, Desiderio carved one of the most admired Madonna and Child reliefs of the period. Characteristic of his pictorial reliefs, this composition shows the nuanced, lively visages of the characters and an evocative, tender interaction. The carving in planes of flat relief animates the wispy tufts of Christ's hair and the crisp folds of the Virgin's gown. Furthermore, their haloes and drapery ingeniously overlap the circular frame so that the figures appear to be focused by, but not enclosed within, its space. Atop the monument stand two angels that support decorative garland strands, and an important addition is the inclusion of shield-bearing putti on either side of the monument's base. The putti are typical of Desiderio's general focus on youth and add a note of youthful optimism to the sobriety of a funerary monument. Virtually all subsequent humanist monuments bear similar figures.

The iconography of the Marsuppini tomb may be largely explained by the principal role of the state

Tomb of Carlo Marsuppini
© Alinari / Art Resource, NY

427

chancellor as representative of the city in matters of foreign affairs. Especially through letters, Marsuppini championed the Florentine republican cause, which saw the city as reviving a Classical model in a new Christian context. Thus, the monument's design is a combination of architectural classicism, being used in contemporary civic architecture, fused with Christian imagery denoting salvation through Christ.

A contemporary Florentine, Luca Landucci, listed the tomb of Carlo Marsuppini as one of the distinguished monuments of the period. Its influence was immediate and pervasive and can be seen in subsequent monuments by Antonio Rossellino, Mino da Fiesole, Matteo Civitali, Francesco di Simone Ferrucci, and Andrea del Verrocchio.

Other aspects of the monument hint at further profound artistic developments that occurred during the course of its execution. Certainly, Desiderio employed many assistants on this work; pairs of similarly designed figures show marked stylistic differences in carving. Documents have yet to reveal the names of these assistants, although Desiderio's brother, Geri, has been proposed, as have other talented sculptors such as Verrocchio. Conservation work has revealed the original appearance of the monument to be more colorful and theatrical than previously assumed. The wall surface around the monument was painted so that the entire monument seemed to be enclosed within a sumptuous cloth canopy. The effects of the background design are a heightened sense of spatial illusionism—by visually disengaging the monument from the wall—and a more dramatic visual presentation of the sculptural monument as it distinguishes itself from the surrounding painted surfaces. Color was also employed to enliven sculpture, and pigment is still visible in areas such as the garlands, coffers, borders of clothing, and bier cloth.

It seems fitting that Carlo Marsuppini's epitaph begins by calling attention to the tomb itself and then to the person it commemorates. Its first line reads, "Stay and see the marbles which enshrine a great sage, one for whose mind there was not world enough." In theory, the impressiveness of the monument denotes the eminence of the individual it commemorates, but in actuality, it more rightly honors the artist who created it. The tomb of Carlo Marsuppini thus anticipates the final line of Desiderio's own epitaph, which concluded, "The life he gave to marble, marble gives to him forever."

ARNOLD VICTOR COONIN

Further Reading

Danti, Christina, et al., "Scultura e affresco: Novità dal restauro del monumento Marsuppini," *OPD Restauro* 10 (1998)

Panofsky, Erwin, *Tomb Sculpture: Its Changing Aspects from Ancient Egypt to Bernini*, New York: Abrams, 1964

Schulz, Ann Markham, "Glosses on the Career of Desiderio da Settignano," in *Verrocchio and Late Quattrocento Italian Sculpture*, edited by Steven Bule, Alan Phipps Darr, and Fiorella Superbi Gioffredi, Florence: Le Lettre, 1992

Weeks, Christopher, "The Restoration of Desiderio da Settignano's Tomb of Carlo Marsuppini in S. Croce, Florence," *The Burlington Magazine* 141 (1999)

CHARLES DESPIAU 1874–1946 *French*

The sculptor and illustrator Charles Despiau came from Mont-de-Marsan, a small, provincial town in the Landes region of southwestern France. Outside his family circle, Despiau's first art instruction was likely with a local drawing teacher by the name of Morin, who may also have modeled or sculpted busts. At the age of 17, Despiau went to Paris, where he enrolled at the École des Arts Décoratifs around 1891. Thereafter he studied at the École des Beaux-Arts.

In 1898 Despiau began to show works in exhibitions sponsored by the Société des Artistes Françaises. He already had an interest in portraiture, and in 1900 he exhibited a bust of his fiancée (Mlle. Rudel), who would become his wife in 1904. In 1900 he began to send work to exhibitions sponsored by the Société Nationale des Beaux-Arts, where he would exhibit until 1923. By 1907 Despiau had come to the attention of Auguste Rodin, who hired him as a studio assistant. Three works after Rodin's design were executed by Despiau: two marble portrait busts and a figural grouping, *The Genius of Eternal Repose* (1914), the latter part of a never-completed tribute that Rodin planned to Pierre Puvis de Chavannes.

During these years Despiau's work received positive, although not always unqualified, praise. In his comments on Despiau's work at the Salon of 1907, for example, André Peraté noted that one of Despiau's pieces was a little too caressed, another a bit cold, but that with his *Paulette* (1907), with its grave eyes and charming mouth, the sculptor approached the ingenuity of certain Egyptian work and perhaps even evoked the spirit of Donatello's *St. John*. Characterizations of Despiau's art ran the gamut over the years as reviewers saw connections with the Classical, the archaic Greek, the Egyptian, the Renaissance (some contemporaries said of Despiau, "C'est notre Donatello"), the Gothic, the art of Fontainebleau (Jean Goujon and Germain Pilon), and even elements of the truly modern.

Despite his association with Rodin, whom he regarded as his spiritual father, Despiau's own sculpture seems closer to work done by other contemporaries, including Aristide Maillol, whose nude figure studies parallel Despiau's own interest in the human body— demonstrated, for example, in his freestanding *Eve*, the shy *Female Faun*, bound to the inert matter of column and architrave, and the more provocatively positioned and seated *Bacchante*. Archetypical images of male and female nudes are recurrent themes in Despiau's art throughout his career.

After Rodin's death in 1917, Despiau set out on his own path. The postwar period offered opportunities for commemorative monuments, and Despiau won the commission for a war memorial planned for the municipality of Mont-de-Marsan. For Despiau, these were years of increasing prosperity and success as he found acknowledgment of his abilities, especially as a portrait artist, both in France and abroad. He created portraits of prominent Parisians, many of them notable women with important art-world connections, such as *Madame André Derain* and *Madame Fauré*.

In 1927 Despiau exhibited at a private gallery in New York. Thereafter, he made portrait busts of notable American subjects, including the wealthy Francophile *Mrs. Chester Dale* and the author *Anne Morrow Lindbergh*. The editor of *Vanity Fair*, Frank Crowninshield, whose personal art collections included works by Renoir and Degas, became one of Despiau's enthusiastic American patrons. He assembled a large collection of Despiau's work that was sold in New York in 1943.

Despiau received numerous honors and awards both in France and elsewhere, including participation in important exhibitions. In 1930 he received a commission to provide figures for the industrialist Emile Mayrish's tomb (1934), designed by notable French architect Auguste Perret. Despiau's formerly close association with Rodin and his growing stature as an important French sculptor of the interwar period earned him a place on the Rodin Museum board in 1934. Despiau, along with Maillol, was also asked to participate in ceremonies associated with the unveiling of Rodin's formerly controversial *Balzac* at the juncture of the Boulevard Raspail on 1 July 1939. That same year, an American patron, Mrs. Simon Guggenheim, presented Despiau's *Assia* to the Museum of Modern Art in New York City; *Time Magazine* reproduced a photograph of the life-size bronze on its art page with the declaration that "not ten classic standing nudes so esthetically satisfactory have been fashioned since the time of Rodin." American art critic Royal Cortissoz also praised Despiau, whose portraiture he regarded as the sculptor's most profound accomplishment. Despiau portrayed his subjects with a reality and grace that was both traditional and modern.

A friendship with German sculptor Arno Breker, who lived in Paris from 1927 to 1933, cast a pall over Despiau's subsequent reputation. Not only did Despiau participate in Nazi-sponsored cultural events in Paris during the Occupation period, but he also traveled to Nazi Germany in 1941, where he visited the atelier of Breker in the company of, among others, Paul Landowski, Kies Van Dongen, Maurice de Vlaminck, and André Derain. The authorship of a book on Arno Breker, composed in the first person with Despiau as the credited writer, is still an embarrassing footnote to Despiau's career. An interview Despiau gave after this trip recorded his positive impressions of what he described as the German genius for order and discipline. Whatever his private feelings about the German occupation of his country, Despiau's wartime utterances and associations did not go unpunished. After the war, the French government placed a two-year moratorium on the exhibition and sale of his work. His sculptures were excluded from the 1944 Salon d'Automne.

MARILYN BAKER

See also **Goujon, Jean; Maillol, Aristede; Pilon, Germain; Rodin, Auguste**

Biography

Born in Mont-de-Marsan, France, 4 November 1874. Moved to Paris and studied at École des Arts Décoratifs under Hector Lemaire, 1891, and at the École des Beaux-Arts under Louis Barrias, 1893–96; exhibited at the Salon des Artists Françaises, 1898–1900, the Salon de la Société Nationale, 1900–23, and the Salon des Tuileries and Salon d'Automne, beginning in 1923; received Chevalier of the Legion of Honor, 1911, Officier, 1926, and Commandeur, 1936; Officer of the Order of Leopold (Belgium), 1924; held foreign memberships in the Académie Royale de Belgique, 1929; the Academy of Fine Arts, Stockholm, Sweden, 1936; appointed professor at Académie Scandinave, 1927. Died in Paris, France, 28 October 1946.

Selected Works

1907 *Paulette*; gilded bronze; Musée Despiau-Wiérick, Mont-de-Marsan, France
1923 *Madame André Derain*; bronze; Musée de L'Annonciade, Saint-Tropez, France
1925 *Eve*; bronze; Musée Nationale d'Art Moderne, Centre Georges Pompidou, Paris, France
1925 *Female Faun*; plaster; Musée Nationale d'Art Moderne, Centre Georges Pompidou, Paris, France
1927 *Madame Fauré*; bronze; Musée Nationale d'Art Moderne, Centre Georges Pompidou, Paris, France
1929 *Bacchante*; bronze; Musée Nationale d'Art Moderne, Centre Georges Pompidou, Paris, France

1934   *Mrs. Chester Dale*; plaster; Musée
        Nationale d'Art Moderne, Centre Georges
        Pompidou, Paris, France

1937   *Assia*; bronze; Museum of Modern Art,
        New York City, United States

1939   *Anne Morrow Lindbergh*; tinted plaster;
        private collection, Paris, France

Further Reading

"Art," *Time Magazine*, 17 April 1939

Butler, Ruth, *Rodin: The Shape of Genius*, New Haven, Connecticut: Yale University Press, 1993

Cone, Michèle C., *Artists under Vichy: A Case of Prejudice and Persecution*, Princeton, New Jersey: Princeton University Press, 1992

Cortissoz, Royal, "Despiau," *New York Herald Tribune* (26 March 1939)

Curtis, Penelope, *Sculpture, 1900–1945: After Rodin*, Oxford: Oxford University Press, 1999

George, Waldemar, *Despiau*, Cologne: Kiepenheur und Witsch, 1954

Judrin, Claude, *Charles Despiau: Sculptures et dessins* (exhib. cat.), Paris: Musée Rodin, 1974

Wilson, Sarah, "Collaboration in the Fine Arts, 1940–44," in *Collaboration in France: Politics and Culture during the Nazi Occupation, 1940–1944*, edited by Gerhard Hirschfeld and Patrick Marsh, Oxford and New York: Berg, 1989

DE VRIES, ADRIAEN

See **Vries, Adriaen de**

DI GIOVANNI, BERTOLDO

See **Bertoldo di Giovanni**

DIRECT CARVING

See **Carving**

MARK DI SUVERO 1933–   *United States*

Although Mark di Suvero was born in Shanghai, China, of Venetian parents, his work exhibits qualities that have come to be critically reflective of an American sculptural aesthetic. The scale (gigantic, mimicking the expanse of geography), industrial design, and improvised raw materials (steel cables, I-beams, wooden ties, and scrap metal) collectively characterize a profound understanding of space as metaphors for freedom, landscape, and working-class values. Di Suvero's large-scale works can only be placed in a setting that allows the viewer to circumnavigate and engage the work. Some historians have described di Suvero as a monumental Minimalist, but he is more accurately a process artist of grand-scale sensibility.

A true postwar Minimalist work (for example Donald Judd's serial and identically sized cubes) revealed neither a discernible touch of the human hand nor the mystic or romantic sources of creation. Minimalist objects were manifestly fabricated using industrial materials voided of emotion and surface nuance or gesture; the presentation was straightforward and objective. In contrast, di Suvero's work concerned the subjective quality of the presentation and manipulation of materials. The sculptural forms revealed the personality of di Suvero through distinctive shapes and forms that managed to be both painterly and linear. Rather than build small-scale models in preparation for a final, finished work, di Suvero developed his sculptures through the process of making, such that explorative gesture became part of the work itself, much like the action paintings of Abstract Expressionists Willem de Kooning, Jackson Pollock, and Franz Kline.

Instead of brushes and paint, di Suvero used found objects, especially early in his career, such as discarded barrels, wood, heavy cables, rope and tires, and later, steel I-beams—all arranged to transcend three-dimensional ideals of symmetry and wholeness. Di Suvero pushed complicated geometry into space (rather than filling space) and encouraged the viewer to interact with the object rather than react to the work as if it were an autonomous structure apart from him or her. In the words of Modernist critic Clement Greenberg, in the new postwar American constructivist-sculpture, "space is there to be shaped, divided, enclosed, but not to be filled" (see Greenberg, 1961). Forgoing the preciousness of traditional sculpture, di Suvero preferred to find a visual language inherited from not only engineering and architecture, but also the prevalent urban "junk aesthetic" of the 1960s. In this respect, he followed Greenberg's dictum that the "new sculptors" ought to exploit the blacksmith's, the welder's, and the carpenter's tools.

Pre-Columbian (1965), an early sculpture constructed of wood, steel, and a rubber tractor tire, revolves like a merry-go-round. It is a functionalist work that marries di Suvero's interest in sculptural form and architectural scale, uniting art object, artist, and the viewer through the comfort of familiar materials and childhood play rituals. The encounter with the work becomes as much about the viewer's associations and physical space as it is about the essential and formal qualities of the materials and the site.

Di Suvero's work celebrates engineering and industry with all the optimistic enthusiasm of Fernand Léger's *The Builders* from about 1950, a time when the activity of post–World War II industrialized labor seemed so promising. Di Suvero's later fervor for working class ideals has fortified his sculpture without a hint of mawkish nostalgia or overt romanticism. Indeed, he is still a member of Local No. 3 of the Operating Engineers Union.

Di Suvero's affinity for these particular materials and techniques such as sawing, welding, and building can be traced his own familiarity with the grand masses and scale of ships and shipyards. His first glimpse of a large ship was as an eight-year-old passenger in 1941, when he fled the soon-to-be-invaded China with his family on the SS *Grover Cleveland*, bound for San Francisco. His father worked in a San Francisco Bay–area shipyard, and as a teenager di Suvero worked in the shipyards as a laborer where he was first introduced to the materials of his artistic oeuvre.

Di Suvero discovered sculpture in college, under the guidance of Stephen Novak, who became a mentor. In 1957 he moved to New York City, and a year later, di Suvero took a job that nearly killed him when a descending elevator failed to stop and crushed him. Although doctors thought he would be in a wheelchair for life, di Suvero was walking without even the aid of crutches by 1965. During the recuperative process, he began to create smaller sculptures that combined wood and steel, using an asbestos apron on his lap and traditional welder's equipment. Works such as *Attic* (1961–62) afforded a new meaning, as the deceptively static-looking piece yielded to the touch, revealing a playful, springy miniature monument. Di Suvero learned to control weight by shifting its center. With help from his artist friends and his brother, he eventually began assembling steel I-beams and other materials, eliminating pedestals and using hydraulic cranes, often with a cherry picker and pulleys for assistance. His work developed into a signature style: that of fabricated, balanced, architecturally scaled, essential cubist shapes that interact in and through time and space to produce stunning visual and three-dimensional effects.

The idea of an intuitive space-time became a critical theme to di Suvero and other artists who opened the Park Place Gallery in 1962 as a countercultural artists' collaborative. Throughout his career, di Suvero has been instrumental in creating public places for art, including People's Park in Berkeley, California, in 1968 and Socrates Sculpture Park (adjacent to his studio in Long Island City, New York), which also provides artists with working space and grants for large-scale works.

By 1967 di Suvero built his first all-crane-assisted piece, the large *Are Years What? (For Marianne Moore)*. It features red steel I-beams soaring majestically several stories high, with a spiderlike design. In one corner, a smaller piece of steel swings from a large chain secured to the top. The sheer physicality of the piece projects a kinetic energy that infers Constructivist optimism but retains its human connection through the easily identifiable visibility of the welded-nuts-and-bolts means of construction. Di Suvero's artistic inspirations have included the Spanish Modernist sculptor Julio Gonzales, who worked aesthetically with iron; David Smith, who transformed steel into strong totemic pieces; Alexander Calder, for his joy in motion; and the Russian Constructivists, for their intentions of the social good.

A retrospective at the Whitney Museum of American Art in New York proved consequential to di Suvero's career because the sculptures were exhibited in all five boroughs of New York City. Viewers could thus see that the content of his work is perceived through physical contact (as opposed to emblematic imagery). In 1985 he exhibited in an optimal bucolic setting: Storm King Art Center, Mountainville, New York, a large park devoted to sculpture, which established him as an American leader in Constructivist and abstract public art.

Jan Arrigo

See also **Abstract Expressionism; Calder, Alexander; Constructivism; Judd, Donald; Minimalism; Public Sculpture; Smith, David**

Biography

Born in Shanghai, China, 18 September 1933. His father was an Italian government official. Spent his early childhood in Tientsin, China, then moved with his family to San Francisco, 1941; worked at a shipyard as a teenager, which influenced the scale and materials of his future work; studied sculpture under Robert Thomas at the University of California, Santa Barbara, 1954–55, and Stephen Novak at the University of California, Berkeley (B.A., philosophy), 1956; moved to New York City, 1957; first solo exhibition at the Green

For Lady Day, 1969
© ART on FILE / CORBIS

Gallery, New York City, 1960; crushed by an elevator and confined to a wheelchair, 1960–62; during recovery period began welding steel on his lap, using a welder's mask and apron; recovered enough to walk again, 1965; moved to Venice, Italy, to protest Vietnam War, 1971–75; first major retrospective, Whitney Museum of American Art, New York City, 1975; founded Socrates Sculpture Park, Long Island City, New York, 1994. Currently lives and works in Petaluma, California, and New York City.

Selected Works

1962–63 *Love Makes the World Go Round*; rope, tire; Storm King Art Center, Mountainville, New York, United States

1965 *Pre-Columbian*; steel I-beam, tire; Storm King Art Center, Mountainville, New York, United States

1967 *Are Years What? (For Marianne Moore)*; steel; Hirshhorn Museum and Sculpture Garden, Washington, D.C., United States

1969–70 *Victor's Lament*; steel I-beams; Baker Center for the Arts, Muhlenberg College, Allentown, Pennsylvania, United States

1977–82 *Arikidea*; Corten steel, wood; Walker Art Center, Minneapolis, Minnesota, United States

1977–84 *Isis*; steel I-beams; Hirshhorn Museum and Sculpture Garden, Washington, D.C., United States

Further Reading

Di Suvero, Mark, *Mark di Suvero: Open Secret: Sculpture, 1990–1992*, New York: Rizzoli, 1993

Gorgoni, Gianfranco, and Giovanni Carandente, *Mark di Suvero a Venezia* (exhib. cat.), Milan: Charta, 1995

Greenberg, Clement, "The New Sculpture," *Art and Culture: Critical Essays*, Boston, Massachusetts: Beacon Press, 1961

Mark di Suvero (exhib. cat.), New York: Danese, 2000

Monte, James K., *Mark di Suvero* (exhib. cat.), New York: Whitney Museum of American Art, 1975

Rose, Barbara, *Mark di Suvero: New Sculpture*, Houston, Texas: Janie C. Lee Gallery, 1978

Sandler, Irving, *Mark di Suvero at Storm King Art Center* (exhib. cat.), Mountainville, New York: Storm King Art Center, and New York: Abrams, 1996

FRANÇOIS DIEUSSART *ca.* 1600–1661

Belgian

Originating in French-speaking southern Belgium, a Roman Catholic land with a rich sculptural tradition, François Dieussart's training is unknown. He was presumably about 20 years old when he was first docu-

mented in Rome, joining the group for expatriate Flemings at the Church of San Giuliano. He was sufficiently mature to have produced a crucifix in an unspecified material for the church. It was probably ivory, a rare and prized material, because seven years later he was documented as carving a statuette of *Christ with the Woman of Samaria* in ivory to crown an ebony cabinet for Cardinal Francesco Barberini. For the same important patron family, that of Pope Urban VIII, he modeled in stucco one of a series of statues designed by Gianlorenzo Bernini for the catafalque of Carlo Barberini. On this commission, Dieussart worked alongside Alessandro Algardi, who is also recorded as having carved in ivory early in his career.

Dieussart was recruited by the great English patron of art, the Earl of Arundel, in 1635, perhaps to restore ancient sculptures and to make some portrait busts. Two busts, depicting Charles I and his nephew Charles Louis, the elector of the Palatinate, are still in the possession of the Howard family at Arundel Castle, Sussex; the busts suggest that Dieussart must have been an accomplished portraitist while still working in Rome. In the case of the king, Dieussart was probably able to benefit from Van Dyck's triple portrait before it was dispatched to Rome for Bernini to work from, but—presumably at the behest of his patron—he clad the monarch in armor in view of the political situation. Charles Louis was also shown in armor, but this was made to resemble *repoussé* work (the method of producing relief metal by hammering and punching chiefly from behind), showing the forge of Vulcan on its breastplate. The busts of Arundel himself and of Prince Rupert of the Rhine are now at the Ashmolean Museum, Oxford. That of Rupert shows him in armor and wearing a sword scarf running diagonally down from a prominent knot on his right shoulder. This recalls a similar motif on Bernini's bust of Charles I, which had in the meantime reached London. The inspiration of the great Roman master enabled Dieussart easily to outdo his French predecessor, Hubert Le Sueur, as court portraitist in London. Dieussart also produced a Baroque, theatrical monstrance for displaying the Blessed Sacrament in the chapel at Somerset House in London that had been built for the Roman Catholic queen, Henrietta Maria (demolished by the Puritans, 1649).

With the outbreak of the Civil War and with a letter of recommendation from the court painter Gerrit Honthorst to Constantijn Huygens, secretary to the prince of Orange, in 1641 Dieussart moved to The Hague. He carved busts of the prince and of Mary Stuart, who had just been married to the prince's heir, William. Next Dieussart carved busts of Queen Elizabeth of Bohemia, the "Winter Queen," and King Frederick, the "Winter King," the mother and deceased father of the two princes whom he had just portrayed in England. Queen Elizabeth was sister of Charles I, and thus there began a pattern of moving in the sculptor's career—like a medieval stonemason or carver—from court to court via recommendations of his patrons and following closely on familial, marital, or political alliances.

Dieussart then moved for a year or so to Copenhagen, where he portrayed Christian V in both marble and bronze, as well as the heir apparent and his ultimate successor. The bust in bronze of the monarch was more sumptuous in appearance and sonorous in mood than Dieussart's previous marble busts and shows the artist evolving a northern European version of the Roman Baroque style that was to profoundly influence his successors in the Netherlands, Artus Quellinus and Rombout Verhulst.

Dieussart returned to the Netherlands to execute an elaborate mural monument to Charles Morgan, the English governor of Bergen-op-Zoom, with full-length portraits of his mourning daughter and grandchildren. These figures corroborate an attribution to Dieussart of an impressive statue of *Judith with the Head of Holofernes* that went with the Arundel marble busts to the Ashmolean Museum, Oxford, as early as the 18th century. Another, smaller, mural monument to Arent and Josina van Dorp in the monastery church in The Hague has recently been attributed to Dieussart. Consisting of two putti standing in front of an aedicule and holding up a cloth of honor inscribed with an epitaph by Huygens, it imitates two monuments by François du Quesnoy in Rome. Probably between 1645 and 1650, Dieussart produced portraits of the Swedish ambassador to the Netherlands, Pieter Spieringh van Silfvercrona, and his wife, Joanna Doré; they also commissioned a bust of their patron, Queen Christina of Sweden (lost). In 1651 the sculptor carved a profile in an oval piece of marble of his supporter, Huygens.

After carving four full-length statues in armor of the princes of the house of Orange for the vestibule of their palace, Huis ten Bosch, and other busts for the same patrons, Dieussart followed the path of a political marriage between Princess Louise Henriette of Orange and the elector of Brandenburg to Berlin. There he carved a statue of the elector, Frederick William, a number of portrait busts of the couple and their relatives, and some statuary for the gardens that the elector was laying out at his country residence, Schloss Sanssouci. Only a few have survived the effects of war, and these are gravely disfigured by weathering.

Dieussart ended his career in Brussels, carving in 1656 a striking bust of Archduke Leopold Wilhelm, regent of the southern Netherlands. Within the next few years, Dieussart also produced some elegant and still more Baroque busts of Charles II during the king's

years of exile in Bruges. The sculptor is recorded as having died in 1661 in London, which suggests that he may have accompanied the king to that country at the time of the Restoration with a view to becoming his court sculptor.

Less well known than he deserves to be as a result of the troubled times that forced him to be unusually itinerant, Dieussart nevertheless set a sound standard for sculpture—especially portraiture—wherever he operated, breaking the mold of the stylized Late Mannerist icons that had previously passed for portraiture in northern Europe. He spread the influence of Bernini through the particular imagery that he adopted and thus laid the groundwork for sculptors of the ensuing generation (for example, Andreas Schluter in Berlin), who were then in a position to develop a fully Baroque style in the various capitals where he had worked.

CHARLES AVERY

See also **Bernini, Gianlorenzo; du Quesnoy, François; Le Sueur, Hubert; Netherlands and Belgium; Quellinus (Quellin) Family; Verhulst, Rombout**

Biography

Born in Arquinghem (near present-day Armentières, France), *ca.* 1600. Training unknown; in Rome, in Brotherhood of San Giuliano dei Fiamminghi, 1622–30; worked for the Barberini family, 1629–30; worked in London, for the Earl of Arundel, Queen Henrietta Maria, and possibly King Charles I, 1636–41; moved to The Hague, the Netherlands, 1641, and carved portrait busts for members of the house of Orange and of Queen Elizabeth of Bohemia; moved briefly to Copenhagen and carved portraits of the royal family, 1644; then returned for five years to The Hague to carve the tomb of Charles Morgan and dynastic statues and busts for the houses of Orange and of Brandenburg; worked in Berlin for the elector of Brandenburg, on a statue of him and on other dynastic portraiture, as well as on garden statuary (mostly lost), 1650–55; moved to Flanders (today Belgium), 1656–60, to carve busts of the regent and of exiled King Charles II; dated a small marble group, the *Pietà,* in Ghent, 1660. Died in London, England, 1661.

Selected Works

ca. 1622 Crucifix, in the Church of San Giuliano
dei Fiamminghi, Rome, Italy; probably
ivory (destroyed)

ca. 1629 *Christ with the Woman of Samaria*; ivory
(lost)

ca. 1630 Catafalque of Carlo Barberini (designed by
Gianlorenzo Bernini); plaster (lost)

ca. 1636 Monstrance to display the Blessed Sacrament (formerly Chapel of Somerset House, London); various materials (lost)

ca. 1636 Bust of Charles I; marble; Arundel Castle, Arundel, West Sussex, England

ca. 1636 Bust of Prince Charles Louis of the Palatinate; marble; Arundel Castle, Arundel, West Sussex, England

1637 Bust of Prince Rupert of the Rhine; marble; Ashmolean Museum, Oxford, England

ca. 1637 Bust of the Earl of Arundel; marble; Ashmolean Museum, Oxford, England

ca. 1637 *Judith with the Head of Holofernes*; marble; Ashmolean Museum, Oxford, England (attributed)

1641 Busts of Frederick V and Queen Elizabeth of Bohemia (also known as "Winter King" and "Winter Queen"); marble; Marienburg, near Hannover, Germany

ca. 1641 Bust of Queen Elizabeth of Bohemia (also known as "Winter Queen"); marble; Victoria and Albert Museum, London, England (attributed)

1641 Bust of Frederick Henry, Prince of Orange; marble; formerly Gotische Haus, Wörlitz, Germany

ca. 1641 Bust of Princess Mary Stuart; marble (lost)

ca. 1644 Bust of King Christian IV of Denmark; marble, bronze; Rosenborg Castle, Copenhagen, Denmark

ca. 1645 Tomb of Charles Morgan; marble; Bergen-op-Zoom, The Netherlands

ca. 1645–50 Busts of Pieter Spieringh van Silfvercrona and Joanna Doré; marble; Rijksmuseum, Amsterdam, The Netherlands

ca. 1646 Mural monument to Arent and Josina van Dorp; marble; monastery church, The Hague, The Netherlands

1646–47 Four statues of the Princes of Orange; marble (destroyed 1945); Royal Palace (Huis ten Bosch) The Netherlands

ca. 1647 Bust of Frederick William, Elector of Brandenburg; marble, Staatliche Museen, Berlin, Germany

1647 Bust of Frederick William and Princess Louise Henriette of Orange, electress; marble; Castle, Doorn, The Netherlands

1648 Princess Sophia; marble; National Portrait Gallery, London, England (attributed)

ca. 1648 Bust of Crown Prince William Henry; marble; Schloss Sanssouci, Potsdam, Germany

ca. 1650 Bust of Queen Christina of Sweden; marble (lost)

1651 Bust of Constantijn Huygens; marble; Gemeentemuseum, The Hague, The Netherlands

ca. 1651 Bust of Frederick William, Elector of Brandenburg; marble, Schloss Sanssouci, Potsdam, Germany

1656 Bust of Leopold Wilhelm; marble; Kunsthistorisches Museum, Vienna, Austria

1656–58 Bust of King Charles II; marble; Gruuthuse Museum, Bruges, Belgium

1656–58 Bust of King Charles II; marble; Guildhall of St. Sebastian's Archers Guild, Bruges, Belgium

1660 *Pietà*; marble; Convent of La Byloke, Ghent, Belgium

Further Reading

Avery, Charles, "François Dieussart in the United Provinces and the Ambassador of Queen Christina," *Bulletin van het Rijksmuseum* 19 (1971)

Avery, Charles, "François Dieussart (c.1600–1661), Portrait Sculptor to the Courts of Northern Europe," *Victoria and Albert Museum Yearbook* 4 (1972); reprint, in *Studies in European Sculpture*, by Avery, London: Christie's, 1981

Avery, Charles, "Dieussart, François," in *The Dictionary of Art*, edited by Jane Turner, vol. 8, New York: Grove, and London: Macmillan, 1996

Bussers, Hélène, "Pietà, 1660," in *La sculpture au siècle de Rubens, dans les Pays-bas meridionaux et la principauté de Liège* (exhib. cat.), Brussels: Musée d'Art Ancien, 1977

Chaney, Edward, "*Thomas Howard, 14th Earl of Arundel*, by François Dieussart," *Apollo* 146 (1996)

Howarth, David, "Charles I, Sculpture and Sculptors," in *The Late King's Goods: Collections, Possessions, and Patronage of Charles I in the Light of the Commonwealth Inventories*, edited by Arthur MacGregor, London: McAlpine, and Oxford: Oxford University Press, 1989

Penny, Nicholas, *Catalogue of the Sculpture at the Ashmolean Museum, 1540 to the Present Day*, 3 vols., New York: Oxford University Press, and Oxford: Clarendon Press, 1992; see especially volume 3

Scholten, Frits, *Gebeeldhouwde portretten; Portrait Sculpture: Rijksmuseum Amsterdam*, Amsterdam: Rijksmuseum Amsterdam, 1995

Scholten, Frits, "Sir Constantijn Huygens and François Dieussart," *The Sculpture Journal* 1 (1997)

Vickers, Michael, "Rupert of the Rhine: A New Portrait by Dieussart and Bernini's Charles I," *Apollo* 107 (1978)

Whinney, Margaret, *Sculpture in Britain, 1530–1830*, London and Baltimore: Penguin, 1964; 2nd edition, revised by John Physick, London and New York: Penguin, 1988

JAMES LEWIS DINE 1935– *United States*

Since the 1960s critics have viewed Jim Dine as a prominent figure in American Pop art. However, as a painter, sculptor, printmaker, performer, and pioneer of assembled Environments and Happenings, Dine has made important and lasting contributions to various aspects of the visual and performance arts far beyond the realms of Pop. His work with found objects in the 1960s has been particularly influential, combining a variety of different techniques, often setting everyday objects against textural, color fields of paint on two-dimensional surfaces.

Characteristically, his work reveals a preoccupation with a series of motifs and symbols and a selection of mundane, even banal, objects in a fashion similar to Jasper Johns, Robert Rauschenberg, and Claes Oldenburg, all of whom were influenced by Marcel Duchamp's readymades. At least one critic has fittingly summed up Dine's sensibility, commenting that the artist had written "a whole page in art history on work dedicated to the seemingly insignificant—a tool, a palette, a robe" (see Shapiro, 1981). Beginning in the 1980s, Dine turned to sculptural forms, as evinced in his reworking of the subject of the Venus de Milo, extensively exploring this powerful icon of the Classical ideal through sculpture, painting, and graphics.

A strong sense of family history and place directly informs Dine's later artwork. Born in 1935, he was raised in Cincinnati, where his father owned a commercial paint and plumbing supply store. Early artistic influences included Cincinnati painters such as Frank Duveneck and Duveneck's pupil John Henry Twachtman, but he found 19th-century painters working in the trompe l'oeil (extreme realism in art; literally "deception of the eye") tradition, such as William Harnett, to be particularly important. According to Dine, their work "made sense in our new history of the found object" (see *Jim Dine: Paintings, Drawings, Sculpture*, 1986).

Dine moved to New York in 1958 and joined a circle of artists that included Rauschenberg, Oldenburg, and Roy Lichtenstein, among other Popists. With Tom Wesselmann, Marc Ratliff, Allan Kaprow and others, Dine founded the Judson Gallery, a makeshift space in the basement of Judson Church on Washington Square in Greenwich Village, New York City. Stressing the "death of easel-painting," the populist Kaprow was an influential figure on the New York art scene at the time, as well as a pioneer of Happenings—unscripted, nontheatrical performance based works that radically severed the relationship among media and reconfigured the artist in the role of an activist. Dine has commented that Kaprow made them all feel like "brave young soldiers being put up in the trenches, the first ones to go over the hill" (see *Jim Dine: Paintings, Drawings, Sculpture*, 1986).

The earliest Happenings usually took place in settings assembled from found objects in sites such as schools, parking lots, auditoriums, galleries, and even the countryside. The artists performed in an impro-

vised sculptural environment, often inviting the audience as well as bystanders to participate. Happenings frequently left behind few objects and scant documentation, and this has posed particular problems for studying them. Nevertheless, they played a seminal role in developing performance art and in taking object-based practice beyond the confines of the pedestal and gallery space and into a collaborative relationship with other art forms and discourses such as theater, poetry, and music.

Between 1959 and 1960, artists staged a number of Happenings at the Reuben Gallery in New York City. The artists included Red Grooms and George Brecht, but the main figures involved in impromptu action and improvised activities were Dine, Kaprow, Oldenburg, and Robert Whitman Jr. In April 1960, as part of his first solo show at the Reuben Gallery, Dine staged *The Smiling Workman*, a bizarre performance lasting 30 seconds that featured the artist daubing himself and drinking red "paint" (actually tomato juice) while writing "I love what I'm doing" on a wall. Drawing on his involvement in two car crashes in 1959, Dine devised his second Happening, *The Car Crash*, in November 1960. This work, part-psychodrama and part-performance, was staged at the Reuben Gallery with accompanying lights and traffic sounds and included girls dancing a deathly "sex-tease." Dine's scripted text and macabre actions evoked speed, motion, and terror, centering on the automobile as a symbol of love, sex, and death. Equally sinister was *The Shining Bed*, performed in December 1960, in which Dine lay on a bed, dressed as Santa Claus and wrapped in cellophane.

Dine collaborated on several projects with Oldenburg. At the Judson Gallery in 1960, Dine presented his assembled environment *The House* with Oldenburg's *The Street*. Dine created his work from junk

Putney Winter Heart
© Pace / Wildenstein and Giraudon / Art Resource, NY

collected from the streets of Manhattan. Only rare documentary photographs remain, together with a few salvaged objects, such as *Bedspring*, a mixed-media assemblage. Dine's second collaboration with Oldenburg, staged at the Judson Gallery that same year, was *Ray-Gun*, whose title was taken from a pulp science-fiction book. At the event, a mimeograph machine turned out comic books with drawings by the artists. These books were sold, poems were recited, and the event ended with ad-lib performances by various artists, including Kaprow and Dine.

From 1960 to 1966 Dine's work was featured in a series of solo exhibitions in New York including the Reuben Gallery, the Martha Jackson Gallery, and the Sidney Janis Gallery. In 1962 he contributed to the ground-breaking International Exhibition of the New Realists, a group show staged by Sidney Janis, an influential emergent dealer of the new American and European art. Although Dine was often associated with Pop artists such as Andy Warhol and Lichtenstein, his work shared the European sensibility of Nouveaux Réalistes such as Yves Klein, Arman, Daniel Spoerri, and Jean Tinguely.

In 1962 Dine moved away from performance-based work and returned to painting and sculpture. His assemblages combined domestic objects such as sinks and lawn mowers with painted backdrops. Accumulations of junk, real articles of clothing, and hardware-store tools consistently appeared in his strange juxtapositions of the real and surreal. Given his family background in retailing hardware, Dine's assemblages and paintings often evoked a strong sense of the artist's personal history.

In 1967 Dine and his family moved to London, where he devoted time to printmaking and drawing. When he returned to the United States in 1971, he continued figure drawing, with his wife as model, but also produced many self-portraits. Since the 1970s, Dine has worked and reworked a familiar set of motifs; bathrobes, tools, and hearts have become signature images in his prints, drawings, and assemblages. In 1982, however, he returned to a more conventional form and iconography of sculpture with a new source of inspiration: the Venus de Milo. This Classical icon of feminine beauty and grace, which has enraptured artists and audiences for centuries, appeared in his paintings from 1977 to 1978. Dine made his initial Venus sculptures in bronze in 1983. In the decade following, he rendered the Venuses in clay, plaster, wood, and stone. Works range in size from the smaller carved works, such as the small bronze *A Lady and a Shovel* (1983), to his monumental versions sited on Avenue of the Americas (Sixth Avenue), New York City, and in Broadgate, London.

Since Dine has dealt with contemporary themes and preoccupations of mass culture—the automobile, billboards, comic strips, movies—his place in the pantheon of Pop art is not surprising. However, the poetic and personal nature of Dine's work in a variety of media and with a wide range of techniques makes for an ambivalent relationship to Pop; and Pop art alone does not account for his important contribution to postwar object-based art. Early in his career Dine pioneered the creation of new forms of artistic expression such as Happenings and Environments that developed directly from an assemblage aesthetic. His later prolific sculptural renditions of the Venus de Milo demonstrate a lifelong trait of the artist—his ability to tirelessly and obsessively explore just a few motifs with poetry, humor, and pathos. By continually revisiting and recycling a series of mundane images and everyday objects, he has reinvested them with symbolism, giving his work multiple layers of meaning and raising important questions about the serial nature of art and sculpture in particular.

GILLIAN WHITELEY

See also **Arman; Assemblage; Duchamp, Marcel; Klein, Yves; Oldenburg, Claes; Performance Art; Spoerri, Daniel;** *Venus de Milo*

Biography

Born in Cincinnati, Ohio, United States, 16 June 1935. Studied at Cincinnati Arts Academy, 1951–53, and Boston Museum School, 1953–57; received B.F.A., Ohio University, 1957; moved to New York, 1958; staged first Happenings with Allan Kaprow and Claes Oldenburg at Judson Gallery, New York, 1959–60; first solo exhibition, Reuben Gallery, New York, 1960; professorships at Yale University, New Haven, and Oberlin College, Ohio, 1960–65; showed at Venice Biennale, 1964; professor, Cornell University, since 1967; lived in London with family, 1967–71; showed at Documenta 4, Kassel, Germany, 1968; moved family to Vermont, 1971, but maintained studios in London and the United States; became member of American Academy and Institute of Arts and Letters, New York, 1980. Currently lives in New York and London.

Selected Works

1959   *Green Suit*; oil, cardboard, man's suit; private collection, New York City, United States

1960   *The Smiling Workman*; performance sites; Judson Gallery and Reuben Gallery, New York City, United States

1960   *Bedspring*; mixed media assemblage on

wire bedspring; Guggenheim Museum of
Art, New York City, United States

1960 *The Car Crash*; performance site; Reuben
Gallery, New York City, United States

1960 *The Shining Bed*; performance site;
Reuben Gallery, New York City, United
States

1962 *Black Bathroom No. 2*; oil paint, canvas,
porcelain sink; Art Gallery of Ontario,
Toronto, Canada

1962 *Five Feet of Colourful Tools*; oil, canvas
board, tools; Museum of Modern Art, New
York City, United States

1962 *Lawnmower*; paint, canvas, lawnmower,
wood base; Aichi Prefectural Museum of
Art, Nagoya, Japan

1983 *The Crommelynck Gate with Tools*;
bronze, paint; Metropolitan Museum of
Art, New York City, United States

1985 *Howard Street Venus*; bronze;
commissioned by the Redevelopment
Agency of San Francisco for Convention
Plaza, San Francisco, California, United
States

1987–88 *The Field of the Cloth of Gold*; bronze,
paint; Pace Wildenstein, New York City,
United States

1989 *East End Venus*; bronze; commissioned by
the Rosehaugh Developments PLC for
Broadgate, London, England

Further Reading

Celant, Germano, and Clare Bell, *Jim Dine: Walking Memory,
1959–1969* (exhib. cat.), New York: Guggenheim Museum,
1999
Feinberg, Jean E., *Jim Dine*, New York: Abbeville Press, 1995
Jim Dine: Paintings, Drawings, Sculpture (exhib. cat.), New
York: Pace Gallery, 1986
Jim Dine's Venus (exhib. cat.), Milan: Electa, 1996
Livingstone, Marco, and Jim Dine, *Jim Dine: The Alchemy of
Images*, New York: Monacelli Press, 1998
Paparoni, Demetrio, "The Memory of Death: Jim Dine," in *Jim
Dine* (exhib. cat.), London: Waddington Galleries, 1989
Shapiro, David, *Jim Dine: Painting What One Is*, New York:
Abrams, 1981

DIPTYCH AND TRIPTYCH

The terms *diptych* and *triptych* describe multipaneled relief sculpture in which the panels are joined together, usually by means of hinges or rings. Diptychs comprise two panels and, strictly speaking, triptychs comprise three, although the latter term is sometimes used to indicate any number of panels greater than two. Further variants exist, including four-paneled quadriptychs and multipaneled polyptychs. When hinged, the panels can be closed, although some large church altarpieces take the diptych or triptych form but are fixed open. In modern art the terms have come to signify works of art consisting of several linked pieces, even when they are not physically joined together.

Diptychs and triptychs have their origins in the ancient world. Diptychs existed in ancient Greece and became extremely common in the ancient Roman period. The earliest diptychs, however, were not sculptural but closer to writing pads, consisting of two or more wooden frames hinged together, with their centers filled with beeswax onto which letters, contracts, and other documents were inscribed using a stylus. Many examples of this style of diptych have been found in England near Hadrian's Wall. The Romans began to use wax diptychs as ceremonial gift-documents for events such as marriages, from which it was only a short step, probably in the 4th century CE, to replace the impermanent wax surface with more durable materials, such as elephant ivory, onto which were carved shallow-relief words and images. An example of this is the 4th-century *Diptych of the Nicomachi and Symmachi* (half of which is in the Musée du Moyen Age, Paris, and half in the Victoria and Albert Museum, London), which is believed to be a marriage diptych. Also common at this time were consular diptychs, which were given by Roman officials to friends and allies to celebrate their promotions.

Early diptychs and triptychs were not necessarily religious, although for both Christians and pagans diptychs could have a religious use. In pagan homes portrait diptychs could commemorate the dead, such as the 4th-century *Symmachorum Diptych* in the British Museum, London. It shows a bearded man riding on a chariot drawn by elephant, while in the sky above he is represented again being greeted by the pagan gods on Olympus. Such diptychs were important in pagan homes, used in elaborate ceremonies of remembrance. Similar considerations may have surrounded the use of diptychs and triptychs by early Christians. The 6th-century Roman diptych *The Six Miracles of Christ* (Victoria and Albert Museum, London) was probably made for private devotional use in a domestic setting rather than in a public space such as a church. In both Christian and pagan households, the relatively small scale of these objects made them extremely portable, and the diptych's ability to be opened, closed, and moved gave it the capacity of transformation, in marked contrast to the stasis of other types of figural sculpture.

Despite their general hostility to pagan imagery, Roman Christians often reused pagan diptychs and even commissioned diptychs that incorporated pagan elements. The 6th-century *Anastasius Diptych*, of which only one leaf survives (Victoria and Albert Museum, London), was probably carved in Christian Constantinople, but it incorporates images believed to show either Amazon women taming horses or events at pagan games. Examples such as these show how the traditions of diptych production that existed in the pagan Roman world lived on in the Christian Roman Empire. Indeed, other than obvious Christian references, the styles of Late Antique pagan and Early Christian diptychs are indistinguishable, as shown by one of the most significant diptychs to survive from the 6th-century, the *Barberini Diptych*, made either in Constantinople or Alexandria (Musée du Louvre, Paris). The surviving leaf is composed of five separate parts in elephant ivory, of which four are intact. The central panel shows a figure on horseback, whom most authorities agree is either the Roman emperor Anastasius I or, more likely, the emperor Justinian I. Justinian may well seem an appropriate assumption given the nature of the representation, as he was instrumental in reconquering many of the Roman lands in western Europe that had been lost to invading Gothic tribes in the previous century, including much of Italy. In form it is similar to the consular diptychs produced in pagan Rome. Also, the figures are extremely fluid, with rhythmic lines that, given its affinities to contemporary Persian and Indian imagery, may be linked to the increasingly oriental perspective of the Roman Empire, which had by this time lost most of its lands in Europe, ceased to have Rome as its capital, and was very much a Middle Eastern state ruled from Constantinople.

Diptychs showing the emperor were made in large numbers and distributed to churches throughout the Roman Empire, where they were treated with quasi-religious reverence. When the Iconoclasts came to power in the 8th century and claimed that the use of images in churches was blasphemous, the only images they tended not to destroy were emperor diptychs, such as the *Barberini Diptych*. As a consequence, when the Iconoclasts were finally defeated by the Orthodox Christians in 843, the tradition of diptych carving that had been practiced continuously since Classical times was still relatively intact, in marked contrast to painting or other forms of sculpture in the Roman Empire. Therefore, Roman diptych manufacture shows less of a break between the Theodosian style of Late Antiquity and the Byzantine style of the Middle Ages.

Outside the Roman Empire the continuing production of diptychs was not as straightforward. Certainly they were in production during the Romanesque period, but before this time they ceased being made outside those areas—such as southern Spain, France, and Italy—that were either under periodic Roman rule or strong Roman influence from the 6th to the 9th centuries. Not until stability returned to western Europe did diptych and triptych manufacture resume. Key to this

Diptych of the Nicomachi and Symmachi, Victoria and Albert Museum, London, England
© Victoria and Albert Museum, London / Art Resource, NY

revival was Charlemagne, king of the Franks, who had himself crowned emperor of the Holy Roman Empire in western Europe in 800. Charlemagne sought to revive Roman traditions in his domain, one consequence being the resumption of diptych production. The 9th-century *Andrews Diptych* (Victoria and Albert Museum, London), made for the Carolingian court, shows how the craftsmen of the Holy Roman Empire sought to emulate Late Antique Roman models, using a form that resembles that of *The Six Miracles of Christ*. Indeed, the stylistic similarities between Late Antique diptychs and Carolingian ones frequently leads to disputes over dating.

Both Late Antique and Byzantine diptychs entered western Europe through a number of channels. Charlemagne populated his court with Roman Greeks from Constantinople, including both ambassadors and artisans, and the growing importance of the Danube-Rhine river link as a conduit for travel, trade, and diplomacy move away from the planar forms, round arches, and hieratic figures of much Late Antique, Byzantine, and Romanesque art toward linear forms, pointed arches, and flowing figures. For example, the stylization of the human figures in the 13th-century *Soissons Diptych* (Victoria and Albert Museum, London), made in Paris, is typical of French Gothic styles found in other art forms of the period, including architectural sculpture and manuscript illumination, with a strong emphasis on the flowing curves of rhythmic lines running throughout. It also places more emphasis on an architectural setting, becoming almost a miniature cathedral in ivory, the carving emphasizing the three-dimensionality of the structure rather than the pictorial qualities of earlier shallow relief. The early 14th-century French *Polyptych of the Virgin and Child* (Metropolitan Museum of Art, New York City) and the mid 14th-century ivory *Diptych with Virgin and Child and Crucifixion* (Walters Art Museum, Baltimore, Maryland) display similar Gothic principles. The figures on the outer four leaves of the former are particularly reminiscent of contemporary manuscript illumination, which is emphasized by their shallow relief, in stark contrast to the almost freestanding figure of the Virgin and Child in the central panel under its Gothic canopy. The *Diptych with Virgin and Child and Crucifixion* also has well-wrought Gothic canopies, but the image of the Virgin in particular relates closely to contemporary freestanding sculptures of the Virgin, such as the French *Seated Virgin and Child* (Victoria and Albert Museum, London). These pieces show a definitive move away from hieratic Byzantine stylization and its replacement by a Gothic style of diptych and triptych production that is well integrated with other Gothic art forms.

As with pre-Gothic diptychs and triptychs, the religious and social symbolism of these pieces was still of the utmost importance. The dominance of images of the Virgin and Child in the Gothic period reflects the Virgin's growing popularity among the Christian laity in the western Church. In the case of the 14th-century *Diptych with Virgin and Child and Crucifixion*, the juxtaposition of images reinforces a central tenet of Christian theology that Christ was born to die on the cross. Portable diptychs and triptychs were also important aids to private devotion in domestic settings.

The Renaissance saw a definite move away from the hinged diptych and triptych form, although church altarpieces and tomb monuments maintained the basic three-paneled form of the triptych, albeit as static pieces. For example, the late 15th-century *Altarpiece with Crucifixion and Saints* by Ferrucci from the Church of S. Girolamo, Fiesole, Italy, comprises a central panel showing the *Crucifixion* and two side panels showing saints, in a typical triptych form, although it

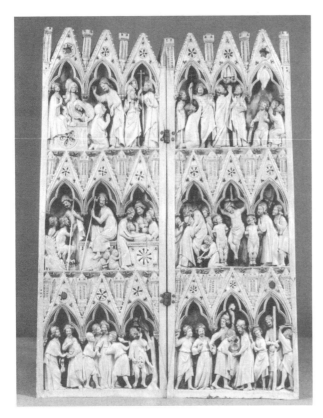

Soissons Diptych, Victoria and Albert Museum, London, England
© Victoria and Albert Museum, London / Art Resource, NY

between western Europe and the Roman (Byzantine) Empire proper reflected the generally cordial relationship between the two "Roman" empires at this time. Western European diptych and triptych production increased after 1095, when western Christians began a series of Crusades to the Near East ostensibly to regain the Christian holy sites in Palestine from the Muslims. The Crusaders also attacked Christian churches and settlements populated by Orthodox Christians loyal not to the pope in Rome but to the Roman emperor in Constantinople, culminating in the Sack of Constantinople in 1204 and the looting of its treasure houses of Classical Roman and Christian art objects. Among the items taken were large numbers of diptychs and triptychs, many of which ended up in western Europe; one example is the triptych the gold *repoussé* (the method of producing relief metal by hammering and punching chiefly from behind) *Reliquary of the True Cross* (Metropolitan Museum of Art, New York), which was constructed from two 11th-century Roman diptychs.

In the west Carolingian, or Romanesque, empire, diptychs and triptychs began as direct emulations of Roman models, but as Romanesque artistic styles gradually evolved into the unique Gothic style, diptychs and triptychs changed as well, reflecting the general

439

is not hinged. This altar corresponds with the changed aesthetic beliefs of Renaissance Classicism, in which the best viewpoint of a work of art was fixed, negating the idea that an altarpiece should move by opening and closing, giving the viewer different viewpoints. Smaller diptychs and triptychs continued to be created in the Renaissance, however, such as the early 15th-century diptych *Scenes from the Life of Christ* from Milan and the early 16th-century German diptych *Martyrdom of Saints Colman and Catherine* (both Victoria and Albert Museum, London). They show clear indications of the rise of Classicism during the Renaissance, with the geometric patterning of the inlaid surround for the Milanese diptych and the Classical naturalism of the figures in the German piece. Both were private devotional objects, and in the case of the *Martyrdom of Saints Colman and Catherine*, the diptych may have been carried like a pendant, as it measures only seven by five centimeters. Similarly sized diptychs were fashionable all over western Europe and by the 16th century were mass-produced for the growing middle classes using protoindustrial methods in areas such as the southern Netherlands. Artists also still created some large-scale hinged triptychs for churches, particularly in Spain and parts of Italy, such as the Tyrolese *Triptych Altarpiece* in wood (Victoria and Albert Museum, London), from the turn of the 16th century. As with other contemporary sculpture from these areas, this altarpiece combines Classical Renaissance techniques, such as the use of perspective, with bright polychromy.

Although most small-scale diptych and triptych manufacture was in ivory, artists also created these works in a variety of other materials. Close in style to ivory diptychs is the mid 13th-century *Polyptych Reliquary of the Cross of Floreffe* (Musée du Louvre, Paris), made of gold, silver, and copper and inlaid with precious stones. Nonetheless, the history of diptych and triptych carving evolved in a continuous line from the ivory diptychs produced in the Classical Roman Empire. The direct use of contemporary and historic Roman models by Carolingian craftsmen to revive diptych manufacture in western Europe in the 9th century meant that the ancient tradition of diptych manufacture did not die away as the Roman Empire slowly collapsed, and although the Roman (Byzantine) Empire finally came to an end in 1453, many of its artistic traditions persisted in western European diptychs and triptychs.

MICHAEL PARASKOS

See also **Altarpiece: Northern Europe; Altarpiece: Southern Europe; Ivory and Bone; Ivory Sculpture: Gothic; Relief Sculpture; Tomb Monument**

Further Reading

Barnet, Peter (editor), *Images in Ivory: Precious Objects of the Gothic Age*, Princeton, New Jersey: Princeton University Press, and Detroit, Michigan: Detroit Institute of Arts, 1997

Beckwith, John, *Early Christian and Byzantine Art*, London: Penguin, 1970; 2nd edition, London and New York: Penguin, 1979

Beckwith, John, *Early Medieval Art*, London: Thames and Hudson, and New York: Praeger, 1964; revised edition, New York: Thames and Hudson, 1994

Calkins, Robert G., *A Medieval Treasury*, Ithaca, New York: Office of University Publications, Cornell University, 1968

Camille, Michael, *Gothic Art*, London: Weidenfeld and Nicolson, and New York: Abrams, 1996

Deuchler, Florens (editor), *The Year 1200*, New York: Metropolitan Museum of Art, 1970

Elsner, Jas, *Imperial Rome and Christian Triumph*, Oxford and New York: Oxford University Press, 1998

Hutter, Irmgard, *Frühchristliche Kunst, byzantinische Kunst*, Stuttgart, Germany: Belser, 1968; as *Early Christian and Byzantine Art*, London: Weidenfeld and Nicolson, and New York: Universe Books, 1971

Kitzinger, Ernst, *Early Medieval Art in the British Museum*, London: British Museum, 1940; as *Early Medieval Art: In the British Museum and British Library*, London: British Museum, 3rd edition, 1983

Williamson, Paul (editor), *The Medieval Treasury: The Art of the Middle Ages in the Victoria and Albert Museum*, London: Victoria and Albert Museum, 1986; new edition, 1998

DISPLAY OF SCULPTURE

The display of sculpture in the history of Western Art has its roots in the ancient world. Interpretations of ancient practices in later centuries played a primary role in the development of display strategies in the early modern period and beyond.

Ancient Greeks built their temples as open exhibition spaces for sculptural decoration and cult images honoring a particular god: relief sculpture appeared in the pediments and the architectural entablature of Greek temples, and temple interiors housed freestanding statues. The interior of the Parthenon consisted of a two-story colonnade designed to allow views of Pheidias' colossal *Athena Parthenos* (446–438 BCE) from all sides. Likewise, the *Aphrodite of Cnidos* (369–364 BCE) by Praxiteles stood in the middle of a circular temple with an open colonnade. Sculptural works also decorated Greek funerary monuments. By the 4th century BCE, Greeks had begun to collect statues and commemorative portrait busts from earlier eras for private and public display.

In ancient Rome, as in Greece, civic buildings and temples contained either freestanding or relief sculpture as decorative or devotional objects. The Pantheon (118–128 CE), where statues of the Olympian gods stood in polychrome marble niches surrounding the outer ring of the rotunda lit from the oculus above, became an influential example of sculpture display during Antiquity and for centuries afterward.

The Romans also collected sculpture—particularly copies or original pieces of Greek origin—to adorn their private homes. Emperors, generals, merchants, and landowners went to great expense and effort to acquire and import treasured statues from other lands for display in their palaces and gardens. Private citizens adapted Roman principles of sculpture display in religious or civic buildings. Romans exhibited statues in their homes in symmetrical arrangements of similar height or subject matter; they would place busts and smaller works in wall niches and over doors. Many palaces contained long halls or open atria with colonnades adorned with freestanding statues on pedestals. As an act of devotion and commemoration, Romans exhibited portrait busts and wax death masks of their ancestors in the atria and on the facades of their homes. They followed rules of decorum, placing statues of athletic heroes in gymnasiums and philosophers in libraries. A favorite device was the display of pendant sculptures, comparative in size, style, or iconographic theme.

The majority of sculpture produced in the Middle Ages was intended for devotional purposes or for civic and political commemoration. During the early 15th century, however, Italian humanists rehabilitated ancient theories of architectural design and decoration; following the ancients' example, humanists installed collections of ancient coins, gems, and statuettes in their studies. They also advocated the public display of sculpture on the facades and in the courtyards of palaces, arguing that such adornments would demonstrate the virtue and noble munificence of the owner to the community. Throughout the 15th century and early 16th centuries, palace and villa gardens became repositories for ensembles of ancient sculptures and inscription fragments, emulating descriptions of ancient villas, such as those owned by Cicero and Pliny the Younger. Humanists saw antiquities collections as a sign of education and good taste in emulation of ancient practice.

Perhaps the most influential exhibition of sculpture was the courtyard of the Vatican Belvedere, completed in 1506. Here, Pope Julius II and later popes displayed ancient masterpieces such as the *Apollo Belvedere* and *Laocoön* in large niches surrounding a courtyard. The center of the courtyard held large river god statues functioning as fountains. The collection and display of antiquities in Roman gardens grew considerably during the 16th century. By midcentury collections could be found in over 50 gardens and palaces in Rome, such as that of the famous Cesi Garden and Palace (now destroyed) near St. Peter's Basilica.

The precepts of sculpture display became firmly established during the late 16th and 17th centuries. Following the perceived historical fashion of Antiquity, Italians articulated walls of a room by sets of columns flanking large and small niches containing statues. They displayed portrait busts most commonly on shoulder-high shelves along the interior walls of a room or on shelves or in niches over doors.

The concept of the sculpture gallery appeared during this period, having evolved from Italian and French architectural design. This room became a standard feature in most great European palaces of the 17th century. The gallery was a long hall, usually decorated with mirrors, frescoes, and tapestries. Freestanding sculpture stood in niches or on plinths placed at regular intervals along a wall, usually arranged in long rows according to size and shape for aesthetic balance, although galleries also featured comparative or contrasting pendant works.

Facades of villas and palaces in Rome during this period also served as display spaces for statuary. The facades of the Villas Medici, Borghese, and Pamphili included ancient relief sculpture and niches containing statues; the courtyards of the Mattei and Giustiniani Palaces displayed fragments of sarcophagi and statues imbedded in the walls for decorative purposes.

Owing to an increasing number of wealthy European travelers in Rome during the 16th and 17th centuries and the dissemination of fashionable artistic trends, Italian concepts of sculpture display spread to other countries. Duke Albert V of Bavaria, for example, built in Munich an antiquarium for sculpture that contained a long gallery space displaying busts and freestanding sculpture in niches. In 1618 Daniel Mijtens painted a portrait of Thomas Howard, second earl of Arundel, shown seated before his gallery lined with ancient statues on pedestals.

During the 18th and 19th centuries the popularity of the grand tour and the increased availability of reproductions of ancient and modern sculpture in the form of plaster casts, copies, and prints meant that Italian sculpture collections continued to influence sculpture arrangements throughout Europe. The overriding aesthetic tone of these collections closely followed the tenets of Neoclassicism. In 1734 Clement XII established the Museo Capitolino in Rome, adding a large number of ancient works to an already existing collection. Statues were organized according to size and subject matter, while busts were evenly arranged on shelves in each room and reliefs were imbedded into the walls in symmetrical patterns. The rooms of sculpture in the Museo Pio-Clementino at the Vatican (1771–93) were organized by subject matter and typology; the museum also featured a rotunda with large statues in niches, modeled on the Pantheon. Sculptures in the galleries at the Villa Borghese (*ca.* 1782) were placed in niches over doors and on large plinths. One of the most influential English collections belonged to Charles Townley. Townley displayed his reliefs and statuary in his London home, lit from skylights and symmetrically arranged before red and blue marbled walls. The British Museum acquired this collection in 1805.

Museum walls, such as those at the British Museum, were at first painted gray, but the dingy color of the sculptures and interest in archaeological correctness led to the use of green and Pompeian red. The darker colors served as a contrast to the sculptures and emphasized their forms. During the 19th century, museums such as the Glypotek in Munich illuminated Greek and Roman sculpture with nature light or lanterns from above. Because the Egyptian works in the British Museum were considered artistically inferior, they were illuminated more casually, from the side. The use of electricity in the early 20th century produced the spotlight and the virtual elimination of natural lighting. Today, museums use both natural and artificial lighting.

Until the mid 19th century, museums arranged sculptures primarily according to type, size, or subject matter. A new emphasis on depicting historical development of style replaced this method, and accordingly museums organized collections chronologically. The early 20th century saw the rise of lighter and brighter museum exhibition spaces: lighter wall colors appeared in galleries, pieces for display were chosen more selectively, and plaster casts were expunged. With their interest in chronological accuracy and archaeological detail, museums began to develop "period rooms" that attempted to display sculpture in its original context or similar environment. At present museums more often organize sculpture display according to relative cultural themes, rather than with the idea of stylistic progression. Instead of imitating ancient temple interiors with plinths and columns for sculpture display, contemporary practice includes a wide variety of cases, stands, and pedestals to facilitate viewing of works in different ways from different angles.

KATHERINE BENTZ

See also Apollo Belvedere; Laocoön and His Sons; Pheidias; Pheidias: Athena Parthenos; Plaster Cast; Praxiteles; Rome, Ancient; Relief Sculpture

Further Reading

Bartman, Elizabeth, "Sculptural Collecting and Display in the Private Realm," in *Roman Art in the Private Sphere: New Perspectives on the Architecture and Decor of the Domus,* *Villa, and Insula,* edited by Elaine K. Gazda, Ann Arbor: University of Michigan Press, 1991

Bober, Phyllis Pray, and Ruth Rubinstein, *Renaissance Artists and Antique Sculpture: A Handbook of Sources,* London: Miller, and New York: Oxford University Press, 1986

Coffin, David R., *The Villa in the Life of Renaissance Rome,* Princeton, New Jersey: Princeton University Press, 1979

Coffin, David R., *Gardens and Gardening in Papal Rome,* Princeton, New Jersey: Princeton University Press, 1991

Haskell, Francis, and Nicholas Penny, *Taste and the Antique: The Lure of Classical Sculpture, 1500–1900,* New Haven, Connecticut: Yale University Press, 1981

Hollingsworth, Mary, *Patronage in Renaissance Italy from 1400 to the Early Sixteenth Century,* Baltimore, Maryland: Johns Hopkins University Press, and London: John Murray, 1994

Jenkins, Ian, *Archaeologists and Aesthetes in the Sculpture Galleries of the British Museum, 1800–1939,* London: British Museum Press, 1992

McDougall, Elisabeth B., *Fountains, Statues, and Flowers: Studies in Italian Gardens of the Sixteenth and Seventeenth Centuries,* Washington, D.C.: Dumbarton Oaks, 1994

Pietrangeli, Carlo, *I Musei Vaticani: Cinque secoli di storia,* Rome: Quasar, 1985

Weil Garris, K., "On Pedestals: Michelangelo's David, Bandinelli's Hercules and Cacus, and the Sculpture of the Piazza della Signoria," *Römisches Jahrbuch für Kunstgeschichte* 20 (1983)

DOMENICO DEL BARBIERE *ca.* 1506–1570/1571 *Italian, active in France*

The Italian Domenico del Barbiere played a significant role in French sculpture of the mid 16th century. Although his impact on his adopted city Troyes was notable, most of his commissions were for the court at Fontainebleau or for noble patrons in the east of France. He often translated principal court artist Francesco Primaticcio's designs into three-dimensional work, but his own fluid style counters Jean Goujon's incisive delineation and leads into Germain Pilon's flowing forms. He practiced in a variety of media: carving stone, marble, and wood; modeling for bronze; making stucco decorations; engraving; and, possibly, painting.

Although his birth in Florence is undocumented, his prints and early *stucchi* (stucco work) suggest training in Italy. His small group of 18 engravings constitutes the work of a lively, independent designer, rather than that of a reproductive printmaker in the school of Fontainebleau. These prints bear some relation to those of Jacopo Caraglio, who engraved Rosso Fiorentino's paintings and drawings in Rome in the 1520s. Domenico's earliest sculptural decorations were executed under fellow Florentine Rosso's direction at Fontainebleau. Giorgio Vasari singles Domenico out as the best *stuccatore* (stucco worker) in the team of artists working on the Gallery of Francis I. Although the *comptes des bâtiments du roi* (royal building accounts) does not confirm his work on this commission, it does cite him as one of two artists who executed the stucco work for the Grotte des Pins (1543–44). Following designs by Primaticcio, Domenico and Jean Picard modeled spirited animals for the ceiling. These are in the tradition of Giovanni da Udine, although the stucco work at the Palazzo del Te, Mantua, Italy, where Primaticcio himself worked, must also be considered as a source.

Exactly when Domenico arrived in France is unclear, but he was definitely involved in the decorations at Fontainebleau for the entry of Emperor Charles V, probably 1539–40, and in 1540 he witnessed a baptism in Troyes, where he settled, married, and resided until his death in 1570 or 1571. Much of his activity in the 1540s was under the direction of Primaticcio at court or elsewhere: he helped create the stucco decorations of the Gallery of Ulysses, the largest decorative program at Fontainebleau, and worked for the Dinteville family to decorate their château at Polisy and to carve an altarpiece for the Abbey Church of Montiéramey, Aube, France (which was probably destroyed by Huguenots on 24 August 1570). In 1545–46 he traveled to Rome to take plaster molds of antique statues, later cast in bronze for the king at Fontainebleau. These copies remain at Fontainebleau.

After King Francis I's death in 1547, Domenico was increasingly employed as an independent sculptor in the east of France. His first major work as designer and principal sculptor was a *jubé* (rood screen) for the Church of Saint-Etienne, Troyes. Although this structure was dismantled after 1791, an engraving reveals that Domenico's design was up to date; it followed the classicizing triumphal arch motif first introduced in Pierre Lescot's and Goujon's rood screen at the Church of St. Germain-l'Auxerrois in Paris. Surviving sculptures of *Faith* and *Charity* demonstrate Domenico's personal style. Carved in the soft *pierre de Tonnere* (limestone), the works exhibit a rumpled drapery, relaxed positioning of the limbs, and ample body type. The recently identified *Virgin* and *St. John Evangelist* exaggerate these tendencies even further, with turbulent drapery that forecasts some aspects of Pilon's late style.

Domenico's most important commission, the tomb of Claude de Lorraine, Duke of Guise in Joinville, France, is contemporaneous with the rood screen of Saint-Etienne. Primaticcio designed the tomb, whereas Domenico acted as its principal sculptor, working with Picard and, possibly, Ligier Richier. Closely following the example of French royal tombs and carved from imported Italian marble, the tomb of Claude de Lorraine was a lavish, multifigured work. *Priants* (praying figures) of Claude and his wife Antoinette surmounted a ledge supported by four caryatid allegories, whereas within the mortuary chapel behind were the *gisants* (reclining figures) of the couple atop a richly carved sarcophagus flanked by reliefs and allegorical figures. Domenico's supple, flowing manipulation of the fine marble is particularly evident in high-relief allegories such as *Charity*. The continuous, undulating surface of the *Triumph of Claude de Lorraine, Duke of Guise*, shows his mastery of Florentine relief style of the generation of Pierino da Vinci and Vincenzo Danti, which is married to Primaticcio's elegant line. Some elements of this now-dismantled tomb's style and design were transferred to the tomb of Henry II (1561–73, Basilica of Saint-Denis, Saint-Denis, France); Domenico was commissioned to create the king's *priant* for this tomb, but it was taken over and executed by Pilon.

Domenico continued to work for the Guise family in the late 1550s and returned to work for the court in the early 1560s. At Meudon he worked with Ponce Jacquio to create a series of stucco decorations for the ceilings of the lower galleries in Cardinal de Lorraine's pleasure house, called the Grotte, probably in 1556–57. At the château of Fontainebleau, he directed the work for a pergola in the Jardin de la Reine (the Queen's Garden) and carved nine of its wooden gods and goddesses. His last significant work was the exuberantly Classicist marble pedestal and the bronze urn for the *Monument to the Heart of Henry II*; Pilon's delicately refined *Three Graces* is the monument's focus, clearly demonstrating the ascendancy of the brilliant young French sculptor. Domenico continued to complete minor work until 1567, several years before his death.

The Italian Domenico had an overwhelming impact on the Champagne region of France; his style diverts regional sculptors from a restrained and simple late Gothic form to an increasingly florid, even inflated, Renaissance form. Indeed, the authors Raymond Koechlin and Marquet de Vasselot blame him for subverting pure French style to decadent Italianism. On a national level, Domenico had a role in the development of relief style from the tight, graphic approach of Goujon to the flowing, more pictorial surfaces exemplified by Pilon's *Entombment* (1588). He was instrumental in importing Italian stucco techniques and style to France, and more than any other artist, he realized Primaticcio's vision in sculptural form.

IAN WARDROPPER

See also **Danti, Vincenzo; Goujon, Jean; Pilon, Germain; Primaticcio, Francesco ("il Bologna")**

Biography

Born probably in Tuscany, Italy, *ca.* 1506. Surname of Ricoveri, Riconuri, or Riconucci; adopted the name Domenico del Barbiere for several engravings, but called Dominique Florentin in France. Likely training and practice in sculpture, probably in stucco, as well as engraving, in Italy; moved to France in the late 1530s; first mentioned in the *comptes des batiments du roi* in records for decorations in honor of Charles V's visit to Fontainebleau, *ca.* 1539; settled by 1540 in Troyes, France; became a leading artist—a status confirmed by his role in organizing decorations for the entry of the king to the city in 1548 and 1564—as well as a man of property; steadily employed at Fontainebleau, in Troyes, or in the east of France, 1540–67; returned to Italy, 1545–46, to take plaster casts of antique sculptures in Rome; naturalized French citizen at Joinville, 10 March 1552; last documented commission repairing column for the city of Troyes, 7 November 1567. Died in Troyes, France, between 1570 and 1571.

Selected Works

ca. 1534–40	Decorations for the Gallery of Francis I; stucco; Fontainebleau, France
1540–47	Decorations for the Gallery of Ulysses, Fontainebleau, France; stucco (destroyed)
1543–44	Decorations for the Grotte des Pins; stucco; Fontainebleau, France
1545	Decorations at the Dinteville château, Polisy, France; stucco (destroyed)
1550–52	*Jubé*; stone; Church of Saint-Étienne, Troyes, France (dismantled): *Faith* and *Charity*, St. Pantaléon, Troyes, France; *Virgin* and *St. John Evangelist*, Musée Historique de Troyes et de la Champagne, Troyes, France; and four reliefs of the *Life of St. Stephen*, Saint-Etienne, Bar-sur-Seine, France
1550–52	Tomb of Claude de Lorraine, duke of Guise; marble; Church of St.-Laurent, Joinville, France (dismantled): caryatids of *Temperance* and *Justice* (attributed); Mairie de Joinville; *Triumph of Claude de Lorraine, Duke of Guise; Attack on a City* (Fuentarabia?); *Battle* (Marignan?); two soldiers; pair of *Geniuses*; armorial of Guise-Lorraine (all in relief), Musée du Louvre, Paris, France; head of Antoinette de Bourbon; *Charity of Claude de Lorraine; Justice of Claude de Lorraine; Faith; Religion; Charity; Liberality* (all relief or high relief), Musée de Chaumont, Chaumont-en-Bassigny, France
1555	Tomb of a cardinal (de Givry?); stone and bronze (lost)
ca. 1556–57	Decorations for the Grotte de Meudon, Seine-et-Oise; stucco (destroyed)
1560–61	Nine gods and goddesses for pergola in the Queen's Garden at Fontainebleau, France; wood (lost)
1560–66	Pedestal and urn, for *Monument to the Heart of Henry II* in Church of the Celestins, Paris, France; marble and (originally) bronze; Musée du Louvre, Paris, France

Further Reading

Beaulieu, Michèle, *Description raisonnée des sculptures du Musée du Louvre*, vol. 2, *Renaissance française*, Paris: Éditions de la Réunion des Musées Nationaux, 1978

L'école de Fontainebleau (exhib. cat.), Paris: Éditions des Musées Nationaux, 1972

Koechlin, Raymond, and Jean-Jacques Marquet de Vasselot, *La sculpture à Troyes et dans la Champagne méridionale au seizieme siecle*, Paris: Colin, 1900; reprint, Paris: Reimpression F. de Nobele, 1966

Wardropper, Ian, *The Sculpture and Prints of Domenico del Barbiere*, (dissertation), New York University, 1985

Wardropper, Ian, "New Attributions for Domenico del Barbiere's Jubé at Saint-Étienne, Troyes," *Gazette des Beaux-Arts* 118 (October 1991)

Wardropper, Ian, "Le style de la sculpture de Dominique Florentin, 1550–1570," in *Germain Pilon et les sculpteurs français de la Renaissance*, edited by Geneviève Bresc-Bautier, Paris: Documentation Française, 1993

Wardropper, Ian, Catalogue entries on Domenico del Barbiere in *The French Renaissance in Prints from the Bibliothèque Nationale de France* (exhib. cat.), Los Angeles: Grunwald Center for the Graphic Arts, UCLA, 1994

Zerner, Henri, *École de Fontainebleau, gravures*, Paris: Arts et Métiers Graphiques, 1969; as *The School of Fontainebleau: Etchings and Engravings*, New York: Abrams, and London: Thames and Hudson, 1969

Zerner, Henri, *L'art de la Renaissance en France: L'invention du classicisme*, Paris: Flammarion, 1996

DONATELLO (DONATO DI BETTO BARDI) 1386–1466 *Italian*

Donatello was a prolific and long-lived Florentine sculptor whose career is well documented in the archives of Florence Cathedral, epicenter of his activity and of the guilds. Significant periods of work in Siena, Rome, and Padua are also recorded. Nevertheless, there are major gaps in our knowledge, among which the most serious is the absence of records of his major work for Cosimo de' Medici, a lifelong patron and supporter. Donatello was a key figure in the generation of artists who in the second and third decades of the 15th century created the Renaissance: he was involved with the architect Filippo Brunelleschi in decorating his structures (such as the Old Sacristy, Church of San Lorenzo, Florence), the theoretician Leon Battista Alberti, and together with the painters Masaccio and Paolo Uccello, in pioneering the application of linear perspective to his narrative reliefs (for example, the marble *Feast of Herod*, Musée des Beaux-Arts, Lille, France).

Barely literate, Donatello was evidently a quick learner and had a fertile imagination, a penetrating eye, and a dexterous hand. With these he explored the whole range of sculptural materials and techniques, from modeling and casting in clay or plaster to carving wood and painting the sculptures so created. He could carve sandstone as well as marble and model wax deftly for preservation by casting into bronze (notably the statues and reliefs for the high altar of the Basilica of St. Anthony, Padua). He even experimented with glass, designing stained-glass windows for the Florence Cathedral and casting a roundel in relief of the *Virgin and Child* (lost). Although Donatello was said to be a prolific draftsman, very few (if any) of his drawings have survived. His versatility distinguishes him from sculptors who preferred particular materials, as Lorenzo Ghiberti did bronze and Michelangelo marble.

Donatello learned the rudiments of modeling from Ghiberti as an apprentice and may have manufactured a number of terracottas—especially images of the Virgin and Child—after he became independent. By 1408 he must have made his name as a marble carver to have been awarded commissions as prestigious as the *David* and the *St. John the Evangelist* for Florence Cathedral. It is presumed that he learned the technique in the workshops at the cathedral; for Ghiberti, a goldsmith, was not qualified to teach him. That Donatello's efforts met with approval is indicated by the steady flow of desirable commissions that ensued: noble statues of patron saints of various guilds for Orsanmichele, hard-bitten, ascetic figures of *Prophets* for the Campanile of Florence Cathedral and several associated panels of narrative carved in the technique of shallow relief (*relievo schiacciato*) that he developed to use the new discovery of linear perspective. During the 1420s he applied himself to modeling all sorts of figures and reliefs in wax for casting into bronze and gilding: a statue of *St. Louis of Toulouse* for Orsanmichele, the effigy of the antipope John XXIII for his tomb, a reliquary bust of San Rossore, and statuettes and reliefs for the Siena Cathedral.

Donatello varied his approach to suit different materials and diverse subjects. For the *Cavalcanti Annunciation* tableau in the Church of Santa Croce, he used Classical types of head and drapery to enhance the calm solemnity of the critical moment, while about the same time he carved in wood and painted a haggard statue of *St. John the Baptist* (1438) for the Florentine colony in Venice. Later he sought similar effects in his *St. Mary Magdalene* and figure of *St. Jerome* (*ca.* 1455?)—both in polychrome wood. He then moved

effortlessly into the very different medium of bronze, exploiting its potential of accurately recording surface textures created in wax, even using real textile impressions on occasion, to make horrifying images of *St. John the Baptist* (1456–57) for the Siena Cathedral and of *Judith Slaying Holofernes* for Cosimo de' Medici's garden. Yet in the same material Donatello could render the suave, almost Hellenistic sensitivity of his nude statue of *David* and his crucifix in Padua. This subtle ambivalence makes his work difficult to date by the normal criteria of stylistic comparison, which assumes a steady evolutionary process: the bronze *David*, for instance, although a key work, has been dated by different scholars at points ranging over two decades (from the mid 1430s to the mid 1450s).

Donatello aimed to communicate ideas forcibly, even shockingly at times, to his viewers, as demonstrated by his movingly emaciated and decrepit images of prophets and hermit-saints. It is even more apparent in his reliefs, when the subjects permitted—or de-

David
The Conway Library, Courtauld Institute of Art

manded—it. His fragmentary panel of the *Lamentation over the Dead Christ* (before 1456) and his several *Crucifixions* attest to the effectiveness of his almost Expressionist approach—one in which the initial dexterity of modeling in wax and the subsequent frenzied chiseling, rasping, or hammering of the bronze in the cold metal betray the artist's intense emotional involvement with the drama and violence of his subjects. In his later years Donatello created an unforgettable and harrowing series of panels for the twin pulpits in San Lorenzo narrating the *Passion of Christ* in all its inhuman brutality. These are complemented by episodes from the *Resurrection* to *Pentecost*, which are scarcely less shocking, inasmuch as he tries to make the beholder empathize with the agitated state of mind of the apostles as these miracles enmeshed their humble lives.

Donatello was a great innovator. If the recent corroboration of an old attribution to him of a painted terracotta bust of *Niccolò da Uzzano* (Museo Nazionale del Bargello, Florence) is correct, Donatello was responsible for reviving the concept of the portrait bust), which until now has been credited to younger marble carvers of the mid 15th century (Mino da Fiesole and Antonio Rossellino) based on signed and dated examples. Furthermore, in his workshop in the 1420s or 1430s, there seem to have originated two characteristic emanations of the Renaissance, the bronze statuette and the plaquette.

Donatello's presence in Siena (twice) and in Padua served to establish in both cities a school of sculpture in bronze that was kept alive by Francesco di Giorgio and Vecchietta in Siena and by Donatello's pupil Bartolomeo Bellano and by Andrea Mantegna, Severo Calzetta da Ravenna, and Il Riccio in Padua. Donatello was respected by Michelangelo, who in his youth had been in contact with Bertoldo di Giovanni (who had helped Donatello finish the reliefs for San Lorenzo, although these were not mounted until 1513). Michelangelo modeled his statue of *Moses* (ca. 1515) on Donatello's *St. John the Evangelist* and admired the psychological power of his *St. Mark*, while the noble youthful head of Michelangelo's *David* (1501–04) owes something to that of Donatello's *St. George*.

CHARLES AVERY

See also **Ghiberti, Lorenzo; Italy: Renaissance–Baroque; Michelangelo (Buonarroti); Modeling; Relief Sculpture; Renaissance and Mannerism; Wax**

Biography

Born in Florence, Italy, *ca.* 1386. Apprenticed to Lorenzo Ghiberti, 1404–07, and worked on bronze doors of Baptistery, Florence; earliest major commissions, for Florence Cathedral, 1408–09; success there led to

many other commissions, including from the Linen Drapers' Guild, 1411, and from the Guild of Armorers, *ca.* 1415, both for statues of patron saints for their niches in the guildhall of the Church of Orsanmichele, Florence; worked in partnership with Nanni di Bartolo, 1420s; went into partnership with Michelozzo di Bartolommeo, 1425–33, for production of important monumental tombs; visited Pisa, 1426, where he was in contact with Masaccio; moved to Rome with Michelozzo, 1430; returned to Florence, where he lived and worked on the site of the projected Medici palace for Cosimo I de' Medici, 1433–43; moved to Padua, 1443; returned to Florence, 1454, to work again for the new palace of Cosimo I; fell ill, 1456, and gave his doctor, Giovanni Chellini, a bronze roundel, the *Virgin and Child* (Victoria and Albert Museum), to pay his bill; moved to Siena, 1457; returned precipitately to Florence in 1459, perhaps to begin work again for Cosimo I. Died in Florence, Italy, 13 December 1466.

Selected Works

1408–09 *David*; marble; Museo Nazionale del Bargello, Florence, Italy

1408–15 *St. John the Evangelist*; marble; Museo dell'Opera del Duomo, Florence, Italy

1411–13 *St. Mark*; marble; Museo di Orsanmichele, Florence, Italy

ca. *St. George* and *St. George and the*
1415–20 *Dragon*; marble; Museo Nazionale del Bargello, Florence, Italy

1415–27 *Prophets*; marble; Museo dell'Opera del Duomo, Florence, Italy

1418–22 *St. Louis of Toulouse*; gilded bronze; Museo dell'Opera di Santa Croce, Florence, Italy

ca. *Feast of Herod* and *Faith, Hope,* and
1423–29 *Putti*; bronze; baptismal font, Baptistery of Siena Cathedral, Siena, Italy

1425–28 Tomb of Baldassare Cossa, Antipope John XXIII (with Michelozzo di Bartolommeo); marble, gilded bronze; Baptistery, Florence, Italy

1433–35 Singing gallery (also known as Cantoria); marble; Museo dell'Opera del Duomo, Florence, Italy

ca. 1435 *Cavalcanti Annunciation*; sandstone; Church of Santa Croce, Florence, Italy

1438 *St. John the Baptist*; gilded and polychrome wood; Church of Santa Maria Gloriosa dei Frari, Venice, Italy

1444–49 Santo Altar reliefs, crucifix, *Virgin and Child* and six saints, *Miracles of St. Anthony*, evangelical symbols, and musician angels; bronze; *Lamentation*;

Nanto stone and glazed terracotta; high altar, Basilica of Sant'Antonio, Padua, Italy

ca. *David*; bronze; Museo Nazionale del
1455? Bargello, Florence, Italy

ca. *St. Mary Magdalene*; gilded and
1455? polychrome wood; Museo dell'Opera del Duomo, Florence, Italy

ca. 1456 *Virgin and Child*; bronze; Victoria and Albert Museum, London, England

1456–57 *St. John the Baptist*; bronze; Siena Cathedral, Italy

ca. 1459 *Judith Slaying Holofernes*; bronze; Palazzo della Signoria, Florence, Italy

ca. 1459 *Passion of Christ, Resurrection,* and *Pentecost*; bronze; Church of San Lorenzo, Florence, Italy

Further Reading

Ames-Lewis, Francis, "Donatello's Bronze *David* Reconsidered," *Art History* 2 (1974)

Avery, Charles, "Donatello's Madonnas Revisited," in *Donatello-Studien*, edited by Monika Cämmerer, Munich: Bruckmann, 1989

Avery, Charles, *Donatello: Catalogo completo delle opere*, Florence: Cantini, 1991

Avery, Charles, *Donatello: An Introduction*, New York: Icon Editions, and London: John Murray, 1994

Avery, Charles, "Donatello and the Medici," in *The Early Medici and Their Artists*, edited by Francis Ames-Lewis, London: Birkbeck College, University of London, Department of the History of Art, 1995

Bennett, Bonnie, and David Wilkins, *Donatello*, Oxford: Phaidon, and Mt. Kisco, New York: Moyer Bell, 1984

Darr, Alan (editor), *Italian Renaissance Sculpture in the Time of Donatello* (exhib. cat.), Detroit, Michigan: The Detroit Institute of Arts, 1985

Dunkelman, Martha, "Donatello's Influence on Italian Renaissance Painting," (dissertation), New York University, 1976

Elam, Caroline, et al., "Donatello at Close Range," *The Burlington Magazine* 129 (1987)

Greenhalgh, Michael, *Donatello and His Sources*, London: Duckworth, 1982

Janson, Horst, *The Sculpture of Donatello*, Princeton: Princeton University Press, 1957; revised edition, 1963

Johnson, Geraldine, "'In the Eye of the Beholder': Donatello's Sculpture in the Life of Renaissance Italy," (dissertation), Harvard University, 1994

Jolly, Anna, *Madonnas by Donatello and His Circle*, Frankfurt and New York: Peter Lang, 1998

Pope-Hennessy, John, *An Introduction to Italian Sculpture*, 3 vols., London: Phaidon, 1963; 4th edition, 1996; see especially vol. 2, *Italian Renaissance Sculpture*

Pope-Hennessy, John, *Donatello: Sculptor*, New York: Abbeville Press, 1993

Radcliffe, Anthony, and Charles Avery, "The Chellini Madonna by Donatello," *The Burlington Magazine* 118 (1976)

Rosenauer, Artur, *Donatello*, Milan: Electa, 1993

Sperling, Christine, "Donatello's Bronze *David* and the Demands of the Medici Politics," *The Burlington Magazine* 134 (1992)

ST. GEORGE

Donatello (Donato di Betto Bardi) (1386–1466)
1416–1417
marble
h. of statue 2.1 m; h. of base 39 cm
Museo Nazionale del Bargello, Florence, Italy

Donatello's *St. George* was part of the sculptural ornamentation of Orsanmichele, a building originally designed and used as a public grain house but eventually transformed into a church. The external niches of Orsanmichele, which host marble and bronze works by Donatello, Lorenzo Ghiberti, Nanni di Banco, Giambologna, and others, constitute the greatest open-air museum of Renaissance sculpture. The *St. George* was originally installed in a tabernacle crowned by a cusp. A pointed arch is inscribed in the cusp and rests on a trilobe. The relief in the cusp area depicts God the Father in a blessing attitude; his left hand braces the Bible, which rests realistically (as always in Donatello's works) on the arch. Over the centuries the *St. George* was shifted from place to place in Orsanmichele (for a while it was installed on the south wall); in 1892 it was moved to the Bargello Museum and replaced by a bronze copy. The predella (painted panel at the bottom of an altarpiece) rejoined the statue only in 1976, and has been replaced by a marble copy.

The date ascribed to the statue is based on a document regarding the marble used for the base. The Armorers' Guild, which commissioned the tabernacle and its internal decoration, bought the stone from the cathedral's Opera in 1417. Understandably, the guild needed a warrior saint in armor. Donatello had already supplied the *St. Mark* for Orsanmichele only a few years earlier, and immediately afterward he made the gilded bronze *St. Louis of Toulouse*, which is now in the Museo dell'Opera di Santa Croce, Florence. As Artur Rosenauer, among others, has noted, the *St. Mark* was the first example of Renaissance sculpture in that it was freestanding and completely self-sufficient, not dependent in any way on the architectural framework.

During this period Donatello began working on several statues for the bell tower (now in the Museo dell'Opera del Duomo). He was thus engaged in wide-ranging experiments with different arrangements of the full human figure in life-size or slightly larger. These experiments certainly included a great variety of movements, but they also showed a full range of expressions, facial features, and psychologies because in Donatello's works the face is always strongly characterized and corresponds to a specific, exactly identifiable, and definable spiritual moment. In this case, the young warrior saint is measuring with preoccupied attention the difficult challenge awaiting him to free the princess, and his gaze is anything but arrogant. Likewise, his pose is that of a person preparing for combat. His feet are planted firmly on the ground with a realistic weight distribution studied from nature, and he projects into the foreground a five-sided shield on which the symbol of Christianity stands out. The textural differentiation is extraordinary; the same marble renders the skin, the metal of the armor, and the cloth of the mantle, with its large knot in front of the right shoulder. It is possible that the figure, like Donatello's bronze *Judith Slaying Holofernes*, originally grasped a now-lost lance or some other metal weapon in his right hand.

The *St. George* has been greatly admired since Donatello's own day. The most extraordinary praise, expressed with critical intelligence and exceptional literary and poetical force, came from Giorgio Vasari, who must have been particularly fond of this saint, his namesake. He wrote that the statue is "extremely vivid," and that "in the head, there may be seen the beauty of youth, courage, and valor in arms, and a proud and terrible ardor." In addition, there is a marvelous suggestion of movement within the stone; in emphasizing this "gesto di muoversi," Vasari recognized the suspense of the moment despite the solidity of the stance, because in an instant the saint would be off to mount his horse and do battle with the dragon. Donatello suggested movement with a very subtle play of twists: the body leans slightly backward to the right and the head turns slightly to the left. Taken as a whole, however, the figure is marked by an accentuated frontality that seems to push it out of the niche together with all its components. This sensation is augmented by the shallowness of the niche. Since the pillar behind it encloses a spiral stairway leading to the upper floor of the building, less depth was left for this niche than for the others. In the last analysis, one may agree with Hans Kauffmann that "with one glance we can embrace the whole thing" (see Kauffmann, 1935).

Donatello presents a figure that is immediately perceived as a whole, one that imposes itself with extraordinary power and realism, as if what is seen were real life in all its physicality. The structure of the tabernacle—unquestionably designed by the sculptor himself—bolsters this immediacy of perception with its severe simplicity. If its date is considered, it is understandable how a figure like the *St. George* really does stand at the beginning of modern Western civilization and how Donatello concentrated in it the cultural values of the Florentine Renaissance, above all the rediscovery of natural observation.

Likewise, the predella scene—considered the first surviving example of a 15th-century bas-relief by Donatello—has always been greatly admired. It is not only the first example by Donatello, but also of the

Saint George
© Arte & Immagini srl / CORBIS

15th century on the whole. At first sight, the painterly effects of the relief are almost disconcerting. Its real depth is no more than two centimeters; the sculptor thus displayed an uncommon technical virtuosity. This is what Vasari called *relievo schiacciato*, crushed relief, where multiple planes are compressed in a play of calculations that render the size and distance of each object with the greatest care. The supreme lightness of the carving does not prevent the sculptor from giving the saint on horseback all the weight necessary to plunge his lance into the dragon's body. From a strictly geometric standpoint, there may be a few mistakes in the linear perspective, as some people have opined. This would be only natural, because the work was created at the very dawn of Renaissance perspective, of which it is the earliest surviving example. But what counts is the sculptor's intelligence in rendering a complex, action-filled scene in two-dimensional perspective. This predella is thus the archetype for later virtuoso marble reliefs such as the ones at the Victoria and Albert Museum in London (*St. Peter Receiving the Keys, ca.* 1430) and in Lille (*The Feast of Herod, ca.* 1435).

GIORGIO BONSANTI

See also **Ghiberti, Lorenzo; Giambologna; Nanni di Banco**

Further Reading

Avery, Charles, "Donatello," in *The Dictionary of Art*, edited by Jane Turner, New York: Grove, and London: Macmillan, 1996

Bonsanti, Giorgio (editor), *Donatello e i suoi: Scultura fiorentina del primo Rinascimento* (exhib. cat.), Florence: La Casa Usher, 1986; with Alan Phipps Darr (editor), Detroit, Michigan: Founders Society, Detroit Institute of Arts, 1986

Cämmerer, Monika (editor), *Donatello—Studien*, Munich: Bruckmann, 1989

Kauffmann, Hans, *Donatello: Eine Einführung in sein Bilden und Denken*, Berlin: Grotesche Verlagsbuchhandlung, 1935

Omaggio a Donatello, 1386–1986 (exhib. cat.), Florence: Museo Nazionale del Bargello, 1985

SANTO ALTAR RELIEFS

Donatello (Donato di Betto Bardi) (1386–1466)

ca. 1447

bronze, partially gilded and silvered

h. 123 cm

High altar, Basilica of Sant'Antonio, Padua, Italy

A series of four panoramic scenes of miracles performed by the name saint of the Basilica of Sant'Antonio in Padua were destined for the predella (panel at the bottom of an altarpiece) of the high altar, with two on the front and two at the back. Above them and under a tabernacle stood life-size figures in bronze of the *Virgin and Child* flanked by saints, some of whom were patrons of the church, such as Francis (founder of the order) and Anthony (his faithful companion), and others of the city of Padua. The reliefs are brilliantly designed and perfectly finished; they rate among Donatello's supreme masterpieces of narrative sculpture. They were intended by their patrons, the Conventual Franciscan friars, to revindicate their claims to supremacy against their new rivals, the Observants.

The use of wax in the preliminary models, which would have been laid out on boards with the architectural surrounds carefully inscribed with rulers and compasses, permitted greater freedom to Donatello than he had enjoyed when working in stucco to create the roundels of the life of St. John the Evangelist in the Old Sacristy of the Church of San Lorenzo, Florence, a few years earlier. The width of the fields allowed his imagination freedom to invent grand schemes of Classical architecture according to his own taste and to provide settings for the medieval stories, which were taken to be literally true in his day. The casting in bronze was delegated to Andrea Conti (known as "of the cauldrons"), a Paduan foundryman.

The pair of panels on the front, mounted directly behind the altar table and thus immediately visible to the priest when celebrating Mass, are probably the *Miracle of the Miser's Heart* and that of the *Repentant Son*, for they have a relatively high viewpoint. The other pair, depicting the *Miracle of the Mule* and the *Newborn Baby*, have the figures thrust well forward, in some cases projecting over the edge of the frame, and are in open-air settings so that they can easily be seen from below, as is the case in the monks' choir behind the altar. Furthermore, there they flank the tabernacle where the Blessed Sacrament is reserved, to which their subjects are more pertinent.

In each case, the crucial episode involving St. Anthony is central, and in three scenes, this is emphasized by the tripartite division of the architecture; in the fourth episode, it is emphasized by the sharply converging lines of a stadium seen in perspective. In this last scene, showing the *Repentant Son*, Donatello opened out in an unorthodox way the perspective of the right foreground so that it would be more readily visible.

Donatello's great achievement is the variety of effect in the four equal panels, where a lesser artist may have been content with a less challenging uniformity. The *Miracle of the Mule*, for instance, is divided precisely into three panels by the Roman barrel vaults that soar above the figures in what would be in reality a most unusual arrangement for the chancel of a Christian basilica. Intriguingly, cavernous spaces are revealed behind the gratings. The saint and the head of the docile beast kneeling to receive the Blessed Sacrament are silhouetted in dark bronze against the radiant gilding on the front of the altar in the scene. From either side, amazed spectators press forward to behold the event, creating a melee of figures, each reacting individually to it; indeed, Henry Moore compared Donatello's abilities as a theatrical director with those of Shakespeare. In the scene with the *Newborn Baby*, the central compartment of the palace is wider than the wings in order to permit a greater crush of courtiers around St. Anthony, the baby, and the blameless mother and the arrogant father in his grand attire. Along the sides, servants rush about in excitement. The protagonist with baby and mother are so posed as to form an isosceles triangle, with a roundel of the Virgin and Child significantly at its apex.

A similar tripartite setting, although now in an exterior space, was used to articulate the *Miracle of the Miser's Heart*. Although the dissection of the miser's corpse is in the center, the focus of the action is in the far left-hand corner, where the heart is discovered in his money chest. In the opposite corner, a young mother comforts two weeping children while other bystanders flee. Donatello provided a number of such appealing vignettes and subsidiary themes, weaving

Detail of *Musician Angels*
© Elio Ciol / CORBIS

them together like a gifted novelist. In the background, the artist amused himself with sketching in an almost proto-Piranesian fantasy of architectonic depths, articulated by staircases and banister rails projected in correct perspective.

In the *Miracle of the Repentant Son*, as St. Anthony kneels on the ground and bends forward to adjust into position the leg that an impetuous youth had severed because he had kicked his mother with it. The drama and high emotion of the story are expressed in a series of triangles formed by the contours of the figures, but then carried through the whole setting in the banister rails of stairs to either side of the foreground, in the receding lines of steps and railings round the arena, and in the projecting triangle formed by the near corner of a distant structure set at 45 degrees to the others.

All the scenes are enlivened by the damascening technique, letting strips of gold or silver into channels in the surface of the otherwise dark bronze so as to catch the light and assist visibility in the flickering candlelight, which was formerly virtually the only illumination in the rather gloomy interior of the basilica. It recalls Donatello's use of gold mosaic behind the marble putti on his singing gallery for Florence Cathedral. Byzantine mosaics were also a prominent feature of church decoration in northeastern Italy, from Ravenna to Venice.

These narrative reliefs formed part of a larger scheme for the decoration of the whole structure of the high altar, comprising a great stone carving of the *Lamentation*, with half-life-size figures; four square

panels with the symbols of the evangelists; *a Dead Christ with Mourning Cherubim*; and 12 upright rectangular panels cast with charming angel musicians.

CHARLES AVERY

See also **Relief Sculpture**

Further Reading

Busignani, Alberto, "Donatello: L'altare del Santo," *Forma e Colore* 11 (1965)
Calore, Andrea, "Andrea Conti 'da le caldiere' e l'opera di Donatello a Padova," in *Contributi Donatelliani*, Padua: Centro Studi Antoniani, 1996

GEORG RAPHAEL DONNER 1693–1741

Austrian

Georg Raphael Donner was one of the most significant artists of the Late Baroque in Central Europe. We know little of his youth. Originally baptized Georg, he adopted the name Raphael as an adult in honor of the Renaissance painter, whom he greatly admired.

Donner's earliest signed and dated surviving work is from the Duchov castle of the Waldstein family, a terracotta *Pietà* group of statues (1721), which bears the influence of his master, Giovanni Giuliani, and that of Italian art. Hardly any of his works produced between 1720 and 1725 are known, although this was presumably the period when he made his first lead sculptures, for example, *Apollo* (Liebieghaus, Frankfurt), *Apollo* (Ruth Blumka Collection, New York City), and *Mercury with Amor* (Stiftsmuseum, Klosterneuburg), inspired by François du Quesnoy.

In 1725 Donner moved to Salzburg, working as a sculptor and medalist with his workshop in the service of Count Franz Anton Harrach, Archbishop of Salzburg. Commissioned by the archbishop, Donner created the staircase sculptures of the Salzburg Mirabell Castle between 1725 and 1727. Among the over-life-size niche statues carved from Untersberg marble, *Paris* is Donner's own work (signed and dated 1726); the rest of the mythological figures and putti on the balustrade were produced in collaboration with his assistants. The themes and form of the statues show mainly antique and Italian Renaissance influences.

Our knowledge of Donner's medal making is based on his works from the Salzburg years, including a silver taler with the portrait of Archbishop Harrach from 1726, a glorifying silver medal with the portrait of Karl Albrecht, Elector of Bavaria, made for a Munich order in 1727, and a gold medal from 1728 with the portrait of Count Leopold Anton Firmian, Archbishop of Salzburg (all Kunsthistorisches Museum, Vienna). They are made in the tradition of his master, Benedict Richter. About the same time he was carving his marble

Fountain of Providence, from the Donner-Brunnen fountain, Vienna, Austria
© Erich Lessing / Art Resource, NY

sculpture *St. John of Nepomuk* in Linz at the request of Joseph Harrach.

Count Imre Esterházy, Prince Archbishop of Hungary, Archbishop of Esztergom, commissioned Donner about 1728 to work on the Chapel of St. John the Almsgiver, which was being built on the northern side of St. Martin's Cathedral in Bratislava. Together with the sculptural decoration, Donner probably also designed the architectural plans, or at least collaborated in the planning. At the end of 1729 he moved to Bratislava, where he, together with his workshop, served Prince Archbishop Esterházy as court sculptor and director of building work (*Baudirektor*). In 1729–32 Donner and his workshop executed the chapel. Donner created two white marble angels standing on both sides of the reliquary altar, the gilded bronze *Pietà* tabernacle relief, six gilded bronze *Passion* predella reliefs (a series of panels at the bottom of an altarpiece), and the praying figure of Prince Archbishop Imre Esterházy as a tomb statue in Carrara white marble and in Hungarian Süttö red marble in 1730–31. Also at this time he cast two bronze candelabra; that these were incorrectly considered to be Italian works of the 16th or 17th centuries clearly demonstrates the influence of Italian Manner-

ism, and specifically Giambologna, on his sculptural and goldsmith works. The chapel, consecrated on 28 October 1732, later served as the burial place of Prince Archbishop Esterházy. With this work, and its rich use of varying shades of marble and gilded bronzes, Donner finally gained recognition within the archbishop's circle, as well as in Vienna, which before this had dismissed him.

Again commissioned by Prince Archbishop Esterházy, Donner cast over-life-size lead sculptures for the main altar of St. Martin's Cathedral in 1733–35. Although the altar was demolished in the 1865–67 Neo-Gothic renovation of the cathedral, the original structure can be reconstructed via photos and contemporary representations. In the middle was the dynamic equestrian statue *St. Martin and the Beggar* (today in the side aisle of the cathedral), while in the foreground to the right and to the left were two adoring angels, today in the National Gallery of Hungary, Budapest. The figures are cast in lead, which before this was rarely used in Central European sculpture. Lead was Donner's favorite material because it was relatively easy to model, enabling him to represent the human body in soft modeling, as well as to produce massive forms. Donner probably learned lead casting in Germany; through him it became a popular process in Austria, Hungary, and Slovakia. Owing to the success of the main altar, he was given several commissions by prince Archbishop Esterházy that were executed by Donner's well-organized workshop.

Executing commissions from Vienna and its environs while he was in the service of Prince Archbishop Esterházy in Bratislava, Donner carved in Carrara marble the *Apotheosis of Emperor Charles VI* for the Breitenfurt castle of Gregor Wilhelm von Kirchner, imperial officer. Its composition and carving is similar in style to that of Balthasar Permoser and of the French Baroque royal portraits. Between 1735 and 1739 Donner created small-size sculptures and reliefs, often making several copies of these in collaboration with his workshop, such as his bust *Emperor Charles VI* on signed oval marble relief, *Count Gundacker Althann* bust on signed oval marble relief, *Mercury* and *Venus* pendant lead sculptures, and *Judgment of Paris* and *Venus at the Forge of Vulcan* pendant lead reliefs.

The commissions of the Viennese City Council (Magistrat) provided Donner with new challenges. He carved for the Magistrat in Carrara marble the signed and dated pendant lavabo reliefs *Christ and the Woman of Samaria* and *Hagar in the Desert* for the lower sacristy of the Viennese St. Stephen's Cathedral (Stephansdom), as well as the cast molds of the sculptures of the Fountain of Providence intended for the Mehlmarkt (today Neuer Markt) in Vienna. As a result of the large-scale commissions of the Magistrat, Donner moved back to Vienna autumn 1739, where he lived until his death.

The Fountain of Providence, unveiled on 4 November 1739, was one of the most important works of Donner's sculptural career. He placed *Providence*, a sitting female figure symbolizing caution and wisdom, in the middle of the fountain on a pillarlike pedestal. Leaning on a shield with a Janus head casting her eyes into the past and the future, the figure holds in her left hand a snake, symbolizing wisdom. Four putti around the pedestal play with fish common in the Danube: catfish, pike, carp, and sturgeon. Originally, water flowed through the mouths of the fish into the fountain, representing the Danube. On the curb of the fountain the dynamically formed figures of the four river gods, *Ybbs*, *Enns*, *March*, and *Traun*, personify the four tributaries of the Danube. The fountain's style may be traced back primarily to Hubert Gerhard's Augustus fountain in Augsburg, as well as French Baroque park statues. The lead sculptures of the fountain were replaced in 1873 with bronze replicas. The original fountain statues are exhibited in the Marble Hall of the Viennese Unteres Belvedere.

After the success of the Fountain of Providence, the Magistrat commissioned Donner to create a wall fountain into the courtyard of the Viennese Town Hall (today Old Town Hall). He worked on this Fountain of Andromeda, also from lead, in 1740–41. The theme of the wall fountain—Perseus releasing Andromeda—represented Vienna's freedom from the threat of the Ottoman Turks. Certain details of the high-modeled relief show the influence of Annibale Carracci and Danese Cattaneo.

Donner was commissioned by Franz Otto Kochler von Jochenstein Provost to make a Holy Cross altar and a new pulpit for the Gurk Cathedral. The middle sculptural group, the *Pietà*, was completed by Donner in 1740, but the rest was finished by his workshop in 1741. The *Pietà* is lyrical in tone; the figures of the four angels and Mary bemoaning the dead Christ powerfully represent the emotional experience of death and mourning. The delicate representation of pain and sympathy shows kinship with the paintings of Donner's friend Paul Troger. The pyramid-like structural arrangement of the figures can be traced back to Nicholas Coustou's work of the same topic in the Cathedral of Notre Dame in Paris. Donner's last signed and dated work was *Count Johann Kaspar von Cobenzl* (1741), a bust on an oval marble relief in the Cathedral of Graz, Austria.

Donner's formal style was promulgated primarily by his younger brother and disciple, Matthäus Donner. The most gifted assistants coming from Donner's workshop to have successful careers include Jakob Christoph Schletterer, Johann Nikolaus Moll and his brother, Balthasar Ferdinand Moll, Adam Friedrich Oeser, Franz Kohl, and Ludwig Gode.

KATALIN HÁMORI

See also **Central Europe; du Quesnoy, François; Fountain Sculpture**

Biography

Born in Essling (present-day Vienna), Austria, 24 May 1693. Studied in Vienna under a goldsmith Prenner, *ca.* 1704, then under the Venetian sculptor Giovanni Giuliani in Vienna and Heiligenkreuz, *ca.* 1706–10; studied with his younger brother, Matthäus Donner (also a sculptor), under the Swedish medalist Benedikt Richter in Vienna, after 1713; traveled to study the works of Balthasar Permoser in Dresden, Germany, 1721; moved to Salzburg, Austria, 1725; worked as a sculptor and medalist with his workshop in the service of Count Franz Anton Harrach, Archbishop of Salzburg, 1725–27; received commissions from Munich and Linz, 1727; returned to Vienna, 1728; moved to Bratislava (Hungarian Pozsony, German Pressburg, capital of the Hungarian Kingdom, current capital of Slovakia), 1729 and worked as a sculptor and director of building work, with his workshop in the service of Hungarian Prince Archbishop Imre Esterházy, 1729–39; received commissions from Vienna and its environs at the same time; moved to Vienna because of commissions from the Vienna City Council, 1739; worked in Vienna, 1739–41; received commissions from Vienna, Gurk, and Graz in this period. Died in Vienna, Austria, 15 February 1741.

Selected Works

1721   *Pietà*; terracotta; National Gallery, Prague, Czech Republic

1725–27 Statues; marble; Mirabell Castle, Salzburg, Austria

1726   *Paris*; marble; Mirabell Castle, Salzburg, Austria

1729–32 Reliquary altar: two standing angels; marble; *Pietà* relief and six reliefs of the *Passion*; gilded bronze; tomb of Prince Archbishop Imre Esterházy; marble; Chapel of St. John the Almsgiver, St. Martin's Cathedral, Bratislava, Slovakia

1733–35 St. Martin's main altar of St. Martin's Cathedral, Bratislavia, Slovakia, lead (demolished 1865–67); fragments include *St. Martin and the Beggar*; lead; St. Martin's Cathedral, Bratislava, Slovakia; two adoring angels; lead; National Gallery of Hungary, Budapest, Hungary

1734   *Apotheosis of Emperor Charles VI*; marble; Österreichisches Barockmuseum, Vienna, Austria

1738–39 *Christ and the Woman of Samaria* and *Hagar in the Desert*; marble; Österreichisches Barockmuseum, Vienna, Austria

1737–39 Fountain of Providence, including figures of *Providence, Ybbs, Enns, March,* and *Traun,* and four putti with different fish; lead; Österreichisches Barockmuseum, Vienna, Austria

1740–41 Fountain of Andromeda; lead; Old Town Hall, Vienna, Austria

1740–41 *Pietà*; lead; Gurk Cathedral, Carinthia, Austria

Further Reading

Balogh, Jolán, *Katalog der ausländischen Bildwerke des Museums der Bildenden Künste in Budapest, IV.–XVIII. Jahrhundert,* 2 vols., Budapest: Akadémiai Kiadó, 1975

Baum, Elfriede, *Katalog des Österreichischen Barockmuseums im Unteren Belvedere in Wien,* 2 vols., Vienna and Munich: Herold, 1980

Blauensteiner, Kurt, *Georg Raphael Donner,* edited by Waltraud Blauensteiner, Vienna: Schroll, 1944; 2nd edition, 1947

Diemer, Claudia, *Georg Raphael Donner: Die Reliefs,* Nuremberg, Germany: s.n., 1979

Krapf, Michael (editor), *Georg Raphael Donner, 1693–1741* (exhib. cat.), Vienna: Österreichische Galerie, 1993

Maué-Diemer, Claudia, "Georg Raphael Donner," in *The Dictionary of Art,* edited by Jane Turner, New York: Grove, and London: Macmillan, 1996

Pigler, Andreas, *Georg Raphael Donner,* Leipzig and Vienna: Hans Epstein, 1929

Pöhl-Maliková, Ma'na, Hana Benediková, and Marta Zipserová (editors), *Georg Raphael Donner und Bratislava (1693–1741)* (exhib. cat.), Bratislava: Slowakische Nationalgalerie, 1992

Schemper-Sparholz, Ingeborg (editor), *Georg Raphael Donner: Einflüsse und Auswirkungen seiner Kunst,* Vienna: Schroll, 1998

Schwarz, Michael, *Georg Raphael Donner: Kategorien der Plastik,* Munich: Fink, 1968

DOORS: BRONZE

Bronze (an alloy of copper and tin) was one of the most prestigious mediums in Antiquity. Bronze doors still survive from Antiquity at the Pantheon in Rome and the Basilica of San Giovanni in Laterano in Rome. These bear no figurative illustrations, however. Important bronze doors that no longer survive are those made for the royal abbey of Saint-Denis, near Paris. Completed for Charlemagne in 775, they depicted the life of St. Denis and the patrons of the Church. These doors plus two further gilt-bronze doors for the west end of the church (1140) depicting the Passion and Resurrection of Christ were melted down in 1794. In the Carolingian period, sculptors revived the casting of bronze doors, such as the doors to the entrance of Charlemagne's Palatine Chapel (now the cathedral) at Aachen, Germany (*ca.* 800). These are quite severe and Classical in design, with distinctive lion-headed door knockers, but they differ from their Classical prototypes in their casting in one piece as opposed to as separate elements.

Germany was an important center for bronze casting in the Ottonian period, as is testified by the doors commissioned by Bishop Bernward of Hildesheim for the Church of St. Michael in Hildesheim. Completed in 1015, according to an inscription, these represent a major landmark in the development of bronze doors. Later, they were moved to Hildesheim Cathedral, where they can still be seen today. The Hildesheim doors are important in two respects: first, each was cast in one piece (a tour de force in bronze casting), and second, they are decorated with an extensive series of narrative illustrations in high relief from the Old and New Testaments. Bishop Bernward had traveled extensively in northern Italy and Rome, where he may have been influenced by the early Christian wooden doors from the Cathedral of Sant'Ambrogio in Milan and the Basilica of Santa Sabina in Rome.

A set of doors with figurative illustrations dating from the 11th century can be found at Augsburg Cathedral. Consisting of 35 separate panel attached to a wooden backing, these differ in both technique and style from the Hildesheim doors. The panels are decorated with largely single subjects, such as *Samson and the Lion* and *King David.* They are executed in a soft, undulating painterly style that looks back to the art of Late Antiquity.

From the 12th century in northern Europe, important sets of bronze doors survive at Novgorod in northwest Russia and Gniezno in Poland. Both of these are thought to have been executed by bronze casters from the Holy Roman Empire. Those at the Cathedral of St. Sophia at Novgorod were probably cast at Magdeburg in Saxony between 1152 and 1154. The doors were originally made for Plock Cathedral in Poland and transferred to Novgorod in the 14th century. They are unusual in featuring portraits of the bronze founders, as well as an image of the probable patron, Archbishop Wichmann of Magdeburg.

The doors for Gniezno Cathedral in Poland, thought to date from the late 12th century, differ in technique, style, and iconography from the Novgorod doors. Cast in one piece, they include illustrations in low relief from the life of St. Adalbert (d. 975), the patron saint of Gniezno and apostle to the Slavs.

Barisanus of Trani, Bronze Doors, 1179, Ravello Cathedral
The Conway Library, Courtauld Institute of Art

Southern Italy did not have an indigenous tradition of bronze casting comparable to that found in Germany in the 11th century. The earliest doors from this region and period were imported from Byzantium. One of the earliest examples of this practice are the bronze doors from the Cathedral of Amalfi in Campania, which carry an inscription indicating their date (1066) and the name of the donor, a man called Mauro, the son of Pantaleone, Count Mauronne. The Mauronne family of Amalfi were wealthy merchants with trading links in Constantinople. Similar doors at the Basilica of San Marco in Venice were obtained from Constantinople. Leo da Molino commissioned the central nave door in 1112 and is himself represented there, prostrate before St. Mark.

The bronze doors of the Church of San Zeno Maggiore in Verona in northern Italy belong to a very different tradition and may have been executed by Saxon artists from northern Europe. They are extraordinarily wide, probably the result of their enlargement at the end of the 12th century. Forty-eight bronze panels decorate the doors; the panels are attached to a wooden backing with figures set in high relief. Two distinct styles can be distinguished in their execution; the earli-

est is roughly contemporary with the construction of the church in the 1130s, whereas the later additions belong to the late 12th century. The doors contain illustrations from both the Old and New Testaments as well as from the life of the titular saint, St. Zeno.

In the second half of the 12th century, bronze casting in Italy developed rapidly and was dominated by two distinctive artistic personalities: Bonanus of Pisa and Barisanus of Trani. Bonanus of Pisa was responsible for the doors for the west facade of Pisa Cathedral, which were completed in 1180 but destroyed by fire in 1595. Bonanus's doors for the south transept (the Porta di S. Ranieri) survive. They contain narrative illustrations from the life of Christ from the Annunciation to Mary to the Ascension, between which are interspersed figures of prophets.

Barisanus of Trani was responsible for executing the cathedral doors (which bear the date 1179) at Ravello. He worked closely within the Byzantine tradition, although he used low relief rather than the silver inlay technique favored by the Byzantines. The doors at Ravello may be taken as representative of his work. They contain largely single-figure subjects, principally the apostles, but also narrative groups from the New Testament, such as the *Deposition*. Barisanus appears to have reused molds, as subjects identical to those found at Ravello recur in other works by him.

Both Bonanus of Pisa and Barisanus of Trani worked on the most prestigious artistic commission of the period: the great monastic church and, later, cathedral in Monreale, near Palermo, which King William II of Sicily commissioned as a mausoleum for himself. Bonanus of Pisa was responsible for the doors for the west portal, which bear the date 1186, and Barisanus of Trani for the doors on the northern side of the church, which provide an entrance to the nave and are normally dated between 1185 and 1189. Those by Bonanus are the largest bronze doors to survive from this period (almost eight meters by four meters). They contain an extensive iconographic program of illustrations from the Old and New Testaments. The doors by Barisanus are less ambitious and have largely single-figure subjects. John White has demonstrated the importance of Bonanus of Pisa's doors at the Pisa and Monreale Cathedrals for later developments in 14th-century narrative art (see White, 1988). They were an important source for Andrea Pisano, who around 1330 was commissioned by the Guild of Wool Importers to provide a pair of bronze doors for the Baptistery of Florence. These are appropriately illustrated with scenes from the life of St. John the Baptist, who was the principal patron saint of Florence. The doors were installed in 1336.

In the Renaissance, the practice of making elaborate, bronze doors continued but was confined to the

Italian peninsula. In 1401 a competition was held to select a sculptor to execute a second set of bronze doors for the Baptistery at Florence. The successful winner was the youthful goldsmith Lorenzo Ghiberti. These doors have as their main theme events from the life of Christ. The casting took three times as long as it had taken the Pisan workmen to make the first set of bronze doors and cost the huge sum of 22,000 florins, of which about 4000 florins went to Ghiberti and his team for labor. Although undertaken in an International Gothic idiom, with individual panels framed in Gothic quatrefoils, the doors are saturated with *all'antica* (after the antique) motifs, placing them firmly in the Renaissance. In 1425 Ghiberti was commissioned to make yet another set of bronze doors for the Baptistery that were even more ambitious than the earlier two and have come to be known as the *Gates of Paradise*, after Michelangelo's description of them. These are now on the eastern side of the Baptistery, which faces the main entrance to the cathedral. They consist of ten square and gilded narrative panels, which have as their theme events from the Old Testament. In a great technical innovation, Ghiberti cast each narrative panel as a whole. Although all the bronzes were cast by 1436, the lengthy subsequent chasing and fire gilding meant that the doors were not installed until the 1450s.

Donatello was also involved in commissions for bronze doors: first, for the Old Sacristy (which also served as the Medici funerary chapel) of the Church of San Lorenzo, Florence, in the 1430s, and later, in the 1450s for Siena Cathedral. However, this last project never came to fruition. The San Lorenzo doors represent a series of martyrs and apostles, two to each panel. They are not static figures but are shown in imaginative poses either in action, in animated discussion, or deep in thought.

In Rome a major program of renovation initiated during the 15th century resulted in the commissioning of bronze doors for the main portal of the Old Basilica of St. Peter from the Florentine architect and sculptor Antonio di Pietro Averlino (known as Filarete). These were even more ambitious in scale than Ghiberti's *Gates of Paradise*, standing at a height of approximately six meters. They depict scenes of specific significance to the papacy, such as the martyrdoms of Sts. Peter and Paul. On the reverse of the door at the base is a panel, dated 1445, which represents Filarete with six members of his workshop.

During the high Renaissance in Italy, only one major bronze door commission came to fruition: the bronze door by Jacopo Sansovino for the sacristy at the Basilica of San Marco in Venice, installed in 1572. It contains reliefs representing the *Entombment* and *Resurrection*.

After a fire destroyed Bonanus's doors for the west front of Pisa Cathedral in 1595, a team of bronze casters working under the guidance of Giambologna replaced these. Between 1568 and 1576 Girolamo and Ludovico Lombardo cast the set of four doors for the Santa Casa, at the Basilica of Santa Maria di Loreto, Italy. A group of bronze sculptors, including Tiburzio Vergelli and Antonio Calcagni, produced a second set between 1596 and 1610 for the same basilica. These all display a richly Mannerist style dependent on Jacopo Sansovino.

The 19th century saw a revival of interest in the casting of bronze doors created for major public monuments. In the newly unified kingdom of Italy, sculptors made spectacular examples for the facades of Florence and Milan Cathedrals. The Art Nouveau style, which arose at the end of the century, with its emphasis on sinuous line, was especially suited to decorative bronze work: an example of bronze doors in this idiom are the doors made by Pier Enrico Astorri for the commemorative monument to Pope Pius X in St. Peter's Basilica, Rome.

The most significant project for bronze doors in the modern period is Auguste Rodin's incomplete *Gates of Hell*, which had as their inspiration Dante's *Inferno* (1314). These were intended to be an analog to Ghiberti's *Gates of Paradise*. Originally commissioned in 1880 as entrance doors to the planned Museum of Decorative Arts in Paris, Rodin's doors lay unfinished at the artist's death in 1917, because of the increasing ambition and spiraling cost of the project. A bronze cast was not made until 1925. The original plaster is preserved in the Musée d'Orsay in Paris.

ANDREAS PETZOLD

See also **Bronze and Other Copper Alloys; Carolingian Sculpture; Filarete (Antonio di Pietro Averlino); Ghiberti, Lorenzo; Rodin, Auguste; Sansovino, Jacopo**

Further Reading

Brandt, Michael, and Arne Eggebrecht (editors), *Bernward von Hildesheim und das Zeitalter der Ottonen* (exhib. cat.), Hildesheim, Germany: Bernward Verlag, and Mainz, Germany: Von Zabern, 1993

Cahn, Walter, *The Romanesque Wooden Doors of Auvergne*, New York: New York University Press, 1974

Cohen, Adam S., and Ann Derbes, "Bernward and Eve at Hildesheim," *Gesta* 40/1 (2001)

Iacobini, Antonio, "Porta," in *Enciclopedia dell'arte medievale*, vol. 9, Rome: Istituto della Enciclopedia Italiana, 1998

Lasko, Peter, *Ars Sacra, 800–1200*, London and Baltimore, Maryland: Penguin, 1972; 2nd edition, New Haven, Connecticut: Yale University Press, 1994

Legner, Anton, *Deutsche Kunst der Romanik*, Munich: Hirmer, 1982

Mende, Ursula, Albert Hirmer, and Irmgard Ernstmeier-Hirmer, *Die Bronzeturen des Mittelalters, 800–1200*, Munich: Hirmer, 1983; new edition, 1994

White, John, "The Bronze Doors of Bonanus and the Development of Dramatic Narrative," *Art History* 11 (1988)

DOORS: WOODEN

The primary function of exterior doors is to connect the building to the space outside, but such doors are also a visible part of the building's facade. So within a representative facade—for example, that of a church—the main portal should be consistent with, even increase, the building's representative character in its function as an exposed place through which the building is entered. A figural sculptured door was considered the appropriate means for serving this function from early Christian times onward. Indeed, the earliest examples still preserved are wooden and date from the 4th or 5th century.

The oak door of the Cathedral Sant'Ambrogio in Milan is traditionally estimated to be a late 4th-century work, although more recent research suggests that it may date from the middle of the 5th century. As is typical for main portals, this door consists of two wings. Each door contains five panels, three small ones and two of double height, surrounded by a heavy framing. Only three of the original reliefs have survived, although severely damaged. Two show scenes from the life of David, suggesting a complete David cycle as the iconographic program; the third carries an ornamental design of two peacocks and a Christogram within a laurel wreath (now exhibited at the Museo di San Ambrogio, Milan). In the 9th century, the panels may have been retouched when the door received a new framing. The current state of the door is the result of a complete rebuilding in 1750, which further complicates the reconstruction of its original arrangement.

Around the year 432, the door of the Basilica of Santa Sabina in Rome was created. The cypress wood reliefs depict scenes from the Old and New Testaments. Compared with the door of Sant'Ambrogio, the framing is rather delicate and leaves more space for the panels—both literally and in the impression it creates. Of the original 28 panels, 18 are left, currently arranged in the original framework in a more or less random order. The four vertical rows, two on each wing, consist of small, oblong panels alternating with large, upright format panels. The presence of scenes from the Old and New Testaments suggests that the original arrangement may have shown a typological program—that is, a formal combination of scenes from the Old Testament with scenes from the New Testament, the former interpreted to announce the latter. Problems in reconstructing the panels' arrangement arise because the surviving panels do not fit the known structure of the door. When the typological cycle is arranged in such a way that one wing shows only scenes from the Old Testament while the other shows only scenes from the New Testament (a pattern known from later examples of doors with a typological program), too many small panels with scenes from the life of Christ result. Wolfgang Kemp suggests that the correspondence is not arranged between the two wings of the door but between the rows; while each horizontal row contains only scenes from either the Old or New Testament, the typological connection is drawn vertically in a complex, multilevel way (see Kemp, 1994).

Derived from the example of the two Italian doors, the door of the Church of St. Maria im Kapitol in Cologne, Germany, was created around 1065. The 26 walnut reliefs—with traces of color—on an oak door show episodes from the life of Christ. The rhythmical and symmetrical composition, containing different kinds of frames that enclose the panels as well as each other, shows a far stricter but also a more balanced order than do its predecessors.

These three doors are without doubt the most important extant wooden doors in Christian art. Further development in sculptured doors continued with bronze doors rather than wooden ones, starting with the door of Bishop Bernward of Hildesheim, which was strongly influenced by the Church of S. Sabina door. Nonetheless, some wooden doors were still produced. For example, two wooden doors from the 12th century can be found in the Abruzzi (southern Italy) at the Church of S. Pietro in Alba Fucens and the Church of S. Maria in Cellis near Carsóli, the latter showing scenes from the life of Christ. The flat, larch-wood door of Gurk Cathedral in Austria (early 13th century) shows a strong influence of linear art forms—stained-glass windows in particular—and shows the *Tree of Jesse* in a unique design in which circular ornaments link the single figures. An astounding Gothic oak door depicting only the life-size figures of the Virgin and Elisabeth, mother of John the Baptist, is also found in Austria; this scene of the *Visitation* is shown on the door of the Church of St. Maria in the small town of Irrsdorf (area of Salzburg). It is datable to shortly before 1408. The doors in the province of Auvergne, France, from the late 12th and early 13th century are apparently independent of the development in Italy (see Cahn, 1974).

As already noted, with the shift toward the use of bronze for highly representative doors in the Middle Ages, wood lost its importance as a material for this purpose. During the Italian Renaissance, the workshop of Giuliano da Maiano, brother of Bendetto da Maiano, produced several wooden doors, none of which carry any figural representation; typically, a coarse structure

Wooden doors, 6th century, Church of Santa Sabina
© Alinari / Art Resource, NY

frames three or four square fields on each wing. The centers of the squares contain precisely symmetrical floral ornaments, often roses that follow antique patterns.

The significance of wooden doors as a representative art form has diminished since the Middle Ages, but even in the 20th century, we can still find examples. Around 1919 the German Expressionist artist Ernst Ludwig Kirchner carved a door for the studio he wanted to build for himself in Davos (now conserved in the Staatliche Kunstsammlung in Kassel, Germany). One of the two wings depicts *Dance between the Women*, the other *Ascent to the Alpine Pastures*, two topics that played an important role in the life and work of the artist.

MARCUS ROSSBERG

See also **Architectural Sculpture in Europe: Middle Ages–19th Century; Bendetto da Maiano; Gothic Sculpture**

Further Reading

Beuckers, Klaus Gereon, *Rex Iubet—Christus Imperat: Studien zu den Holztüren von St. Maria im Kapitol und zu Herodesd-*
arstellungen vor dem Investiturstreit, Cologne, Germany: SH-Verlag, 1999
Cahn, Walter, *The Romanesque Wooden Doors of Auvergne*, New York: New York University Press, 1974
Dellbrueck, Richard, "Notes on the Wooden Doors of Santa Sabina," *Art Bulletin* 34 (1952)
Jeremias, Gisela, and Franz Xavier Bartl, *Die Holztür der Basilika S. Sabina in Rom*, Tübingen, Germany: Wasmuth, 1980
Kemp, Wolfgang, *Christliche Kunst: Ihre Anfänge, ihre Strukturen*, Munich: Schirmer, 1994
Kirchner, Ernst Ludwig, *Ernst Ludwig Kirchner, 1880–1938* (exhib. cat.), Berlin: Nationalgalerie, 1979
Lambertini, Daniela, Marcello Lotti, and Roberto Lunardi (editors), *Giuliano e la bottega dei da Maiano*, Florence: Octavo, 1994
Mroczko, Teresa, "The Original Programme of the David Cycle on the Doors of San Ambrogio in Milan," *Artibus et historiae* 3/6 (1982)
Salomi, Salvatorino (editor), *Le porte di bronzo dall'anichità al secolo XIII*, 2 vols., Rome: Istituto della Enciclopedia Italiana, 1990
Volbach, Wolfgang Friedrich, and Max Hirmer, *Frühchristliche Kunst: Die Kunst der Spätantike in West- und Ostrom*, Munich: Hirmer, 1958; as *Early Christian Art*, translated by Christopher Ligota, New York: Abrams, 1961

JACQUES DU BROEUCQ *ca.* 1505–1584
Franco-Flemish

Jacques Du Broeucq belonged to the second generation of Italian-influenced Renaissance sculptors of the Low Countries. Like most of the important artists of his time, he also became active as an architect. Unlike his contemporary, Cornelis II Floris, with whom he was in competition for the design of the Antwerp town hall in 1560, Du Broeucq never seems to have operated a large and exporting workshop. The reason for this can be found in the fact that he was employed by the Habsburg court in the Low Countries from around 1540 to around 1560.

The study of Du Broeucq is obstructed by the fact that his early career is not documented and that most of his later works were destroyed during the Habsburg-French wars in the mid 16th century or during the French Revolution. Du Broeucq, however, seems to have visited Italy, most probably between 1530 and 1535. Central in his career was the commission for the sculptural program of the rood screen for the Church of St.-Waudru in Mons (now in Belgium). Destroyed during the French Revolution, an important part of the sculptures was preserved, together with a drawing showing the entire work. Differences between the iconographic program of the drawing, dated 1535, and the preserved sculpture suggest that the drawing must be viewed as an early proposal not entirely followed during the execution of the sculpture. The assumption made by most scholars that the 1535 drawing, showing a revolutionary design by a master well acquainted with Italian architecture, was done by Du Broeucq cannot, however, be proved. The date corresponds with that of the contract between the chapter and the stonemason Hubert Nonon, commissioning black marble, but the fact that the iconographic program depicted in the drawing relating the Creation and Genesis was changed into the representation of the Passion and the life after the Passion could be owing to the fact that only later on, when the architectural part of the rood loft was already executed, Du Broeucq became involved and suggested the new subject. If so, the partly preserved tomb of Eustache de Croij in the old Church of Notre-Dame at Saint-Omer must be considered the oldest work by Du Broeucq that is known. This type of mausoleum—with the deceased represented in prayer before a *transi* (sculpture representing the corpse)—was at the time an innovation for the Low Countries. Du Broeucq may have seen this type of monument in Italy and perhaps in France (for instance, the monument of Louis XII and Anne of Brittany by Jean I Juste [Giovanni di Giusto Betti] in Saint-Denis, near Paris). The sculpture of the rood loft shows more immediate Italian 15th- and 16th-century influence and announces Giambologna's compositions (such as his *Flagellation* and *Charity* in the Grimaldi Chapel, Genoa). Because Giambologna was later reported to have been Du Broeucq's pupil, it is possible that he was involved in the execution of these sculptures.

In 1539 Du Broeucq also became active as an architect for the Château de Boussu (in Belgium, near the French border). Between 1544 and 1560 architecture seems to have been the more important of his occupations. He was involved in designing the châteaus of Mariemont, Binche, Brussels, and Ghent; the fortresses of Philipville and Mariembourg; and the town halls of Bavai, Beaumont, Ath, and Antwerp. Fragments of sculpture preserved in Mariemont and the Church of St.-Waudru (said to come from the Château de Boussu) suggest that his workshop also provided sculptural decoration for these projects. Those for Mariemont, Binche, Philipville, Brussels, and Ghent were commissioned by Mary of Hungary or her brother, Emperor Charles V, and Du Broeucq was rewarded with the title of *maître-artiste de l'empereur* in 1555. The departure of Philip II for Spain in 1559 and the wars of religion that followed soon afterward possibly gave Du Broeucq's career a new turn. As the quality of the sculpture for the Altar of St. Mary Magdalene of 1550 in the Church of St.-Waudru establishes that it was executed by the workshop, later works show the work of the master himself. In 1572 Du Broeucq was forced to deliver a statue of St. Barthélemy for adherence to Protestantism during the occupation of Mons by Louis of Nassau. Compared with his earlier work, St. Barthélemy is less Mannerist and made in a more mature, and even pre-Baroque, style. The head of the apostle

nevertheless still shows the influence of Italian masters (such as Donatello and his *Christ Giving the Keys to St. Peter*, 1420s). The tomb of Philips de St.-Aldegonde in Saint-Omer, unfortunately, was not preserved. Du Broeucq died in Mons on 30 September 1584.

JAN VAN DAMME

See also **Donatello (Donato di Betto Bardi); Giambologna**

Biography

Born in Saint-Omer, France, or Mons, now in Belgium, *ca.*1505. Traveled in Italy, 1530–35; back by 1535 in Mons, where charged with important architectural and sculptural commissions; had the young Jean de Boulogne (Giambologna) as a pupil and collaborator; worked as a sculptor and architect for Habsburg governor of the Low Countries, Queen Mary of Hungary, and her brother Emperor Charles V; *maître-artiste de l'empereur* of Charles V and Philip II, starting 1555. Died in Mons, now in Belgium, 30 September 1584.

Selected Works

1535–48 Rood screen, for Church of St.-Waudru, Mons; stone (destroyed, French Revolution); fragments: *Theological Virtues* (attribution disputed), *Cardinal Virtues*, *Holy Trinity*, *Passion*, and *Resurrection*, Church of St.-Waudru, Mons, Belgium; architectural parts: Harlaxton Castle, Lincolnshire, England

1538–44 Designs for choir stalls (executed by Jean Fourmanoir); stone; Church of St.-Waudru, Mons, Belgium

1539–62 Sculptural decoration, for Château de Boussu; stone (destroyed); fragments: Church of St.-Waudru, Mons, Belgium

1539–62 Tomb of Eustache de Croij, bishop of Arras; alabaster; Church of Notre-Dame, Saint-Omer, France

1550 Altar of St. Mary Magdalene; stone (destroyed 1797, largely rebuilt); Church of St.-Waudru, Mons, Belgium

ca. 1562 Tomb of Jean de Hennin-Liétard, comte de Boussu; stone; Boussu, Belgium

1572 *St. Barthélemy*; stone; Church of St.-Waudru, Mons, Belgium

1574 Tomb of Philips de St.-Aldegonde (three fragments); alabaster; Church of Notre-Dame, Saint-Omer, France

Further Reading

De Jonge, Krista (editor), *Le château de Boussu*, Namur, Belgium: MRW, Division du Patrimoine, 1998

Didier, R., *Jacques Dubroeucq, sculpteur et maître-artiste de l'empereur (1500/1510–1584)*, Brussels: Ars Libris, 2000

Hedicke, Robert, *Jacques Dubroeucq de Mons*, Strasbourg, Germany: Heitz, 1904

Jacques Du Broeucq, sculpteur et architecte de la Renaissance, Mons, Belgium: Europalia 85 España, 1985

Kavaler, Matt, "The Jubé of Mons and the Renaissance in the Netherlands," in *Beelden in de late middeleeuwen en Renaissance*, edited by Reindert Falkenburg, Zwolle, The Netherlands: Waanders, 1994

Popham, A.E., "The Authorship of the Drawings of Binche," *Journal of the Warburg and Courtauld Institutes* 3 (1939–40)

Steppe, Jan, *Het koordoksaal in de Nederlanden*, Brussels: Paleis de Academiën, 1952

Wellens, Robert, *Jacques Du Broeucq, sculpteur et architecte de la Renaissance, 1505–1584*, Brussels: Renaissance du Livre, 1962

FRANÇOIS DU QUESNOY 1597–1643

Flemish

François du Quesnoy, son of Jérôme du Quesnoy the Elder (the creator of the famous fountain of *Manneken-Pis*) and elder brother of Jérôme du Quesnoy the Younger, was the most illustrious member of this family of sculptors from Brussels. He was taught by his father and initially worked alongside him, although no work from this period has been identified with certainty. It was in Rome, where he lived from 1618 until just before his death in 1643, that he made his career under the pseudonym Il Fiammingo. Du Quesnoy was one of the four most important sculptors of the first half of the 17th century, along with Gianlorenzo Bernini, Alessandro Algardi, and Francesco Mochi, and one of the foremost representatives of the classicizing tendency that developed around the 1630s. His very restricted oeuvre includes only two monumental statues and consists, for the most part, of small sculptures intended for private collections; nevertheless, both the subject matter and the style of his sculptures immediately won over his contemporaries and earned him lasting success.

Du Quesnoy's output from his first ten years in Rome is still somewhat imperfectly identified and difficult to date. Consisting essentially of small-format works in wood, ivory, or bronze, and intended for a clientele of private collectors, his work was characteristic of the activity of a foreign sculptor who needed to earn a living and make a name for himself. Nonetheless, the artist almost immediately succeeded in developing a new style within a traditional genre—that of the infant figure—which earned him the nickname *Fattore di putti* (maker of children) and decisively established his reputation. In the reliefs of *Divine Love Overcoming Profane Love* and the *Bacchanal of Putti*, on

the epitaphs of Adrian Vryburg and Ferdinand van den Eynde, and again in his *Cupid Carving his Bow*, du Quesnoy portrayed very young children and succeeded in representing in marble the delicacy of their smooth and soft flesh, drawing inspiration both from nature and from Titian's putti. Du Quesnoy had studied Titian's painting *The Offering to Venus* (1519; Museo del Prado, Madrid), which at that time formed part of the Ludovisi Collection in Rome. This striving after an illusionistic portrayal of life, for which the Flemish realist tradition had prepared him, is characteristic of 17th-century Roman art, and in particular of the sculptures of Bernini.

Du Quesnoy's sculpted children were enormously successful, and little by little his work list was artificially swollen by a large number of variants and replicas. They were used as models in the workshops of contemporary artists, and his reliefs of putti were endlessly alluded to in Flemish paintings of the mid 17th

Detail from the *Mannekin-pis* (Boy pissing) fountain, Brussels, Belgium (Jérôme du Quesnoy the Elder)
© Kavaler / Art Resource, NY

century and also the 18th century (by Frans van Mieris the Jounger and the Elder, Willem van Mieris, and/or Matthijs Naiveu), then by the French painters of the following century, including Jean-Baptiste Siméon Chardin, Pierre Subleyras, and Louis-Léopold Boilly. The collectors themselves, in the 17th and particularly in the 18th centuries, prized his figures of children especially, thereby ensuring him a lasting reputation.

Du Quesnoy is not famous, however, for his putti alone: he succeeded in deriving a convincing modern style from his extensive study of antique models (a practice widespread among 17th-century artists) and in establishing himself as the foremost classicizing sculptor ahead of Algardi and in opposition to Bernini. For a foreign artist, making the journey to Rome meant coming to study not only the Renaissance masters, but also the works of the Classical period, then essentially preserved in the form of sculptures. Du Quesnoy's biographers relate that he set himself to measure the famous statues of the Belvedere in Rome—the antique *Antinous*, the *Laocoön and His Sons*, and the *Belvedere Torso*. A knowledge of Antiquity was also gained through the restoration of sculptures uncovered by the numerous excavations scattered throughout the city. These were avidly sought by connoisseurs, who, however, only fully appreciated them once they had been reconstructed. The restoration of antiquities was not only a chance for sculptors to give proof of their skills—and du Quesnoy was among the most renowned in this field—but also offered a stimulating opportunity to compete with the ancient masters. The restoration of the *Rondinini Faun* attests to a concern to show an archaeologist's respect for the ancient torso: du Quesnoy followed the original design, as indicated by the faun's tail preserved in the small of the back; yet for the new portions, he chose a marble with texture and shade that matched the ancient material, and in sculpting the head he drew inspiration from those of antique fauns. By the sensitivity of his rendering of the skin and the figure's movement, he breathed into the statue; however, in so doing, he transformed it into a modern work.

In more general terms, du Quesnoy's sculpture betrays the influence of antique models in his selection of iconographical themes, as well as in the style he adopted. His reliefs of putti were inspired by bacchanal scenes from ancient sarcophagi; his dozing children were variations on the theme of the sleeping Cupid, of which the ancients were fond; and the bronze *Mercury and Cupid* and *Apollo and Cupid* took up the model of the Belvedere *Antinous*. In addition, du Quesnoy played an especially active role in Roman circles with a passionate interest in antiquities, working with artists such as the painters Nicolas Poussin, Andrea Sacchi, and Joachim von Sandrart, and either for scholars such as Cassiano dal Pozzo or collectors such as the Marchese Vincenzo Giustiniani. The bronze *Mercury and Cupid*, which du Quesnoy produced for Giustiniani was the only modern work among the antiques of this renowned collection. At the beginning of the 1630s, du Quesnoy's Classicism reached its peak with the statue of *St. Susanna:* the sculptor now appeared as the leader of the classicizing movement in sculpture, in opposition to the Baroque tendency led by Bernini.

His capacity to combine idealization and naturalism also warrants du Quesnoy a far from negligible place alongside the likes of Bernini, Algardi, and Giuliano Finelli in the evolution of portrait sculpture in Rome during the second quarter of the 17th century. The posthumous bust of the poet John Barclay is undoubtedly idealized but animated by a discreet smile, whereas that of Cardinal Maurizio di Savoia presents a perfect balance between the realistic rendering of a portrait sculpted from life and the suggestion of ideal nobility necessitated by the subject's high standing.

Over the years 1629 through 1640, du Quesnoy had the privilege of producing one of the four colossi in the niches of the transept crossing of St. Peter's Basilica in Rome: the commission for the *St. Andrew* is in itself testimony to the Flemish artist's renown. The statue, inspired by the model of a Classical Jupiter, represents the saint lost in mystical conversation with the Divine. The power of du Quesnoy's sculpture caused it to be universally preferred to Bernini's *St. Longinus*, which occupies the neighboring niche. Louis XIII is known to have offered du Quesnoy the post of royal sculptor, but his premature death prevented him from taking this office.

MARION BOUDON

See also **Algardi, Alessandro; Antinous; Belvedere Torso; Bernini, Gianlorenzo;** *Laocoön and His Sons;* **Netherlands and Belgium**

Biography

Born in Brussels, Belgium, 1597. From family of sculptors. Trained and worked with sculptor father, Jérôme the Elder, creator of the fountain of *Mannekenpis*; elder brother to Jérôme the Younger, sculptor and architect; traveled to Rome on scholarship from Archduke Albert, 1618; entered workshop of Claude Poussin, 1621; remained in Rome until 1643; known as Il Fiammingo; summoned by Louis XIII of France to become royal sculptor, 1639; 20-year sculpting career included many commissions, primarily for churches. Died in Leghorn, Italy, July 1643.

Selected Works

1620s   *Rondinini Faun* (restoration); marble; Victoria and Albert Museum, London, England

1626   *Bacchanal of Putti*; marble; Galleria Doria-Pamphili, Rome, Italy

1628   *Guglielmi*; marble; Basilica of San Lorenzo fuori le Mura, Rome, Italy

1628   *John Barclay*; marble; Convent of Sant'Onofrio, Rome, Italy

1629   Funerary monument of Adrien Vrijburgh; marble; Church of Santa Maria dell'Anima, Rome, Italy

late   *Cupid Carving his Bow*; marble; Bodemus,
1620s   Berlin, Germany

1629–33 *St. Susanna*; marble; Church of Santa Maria di Loreto, Rome, Italy

1629–40 *St. Andrew*; marble; St. Peter's Basilica, Rome, Italy

ca. 1630 *Divine Love Overcoming Profane Love*; marble; Galleria Doria-Pamphili, Rome, Italy

ca.   *Mercury and Cupid* and *Apollo and Cupid*;
1630–40 bronze; collection of Prince of Liechtenstein, Vaduz, Liechtenstein

1633–34 *Dwarf of Créqui*; marble; Galleria Nazionale di Palazzo Barberini, Rome, Italy

1633–40 Funerary monument of Ferdinand van den Eynde; marble; Church of Santa Maria dell'Anima, Rome, Italy

after   Funerary monument of Jacques de Hase;
1634   marble; Church of Santa Maria della Pietà, Rome, Italy

1635   *Cardinal Maurice of Savoy*; terracotta; Museo di Roma, Rome, Italy; marble; Galleria Sabauda, Turin, Italy

1640–42 *Concert of Angels*; marble; Church of Santi Apostoli, Naples, Italy

Further Reading

Bacchi, Andrea, *Scultura del '600 a Roma*, Milan: Longanesi, 1996

Hadermann Misguish, Lydie, "du Quesnoy: François," in *The Dictionary of Art*, edited by Jane Turner, New York: Grove, and London: Macmillan, 1996

La sculpture au siècle de Rubens: Dans les Pays-Bas méridionaux et la principauté de Liège (exhib. cat.), Brussels: Musée d'art Ancien, 1977

Lavin, Irvin, "Duquesnoy's 'Nano di Crequi' and Two Busts by Francesco Mochi," *Art Bulletin* 52 (1970)

Radcliffe, Anthony, "Mercury and Cupid, Apollo and Cupid," in *Renaissance and Later Sculpture: With Works of Art in Bronze*, London: Wilson, 1992

Wittkower, Rudolf, *Art and Architecture in Italy, 1600–1750*, London and Baltimore, Maryland: Penguin, 1958; 6th edition, 3 vols., revised by Joseph Connors and Jennifer Montagu, New Haven, Connecticut: Yale University Press, 1999

ST. SUSANNA
François du Quesnoy (1597–1643)
1629–1633
marble
h. 2.3 m
Church of Santa Maria di Loreto, Rome, Italy

The *St. Susanna* is one of only two large-scale marble sculptures now known as the work of François du Quesnoy; it is a work whose quality earned him immediate success and decisively established his reputation. *St. Susanna* is the finest sculptural example of the classicizing current that developed in Rome in opposition to the Baroque tendency at the beginning of the 1630s, and for this reason, it represents a milestone in the history of art.

In 1627 the Guild of Bakers in Rome decided to provide monumental sculptures to decorate the Chapel of the Virgin in the Church of Santa Maria di Loreto near Trajan's Forum. The *St. Susanna*, sculpted between 1629 and 1633, is one of four statues of virgin martyrs that adorn the sanctuary—along with Giuliano Finelli's *St. Cecilia* (1629–33), Domenico Rossi's *St. Flavia Domitilla* (1628–30), and Pompeo Ferrucci's *St. Agnes* (1628–30). This iconographical cycle is typical of Counter Reformation art, which aimed, in particular, to revive the cult of the Christian martyrs for Roman Catholic preaching. With *St. Susanna*, however, du Quesnoy responded to the demands of Tridentine art in order to arouse the emotion of the viewer not so much by a direct evocation of her martyrdom (her attribute, the sword with which she was decapitated, is barely visible; it has been laid at her feet on the plinth and half-covered by drapery) as by the image of piety that she represents. Both her stance and her facial expression are full of humility, in keeping with her status as a virgin martyr. Above all, by her gesture—she was originally located in the first niche on the right, her head turned toward the entrance of the chapel, and with her hand pointing toward the altar—she performed the role of a guide to the faithful as they approached the sanctuary.

Early sources make it clear that du Quesnoy drew inspiration for his statue from a celebrated work of Antiquity, the Capitoline *Urania*, but other Antique statues also influenced the statue. The Classical influence is indeed evident in the choice of clothing (that of a vestal or muse); in the type of drapery that reveals the body; and in the depiction of the face, a beautiful oval with blank eyes. Du Quesnoy's originality is to be found not in the principle of drawing on Antiquity as a creative source, which was common to all the artists of his time, but rather in what he made of it. Compared with other contemporary feminine statues such as Gianlorenzo Bernini's *St. Bibiana* (1624–26), Alessandro Algardi's *St. Mary Magdalene* (1628–29), or Francesco Mochi's *St. Veronica* (1629–40), the *St. Susanna* stands out for the rigorous balance of its pose as much as of its expression. The drapery is undoubtedly the element that, more than any other, enables us to appreciate the work's originality: rather than fluttering in disdain of the laws of gravity, as is the case with most statues of the time, the clothing of the *St. Susanna* falls harmoniously, emphasizing the contours and movement of the body without any independent or arbitrary effect. From the 17th century onward, this statue was considered a model for the depiction of the clothed woman, on a par with the examples provided by Antiquity.

At the same time that du Quesnoy was sculpting the *St. Susanna*, Andrea Sacchi was painting his *Divine Wisdom* on the ceiling of the Palazzo Barberini, and Nicolas Poussin was painting his *Inspiration of the Poet* (Musée du Louvre, Paris). These three works marked the birth of the classicizing movement in Rome about 1630, in opposition to the output of figures by Bernini, Pietro de Cortona, and Francesco Borromini, which would later be referred to as Baroque. The theorist of Classicism, Giovan Pietro Bellori, recognized the importance of the *St. Susanna* in 1672: in the section of his *Lives of the Modern Painters, Sculptors, and Architects* focusing on du Quesnoy, Bellori wrote an entire paragraph to the statue and, the better to emphasize its significance, went so far as to alter historical truth by claiming that it was thanks to the success of the *St. Susanna* that du Quesnoy had obtained the commission for another major statue, the *St. Andrew* produced for St. Peter's Basilica in Rome (whereas, in fact, the sculptor was already working on the latter when the statue in Santa Maria di Loreto was unveiled). This inaccurate chronology was subsequently adopted wholesale by art literature, further underlining the statue's importance.

The success of the *St. Susanna* was immediate and lasting. The sculptor himself produced a bronze bust of the piece, of which numerous replicas are known today, for his friend the painter Joachim von Sandrart. The Classicist painter and friend of du Quesnoy, Sacchi, paid homage to the statue by depicting it in his painting of *St. Anthony of Padua* produced during the same period (1632–33; Church of Santa Maria della Concezione, Rome). The influence of the *St. Susanna* on 17th-century Roman sculpture was significant, but it was also felt beyond the borders of Italy, thanks in

St. Susanna
© Alinari / Art Resource, NY

particular to the dissemination of the original by way of engravings and casts, and also of marble replicas such as the one produced by Guillaume Coustou II in 1736 (now at Versailles, France) and Pierre-François Leroy, which was kept during the 18th century in the chapel of the royal château of Laeken in Brussels, and from 1836 to the present in the castle of Zidlochovice in the Czech Republic. The *St. Susanna* was also occasionally reproduced by painters: for example, a reduced model of the statue appears twice in works by Pierre Subleyras, in *The Attributes of the Arts* (or *The*

Five Senses, ca. 1735; Musée des Augustins, Toulouse) and the *Self-Portrait in the Studio* (*ca.* 1746; Académie des Beaux-Arts, Vienna).

With the *St. Susanna*, du Quesnoy succeeded in transforming the models offered by Antiquity into a modern language. The statue's Classicism is expressed through its graceful posture, which is not without sensuality, and the gentle lyricism that radiates from the figure's face. Like the sculptures of Bernini, albeit by a different route, it comes to life, breaking from the confined space of the niche and establishing direct contact with the viewer. With this work, du Quesnoy showed himself a worthy rival to the ancients and earned himself a place alongside the greatest Roman sculptors of the 17th century.

MARION BOUDON

Further Reading

Benedetti, Sandro, *Santa Maria di Loreto*, Rome: Marietti, 1968

Huse, Norbert, "Zur 'S. Susanna' des Duquesnoy," in *Argo: Festschrift für Kurt Badt zu seinem 80. Geburtstag am 3. März 1970*, edited by Martin Gosebruch and Lorenz Dittmann, Cologne: DuMont Schauberg, 1970

Mahon, Denis, "Poussiniana: Afterthoughts Arising from the Exhibition," *Gazette des Beaux-Arts* 60 (1962)

JEAN DUBUFFET 1901–1985 *French*

Jean Dubuffet's first sculptures reveal an enormous interest in unusual materials from the surrounding world. In 1954 he presented *Petites statues de la vie précaire* (Small Statues of the Precarious Life), 44 works made of iron residue, charcoal, sponges, and other common substances (for example, *Le Morvandiau* and *Pleurnichon*), at an exposition organized by René Druouin in the Cercle Volney, Paris. The intent was to bestow an intense expressive language representing spiritual phenomena onto the ordinary materials of the works, materials that had been ignored in Classical statuary. In these sculptures, Dubuffet's intervention was minimal, given the elementary simplicity of the compositional technique; instead, he preferred to trust chance in his precarious and transitory forms, which opposed the fixed canons of Classical statuary.

Only a few critics recognized the importance of this event, which anticipated all of the movements of the 1960s and 1970s in which artists presented discarded materials directly as art. In fact, Dubuffet is commonly regarded by contemporary critics as one of the most important precursors of Nouveau Réalisme in France (a movement that included Yves Klein, Fernandez Arman, César, and Daniel Spoerri), *arte povera* (an Italian movement often characterized by the use of ephemeral materials) in Italy (Mario Merz, Piero Man-

zoni, and Jannis Kounellis), and Neo-Dada (Robert Rauschenberg and Jasper Johns) and Junk art (John Chamberlain) in the United States. With respect to these artists, however, Dubuffet maintained a strong connection to his artistic roots because of his willingness to continue to represent the world with the symbols of art, rather than present unmediated reality.

Dubuffet's conception of *art brut*, or crude and spontaneous art, shares the total rejection of high and official culture with the antiart stance of the French Dada movement of the 1920s. Dubuffet continued Marcel Duchamp's idea of abandoning the traditional techniques and instead using whatever was best suited to the situation. All of Dubuffet's work is based on the idea of art which is free from intellectual conception and closer to an organic expression of nature.

Between October 1959 and 1960, Dubuffet created a new series of sculptures in papier mâché, cork, and silver foil. In these works, he abandoned materials found directly in nature and appeared to come closer to the traditional techniques of sculptural modeling. The ever-present contrast in Dubuffet's work between the material force and the expressiveness of the surface reached its culmination in the four papier-mâché heads

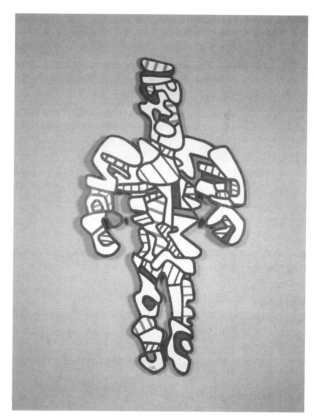

Le Sergent (The Sergeant)
© 2001 Artists Rights Society (ARS), New York, ADAGP, Paris, and Art Resource, NY

(e.g., *Oberon*), which seem as heavy as stones. Dubuffet's primitive technique of violently tracing features on flat surfaces corresponds to the coarse materials he used. In this way he obtained a decidedly grotesque effect, recalling ancient or archaic sculptures. In the same period, Dubuffet created simply assembled works out of driftwood.

From 1966 on, Dubuffet's work underwent a decisive turning point. Along with his pleasure in experimenting with what the dominant culture rejected, he opted for a more open and fanciful explosion of imagination, which was completely independent of nature. He decided to apply his characteristic flat graphics, or "Horloupe," on a very light sculpture in expanded polystyrene. Horloupe is a type of automatic writing with a cell-like structure in red and blue, which simulates the proliferation of nature. It is a double challenge to both the rigidity of human rationality and the vitality of nature. In order to cut the polyester in irregular forms, Dubuffet used a heated electric wire.

Initially these *peintures monumentées* (monumental paintings) are barely freed from the two-dimensional plane of painting because of our instinctive diffidence toward perspective, understood as a system of rational rules that were established in the Renaissance. In the language of Horloupe, the optical relationship between red and blue, underlined by white backgrounds, instead creates a slight distortion of space that suggests a potential relief. In the first series of this period, *Logos Milestone*, Dubuffet created objects that were too subtle to be considered true sculpture. In the *Amoncellements* series he grouped various objects, thereby obtaining extremely interesting results. In *Table porteuse d'instance, d'objets et de projets* (Table Carrying Authority, Objects, and Projects), Dubuffet mixed unidentifiable objects in completely abstract forms. With *Paysage portatif* (Portable Landscape), he obliterated every reference to reality by arranging a group of unlikely elements. The *peintures monumentées*, produced with various assembled elements, constitute the basis for large-scale architecture for Dubuffet, conceived as practical interiors like real dwellings but in which all traditional construction principles have been dismantled. Dubuffet takes from the Dadaist Kurt Schwitters the concept of irrational architecture manifested in the "Merzbau" of 1922. To produce his "Edifices," Dubuffet progresses to the use of expanded resin polystyrene. Like in a primitive cave the walls, floor, and ceiling are decorated with characteristic Horloupe, which in this way enormously accentuates their power of aberration.

Cabinet Logologique was Dubuffet's first monumental work. It is articulated in four panels arranged to form a room with two doors. Created exclusively for the imagination, within it the mind loses every real reference. To give permanent shelter to the *Cabinet*, Dubuffet began the construction of the *Villa Falbala* at Périgny-sur-Yerres, in the country near Paris, after which followed the *Closerie Falbala*, his largest architectural production and one of the peaks of his oeuvre.

Group of Four Trees, an installation from 1972 commissioned by David Rockefeller for the heart of Wall Street, was rich in suggestions for the American art scene. The insertion of a work of feverish graphic qualities in an urban context, which is a symbol of the world's economic rationality, created a notable contrast. Dubuffet had not had any direct contact with American artists in his many trips to the United States, but his original work offered new and interesting prospects. In spite of the reservations of some American critics, who were busy defending the superiority of American abstract art over that from Europe, Dubuffet's celebrated lecture at the Arts Club of Chicago in 1951, and his retrospectives in 1962 and 1968 at the Museum of Modern Art in New York City and at the Guggenheim Museum of Art in 1966 and 1973, helped to consecrate Dubuffet as a protagonist on the international art scene. Dubuffet's shows were always met with enthusiasm by a smaller number of critics and the public while they scandalized most others. Only belatedly have the European museums received him without reserve, and after his death in France, the Fondation Dubuffet was established in Périgny-sur-Yerres.

In general, critics have always been divided in their evaluation of Dubuffet's work, but they are in agreement in assigning him a fundamental role in having influenced sculpture with fertile and clever ideas for two successive decades, due above all to his intense theoretical activity. Dubuffet therefore contributed to creating the aesthetic conditions necessary for the birth of Junk art and Pop art, demolishing the traditional boundaries between the beautiful and the ugly.

CATERINA BAY

See also **Arman (Fernandez); César (Baldachini); Klein, Yves; Kounellis, Jannis; Manzoni, Piero; Merz, Mario; Schwitters, Kurt; Spoerri, Daniel**

Biography

Born in Le Havre, France, 31 July 1901. After attending high school, enrolled in the École des Beaux-Arts, Le Havre, 1916; moved to Paris, where he enrolled in the Académie Julien, 1918; left Académie after six months and began working in his own studio; did not work as an artist from 1924 to 1942; first solo exhibition at Galerie René Drouin, Paris, 1944; lived and worked in New York City, 1951–52, while his dealer, Pierre Matisse, organized many shows in the United States; lived in Vence, France, 1955–61; retrospectives in Italy, Germany, Holland, and France, 1960; the Museum of Modern Art in New York City dedicated a large retrospective to him, 1962; lived in both New York City and Vence from the 1960s on; retrospectives at Guggenheim Museum of Art, New York City, 1966 and 1973; retrospective at the Art Institute of Chicago, 1970. Died in Paris, France, 12 May 1985.

Selected Works

1954   *Le Morvandiau*; charcoal; private collection, Paris, France

1954   *Pleurnichon*; sponge, cement; Collection Sonnabend, New York City, United States

1959   *L'Aveugle* (The Blind Man); silver foil; private collection, New York City, United States

1960   *Oberon*; papier mâché with glue, mica, wood chips; Hirshhorn Museum and Sculpture Garden, Washington D.C., United States

1966   *Logos Milestone VII*; expanded polyester; Albright-Knox Art Gallery, Buffalo, New York, United States

1968   *Table porteuse d'instance, d'objets et de projets* (Table Carrying Authority, Objects, and Projects); expanded polyester; Fondation Dubuffet, Périgny-sur-Yerres, France

1969   *Cabinet Logologique*; epoxy paint on polyurethane; Fondation Dubuffet, Périgny-sur-Yerres, France

1969   *La Foret* (The Drill); epoxy paint on polyurethane; Art Institute of Chicago, Illinois, United States

1969   *Paysage portatif* (Portable Landscape); expanded polyester of 14 elements; Museum Ludwig, Cologne, Germany

1970–73 *Villa Falbala* and *Closerie Falbala*; stratified resin painted in polyurethane, painted sculpted concrete; Fondation Dubuffet, Périgny-sur-Yerres, France

1972   *Group of Four Trees*; epoxy paint on polyurethane over metal sculpture; Chase Manhattan Plaza, New York City, United States

Further Reading

Cordier, Daniel, *Les dessins de Jean Dubuffet*, Paris: Ditis, 1960; as *The Drawings of Jean Dubuffet*, translated by Cecily Mackworth, New York: Braziller, 1960

Dubuffet, Jean, *Prospectus et tous les écrits suivants*, 2 vols., Paris: Gallimard, 1967

Dubuffet, Jean, *Asphyxiante culture*, Paris: Pauvert, 1968

Dubuffet, Jean, *Edifices*, Paris: Bucher,m and Basel: Beyeler, 1968; as *Jean Dubuffet: Edifices*, New York: Museum of Modern Art, 1968

Dubuffet, Jean, and Mildred Glimcher, *Jean Dubuffet: Towards an Alternative Reality*, edited by Marc Glimcher, New York: Pace, and Abbeville Press, 1987

Franzke, Andreas, *Jean Dubuffet*, Basel, Switzerland: Beyeler, 1975; as *Dubuffet*, translated by Robert Erich Wolf, New York: Abrams, 1981

Franzke, Andreas, *Jean Dubuffet: Petites statues de la vie précaire; Kleine Statuen des unsicheren Lebens* (bilingual French-German edition), Bern, Switzerland: Gachnang und Springer, 1988

Limbour, Georges, *Tableau bon levain à vous de cuir la pate: L'art brut di Jean Dubuffet*, Paris: Drouin, and New York: Matisse, 1953

Loreau, Max (editor), *Catalogue des travaux de Jean Dubuffet*, Paris: Pauvert, 1964–

Ragon, Michel, *Jean Dubuffet: Paysage du mental*, Paris: Galerie Jeanne Bucher, and Geneva: Skira, 1989

Seghers, Pierre, *L'homme du commun ou Jean Dubuffet*, Paris: Éditions Poésie, 1944

Selz, Peter Howard, *The Work of Jean Dubuffet*, New York: Museum of Modern Art, 1962

Sypher, Wylie, *Loss of the Self in Modern Literature and Art*, New York: Random House, 1962

MARCEL DUCHAMP 1887–1968 *French*

Famous for his "readymades", a term and a concept that he coined, Marcel Duchamp has been widely considered the first conceptual artist of the 20th century. His "readymade" was conceived as an ordinary object, usually manufactured, which the artist by the virtue of his selection elevated it to the level of high or fine art. With the execution of his readymades, Duchamp paved the way for the unlimited introduction of found objects into the realm of art.

This strategy for object-based sculpture was adopted by the avant-garde Dadaists in Berlin and Zürich in the early decades of the 20th century. Duchamp was attracted to Dada because it was a way of interjecting humor into a world gripped by the violence of war, fear, and anxiety. The execution of a readymade was a deliberate activity, weaving humor and the play of mental associations into the realm of art and aesthetics, which had heretofore been characterized by either academicism or intellectualism. Although associated with the Dadaists, Duchamp refused to confine himself within any art movement or philosophy, and his oeuvre is marked therefore by ambiguity, disparity and a wide ranging treatment of materials and approaches ranging from painting and sculpture to conceptual and performance-related works.

Unlike the Dadaists, Duchamp neither intended to transform everyday objects into objects of art nor to undermine the foundations of conventional artistic practice. Rather, he sought to create art that was devoid of aesthetics. By nullifying the visual pleasures of an art piece, such as color, composition, and form, he hoped to convey a symbolic intention to the viewer, rather than to indulge him or her in a purely visual experience. The pleasure, rather, was to be found in the mind; hence Duchamp is often associated with later Conceptual artists and movements that sprang up in the wake of World War II.

Duchamp began his career between 1911 and 1912, when he practiced Cubist painting after having joined the Puteaux group through his brother Raymond Duchamp-Villon's influence. Duchamp's *Nude Descending a Staircase No. 2* (1912), which demonstrates the pictorial influences of Cubism and Futurism, established him as a major independent figure on the contemporary scene. After some forays into painting, however, Duchamp put aside his brushes and constructed the first of his readymades, *Bicycle Wheel*, in 1913. This work consisted of a bicycle wheel attached to the seat of a nondescript wooden stool. Duchamp was interested in an element of movement in his work as well as the creation of an object devoid of aesthetic value. The mystique of *Bicycle Wheel* was that when spun it was an object with visual resonance but no aesthetic component.

The second of Duchamp's readymades was executed a year later in 1914. Critics of his time called *Bottle Rack* beautiful. Duchamp found this assessment surprising and amusing. In later life, he discussed the difficulty of the readymade selection process. The object had to be something he neither liked nor disliked. In fact, it had to be something that he was indifferent about, something absent of good or bad taste. Not surprisingly, taste was associated with the bourgeois in the mind of the Surrealists, who disregarded notions of "good" or "bad" taste in favor of the taboo. The emotional flatness or neutrality of Duchamp's selections resonated with an absurdity that echoed Surrealist art and literature of the day, but also a deadpan irony that would deeply inform later postwar Conceptual practices in Europe and America.

By displacing objects from their material and societal context, Duchamp forced his audience to view them in a different way, raising the question of aesthetics, spectatorship, and the meaning of art as a whole. He also realized that for a readymade to retain its power as an art object, it must have a certain quality of rarity; thus, he deliberately limited his output to just one or two pieces per year. Duchamp's readymade selection and production methods varied. An object could be chosen, given a title, and signed. For example, he caused a scandal in 1917 by presenting *Fountain*, a urinal that he signed "R. Mutt," at the exhibit of the Society of Independent Artists in New York City. ("R. Mutt" was a pseudonym for the artist and also the name of a German manufacturing firm, further confounding the association between the fine art object and the manufactured or mass-produced object.)

A readymade could also be planned. For instance, a note in his *Green Box* (1934) includes a written instruction to "buy a pair of tongs as a readymade." His *Unhappy Readymade* (1919) was actually produced by proxy. Duchamp sent a note from Buenos Aires to his sister in Paris instructing her to produce a readymade, a geometry book, which was hung from the balcony of her apartment.

Duchamp also conceptualized the reciprocal readymade. He would instruct a participant, for example, to take a painting by Rembrandt and use it as an ironing board. Another type, the assisted readymade, was open to wider interpretation. These works consisted of objects composed of found items but arranged (or "assisted" or adapted in some way) by the artist. One of the most famous of his assisted readymades was *Why Not Sneeze, Rrose Sélavy?*, created in New York in 1912. The work comprised a birdcage containing small marble blocks (simulating sugar cubes), a cuttlefish bone, and a thermometer. The assisted readymades enchanted Surrealists such as Man Ray, André Breton, and Joan Miró who were experimenting with what they called surrealist objects (as sculpture) at the time. Duchamp's attitude toward Surrealism resembled his attitude toward Dada. He largely infused the Parisian scene with a Dada element, and after his arrival in New York in 1915, which prompted meetings with Louise and Walter Arensberg (nascent collectors of modern art), Man Ray, and many other American artists and poets, Duchamp dominated Dada activities there as he worked on the *Large Glass*, also known as *The Bride Stripped Bare by Her Bachelors, Even* and considered the penultimate statement in his artistic oeuvre. In both cases, Duchamp served as an vital influence and precursor; however, he believed that Dada and Surrealist techniques lacked the subtlety and grace he strove for in his own work.

Duchamp published three groups of his notes in 1914, 1934, and 1967. The first of these, the *Box of 1914*, consisted of 16 proposals written between the years 1912 and 1914. The work was produced in an edition of three. Twenty years later, the *Green Box*, produced in an edition of 320, contained 94 items, including fragmentary manuscripts of the *Large Glass*, notes for readymades, ideas for a new language, and other miscellaneous projects. His third box, *In the Infinitive*, was produced in an edition of 150.

Many people assumed that in the last 20 years of his life, Duchamp gave up art entirely to perfect his game of chess. In actuality, he was working on his final piece, *Etant Donnés*, or *Given: 1. The Waterfall 2. The Illuminating Gas*, which was not discovered until after his death. Duchamp worked on the piece intermittently between 1944 and 1966, and he left a book with carefully written instructions for its installation, as well as snapshots and drawings. Following his notes, the work was constructed in the Philadelphia Museum of Art in 1969. The work is a complex installation in a darkened space (that is, a diorama) that must be viewed through a peephole by only one person at a time, in effect, stressing the role of the viewer as a voyeur. The viewer peers through what appears to be a wood and brick-framed door to a mysterious space only to be confronted with a strangely surreal and fragmented image of a naked woman in a natural landscape, seemingly referencing erotic symbols, dreams, as well as the art historical genre of the female nude in the landscape. *Etant Donnés*, similar to much of Duchamp's oeuvre, remains inextricably inscrutable; its quietly violent imagery and its power to entice and even seduce the viewer has been its most disturbing legacy.

Duchamp was one of the most influential modernists on the contemporary, postwar art world. Even in his supposed retirement, he continued to be a dominant influence on the avant-garde well into the 1960s.

CECILIA HAE-JIN LEE

See also **Modernism; Performance Art; Postmodernism; Surrealist Sculpture**

Biography

Born in Blainville-Crevon (Seine-Inférieure), near Rouen, France, 28 July 1887. Began his first work, *Landscape at Blainville*, 1902; graduated from École Bossuet, the *lycée* in Rouen, 1904; studied painting at Académie Jullian, Paris, until July 1905; intermittently drew cartoons for *Courrier Français* and *Le Rire*, 1905–10; exhibited for first time at the Salon des Indépendants, 1909; moved to New York and began *Large Glass*, 1915; returned to Paris, 1919; founded *Societé Anonyme* with Katherine Dreier and Man Ray, and assumed pseudonym of Rrose Sélavy, 1920; returned to New York to continue work on *Large Glass*, 1922; abandoned work on *Large Glass* and returned to Paris, 1923; first Surrealist Manifesto appeared in *Entr'acte*, a film by René Clair, 1924; traveled through Italy and completed his second optical instrument, *Rotary Demisphere*, 1925; *Large Glass* exhibited for first time, 1926; exhibited in international Surrealist Exhibition, London, and visited New York to undertake restoration of *Large Glass*, 1936; first one-man exhibition of nine works, Art Club of Chicago, 1937; participated in the International Surrealist Exhibition in Paris, returned to New York, collaborated with Breton, Sidney, Janis, and R.A. Parker on *First Papers of Surrealism* exhibition, 1938; permanent exhibition of Arensberg Collection opened at Philadelphia Museum of Art, 1954, with 53 of Duchamp's works; major exhibition of Duchamp

and brothers, also sculptors, at Solomon R. Guggenheim Museum, New York City. Died in Neuilly, Paris, France, 1 October 1968.

Selected Works

1913   *Bicycle Wheel*; readymade: bicycle wheel on wooden stool (lost); 1964, eight replicas, produced by Gallery Swarz, Milan, Italy

1914   *Bottle Rack*; readymade: galvanized iron (lost); 1964, replica, Philadelphia Museum of Art, Pennsylvania, United States

1915   *In Advance of a Broken Arm*; readymade: wood and metal snow shovel (lost); 1964, replicas, Yale University Art Gallery, New Haven, Connecticut, United States; Musée National d'Art Moderne, Centre Georges Pompidou, Paris, France

1915–23 *Large Glass* (also known as *The Bride Stripped Bare by Her Bachelors, Even*); oil, lead, wire, foil, dust, and varnish on glass with wood and steel frame; Philadelphia Museum of Art, Pennsylvania, United States

1916   *With Hidden Noise*; ball of twine between two brass plates containing an unknown object; Philadelphia Museum of Art, Pennsylvania, United States

1917   *Fountain*, for Society of Independent Artists exhibit, New York City, United States; readymade: porcelain urinal signed "R. Mutt" (lost)

1918   *To Be Looked At (from the Other Side of the Glass) with One Eye, Close To, for Almost an Hour*; readymade: glass, lead wire, oil paint, magnifying lens, and silver leaf, mounted between two panes of glass in a standing metal frame on painted wood base; Museum of Modern Art, New York City, United States

1919   *Air of Paris*; readymade: 50 cm^3 of Paris air in glass; Philadelphia Museum of Art, Pennsylvania, United States

1919   *L.H.O.O.Q.*; rectified readymade: pencil on reproduction of the *Mona Lisa*; private collection, Paris, France

1919   *Unhappy Readymade*; geometry textbook exposed to the wind on the balcony of his sister, Suzanne (destroyed)

1921   *Why Not Sneeze, Rrose Sélavy?*; assisted readymade: small painted birdcage, marble (sugar) cubes, thermometer, and cuttlefish bone; original: Philadelphia Museum of Art, Pennsylvania, United States; 2nd version: 1963, Ulf Linde, Stockholm, Sweden; 3rd version: Galleria Schwarz, Milan, Italy

1934 *Green Box*; facsimile notes and reproductions in a box; Collection of Angelo Calmarini, Milan, Italy

1946–66 *Etant Donnés* or *Given: 1. The Waterfall 2. The Illuminating Gas*; mixed media assemblage; Philadelphia Museum of Art, Pennsylvania, United States

Further Reading

Ades, Dawn, Neil Cox, and David Hopkins, *Marcel Duchamp*, New York and London: Thames and Hudson, 1999

Bonk, Ecke (editor), *Joseph Cornell, Marcel Duchamp—in Resonance*, Houston, Texas: Menil Collection, Philadelphia: Philadelphia Museum of Art, and Ostfildern-Ruit, Germany: Cantz, 1998

Cabanne, Pierre, *Entretiens avec Marcel Duchamp*, Paris: Belford, 1967; as *Dialogues with Marcel Duchamp*, London: Thames and Hudson, and New York: Viking Press, 1971

De Duve, Thierry, *The Definitively Unfinished Marcel Duchamp*, Cambridge, Massachusetts: MIT Press, 1991

Hulten, Karl Gunnar Pontus (editor), *Marcel Duchamp: Work and Life*, Cambridge, Massachusetts: MIT Press, and London: Thames and Hudson, 1993

Jacobs, Lewis, *Marcel Duchamp in His Own Words* (video-recording), Northbrook, Illinois: Roland Collection of Films on Art, 1982 (based on tape recordings of Duchamp made in Cadaques, Spain, August 1968)

Joselit, David, *Infinite Regress: Marcel Duchamp, 1910–1941*, Cambridge, Massachusetts: MIT Press, 1998

Naumann, Francis M., *Marcel Duchamp: The Art of Making Art in the Age of Mechanical Reproduction*, New York: Achim Moeller Fine Art, and Ghent, Brussels: Ludion Press, 1999

Paz, Octavio, *Marcel Duchamp: Appearance Stripped Bare*, New York: Seaver Books, 1981

Ramirez, Juan Antonio, *Duchamp: El amor y la muerte, incluso*, Madrid: Ediciones Siruela, 1993; 2nd edition, 1994; as *Duchamp: Love and Death, Even*, translated by Alexander R. Tulloch, London: Reaktion Books, 1999

Seigel, Jerrold, *The Private Worlds of Marcel Duchamp: Desire, Liberation, and the Self in Modern Culture*, Berkeley: University of California Press, 1995

Tomkins, Calvin, *Duchamp: A Biography*, New York: Holt, 1996; London: Chatto and Windus, 1997

LARGE GLASS (THE BRIDE STRIPPED BARE BY HER BACHELORS, EVEN)

Marcel Duchamp (1887–1968)

1915–1923

oil, lead, wire, foil, dust, and varnish on glass (cracked) mounted between two glass panels in a wood and steel frame

h. 2.78 m; w. 1.75 m

The Louise and Walter Arensberg Collection, Philadelphia Museum of Art, Pennsylvania, United States

The *Large Glass* may be one of the most complicated and pondered art objects of the 20th century. The work

was Marcel Duchamp's primary focus from 1913 to 1915 and included several preliminary studies and some related works that he painted in Munich in 1912. By 1915 he had prepared the first sketches and began working on the *Large Glass*. Although he created many related pieces, he considered the *Chocolate Grinder* (also known as *Chocolate Grinder No. 1*, 1913) to be the origin of the *Large Glass*.

Duchamp executed the *Large Glass* in New York from 1915 to 1923. The work consists of oil paint, lead wire, foil, dust, and varnish encased in two large pieces of glass. He chose glass as a support for this two-dimensional work that truly functions three-dimensionally because of its purely abstract and aesthetic effects. According to his notes, Duchamp wanted to make a painting on glass so that it would have neither a front nor back, top nor bottom—to create a three-dimensional object that existed in four dimensions. The finished work—which is transparent—can be viewed from both the front and the back, creating, in effect, a sculpture in the round. He had made use of a glass palette in previous years and was influenced by the brilliance of the pigment pressed up against the material surface. This resulted in a flat, exact shape, as is demonstrated in the *Chocolate Grinder*. Onto the wet paint Duchamp pressed a layer of lead foil, which isolated it from the surrounding air. This sealed the paint from oxidation, thus allowing it to retain its original luminosity.

The *Large Glass* is divided into two sections by a horizontal metal bar. The top half is the realm of the bride, a surreal environment that resembles an internal combustion engine. The bride is a mechanical figure, derived from Duchamp's memory of county fair games and expressed in machinelike elements and visceral forms. She is the summation of all of the female figures in his work; however, she originates from two particular works. The first is a small drawing designed as an accompaniment to Jules Laforgue's poem *Encore à Cet Aster*. This drawing subsequently led to two versions of his major painting *Nude Descending a Staircase* (1911/12; Philadelphia Museum of Art, Pennsylvania). The presence of the nude figure in the *Large Glass* is thus developed from more traditional iconographies and yet is transformed into a modern interpretation of femininity, albeit a machine-like conception of love and sex.

Although the bride retained certain visual links with the world of Cubism, the bachelors were derived from the concept of the readymade. The bachelor-machines, the chocolate grinder, and the water mill resemble Duchamp's earliest readymades in that they retain a degree of formal elegance despite Duchamp's intention to remove their aesthetic element. His *Coffee Mill* (1911; Tate Gallery, London) is a significant precursor.

Although it was a painting he executed for the kitchen of one of his brothers (and therefore not intended for public exhibition), the work demonstrated Duchamp's fascination with the artistic possibilities of everyday objects.

In the *Chocolate Grinder No. 1* (1913), the first elements of the bachelor mechanism become apparent. The bride is not partnered by the chocolate grinder, however, but instead by the bachelors, which are represented by the nine malic molds. A definitive model was executed on glass in Paris during 1914–15. Another related work is *Glider Containing a Water Mill in Neighboring Metals*, executed between 1913 and 1915 (Philadelphia Museum of Art, Philadelphia, Pennsylvania). It is the only one of Duchamp's works on glass that remains unbroken.

Some critics believe that the *Large Glass* should be viewed as an explanatory diagram, such as an instruction or operating manual. Duchamp had at one point considered the idea of supplementing the work with text, creating notes like a guidebook to accompany the visual experience. Despite eight years of work, however, he never finished his notes; a collection of them was published in 1934 as the *Green Box*, which included a compilation of documents, plans, sketches, and notes made between 1912 and 1915 in connection with the *Large Glass*, providing some explanatory and theoretical text. In fact, Duchamp abandoned work on the *Large Glass* in 1923, choosing to leave the work in its unfinished state. Duchamp has said of the *Large Glass* that it "is not to be looked at for itself but only as a function of a catalog I never made." In some sense, the *Large Glass* therefore functions as an index of the artist and his oeuvre, or as an inscrutable reference for a body of work that resists meaningful interpretation.

The studies, projects, and notes that culminated in the *Large Glass* held supreme importance to the emergence of both the Dada and Surrealist movements. The appearance of the *Green Box* provoked André Breton to write an essay (*Phare de la Marée*) in the 1953 issue of the Surrealist periodical, *Minotaure*, describing the *Large Glass* as a "mechanical and cynical interpretation of the phenomenon of love." Breton suggested that the bride and her bachelors attempt to consummate a physical union that they desire but that they recognize is impossible to achieve. The poet Octavio Paz, on the other hand, accepted that the *Large Glass* was designed as in insoluble enigma.

In his own notes, Duchamp describes the piece as a "wedding of mental and visual concepts." Eroticism was a subject of fascination for Duchamp, and *Large Glass* manifests the artist's passions as well as frustrations and perhaps even anxieties. The bride acknowledges the activity of the bachelor apparatuses beneath her by allowing her robe to fall away. At her base is

her "love gasoline" that is distributed to a series of motors with feeble cylinders. The bachelor mechanism, in turn, produces a gas that first filters through the seven conical sieves and then is thrust upward through a series of circular devices (or "oculist witnesses"). The number of bachelors was originally set at eight, as seen in a preliminary drawing, before Duchamp decided on the more agile number nine. A written key identifies the molds in terms of their respective uniforms as a policeman, a priest, and an undertaker, among others. Critically read as metaphor for coitus interruptus, the *Large Glass* indeed depicts the failure to consummate the sexual passions. The bachelors' love gasses—represented by specks of dust the artist allowed to collect between the panes of glass—never reach their final destination. Whether is was meant as cynicism, as Breton describes it, or an enigmatic musing on the futility of love, as Paz might have intended, the work remains a critical example of early 20th century Modernism. Oddly unerotic for a work whose subject is carnal eroticism, the *Large Glass* reflects the ambivalence and anxiety of the human psyche.

After its first public appearance at the International Exhibition of Modern Art at the Brooklyn Museum, New York, in 1926, the *Large Glass* was shattered. When first informed of the disaster, Duchamp expressed only some amusement; ten years later, however, he spent several months piecing the fragments together again. Duchamp later said that the cracks "brought the work back into the world." As he restored the work, the original glass became encased in a new metal frame.

From 1943 to 1944, the *Large Glass* was exhibited again at the Museum of Modern Art in New York before finding its permanent home in 1953 at the Arensberg Collection of the Philadelphia Museum of Art. Because of its fragile condition, it will probably never travel again.

CECILIA HAE-JIN LEE

Further Reading

Adcock, Craig E., *Marcel Duchamp's Notes from the Large Glass: An N-Dimensional Analysis*, Ann Arbor, Michigan: UMI Research Press, and Epping, Essex: Bowker, 1983

Golding, John, *Marcel Duchamp: The Bride Stripped Bare by Her Bachelors, Even*, New York: Viking Press, 1972; London: Allen Lane, 1973

Henderson, Linda Dalrymple, *Duchamp in Context: Science and Technology in the Large Glass and Related Works*, Princeton, New Jersey: Princeton University Press, 1998

Matisse, Paul, *Marcel Duchamp, Notes*, Paris: Centre Georges Pompidou, 1980; as *Marcel Duchamp, Notes*, Boston: G.K. Hall, 1983

Hopkins, David, *Marcel Duchamp and Max Ernst: The Bride Shared*, Oxford: Clarendon Press, and New York: Oxford University Press, 1998

RAYMOND DUCHAMP-VILLON 1876–1918 *French*

Raymond Duchamp-Villon was one of the most innovative and versatile artists of the early Parisian avant-garde. Self-taught and without any formal training, his impact on modern sculpture is disproportionate to his output during a short career that preempted many later attempts at introducing Modernist notions of time and space into the sculptural process. He was, with Alexander Porfirevich Archipenko, the first to explore in depth the implications of Futurism and Cubism for sculpture, finding ways of expressing the dynamism of modern life through the counterbalance of solid form and void, of stable structures and animated line.

Duchamp-Villon's skill lay particularly in his ability as a draftsman and the clarity of design that arose from his interest in architecture. He was unusual for the time in his stark simplification of sculptural planes and his way of describing the energy of the human body by reducing it to abstract modular segments that combined into an organic, free-flowing pattern suggesting continuous movement. Perhaps his greatest innovation was to see modeling in sculpture as outmoded for the modern sensibility, supplanting this with a more truly three-dimensional technique that cut deeply into the center of the form. He believed that sculpture should follow "the logic of its material," using the Eiffel Tower as a model of simplicity and austerity, its powerful metal shafts slicing and fracturing space but also drawing it together.

Duchamp-Villon's interest in architecture and its relationship with sculpture was the aspect of his work most admired by his contemporaries. It was discussed in terms of the desire within his circle for a more "analytic" art exposing the hidden structure of objects and in terms of Duchamp-Villon's own architectural projects. The most notable of these was his *Design for a Cubist House*, made at André Mare's request for the 1912 Salon d'Automne. The series of maquettes and drawings that the sculptor produced combined a stylized Cubism with traditional decorative detail. From this moment the French press turned their attention onto Duchamp-Villon, and in the *Paris Journal* of 14 November 1913, he was proclaimed the principal exponent of Cubist sculpture.

It was in 1912 that Duchamp-Villon embarked on his most ambitious and acclaimed sculptural theme, that of *The Horse*. His development of this subject typifies the way his initial ideas had a protracted evolution. His definitive study in plaster of 1914 is considered to be his last major sculpture. Although Duchamp-Villon was planning a reinvention of the traditional equestrian monument well before the outbreak of World War I, his ambition was enhanced by his war-time posting as a cavalry medical officer, and he was by all accounts an accomplished horseman. His early *Horse and Rider* maquettes bear out one of his key tenets, that artistic expression should be rooted in the observation of nature. As the limbs of man and beast increasingly merge through the series of studies to become one great heaving machine of turning cogs and pistons, the structure remains an analysis of an animal in motion. Indeed, among Duchamp-Villon's inspirations for *The Horse* were Eadweard Muybridge's photographic investigations into *The Horse in Motion* (1872). The work also clearly incorporates the sculptor's experiences of modern warfare and the searing disjunction of life at the front.

Yet the reason *The Horse* remains an icon of modern sculpture lies rather in its use of metaphor. It abandons the linear logic requiring that horse and rider should be clearly definable, carrying easily recognizable features. Only aspects of each remain, and these are developed with such poetic freedom that a totally new object emerges that describes both entities and yet is a thing unto itself.

Duchamp-Villon applied the same freedom to portraiture. In the portraits *Baudelaire*, *Maggy*, and *Professor Gosset*, the dense volume, ruthless paring down, and exaggerated hollows of the head give each work an otherworldly aura, most startling in the final work. *Gosset* becomes a living skull, an image of imminent death and fear of loss, a vision from beyond the grave.

The device Duchamp-Villon used with great originality to enhance the solidity of his figures was to bring the space around an object into the heart of its construction. He developed this technique through a series of reliefs, from 1911 to 1913, culminating in the relief of

Raymond Duchamp-Villon, *The Horse*, 1914, bronze (cast 1930–31) 101.6 × 100.3 × 56.8 cm. Museum of Modern Art, New York, Van Gogh Purchase Fund
© 2000 the Museum of Modern Art, New York and Art Resource, New York

The Lovers. Here the rhyming segments that describe the figures are punctuated by intervals instead of joints, creating a lively and highly decorative schema. Convex and concave are stressed so as to be almost interchangeable. The figures and the space around them appear equally substantial and all the more resonant.

The fertile context in which Duchamp-Villon's ideas matured was that of the Puteaux group, those friends with whom he met, during 1910–11, to debate the latest aesthetic theories—his brother Marcel Duchamp, František Kupka, Jean Metzinger, Albert Gleizes, Francis Picabia, Roger de la Fresnaye, and occasionally, Guillaume Apollinaire. Within this group Duchamp-Villon stands out as having been a strikingly adept proselytizer for modern sculpture. He had a gift for composing compelling manifestos, and his progression through the committees of the Salon d'Automne, the place for up-and-coming sculptors to exhibit, demonstrates how ambitious he was for his own work and that of his associates.

In this position at the sharp end of the avant-garde, Duchamp-Villon still retained his respect for the oldest traditions of sculpture, and he is representative of the Cubist sculptors working in Paris in his insistence that his work did not break with, but rather expanded, those traditions. With his fellow Puteaux artists, he believed that Modernist practice should revive the great canons of the past. His enthusiasms included Leonardo da Vinci and Albrecht Dürer, Dürer especially for his economy, clarity, and analysis of proportion. Writing to Walter Pach about his own work in March 1914, the sculptor suggested how it could be read in terms of the French Gothic primarily for what it shared with that style in its underlying spirit and emotion.

CATHERINE PÜTZ

See also **Archipenko, Alexander Porfirevich; Duchamp, Marcel**

Biography

Born in Damville, Eure, France, 5 November 1876. Maternal grandfather an artist; brother of the artists Jacques Villon and Marcel Duchamp. Moved with Villon to the rue des Écoles, Paris, 1895; abandoned medical studies due to ill health, 1898, and took up sculpture during convalescence; had first Paris studio, shared with Arthur Bullard, 1900–01; first exhibition, 1902, at the Société Nationale des Beaux-Arts; exhibited annually at the Salon d'Automne, 1905–13, becoming a committee member, 1908, and vice president of the jury, 1910; moved to Puteaux, Paris, 1907, and set up studio he used for the rest of his life near those of Villon and František Kupka; began fruitful collaboration with designer André Mare, 1911; contributed to

Section d'Or exhibition at Galerie La Boétie, Paris, 1912; same year made first contacts with American collectors via new friend Walter Pach; exhibited at the Armory Show, New York City, 1913; conscripted by the French army, 1914, and assigned to the 11th Cuirassiers Regiment as a medical auxiliary; posted to Saint-Germain-en-Laye, 1914–15, then sent to front at Champagne; contracted typhoid, 1916; continued sketching ideas for sculpture; eventually succumbed to septicemia. Died in Cannes, France, 7 October 1918.

Selected Works

1907   *Torso of a Woman*; bronze; Musée Nationale d'Art Moderne, Centre Georges Pompidou, Paris, France

1910   *Pastoral* (also known as *Adam and Eve*); plaster; Musée Nationale d'Art Moderne, Centre Georges Pompidou, Paris, France

1910   *Torso of a Young Man*; plaster; Hirshhorn Museum and Sculpture Garden, Washington, D.C., United States

1911   *Baudelaire*; bronze; Museum of Modern Art, New York City, United States; plaster versions: Musée Nationale d'Art Moderne, Centre Georges Pompidou, Paris, France; Philadelphia Museum of Art, Pennsylvania, United States; Nasher College, Dallas, Texas, United States; Musée d'Art et d'Histoire, Saint-Denis, France

1912   Facade for a Cubist house; plaster maquette (destroyed)

1912   *Maggy*; plaster; Musée Nationale d'Art Moderne, Centre Georges Pompidou, Paris, France; cast: Galerie Dina Vierny, Paris, France

1913   *The Lovers*; plaster; Musée Nationale d'Art Moderne, Centre Georges Pompidou, Paris, France; other casts: Philadelphia Museum of Art, Pennsylvania, United States; Museum of Modern Art, New York City, United States

1914   *Horse*; plaster; Philadelphia Museum of Art, Pennsylvania, United States; cast: Musée des Beaux-Arts de Grenoble, France

1914   *Horse and Rider*; bronze maquette; Musée Nationale d'Art Moderne, Centre Georges Pompidou, Paris, France; private collection, England

1914   *Seated Woman*; plaster (lost); bronze casts: 1914–15, Yale University Museum, New Haven, Connecticut, United States; Rhode Island School of Design, Providence,

Rhode Island, United States; Museum
Ludwig, Cologne, Germany
1917–18 *Professor Gosset*; plaster; Philadelphia
Museum of Art, Pennsylvania, United
States; cast: Musée des Beaux-Arts de
Rouen, France

Further Reading

Cork, Richard, *A Bitter Truth: Avant-garde Art and the Great
War*, New Haven, Connecticut: Yale University Press, 1994
Duchamp-Villon, Raymond, *Raymond Duchamp-Villon, Sculp-
teur*, Paris: Povolozky, 1924
Duchamp-Villon, Raymond, *Raymond Duchamp-Villon, 1876–
1918* (exhib. cat.), New York: Walker, 1967
Duchamp-Villon, Raymond, *Duchamp-Villon: Collections du
Centre Georges Pompidou, Musée nationale d'art moderne
et du Musée des Beaux-Arts de Rouen*, Paris: Centre Georges
Pompidou, and Réunion des Musées Nationaux, 1998
Elsen, Albert, "The Sculpture of Duchamp-Villon: His First
Retrospective Opens at Knoedlers' This Month," *Artforum*
6 (6 October 1967)
Giedion-Welcker, C.G., "Verankerung und Vorstoss bei Ray-
mond Duchamp-Villon," *Werk* 5/8 (April 1964)
Janneau, Guillaume, *L'art Cubiste: Théories et réalisations*,
Paris: Moreau, 1929
Pradel, Marie-Noëlle, "Raymond Duchamp-Villon, la vie et
l'oeuvre," (thesis), Paris: École du Louvre, 1960
Salmon, André, *La jeune sculpture française*, Paris: Société des
Trente, 1919
Villon, Jacques, "Duchamp-Villon: 1876–1918," in *Les sculp-
teurs célèbres*, edited by Pierre Francastel, Paris: Mazenod,
1954
Zervos, Christian, "Raymond Duchamp-Villon," *Cahiers d'art*
(1931)

DUPRÉ FAMILY *Italian*

Giovanni Dupré 1817–1882

Because of the foresight of Amalia Dupré, who turned
the studio she had shared with her father, Giovanni
Dupré, into a museum upon his death in 1882, much
of the output of these two sculptors has been preserved
as testimony to an important, but underplayed, moment
in Italian sculpture history. The scope of the extant
sketches and plaster casts in the Villa Dupré, Fiesole,
indicates the intensive studio production and stylistic
verve of the Duprés, who produced work for churches,
public monuments, and private clients throughout Italy
and Europe during a period well exceeding 50 years.

Giovanni Dupré trained as a woodcarver with his
father, later becoming foreman in Paolo Sani's intaglio
workshop in Florence, an experience that perhaps provided him with the discipline to execute a large number
of commissions at an early stage in his career. His first
acclaimed work, *Dying Abel*, shown at the Florence
Academy, produced buyers for marble and bronze ver-

sions and for a companion piece, the standing figure
of *Cain*. Giovanni's background as a craftsman, rather
than an academician, has been cited as permitting the
naturalistic modeling of the prone *Dying Abel*, apparent in the prominent detailing of the figure's rib cage
and exposed underarm hair. Critics accused the young
sculptor of casting the model from life, a claim he was
able to disprove. This early venture to find "il bello
nel vero" (the beauty in truth), supported by fellow
sculptor Lorenzo Bartolini and emphasized later in Dupré's *Ricordi Autobiografici* (1879–82), suggested a
move toward an art that hoped to embrace the modern.

Nonetheless, Giovanni Dupré's work of the next
years, influenced by a trip to Rome in 1844–45, did
call upon Classical form, and this was paramount in
his later work *Sappho*, which depicts the contemplative
mood of the Greek poet moments before her suicide.
The choice of subject matter, the supporting object of
the lyre, and the figure's idealized features conform to
neo-Greek interests in the antique, and art historian
Augusto Conti cited the Neoclassical emphasis on
ideal forms of nature: "The breast, the torso, the shoulders, arms, hands, and feet and finally the face . . .
show us that the artist is a disciple of beautiful nature"
(see Frieze, 1886).

By the 1860s, Giovanni Dupré was running an enormously successful studio, counting among his pupils
his daughter Amalia. His prominence in the Florentine
art world ensured sculpture commissions for several
architectural restoration projects in the city, including
the facade of the Church of Santa Croce (architect,
Niccola Matas, completed in 1863), for which Giovanni, along with two pupils, executed low-relief
panels. In the central tympanum, *Exaltation of the Holy
Cross*, Dupré blended appropriate religious symbolism
in the rays emanating from the cross with mediating
angels and a reading of Christian history in the semicircular arrangement of figures below. Dupré's treatment
of the generalized barbarian and freed slave, both centrally positioned among familiar Christian historical
figures, invite attention. Their inclusion as representatives of designated types referenced prevalent European discourses on physiognomy, which can be seen
in the differentiation between the elongated, slender
forms of the angels and the less refined limbs of the
barbarian.

Giovanni Dupré's funerary monument the *Pietà*, exhibited in the 1867 Exposition Universelle in Paris and
awarded the Grand Medal of Honour, combines Neo-
Renaissance composition with the perfected naturalism of the dead Christ's body, prompting critics to
note a tension in the work between the ancient and
the modern. His international renown (he had earlier

entered the London competition for the monument to Wellington in 1857) was reinforced in the London *Art Journal* (1868), which praised his contribution as "vigorous, naturalistic, and masterly."

As a leading national sculptor, Giovanni executed numerous works of portraiture, his most renowned being the memorial statue to Risorgimento leader Camillo Benso, conte di Cavour, unveiled in 1873 in Turin and paid for by public subscription. His decision to represent the national hero in a toga with a seminude personification of Italy caused much discussion in the press, indicating a change in public taste that the sculptor had previously gauged so well. The supporting allegorical groups, *Right*, *Duty*, *Statesmanship*, and *Independence*, have received scant attention. Together with the bas-reliefs of Sardinian troops returning from the Crimea and the 1856 Congress of Paris, the groups were a significant contribution to the narrative of a new Italian nationhood and placed Giovanni Dupré alongside his contemporaries in secular art production, Vincenzo Vela and Carlo Marochetti. In his later output, Giovanni concentrated on Christian subject matter, particularly in tomb sculpture and statuary.

Amalia Dupré, *Saint Peter in Chains*
© Alinari / Art Resource, NY

Giovanni Dupré, *Sappho*
© Alinari / Art Resource, NY

Amalia Dupré 1842–1928

By the time of Giovanni Dupré's last work, *St. Francis* (one of several commissions for the Cathedral of the San Rufino, Assisi), his daughter Amalia, who finished the statue in marble, had been working in the studio since at least 1862. In his *Ricordi Autobiografici* Giovanni reports that because Amalia had manifested an early inclination for sculpture, he began her training, which included access to live nude models—a significant advantage over many of her female contemporaries, to whom life drawing and anatomy classes were closed. The working relationship was a close one, and along with *St. Francis*, Amalia undertook Giovanni's other unfinished figure, *St. Zenobius*, for the central facade portal of Florence Cathedral, adding the companion pieces *St. Clare* and *St. Reparata*.

In addition to meeting the preeminent Florentine artists of the day in her father's studio, Amalia Dupré accompanied Giovanni to Turin, Rome, and Paris, thereby gaining exposure to a wide range of national and international artistic production. Her marble *Giotto as a Boy* was exhibited with some success in Paris in 1867, although it was omitted from the London *Art Journal* report of the exhibition. Nevertheless, the plaster original of *Giotto as a Boy* reveals the artist's acute observation of the supple curve of her boy model's back and of the youth's gaunt wiriness.

Amalia Dupré's other early works can be described as strictly Neoclassical. Marble relief panels of five *Saints*, the *Virgin*, and the *Risen Christ* for the pulpit in San Miniato Cathedral show clear and direct forms, with reductive profiles and uncomplicated drapery against plain backgrounds in extremely shallow relief. Four funerary monuments along the nave in the same cathedral consist of busts of the deceased surmounting framed reliefs of themes from their careers. Again, these reliefs display an extreme cleanliness of line and spatial form, although the portrait busts merit attention for their vividness and individuality.

Amalia Dupré's skill in these varying areas is strikingly illustrated by a monument to her father of 1882. The "idealized realism" of the life-size figure of a mature but not yet aging man in modern dress contrasts starkly with the rendering of figures in the bas-relief panels of scenes from Giovanni's life that recall the stylized compositions, stasis, and truncated proportions of late imperial and early Christian relief carving.

Two of Amalia Dupré's later works, *Virgin and Child* in the parish of Casacalenda and the *Madonna of the Rosary* in the Church of San Marco in Florence, both painted terracotta life-size figures in the round, reflect a more mature, neo-15th-century style, referred to as Purist or Robbian. Here, Amalia tempered the rigidity of her early Neoclassicism and the emotionalism of her more Romantic tendencies to yield moving, yet not maudlin, devotional figures.

Although religious works predominate in her oeuvre, Amalia Dupré also produced portrait busts and work with secular themes. Pious to an extreme, Dupré did little to promote herself and her work, even though Angelo De Gubernatis, director of the Esposizione Beatrice in 1890—a national exposition of women's arts and industries in Florence—wrote several times to Dupré, begging her to contribute.

Giovanni Dupré reported that Amalia, who did not need to support herself through her sculpting, frequently donated her work to churches and religious groups. Although this situation may have contributed to her disappearance from the annals of professional artists, it also meant that she could sculpt most of her work herself, rather than relying on the support of studio workers. Such intimacy with her material led to an increasing freeness in the rendering of both poses and surfaces, best seen in the plaster maquettes of her late works *Three Cardinal Virtues* and *Baptism* (after 1890), which introduce a Modernist dynamism to traditional religious themes.

Late in life, Amalia Dupré trained the young sculptor Carmela Adani for three summers, between 1922 and 1925; the Dupré family is also represented in the early 21st century by a descendant, the sculptor Amalia Ciardi-Dupré, who works largely with Christian imagery and themes.

MIRANDA MASON and NANCY PROCTOR

See also **Bartolini, Lorenzo; Neoclassicism and Romanticism; Vela, Vincenzo**

Giovanni Dupré

Biography

Born in Siena, Italy, 1 March 1817. Family settled in Florence by 1827; worked in father's wood carving workshop, also with Paolo Sani and other renowned intaglio masters; briefly attended Instituto di Belle Arti in Siena; met sculptor Lorenzo Bartolini; first works in wood and plaster; plaster model of *Dying Abel* exhibited at Accademia di Belle Arti in Florence, 1842; traveled to Rome, 1844–45; to Naples, 1853–54; traveled to London for international competition for Wellington monument, 1857; exhibited at Exposition Universelle, Paris, 1867; president of sculpture jury at International Exhibition in Vienna, 1873. Pupils included Augusto Rivalta and own daughter Amalia Dupré, with whom he shared studio until his death. Published autobiography, 1879, and various treatises on art; some periods of illness due to overwork. Died in Fiesole, Italy, 10 January 1882.

Selected Works

1845	*Dying Abel*; marble; Hermitage, St. Petersburg, Russia	
1845	*Giotto*; marble; Galleria degli Uffizi, Florence, Italy	
1847	*Cain*; marble; Hermitage, St. Petersburg, Russia	
1850	*Cain*; bronze; Palazzo Pitti, Florence, Italy	
1850	*Dying Abel*; bronze; Palazzo Pitti, Florence, Italy	
1850	*Nymph with a Scorpion* (originally by Lorenzo Bartolini, completed by Dupré on his death); marble; Hermitage, St. Petersburg, Russia	
1850	*Nymph with a Serpent* (originally by Lorenzo Bartolini, completed by Dupré on his death); marble; Fondazione Magnani-Rocca, Reggio Emilia, Italy	
1859	*Festive Bacchus*; marble; Palazzo Pitti, Florence, Italy	
1861	*Sappho*; marble; Galleria Nazionale d'Arte Moderna, Rome, Italy	
1862–68	*Pietà*; marble; Misericordia Cemetery, Siena, Italy	

1864	Monument to Berta Moltke Ferrari Corbelli; marble; Church of San Lorenzo, Florence, Italy
1873	Monument to Camillo Benso, Conte di Cavour; marble; Piazza Carlo Emanuele II, Turin, Italy
1877	Monument to Fiorella Favard; marble; Villa Favard, Rovezzano, Italy
1880	*Pius IX*; marble; Piacenza Cathedral, Piacenza, Italy

Amalia Dupré

Biography

Born in Florence, Italy, 26 November 1842. Trained by her father, Giovanni Dupré; traveled with him to Rome and later exhibited with him at Exposition Universelle, Paris, 1867; founded museum after her father's death (1882); exhibited Esposizione Beatrice, Florence, 1890; sculptor Carmela Adani her pupil during summers, 1922–25. Died in Florence, Italy, 23 May 1928.

Selected Works

1862	*Giotto as a Boy*; plaster; Villa Dupré, Fiesole, Italy
1869	*St. Peter in Chains*; plaster; Museo dell'Accademia, Montecatini, Italy
before 1871	*Saints*, *Virgin*, and *Risen Christ*; marble; San Miniato Cathedral, San Miniato, Italy
1872	Monument to Luisa Dupré; marble; Fiesole Cemetery, Italy
1879	*Angel of Peace*; bronze; Villa Camerini, Piazzola sul Brenta, Italy
ca. 1882	*St. Zenobius*; marble; Cathedral of Santa Maria del Fiore, Florence, Italy
1882	*St. Francis*; marble; Cathedral of San Ruffino, Assisi, Italy
after 1882	*Giovanni Dupré*; plaster; Villa Dupré, Fiesole, Italy
ca. 1887	*St. Reparata*; marble; Cathedral of Santa Maria del Fiore, Florence, Italy
1888	*St. Clare*; marble; Cathedral of San Ruffino, Assisi, Italy
after 1890	*Virgin and Child*; painted terracotta; Sanctuary of Santa Maria della Difesa, parish of Casacalenda, Campobasso, Italy
after 1890	*Madonna of the Rosary*; painted terracotta; San Marco, Florence, Italy

Further Reading

Da Antonio Canova a Medardo Rosso: Disegni di scultori italiani del XIX secolo (exhib. cat.), Rome: De Luca Editore, 1982

Dupré, Giovanni, *Pensieri sull' arte e ricordi autobiografici*, Florence: Le Monnier, 1879; as *Thoughts on Art and Autobiographical Memoirs*, translated by E.M. Peruzzi, Edinburgh and London: Blackwood, 1884; Boston: Roberts, 1886

Finn, David, "Discovering Giovanni Duprè," *Sculpture Review* 41 (1992)

Frieze, Henry Simmons, *Giovanni Duprè*, New York: Scribner and Welford, and London: Sampson Low Searle and Rivington, 1886

Santa Croce nell'800 (exhib. cat.), Florence: Alinari, 1986

Sisi, Carlo, Ettore Spalletti, and Giuliano Catoni (editors), *La cultura artistica a Siena nell'Ottocento*, Siena, Italy: Monte dei Paschi di Siena, 1994

SUSAN D. DURANT early 1820s–1873
British

A progressive 19th-century Englishwoman, Susan D. Durant championed enfranchisement for women, the improvement of female education, and woman's self-sufficiency through professional work. She came to sculpture as an amateur but soon took it on as a profession and was a critical and financial success until her untimely death. Many contemporaries considered her one of England's most accomplished women sculptors.

Born in Devon, Durant first became interested in art during a visit to Italy with her parents. She had intended to study sculpture only as a hobby, but the expense of sculpting caused her to make a life-changing decision to devote herself professionally as a sculptor. Like other 19th-century Neoclassical sculptors active at midcentury, Durant's oeuvre consists mostly of portraiture, both in the round and in relief, and ideals, often taken from literary sources such as Classical literature, English literature, and the Bible. She worked in both England and France, studying in Paris with Baron Henri de Triqueti.

Durant contributed a total of 40 works to the Royal Academy, exhibiting almost annually between 1847 and 1873. Her portraits included *Self-Portrait*, a bust titled *Harriet Beecher Stowe* (1857), and the medallion *George Grote*. Her last Royal Academy exhibition was the bust *Dr. Elizabeth Garrett Anderson*, shown posthumously in 1873.

Durant's early portraits, such as that of Harriet Beecher Stowe (1857), which established her reputation, successfully combine the hallmarks of the then-popular Neoclassical style with an accurate likeness, subtle detail, and expression of the sitter's character. Neoclassical in the formal pose, calm, reserve, smooth surface treatment, and introspective countenance, Durant's portraits are idealized only enough to possess Classical beauty but not to obscure the individuality of the person portrayed. Providing a fine likeness within a Classical semblance would have made Durant's style and ability quite popular with her sitters.

Durant exhibited her ideals, based on a variety of literary subjects and often not commissioned, to attract the attention of potential patrons. These works received high praise from critics for both their level of composition and their execution. All exhibited at the Royal Academy, they included *The Chief Mourner, Statue of a Girl*, also displayed at London's Great Exhibition of 1851; the statuette *Robin Hood* (1856), also exhibited at the Art Treasures of Great Britain exhibition in Manchester (1857); a work inspired by the First Idyll of Theocritus, titled *The Negligent Watchboy of the Vineyards, Catching Locusts*, also exhibited at the British Institution (1860); and *Constance* (1866) from Chaucer. Durant also contributed a variety of works to the Society of Female Artists exhibitions, including three related marbles in bas-relief depicting scenes from the myth of Achilles: *Thetis Dipping Achilles in the Styx*, *Thetis Receiving from Vulcan the Arms of Achilles*, and *Thetis Mourning over the Dead Body of Achilles*.

In 1863 Durant won the competition and £500 prize from the Corporation of London for an ornamental statue for Mansion House. Her contribution to their English literature series was the ideal *The Faithful Shepherdess*, based on John Fletcher's retelling of the story of Daphnis and Chloe. Durant exhibited *The Faithful Shepherdess* at the Royal Academy before it was installed at Mansion House. It is the only ideal figure by Durant to be located.

Introduced into the court of Queen Victoria in about 1865, Durant became one of the queen's favorite sculptors. Her portraits exhibited at the Royal Academy beginning in 1866 consist mostly of her large number of busts and medallions of members of the royal family. Two major royal commissions included the cenotaph to King Leopold I of Belgium for St. George's Chapel (now Esher Church, Surrey) and the restoration of Wolsey's Chapel. Queen Victoria commissioned the cenotaph to King Leopold I to honor her uncle the year after his death. A memorial in a less formal manner, emulating the French style, it depicts Leopold on his deathbed, his relaxed right hand on the mane of the Belgian lion by his side. Two angels, bearing shields displaying the arms of England and Belgium, are to the left. Contemporary critics noted the group's effect of peace and calm in contrast to Leopold's active life. For the restoration of Wolsey's Chapel, now Albert Memorial Chapel, Windsor Castle, Durant assisted her teacher Triqueti. She contributed seven marble portrait medallions of the royal family, carved in high relief and set in polychrome marble and inlaid floral motifs to integrate with Triqueti's inlaid commemorative murals.

In addition to her royal commissions, Durant gave instruction in sculpting to the queen's daughter, Princess Louise. Durant's plaster relief *Princess Louise*, an example of the sculptor's later portrait style, exhibits the characteristics that made her a popular Neoclassical portraitist. Although she placed the head of the princess in profile, the torso is at three-quarter view to provide a natural and pleasing turn to the body. This subtle twist implies animation, as if the sitter could turn toward the viewer in the next moment, and counteracts the often-static effect of profile relief. The carefully done face presents the individual facial features of Princess Louise. The hair, in a pseudo-Classical wrap, provides only a suggestion of Antiquity and is not out of place with the contemporary jewelry and bodice that complete the medallion design.

So much of Durant's sculpture is untraced that it is difficult to study fully her artistic development. In addition, biographical information is incomplete. Arthur Munby fortunately provides a description of Durant, which depicts a strong, intelligent, attractive woman who would have fit well into the social circle of her many patrons:

> Miss Durant is a very striking person: she was alone; she sailed in upon us . . . a tall & very comely young woman; . . . erect, high-couraged, and superbly drest [sic]. And her talk was worthy of all this; she dwelt with airy ease, but without parade of learning, upon art works, art subjects. . . . And whithal she was full of graceful fun, and told happy stories of the Queen & Princesses, with whom it seems she is a favourite. (Hudson and Munby, 1972)

CHARLENE G. GARFINKLE

See also **Women Sculptors**

Biography

Born in Devon, England, early 1820s. Studied sculpture independently in Rome and with Baron Henri de Triqueti in Paris; independent studio in London, 1847; frequent trips to France; exhibited at Royal Academy, London, 1847–53, 1856–60, 1863–64, 1866–69, 1872–73; Great Exhibition, London, 1851; Art Treasures of Great Britain exhibition, Manchester, 1857; Society of Female Artists, London, 1858, 1863; British Institution, London, 1860; known for Neoclassical portraiture and ideals based on literary sources; introduced to court of Queen Victoria, *ca.* 1865; one of Queen Victoria's favorite sculptors; executed busts and medallions of royal family; instructed Princess Louise in sculpture. Died in Paris, France, 1 January 1873.

Selected Works

1850   *The Chief Mourner, Statue of a Girl* (untraced)

1857	*Harriet Beecher Stowe*; plaster; Castle Howard, Yorkshire, England; marble version (untraced)
1858	*The Negligent Watchboy of the Vineyards, Catching Locusts*; marble (untraced)
ca. 1858	*Thetis Dipping Achilles in the Styx, Thetis Receiving from Vulcan the Arms of Achilles*, and *Thetis Mourning over the Dead Body of Achilles*; marble (untraced)
1863	*The Faithful Shepherdess*; marble; Mansion House, London, England
1863	*George Grote*; marble; University College, London, England
ca. 1863	*Harriet Beecher Stowe*; marble; Harriet Beecher Stowe Center, Hartford, Connecticut, United States
1866	*Princess Louise*; plaster; Royal Collection, England
1866	*Queen Victoria*; marble; Windsor Castle, Berkshire, England
1866–67	Cenotaph to King Leopold I of Belgium; marble; Esher Church, Surrey, England
1866–69	Portrait medallions of the royal family; marble; Albert Memorial Chapel, Windsor Castle, Berkshire, England
1869	*Ruth*; marble (untraced)

Further Reading

Amberley, John Russell, and Katharine Louisa Stanley Russell Amberley, *The Amberley Papers: The Letters and Diaries of Bertrand Russell's Parents*, 2 vols., edited by Bertrand Russell and Patricia Russell, London: Hogarth Press, and New York, Norton, 1937

C.A.H.C., "Susan Durant: The Sculptor," *Queen*, 11 January 1873

Dunford, Penny, *A Biographical Dictionary of Women Artists in Europe and America since 1850*, Philadelphia: University of Pennsylvania Press, 1989; London and New York: Harvester Wheatsheaf, 1990

Graves, Algernon, *The Royal Academy of Arts*, 8 vols., London: Graves, 1905–06; reprint, New York: Franklin, 1972; see especially vol. 1

Gunnis, Rupert, *Dictionary of British Sculptors, 1660–1851*, London: Odhams Press, 1953; Cambridge, Massachusetts: Harvard University Press, 1954; revised edition, London: Abbey Library, 1968

Hudson, Derek, and Arthur Joseph Munby, *Munby, Man of Two Worlds: The Life and Diaries of Arthur J. Munby, 1828–1910*, Boston: Gambit, and London: Murray, 1972

Hurtado, Shannon Hunter, "The Company She Kept: Susan D. Durant, a Nineteenth-Century Sculptor and Her Feminist Connections," (Master's thesis), University of Manitoba, 1995

Hurtado, Shannon Hunter, "Durant, Susan (D.)," in *Dictionary of Women Artists*, edited by Delia Gaze, London and Chicago: Fitzroy Dearborn, 1997

Mackay, James Alexander, *The Dictionary of Western Sculptors in Bronze*, Woodbridge, Suffolk: Antique Collectors' Club, 1977

"[Obituary]," *Art Journal*, 25 March 1873

Redgrave, Samuel, *A Dictionary of Artists of the English School*, London: Longman, 1874; 2nd edition, London: Bell, 1878; reprint, Amsterdam: Hissink, and Bath, Somerset: Kingsmead, 1970

Yeldham, Charlotte, *Women Artists in Nineteenth-Century France and England*, 2 vols., New York: Garland, 1984

DYING GAUL

Anonymous

Roman copy of an original of ca. 230–220 BCE

marble

life-size

Musei Capitolini, Rome, Italy

Dying Gaul is a marble replica of a lost Hellenistic bronze from the city of Pergamon (Pergamum) in Asia Minor. The Pergamene bronze statue was part of a large, multifigured monument erected in the 220s BCE to commemorate Pergamon's victory over the Gauls (Galatians) a decade earlier. The marble copy of the statue was first recorded in a 1623 inventory of the collection of the Ludovisi family in Rome; it was most likely recovered during the construction of the family's villa earlier that century. In Antiquity, this villa's grounds were occupied by the Horti Sallustiani, a large private estate with expansive gardens; the replica was only one of numerous sculptures that made up the collection of this estate. *Dying Gaul* is now in the collection of the Musei Capitolini in Rome; a torso in Dresden, Germany, may reflect a second, more fragmentary replica of the same statue type.

Dying Gaul represents a muscular, nude warrior who has fallen in battle. The figure supports himself with his right arm, while his left arm presses against his right leg. The Gaul's muscles strain to support his body's weight, and his downwardly turned face grimaces with pain as blood flows from the mortal wound in his chest. Restorations made to the statue soon after its discovery include the right arm (in legend attributed to Michelangelo, thus adding to the statue's fame) and large portions of the plinth. The statue embodies the drama and pathos characteristic of the Hellenistic Baroque style, which was favored by the Attalid kings of Pergamon for many of their sculptural commissions.

The figure is clearly identifiable as a Gaul of noble lineage both by physical appearance and attributes. The torque worn around the neck, which serves as a badge of Gallic nobility, offsets the figure's muscular nudity, and the distinctive forms of a Gallic shield and a curved battle trumpet are visible on the plinth. The physical characteristics of the figure also conform to a description of the Gauls provided by the historian Diodorus Siculus in his *World History* (*ca.* 60–30 BCE). Diodorus described the Gauls as tall and muscular, with heavy, coarse hair, similar to a horse's mane, that resulted from being washed in lime water. He further recorded that Gallic nobles shaved their cheeks but grew long mustaches. The muscular physique, the coarse, manelike locks (the tips of which are now broken, giving the head a more bristly appearance than intended), and the beardless mustache described by the historian are all represented in the statue *Dying Gaul*.

The Hellenistic bronze statue on which *Dying Gaul* is based is considered by many scholars to be the work of the Pergamene court sculptor Epigonos, who is recorded in Pliny the Elder's *Natural History* (77 CE) as the creator of a bronze trumpeter. Pliny also makes note of a sculptor Isogonos, who represented the battles of the Pergamene king Attalos (Attalus) I against the Gauls. The two names appear closely together in Pliny's text and are often considered to refer to the same artist. (The name Isogonos, otherwise unknown, most likely reflects a misreading of Epigonos.) The sculptor Epigonos is also known from inscribed statue bases found at Pergamon, including a long base that may have held the bronze trumpeter.

The Hellenistic prototype for *Dying Gaul* was created as part of a monument to commemorate the victory of the Pergamene king Attalos I (*r.* 241–197 BCE) over Gallic tribes in the 230s BCE. Several tribes of Gauls from northern Europe had settled in Asia Minor during the 3rd century BCE. Warriors from these tribes marauded local Greek cities and extorted payments from them; they also served as mercenaries for enemy kings. The successful campaign of Attalos I against the Gauls was instrumental to Pergamon's political and cultural rise in the late 3rd and 2nd centuries BCE, and the significance of this victory is affirmed by the im-

pressive sculptural votive monuments set up by Attalos I, both in Pergamon and in Athens.

The Hellenistic bronze was part of the victory monument that was erected in the Sanctuary of Athena on the Pergamene acropolis. The monument set up in Athens included a similar, but smaller, version of the statue. The Athenian monument was composed of under-life-size figures representing Giants, Amazons, Persians, and Gauls that were set up on the south side of the Acropolis. (For figures from this monument that survive in marble versions, see Palma, 1981). In addition to *Dying Gaul*, several other sculptures can be associated with the monument installed at Pergamon, of which the best known is the Ludovisi *Gaul* group, a dramatic marble group representing the double suicide of a Gallic chieftain and wife (which was also part of the Ludovisi collection and now is in the Museo Nazionale Romano). A head of a hooded *Persian* (603; Museo Nazionale Romano, Rome) and a head of a bearded *Gaul* (1271; Vatican Museums, Rome), both carved marbles found in Rome, also have been associated with this monument.

The precise form of the sculptural monument to which the Hellenistic bronze belonged, however, has not been established with certainty, with scholars divided between placing the statues on a tall, round base or a long, narrow base. Archaeological evidence for both a round monument and a long monument has been uncovered in the Sanctuary of Athena, making both options viable. In the reconstruction of the round victory monument, which measures approximately 3 meters in diameter, several statues of fallen Gauls, including *Dying Gaul*, are restored in a circle around the central Ludovisi *Gaul* group. The long monument, which measures approximately 20 meters, divided into eight sections, would have included significantly more figures. Its base preserves a fragmentary inscription that has been reconstructed to read the "work of Epigonos," thus further connecting the Gauls with the Pergamene court sculptor.

The surviving marble version of the statue in the Musei Capitolini was manufactured for display in Rome, where it may have been installed alongside the Ludovisi *Gaul* group. The *Dying Gaul* was enthusiastically received from the time of its discovery, and its appeal remained steady throughout the 18th and 19th centuries. It was praised for both its anatomical exactness and its heroic pathos, and numerous replicas and engravings of the figure were made for connoisseurs and collectors across Europe.

JULIE VAN VOORHIS

Dying Gaul
© Alinari / Art Resource, NY

See also **Pergamon Altar (Great Altar of Pergamon)**

Further Reading

Coarelli, Filippo, "Il 'Grande Donario' di Attalo I," in *I Galli e l'Italia*, edited by Paulo Santoro, Rome: De Luca, 1978

de Grummond, Nancy T., and Brunilde S. Ridgeway (editors), *From Pergamon to Sperlonga: Sculpture and Context*, Berkeley: University of California Press, 2000

Haskell, Francis, and Nicholas Penny, *Taste and the Antique: The Lure of Classical Sculpture, 1500–1900*, New Haven, Connecticut: Yale University Press, 1981 (for the post-Antiquity history of the statue)

Künzl, Ernst, *Die Kelten des Epigonos von Pergamon*, Würzburg, Germany: Triltsch, 1971

Mattei, Marina, *Il Galata capitolino: Uno splendido dono di Attalo*, Rome: L'Erma di Bretschneider, 1987

Palma, Beatrice, "Il piccolo donario pergameno," *Xenia* 1 (1981)

Wenning, Robert, *Die Galateranatheme Attalos I*, Berlin: De Gruyter, 1978

E

EARLY CHRISTIAN AND BYZANTINE SCULPTURE (4TH–15TH CENTURY)

From the 4th to the 7th centuries, few examples of early Christian and Byzantine statuary survive from what was scant production compared with that of antiquity. Sculpture in the round was mainly reserved for imperial portraits. Numerous early 4th-century marble examples of Constantine I (mostly fragments) survive (such as those in the collection of the Metropolitan Museum of Art, New York City, and the Belgrade National Museum, as well as the colossal statue in the Musei Capitolini, Rome). The bronze colossus in Barletta has been identified as Marcian or Leo I. Marble portraits of empresses include the statuette of Aelia Flacilla (*ca.* 380–390; Cabinet des Médailles, Bibliothèque Nationale de France, Paris), and the head of Theodora (*ca.* 500–548; Castello Sforzesco, Milan, Italy). The last honorific statue to be erected in Constantinople was that of a cousin of Emperor Heraclius, about 614. Nonimperial portraits from the late 4th through the 6th century include the bust of Eutropios (Kunsthistorisches Museum, Vienna, Austria) and the statue of a male figure (Archaeological Museum, Istanbul, Turkey) found at Aphrodisias. Stylistically, these sculptures tend toward a serene abstraction and away from observation of naturalistic detail.

Religious statuary is scarce and consists primarily of a few examples of the Good Shepherd and youthful standing portraits of Christ. An exceptional series of five marble statuettes, found together with three pairs of male and female portraits, represents the Good Shepherd and four episodes of the Jonah story (*ca.*

260–275; Cleveland Museum of Art, Ohio). Although some researchers have questioned their authenticity, they are thought to come from a tomb or a baptismal or domestic setting.

Early Christian sculpture is predominantly relief sculpture, falling into four main categories: funerary, triumphal monuments, architectural decoration (primarily interior), and church furniture. Sarcophagi or sarcophagus slabs constitute the most abundant group of 4th- and 5th-century sculpture, with Rome and Ravenna as the main centers of production. After Rome, the most abundant locus of early Christian sarcophagi is Arles, France; scholars disagree on whether these were imports from Rome or of local production.

During the 3rd and 4th centuries, the same workshops may have produced pagan, Christian, and Jewish sarcophagi. The earliest Christian examples used elements derived from antique sepulchral symbolism. A sarcophagus (*ca.* 270) in S. Maria Antiqua, Rome, was the first to show neutral motifs alongside Christian scenes: an *orans* figure (with arms outstretched in prayer), a philosopher, and a man carrying a ram appear next to scenes of the baptism of Christ and Jonah under the gourd. Following the Edict of Milan in 313, the range of imagery on sarcophagi expanded to new themes from the Old and New Testament. Early sarcophagi depict scenes generally based on concepts concerning the afterlife. Images stressed the hope of salvation (illustrated by the story of Daniel in the lions' den) or rest after death (Jonah under the gourd). From about the mid 4th century, hierarchic centralized compositions were more popular, as on columnar and citygate sarcophagi. Influenced by Roman triumphal iconography, an enthroned Christ as the ruler of the kingdom of God frequently appears in the center.

Tomb slabs and sarcophagi were exported from Rome to provincial centers in Italy, the Dalmatian coast, southern Gaul, North Africa, and the Iberian Peninsula, where they influenced the form and iconography of locally produced sarcophagi. From the early 5th century to the first quarter of the 6th, numerous sarcophagi were carved of marble from St. Béat in the Pyrenees. These are mainly in Toulouse and Bordeaux. Some sarcophagi were decorated with Old and New Testament figural themes, but most were strigillated or displayed symbolic plant ornamentation. Generally in low relief, popular imagery included a central *chi-rho* (monogram of the name of Christ combining the first two letters of the Greek name) within a wreath surrounded by vine tendrils, ivy, and acanthus leaves stylized as the tree of life.

During the period called early Christian, non-Christian religious sculpture continued to be produced throughout the lands formerly under the influence of the Roman Empire. Relief carving decorated sanctuaries of various cults, such as plaques of Mithras slaying the bull (found in S. Stefano Rotondo and S. Clemente in Rome). Sarcophagi with representations from Classical mythology abound. Examples of sculpture in Jewish contexts include a 3rd-century sarcophagus with a menorah (Museo Nazionale Romano), and a fragment from a synagogue screen (6th–7th century; Israel Museum, Jerusalem).

In Egypt, a distinct form of funerary art was the carved niche head of tombs. A wealth of 4th- to 5th-century material survives from Herakleopolis Magna (Coptic Museum, Cairo, Egypt), and Oxyrhincos (Graeco-Roman Museum, Alexandria, Egypt). Imagery from Graeco-Roman culture, such as nymphs, Leda and the swan, and Hercules, were used for non-Christian burials, whereas angels, crosses, and portraits were common in Christian tombs. Shared vocabulary of ornament and carving style indicate common workshops for these two groups.

The most important example of state-sponsored sculpture in Rome during this period is the Arch of Constantine (*ca.* 315). The arch's frieze shows events before and after Constantine's triumph over Maxentius in 312. Although it adheres to the tradition of official state art, the reliefs contrast stylistically from the Classical formal ideal. Hieratic scenes in low relief show frontal figures arranged isocephalically (with their heads all in a row). These reliefs are combined on the arch with reused elements, or *spolia*, sometimes recarved from earlier imperial monuments.

A classicizing trend culminated in the refined court style of Theodosios I. The base of the Egyptian obelisk reerected in the hippodrome of Constantinople (*ca.* 390–391) was commissioned by the city prefect Proculus in the emperor's honor. The lower level shows the obelisk and a chariot race, with Greek and Latin inscriptions referring to the emperor's victories. Above, four large panels express Theodosios's claim to universal power, depicting him in official functions: at court, in state, receiving an embassy of barbarians, and at the circus. Hieratic compositions consistently portrayed the imperial family in the central uppermost field. Typical features are rigid frontality of the main figures, elongated bodies, and individualized facial features.

Increasingly important in early Christian and Byzantine architectural sculpture is polychromy: the use of different colored marbles for revetment of all surfaces from floor to vault and inlays of contrasting material (niello, glass paste, stone) in carved decoration. Architectural sculpture frequently relied on *spolia* of ancient Roman buildings (particularly capitals). A gradual shift from the Graeco-Roman heritage toward truly Byzantine forms, with a new ornamental vocabulary partially indebted to Sasanian influence, appears in architectural sculpture in the time of Justinian I (such as the fragments of the destroyed Church of St. Polyeuktos, 524–527; Archaeological Museum, Istanbul, Turkey).

Corinthian and composite capitals were most common, particularly the so-called Asiatic acanthus. The dematerialization of the capital, often merged with the impost, is evident in the churches of SS. Sergios and Bachus (527–536) and the Hagia Sophia (532–537), where extensive use of the drill transformed capitals, imposts, and architraves into lacelike decoration whose roots in the acanthus leaf of Corinthian capitals are still discernible. At S. Vitale, Ravenna (546–548), the deeply *champhered* (beveled off) imposts appear to float unsupported above the capitals. Another variation of the capital combines acanthus leaves in the lower zone with animal *protomes* (bust of front part of animal) above. The earliest dated examples of the basket capital are found at St. Polyeuktos alongside motifs derived from Eastern textiles and metalwork. From the first half of the 6th century, various elements are found on capitals: cornucopia, leaf-masks and gorgons, seraphim, and personifications or inhabited vine scrolls.

In the niches of the lower entablature at St. Polyeuktos, fantailed peacocks against a background of vines are among the finest examples of Byzantine sculpture. Also notable from this site is a series of marble icons of Christ and the apostles. A rich body of work is also preserved in the Cathedral of Eufrasius, Porec, in Croatia (*ca.* 550; Parentium, Parenzo). Capitals, soffits of the nave arcade, and church furnishings are beautifully carved with bird and animal motifs, as well as foliate and geometric designs. Examples of carved columns in the West include those from La Daurade, Toulouse (Metropolitan Museum of Art, New York City; Musée du Louvre, Paris).

In the service of the newly recognized Christian religion, new elements were introduced in the architectural decoration of churches, such as *transenna* (marble latticework enclosing shrine or sanctuary) panels, parapet reliefs, ambos, ciboria, episcopal thrones, and altar tables. Decorative motifs tended to be crosses, monograms, foliate, and geometric ornament. Plaques from screens or parapets usually had a central motif (such as cross or *chi-rho* monograms) inscribed on a disk or a lozenge. Animals frequently flank a central vase or cross. Rare examples of human figures are Daniel in the lions' den and Hercules (S. Apollinare Nuovo, Ravenna; Museo Nazionale, Ravenna, Italy). Altar tables were rectangular, round, or sigma-shaped and commonly carved with a multilobed border and symbolic Christian imagery (*Sigma-shaped Table*, 5th–6th century, Metropolitan Museum of Art, New York City).

Church furniture is closely related to architectural sculpture and was often exported all around the Mediterranean from the same Constantinopolitan workshops. Most impressive are the ambos, either with a large monolithic stairway or two stairways flanking a platform. They were decorated with crosses, animals, and occasionally scenes of the sacrifice of Isaac and the Good Shepherd (Archaeological Museum, Istanbul; Ephesos Archaeological Museum, Selçuk, Turkey). An outstanding example is the fan-shaped ambo from Hagios Georgios (500–530), Thessaloníki, which has a curved double stairway. The niches in the lower register display an adoration of the Magi scene surrounded by architectural and foliate motifs.

Although most sculpture was of marble or stone, other materials were utilized. Written sources (such as Eusibius's descriptions of Constantine I's donations) and rare fragments bear witness to silver statues and metalwork revetment of sculpture in churches. In the Orthodox Baptistery in Ravenna, stucco decoration includes arcades framing prophets and rich acanthus vine scrolls (*ca.* 450). Other important media of early Christian and Byzantine sculpture are ivory and steatite.

The pair of cypress door leaves at Santa Sabina in Rome (*ca.* 430) displayed Old and New Testament scenes in 28 relief panels whose original arrangement remains speculative. The 18 surviving panels have been compared with ivory carving of the late 4th to early 5th century that is probably from Rome. The tie-beam roof casings over the nave of the church (548–565) of St. Catherine's Monastery, Sinai, are impressive examples of wood sculpture. Some are carved with vine scrolls; others have a central wreathed cross flanked by friezes of animals, birds, and plants framed by ornamental panels. These representations have been interpreted as an allegory of the messianic paradise of peace on earth (Isaiah 35; see Drewer, 1971) or as a literal depiction of the divisions of the Creation (see Maguire, 1987).

From around the middle of the 7th century onward, production of sculpture in the round ceased. In 10th-century Constantinople, a new type of monumental sculpture appeared, which was to become the dominant form of relief sculpture following the iconoclasm period: the relief icon. Icons, such as that of the Virgin Orans (mid to late 12th century; Museo Regionale, Messina) and Christ Evergatês ("The Benefactor," possibly late 13th century; Metropolis, Serres), probably covered the walls of churches and were also mounted on piers flanking the iconostasis. The Serres Christ, which was carved in a flat, two-dimensional technique, is likely based on an earlier painted or mosaic icon. Subjects were mainly individual portraits of Christ, the Virgin, archangels, and saints; in the later period Christological scenes such as the Deësis (Christ flanked by the Virgin Mary and John the Baptist extending hands in a gesture of entreaty for intercession) were also portrayed. The reliefs were mostly painted marble, with the figure set against a smooth background surrounded by a frame. Also popular were icons made of stone and colored glass paste inlays inserted into a marble matrix resembling enamel work, such as the St. Eudokia (early 10th century, from the Lips monastery in Constantinople; Archaeological Museum, Istanbul). This type of inlaid decoration was also used for iconostases and altar tables from the 10th to the 13th century.

Funerary monuments of the later period were mainly sarcophagi faced with marble slabs. A more ambitious type, tomb *arcosolia* (arched niches carved out of or built in front of a wall) dressed in marble, appeared in 14th-century Constantinople, with rich sculptural decoration around the arch of the niche. Busts of Christ, the apostles, and angels, although defaced, can still be seen on *arcosolia* at the Church of Christ the Savior in Chora (Kariye Camii, Turkey). This arrangement of crowning an archivolt was copied in Venice above the doors of San Marco.

The development of architectural sculpture can be found in numerous monuments in Constantinople, along the coast of Asia Minor, and in Greece. Late 9th- to 11th-century *templa* (screens separating the nave from the sanctuary), capitals, cornices, slabs, icon frames, and door frames display mainly crosses, geometric and foliate ornamentation, but rarely animals or birds. Marble fragments of the 10th-century sanctuary screen of the Monastery of Vatopaidi, Mount Athos, were reused to frame the royal doors of the Chapel of the Holy Girdle. These are mainly panels of geometric ornamentation. From the 12th century, a renewed interest in sculpture was accompanied by a more varied repertory, including mythological subjects, heraldic compositions, and animal combat, the human form being only rarely employed and found mainly in Palaeologan Constantinople. The same ornamental repertory is found in the few preserved examples of church furniture. Ciboria became increasingly scarce during this period. The carved archivolts once used to decorate them were employed instead as surroundings for mural icons or as *arcosolia* reliefs.

Parapet plaques were richly decorated with omnipresent interlace, frequent crosses, and animal motifs. The wide range of animals includes confronted or single peacocks, griffins, *senmurvs* (Sassanian mythological beast, often represented as the combination of a bird and either a dog or a lion), and an eagle snatching a hare. Mythological and allegorical subjects were also portrayed, such as *Hercules and the Nemean Lion* (Museum of Byzantine Culture, Thessaloníki, Greece), and the *Apotheosis of Alexander* (Archaeological Museum, Istanbul, Turkey).

The two churches of Hosios Loukas in Phokis (Greece) constitute an important ensemble. The drum of the Theotokas dome (*ca.* 946–955) is covered with marble plaques decorated with crosses against fields of ornament and lion-head waterspouts. Palmettes or acanthus and some cherubim adorn the interior capitals. The iconostasis is decorated with arabesques surrounding palmettes and cruciform motifs. Pseudo-Kufic lettering and acanthus scrolls imitating early Christian vine scrolls decorate the semicircular surrounds above the icons on the piers. In the *katholikon* (main church of the monastic complex) the iconostasis is decorated with archivolts enclosing palmettes, a central cross, and interlacing circles containing high-relief ornament. Griffins flank the architrave's main section, while exterior plaques beneath the windows imitate early Christian screens.

Portions of sculptural ensembles survive from the Komnenian period (late 11th to 13th century). The 12th-century Church of Christ the Savior in Chora is more indicative of later ornamentation, since it was redecorated about 1316–21 by Theodore Metochites. Its sculpture imitates early Christian models. Some capitals have busts of saints or angels that have been attributed to the early Komnenian phase (*ca.* 1080). Subsequently, several capitals, consoles, and imposts in the same church were carved with representations of the Evangelists, St. John the Baptist, and military saints. Unfortunately, these are badly damaged. Fragments of marble parapet panels and *colonnettes* (small columns) of the iconostasis remain in the church of St. Panteleimon, Nerezi (Macedonia), which was begun in 1164. Most impressive here is the stucco frame of

the south *proskynetarion* (pier icon of a patron saint). Above a trilobed arch of interlace, vine scrolls and palmettes spring from a central vase surrounded by pheasants.

Although exterior sculptural decoration is minimal on churches in the Byzantine Empire, it is found extensively in Armenia, Kievan Rus', and Serbia. Armenian churches are rich in exterior figural sculpture. On the Church of the Holy Cross, Aght amar (915–921; present-day Turkey), the patron King Gagik I Artsruni holds a model of his church. With Christ, he flanks angels holding a cross-decorated medallion among other figural and ornamental reliefs. Two reliefs of mounted military saints slaying dragons and an enemy survive from the Cathedral of the Mykailivs'kyi Zolotoverkhyi Monastery in Kiev, Ukraine. Carved in red schist, it is unclear whether they were originally part of the exterior or interior decoration (mid 11th to early 12th century; State Tretyakov Gallery, Moscow, Russia; National Architectural Conservation Area, Kiev, Ukraine). Late 14th- and early 15th-century churches of the Morava school, such as Ravanica and Kalenic, display variations of pierced interlace rosettes and relief carvings of interlace, griffins, birds, and figures.

As for secular reliefs, only two imperial portraits survive from this period (Dumbarton Oaks, Washington, D.C.; Campiello de Ca' Argheran, Venice, Italy). Both come from the Veneto and are frontal portraits in full regalia set within tondi; they are tentatively dated to the end of the 12th century.

During the Latin occupation of Constantinople (1204–61), many works of art, including stone reliefs and icons, were looted by the crusaders and transported to Italy. Italian carvers, particularly those in Venice, copied these works so faithfully that it is often difficult to distinguish between Byzantine and Byzantinizing works. In addition to the diverse traditions of sculpture in the provinces and in the states neighboring the Byzantine Empire, a stylistic trend emerged during the Palaeologan period (1261–1453) that reflected a conscious reduction in the use of sculptural techniques, as in the front slab of the tomb of Theodora in the narthex of Hagia Theodora, Arta (*ca.* 1270). Another trend in Palaeologan sculpture favored increased modeling of figures.

Wood was also used in architectural decoration and church furnishings. The 12th-century outer narthex doors of St. Catherine's in Sinai show the Transfiguration amid other Old and New Testament scenes. The surrounding polygonal design of interlocking pieces is similar to both Christian and Islamic wood relief in late 12th-century Egypt.

The sanctuary doors of the church of the Virgin (al-'Adra) at the monastery of the Syrians (es-Suriani), Wadi Natrun (913–914; Egypt), made of ebony with ivory inlay, depict Christ Emmanuel and the Virgin flanked by Fathers of the Coptic and Syrian Churches. The choir doors (926–927) show the Virgin and Christ trampling on a lion and a dragon flanked by paradisiacal trees above geometric motifs and foliate crosses. The images of the Virgin and saints interceding with Christ relate to the iconography of Byzantine iconostases; their content and technique have been compared with the Byzantine bronze doors of the Cathedral of Amalfi (*ca.* 1060; see Frazer, 1973).

Byzantine wooden sculpture absorbed Western influences during the Crusades, such as a 13th-century painted sculpture from Kastoria of St. George shown in profile at prayer. He wears a military uniform, and his shield displays a red and blue armorial design. Scenes of his life and martyrdom form the frame in the manner of a vita icon. An earlier example of a St. George vita icon, also of carved and painted wood, probably came from the Monastery of St. George in Balaklavi on the Crimean Peninsula (late 12th to mid 13th century; National Art Museum, Kiev). The same saint is depicted as a frontally facing two-thirds statue in a niche in Hagios Georgios at Gallista, near Kastoria. This sculpture retains traces of paint and was probably made locally when the church was founded in 1286–87.

Fifteenth-century sculpture is found primarily in states surrounding the Byzantine Empire, rather than in Constantinople. Wooden doors dated 1453 from the Snagov Monastery, now in the Bucharest National Museum, were carved in six panels and surrounded by inscriptions. The panels depict the Annunciation flanked by David and Solomon, four liturgical saints, and two military saints on horseback.

LESLIE BUSSIS TAIT

See also **Ambo; Polychromy; Relief Sculpture; Sarcophagus**

Further Reading

Belting, H., "Zur Skulptur aus der Zeit um 1300 in Konstantinopel," *Münchner Jahrbuch der bildenden Kunst*, 3rd series, 23 (1972)

Briesenick, Brigitte, "Typologie und Chronologie der südwestgallischen Sarkophage," *Jahrbuch der Römanische-Germanische Zentmus* 9 (1962)

Ćurčić, Slobodan, "Some Uses (and Reuses) of Griffins in Late Byzantine Art," *Byzantine East, Latin West: Art-Historical Studies in Honor of Kurt Weitzmann*, edited by Christopher Moss and Katherine Kiefer, Princeton, New Jersey: Department of Art and Archaeology, Princeton University, 1995

Drewer, L., "The Carved Wooden Beams of the Church of Justinian, Monastery of St. Catherine, Mt. Sinai" (dissertation), University of Michigan, Ann Arbor, 1971

Evans, Helen C., and William D. Wixom (editors), *Glory of Byzantium: Art and Culture of the Middle Byzantine Era, A.D. 843–1261* (exhib. cat.), New York: Metropolitan Museum of Art, 1997

Firatli, Nezih, *La sculpture Byzantine figurée au Musée archéologique d'Istanbul*, Paris: Librairie d'Amerique et d'Orient Adrien Maisonneuve, 1990

Frazer, Margaret E., "Church Doors and the Gates of Paradise: Byzantine Bronze Doors in Italy," *Dumbarton Oaks Papers* 27 (1973)

Grabar, André, *Sculptures byzantines du Moyen Âge: XIᵉ–XIVᵉ siècle*, Paris: Picard, 1976

Harrison, R. Martin, *A Temple for Byzantium: The Discovery and Excavation of Anicia Juliana's Palace-Church in Istanbul*, London: Miller, and Austin: University of Texas Press, 1989

Immerzeel, Mat, and Peter Jongste, "Import and Local Production of Early Christian Sarcophagi in France," *Boreas* 16 (1993)

Lange, Reinhold, *Die byzantinische Reliefikone*, Recklinghausen, Germany: Bongers, 1964

Maguire, Henry, *Earth and Ocean: The Terrestrial World in Early Byzantine Art*, University Park: Pennsylvania State University Press, 1987

Thomas, Thelma K., *Late Antique Egyptian Funerary Sculpture: Images for This World and for the Next*, Princeton, New Jersey: Princeton University Press, 2000

Weitzmann, Kurt, et al., *The Age of Spirituality: Late Antique and Early Christian Art, Third to Seventh Century* (exhib. cat.), New York: Metropolitan Museum of Art, 1979

EGYPT, ANCIENT: INTRODUCTION; PREDYNASTIC–OLD KINGDOM (*ca.* 3000–2150 BCE)

Introduction

The art form of sculpture in Pharaonic Egypt developed and was maintained essentially in the service of religion and state. The purposes of paying homage to and glorifying the gods and the ruler in one context and of providing the preparation for the continuation of life after death in another (i.e., sculpture for temple or tomb) underlay all examples of what would now be considered or categorized as artistic expressions. Very little of a frivolous nature has been preserved from this civilization. Even seemingly mundane woodcarvings of what scholars had thought to be decorative subjects have been reinterpreted in the light of intense research as having religious or mythological significance. In Egyptian art, even the most common of decorative motifs such as the lotus blossom alluded to the cycle of life or death and resurrection.

Almost without exception, Egyptian sculpture in all periods adhered to two basic principles: it may be described as cubic and frontal. Stone to be used for sculpture was detached from the quarry in the appropriate size for a project in neatly shaped blocks. In the developed form of all Egyptian stone sculpture, the basic cubic shape of the block from which it was carved was maintained and remains obvious. From numerous

485

unfinished examples, it is apparent that sculptors transferred the designs for a work to the front and the sides of the stone; the initial roughing out of the statue was simply a matter of cutting away anything outside the outlines, one of the simplest methods of translating two-dimensional design into three dimensions. In addition to the unfinished statues, sculptors' working models also attest to this practice. The form resulting from this method of constructing the image retained or recalled much of its cubic origin throughout 3,000 years of Pharaonic history. As a practical consideration, the sculptor often did the initial roughing out of the form in advance at the quarry in order to reduce the weight of the material for transport.

Frontality, the second general characteristic of Egyptian sculpture, was directly related to the conceptual notion that all art was symbolic, hence not reflecting any aspect of time, and meant to be eternal. Artists did not intend sculpture, painting, and other arts to convey any sense of the ephemeral. The arts all served to create images for which neither the words *substitute* nor *symbol* fully conveys the total meaning of the art form, which was intended to last for eternity. The frontal view of the statue was the most important aspect, the sides less so; the back was only important as a supporting pillar that could also carry a dedicatory or identifying inscription. As a result, Egyptian sculpture has been criticized as reserved or stiff, particularly in comparison with Western sculptural form, from the time of the Greeks on. Unlike much of Classical sculpture, which attempts to convey a sense of movement in space, Egyptian sculpture was symbolically static. Because it was never meant to reproduce a momentary impression, a piece of Egyptian sculpture was generally organized as a carefully balanced, fully integrated composition that intentionally negated movement.

Some standard elements that governed representation in art throughout Egyptian history include the use of a fixed canon of proportion, a set of strict rules of presentation, and a standard method for the adaptation of the rules to various materials. The proportional system on which the representation of the human body was based had been developed and refined early in Egyptian history. Artists created three-dimensional sculpture using the same proportional system as employed in painting or relief, based on a division of the human figure into 18 equal units measured from the sole of the foot or ground line to the hairline above the eyes. The variety of wigs and crowns represented precluded measuring to the top of the head. Scholars have found evidence for the use of this proportional system in unfinished sculpture and wall painting, as well as in artists' preparatory materials and models. During the Late Period (perhaps as early as Dynasty XXI) in Egyptian history, the 18-square canon was

reformed, but the proportions of figures did not change remarkably.

In the standard methods of representing the human figure in sculpture, the male, when standing, is usually shown stiffly erect, left foot advanced, hands clasped at his sides. The female, in contrast, generally has feet together, although for iconographic purposes, the left foot may be slightly advanced in some cases, with the hands flat at the sides in most instances. In the developed convention, seated figures have their hands on their knees, most usually with one flat palm down and the other closed or clenched. A number of variations of pose developed for specific purposes, including typical formats such as the cross-legged seated position of the scribe who holds a papyrus on his lap and various postures of presentation in which the image of ruler or noble is holding offerings, statues, shrines, or other objects. Sculptors often carved multiple images of husband and wife ("pair statues") or other family groupings ("group statues") from the same block. A further specialized form was the "block statue," in which the figure is shown seated, knees pulled up to the chest, reducing the image to a near cube with a head. This

King Mycerinus
© Roger Wood / CORBIS

economical use of the material also provided greater surface for dedicatory inscriptions.

Sculptors conveyed a strict hierarchy of importance in images by the use of relative size. They depicted deities on a larger scale than humans, rulers larger than nobility, and males larger than females, with servants, slaves, and animals at the lower end of the scale. To a large degree, artists also applied the strict formality of presentation according to ranking, so that images of field-workers, for example, were considerably less formally arranged than those of their masters.

Materials

An important convention in Egyptian stone sculpture was the use of "connectives" to strengthen the statue. The virtual lack of complete undercutting in the carving meant that the spaces between torso and arms and between the two legs—as well as other smaller cavities—were not carved away. In painted sculpture, the artist usually colored these spaces black and simply considered them as not represented. In earlier Egyptian sculpture, the lower legs of figures are often disproportionately heavy, probably a result of overcompensation on the part of the sculptor in a further effort to strengthen the figure. The use of connectives and such distortion were not necessary when material other than stone was used. In wood or metal, the strength of the statue did not depend on the additional support provided, so the stance of figures in these materials appears less rigid and more naturalistically rendered.

The clenched fist of male figures is usually filled with a nondescript object for which there may be three possible explanations and on which scholars do not agree. These objects may simply be space fillers, they may be representations of a stylized kerchief, or they may be symbolic of staves or batons impossible to render in stone. In some instances, these objects contain further decoration on the butt with the name of the ruler in a cartouche, suggesting a seal or stamp. In others, the cloth of a kerchief can be seen clearly delineated as draped from the back of the fist. Because this representation of cloth can be demonstrated in some examples, the tendency is to identify all of the variations as a kerchief.

Some sculptural types that are standard in other cultures are rare or almost absent in ancient Egypt. The portrait bust is seldom seen, except as a special funerary object in the Old Kingdom (2650–2150 BCE) or as part of an ancestor cult in later periods. The nude as a sculptural type is also rare and, when present, suggests that the figure was meant to be covered with real clothing, although some images of females are clothed in such form-fitting garments that it is difficult to distinguish them from intentional nude figures.

Throughout Pharaonic history, sculpture in the round seems for the most part to have been reserved for images of gods, sacred animals, rulers, and the nobility. The major exception comes from the late Old Kingdom, when a number of servant statues were made for the tomb. Carved in limestone, these figures represented individuals occupied in various trades. An extension of this idea occurred in the Middle Kingdom (2040–1640 BCE) when these single figures expanded into miniature tableaux representing not individuals but complete workshops. By contrast, in relief carving for tombs and temples, countless representations of the lesser classes depict a wide variety of daily activities throughout Egyptian history.

Predynastic Period (before *ca.* 3000 BCE)

The era immediately preceding the unification of Egypt, the formation of the state, and the advent of writing is called the Predynastic period (before *ca.* 3000 BCE). The art forms in general at this time indicate a distinctly formative stage. Sculpture in particular was at a very basic level of development. The sculptural objects that have been preserved from this period are for the most part made of bone or ivory, ceramic, and small pieces of stone. The terracotta figurines that have been found are generally of female figures, with stylized and exaggerated sexual identity, perhaps related to some aspect of a fertility cult. These female images can sometimes be gracefully designed and visually appealing in their simplicity. It is possible that they relate to similar stylized figures painted on pottery characteristic of the same period. Other clay objects depict animals such as the hippopotamus, baboon, and crocodile, among others. The interest in animal sculpture began early and continued throughout Egyptian history, in part because of the importance of the so-called sacred animals related to various deities.

Stone palettes for the grinding of cosmetics were often carved in the shape or contour of animal, bird, and fish forms. Stone containers for what were probably cosmetic materials may qualify as sculpture simply because these classes of objects were also frequently carved in animal form. The stone used for them was often hard and variegated, chosen undoubtedly for the color as well as for its enduring quality.

Fragments of standing male figures found at Coptos suggest some attempt to institute the production of large-scale images of gods. Although the dating of these figures is uncertain, the rudimentary style in which they were carved suggests a "preformal" attempt at colossal sculpture. One reconstruction makes these figures around 4 meters tall. They were male images, presumably of the fertility god Min, socketed for the addition of an erect phallus, to be added in a separate piece of stone.

Archaic Period (First and Second Dynasties, *ca.* 3000–2650 BCE)

The natural descendants of the utilitarian stone palettes of the Predynastic period are the so-called ceremonial palettes, made at the beginning of dynastic history (*ca.* 3000–2650 BCE). Sculptors carved these important objects, apparently created as commemorative records, in low relief. The most famous, and one of the most formal, of these objects is the palette of King Narmer, a two-sided relief on which he is identified by name in hieroglyphs. He is depicted as a conquering ruler of the south in the act of subjugating the peoples of the north. The importance of this and other such palettes to the history of art is the manner of representation in which they were conceived. The image of Narmer at this early stage in the development of Egyptian art is a fully realized male figure in relief. The conventions of sculptural representation in two dimensions and the canon of proportion that was to become standard throughout most of Pharaonic history are here almost completely developed and refined. The stock image of "the king smiting the enemy," already worked out and destined to change little except in small details from this early time to well into the period of Roman occupation 3,000 years later, illustrates that certain formulas of representation had also been codified.

The emergence of a formal sculpture in the round, distinct from the "primitive" work of the predynastic period, cannot be documented to any extent before the end of the second dynasty (2770–2650 BCE). The early evidence mainly consists of a pair of preserved images of King Khasekhem found at Hierakonpolis. The obvious cubic quality that would be a hallmark of Egyptian sculpture throughout history is clearly evident; however, the sculptor has been able to realize a convincing figure of a seated king. In both examples, he is shown wearing the crown of Upper Egypt, is clothed in what can be identified as a festival garment, and has his left arm clenched across his abdomen. This position of the arm would later be modified in most sculpture likely because it was deemed to be disruptive to the symmetry or formalistic balance of the figure. The figure and support are clearly integrated, although at this stage a relief representation decorating the "throne" identifies it as a chair. The two figures of Khasekhem were carved in two different stones, limestone and schist or slate, indicating either a spirit of experimentation in a variety of materials or a calculated choice, perhaps for iconographic reasons.

Old Kingdom (Third to Sixth Dynasties, 2650–2575 BCE)

One of the most arresting images of the Old Kingdom comes from the Third Dynasty (2650–2575 BCE) and shows the early development of Egyptian sculpture. The figure of Zoser (Djoser), approximately life-size, was found in a closed chamber in front of the king's step pyramid at Saqqara. The image conveys a distinct feeling of gravity and majesty through the use of a massive treatment of the wig cover, the heavy false beard, the graphically carved facial features, and the careful integration of the figure and throne. One arm is raised across his chest, continuing the pose seen in the earlier figures of Khasekhem. However, a new element can be observed. The eyes were once inlaid with other materials, signaling an artistic elaboration much used in the Old Kingdom. Artists crafted inlaid eyes from a variety of colored stones, including rock crystal, presumably to create the illusion of more depth and vitality. This tradition, unfortunately, resulted in damage done by tomb robbers attracted by the precious materials, as in the case of the Zoser statue. Even with the damaged face, however, one can see that the statue of this king marks a step in the depiction of the ruler toward a representation that is not only idealized, but iconic, and therefore superhuman. Three unfinished whole and fragmentary statues of Zoser also found in his pyramid complex offer direct evidence of the progressive stages of sculptural production during the Third Dynasty.

Two images representing a nobleman and wife, Rahotep and Nofret, illustrate an early mode of direction in private sculpture. Created shortly after the time of Zoser, and depicting nobility rather than royalty, they display much of the same imposing character. An exceptional feature of these two statues, carved separately but meant to be seen as one piece, is the remarkable preservation of the polychromy. These two figures stand as an outstanding example of the way most Egyptian sculpture was meant to be seen, although many have lost their original color.

Evidence of relief sculpture from the Third Dynasty is best characterized by the multiple images of a nobleman named Hesi-re, preserved in a series of carved wood panels, made as decoration to be set into the facade of his mastaba tomb. The panels represent Hesi-re in a variety of different formal poses and costume. These woodcarvings, preserved by chance, demonstrate in their subtle use of shallow relief a level of skill and sophistication unexpected at such an early stage in the development of relief sculpture. The carving of the signs in the inscription in high relief further displays the artist's skill. Each hieroglyph is a miniature composition in its own right.

The Fourth Dynasty (2575–2465 BCE), the age of the Giza pyramid builders and the height of architectural accomplishment during the Old Kingdom, is also the period in which the art of sculpture reached its highest level. Sadly and mysteriously lacking are large-scale representations of Cheops (Khufu), the builder of the Great Pyramid. The only generally acknowledged image of this king is a small ivory carving found at Abydos. A large stone head preserved in the Brooklyn Museum of Art (New York City) has also been thought to represent Cheops, although it may be an image of another ruler from about the same time. Massive in its conception, the head suggests a transitional stage from the intentionally monumental to an idealized and perfected image of divine rulership exemplified by later images of Khephren and Mycerinus. From the time of Cheops is preserved an imposing life-size statue of his nephew, Heniunu. High ranking in the administration of the king, and probably the overseeing architect of the Great Pyramid, Heniunu had himself depicted as a corpulent middle-aged man rather than at the peak of physical perfection, the more normal mode of representation. This choice exemplifies the possibility of a dual approach to the eternal image made as an "alternate body" or "resting place" for the spirit in the tomb. Images of males from the Old Kingdom could be shown either as young at the height of their physical form or middle-aged at the height of their power and importance. Both were deemed symbolic of the essence of the individual depicted.

A seated statue of King Khephren exemplifies the classic and standard image of the ruler in the Old Kingdom. It is one of the few whole images preserved from a large number created for the king's funerary complex at Giza. He is shown seated on a high-backed chair, itself carefully detailed to describe the decorative elements of the furniture piece. Behind his head is the falcon of the god Horus, symbolizing that the king is in fact "the living Horus" on earth, an additional reminder that Egyptian art is meant to be read as a series of potent symbols, not as a realistic depiction of any person or object. The anatomic detail in the figure's rendering indicates a new level of anatomic knowledge capable of conveying the conception of the superhuman or perfected image of kingship. The placement of both hands on the knees, one flat and one clasped, emphasizes the balance of the figure. The total effect is of a majestic and awe-inspiring image of the godlike ruler.

A pair statue of King Mycerinus with his queen and a series of triad statues of the king in the company of deities, found together as a group in his mortuary complex, exemplify the art of sculpture in the Old Kingdom at its height. The sculptor (more likely sculptors; such work was usually a group project) achieved

a high degree of proficiency in the use of carving and polishing tools. Knowledge of anatomy by this time had advanced to a stage where the bone structure and musculature were carefully realized and acknowledged, if not completely indicated. Mycerinus is depicted as the idealized human, young, muscular, and virile. The representation of his wife and the images of the deities imitate his facial features, suggesting the use of his appearance as a model of perfection. In about 200 years, the art of sculpture had advanced from its tentative beginnings to a standard of perfection to be acknowledged and imitated later in Egyptian history.

In the Fifth Dynasty (2465–2323 BCE), private statues generally had become smaller in scale. Curiously, as well, few examples of large-scale royal sculpture from this period exist. In two-dimensional art, relief carving flourished for temple or tomb wall decoration. Artists used color to enhance the subtlety of the rendering in shallow relief, and numerous private tombs evidence the skill maintained under the example of royal workshops. These general characteristics carried over into the Sixth Dynasty (2323–2150 BCE), which saw a decline in the arts as the country began to lack strong centralized leadership. Notable among preserved examples of royal sculpture from the Sixth Dynasty is a miniature figure in alabaster of Pepi I in the collection of the Brooklyn Museum of Art. A figure of the same king, with one of his sons, both in the Cairo Museum, are rare examples of copper sculpture from the Old Kingdom. These figures suggest that more images in metal may have existed but have not been preserved.

WILLIAM PECK

Further Reading

Aldred, Cyril, *Egyptian Art: In the Days of the Pharaohs, 3100–320 B.C.*, London: Thames and Hudson, 1980

Egyptian Art in the Age of the Pyramids (exhib. cat.), New York: Metropolitan Museum of Art, 1999

Fazzini, Richard, et al., *Ancient Egyptian Art in the Brooklyn Museum*, Brooklyn, New York: The Brooklyn Museum, 1989

Harris, James R., *Egyptian Art*, London: Spring Books, 1966

Lucas, Alfred, *Ancient Egyptian Materials and Industries*, London: Arnold, 1926; 4th edition, Mineola, New York: Dover, 1962

Peck, William H., *Drawings from Ancient Egypt*, London: Thames and Hudson, 1978

Robins, Gay, *Proportion and Style in Ancient Egyptian Art*, Austin: University of Texas Press, 1994

Saleh, Mohamed, and Hourig Sourouzian, *The Egyptian Museum, Cairo: The Official Catalogue*, Munich: Prestel-Verlag, and Mainz, Germany: Von Zabern, 1987

Schäfer, Heinrich, *Von ägyptischer Kunst besonders der Zeichenkunst: Eine Einführung in die Betrachtung ägyptischer Kunstwerke*, 2 vols., Leipzig: Hinrichs, 1919; as *Principles of Egyptian Art*, translated by John Baines, edited by Emma Burner-Trait, Oxford: Clarendon, 1986

Smith, William Stevenson, *A History of Egyptian Sculpture and Painting in the Old Kingdom*, London: Oxford University Press, 1946

Smith, William Stevenson, *The Art and Architecture of Ancient Egypt*, Baltimore, Maryland: Penguin, 1958; revised edition, with additions by William Kelly Simpson, New Haven, Connecticut: Yale University Press, 1981

Wilson, John A., "The Artist of the Egyptian Old Kingdom," *Journal of Near Eastern Studies* 6 (1947)

EGYPT, ANCIENT: FIRST INTERMEDIATE PERIOD–MIDDLE KINGDOM (*ca.* 2150–1650 BCE)

During the course of the Old Kingdom, the crafting of sculpture was a canonical enterprise, the supervision of which was placed into the hands of able administrators by the crown. These administrators led expeditions into various regions in order to obtain a variety of stone in quarries, all of which were under the pharaoh's direct control. Ancient texts reveal that these expeditions were dispatched only by pharaoh's direct command and that the opening and closing of the quarries were religiously sanctioned. The design of any given statue was predetermined by the pharaoh and his delegates so that the individuals who actually sculpted the statues had no independent authority. They were paid in kind at exponentially lower rates than were their overseers and labored under the most primitive conditions. Furthermore, the right to a statue of one's self was dependent upon the pharaoh's permission. These circumstances generally held for the entire history of ancient Egyptian sculpture but were altered from time to time due to changed political circumstances.

The collapse of central authority at the end of the Old Kingdom caused one such alteration. The rise of competing local elites witnessed the end of royal patronage for sculptors and an end to the creation of canonical, royal models. Local administrators seem to have lost access to quarries, many located within the nomes of their rivals, and the efficient system of distribution that contributed to the construction projects of the pyramids of the Old Kingdom appears to have disintegrated. By the end of Dynasty X (*ca.* 2040 BCE), stone sculpture virtually vanishes from the cultural record, as wood became the chosen material throughout the First Intermediate Period (*ca.* 2155–2061 BCE).

The First Intermediate Period witnessed a burgeoning of wooden funerary models intended to serve the needs of the deceased in the afterlife. Two remarkable examples, both now in the Egyptian Museum Cairo, come from the tomb of Mesehti and represent a group of 40 Nubian archers and a similar number Egyptian pikemen, respectively. They are meticulously detailed and neatly painted, and their presence in his tomb may be indicative of the strife that characterized this period and that may have been thought to extend to the afterlife.

Funerary statues of the deceased are no less impressive, as seen in the representations of Wepwawet-em-hat in Boston (Museum of Fine Arts) and of Nakht in Paris (Musée du Louvre). The Boston Wepwawet-em-hat measures more than 1.5 meters tall and, compared with canonical models of the Old Kingdom, has physiognomic features that include disproportionately large eyes and lips with an equally discordant distance between the wings of the nose and the upper lip.

Stone sculpture was gradually reintroduced during the early course of Dynasty XI, as seen for example in a statue of Mesehty, once on loan to Boston (Museum of Fine Arts), which seems to have taken as its canonical model that used for statues of Idy of Dynasty VI (*ca.* 2390/2290–2155 BCE). The resurgence of stone sculpture appears to be linked to successful political attempts to reunite the country, particularly under Pharaoh (Nebhepetre) Montuhotep II, who succeeded in the task. One of his statues from Deir el-Bahari now in New York (Metropolitan Museum of Art), although altered by subsequent pharaohs, still retains much of its original features. Enthroned and wearing a costume identified as jubilee related, the figure is massive and

Sesostris III
© Gianni Dagli Orti / CORBIS

solid, with its flesh painted black, the symbolic color both of Osiris, god of the dead, and the fertile alluvial soil. Despite the rather summary treatment of the legs and kneecaps, the treatment of the face is fine and exhibits a degree of symmetry and physiognomic proportion lacking in the face of Wepwawet-em-hat.

Some of the most hauntingly evocative images of pharaohs ever created in Egypt were those sculpted during Dynasty XII (*ca.* 1991–1785 BCE). Their genesis may be the result of a royal appropriation of an idiom first developed by a competing elite. As the dynasty began, the faces of royal images were both bland and idealizing, in keeping with canonical conventions of the Old Kingdom. The series of ten like images of Sesostris I now in Cairo (Egyptian Museum) are exemplars. Concurrently, competing elites began to introduce images of themselves characterized by signs of age such as the depiction of both folds and wrinkles in the face; the images associated with the sanctuary of Heka-ib at Elephantine seem to be among the first of this type. In time the crown appropriated this visual vocabulary and commissioned statues such as those of Sesostris III (Metropolitan Museum of Art, New York) and Amenemhat III (Egyptian Museum, Cairo), in which naso-labial furrows and knotted brows prevail. These features can also be seen in the faces of a few statues of women created during the reign of Amenemhet III. As a measure of protection from competing elites, royal statues characterized by such signs of age were often accessorized with amulets, as seen in a statue of Sesostris III in Cairo (Egyptian Museum). By the time of Dynasty XIII (*ca.* 1785–1650 BCE), this style became ossified and the physiognomy, now dominated by the lips turned down into a frown, as if the visage were a caricature, as seen in the statue of Senpu in Paris (Musée du Louvre).

Innovations introduced during the Middle Kingdom also included an egg-shaped head, the artistic antecedent of that reintroduced in the later Amarna age, as well as changes in the treatment of the male torso. The torso was treated in one of three ways: as traditional bipartition, in which the pectoral region, rib cage, and lower abdomen are sculpted as a unity without differentiating it from the rib cage. The entire torso is articulated only by the body's vertical axis of symmetry; as tripartition, in which the same three zones are subtly indicated; or as corpulence, always a sign of rank in ancient Egyptian art, either as a series of accordion folds running horizontally across the lower abdomen, as seen in the statue of Montuhotep in Paris (Musée du Louvre) or as an undulating curve under the pectoral muscles. Group statues, better termed statuettes, commemorating members of the elite and their families proliferated and included as many as five family members. In addition, the block statue, named because it resembles the cubic block of stone from which it was carved, gained wide currency, and copper seems to have been used on a larger scale for statues than heretofore thought.

These strides were soon interrupted by the continuing competition of rival elites that brought the Middle Kingdom to a close and witnessed the first documented foreign occupation of the Delta at the close of Dynasty XIII (*ca.* 1650 BCE). The development of sculpture in the round was halted until the wars of liberation beginning late in Dynasty XVII (*ca.* 1600–1550 BCE) enabled Egypt to become united again under a native pharaoh.

ROBERT STEVEN BIANCHI

See also **Ancient Egypt: Old Kingdom**

Further Reading

Bourriau, Janine, *Pharaohs and Mortals: Egyptian Art in the Middle Kingdom* (exhib. cat.), Cambridge: Cambridge University Press, 1988

Davis, Whitney, *The Canonical Tradition in Ancient Egyptian Art*, Cambridge: Cambridge University Press, 1989

Delange, Elisabeth, *Catalogue des statues égyptiennes du Moyen Émpire, 2060–1560 avant J.–C.*, Paris: Éditions de la Réunion des Museés Nationaux, 1987

James, T.G.H., and W.V. Davies, *Egyptian Sculpture*, Cambridge, Massachusetts: Harvard University Press, 1983

Robins, Gay, *Beyond the Pyramids: Egyptian Regional Art from the Museo Egizio, Turin*, Atlanta, Georgia: Emory University Museum of Art and Archaeology, 1990

Spanel, Donald, *Through Ancient Eyes: Egyptian Portraiture* (exhib. cat.), Birmingham, Alabama: Birmingham Museum of Art, 1988

Valbelle, Dominique, "Craftsmen," in *The Egyptians* edited by Sergio Donadoni, Chicago: The University of Chicago Press, 1990

EGYPT, ANCIENT: SECOND INTERMEDIATE–NEW KINGDOM PRE-AMARNA (*ca.* 1715–1554 BCE)

During the course of the Middle Kingdom, Egyptian kings founded a city in the eastern Delta at Tell el-Daba called Avaris and enlisted the assistance of a large number of Canaanites to serve in various positions, including some as highly placed officials within the Egyptian bureaucracy. Excavations have revealed the remains of an over-life-size limestone statue that include a head and upper part of the shoulders of a male figure, excavated by the Austrians at the eastern Delta site of Tell el-Daba (now in the Egyptian Museum, Cairo), with coiffure intact, but facial features damaged, and part of its right shoulder with the remains in raised relief of part of a clublike throw stick. The coiffure identifies the statue as a depiction of a Canaanite official, an identification reinforced by traces of yellow pigment on the face. The political instability during the course of Dynasty XIII (*ca.* 1785–1650 BCE) plunged Egypt once again into anarchy, from which the Canaanites eventually became the first nonnative rulers of Egypt and established a dynasty that lasted just over a century, intercalated into the many competing local dynasties of the Second Intermediate Period (Dynasties XIV–XVII, *ca.* 1715–1554 BCE).

Very little sculpture has survived from this epoch, and virtually none in stone. The most ubiquitous statue type is that of a small-scale female figurine in terracotta, generally termed a bride of the dead but more properly described as a fecundity figure. Abstracted in the extreme, with great emphasis placed on breasts and pubic region, and depicted with a disproportionately large head, beaklike nose, large ears generally sporting earrings, and a flat, mortarboard-like crown of the head to which secondary materials have been added as hair and ornaments, these figures enjoyed a wide distribution from Thebes to the mountains of the eastern desert.

During the New Kingdom (Dynasties XVIII–XX, *ca.* 1554–1080 BCE), after Egypt was freed of foreign domination, the reemergence of sculpture at the beginning of Dynasty XVIII (1554–1305 BCE) looked to Dynasty XII (*ca.* 1991–1785 BCE) for canonical models. The rise of statues representing women reflected the fact that the elite women now played a more prominent role in state affairs. For example, the painted limestone statue of Mutnofret in Cairo (Egyptian Museum) was among the first life-size statues created during this time. The simplicity of the carving suggests that found in female statues of the Middle Kingdom; the tightly fitting sheath is not modeled, and the elements of the tripartite wig are arranged in a style first encountered during that period. A second example, of an anonymous royal woman (Metropolitan Museum of Art, New York City) is likewise indebted to Middle Kingdom canons, particularly in the physiognomy and the treatment of the wig. These recall a type represented by Nofret (Egyptian Museum, Cairo), a queen of Sesostris III.

The corpus of statues of Hatshepsut represents the largest number for a female monarch to have survived. In keeping with canonical conventions, most of her representations depict her in male guise, bare-chested and false-bearded, because the theological basis of ancient Egyptian kingship recognized the dual and equal nature of the male and female principals but relied on male visual conventions for visual expression. Large in scale, the images depict the female pharaoh with idealizing features, including an aquiline nose, a small mouth with full lips, and open almond-shaped eyes aligned horizontally across the face. These facial features, which represent a departure from Middle King-

dom canonical norms, dominated, with some deviation, the physiognomies of royal representations throughout the early reigns of Dynasty XVIII, often with subtle variations, as seen, for example, on two statues of Tuthmosis III in Cairo (Egyptian Museum). Although a distinguishing feature seems to be the treatment of the lower eyelid, relatively horizontal in images for Hatshepsut but often sinuously curved in those inscribed for Tuthmosis, it is often difficult to identify which Tuthmoside pharaoh is being represented without an accompanying inscription. A degree of individualization can be found in a statue of Hatshepsut (Metropolitan Museum of Art, New York City) that represents the queen as a woman, with a more slender appearance consistent with her subtly rendered, small breasts.

The first perceptible change in the physiognomic design of a royal face occurs in depictions of Tuthmosis IV, evident in the pair statue in which he is enthroned with his mother (Egyptian Museum, Cairo). The lips are now pursed into an Egyptian equivalent of a Greek archaic smile, and the almond-shaped eyes are proportionally smaller and more elongated than in earlier Tuthmoside representations. A second statue of this same monarch, also in Cairo (Egyptian Museum), places the almond-shaped eyes at an angle so that the outer rim is at a higher level than the lower. This feature, fully exploited in royal images, first appeared earlier in the dynasty in depictions of nonroyal members of the elite as a marker of their status.

The smile first introduced in images of Tuthmosis IV became larger and lips fuller in depictions of Amenhotep III. Representations of Amenhotep III also introduced a fold, rendered as two incised lines in the upper eyelid, a feature exclusive to images of this pharaoh. Depictions known to have been created late in his reign intentionally portrayed him as younger in appearance than he would have been in life, which conforms to his elaborate ideological program centering on rejuvenation.

These royal representations were not meant to be portraits in the Western sense of the word. Each image has been justifiably described as a hieroglyph, the face designed with features sanctioned by the elite. Accompanying regalia, such as a headdress or crown decorated with a serpent, proclaimed the identity of such images as depictions of pharaohs. The images were ritually animated in either temple or funerary cults and could be the recipients of both prayers and offerings. The materials from which they were sculpted had symbolic meaning, often coincident with the function served by the statues. For example, quartz and rose granite, because of their predominantly red, orange, and yellow hues, were associated with the sun god.

The statuary of nonroyal members of elite status developed in Dynasty XVIII in tandem with royal representations, using as sources canonical models from the Middle Kingdom. A wooden statue of Sanehem (Musée du Louvre, Paris, France), for example, reflects the so-called attenuated style in vogue during Dynasty XI (*ca.* 2134–1991 BCE), while a cloaked, seated figure of Ahmose (Brooklyn Museum of Art, New York, United States) reflects the style, costume, and attitude common to Dynasty XII sculpture. Nowhere is this indebtedness more marked than in the statue of Amenhotep, son of Hapu (Egyptian Museum, Cairo), who served under Amenhotep III. The statue type, costume, gesture, physiognomy (marked by signs of age), and torso (characterized by corpulence) are so indebted to Middle Kingdom canonical norms that some scholars have erroneously suggested that this statue was usurped. However, the treatment of the eyes, details of the wig, and treatment of the mouth derive from prevailing Dynasty XVIII canonical norms, harmoniously integrated into the earlier norm. That the ancient Egyptians used earlier canonical models to serve contemporary purposes is also demonstrated by a slate palette (Brooklyn Museum of Art, New York City, United States) dated to the very beginning of Egypt's Dynasty I (*ca.* 3200 BCE), which was reinscribed with the name of Tiye, chief queen of Amenhotep III, perhaps as part of the king's rejuvenation program late in his reign.

Often new forms first appeared in statuary created for the nonroyal elite, such as the signs of age encountered on the physiognomies of Middle Kingdom individuals and the designs of the eyes first exhibited in Dynasty XVIII in the statue of Djuhty. Similarly, images of other members of the elite created during the first half of Dynasty XVIII first included the double wig.

An examination of the statues created for Senenmut, an individual of humble origins who rose to power under Hatshepsut, provides one glimpse into the mechanisms of this sculptural program. More than two dozen statues inscribed with his name have survived, including several showing him with the young princess Neferure, daughter of Hatshepsut and Tuthmosis II. In his autobiographical texts, Senenmut states that he introduced composite hieroglyphs, which appear on a number of his statues. These signs seem to have been the basis for the designs of a number of his statues that feature a rebus, or sculptural pun. One such statue of Senenmut is indebted to the Middle Kingdom for the lower abdominal accordion folds of fat, yet partakes of the Tuthmoside design of the aquiline nose and wide-open eyes. The kneeling figure offers a uraeus, cradled between upraised arms, and wears a horned framed sun disk as an attribute. The statue's inscriptions state that the image is that of the goddess Renenutet, a fecund deity associated with harvests. Yet the component elements of the image are individual hieroglyphs that spell the throne name of Hatshepsut. Senenmut therefore simultaneously offered an image of Renenutet and elevated his ruler's name to Montu, the deity at Armant in which this statue was found. Designers of statues of Rameses II from Dynasty XIX (*ca.* 1305–1196 BCE) would further exploit the rebus statue.

The design elements introduced into the repertoire of sculpture during the reign of Amenhotep III and the ability of the ancient Egyptians to identify and employ canonical models from earlier periods developed in an extraordinary way in other statues created for Amenhotep III and his son and successor, Amenhotep IV, more commonly known as Akhenaten.

ROBERT STEVEN BIANCHI

Further Reading

Bianchi, Robert Steven, "An Elite Image," in *Chief of Seers: Egyptian Studies in Memory of Cyril Aldred*, edited by Elizabeth Goring, Nicholas Reeves, and John Ruffle, London: Kegan Paul International, 1997

Fazzini, Richard, et al., *Ancient Egyptian Art in the Brooklyn Museum*, Brooklyn, New York: The Brooklyn Museum, 1989

Kozloff, Arielle P., and Betsy M. Bryan, *Egypt's Dazzling Sun: Amenhotep III and His World*, Cleveland, Ohio: The Cleveland Museum of Art, 1992

Pharaonen und Fremde: Dynastien im Dunkel (exhib. cat.), Vienna: Eigenverlag der Museen der Stadt Wien, 1994 (with a brief English summary)

Redford, Donald B., *Pharaonic King-Lists, Annals, and Day-Books: A Contribution to the Study of the Egyptian Sense of History*, Mississauga, Ontario: Benben Publications, 1986

Saleh, Mohamed, and Hourig Sourouzian, *The Egyptian Museum, Cairo: Official Catalogue*, Mainz, Germany: Von Zabern, 1987

EGYPT, ANCIENT: NEW KINGDOM: AMARNA (*ca.* 1554–1347 BCE)

Ancient Egyptian art was a canonical enterprise, relying on tradition and introducing innovation as the need arose. It served as visual signs of decorum by which members of the elite could be visually identified. Nonroyal elite groups first developed the egg-shaped cranium for their depictions during the Middle Kingdom because the pharaoh was never represented bareheaded, the traditional headdresses and wigs effectively concealing the shape of the skull. They further developed the canonical model of corpulence, already evident in the Old Kingdom in statues such as that of Ka-aper in Cairo (Egyptian Museum). During the course of the first part of Dynasty XVIII (*ca.* 1554–1305 BCE), these traditions were already well established. Statues of Amenhotep III depict the pharaoh not only as an obese old man with a face marked with signs of age in the form of folds and wrinkles but also in a series of unusual images clothed in equally unusual garments. One such inscribed example (Metropolitan Museum of Art, New York City) depicts Amenhotep III as a fertility deity, with the swollen stomach and pendulant breasts characteristic of the images of such deities. A remarkable statue discovered in Thebes (Luxor Museum, Luxor) depicts Amenhotep III as a statue; its text explicitly identifies him with the Aten (the name by which the sun god was both known and worshiped during the Amarna Period)

All of the elements associated with the Amarna revolution of Amenhotep IV, later known as Akhenaten, seem to have already been in place during the reign of his father, Amenhotep III. Because of the paucity of contemporary texts, many purposefully destroyed in the pogrom condemning Akhenaten's memory, the period's history remains opaque. It would appear that Amenhotep III formulated a religious doctrine in which he, his wife, Tiye, and their son, Akhenaten, were major figures. When the city of Tell el-Amarna in middle Egypt, which became the capital of the country under Akhenaten, was excavated in the late 19th century, extraordinary images of Akhenaten were revealed for the first time in modern times; continued excavations, particularly at Thebes in the 1920s, enriched the corpus of his depictions. Removed from the entire corpus of ancient Egyptian statuary, these images of Akhenaten appeared to scholars to be unique and so imbued with a pronounced degree of nonidealizing qualities that they were immediately assumed to be graphic visual depictions of any number of pathological disorders. In addition, philologists recognized certain similarities between hymns, composed by Akhenaten himself, to his god, the Aten, and passages in certain books of the Old Testament, and some incorrectly identified Akhenaten as the pharaoh mentioned in Genesis in relation to Joseph. Serious scholars beginning in the late 20th century have engaged in separating fact from fiction regarding this period in art.

Early images of Akhenaten from Thebes (Egyptian Museum, Cairo) show that the design of the eyes and lips developed from stylistic features already in place during his father's reign. The seemingly gaunt expression on his face is a variation on the signs-of-age physiognomies developed during the Middle Kingdom and served as a marker distancing him from the policies of earlier monarchs of the dynasty. His corpulence, too, is indebted to that developed for images of his father.

Recent exhibitions have done much to advance identifications of many of the uninscribed statues from this period, including the images of women. Subtle differences in modeling and emphasis distinguish im-

Bust of Queen Nefertiti
© Ägyptisches Museum, Berlin, Germany. Photo by Margarete Büsing

ages of Queen Nefertiti from those of her husband Akhenaten, but the identity of other individuals—for example, the fine fragment of a face in yellow jasper (Metropolitan Museum of Art, New York City) and a magnificent torso of a princess in red quartzite (Musée du Louvre, Paris)—remains unresolved.

These same exhibitions have cast new light on the series of remarkable plaster heads (Ägyptisches Museum, Berlin) excavated in archaeological contexts at Amarna associated with the workshop of a sculptor named Thutmose. Not taken from life and clearly worked by hand, the purpose and function of examples in this group remain debatable, particularly since they find no exact parallels in any of the period's other sculpture in any other medium.

Perhaps the most aesthetically satisfying examples of Amarna art from a Western vantage are the egg-shaped heads of the Amarna princesses. Many are equipped with either mortises or tenons, indicating that they were pieced together in order to form composite statues, the component parts of which were crafted from different materials. The meaning of these images remains enigmatic. Equally enigmatic is the famed bust identified as that of Nefertiti, Akhenaten's wife (Ägyptisches Museum, Berlin), which is sculpted from limestone with plaster additions and painted, its right eye perfectly inlaid, its left socket empty but finished. Termed a model from which apprentice sculptors might learn, the bust appears too accomplished for that purpose. Its design is unlike anything else from ancient Egypt. Viewed in profile, the face lunges forward, like a streamlined wedge, but retains its equilibrium; its center of gravity aligns with the base, preventing it from toppling.

The appealing statuary of this period still captivates a modern audience and has fueled an industry of forgeries.

ROBERT STEVEN BIANCHI

See also **Forgeries and Deceptive Restorations**

Further Reading

Arnold, Dorothea, *The Royal Women of Amarna: Images of Beauty from Ancient Egypt*, New York: The Metropolitan Museum of Art, 1996

Berman, Lawrence Michael, *The Art of Amenhotep III: Art Historical Analysis*, Cleveland, Ohio: The Cleveland Museum of Art, 1990

Bianchi, Robert Steven, "On the Nature of Forgeries of Ancient Egyptian Works of Art from the Amarna Period," *SOURCE: Notes in the History of Art* 20 (2000)

David, A. Rosalie, *Cult of the Sun: Myth and Magic in Ancient Egypt*, London: Dent, 1980

Freed, Rita E., Yvonne J. Markowitz, and Sue H. D'Auria (editors), *Pharaohs of the Sun: Akhenaten, Nefertiti, Tutankhamen*, Boston: Museum of Fine Arts, 1999

Kozloff, Arielle P., and Betsy M. Bryan, *Egypt's Dazzling Sun: Amenhotep III and His World*, Cleveland, Ohio: The Cleveland Museum of Art, 1992

Redford, Donald B., *Akhenaten: The Heretic King*, Princeton, New Jersey: Princeton University Press, 1984

EGYPT, ANCIENT: NEW KINGDOM POST-AMARNA–THIRD INTERMEDIATE PERIOD (*ca.* 1347–720 BCE)

The events subsequent to the death of Nefertiti, the initial principal wife of Akhenaten, are opaque, but the repudiation of the cult of the Aton and the country's return to orthodoxy occurred during the reign of Tutankhaton, who within a year of his reign (*ca.* 1347–46 BCE) abandoned Tell el-Amarna and reestablished Thebes as the nation's capital. To mark this event, both he and his wife, Ankhensenpaaten, a daughter of Akhenaten and Nefertiti, changed their names to Tutankhamon and Ankhensenpaamun, respectively. The ascendancy once again of the god Amun, diety of invisibility, who was now worshiped on a national level as a state god, did not, however, erase certain features associated

with the art of Amarna. That this was so is not surprising given the canonical nature of Egyptian art in general and the hereditary nature of the professions in which its craftsmen worked. A head of the god Amun (Metropolitan Museum of Art, New York), with its round face, naturalistically modeled ears, and full lips, for example, is indebted to the art of the late Amarna period (*ca.* 1347–1305 BCE) and may reflect features of Tutankhamon. The characteristic egg-shaped cranium of the Amarna princesses continued into Dynasty XIX (*ca.* 1305–1196 BCE) in small anthropoid busts from Deir el Medinet in western Thebes, many used in household shrines honoring the spiritual aspect of deceased relatives and abounding in two-dimensional representations of the period, not only in the tomb paintings at Deir el Medinet but also in the figural style of the reliefs of Pharaoh Seti I at Abydos.

Other sculpture created under Tutankhamon sought its antecedents in canonical traditions antedating the move to Amarna. One such example is a group statue in which a larger, enthroned depiction of Amun places his hands on a smaller, headless figure of Tutankha-

Head of a Satyr
© Jonathan Blair / CORBIS

mon standing between his feet (Musée du Louvre, Paris). Nothing sculpturally extraordinary was discovered among the finds in the tomb of this pharaoh save for a series of alabaster vessels, popularly called spaghetti jars because their lacelike, intricate motifs were carved from single pieces of stone.

Few sculptural monuments can be associated with Horemhab (1332–1305 BCE), the last pharaoh of Dynasty XVIII, or with the official who served under him, Rameses I (1305–1303 BCE), who became the first pharaoh of Dynasty XIX. Surviving statues of Seti I, who succeeded Rameses I, are also rare but include at least two. The first, in the Egyptian Museum, Cairo, depicts him in a wig of late Dynasty XVIII (*ca.* 1403–1305 BCE) design and in a voluminous, pleated costume apparently without parallel. Despite modern restoration to the face, a second statue in the Metropolitan Museum of Art, New York, depicts the king with two rings of Venus on his throat, the wings of the nose designed in such a way that the nostrils are evident, and with buttonhole eyes evocative of the eyes first introduced under Tuthmosis IV of Dynasty XVIII (*ca.* 1413–1403 BCE). The style of the statue passes over the stylistic characteristics of the Amarna period in favor of those of the period immediately before. The design was conscious, meant to suggest that the Amarna period never occurred.

Of the statuary created for Seti I's son and successor, Rameses II, none is finer than the seated representation in the Museo Egizio, Turin, Italy. It is indebted to the canonical style of his father's statue now in New York, particularly in the profile of the face, but the design is so accomplished that the ends of the garment's flaring sleeves and the tip of the scepter jut out into space in a remarkable, unprecedented way. The naso-labial furrows are designed in such a way that the jowl is emphasized, a feature exaggerated on a head in the Nicholson Museum, Sydney, Australia, and perhaps adopted from representations of Seti I. New types of sculpture were introduced into the repertoire, such as a statue in the Egyptian Museum, Cairo, that depicts Rameses II in a kneeling, prostrate pose offering an altar. Over the course of his long reign, Rameses II usurped scores of monuments of earlier kings and both recut and reinscribed them. On the other hand, one of the most innovative architectural complexes ever designed in ancient Egypt are the two rock-cut temples of Abu Simbel, which contain perhaps the best-known colossal images of this ruler. The niche over the doorway of the great temple contains an image of a falcon-headed deity holding attributes that serve as hieroglyphs for the pharaoh's name, recalling the rebus of the Senenmut statue of Dynasty XVIII (*ca.* 1490–1468 BCE) (Brooklyn Museum of Art, New York City, United States), a device used again on a colossal scale

in a statue in the Egyptian Museum, Cairo, depicting Rameses II as an attribute holding a child squatting against the breast of a colossal falcon.

Dynasty XX witnessed successive waves of foreigners, the Sea Peoples, attempting to invade Egypt, which Rameses III successively repelled. A head in the Museum of Fine Arts, Boston, Massachusetts, now known to have come from an inscribed statue still in place in Thebes, depicts Rameses III in a style evocative of the late Amarna period, but the features are exaggerated to the point of verging on the grotesque. A second statue of Pharaoh Rameses II in the Egyptian Museum, Cairo, is likewise a throwback to the Amarna period, particularly in the design of the eyes and in the type of wig. Canonical types established during the Amarna period, although subsequently proscribed, still remained within the repertoire and could be placed into the service of designers at will.

Although Egypt survived the repeated assaults of the Sea Peoples, internal disturbances in the late Ramesside period, including the looting of royal tombs in the Valley of the Kings, and a mass immigration into the country of individuals of Libyan descent undermined central authority; a divided Egypt plunged into the Third Intermediate Period (Dynasties XXI–XXIV, *ca.* 1080–720 BCE). The Libyans appear to have been so mesmerized by Egypt's material culture and traditions that they masked their ethnic identity with an Egyptian veneer. They established themselves in the delta, while native dynasts occupied the south. The images of the kinglets of Dynasty XXII (*ca.* 946–720 BCE) reverted to a variety of canonical Dynasty XVIII models. An image of Osorkon I (Musée du Louvre, Paris, France) depicts this monarch with a wig first introduced under Horemhab, whereas one of Osorkon II (University of Pennsylvania, Museum of Archaeology and Anthropology, Philadelphia) could easily be mistaken at first glance for that of a Tuthmoside monarch.

The Third Intermediate Period was far from impoverished, as the discovery of gold and silver within the unplundered royal tombs of monarch of Dynasty XXI (*ca.* 1080–946 BCE) and their selected officials at the delta site of Tanis revealed. Technology was also highly advanced. The art of mummification, for example, achieved levels of perfection unsurpassed either before or after. And metallurgical skills, revealed by the treasures of Tanis, were extraordinary, particularly in the casting of bronze by the lost-wax method, as seen in the remarkable series of statues inlaid with precious metals such as that of Karomama in the Musée du Louvre, Paris, France, or Takushite in the National Archaeological Museum, Athens. The Greeks of Samos would be the first to adopt this technology during the late 8th and early 7th centuries BCE. Bronze statuettes, excavated on that island's Sanctuary of the Goddess Hera, represent Egyptian imports, suggesting that the island's legendary metalsmith, Theodorus, who is universally credited by the Greeks with the development of bronze casting, learned his trade from his contemporary Egyptian masters.

ROBERT STEVEN BIANCHI

See also **Bronze and Other Copper Alloys**

Further Reading

Bianchi, Robert Steven, "Egyptian Metal Statuary of the Third Intermediate Period (*ca.* 1070–656 B.C.), from Its Egyptian Antecedents to Its Samian Examples," in *Small Bronze Sculpture from the Ancient World*, Malibu, California: The J. Paul Getty Museum, 1990

Fazzini, Richard A., *Egypt Dynasty XXII–XXV*, Leiden: Brill, 1988

Freed, Rita, *Ramesses the Great*, Memphis, Tennessee: The City of Memphis, 1987

Hope, Colin A., *Gold of the Pharaohs*, Sydney: International Cultural Corporation of Australia, 1988

Kitchen, Kenneth A., *The Third Intermediate Period in Egypt, 1100–650 B.C.*, Warminster, Wiltshire: Aris and Phillips, 1973; 2nd edition with supplement, 1986

Kitchen, Kenneth A., *Pharaoh Triumphant: The Life and Times of Ramesses II, King of Egypt*, Warminster, Wiltshire: Aris and Phillips, 1982

EGYPT, ANCIENT: LATE PERIOD–ROMAN PERIOD (*ca.* 720 BCE–395 CE)

The history of the Late Period (Dynasty XXV to the Roman Imperial Period, *ca.* 720 BCE–CE 395) is characterized by successive waves of foreign occupation with a periodic return to independence under native pharaohs. The resilience of the material culture of ancient Egypt may be observed in the way each foreign ruler repudiated his national artistic styles and cloaked himself in the canonical styles of the Egyptian elite, effectively masking his own cultural identity. Egyptian sculptors created these statues according to designs provided by the elite in concert with their overlords; the statues often contain particular details, usually in the form of a characteristic accessory, which were reproduced in accordance with Egyptian design tenets, never betraying signs of foreign influence. The ability of the ancient Egyptians to borrow from the past is evident, and they habitually transformed what they borrowed into new canonical models required to serve the needs of the current political situation.

After the Kushites wrested control of the south from the Egyptians (Dynasty XXV, *ca.* 720–664 BCE), several concurrent styles appear to have been available to represent the Egyptians' new sovereigns. One was bland and idealizing, which characterized much of the nondescript art of the Third Intermediate Period (*ca.* 1080–720 BCE), perpetuated for images such as that of the Kushite pharaoh Taharqa (Dynasty XXV, *ca.* 690–664 BCE) (the statue is in Khartoum, Sudan National Museum, Sudan). A second seems to involve the adaptation of Kushite traditions to Egyptian norms, as the abstracted forms of a sphinx of that same pharaoh seem to suggest. A third, found on yet another image of Taharqa (Egyptian Museum, Cairo), exhibits a round face and the so-called Kushite fold, by which the cheekbones of the face are accentuated. The impetus for this physiognomic detail is doubtless the signs of age introduced into the canon during the Middle Kingdom. These Kushite monarchs are regularly depicted wearing a cap-crown; whether it is a head covering or just a convention for natural hair cut short is open to question. Kushite royal regalia included the double uraeus as well as a lanyard, with ram's head amulets at its ends and center symmetrically draped around the shoulders and adorning the chest, such as in a consummately crafted bronze statuette of the Kushite pharaoh Shabaqo (Dynasty XXV, *ca.* 713–698 BCE) (National Archaeological Museum, Athens, Greece). The significance of the double uraeus is unclear, but the ram's head is a symbol of the god Amun, tutelary deity of the Kushites, and lord of Karnak, seat of their religious power in Egypt.

While the representations of Kushites as pharaohs relied almost exclusively on the Kushite fold as a marker of identity, images of elite members of their administration were more graphically marked by signs of age and corpulence. The full effects of the application of these models, termed *archaizing*, on contemporary creations can be seen in the obese torso of Harwa and in a head of Montuemhat and combined in a complete statue of Harwa (all in the Egyptian Museum, Cairo). The statue of yet another member of the elite, Ariketekana (Egyptian Museum, Cairo), with his egg-shaped cranium and pendulant breasts, might at first glance be taken for a woman, inviting comparison with depictions from Amarna, if it were not for the signs of age sculpted into his face and the inscription.

When the Kushites were finally removed from Egypt and ensconced in Nubia, Psametik I gained control of Egypt. Some of the sculpture created for the elite during Dynasty XXVI (664–525 BCE), inaugurated by Psametik I, continued to rely on the signs of age introduced during Dynasty XXV (*ca.* 720–664 BCE), as seen on the faces of elite members of this dynasty such as those of the officials Djedasteriufankh (Egyptian Museum, Cairo) and Petamenophis (Egyptian Museum, Cairo). This style coexisted with a bland and idealizing idiom that was to characterize much of Saite statuary later in the dynasty. A second statue of Petamenophis as a cross-legged seated scribe (Egyptian Museum, Cairo) stands at the beginning of this tradition. Its canonical model can be traced to that used to create images of the elite during the Old Kingdom in the region of Memphis. The archaistic tendencies of the Late Period (*ca.* 720 BCE–395 CE) in general and of the Saite Period (another designation for Dynasty XXVI, 664–525 BCE, so named because its pharaohs ruled Egypt from the delta city of Sais) in particular were so faithful to the earlier canonical types that it is often difficult to assign a sculpture to its correct period.

Saite Egypt fell to the advancing Persian armies during the last quarter of the 6th century BCE and was subsequently incorporated as a satrapy, or province, within the Achaemenid Empire. The Persians established a precedent of ruling in absentia, co-opting members of the Egyptian elite as their administrators. A headless statue of Wedjahorresnet, a member of the Egyptian elite in the service of his Persian overlords (Museo Gregoriano Egizio, Vatican City, Rome, Italy) is depicted wearing a characteristically Persian-styled skirt wrapped around a typically Persian garment with flared sleeves. Reliefs at Persepolis often depict this garment, which is so convincingly rendered on this statue that it raises the question of whether Egyptians worked for the Persians on that project, since the wraparound garment is represented in Egyptian art on monuments that predate the Persian invasion. A second statue depicting its owner in the same costume is that of Ptahhotep (Brooklyn Museum of Art, New York City), another member of the Egyptian elite serving the Persians as a highly-placed treasury, with the addition of a Persian torque, the design of the ram's-head terminals of which have been rotated in accord with Egyptian conventions.

Egypt gained its independence once again in 404 BCE, and after the collapse of Dynasties XXVIII and XXIX, the later falling in 380 BCE, a powerful elite family from Sebennytos in the delta established themselves as rulers of Egypt. The art of Dynasty XXX (380–342 BCE) often invokes canonical models in its archaizing tradition. This archaistic process is more noticeable in two-dimensional representations than in statuary, which was still indebted to Saite norms. A statue of Nectanebo II of Dynasty XXX in the Metropolitan Museum of Art, New York City, depicts him nestled against the breast of a falcon holding attributes that spell his name in a rebus, recalling those of Rameses II of Dynasty XIX (*ca.* 1290–1224 BCE). The Dattari statue, named after its former owner, a notable art collector, depicting an elite member of the administration of Dynasty XXX (Brooklyn Museum of Art, New York City), indebted to canonical norms of the Old Kingdom for the classic type of the striding male figure, is designed with a torso that exhibits tripartition first encountered during the Middle Kingdom. Its idealizing face with full cheeks and chin set off from the

jaw would later characterize most faces created during the Ptolemaic period (305–30 BCE). The head of the statue of Wesirwer (Brooklyn Museum of Art, New York City), the body of which is in Cairo (Egyptian Museum), reveals how the designs of some works of the period, while relying on earlier models, are unique and without contemporary parallels. Although the wrinkle of the brow and smoothly polished surfaces of the skin derive from the canons of Dynasty XXV and XXVI, the broad and squat shape of his skull are without precedent.

A remarkable limestone head in a private collection may well be one of the only Egyptian statues of Alexander the Great, who established control over Egypt in the second half of the 4th century BCE. It portrays him with ideal features wearing a *kausia*, a particular type of cap associated with traditional Macedonian garb (that doubtless serves as the model for the type of cap worn today by modern Afghanis), rendered in Egyptian idiom, fronted by a serpent. Within two decades, his general, Ptolemy, who had governed Egypt as regent, declared himself pharaoh and inaugurated a dynasty that lasted until Cleopatra VII. Society in Ptolemaic Egypt, consisting of Greek overlords and native Egyptians, was separate and unequal, although individuals could work the system and fluidly operate in both spheres. Canonical art created for that elite remained true to its traditions. The statue of Amunpayum (Cleveland Museum of Art, Cleveland, Ohio) belongs to the canon on which the Dattari statue depends, and a block statue of Wahibre (private collection, Hater Family Trust) is so indebted to canonical traditions that it was believed to date to the period before Dynasty XXVII (525–404 BCE) until its date to the Ptolemaic period was unequivocally established.

Statues of the elite wearing tripartite costumes consisting of short-sleeved shirts, fringed wraparound skirts, and fringed shawls draped asymmetrically around the body over the left shoulder appear in stone in numbers for the first time during this period. Long considered the product of a mixed school exhibiting an interaction between Greek conventions and Egyptian canonical traditions, the statues have since proved to be exclusively indebted to the latter. Other sculptures from this period also show exclusive indebtedness to the Egyptian canon, which is consistent with the societal division of Egypt and underscored by temple inscriptions in hieroglyphs over entrances, such as that at Dendera, which explicitly prohibit the entry of all foreigners, Greeks included. The inclusion of an epitome in Greek often found on a canonical creation explaining the nature of the statue viewed demonstrates that the elite and the sculptors in their employ understood the differences between canonical Egyptian images and Greek creations. When found on these canonical images, folds, both in the physiognomies of individuals and in the costumes of elite men and women, should be understood in terms of Egyptian tradition, independent of any foreign influence.

The death of Cleopatra VII and the victory of Octavian (later Rome's first emperor Augustus) in 30 BCE changed the face of Egypt forever. His agents cooperated with the elite at Aswan in the construction of several temples, one originally at Dendur (now in the Metropolitan Museum of Art, New York City), on the walls of which Augustus is depicted as an idealized Egyptian pharaoh offering to the deities of the region. Canonical sculpture in the round continued, predominantly in the form of statuettes of seated officials, often with inlaid eyes; its production seems to cease altogether about 50 CE, although the tradition may have continued sporadically for another century.

The cessation of a four-millennia-old canonical, sculptural tradition in the middle of the 1st century CE is not difficult to explain. This tradition depended on the pharaoh, who with his delegates designed the models that the sculptors followed. Egypt therefore experienced a sculptural crisis each time the central authority collapsed. Canonical sculpture in Egypt had always been the visual manifestation of ideology, hence the appearance of signs of age in the Middle Kingdom and the seemingly aberrant depictions of Akhenaten and his court in the New Kingdom. The elite no longer needed such images because political activism on the local level had been squashed by the Romans, who put an end to nomarchal competition for hegemony over all of Egypt. The function that canonical sculpture served thus ceased to exist.

ROBERT STEVEN BIANCHI

Further Reading

Bianchi, Robert Steven, *Cleopatra's Egypt: Age of the Ptolemies*, Brooklyn, New York: The Brooklyn Museum, 1988

Bianchi, Robert Steven, "The Cultural Transformation of Egypt as Suggested by a Group of Enthroned Male Figures from the Faiyum," in *Life in a Multi-Cultural Society: Egypt from Cambyses to Constantine and Beyond*, edited by Janet H. Johnson, Chicago: Oriental Institute of the University of Chicago, 1992

Bothmer, Bernard V., Herman de Meulenaere, and Hans Wolfgang Müller, *Egyptian Sculpture of the Late Period, 700 B.C.–A.D. 100*, Brooklyn, New York: The Brooklyn Museum, 1960

Wildung, Dietrich (editor), *Sudan: Ancient Kingdoms of the Nile*, Paris: Flammarion, 1997

ÉMAIL EN RONDE BOSSE

Enameling is the process of fusing glass, a vitreous substance, to a metal surface. No single culture is credited with the discovery of enameling on metal, but the earliest known examples are found decorating Mycenean (1450 BCE), Assyrian (700 BCE), and Greek (600 BCE) jewelry.

Historically applied only to objects fashioned from precious metals—gold and silver—enamel is created by first mixing silica—white sand or flint—with sodium, lime, borax, and lead, and heating the mixture to form a translucent base called flux. Color is derived from metallic oxides—green from copper, blue from cobalt, red and brown from iron, and opaque white from tin oxide—that are added to the flux. The final product is smelted at high temperatures to form a lump of raw color known as frit. To prepare the enamel for application to metal, a lump of frit is placed in a bowl, covered with water, and ground into powder to form a paste that is applied wet or left to dry and stored for later use. Once the wet enamel applied to the object is completely dry, it is placed in a kiln or furnace heated to temperatures ranging from 300 to 850 degrees Celsius to fuse the prepared glass paste to the metal object. Gold, a material that does not oxidize (turn a darker color) when heated, was traditionally a popular choice for enameling because it did not affect the brightness of a translucent enamel color.

Translated as enamel on a round relief, *émail en ronde bosse* describes the technique used to apply enamel to small-scale objects cast or chased in the round from gold or silver. Great skill in both chasing the gold and applying the enamel was required of the goldsmith to produce a successful example. Figures worked in the round were chased in separate pieces from thin sheets of gold and soldered together before enameling. Next, the craftsman applied enamel paste in a thin, even coating to the gold surfaces, which were roughened to hold the enamel in place. Firing was done in two stages to allow the goldsmith to remove accumulated enamel from the depressions in the figure and to fill in gaps before the final firing. In two chapters of his *Treatise* on goldsmithing, Benvenuto Cellini described the labor involved in successfully fashioning and enameling minute gold figures. The greatest difficulty was supporting the figure in the kiln while it was being fired; the support material could damage the enamel in progress.

The earliest examples of this style, also referred to as encrusted enamel, date from late 14th-century France. Thought to have originated in Paris, objects enameled in the round were incorporated into sculptural works of unrivaled luxury to satisfy the extravagant taste of the courts of the kings of France and the Dukes of Burgundy. Nearly all works of art created in 14th- and 15th-century France, whether religious or secular, were functional. Enameled precious metal sculptures such as *nefs*, elaborate boat-shaped containers made to hold the personal table utensils of a king, or table fountains cast in fantastic shapes functioned as magnificent serving pieces on the banquet tables of French royalty. The motifs of these creations reflect the Gothic desire to produce sculptural objects that were more naturalistic, a movement reflected in the development of the pink and white skin tones found in *ronde bosse* enameled figures. In these figures, the goldsmiths of Paris continued the trend of naturalism, which they derived from polychrome statues of the period. The only surviving example of a 14th-century *nef* is the *Nef of St. Ursula*, which has been converted to a reliquary. The nine figures enameled in *ronde bosse* are easily visible standing on the deck of the great ship.

Other examples of the virtuosity of the French goldsmith/sculptor exist in devotional objects. Two of the finest examples that include *émail en ronde bosse* figures are the *Goldenes Rössl*, a devotional sculpture commissioned in 1385 by Queen Isabel as a gift to her husband, King Charles VI of France. The name is derived from the figure of the golden horse, enameled in pure white, held by its groom at the base of the sculptural grouping. The second example, the *Holy Thorn Reliquary*, commissioned from a Paris goldsmith by Jean, Duke of Berry, in 1405, is a masterpiece of sculptural enameling. Echoing the hierarchy found in Byzantine mosaic apse decorations, this reliquary depicts God the Father, enthroned and flanked by two angels, seated on an arch surrounded by the 12 apostles. Inside the arch is a seated Christ, in the traditional posture of blessing, the cross at his back and the world at his feet. The rock crystal container holding the Holy Thorn is at the base of the cross.

The practice of *émail en ronde bosse* was continued throughout Renaissance Italy and Germany, where goldsmiths produced many of the finest small examples of encrusted enamel in jewelry. However, the large sculptural application of the technique was not revived until the early 18th century with German goldsmith Johann Melchior Dinglinger. Appointed court jeweler to Augustus the Strong in 1698, he supplied most of the treasury pieces commissioned by Augustus II. His masterwork, the *Court of Aurangzeb* (Grünes Gewölbe, Dresden, Germany), begun in 1701 and finished in 1708, contains 165 gold figures enameled in *ronde bosse*, arranged on a silver-gilt stage before a facade representing the buildings of the oriental court.

The revivals of the 19th century reawakened interest in the *ronde bosse* technique. Examples are found in the work of Italian jewelers Castellani and Giuliano, Parisian jeweler François-Désiré Froment-Meurice, and Russian jeweler Peter Karl Fabergé. Jeweler to the Russian Imperial Court from 1870 on, Fabergé's *Resurrection Egg*, commissioned by Alexander III around 1886, recalls the exquisitely detailed *ronde bosse* enamelwork found in the *Holy Thorn Reliquary*. The egg, carved from rock crystal, contains the enameled figures of Christ rising from the tomb flanked by two angels.

KAREN YORK

See also **Cellini, Benvenuto; Goldenes Rössl (Golden Horse) of Altötting; Greece, Ancient**

Further Reading

Campbell, Marian, *An Introduction to Medieval Enamels*, London: HMSO, 1983

Cellini, Benvenuto, *The Treatises of Benvenuto Cellini on Goldsmithing and Sculpture*, translated by C.R. Ashbee, London: Arnold, 1898; reprint, New York: Dover, 1967

Cherry, John F., *Goldsmiths*, Toronto: University of Toronto Press, 1992

Gere, Charlotte, *The Art of the Jeweller: A Catalogue of the Hull Grundy Gift to the British Museum: Jewellery, Engraved Gems, and Goldsmiths' Work*, edited by Hugh Tait, London: British Museum Publications, 1984

Lightbown, R.W., *Secular Goldsmiths' Work in Medieval France: A History*, London: Society of Antiquaries of London, 1978

Middeldorf, Ulrich, "On the Origins of Émail sur ronde bosse," *Gazette des Beaux-Arts* 6/55 (April 1960)

Speel, Erika, *Dictionary of Enamelling*, Aldershot, Hampshire, and Brookfield, Vermont: Ashgate, 1998

ENGLAND AND WALES: ANCIENT

This survey of ancient sculpture from the Neolithic or New Stone Age (*ca.* 5000 BCE) through the Dark Ages (*ca.* 1000 CE) includes three-dimensional monuments and objects that may have held some ritualistic purpose or contained a highly defined aesthetic and those with significance beyond the utilitarian. Mystery surrounds many of the ancient monuments of Great Britain, which is perhaps the secret to their enduring power.

Burial monuments were extremely important to the Neolithic people. Many ritual burial sites can be found throughout the British Isles, including the well-known causewayed camps in southern and eastern England, large circular or oval enclosures defined by concentric rings of earthen banks and ditches. Major camps were built at Bryn Celli Ddu, Anglesey, Wales, and at Windmill Hill, Wiltshire. Alongside regular meetings and ceremonial feasts, the ritual exposure of bodies is thought to have taken place. Bones were then inhumed in communal tombs, earthen mounds known as long barrows in England and cairns in Wales, which are found throughout the countryside (one at Maiden Castle, Dorset, measures almost 0.5 kilometers). From about 4000 to 2500 BCE, larger burial monuments constructed of huge stones (megaliths) appeared, particularly in Wales, with massive capstones at both Tinkinswood and St. Lythans, South Glamorgan.

In the thousand years between about 2500 and 1500 BCE, stone circles and henges appeared. Why these sites were built and what took place there remains unknown. One of the earliest, largest, and most spectacular stone circle sites, Long Meg and Her Daughters, is found in Cumbria in the north of England. Another great stone circle is at Avebury in the south. The best-known henges in Wales are in Llandegai, opposite the Isle of Anglesey.

Yet the most famous circle of this type, one of Europe's greatest monuments, is Stonehenge on Salisbury Plain in southern England. Stonehenge is a complex ritual site that remained a focus of activity for more than 1500 years. This technical and engineering marvel was originally constructed about 3100 BCE and went through two major renovations. The earliest phase (Stonehenge I) consisted of the outer bank and ditch with a circle of holes on the inside. These holes were originally used for burial but were filled in during Stonehenge II (ca. 2100 BCE), when a circle of blue stones from Wales was erected. It is believed that these stones were ferried across the Bristol Channel on rafts and then moved on rollers overland. The last phase (Stonehenge III, ca. 2000 BCE) saw the raising of the great trilithons that now dominate the site. These huge *sarsens* (large sandstones), many weighing nearly 50 tons, were dragged 32 kilometers overland from the Marlborough Downs before being laboriously pounded smooth with stone hammers. Another wonder of the ancient world, the Great Pyramid of Cheops in Egypt, was built contemporaneously (*ca.* 2500 BCE).

Many theories link the stone circles to the sun and the moon, and markings made up of cup and ring motifs of spiraling or concentric circles thought to symbolize these celestial bodies can be found on some of the stones. These forms, also found carved on rocks, particularly in northern England, were mainly executed between about 2500 and about 1500 BCE. Also during this period, distinctive pottery was made by the Beaker Folk, originally from the Low Countries, who emigrated to the British Isles early in the 2nd millennium BCE. They buried their dead in individual graves (instead of communal tombs) with the coil-built pots covered with crosshatched patterns that gave them their name.

Deteriorating climatic conditions (*ca.* 1200 BCE) exacerbated by ash from a major volcanic eruption in Iceland led to the decline of this society and the emergence of the Celts as a major presence. Various communities of Celts emigrated to Britain from Europe starting around the 1st millennium BCE, building hill forts—massive defensive hilltop settlements ringed by impressive earthworks—and bringing advanced iron-working techniques and an abstract visual language. The Hallstatt style of geometric decoration was at its peak during the end of the Bronze Age (*ca.* 1300–800 BCE), but as the Iron Age developed, a new decorative style, the La Tène, emerged, incorporating flowing curved lines of floral designs and zoomorphic motifs. The production of fine decorated metalwork such as gold and silver jewelry, swords and scabbards, shields inlaid with enamel, bronze mirrors, and wood and ceramic containers reached new heights in Britain with this style. Examples were found either with burials or in hoards, caches of ritual items deliberately placed in the ground or submerged in bodies of water. One such ritual item, the Waterloo Helmet, a horned helmet with curvilinear decoration, was dredged from the river Thames.

In about 55 BCE the Romans invaded, and sculptural relics in the Roman tradition can be found throughout Great Britain, including what many consider one of the finest mosaics in the country: the floor of the Orphic temple at Littlecote. Under the 400 years of Roman rule, Roman classicism mingled with Celtic design, as is seen in the Gorgon-headed Medusa centerpiece of the pediment on the main temple in Bath.

Throughout the Iron Age the Celts sculpted simple stone and wood heads, often with only the nose and eyes delineated—the nose frequently representing a phallus and the eyes, testes—and a menacing expression. After the Roman invasion, the style of the head became increasingly influenced by Roman realism, but the sense of menace remained. Celtic forms and influence lasted into the Dark Ages and beyond, with relics of Celtic heads found in the grotesque masks and gargoyles of some medieval churches and a frieze of Celtic-style carvings found on an arch from the Norman period in the church at Adel, Yorkshire.

Another major legacy of the Celts is the stone crosses found throughout Britain. With Christianity taking hold in the 7th century CE, in the wake of St. Augustine, stone crosses, originally on unshapen stone pillars, were refined into freestanding crosses. Many of these crosses can be found in Cornwall; one of the finest, a 10th-century cross, is at Cardingham. The crosses are the most numerous and prominent of the surviving Dark Age monuments, signaling the end of the ancient pagan monuments and the beginning of the age of sculpture based on Christian iconography.

AMY BERK

Further Reading

Burgess, Colin, *The Age of Stonehenge*, London: Dent, 1980

Burl, Aubrey, *Rings of Stone: The Prehistoric Stone Circles of Britain and Ireland*, edited by Josephine Christian, London: Lincoln, 1979; New Haven, Connecticut: Ticknor and Fields, 1980

Burl, Aubrey, *Great Stone Circles: Fables, Fictions, Facts*, New Haven, Connecticut: Yale University Press, 1999

Chippindale, Christopher, *Stonehenge Complete*, Ithaca, New York: Cornell University Press, and London: Thames and Hudson, 1983; revised edition, London and New York: Thames and Hudson, 1994

Cunliffe, Barry W., *The Celtic World*, New York: McGraw-Hill, and London: Bodley Head, 1979

Cunliffe, Barry W., *The Ancient Celts*, Oxford and New York: Oxford University Press, 1997

Fowles, John, and Barry Brukoff, *The Enigma of Stonehenge*, New York: Summit Books, and London: Cape, 1980

Hadingham, Evan, *Circles and Standing Stones: An Illustrated Exploration of Megalith Mysteries of Early Britain*, London: Heinemann, and New York: Walker, 1975

Legg, Rodney, *Romans in Britain*, London: Heinemann, 1983

Megaw, M. Ruth, and J.V.S. Megaw, *Celtic Art: From Its Beginning to the Book of Kells*, New York and London: Thames and Hudson, 1989

Somerset Fry, Plantagenet, *Roman Britain: History and Sites*, Newton Abbot, Devon: David and Charles, and Totowa, New Jersey: Barnes and Noble Books, 1984

Thomas, Julian, *Rethinking the Neolithic*, Cambridge and New York: Cambridge University Press, 1991; revised 2nd edition, as *Understanding the Neolithic*, London and New York: Routledge, 1999

ENGLAND AND WALES: ROMANESQUE (*ca.* 1066–1160)

The Romanesque style in England is conventionally taken as beginning in 1066 with the Norman Conquest, although its manifestations have been detected in the preceding two decades, most significantly in the work undertaken by Edward the Confessor at Westminster Abbey. Far less Romanesque sculpture survives in England than in other regions of Europe due to the iconoclasm of the Reformation and the reforming zeal of the Puritans during the civil war in the 17th century.

The most important consequence of the Norman Conquest for the arts was a massive building program, with the construction of great churches and castles in stone that provided the background for developments in architectural sculpture. Sculpture within these buildings tended at first to be confined to carving on capitals. The adaptation from Germany at the end of the 11th century of the cubic capital with its four smooth surfaces provided an ideal surface for innovative, figurative carving. This form of capital can be seen side by side with the more traditional Corinthian type in the extensive crypt built underneath the Cathedral of Canterbury at the end of the 11th century. The capitals at Canterbury were decorated by a group of stonemasons, the most proficient of whom has been named the "Gabriel Chapel Master." His subjects include the conceit of animals playing musical instruments. Later capitals incorporated one or more narrative illustrations—a type of capital known as *historiated*. A characteristic example, portraying *Christ Calling Saint Peter* (*ca.* 1120), survives from Lewes Priory in Sussex (which was dedicated to Saint Peter and a royal foundation) and is now preserved in the British Museum.

Another innovative form of Romanesque sculpture was the tympanum. Although none in England compares in scale to the impressive tympana that survive in France and Spain, one of the earliest examples of a tympanum in northern Europe can be found at Chepstow Castle (*ca.* 1070) in Wales (albeit with geometric rather than figurative decoration). The tympanum above the Prior's Doorway at the Cathedral of Ely is one of the most impressive to survive in England from a major foundation. The piece represents *Christ in Majesty*, who is enclosed in a mandorla that is supported by two angels. Countless minor churches also retain their original tympanum. The Church of Barfreston in Kent, with its tympanum portraying *Christ in Majesty*, is a characteristic example. More unusual is the Church of Quenington in Gloucestershire, which has tympana over both its entrances, one representing the *Harrowing of Hell* and the other representing the *Coronation of the Virgin*, one of the earliest examples of this iconography.

Another form of sculptural relief prevalent in Romanesque sculpture that has its antecedents in antiquity is the narrative frieze. The most notable example of this genre in England is the frieze on the west front of

Crypt Capital, Cathedral of Canterbury, England
The Conway Library, Courtauld Institute of Art

the Cathedral of Lincoln, which was commissioned by Bishop Alexander of Lincoln in the 1140s and inspired by Wiligelmo's earlier frieze on the Cathedral of Modena in Italy.

Within the interior of a church the nave would have been separated from the rest of the church by means of a rood screen, which was often the object of an elaborate sculptural program. Some of the most impressive fragments of Romanesque sculpture originally formed part of a rood screen. The relief carvings at Chichester (*ca.* 1130) and Durham (*ca.* 1155) fall into this category. The two carvings at the Cathedral of Chichester represent respectively *Christ at Bethany* and the *Raising of Lazarus* and rank among some of the most emotionally powerful religious art ever produced in England. Their closest stylistic and iconographic antecedents are in German art, although certain elements, such as the grave diggers with their grotesque faces, are characteristically English.

Within the church interior would also have been a large number of portable objects used in the liturgy that were the subject of sculptural relief. Of these the most important category to survive in England are fonts made not only of stone but also lead. They are frequently decorated with interesting iconographic programs. The font at Burnham Deepdale in Norfolk, for example, is decorated with a series of illustrations representing the 12 occupations of the months. A distinctive category of fonts, made of black Tournai marble, was imported from Flanders by Henry of Blois, bishop of Winchester and brother of King Stephen. Very little wooden sculpture survives from this period. Two fragments of a wooden crucifix from the Church of South Cerney in Gloucestershire, for example, are all that survive of Romanesque wooden crucifixes in England but give an indication of the quality of such work.

A further consequence of the Norman Conquest was a greater receptiveness to influences from the Continent, which were frequently combined in a creative manner with indigenous artistic traditions. Romanesque sculpture in the British Isles is characterized by considerable stylistic heterogeniety. Influences have been detected from, among other places, northern Italy (notably in the Prior's Doorway at Ely), northern Germany (in the Chichester reliefs), and southwest France (such as the porch at Malmesbury, *ca.* 1160). In the second half of the 12th century, Byzantine influence also became increasingly important. This can be seen, for example, in the beautiful *Virgin and Child* relief, carved in limestone, at York Minster, which has been dated to the mid 12th century.

Scholars of English Romanesque sculpture have isolated certain regional schools. Of these one of the most interesting is that based in the west of England

in Herefordshire. It has been argued that the principal sculptor of this school accompanied Oliver de Merlimond, the lord of the manor and founder of Shobdon Church, on a pilgrimage to Santiago de Compostela in northwest Spain and was influenced by the monuments along the way that came to provide the basis for his own work. The best-preserved church from this school is that of Kilpeck, which was built in the 1140s. The structure has carving on its doorway (complete with a tympanum representing the *Tree of Life*), chancel arch, and west window, as well as a series of amusing carved corbels placed beneath the eaves of the roof on the exterior apse of the church. The doorway of Kilpeck Church reflects the influence of Scandinavian art and with its radiating voussoirs, figurated medallions, and figures placed one on top of another, has close parallels with certain churches in southwest France.

The Romanesque style continued to be practiced in parts of England until the end of the 12th century. But by the 1160s the earliest manifestations of the more naturalistic Gothic style, transplanted from the Île-de-France region in northern France, can be seen in certain cosmopolitan centers. The west portal at the Cathedral of Rochester with its column figures is an early example.

Andreas Petzold

Further Reading

Bond, Francis, and Frederick Charles Eden, *Fonts and Fontcovers*, London, New York, and Toronto, Ontario: Frowde, 1908

Kahn, Deborah, "La sculpture romane en Angleterre: État des questions," *Bulletin Monumental* 146 (1988)

Kahn, Deborah, *Canterbury Cathedral and Its Romanesque Sculpture*, London: Miller, and Austin: University of Texas Press, 1991

Thurlby, Malcolm, *The Herefordshire School of Romanesque Sculpture*, Herefordshire: Logaston, 1999

Zarnecki, George, *Studies in Romanesque Sculpture*, London: Dorian Press, 1979

Zarnecki, George, Janet Holt, and Tristram Holland (editors), *English Romanesque Art, 1066–1200*, London: Weidenfeld and Nicholson, 1984

ENGLAND AND WALES: GOTHIC (*ca.* 1150–1500)

Any study of English Gothic sculpture must consider that the overwhelming majority of religious imagery created during this period has been destroyed, mostly during the 16th-century iconoclasm accompanying the dissolution of the monasteries under Henry VIII. Despite these historical circumstances, scholars have reconstructed the general outline of the production of English Gothic sculpture. Much of the sculpture that remains is architectural, and most of this, unfortunately, has been highly restored. Evidence indicates that almost every sculpture produced in England during this period was painted, whether it was produced in stone, ivory, or wood. Little Welsh sculpture remains from this period apart from a few grave slabs and effigies from North Wales carved between 1250 and 1440. This work is usually highly decorative relief carving that displays heraldic symbols but few figural images.

Some of the earliest sculptures that can be considered Gothic are the life-size figures originally found on a portal (now destroyed) of St. Mary's Abbey, York, in the late 12th century (Yorkshire Museum). Representing biblical figures, probably apostles, they are softly modeled and enticingly tactile. In order to find

Portal figure, St. Mary's Abbey, York, England
The Conway Library, Courtauld Institute of Art

the beginnings of a thoroughly English Gothic style, however, one must look to the West Country in the early 13th century. The transepts at the Cathedral of Wells display excellent examples of this early English Gothic sculpture, especially in the prototypical English "stiff-leaf" foliage found on many capitals. In these sculptures, small human figures cavort among abstracted, sharply curving foliage. In 1229 a large workshop was assembled to create the west facade of the Cathedral of Wells, a massive undertaking—originally including more than 175 statues and almost 50 biblical reliefs—stretching like a large screen across the end of the building. Its intense sculptural decoration emphasizes fluid and sweeping garments that can seem heavy and stiff in some examples while excitedly mobile in others. Such enthusiasm for the decorated surface only increased throughout the Gothic period.

English Gothic sculpture changed again at Westminster Abbey, in the new church begun in 1246 by Henry III. The sculptural decoration here presents a more idealized conception of the human form than in past English Gothic sculpture. The highly praised angels found in the triforium spandrels of the transepts look out over the church with serenely idealized expressions and thin, flowing garments as they turn their bodies to swing their censers over the architectural space. The Westminster angels stand at the beginning of a long English tradition of decorating architectural spaces with angels, typified by the late 13th-century Angel Choir of the Cathedral of Lincoln. Its sculptures bear a striking resemblance to contemporary work in France marked by complacent smiles and swaying bodies. The Cathedral of Lincoln also houses one of the earliest surviving English Easter sepulchers (*ca.* 1290). Important remnants of a particular 13th- and 14th-century English Gothic sculpture, these sculptures are permanent re-creations of the tomb of Christ used in the liturgical events surrounding Easter.

In the 14th century, English Gothic sculpture became markedly more profuse and ornamental. Figures surrounded by increasingly decorative niches propagated across any and every surface. The Lady Chapel at Ely contains ornate sculptural decoration that does not simply ornament the walls but also forms a complete decorative shell around the chapel. Some of the most remarkable 15th-century sculpture is found at the chantry chapel of Henry V at Westminster Abbey, which has survived almost entirely intact. The sheer quantity of intricate decoration is astounding.

English Gothic sculpture also included many masterful effigy sculptures in stone, bronze, and brass; the secular nature of these figures spared them from much of the iconoclastic destruction of the 16th century. The Cathedral of Wells houses early 13th-century examples of stone tomb effigies representing a set of Anglo-

Saxon bishops. Many early 13th-century effigies are incised or carved in low relief in the deep brownish-purple limestone known as Purbeck "marble." Later, figures emerge from the flat surface to become more agitated and engaging, as exemplified by the cross-legged position assumed by the late 13th-century knight at Dorchester Abbey (Oxfordshire). After 1291, when Edward I commissioned gilt-bronze effigies of Henry III and Eleanor of Castile from a London gold-smith named William Torel, this medium became popular for royal tomb sculpture. Eleanor was also publicly memorialized in a series of 12 stone crosses commissioned by Edward, her bereaved husband. Only three remain, and two have identifiable sculptors: William of Ireland, who carved the Northampton cross, and Alexander of Abingdon, who carved the Waltham cross and also made the base of Queen Eleanor's tomb in the Cathedral of Lincoln. The quality of incised monumental brass tomb effigies reached a peak in the late 14th and early 15th centuries.

It is difficult to identify particular sculptures in ivory with English workshops during the Gothic period. As a rule, Paris was the source of most worked ivory from this time, and even objects made elsewhere look Parisian. A set of ivory devotional panels made for Bishop John Grandisson of Exeter in the 1330s (British Museum, London) testifies to the type of ivory carving popular in England at that time, even if it may not have been carved by English masters.

Alabaster sculptures carved by English artisans were extremely popular across Europe after about 1340. Artists most often fashioned these images into altarpieces or effigy sculptures. The most impressive of these sculptures may be the 14th-century Nottingham or Flawford alabasters (Nottingham Castle Museum). These images—originally painted, gilded, and carved within large rectangular panels—are among the earliest English alabaster images to survive. By the end of the 14th century, English alabaster sculpture was mass-produced, and the imagery became repetitive.

An ever-increasing use of ornament and attention to complex detail marked English Gothic sculpture from 1150 to 1500. Unique sculptural expressions, such as the Wells transepts and the 13th-century tomb sculpture, dominated at first, but by the close of the period, distinctively English images gave way to a more formulaic pan-European style, as displayed by the Lady Chapel at Ely and the late 14th-century alabasters.

ALISON LANGMEAD

Further Reading

Alexander, Jonathan J.G., and Paul Binski (editors), *Age of Chivalry: Art in Plantagenet England, 1200–1400* (exhib. cat.), London: Royal Academy of Arts, 1987

Cheetham, Francis W., *English Medieval Alabasters: With a Catalogue of the Collection in the Victoria and Albert Museum*, Oxford: Phaidon-Christie's, 1984
Gresham, Colin A., *Medieval Stone Carving in North Wales: Sepulchral Slabs and Effigies of the Thirteenth and Fourteenth Centuries*, Cardiff: University of Wales Press, 1968
Prior, Edward Schröder, and Arthur Gardner, *An Account of Medieval Figure-Sculpture in England*, Cambridge: Cambridge University Press, 1912
Stone, Lawrence, *Sculpture in Britain: The Middle Ages*, London and Baltimore, Maryland: Penguin, 1955; 2nd edition, 1972
Williamson, Paul, *Gothic Sculpture, 1140–1300*, New Haven, Connecticut: Yale University Press, 1995

ENGLAND AND WALES: RENAISSANCE (*ca.* 1510–1625)

The term "Renaissance" (from the Italian *Rinascimento*, or rebirth) is not a term usually applied to English and Welsh art. Although it generally denotes a period of time from the end of the 14th to the 16th centuries, it is usually established as indicating Italian, and to some extent Netherlandish, art of this period. In discussions of Renaissance cultures outside Italy, British art does not generally feature. England and Wales had no sculptors equivalent to such Italian sculptors as Ghiberti, Donatello, or Michelangelo Buonarroti. Nor was there the level of patronage found among the merchants of Florence or the court of Francis I of France. Nonetheless, Renaissance culture did impinge upon England and Wales, although often in a hybrid or idiosyncratic form, frequently incorporating older styles, including Gothic. However, there is a frequent tendency for admirers of both Italian-style Renaissance Classicism and medieval Gothic to dismiss the Renaissance in England and Wales as either Classicism corrupted by Gothic, or Gothic corrupted by Classicism.

The term "English Renaissance" is used, however, although this did not apply to art of the period paralleling the Italian Renaissance but to the work of late 17th century figures such as Nicholas Stone and the architect Christopher Wren. English art of this period is probably best seen as belonging to the Baroque. Certainly 16th-century England and Wales had a ruler who was cultured, patronized the arts, and, most significantly in this context, commissioned sculptural works that are Classical in form. Henry VIII, despite his "roast beef and olde England" characterization in popular culture, was considered at the time a quintessential Renaissance prince. Among his most notable sculptural commissions was the double tomb for his father, Henry VII, and Elizabeth of York in Westminster Abbey, London, made by the Florentine sculptor Pietro Torrigiano between 1512 and 1518. Torrigiano trained alongside Michelangelo in the studio of Ghirlandaio, but according to Giorgio Vasari, he had to leave Florence in disgrace after having broken the nose of Michelangelo in a fight. After this he is known to have worked in the Netherlands before arriving in England around 1510. The tomb betrays this Florentine connection openly, with the recumbent figures of the king and queen modeled in a Classical style and a classically formed sarcophagus with four fully rounded, putti-like angels seated at the corners. Such classically influenced sculpture was wholly new in England where the Gothic style still dominated, but even Torrigiano's English work is marked by Gothic influence, possibly to accommodate the dominant style of Westminster Abbey. It is even apparent in another tomb in Westminster Abbey by Torrigiano, the tomb of Lady Margaret Beaufort, which has a Gothic canopy. The tomb of Dr. Young, generally attributed to Torrigiano in the Public Records Office Museum in London, was realized in a fully formed Florentine manner.

Other Florentine sculptors working in England during this period include Benedetto da Rovezzano, who was probably responsible for the wooden screen in King's College Chapel, Cambridge, about 1533–36. Two stories tall, the ground floor of the screen comprises elegant, Classical, semicircular arches and the first floor a Florentine-style balcony, perhaps partially inspired by the *Cantoria* galleries from the Cathedral of Florence, which were designed by Luca della Robbia (1431) and Donatello (1433–39). A third Florentine artist active in England was Giovanni da Maiano, who was patronized by Cardinal Wolsey. Da Maiano produced for the cardinal a series of terracotta roundels for his new palace at Hampton Court, Surrey, about 1521. Placed on the external walls of the gatehouses, these depict the heads of Roman emperors with a naturalism in the antique style.

Benedetto had previously worked in France and through this route brought foreign cultural ideas to England. In the case of Torrigiano, this came via the Netherlands. Although Italian Renaissance artists working in England were relatively rare, French and Dutch sculptors were relatively common. It is preferable to consider the Renaissance in England and Wales not as a poor emulation of Italian Renaissance art but as part of a general northern European phenomenon in which there was a growing interest in Classical forms and ideas. Good evidence for this can be seen in the tomb of Sir Robert Dormer at Wing, Buckinghamshire (*ca.* 1522), which shows strong French influence in its Classical columns and canopy and suggests that the unknown maker may have been a French sculptor. Netherlandish influence is more apparent in the tombs of the earls of Rutland and in the Church of St. Mary, Bottesford, Leicestershire. The tomb of the first Earl of Rutland (*ca.* 1543) by Richard Parker

consists of a double-effigy tomb that shows a typical mixture of Gothic and Classical elements, with the Gothic effigies of the Earl and his wife recumbent and praying on the top of the sarcophagus combined with the Classical pilasters, swags, and naturalistic relief figures. In the same church is the tomb of the fourth Earl of Rutland and his son Nicholas (*ca.* 1591) by Gerard Johnson, a Dutch immigrant sculptor from Amsterdam, in which the effigies lie under a grand and fully Classical canopy comprising two full columns with Corinthian capitals, a Classical entablature, and double Classical semicircular arches. The kneeling figures surrounding the tomb still appear incongruous, however, because of their diminutive size, showing that aspects of the northern Gothic tradition were not wholly abandoned by the end of the 16th century. The Johnsons were capable of using a much more recognizable Italian Renaissance style, as shown by the tomb of Sir Thomas and Lady Sondes (1584–92; Throwley, Kent). Here the figures are upright and kneeling in prayer and represented in plain white marble, and the sarcophagus itself is in a restrained form of Classicism with plain pilasters and shields.

The Johnson's tomb at Bottesford represents the style of sculpture that came to dominate in early 17th-century England, and given that it was generally practiced by local sculptors rather than itinerant foreign ones, it might legitimately be labeled English Renaissance. Foreign influence was still strong, however, as the period saw a new and more profound settlement of sculptors from Holland in England. Many artists were fleeing religious persecution at the hands of the Catholics in the Spanish-controlled Netherlands. The Anglo-Dutch style they imported can be seen in tombs and monuments all over England and Wales: in York Minster, for example, an impressive example is the tomb to Matthew Hutton, archbishop of York (1606), comprising a single semicircular arch flanked by two Classical Corinthian columns, with the archbishop represented lying on his side, his head propped up on his left hand. Two other monuments of this period in York Minster include those of Sir William Ingram of 1623 and Henry Swinburne of 1624, both comprising a single centered arch in which the effigies are placed, supported by Classical allegorical figures to each side. The representation of the figures is stiff and unnaturalistic, yet they are set within a general Classical framework, including Classical entablature and decorative detailing. The Swinburne monument, however, still retains recognizably Gothic elements in the canopies over the two allegorical figures, which is in marked contrast to the fully realized caryatids that flank the effigies of Sir William and Lady Catherine Ingram.

This type of tomb and monument sculpture can also be related to architectural sculptural works in secular settings. An anonymous fireplace at Raglan Castle, Gwent, in Wales, dating from the late 16th century, is a good illustration of how un-Italian the use of Classical forms in England was at this date. The sources for this are probably Netherlandish. Extremely ornate, the fireplace has Classical columns, pilasters, and niches and is symmetrical. Although the caryatid figures on either side of the grate are superficially Classical and stiff and hieratic in appearance, other, smaller figures that writhe around the fireplace might almost have been transposed from a Gothic misericord. The Netherlandish influence in this work is also echoed by the example of an oak screen at Knole House in Kent, carved by William Partinton (*ca.* 1605). This also has similar grotesque forms, including caryatids in an un-classicizing style, which are probably based on Flemish pattern books by either Wendel Dietterlin or Marten de Vos, important sources for much English sculptural ornament.

Despite the strength of this northern European Renaissance culture and its reinforcement in England by the presence of Dutch refugees, sculpture in England and Wales was soon to start on a path toward a very different type of Classicism. There are intimations of this even in the late 16th century in the work of another sculptor of Dutch descent, William Cure. Cure established a dynasty of craftsmen sculptors; his son, Cornelius, was master mason to the court of Elizabeth I. Subsequently, Cornelius's son, also called William, worked for the crown, which under the Franco-Scottish Stuart dynasty was increasingly influenced by French Classical tastes. The Cure workshop seems to have been more aware of French forms of tomb sculpture judging by the consistency and greater simplicity in their use of Classical forms and absence of grotesques in the tomb of Sir William Pickering (*ca.* 1574; St. Helen, Bishopgate, London) and the tomb of First Baron Burghley *ca.* 1598; St. Martin's Church, Stamford, Lincolnshire). Northern European styles that had dominated the late 16th and early 17th centuries gave way to a more familiar Latinate Classical style, which bears a much closer comparison with Italian or French contemporary modes than the "Artisan Mannerism" of Partinton and others. This change would lead to a more recognizable Classical style in the work of later sculptors, such as Maximilian Colt and Nicholas Stone.

MICHAEL PARASKOS

See also **Colt, Maximilian; Stone, Nicholas; Torrigiani, Pietro**

Further Reading

Chancellor, Edwin Beresford, *The Lives of the British Sculptors, and Those Who Have Worked in England from the Earliest Days to Sir Francis Chantrey*, London: Chapman and Hall, 1911

Ford, Boris (editor), *Renaissance and Reformation*, Cambridge and New York: Cambridge University Press, 1988

Galvin, Carol, and Phillip Lindley, "Pietro Torrigiano's Tomb for Dr. Young," *Church Monuments* 3 (1983)

Kemp, Brian, *English Church Monuments*, London: Batsford, 1980

Molesworth, Hender Delves, *Sculpture in England: Renaissance to Early XIX Century*, London and New York: Longmans, 1951

Patterson, Ian, and Hugh Murray, *Monuments in York Minster*, York, England: Dean and Chapter of York Minster, 2000

Underwood, Eric Gordon, *A Short History of English Sculpture*, London: Faber and Faber, 1933

Wells-Cole, Anthony, *Art and Decoration in Elizabethan and Jacobean England: The Influence of Continental Prints, 1558–1625*, New Haven, Connecticut: Yale University Press, 1997

Whinney, Margaret, *Sculpture in Britain, 1530–1830*, London and Baltimore, Maryland: Penguin, 1964; 2nd edition, revised by John Physick, London and New York: Penguin, 1988

White, Adam, "England *c.* 1560–*c.* 1660: A Hundred Years of Continental Influence," *Church Monuments* 8 (1992)

ENGLAND AND WALES: BAROQUE–NEOCLASSICAL (*ca.* 1625–1800)

Nicholas Stone, the son of a quarry man, trained in the early 17th century with Hendrick de Keyser in Amsterdam, where he came into contact with ambitious Continental sculptural projects. He became the preeminent mason-sculptor in England, infusing British sculpture with new vigor and originality. His workshop received many commissions from Charles I and the city of London. His work reveals a response to the style of Italian sculpture he had seen and studied in the royal collections. Many English sculptors traveled abroad to obtain training and experience during the reign of Charles II, and the influence of both Gianlorenzo Bernini and the French favorite of Charles I, Hubert Le Sueur, can be traced in the work of the successful Englishman John Bushnell.

Although Caius Gabriel Cibber developed Stone's workshop in the 17th century and produced highly original and prestigious Baroque works for the city of London, such as his *Monument to the Great Fire of London* (1673–75), Grinling Gibbons became, with the assistance of Artus III Quellinus, more successful in achieving major commissions, for example, the chapel at Whitehall Palace; Gibbons attained the prime post of master sculptor to the crown in 1684. His name is associated with virtuoso woodcarving, but his workshop also produced many major monuments and stone reliefs. Francis Bird designed more daring and dramatic tombs, although the quality of his work varied. Edward Pierce—mason, carver, architect, and sculptor—had a high reputation as a decorative woodcarver but also produced some remarkable Baroque portrait busts in the manner of Bernini. The most lively, individual, and expressive of these is the *Bust of Sir Christopher Wren* (1673), at the Ashmolean Museum, Oxford, England.

A new spirit supporting the return to order of Classical forms and proportions in art and architecture found expression in the writings of the third Earl of Shaftesbury and Lord Burlington. Patrons and connoisseurs traveling on the Continent used Jonathan Richardson's *Account of the Statues, Bas-Reliefs, Drawings, and Pictures in Italy, France, etc.* (1722) as a guide to study of the antique. Sculpture flourished in England, achieving its most distinguished expression in the 18th century in the work of three foreigners, Michael Rysbrack, Peter Scheemackers, and Louis-François Roubiliac. Rysbrack transformed the English portrait bust by combining an increasingly realistic treatment of facial features with Classical Baroque poses. His many monuments drew on Classical models and were executed in a refined and sophisticated technique unmatched by his contemporaries. Roubiliac, an original and accomplished sculptor from Lyons, challenged Rysbrack's leading position and introduced an informality of pose into portrait sculpture in England, exemplified by his full-length statue of George Frideric Handel for Vauxhall Gardens in 1738 (later moved to Victoria and Albert Museum, London, England), which attained instant success. Many of the most theatrical tombs in Westminster Abbey come from his hand. Roubiliac also received commissions from the Baillie family in Scotland (*Lady Grizel Baillie*, 1746, Earl of Haddington collection) and the Middleton family in Wales (*Miss Mary Myddelton* monument, 1750, Wrexham, Denbigh). Sir Henry Cheere, who was instrumental in founding the Royal Academy of Art, London, ran a large successful sculpture workshop at Old Palace Yard, Westminster, and worked for most of the major British patrons until 1770. His monument to Admiral Sir Thomas Hardy (1732) at Westminster Abbey and the more elaborate monument to the Earl of Kildare (1743) in Christ Church Cathedral, Dublin (with reclining and standing figures), combine Classical motifs with Rococo detail. His brother John Cheere maintained a flourishing independent sculpture yard, which produced a range of Rococo garden sculptures and busts for the provinces.

Excavations of Classical sites at Herculaneum and Pompeii commanded great interest among artists and cognoscenti in England, who displayed and discussed ancient artworks; major collectors such as Sir William Hamilton and Charles Townley bought Classical works. In 1765 Henry Fuseli translated into English the seminal treatise by Johann Joachim Winckelmann, *Reflections on the Painting and Sculpture of the Greeks*. Sir Joshua Reynolds, president of the Royal Academy of Art, promoted the grand style in his *Discourse X* to the Royal Academy in 1780; this discourse is the one original English text from this period on sculpture. In it he denounces the use of contemporary dress in sculpture as becoming too rapidly outmoded, but at the same time he severely criticizes the classically nude statue of Voltaire (1776) by Jean-Baptiste Pigalle as inviting ridicule. Reynolds asserted that portrait sculpture should remain true to the permanent and grand nature of stone by presenting the sitter in an ideal rather than a naturalistic manner without falling into "inanimate insipidity." His writings and those of Winckelmann profoundly affected the work of the next generation of sculptors.

Two other factors developed the taste for Classical forms in England and Wales at the beginning of the 19th century: the display in London in 1806 of the Parthenon Marbles retrieved from the Acropolis in Athens by Lord Elgin (the so-called Elgin Marbles) and the contemporary work of Antonio Canova. The designs of Canova, Europe's most famous and influential Neoclassical sculptor, became known in England through the works he exhibited at the Royal Academy between 1817 and 1823 and by works acquired by English collectors, such as the *Three Graces*. A three-volume set of Canova's engravings published by Henry Moses in 1822–24 profoundly affected the development of British monumental sculpture. Canova gave evidence to a select committee formed in London in 1816 to consider the importance of the Elgin Marbles and helped Benjamin Robert Haydon persuade the government of their quality and importance in stimulating the development of British art. John Flaxman

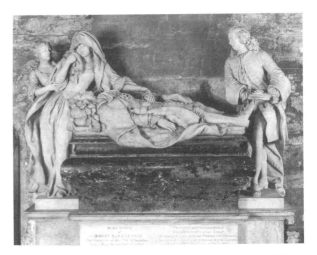

Sir Henry Cheere: Monument to Robert, first Earl of Kildare, *ca.* 1743; Christ Church Cathedral, Dublin, Ireland
The Conway Library, Courtauld Institute of Art

was one of many British artists who visited Canova's studio while studying in Rome.

A committee of taste initiated a project commemorating military heroes at St. Paul's Cathedral in London, for which Thomas Banks produced Neoclassical monuments to two naval heroes, Captain Burgess (1802) and Captain George Westcott (1805). The new style Banks used to represent these modern heroes—one practically nude, the other in a Classical chiton—outraged public opinion. Flaxman interpreted the messages of Canova and the Elgin Marbles more successfully in his monument to Lord Nelson (1808–18) and became adept at rendering heroism, pathos, and restrained human emotion through a refined use of linear values in a more acceptable allegorical form. Flaxman's efforts to communicate in his lectures to the Royal Academy his ideas on expressing deep sentiment through Neoclassical forms were not always as lucid as his sculptural examples. His spare, fluent line illustrations to editions of *The Iliad* and *Odyssey*, influenced by the decorated vases from William Hamilton's collections, were even more persuasive imagery and influenced painters, crafts, and collectors, as well as sculptors. Joseph Nollekens, Richard Westmacott and his studio, Francis Chantrey, and Richard Wyatt continued the Neoclassical tradition until John Gibson became the favored Regency sculptor and a more Romantic style prevailed.

Gibson was born in Wales, near Coventry, but like most ambitious Welsh masons and sculptors before the mid 19th century, he had to train in London before he went to Rome. He undertook no major monuments for Welsh patrons but his work is represented in the National Museum at Cardiff. A pupil of Canova, Gibson was noted for the purity of his design, based on that of his teacher. He won international acclaim and his example stimulated the next generation of Welsh sculptors. After his death a British school of sculptors developed interests in the realistic detail and dramatic effects that could be achieved by different techniques such as modeling, and the New Sculpture movement emerged.

J. PATRICIA CAMPBELL

See also **Banks, Thomas; Bushnell, John; Chantrey, Sir Francis (Legatt); Cibber, Caius Gabriel; Flaxman, John; Gibbons, Grinling; Gibson, John; Nollekens, Joseph; Rysbrack, Michael; Stone, Nicholas**

Further Reading

Boase, Thomas Sherrer Ross, *English Art, 1800–1870*, Oxford: Clarendon, 1959

Esdaile, Katherine Ada McDowall, *English Monumental Sculpture since the Renaissance*, London: Society for Promoting Christian Knowledge, and New York and Toronto, Ontario: Macmillan, 1927

Flaxman, John, *Lectures on Sculpture*, London: Murray, 1829; 2nd edition, London: Bohn, 1838

Gunnis, Rupert, *Dictionary of British Sculptors, 1660–1851*, London: Odhams Press, 1953; Cambridge, Massachusetts: Harvard University Press, 1954; revised edition, London: Abbey Library, 1968

Kemp, Brian, *English Church Monuments*, London: Batsford, 1980

Mercer, Eric, *English Art, 1553–1625*, Oxford: Clarendon, 1962

Penny, Nicholas, *Church Monuments in Romantic England*, New Haven, Connecticut: Yale University Press, 1977

Reynolds, Joshua, *Discourses on Art* (1797), edited by Robert R. Wark, New Haven, Connecticut: Yale University Press, 1997

Stone, Nicholas, *The Note-book and Account Book of Nicholas Stone, Master Mason to James I and Charles I*, edited by Walter Lewis Spiers, Oxford: University Press, 1919; reprint, London: Dawson, 1969

Walpole, Horace, *Anecdotes of Painting in England*, 4 vols., London: Farmer, 1762–71; reprint, New York: Arno Press, 1969

Whinney, Margaret, and Oliver Millar, *English Art, 1625–1714*, Oxford: Clarendon Press, 1957

Whinney, Margaret, *Sculpture in Britain, 1530–1830*, London and Baltimore: Penguin, 1964; 2nd edition, revised by John Physick, London and New York: Penguin, 1988

ENGLAND AND WALES: 19TH CENTURY–CONTEMPORARY

The Neoclassical movement, dominant in the late 18th century, remained a major strand of British sculpture well into the 19th century. It is seen in the work of the John Bacon father-and-son dynasty, Richard Westmacott, and John Flaxman, particularly in their public and church monuments. The early 19th century also witnessed an upsurge of state patronage commemorating Napoleonic War leaders, seen in a series of stolidly Neoclassical monuments in St. Paul's Cathedral, London, and in Lord Nelson's Column (1839–67) in Trafalgar Square, London, with its statue of Nelson by E.H. Baily (1788–1867). Francis Legatt Chantrey (1781–1841) monopolized portraiture; his many commissions for busts, statues, and monuments made him extremely wealthy. He owed his success to a mastery of fleshy textures and pragmatic adaptation of form and costume to sitters' appearances. The conservatism of British sculpture in this era was reflected in the claim of Henry Weekes (1807–77), Chantrey's former assistant and later a professor at the Royal Academy, that it was "an art that is limited and can never be popular" (see Read, 1982). Imaginative, "ideal" sculpture aroused relatively little interest in Britain and secured few commissions. Its principal exponent was the internationally admired and uncompromisingly Neoclassical John Gibson (1790–1866).

In the mid 19th century, John Henry Foley (1818–74) developed from idealized Classicism to self-confident, timeless realism in his *Prince Albert* statue

509

(1868–74; Hyde Park, London). The latter forms part of the Albert Memorial, the most significant sculptural commission of the period, which H.W. Janson has described as "Late Neoclassic modified by zoological and ethnographical realism" (see Janson, 1985). The Pre-Raphaelitism of Thomas Woolner (1825–92) and Alexander Munro (1825–71) is evident in the scrupulously rendered flowers of Woolner's William Wordsworth monument at Grasmere (1851) and Munro's lyrical, Rossetti-like *Paolo and Francesca* (1851). Alfred Stevens (1817–75) remains the most admired British sculptor before 1880, largely because of his Wellington Monument figures (1857–1912), a sensitive interpretation of Michelangelo. Stevens bridged earlier Victorian sculpture and what became known as the New Sculpture movement of the 1880s. William Hamo Thornycroft (1850–1925) placed new emphasis on realism, which was complemented by the imaginative symbolism of Alfred Gilbert (1854–1934) and George Frampton (1860–1928). Thomas Brock (1847–1922) united both these strands in his Queen Victoria Memorial (1903–24). Both in rejecting Neoclassical conservatism and in raising British sculpture to new levels, the New Sculpture was a considerable achievement. Its legacy continued well into the 20th century, especially with World War I memorials. Although they were generally stylistically conservative, the memorials sometimes combined admirable execution with imaginative creativity, for example in the works of William Goscombe John (1860–1952) and Charles Sargeant Jagger (1885–1934).

Modern sculpture first appeared in Britain shortly before World War I with Jacob Epstein (1880–1959), Henri Gaudier-Brzeska (1891–1915), and, less radically, Eric Gill (1882–1940). Epstein's public sculpture created considerable media controversy because of its deliberate primitivism and sexuality, as well as its rejection of Classical conventions. Frank Dobson (1886–1963) represented the more reticent and acceptable face of modern sculpture in the 1920s and early 1930s, winning admiration over Epstein from critic Roger Fry. The gulf between most "modern" and "academic" sculpture at this time has been exaggerated. Dobson, Gill, and Maurice Lambert (1902–64) did not aim to shock and remained fundamentally figurative. Conversely, the leading academic sculptors Gilbert Ledward (1888–1960) and Charles Wheeler (1892–1974) experimented with modern methods of direct carving and incorporated stylized Art Deco elegance into their work.

The early 1930s witnessed a turning point as significant as the advent of the New Sculpture 50 years earlier. Henry Moore (1898–1986) and Barbara Hepworth (1903–75) rejected cautious Modernism, turning instead to Continental influences such as Pablo Picasso, Hans Arp, and Constantin Brancusi. Whereas Moore's sculpture usually employs the reclining figure and relates in style, scale, and site to nature and the landscape, Hepworth's works are more uncompromisingly abstract. Moore attracted great critical and institutional prestige, particularly through the efforts of his biographer and friend Herbert Read. By 1948, when Moore won the sculpture prize at the Venice Biennale, he was internationally famous, and by the following decade, he was synonymous with "modern sculpture."

After a period in the 1950s during which the spiky, existentialist work of Kenneth Armitage (*b.* 1916), Reg Butler (1913–81), and Lynn Chadwick (*b.* 1914) won critical accolades, Anthony Caro (*b.* 1924) dominated current British sculpture. A former assistant to Moore, Caro, after visiting the United States, where he admired the work of David Smith, rejected the modeled figure. Instead, he made purely abstract sculpture constructed from industrial components, which he painted brightly. Caro claimed that his "big break" was in "challenging the pedestal, killing statuary, bringing sculpture into our own lived-in space." As a teacher at Saint Martin's School of Art, London, he made considerable impact on the younger, so-called New Generation of abstract sculptors, which included Phillip King (*b.* 1934) and William Tucker (*b.* 1935). In the late 1960s, Caro's influence was itself challenged by the Conceptual "living sculptors" Gilbert and George, the

Barbara Hepworth, *Pelagos*, 1946
© Henry Moore Foundation, Tate Gallery, London / Art Resource, NY

"soft art" forms of Barry Flanagan (*b.* 1941), and the land art of Richard Long (*b.* 1945). The latter-day Surrealism of Eduardo Paolozzi (*b.* 1924) made sinister use of found objects and represented a strand in British sculpture that complemented Caro's approach.

In the late 20th century, British sculpture underwent significant, indeed bewildering, changes. Stylistic battles of previous generations yielded to Postmodern pluralism, with no single figure exerting the dominance of Moore midcentury or Caro in the 1960s. Some sculptors, such as Michael Sandle (*b.* 1936) and Glynn Williams (*b.* 1939), have worked in overtly historicist modes, unthinkable in the eras of Moore or Caro. The "New British Sculptors," Tony Cragg (*b.* 1949) and Bill Woodrow (*b.* 1948) make imaginative use of junk, the former by constructing maps and flags from plastic shards, the latter by painting and rearranging disused whiteware components. Rachel Whiteread (*b.* 1963) created a poignant work in *Untitled (House)* (1993; destroyed), a ghostly concrete cast of an entire house due for demolition in London's East End. Probably the most familiar sculpture of late 20th-century Britain is the *Angel of the North* (1996) by Antony Gormley (*b.* 1950), a monumental steel figure that received the accolade of being imitated by the soccer player Alan Shearer. Since the late 1980s, the sculptural limelight has been captured by the so-called Young British Artists (YBAs), sculptors whose gifts for publicity and the "shock of the new" arguably exceed traditional crafting or even conceptual skills. Their leading protagonists include Damien Hirst (*b.* 1965), celebrated for his tanks containing dead fish and severed parts of cows, and Tracey Emin (*b.* 1963), whose autobiographical installation *Everyone I Have Ever Slept With* (1995) records the names of these bedfellows. Conservative critics have questioned whether such works are "sculpture," but according to Richard Cork, the fact that in Britain the art continues to undergo such "momentous and often bewildering changes testifies to vigour rather than redundancy" (see Marshall, 1997).

MARK STOCKER

See also **Bacon, John; Butler, Reg (Reginald Cotterell); Caro, Anthony; Chantrey, Sir Francis (Legatt); Cragg, Tony; Epstein, Jacob; Flanagan, Barry; Flaxman, John; Frampton, George; Gibson, John; Gilbert, Alfred; Gill, Eric; Gormley, Antony; Hepworth, Barbara; Jagger, Charles Sargeant; Long, Richard; Moore, Henry; Stevens, Alfred**

Further Reading

Beattie, Susan, *The New Sculpture*, New Haven, Connecticut: Yale University Press, 1983

Causey, Andrew, *Sculpture since 1945*, Oxford and New York: Oxford University Press, 1998

Compton, Susan (editor), and Dawn Ades, *British Art in the Twentieth Century: The Modern Movement* (exhib. cat.), London: Lund Humphries, and Munich: Prestel, 1987

Curtis, Penelope, *Sculpture, 1900–1945: After Rodin*, Oxford and New York: Oxford University Press, 1999

Farr, Dennis, *British Sculpture since 1945*, London: Tate Gallery, 1965

Fine Art Society, *British Sculpture, 1850–1914* (exhib. cat), London: Fine Art Society, 1968

Hammacher, Abraham Marie, *Modern English Sculpture*, London: Thames and Hudson, 1967

Janson, Horst Woldemar (editor), *La scultura nel XIX Secolo; La sculpture du XIXᵉ siécle; Nineteenth-Century Sculpture* (trilingual Italian-French-English edition), Bologna, Italy: CLUEB, 1984; London, Thames and Hudson, and New York: Abrams, 1985

Livingstone, Marco, "England: IV. Sculpture, 5. After *c.* 1914," in *The Dictionary of Art*, edited by Jane Turner, vol. 10, New York: Grove, and London: Macmillan, 1996

Lucie-Smith, Edward, *Sculpture since 1945*, Oxford: Phaidon, and New York: Universe, 1987

Marshall, Catherine (editor), *Breaking the Mould: British Art of the 1980s and 1990s, the Weltkunst Collection*, London: Lund Humphries, and Dublin: Irish Museum of Modern Art, 1997

Nairne, Sandy, and Nicholas Serota (editors), *British Sculpture in the Twentieth Century* (exhib. cat.), London: Whitechapel Art Gallery, 1981

Neff, Terry A. (editor), *A Quiet Revolution: British Sculpture since 1965* (exhib. cat.), London and New York: Thames and Hudson, 1987

Read, Benedict, *Victorian Sculpture*, New Haven, Connecticut: Yale University Press, 1982

Read, Benedict, and Peyton Skipwith, *Sculpture in Britain Between the Wars* (exhib. cat.), London: Fine Art Society, 1986

Spalding, Frances, *British Art since 1900*, London and New York: Thames and Hudson, 1986

Whinney, Margaret, *Sculpture in Britain, 1530–1830*, London and Baltimore, Maryland: Penguin, 1964; 2nd edition, revised by John Physick, London and New York: Penguin, 1988

ENGRAVED GEMS (INTAGLIOS AND CAMEOS)

Intaglio engraving of small stones for the practical purpose of sealing can be traced back at least seven millennia; but a new era in the history of this craft dawned in 8th-century BCE Greece, with green serpentine "Island Gems" from the Cyclades incised with animals and hybrid monsters and worn on cords as amulets or jewels. By the 6th century BCE, scarab and simplified domed scaraboid shapes engraved with satyrs, animals, and sphinxes on harder quartzes, which required more sophisticated cutting techniques, were introduced from the Near East. Since that time, from which we may date the rise of gem engraving as an art, the principal stones employed as well as the tools and the technique used to engrave images on gemstones have remained basically the same: engravers incise lines and hollows in hard stones with metal drills coated with a hard gemstone powder in a liquid solution. Early tools were fast-revolving vertical bow drills, eventually supplanted by a horizontally mounted spindle moved by a foot-driven lathe, with exchangeable tips of varying shapes and sizes. The 18th-century engraver is depicted seated at just such a lathe, whereas the 20th-century engraver has exchanged foot power for electric power.

Toward the end of the 6th century BCE, depictions of young boys and girls show considerable artistry in rendering anatomical features and complicated poses, and some stones bear the signatures of artists. During the subsequent Classical Greek period of the 5th to 4th century BCE, gem engraving reached heights comparable to the major arts. Engravers depicted divinities and humans, animals, and mythical monsters mostly on large whitish, gray, or blue chalcedony scaraboids. Longitudinally pierced and mounted on swivels, they were worn as rings or pendants and prized as jewels for their beauty, as were similarly engraved gold rings, while bronze rings fulfilled the practical purpose of sealing. The mid 5th century BCE engraver Dexamenos of Chios signed studies of waterbirds, a portrait head, and a scene of a lady with her maid, which rank with the finest examples of major sculpture. Toward the end of the period, exquisitely engraved figures parallel the styles of Praxiteles and Lysippos; Graeco-Persian gems from the Near East depict figures in Persian costume, cut in Greek style and technique, whereas in Etruria, the craft underwent a separate development with the use of elaborate scarab shapes in dark red cornelian engraved with athletic figures, legendary heroes, animals, and monsters.

Gem engraving received a new impetus during the luxurious palace civilization that originated with Alexander the Great and continued in the successor states, notably Ptolemaic Egypt. Alexander is said to have permitted only the engraver Pyrgoteles (none of whose works has survived) to cut his portrait, but many portraits of the later dynasts have survived. Standing figures in a delicate classicizing style are now found engraved on slender, elongated, colorful stones, such as aquamarine, garnet, and amethyst, introduced from the East with the expansion of Alexander's empire. Moreover, a far-reaching innovation, the introduction of cameos, underlines the fact that engraved gems were now regarded primarily as jewels. Engravers did not incise these images into the stones but cut them as raised reliefs, often against contrasting backgrounds on layered stones such as reddish-brown and white sardonyx. The first recorded collections demonstrate that engraved gems were cherished as works of art: that of Mithradates VI of Pontus, captured by Pompey the Great, was dedicated about 62 BCE on the Capitol in Rome.

In Italy intaglio seal stones and their cheaper imitations in molded glass were already commonly worn in finger rings, but migrating Greek engravers introduced a more sophisticated art in the 1st century BCE. Dioscourides, Augustus's court artist, his three sons, and their contemporaries signed many of their stones, as did Romans such as Felix and Rufus. But the most important gems of the period are the two large, multi-figured sardonyx cameos known as the Gemma Augustea (in the Kunsthistorisches Museum, Vienna) and the Gemma Tiberiana in the Cabinet de Médailles of the Bibliothèque Nationale, Paris, France. The first, more than 18 centimeters tall, depicts in the center Augustus as Jupiter, seated with Roma and crowned by Oecumene (the inhabited Earth); the second, an even larger stone, centers on Tiberius and his mother Livia.

In addition to such extraordinary luxury objects and state cameos of succeeding emperors, the Roman world produced a plethora of intaglios, molded-glass gems, and more rarely, cameos, worn by the mass of the population and with an enormous variety of images, ranging from deities and legendary heroes to portraits, scenes from daily life, animals, and lucky symbols. During the 1st centuries CE, sard and cornelian

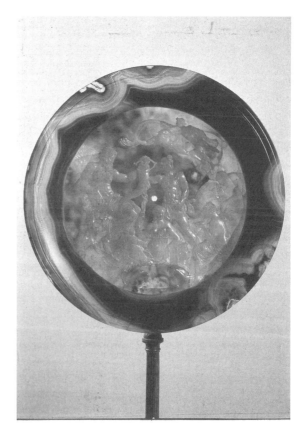

Nile with other figures, Farnese cup, Sardonyx cameo, Hellenistic, 3rd–2nd centuries BCE© Scala / Art Resource, NY

512

gave way to opaque stones such as red jasper and two-layer dark and pale blue nicolo, which were later supplanted by unengraved ring stones in bright colors. One quite different type of engraved stone, however, took their place in the wider empire: magical amulets with distinctive, mostly Gnostic devices and inscriptions. Beside them, small gemstones bore Christian symbols; but Christian devotional gems in the form of cameos of Christ, the Virgin, and saints became a major area of production in the later Byzantine Empire.

During the Early Middle Ages, gem engraving in the West lost its former dominance, but surviving ancient stones were greatly cherished, reappearing in precious settings, whether as ring stones with circumscriptions cut in their gold surrounds or incorporated in sumptuous liturgical objects, most strikingly the 300 stones originally mounted on the 13th-century shrine of the Magi in the Cathedral of Cologne, Germany. But practical knowledge of the craft was by no means lost, as sporadic revivals demonstrate. Some of considerable artistic importance, such as Carolingian rock crystal intaglios, notably the large 9th-century Lothair Crystal, illustrating the story of Susanna and the Elders, and a group of multifigured cameos, some with Hebrew inscriptions, have been attributed to 13th-century engravers working for Emperor Frederick II.

The surge of interest in the arts of Antiquity during the Renaissance of the 15th century fueled a far more widespread revival, in which both artists and collectors avidly sought ancient stones. Pope Paul II probably acquired, among many other gems, the Hellenistic cameo-engraved tazza, which passed into the collection of Lorenzo the Magnificent in Florence and was later called the Tazza Farnese after its eventual ownership by the Farnese family. In the wake of this passion, craftsmen in Italy, where both intaglio and cameo cutting flourished, began to emulate Classical examples. Renaissance engravers such as Francesco Arichini and Pietro della Pescia, however, did not slavishly copy Classical models but invented their own images of Classical and biblical subjects. They also created striking portraits, such as those of Girolamo Savonarola, Lodovico il Moro, and Lorenzo de' Medici, as well as the rulers of France and England. During the 16th century, engraved stones became ever more luxurious, with large cameo busts reminiscent of the art of Tullio Lombardo, others executed in a mosaic of colored stones, and small, cursorily executed cameos used to decorative effect on vessels and mirrors; a favorite set of images were cameos of the Twelve Caesars.

The grandest objects, however, were the cases incorporating sets of large reverse-engraved intaglio plaques by Valerio Belli of Vicenza and Giovanni Bernardi of Castel Bolognese. Their work, like that of their contemporaries, is frequently found copied in metal plaquettes. The last great collector of the period was the Habsburg emperor Rudolf II, who established the Miseroni family of engravers in his residence in Prague; many of the magnificent Rudolfine gold-enameled gem mounts have been preserved in the collection now in the Kunsthistorisches Museum in Vienna, Austria. Large cameo busts of Christ and the Virgin, many on bloodstone, after medals by Antonio Abondio, date from the 17th century, during the Counter Reformation, although newer luxuries such as carved ivory and engraved glass now largely displaced gem engraving. Carvings on large shells, whereby the layers were used to imitate those of much more laboriously engraved sardonyx, decorated *Kunstkammer* (cabinet of rarities) objects. Engravers used other easily cut substances such as ivory and coral for series of small portraits of whole dynasties such as the Habsburgs, although the Baroque age also produced a small number of ostentatious court portraits in precious stones such as sapphire, emerald, the very hard ruby, and even the odd laboriously engraved diamond.

In the 18th century, the art of gem engraving experienced a last great revival, once again stimulated by admiration of the arts of Antiquity. As visitors flocked to Italy to view extant old collections and acquire gems for themselves from the many dealers who set up to cater to them, a number of new workshops began to spring up, especially in Rome, which remained the center of this craft for a century. The engravers of this period successfully copied or varied the imagery of ancient, primarily Roman, gems, cutting their stones in a most accomplished technique on the traditional quartzes, so that it would often be difficult to distinguish between ancient and 18th-century gems, were it not that many of these Neoclassical artists were sufficiently self-confident to sign their stones; but they also practiced new genres, such as portraits of *uomini illustri*, famous men of bygone centuries, the equivalents of library busts, and also executed likenesses of visitors to Rome, as in contemporary busts often depicted *all'antica* (after the antique).

A most important branch of their art consisted of cutting copies of the famous ancient sculptures that were Italy's prime attraction, such as the Apollo Belvedere and the Hercules Farnese, for ring stones and medallions; to these they later added works by the most celebrated moderns, Antonio Canova, Bertel Thorvaldsen, and John Gibson. The most famous Roman workshop during this period was that of the Pichler family, of which the most illustrious members were Giovanni and his brother Luigi. The popularity of the Grand Tour among the British materially contributed to establishing another important center for gem engraving in London; both Edward Burch and his pupil Nathaniel Marchant, who studied and worked in Rome for 16 years, were elected Royal Academicians; in Paris the engraver Jacques Guay was patronized by Madame de Pompadour.

This all-encompassing passion for engraved gems, which pervaded a vast swath of literate Europe, lasted well into the 19th century. Manufacturers of molded impressions in sulfur or plaster catered to collectors eager to study as many examples of the art as possible. Mounted in small sets of drawers, or in fictive "folio volumes" and hanging frames for the library, these impressions made treasured souvenirs. James Tassie in London eventually overtook manufacturers in Rome and Germany. Subsidized by Catherine the Great of Russia, the greatest collector of the age, Tassie offered almost 16,000 models in red sulfur, a white, glassy "enamel," and colored-glass pastes, imitation intaglio stones. Because sealing with a finger ring or pendent fob seal had become common, when fashion decreed the wearing of numerous little seals with different meaningful images, glass pastes came into their own, so much so that they are usually known by the generic name of *tassies*. For ladies' jewelry, cameos became increasingly the fashion around the turn of the 19th century, not least through the influence of Napoléon and his consort, Josephine de Beauharnais. A further consequence of the demand for cameos was the revival of imitative shell cutting, with many specialist workshops and even stone engravers offering cheaper versions of their gems in shell. Shell cameos were enormously popular throughout the 19th century and have remained a flourishing industry to the present day, even if the images became more and more repetitive busts of Bacchus, Ceres, and Flora.

True stone cameo cutting, also of a repetitive kind, flourished again in Second Empire Paris, with large profile busts of ladies set in handsome gold and pearl mounts; intaglio engraving experienced a special revival in work for the refined and precious "archaeological jewelry" of the firm of Castellani and his compeers. Even today, a few engravers cater to the demands of rare enthusiasts, and collectors appreciative of an art that has left us many masterpieces during the more than two millennia of its history eagerly compete for those antique examples that have not found a permanent home in museums.

GERTRUD SEIDMANN

See also **Apollo Belvedere**; **Canova, Antonio**; **Thorvaldsen, Bertel**

Further Reading

Boardman, John, *Greek Gems and Finger Rings: Early Bronze Age to Late Classical*, London: Thames and Hudson, 1970; New York: Abrams, 1972

Bonner, Campbell, *Studies in Magical Amulets, Chiefly Graeco-Egyptian*, Ann Arbor: University of Michigan Press, 1950
Brown, Clifford Malcolm (editor), *Engraved Gems: Survivals and Revivals*, Washington, D.C.: National Gallery of Art, 1997
Dalton, O.M., *Catalogue of the Engraved Gems of the Post-Classical Period in the Department of British and Mediaeval Antiquities and Ethnography in the British Museum*, London: British Museum, 1915
Henig, Martin, *The Content Family Collection of Ancient Cameos*, Houlton, Maine: Content, and Oxford: Ashmolean Museum, 1990
Kagan, Julia Osval'dovna, *Western European Cameos in the Hermitage Collection*, Leningrad: Aurora Art Publishers, 1973
Kornbluth, Genevra Alisoun, *Engraved Gems of the Carolingian Empire*, University Park: Pennsylvania State University Press, 1995
Plantzos, Dimitris, *Hellenistic Engraved Gems*, Oxford and New York: Clarendon Press, 1999
Richter, Gisela Marie Augusta, *Engraved Gems of the Greeks, Etruscans, and Romans*, 2 vols., London: Phaidon, 1968–71
Seidmann, Gertrud, *Nathaniel Marchant, Gem Engraver*, London: The Walpole Society, 1989

ENTOMBMENT GROUP

See **Lamentation and Deposition Group**

JACOB EPSTEIN 1880–1959 *United States, active in England*

A pioneer of direct carving and primitivism, the dominant sculptor of the British prewar avant-garde, and an original architectural sculptor, Jacob Epstein was also the leading portrait sculptor of his day. He was a supporter of and influence on the young Henry Moore and has also been acknowledged by contemporaries, including Antony Gormley and Michael Sandle. In Epstein's obituary Henry Moore described the sculptor as having "taken the brickbats for modern art." Epstein is as important for the media and academic controversies that centered on his identity and work as for the works themselves.

The conservatism of Edwardian England made the uninhibited, if austere, vigor of Epstein's nude male and female figures for the British Medical Association Building (architect Charles Holden) appear shockingly radical. Though naturalistic and Classically inspired, they marked his rejection of the ornate, anodyne Classicism of much contemporary public sculpture. The sexual candor, especially of the pregnant *Maternity* (1910), provoked an outcry and inaugurated Epstein's notoriety, which escalated as a result of the repeated provocation to media and popular public taste, prudery, literalism, and religious sentiment that his large carvings and bronzes presented. Pregnancy is a recurrent theme in the voluptuous Indian-inspired *Maternity*; his *Female Figure in Flenite*; *Figure in Flenite*; the two versions of *Venus*; and, most controversially, *Genesis*. The elemental power and heroic masculinity of his Whitmanesque *Adam*, which embodied the generative force of humankind, was similarly confrontational.

Epstein had early discovered non-European sculpture in the Trocadéro, Musée Guimet, and Musée Cernuschi in Paris and in the British Museum. From about 1912 he began to collect African and Oceanic sculpture, one of the first to do so in Great Britain. Both his carvings and to a lesser extent his bronzes reflect the formal and symbolic influence of these sculptures. He amassed a superb collection, which was exhibited at the Tate Gallery in London in 1960 before its dispersal.

During a brief but intense friendship with Eric Gill between 1910 and 1912, Epstein began to carve directly in stone and to develop simplified, geometric styles of great mass and presence, drawing inspiration from ancient Egyptian and Assyrian, Indian, and African sculpture. *Sun God*, begun in 1910, *Maternity*, and the tomb of Oscar Wilde all date from this developmental period. The Assyrian-inspired Wilde tomb, with its winged male nude in flight emerging from within a massive stone block, represented a break with funerary sculpture traditions comparable to Constantin Brancusi's Tania Rachevskaia monument (*The Kiss*, 1907).

The formal lucidity, repetition, and direct technique of Brancusi's and Amedeo Modigliani's sculpture, which Epstein encountered in Paris in 1912, acted as a catalyst to the increasingly abstract and formalized direction of his work: *Sunflower* (1913), the three pairs of mating *Doves*, the two flenite figures, and the two Africanized *Venus* figures. During 1913 through 1915 Epstein associated himself with the group around Wyndham Lewis at the Rebel Art Centre in London but was closest to the philosopher and aesthetician T.E. Hulme, who saw in Epstein and the painter David Bomberg the emergence of a distinctively modern art based on geometric forms. Epstein's *Rock Drill*, a towering white, mechanistically stylized male figure mounted astride a real rock drill, appeared to realize Hulme's vision. Epstein later claimed to have considered making the figure kinetic. It is now widely seen as one of the most important British sculptures of the 20th century, but in 1915 it was ignored or ridiculed as "the Prussian war god," its inspiring optimism about the machine age destroyed by the mass slaughter of the trenches. The work is often associated with the ethos and aggressive virility of Vorticism, which came into being through Lewis and Ezra Pound in 1914, but Epstein neither signed the Vorticist Manifesto nor published in its journal, *Blast*. It was his younger contemporary and acolyte, Henri Gaudier-Brzeska, who became one of the movement's leaders.

After 1918 Epstein never returned to the extreme formal radicalism of the prewar years, although many of the themes and primitivizing and totemic elements recur. His commissioned carvings during the 1920s—the *Rima* relief and his starkly architectonic *Night* and *Day* for the London Underground Electric Railway (now London Transport) headquarters (architect C. Holden)—are characterized by symmetrically composed masses and the synthesis of non-European stylistic elements with traditional Western subjects and compositions; *Night* is a pietà in all but name. Both these public works gave rise to controversy; supporters such as R.H. Wilenski saw them as major contributions of modern architectural sculpture, while opponents, including several of the New Sculptors, accused the works of being ugly and barbaric. They were also subjected to anti-Semitic attacks. Criticism was not confined to his carved works; *Risen Christ*, an over-life-size bronze redolent of Donatello and medieval cathedral jamb figures, was excoriated for its radical rethinking of sacrosanct cultural and visual clichés.

The primitivist and iconoclastic tendencies manifest in his works from the 1920s are even more apparent in the uncommissioned carvings produced during the 1930s—*Genesis*, *Primeval Gods*, *Behold the Man*, *Consummatum Est*, *Adam*, and *Jacob and the Angel*. These works gave rise to populist and highbrow criticism that conflated hostility to primitivism, fears of "barbarism" and political subversion, and the artist's Jewish origins into insidiously anti-Semitic art criticism, feature articles, cartoons, and doggerel verse. By contrast, his modeled portraits, many of which were commissioned, were widely acclaimed for their insight and expressive vitality, although they have subsequently been sidelined by the dominant modernism of art historical discourse. His 500 or so portraits ranged from commissions from the beautiful, great, and good to the social outcasts, nightclub performers, and eccentrics whom he invited to sit. Some of his favorite models were South Asian, Chinese, African, and African American.

The disconcerting dichotomy contemporaries perceived between the realism of Epstein's bronzes and the formal distortion and primitivism of his carvings was not anomalous to the sculptor. He rejected the fashionable tendency to rate carving above modeling; his own "truth to materials" was that clay lent itself to observation and realism, while stone better expressed abstract ideas.

The most successful works of Epstein's last decade, with the exception of *Lazarus* and the war memorial for the Trades Union Congress, were monumental modeled figures commissioned as part of the recon-

515

struction of damaged religious buildings after World War II. His *Madonna and Child* was a critical and public success and led to a late flood of public commissions, including *Christ in Majesty* for the Cathedral of Llandaff in Wales and *St. Michael and Satan* for the new Cathedral of Coventry.

EVELYN SILBER

Biography

Born in New York City, United States, 10 November 1880. Educated at The Art Students League, New York, where he studied under George Grey Barnard; moved to Paris in 1902 and studied briefly at the École des Beaux-Arts and for about a year at the Académie Julian; moved to London, 1905; naturalized British citizen, 1910; associated with Rebel Art Centre, London; conscripted into Royal Fusiliers, 1917, and discharged, 1918; began to collect African and Oceanic sculpture, *ca.* 1912; a founding member of the London Group, 1914. Honorary Ph.D., University of Aberdeen, 1938; knighted 1954; honorary D.C.L., Oxford University, 1955. Died in London, England, 19 August 1959.

Selected Works

1908 Eighteen figures; Portland stone; Zimbabwe House, The Strand, London, England

1910 *Maternity*; Hoptonwood stone; Leeds City Art Gallery, England

1910 *Sun God* (completed 1933); Hoptonwood stone; Metropolitan Museum of Art, New York City, United States

1912 Tomb of Oscar Wilde; Hoptonwood stone; Père-Lachaise Cemetery, Paris, France

1913 *Doves No. 2*; marble; Israel Museum, Jerusalem, Israel

1913 *Female Figure in Flenite*; serpentine; Tate Gallery, London, England

1913 *Mother and Child*; marble; Museum of Modern Art, New York City, United States

1914 *Rock Drill*; plaster, readymade drill (dismantled by sculptor); reconstruction: 1973, Birmingham Museum and Art Gallery, England; bronze; 1914–16, Tate Gallery, London, England

1915 *Torso in Metal* from the "*Rock Drill*"; gunmetal; National Gallery of Canada, Ottawa, Canada; other casts in bronze: Tate Gallery, London, England; Museum of Modern Art, New York City, United States; Art Gallery, Auckland, New Zealand

1916 *Venus No. 2*; marble; Yale University Art Gallery, New Haven, Connecticut, United States

1919 *Risen Christ*; bronze; Scottish National Gallery of Modern Art, Edinburgh, Scotland

1925 *Rima* (W.H. Hudson memorial); Portland stone; Hyde Park, London, England

1929 *Night* and *Day*; Portland stone; London Underground Headquarters, St. James's Park Station, London, England

1930 *Genesis*; marble; Whitworth Art Gallery, Manchester, England

1936 *Consummatum Est*; alabaster; Scottish National Gallery of Modern Art, Edinburgh, Scotland

1939 *Adam*; alabaster; Harewood House, Leeds, England

1941 *Jacob and the Angel*; alabaster; Tate Gallery, London, England

1948 *Lazarus*; Hoptonwood stone; New College Chapel, Oxford, England

1952 *Madonna and Child*; lead; Heythrop College, University of London, Cavendish Square, London, England

1953 *Social Consciousness*; bronze; Fairmount Park, Philadelphia, Pennsylvania, United States

1955 *Christ in Majesty*; aluminium; Cathedral of Llandaff, Wales

1956 *War Memorial*; Trades Union Congress, Great Russell Street, London, England

1958 *St. Michael and Satan*; bronze; Cathedral of Coventry, England

Further Reading

Buckle, Richard, *Epstein Drawings*, London: Faber, 1962

Buckle, Richard, *Jacob Epstein, Sculptor*, London: Faber and Faber, 1963

Cork, Richard, *Vorticism and Abstract Art in the First Machine Age*, 2 vols., London: Gordon Fraser, 1976

Cork, Richard, *Art beyond the Gallery in Early 20th-Century England*, New Haven, Connecticut: Yale University Press, 1985

Cork, Richard, *Jacob Epstein*, London: Tate Gallery, and Princeton, New Jersey: Princeton University Press, 1999

Dieren, Bernard van, *Epstein*, London and New York: John Lane, 1920

Hapgood, Hutchins, *The Spirit of the Ghetto: Studies of the Jewish Quarter in New York*, New York: Funk and Wagnalls, 1902; reprint, Cambridge, Massachusetts: Harvard University Press, 1983

Haskell, Arnold, and T.E. Hulme, *The Sculptor Speaks: Jacob Epstein to Arnold L. Haskell, a Series of Conversations on Art*, London: Heinemann, 1931

Powell, L.B., *Jacob Epstein*, London: Chapman and Hall, 1932

Silber, Evelyn, *The Sculpture of Epstein: With a Complete Catalogue*, Oxford: Phaidon, and Lewisburg, Pennsylvania: Bucknell University Press, 1986

Silber, Evelyn (editor), *Jacob Epstein: Sculpture and Drawings* (exhib. cat.), Leeds, West Yorkshire: Leeds City Art Galleries, and London: Whitechapel Art Gallery, 1987

Wellington, Hubert, *Jacob Epstein*, London: Benn, and McPherson, Kansas: Smalley, 1925

ROCK DRILL

Jacob Epstien (1880–1959)

1913–1916

bronze

h. 94 cm

Tate Gallery, London, England

Rock Drill, Jacob Epstein's most astonishing work, has never been repeated or reproduced. It remains the most mechanistic of all Epstein's major sculptures, its origins lying in his enthusiasm for primitivism and the power of totemic structures.

Rock Drill was shown in the March 1915 London Group exhibition and attracted the same reaction as Marcel Duchamp's *Bicycle Wheel* when it was exhibited as a work of art. The reception of Epstein's work, however, was affected by World War I. Several critics were disturbed by the juxtaposition of the black drill and the white robot-man. An article by P.G. Konody in the *Observer* (14 March 1915), for instance, stated that *Rock Drill* had "only the remotest connection with the art of sculpture" and declared "the whole effect unutterably loathsome." The *Manchester Guardian* (15 March 1915), on the other hand, appreciated the work as "a real piece of invention, a synthetic shape which has a swift, significant interest, even beauty, all its own."

All the preparatory studies for *Rock Drill* incorporated the drill, which served as the most important element of the design. In these studies Epstein added new elements, including a tensioned body conveyed by a judicious use of semiorganic forms akin to the stripped muscles of anatomic studies. In the center of the drawings he placed a commanding angular piece, consisting of a woman pierced by a man inverted below her. The tension of the embrace leads to an amalgamation of the male and female figures, expressing the idea of copulation much more clearly than does the allusion in Constantin Brancusi's *The Kiss* (1907). Epstein took the opportunity to explore the possibility of not only a monumental embodiment of masculinity but also an exacerbation of the male force before a machine. Half human and half automaton, the figure appears to be the harbinger of a different, harsher, and more disturbing world.

Encouraged by T.E. Hulme, Epstein wanted to express his passionate concern with sexuality and procreative forces, revealed in the preparatory drawings of this period. At the same time, the creation of *Rock Drill* recalled also the prewar days of 1913, which stressed the power of the machine on humankind. Viewed from behind, the drilling rides far above the ground and a cloud floats from the side of the drill as if to emphasize its airborne dimensions.

During the realization of his preparatory drawings, Epstein situated the figures between totemic idols and Cubist forms in the process of creating the sculpture. He attached a great importance to symbolism and began to question the metamorphosis of his concept from the idea of love and procreation to the dehumanized robot as the drilling figure itself.

At the beginning, Epstein meant *Rock Drill* to be an optimistic statement, a metaphor of the heroic modern figure: the driller epitomizes humankind's command of superhuman power. The horrors of World War I, however, contributed to a shift from the positive to the negative, as Epstein understood it:

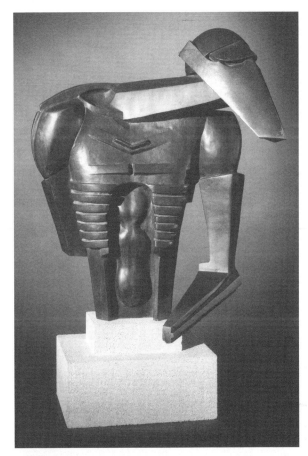

Rock Drill
© Tate Gallery, London / Art Resources, NY

517

It was in the experimental pre-war days of 1913 that I was fired to do the rock drill, and my ardour for machinery (short-lived) expended itself upon the purchase of an actual drill, second-hand, and upon this I made and mounted a machine like robot, visored, menacing, and carrying within itself its progeny protectively ensconced. Here is the armed, sinister of to-day and to-morrow. No humanity, only the terrible Frankenstein's monster we have made ourselves into. (Epstein, 1940)

The critical and public interpretations of *Rock Drill* as an aggressive menace had discouraged the sculptor, who hated the war. Epstein was saddened at such interpretations. Two of his best friends, Henri Gaudier-Brzeska and Hulme, were killed during the war, and Epstein himself suffered a "complete break-down" later in 1918.

Affected by these interpretations, Epstein concluded that *Rock Drill* should be excluded from his oeuvre. Richard Cork (1987) notes that Epstein's widow recalled the sculptor explaining "that he abandoned the drill because he hadn't made it himself, it was just a machine."

By 1916, however, Epstein had reflected on the controversial status of the readymade in his art, which differed from Duchamp's. He decided to retain only the man-made of his *Rock Drill* and cast it in metal. The sculpture was exhibited at the London Group show in the summer of 1916 under the title: *Torso in Metal from the "Rock Drill."* Trying to humanize the machine, the artist did not change the symbol of his work but created instead a unique sculpture in his long career.

DOÏNA LEMNY

Further Reading

Babson, Jane F., *The Epsteins: A Family Album*, Chearsley, Aylesbury: Taylor Hall, 1984
Black, Robert, *The Art of Jacob Epstein*, Cleveland, Ohio: World, 1942
Cork, Richard, "Vorticism," in *Vorticism and Its Allies* (exhib. cat.), London: Hayward Gallery, 1974
Cork, Richard, "1913–1916. Rock Drill," in *Jacob Epstein, Sculpture and Drawings*, London: Whitechapel Art Gallery, 1987
Epstein, Jacob, *Let There Be Sculpture*, New York: Putnam, 1940
Ireland, Geoffrey, *Epstein: A Camera Study of the Sculptor at Work*, London: Deutsch, 1957
James, Philip, "Introduction," in *Epstein, Book of Illustrations, Including a Number of Works Not Exhibited*, London: Arts Council of Great Britain, 1952
Rothenstein, John, "Introduction," in *Epstein*, London: Arts Council of Great Britain, 1961
Schinman, Edward P., and Barbara Ann Schinman (editors), *Jacob Epstein: A Catalogue of the Collection of Edward P. Schinman*, Rutherford, New Jersey: Fairleigh Dickinson University Press, 1970
Silber, Evelyn, *Rebel Angel: Sculpture and Watercolours by Sir Jacob Epstein, 1880–1959*, Birmingham: City Museum and Art Gallery, 1980

EQUESTRIAN STATUE

An equestrian statue is a monumental sculpture of a horse and rider that serves a public purpose. The rider is typically a portrait, usually of an emperor, ruler, monarch, or other military leader. Typically, these monuments commemorate and convey the authority and dignity of the rider. Ideally, the equestrian statue is freestanding, although some use artfully conceived external supports. The complexity of the composition depends on whether the horse is still, striding, or rearing and whether it is freestanding or requires additional supports. The challenge for the sculptor is to support the massive weight of the body of the horse surmounted by a rider on four slender, vertical structures: the legs. Equestrian sculpture makes use of a variety of materials, including marble and wood. The most dynamic examples are constructed of bronze, because the material's tensile strength allows for more elaborate compositions; the presence of an internal armature extending from within the horse into the base or pedestal of the entire work allows for a truly freestanding work. A description of seminal examples of equestrian statuary from its Antique origins through its rise in the Renaissance to its decline in the 19th and 20th centuries illustrates the development and evolution of the genre.

Equestrian monuments were certainly the greatest sculptural challenge in Antiquity. Although no Greek examples survive, their existence is known through ancient literature, such as Pliny's *Natural History* (1st century CE) as well as fragmentary evidence and statuettes such as the one at the National Museum of Naples (Museo Archeologico Nazionale), presumably of Alexander the Great. Other images of a rider on his horse, such as those depicted on grave stelae, are believed to have commemorated the rider's heroic victory during either battle or competition.

The few surviving examples from the Roman era tremendously impacted the future of the genre. Although the Marcus Aurelius monument (161–80 CE) was not the only equestrian statue from the Roman era, it was the most significant. A few equestrian monuments from the Roman republican period (509–27 BCE) were discovered at Pompeii and Herculaneum during the excavations of those cities in the mid 18th century. During the Roman imperial period (27 BCE–323 CE), however, bronze was reserved for the emperor as a visual statement of his authority. The over-life-size bronze of the Roman emperor Marcus Aurelius was originally gilt. It is the only bronze imperial example to have survived from Antiquity, perhaps because it was once believed to represent Constantine, the first Christian emperor. Its prominent location, originally on the grounds of the Lateran Palace, papal property given by Constantine, may have also added to the sustained influence of this work through the centuries. The group was transferred to the Piazza del Campidoglio in Rome in the 16th century. The bearded emperor wears a tunic, rather than a military uniform, and rides without stirrups or saddle. He gestures with his right hand either to command or to pacify. The group is contemplative, rather than militaristic. The dignified authority conveyed by the rider is echoed by the steady forward movement of the horse, which is midstride with a raised right front hoof.

The *Regisole* (Sun King) is the only other equestrian statue to have survived through Antiquity. The group was transferred from Ravenna to Pavia. Had it been in Rome, perhaps more depictions of the *Regisole* would exist. Instead, only a 1505 woodcut and a few descriptions of this work, which was destroyed in 1796, survive. Suggestions for its date range from the 3rd to 6th centuries CE. Also uncertain is the identity of the rider, who may have been one of a number of possible emperors. The horse's natural gait, described as a high trot, appears to have been the most significant feature of the work for subsequent generations. Leonardo da Vinci, in particular, was profoundly influenced by this work when planning the Sforza and Trivulzio equestrian monuments.

Another influential Antique group, although without riders, was the *Horses of San Marco*. The dating of this bronze group of four horses is still controversial but is somewhere between 300 BCE and 400 CE. The group was looted from Constantinople in 1204 and displayed on the facade of the Basilica of San Marco in Venice about 1265.

Few equestrian monuments were executed during the Middle Ages, and it is possible that economic and symbolic factors, as well as a loss of technological knowledge necessary to cast such life-size works, were reasons for the decline of this genre during the Medieval period. Because few personal monuments were erected in the Middle Ages, among them the equestrian statuette of Charlemagne (Carolingian sculpture), there are also few examples of large-scale equestrian monuments. The majority of these are in Italy and were intended for tombs or funerary monuments. Fewer still were made in northern Europe and often had less to do with an individual and more to do with personifying virtues. The interest in equestrian statues north of the Alps may have been inspired by the Holy Roman Emperor Frederick II, who was fascinated by Italian culture, art, and politics.

One example from northern Europe is the Bamberg *Rider* (1230–37), a sandstone, life-size group in the nave of the Cathedral of Bamberg, Germany. Placed on a large socle attached to a pier, the work is very much a part of its architectural setting. The identity of the rider is disputed. Some argue that it is a literal representation of a ruler, such as Stephen I, king of Hungary, or Frederick II. The rider's frequent association with Frederick II can be attributed to his patronage of the cathedral and residence in Germany at the time of the Bamberg *Rider*'s creation. Others claim that the figure is a personification of Virtue based on an actual, historical person. However, if the Bamberg *Rider* does indeed represent Frederick II, it is not a literal likeness, but an allegorical representation of the contemporary emperor as worldly ruler. The figure wears fashionable, courtly attire with a crown in order to create an aristocratic demeanor of a contemporary ruler within an ecclesiastical context, rather than one with a militaristic or imperial sensibility. The horse and rider show little sense of movement or implied movement.

The Magdeburg equestrian statue (or Magdeburg *Rider*) was executed at approximately the same time as the Bamberg *Rider* and also has been identified with a variety of historical figures. The work is a life-size, freestanding statue carved in stone and stands under a baldachin within an architectural framework. Unlike the Bamberg *Rider*, the statue in Magdeburg, Germany, is displayed in a public, secular context in the old market square in front of the town hall. In addition to possibly representing Otto I, the founder of Magdeburg, or the contemporary ruler Frederick II, some have suggested that it personifies the Holy Roman Empire or symbolizes the judicial and legal authority of a ruler. The group includes two accompanying female allegorical figures. As in the Marcus Aurelius monument, the Magdeburg statue dons everyday attire typical of its time. Unlike the Antique group, however, the Medieval work fails to convey a strong sense of movement. The original sculpture has been moved indoors, and a bronze replica of the group from the 1960s stands in its place.

The majority of Medieval equestrian statues in Italy commemorated individuals primarily in the form of funerary monuments. A possible early source for this trend is seen in a marble relief from the tomb of Guglielmus (Church of Santissima Annunziata, Florence), who died in 1289 in the Battle of Campaldino. It depicts the deceased in full armor on horseback charging into battle. The relief honors a vigorous military hero, not an emperor or ruler, thus beginning a trend of honoring military heroes and condottieri with equestrian statues in tomb monuments. Even painted equestrian images adorned tombs of fallen condottieri, such as the equestrian portrait of Sir John Hawkwood in the

Cathedral of Florence (original fresco by Agnolo Gaddi, replaced by Paolo Uccello in 1436).

The Veronese Scaligeri family of the 14th century adorned their tombs with equestrian statues. The most notable example is the stone equestrian statue for the tomb of Cangrande I, who died in 1329. The original group is now in the museum of the Castelvecchio, Verona, with a copy in its place. Like the riders of the Scaligeri tombs to follow, Cangrande is shown in full armor with raised sword and his helmet cast behind him. He is depicted as a victorious warrior or condottiere, full of confidence, if not arrogance, expressed by his broad grin. The horse is motionless and freestanding with the weight of the group carried by the horse's legs, which have been structurally enhanced by the "drapery" covering the legs to create broader support. Few medieval equestrian statues rival the boldness of this group. A statue of a later member of the Scaligeri family, Cansignorio I, similarly shows the figure in full armor atop his tomb, but here the weight of the stone group is supported by an obvious post directly beneath the body of the horse. Although affiliated with churches, the large scale of these tomb monuments necessitated their placement outdoors, which gave them a secular and public forum as well.

The equestrian statue and tomb for Paolo Savelli (1405; Church of Santa Maria Gloriosa dei Frari, Venice) commemorates the Venetian citizen who fought against the Paduans and died on 3 October 1405. The monument, which some have attributed to Jacopo della Quercia, is significant for its construction in wood, a lighter and more easily carved material than stone, but less enduring; the wood was covered in gesso and the group was colorfully painted. Although it is a freestanding group, it is so closely connected to the marble wall tomb on which it rests that it cannot be appreciated in the round. The horse's implied mobility is controlled by the rider. Like the Veronese Scaligeri statues, the figure also wears armor, which here is draped with a mantle.

The renewed interest in Antiquity during the Renaissance revived the tradition of equestrian statues, paving the way for further development of the genre. The revival of portraiture and of successful bronze casting techniques during the Renaissance helped promote a new wave of equestrian monuments. Although Renaissance artists looked to Antique works such as the Marcus Aurelius monument and the *Horses of San Marco* for inspiration, their immediate, Italian past was also influential. Renaissance artists and patrons, like their medieval counterparts, did not exclusively reserve the genre for rulers and honored their military heroes with equestrian statues. The merging of these two distinct traditions created the Renaissance equestrian statue, often considered the height of the genre.

It is frequently assumed that Donatello's *Gattamelata* (1447–53) was the first bronze equestrian statue since Antiquity. This credit actually goes to Niccolò Baroncelli and Antonio di Cristoforo, who in 1441 erected the bronze statue of Nicolò d'Este of Ferrara on horseback (destroyed in 1796). However, this life-size bronze group did not have the impact of Donatello's *Gattamelata*, because it retained many medieval qualities and was not truly freestanding like the Marcus Aurelius monument.

Donatello's *Gattamelata* was executed in Padua for one of the Venetian Republic's condottieri, Erasmo da Narni, who died in 1443. Instead of a realistic portrait of the aged and ailing Narni, Donatello idealized him, depicting him in the prime of life. *Gattamelata* nearly meets the technical challenge of supporting a large bronze horse and rider on four slender legs. However, Donatello placed a cannonball beneath the raised front hoof for added stability and as an example of modern artillery. Although it was neither the first bronze equestrian since Antiquity, nor the first equestrian statue dedicated to a military hero, it was the first bronze equestrian statue honoring a commander, rather than an imperial leader or sovereign. Because of its overt associations to a Roman emperor, the Venetian Senate was quite perturbed. Like its medieval predecessors, *Gattamelata* was not completely independent of funerary associations, given that its location was in the Church of St. Anthony's cemetery and the base of the statue includes Classical associations with Antique sarcophagi. Classical details also adorn the armor of *Gattamelata*. Nevertheless, the primary function of *Gattamelata* was to commemorate and immortalize the general's fame and heroism, and the figure appears to survey his troops on the battlefield. His baton alludes to his authority. However, unlike the Marcus Aurelius monument, *Gattamelata* has stirrups and a saddle and Donatello's horse is much larger and stockier in proportion to the rider. The fame of Donatello's monument quickly spread and inspired another generation of artists and patrons in this genre.

Andrea del Verrocchio's equestrian statue of Bartolomeo Colleoni in Venice sought to rival both the Marcus Aurelius monument and *Gattamelata*. Verrocchio began the Colleoni statue in 1479, but following his death, it was completed by Alessandro Leopardi, who cast the group based on Verrocchio's model. The equestrian statue was in place by 1494. Colleoni, also a condottiere for Venice, left a portion of his estate to the republic and stipulated that an equestrian monument be erected in his honor on the Piazza San Marco, although the Senate placed the group in the Piazza Santi Giovanni e Paolo. Colleoni clearly saw himself as a challenger to the actual Gattamelata (Narni) and therefore believed he should have an equally elaborate monument. This equestrian statue, which originally was gilded, was more contemporary than Donatello's Classical statue and is without funerary associations.

The group's overall composition is far more dynamic, active, and open—and slightly larger—than the more restrained and stately *Gattamelata*. Verrocchio adjusted the proportions, making the commander larger by slightly reducing the size of the horse, which resulted in a depiction of Colleoni as a fearsome and physically imposing warrior who commands the horse and the surrounding space. Verrocchio achieved this in part by having the rider stand in his stirrups with a *contrapposto* (a natural pose with the weight of one leg, the shoulder, and hips counterbalancing one another) posture. The rider appears to react to the vigorous movement of the horse, and both horse and rider unite in implied forward movement. Verrocchio's Colleoni monument also owes a debt to the painted equestrian group of Niccolò da Tolentino by Andrea del Castagno in Florence (1456).

Leonardo da Vinci's drawings for two equestrian statues, the Sforza and the Trivulzio monuments, also fall into the military equestrian category, although neither project was ever completed. From 1482 to 1490, Leonardo executed a number of studies for the monument to Ludovico Sforza, the Duke of Milan and condottiere for the Visconti rulers of Milan. Leonardo initially planned an equestrian group with a horse rearing over a fallen enemy, which would have provided more stability to the group. Had this been executed, it would have been an astonishing achievement, but ultimately Leonardo modified his designs into a striding horse. The Antique *Regisole* in Pavia (destroyed in 1796), with its natural gait, greatly influenced Leonardo's design. To achieve this challenging design, Leonardo devised a piece-mold casting process to preserve the model and to cast the work in a single piece, something that could not be achieved for such a monumental work through the lost-wax bronze casting method. For this work he created a full-scale terracotta model (1489–93). After the French invaded in 1499, French troops used it for target practice and it was ultimately destroyed, with no further mention after 1501. Although this revised plan was abandoned, the designs for the rearing horse remained influential until the genre's next great development in the 17th century.

After the Sforza monument was abandoned, Leonardo was requested to work on another tomb statue in Milan for Gian Giacomo Trivulzio. The artist's designs for this monument date between 1506 and 1511, and again these include a rearing horse over a fallen victim. Once more, the plans were modified into the *Regisole*-type trotting horse used in his Sforza monument designs. Like so many of Leonardo's works, the Trivulzio monument was also abandoned, but its significance endured.

Despite interest in equestrian statuary during the 15th century, as expressed by at least two of the most enduring examples of the genre, the popularity of equestrian monuments waned during the 16th century. There were many commissions, but not a single project was completed. Instead of honoring victorious military heroes, as it had in the Middle Ages and the Renaissance, the equestrian statue reclaimed its imperial Roman purpose by becoming a public symbol of sovereign power and a statement of political propaganda. It is likely that the catalyst for this renewed association was the move of the Marcus Aurelius monument to the seat of Rome's government and its rulers at the Campidoglio.

On the death of King Henry II of France in 1559, his consort, Catherine de' Medici, sought to commemorate the king with a bronze equestrian monument. Although she desired Michelangelo to undertake the project, the commission went to Daniele da Volterra in 1560, and the design relied on the Marcus Aurelius statue and a drawing by Michelangelo. Catherine stipulated that the horse be larger than that of the Marcus Aurelius and that it be cast in one piece, as in Leonardo's example. Only the horse was completed at the time of Volterra's death in 1566. The horse remained in Rome until 1622, when it was moved to Paris. By 1639 the rider was added, now in the form of King Louis XIII and designed by Pierre II Biard, and it was installed in the Place Royale. Like many other equestrian monuments, this group was destroyed during the French Revolution. The work is an important step in the evolution of the equestrian monument in Italy and in France, where it furthered an Italian influence upon the genre.

The genre's next proponent was Giambologna and his equestrian statue of Duke Cosimo I de' Medici (1590–92) for the Piazza della Signoria in Florence, the city's seat of government. Giambologna's work was a response to and culmination of his studies of the equestrian statue of Marcus Aurelius, the monuments by Donatello and Verrocchio, and his own studies of horses. The equestrian monument to Cosimo I is a compact, refined, and noble group. The horse, in midstride, is animated primarily by its untamed mane. The Duke, with his attributes, epitomizes control and authority, not only over the horse, but also over the citizens of Florence. The implied authority is made explicit in the three bronze reliefs on the base of the equestrian group, which illustrate highlights from the duke's career. This work inspired many versions by Giambologna and other artists whose patrons sought to capture their sovereignty and authority in a similar fashion, such as Giambologna's equestrian statue of Ferdinando I de' Medici , which was finished in 1638 by his student Pietro Tacca. Other examples include the equestrian statues of Rannuccio Farnese I (1620) and Alessandro Farnese (1625) by Francesco Mochi. With a stronger sense of dynamism and movement, this pair of equestrian statues builds upon Giambologna's example by conveying the same sense of dynastic authority.

Giambologna's chief assistant and eventual successor to his workshop was Tacca. King Philip III of Spain commissioned an equestrian monument from Giambologna's workshop in 1606, which was begun by Tacca in 1610 after the master's death. King Philip IV would later commission Tacca to cast another bronze equestrian statue, which would meet Leonardo's technical challenge to become the first monumental rearing equestrian statue and one of the supreme examples of equestrian statuary. The latter group was begun in 1634, cast in 1639–40, and shipped to Spain for assembly in 1640. Although influenced by Leonardo's designs, Tacca's unprecedented bronze equestrian monument of a rider on a rearing horse was also based on Peter Paul Rubens's now-lost painting *Philip IV on Horseback* (1628). Tacca, with the assistance of Galileo, resolved the technical difficulties of supporting the weight of a rearing horse with rider by using the horse's long flowing tail as an additional support to the two legs and concealing the required internal armature. The work was originally erected in the garden of Buen Retiro, Madrid, and is now in Madrid's Plaza de Oriente.

Gianlorenzo Bernini's *Constantine the Great* depicts the first Christian emperor on a rearing horse. The group was originally commissioned by Pope Innocent X in 1654 but languished after the pope's death. Eventually the commission was completed and the work was finally displayed in 1670. It is characteristically Baroque in its sense of drama and action, with natural light highlighting the group. The statue is carved out of marble and, therefore, is not freestanding because of its material and ambitious rearing-horse composition. The group is attached to the wall as if an extremely high relief, the attachment of which is ingeniously concealed with colored marble carved as billowing drapery. Bernini depicted Constantine at the pivotal moment of his conversion to Christianity. The rearing horse and the rider are caught in a specific and historically significant moment, which broadens the traditional notion of the equestrian portrait. The work is less a portrait of the emperor than an emblem of the significance of this event, which transformed the course of Christian history.

King Louis XIV of France commissioned an equestrian portrait group with a rearing horse (1670–73) from Bernini as a means of emphasizing his royal authority and command. The statue of King Louis XIV on a rearing horse as intended by Bernini is known only through a terracotta model because the king was so displeased with Bernini's finished marble product that he ordered François Girardon to recarve it as a group featuring Marcus Curtius. Bernini needed to devise a way to artfully disguise the support for the rearing horse because the work was in marble. The surviving terracotta model illustrates his solution by having the horse in the act of riding up a mountainous slope, the rocks of which serve as a support beneath the horse. The king's decision to reject the rearing-horse equestrian theme did not dissuade him from commissioning other equestrian statues from other sculptors, such as Girardon, Antoine Coysevox, and Martin Desjardins. These were all destroyed during the French Revolution. Louis XIV preferred the Classical equestrian portraits, as these were intended to convey a specific political message. Louis XIV rejected the challenging, rearing-horse type by Bernini because it simply was not suited for the replication required of a large-scale, prolific, and public political symbol. Although the large-scale examples based on Girardon's equestrian monument of Louis XIV were all destroyed during the French Revolution, models, statuettes, and engravings survive.

A direct relative of the equestrian statues created for Louis XIV might be the monument to Frederick Wilhelm, Grand Elector (1696–1709) by Andreas Schlüter. *The Great Elector of Brandenburg*, as it is also known, is the most important example of the genre in the German Baroque style. The work is a symbol of political authority and also reflects the Italian influences of Bernini and Mochi. The monumental work was cast by Johann Jakobi.

Étienne-Maurice Falconet's bronze equestrian monument of Peter the Great (1766–82) was commissioned by Catherine (II) the Great. The French author Denis Diderot probably suggested to Empress Catherine that Falconet be the artist to carry out the commission. The sculpture's inscription not only honors Peter the Great, but also refers to his daughter Catherine as his rightful successor: "*Petro Primo/Catherina Secunda.*" It is a powerful group that is more than twice life-size, and for it Falconet revived the rearing-horse type. Peter the Great is not presented as emperor or king, but as legislator and leader. Its novel, granite base mimics a steep, mountainous precipice. The upward motion of the base parallels the rearing motion of the horse, which augments the strength and drama of the work. In addition to the hind legs of the horse, the group is supported by its tail, which is also attached to the snake of Envy, thus giving the group three points of support.

After the French Revolution, the power and potency of equestrian statues as portraits of imperial authority and supremacy lost its vitality. Popular or elected leaders could not very well commemorate themselves in the manner of royalty, monarchs, or emperors. Nevertheless, many equestrian statues continued to be made throughout the 19th century. In fact, equestrian statues, often of military commanders, are found in nearly every major Western city, but these later examples are no longer as rare and no longer forge in new directions. These works typically convey bravery, are allegorical, or simply show an interest in verisimilitude, rather than demonstrate dynastic authority or power.

Carlo Marochetti made a name for himself in the genre of equestrian statuary with his bronze monument to Duke Emanuele Filiberto of Savoy (1838). The statue represents the Duke of Savoy returning from battle. While living in England, Marochetti also created a romantic and dynamic equestrian statue of Richard I (the Lionhearted) (*ca.* 1860). Both monuments are of distant past leaders and promote a sense of civic or national pride. Augustus Saint-Gaudens's bronze Sherman Monument (1892–1903) in Central Park, New York City is an equestrian statue of the United States Civil War general by one of America's best sculptors. The general, led by an allegorical figure of Victory, is shown on his march through Georgia during the war.

Few equestrian statues were made during the 20th century. Heroes and military or political leaders are now rarely depicted on horseback, thus bringing to an end the popularity of the equestrian statue.

STEPHANIE R. MILLER

See also **Bernini, Gianlorenzo; Coysevox, Antoine; Donatello (Donata di Betto Bardi); Falconet, Étienne-Maurice; Giambologna; Girardon, François; Jacopo della Quercia; Mochi, Francesco; Tacca Family**

Further Reading

Boström, Antonia, "Daniele da Volterra and the Equestrian Monument to Henry II of France," *The Burlington Magazine* 809 (December 1995)

Covi, Dario, "The Italian Renaissance and the Equestrian Monument," in *Leonardo da Vinci's Sforza Monument Horse: The Art and Engineering*, edited by Diane Cole Ahl, Bethlehem, Pennsylvania: Lehigh University Press, and London: Associated University Presses, 1995

Glorious Horsemen: Equestrian Art in Europe, 1500–1800, Springfield, Massachusetts: Museum of Fine Arts, 1981

Hibbard, Howard, *Bernini*, London and Baltimore, Maryland: Penguin, 1965

The Horses of San Marco, Venice (exhib. cat.), translated by John Wilton-Ely and Valerie Wilton-Ely, Milan and New York: Olivetti, 1979

Janson, H.W., "The Equestrian Monument from Cangrande Della Scala to Peter the Great," in *Aspects of the Renaissance: A Symposium*, edited by Archibald R. Lewis, Austin: University of Texas Press, 1967

Janson, H.W., "The Revival of Antiquity in Early Renaissance Sculpture," in *Looking at Italian Renaissance Sculpture*, edited by Sarah Blake McHam, Cambridge and New York: Cambridge University Press, 1998

Kaufmann, Virginia, "The Magdeburg Rider: An Aspect of the Reception of Frederick II's Roman Revival North of the Alps," in *Intellectual Life at the Court of Frederick II Hohenstaufen*, edited by William Tronzo, Washington, D.C.: National Gallery of Art, and Hanover, New Hampshire: University Press of New England, 1994

McHam, Sarah Blake, "Public Sculpture in Renaissance Florence," in *Looking at Italian Renaissance Sculpture*, edited by McHam, Cambridge and New York: Cambridge University Press, 1998

Pope-Hennessy, John, *An Introduction to Italian Sculpture*, 3 vols., London: Phaidon, 1963; 4th edition, 1996

Sauerländer, Willibald, "Two Glances from the North: The Presence and Absence of Frederick II in the Art of the Empire: The Court Art of Frederick II and the Opus Francigenum," in *Intellectual Life at the Court of Frederick II Hohenstaufen*, edited by William Tronzo, Washington, D.C.: National Gallery of Art, and Hanover, New Hampshire: University Press of New England, 1994

Valentiner, W.R., "The Equestrian Statue of Paolo Savelli in the Frari," *Art Quarterly* 16 (Winter 1953)

EQUESTRIAN STATUE OF MARCUS AURELIUS

Anonymous

ca. 161–180 BCE

bronze, originally gilded

h. 4.24 m

Musei Capitolini, Rome, Italy

The Capitoline statue of horse and rider known as the Equestrian Statue of Marcus Aurelius is almost two times life-size and is made of gilded bronze. Its genre, colossal size, and medium, combined with the fact that it has never been buried or lost, have made it one of the most continuously celebrated and influential statues in Western art.

By 1600 the rider was correctly identified as the 2nd-century Roman emperor Marcus Aurelius. The physiognomy, hairstyle, and beard of the portrait correspond to numismatic representations that are identified by their legends as Marcus Aurelius. In all details except the long shape of the face and the arrangement of individual locks of hair at the back and sides of the head, the Capitoline portrait closely reproduces the official portrait of Marcus Aurelius created when he became emperor in 161 CE and that is preserved in at least 50 other ancient sculpted versions. The large scale of the head may have permitted the sculptor to diverge from the smaller official portrait model. Interestingly, the alteration of the hair and the elongation of the face recall the official portrait designed for Marcus' son Commodus, when he became emperor in 180. The Capitoline statue may have been created after Marcus' death during the reign of Commodus and the variation in Marcus' portrait a deliberate attempt to connect the son to his illustrious father. The portrait of the Capitoline statue can be securely dated after 161 and probably before the end of the reign of Commodus in 192.

During the Roman Empire an equestrian statue was considered to be one of the greatest honors that could be awarded to emperors, senators, and local dignitaries. Imperial equestrian monuments were distinguished by their prominent locations and considerable size. For instance, a colossal equestrian statue (*ca.* 89–93 CE) of the Emperor Domitian was erected in the Roman Forum, and a similar statue of Trajan (112 CE) was the centerpiece of the Forum of Trajan in Rome.

In the Capitoline monument, Marcus Aurelius wears a *tunica* (undergarment) and a *paludamentum* (cloak), practical clothing that he would have worn when traveling, especially on military campaigns. In addition, he wears senatorial shoes (recognizable by their double straps and two knots) and a ring on the ring finger of his left hand. The emperor commands order with his outstretched right arm while holding the now-missing reins in his left hand. The powerful horse, decorated with parade paraphernalia and constrained masterfully by the bridle, steps forward. Near the horse's raised right leg was originally the figure of a kneeling barbarian, lost before the Renaissance. The image expresses Marcus Aurelius' military prowess (understood from the emperor's dress and the defeated barbarian) and his firm political control (the restrained horse and gesture), obtained and sustained through military strength.

The precise date for the erection of the statue is uncertain. Probably this type of statue would have been dedicated to commemorate a military victory. Medallions from 162 and 177 and coins from 172 to 174 and 177 depict equestrian images of the emperor. The issues of 172–174 and 177 could plausibly correspond to monuments erected to commemorate either the ephemeral victory over the Germans in 172 or the victory over the Marcomanni and Sarmatians in 176.

The asymmetrical construction of the monument may support another theory of dating, one based on the proposition that the statue was part of a monument featuring two equestrian statues. By this hypothesis, the Capitoline statue represented a victory monument pairing Marcus with his coruler Lucius Verus (161–169) or his son Commodus (either during Marcus' reign or posthumously during the reign of Commodus). The last possibility is intriguing, given the portrait's resemblance to Commodus and the lack of an appropriate event during Marcus' coregency with Lucius.

At the time of Charlemagne's first visit to Rome (781–782), the statue was located on the Lateran hill near a basilica constructed by Constantine and adjacent to the papal palace. Two theories that assume the statue

Equestrian Statue of Marcus Aurelius
© Archivio Fotografico dei Musei Capitolini, Rome, Italy

was always on the Lateran—either on property belonging to the family of Marcus Aurelius or in a military barracks—are generally refuted because the monument's size and iconography contradict a private context and the remains of the barracks found in that area postdate Marcus Aurelius. Because the reuse and moving of earlier statues is frequently documented in Late Antiquity, it is possible to imagine that this statue, which exudes majesty and power, was deliberately brought from elsewhere to the important Christian center at the Lateran. The statue's placement next to Constantine's basilica and the papal palace as a symbol of the Church's authority explains why it escaped destruction and why for centuries the rider was misidentified as Constantine.

In the early 15th century, the statue and its conservation became a concern for the popes and their artists. The statue appears in 15th-century drawings (Pisanello), paintings (Filippo Lippi), and small-scale copies (Filarete). Moreover, it heavily influenced Renaissance equestrian designs—for instance, Donatello's Gattamelata monument in Padua (1447–53), Andrea del Verrocchio's Colleoni monument in Venice (1480–88), and Leonardo's sketches for a monument to Giangiacomo Trivulzio (1508–11).

Marking the culmination of papal interest, Pope Paul III moved the statue to the Capitoline in 1538 and commissioned Michelangelo to create a worthy installation for it. Michelangelo constructed a new marble base from large fragments of ancient architecture and set the statue in the center of a geometrical design as the focal point of an entirely new piazza, Piazza Campidoglio. This glorious setting further enhanced the statue's fame, which reached its peak between the mid 17th and early 18th centuries. Among the many important equestrian statues indebted to it are Andreas Schlüter's statue (1696–1700) of the Great Elector Friedrich Wilhelm for Charlottenburg in Berlin, François Girardon's statue of Louis XIV erected in 1699 in Place Louis-le-Grand (modern Place Vendôme) (destroyed 1792), Antonio Canova's statue designed originally for Napoléon and then changed to Charles III of Spain in Naples, and Bertel Thorvaldsen's statue of Joszef Poniatowski erected in 1826–27 in Copenhagen.

By the end of the 18th century, however, admiration ceased to be unanimous. In 1771 Étienne-Maurice Falconet responded to criticism of his non-Classical equestrian monument for Peter the Great by denigrating the Marcus Aurelius, which he had studied from a cast. An early 19th-century observer, summarizing contemporary views, wrote that "the great statue of Marcus Aurelius, or rather of his horse, which was once the idol of Rome, is now a subject of contention. Some critics find the proportion of the animal false, and his attitude impossible. One compares his head to an owl's; another his belly to a cow's" (see Haskell and Penny, 1981).

In 1981 the statue was removed from its base for documentation and restoration. Strikingly, a gilt surface, probably of a medieval or Renaissance restoration, was revealed. After great debate about art, the environment, and the integrity of context, the cleaned statue was installed inside the Musei Capitolini in 1990, and a copy made from a cast was erected on Michelangelo's base in Piazza Campidoglio.

JULIA LENAGHAN

Further Reading

Bergemann, Johannes, *Römische Reiterstatuen: Ehrendenkmäler im öffentlichen Bereich*, Mainz, Germany: Von Zabern, 1990

Bergemann, Johannes, "Marc Aurel als Orientsieger? Noch einmal zur Ikonographie der Reiterstatue auf dem Capitol in Rom," *Archäoligische Mitteilungen aus Iran* 24 (1991)

De Lachenal, Lucilla, "Il gruppo equestre di Marco Aurelio e il Laterano: Ricerche per una storia della fortuna del monumento dall' età medievale sino al 1538," *Bollettino d'arte* 61 (1990)

Fittschen, Klaus, and Paul Zanker, *Katalog der römischen Porträts in den Capitolinischen Museen und den anderen kommunalen Sammlungen der Stadt Rom*, Mainz, Germany: Von Zabern, 1983–; see especially vol. 1, 1985

Hannestad, Nils, *Romersk kunst som propaganda*, Højbjerg, Denmark: Jutland Archaeological Society, 1986; as *Roman Art and Imperial Policy*, translated by P.G. Crabb, Aarhus: Aarhus University Press, 1988

Haskell, Francis, and Nicholas Penny, *Taste and the Antique: The Lure of Classical Sculpture, 1500–1900*, New Haven, Connecticut: Yale University Press, 1981

Kleiner, Diana E.E., *Roman Sculpture*, New Haven, Connecticut: Yale University Press, 1992

Liedtke, Walter, *The Royal Horse and Rider: Painting, Sculpture, and Horsemanship, 1500–1800*, New York: Abaris, 1989

Melucco Vaccaro, Alessandra, and Anna Mura Sommella (editors), *Marco Aurelio: Storia di un monumento e del suo restauro*, Cinisello Balsamo (Milan): Silvana, 1989

Mura Sommella, Anna, and Claudio Parisi Presicce (editors), *Il Marco Aurelio e la sua copia*, Cinisello Balsamo (Milan), Italy: Silvana, 1997

Stemmer, Klaus, *Kaiser Marc Aurel und seine Zeit*, Berlin: Abgüss-Sammlung Antiker Plastik, 1988

GREGOR ERHART *ca.* 1470–1540 *German*

Gregor Erhart, called in a contract an *ingeniosus magister*, or talented master, is a highly problematic figure, a transplanted descendant of the Ulm school of Late Gothic sculpture who is simultaneously a representative of the German Renaissance. The son of Ulm's leading sculptor, Michel Erhart, Gregor moved in 1494 to Augsburg, which with its close business connections to Italy and its rich economy was a major port of entry of the new Italianate style into Renaissance Germany. Gregor rapidly became the city's most important sculptor, producing innovative works within the native German vocabulary while absorbing Italian characteristics. This influence is particularly evident in the greater mass of Gregor's figures, a thoroughly believable weightiness traditionally associated with Italian artistic developments.

While Gregor's work clearly comes out of Ulm traditions, his emergence and evolution away from this background fuel the main scholarly disagreements concerning this artist. The dating of certain works covers a wide range, depending on whether a particular scholar views Gregor either a last representative of the Late Gothic or a timely champion of the new Renaissance style. Treatments of Gregor thus participate in an argument about what precisely the Renaissance means in Germany and whether Italianate German works carry equal value to the art that came before.

Part of the problem lies within Gregor's oeuvre itself. The only surviving signed and dated work is a heavily illustrated 1533 treatise on fencing. Sculptures for which documentation still exists have long since vanished. Moreover, scholars originally based attributions to Gregor on a *Virgin of Mercy* presumed to be the 1502–04 Virgin from Kaisheim Abbey, a work that burned in Berlin during the closing days of World War II. It is unknown, in fact, whether any of the works attributed to Erhart truly are indeed by him. The greatest consensus, however, surrounds the wood sculpture. The information concerning the apparently large portion of Gregor's oeuvre created in stone remains totally unclear. Documents record that he sometimes shared quarters with carvers in stone and mention some of his own work in that medium. One was a 1509 life-size equestrian figure of Maximilian I; Gregor never completed it, and even the rough block out of which it was to be carved is gone. The attributions to Gregor of works in stone remain heavily disputed.

Nonetheless, scholars have long agreed on assigning to Gregor a particular body of works in the limewood typical of south German sculpture. These pieces tend to be over-life-size and to have highly naturalistic polychromy, some of it possibly by Gregor's erstwhile collaborator, the painter Hans Holbein the Elder, to whom the sculptor was related by marriage. Gregor is particularly known for his female figures, and they have strikingly similar features: a beautifully regular, long oval face with half-closed eyes, a high, straight nose, a full lower lip, and a cleft chin. An Erhart woman radiates an intense sweetness without being saccharine.

The central Virgin of the great Blaubeuren altarpiece commissioned from Michel Erhart hints at Gregor's future. Gregor worked with his father on the multiple figures of the altarpiece. It is difficult to determine which parts the young artist may have carved, but the Virgin has the typical facial features and otherwise seems in her greater volume to presage later figures by Gregor. However, some scholars assign this important sculpture to Michel, while others give it only to his workshop.

Gregor certainly borrowed from his father for the Kaisheim Virgin's tight composition, which was very like that of Michel's *Virgin of Mercy* in Berlin, with its faithful gathered closely under the Virgin's cloak. Simultaneously, however, the Kaisheim Virgin had the sweet face of Gregor's other works, as well as a Renaissance, not Late Gothic, solidity. The strong lines of the plump and extremely naturalistic Christ child lying across his mother's arms and his horizontal contrast to the praying, vertical figures clustered at Mary's feet visually underline this weight.

The most important surviving Virgin of Gregor is the *Virgin of Mercy* at the pilgrimage church of Frauenstein in Austria. A composite Virgin of Mercy and Virgin Enthroned, with echoes of the Virgin of the Rosary, the Frauenstein *Virgin of Mercy* is a massive, quiet figure. She wears a heavy crown, the apex of a strongly pyramidal and diagonal composition. The sculptor further emphasized her head by curling her scarf around it and then letting it cascade down her shoulder in a manner reminiscent of similarly dramatic headdresses in his father's work. Mary holds the Christ child on her knee, and he in turn clasps a garland of roses, while other figures kneel in prayer under the Virgin's cloak. Among these are recognizable portraits that include Maximilian I and his second wife; Maximilian may have commissioned this sculpture around 1514, although its dating is controversial. The Virgin and Child are oblivious to these figures.

Gregor's slightly over-life-size *Mary Magdalene* is likewise a variation on an old theme. The nude *Mary Magdalene*, covered only by her hair, is a frequent subject in German art of the period; scholars have commented on what seems to be the relation of this figure to a print by Albrecht Dürer. Gregor's work is a three-dimensional version of this well-known iconographic type and would have obtained additional drama from her original halo (now gone) and from the angels who must have surrounded her, as in Tilman Riemenschneider's earlier Münnerstadt *Magdalene* (ca. 1490–92). Uniquely, Gregor did not mean his *Mary Magdalene* to stand, as it does today, but to hang from the ceiling of a church, much like better-known images of the Virgin by Riemenschneider and Veit Stoss. Therefore Gregor worked it fully in the round, also giving his German saint, with her delicately twisted pose, an Italian *contrapposto* (a natural pose with the weight of one leg, the shoulder, and hips counterbalancing one another).

Gregor Erhart adapted native subjects and styles to suit a new period by adopting some Italian concepts. The next, much more overtly Italianate development of the hybrid style appeared in the work of his nephew and pupil, Hans Daucher.

LISA KIRCH

Biography

Born probably in Ulm (now in Germany), *ca.* 1470. Son of the sculptor Michel Erhart. Moved to, and obtained citizenship in, Augsburg (now in Germany), 1494; his sister had married Adolph Daucher, a joiner in Augsburg, with whom he then lived and worked; married Anna Mair, daughter of Hans Mair (presumably the painter Mair of Landshut) and cousin of Hans Holbein the Elder, 1496; worked with Holbein on commissions for Kaisheim, 1502–04, and the Church of St. Moritz, Augsburg, 1502–08. Sebastian Kriechbaum and Gregor's nephew Hans Daucher recorded among his apprentices; turned workshop over to son, Paulus, 1531. Died in Augsburg (now in Germany), 1540.

Selected Works

1493–94 Blaubeuren altarpiece; wood; Blaubeuren
        Abbey, Germany
ca. 1500 *Christ Child*; wood; Hamburger Museum
        für Kunst und Gewerbe, Hamburg,
        Germany
ca. 1500 *Virgin and Child*; wood; Bayerisches
        Nationalmuseum, Munich, Germany
ca. 1500 *Virgin of Mercy*; wood; Pilgrimage
or after Church, Frauenstein, Austria
1515
1502–04 *Virgin of Mercy*, for Kaisheim altar; wood
        (destroyed in World War II)
ca. 1510 *Mary Magdalene*; limewood; Musée du
        Louvre, Paris, France

Further Reading

Baxandall, Michael, *The Limewood Sculptors of Renaissance Germany*, New Haven, Connecticut: Yale University Press, 1980

Broschek, Anja, *Michel Erhart: Ein Beitrag zur schwäbischen Plastik der Spätgotik*, Berlin and New York: De Gruyter, 1973

Guillot de Suduiraut, Sophie, *Gregor Erhart, Sainte Marie-Madeleine*, Paris: Éditions de la Réunion des Musées Nationaux, 1997

Otto, Gertrud, *Gregor Erhart*, Berlin: Deutscher Verein für Kunstwissenschaft, 1943

Schneckenburger-Broschek, Anja, "Gregor Erhart," in *The Dictionary of Art*, edited by Jane Turner, vol. 10, New York: Grove, and London: Macmillan, 1996

MICHEL ERHART *ca.* 1440–1522 *German*

After Hans Multscher had brought artistic recognition to the city of Ulm, Michel Erhart established the reputation as his preeminent successor. The robust economy of Germany during the latter half of the 15th century fostered the prolific output by sculptors working more independently than had their predecessors. Within such a context, Erhart and his contemporaries developed their own methods of expression using the conventions of the Late Gothic style. Yet although written records amply account for Erhart's activity, only one piece bears his name. The later work of his son Gregor also makes proper attributions difficult. The stylistic influences and attributions of those works that survive by one of the most active workshops in Germany reveal a strong legacy from Erhart's oeuvre during the rich transitional phase for German sculpture during the Late Gothic period.

Although there is no consensus regarding authorship, scholars agree that Erhart had an active role in the choir-stall busts for the Cathedral of Ulm, based on several factors, including the relationship between Erhart and Jörg Syrlin. Erhart is listed on the Ulm tax rolls as a sculptor when work began in 1469. Syrlin received the commission as a joiner, requiring Erhart and other sculptors for the sizable number of busts. Some of the busts also demonstrate the strong influence of a Netherlandish style. After a presumed internship with a master carver from the north, Erhart's work would have shown the influence of the Low Countries. In 1473 the relationship between Erhart and Syrlin was established with the commissioning of the high altar for the Cathedral of Ulm. It is evident that by 1474, with the formation of his own workshop, Erhart had become established as a master carver in Ulm, responsible for most of the statuary in the cathedral.

Erhart's *Virgin of Mercy* is one of the earliest examples of the sculptor's mature style. The precedent for a sculpture of this type is rare, most commonly depicted two-dimensionally. Particularly challenging to the sculptor was the representation of the smaller figures beneath the Virgin's cloak. The proximity of these figures in a tightly compressed space demanded a design that avoided the appearance of a relief, by which their impact would have been lost in contrast to the Virgin. The result is a subtle artifice, illusory, graceful, and yet attentive to both nuance and detail. The Virgin's curvilinear movement terminates in the head, with a sincere and gracious expression. Although the proportions and features reference the style of Flemish painter Rogier van der Weyden, the expressive design and linear composition are of Erhart's own mastery and invention.

Erhart received a commission in 1487 to create an altarpiece for the St. Dionysius Chapel adjacent to the Church of Sts. Ulrich and Afra in Augsburg. Although it has not survived, the sculpture's location signaled the beginning of a shift in cultural prominence from Ulm to Augsburg. Erhart expanded his influence well beyond the Swabian region; evidence of a defined workshop style dates from the 1490s, when Erhart was most productive. In contrast to his soft and curvilinear style, Erhart created one of his more severe yet expressive pieces for the Church of St. Michael in Schwäbisch Hall. His only dated and signed work, the crucifix of 1494 is by comparison different from his earlier work. Strong undercutting and linear patterning in the loincloth and hair coexist alongside his expressive vision of Christ's suffering. It is one of many crucifixes his workshop produced throughout the remainder of his approximately 50 years of activity.

During the 1490s Erhart's son Gregor began to work more independently. In 1494 Gregor became a burgher in Augsburg and shortly thereafter established his own workshop. The exact influence exerted by his father's workshop is unknown. A demarcation in style from Michel is nonetheless noted in their monumental altarpiece for the Benedictine monastery of Blaubeuren. The altarpiece is one of the best-preserved examples of the *Schnitzaltar*, a complex sculptural program incorporating sculpture and architecture for ritual and devotional purposes. Comprising four sections, the central shrine is flanked by two movable wings with painted reliefs of the Nativity and Adoration of the Magi, and a carved *predella* (a painted panel at the bottom of an altar piece) beneath. The ornately carved and gilded shrine would have been opened on feast days, particularly those associated with the Virgin or the saints. As a slight deviation from Michel's sculptural type, the saints rest on their own bases projecting obliquely forward from the frontal plane. Their relative independence anticipates later developments in German sculpture. In contrast, the combination of movement and gesture in the figures appears schematic. Devoted to Late Gothic ideals, Erhart balanced the composition, creating the meditative and tranquil quality that infuses the altarpiece.

Michel and Gregor Erhart, high altar, Abbey Church, Blaubeuren, Germany
© Foto Marburg / Art Resource, NY

Erhart's approach to this altar shows both continuity and variety from his earlier work. He clearly maintained the refinement, precision, and subtlety in his figures' hands, heads, and drapery. The Virgin especially emulates these qualities, providing a stylistic link to other similarly attributed works, including *Vanity*, *The Seated Virgin*, and in particular the *Virgin and Child* in the Detroit Institute of Arts, Michigan, United States. Common attributes in the moon, the attitude of the reaching child, and the pose show the direct involvement of either Michel or his workshop.

Although not considered an innovator in German sculpture, Michel Erhart and his workshop were responsible for a large body of work found throughout Germany, Austria, Switzerland, and parts of France. His conventional yet attentive approach influenced Veit Stoss and Tilman Riemenschneider, both of whom placed themselves outside the well-accepted tradition. When Erhart received the commission in 1517 to create a monumental Mount of Olives in limestone and wood, the height of German Gothic sculpture would soon begin to wane. Coincidental with this date was the advent of political and religious forces that would seriously alter the basis for much of the sculpture created by Michel and his contemporaries. It would be another 100 years before German religious sculpture reemerged in a radically new context.

BARRON NAEGEL

See also **Erhart, Gregor; Syrlin, Jörg, the Elder**

Biography

Born in Ulm, *ca.* 1440. May have apprenticed with wood sculptor in the Netherlands, 1460–65. Married Margarethe Ensinger, daughter of architect Vincenz Ensinger; sons Gregor and Bernhard became sculptors. Established workshop in Ulm, 1474; prior to 1490 (with exception of high altars for Ulm and Augsburg), surviving work is small in scale but rich in stylistic invention; Blauberen altarpiece of 1493 considered most notable work; importance based on demonstrating conventions of his workshop; few of his works remain. Died in Ulm, Germany, after 8 Dec 1522.

Selected Works

1469   Eighteen busts (under Jörg Syrlin); wood; choir stalls, Cathedral of Ulm, Germany
1473   High altar, for Cathedral of Ulm, Germany (under Jörg Syrlin); wood (destroyed)
ca. 1480 *The Seated Virgin*; polychromed wood; Staatliche Museen, Berlin, Germany (attributed)
ca. 1480 *Vanity*; polychromed wood;

Kunsthistorisches Museum, Vienna,
Austria (attributed)

ca. 1480 *Virgin and Child*; polychromed wood; The
Detroit Institute of Arts, Michigan, United
States (attributed)

ca. 1480 *Virgin of Mercy*; polychromed wood;
Staatliche Museen, Berlin, Germany

1487 High altar, for St. Dionysius Chapel,
Church of Sts. Ulrich and Afra, Augsburg,
Germany; polychromed wood (destroyed)

1493–94 High altar (with Gregor Erhart);
polychromed wood; Abbey Church,
Blaubeuren, Germany

1494 Crucifix; polychromed wood; Church of
St. Michael, Schwäbisch Hall, Germany

1517 Sculptures for Mount of Olives, Ulm,
Germany; limestone, wood (destroyed);
fragments: Ulm Museum, Germany

Further Reading

Barnet, Peter, "Late Gothic Wood Sculptures from Ulm," *Bulletin of the Detroit Institute of Arts* 64/4 (1989)

Baum, Julius, *Die Ulmer Plastik um 1500*, Stuttgart, Germany: Hoffmann, 1911

Baxandall, Michael, *The Limewood Sculptors of Renaissance Germany*, New Haven, Connecticut: Yale University Press, 1980

Chapuis, Julien, and Michael Baxandall, *Tilman Riemenschneider: Master Sculptor of the Late Middle Ages*, New Haven, Connecticut: Yale University Press, 1999

Deutsch, W., "Der ehemalige Hochaltar und das Chorgestuhl, zur Syrlin- und zur Bildhauerfrage," in *600 Jahre Ulmer Münster: Festschrift*, edited by Hans Eugen Specker and Reinhard Wortmann, Stuttgart, Germany: Kohlhammer, 1977; 2nd edition, 1984

Müller, Theodor, *Sculpture in the Netherlands, Germany, France, and Spain, 1400 to 1500*, translated by Elaine Robson Scott and William Robson Scott, London: Penguin, 1966

Osten, Gert von der, and Horst Vey, *Painting and Sculpture in Germany and the Netherlands, 1500–1600*, London: Pelican, 1969

Valentine, Wilhelm R., "Late Gothic Sculpture in Detroit," *Art Quarterly* 6 (1943)

MAX ERNST 1891–1976 *German, active in France and the United States*

Max Ernst is especially recognized as a great innovator of artistic language in the field of painting, although his interest for the plastic arts never left him and continued to resurface and give rise to many sculptures throughout his long career.

Ernst began by experimenting with collages during his Dadaist period and later during his Surrealist period. From the end of the 1920s, his interest in sculpture as a separate discipline became more apparent, and his plastic output became independent of his paintings. His sculpture placed greater emphasis on space and rhythm, with strong constructional overtones, an approach underscored by his use of stone and bronze as basic materials. His sculpture affords the image a totemic nature. His works are like symbols of a coded language of a personal and undecipherable holiness.

Ernst's sculpture was first shown in thematic exhibitions in the 1960s. In the interviews and texts accompanying these shows, Ernst drew attention to the playful aspects of his sculpture and his relationships to the games of children in the sand and indicated that he created individual group of works, such as the granite sculptures from Maloja and the plaster sculptures on Long Island, while on holiday or in places far from city life in Paris and New York.

Ernst began decorating his houses in Saint-Martin-d'Ardèche, France, and Sedona, Arizona, with numerous sculptures in cement. Later, when he took up residence in France in Huismes and Seillans, he began to carve in plaster and in stone. However, assemblage objects formed an accompaniment to the Dadaist work in Cologne and Surrealist activity in Paris.

Ernst's earliest sculpture, *Les Amoureux* (The Lovers) (1913) was first exhibited in his 1959 retrospective at the Musée Nationale d'Art Moderne in Paris. Toward the end of 1919 Ernst made his *Relief 123*, an assemblage containing three wooden quadrangles situated in different positions; they are joined at their corners by diagonal lines, the artist painting over the resulting triangular areas. Borrowing from Alexander Archipenko's poster the inscription "sculpto-peinture," Ernst explained his manner, which consisted, particularly at the beginning, of painted forms. He also justified his discovery as deriving from collages he painted during his time in Cologne.

Ernst moved to Paris in 1922, undertaking the assemblages *Bird*, *Two Children Are Threatened by a Nightingale*, and *Dadaville*, all from 1924, the year in which André Breton published his *Manifesto of Surrealism*. All three works hark back to Dadaism. The first features two flat pieces of wood with rounded contours—to suggest the side view of a bird's head like the one shown in the painted wood relief *Two Children Are Threatened by a Nightingale*. These works illustrate the way in which Ernst abolished the distinctions between genres and tried to abolish the separation between illusion and reality; the nine strips of cork of *Dadaville* are mounted vertically side by side, the microstructure of the cork turning into the macrostructure of a forest.

In 1934 Ernst spent the summer as a guest at Alberto Giacometti's house in Swiss Bergell, during which time Giacometti introduced him to the techniques of carving. Ernst benefited from this apprenticeship,

The King Playing with the Queen
The Conway Library, Courtauld Institute of Art

which allowed him to continue his meditations on ovals and spheres, and he worked on over 20 sphere-shaped and egg-shaped stones. In these one notices an interplay between the smooth and structured areas of the rounded stones. Ernst painted certain of the granite blocks with red and black oil colors. He also added to his assemblage *Loplop Introduces a Young Girl* a painted stone.

Back in Paris the winter of 1934, Ernst began working on a series of freestanding sculptures in plaster, using smooth, tapering, truncated cones as a reminder of his Dada period. The best known of these sculptures is the *Habakuk*—a complex combination of different figures from which he cast *Oedipus I* and *Oedipus II*, likewise assembled from casts of flowerpots. This period is also characterized by several anthropomorphic constructions that make allusion to mythology or ancient history.

After his participation in May 1936 in the Exposition surréaliste d'objets with *Mobile Object Recommended for Family Use* (1934), which opened a large debate in the 1936 double issue of the periodical *Cahiers d'Art* (devoted to the object and to the "Crisis of the Object"), Ernst created his own "surrealist palace" in Saint-Martin-d'Ardèche. Accompanied by Leonora Carrington, he filled their house with bas-reliefs, wall paintings, and freestanding sculptures. He created hybrids of human beings, animals, and birds constructed by piecing together readymade body parts and joining them with limbs. Two circular masks surrounded the door opening onto the staircase, for which he created as pendants *Lunar Asparagus*.

After a brief marriage to Peggy Guggenheim, Ernst met the artist Dorothea Tanning toward the end of 1942, with whom he found an old house in Sedona. He transformed the abandoned house into a workshop, where he worked on several sculptures concurrently. He continued to create his strange composite figures cast of individual objects, such as buckets, bowls, boxes, tubes, and tins, and also left in plaster some expressive and complicated figures such as *Young Woman in the Shape of Flower* (1944) and *White Queen*, the latter also known as *Young Woman in the Shape of Moon* (lost today; documented only in a photograph by Man Ray). With *Moonmad* he attempted a more complex structure in order to express how open and closed forms follow each other in close succession: he refers to the crescent moon, the full moon with its halo, the half moon, the chubby face of the moon, and the friendly moon from children's books.

Among his anthropomorphic constructions, Ernst's *The Table Is Set* recalls Giacometti and anticipates Ernst's highly complex sculpture *The King Playing with the Queen*. The king, as both a chess player and the artist himself playing with forms, dominates the group through his size and the all-encompassing sweep of his arms. This work anticipates *Capricorn*, first created in cement in Sedona in 1948, as the good spirit of the house, which he decorated with several friezes of masks and figures. The exterior walls of Ernst's and Tanning's house in Arizona were decorated with 36 frieze blocks with heads, gargoyles, masks, animals, constellations, and signs. Twenty years later, he cast some of these stone reliefs in bronze.

Ernst's final Parisian period (in the 1960s) is best characterized by *The Spirit of the Bastille*. The height of the stalk that carries and presents the principal image dominates, transforming itself into a symbolic column.

DOÏNA LEMNY

Biography

Born in Brühl (near Cologne), Germany, 2 April 1891. Studied philosophy, psychiatry, art history at University of Bonn, 1909–12; collaborated on first Salon d'Automne organized by *Der Sturm* in Berlin, 1913; served in German Army, 1914–18; exhibition of his works organized by *Der Sturm*, 1916; second exhibition organized by Galerie Dada in Zurich, 1917; exhibition of collages, Paris, 1921; settled in Paris, 1922, and participated actively in Surrealist movement; exhibition at Galerie Georges Bernheim, 1928; made film *L'âge d'or* with Buñuel and Dalí, 1930. Settled in Sedona, Arizona, 1943, where he created wall sculpture; became American citizen, 1948; traveled through Europe, 1949; settled in Paris, 1953; won first prize for painting at the 27th Venice Biennale for painting, 1954; became French citizen, 1958; one year later, first retrospective at the Musée National d'Art Moderne, Centre Georges Pompidou, Paris; further retrospectives at Museum of Modern Art in New York City, Tate Gallery in London, and at Kunsthalle in Zürich; received several prizes in Europe such as Lichtwark prize, Hamburg, 1964; awarded Legion of Honour, 1966; exhibition of paintings and sculptures at Jewish Museum in New York City, 1966; major retrospective at Guggenheim Museum, New York City, 1975. Died in Paris, France, 1 April 1976.

Selected Works

1924   *Dadaville*; painted cork, plaster; Tate Gallery, London, England

1924   *Two Children Are Threatened by a Nightingale*; painted wood; Museum of Modern Art, New York City, United States

1930   *The Sphynx Eye*; stone, box; The Capricorn Trust, Cavaliero Fine Arts, New York City, United States

1930–66 *Loplop Introduces a Young Girl*; wood, plaster, objects; Musée Nationale d'Art Moderne, Centre Georges Pompidou, Paris, France

1934   *Habakuk*; bronze; Skulpturenmuseum Glaskasten, Marl, Germany

1934   *Oedipus I*; plaster; Kunstsammlung Nordrhein-Westfalen, Düsseldorf, Germany

1934   *Oedipus II*; bronze; Kunstmuseum Bonn, Germany

1934–35 *Bird Head*; bronze; Museum of Modern Art, New York City, United States

1934   *Lunar Asparagus*; bronze; private collection

1944   *The King Playing with the Queen*; bronze; The Menil Collection, Houston, Texas, United States

1944   *Moonmad*; bronze; Hirshhorn Museum and Sculpture Garden, Washington, D.C., United States

1944   *The Table Is Set*; bronze; Hirshhorn Museum and Sculpture Garden, Washington, D.C., United States

1960   *The Spirit of the Bastille*; bronze, stone; Cavaliero Fine Arts, New York City, United States

1967   *Big Turtle*; plaster; The Capricorn Trust, Cavaliero Fine Arts, New York City, United States

Further Reading

Bosquet, Alain, *Max Ernst: Oeuvre sculpté, 1913–1961*, Paris: Galerie Le Point Cardinal, 1961

Giedion-Welker, Carola, *Max Ernst*, Cologne, Germany: Wallraf-Richartz-Museum, 1962

Holeczek, Bernhard, *Max Ernst: Gemälde, Skulpturen, Collagen, Frottagen, Zeichnungen, Druckgraphik und Bücher: Verzeichnis der Bestände*, Hanover, Germany: Kunstmuseum Hannover mit Sprengel Museum, 1981

Jouffroy, Alain, "Max Ernst, Sculptor," in *Max Ernst: The Sculpture*, edited by Fiona McLeod, Edinburgh: Fruitmarket Gallery, 1990

Pech, Jürgen, "Mythology and Mathematics: Max Ernst's Sculpture," in *Max Ernst: Sculture; Sculptures* (bilingual Italian-English edition), edited by Ida Gianelli, Milan: Charta, 1996

Russell, John, "Die Skulptur," in *Max Ernst: Leben und Werk*, by Russell, Cologne, Germany: DuMont Schauberg, 1966; as *Max Ernst: Life and Work*, New York: Abrams, and London: Thames and Hudson, 1967

Spies, Werner, "Skulptur und Montage," in *Die Rückkehr der schönen Gärtnerin: Max Ernst, 1950–1970*, Cologne, Germany: DuMont Schauberg, 1971; as *The Return of La Belle Jardinière: Max Ernst, 1950–1970*, New York: Abrams, 1971

Spies, Werner, Günter Metken, and Sigrid Metken, *Max Ernst, Oeuvre-Katalog*, 6 vols., Houston, Texas: Menil Foundation, and Cologne, Germany: DuMont Schauberg, 1975–98

ETRUSCAN SCULPTURE

Despite the fact that from the late 8th to the 5th centuries BCE the Etruscans exercised a political and territorial control in Italy similar to that of the Greeks to the east and the Phoenicians in northern Africa, their art was not, until fairly recently, accorded the same kind of scholarly attention garnered by their Mediterranean neighbors. Part of the reason for this lies with their elusive origins and a language that, like the Etruscan culture itself, has yet to be fully understood. As a result, the Etruscans were commonly regarded as substandard imitators within the Graeco-Roman context. They have in addition been seen as the antithesis of Roman aggression: "sensitive, diffident . . . altogether without sternness or natural will-to-power," as characterized by the writer D.H. Lawrence in the 1920s. As late as the mid 20th century, their unique position in the ancient world branded them as "one of the strangest civilizations in the records of mankind."

Herodotus' claim that the Etruscans migrated to the Italian peninsula from Asia Minor in the 12th century BCE was the traditionally accepted theory of their origin. Recent scholarship, however, argues that the Etruscans did not migrate but were indigenous to Italy.

This view was actually put forth by Dionysius of Halicarnassus as early as the reign of Emperor Augustus (*r.* 27 BCE–14 CE), and it is one that is more widely accepted today. Their beginnings can be found in an earlier Iron Age people, the Villanovans, who inhabited the Po River area from about 1000 to 750 BCE. From their villages, which gradually extended from the north central to the central western coast of Italy, a dozen powerful, independent Etruscan cities, including Veii, Cerveteri, Tarquinia, and Vulci, emerged. Among the artists working in these and other Etruscan locations were Greek artisans who had settled on the peninsula as early as the 8th century BCE. Etruscan harbors sent and received trading vessels from northern Africa and the Near East, thereby bringing Phoenician and eastern orientalizing along with Greek influences into early Etruscan metalwork. For these reasons, common judgments were that their production in art was dispassionately copied from these cultures. In spite of these diverse influences, seeing Etruscan art as merely derivative only encumbers any meaningful assessment and appreciation of this work. Etruscan artists drew from these sources, and with the rich natural resources of metals on the Italian peninsula, they created sculptural forms of unprecedented vitality and terse verity largely unfettered by the developing idealism that was a primary characteristic of contemporary Greek Archaic and Classical period sculpture.

From the very beginnings of their history, the Etruscans reflected an obsession with an uninterrupted continuity of life beyond the grave. Their conceptions of the afterlife, still not fully understood, seem nearly as well developed as those in Egypt. They probably contributed to that most famous depiction of the shadowy underworld described by Virgil in book 6 of *The Aeneid*, which was the source for the later Christian hell of Dante's *Inferno*. Virgil himself appears to have been of Etruscan descent, and his city, Mantua, was said to derive from the powerful mates Mantus and Mania, king and queen of the Etruscan underworld. The fascination with death informed the earliest proto-Etruscan three-dimensional works. These are the Villanovan ash urns produced from the 8th to 7th centuries BCE in forms that vary from simple two-piece ("biconical") pots to human-headed forms that recall Egyptian canopic jars, most ranging from about 60 to 90 centimeters high. These vessels formed a humanlike container for cremated remains made to ensure a continued existence of the human spirit following its separation from the body. The materials used to form them were terracotta and hammered and riveted bronze sheets used independently or in combination. Later Etruscan sculpture was primarily formed of these two materials.

One example resides in the Etruscan Museum at Chiusi. A terracotta throne supports a bronze urn, which in turn is surmounted by a terracotta portrait head. Another curious type of ash vessel takes the form of simple huts or more elaborately decorated houses or palaces. These bear out the interest in an art with the primary function of providing familiar "living rooms" for the dead. The idea is elaborated in the many painted tomb chambers, such as those at Tarquinia, with scenes of industrious workers and ecstatic dancers, but in sculpture, a life-size version in relief is the rock-cut burial chamber of the Banditaccia necropolis ("city of the dead") at Cerveteri called the *Tomb of the Reliefs*, which dates from the late 4th century to the early 3rd century BCE. The painted stucco applied to tufa stone recreates an interior living space and is decorated with a vast array of utilitarian objects such as rope, tools, jars, shields, and other armor. The household for an entire family of over 40 members, complete with pets, is recreated. Linens, neatly folded and stored, and pillows leaning against nonstructural piers suggest the eternal rest accorded to the tomb inhabitants. This remarkable space provides not only insight into Etruscan funerary practice but also an invaluable view into their daily lives and information about their home interiors, none of which has survived.

Works such as these are generally in keeping with the ancient belief that the ghosts of the dead longed to rejoin the world of the living to enjoy the pleasures that death had stolen from them. When interment of the body gradually replaced cremation in the 6th century, a totally original form of sculpture emerged from Etruscan workshops. These were painted terracotta sarcophagi surmounted by single figures or couples. With smiles derived from contemporary archaic Greek statuary, these figures relax atop couchlike furniture in the manner of the social and convivial Greek *symposium*, literally "drinking together." In the remarkable *Sarcophagus of the Married Couple* from Cerveteri, the figures are actively celebrating life. Herodotus wrote that Etruscan women enjoyed unprecedented privilege in the ancient world, participating in all manner of public spectacle with equity; this and other Etruscan art serve to substantiate his claim. The hands of the couple form animated essays of lifelike gestures of embrace and offering while presenting objects that activate space with a flurry of motion so unlike the static nature of the contemporary archaic sculpture produced in Greece. The male figure appears to have held a small object delicately between the thumb and forefinger, probably an egg.

Egg imagery may be found in many painted funerary banquet scenes of reclining figures—such as those at Tarquinia—to symbolize the newly emerged life that tomb inhabitants so fully appear to enjoy. Even lacking its original, richly painted surface, the whole arrangement of this and other Etruscan tomb sculptures conveys an ecstatic, lifelike energy that seems more contemporary than ancient. A humanized and more intimate version of this type emerged by the early 3rd century BCE. In the limestone relief *Sarcophagus of Ramtha Visnai* from Vulci, for example, the couple embrace under a thin sheet. The joyous tone of celebration seen in the *Sarcophagus of the Married Couple* from Cerveteri is absent. The male figure looks distant, even preoccupied with worry, whereas the woman appears focused on rendering compassion for his concern. The somber mood conveyed in this work reflects the harsh realities of encroaching Roman domination.

Vulca of Veii is today the only Etruscan sculptor whose name we know. Pliny the Elder wrote that he was summoned from his hometown in order to create "the most praiseworthy images of deities of that era." One of these images is believed to be the 1.8-meter, fully painted, terracotta *Apollo*, originally part of a group positioned on the gable across the top of the early 6th century BCE Pontonaccio Sanctuary at Veii. The god is depicted in pursuit of Herakles and the Ceryneian deer. Originally clutching a bow, Apollo lunges forward, his weight propelled by the tensed left leg as he reaches to rescue the sacred animal from the grasp of Herakles. While the stride forward, the flat, zigzag drapery, and the large eyes and formal smile relate to contemporary archaic Greek kouros and kore statuary, the dramatic physical action and forms thrusting into space anticipate later works, such as the Hellenistic *Nike of Samothrace* by a full three centuries. This unprecedented and remarkable vitality of the human form in freestanding sculpture is without rival at this time in the ancient world.

The so-called *Orator*, a bronze portrait statue of an Etruscan nobleman, was produced about the time the Etruscans were forced to accept Roman citizenship early in the 1st century BCE. The orator's name, Aulus Metellus, is notably inscribed in Latin with Etruscan characters on the hem of the garment. This kind of cross-cultural fusion of type is common in the late period, and it anticipates the frequently noted stylistic similarity between the *Orator* and the Roman *Augustus of Prima Porta*. Livy, historian and protégé of Emperor Augustus, said that "Etruria filled the whole length of Italy," and the erudite Emperor Claudius, whose wife was of Etruscan descent, wrote an extensive multivolume history of her ancestors in the next century. Although the language that the *Orator* spoke was as clearly understood by the Roman citizenry as its visual language, only the latter survives today. This Etruscan visual language experienced the first of many revivals when the *Orator* was discovered in 1566 during Cosimo I de' Medici's rise to power in Florence in the late Renaissance period following Michelangelo's death.

Exactly contemporary with the *Apollo* of Veii is arguably the world's most famous animal sculpture and a monument to Etrusco-Roman artistic fusion. The fame of the *She-wolf* rests partially on its association with the legendary story of Rome's founding by the twin sons of Mars, Romulus and Remus, whereas the name of the primary Etruscan god Tinia is inscribed in Etruscan on the right foreleg. Cast in the lost-wax process, the work also represents a high point in Etruscan bronze technique. The muscle tension of the protective animal's torso, fiercely snarling jaws, and alert eyes and ears indicates that the sculptor must have carefully observed animals in the environment. This realism, offset by the orientalizing pattern seen in the mane and braid plaiting along the spine and down to the front legs, combines naturalism and cultural borrowings with a high degree of originality. In the bronze *Wounded Chimaera* of a century later, the conception is controlled by imaginative fantasy. The mythical creature is described by Homer in the *Iliad* as "a lion in its foreparts with a serpent's tail and in the middle a goat, and it breathes fire." From this scant reference, an unknown Etruscan sculptor managed to create one of Western art's great transformations from literary to visual form. The mane of the chimera bristles as she recoils from a fatal wound inflicted to the head of the goat by the pursuing Corinthian hero Bellerophon. The intensity of energy is given added emphasis in the whiplash formed by the serpent tail and the horns of the goat. Together with the *She-wolf*, the *Wounded Chimaera* occupies a key position in the history of bronze animal sculpture.

The Etruscans were the first major producers of sculpture on the Italian peninsula during the ancient period. Like the Minoans a millennium earlier, an unknown language shrouds them in mystery, and similarly their culture succumbed to their more aggressive neighbors. Decline began in the late 5th century, and in 281 the last reference to their struggle with the Romans was recorded.

The Etruscans were much like a large feuding family, never fully able to unite the cultural aims of their dozen cities into a single polity. As a result, they were left in a vulnerable position during the Roman rise to power, and in the *Lex Julia* of 87 BCE, no options were open to the Etruscans but to accept citizenship. Yet through transmission of Greek and other ideas, as well as by the sheer power of originality, they in large part provided the impetus for the manner in which their Roman conquerors would rule, what they would believe, and the appearance of their sculptural forms. The Etruscan creative spirit was to be rekindled in the work of Donatello, Giambologna, Benvenuto Cellini, and others who worked on Etruscan soil. In assessing the sculptural contributions of the Etruscans, one would do well to keep in mind the idea of one of the important early 20th-century scholars: that the lands of the Etruscans would become the homeland of the Italian Renaissance.

JAMES SLAUSON

Further Reading

Bloch, Raymond, *Etruscan Art*, Greenwich, Connecticut: New York Graphic Society, 1959; London: Barrie and Rockcliff, 1966

Boëthius, Axel, *Etruscan Culture, Land, and People*, New York: Columbia University Press, 1962

Bonfante, Larissa (editor), *Etruscan Life and Afterlife: A Handbook of Etruscan Studies*, Detroit, Michigan: Wayne State University Press, 1986

Del Chiaro, Mario Aldo, *Etruscan Art from West Coast Collections*, Santa Barbara: University of California Art Gallery, 1967

Hamblin, Dora Jane, *The Etruscans*, New York: Time-Life Books, 1975

Mansuelli, Guido Achille, *The Art of Etruria and Early Rome*, translated by C.E. Ellis, New York: Crown, 1964; revised edition, New York: Greystone Press, 1967

Richardson, Emeline Hill, *The Etruscans: Their Art and Civilization*, Chicago: University of Chicago Press, 1964

Spivey, Nigel Jonathan, *Etruscan Art*, New York: Thames and Hudson, 1997

EXPRESSIONISM

See **Abstract Expressionism; Germany: 20th Century–Contemporary**

F

FAKES

See **Forgeries and Deceptive Restorations**

ÉTIENNE-MAURICE FALCONET 1716–1791 *French, also active in Russia*

Étienne-Maurice Falconet can be associated with those artists whose work is still too little studied and therefore probably underappreciated. For a description of the master, one must consider both his plastic works and his literary works, which included theoretical writings and correspondence with the Russian empress Catherine II. The latter shows Falconet's exceptional individuality not only as an artist, but also as an original philosopher and a genuine son of the Enlightenment.

It is possible that the underestimation of Falconet is tied to the fact that the sculptor spent 12 years of his life in Russia, which was also home to his most significant work—the equestrian monument of Peter the Great, unanimously acknowledged as a masterpiece of 18th-century sculpture. At the very least, the conclusion of the contract for this monument and Falconet's arrival in Russia in 1766 clearly divide his work into two sharply distinguished periods.

Falconet's first work, *Milo of Crotona*, appeared in plaster in the Acadèmie Royale in Paris in 1744 and showed its creator to be an artist with tendencies toward expression, the communication of strong feelings, and tragic pathos. Thereafter he produced, besides a few portraits, a series of chamber works that were masterfully executed but completely in accor-

dance with the taste of their time. It was probably this very correspondence with the spirit of the epoch that secured for Falconet the patronage of the Marquise de Pompadour, a favorite of Louis XV. Such well-known statues by Falconet as *Genius of Music* and *Menacing Cupid* were created for her. Similar works guaranteed the sculptor not only fame, but also an important post at the porcelain factory in Sèvres, where from 1757 until his departure for Russia he managed the sculpture studios. Falconet's later compositions—the group *Pygmalion at the Feet of His Statue* and *Sweet Melancholy*—are in that same style. Such works were very popular throughout Europe during the second half of the 18th century. They spawned a multitude of imitations, from which the oeuvre of Falconet has not freed itself to this day. Perhaps only the marble statue *Winter*, begun in 1765 and finished in Russia, shows some evolution in the direction toward the Neoclassical style.

It may be assumed that the most significant and crucial commission of Falconet's French period was that of the statues created for the Church of St. Roch in Paris. These included the figures of Mary and the archangel Gabriel from the composition *Annunciation*, as well as the *Crucifixion* with its portrayal of a weeping Mary Magdalene at the foot of the cross. Unfortunately, the majority of these statues were destroyed during the French Revolution, and only the figure *Christ in Agony* was preserved. It may be surmised that this ensemble continued the tradition of Baroque Italian sculpture with its clearly expressed theatricality, rather than opening new paths in art. However, there is no doubt that Falconet solved difficult problems on a very high artistic level, thus demonstrating his multifaceted talent.

Nonetheless, the perspicacity of Denis Diderot is intriguing. He saw in his friend, Falconet, a master craftsman capable of creating the equestrian monument of Peter the Great, a work that not only completed the evolution of the Classical equestrian monument, but also opened a new page in the history of European sculpture. In his time, Louis Réau correctly formulated the innovative character of the monument in five points: the czar is represented seated on a rearing horse; natural cliffs of irregular form take the place of a pedestal; the hero is treated as legislator and benefactor of the people, rather than military leader and conqueror; allegory is almost completely absent; and the inscription is remarkable for its laconic brevity. To this can be added that, using the experience of his predecessors and being more or less familiar with the majority of equestrian monuments placed in other European countries, Falconet could create one of those eternal works of art whose style is impossible to define. Although it possesses the external marks of the Baroque style (the rearing horse and stone sculpted to resemble primeval cliffs), the monument goes far beyond the framework of a single style, reflecting in various ways the Classical tendencies of the age. The image of Peter the Great as a legislator born of the Enlightenment and capable of founding St. Petersburg largely defined its time and turned out to be prophetic for the St. Petersburg of the first half of the 19th century, which is considered the Golden Age of Russian culture and literature. In this amazing image, Falconet foresaw not only the future ensemble of the Senate Square (with the later construction of the Admiralty buildings, as well as the Senate and Synod), but also the flourishing of Russian art during the Pushkin period. And it seems hardly accidental that the monument Aleksandr Pushkin called "The Bronze Horseman" became the hero—alongside the historical Peter the Great—of an ingenious poem about the city, also entitled "The Bronze Horseman."

Thus although almost nothing remains of Falconet's St. Petersburg period (during this time he completed the statue Winter and cast a bronze replica of the antique Boy Removing a Splinter, 1772), these 12 years were a time when his talent rose to a new height and he created a work that forever inscribed his name Selectedamong the most significant sculptors of the 18th century.

SERGEI ANDROSSOV

Biography

Born in Paris, France, 1 December 1716. Studied under Jean-Baptiste Lemoyne for almost ten years; worked at the Sèvres manufactory, from 1757, as director of the models studio, for which he completed more than 100 models; worked in St. Petersburg, Russia, on the equestrian monument of Peter the Great, 1766–78; upon returning from Russia, spent two years in the Netherlands enjoying the hospitality of the Russian envoy Dmitry Golitsyn; returned to Paris, 1780, where due to a stroke he rarely worked as a sculptor. Died in Paris, France, 25 January 1791.

Selected Works

1744   Milo of Crotona, for Académie Royale, Paris, France; plaster; Hermitage, St. Petersburg, Russia; marble version: 1754, Musée du Louvre, Paris, France

1750–51 Genius of Music; marble; Musée du Louvre, Paris, France

1753–66 Christ in Agony; stone; Church of St. Roch, Paris, France

1753–66 Figures of Mary and the Archangel Gabriel, and Crucifixion, for Church of Saint Roch, Paris, France; marble (destroyed)

1757   Standing Bather; marble; two versions: Musée du Louvre, Paris, France; Victoria and Albert Museum, London, England

1757   Menacing Cupid; marble; Rijksmuseum, Amsterdam, The Netherlands

1761   Sweet Melancholy; plaster (lost or destroyed); marble version: 1763, Hermitage, St. Petersburg, Russia

1763   Pygmalion at the Feet of His Statue; marble; Musée du Louvre, Paris, France

1765–71 Winter; marble; Hermitage, St. Petersburg, Russia

1766–82 Equestrian monument of Peter the Great; bronze; Decembrists' Square, St. Petersburg, Russia

Further Reading

Diderot, Denis, and Étienne-Maurice Falconet, Le pour et le contre: Correspondance polémique sur le respect . . . [de] Diderot et Falconet, edited by Yves Benot, Paris: Éditeurs Français Réunis, 1958

"Falconet, Étienne-Maurice," in The Dictionary of Art, edited by Jane Turner, vol. 10, New York: Grove, and London: Macmillan, 1996

Levitine, George, The Sculpture of Falconet, Greenwich, Connecticut: New York Graphic Society, 1972

Réau, Louis, Étienne-Maurice Falconet, 2 vols., Paris: Demotte, 1922

Zaretskaia, Zinaida, Fal'kone, Moscow: Sov. Khudozhnik, 1965

EQUESTRIAN MONUMENT OF PETER THE GREAT (*THE BRONZE HORSEMAN*) 1766–1782

Étienne-Maurice Falconet 1716–1791

bronze

twice life-size

Decembrists' Square, St. Petersburg, Russia

Equestrian Monument of Peter the Great (*The Bronze Horsemen*), St. Petersburg, Russia
Courtesy Sergei Androssov

Catherine II decided in the autumn of 1763 to create an equestrian monument dedicated to Peter the Great. Having secured the Russian throne after the overthrow of Czar Peter III, her husband and Peter's grandson, the empress was especially interested in showing her succession from the famous reformer, who, according to Pushkin, had cut "a window to Europe." A year later, the empress inspected an equestrian statue executed from 1743 to 1755 according to the plans of Bartolomeo Carlo Rastrelli; she rejected it.

At that time, Russia did not have professional sculptors trained for such crucial work. Therefore, a sculptor had to be invited from abroad. With the recommendation of Denis Diderot, a correspondent and consultant of Catherine II, the choice fell to Étienne-Maurice Falconet. On 26 August 1766, Dmitry Golitsyn, the Russian envoy to Paris, drew up a contract with the sculptor for eight years of work. On 15 October of that same year Falconet, together with his young student, Marie-Anne Collot, arrived in St. Petersburg.

Judging from the evidence, Falconet had already completed the first study of the future monument while in Paris. Diderot knew of this study; his approval influenced the empress's support for the project. In keeping with the tone of his era, Falconet treated Peter the Great above all as legislator and benefactor of his country.

Falconet had already made a small model of the statue in the first half of 1767. On 1 February 1768, he set to work on a large model, which he completed in June of the following year. A plaster version was presented for general review and discussion in late May 1770. Some of the opinions of the Russian public, which was unprepared to judge a work of sculpture, enraged Falconet. However, the empress approved the statue and ordered that the work continue.

Falconet rejected many of the canons accepted by past French sculptors working on equestrian monuments. He chose not to depict a victorious military leader on a proud, heavy, charging horse. Rather, he portrayed a young hero in light, conventional dress, seated on a rearing horse that has just reached the top of an ornate cliff. The image can be traced to a motif by Leonardo da Vinci. This type of equestrian statue was often encountered in models for monuments and small-scale statuettes in the late 17th and early 18th centuries. However, it is more likely that Falconet was familiar only with the equestrian monument of King Philip IV of Spain, which was created by Pietro Tacca in Madrid between 1634 and 1640. Indeed, the Frenchman probably knew of this work only through an engraving. The image created by Falconet greatly surpassed the statue from Madrid in expressiveness, namely because of the new treatment of the hero and the mastery of the artist's execution. A slight technical refinement also showed itself to be an important peculiarity: the tail of the horse is supported not by the ground (as with Tacca's work), but by the figure of a serpent embodying Envy.

Work on Peter's head caused Falconet definite difficulties, as it was necessary to compose the likeness of a portrait with expression characteristic of monumental statuary. According to the testimony of the sculptor himself, the czar's head was completed by Collot, who specialized in plastic portraiture. A plaster head of Peter the Great, now preserved in the Russian Museum in St. Petersburg, and a small bronze bust of the czar that was signed by Collot, now in the Hermitage in St. Petersburg, serve as evidence of her work on the monument.

The choice of a pedestal in the form of natural cliffs was also innovative. The search for the appropriate stone had already begun in the late 1760s and was the source of many problems for Falconet. In 1768 an enormous, satisfactory stone was located in the forest near the settlement of Lakhta. With great concentration of power and the use of all the technology available at the time, the monolithic stone was moved to the Gulf of Finland over the course of a year. There it was loaded on a special ship and taken by water to Senate Square (now called Decembrists' Square), the chosen site for the monument.

Falconet encountered major problems during the casting of the monument. During the summer of 1768, a site had been outfitted for the casting studio, and a search had begun for an experienced master caster (Falconet did not possess the necessary experience). Two masters arrived in St. Petersburg from Italy at the end of 1770, but Falconet considered them insufficiently prepared and refused their services. In March of 1773, a contract for the casting was made with the master Benoit Ersman of France. However, this caster could not get along with Falconet and was fired during the summer of 1774. In the end, Falconet decided to carry out the project himself, supported by the experienced Russian master Emelyan Khailov, who had worked at the Arsenal in St. Petersburg. The first casting was produced in August 1775 and almost ended in catastrophe because of a worker's carelessness. The situation was saved by Khailov, whose selflessness and daring Falconet especially emphasized in his writings. Although the results of the first casting were satisfactory, a second was ordered and produced in July 1777. Thereafter, the equestrian monument was basically ready.

During this time, Falconet's position in Russia was becoming more and more difficult. An artist with a difficult and uncompromising character, he possessed no diplomatic skills. His relationship with Ivan Betskoy, head of the bureau for construction and president of the Academy of Arts in St. Petersburg, was complicated from the very beginning, but it eventually entered a phase of open conflict. Betskoy, in particular, blamed Falconet for a deliberate delay in the work. Obviously, Betskoy was able to exert a certain influence even on Catherine II, who had initially shown Falconet personal patronage and even corresponded with him (thereby furnishing the most important sources for the history of the monument). The empress did not find time even to review the cast monument, a fact that must have provoked dissatisfaction in the artist. Falconet finally abandoned St. Petersburg in the fall of 1778, not waiting for the engraving and mounting that would complete the work.

The Russian architect Yury Velten then took charge of the work. To him fell the duty of systematizing the Senate Square, preparing the pedestal and final mounting, and supervising the engraving. The completion of work was set to coincide with the centenary anniversary of Peter the Great's birth. On 7 August 1782 the monument was solemnly unveiled in the presence of Catherine II, who also immortalized herself in the inscription on the pedestal in Russian and Latin: "Pietro Primo/Catherina Secunda/MDCLXXII." Falconet was not invited to its unveiling and was only later sent a medal commemorating the event.

Nevertheless, Falconet entered the history of art as a first-class sculptor because of his monument to Peter the Great—a model work and a worthy completion of the evolution of the equestrian monument in the history of Classical art.

SERGEI ANDROSSOV

Further Reading

Arkin, David, *Mediny Vsadnik: Pamiatnik Petru I v Leningrade* (The Bronze Horseman: The Monument to Peter I in Leningrad), Leningrad and Moscow: Iskusstvo, 1958

Ivanov, Georgii, *Kamen'-grom* (Stone-Thunder), St. Petersburg: Stroiizdat SPb, 1994

Kaganovich, Avraam L., *"Mednyi Vsadnik": Istoriia sozdaniia monumenta* ("The Bronze Horseman": The History of the Creation of the Monument), Leningrad: Iskusstvo, 1975

Levitine, George, *The Sculpture of Falconet*, Greenwich, Connecticut: New York Graphic Society, 1972

JEAN-ALEXANDRE-JOSEPH FALGUIÈRE 1831–1900 *French*

Known only to specialists today, Alexandre Falguière was one of the most celebrated French sculptors of the last third of the 19th century. Counterfeit reproductions of his works were hawked on Parisian sidewalks along with cheap Venus de Milos. Falguière swiftly achieved success through academic channels, garnering every official honor; only later did this friend of Jean-Baptiste Carpeaux and Auguste Rodin pursue more individualistic directions.

Falguière came from a family of artisans in Toulouse and arrived in Paris with a modest scholarship from his native city; he compensated for his lack of material advantages with ebullient energy and talent. His first masterpiece, *The Winner of the Cockfight*, sent from Rome to the Paris Salon of 1864, reveals the influence of antique bronze sculptures such as the 4th-century-BCE *Thornpuller* and of Italian Renaissance bronzes, then enjoying a revival. Soon afterward, Falguière created a second unanimously admired sculpture, and his most famous, *The Christian Martyr Tarcisius*. The work depicts an early Christian altar boy—a poignant waif reminiscent of Carpeaux's youths in *Count Ugolino and His Sons* (1857–61)—who preferred to be stoned to death rather than yield the consecrated host to the pagans.

In the winter of 1870, Falguière's battalion was stationed on the ramparts of Paris, awaiting the German invasion. There he modeled an allegorical figure out of snow, a colossal nude woman seated in a defiant pose by a cannon, and called it *Resistance* (1870). Commemorated in etchings and poems, as well as in a reduced bronze edition from the 1890s, the piece enjoyed a fame that belied its transience.

In the three immensely productive decades that followed, Falguière exhibited at every Salon, usually placing the "Falguière of the year" at the entrance to the Palais de l'Industrie. Critics marveled at his ability to endow inert matter with a sense of palpitating life and movement. His sculptures and monuments still ornament Parisian institutions, such as the Collège de France, Grand Palais, Opéra, Opéra Comique, Panthéon, Sorbonne, and Théâtre Français, and such French cities as Abbeville, Cahors, Carcassonne, Mâcon, Nîmes, Rouen, and Toulouse, as well as Athens, Biskra (Algeria), Buenos Aires, and Washington, D.C. Falguière was able to embody a hero's salient character traits and moral qualities in simple, natural, yet highly expressive gestures. By 1880 he was turning away commissions, and in the 1890s only Rodin's studio rivaled his in its intense activity. Falguière trained and employed a cohort of young sculptors, many from Toulouse, including Antonin Mercié.

Some of Falguière's most interesting works were, like *Resistance*, ephemeral or incomplete. For the 1878 International Exposition, he created a multifigured fountain, the *Seine and Its Tributaries*, at the Trocadéro Palace; composed of plaster, it eventually crumbled away. In 1882 he designed a complex neo-Baroque sculptural group, *The Triumph of the Revolution*, for the Arc de Triomphe, which boasted many figures, a chariot, and four furiously energetic horses. The plaster model remained atop the arch for four years, slowly disintegrating, while committees debated, eventually rejecting the massive, too-diffuse form. In 1890 Falguière received another commission to honor the Revolution, this time for the Panthéon. It too was never completed, although he produced at least four successive projects, all of which either displeased the authorities, the press, or the artist. An accomplished portraitist, Falguière modeled almost 50 busts with a lively touch that resembles Carpeaux's. Among the finest are those of the statesman Léon Gambetta (1884) and the sculptor Paul Dubois (1891).

Of all Falguière's works, his nude female sculptures brought him the most notoriety—and, in their multiple editions, the most income. The first was his 1882 plaster *Diana*, the goddess of the hunt, soon followed by *Hunting Nymph* (1888); *Woman with a Peacock* (1890); *Diana/Callisto* (1892); *Heroic Poetry* (1893); and *Dancer (Cléo de Mérode)* (1895). These were all fleshy nudes of almost uncomfortable naturalism. His admirers considered the creation of the modern nude to be Falguière's most important innovation: the provocative, sensual, and highly fin de siècle French nude. More representational than Rodin, Falguière created the illusion of exquisitely soft flesh. Detractors complained that Falguière had not even idealized the heads, which were astonishingly accurate portraits of specific

Diana
Courtesy Daniel Martin

studio models, complete with contemporary hairstyles and—most shocking—traces of the modern corset.

Clay was Falguière's favorite medium; it satisfied his incessant need to create and suggested the energy of living beings. Plaster and bronze translate his works most faithfully, substantiating his contemporaries' claim that he was a "colorist" in sculpture, concerned, like Rodin, with the nuances of light and shade playing across surfaces. His marbles, executed by *praticiens* (skilled stonecarvers) are sometimes less successful; in his haste to move on to his next project, he did not always provide adequate supervision of the last.

Often content to recycle conventional elements, Falguière lacked Rodin's inventive genius. He was exceptionally gifted, however, at translating his perceptions into three-dimensional modeled form. His sculptural process, like the literalism of his Dianas, demonstrates this tendency to create by copying: he used models posing in tableaux vivants, mannequins fashioned out of clay and clothed with rags, photographs of models, and even life casts, a controversial procedure. At the Salon of 1896, a scandal erupted when Falguière showed his *Dancer (Cléo de Mérode)*, a nude figure of stunning realism for which the well-known beauty Cléo de Mérode had allowed him to take casts. Curiously, 16 years earlier, Falguière had come to Rodin's defense by rebutting charges that the latter's *The Age of Bronze* (1876; Musée Rodin, Paris, France) was only a cast from life. In their late years, however, both sculptors experimented with casts as part of their creative process.

In 1898, after the Société des Gens de Lettres rejected Rodin's monument to novelist Honoré de Balzac, Falguière took on the commission, but not before striving in vain to support Rodin. (Rodin's and Falguière's portrait busts of one another date from 1899 and 1900.) Falguière approaches Rodin most closely in a few late works. In *Bacchantes Fighting*, two nude women grapple brutally with each other. *Cain Carrying the Dead Abel*, an evocation of primitive violence, was so radical in its naturalistic modeling of a corpse that it was never exhibited in Falguière's lifetime. Finally, the eight terracotta reliefs on mythological themes that ornamented the house of Baron Vita, at Evian-les-Bains (Haute-Savoie), featured close-up views of nude figures in antiacademic poses. Symbolists appreciated this side of Falguière, as well as his evocation of the mysteries of *la femme* and his suggestively unfinished clay maquettes. Although he was faithful to Classical tradition and a major purveyor of public statuary, Falguière nonetheless sought to energize a static medium and, with his earthy nudes, test the boundaries of naturalism.

LYNNE D. AMBROSINI

See also **Rodin, Auguste**

Biography

Born in Toulouse, France, 7 September 1831. Studied at the École Régionale des Beaux-Arts, Toulouse, 1844; moved to Paris to study sculpture, first in the studios of Albert Carrier-Belleuse and Jean-Louis Chenillion; entered the École des Beaux-Arts under François Jouffroy, April 1854; first exhibited at Salon, 1857; won Prix de Rome, 1859; returned to Paris, 1865, settling at 68 rue d'Assas, and remained for 35 years; government purchased *The Winner of the Cockfight*, 1864; served in National Guard, Franco-Prussian War, 1870–71; fulfilled over 30 monumental and decorative commissions, primarily in France, but also abroad; received medals at the Salons of 1864, 1867, 1868, and 1875, and at the Expositions Universelles of 1867 and 1878; received the Legion of Honor, 1870; named Officer and Commander of the Legion, 1878 and 1889; became professor at École Nationale des Beaux-Arts, and named to a seat at Académie des

Beaux-Arts, 1882; showed first of his sculptures of nude mythological goddesses, 1882; exhibited portrait busts throughout his career. Died in Paris, France, 19 April 1900.

Selected Works

1864	*The Winner of the Cockfight*; bronze; Musée d'Orsay, Paris, France
1868	*The Christian Martyr Tarcisius*; marble; Musée d'Orsay, Paris, France
1877	*Alphonse de Lamartine*; bronze; Esplanade Lamartine, Mâcon, France
1878	*Pierre Corneille*; marble; Comédie Française, Paris, France
1879	*St. Vincent de Paul*; marble; Panthéon, Paris, France
1882	*The Triumph of the Revolution* for the Arc de Triomphe, Place de l'Etoile, Paris; France; plaster (destroyed); wax model, Musée des Beaux-Arts de Grenoble, France
1884	*Léon Gambetta*; bronze; Place d'Armes, Cahors, France
1886	*Bacchantes Fighting*; plaster; Musée des Beaux-Arts, Calais, France
1887	*Diana*; marble; Musée des Augustins, Toulouse, France
1888	*Hunting Nymph*; marble; Musée des Augustins, Toulouse, France
1880s	*Cain Carrying the Dead Abel*; plaster; Ivry Storage, Collection of the City of Paris, France
1892	*Diana/Callisto*; marble; Ny Carlsberg Glyptotek, Copenhagen, Denmark
1890s	Eight mythological bas-reliefs; terracotta; Baron Vita's house; Evian-les-Bains, France (other locations unknown)
1893	*Heroic Poetry*; marble; Salle des Illustres, Capitole, Toulouse, France
1897	*Pegasus Carrying the Poet toward the Regions of the Dream*; bronze; Square de l'Opéra, rue Boudreau, Paris, France

Further Reading

Bénédite, Léonce, *Alexandre Falguière*, Paris: Librairie de l'Art Ancien et Moderne, 1902

Butler, Ruth, and Jane Van Nimmen, *Nineteenth-Century French Sculpture: Monuments for the Middle Class*, Louisville, Kentucky: J.B. Speed Art Museum, 1971

Fusco, Peter, "Falguière, the Female Nude, and 'La Résistance,'" *Los Angeles County Museum of Art Bulletin* 23 (1977)

Fusco, Peter, and H.W. Janson, *The Romantics to Rodin: French Nineteenth-Century Sculpture from North American Collec-*

tions, Los Angeles: Los Angeles County Museum of Art, and New York: Braziller, 1980

Lami, Stanislas, *Dictionnaire des sculpteurs de l'école française au dix-neuvième siècle*, 4 vols., Paris: Champion, 1914–21; see especially vol. 2, 1916

La plume 219–23 (1 June 1898) (special issue on Alexandre Falguière)

Levkoff, Mary L., *Rodin in His Time*, New York: Thames and Hudson, 1994

Pingeot, Anne, "Le fonds Falguière au Musée du Louvre," *Bulletin de la Société de l'histoire de l'art français* (1978)

Wasserman, Jeanne, "In Search of Diana," in *Shop Talk: Studies in Honor of Seymour Slive*, edited by Cynthia P. Schneider, William W. Robinson, and Alice L. Davies, Cambridge, Massachusetts: Harvard University Art Museums, 1995

DOMENICO FANCELLI 1469?–1519

Italian, active in Spain

Domenico Fancelli was one of the earliest artists, if not the first, to introduce Italian Renaissance sculpture to Spain. His most celebrated works consist of tombs carved in an elegant central Italian style, evident particularly in the refined handling of the effigies and reliefs. Erected for some of the most important Spanish patrons, these monuments established a new trend in funeral art. His talent has frequently been overlooked: Spanish art historians have considered him a foreign exponent of the Italian Renaissance, whereas those studying the art of Italy have focused on the work of other sculptors.

Little is known of Fancelli's career before he arrived in Spain. In two different wills (one of 1512 and another of 1519), he is described alternately as a native of Settignano and Florence. He probably learned his art in Florence, although he may have subsequently worked in Rome. The exact nature of his training in Italy can only be deduced from his Spanish works; in type these recall Antonio Pollaiuolo's tomb of Pope Sixtus IV (1484–93) and Giovanni Dalmata and Mino da Fiesole's tomb of Pope Paul II (1474–75); stylistically they resemble the works of sculptors such as Andrea Bregno and Andrea Sansovino.

Therefore, it is unclear where he was working in Italy when Spanish patrons found him, but the Mendoza family, which commissioned his first works in Spain, had contacts in Rome. Fancelli's first work in Spain may well have been the tomb of Cardinal Pedro González de Mendoza. The attribution is based on the close similarity between this effigy and that which he sculpted on the tomb of Cardinal Diego Hurtado de Mendoza (see Lenaghan, 1998). On stylistic grounds, it seems that a team of local artists created the remainder of the tomb (figures, reliefs, and architectural details), but they were presumably working under Fancelli's supervision. According to this hypothesis, Fancelli also designed the tomb's composition, which is striking for its combination of Italian motifs in a two-tiered triumphal arch. This solution, although unusual in Italy, probably resulted as a compromise between the conflicting desires of the patron, artist, and the cathedral chapter. When each level is considered separately, however, a stylistic indebtedness to the works of the central Italian tradition of Bregno and Sansovino becomes apparent.

In effect, Fancelli designed the tomb that introduced the Italian Renaissance style to Spanish patrons who had up to that point known only the Gothic. This alone might have guaranteed his position in the history of art, but the new style was well received, and Fancelli soon found himself carving more works. The Mendoza family obviously prized the artist, and the Count of Tendilla turned to the artist for his next project, the tomb of Cardinal Diego Hurtado de Mendoza. Typologically, this work replicates Dalmata and Mino's tomb of Pope Paul II, with changes only to accommodate iconographic details appropriate to the deceased. The quality fineness of the relief carvings on the tomb would have been exceptional in early 16th-century Spain.

This project also marks a significant shift in workshop practice. Whereas Fancelli had carved the first tomb in Spain using stone (alabaster) found in the region and a team of local sculptors, he carved the second monument in Italy and then supervised its shipping to Seville and installation in the cathedral. He would follow this practice in the remaining monuments he carved for Spanish patrons.

With the support of the Mendoza family—the letter of recommendation from the Count of Tendilla survives—Fancelli was awarded the commission for the tomb of Prince John. In this work, the sculptor emu-

Tomb of the Catholic Kings (Tomb of Ferdinand and Isabella)
The Conway Library, Courtauld Institute of Art

lates Pollaiuolo's tomb of Pope Sixtus IV in St. Peter's Basilica by creating a catafalque that tilts pyramidally, but Fancelli departs from this model by designing a taller bier. Interestingly, the type proved popular in Spain, whereas few patrons and sculptors in Italy would choose to follow its example. Fancelli carved the effigy with an idealized, almost classicizing, beauty that distinguishes it from contemporary works in Spain. Similarly, the dramatic placement of large griffins at the corners of the tomb marks another of the artist's innovations.

After installing this tomb in late 1512 or early 1513, Fancelli received the commission for his next work, the tomb of the Catholic Kings (also known as the tomb of Ferdinand and Isabella). The tomb was shipped to Spain in 1517 and was probably installed directly in front of the high altar shortly afterward. The tomb remained in this position until it was shifted to the right in 1603 to make room for Bartolomé Ordóñez's tomb of King Philip the Fair and Queen Joanna the Mad (1519–26).

The tomb of Ferdinand and Isabella follows the type established in Prince John's tomb in which the deceased lies on a pyramidal base. Fancelli, however, separated the base into two levels more forcefully by emphasizing the cornice, which divides the base, and by heightening the second level. This tomb, therefore, is taller and has a greater surface area on which to place attributes. Notable among these are the figures of the Apostles and tondi of the *Baptism of Christ* and *Resurrection*; the latter, in particular, offer an impressive demonstration of relief sculpture with some figures almost fully round and others barely indicated. Seated at the corners are four doctors (teachers) of the Roman Catholic Church, whose presence marks another break from 14th- and 15th-century tombs in Spain.

When Fancelli returned to Spain to install the tomb of Ferdinand and Isabella, Charles V awarded him the contract for the tomb of Philip and Joanna, and on 14 July 1518, Francisco Ximénez de Cisneros's executors hired Fancelli for the tomb of the cardinal. The tomb of the Catholic Kings had become such a success that both of these contracts now specified it as a model. Fancelli, however, died in Saragossa in late April 1519 before he could return to Italy to begin these projects.

PATRICK LENAGHAN

Biography

Born probably in Settignano, Italy, perhaps 1469. Came from a family of sculptors and masons. Information regarding his training scarce, but probably worked in Florence and Rome; called to Spain to work for the Mendoza family, perhaps as early as 1503; established

himself there, specializing in funerary sculpture; returned to Italy, *ca.* 1508; produced funerary monuments to be shipped back to Spain and installed under his supervision. Died in Saragossa, Spain, April 1519.

Selected Works

ca. 1503– *ca.* 1508	Tomb of Cardinal Pedro González de Mendoza; alabaster; Cathedral of Toledo, Spain (attributed)
1508–10	Tomb of Cardinal Diego Hurtado de Mendoza; marble; Cathedral of Seville, Spain
1511–13	Tomb of Prince John; marble; Convent of Santo Tomás, Ávila, Spain
1514–17	Tomb of the Catholic Kings (Tomb of Ferdinand and Isabella); marble; Royal Chapel, Granada, Spain

Further Reading

Andrei, Pietro (editor), *Sopra Domenico Fancelli Fiorentino e Bartolammeo Ordognes Spagnolo e sopra altri artisti loro contemporanei che nel principio del secolo decimosesto coltivarone e propagarono in Ispagna: Le Arti Belle italiane: Memorie estratte da documenti inediti*, Massa, Italy: Frediani, 1871

Gómez-Moreno, Manuel, *La escultura del renacimiento en España*, Florence: Pantheon Casa Editrice, 1931; as *Renaissance Sculpture in Spain*, translated by Bernard Bevan, Florence: Pantheon, 1931; reprint, New York: Hacker Art Books, 1971

Hernández Perera, Jesús, *Escultores florentinos en España*, Madrid: Instituto Diego Velázquez del Consejo Superior de Investigaciones Científicas, 1957

Justi, Carl, *Miscallaneen aus drei jahrhunderten spanischen Kunstslebens*, 2 vols., Berlin: Grote, 1908; see especially vol. 1

Lenaghan, Patrick, "Reinterpreting the Italian Renaissance in Spain: Attribution and Connoisseurship," *The Sculpture Journal* 2 (1998)

Proske, Beatrice Gilman, *Castilian Sculpture: Gothic to Renaissance*, New York: The Hispanic Society of America, 1951

Redondo Cantera, María José, *El sepulcro en España en el siglo XVI: Tipología e iconografía*, Madrid: Ministerio de Cultura, 1987

FRANCESCO FANELLI 1577–after 1662?
Italian

The Florentine Francesco Fanelli was one of the principal European bronze sculptors in the first half of the 17th century, and together with Hubert Le Sueur, he was the leading sculptor active in England in the age of King Charles I. Born in 1577, he received at least part of his training in the studio of Giovanni Bandini (called Giovanni dell'Opera), who in his will honored an agreement to allow his sculptural models to be used by Fanelli, a former member of his workshop.

Before 6 August 1605, Fanelli had settled in Genoa, where on that day his son was baptized; the painter Agostino Tassi was his godfather. The sculptor is regularly documented in the Ligurian capital up to and including 1630. Although his early Genoese works remain untraced, some important commissions are documented, such as his life-size bronze *Crucifix*, commissioned in 1609 by Giovan Domenico Spinola. In the contract for this work, the painter Giovanni Battista Paggi acted as a guarantor for Fanelli. From 1615 to 1617, Fanelli carved six marble angels for the lateral portals of the sanctuary of the Church of Madonna della Misericordia in Savona (*in situ*). From 1620 on, he worked on the decoration of the Chapel of the Virgin in the Church of Nostro Signore delle Vigne, where in 1627 he was paid for some gilded bronze capitals and in 1629 for two gilded bronze angels. In 1619 his *St. John the Evangelist* was put up in the choir of the Church of the Gesù, and in 1625 he was paid for the statues of *Christ the Redeemer* and *Ecce homo* for the Raggi Chapel in the same church. These three large marble sculptures, as well as the convincingly attributed *Madonna with the Christ Child* now in the Church of Parodi Ligure, clearly reveal—particularly in their drapery style—the influence of Giovanni Battista Caccini, the leading marble sculptor active in Florence around 1600.

Fanelli must have arrived in England at the latest by 1632 because in 1634 he was paid a pension or retainer fee on behalf of Charles I, which was backdated by two years and renewed in 1635. According to Joachim von Sandrart, an ivory statue representing Pygmalion gained him the attention of the king. But neither this nor any other carvings in this material are extant. Noteworthy, however, was his production of small bronzes, which circulated greatly not only in England but also on the continent. For instance, Sandrart himself kept several of these in his private collection in Nuremberg. In his *Deutsche Akademie* (German Academy) (1675), he praised Fanelli's skills in casting bronzes that were so precise that it was not necessary to chase and polish them subsequently. As evidence of his technical mastery, Sandrart recorded one case when Fanelli cast a huge, hollow statue with a bronze skin as thin as a medal. Because small bronzes by Fanelli are included in some inventories of Genoese citizens, this branch of his activity must have been of appreciable importance already in his earlier years in Italy. The 17th-century inventory of small bronzes at Whitehall attributed to "ffrancisco ffanello" (also called the "one-eyed Italian," pointing to a physical handicap), as well as the 18th-century list of Fanelli's bronzes at Welbeck Abbey drawn up by George Vertue, permit us to identify a number of types produced by the sculptor and show his fondness for equestrian themes; apart from various single *Horses* whose poses range from standing to pacing to galloping, he created a *Cupid on Horseback*, a *St. George on Horseback Fighting a Dragon*, a *Turk on Horseback Attacked by a Lion*, and the *Nessus with Deianira*. Typologically, the equestrian hunting and battle groups have a model in Giovanni Bandini's *Hunt of Meleager* (1583).

Fanelli, like his teacher, was a master in the genre of the portrait bust. His only signed and dated work is the bronze bust of Charles, Prince of Wales (later Charles II), at Welbeck Abbey. It bears an inscription on the front of the base reading "Carolus Princeps Walliae 1640" and one on the reverse reading "Fran(cis)cus Fanellius Florentin(us) Sculptor Magn(a)e Bri(tannia)e Regis." To judge from the age of the sitter, the bronze bust of his patron Charles I must be a few years earlier. Both royal personalities wear precious armor, and in the portrait of the prince, a strong interest in the naturalistic rendering of flesh and hair can be discerned. Significantly, in 1641 Thomas Howard, Earl of Arundel, disposed in a draft will that Fanelli should create his own memorial (not executed), indicating perhaps a certain fame of Fanelli's for such artistic tasks. In the field of tomb sculpture, however, the bronze effigy of Sir Robert Aiton in Westminster Abbey is Fanelli's only generally accepted work. The bronze bust of Richard, Earl of Portland (about 1631/32), in Winchester Cathedral, with its markedly naturalistic features, is also likely by Fanelli.

In his bronze reliefs, Fanelli shows his familiarity with the most recent accomplishments of Florentine court sculpture, especially with the style of Pietro Tacca. Fanelli's most popular work in this genre is a pair showing *The Holy Family in the House of the Robber* and *Christ on the Road to Calvary*, examples of which can be found in several museums and private collections. Two suites of engravings after his drawings, showing *Fountains* (1661) and *Grottoes* (undated), were published in Paris and might be evidence of a French stay. According to Vertue, Fanelli "dyd in England." On the basis of the fact that Cornelis de Brie in his *Gulden Cabinet* (manuscript from 1657, printed in 1661 and 1662) cites him as if he were still alive, it has been concluded that he died only after 1662. However, the artist's later years remain obscure. His son Virgilio, who worked with him in his Genoese studio in 1630, later had a remarkable career as a goldsmith and metal sculptor in Bologna and Toledo.

EIKE D. SCHMIDT

Biography

Born in Florence, Italy, 17 December 1577. Trained in part by Giovanni Bandini (also called Giovanni dell'Opera); documented as active in Genoa, *ca.* 1605–30; traveled to England, *ca.* 1632; appointed sculptor to Charles I, King of England, from 1632; only signed and dated work is *Charles II as Prince of Wales*, 1640; later years remain obscure. Died in England (city unknown), perhaps after 1662.

Selected Works

1615–17 Six angels; marble; Church of Madonna della Misericordia, Savona, Italy

1619 *St. John the Evangelist*; Church of the Gesù, Genoa, Italy

1625 *Christ the Redeemer* and *Ecce homo*; Raggi Chapel, Church of the Gesù, Genoa, Italy

ca. *Charles I, King of England*; bronze;
1635–40 Victoria and Albert Museum, London, England

1640 *Charles II as Prince of Wales*; bronze; Welbeck Abbey, Nottinghamshire, England

Further Reading

Franchini Guelfi, Fausta, "Fanelli, Francesco," in *Dizionario biografico degli Italiani*, vol. 44, Rome: Istituto della Enciclopedia Italiana, 1994

Howarth, David, "Charles I, Sculpture and Sculptors," in *The Late King's Goods: Collections, Possessions, and Patronage of Charles I in the Light of the Commonwealth Sales Inventories*, edited by Arthur MacGregor, London: McAlpine, and Oxford: Oxford University Press, 1989

Motture, Peta, "Victoria and Albert Museum, London, Francesco Fanelli, Bust of King Charles I," *National Art-Collections Fund Review* (1999)

Pope-Hennessy, John, "Some Bronze Statuettes by Francesco Fanelli," *Burlington Magazine* 95 (1953)

Radcliffe, Anthony, and Peter Thornton, "John Evelyn's Cabinet," *Connoisseur* 197/794 (1978)

Schmidt, Eike D., "Giovanni Bandini tra Marche e Toscana," *Nuovi studi* 6 (1998) (on Fanelli's early Florentine period)

Whinney, Margaret, *Sculpture in Britain, 1530–1830*, London and Baltimore, Maryland: Penguin, 1964; 2nd edition, revised by John Physick, London and New York: Penguin, 1988

White, Adam, "A Biographical Dictionary of London Tomb Sculptors, c. 1560–c. 1660," *Walpole Society* 61 (1999)

COSIMO FANZAGO 1591–1678 *Italian*

Cosimo Fanzago is the most important figure of the Neapolitan Baroque period. He was chiefly a marble sculptor, in statue and decorative carving, and he was an architect of ecclesiastic and civil works. He also produced many projects, however, for liturgical jewelry, bronze sculpture, marble decoration, and wood furnishings.

Fanzago's activity consisted primarily of directing large workshops. He would carry out many works contemporaneously, frequently traveling as well as sending works or collaborators to different places. Fanzago occasionally collaborated with the sculptors Ercole Ferrata and Andrea Bolgi. Giuliano Finelli frequently meddled in Fanzago's work, and the relationship between them is characterized by Finelli's ancient biographers, Giambattista Passeri and Lione Pascoli, as an acute rivalry that also involved the painter Giovanni Lanfranco.

The conception of an integration and a correspondence between architectonic, decorative, and sculptural elements is a main feature of Fanzago's style. In fact, it is difficult to make a clear distinction between his architectural and sculptural works, because Fanzago always merged the two techniques, usually requalifying the architectonic interiors with marble decoration. Fanzago's work consistently featured spectacular effects created through illusionistic perspective games and the richness and splendor of the whole.

More representative of Fanzago's decorative style is the interior decoration mainly of floral motifs done with marble encrustation, or *tarsia*, of polychrome marbles with the assured distribution of different colors and types of materials. One example is the interior of the Church of the Certosa di San Martino in Naples. The extraordinary creativity by which Fanzago developed this decorative style, and the enrichment of it with figural sculpture, was influential in the decoration (*ca.* 1660) of the Spada Chapel in the Church of San Girolamo della Carità in Rome by the architect Francesco Borromini.

In Fanzago's work, the virtuosity in decorative details and the creative approach to technical problems are the heritage of the great artisan tradition from which he emerged. A small but significant example of Fanzago's manual dexterity was the decorative solution of the *Crowned Skulls*, which was a termination of the marble balustrade of the monks' cemetery in the Chiostro Grande (grand cloister) of the Certosa di San Martino in Naples.

The Certosa di San Martino workshop in Naples was the greatest work directed by Fanzago; he not only directed it, but also intervened and executed much of the work himself. He is documented as working there from 1623 to 1656, and in 1630 he became the chief master, succeeding the Florentine architect Giovanni Antonio Dosio and the Neapolitan architect Giovanni Giacomo di Conforto. Here the most important works guided by Fanzago's design and direction are the Chiostro Grande and the interior decoration of the church of the Certosa. The sculptural works of the Chiostro Grande are remarkable mainly for the decorative solution of the corner doors of the court. Each door is surmounted by an oval niche in which a marble bust of a Carthusian saint or blessed resides. The most extraordinary sculptures of this group are the three commonly attributed to the master's hand: *Blessed Nicolò Albergati, San Gennaro*, and *San Bruno*. Each of these extraordinary figures possesses a sculptural virtuosity that is revealed in the drapery and the strong human and psychological characterization. This is emphasized by the studied dynamic postures of the figures, which emerge from open space and are carefully calibrated to their architectonic frame. The posture of the figures is conceived to emphasize their lateral view, which is the most usual in the passageway of the court open galleries.

Fanzago's role in the Baroque reshaping of Naples cannot be underestimated. The extreme breadth of his work shows the extent and importance of his activity and the range of his influence. Fanzago's catalogue is astonishing in the number and types of works, since the main part of it consists of monumental decorations such as high altars, pulpits, and fountains, such as the Medina (1634–40) and Sebeto (1635–39) fountains in Naples. But one of the most common characteristics of Fanzago's inventions in the urban texture, which are significant especially for their marked spectacular effect, are the *guglie* (spires), the first of which was the *Guglia di San Gennaro*. *Guglie* are sculptural composite colossi, sorts of obelisks covered with very rich sculptural decoration. At first glance they reveal their influence from ephemeral decorations, with the ingenious application of their decorative details applied to permanent monuments. Fanzago's activity in creating ephemeral decorations for holidays is documented.

The omnipresence of Fanzago's workshop is partly due to a remarkable socioeconomic aspect of his complex personality; he was an entrepreneur and a speculative contractor who was always looking to obtain the largest number of contract works for big profits. He was also involved in the sale of painting. The unique ancient biography dedicated to this great protagonist of Baroque art was written by Bernardo de Dominici, the Neapolitan art historiographer of the 18th century. It is a highly praising document that explores the primary qualities of Fanzago's style: creativity, expression, and an interweaving of realistic detail with decorative embellishment. De Dominici allusively refers to Borromini as relative and moderate and looks at Fanzago's unusual inventions as the positive term of comparison. He counters Fanzago's ingenuity to Borromini's absolute irregularity. This critical position is interesting if compared to 19th-century historian Leopoldo Cicognara's, who negatively views Fanzago as a contributor to the century of decadence and points

to him as a leader in the definition and establishment of the corrupted taste in art.

FRANCESCA PELLEGRINO

Biography

Born in Clusone, Bergamo province, Italy, 1591. From a family of sculptors and engineers active in Clusone and Bergamo in the 16th century; uncle Pompeo Fanzago was a sculptor working in Naples. Moved to Naples, 1608, and remained until 1647; trained in his uncle's workshop; junior partner with the Tuscan sculptor Angelo Landi, 1612–20; traveled extensively through Italy for work; active in workshop of the Certosa di San Martino, Naples, 1623–29, and from 1630 to 1656 as chief master. Also documented in Puglia, 1619–20; Abruzzi, Monte Cassino, 1626–31; Venice, 1629–30; Bergamo, 1630; Calabria, 1631; Rome, 1638 and 1647–1651; and Salamanca, Spain, 1636; named Cavaliere, 1627; named first engineer of the Kingdom of Naples, 1645; sued by the Carthusians of San Martino regarding the Certosa di San Martino workshop (lawsuit continued against his heirs), 1656–1700. Died in Naples, Italy, 13 February 1678.

Selected Works

1617   Memorial to Ottavio Brancaccio; marble; Church of Sant'Angelo a Nilo, Naples, Italy

ca. 1620 Monument to Gerolamo Flerio; marble; Church of Santa Maria di Costantinopoli, Naples, Italy

1626   Floor; polychrome marble; San Martino Chapel, Church of the Certosa di San Martino, Naples, Italy

1628–43 *Crowned Skulls*; marble; Monk's Cemetery, Chiostro Grande, Certosa di San Martino, Naples, Italy

1629–68 Gate with bust of San Gennaro (with Giuliano Finelli); gilded bronze, brass; Cappella del Tesoro di San Gennaro, Cathedral of Naples, Naples, Italy

1631–56 Busts of *Blessed Nicolò Albergati, San Gennaro, San Bruno, Blessed Landino*, and *Sant'Ugo*; marble; Chiostro Grande, Certosa di San Martino, Naples, Italy

1635–41 High altar; polychrome marble; Church of Santi Severino e Sosio, Naples, Italy

1636–65 *Guglia* (spires) *di San Gennaro* (with Giuliano Finelli); marble, bronze; Piazza Cardinale Sisto Riario Sforza, Naples, Italy

1639–50 High altar and statues of *Saint Roch* and

Saint Sebastian; marble; Church of Santa
Maria di Costantinopoli, Naples, Italy

1646–50 Statues of *Isaiah* and *Jeremiah*; marble;
San Francesco Saverio Chapel, Church of
the Gesù Vecchio, Naples, Italy

1651 *Immaculate Conception*; marble;
Seminario Arcivescovile, Naples, Italy

1656–58 *Guglia* (spire) *of San Domenico*; bronze;
Piazza San Domenico Maggiore, Naples,
Italy

Further Reading

Blunt, Anthony, "Naples as Seen by French Travellers, 1630–
1780," in *The Artist and the Writer in France: Essays in
Honour of Jean Seznec*, edited by Francis Haskell, Anthony
Levi, and Robert Shackleton, Oxford: Clarendon Press, 1974

Blunt, Anthony, *Neapolitan Baroque and Rococo Architecture*,
London: Zwemmer, 1975

Bosel, Richard, "Fanzago, Cosimo," in *The Dictionary of Art*,
edited by Jane Shoaf Turner, vol. 10, New York: Grove and
London: Macmillan, 1996

Brauen, Fred, "Cosimo Fanzago and Seventeenth-Century Neapolitan Marble Decoration" (dissertation), New York: Columbia University, 1973

Brauen, Fred, "The High Altar at S. Pietro a Maiella: Fanzago,
the Ghetti, and the Celestine Fathers in Naples," *Storia dell'
arte* 35 (1979)

Cantone, Gaetana, *Napoli barocca e Cosimo Fanzago*, Naples:
Banco di Napoli, 1984

Cassani, Silvia, *Civiltà del Seicento a Napoli* (exhib. cat.), 2
vols., Naples: Electa, 1984; see especially vol. 2

Wittkower, Rudolf, *Art and Architecture in Italy, 1600–1750*,
London and Baltimore, Maryland: Penguin, 1958; 6th edition, 3 vols., revised by Joseph Connors and Jennifer Montagu, New Haven, Connecticut: Yale University Press, 1999

Zanuso, Susanna, "Cosimo Fanzago," in *Scultura del '600 a
Roma*, edited by Andrea Bacchi and Susanna Zanuso, Milano: Longanesi, 1996

FÉLICIE DE FAUVEAU 1801–1886

French

Considered in her time one of the most promising
sculptors of the new French Romantic school (along
with David d'Angers, A.L. Barye, Auguste Préault,
Henri de Triqueti, and Antonin Moine), Félicie de
Fauveau has long since been forgotten. This is surprising, since Fauveau, a passionate woman, sculptor of
great talent, and political exile with exceptional courage, was the archetypal Romantic figure. Like the Na-
zarenes in Rome and later the Pre-Raphaelites in England, Fauveau belongs to the early Gothic Revival
movement in Europe, which rejected the primacy of
the High Renaissance, Mannerism, and Baroque in
favor of the Italian Gothic and Early Renaissance.

Fauveau was a multifaceted artist in the tradition of
the Middle Ages and early Renaissance. She was not
only a sculptor but also an architect, jeweler, silver-

smith, armorer, and interior designer. Besides traditional marble sculptures, her oeuvre includes a remarkable variety of objects produced from a variety of
materials. These range from jewels, silver bells, dag-
gers, spurs, and letter openers to furniture, mirror
frames, fireplaces, fountains, and ecclesiastical objects. Fauveau often incorporated her sculptures into
ornate architectural frameworks that were further embellished with mottoes in Latin or Old French or poems
by Dante or Clément Marot. A devout Roman Catholic,
Fauveau was also an advocate of Christian art. Following ideas earlier expressed by Chateaubriand in his
Génie du Christianisme (The Genius of Christianity;
1802), she strongly believed in the importance of religious sentiment in art, and her work is replete with
references to Catholic imagery. A friend of Auguste
Rio (author of *De la Poésie Chrétienne* [On Christian
Poetry]; 1836) and Lord Lindsay (author of *The
Sketches of History of Christian Art*, 1847), Fauveau
played an active role in the conception of their books
on Christian art.

Born in Florence to French parents, Fauveau returned with them to Paris to study drawing with the
painters Louis Hersent and Bernard Gaillot. She first
exhibited at the Paris Salon of 1827, where she showed
two reliefs, one representing *Queen Christina and Monaldeschi* and the other *The Abbot*, after a novel by
Sir Walter Scott. In 1830 she executed one of her most
famous sculptures, the monument to Dante: *Paolo
(Malatesta) and Francesca* (da Rimini), for the banker
and famed collector Count James de Pourtalès-Gor-
gier. Her artistic career was interrupted by the revolution of 1830. An ardent royalist and a fervent legitimist,
Fauveau was arrested and jailed for having conspired
against King Louis-Philippe following the overthrow
of Charles X. Although she was acquitted after a trial in
Poitiers, Fauveau revived her conspirational activities
when the Duchess of Berry attempted to incite the
Vendée to revolt in 1832. Condemned to life imprisonment, Fauveau escaped to Switzerland and then to
Florence, where she remained an exile until her death
in 1886.

In Florence, Fauveau opened a studio in a former
convent and worked with her brother Hypolite for an
exclusive group of conservative Russian, Italian,
French, and English aristocrats who opposed the rising
power of the new bourgeoisie. The group included the
czar of Russia (for whom she created a fountain for
his neo-Gothic pavilion at Peterhof) and his daughter,
Princess Maria of Leuchtenberg; the Grand Duchess
of Tuscany; the kings of Naples and Sardinia; the
Duchess of Berry; the Duke of Rohan; the Countess
of La Rochejacquelein; Lord Lindsay; and Lord Lon-
donderry. In the late 1830s Fauveau worked for the
Russian connoisseur Anatole Demidoff at his Floren-

Clémence Isaure Instituting the Floral Games
The Conway Library, Courtauld Institute of Art

From 1851 to 1852 Fauveau worked for Count Edmund Zichy, a young Hungarian aristocrat living at the time in Florence, creating for him a Hungarian costume comprising several elements in silver, among them a collar, belt, sword, and spurs. Fauveau also realized a number of funerary monuments, including the monument to the painter Gros and his wife, commissioned by her friend the landscape painter Sarazin de Belmont; the funerary monument of Louise de Favreau erected in 1855 in the Medici Chapel in Santa Croce in Florence; the monument in memory of her mother Anne de Fauveau (1859), today in the cloister of Santa Maria delle Carmine; and in 1865 and 1866 the tombs of Count Henri de Larderel, a rich industrialist of French origin (Chapel of Pozzo Latico, Italy), and the Duke of Duras, the father of Fauveau's lifelong friend, Félicie de La Rochejacquelein (Chapel of the Château d'Ussé, France). In 1852 Fauveau exhibited the relief *Le Combat de Jarnac et de la Chataigneraie*, commissioned by the Duke of Rohan. At the Paris Exposition Universelle of 1855 she exhibited sculptures of *St. Dorothy* (commissioned by Dorothée de Talleyrand-Périgord, Duchess of Dino and Sagan) and *St. Elisabeth*. An indefatigable worker throughout her life, Fauveau continued to create sculptures until she died in Florence in 1886 at the age of 85. Her last work seems to be her own epitaph, on which, in memory of a woman for whom "her political ideas had been more important than her art," she wanted the following words to be inscribed: "Vendée, Labeur, Honneur, Douleur" (Vendée, labor, honor, sorrow).

CHARLES JANORAY

Biography

Born in Florence, Italy, 1801. Daughter of French parents, returned with them to Paris and studied drawing with painters Louis Hersent and Bernard Gaillot; established studio on rue de La Rochefoucault, Paris; befriended Ingres, Paul Delaroche, and Ary Scheffer (who painted her portrait, now in the Louvre); exhibited at Paris Salon of 1827, receiving a *seconde médaille*; arrested and jailed for conspiring against King Louis-Philippe, following the overthrow of King Charles X; acquitted after trial in Poitiers; joined the Duchess de Berry in Vendée, France, 1832, as a conspirator; condemned to life imprisonment; escaped to Switzerland and then to Florence, 1833; opened a studio first on via della Fornace and later on via de Serragli; worked principally as a sculptor, but also as an architect, jeweler, silversmith, and interior designer; received commissions mainly from French, Italian, English, and Russian aristocrats; exhibited at the Paris Salons of 1842 (*Judith*) and 1852 (*Le Combat de Jarnac et de la Chataigneraie*); participated at the 1855

tine villa of San Donato, realizing for him a series of allegorical picture frames for paintings by Delaroche (*The Execution of Lady Jane Grey* [National Gallery, London, England]), Delacroix, Granet, Gudin, and Marilhat. In 1843 her elaborate Louis XIII–style wood *Miroir de la Vanité* (location unknown) was deemed a piece of furniture and rejected from the Paris Salon because it did not fall within the traditional categories accepted by the Academy. In 1840, when the Comte de Chambord (Henry V—son of the Duke of Berry and grandson of Charles X) came to Rome to obtain political support from the pope for the reestablishment of the Bourbons on the throne of France, Fauveau carved several versions of the count's portrait in marble. She also executed a bust of his mother, the Duchess of Berry, for whom she carved a marble statue of *Sainte Geneviève* for the Duchess's private chapel.

Exposition Universelle in Paris. Died in Florence, Italy, 12 December 1886.

Selected Works

1827   *Queen Christina and Monaldeschi*, for Paris Salon of 1827; plaster; Musée Municipal, Louviers, France

1830–36 *Paolo and Francesca*; marble fragments; private collection, Paris, France

1840   *Comte de Chambord*; marble; private collection

1841   *Sainte Geneviève*; marble; private collection

1843   *Miroir de la Vanité*; wood (lost)

1847   Monument to the painter Gros and his wife; marble; Musée des Augustins, Toulouse, France

1849   Holy water stoup for Princess Maria of Leuchtenberg; marble (lost)

1850   *Dagger*; silver; Musée du Louvre, Paris, France

1850   *Formal de Monseigneur de Bonald*; silver; Trésor de la Primatiale, Lyons, France

1852   Holy water stoup; marble; Musée Municipal, Douai, France

1855   Fountain; marble; Peterhof, St. Petersburg, Russia

1855   Monument of Louise de Favreau; marble; Church of Santa Croce, Florence, Italy

1859   Monument to the memory of Anne de Fauveau; marble; Cloister of Santa Maria delle Carmine, Florence, Italy

1869   *Ondine*; marble (lost)

Further Reading

Benoist, Luc, *La sculpture romantique*, Paris: La Renaissance du Livre, 1928; new edition, edited by Isabelle Leroy-Jay Lemaistre, Paris: Gallimard, 1994

Brigstocke, Hugh, *Lord Lindsay as a Collector and the Sketches of the History of Christian Art*, Manchester: John Rylands University Library of Manchester, 1982

Easterday, Anastasia, "Labeur, Honneur, Douleur: Sculptors Julie Charpentier, Félicie de Fauveau, and Marie d'Orléans," *Woman's Art Journal* 18 (Fall 1997–Winter 1998)

Schiff, Gert, "The Sculpture of the 'Style Troubadour,'" *Arts Magazine* (1984)

Yeldham, Charlotte, *Women Artists in Nineteenth-Century France and England*, 2 vols., New York: Garland, 1984

LUCAS FAYDHERBE 1617–1697 *Flemish*

Unlike sculptors of the previous generation (such as Hans van Mildert and the de Nole family) who executed sculpture to designs by Peter Paul Rubens but who are rarely associated with the name and fame of Rubens, Faydherbe is always mentioned as his sole pupil sculptor. Indeed, he completed his training by spending three years in the workshop of Rubens, after which he got married. To render Faydherbe's professional settling in at Mechelen (Malines), Belgium, smoother, Rubens wrote a certificate commending Faydherbe to city magistrates and praising his work in ivory as well as his monumental *Mater Dolorosa* "for the Begijnhofkerk at Mechelen which he, alone and at my house (without anybody else touching it), made so perfectly beautiful, that I do not think that any sculptor in the whole country could improve it" (see De Nijn et al., 1997). The *Mater Dolorosa* is filled with the aesthetic Rubens gave to his painted figures in the 1630s: a chubby and fleshy face and neck and a slight *contrapposto* (a natural pose with the weight of the legs, the shoulder, and hip counterbalancing one another) largely hidden by copious and heavy drapery enlivened with small creases.

From Faydherbe's early years also date three monumental pier statues (which also functioned as epitaphs with inscribed consoles) representing *St. Simon*, *St. James the Greater*, and *St. Andrew* for the Cathedral of Brussels. Their heavy static monumentality is emphasized by drapery with few but generous folds. These have long been seen to epitomize so-called Flemish Rubensian realism, as contrasted with François du Quesnoy's greater Classicism, particularly noticeable in his brother Jérôme du Quesnoy II's pier statue of *St. Thomas* (ca. 1645) in the same cathedral. This contrast exaggerates the differences between the 12 pier statues of the cathedral and reminds of Belgian nationalistic style discussions of the 19th century, which saw Faydherbe as a champion of national sculpture in Belgium and, as the 19th century drew to a close, in Flanders alone.

Faydherbe's career developed exponentially in the 1660s, after he had gradually come to terms with Rubens's legacy. The number of commissions Faydherbe obtained increased substantially, as did the variety of and personal input in his works. He also began to concern himself with important architectural projects such as the Leliëndaal and Hanswijk churches.

One of Faydherbe's masterpieces is the tomb monument to Archbishop Andreas Cruesen in the Cathedral of St. Rombout in Mechelen. The tomb was planned years before the prelate's death in 1666 and clearly emulated the similar setup at the cathedral of Ghent, where the bishops' tomb monuments were also placed between the pillars separating the high altar from the ambulatory. Moreover, Jérôme du Quesnoy II had erected a monument to bishop Antonius Triest (1651–54) with a similar architectural framework and iconography, and similarly including a figure of the *Risen*

Christ, which itself was a reinterpretation of Michelangelo's statue in Santa Maria sopra Minerva (Rome, Italy). Stylistically, Faydherbe's monument to Andreas Cruesen marks a turning point in the sculptor's career. No longer under the yoke of Rubens's aesthetic, with his earlier, more superficial use of the elder's motifs, Faydherbe achieved a monumentality infused with refined power and improved the anatomical structure of his figures. With this monument Faydherbe asserted his stylistic independence while affirming his professional success with a major commission.

Archbishop Cruesen also commissioned a high altar for his cathedral, St. Rombout's in Mechelen. Designed by the Jesuit architect Willem Hesius, the altar was executed by Faydherbe. Of extraordinary proportions (18 meters high), and despite its structural simplicity, the altar remarkably integrates the architectural and sculptural parts. The focus is on the top figure, a double life-size *St. Rumoldus*, which idealizes the image of the bishop in the cathedral of the main archbishopric of the Netherlands above the two villains "subjected" to the broken pediment.

Further semiarchitectural works include the two high reliefs decorating the dome of the Hanswijk Church in Mechelen, which represent *The Adoration of the Shepherds* and *The Road to Calvary*. Unique in Faydherbe's oeuvre for their size (about eight meters wide) and material (stucco), their placement within the architecture of a church designed by the sculptor himself is obviously significant; few sculptors had the opportunity to work out narrative compositions on this scale. The intelligent use of the relief's shape within the composition—creating a purposeful movement that enhances the meaning of the subject—together with the perspectival and actual gradations in depth make the reliefs particularly successful. Representing respectively the *Fourth Joy* (of seven) and the *Fourth Sorrow* of the Virgin, their iconography was particularly well suited to the pilgrimage church of an order of stout devotees of the Virgin. The *Adoration of the Shepherds* (as opposed to that of the Magi) and the Marian emphasis firmly place these works in the realm of Counter Reformation art. The production history of the reliefs is also noteworthy. Initially planned to be executed in Avesnes stone, this idea was discarded when Faydherbe realized that the weight of the material would not be borne by the architectural structure beneath. He resolved the difficulty by using stucco, which he could use in lesser quantities compared to the stone.

A number of terracotta models, many of them preparatory to extant works, have survived from Faydherbe's workshop, handed down through many generations of his descendents but now scattered among Belgian public and private collections. Other terracotta sculptures also left his productive workshop, especially mythological terracotta busts. These now remain elusive as to their original function and market. Particularly difficult to interpret is how Faydherbe organized his workshop to produce similar, but not identical, terracottas in relatively large series. A prime example of this production is the bust of *Hercules* now at the Victoria and Albert Museum in London.

Although it may appear that Faydherbe, who was the virtually unrivaled master of sculpture in Mechelen in the 17th century, was allowed to prosper without trouble, quite to the contrary, his proud and stubborn character, combined with the often difficult and always lengthy and costly business of carving sculpture and erecting altars, meant that he often had to fight for his cause. Moreover, some of his architectural projects suffered from technical deficiencies, which led to a few accidents. Rows not infrequently had to be settled in court.

LÉON E. LOCK

Biography

Born in Mechelen, Spanish Netherlands (present-day Belgium), 19 January 1617. Son of Hendrik Faydherbe (1574–1629), a painter and sculptor, who died when Lucas was 12; trained under his stepfather, Maximiliaan Labbé, 1630–36; trained under Peter Paul Rubens in Antwerp, 1636–40, especially in ivory carving but also in monumental sculpture (the only Flemish sculptor to train in Rubens's studio); married in 1640, settled in Mechelen, so canceled his plans for a trip to Italy; became a master in the guild of St. Luke, 1640. Died in Mechelen, Spanish Netherlands, 31 December 1697.

Selected Works

ca. *Mater Dolorosa* (Sorrowing Mother);
1639–40 sandstone; Church of the Begijnhof, Mechelen, Belgium
ca. 1640 *Putti Dancing around Pan*; ivory; Museo Nacional del Prado, Madrid, Spain
ca. *Hercules*; terracotta; Victoria and Albert
1640–50 Museum, London, England
ca. *St. Simon, St. James the Greater*, and *St.*
1641–44 *Andrew*; stone; Cathedral of Brussels, Brussels, Belgium
1659–66 Tomb of Archbishop Andreas Cruesen; marble, Avesnes stone, brass; Cathedral of St. Rombaut, Mechelen, Belgium
1660–83 High altar; marble, Avesnes stone, gilded wood; Cathedral of St. Rombaut, Mechelen, Belgium

1662–70 Onze Lieve Vrouw Leliëndaal convent church, Mechelen, Belgium

1675–77 *Adoration of the Shepherds*; stucco; Church of Onze Lieve Vrouw van Hanswijk, Mechelen, Belgium

1675–77 *Road to Calvary*; stucco; Church of Onze Lieve Vrouw van Hanswijk, Mechelen, Belgium

Further Reading

De Nijn, Heidi, Hans Vlieghe, and Hans Devisscher (editors), *Lucas Faydherbe, 1617–1697: Mechels beeldhouwer en architect* (exhib. cat.), Mechelen, Belgium: Stedelijk Musuem Hof van Busleyden, 1997

De Smedt, Raphaël, "De aura van Lucas Faydherbe, 1617–1697: Een bibliografisch onderzoek," *Handelingen van de Koninklijke Kring voor Oudheidkunde, Letteren en Kunst van Mechelen* 101 (1997) (a complete bibliography on Faydherbe until 1997)

Lock, Léon E., "Lucas Faydherbe's Tercentenary Celebrations in Mechelen," *Sculpture Journal* 2 (1998)

Van Riet, Sandra, "Twee werken van Lucas Faydherbe nader onderzocht," *Handelingen van de Koninklijke Kring voor Oudheidkunde, Letteren en Kunst van Mechelen* 98 (1994)

Van Riet, Sandra, "Lucas Faydherbe als beeldhouwer en altaarbouwer: Nieuwe gegevens en documenten," *Jaarboek Koninklijk museum voor schone kunsten Antwerpen* (1996)

GREGORIO FERNÁNDEZ 1576–1636

Spanish

Gregorio Fernández dominated the sculpture of 17th-century Valladolid and Castile with religious statues that are characterized by an impressive vividness and an almost Classical sense of form.

Apart from his artistic projects, Fernández's biography is simple, and most surviving documentation relates to his profession. Little is known of his youth and training. He was born in Sarria (province of Lugo in Galicia), where he probably received his initial instruction from his father, also a sculptor named Gregorio. Through the connections Fernández established in his native region, he came into contact with artists active in Valladolid and eventually moved there, although he may have first spent time in Madrid. On his arrival in Valladolid, he worked for the preeminent sculptor Francisco Rincón, whose style shaped that of Fernández. Although an early source claims Rincón was his teacher, it seems more likely that Fernández entered Rincón's workshop as a fully trained artist. The tie between the two must have been close; when Rincón died, Fernández became the guardian of his son.

Valladolid was at the time a thriving city and an active center of sculpture. While Fernández's work reflects the various examples he saw there, he maintained his own style from the outset. Perhaps the most cele-brated artist in the city then was the official court sculptor Pompeo Leoni, whose elegant, classicizing manner may have influenced Fernández. Most notably, Fernández's tombs of the Count and Countess of Fuensaldaña reflect Leoni's kneeling figures of the Duke and Duchess of Lerma. Fernández's work also evokes sources beyond Rincón and Leoni. For instance, his statue of the nude *Archangel Gabriel* recalls Giambologna's bronze statue of *Mercury*. Since Fernández, like most Spanish sculptors, had not traveled to Italy, he probably learned of the composition through print sources. Here and elsewhere, when drawing on Flemish or northern sources, he worked with a naturalism and restraint that distinguishes his work from the elongated compositions of his models. Such traits also characterize his response to his Spanish predecessors, particularly Juan de Juni. The relation with this sculptor has particular appeal for art historians since Fernández lived in houses that Juan de Juni had owned. Comparisons of their work, particularly suffering Christs or the Pietà, reveal similarities, but Fernández consistently carves slimmer figures that turn and move in space more freely and with less contortion while still evoking a strong emotional impact.

By 1605 Fernández had attained such recognition in Valladolid that he received the commission for statues for an ephemeral structure built in the royal palace as part of the celebrations held for the birth of the royal heir, Philip IV.

After Philip III left for Madrid in 1606, Fernández remained behind, receiving numerous commissions in Valladolid from the court and prominent aristocrats. Among them, the Duke of Lerma, the favorite of Philip III, commissioned the sculptor for a statue of the *Dead Christ* for the Church of San Pablo, where the Duke intended to be buried. Members of Lerma's family and

Pietà
© Scala / Art Resource, NY

other noblemen almost invariably desired polychromed wood statues of religious subjects, but in one notable exception Fernández carved the alabaster tombs of the Count and Countess of Fuensaldaña for the Church of San Miguel, Valladolid.

Fernández gradually established himself in Valladolid as the most important sculptor of religious figures, altars, and *pasos*—figures and multifigural ensembles designed to be taken out in procession during Holy Week. In the 1620s prelates, important churchmen, and confraternities turned to the artist in growing numbers for religious works. To meet the increasing demand, Fernández expanded his workshop, which had already been active on a large scale. His workshop was still able to perform at a high level because he carefully supervised the carving, installation, and polychroming of the pieces.

Fernández excelled at subjects such as the Immaculate Conception, Christ at the Column, the Dead Christ, and the Crucifixion. His images of Christ's Passion rank among his greatest achievements for their evocation of suffering and compassion. He also designed statues of Saint Francis and Mary Magdalene, which in turn inspired Pedro de Mena; several versions of Saint Francis remain, but Fernández's images of Mary Magdalene survive only in copies, unless the one in the Convento de las Reales Descalzas (Madrid) comes from his hand.

Fernández oversaw the sculpture for many monumental altars, frequently creating large reliefs of exceptional inventiveness and immediacy. His talent in this regard appears in his striking images of *Christ Embracing St. Bernard* and the *Baptism of Christ*. Between 1625 and 1632 he undertook the largest of his monumental projects, the reliefs and single figures for the high altar of the Cathedral of Plasencia, and about 1635 he created the impressive relief of *Saint Teresa's Vision of the Virgin and Saint Joseph* for the Convento de Sta. Teresa, Avila. Fernandez's ability to carve multifigural groups found expression in *pasos*, many of which are still used today. He began carving these early in his career with works such as his *St. Martin and the Beggar*. More elaborate *pasos*, such as his *Descent from the Cross*, demonstrate an accomplished understanding of drama realized in three-dimensional works. His *Pietà*, with its accompanying figures and statues of the good and bad thieves still on the cross, may represent his most moving work in this genre. In some cases he only carved selected figures, and in others subsequent alterations made when confraternities sought to update them have obscured the sculptor's contribution.

According to documents from the mid 1620s, Fernández's health had begun to decline, yet he continued to produce works of exceptional quality and size. At the time of his death, he had effectively placed his stamp on the sculpture of Valladolid and, more broadly, Castile and northern Spain. Significantly, however, his work is conspicuously absent in Catalonia and Andalucía.

PATRICK LENAGHAN

See also **Giambologna; Leoni Family; Juni, Juan de**

Biography

Born in Sarria, Galicia, Spain, April 1576. Son of Gregorio a sculptor. Moved to Valladolid after possible stay in Madrid, *ca.* 1605; probably entered workshop of the preeminent sculptor Francisco Rincón, whose style influenced him; received royal commission, 1605; gradually established himself in Valladolid as a religious sculptor; worked in Valladolid for the remainder of his life carving statues, altars, and *pasos* for aristocrats, prelates, and confraternities; patrons included Philip III, Philip IV, and Carmelite, Franciscan, and Jesuit orders. Died in Valladolid, Spain, 22 January 1636.

Selected Works

1606   *St. Martin and the Beggar*; polychromed wood; Museo Catedralicio, Valladolid, Spain

ca. 1611 *Archangel Gabriel*; polychromed wood; Museo Catedralicio, Valladolid, Spain

1612   *I Thirst* (attributed); polychromed wood; Museo Nacional de Escultura, Valladolid, Spain

1613–16 *Christ Embracing St. Bernard*; polychromed wood; high altar, Convento de las Huelgas Reales, Valladolid, Spain

1614–15 Figures of *Simon of Cyrene, Veronica*, and *Sayones*, for *Camino del Calvario*; polychromed wood; Museo Nacional de Escultura, Valladolid, Spain

1616   *Pietà*; polychromed wood; Museo Nacional de Escultura, Valladolid, Spain

ca. 1617 Tombs of the Condes de Fuensaldaña; alabaster; Church of San Miguel, Valladolid, Spain

1620–25 *Dead Christ*; polychromed wood; Convento de la Encarnación, Madrid, Spain

1621   *Ecce homo*; polychromed wood; Museo Catedralicio, Valladolid, Spain

1623   *Descent from the Cross*; polychromed wood; Church of Vera Cruz, Valladolid, Spain

1624   *Baptism of Christ*, for Convento del

Carmén, Valladolid, Spain; polychromed wood; Museo Nacional de Escultura, Valladolid, Spain

1625–30 *Dead Christ*; polychromed wood; Museo Nacional de Escultura, Valladolid, Spain

1625–32 High altar; polychromed wood; Cathedral of Plasencia, Province of Cáceres, Spain

ca. *Christ at the Column*; polychromed wood; 1630–35 Convento de Sta. Teresa, Avila, Spain

ca. 1635 High altar; polychromed wood; Convento de Sta. Teresa, Avila, Spain

Further Reading

Brooks, Joseph C., "The Pasos of Valladolid: A Study in Seventeenth-Century Sculpture" (dissertation), Chicago: University of Chicago, 1974

Gómez-Moreno, Manuel, and Maria Elena Gómez-Moreno, *The Golden Age of Spanish Sculpture*, Greenwich, Connecticut: New York Graphic Society, and London: Thames and Hudson, 1964

Gregorio Fernández, 1576–1636 (exhib. cat.), Madrid: Fundación Central Hispano, 1999

Martín González, Juan José, *El escultor Gregorio Fernández*, Madrid: Ministerio de Cultura, Dirección General del Patrimonio Artistico, Archivos y Museos, Patronato National de Museos, 1980

Martín González, Juan José, *Escultura barroca en España, 1600–1770*, Madrid: Ediciones Cátedra, 1983; 2nd edition, 1991

Pasos restaurados (exhib. cat.), Madrid: Subdirección General de Promoción de las Bellas Artes, 2000

Proske, Beatrice Gilman, *Gregorio Fernández*, New York: The Hispanic Society of America, 1926

Trusted, Marjorie, "Moving Church Monuments: Processional Images in Spain in the Seventeenth Century," *Church Monuments* 10 (1995)

ERCOLE FERRATA 1610–1686 *Italian*

Ercole Ferrata, one of the leading sculptors in seicento (17th-century) Rome, is today mainly remembered as the teacher of the greatest Italian sculptors of the late 17th and early 18th centuries. Born in Pelsoto (now Pellio Inferiore) near Como, Ferrata received his early training in Genoa under the minor sculptor Tommaso Orsolino. According to his biographer, Filippo Baldinucci, while in Genoa, Ferrata learned to "model, carve, and polish" marble. In 1637, after spending seven years in Orsolino's studio, Ferrata made his way to Naples, where he engaged primarily in decorative work until 1641, when he collaborated with Cosimo Fanzago on the high altar of Chiesa dell'Annunziata.

In 1646 Ferrata left Naples to work in L'Aquila and make a short trip to Rome with Monsignor Virgilio Spada, a member of the Reverenda Fabricca of St. Peter's Basilica. When he returned to Rome the following year, Gianlorenzo Bernini hired him to assist with dec-

orations for the nave of St. Peter's. The high quality of Ferrata's work led Bernini to employ him on the crypt of S. Francesca Romana, for which he carved a medallion of the saint, and on the tomb of Cardinal Domenico Pimental, where he carved a statue of the deceased. Over the next two decades, Ferrata worked with Bernini on a number of projects, including the *Cathedra Petri*, the Ponte Sant'Angelo, and the Chigi Chapel, where his statue *St. Catherine of Siena* served as a counterpart to Bernini's *St. Mary Magdalene* and *St. Jerome* (both 1662).

During his early years in Rome, Ferrata also worked as an assistant in the studio of Alessandro Algardi. Although Baldinucci claimed that Ferrata was responsible for the figure of *Liberality* on Algardi's tomb of Pope Leo XI (1634–44; St. Peter's Basilica, Rome), he did not arrive in Rome until after its completion. Evidence suggests that he did, however, participate in the execution of the monumental relief *Pope Leo Driving Attila from Rome* (1646–53), after which he modeled a reduced replica from which numerous copies were made. This replica appeared in an inventory of Ferrata's studio conducted after his death in 1686, which also lists several works by Algardi, who left his molds and models to his four leading assistants, including Ferrata.

This inheritance proved to be valuable: Ferrata was left to complete a number of Algardi's unfinished works, such as the high altar of the Church of San Nicolò da Tolentino (1651–55). In the course of completing these monuments, he adopted the Classical style of Algardi, with his early work exhibiting an interest in clarity and artistic decorum. His statue of *St. Agnes on the Pyre* recalls Algardi's *St. Mary Magdalene* (ca. 1628; Church of S. Silvestro al Quirinale, Rome) in both its *contrapposto* (a natural pose with the weight of the leg, the shoulder, and hip counterbalancing one another) and serene expression. Ferrata's arabesque drapery also reveals a debt to Bernini, especially in the stray fabric billowing behind her, taken from his *Longinus* (1629–38; St. Peter's Basilica, Rome). Yet Ferrata's compositions remained closer to Algardi, as in his *Martyrdom of St. Emerenziana*, which has the same unusual curved surface as the altar of the Church of S. Nicolò da Tolentino.

As Ferrata's work matured, his style became increasingly classicizing, visible in his statue of *Faith* for the Falconieri Chapel in the Church of S. Giovanni dei Fiorentini. Here all decorative features are removed and the drapery clings to the figure, revealing the form beneath in a manner reminiscent of antique statuary. Even when working from designs supplied by Bernini, as with the *Angel Carrying the Cross*, Ferrata kept the emotion of his figures to a minimum, significantly reducing the movement of their drapery and the

Portrait Bust of Ottaviano Acciaiuoli
Founders Society Purchase, the Jennifer C. Stoddard
Foundation, the General Membership Fund, with funds from
the Visiting Committee for European Sculpture and
Decorative Arts; gifts from Edsel B. Ford, Julius
Goldschmidt, the Italian-American Citizens of Detroit; the
Estate of W. Hawkins Ferry, Cameron D. Waterman, Miss
Alma L'Hommedieu, City of Detroit © 1998 The Detroit
Institute of Arts

During his final years, Ferrata also completed a number of commissions begun by his students, such as the *Martyrdom of St. Eustace* (1660–72) and the *Charity of St. Thomas of Villanova* (1662–71), both of which were begun by Melchiorre Caffà. Ferrata's activity as a teacher is well documented. In 1667 Grand Duke Cosimo III of Tuscany appointed Ferrata and Ciro Ferri as instructors in the newly established Florentine Academy in Rome. Through his involvement with the academy and the students in his own studio, Ferrata trained many of the most important sculptors of the following generation, including Caffà, Giovanni Battista Foggini, and Camillo Rusconi. A large part of their training consisted of copying works by Algardi and Bernini, making Ferrata a vital link to the Baroque.

DAVID L. BERSHAD AND GABRIELLA SZALAY

See also **Bernini, Gianlorenzo; Caffà, Melchiorre; Foggini, Giovanni Battista; Rusconi, Camillo**

Biography

Born in Pelsoto (now Pellio Inferiore), Italy, 1610. Moved to Genoa in 1630 to study sculpture under Tommaso Orsolino; departed for Naples, 1637; employed as marble worker for Corporazione di Scultori e Marmori, 1646–47; moved to Rome and was introduced to Gianlorenzo Bernini; worked as assistant to Bernini and Alessandro Algardi on decorations for St. Peter's Basilica, Rome, 1647–54; established own studio; appointed instructor at Accademia Fiorentina, Rome, by Cosimo III, Grand Duke of Tuscany, in 1667. Died in Rome, Italy, 11 April 1686.

Selected Works

1641   High altar (with Cosimo Fanzago), for
        Church of the Annunziata, Naples, Italy
        (destroyed by fire in 1757)
1649–50 Medallion of St. Francesca; marble;
        Church of S. Francesco Romana, Rome,
        Italy
1651–55 *S. Nicola da Tolentino*; marble; Church of
        San Nicolò da Tolentino, Rome, Italy
ca. 1654 Tomb of Cardinal Domenico Pimentel
        (with Gianlorenzo Bernini); polychromed
        marble; Church of Santa Maria sopra
        Minerva, Rome, Italy
1657–59 *Pope Leo Driving Attila from Rome*;
        silver; Royal Palace, Madrid, Spain
1657–60 *Cathedra Petri* (with Gianlorenzo
        Bernini); gilt bronze; St. Peter's Basilica,
        Rome, Italy
1660   *St. Agnes on the Pyre*; marble; Church of
        Sant'Agnese in Agone, Rome, Italy

breadth of their gestures. This increased severity not only reflects Ferrata's extensive knowledge of Classical art, of which he was a leading restorer, but is also indicative of a certain lack of creative ingenuity typical of his work.

Consequently, Ferrata often relied on other artists to provide him with designs for major projects. For example, his figure of *Charity* for the tomb of Pope Clement IX and his statue *Pope Clement X* for the pope's tomb are based on designs by Carlo Rainaldi and Mattia de Rossi, respectively. Despite this tendency, he maintained his own style, although his figures became more angular and two-dimensional toward the end of his career. The nature of this change appears in his statue *Time* for the tomb of Monsignor Giulio del Cornu, whose physique is in keeping with Classical conventions but is flattened and twisted onto a single plane. A similar development occurred in his statue *St. Elizabeth*, based on his *St. Agnes on the Pyre* but not as developed in the round and more angular in its drapery patterns.

1660–72 *Martyrdom of St. Emerenziana* (completed by Leonardo Retti); marble; Church of Sant'Agnese in Agone, Rome, Italy

1662–63 *St. Catherine of Siena*; marble; Chigi Chapel, Cathedral of Siena, Siena, Italy

1665–85 *Faith*; marble; Falconieri Chapel, Church of S. Giovanni dei Fiorentini, Rome, Italy

1668–69 *Angel Carrying the Cross*; marble; Ponte Sant'Angelo, Rome, Italy

1671 *Charity*, for tomb of Pope Clement IX; polychrome marble; Basilica of Santa Maria Maggiore, Rome, Italy

1676–86 *Pope Clement X*, for tomb of Clement X; marble; St. Peter's Basilica, Rome, Italy

1679–83 *St. Elizabeth*; marble; Cathedral of Breslau (now Wrocław), Wrocław, Poland

ca. 1681 *Time*, for tomb of Monsignor Giulio del Cornu; polychromed marble; Church of Gesù e Maria, Rome, Italy

Further Reading

Baldinucci, Filippo, *Notizie de' professori del disegno da Cimabue in qua*, 6 vols. in 5, Florence: Santi Franchi, 1681–1728; edited by Ferdinando Ranalli, 5 vols., Florence: Batelli, 1845–47; reprint, 7 vols., Florence: S.P.E.S., 1974–75; see especially vol. 5

Bershad, David L., "Some New Documents on the Statues of Domenico Guidi and Ercole Ferrata in the Elizabeth Chapel in the Cathedral of Breslau (now Wrocław)," *Burlington Magazine* 118 (1976)

Ferrari, Oreste, and Serenita Papaldo, *Le sculture del Seicento a Roma*, Rome: Ugo Bozzi, 1999

Montagu, Jennifer, *Alessandro Algardi*, 2 vols., New Haven, Connecticut: Yale University Press, 1985

Montagu, Jennifer, *Roman Baroque Sculpture: The Industry of Art*, New Haven, Connecticut: Yale University Press, 1989

Preimesberger, Rudolf, and Mark S. Weil, "The Pamphili Chapel in Sant'Agostino," *Römisches Jahrbuch für Kunstgeschichte* 15 (1975)

Weil, Mark S., *The History and Decoration of the Ponte S. Angelo*, University Park, Pennsylvania: Pennsylvania State University Press, 1974

JOSEPH ANTON FEUCHTMAYER 1696–1770 *Austrian, active in Germany, Austria, Switzerland*

Feuchtmayer has to be regarded as one of the most innovative and versatile sculptors of 18th-century Germany. He surpassed the craftsmanship of contemporary masters by increasing his skills in reflecting international ideas on art in his works. Striving for the ideal of a "total work of art," he was influenced by the successful Italian stuccoist-architects and by French ornamental prints. For reasons of artistic independence, he avoided guild restrictions by situating his workshop on the land of the monastery at Salem in Bavaria and never strove for any master status.

Although rediscovered by art historians in the era of German Expressionism in the 1920s because of his peculiar expressivity, Feuchtmayer has come to personify the airy Rococo style of the Lake Constance region. Nonetheless, his sculptures range from the sweetness of his putti to an almost ugliness in his *Diogenes*. He always fit his creations to the subject being illustrated. Except in documents of his patrons, Feuchtmayer is missing in contemporary art literature, although followers continued his style for a long period. Lacking any personal and temporal context, some of his main works were destroyed, especially in the second half of the 19th century, because of their supposedly dubious decorum.

The latest restoration of Feuchtmayer's *Virgin* in Berlin makes evident that she and his *Angel Playing a Lute* are surviving fragments from organ decorations for the Abbey of Salem from around 1719. A painting of the statues executed by Feuchtmayer's brother Gervasius, who lived at the abbey, provides evidence for the statues' original state. These statues are the earliest works by Feuchtmayer made after the death of his father Franz Joseph in 1718. The elder Feuchtmayer had worked as a stuccoist and sculptor on almost all the important contemporary cloister projects in Upper Austria influenced by Italian artists before situating his workshop near Salem about 1708. In addition to the influence of his father's works, Joseph Anton likely gained experience drawing the nude at the Academy of Augsburg. His works from this period, which demonstrate unusual and unclassical attitudes, are still influenced by the kinetic style of late Gothic sculpture and the reduced shape of almost-dispassionate faces with slit eyes.

In the 1720s Feuchtmayer worked on the choir stalls at Weingarten. In his figures of saints, the shape of the garment has become more voluminous and the bodies more plastic and naturalistic.

A characteristic of Feuchtmayer's work is to give a statue of a certain material the finish and appearance that would have been appropriate to another material. For example, he provided the stucco figures for Kissleg Castle with a polished but artificially imperfect surface to give them the look of stone. The paint on the wood statues for the stable of Salem imitates sandstone, while the shapes of the figures assume the appearance of freely added plaster. His technique of carving in the not-yet-hardened plaster originated from woodworking.

From the sibyls in the niches at Kissleg to the original founder figures of the Zaehringer in the Church of St. Peter in the Black Forest, one can see a tendency in Feuchtmayer's work to move away from the wall, an

Putti from nave decoration, Pilgrimage Church of Neubirnau
The Conway Library, Courtauld Institute of Art

interplay of figure and space in freestanding sculpture. With the commission for the chapel of Bachhaupten, Feuchtmayer was able for the first time to design a whole ensemble. The plasterwork shows strong influences from the French prints of Jean Bérain and from the architectural theoretician Paul Decker.

Feuchtmayer was also influenced by the architectural treatise *Perspectiva pictorum et architectorum* by Andrea Pozzo, first published in 1693, as well as Charles Le Brun's *Methode pour apprendre a dessiner les Passions* (1698). He may have learned of these works from his uncle Johann Michael Feuchtmayer, who was a court painter in Constance. In his works for Mainau and Merdingen, Joseph Anton formed this theory of physiognomy into a three-dimensional reality similar to Gianlorenzo Bernini. While laying stress on mimic expression, the character of Feuchtmayer's sculptures in Meersburg is more closed.

In opposition to that strong inner expression, Feuchtmayer ornamented his figures in the form of rocaille details of the clothing and a corresponding treatment of the hair and faces. One sees this quality first in his *Crucifix* of the High Altar in Meersburg, where Feuchtmayer was one of the first artists in Germany to use rocaille decoration. Prints of the French picturesque genre surely inspired his manner of blending rocaille, sculpture, and architecture. He may have also traveled to Augsburg and Strasbourg, which would have intensified that tendency and also prompted him to produce his own ornamental prints.

Since Feuchtmayer's works for the altars of Engelberg are now lost, the designs for the pilgrimage church of Neubirnau classify as the main works in his oeuvre. Although interacting in the architectural plans, Feuchtmayer built a sort of anti-architecture with his rocaille altars. Sculpture dominates the interior in a way such that only the ensemble of his own works is worthy of the denotation "total work of art." That competition originated from problems of cooperation between the regional craftsmen-architects and internationally orientated decorative artists.

The size of the Neubirnau commissions meant that Feuchtmayer had to enlarge his steadily growing workshop, which had been situated in Salem since 1730, engaging the Dirr brothers for their skill in woodwork. It is sometimes difficult to differentiate between Feuchtmayer's and the Dirrs' works from this period. As in the reliefs for the Neubirnau pulpit and in the works for St. Gall, Feuchtmayer created depth more by the plasticity of the figures and less by perspective.

Feuchtmayer's late style can be seen in his works for Neubirnau after 1755, exemplified in less movement and more stereotyped features, which may be the influence of French Classicism, a style preferred by some important patrons. The choir stalls, confessional, and facade relief for the Abbey Church of St. Gall were the greatest of his late works. In the busts of saints over the confessionals, he brought his idea of blending garment, body, and hair to perfection. In his last years he tried to conform to the new taste for Classicism but received no more important commissions.

INGOLF PATZ

Biography

Born in Linz, Austria, 3 June 1696. Father Franz Joseph a sculptor and stuccoist; brother Gervasius a polychromatist; uncle Johann Michael a painter. Moved to Mimmenhausen near Salem with family, *ca.* 1708; first trained in father's workshop in Mimmenhausen; collaborated on altars for Salem Monastery, 1714; in Augsburg, possibly attended the academy, 1715; had own workshop in Salem, from *ca.* 1730; worked at Neubirnau, 1748–50, and at St. Gall, 1761. Died in Mimmenhausen, Germany, 2 January 1770.

Selected Works

ca. 1718/19	*Angel Playing a Lute*; wood; Badisches Landesmuseum, Karlsruhe, Germany
ca. 1718/19	*Virgin*; wood; Staatliche Museen, Berlin, Germany
1720–24	Figures of saints; wood; choir stalls, Monastery Church, Weingarten, Germany
1726	Sibyls; stucco; staircase, Schloss Kissleg, Germany
1728–31	Figures and statues; stucco, stone; interior and facade, Abbey Church, St. Peter in the Black Forest, near Karlsruhe, Germany
1729–30	Chapel (ceiling, altars, pulpit); stucco, stucco-marble, wood; St. Michael, Bachhaupten, Germany
1730–34	Altars (with Diego Francesco Carlone); stucco-marble, scagliola; Monastery and Pilgrimage Church, Einsiedeln, Switzerland
1735–36	Statues; wood; stable, Salem Monastery, Germany
1736	*Diogenes*; stucco; Schloss Maurach, Germany
1737–38	Chapel (altars, pulpit, busts); stucco, wood, lead; Schloss Mainau, Germany
1740–41	Altars and pulpit; stucco; Parish Church, Merdingen, Germany
1741–43	Chapel (walls, altar pulpit, oratorio, putti); stucco, stucco-marble; Schloss Meersburg, Germany
1748–55	Pilgrimage church (altars, pulpit, confessional, reliefs, putti, busts); stucco, stucco-marble, wood; Birnau, Germany
1757	Statues of *St. Wendelin* and *St. Blasius*; wood; nave chapels, Birnau, Germany
1761–69	Choir stalls, confessional, relief; wood; Abbey Church, St. Gall, Switzerland

Further Reading

Boeck, Wilhelm, *Joseph Anton Feuchtmayer*, Tübingen, Germany: Wasmuth, 1948

Boeck, Wilhelm, *Feuchtmayer Meisterwerke*, Tübingen, Germany: Wasmuth, 1963

Boeck, Wilhelm, *Joseph Anton Feuchtmayer: Der Bildhauer, Altarbauer und Stukkator*, Friedrichshafen, Germany: Gessler, 1981

Buczynski, Bodo, and Ulrich Knapp, "Die Berliner Marienfigur: Ein umstrittenes Werk von Joseph Anton Feuchtmayer," *Jahrbuch der Berliner Museen* 40 (1998)

Knapp, Ulrich, *Die Wallfahrtskirche Birnau: Planungs- und Baugeschichte*, Friedrichshafen, Germany: Gessler, 1989

Knapp, Ulrich, *Joseph Anton Feuchtmayer, 1696–1770*, Constance, Germany: Stadler, 1996

FILARETE (ANTONIO DI PIETRO AVERLINO) *ca.* 1400–*ca.* 1469 *Italian*

The artistic reputation of Antonio di Pietro Averlino, known as Filarete, was built in two fields, sculpture and architecture, but his achievements have been tarnished ever since Giorgio Vasari disparaged his talent and work in the 16th-century *Lives of the Painters, Sculptors, and Architects*. Although Florentine by birth, Filarete created his most important sculpture in Rome and Milan. In Rome he used the direct knowledge gained of Italy's Classical heritage imaginatively throughout his career. Contact with works of antiquity also influenced his architecture and culminated in a theoretical treatise on architecture. Although fortuitous circumstances placed Filarete in charge of a major commission for the bronze door for the Old Basilica of St. Peter in Rome, its conservative and seeming archaic quality of Classicism has relegated him to a rank below the leaders of the Italian Renaissance.

Filarete is believed to have been one of Lorenzo Ghiberti's assistants on the bronze doors for the baptistery of Florence. His possible association with Ghiberti, but more important, the unavailability of Ghiberti and Donatello, may explain Pope Eugenius IV's surprising choice of Filarete to create the single, major artistic work of the pope's reign, the bronze door for the Old Basilica of St. Peter's Vasari reported that the bronze door occupied Filarete and his assistant, Simone di Giovanni Ghini, for 12 years. Since the door was completed in 1445 (signed and dated), Vasari's chronology puts Filarete in Rome by 1433. Other than perhaps assisting Ghiberti, nothing is known of Filarete's work during his initial Florentine period. His relatively small oeuvre of sculpture, built around a few signed and dated pieces, consists mostly of attributions grouped either at the start of the bronze door or at its completion.

Eugenius IV commissioned the bronze door for the Old Basilica of St. Peter's to enhance the venerable but decrepit structure and to reassert papal claims to the heritage of the authority of the Apostle Peter and the Roman Empire. The completed door, which was set in place in 1452, was destined for the central portal, the Porta Argentea, and when the new basilica was completed, it was reinstalled in the same position (1620). Two strips of bronze were added at the top (bearing an inscription of Pope Paul V) and at the bottom in order to adjust the door to the height of the portal in the new basilica. The door consists of two wings cast in bronze, which were originally gilded (although no trace survives) and ornamented with champlevé enamel. The latter was apparently a customary practice in Filarete's studio, and traces of blue, red, and white enameling survive. The two wings are identical in layout, each with three framed panels of unequal size. The top panels show Christ enthroned (left) and the Virgin enthroned (right) as king and queen of heaven. The large central panels depict standing figures of St. Paul holding a sword and book (left) and St. Peter with the keys and book (right). Eugenius IV kneels before St. Peter and clutches the keys, symbol of the authority invested in the Apostle by Jesus and claimed by the popes. The bottom panels present scenes of the martyrdoms of St. Paul (left) and of St. Peter (right). Between the panels of each wing are four small narrative scenes devoted to historical events in the life of Eugenius IV between 1438 and 1440. These scenes were inserted in the wings after the main panels were cast and therefore do not support a date of 1439 for the start of the commission. Above St. Paul is *The Arrival of Emperor John VIII Paleologus and His Reception by Eugenius IV at Ferrara.* Below is the *Coronation of the Emperor Sigismund and the Procession of the Pope and the Emperor to Castel Sant'Angelo.* Above St. Peter is the *Council of Florence and the Embarkation of the Greeks at Venice.* Below is *Abbot Andrea of the Order of Sant'Antonio in Egypt Receiving the Bull of the Union of the Eastern and Western Churches from the Pope and the Arrival of the Abbot at Rome to Visit the Tombs of the Saints Peter and Paul.* The framed panels of each wing are surrounded by a complex border of leafy scrolls containing animals, bacchanalian figures, and scenes from Greek mythology, Roman history, and other Classical subjects based on texts by Ovid, Livy, Valerius Maximus, and Virgil. Filarete's name appears four times on the door, once with the date. In a small narrative scene on the back of the door (now at the top but originally at the foot), Filarete depicted himself with his assistants, six of whom are named elsewhere on the door.

All of the stylistic features of Filarete's signed sculptures are evident in the bronze door. The sculptor used a flattened relief, like that of Donatello, but without deep illusionistic recesses of space. Filarete's blocky, squat figures simply adhere to the surface of the relief and seldom display true volumetric form. Instead of receding into depth, figures and architecture pile up on the surface of the relief, for example, in the two scenes of martyrdom. The effect of Filarete's relief sculpture is similar to that of early Christian ivory carvings and some ancient Roman reliefs, such as on Trajan's column. Filarete's figures are generally enveloped by a light drapery arranged with repetitive, elliptical folds. While the figures are often expressive in their poses and gestures, their odd bodily proportions, especially the overly large heads, make them seem awkward and graceless, lending credence to Va-

Bronze door, St. Peter's Basilica, Rome
© Alinari / Art Resource, NY

sari's criticisms. Nonetheless, vivid detail such as that on the foliate border enlivens the surface texture and gives variety to the relief.

Filarete's bronze door is frequently compared unfavorably to Ghiberti's east door (*Gates of Paradise,* 1429–37) for the Florentine Baptistery. However, the requirements of Filarete's commission, which combined pagan and Christian subject matter and ancient and medieval iconographic models, fulfilled a Roman, and especially papal, program of propaganda that responded to the tenuous and dangerous position of Eugenius IV and the papacy in exerting control over the Church and Rome. Indeed, the pope was in exile from Rome during most of the period of the door's creation. Within his artistic abilities Filarete responded imaginatively and effectively to create a substantial work of art for the Old Basilica of St. Peter that set a conceptual, though not stylistic, pattern for papal commissions until the end of the 15th century.

Other attributions to Filarete during his Roman period include the bronze relief of the *Triumph of Caesar,* which recalls the historical scenes of Eugenius IV. Squat figures, with large heads in low relief, parade across the surface. Details of the Roman armor and the intricately stylized border enrich the scene, although deficiencies in the figures' anatomy and proportion illustrate the artist's vague grasp of these essentials.

Vasari states that during Filarete's sojourn in Rome the sculptor created tombs for popes and cardinals but that these were destroyed when the Old Basilica of St. Peter's was demolished. The tomb monument of the Cardinal of Portugal, Antonio Chiaves (d. 1447), in St. John Lateran may have been commissioned from Filarete, and he may have contributed to the design, but the surviving parts are by other sculptors, possibly including Isaia da Pisa. The bronze plaquette of the *Battle of Odysseus and Iros* presents nude and clothed figures in a Classical architectural setting, nimbly delineated by linear perspective, although the figures still lack convincing volumetric form. Before he departed to Florence from Rome in 1447, prompted by the accusation that he had stolen relics from St. John Lateran, Filarete completed a bronze statuette of the *Equestrian Monument to Marcus Aurelius* (before 1447 [dated 1465]; Albertinum, Dresden, Germany). This was a gift to Piero de' Medici. The statuette is literally adapted from the Roman monument that then stood in front of St. John Lateran but which is now on the Campidoglio.

After Filarete returned to Florence, he also traveled to Todi, Rimini, Mantua, and Venice, where he completed a silver and gilded bronze processional cross for the Cathedral at Bassano. The front of the cross presents the crucified Christ, and in the quatrefoils terminating the four ends of the cross are Mary Magdalene, the Virgin Mary, St. John the Baptist, and an angel, the symbol of St. Matthew. The back depicts the Virgin and Child with symbols of the other three Evangelists and a pelican in the terminating quatrefoils. The figures are more accomplished and well proportioned than any of the figures of the bronze door.

In 1451, at the request of Duke Francesco Sforza, Filarete went to Milan to build the Ospedale Maggiore. Until the Duke's death in 1466, when Filarete returned again to Florence, he was engaged primarily with architecture and with composing his treatise, the *Trattato d'Architettura* (Treatise on Architecture, 1461–64), which he dedicated to Piero de' Medici in 1465. Among his last sculptures is a bronze statuette of *Hector*. Despite the discrepancy of scale between horse and rider, the equestrian group is lively and fully modeled with Filarete's characteristic attention to textural detail. It also shows both an inventiveness and conservatism that are independent of the stylistic influence of the major masters.

JOHN HUNTER

See also **Ghiberti, Lorenzo**

Biography

Born probably in Florence, Italy, *ca.* 1400. Believed to have been one of Lorenzo Ghiberti's assistants; active career began in Rome, 1433–45, with work on the bronze door of the Old Basilica of St. Peter; designed tomb monuments for popes and cardinals; left Rome charged with the theft of relics and returned to Florence, 1448; visited Todi, Rimini, Mantua, and Venice; moved to Milan, 1451, to work on architectural projects and his treatise *Trattato d'Architettura* (Treatise on Architecture) until 1466, when he returned to Florence. Died in Rome, Italy, *ca.* 1469.

Selected Works

ca. 1433   *Peace*; gilded wood; Church of S. Stefano, Linari (Barberino Val d'Elsa), Italy

after 1433   *Triumph of Caesar*; bronze; Musée du Louvre, Paris, France

1433–45   Door; bronze; St. Peter's Basilica, Rome, Italy

before 1439   *Ploughman*; bronze; formerly Paul Garnier Collection, Paris, France (current location unknown)

before 1445   *Battle of Odysseus and Iros*; bronze; Kunsthistorisches Museum, Vienna, Austria

1445   *Nero Witnessing the Death of Seneca*; bronze; National Gallery of Art, Washington, D.C., United States

ca. 1445   *Christ of the Passion*; gilded bronze; Kunsthistorisches Museum, Vienna, Austria

1445?   *Virgin and Child with Angels*; bronze; Musée du Louvre, Paris, France

after 1445   *Bull and Lion*; bronze; Hermitage, St. Petersburg, Russia

before 1447   Equestrian monument to Marcus Aurelius; bronze; Albertinum, Dresden, Germany

1449   Processional cross; silver and gilded bronze; Santa Maria del Colle Cathedral, Bassano del Grappa, Vincenza, Italy

1456   *Hector*; bronze; Museo Arqueológico Nacional, Madrid, Spain

Further Reading

Cable, Carole, *Filarete (Antonio di Piero Averlino): Renaissance Architect and Theoretician*, Monticello, Illinois: Vance Bibliographies, 1983

Cannata, Pietro, "Le placchette del Filarete," *Studies in the History of Art* 22 (1989)

Coppel, Rosario, "A Newly-Discovered Signature and Date for Filarete's 'Hector,' " *The Burlington Magazine* 129 (December 1987)

King, Catherine, "Filarete's Portrait Signature on the Bronze Doors of St. Peter's and the Dance of Bathykles and His Assistants," *Journal of the Warburg and Courtauld Institutes* 53 (1990)

Pope-Hennessy, John, *An Introduction to Italian Sculpture*, 3 vols., London: Phaidon, 1963; 4th edition, 1996; see especially vol. 2, *Italian Renaissance Sculpture*

Roeder, Helen, "The Borders of Filarete's Bronze Doors to St. Peter's," *Journal of the Warburg and Courtauld Institutes* 10 (1947)

Seymour, Charles, *Sculpture in Italy: 1400 to 1500*, London and Baltimore, Maryland: Penguin, 1966

Spencer, John R., "Filarete's Bronze Doors at St. Peter's," in *Collaboration in Italian Renaissance Art*, edited by Wendy Stedman Sheard and John T. Paoletti, New Haven, Connecticut: Yale University Press, 1978

Spencer, John R., "Filarete, the Medallist of the Roman Emperors," *The Art Bulletin* 61 (1979)

Spencer, John R., "Speculations on the Origins of the Italian Renaissance Medal," *Studies in the History of Art* 21 (1987)

GIULIANO FINELLI 1601–1653 *Italian*

In the sculptors' workshops of Baroque Rome, jobs were routinely assigned to assistants, and often even master sculptors retained specialists to carve certain details. Gianlorenzo Bernini himself exploited Giuliano Finelli's technical proficiency to obtain virtuoso effects in some of his most celebrated sculptures of the 1620s. Using a drill and delicate taps of his chisel, Finelli could alter the very essence of marble—transforming the stone into a malleable and highly ductile material and thinning it until it became translucent—as in Bernini's *Apollo and Daphne* (1622–24), upon which he worked. In her vain attempt to escape the lustful young god, Daphne is being turned into a tree: the branches shooting out from her fingers, the roots securing her forever to the ground, and the bark beginning to cover her legs and sides are all rendered in Finelli's sublime technique, which was similar in some ways to a goldsmith's, yet produced mimetic effects so extraordinary that they can be likened to painting.

The son of a marble merchant, Finelli became familiar with marble and the tools of the trade when he was a boy; in 1611 his uncle Vitale, a sculptor, took him to work at his shop in Naples. Two years later, Finelli moved on to the shop run by the more famous Michelangelo Naccherino, where he remained until the master became sick in 1618; Finelli then returned to his uncle's workshop. Dissatisfied with the commissions Vitale procured for him and determined to pursue his studies in Rome, Finelli left Naples in 1622 for Rome. There he began to work under the sculptor Sante Ghetti, who set him to carving two putti for the tomb of Ottaviano Ubaldini della Gherardesca in Santa Maria sopra Minerva. Pietro Bernini took notice of his work and brought the young sculptor into his own shop. Finelli collaborated with him on the tomb of Cardinal Roberto Bellarmino (1623–24) in the Church of the Gesù, Rome; he then went on to work side by side with the celebrated Gianlorenzo Bernini. Besides the *Apollo and Daphne*, Finelli's hand is evident in the statue of St. Bibiana in the Roman church dedicated to her (1624–26), in the angels on the altar in S. Augustino (1626–28), and in the bust of Maria Barberini Duglioli (1626–27, formerly in Palazzo Sciarra). In 1628, again under Bernini's supervision, Finelli worked on the great bronze baldachin erected above the papal altar in St. Peter's Basilica in Rome: he helped to execute the canopy and the angels atop the columns. However, Finelli's relations with Bernini soured because the master favored another assistant, Andrea Bolgi, whom he selected for the execution of the *St. Helena* that was to be placed in one of the four niches at the base of the piers supporting the dome in St. Peter's Basilica. Embittered by the loss of this great opportunity, in 1629 Finelli set up his own workshop, which was supported by the affection and esteem of friends like the painters Pietro da Cortona, whom he had met while working at S. Bibiana, and Giuseppe Cesari (known as the Cavalier d'Arpino), who procured Finelli the commission for a statue of *St. Cecilia*. Although the work is still imbued with Bernini's manner, *St. Cecilia* shows Finelli moving closer to the sculptural style of Alessandro Algardi and the manner of Pietro da Cortona, an influence that was also noted by early commentators. In 1736 Lione Pascoli wrote that in this work Finelli "acquitted himself quite well and reaped universal applause, though he had abandoned his usual manner, perhaps to distance himself from Bernini's and come closer to Cortona's."

Finelli received an important new commission from Naples, and in 1634 he moved there to execute the statues *St. Peter* and *St. Paul* that were to flank the entrance to the Chapel of the Treasure of San Gennaro in the Cathedral of Naples. Finished between 1639 and 1640, these two colossal figures (over four meters) mark a new departure in Finelli's style. In this Neapolitan debut, he drew on the representational culture and the strong naturalism of the Spanish painter Jusepe de Ribera (known as Spagnoletto), who had been working in Naples since 1616. The Treasury council then awarded Finelli another prestigious commission, a series of 13 bronze statues of the patron saints of Naples for the niches of the tribune in the Chapel of the Treasure of San Gennaro. To help in this complex enterprise, completed only in 1648, Finelli called on first-rate sculptors such as Ercole Ferrata, his nephew Domenico Guidi, and Gregorio de Rossi, an artist who had become an expert in the art of casting bronze while assisting Bernini on the great works at St. Peter's Basilica, Rome.

Finelli spent the final years of his career back in Rome, where he had been sent by the viceroy of Naples to supervise the execution of 12 bronze lions commissioned by the King Philip IV of Spain. According to the documents, his task on the project was limited to assisting and approving the work of Matteo Bonarelli, who did the clay models and signed the castings.

Based on new documentary evidence and recently identified works, art historians today draw attention to Finelli's fundamental stylistic and typological contribution to portraiture and funerary sculpture. The portraits he did during his first sojourn in Rome are distinguished by their extreme formal refinement and the artist's capacity for deep psychological penetration. His bust of Cardinal Domenico Ginnasi, for instance, seems nearly to come to life, so intense is his expression and so piercing his gaze. Cheeks hollowed by age and with mouth agape, Ginnasi is captured in the intimacy of his meditations, but Finelli's tour de force is in the treatment of the beard. Working with a drill, he created an expanse of curly tufts that looks almost like lace. The same vitality, translated in terms of pious devotion and mystic meditation, marks the figures Finelli sculpted for funerary monuments, where he attained heights of originality. In those executed for Roman patrons, Finelli modernized Algardi's standard designs with their half-busts of the deceased in prayer. In the tomb of Cardinal Giulio Antonio Santorio in the Basilica of St. John Latern in Rome, where the cardinal is shown praying in the direction of the altar, one has the impression that he is there kneeling at his prie-dieu, hands clasped together and forearms resting on a realistic cushion. In Naples, Finelli adapted his art to local taste—often less refined than that of his sophisticated Roman patrons—and proposed instead a tomb model (already worked out by Naccherino, his first master) in which a full figure of the deceased kneels in the direction of the altar, as in the monument to Viceroy Emanuel de Fonseca y Zúniga and his wife Leonora de Guzmán y Olivares, today in Salamanca, Spain, and the monument to Cesare Firrao in the Neapolitan church of San Paolo Maggiore.

CRISTIANO GIOMETTI

See also **Bernini, Gianlorenzo**

Biography

Born in Carrara, Italy, 1601. Son of marble merchant Domenico Finelli. Moved to Naples to join the workshop of his uncle, sculptor Vitale Finelli, 1611, then entered Michelangelo Naccherino's workshop; active in Rome from 1622; collaborated first with Pietro Bernini, then with Gianlorenzo Bernini, under whose direction took part in execution of works such as *Apollo and Daphne* (1622–24) in Galleria Borghese and the baldachin (1623–34) in St. Peter's Basilica; broke with Bernini and began to work independently in Rome, 1629; returned to Naples, 1634; returned to Rome, late 1650, to supervise execution of sculptures commissioned by the king of Spain (Philip IV). Died in Rome, Italy, 16 August 1653.

St. Paul, Chapel of the Treasure of San Gennaro, Cathedral of Naples, Italy
The Conway Library, Courtauld Institute of Art

Selected Works

1628–29 Bust of Cardinal Domenico Ginnasi; marble; Galleria Borghese, Villa Borghese, Rome, Italy

1629–33 *St. Cecilia*; marble; Church of Santa Maria di Loreto, Rome, Italy

1630 *Michelangelo Buonarroti the Younger*; marble; Casa Buonarroti, Florence, Italy

1630–31 Bust of Francesco Bracciolini; marble; Victoria and Albert Museum, London, England

1632 Bust of Cardinal Scipione Borghese; marble; Metropolitan Museum of Art, New York City, United States

1633–34 Tomb of Cardinal Giulio Antonio
Santorio; marble; Basilica of St. John
Latern, Rome, Italy

1634–37 Monument to Viceroy Emanuel de
Fonseca y Zúniga and his wife Leonora de
Guzmán y Olivares; marble; Church of
Las Agustinas Descalzas, Salamanca,
Spain

1634–40 *St. Peter* and *St. Paul*; marble; facade,
Chapel of the Treasure of San Gennaro,
Cathedral of Naples, Italy

1635–48 Statues of the patron saints of Naples (Sts.
Andrea Avellino, Dominic, Gennaro,
Asperno, Thomas Aquinas, Agnello,
Severo, Agrippino, Euphebius, Giacomo
della Marca, Patricia, Francis of Paola, and
Blaise); bronze; tribune, Chapel of Tesoro
di San Gennaro, Cathedral of Naples, Italy

1640–42 Monument to Cesare Firrao; marble;
Church of San Paolo Maggiore, Naples,
Italy

1640–45 Tomb of Cardinal Domenico Ginnasi;
marble; Church of Santa Lucia dei
Ginnasi, Rome, Italy

1649–50 Tomb of Gennaro Filomarino; marble;
Church SS. Apostoli, Naples, Italy

1650–51 *Twelve Lions*; bronze; Museo del Prado,
Madrid, Spain; Royal Palace, Madrid,
Spain

Further Reading

Bacchi, Andrea, *Scultura del '600 a Roma*, Milan: Longanesi, 1996

Cassani, Silvia, *Civiltà del seicento a Napoli*, 2 vols., Naples: Electa, 1984–98

Coliva, Anna, and Sebastian Schütze, *Bernini scultore: La nascita del barocco in casa Borghese*, Rome: Edizioni De Luca, 1998

Dombrowski, Damian, *Giuliano Finelli: Bildhauer zwischen Neapel und Rom*, Frankfurt and New York: Lang, 1997

Montagu, Jennifer, *Alessandro Algardi*, 2 vols., New Haven, Connecticut: Yale University Press, 1985

Montagu, Jennifer, *Roman Baroque Sculpture: The Industry of Art*, New Haven, Connecticut: Yale University Press, 1989

Pascoli, Lione, *Vite de pittori, scultori ed architetti moderni*, edited by Valentino Martinelli, Perugia, Italy: Electa Editori Umbri, 1992

Pope-Hennessy, John, *An Introduction to Italian Sculpture*, 3 vols., London: Phaidon, 1963; 4th edition, 1996; see especially vol. 3, *Italian High Renaissance and Baroque Sculpture*

Pope-Hennessy, John, *Catalogue of Italian Sculpture in the Victoria and Albert Museum*, 3 vols., London: Her Majesty's Stationery Office, 1964

Wittkower, Rudolf, *Gian Lorenzo Bernini: The Sculptor of the Roman Baroque*, New York: Phaidon, 1955; 3rd revised edition, London: Phaidon Press, 1981

Wittkower, Rudolf, *Art and Architecture in Italy, 1600–1750*, London and Baltimore, Maryland: Penguin, 1958; 6th edition, 3 vols., revised by Joseph Connors and Jennifer Montagu, New Haven, Connecticut: Yale University Press, 1999

FINLAND

See **Scandinavia**

BARRY FLANAGAN 1941– *Welsh*

Barry Flanagan's artistic career has been one of continuing alternation. From his earliest sculptural forays, he has struggled between an adherence to tradition and a rejection of his sculptural heritage in favor of artistic innovation. Aligned with this struggle is the periodic alternation in his work between attitudes of seriousness and whimsy. Similarly, he moves easily between works of abstraction and figuration. The dualities in his career testify both to his debt to 20th-century British sculpture and to his success in charting his own path.

Flanagan's struggles with tradition are evident even from his days as a student at St. Martin's School of Art in London. From 1964 to 1966 he studied sculpture under Phillip King and Anthony Caro, challenging their artistic norms from the outset. While his teachers explored the sculptural potential of plastics, metals, and other rigid, permanent materials, Flanagan labeled himself a heretic as he opted instead for pliable bits of ephemera. His *aaing j gni aa*, cloth bags filled with sand and plaster, exemplifies his explorations during this period. In works such as *Heap (1)* and *four casb 2'67, ring I 1'67, rope (gr2sp60) 6'67*, he arranged lengths of rope on the floor, filled cloth with sand, and draped fabric from suspended strings. His materials added a transient quality to his sculpture, a genre more often recognized for its resistance to the passage of time. Throughout much of the 1960s he focused on the process of creation rather than on a permanent, final product, rejecting the artistic authority of his professors. Still, some influence seems to have occurred despite Flanagan's rebellion, as the conical shape found in much of his early sculpture was also favored by King.

Flanagan's focus on process rather than the final product naturally resulted in works of abstraction lacking real-world referents. His titles, inspired by Alfred Jarry's artistic and literary absurdities, often reflect this abstraction. Flanagan's attention to process also indicated an affinity with the works of Richard Serra and Eva Hesse, with whom he exhibited in the 1969 show *When Attitudes Become Form*. All three sculptors experimented with soft, malleable materials, suggesting impermanence and sometimes labeled antiform. In the same vein, Flanagan's early work also implied connections with *arte povera* (an Italian movement often characterized by the use of ephemeral materials).

Despite his break with the artistic ideas of his professors, Flanagan embraced concepts espoused by Henry Moore, perhaps in part because his professors renounced that same influence. Moore's belief in a "truth to materials," or an attention to a material's inherent properties, resonated for Flanagan, who believed that the material's characteristics would reveal themselves through the sculptor's actions.

Later decades saw a shift in Flanagan's materials. In the early 1970s, he moved away from soft sculpture and adopted more durable, traditional materials. His interest moved first to carving in and on stone. In *A Nose in Repose*, Flanagan carved curvilinear designs onto a block of rough-hewn Hornton stone, a material much favored by Moore. Although much of Flanagan's work still appeared abstract, suggestively figurative titles gave a hint of the more pronounced figuration to come. He began his alternation between abstraction and figuration in the 1980s. Early in the decade, he began creating abstract forms in soft clay, which he then commissioned Italian carvers to interpret and enlarge in marble. Although he also continued his abstracted stone carvings, he returned to another traditional material—cast bronze—when experimenting with recognizable figures.

Although Flanagan's earlier abstract work had garnered him some attention, with his first solo exhibition in 1966 at the Rowan Gallery, his bronze works from the 1980s earned him both popular and critical acclaim. Even when appearing to return to a tradition of figurative sculpture, however, he could not help but digress. Rather than portraying human subjects, he depicted animals in bronze, but he endowed them with such anthropomorphic qualities as to render them nearly human. While the art world experienced a general revival of human figuration during the 1980s, Flanagan paralleled the trend with an eccentric twist.

Leaping Hare was the first of many variations on a theme of anthropomorphized animals. Although Flanagan cast a range of animals, such as elephants, horses, and dogs, he returned again and again to the form of the hare. He partially explained this choice when he stated that he found the creature to have incredible expressive potential, particularly in its long ears. Many of his hares stand on their hind feet and function almost as human surrogates as they dance, box, and play cricket. By selecting an animal to exhibit human qualities, Flanagan teases the viewer with hints of a figural tradition, only to reject that seriousness with a playful response.

Flanagan also creates dichotomous juxtapositions in his hare sculptures. He most often pairs his hares, which appear vital and lifelike in their poses, with casts of rigid, inanimate objects, positioned as bases for the animals. Such bases as anvils and bells make specific reference to the practice and tradition of bronze casting while also providing a serious counterpart to the whimsical hares. *Hare on Helmet II* epitomizes this opposition: an inquisitive and lively hare, its ears perked up in alertness, stands on its hind legs atop a helmet, a weighty object with connotations of work and war.

Throughout his career, Flanagan has struggled with sculptural traditions regarding materials, methods, and subject matter. From an early iconoclasm in the 1960s, he has since developed a stylistic pluralism and in the process has gradually carved out a place for himself within British sculptural history.

RACHEL EPP BULLER

Hare
The Conway Library, Courtauld Institute of Art

Biography

Born in Prestatyn, North Wales, 11 January 1941. Studied architecture at Birmingham College of Art and Crafts, 1957; attended classes under Anthony Caro at St. Martin's School of Art, 1960, where he enrolled full-time to study with Caro and Phillip King, 1964–66; held first solo exhibition at Rowan Gallery, London, 1966; moved to Ibiza, Spain, 1987. Lives and works in Dublin, Ireland.

Selected Works

1965   *aaing j gni aa*; sand, plaster, hessian; Tate Gallery, London, England

1967   *four casb 2'67, ring 1 1'67, rope (gr2sp60) 6'67*; cloth, rope, linoleum, sand, plastic; Tate Gallery, London, England

1968   *Heap (1)*; canvas and sand (location unknown)

1977–79 *A Nose in Repose*; Hornton stone, elmwood; Tate Gallery, London, England

1980   *Leaping Hare*; bronze; Waddington Galleries, London, England

1981   *Hare on Helmet II*; bronze; Tate Gallery, London, England

Further Reading

Barry Flanagan (exhib. cat.), Eindhoven, The Netherlands: Van Abbemuseum, 1977; London: Serpentine Gallery, 1979

Barry Flanagan: Recent Sculpture, Chicago: Richard Gray Gallery, 1995

Barry Flanagan: Sculpture (exhib. cat.), Venice: Venice Biennale Internazionale d'Arte, and London: British Council, 1982

Beal, Graham, "Barry Flanagan: 'Twice As Hard in a Negative Way,'" in *A Quiet Revolution: British Sculpture since 1965*, edited by Beal and Mary Jane Jacob, Chicago: Museum of Contemporary Art, 1987; edited by Terry A. Neff, London: Thames and Hudson, 1987

Live in Your Head: When Attitudes Become Form: Works, Concepts, Processes, Situations, Information (exhib. cat.), London: Institute of Contemporary Arts, 1969

JOHN BERNARD FLANNAGAN 1895–1942 *United States*

John B. Flannagan was an important proponent of direct carving (*taille directe*) in the United States in the early part of the 20th century. Between 1910 and 1940 this sculptural technique represented a Modernist alternative to the tradition of monumental cast sculpture that had dominated public awareness in the United States since the 19th century. Flannagan rejected the large-scale commemorative sculpture encouraged by the academic competitions and instead favored a smaller, much more intimate conception. While not as influential as his contemporaries William Zorach and Robert Laurent, Flannagan formulated what many consider one of the most cogent statements on direct carving ever written, "The Image in the Rock" (1942).

During the 1920s and 1930s Flannagan worked predominantly in and around New York City. From 1914 to 1917 he studied academic painting at the Minneapolis School of Art in Minnesota, together with Wanda Gág, Adolf Dehn, and Harry Gottlieb, all of whom also moved to New York. Flannagan was aware of international crosscurrents in sculpture and most certainly of the work of Constantin Brancusi. Like Brancusi, Flannagan sought to capture the essence of his subject more than its specific attributes. However, Flannagan did not resort to such radical simplifications of form. His sculptures are stylized but not abstract. For Flannagan, the artist's unmediated relationship with the material governed the creative process. He conceived of stone as the bearer of a hidden natural reality; the sculptor's role was to release it. Although he concentrated on a limited number of subjects—religious iconography, single figures, mother and child groups, and, most characteristically, animals—these were made to stand for such universal themes as birth, growth, death, and regeneration.

Flannagan first exhibited with the Society of Independent Artists in 1919 and 1921, the same year that *The Dial*, the distinguished literary journal of the 1920s, published one of his brush-and-ink drawings. In the early years of the 1920s, he worked mainly in wood, beginning a tendency toward self-conscious primitivizing that may also be considered quite modern. Like Zorach, Flannagan combined an interest in outside sources with the aesthetic of truth to materials. His first important group show in 1923 at the Montross Gallery, with Arthur B. Davies, William Glackens, Maurice and Charles Prendergast, Charles Sheeler, and Walt Kuhn, included two wax paintings, along with carved works of religious subjects. Davies, who, at the behest of a mutual acquaintance, had allowed Flannagan to stay at the Davies farm in Congers, New York, in 1922–23, presumably encouraged the younger artist.

Throughout his life Flannagan gravitated to rural, secluded locations outside New York City where he felt a communion with nature. Emotionally scarred from childhood experiences of abandonment, he suffered from depression and alcoholism. After 1923 he lived and worked both in New City, New York, and Woodstock, New York, where he carved the famous *Maverick Horse*, a symbol of the artist's colony founded in 1905 by Hervey White. Unable to afford quarried stone, around 1925 Flannagan began to carve fieldstone; henceforth, stone was his preferred medium. This year also saw the beginning of his relationship with Juliana Force, who was instrumental in helping to form the collection of the Whitney Museum of American Art in New York City; he exhibited with four other artists at the Whitney Studio Club, an early precursor to the museum.

In 1928 Erhard Weyhe of the Weyhe Bookshop and Gallery in New York City offered Flannagan a stipend in exchange for a certain number of sculptures a year. This agreement proved pivotal for Flannagan's career and continued for almost ten years. Carl Zigrosser, Flannagan's dealer at the Weyhe Gallery, was a valuable supporter and loyal friend. Six solo shows followed Flannagan's first solo show at the Weyhe Gallery in 1927. Weyhe also financed the artist's first trip to Ireland in 1930–31, allowing Flannagan direct exposure to medieval and Gothic influences and ultimately enabling him to do some of his best work. He returned to Ireland in 1932–33 on a Guggenheim fellowship.

Colt
© Francis G. Mayer / CORBIS

Mother and Child (also called *Design for Skyscraper Court*), his first attempt at public sculpture, is based on a work of the same name that Flannagan had carved in Ireland.

Flannagan's professional standing began to increase in 1930, the year of his third solo show at the Weyhe Gallery. The works he produced in Ireland, mostly sculptures of animals and large figural works, further solidified his reputation. In 1933 he received a commission to sculpt a large-scale figure for the Samuel Memorial in Fairmount Park, Philadelphia. Unfortunately, in 1934 he suffered a nervous breakdown and was institutionalized for seven months. Unable to work in his preferred technique, he experimented with metal casting, which is interesting in the context of his mixed-material piece from Ireland, *Figure of Dignity*.

In 1937 Flannagan worked part of the year near Ridgefield, Connecticut, and sculpted two of his best-known pieces, *Jonah and the Whale* and *Triumph of the Egg, I* using direct carving. After being struck by a car in 1939, however, he underwent four brain operations, and doctors urged him against the physical strain of direct carving. In the early 1930s Flannagan had

begun to authorize casts of his original works. He continued this practice with increasing frequency from the time of his accident up until his death. Unable to work with the vigor that had characterized his earlier years, Flannagan took his own life in 1942 on the eve of an important retrospective showing of his sculpture at the Buchholz Gallery in New York City.

Although largely forgotten today, Flannagan produced a body of work believed to include some 200 sculptures, many in major collections throughout the United States. Less a pioneer of modern sculpture than a revitalizer of an existing aesthetic, he falls outside the mainstream of modern art. In his singular facility for both the sculptural medium and the written word, he was surely unique.

KATHERINE RANGOON DOYLE

See also **Brancusi, Constantin**

Biography

Born in Fargo, North Dakota, United States, 7 April 1895. Studied painting under Robert Koehler at Minneapolis School of Art, 1914–17; Guggenheim Fellowship, 1932–33; Public Works of Art Project, December 1933–March 1934; member, Sculptors Guild, 1938; exhibited at New York World's Fair, 1939; awarded the Alexander Shilling Prize, 1940. Died in New York City, United States, 6 January 1942.

Selected Works

1924   *Maverick Horse*; chestnut; Woodstock Artists Association, Woodstock, New York, United States
1925   *Christ*; wood; National Gallery of Art, Washington, D.C., United States
1929–30 *Elephant*; bluestone; Whitney Museum of American Art, New York City, United States
1932   *Figure of Dignity*; granite, cast aluminum; Metropolitan Museum of Art, New York City, United States
1932–33 *Mother and Child*; limestone; Hugh Lane Municipal Gallery of Modern Art, Dublin, Ireland
1934–35 *Mother and Child* (also known as *Design for Skyscraper Court*); sandstone; Fogg Art Museum, Cambridge, Massachusetts, United States
1937   *Jonah and the Whale*; bluestone; Brooklyn Museum of Art, New York City, United States
1937   *Triumph of the Egg, I*; granite; Museum of Modern Art, New York City, United States

1938	*The Gold Miner*; limestone; Samuel Memorial, Fairmount Park, Philadelphia, Pennsylvania, United States
1938	*Gorilla*; stone; National Gallery of Art, Washington, D.C., United States
1940	*Not Yet*; wrought bronze; Minneapolis Institute of Art, Minnesota, United States

Further Reading

Flannagan, John Bernard, "The Image in the Rock," *The Sculpture of John B. Flannagan* (exhib. cat.), edited by Dorothy Miller, New York: Museum of Modern Art, 1942

Flannagan, John Bernard, *Letters of John B. Flannagan*, New York: Valentin, 1942

Flannagan, John Bernard, *John B. Flannagan: Sculpture/Drawings, 1924–1938* (exhib. cat.), Saint Paul, Minnesota: Minnesota Museum of Art, 1973

Forsyth, Robert Joseph, "John B. Flannagan: His Life and Works" (dissertation), University of Minnesota, 1965

Tarbell, Roberta K., "Direct Carving," in *Vanguard American Sculpture, 1913–1939*, by Joan M. Marter, Tarbell, and Jeffrey Wechsler, New Brunswick, New Jersey: Rutgers University, 1979

Zilczer, Judith, "The Theory of Direct Carving in Modern Sculpture," *The Oxford Art Journal* (November 1981)

JOHN FLAXMAN 1755–1826 *British*

John Flaxman, a figure of central importance during the Neoclassical movement, was a remarkably versatile artist whose style lent itself to a variety of media. As a sculptor, his church monuments were innovative in their sentiment, piety, and humanity. His illustrations for the works of Dante, Homer, and Aeschylus earned him international influence and fame. Also significant were his designs for Wedgwood ceramics and precious metalwork, which established him as a pioneering artist during the Industrial Revolution. Margaret Whinney claimed that his achievements reflected "perhaps better than any European sculptor of his day, the crosscurrents of taste affecting artists at the opening of the 19th century" (see Whinney, 1956).

The son of a London plaster-cast dealer, Flaxman showed precocious sculptural talents and entered the newly established Royal Academy Schools at age 14, where fellow pupils included his lifelong friends William Blake and Thomas Stothard. He received regular commissions for ceramic designs from Josiah Wedgwood. Although such work did not fully satisfy Flaxman's ambitions, it deepened his interest in antiquity and helped to develop his distinctive, linear style. His Wedgwood designs include jasperware reliefs of *The Dancing Hours* and the *Apotheosis of Homer* (both 1778), which have rarely been out of production. During this period, Flaxman established his career as a sculptor. His relief monument to Sarah Morley is an

uncertain mixture of Gothic, late Baroque, and Neoclassical elements. Yet as Allan Cunningham, Flaxman's assistant and biographer, claimed, "it elevates the mind and not without tears."

In 1787 Flaxman left for Rome, where he spent seven years. In 1790 he received his first commission for a major imaginative sculpture, the *Fury of Athamas*, which was strongly influenced by the *Laocoön*. This was followed by the relief *Apollo and Marpessa*, which is unusually delicate in carving and sensitive in finish. In 1792 Flaxman was commissioned by Thomas Hope to draw illustrations for Dante's *Divine Comedy*, and he subsequently produced illustrations for Homer's *Iliad* and *Odyssey* (1793) and the works of Aeschylus (1795), all of which were published as engravings. Their sources included Greek vase figures and 14th-century Italian painting, but the results were original in their minimalism and primitivism. Flaxman minimized perspective and modeling and instead stressed simple, expressive outlines. George Romney believed that "they look as if they had been made in the age when Homer wrote." Romney's admiration was echoed by other major artists, including Jacques-Louis David, Francisco de Goya, Jean-Auguste-Dominique Ingres, and François Rude, as well as the critics August Wilhelm von Schlegel and Johann Wolfgang von Goethe.

Flaxman underrated his illustrations and, in reference to Schlegel, wished that "the Germans had something better to exercise their critical talent upon." He claimed that his vision did not "terminate in giving a few outlines to the world," and intended the illustrations to serve as blueprints for relief sculptures—although few recognizably did so (see Symmons, 1984). On his return to England in 1794, he dedicated his subsequent career to sculpture. His work was monopolized by monuments, several of which were on a large scale. Two of the best known commemorate Lord Mansfield and Lord Nelson. The grieving figure of a genius of death at the rear of the Mansfield monument and the Britannia figure urging two young midshipmen to look up toward Nelson as a role model are both emotionally effective. Two unexecuted designs for colossal civic monuments to Britannia reflect Flaxman's visionary Neoclassicism. Generally, however, he was happier with simpler and smaller church monuments whose predominantly relief formats had closer affinities with his illustrations.

Flaxman's most famous church monument, that to Agnes Cromwell, is an idealized representation of the young woman carried heavenward by angels. The emphasis on eternal life reflects Flaxman's adherence to the doctrines of the mystical philosopher Emanuel Swedenbourg. The monument also conveys Flaxman's belief that "sentiment is the life and soul of fine art; without which it is all a dead letter!" Art historians

Monument to Agnes Cromwell
The Conway Library, Courtauld Institute of Art and M.H.
Ridgway

have labeled such works as "Romantic Classicism": they are Neoclassical in their formal and Romantic in their emotional qualities. Flaxman's monument to the headmaster Joseph Warton is a charming fusion of Classicism and realism. The former is evident in its background representations of Homer and Aristotle, and the latter in the group of boys being taught by the learned and kindly Warton. The success of the Warton monument was reflected in a more ambitious monument carved in the round commemorating Susan, Viscountess Fitzharris. This portrays a young mother reading to two of her children and nursing the youngest on her lap. It reflects Flaxman's attraction to Madonna themes and his belief in maternal affection as an admirable sentiment—both in sculpture and in life. Other major monuments include one to the orientalist Sir

William Jones (1796), which blends exoticism and realism; a series of three wall panels to members of the Baring family illustrating the Lord's Prayer (1809–10); and two classicized monuments showing the bestowal of charity, which commemorate members of the Yarborough family (1803–06) and Georgiana, Countess Spencer (1816–19).

Flaxman's relatively few imaginative works vary in quality. The early *Fury of Athamas* and *Hercules and Hebe* are compositionally awkward, whereas the plaster relief *Mercury Bearing Pandora to Earth* has an ethereal exquisiteness reminiscent of the monument to Agnes Cromwell. Flaxman's contemporaries warmly praised his last major sculpture, *St. Michael Overcoming Satan*, which was influenced by Giambologna. At the 1979 Flaxman exhibition at the Royal Academy, his silverwork designs for Rundell, Bridge, and Rundell captured public and critical attention. The *Trafalgar Vase*, a centerpiece (1809; Royal Collection, Windsor Castle, England), and the 600-ounce *Shield of Achilles* are massive pieces, contrasting with the delicacy and intimacy usually encountered in his art.

In 1810 Flaxman was elected as the first professor of sculpture at the Royal Academy. His *Lectures on Sculpture* (1829) were conscientious, earnest, and morally purposeful, yet were justly criticized by William Hazlitt as "dogmatic, rather than philosophical" and frequently "weak, warped, insufficient, and contradictory" in argument. Flaxman was at his most persuasive when expressing moral and patriotic enthusiasm for English medieval sculpture and damning the Baroque for its exaggeration and theatricality. When he died, Flaxman was lauded for his artistic and personal qualities and was dubbed "the Fra Angelico of sculpture" and "our Phidias." Although admired throughout the 19th century, his reputation suffered when Modernism was ascendant. This changed when Robert Rosenblum revealed the radical, abstract implications of Flaxman in *Transformations in Late Eighteenth-Century Art* (1967). As a sculptor, Flaxman's standing would be greater but for his inconsistency. Too often his plaster models were delegated in their carving to untalented assistants. Nicholas Penny called some designs "extraordinarily clumsy" and considered "many signed works deplorably executed" (see Penny, 1977). Yet Flaxman repeatedly displayed, as David Bindman wrote, a "special ability to infuse the conventions of Neoclassicism with warmth" (see Bindman, 1979).

MARK STOCKER

Biography

Born in York, England, 6 July 1755. Father a London plaster-cast maker and dealer. Studied and exhibited at Royal Academy Schools, London, *ca.* 1770–73; designed for firm of Wedgwood and Bentley, 1775–87; lived in Rome, 1787–94; after recommendations by Antonio Canova, received commissions from Thomas Hope, Mrs. Georgiana Hare-Naylor, and the dowager Georgiana, Countess Spencer, for illustrations to the classics, *Iliad, Odyssey, Divine Comedy*, and works by Aeschylus, all of which attracted international attention; returned to London, 1794; concentrated on sculpture and church monuments; elected associate of the Royal Academy of Arts, London, 1797, and to full membership, 1800; visited Paris, 1802; designed silverwork, mostly for Rundell, Bridge, and Rundell, 1805–25; appointed first professor of sculpture at Royal Academy, 1810; lectured on history of sculpture at Royal Academy, 1811 (published posthumously, 1829). Died in London, England, 9 December 1826.

Selected Works

1784   Monument to Sarah Morley; marble; Gloucester Cathedral, England

1790–94 *Apollo and Marpessa*; marble; Royal Academy of Arts, London, England

1790–94 *Fury of Athamas*; marble; Ickworth House, Suffolk, England

1795–   Monument to Lord Mansfield; marble;
1801   Westminster Abbey, London, England

1799–   Monument to Agnes Cromwell; marble;
1800   Chichester Cathedral, England

1804   Monument to Dr. Joseph Warton; marble; Winchester Cathedral, England

1804–5 *Mercury Bearing Pandora to Earth*; plaster; Ny Carlsberg Glyptotek, Copenhagen, Denmark

1808–18 Monument to Lord Nelson; marble; St. Paul's Cathedral, London, England

1816–17 Monument to Susan, Viscountess Fitzharris; marble; Christchurch Priory, Dorset, England

1817–21 *Shield of Achilles*; silver gilt; Royal Collection, Windsor Castle, Berkshire, England

1819–26 *St. Michael Overcoming Satan*; marble; Petworth House, Petworth, West Sussex, England

Further Reading

The Age of Neo-Classicism (exhib. cat.), London: Arts Council of Great Britain, 1972

Bindman, David (editor), *John Flaxman, R.A.* (exhib. cat.), London: Thames and Hudson, 1979

Bindman, David, "John Flaxman," in *The Dictionary of Art*, edited by Jane Turner, vol. 11, New York: Grove, and London: Macmillan, 1996

Constable, William George, *John Flaxman, 1755–1826*, London: University of London Press, 1927

Flaxman, John, *Flaxman's Illustrations to Homer*, edited by Robert Essick and Jenijoy LaBelle, New York: Dover, 1977

Flaxman, John, *John Flaxman: Mythologie und Industrie*, edited by Werner Hofmann, Hamburg, Germany: Kunsthalle, 1979

Irwin, David, *John Flaxman, 1755–1826: Sculptor, Illustrator, Designer*, London: Studio Vista, 1979

Irwin, David, *Neoclassicism*, London: Phaidon, 1997

Janson, Horst Woldemar, *19th-Century Sculpture*, New York: Abrams, 1985

Penny, Nicholas, *Church Monuments in Romantic England*, New Haven, Connecticut: Yale University Press, 1977

Reilly, Robin, *Wedgwood*, 2 vols., New York: Stockton Press, 1989

Rosenblum, Robert, *Transformations in Late Eighteenth-Century Art*, Princeton, New Jersey: Princeton University Press, 1967

Symmons, Sarah, *Flaxman and Europe: The Outline Illustrations and Their Influence*, New York: Garland, 1984

Whinney, Margaret, "Flaxman and the Eighteenth Century," *Journal of the Warburg and Courtauld Institutes* 19 (1956)

Whinney, Margaret, *Sculpture in Britain, 1530–1830*, London and Baltimore, Maryland: Penguin, 1964; 2nd edition, revised by John Physick, London and New York: Penguin, 1988

Whinney, Margaret, and Rupert Gunnis, *The Collection of Models by John Flaxman, R.A., at University College London: A Catalogue and Introduction*, London: Athlone Press, 1967

CORNELIS II FLORIS DE VRIENDT *ca.* 1513/14–1575 *Netherlandish*

Cornelis II Floris de Vriendt was born into a family of stonemasons. His grandfather (Jan), father (Cornelis I), and an uncle (Pieter) were active in that trade. Another uncle, the sculptor Claudius, probably initiated Cornelis II into the profession. Three of Cornelis II's brothers became artists as well: Frans was a well-known painter, Jacob was a ceramist, and Hans was a glass painter. Most likely it was Claudius, who sometimes called himself Clauderio, and Lambert Lombard, with whom Frans studied, who interested Cornelis II in the new Renaissance style. In 1538 he was in Rome. One year later he was back in Antwerp and became, like his uncle, a member of the guild of Saint Luke. At that time Claudius was in dispute with the guild of the stonemasons, which did not want sculptors who worked in stone to become members of the artists' guild of Saint Luke instead of the Vier Gekroonden, which united most of the building trades. The dispute clearly shows that the Renaissance ideas of art and the artists' social position as part of the liberal arts had not yet been accepted in Antwerp.

Floris nevertheless succeeded in setting up an Italian-style workshop with several assistants, probably reserving designing and management for himself. His earliest documented works consist of drawings for a frieze or invention for a print, dated 1543, and a series of ornamental initials in the guild *Liggeren* (books containing the financial records of the guild, including lists of the names of the members). Beginning in 1548, several important series of ornamental prints after his invention were published. These prints soon became quite influential, being used as the immediate source of much ornamental sculpture in the Low Countries, northern Germany, and Denmark. In 1549 Floris received a commission for the sepulchral monument for Dorothea of Denmark, wife of Duke Albrecht of Prussia, for the Cathedral of Königsberg. More such monuments followed, most of them for churches in Denmark or northern Germany. The output of the workshop consisted in large part of sepulchral monuments, some for kings and others for rich citizens. Examples of these that survived the iconoclastic movement of the 1560s can be found in the Grote Church in Breda, the Netherlands. The *Spencer Album* (New York Public Library, Spencer Collection), which contains more than a hundred inventions for sepulchral monuments, can be regarded as a kind of catalogue of the workshop. Several of the drawings represent monuments executed by Floris. The catalogue also contains inventions for larger works as well as for less-important and smaller monuments. The shop also helped produce *Sacramentstorens* (towers for Eucharistic reservation) and an important rood loft for the Cathedral of Tournai. About 1562 Philip II commissioned Floris for an important altar for the cloister of San Jéronimo el Real in Madrid.

By the late 1550s, Floris had also become active as an architect. His projects for a porch for the town hall of Cologne are dated 1558. From 1561 to 1565 he was active as the main architect for the Antwerp town hall, while his workshop executed parts of the sculptural decoration of the same building. He was also responsible for at least part of the Oosters Huis, a commercial complex built by the Hanze merchants in Antwerp.

JAN VAN DAMME

Biography

Born in Antwerp, Belgium, *ca.* 1513/14. Traveled to Mechelen to become court sculptor to Margaret of Austria, by 1524; visited Rome, 1538; became master, guild of Saint Luke in Antwerp, 1539; served as dean of guild, 1547–49; period of most intense activity began *ca.* 1548; published engravings; executed tombs for Danish royal family; produced decorations for triumphal entry of Philip II into Antwerp; also worked on the Cathedral of Tournai and Church of St. Leonard (Zoutleeuw). Died in Antwerp, Belgium, 20 October 1575.

Selected Works

1548–49 Epitaph of Dorothea of Denmark, for the Cathedral of Königsberg; stone (dismantled)

1549–52 Eucharist tower; stone; Church of St. Leonard, Zoutleeuw, Belgium

1551–53 Tomb of Frederick II of Denmark; alabaster and marble; Cathedral of Schleswig, Germany

1553–54 Tomb of Jan Van Merode and Anna van Gistel; alabaster and marble; Church of Saint Dymphna, Geel, Belgium

1555 Epitaph of Jan van Dendermonde; stone; Grote Church, Breda, The Netherlands

1555–57 Eucharist tower; parish church, Zuurbemde, Belgium

1557–61 Tomb of Archbishop Anton von Schauenburg; alabaster and marble; Cathedral of Cologne, Germany

after Epitaph of Nicholas Vierling; stone; Grote
1557 Church, Breda, The Netherlands

1566–68 Epitaph of Herluf Trolle and Birgitte Goye; alabaster and marble; Church of Saint Oli, Helsingør, Denmark

1566–68 Tomb and epitaph of Herluf Trolle and Birgitte Goye; alabaster and marble; Cloister Church, Herlufsholm, Naestved, Denmark

1568–75 Tomb (Mausolea) of Christian III and Frederick II of Denmark; Cathedral of Roskilde, Denmark

1570–73 Rood-loft; alabaster and touchstone; Cathedral of Tournai, Belgium

Tomb of Christian III
The Conway Library, Courtauld Institute of Art

Further Reading

Bevers, Holm, *Das Rathaus von Antwerpen (1561–1565): Architektur und Figurenprogramm*, New York: Olms, 1985

Hedicke, Robert, *Cornelis Floris und die Florisdekoration: Studien zur niederländischen und deutschen Kunst im XVI. Jahrhundert*, Berlin: Julius Bard, 1913

Huysmans, Antoinette, et al., *Cornelis Floris, 1514–1575, beeldhouwer, architect, ontwerper*, Brussels: Gemeentekrediet, 1996

Velde, Carl van de, "The Grotesque Initials in the First Ligger and in the Busboek of the Antwerp Guild of Saint Luke," *Bulletin van de Koninklijke musea voor kunst en geschiedenis* 45 (1973)

Velde, Carl van de, "Floris (Vriendt de): Cornelis Floris II," in *The Dictionary of Art*, edited by Jane Turner, vol. 11, New York: Grove, and London: Macmillan, 1996

PETER FLÖTNER *ca.* 1490/1495–1546

German

Peter Flötner was one of the most important artists of the German Renaissance and, next to Albrecht Dürer, also one of the most versatile and stimulating. He was active in small-scale sculpture and woodworking as well as in woodblock carving, drawing, and illustrating. His ornamental designs and plaques achieved the greatest fame. Hardly any information is known about his life, however. He was born in Thurgau in Switzerland and possibly did part of his training in Augsburg. It has been conjectured that he belonged to the workshop of the important Augsburg sculptor Adolf Daucher and that he took part in the work on the Fugger chapel in the Church of Saint Anna; however, there is no evidence for this speculation. His study trip possibly brought him to Italy, although no evidence supports this conjecture either. In 1523 he received citizenship in Nuremberg by swearing the civic oath. Documentary sources refer to him as "Meister Peter" and "the foreign sculptor from Ansbach." This indicates that he had been working before in the middle Franconian royal seat, perhaps in the service of the margrave.

In Nuremberg, Flötner initially created small-scale sculptures as well as graphic and plastic models for bronze sculptures. Among the latter is a sculpture of Adam. A small limewood carving of the apostle Andrew was possibly the model for the lost silver *Andrew* reliquary of the Hallesches Heiltum, one of Cardinal Albrecht von Brandenburg's great reliquary collections. The model for a small horse cast in bronze about that time is also attributed to Flötner. A design also survives in the Staatliche Museen in Berlin for a grotto fountain that has not been preserved.

The most famous of Flötner's works from this time is the Apollo fountain, which was cast in 1532 in the Nuremberg shop of Pankraz Labenwolf. The fountain column was created on commission from the Nuremberg Guild of Crossbowmen, who installed it at their guildhall in the Herrenschiessgraben, the section of ditch belonging to the city fortifications that was used for practice grounds. On top of the richly ornamented pedestal, adorned with four masks and four putti riding on dolphins, stands the nude figure of Apollo, the young Greek sun god, shooting an arrow with a bow. He is depicted in Classical *contrapposto* (a natural pose with the weight of one leg, the shoulder, and hips counterbalancing one another) in the moment at which the string is tensed. That Flötner was the figure's creator can be determined from the correspondence between the bishop of Trent, Cardinal Bernhard von Cles, and the Nuremberg patrician Christoph Scheurl. Inspired by the design or model of the fountain, the cardinal ordered a similar work—also to be designed by Flötner and cast by Pankraz Labenwolf—for his castle in Trent, the Castello del Buon Consiglio.

Flötner's pen-and-ink drawing kept in the Grand Duke of Weimar's collection until World War II and dated to 1531, which is also one of the most impressive accomplishments of Dürer's successors, was possibly the very sketch mentioned by the cardinal. It was received by the cardinal for viewing in 1532 and, according to the correspondence, sent back again to Nuremberg. The figure on the Nuremberg fountain displays Flötner's mature style, which reveals the influence of the great wealth of forms in Italian art. This has prompted scholars to assume that the sculptor made a trip to Italy and to attribute his knowledge and abilities to an intensive study of the Paduan sculpture of Andrea Riccio and his successors. Graphic models—including Jacopo de' Barbaris's *Apollo and Diana* print (1503/04) and Dürer's print of *Adam and Eve* (1504)—certainly influenced this composition. What the sculpture makes especially manifest, however, is the inspiration of the *Apollo Belvedere* discovered in the Tusculum area of antiquity, near Frascati. The *Apollo Belvedere* was one of the most important Roman sculptures and has deeply influenced Western sculpture in conveying the Classical understanding of the body. The sculpture of the Apollo fountain is unique in its conception and execution. It not only belongs to the major works of Nuremberg brass founding of the mid 16th century but is also the first German sculpture intended to be viewed from all sides. It therefore occupies a central position in the history of northern European Renaissance sculpture.

Flötner was also active designing the interior decoration and furnishings for the Tucher family's palace in Nuremberg, begun in 1533. In 1533–34 the Hirsvogelsaal (Hirsvogel Hall) was built, probably under his direction. It is assumed that Flötner conceived the fa-

Plaquettes depicting Four Music-Making Angels
The Conway Library, Courtauld Institute of Art

cade, the splendid wall paneling, and the chimney, which was richly decorated with figural and ornamental carving. This building fell victim to the bombing of World War II, although some of the furnishings were saved, now installed in an addition built on the Tucher palace. The hall is unique in the perfect purity of its Renaissance forms; such rigorous purity was without precedent in German art. The construction was conceived as a *Gesamtkunstwerk* (total work of art), thereby reflecting Flötner's significance as a versatile and highly talented artist.

In 1534–35 Flötner delivered sketches for the famous silver altar in the Cathedral of Wawel in Kraków, a project that involved several Nuremberg artists. Flötner was also one of the most important German masters of plaquette making. His lead and bronze plaquettes demonstrate a high degree of deftness and virtuosity in depicting figures and landscapes. The frequency with which the motifs he created were used by goldsmiths indicates their popularity. One can find his small-scale relief casts on mortars and goblets from the workshop of the famous Nuremberg goldsmith Wenzel Jamnitzer. Flötner's series the *Die neun Musen* (The Nine Muses), *Die ältesten deutschen Könige* (The Old-

est German Kings), and *Die Tugenden und die Laster* (The Virtues and the Vices), all around 1540, were apparently collected by humanistically educated scholars, townspeople, and clergymen. That the stone relief for the casting of the plaquette of *Caritas* (*ca.* 1540) found in the Kunsthistorisches Museum, Vienna carries Flötner's rare signature illustrates the high esteem held for his works, as well as his self-confidence as an artist. From a historiographical perspective, it is interesting to note that the extensive array of otherwise unsigned plaquettes attributed to Flötner on stylistic grounds were ascribed to him based on this very stone mold.

Flötner also created many woodcuts for book illustrations and leaflets. Most of the drawings and woodcuts were probably commissioned by his publisher to serve as models for works by goldsmiths and other craftsmen. One of the most magnificent designs in this regard is the one for the "coconut goblet" of the Nuremberg patrician family Holzschuh, perhaps created by the goldsmith Melchior Baier. The coconut reliefs and the images on the cast-silver figured pedestal are also attributed to Flötner's hand. With his models Flötner played an essential and defining role in the development of Renaissance forms. He had a formative influence on the crafts and on architectural ornament as well, above all in southern Germany, into the 17th century. In addition, Flötner is to be counted among those masters who were also involved in the deliberate and artistic design of furniture.

For his contemporaries, as well as for the next two or three generations, Flötner's figural and ornamental models were such novel creations in both form and content and were of such unsurpassable perfection that they were employed repeatedly by goldsmiths, workers in pewter, coppersmiths, and potters. His virtuosic mastery and modification and development of the ornamental forms of the Italian Renaissance guaranteed the master an important place in the history of German crafts.

FRANK MATTHIAS KAMMEL

See also **Apollo Belvedere; Plaquette**

Biography

Born probably in Thurgau, Switzerland, *ca.* 1490/95. Received training or perhaps was active for a short time in Augsburg, Germany; was later active in Ansbach, Franconia, Germany; received citizenship in Nuremberg, 1523, where he worked for the rest of his life; active designing decorative ornaments and furnishings, Tucher family palace, Nuremberg, 1533; created many popular plaquette designs for relief work on mortars and goblets, 1530s. Died in Nuremberg, Franconia, Germany, 13 October 1546.

Selected Works

1525   *Adam*; wood; Kunsthistorisches Museum, Vienna, Austria

1530   *Apostle Andrew*; limewood; Museum für Kunst und Gewerbe, Hamburg, Germany

ca. 1530 Small horse; bronze; Württembergisches Museum, Stuttgart, Germany

1532   Apollo fountain (design; casting done by Hans Vischer or Pankraz Labenwolf); bronze; Stadtmuseum Fembohaus, Nuremberg, Germany

1533–34 Paneling and fireplace of Hirsvogel Hall; wood, limestone; Tucherschloss, Nuremberg, Germany

ca. 1540 *Die ältesten deutschen Könige* (The Oldest German Kings); plaquette series in lead, bronze, silver; Kunsthistorisches Museum, Vienna, Austria; Bayerisches Nationalmuseum, Munich, Germany; Museum für Kunsthandwerk, Dresden, Germany; Germanisches Nationalmuseum, Nuremberg, Germany

ca. 1540 *Die neun Musen* (The Nine Muses); plaquette series in lead, bronze; Bayerisches Nationalmuseum, Munich, Germany

ca. 1540 *Die Tugenden und die Laster* (The Virtues and the Vices); plaquette series in lead, bronze; Historisches Museum, Basel, Switzerland

ca. 1540 The Holzschuher covered goblet; silver; Germanisches Nationalmuseum, Nuremberg, Germany

Further Reading

Angerer, Marin, *Studien zu Peter Flötner: Peter Flötners Entwürfe: Beiträge zum Ornament und Kunsthandwerk in Nürnberg in der ersten Hälfte des 16. Jahrhunderts*, s.l.: s.n., 1983

Bange, Ernst Friedrich, *Peter Flötner: Meister der Graphik*, Leipzig: Klinkhard und Biermann, 1926

Kuhn, Charles Louis, "An Unknown Relief by Peter Flötner," *The Art Quarterly* 17 (1954)

Peter Flötner und die Renaissance in Deutschland: Ausstellung anlässlich des 400. Todestages Peter Flötners (exhib. cat.), Nuremberg, Germany: Verlag Die Egge, 1947

Von der Osten, Gert, and Horst Vey, *Painting and Sculpture in Germany and the Netherlands, 1500 to 1600*, London and Baltimore, Maryland: Penguin, 1969

Weber, Ingrid, *Deutsche, niederländische und französische Renaissanceplaketten, 1500–1650: Modelle für Reliefs an*

Kunst-, Prunk- und Gebrauchsgegenständen, 2 vols., Munich: Bruckmann, 1975

GIOVANNI BATTISTA FOGGINI 1652–1725 *Italian*

Giovanni Battista Foggini was one of the most important sculptors of late 17th-century Florence, being chiefly responsible for the introduction and dissemination of the Roman Baroque style into that city. As court sculptor and architect to Grand Duke Cosimo III de' Medici, he carried out many important projects for churches, chapels, altars, and tomb monuments (usually including important sculptural elements) and freestanding religious and secular statues and busts, and he provided designs for the extensive range of crafts practiced in the grand ducal workshops. Despite his prodigious output of plans, models, and designs, Foggini also modeled and cast numerous small bronzes with the high quality of craftsmanship typical of his predecessors Giambologna and the Tacca family.

Foggini's skill as a draftsman testifies to his earliest training as an artist. After turning to sculpture about 1664/65, his talents were noticed by Grand Duke Ferdinando II de' Medici, but his main artistic formation was in the Accademia Fiorentina in Rome. This academy was founded in 1673 by Cosimo III to reinvigorate and modernize the arts in Florence so that they might be employed once more for dynastic propaganda. In the academy (held at the Villa Madama), the students were instructed by the artist and architect Ciro Ferri (heir to the painter Pietro da Cortona) and the sculptor Ercole Ferrata, former assistant of both Alessandro Algardi and Gianlorenzo Bernini. Ferrata had been chosen to instruct the young Florentines because of his affinity with Algardi, whose style was to be an important formative influence upon them, but Foggini, conscious of his own place within the traditions of Florentine sculpture, was responsible for the continuation of many typically Florentine art forms in the spirit of the Roman Baroque.

Foggini's last months in Rome were spent preparing for the execution of a commission for a bronze equestrian portrait statue of Charles II, king of Spain, which was received from Spain in March 1676. The commission, supervised by the court sculptor Ferdinando Tacca, was abandoned soon after Foggini's return to Florence in June 1676.

In the following years, the munificent patronage of Cosimo III allied to Foggini's prolific powers of invention in the Roman Baroque idiom, and his facility in drawing and modeling, was to establish Florence once more as an artistic center. On his return to Florence, Foggini was immediately commissioned by the Corsini family to introduce a new and essentially Roman form of decoration to Florence, manifested in three large marble reliefs figuring scenes from the life of St. Andrea Corsini in the Church of Santa Maria del Carmine to adorn the family chapel in the style made famous by Algardi's great relief of *Pope Leo Driving Attila from Rome* (1646–53) in St. Peter's Basilica, Rome. However, where in Algardi's relief the drama is restrained, Foggini's relief of *The Battle of Anghiari* (1684–89), also commissioned by the Corsini family, has all the exuberance of the sculptures of Bernini. The steep diagonal design of the composition from the sword-brandishing saint at the top right-hand corner down to the headlong flight of the Pisan army out of the lower left-hand corner and into the chapel—enhanced by a sure control of anatomy and perspective—amply demonstrates the youthful sculptor's skills. The horses that project and fall dramatically out of the wall plane testify to Foggini's studies of equine anatomy in his last months at the Florentine academy.

The pressure of commissions throughout Foggini's life would rarely allow him to match the intensity and ambition of this early relief (which may have been too close in style to Bernini for his grand ducal patron), but many other important architectural and sculptural ensembles followed. The reliefs for the Chapel of St. Francis Xavier in Goa, India, and the Feroni Chapel, Florence, Italy, are among the most notable. Foggini's models for the antependium relief of the high altar of Santissima Annunziata seamlessly integrate an altar ensemble in the Florentine tradition of exquisite refinement of detail—carried out in precious metals that contrast with the colors of hard stone inlay—into the Roman Baroque taste for opulence and polychrome combinations of materials.

The graphic fluency of Foggini's relief style here, which links it directly with his drawings, is interestingly contrasted with that of his four bronze reliefs depicting the life of St. Francis Xavier. These follow the traditional form of Florentine pictorial relief cycles in which the figure composition stands out boldly against a landscape and whose style had last been seen in Ferdinando Tacca's antependium relief of the *Stoning of St. Stephen* (1649–56). Foggini's appreciation of the work of the younger Tacca also extended to his small bronze two-figure groups representing mythological and literary lovers as miniature theatrical tableaux developed along a frontal plane. His bronze statuette groups of *The Baptism of Christ* and *David and Goliath* form part of an important set of 12 groups made by Florentine sculptors between 1722 and 1725 for Anna Maria Luisa de' Medici, Electress Palatine, that clearly demonstrate the aesthetic principles of late Florentine Baroque sculpture. These groups include architectural and landscape elements, thereby enhancing

the fusion of the sculptural forms of the freestanding figure and the pictorial relief initiated by Tacca. Other small-scale works by Foggini, now missing, are recorded by their molds sold by his heirs to the porcelain manufactory of Doccia.

Most of Foggini's designs for furniture, both ecclesiastical and secular, include significant sculptural elements. The rarity of precedents for his daring design for a tabernacle in the Cathedral of Pisa (1678–86; Cappella del Sacramento) borne by flying angels may well be because of the difficulty of maintaining the illusion, a problem Foggini did not fully overcome.

When Foggini succeeded Ferdinando Tacca as court sculptor in 1687, he took over the Borgo Pinti foundry. This was the center of official Florentine bronze production, a facility he would fully exploit when in 1694 he received the title of court architect and became director and chief designer of the court workshops for the manufacture of furniture and hard stone ornamentation. In his design for the cabinet of the Elector Palatine, a type of furniture produced for over a century, Foggini combined the traditional materials of ebony and hardstone inlay with exquisitely modeled figurines and decorative detail in gilt bronze. This blend of Florentine and Baroque elements represented the triumph of the prince, whose effigy of combined bronze and carved hardstone is seated in the center of the ensemble.

Foggini adapted the ancient craft of hardstone carving to the Baroque style of his furniture by designing applications of miniature fruit and flowers both in high relief and fully in the round so that, combined with the abundant use of gilt-bronze figurines, they would play a more dominant role in the total ensemble and endow it with a new sculptural quality.

With a style that emphasizes humanity, Foggini's portrait of Grand Prince Ferdinando de' Medici softens the magniloquence of the heavy-limbed elector and recalls Foggini's dignified equestrian portrait of the unpromising figure of Charles II. The portrait formerly surmounted an ebony base with four bronze angle figures representing the continents (these are now lost; a set of plaster casts exists in the Museo Civico, Livorno, Italy). Here again Foggini adapts another early Florentine form of portraiture, the rearing equestrian portrait statuette created by Pietro Tacca, for a different age. Since Foggini did not carve in marble himself, his portrait busts are uneven in quality, but his moving representation of his grand ducal patron in old age (*Cosimo III de' Medici, Grand Duke of Tuscany*) is among the most remarkable portraits of 18th-century Florence.

ANTHEA BROOK

See also **Tacca Family**

Biography

Born in Florence, Italy, 25 April 1652. First studied drawing with Vincenzo Dandini but turned to sculpture, *ca.* 1664; apprenticed to uncle Jacopo Maria Foggini, a minor sculptor in wood; one of the first students of the Accademia Fiorentina in Rome (newly founded by Cosimo III de' Medici, Grand Duke of Tuscany), 1673; returned to Florence, 1676; practiced in Florence thereafter as independent sculptor and architect, working for the Medici and other leading Florentine families; recorded among artistic directors of the Accademia del Disegno by 1684; responsible for training of most sculptors and many architects of next generation; appointed court sculptor, 1687; appointed court architect and designer to Medici mausoleum in San Lorenzo and Galleria dei Lavori (grand-ducal workshops), 1694. Died in Florence, Italy, 12 April 1725.

Selected Works

1677–1701	Scenes from the life of St. Andrea Corsini; marble; Corsini Chapel, Church of Santa Maria del Carmine, Florence, Italy
1678–82	Models for *The Last Supper* and other reliefs for the antependium (executed by H. Brunick); silver; Church of Santissima Annunziata, Florence, Italy
ca. 1685	*Grand Prince Ferdinando de' Medici*; marble; Metropolitan Museum of Art, New York City, United States
ca. 1687–94	*Hercules and Iole*; bronze; Victoria and Albert Museum, London, England
1689–97	Scenes from the life of St. Francis Xavier; bronze; Chapel of St. Francis Xavier, Church of Bom Jesus, Goa, India
1698	*Charles II, King of Spain*, in Museo del Prado, Madrid, Spain; bronze (lost); plaster casts: Museo Civico, Livorno, Italy
1702	Tomb of Donato dell'Antella; marble; Church of Santissima Annunziata, Florence, Italy
1707–09	Cabinet of Anna Maria Luisa de' Medici, Electress Palatine; wood; Museo degli Argenti, Florence, Italy
before 1716	*Apollo and Marsyas*; bronze; Bayerisches Nationalmuseum, Munich, Germany; another cast: Victoria and Albert Museum, London, England
before 1716	*Mercury Freeing Prometheus*; bronze; Victoria and Albert Museum, London, England
1722	*David and Goliath*; bronze; Pushkin Museum, Moscow, Russia
ca.	*The Baptism of Christ*; bronze; Palazzo
1722–25	Pitti, Florence, Italy
ca. 1723?	*Cosimo III de' Medici, Grand Duke of Tuscany*; marble; National Gallery of Canada, Ottawa, Canada

Further Reading

Avery, Charles, "Foggini, Giovanni Battista," in *The Dictionary of Art*, edited by Jane Turner, vol. 10, New York: Grove, and London: Macmillan, 1996

Brook, Anthea, "Dynastic Statuary for Charles II of Spain," in *La scultura: Studi in onore di Andrew S. Ciechanowiecki*, Turin, Italy: Allemandi, 1994

Costantini, M., "Foggini, Giovanni Battista," in *Dizionario biografico degli italiani*, vol. 48, Roma: Istituto della Enciclopedia Italiana, 1997

Detroit Institute of Arts, *The Twilight of the Medici: Late Baroque Art in Florence, 1670–1743* (exhib. cat.), Florence: Centro Di, 1974

Fabbri, M.C., "La cappella Corsini," in *La chiesa di Santa Maria del Carmine a Firenze*, edited by Luciano Berti., Florence: Giunti, 1992

Krahn, Volker (editor), *Von allen Seiten schön: Bronzen der Renaissance und des Barock: Wilhelm von Bode zum 150. Geburtstag* (exhib. cat.), Berlin: Edition Braus, 1995

Lankheit, Klaus, *Die Modellsammlung der Porzellanmanufaktur Doccia: Ein Dokument italienischer Barockplastik*, Munich: Bruckmann, 1982

Montagu, J., "*Hercules and Iole* and Some Other Bronzes by Foggini," *Apollo* 87, no. 73 (1968)

Pratesi, Giovanni (editor), *Repertorio della scultura Fiorentina del Seicento e Settecento*, 3 vols., Turin, Italy: Umberto Allemandi, 1993; see especially vols. 1 and 2

Visonà, M., "Un ritratto di Anna Maria Luisa de' Medici bambina e i lari del Poggio Imperiale (riflessioni sul Foggini)," *Paragone* 49/585 (1998)

FERONI CHAPEL
Florence, Italy, 1691–1693

The Feroni Chapel represents for Florentine ecclesiastical architecture the culmination of a stylistic progression during the course of the 17th century, from the late Renaissance to an embracing of the flamboyant Baroque style of Gianlorenzo Bernini to a degree never seen there before or after. The Medici mausoleum (the Cappella dei Principi) in the Church of S. Lorenzo was the paradigm of the *cappella gentilizia* (chapel of a noble family), a structure deployed during the 17th century to serve more as a vehicle of expression for the aspirations of the Florentine nobility than for its essential function. Marquis Francesco Feroni, the patron of the Feroni Chapel, was atypical of the high officials of the Medici court; born in 1614 into a family of wool dyers in Empoli, he left that profession to establish himself as a merchant banker from about 1640 in Amsterdam, owning ships that traded most profitably between the African coast and the Spanish New World and acquiring fabulous wealth. In 1673 the newly acceded Grand Duke Cosimo III de' Medici persuaded Feroni to return to Italy, offering him the post of Depositario Generale (minister of finance) and a marquisate. The favor of his ruler, his high office, and unlimited financial means opened all doors, yet Feroni sought to outdo the old families of the aristocracy through the splendor of his way of life and to confirm, by the construction of a family chapel, his arrival among their ranks.

Feroni's first choice of a site for his family chapel—opposite that of the Corsini (Florence's leading family after the Medici) in the Church of S. Maria del Carmine—was the Brancacci Chapel, whose frescoes by Masaccio he offered to detach. Forced to renounce this plan, he acquired a smaller chapel in the Church of SS. Annunziata in June 1691 and commissioned Giovanni Battista Foggini, Florence's most fashionable architect, to carry out the project within a year. Work began in July 1691, and on 21 March 1693 the chapel was inaugurated. Feroni's intention that it surpass that of the Corsini both in magnificence and stylistic novelty determined the chapel's appearance, and it is a measure of Foggini's creative and organizational skills that he met this challenge within constricted time and space. Such a feat could only be achieved by the deployment of all available resources: Foggini's team included the distinguished sculptor Massimiliano Soldani and seven other sculptors who had either, like himself, attended the Florentine Academy in Rome (Giuseppe Piamontini, Carlo Marcellini, Antonio Andreozzi, and Camillo Cateni) or worked in his own studio (Giovacchino Fortini, Isadore Franchi, and Lorenzo Merlini).

The sophisticated court milieu would have recognized and enjoyed the references the Feroni Chapel makes to the masters of the Roman Baroque—Bernini, Alessandro Algardi, and Ciro Ferri—within its diminutive interior. Foggini created the illusion of space by exploiting its height, and the construction of a cupola signals its monumental pretensions. The dual messages of its iconography (provided by the scholar Anton Maria Salvini) make clear that the patron contributed to the program. The main theme appropriately concerns the "good death" and the life hereafter, as represented by Johann Loth's altarpiece of the *Death of St. Joseph*, the chapel's keynote. The drama unfolds with the upward impulse of the spiral columns of the Berninesque baldachin propelling the saint's soul to its radiant subsumption in the Holy Ghost in the form of a dove, seen in a sunburst of rays in the window above the altar and joyfully witnessed by pairs of marble angels hovering in the pendentives beneath the cupola. The dove's hypothetical flight continues along the gilt stucco rays above the window into the cupola, where it must navigate fluid gilt stucco decoration and lively stucco cherubim and finally escape through the opening of the central oculus, whose unifying light streams down from the lantern above.

Two marble figures, prestigious intercessionaries for Feroni's soul, emerge from niches in the side walls above the sarcophagi and also witness the drama: *St. Francis of Assisi* (by Cateni) and *St. Dominic* (by Marcellini). The iconography of the subsidiary prologue to this spiritual drama concerns the earthly status of the marquis: Soldani's pair of large oval bronze high reliefs (by far the finest works of art in the chapel) receive the greatest prominence within the chapel, representing (left) a profile portrait of the marquis, whose features are represented with unflinching realism, and (right) a heavily armed trading vessel, a miniature in remarkable detail of one of the ships that ferried the black slaves of Feroni's trade to the New World. In an original touch, the pairs of marble allegorical statues seated to either side of the sarcophagi, representing the Virtues judged by Feroni to have enabled him to attain his ambitions, support these medallions. Those on the left, representing *Diligence* and *Fidelity* (by Andreozzi and Franchi), refer to Feroni's fulfillment of his ministerial duties to his Medici patron, while the felicitous

Feroni Chapel, Florence, Italy
The Conway Library, Courtauld Institute of Art

574

combination of those on the right, *Nautical Fortune* and *Cogitation* (by Piamontini), had resulted in his mercantile success. Piamontini's idiosyncratic *Cogitation* is the only one of the four allegorical sarcophagus statues to refer to their illustrious source in Michelangelo's tomb figures for the new sacristy at the Church of San Lorenzo (1520–34). In other words, the appearance of paired allegorical figures upon opposed tomb sarcophagi finds root precisely in Michelangelo's tombs for Giuliano and Lorenzo de' Medici. The figures adorning the Feroni Chapel recall Michelangelo stylistically as well, particularly in their classicizing nudity and referential physical depictions.

Highly technically accomplished, all four figures possess a wealth of picturesque detail (for example, *Nautical Fortune*'s cornucopia of shells and the dog of *Faithfulness*). The gracefully balletic attitudes of the adolescent angels (by Andreozzi/Franchi, Andrea Vacca, Fortini, and Merlini) and the chubby infants supporting prominent coats of arms (by Andreozzi/Franchi and Paolo Monacorb) confirm the genial mood. Foggini's enjoyment in the creation of this little theater ameliorates the sober keynote of the chapel set by Loth's altarpiece; Foggini alone was responsible for the chapel's picturesque and disarmingly festive impression, although Soldani, Piamontini, and Marcellini, important artists in their own right, asserted their own personalities in their contributions.

The use of natural light in the dramatic enactment of a sacred mystery and the involvement of the spectator in that event define the chapel's style as Berninesque. Lacking depth within the chapel, Foggini used the novel device of placing the main viewpoint in the nave beyond, whence a unified vision of the design might be obtained, employing the persuasive gestures of the sarcophagus figures and of *St. Dominic* to draw the spectator inside the chapel to be then caught up in the vertical momentum of the altar wall.

Perceptions of the Feroni Chapel have differed widely since its completion, when it attracted considerable attention for its magnificent embellishment and (for Florence) stylistic novelty. In his biography of Foggini (*ca.* 1725–30), however, Francesco Saverio Baldinucci also expressed a more sophisticated current opinion that the chapel was too small to display its wealth of detail effectively, "so that the result was certainly rich, but confused and extravagant, and so filled with statuary of every dimension that it looked more like a sculptor's studio than a holy chapel." In the course of changing tastes in subsequent centuries, the Feroni Chapel was forgotten until Klaus Lankheit published the first full enquiry into Late Baroque sculpture in Florence (see Lankheit, 1962) and M. Visonà's detailed analysis permitted a balanced assessment of the chapel's artistic merits (see Visonà, 1990). Visonà concludes from the negative criticism of the chapel that certain factors compromised Foggini's design: the numbers of sculptors required to complete the project in the required time inevitably affected its qualitative and stylistic unity and, above all, the determination of the parvenu Feroni to surpass the Corsini in a display of wealth forced the designer into a superintensity of figurative and ornamental elements, including 14 over-life-size statues. However, the restoration of the chapel in 1998 has completed the rehabilitation of its reputation as an exemplary anthology of Late Baroque Florentine sculpture within a design whose formal expression was driven as much by sociological factors specific to the Florentine society of the day as by stylistic fashion.

ANTHEA BROOK

Further Reading

Casazza, Ornella, "La Cappella Feroni alla SS. Annunziata e il suo restauro," in *La Collezione Feroni: Dalle province unite agli Uffizi*, edited by Caterina Caneva, Florence: Centro Di, 1998

Chigiotti, Giuseppe, [Introduction to the architectural section], in *The Twilight of the Medici: Late Baroque Art in Florence, 1670–1743*, (exhib. cat.), Florence: Centro Di, 1974

Lankheit, Klaus, *Florentinische Barockplastik: Die Kunst am Hofe der letzten Medici, 1670–1743*, Munich: Brückmann, 1962

Martellazzi, R., "Cappelle gentilizie dalla controriforma alla fine del seicento: Storia, tipi e linguaggi formali," in *Architetture nell'architettura: Cappelle gentilizie nelle chiese fiorentine, 1576–1693*, by Marco Bini and Rosamaria Martellacci, Florence: Alinea, 1997

Paatz, Walter, and Elisabeth Paatz, *Die Kirchen von Florenz: Ein Kunstgeschichtliches Handbuch*, 6 vols., Frankfurt: Klostermann, 1940–54; see especially vol. 1, 1940

Rudolph, Stella "Florentine Patronage during the Late Seventeenth and Early Eighteenth Centuries: I. The Private Patrons," *Arte illustrata* 5/49 (1972)

Visonà, M., "Cappella Feroni nella SS. Annunziata," in *Cappelle barocche a Firenze*, edited by Mina Gregori, Cinisello Balsama, Italy: Silvana, 1990

FONT

See **Baptismal Font**

LUCIO FONTANA 1899–1968 *Italian*

Lucio Fontana was a consummate artist who singularly explored the problem of space in three-dimensional art. In Milan in 1947, Fontana founded the *Movimento spaziale* (Spatial Movement) and, together with other artists and intellectuals, published his *Primo Manifesto dello Spazialismo* (First Manifesto of Spatialism). The germination of this idea appears in his initial artistic endeavors that included figurative works in clay and painting and his later sculptures elaborate the concept in manifold ways. Fontana was preoccupied throughout his career with searching for a synthesis of the physical aspects or elements of art, including color, sound, movement, and space. *Spazialismo* evinced his efforts to achieve a unity of matter, space, and time that remained both physical (concrete) and metaphysical (spiritual). Similar to the French Nouveaux Réaliste Yves Klein, who concurrently was developing a conceptual body of work focused on the vitality and transcendence of matter and the human body, Fontana's manifesto-inspired work retained a strong romantic overtone despite its apparent iconoclasm.

Fontana's earliest sculptures, made between 1926 and 1931, were plaster, bronze, and terracotta pieces with Classical subject matter, both representational and abstract. Working with motifs consisting of nudes, reclining figures, upright figures, and mythological themes, Fontana shifted from quasi-Cubist figurative works such as *Nude* (1926) to the increasingly abstract *Cavallo rampante* (1929, Rampant Horse) and *Vittoria* (1930, Victory).

The development from this early period to *Spazialismo* encompassed painting, drawing, freestanding and wall relief sculpture, and "spatial environments"; in fact, Fontana's refusal to limit artistic creation to either the two- or the three-dimensional remained a hallmark of his hybrid aesthetic. For instance, Fontana's first purely abstract sculpture, made in two series titled *Tavoletta grafita* (1931–34, Tablet with Graffiti) and *Scultura* (1931–34, Sculpture), emphasized planarity and two-dimensionality. This series undermined established sculptural conventions and demonstrated at an early date what would be germane to Fontana's overall artistic trajectory: constant experimentation with new media and forms.

Perhaps the most radical works within his corpus were a series of monochrome paintings—each titled *Concetto spaziale* (Spatial Concept)—whose surfaces Fontana had sliced and punctured with a razor blade. Here "spatial concept" is meant to be a kind of analogue or sign of real or actual space, although Fontana represented space through otherness, or even emptiness, namely the voids left by his gashes, slices, and stab marks. Fontana's violation of the surface of the painting suggested an attempt to introduce spatial concerns that were conventionally the province of sculpture, namely the interior and the exterior of the forms. Fontana believed that the canvas, rather than function as a surface upon which to represent, was meant to show that we can look and move through it, almost as if the canvas functioned as a porthole or a looking glass. The punctured surfaces evoked the integration of theoretical or represented space (the image on the surface of the painting) and the tangible space that surrounded them, that is, the viewer's space.

Although he created figurative works after 1931, Fontana's sculpture after his first solo exhibition in 1930 increasingly engaged abstraction, but from a painterly perspective. The *Tavoletta grafita* series consisted of horizontal rectangles of polychrome plaster and cement inscribed with childlike gestures, which can be seen as precursors to his slashed, punctured, and agitated works. The link with painting is evident in his disparate formal influences that included the Futurist paintings of the Italians Umberto Boccioni and Giacomo Balla, and the random surface textures and gestures of Surrealist automatism. These two pictorial influences came to the fore after the mid 1930s in Fontana's ceramic sculptures.

The ceramic sculptures comprised possibly the most pivotal period of Fontana's work. Using mixed media such as glass, ceramic and wood, he fully articulated a vocabulary of tactility that would be his signature style in both sculpture and painting. He imbued works such as *Icaro* (1936, Icarus), *Leoni* (1937, Lions), and *Medusa* (1941) with expressive surfaces heightened by a tonal palette that runs the spectrum from subdued opacity to a high key brilliance. The infusion of color in the ceramic pieces demonstrates a texture or skin akin to a painterly impasto and moreover symbolizes Fontana's belief in the energetic quality of matter.

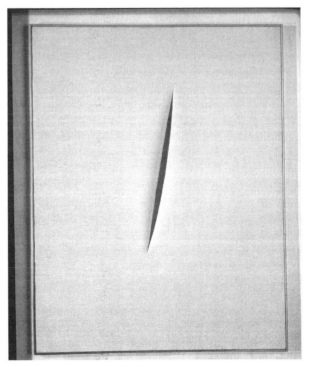

Concetto spaziale (Spatial Concept)
© Tate Gallery, London / Art Resource, NY

In his *Spaziali* (*Second Spatialist Manifesto*; 1958–59) Fontana explained, "What we want to do is unchain art from matter." Matter for Fontana meant energy made manifest; matter was to be sculpted to embody what previous art could never capture, that is, the ideal synthesis of the physical world in time and space. For Fontana, *Spazialismo* recalled the sublime and immeasurable space of the cosmos, the very idea of the infinite. In 1946 Fontana published the *Manifesto Blanco* (White Manifesto) with his students in Argentina, in which he wrote, "What is necessary is to overcome painting, sculpture, poetry and music. We need a more comprehensive art that meets the requirements of the new spirit." Like the proto-conceptualist Marcel Duchamp, the Nouveaux Réalistes, and the later American neo-Dadaists Jasper Johns, Robert Rauschenberg, and Jim Dine, the tendency to dissolve art into life was imbued with the drama of the self.

After 1947 Fontana began to construct painted and neon sculptures that he called *Ambienti spaziali* (Spatial Environments). The first of these (*Ambiente Spaziale a Luc Nera*, 1949) was installed in the Galleria del Naviglio in Milan and comprised an abstract sculpture that Fontana had painted with phosphorescent varnish and lit by a neon lamp. An early form of Installation art, the *Ambienti spaziali* merged the space of the sculptural object with that of the viewer through the vicissitudes of light, space, scale and movement.

The concept of the spatial environment is crucial in understanding the formal and conceptual operations that underline Fontana's oeuvre. One of its main aims was to dissolve the boundaries between art and life evidenced by the separation of media (painting versus sculpture) and the experience of viewing the work of art as a performance rather than a stable, autonomous object. Like Yves Klein and Piero Manzoni, Fontana's strategy involved the architecture of the exhibition space, which he thought of as a microcosm of the world, even the cosmos, in confluence with physical matter and kinetic energy. The evolution of art relied upon, for Fontana, primarily conceptual and philosophical rather than visual phenomena.

RAÚL ZAMUDIO AND LYNN M. SOMERS

See also **Assemblage; Installation; Klein, Yves; Manzoni, Piero; Surrealist Sculpture**

Biography

Born in Rosario, Santa Fe, Argentina, 1899. Son of Milanese sculptor Luigi Fontana and an Argentinean mother. Moved to Milan, 1905, and later apprenticed to an artist; first group exhibition in Rosario, Santa Fe, Argentina, 1926; returned to Milan, 1928, and studied sculpture at Accademia di Brera for two years; presented *Eroe che doma il cavallo* (Hero Taking a Horse) as his final thesis; first solo exhibition, 1930; showed two sculptures at Venice Biennale, 1930; developed aesthetic theory called *Spazialismo* (Spatialism), mid 1940s to early 1950s; established Academia d'Altamira art school in Buenos Aires, 1946; included in 1949 exhibition *Twentieth-Century Italian Art*, Museum of Modern Art, New York City, United States; solo exhibition at 29th Venice Biennale, 1958; participated in Documenta II, Kassel, Germany, 1959; received International Grand Prize at Venice Biennale, 1966. Died in Comabbio, Italy, 7 September 1968.

Selected Works

1926   *Nude*; plaster; Teresa Fontana collection, Milan, Italy
1929   *Cavallo rampante* (Rampant Horse); bronze-nickel alloy; private collection, Florence, Italy
1930   *Vittoria* (Victory); bronze; Fondazione Lucio Fontana, Milan, Italy
1931–34   *Scultura* (Sculpture) series; example in scratched cement: private collection, Milan, Italy
1931–34   *Tavoletta grafita* (Tablet with Graffiti) series; example in colored cement: private collection, Milan, Italy
1936   *Icaro* (Icarus); ceramic, heat-resistant material; Mazzoti collection, Albisola Marina, Liguria, Italy
1937   *Leoni* (Lion); ceramic; Rognoni collection, Milan, Italy
1941   *Medusa*; ceramic; R. Soldi collection, Buenos Aires, Argentina
1949–67   *Ambiente spaziali* (Spatial Environment) series; example in neon: temporary installation realized at Milan Triennial, Milan, Italy
1957   *Concetto spaziali* (Spatial Conception); bronze; private collection, Milan, Italy
1960–61   *Concetto spaziali* (Spatial Conception) Nature Cycle; terracotta; Fondazione Lucio Fontana, Milan, Italy
1968   *Scultura-contenitore* (Sculpture-Container), for the Otto Hahn opera *Portrait of Antonin Artaud*; mixed media; Le Soleil Noir, Paris, France

Further Reading

Ballo, Guido, *Lucio Fontana*, New York: Praeger, 1971
Crispolti, Enrico, and Rosella Siligato (editors), *Lucio Fontana*, Milan: Electa, 1998
Lucio Fontana, 1899–1968: A Retrospective (exhib. cat.), New York: Solomon R. Guggenheim Foundation, 1977

Lucio Fontana: Profeta del espacio, Buenos Aires: Centro Cultural Borges, and Museo Juan B. Castegnino, 1999

Van der Marck, Jan, and Enrico Crispolti, *Lucio Fontana*, 2 vols., Brussels: La Connaissance, 1974

Whitfield, Sarah, *Lucio Fontana*, London: Hayward, 1999

FORGERIES AND DECEPTIVE RESTORATIONS

The use of the terms *fake, fraud*, and *forgery* all imply with various shades of conviction the deliberate attempt to deceive by the production of a work of art in a style or material not genuine by an artist or craftsman who imitates the work of others. The usual or more obvious motive for fakery is simple financial profit. However, pride of accomplishment in an imitative skill and the ability to deceive the expert have also played a considerable part in the history of forgery. A wide range of sculptural types have lent themselves to the practice of the clever faker throughout the history of art, including work in most of the materials that can be carved, cast, or modeled.

The various categories of fraudulent sculpture, as in the visual arts as a whole, are of basically three types. The first and most obvious is the intentional fake, meant simply to deceive and defraud, for whatever motive. Next is the innocent copy, meant as a frank imitation by a student or even a skilled artisan for various reasons but later passed off, often by a third party, as original. Third is the pastiche, the uniting of unrelated parts of real works or real with false parts in order to create an object that appears whole and genuine. The Late Archaic Greek sculptures of the early 5th century BCE from the temple of Aphaia at Aegina were dramatically restored by Bertel Thorvaldsen, for example, with the addition of heads and limbs in an effort to make the ancient statues appear complete. These additions have been removed in recent years and have been exhibited as examples of Neoclassical art. Another example of parts apparently united in antiquity is a figure of Isis in the Egyptian Collection, Munich. Discovered at Hadrian's Villa at Tivoli, the work combined a female body with a male head, probably both of the Ptolemaic period, but slightly differing in date. These two parts have also been disjoined in modern times.

The possibility of falsification in the art of the sculptor may be said to have had its origins in remote antiquity. The ancient Egyptians, paying homage to their own remote ancestors and influenced by the strength of tradition, carefully imitated the canon and rules of proportion laid down in the Old Kingdom in works produced as much as 2,000 years later. This deliberate imitation of earlier styles was not an attempt to deceive but rather was an outright return to methods of representation honored by the sanctity of supposed origins in the time "of the gods." Although that pious imitation was not meant to deceive, archaism can lead to a later confusion in which the more recent works may be mistaken for productions dating from the time of the earlier prototypes. This cannot be taken as a prime example of intentional fraud, but it does suggest the complexity of the problem—that is, determining what is intentionally fake, forgery, or fraud in the art of sculpture and what is the result of the misrepresentation.

A classic, and perhaps apocryphal, story illustrates the venerable tradition of the intentional faker in Western art. In his 16th-century *Lives of the Painters, Sculptors, and Architects*, Giorgio Vasari relates the story of the young Michelangelo, who was persuaded that his carving of a sleeping cupid could be passed off as an ancient sculpture and thereby make a greater profit. All that was necessary was to bury it in the earth to give it the look of age. This done, the piece was sold at Rome, and for a time it fooled the purchaser. The intense interest in the art of Antiquity during the Renaissance led to a flood of imitations, copies, and outright frauds. Many pieces that began life as innocent homage or allusion to the art of the ancients could easily be mistaken and misattributed as genuinely ancient after the fact.

In a history of faked and forged sculpture, some specific cases may serve as general examples. While traveling in Egypt in the 1870s, Amelia Edwards, English novelist and later a cofounder of the Egypt Exploration Fund, inadvertently discovered a faker's workshop in Luxor. Before the mistake was revealed, she was able to examine the tools of the faker as well as the fragments of ancient wood from coffins and tomb furniture already prepared for the production of fake sculpture. The use of the ancient materials would have given carvings made from them a genuine appearance and "feel," the easy solution to a technical problem all forgers face. The art of forgery in Egypt has had a long history and has been practiced ever since there have been tourists to be deceived. The use of old materials and clever methods of aging new works has resulted in numerous Egyptian "antiquities" that have long escaped detection. The types of forgeries Edwards saw now have considerable age in their own right and consequently are even more difficult to detect. The art of the faker in modern Egypt has continued to the present, but the products of such workshops are intended for the most part for the unwary tourist.

The taste of 19th-century Europe and a revived interest in the arts of antiquity also gave rise to a wave of virtuoso stone carvers in Italy, many of them frankly imitative or decorative sculptors and not originally intentional fakers. The career of Giovanni Bastianini provides a classic example of this skill taken a step further and turned to forgery. A talented and skillful sculptor in his own right, he specialized in work of the Renaissance in the styles of Mino da Fiesole and Desiderio da Settignano, and his works were readily accepted as genuine products of the Renaissance. It was generally believed that it was not the artist who misrepresented his work as antique but others who did so for profit. In 1886 the Louvre purchased a portrait bust by Bastianini for a reputed 14,000 francs in the belief that it was a Renaissance work by someone of the stature of Donatello or Andrea del Verrocchio. When it was revealed that the work was a contemporary product by a relatively unknown Italian artist, the experts who praised it were loath to admit that they had been fooled. Alceo Dossena, a spiritual descendant of Bastianini, was an even more infamous Italian sculptor of the 20th century. He was also one of the best-known recent examples of a versatile forger able to imitate many styles of sculpture, from ancient Greek and Etruscan prototypes to works of the Italian Renaissance. Dossena maintained that the dealers who sold his "imitations" as genuine duped him, but he always produced his work, as far as he was able, with careful attention to material and technique, as well as to fidelity to period style. Museums acquired a number of his and Bastianini's pieces for their collections with the full faith that they were authentic.

The case involving a group of colossal terracotta figures in Etruscan style illustrates an example in more recent memory from another cultural tradition. Long treasured in the Metropolitan Museum of Art (New York City), they were eventually proved to be produced by Italian ceramic workers early in the 20th century. Small ancient terracotta prototypes provided the inspiration and design for these pieces. The large forgeries were intentionally damaged to give the appearance of age. Eventually, scholars cast doubt on them for stylistic reasons and not at first on scientific evidence.

In the history of fraud, the first line of examination has usually been the experience of the art expert and knowledge of the history of style. Only in the 20th century were scientific methods further developed to test accurately the materials and techniques employed by the forger of sculpture, but these are generally considered as aids and not ends in themselves. The use of advanced scientific techniques has certainly made it more possible to prove the fraudulence of some modern faking of ancient material. Microscopic examination of the surface of stone sculpture, for example, will reveal much about supposed old surfaces, patinas, tools, and carving techniques employed. Minute analysis of the surface will also identify the material of which the tools were made. Examination by ultraviolet and infrared illumination will often give further evidence of surface condition and structural damage. X-ray defraction and metal sampling for spectroscopic analysis may help to determine the alloy constituents of metal sculpture.

Other recent and memorable examples of fraudulent art show that the art of the faker is still very much alive. In the 1920s a carver thought to have worked in Berlin, who specialized in ancient Egyptian reliefs, produced work in styles ranging from the Old Kingdom to the Late Period in wood and several different types of stone. He was unable, however, to conceal his own hand regardless of the period he imitated. When scholars identified his personal style nearly half a century later, it became clear that his pieces shared other characteristics. Most of his products were single heads in relief, and almost all were of a type that can be termed a "neat fragment"—that is, a piece made as a fragment of a larger composition with no significant parts of the design damaged.

In the 1960s stone sculpture from the Cycladic Islands dating from the 3rd millennium BCE and terracotta animal figures from northwest Iran from the early 1st millennium both became popular subjects for the faker. In both instances, the abstract quality of the ancient originals appealed to a modern aesthetic as much as their apparent simplicity of form facilitated the imitation of the styles. The clay of the figures from Iran could be tested for age; the stone of the spurious "Cycladic" figures was a more difficult material to test because only the surface can be demonstrated to have aged or acquired a patina, and most of these objects had apparently been subjected to harsh cleaning. The specialized study of the artistic style of these "Cycladic" figures, developed by art historians only in recent decades, in combination with intense scientific scrutiny, led to the uncovering of some of the frauds. The revelation of fakes in sculpture, as in the other visual arts, depends on a certain amount of detective work. The skills of the art historian and the eye of the connoisseur, supported by the advanced scientific aids now available, have made the task somewhat more certain. Even so, many questionable works of art still remain in museum and private collections, for which authenticity (or the lack of it) has yet to be proven.

WILLIAM PECK

Further Reading

Arnau, Frank, *Kunst der Fälscher, Fälscher der Kunst: Dreitausend Jahre Betrug mit Antiquitäten*, Düsseldorf, Germany: Econ Verlag, 1959; as *The Art of the Faker: Three Thousand Years of Deception*, translated by J. Maxwell Brownjohn, Boston: Little Brown, 1961

Ashmole, Bernard, *Forgeries of Ancient Sculpture: Creation and Detection*, Oxford: Blackwell, 1962

Dutton, Denis (editor), *The Forger's Art: Forgery and the Philosophy of Art*, Berkeley: University of California Press, 1983

Fleming, Stuart James, *Authenticity in Art: The Scientific Detection of Forgery*, New York: Crane Russack, 1975

Haywood, Ian, *Faking It: Art and the Politics of Forgery*, New York: St. Martin's Press, 1987

Kurtz, Otto, *Fakes: A Handbook for Collectors and Students*, New Haven, Connecticut: Yale University Press, 1948

Mendax, Fritz, *Aus der Welt der Fälscher*, Stuttgart, Germany: Kohlhammer, 1953; as *Art Fakes and Forgeries*, translated by H.S. Whitman, London: Laurie, 1955

Nobili, Riccardo, *The Gentle Art of Faking: A History of the Methods of Producing Imitations and Spurious Works of Art from the Earliest Times up to the Present Day*, Philadelphia, Pennsylvania: Lippincott, and London: Seeley Service, 1922

Picker, Günther, *Fälscher, Diebe, Betrüger: Die Kehrseite des Kunst- und Antiquitätenmarkts*, Munich: Bruckman, 1994

Radnóti, Sándor, *The Fake: Forgery and Its Place in Art*, translated by Ervin Dunai, Lanham, Maryland: Rowman and Littlefield, 1999

Rieth, Adolf, *Vorzeit Gefälscht*, Tübingen, Germany: Wasmuth, 1967; as *Archaeological Fakes*, translated by Diane Imber, London: Barrie and Jenkins, 1970

Sox, H. David, *Unmasking the Forger: The Dossena Deception*, London: Unwin Hymand, 1987

Türr, Karina, *Fälschungen antiker Plastik seit 1800*, Berlin: Mann, 1984

Von Bothmer, Dietrich, and Joseph V. Noble, *An Inquiry into the Forgery of the Etruscan Terracotta Warriors in the Metropolitan Museum of Art*, New York: Metropolitan Museum of Art, 1961

Wakeling, T.G., *Forged Egyptian Antiquities*, London: Black, 1912

FOUND OBJECT

See **Assemblage**

FOUNTAIN SCULPTURE

Fountains unite imaginative design with water, one of nature's most essential resources. Originally, the word *fountain* referred to a natural spring, but it has come to mean a sculptural or architectural structure that contains and moves water to provide refreshment and aesthetic pleasure. Artists and architects, with hydraulic experts, have designed decorative fountains to manipulate and shape the fluidity of water into delicate or grand jets and sprays or to channel it into refined or thundering flows and falls, which cascade into one or more containers. Since Antiquity, fountains have served practical or ornamental purposes in public and private settings—in plazas, courtyards, gardens, and parks.

In many fountains the water action is secondary to the sculpture or architectural structure. Such fountains are aesthetic even without water running. When flowing water is present the fountain gains added vitality from the constantly changing kinetic motion, sparkling effects, and splashing sounds. Renaissance fountains by Florentine sculptors featured statues as the main fountain element, such as Bartolomeo Ammanati's Fountain of Neptune (*ca.* 1560–75) in Florence. In other fountains the aesthetic impact depends chiefly, if not exclusively, on rising and falling water as jets or cascades, either as a singular feature or as a series of various water movements. These fountains, such as in the 18th-century cascades at Caserta, are less attractive when dry.

Every fountain has two basic components: the source or genesis of the water flow or trajectory and the basin or pool capturing and containing the water flow or trajectory. Sculptural fountains are either wall fountains (often set in niches or against architectural facades), and thus best viewed from the front, or freestanding fountains with sculpture that can be appreciated in the round. Many freestanding sculptural fountains present a central figure or group of figures raised above one or more basins. The candelabrum type of fountain, originating in the Renaissance, features a statue crowning a series of ornamented basin tiers (decreasing in size as they approach the top) supported by a richly decorated shaft. Many fountains display humans, animals, or imaginary creatures whose mouths serve as fountain spouts or faucets.

Until the 20th century texts, prints, and drawings were the primary means of transmitting practical hydraulic information and fountain design ideas. The first influential book was by Salomon de Caus, renowned throughout Europe for his ingenious water features. His pioneering *Les Raisons des forces mouvantes* (The Principles of Moving Forces; 1615) was long regarded the fundamental text on hydraulics, water distribution methods, and aspects of fountain design, including playful water automata, water organs, and grottoes. As mechanical pumping and other fountain devices evolved in the 17th and 18th centuries, others documented diverse fountain effects and aesthetic styles or otherwise expanded scientific knowledge about controlling water's movement and power. After the industrial revolution hydraulics technology based on electricity and computers developed extensively, making possible more complex fountains in many more places.

Besides furnishing fresh water, fountains can provide meaning through symbol and metaphor and have been long associated with mythology or religious beliefs. Some fountain sculptures, drawing on the lifegiving and restorative properties of water, symbolize spiritual purification, love, wisdom, or the fountain of life. Patrons beginning in the Renaissance commissioned sculptors and architects to create fountains as impressive landmarks broadcasting images of strength, power, prosperity, and glory. Classical myths provided heroic subjects for fountain iconography: Pegasus supposedly created the first fountain by tapping his hoof over a hidden spring, thereby releasing a jet of water. Thus, Pegasus and the Muses, deities of springs and streams, are regarded the sources of artistic inspiration. The 16th-century Pegasus fountain, which still survives at the Villa d'Este in Tivoli, alludes to this myth. For centuries, the potent symbolism of the gods Neptune and Oceanus personified the ultimate power of water, along with an entourage of nereids, tritons, and other marine creatures. River gods, symbols of life's seasonal renewal, and nymphs were also revered as life-nourishing forces. The prototype for Renaissance and Baroque reclining river gods was undoubtedly inspired by Classical models.

Local legend and secular history have also inspired many fountain sculptures. Throughout city centers of central Europe, freestanding fountains with figurative statuettes frequently represented local saints, heroes, or model citizens. For example, Nuremberg's Geesebearer fountain (*ca.* 1540) by Pankraz Labenwolf features a small statue of a farmer bringing two fat geese to town, where he will be rewarded for his labors. In Bern many such fountains represent aspects of its cultural history, including the child-devouring Ogre fountain sculpted in 1542–46 by Hans Gieng. In

Gianlorenzo Bernini, Fountain of the Four Rivers, Piazza Navona, Rome
© Scala / Art Resource, NY

Brussels the popular Manneken-Pis (sometimes called "petit Julien") is part of local lore dating back to the 12th century. In 1618 Jérôme du Quesnoy sculpted this *putto pissatore* (technically "pissing putto") statuette (replaced several times subsequently), which is costumed for festive occasions.

In Islamic mosques, fountains and basins were located near entrances so that the worshipers could perform ritual ablutions. Islamic, Mughal, and Persian enclosed gardens were divided into four parts by prominent water channels symbolizing the four sacred rivers of Paradise, as cited in the Koran. The water display emphasized the essential source of life. Reflecting pools and low, circular (or hexagonal) basins with gently gurgling water jets accented the long watercourses. The fountains provided an ideal oasis where water's refreshing aesthetic effects could function even with a minimal supply. At the Alhambra in Granada, Spain, the Fountain of the Lions in the 14th-century Court of the Lions is at the heart of the palace. Placed at the intersection of four shallow water channels, the fountain's 12 marble lions (11th century), each spouting water, support a large basin (14th century) with a single, low jet. The Arabic inscription carved on the basin's brim praises the beauty of the palace and its plentiful water supply.

Monumental medieval fountains erected in European town squares tended to be architectural in form, yet richly embellished with relief sculpture. A stellar example is the marble and bronze Fontana Maggiore (1277–78), designed and sculpted by Nicola Pisano with his son Giovanni, in Perugia. On the sides of the almost-circular fountain are religious and pagan sculpture, as well as episodes of Roman history evoking the city's heritage, its well-being, and civic aspirations. In the market square of Nuremberg, the Beautiful Fountain (*Schöner Brunnen*; begun in 1386, then destroyed in World War II but since rebuilt) is an ornate, Gothic spire structure, adorned with 30 figures—Christian, Jewish, and pagan heroes, the four church fathers, the four evangelists, and seven imperial electors—arranged in four tiers and representing a complex historical iconography.

The Fountain of Joy (*Fonte Gaia*; 1414–19), so named because of the celebrations surrounding the completion of the first public water system supplying Siena's city center, was prominently placed in the Piazza del Campo. Jacopo della Quercia designed the fountain as a large rectangular basin, into which water poured from a row of spigots located on the surrounding balustrade. The fountain's decoration, which includes the Virgin and Child flanked by angels and the Virtues, integrated a strong spiritual message with civic symbolism. The original fountain, now preserved inside the Palazzo Pubblico, was replaced in 1868 with a copy by sculptor Tito Sarrocchi.

In Paris the Fountain of the Innocents (1547–49) was erected on Henry II's royal processional route. Architect Pierre Lescot and sculptor Jean Goujon designed the three-sided fountain to recall both an elegant loggia and a triumphal arch. Goujon's graceful sculptural reliefs symbolically evoked water, as compensation for the meagerness of its actual presence in faucets at street level. To turn the work into a freestanding fountain in the midst of a newly established Market of the Innocents, Augustin Pajou in the late 18th century created the sculptural decoration on the fountain's newly added fourth side. In the mid 19th century the revered fountain was moved to a site near the Les Halles market (now the Centre Pompidou area) and transformed so that water abundantly cascades down a four-sided stepped pedestal to a circular pool.

In 16th-century Italy the development of luxurious private palaces and villas contributed to the rise of pleasure fountains. Grand Duke Cosimo I de' Medici launched the most impressive projects, commissioning elaborate gardens filled with sculpture and fountains created by the foremost sculptors and architects of his day. The innovative Tuscan fountains emphasized figurative sculpture in marble and bronze, partly because the water supply was not abundant enough to sustain a continuous water display beyond a trickle. Niccolò Tribolo masterminded the design of the garden of the Villa Medici at Castello and the Boboli Gardens in Florence, together with their major fountains. Although many of his schemes were carried out before his death, other sculptors, notably Bartolomeo Ammanati and Giambologna, executed the fountains based on his models.

Greatly admired since its completion, the Hercules and Antaeus fountain, designed by Tribolo around 1543, is a dramatic focal point of the garden at the Villa Medici at Castello. Ammanati executed the terminal bronze figures in 1559–60. Hercules is shown lifting and squeezing the struggling Antaeus, whose head is thrown back. A geyser, symbolizing Antaeus' last gasps, gushes upward from his mouth to great height. Ammanati's most renowned sculpture is the Fountain of Neptune (ca. 1560–75) in the Piazza della Signoria, Florence, which celebrates Cosimo's role in providing the aqueduct to increase the city's water supply. Thus, for the first time, a large city fountain could continuously flow with water. Even though Neptune is shown riding the waves of his sea domain (suggested by multiple water jets), Ammanati's statue is static compared to the more animated monumental Neptune fountain sculpture Giambologna created in Bologna.

Pope Pius IV commissioned Giambologna's Fountain of Neptune (1566), among the most esteemed of Italian sculptural fountains, to commemorate Bologna's improved public water supply and the conclusion of the Council of Trent. The sculptor's imaginative treatment of Neptune, the subsidiary figures, and the fountain ornamentation encourage viewing the fountain on all sides. In the Boboli Gardens in Florence, Giambologna's powerful marble Fountain of Oceanus (1571–75), reminiscent of the Bologna Neptune, reigns over the Nile, Ganges, and Euphrates river gods. This impressive sculptural group dominates the fountain's monolithic tazza.

In 1571–72 Giambologna finished Castello's Fountain of the Labyrinth, the great candelabrum fountain originally designed by Tribolo for the villa's labyrinth garden (now at Villa Petraia). The nude bronze of Florence, personifying the city, is shown wringing water from her hair (from which water actually streams to start the fountain flow), a motif inspired by the Classical Venus Anadyomene, recreated in an engraving by Marcantonio Raimondi (1506). Followers of Giambologna and later artists so admired this sculpture's beautiful rendition that they made copies and versions of it.

The enchanting fountains and surprising water jokes devised in the 16th century at the Villa d'Este in Tivoli would inspire later designers to conjure theatrical fountains and water extravaganzas. Pirro Ligorio, architect, archeologist, and antiquarian, devised the garden's complex design, iconography, and realization between 1550 and 1572. Centrally placed in the garden, the dramatic Fountain of the Dragons explosively emitted tall jets to mimic fiery snorts. Another prominent focal point, sited at one end of a major terraced axis, is the elegant Fountain of Tivoli. Its graceful veil of water falls into an oval basin, embraced by a semicircular arcade adorned with nymph sculptures. At the other end of this garden axis is the Fountain of Rome, which recreated in microcosm the city's seven hills and Tiber River. Linking the two fountains is the impressive Avenue of the Hundred Fountains, with three tiers of fanned jets and rows of arched water spouts along the entire promenade, accentuated by statuettes of the Este Eagle.

A severe water shortage in Renaissance Rome led Pope Sixtus V to restore the ancient aqueduct Alexandrina, which he renamed Acqua Felice. The Fountain of the Acqua Felice (1588), also called the Fountain of Moses, was the first monumental fountain erected in Rome since antiquity. The architect-engineer Domenico Fontana designed it to recall the great Roman triumphal arches, boldly announcing the successful arrival of water to the area. Besides providing local citizens with water, the Acqua Felice also supplied fountains elsewhere in the city; Roman fountains were distinguished by their profuse water display, usually in architectural settings complemented by antique sculpture. Within the central arch of the Fountain of the Acqua Felice is an oversized statue of Moses, completed by Leonardo Sormani after Prospero Antichi. In the flanking niches are reliefs by other sculptors depicting biblical episodes associated with water.

In Baroque Rome, Gianlorenzo Bernini was the great innovator of sculptural fountains that appeared to interact with the water action. He endowed his sculpture with a liberating sense of movement, and his fountains were unprecedented masterpieces. For the freestanding Triton fountain (1642–43), created for Pope Urban VIII, Bernini infused a convincing vigor into the torso of the mythological creature summoned by Neptune to blow the conch shell so mightily that even the most distant turbulent waves would hear the command to restore calm. Perched on a scallop shell on top of the tails of four dolphins, the kneeling Triton "blows" a forceful jet skyward, a hydraulic visualization of colossal sound, reminiscent of the effect created by Castello's Hercules and Antaeus fountain.

Bernini's Fountain of the Four Rivers (1648–51) is the central landmark in Rome's Piazza Navona. Commissioned by Pope Innocent X Pamphilj as a symbol of the pope's global triumph, Bernini's design united the four rivers (Nile, Ganges, Danube, and Plata) representing the original rivers of Paradise that divided the world into four continents. Seated at the base of an obelisk (a stylized sun ray), the river gods twist, gesticulate, or look away as if to shield themselves from blinding light; water copiously streams from the rocky base beneath them. Surviving drawings, models of the fountain, and terracotta *bozzetti* (small sculptures made as preparatory studies or models for full-scale works) of the river gods Nile and Plata reveal Bernini's extraordinary vision and design process for this grand monument celebrating the pope's extension of the Acqua Vergine to this plaza. Several sculptors assisted in the carving of the fountain.

Between 1662 and 1680 Louis XIV spent enormous sums on various hydraulic projects at Versailles before enough water was available to create the 1,000 royal fountains (of which 300 remain) at the palace's riverless site. The garden designer André Le Nôtre and artist Charles Le Brun directed the transformation of the unsuitable topography into a landscape reflecting the king's glory. The Latona fountain (1668–70), with sculpture by Gaspard and Balthazar Marsy, sited near the palace, marked the best place to view an impressive vista of the garden. According to mythology, when Latona was taunted by Lycian peasants, she called on the gods to punish them, so they were changed into semiaquatic creatures.

Apollo, the sun god, became the brilliant symbol for Louis XIV, the Sun King. Located on Versaille's main axis, the Apollo fountain (1671) has been the crowning centerpiece in the royal park since its completion. Jean-Baptiste Tuby's sculpture shows Apollo in his chariot rising to create a new day and, thus, enlightenment. When the water action is off, the tranquil surface of the pool mirrors the limitless expanse of the sky that is Apollo's domain. The Apollo fountain created a waterworks spectacle unprecedented in 17th-century France, as did the explosive splashing and the colossal column of water of the nearby Fountain of Enceladus (1675–76), with fountain sculpture by Gaspard Marsy after Le Brun's design. The majestic formal gardens and fountains of Versailles inspired royal gardens with sculptural fountains throughout Europe, including Sweden's Drottningholm (1690s); Peter the Great's Peterhof (begun 1709), St. Petersburg; and Philip V's La Granja (1720–39) near Segovia.

Rome's Trevi fountain (mid 18th century) is the most celebrated of all fountains. Renowned for the purity of its water, its history dates to 19 CE, when Marcus Vipsanius Agrippa first completed the Aqua Virgo. The original Trevi fountain, located at an intersection of three streets, which probably gave the fountain its name, marked the aqueduct's terminus. Although Pope Nicholas V restored the Aqua Virgo in the 15th century, its unpretentious water basin belied its importance as the city's sole fountain until the completion of the Acqua Felice in 1588. In 1643 Urban VIII had the 15th-century fountain razed to accommodate a new design by Bernini. Yet his project, and many later ones by others, failed to materialize. In 1730–32 Pope Clement XII held a competition to complete the Trevi. Architect Nicola Salvi's winning proposal successfully incorporated the elegant facade of the Palazzo Poli as the backdrop for a prominent statue of Oceanus, who stands in a dignified pose of benevolent authority above animated Tritons and sea horses. Salvi died in 1751, followed soon after by the death of the chief sculptor Giovanni Battista Maini; the architect Giuseppe Panini and sculptor Pietro Bracci, who carved the central group in marble after Maini's models, supervised the completion of the Trevi fountain. Filippo della Valle sculpted the statues of *Fertility* and *Health* in the lateral niches; beneath are other sculptures representing the origins of the Acqua Virgo and the bounty of nature. Beneath Oceanus the impressive naturalistic cascade and large basin transform the plaza into an aqueous amphitheater animated by water sounds and motion.

Commissioned by the city of Paris, Edme Bouchardon designed the Fountain of the Four Seasons (1739–45) to introduce a water supply to the fashionable rue de Grenelle area. As part of his political agenda, Louis XV wished the fountain to proclaim the glory of Paris.

Still *in situ*, this splendid fountain featuring a central statue of the city of Paris flanked by the Seine and Marne River gods as well as sculpture for each season, ranks among the great masterpieces of the 18th century.

The Bourbon king Charles VII of Naples built his grandiose Palazzo Reale (1752–72) in Caserta, near Naples, to rival Versailles. Martin Biancour designed the formal gardens under the supervision of palace architect Luigi Vanvitelli. Dominating the garden panorama is an immense canal and cascading waterway accented by dramatic, life-size marble sculptural tableaux: *Diana and Her Nymphs* paired with *Actaeon Attacked by His Hounds* (1785–89), mainly by Paolo Persico and Angelo Brunelli after Persico's models; and *Venus and Adonis* (1784–89) by Gaetano Salomone. After 1759, when the king left for Madrid (as Charles III of Spain), he transformed a previously undistinguished area of that city with sculptural fountains, inspired by Italian and French models. Architect-engineer José de Hermosilla designed the Paseo del Prado (1767–82) as a park promenade adorned with splendid fountains, designed by architect Ventura Rodríguez. The Fountain of Cybele (1780–86) is sited between the Fountain of Neptune and the Fountain of Apollo with the Four Seasons. Riding a chariot pulled by two lions, showing her dominion over wild beasts, Cybele, sculpted by Francisco Gutierrez, symbolizes the abundant fertility of the region.

The Industrial Revolution further advanced hydraulic technology, and fountain design activity increased throughout Europe and the United States in the 19th century to fulfill ambitious urban embellishment projects. In addition, sidewalk drinking fountains proliferated.

In Paris the architect Jacques-Ignace Hittorff received the prestigious commission to redesign the Place de la Concorde. A Ramses II obelisk, a gift from Egypt's viceroy to King Louis-Philippe, was to be the monumental centerpiece. Inspired by Rome's Piazza of St. Peter, with its obelisk flanked by fountains, Hittorff conceived the design of two grand fountains embellished with sculpture, which were created by a team of artists. The maritime fountain (on the south, or Seine side) features two allegorical figures of the Atlantic Ocean and the Mediterranean Sea, and additional sculptures symbolize aspects of maritime industry and commerce. The north fountain features figures symbolizing the two great French rivers, the Rhône and the Rhine, along with personifications of various harvests. At the periphery of the fountain, tritons and nereids hold fish casting water in backward arcs toward the center.

Among the stately Paris fountains designed by architect Louis Visconti is the Fountain of the Sacred Orators in Place Saint Sulpice (1848), commemorating four great French theologians active during the reign of Louis XIV. Atop a two-tiered cascade, a French-Renaissance style temple with niches shelters the seated statues of each bishop, arranged on the cardinal compass points.

The Observatory fountain (1867–84), its overall design supervised by architect Gabriel Davioud, who worked with a team of artists including Jean-Baptiste Carpeaux, is a monumental focal point on a grand allée in Paris's Luxembourg Gardens. Carpeaux's sculpture *The Four Parts of the World* supports an armillary celestial sphere (containing the terrestrial world). The sculpture's symbolism refers to the nearby Observatory (erected 1668–72), with each of its four walls precisely facing one of the four cardinal directions, while within, scientists expanded knowledge of the universe.

The architects Calvert Vaux and Jacob Wrey Mould designed New York's Bethesda fountain (1873), sited in Central Park, one of the United States' most important 19th-century fountains. Emma Stebbins, a little-known sculptor who had studied in Rome, created the bronze *Angel of Waters*. The statue holds lilies, symbols of purity, in its left hand, while its right arm reaches out to bestow water's rejuvenating powers on visitors to the fountain.

Frédéric-Auguste Bartholdi sent a nine-meter-high cast-iron fountain to the 1876 U.S. Centennial Exhibition in Philadelphia. The Bartholdi fountain presents three Neoclassical caryatids supporting the main upper basin trimmed with gas lamps, above which three tritons crouch. At night, the novelty of gas lamp illumination created a shimmering spectacle. The U.S. government purchased the fountain, erecting it in 1878 on the grounds of the Botanic Garden, Washington, D.C., until 1932, when it was resited to a small park near the nation's Capitol building.

Alfred Gilbert designed the Shaftesbury Memorial (1893), commonly known as the Eros fountain, for London's Piccadilly Circus. It honors Anthony Ashley-Cooper, Earl of Shaftesbury, a champion of social and educational reform. Breaking with the Victorian tradition of portrait statues, Gilbert used the god Eros as the symbol of selfless love and the overflowing fountain to represent Shaftesbury's abundant philanthropy. Giambologna's *Flying Mercury* (1564) and the figure of Bacchus in Titian's painting *Bacchus and Ariadne* (1522–23) inspired the pose for Eros. Despite initial criticism of the composition and imagery, public opinion of the fountain eventually transformed to fondness. The Eros fountain remains a charming focal point in one of the busiest intersections of central London and a spirited commemorative monument.

In 20th-century Scandinavia major sculptural fountains reinforced either national legends or universal themes about life. Copenhagen's robust Gefion fountain (1908) by Anders Bundgaard shows a heroic woman commanding a great plow pulled by mighty oxen. She presides over a rocky cascade to depict the origins of the largest Danish island, Zealand. According to myth, the Swedish king Gylfe granted the fertility goddess Gefion the right to use as she wished any Swedish land she could plow in one day and one night. By night's end she had dug up enough to form a large lake, and with the displaced earth she built part of Denmark. Ville Vallgren sculpted for Helsinki the popular Havis Amanda fountain (1908), a nude mermaid surrounded by spouting seals. In Oslo, Gustav Vigeland, inspired by Auguste Rodin, devised for his Vigeland Park the *Cycle of Life* (1907–14), a monumental granite fountain carved with 60 reliefs surrounded by 20 figure groups of all ages.

Beginning in the 1890s American architects and civic leaders promoted beautifying U.S. cities with European-style plazas, parks, and gardens and strategically placed fountains as elegant focal points. The Court of Neptune fountain (1897–98) in front of the Library of Congress in Washington, D.C., for example, is in a Classical Revival style inspired by Italian Renaissance fountains and designed by J.L. Smithmeyer and others, with sculptor Roland Hinton Perry. In New York the sculpture of *Pomona* by the Viennese sculptor Karl Bitter graces the large Italian Renaissance candelabrum-style Pulitzer Fountain (1913–16) as a benevolent symbol of nurtured abundance and cultural well-being. In Detroit, Michigan, the Scott Memorial fountain (1925) commemorates James Scott, a ruthless citizen in life, who left the city his entire estate in order to erect a fountain in his name on Belle Isle, an urban park situated on the strait between U.S. and Canadian shores. Architect Cass Gilbert's design, inspired by the great fountains of Perugia, Florence, Rome, Versailles, and Caserta, incorporates imagery from Detroit's early fur-trapping history. The white marble and bronze fountain, completed in collaboration with the sculptors Herbert Adams and Robert Aitken, features a central column of water encircled by a crown of low jets.

Chicago's Clarence Buckingham Memorial fountain (1927; renovated 1994), with enormous tiers of pink Georgian marble, surpassed every U.S. fountain and even rivaled those in Europe with its intricately engineered water spectacles. Architect Edward H. Bennett designed the fountain, which honors a Chicago philanthropist, as a regal focal point within Grant Park, near the Lake Michigan shore. In Rockefeller Center, New York City, Paul Manship's sleek, gilded bronze Prometheus fountain (1934) symbolizes the heroic aspirations of a modern capitalist empire. An important and popular city landmark of the early skyscraper era, this fountain was a tribute to skill, imagination, and a strong economic democracy.

In St. Louis, Missouri, Carl Milles created a spectacular fountain landmark with 14 bronze figures as a wedding entourage of water creatures symbolizing the merging of the mighty Mississippi and Missouri Rivers, titled The Meeting of the Waters fountain (1940). Kansas City, Missouri, which dubs itself the "City of Fountains," boasts that it has as many fountains as Rome, including the J.C. Nichols memorial fountain (dedicated 1960), honoring the real estate magnate who developed much of the city, including the Country Club Plaza area where the fountain is located. Rather than commissioning a new fountain, the city opted to restore a neglected fountain with sculpture by the French artist Henri Greber originally executed in 1910 for a Long Island (New York) estate. Four dramatic equestrian figures represent the Mississippi, Volga, Rhine, and Seine Rivers.

Since the late 1950s fountain sculpture has tended to be more abstract. The Seattle-based sculptor George Tsutakawa, for example, drew on his heritage of Asian art and philosophy, where aspects of nature are in harmony with the universal whole. For the Fountain of Wisdom at the Seattle Public Library (1958–60), Tsutakawa stacked hollowed, abstract forms inspired by Tibetan rock mounds. The flowing water is alternatively separated and united by each of the sculptural shapes, evoking the harmonious balance of the world's liquid and solid elements and the integration of one life cycle with another.

Water that suggests tree or plant shapes is another popular type of fountain, originating in Islamic gardens and Renaissance villa water joke fountains, exemplified by Chatsworth's Willow Tree fountain (originally 1693, since rebuilt). Modern dandelion fountains can be found in cities around the world, including Sydney, Minneapolis, New York, and Paris. Australian architect and fountain designer Robert Woodward is credited with designing the first modern dandelion fountain. His El Alamein Memorial fountain (1959–61) in Sydney was a spherical arrangement of 211 bronze pipes spreading radially from a central core. At the tips of the pipes specially designed nozzles projected fine radiating sprays, so that the resulting fountain resembled a huge fuzzy dandelion.

New York's Lincoln Center for the Performing Arts Plaza fountain (1964) is like a dazzling chandelier in its cultural urban setting. The grand circular fountain, designed by architect Philip Johnson with Richard Foster, contains 577 nozzles and 88 spotlights within its nearly 13-meter diameter, and it was programmed (in precomputer days via tape) to provide a constantly jumping water dance.

Since the mid 1960s, San Francisco–based landscape architect Lawrence Halprin has been a leader in reviving waterfall fountains to create an urban oasis full of vigorous water movement and sounds, basing his designs on close observation of water movement in mountain streams and on coastal shores. Portland, Oregon's Ira's fountain (1970), named for Ira Keller, a local industrialist and civic leader, is a six-meter-high cataract that on warm days invites people to interact with the water. Other Halprin-designed public spaces with major water features are in Seattle, San Francisco, and Los Angeles. For his Washington, D.C., memorial to U.S. president Franklin Delano Roosevelt (completed in 1997), he created a sequence of four landscaped rooms (each with a slightly different waterfall) representing the main achievements of the president's four terms (1932–45) and the four freedoms: freedom of speech, freedom of worship, freedom from want, and freedom from fear.

Isamu Noguchi created three major projects that were innovative in their use of water combined with sculpture. The Chase Manhattan Bank Plaza Water Garden (1961–64) in New York's financial district recalls a Japanese-style Zen meditation garden. In 1970 Noguchi was invited to design fountains for the Japan World Exposition in Osaka, the first international exposition in Asia. The Pond of Dreams, with Noguchi's nine fountain sculptures, evoked gyrating cosmic forces. Futuristic stainless-steel sculptural forms emitted masses of water or mist to suggest rockets, orbits, comets, hurricanes, or nebulae. The Horace E. Dodge and Son Memorial fountain (1979) in Detroit, commissioned to help revitalize the city's downtown riverfront, is an industrial-scale stainless-steel ring supported by two inclined cylinders above a circular basin. Noguchi designed this sculpture to be programmed with powerful, changing waterworks sequences surging with energy and strength appropriate to the "Motor City," a fountain proclaiming hydraulic force without any traditional references to sea and river deities.

Some designers deliberately exploit water in its nonliquid states to create structures that further expand the traditional notion of a fountain. Inspired by the natural beauty of the craggy rocks, water seepage, snow banks, and ice in his homeland, the Norwegian artist Carl Nesjar began to design fountains in the 1960s that would function in every season, particularly in northern climates. For the 1980 Winter Olympics at Lake Placid, he created his first ice fountain in the United States—a memorial to Norwegian ice-skating champion Sonja Henie. Nesjar has also created ice fountains in Anchorage, Alaska; Minneapolis, Minnesota; and Buffalo, New York, as well as in the French Alps and Norway.

While most sculptors prefer water to move about a static sculpture, some have introduced kinetic movement to the fountain's solid elements. Constructivist Naum Gabo's Revolving Torsion fountain (1972–75), installed at St. Thomas's Hospital, London, recalls early experiments with nonobjective form and space as a volumetric part of the structure. During the fountain's slow ten-minute revolution, the water jets torque and become lines of light defining the fountain's negative space.

In the 1960s Jean Tinguely, noted for his imaginative mechanical kinetic sculptures, was inspired by lawn sprinklers to create large-scale, rotating fountain sculptures emitting water in a variety of erratic sprays and squirts. For the Carnival fountain (1977) in Basel's State Theater Plaza, Tinguely fashioned rubber tubes, nozzles, scrap iron, wheels, and electric motors into ten playfully spraying, kinetic structures that sway and squirt in idiosyncratic ways. When the composer Pierre Boulez saw Basel's Carnival fountain with its own special music, he promoted the creation of a similar fountain in Paris for the plaza near the Centre Pompidou honoring the composer Igor Stravinsky. Tinguely collaborated with Niki de Saint-Phalle to create the Igor Stravinsky fountain (1983). Each devised eight fountain elements to create a circuslike tribute inspired by Stravinsky's music and ballets. Among the figures cavorting in the pool are a large *G Clef*, *Ragtime*, *Love* (shown as red lips), and the *Firebird*, a grand diva with plume-like sprays jetting from her head.

Some fountains exploit the fluid qualities of water as metaphoric currents of commemoration. The Southern Poverty Law Center in Montgomery, Alabama, commissioned Maya Lin to design the first monument dedicated to civil rights achievements. The Civil Rights Memorial fountain (1989) presents a black granite wall behind a low table basin, each constantly bathed with a smooth veil of water. The continuous water motion over this memorial evokes a calm invincibility that belies the turbulent history of racial injustice. The wall is inscribed with the words of Martin Luther King, Jr.—"until justice rolls down like water and righteousness like a mighty stream"—his famous variant on the biblical passage (Amos 5:24) that rallied people to civil rights action. Encouraging introspection and connection, the fountain invites visitors to touch the memorialized names through the water.

Tony Cragg's *Archimedes Screw* (1993), a mechanical fountain in 's-Hertogenbosch, the Netherlands, refers to the ancient water-moving machine invented by the 3rd-century-BCE Greek scientist and mathematician Archimedes. Its presence in Holland alludes to the pumps and dikes that helped reclaim the countryside from the sea.

In recent decades, as sculpture has mediated between traditional and less traditional forms, many fountains are hybrids of art, architecture, landscape design, and performance, combined with an increasingly advanced technology. To gain the attention of a global audience, waterworks extravaganzas have become major entertainment features that astonish beholders with dramatic scale and hydraulic wizardry, particularly at international expositions and recreational destinations. For example, a popular attraction at Las Vegas's Bellagio Casino (1998) is a sweeping mile-long spectacle of choreographed water jets performing like theatrical superstars. As in the past, some fountains today are thrilling spectacles, while others offer an experience of soothing tranquility.

MARILYN SYMMES

See also **Ammanati, Bartolomeo; Bartholdi, Frédéric-Auguste; Bouchardon, Edme; Bracci, Pietro; Carpeaux, Jean-Baptiste; du Quesnoy, François; Giambologna; Gilbert, Alfred; Goujon, Jean; Jacopo della Quercia; Lin, Maya; Manship, Paul; Milles, Carl; Noguchi, Isamu; Pajou, Augustin; Saint Phalle, Niki de; Tinguely, Jean; Tribolo, Niccolò; Valle, Filippo della; Vigeland, Gustav**

Further Reading

Berger, Robert W., *In the Garden of the Sun King: Studies on the Park of Versailles under Louis XIV*, Washington, D.C.: Dumbarton Oaks Research Library and Collection, 1985

Coffin, David R., *Gardens and Gardening in Papal Rome*, Princeton, New Jersey: Princeton University Press, 1991

De Andia, Beatrice, et al., *Paris et ses fontaines: De la Renaissance à nos jours*, Paris: Délégation à l'Action Artistique de la Ville de Paris, 1995

D'Onofrio, Cesare, *Le fontane di Roma*, Rome: Staderini, 1957; 2nd edition, 1962

Lazzaro, Claudia, *The Italian Renaissance Garden: From the Conventions of Planting, Design, and Ornament to the Grand Gardens of Sixteenth-Century Central Italy*, New Haven, Connecticut: Yale University Press, 1990

MacDougall, Elisabeth B. (editor), *Fons Sapientiae: Renaissance Garden Fountains*, Washington, D.C.: Dumbarton Oaks Trustees, 1978

Millon, Henry A. (editor), *The Triumph of the Baroque: Architecture in Europe, 1600–1750*, New York: Rizzoli, 1999

Miller, Naomi, *French Renaissance Fountains*, New York: Garland, 1977

Miller, Naomi, "Piazza Nettuno, Bologne: A Paean to Pius IV," *Architectura* 7 (September 1977)

Symmes, Marilyn (editor), *Fountains: Splash and Spectacle, Water and Design, from the Renaissance to the Present*, New York: Rizzoli, 1998

Weber, Gerold, *Brunnen und Wasserkünste in Frankreich im Zeitalter von Louis XIV*, Worms, Germany: Werner'sche Verlagsgesellschaft, 1985

Wiles, Bertha Harris, *The Fountains of Florentine Sculptors and Their Followers, from Donatello to Bernini*, Cambridge, Massachusetts: Harvard University Press, 1933

GEORGE FRAMPTON 1860–1928 *British*

> Mr. Frampton is one of the most versatile and most original artists of the present day, thoroughly "in the new movement," which he has done so much to direct. Highly accomplished and firmly based on the true principles of his art, he is at home in every branch of it—portraiture, decoration, ideal work, metalwork, goldsmithing, jewelry, enamel, and furniture; indeed he covers the whole field.

So wrote Marion Spielmann, a leading art critic of the time (see Spielmann, 1901). The New Sculpture movement in which George Frampton was a key figure brought a dynamism and creativity to British sculpture in the 1880s and 1890s, which it had lacked for 80 years, and ended the dominance of the Neoclassical tradition. The sculptors of this movement were linked by an interest in modeling and an admiration of both contemporary French sculpture (in particular the work of Aimé-Jules Dalou) and that of the Renaissance—many were also under the spell of the poetic medieval vision of Sir Edward Burne-Jones and William Morris.

While at the Royal Academy Schools, Frampton won a gold medal and traveling scholarship that enabled him to study painting and sculpture in Paris. His work was relatively conventional until the early 1890s, when it took on a highly personal, symbolist character reflecting several influences, in particular Italian 15th-century sculpture and the work of Burne-Jones and Moreau Vauthier. This made Frampton one of the most discussed sculptors of the day. Perhaps his 1893 marriage to a fellow student and the birth the following year of their son (the future painter Meredith Frampton) sparked the visionary intensity of his work at this time. The masterpiece from this brief phase is the tinted plaster *Mysteriarch*.

With its pent-up emotion heightened by the dreamy, almost frontal gaze of the figure, *Mysteriarch* puzzled many viewers when it was exhibited at the Royal Academy in 1893. The sculpture attempts to express the essence of mystery through "a disquieting androgynous figure with a cuirass and helmet like that of a Verrocchio" (see Phillips, 1893). When Frampton showed *Mysteriarch* at the first exhibition of *La Libre Esthétique* in 1894, in a review in *La revue encyclopédique*, Roger Marx declared, "the fight for spiritual expression was taken up in England by Watts . . . and is now continued by another artist from across the channel, Mr. George Frampton, a sculptor-decorator obsessed with dream and mysticism."

Frampton's most elaborate essay in his symbolist manner was the bust of *Lamia*, which was inspired by the snake-enchantress of John Keats's poem "Lamia." The sculpture is a tour de force with ivory for the flesh, bronze for the dress and headdress, and bronze jewelry set with opals—traditional symbols of misfortune. As Frampton told *The Art Journal* in 1897, he preferred to be known as an art worker rather than a sculptor. Indeed, for he had joined the Art Workers Guild in 1887.

Among the New Sculptors' most innovatory traits was their eagerness to collaborate with architects in order to give architectural ornament on buildings a new vitality. While a student, Frampton had worked with a firm of monumental masons, and designing and carving sculpture for buildings always remained one of his primary interests. His first major collaboration with an architect was with J.W. Simpson on the Glasgow Art Gallery (finished 1907), for which Frampton modeled *St. Mango as Patron of the Arts.*

Outstanding in this genre are Frampton's friezes and figures for Lloyds Registry of British and Foreign Shipping in London, which he did in collaboration with the architect T.E. Collcutt. The original and harmonious balance achieved between sculpture and architecture is exactly what the New Sculptors sought. Modern maidens, dressed in embroidered medieval-style gowns, hold and discuss both modern and ancient ships. The figures are arranged using a system of parallel planes that preserved the flatness of the building and heightened the air of mysterious activity.

No contemporary could challenge Frampton's mastery of the art of the relief. A thorough study of 15th-century Italian techniques, in particular of *relievo schiacciato* (the method of pictorial relief perfected by his hero, Donatello), gave him unrivaled technical mastery, as can be seen in the bronze relief of *St. Christina* and the series of commemorative medals inspired by Renaissance examples. In the memorial to the shipbuilder Charles Mitchell in St. George's Church in Newcastle—perhaps his most inventive relief—Frampton preserved the conventional layout of a wall monument but articulated it by using low-relief tree trunks for columns, roots for bases, and branches with leaves and apples as capitals. Characteristically he contrasts areas of complex minute detail with simple plain surfaces. To evoke Mitchell's career, two Arthurian-style ships under straining canvas appear to set sail from the principal ledge.

Frampton was much in demand for public monuments, particularly to Queen Victoria following her Diamond Jubilee of 1897 and death in 1901. Statues were commissioned by, among other towns, Leeds and Newcastle-upon-Tyne in Britain and Calcutta and Winnipeg in the British Empire. Each work evokes an appropriately imperial image, although Frampton often reused the figure of the queen and other elements.

Frampton's ability to breathe life into statues commemorating local public figures shines out in the bronze statues of worthies he undertook in Liverpool, notably *William Rathbone*, where a plaque illustrates the benefits of district nursing, which Rathbone had supported. Frampton's most popular public work was *Peter Pan*, which was commissioned by the author J.M. Barrie and installed in Kensington Gardens in 1912. Peter plays a pipe while standing on a vast tree trunk from which fairies and animals emerge.

In his artistic approach, there was in Frampton a strong sense of practicality. After the 1890s he rarely made a piece unless specifically commissioned; he apparently needed this discipline to spark his creativity. The Arts and Crafts movement particularly admired appropriateness of purpose, and this was a quality that characterized Frampton's work whether in the carefree figure of *Peter Pan*, the maidens with their ships on Lloyds Registry, or the memorial to Nurse Cavell, where the choice of Portland stone reflects her steadfastness.

TIMOTHY STEVENS

See also **Dalou, Aimé-Jules**

Biography

Born in London, England, 16 June 1860. Worked in architect's office, then studied modeling under W.S. Frith at Lambeth School of Art; entered Royal Academy Schools, 1881; worked for firm of architectural carvers while studying; exhibited at Royal Academy from 1884; won Royal Academy Gold Medal and traveling scholarship and joined Art Workers Guild, 1887; Master, 1902; went to Paris; studied under sculptor Antonin Mercié and painters P.A.J. Dagnan-Bouveret and Gustave Courtois, 1887 (or 1888); silver medal at Paris Salon for *The Angel of Death*, 1890; showed abroad at first Vienna Secession, with "La Libre Esthétique"; much employed on public commissions but continued to undertake architectural sculpture commissions after 1900; elected Associate of the Royal Academy, 1894, and Royal Academician, 1902; knighted, 1908. Died in London, England, 21 May 1928.

Selected Works

1889   *St. Christina*; bronze; Walker Art Gallery, Liverpool, England

1892   *Mysteriarch*; plaster; Walker Art Gallery, Liverpool, England

1894   *My Thoughts Are My Children*; plaster (untraced); bronze version, about 1900, Walker Art Gallery, Liverpool, England

1897   Jubilee Monument to Queen Victoria; bronze; outside the Victoria Memorial Hall, Calcutta, India

1897   Monument to Charles Mitchell; bronze,

	copper, marble, enamel; St. George's Church, Newcastle-upon-Tyne, England
1898– 1901	Friezes of *Trades, Commerce*, and *Shipping*; stone; Lloyds Registry of Shipping, London, England
1899	*William Rathbone*; bronze; St. John's Gardens, Liverpool, England
1899– 1900	*Lamia*; bronze, ivory, opals; Royal Academy of Arts, London, England
ca. 1900	*St. Mango as Patron of the Arts*; bronze; Glasgow Art Gallery, Scotland
1901–05	Monument to Queen Victoria; bronze; Leeds, England
1910	*Peter Pan*; bronze; Kensington Gardens, London, England
1914	Recumbent Lions; Portland stone; British Museum, London, England
1920	Monument to Nurse Edith Cavell; Portland stone; St. Martin's Place, London, England

Further Reading

Beattie, Susan, *The New Sculpture*, New Haven, Connecticut: Yale University Press, 1983

E.B.S., "Afternoons in Studios: A Chat with Mr. George Frampton ARA," *The Studio* 6 (January 1896)

Miller, Frederick, "George Frampton A.R.A., Art Worker," *Art Journal* (1897)

Phillips, Claude, "Sculpture of the Year," *Magazine of Art* (1893)

Spielmann, Marion H., *British Sculpture and Sculptors of Today*, London and New York: Cassell, 1901

Stevens, Timothy, "George Frampton," in *Patronage and Practice: Sculpture on Merseyside*, edited by Penelope Curtis, Liverpool, Merseyside: Tate Gallery Liverpool, National Museums and Galleries on Merseyside, 1989

Wilton, Andrew, and Robert Upstone (editors), *The Age of Rossetti, Burne-Jones, and Watts: Symbolism in Britain, 1860–1910*, Paris and New York: Flammarion, and London: Tate Gallery, 1997

PIETRO FRANCAVILLA 1548–1615

Franco-Flemish

Pietro Francavilla's well-to-do father discouraged him from taking up sculpture as a career and insisted on an academic education. The young Francavilla, however, apprenticed himself briefly (*ca.* 1564) to an unidentified "good sculptor" in Paris, where his father had let him go to further his education; he then proceeded to Innsbruck. He stayed there for six years working with Alexander Colin on the narrative reliefs for the tomb of the Emperor Maximilian in the Hofkirche (Court Church) and on the decoration of Ambras Castle (1563–70) in the Tyrol. Colin imbued Francavilla with knowledge of the modern Renaissance style and enhanced his skill in carving. Francavilla also may have

experimented with casting bronze, of which Innsbruck was a center. He was employed by Archduke Ferdinand of Tyrol, with whom he even went mountain climbing and who recommended him to the Medici Grand Dukes in Florence and to the Flemish sculptor Giambologna. Once in Florence (*ca.* 1571), Francavilla rapidly became the right-hand man of his older compatriot, assisting him with carving marble in order to help conserve his master's energies and time for more creative activity; this may explain why Giambologna handed over to him an attractive commission for garden statuary for Villa Bracci, although the master probably supplied the majority of the models. In 1576, Francavilla was portrayed holding a wax model for a flayed anatomical figure, an example of which is cast in bronze and survives with two others in the Jagiellonian University Library, Cracow, Poland.

After unspecified assistance to Giambologna on the Grimaldi Chapel in Genoa (*ca.* 1579), Francavilla was commissioned by Luca Grimaldi to carve two colossi of Janus and Jupiter, which are heavily muscled variations on poses invented by Giambologna, for his palace. Francavilla continued his activity in Genoa with six statues depicting the four Evangelists, St. Ambrose, and St. Stephen for the Senarega Chapel in the cathedral.

Returning to Florence, Francavilla carved five statues for the Niccolini chapel in Santa Croce. Of these, the models for the powerful and intense seated figures of Moses and Aaron (both indebted to Michelangelo's *Moses*, *ca.* 1515) are by Giambologna (Museo Nazionale del Bargello, Florence, Italy). The other three statues, depicting Christian Virtues, may be Francavilla's own variations on those by his master, which are in the Grimaldi Chapel in Genoa. Next, Francavilla carved six statues of saints for Giambologna's Salviati Chapel in San Marco, of which at least the St. John the Baptist is from a model—also known from a cast in bronze—by Giambologna. In 1589, Francavilla contributed six colossi in ephemeral materials for the joyous entry into Florence of Christine of Lorraine, bride of Ferdinando I de' Medici. A portrait of the same year by Giovanni Battista Paggi (once owned by Filippo Baldinucci and still in private hands) shows the sculptor smartly dressed with the instruments of an architect on a table and holding open a book with a plan for a church in one hand and a model for a figure of Fame trumpeting in the other. This portrait may have been commissioned to celebrate Francavilla's 40th birthday and his marriage, as well as his prospects as court sculptor to the new grand Duke.

Even so, Francavilla continued his partnership with Giambologna (who by then was over 60 years old), carving from his models (Victoria and Albert Museum, London, England; Musée du Louvre, Paris, France) statues of Ferdinando I de' Medici for two major provincial cities in Tuscany, Arezzo and Pisa, and of Cosimo I de' Medici—complete with a fountain with grotesque ornament below it—in the Piazza dei Cavalieri in Pisa, Italy. In Pisa he also attended classes in anatomy at the recently founded university and produced teaching models with removable organs in colored papier mâché. A statue of St. Matthew for the Cathedral of Orvieto was virtually a replica of his master's statue of St. Luke for Orsanmichele, Florence. Francavilla continued to make mythological statues for private patrons, which were well received, among them that of *Orpheus and Cerberus* that was designed for export to Paris (with attendant animals by Romolo del Tadda) for the garden of Girolamo Gondi. Admired by Henri IV of France, these works encouraged the king to recruit the sculptor, but this was no easy matter because neither the Grand Duke nor Giambologna wanted to lose Francavilla's services.

After a couple of preliminary visits, Francavilla did eventually move to Paris with his family in 1607; it was perhaps intimated that Pietro Tacca and not Francavilla was to succeed Giambologna as court sculptor after the latter's demise. Francavilla was lodged in the Louvre Palace in Paris and received a high salary as *premier sculpteur du roi* (court sculptor). He also took two Italian apprentices, one of whom, Francesco di Bartolomeo Bordoni, became his son-in-law in 1611 and eventually inherited his title and business. Francavilla's first work in France was a marble statue of Henri IV (now at Pau), followed by a spectacular 1609 marble group of *Time Abducting Truth* for the gardens of the Tuileries Palace and a 1612 statue of *David with the Head of Goliath*. There are several painted portraits, a drawing, and an engraving of the sculptor who, by birth an armigerous gentleman, had been made an honorary citizen of Pisa and a privileged court favorite in Paris. His studies of anatomy also led him to be highly regarded as a scientist and intellectual. He was also a competent painter, as is proven by his only canvas identified thus far, a full-length portrait of Giambologna (*ca.* 1575) in his studio.

Francavilla was an important sculptor who has been underrated because for most of his career he played second fiddle to Giambologna, whose reputation was, justifiably, international. Yet without Francavilla's timely and diligent assistance with carving statues accurately from his models and his installation of the architectural components of his chapels, Giambologna could never have achieved the phenomenal output of marble sculpture that was essential to his fame and fortune. It remains to disentangle Francavilla's personal contributions and achievements from those of his master. Once that is done, he may prove to deserve more of the credit for their joint projects than he has been allowed thus far.

From his period of training in Paris, Francavilla brought to Florence a more intimate knowledge of the sculpture of the Fontainebleau school than Giambologna had, including the stuccoes by Rosso Fiorentino and Francesco Primaticcio and Benvenuto Cellini's various statues. This knowledge accounts for the etiolated elegance of his figures and their emotional coolness, which was even more extreme than Giambologna's. Furthermore, his late work in France has not been seriously studied, but his *Time Abducting Truth* antedates Gianlorenzo Bernini's projected group in Rome by several decades and is a major contribution to the development of the sculptural group in northern Europe. His bronze slaves for the monument to Henri IV were also an inspiration to later sculptors, such as Hubert Le Sueur in his mourners for Westminster Abbey in the 1630s. A statuette of the caliber of *Saturn Devouring His Children* (date unknown), which later belonged to André Le Nôtre and King Louis XIV, indicates another field of which he was master and where further works may well remain to be identified.

CHARLES AVERY

See also **Colin, Alexander; Giambologna**

Biography

Born in Cambrai, French Flanders (present-day France), 1548. Moved to Paris, *ca.* 1564, and apprenticed as a sculptor; moved to Innsbruck for six years in 1566, and worked as Alexander Colin's assistant; moved to Florence, *ca.* 1572, and helped Giambologna complete the carving of the marble version of *Florence Triumphant over Pisa* (*ca.* 1567–72); delegated to carve 13 statues for Villa Bracci, 1575; helped Giambologna install a series of bronze statues and reliefs in the Grimaldi Chapel in Genoa, *ca.* 1579; signed and dated a pair of colossal statues of Jupiter and Janus for the Grimaldi Palace, 1585; produced six statues of Christian allegories for Genoa Cathedral, 1585; returned to Florence, *ca.* 1586; elected to the Accademia del Disegno, Florence, 1586; one of the court sculptors to Ferdinando I de' Medici by 1590; worked in Pisa and Arezzo, 1594–1600; summoned to Paris to serve King Henri IV, 1600, and stayed until 1602; moved back to Paris, 1607, where he became *premier sculpteur du roi*, and lived in the Louvre Palace. Died in Paris, France, 25 August 1615.

Selected Works

1575–80 Statues (originally in the gardens of Villa Bracci, Rovezzano, Italy); marble;

dispersed: *Apollo and Zephyr*; Victoria and Albert Museum, London, England; statues of *Pomona*, *Flora*, *Syrinx*, and *Diana*; The Orangery, Kensington Palace London, England; others: Wadsworth Athenaeum, Hartford, Connecticut, United States

ca. 1576 Three flayed anatomical figures; bronze; Jagiellonian University Library, Cracow, Poland

1585 *Jupiter* and *Janus*; marble; Palazzo Rosso, Genoa, Italy

1585 *Four Evangelists*, *St. Ambrose*, and *St. Stephen*; marble; Senarega Chapel, Cathedral of Genoa, Italy

1586 *St. John the Baptist* (from model by Giambologna), *St. Dominic*, *St. Thomas Aquinas*, *St. Anthony*, *St. Philip*, and *St. Edward*; marble; Salviati Chapel, San Marco, Florence, Italy

1588 *Moses*, *Aaron* (from models by Giambologna), *Humility (St. Agnes)*, *Virginity*, and *Prudence*; marble; Niccolini Chapel, Church of Santa Croce, Florence, Italy

1589 *Jason and the Golden Fleece*; marble; Museo Nazionale, del Bargello, Florence, Italy

1591 *Apollo and Python*; marble; Walters Art Museum, Baltimore, Maryland, United States

1593 *Primavera* (Spring); marble; Ponte Santa Trinità, Florence, Italy

1594 *Ferdinando I de' Medici* (from model by Giambologna); marble; Piazza del Duomo, Arezzo, Italy

1594 *Ferdinando I de' Medici Raising Pisa* (from model by Giambologna); marble; Piazza Carrara, Pisa, Italy

1595–1600 *St. Matthew* (from model by Giambologna); marble; Museo del Duomo, Orvieto, Italy

1598 *Orpheus and Cerberus*; marble; Musée du Louvre, Paris, France

1600 *Venus with a Nymph and Satyr*; marble; Wadsworth Athenaeum, Hartford, Connecticut, United States

1604 *The Active and the Contemplative Life*; marble; mortuary chapel of Giambologna, Church of Santissima Annunziata, Florence, Italy

1604 *Mercury with the Head of Argus*; marble; Palazzo Pitti, Florence, Italy

1609 *Time Abducting Truth*, for the Tuileries Gardens, Paris, France; marble: Château de Pontchartrain, near Paris, France

1610–15 Models for four captives for monument to Henri IV; terracotta, wax (lost); casts by Francesco Bordoni: 1618, Musée du Louvre, Paris, France

1612 *David with the Head of Goliath*; marble; Musée du Louvre, Paris, France

Further Reading

Avery, Charles, "Pietro Francavilla's Drawings of Giambologna's Models," *Apollo* 152 (2000)

Francqueville, Robert de, *Pierre de Francqueville, sculpteur des Médicis et du roi Henri IV (1548–1615)*, Paris: Picard, 1968

Walpole, Horace, *The Yale Edition of Horace Walpole's Correspondence*, 48 vols., New Haven, Connecticut: Yale University Press, 1937–83; see especially vols. 4–6

Wiles, Bertha, "Pietro Francavilla," *Bulletin of the Fogg Art Museum* 1/4 (May 1932)

STATUES FROM VILLA BRACCI
Pietro Francavilla (1548–1615)
1575–ca. 1600
marble
h. 170–254 cm

Two statues, Victoria and Albert Museum, London, England; four statues, The Orangery, Kensington Palace, London, England; one statue, Wadsworth Athenaeum, Hartford, Connecticut, United States; one fragmentary statue, private collection, United States

In 1575 a series of 12 or 13 marble statues of Classical deities was commissioned from Pietro Francavilla for a walled garden that Abbot Antonio di Zanobi Bracci was building at his newly acquired villa in Rovezzano, Italy (Il Palagio di Ponte a Mensola). Of these, six survive complete, though severely weathered, in the British Royal Collection (Victoria and Albert Museum, London, England), and one can be found in the Wadsworth Athenaeum in Hartford, Connecticut. The remainder, including three statues bearing signatures of Francavilla, were regrettably allowed to fall into disrepair while in the gardens of Windsor Castle in England; they have since been disposed of.

The carving of the series was proposed first to Giambologna, the grand ducal sculptor of the day, who was famed by then throughout Europe, but he was too busy and suggested that the project be delegated to Francavilla. A contract signed on 22 January 1575 specified that Francavilla was to earn five gold scudi per month in addition to his keep and materials. This agreement ran until June 1577, but the commission was not complete by then and several of the statues bear later dates. Presumably they were paid for by the piece.

According to Florentine art historian Filippo Baldinucci, these latter statues represented *Apollo*, the sun, and *Diana*, the moon, which flanked the entrance to the closed garden; *Ceres*, the goddess of corn (1576), and *Bacchus*, god of wine; *Flora* (signed) and *Zephyr*, which symbolized the germination of flowers; *Pomona* and *Vertumnus*, symbolizing orchards and gardens; *Pan* (1580?) and *Syrinx*, for wild woods; and *Nature* and *Proteus* (1576), for mother nature and the art of gardening. Finally, a larger group of statuary, 4.5 *braccia* (2.6 meters) high, is *Venus with a Nymph and Satyr* (the satyr, Pan, symbolized the pleasures of the flesh, whereas the girl stood for procreation). The *Nature* and *Proteus* groups remained in the courtyard of the Bracci Palace in via dei Ginori, Florence, and the *Venus* group, dated as late as 1600, is now at the Wadsworth Athenaeum.

Although Francavilla definitely carved the groups—indeed, it was in that capacity that he was employed by Giambologna on the Grand Duke's group of *Florence Triumphant over Pisa*—it is almost as certain that Giambologna designed them, probably purveying small models in wax or terracotta for his protégé's benefit and Bracci's approval. In 1582 Giambologna was reported as saying that Francavilla "had never made anything out of his own head, but had always worked from the master's models," and given the date, he was almost certainly thinking of the Bracci commission, which might otherwise have been regarded on the basis of the prominent signatures as entirely Francavilla's own work.

Mastrorocco has convincingly demonstrated that a complex and multilayered intellectual scheme lay behind the choice of deities to populate Bracci's new garden, reflecting contemporary beliefs in science, alchemy, and the understanding of the processes of nature (see Mastrorocco, 1981). Each statue in this out-of-doors environment had several meanings: Ceres, Bacchus, Flora, Zephyr, Pomona, and Vertumnus are all Classical tutelary deities of the fecundity of nature and symbolize in various ways the eternal cycle of renewal, as well as the linkage between astrological time and the affairs of men. Nature, Apollo, and Diana also correspond to the three components of a human being: body, mind, and spirit. Furthermore, several of the deities correspond to the main metals in the alchemical program: Apollo, the sun, stands for gold; Diana, the moon, for silver; and Venus for copper. Pan symbolizes the life force, whereas in the legend concerning Syrinx, the sadness and desperation that often accompany imperfect, human love are duly adumbrated. Bacchus and Ceres symbolize the rhythm of decay, death, and renewal in the passing of the seasons.

All of the statues form easily identifiable pairs, and they probably faced one another across the garden from the brick and stone niches built symmetrically into the walls enclosing the garden (which still survive at Rovezzano, albeit in a ruinous state). The huge group of Venus and her companions, which, although frontally designed, was intended to be freestanding and set in or behind a pool into which her symbolic dolphins could spout water, was designated for the focal point of the scheme in order to represent the fountain of Youth and of Life. This was in itself a symbol of the continual cycle of renewal of life through procreation in man, animals, and plants, of which water represents the essential liquid responsible for fertility and growth.

Mastrorocco cites a poetic intermezzo on this very theme, mentioning Proteus and Zephyr from Torquato Tasso's *Aminta*, which perfectly exemplifies the thought patterns of Francavilla's day that would have been evoked by the contemplation and enjoyment of nature. An educated visitor could thus have "read" the statuary around the walls of the enclosed garden, as well as the plants that it contained, in an intellectual way, as well as enjoyed them for their own sake through the senses. A later study by Lazzaro, although not referring to the scheme of Bracci's dispersed garden, provides further clues as to how a modern viewer needs to set aside simplistic preconceptions when considering such a garden of the late Renaissance (see Lazzaro, 1998).

The series has had a remarkably eventful and checkered history. Abbot Bracci died on 25 January 1586 before the last statues had been carved, and they were inherited by his nephew Filippo. A prominent antique dealer, Filippo viewed the statues as a potential source of profit, although his and his successor's greed stymied their prospects until the mid 18th century. Duchess Sforza tried to negotiate a sale to Queen Marie de Médicis in Paris for the sum of 16,000 or 18,000 crowns. In 1660 the statues were offered via the Abbot Luigi Strozzi first to Cardinal Jules Mazarin, who judged the price "very high, seeing that they are modern statues and not very big," and then to Jean-Baptiste Colbert on behalf of King Louis XIV, as being in effect works by the great Giambologna. Having received a drawing of two of the series, advice that they were really by Francavilla, and an independent estimate of their value, Colbert rejected them in December 1664 as being exorbitantly priced.

According to a letter of 1761 from Sir Horace Mann (British representative at the court of the Grand Dukes of Tuscany) to Horace Walpole (from which other data as to would-be buyers are also derived), the statues were considered by the Duke of Marlborough for Blenheim Palace about 1712, "but he squabbled about a few hundred crowns."

Eventually, in 1750, the statues were purchased on the instructions of George Bubb Doddington by Mann on behalf of Frederick Louis, Prince of Wales, for 5,500 crowns, a sum thought to be well below their real value. The latter's death in 1751 led to a history of disgraceful neglect, and they remained crated in a shed at Kew Palace from 1752 until the early 19th century. In Florence, meanwhile, their export had caused an outcry that culminated in the ratification of a bill on 29 December 1754 to prevent further depredations on the patrimony of ancient monuments in Tuscany.

In 1816, four of the statues (*Diana*, *Flora*, *Pomona*, and *Syrinx*) were sent to decorate Hampton Court Palace, but they were rapidly transferred to Sir Jeffry Wyatville's newly laid out East Terrace Garden of Windsor Castle and remained there from 1829 to 1990. Recarved in 1856 by John Thomas, they were transferred in the late 20th century to The Orangery at Kensington Palace, London, to prevent further weathering. The remainder were disposed about the gardens of Royal Lodge, in Windsor Great Park, or around Virginia Water. The *Venus* group, *Apollo*, and *Zephyr* were then lent by the prince consort to the Royal Horticultural Society in London for display in the East Pavilion of the Albani Arcade in Kensington Gardens (1861–82). The statues were removed to the vinery of the society's garden at Chiswick until 1891, when the two male figures were displayed in a greenhouse in the Botanical Gardens at Kew. Finally, the latter two were transferred for safe keeping to the Victoria and Albert Museum in London.

The *Venus* group, meanwhile, had become separated from the others and may have been exhibited in the Crystal Palace at Sydenham in about 1914. Thereafter, it was "dug up" in a garden in Croydon around 1919. It was acquired by Durlacher Brothers, who exhibited it in London in 1924 and then in the London Museum until 1926; it was then transferred to the Fogg Art Museum in Cambridge, Massachusetts, and published in the museum's bulletin in 1932. Acquired in the following year by the Wadsworth Athenaeum, Hartford, Connecticut, the piece was mounted in the courtyard of the museum's new building as the centerpiece of a functioning fountain. The remnants of the series of statues were rediscovered badly damaged amid undergrowth near Royal Lodge in 1935 and again in 1955.

CHARLES AVERY

Further Reading

Gentilini, G., *Per la storia della scultura* (exhib. cat.), Turin, Italy: Antichi Maestri Pittori, 1992
Lazzaro, Claudia, "Gendered Nature in Sixteenth-Century Garden Sculpture," in *Looking at Italian Renaissance Sculpture*, edited by Sarah Blake McHam, Cambridge: Cambridge University Press, 1998
Lewis, W.S. (editor), *Horace Walpole's Correspondence*, 48 vols., New Haven, Connecticut: Yale University Press, 1937–83; see especially vols. 4–6
Mastrorocco, Mila, "Il giardino della Villa Bracci di Rovezzano: L'intermezzo pastorale: Accademismo e suggestioni magiche," in *Le mutazioni di proteo*, by Mastrorocco, Florence: Sansoni, 1981
Scott-Elliot, Ann H., "The Statues by Francavilla in the Royal Collection," *The Burlington Magazine* (1956)

FRANCE: ROMANESQUE–GOTHIC

Romanesque 1100–1150

The production of monumental stone sculpture was almost nonexistent during the years between the fall of the Roman Empire and the end of the 11th century. Although stone carving did continue during those years, it was limited for the most part to very two dimensionally conceived ornamental work on capitals or screens. Plastic renderings of the human figure were almost entirely absent. Carving in other materials, such as ivory, was practiced, as was metalwork, particularly in the imperial workshops of the Carolingian rulers. However, these works were miniature in scale, and the precious materials used meant that the sculpture produced had a limited audience.

In contrast, a sudden and prolific revival of monumental stone carving began shortly before 1100. Large-scale figures appeared in prominent public locations of buildings, such as the tympana and jambs of portals. Sculptors expanded their repertoires of subjects, introducing ambitious narratives composed of many figures. Romanesque sculptors also produced cult images of the Virgin and Child or saints, carved in wood and painted. The tradition of making such figures, to be placed on altars or carried in processions, goes back to the pre-Romanesque period, but they became immensely popular in the 12th century.

Because Romanesque sculptural production is characterized by a wide variety of styles, it is difficult to generalize the period. However, in contrast to Classical sculpture, that of the 11th and 12th centuries is generally less three-dimensional in conception and more closely tied to its architectural setting. Drapery folds are often rendered in linear fashion as sharp ridges or engraved lines, rather than as three-dimensional shapes. Pattern rather than naturalistic imitation often dominates the carving of hair, beards, and drapery folds. Much Romanesque sculpture is expressive, even distorted in proportion or pose, rather than naturalistic or idealized.

Many of the important monuments of French Romanesque sculpture are not firmly dated. The material is most often organized according to regional schools, as divergent styles and seemingly independent developments are evident in the various regions of France. Contemporary and earlier developments in Italy and Germany are not directly related to work in France. However, very close connections between southern France and northern Spain have long been observed, where the pilgrimage to Cathedral of Santiago de Compostela in Galicia fostered interactions.

Notable examples of facade sculpture prior to 1100 are found in Roussillon: at the abbey Church of Saint-Genis-des-Fontaines, at the Church of Saint-André-de-Sorède, and on the Church of Sainte-Marie at Arles-sur-Tech. The Saint-Genis-des-Fontaines relief (1019–20) bears figures of an enthroned Christ and six apostles in very flat relief with essentially two planes: that of the background and that of the silhouetted figures. Details are incised rather than modeled in three dimensions. In capital sculpture, simplified versions of Classical forms, especially the Corinthian, survived throughout the early Middle Ages. Sculptors working on the porch portal at the Church of Saint-Benoît-sur-Loire expanded the range of forms and plasticity of carving on their capitals, possibly as early as the 1030s. These sculptures are characterized by relatively high relief that is packed tightly on the surfaces of the capitals and that includes narrative subjects.

More extensive programs of decoration appeared on the large churches built at pilgrimage sites and for monastic communities in approximately 1100. Although firm dates are rare, the earliest among these programs is dated: the set of seven reliefs and the altar table for the Church of Saint-Sernin in Toulouse carved by Bernardus Gelduinus and his workshop. The altar's inscription refers to the consecration of the sanctuary, which was performed in 1096 by Pope Urban II. All four edges of the table are decorated with heads of imposing three-dimensionality despite their small scale. The reliefs, at nearly life-size, may have been intended to be part of a sanctuary program, but their planned installation remains a mystery.

Other sculpture along the pilgrimage routes in Languedoc and northern Spain is stylistically related to the Gelduinus workshop products. The cloister decoration at the Abbey of Saint-Pierre in Moissac, dated by inscription to 1100, includes pier reliefs of apostles and Abbot Durand and an extensive group of capitals with vegetal forms, animals, monsters, and narrative scenes. At the same time, closely related capitals were carved for the cloister at La Daurade in Toulouse. Saint Sernin in Toulouse is the site of two early portal programs: the Porte des Comtes around 1096, has carved capitals on the jambs, and the Porte Miègeville, around 1100, includes a tympanum and lintel representing the *As-*

Virgin and Child, Ste. Chapelle, Paris, ivory, beginning of the 14th century
© The Louvre, Paris, France

cension of Christ and relief plaques of St. James and St. Peter in the spandrels.

The south porch portal at Moissac (1125–31) exemplifies the extended portal designs that developed after 1120. The tympanum depicts the *Apocalyptic Vision of Christ*, which is surrounded by the four beasts of the Evangelists and the 24 Elders. The jambs on either side have relief statues of St. Peter and Isaiah, whereas the *trumeau* (central doorpost) carries figures of Jeremiah, St. Paul, and three pairs of lionesses. The walls of the projecting porch are also covered with reliefs: on the left, the parable of Lazarus and Dives, and on the right, the Infancy of Christ (*Gabriel of the Annunciation* is a 19th-century restoration). In contrast to the austere, still figures of the apostles and Durand in the cloister at Moissac, the later portal figures twist and turn, crossing their long slender limbs and in some cases contorting themselves to fit into the space allotted them. Stylistically similar work can be seen at the abbey church of Saint-Pierre at Beaulieu-sur-Dordogne and at the abbey church in Souillac.

A new generation of sculptors in Toulouse produced a series of monumental capitals carrying a complex Passion cycle for the cloister of La Daurade (1115–30). In addition, at the Cathedral of Saint-Étienne in Toulouse a group of narrative capitals were made for the cloister and reliefs of the Twelve Apostles for the chapter house (1130s and 1140s).

In Burgundy, the earliest Romanesque tympanum is most likely that of the Church of Saint-Fortunat at Charlieu priory (1100). An ambitious and influential project was executed for the third abbey church at Cluny sometime during 1080–1115. The eight capitals carved for the hemicycle at Cluny, now preserved in the Musée du Farinier in Cluny (on the grounds of the former abbey), bear figural scenes representing Adam and Eve, Musical Tones, and Virtues, among other subjects. Scholars have looked for a coherent program, but a satisfactory explanation has remained elusive. The sculpture made for the entrance to the nave, now surviving only as fragments, included a massive tympanum with Christ in a *mandorla* (almond-shaped glory) flanked by angels, two seraphim, and the four symbols of the Evangelists.

Many portal programs related to Cluny's are found in Burgundy, such as those at Perrecy-les-Forges and Montceaux l'Étoile. The narthex portals of the Church of Sainte-Madeleine at Vézelay present a coordinated program of tympana across the three doors (1125–35). The expressive and dramatic style of these sculptures shows clear relationships to that of the Cluny fragments. On the central portal tympanum, Christ in a *mandorla* is surrounded by his apostles. Additional figures appear in compartments along the side of the tympanum, and two archivolts surround the whole, a vine scroll on the inner one and the Labors of the Months and Signs of the Zodiac on the outer one. Apostles are carved on the embrasures and *trumeau*, and a figure of St. John the Baptist, whose plasticity approaches that of the early Gothic column statues at the Basilica of Saint-Denis and Cathedral of Chartres's west portal, stands before the *trumeau*. Tympana and decorative archivolts were made for the side portals as well. Interior capitals at Vézelay from the nave (1120s) and the narthex (1140s) continue the tradition of variety: narrative, figural, and vegetal forms, with no two alike.

At the Church of Saint Lazare (now the Cathedral of Autun), the *Last Judgment* (1125–35) of the west portal is signed, "Gislebertus hoc fecit" (Gislebertus made this), and it is thought that this sculptor is almost single-handedly responsible for the series of narrative capitals in the interior of the church. One figure survives from the north portal, the famous fragmentary lintel depicting the recumbent Eve picking the fruit in the Garden of Eden in the Musée Rolin in Autun.

The Church of Sainte-Foy at Conques, in the Rouergue, has an important *Last Judgment* tympanum (ca. 1135). Christ in a *mandorla* is flanked on either side by three registers divided from one another by bands carrying carved inscriptions; the blessed are on his right, and on his left are the damned among the devils in Hell. The figures are stocky with round faces and simple garments. Although tightly spaced, they are neither distorted like contemporary work in Languedoc, nor do they share the attenuated linear forms of Burgundy. Traces of red and blue paint are still quite visible in the crevices of the relief.

Extensive sculptural programs appear on the churches of western France; however, on exteriors the tympanum is not much used. Reliefs are found on archivolts, friezes, blind arcades, and panels inserted into the fabric of the wall. The facade of the Cathedral of Saint Pierre at Angoulême (1110–30) has a series of panels and friezes culminating in an *Ascension/Second Coming* inserted within a blind arch in the upper level of the facade. The Church of Saint-Pierre at Aulnay (1130–50) has a smaller example of such a facade. The blind arcades on either side of the central door carry the *Crucifixion of St. Peter* on the left and Christ between Sts. Peter and Paul on the right surrounded by multiple patterned archivolts. On the central doorway, four archivolts surround the opening, depicting the Lamb of God with angels, the Virtues and Vices, the Wise and Foolish Virgins, and the Months and Zodiac. Lively archivolts also decorate the south portal at Aulnay. The Church of Notre-Dame-la-Grande in Poitiers (1130s) has figures in blind arcades surrounding the central window above the portal. Narrative scenes are carved into the spandrels surrounding the central door and the two blind arches flanking it, and under the high gable, a *mandorla*-shaped frame encloses the *Ascension*.

In Provence, Romanesque sculpture developed around the mid century. On the portals of the Abbey Church of Saint-Gilles-du-Gard and the Church of Saint-Trophîme in Arles, figures on tall relief plaques flank the doors. Above, a frieze bearing narratives spreads across the facade and tympana surmount the doors, carved with large figures in relatively spacious settings. Saint-Trophîme at Arles also has a richly decorated cloister, including narrative and vegetal capitals, and both narrative relief panels and large-scale figures are attached to the piers. In all cases, the sculpture is clearly influenced by Classical Roman work, which was present in large quantities in Provence.

Gothic *ca.* 1140–*ca.* 1400

Around 1140 sculpture in the Île-de-France began to exhibit features that separate it from the Romanesque style. Gothic sculpture remained predominantly architectural through the 12th and 13th centuries, and like its Romanesque predecessors, it was typically carved before being set in place and was almost invariably painted. Early Gothic sculpture evidences a greater regularity of forms than does Romanesque work. Statue columns line the jambs of portals in even rows, and tangentially arranged archivolt figures enhance the sense of order. The sculptures are calmer, lacking the tension and twisting of figures from the first half of the 12th century. The introduction of the pointed arch produces a more vertical tympanum, and horizontal registers regularize and order the figures within them.

Although the west portals of the Basilica of Saint-Denis (1135–40) have suffered heavy damage and much restoration, a substantial amount of original sculpture remains in place. Fragments are preserved in museums (especially heads from the statue columns now in the Walters Art Museum in Baltimore, Maryland; the Fogg Art Museum in Cambridge, Massachusetts; and the Musée National du Moyen Age in Paris, France) and drawings were made before the French Revolution. Although the jamb figures were confined to the columns behind them, they possessed greater three-dimensionality and weight than their Romanesque counterparts. Perhaps even more important is the unifying effect of the placement of these figures across the triple portals. The slightly later west portal program at the Cathedral of Chartres (1145–55) is much more completely preserved. The statue column of a king now in the Metropolitan Museum of Art in New York City indicates that figural decoration was made about 1150 for the now-destroyed cloister at Saint-Denis. Other projects related stylistically to the Saint-Denis and Chartres west portals include the following: the south portal at Notre-Dame, Étampes (*ca.* 1145), the north and south portals at the Cathedral of Bourges (1155–60), and sculpture made for Cathedral of Notre-Dame in Paris (1150–60), which is now installed on the Portail Sainte Anne.

The facade of the Cathedral of Notre-Dame at Senlis (1165–70) follows the model of three-dimensional figures set into archivolts and tympanum and statue columns on jambs, but it also introduces a new style. The *Coronation of the Virgin* in the tympanum, surrounded by a *Tree of Jesse* in the archivolts, reflects the emerging importance of the Virgin in Christian devotion. In contrast to the rigid and confined gestures and patterned drapery of Saint-Denis and Chartres, these sculptures exhibit a fluidity often seen in Mosan metalwork of the period. The Porte des Valois at Saint-Denis (*ca.* 1170), now on the north transept, is close in style.

It was once thought that the cloister programs of the Romanesque period gave way to purely decorative carving after 1150. However, excavations at the Church of Notre-Dame-en-Vaux at Châlons-sur-Marne yielded evidence to the contrary. Around 1180, a major ensemble of some 50 statue columns and as many capitals, some with narrative scenes, was executed for the cloister. As with the Senlis sculpture, stylistic connections with Mosan metalwork are apparent in the smooth, polished surfaces and graceful curving forms of these carvings.

In the years between 1180 and 1200, the mature Gothic style emerged, evident on the north and south transepts of the Cathedral of Chartres. A significant shift in the conception of the statue column occurred. Figures flanking the *Infancy Door* (1205–10) were released from the architectonic structure of the portal; the *Annunciation* and *Visitation* pairs turn toward one another, breaking up the columnar effect of earlier jamb ensembles.

Two portals were carved for the west facade of the Cathedral of Notre-Dame in Paris (1210–20). The central portal tympanum bears an enormous enthroned Christ presiding over the *Last Judgment*, and two broad lintels depict the blessed and damned on either side of St. Michael and the dead rising from their tombs. Small figures multiply across the enormous, splayed archivolts, replacing the more substantial early Gothic ones. In addition to jamb apostles and a blessing Christ on the *trumeau*, reliefs of the Virtues and Vices are introduced on the socle zone, bringing the moral lesson of the *Last Judgment* down to the viewer's eye level. The north portal tympanum depicts the *Assumption* and *Coronation of the Virgin*. The 28 figures from the Gallery of the Kings above (*ca.* 1230) were removed during the French Revolution. However, 21 heads were recovered in 1977 and preserved in the Musée Nationale du Moyen Age.

A double portal on the south transept of the Cathedral of Strasbourg (1225–30) shows significant influence from the classicizing styles of the Germanic empire and the more naturalistic carving of the transept portals at Chartres. In the tympanum depicting the *Death of the Virgin*, figures clad in soft draperies, their bodies clearly visible beneath, cluster in a poignant and emotional scene unparalleled elsewhere. The accompanying tympanum of the *Coronation of the Virgin* is more neutral in tone. Although the column statues of apostles originally flanking these two portals are gone, the figures of Ecclesia and Synagoga survive in the Cathedral Museum in the Strasbourg Cathedral. They are related to figures from the south transept portal at Chartres. The highly unusual *Angel's Pillar* in the south transept at Strasbourg also is of interest because it retains much of its original paint surface.

Variations in style among the sculptures at the Cathedral of Reims reflect interruptions during construction. Prior to 1233, sculpture similar to that of the Chartres transepts mixed with other work strongly influenced by direct study of Roman antiquities. A later workshop produced sculpture that reveals the refined features, curly hair, and expressive faces characteristic of the second half of the 13th century.

A major program was under way at the Cathedral of Amiens in 1225–35. The central door depicts the *Last Judgment*, the south door the *Coronation of the Virgin*, and the north portal is dedicated to St. Firmin, first bishop of Amiens. Close parallels exist with the 13th-century sculpture from the Cathedral of Notre-Dame in Paris's west portal, but the three doors are more closely knit together than on any previous facade. Scenes in quatrefoils are carried over all three doorways at the socle zone, reinforcing and strengthening the visual ties made by the statue columns above. On the Virgin portal, figures from the Infancy cycle on the jambs assert almost complete independence from architectural constraints.

Although interior programs are rare, figures of the Twelve Apostles were carved for the Sainte-Chapelle in Paris (1248; some are *in situ* and others are in the Musée Nationale du Moyen Age). They are highly elegant, with delicate features and softly curling hair. Their drapery falls in broad folds, nearly concealing the form beneath. Placed in front of the main piers, these figures exhibit striking independence from the architecture and a great degree of individuality. Another interior program of note is the western wall of the nave at the Cathedral of Reims, where an immense registered screen of figures standing within trilobed niches was executed in 1260–70.

During the 14th century, freestanding statues became more popular. Sculpted tombs, carved retables, and other church furnishings were produced in large numbers. Under courtly patronage, precious materials such as ivory and gilded silver became the media of choice. Figures strike elegant and refined poses, and drapery falls in sweeping curves that often disguise, rather than reveal, the form underneath. At the same time, an increase in representations of contemporary figures, as donors and on tombs, preserves the interest in naturalism so evident in Claus Sluter's work for the Duke of Burgundy at the end of the century.

Images of the Virgin and Child often emphasize their human relationship, as is the case with the silver-gilt statuette given to the Abbey of Saint-Denis by Jeanne d'Evreux in 1339, or the alabaster figure from the Cistercian abbey of Pont-aux-Dames now in the Metropolitan Museum of Art in New York City. The child sometimes reads from a breviary (1330–40; Musée de Cluny, Paris, France), plays with a bird (mid 14th century; Church of Dommarien, Langres, France), or even nurses (late 14th century; Cistercian abbey of Royaumont, Oise, France).

A number of figures survive from those commissioned by Jean Tissendier for the Chapelle de Rieux of the Convent of the Corderliers in Toulouse (1333–44; Musée des Augustins, Toulouse, France). A portrait of the kneeling donor holding a model of the chapel has lively features, and polychromy increases the sense of immediacy. Other figures from the chapel include 11 apostles, St. Louis of Toulouse, and an *Annunciation*. The figures of saints are more mannered than that of Tissendier, with tilted heads and long, graceful hands.

An extensive narrative retable was commissioned by Jeanne d'Evreux for the Cistercian abbey of Maubuisson about 1340. Fragments attributed to Evrard d'Orléans include four prophets, Moses and David, and a scene of the *Communion of St. Denis* in the Musée du Louvre, Paris, and a *Last Supper* in the main altar of the Church of Saint-Joseph-des-Carmes, Paris. Statues of the king and queen, their daughters Marie and Blanche, and St. Paul and St. Catherine once surrounded the altar. A damaged but complete retable in the Musée de Cluny in Paris depicts six Passion scenes, each framed by an elaborately traceried niche.

The *gisant* (reclining figure) of Charles V in Saint-Denis is the only known work of the sculptor André Beauneveu, which was carved in 1364–66. It is the earliest such figure sculpted for a living monarch, as the specificity of the king's features, in no way flattering, attests. A bust from the *gisant* of Marie de France, although carved by Jean de Liège after her death about 1380, nonetheless presents a convincingly naturalistic image of the young princess.

As is true for the Romanesque period, sculpture from the Gothic age displays a number of different stylistic trends. Although figures in some cases are highly idealized and conform to a canon of proportion that is almost mannered, in other cases, the sense of realism is extremely strong. It is clear, however, that an increased plasticity and a greater sense of motion are inherent in most works made after 1200. The shift in the function of sculpture apparent after 1300—to freestanding figures, tombs, and church furnishings and away from the decoration of major architectural settings—continued into the Renaissance period.

MARJORIE J. HALL

See also **Chartres Cathedral**

Further Reading

Hearn, M.F., *Romanesque Sculpture: The Revival of Monumental Stone Sculpture in the Eleventh and Twelfth Centuries*, Ithaca, New York: Cornell University Press, and Oxford: Phaidon, 1981

Lyman, Thomas W., and Daniel Smartt, *French Romanesque Sculpture: An Annotated Bibliography*, Boston: G.K. Hall, 1987

Rupprecht, Bernhard, Max Hirmer, and Albert Hirmer, *Romanische Skulptur in Frankreich*, Munich: Hirmer, 1975; 2nd edition, 1984

Salvini, Roberto, *Medieval Sculpture*, Greenwich, Connecticut: New York Graphic Society, and London: Joseph, 1969

Sauerländer, Willibald, *Gotische Skulptur in Frankreich, 1140–1270*, Munich: Hirmer, 1970; as *Gothic Sculpture in France, 1140–1270*, translated by Janet Sondheimer, New York: Abrams, 1971; London: Thames and Hudson, 1972

Vergnolle, Éliane, *L'art roman en France: Architecture, sculpture, peinture*, Paris: Flammarion, 1994

Williamson, Paul, *Gothic Sculpture, 1140–1300*, New Haven, Connecticut: Yale University Press, 1995

FRANCE: RENAISSANCE–early 19TH CENTURY

Renaissance (*ca.* 1475–1600)

In sculpture, as in the other arts, the influence of Italy pervaded France throughout the 16th century, predominating by the middle of the century. Military campaigns against Italy under Charles VIII, Louis XII, and Francis I from 1483 to 1545 brought the French into contact with Italian art forms and humanistic thought. Francis I methodically began to centralize power, and the court became the principal patron of the arts. The king collected Italian painting and sculpture and invited Italian artists, including Leonardo da Vinci, to work in France on a major program of carefully calculated building, decoration, and refurbishment in an experimental Franco-Italian style known as the "Francis I" style.

The tomb of Louis XII (1515–31) at the Basilica of Saint-Denis is typical of the early 16th-century transitional style. Its Gothic-Florentine framework includes allegorical figures probably created by two Italian sculptors, Antonio and Giovanni Giusti, although realistic figures of the king and queen in the tomb show marked northern traits of precise observation and are possibly by a French sculptor. Kneeling figures of the king and queen on top of the tomb are usually attributed to Michel Colombe, a French sculptor much influenced by calm, idealized Florentine models. His most famous work is the highly personal altar relief of *Saint George and the Dragon* (1508–09) for the palace at Gaillon (now at the Musée du Louvre, Paris).

The lavish combination of stucco and paint that characterizes the decorations from the 1530s at the royal palace of Fontainebleau introduced forms of Italian Mannerism to France and inspired a generation of French sculptors. Two Italian refugees from the sack of Rome in 1527, the painter Giovanni Battista Rosso and the sculptor, architect, painter, and interior designer Francesco Primaticcio, carried out the work. Figures with elongated bodies, small refined heads, and delicately pleated draperies characterize their sophisticated style, as illustrated in the enigmatic statue called *Diana of Anet* and in Primaticcio's remaining stucco figures at Fontainbleau, in the Chambre de la Duchess d'Etampes, about 1541–45. Works by French exponents of this style are difficult to attribute; scholars usually group them under the general designation of the School of Fontainebleau. Benvenuto Cellini also made a series of virtuoso and extremely influential works in precious metals during his stay in France between 1540 and 1545. Little survives save his masterpiece, an elaborate gold saltcellar for Francis I (Kunsthistorisches Museum, Vienna, Austria). Reliefs by Jean Goujon from the Fountain of the Innocents

Hoyau, Charles: St. Cecilia, 1663, Cathedral of Le Mans
The Conway Library, Courtauld Institute of Art

(1547–49) combine the elegance of these Italian influences with an entirely French Classical restraint, evident in the drapery. Originally from Rouen, Goujon was a master of the fluent, carved line and had full understanding of the relationship of sculptural to architectural forms. He worked with the architect Pierre Lescot at the Louvre until 1562. Goujon's best-known works, the *Pietà* (1544–45) originally on the rood screen for the Church of St. Germain-l'Auxerrois and designed by Lescot and *Nymph and Triton* (1547–49) from the Fountain of the Innocents (both now at the Musée du Louvre, Paris), demonstrate his knowledge of Classical prototypes, which he perhaps gained through prints by Marcantonio Raimondi and Parmigianino. Pierre Bontemps also worked on decorative rather than monumental sculpture at Fontainebleau and at the Louvre on decorative projects and on an elaborate monumental urn to contain the heart of Francis I (1550, Basilica of Saint-Denis). In the provinces where more latitude in self-expression was possible than in court circles, sculptors embellished castles; Ligier Richier, for example, worked for the Dukes of Lorraine and produced much grimmer personifications of Death on his tomb sculpture (for example, his tomb of René of Châlon [*ca.* 1544], at the Church of St. Etienne, Bar-le-Duc, Meuse) than would have been acceptable in Paris.

After a formative period in the Fontainebleau style, Germain Pilon developed a new style of funerary sculpture in courtly circles; he vividly contrasted the pathos of deterioration and death with the beauty and power the deceased had had in life. His tomb of Valentine Balbiani (1572–73), the wife of the Milanese chancellor of France, for example, portrays a richly attired young woman of great beauty, embodying symbols of worldly aspiration and power. She is recumbent, above an emotive *gisant* (reclining figure) relief of staggering poignancy. Emaciated and helpless, the corpse from which the spirit has fled still retains reminders of mortal grace in Valentine's thickly flowing hair and delicate, aristocratic, long finger bones.

Baroque (*ca.* 1600–*ca.* 1700)

Pietro Francavilla (Pierre Francqueville) (1548–1615) was a much traveled and accomplished sculptor from Cambrai who trained in Paris and Innsbruck before becoming a partner of Giambologna in Florence about 1570, an association that lasted more than 30 years. He thoroughly assimilated Giambologna's Mannerist style in his grand scale Classical works such as the Orpheus and Cerberus, 1598, at the Musée du Louvre. He shared a keen interest in anatomy with Giambologna, making several bronze ecorche statuettes. He was recalled to Paris in 1604 by Marie de Medici to

Pajou, Augustin: *Madame Du Barry*, 1773
© Archivo Iconografico, S.A. / CORBIS

work on four sophisticated figures in the Mannerist style, slaves for the pedestal of Giambologna's influential bronze equestrian statue of Henry IV. The statue was finally installed on the Pont Neuf, Paris, in 1614. Before it was destroyed in 1796, it spawned a series of triumphal equestrian statues of French monarchs that derived from the 2nd century Classical statue of Marcus Aurelius in Rome. Francavilla's elegant marbles that he produced in Paris maintained the primacy of Italian influence on French sculpture until his death.

During the reign of Louis XIV, Jean-Baptiste Colbert, *surintendent des bâtiments* (superintendent of buildings), extended the program of centralization. This resulted in complete state control of the arts through a dogmatic program of theoretical teaching at the Academy of Painting and Sculpture, reorganized in 1663 under the directorship of the *peintre du roi* (king's painter), Charles Le Brun. Le Brun had trained in Rome under the Classicist Nicolas Poussin and became virtual dictator of all the arts, arbitrating taste via lectures on the virtues of Classical proportions and ideas and controlling the awarding of commissions to artists in Paris and at Versailles until the death of his patron Colbert in 1683.

François Girardon, a close associate of Le Brun, worked on many of the grand decorative projects at Versailles when the palace became the major focus of French artistic activity. Like most successful 17th-century sculptors, Girardon had visited Rome and was familiar with both the sculpture of Classical antiquity and contemporary Italian sculpture, in particular that of Gianlorenzo Bernini. Underpinned by a profound interest in and understanding of Classical models, Italian Baroque sculpture exhibits exuberant movement, powerful *contrapposto* (a natural pose with the weight of one leg, the shoulder, and hips counterbalancing one another), dramatic poses, careful representation of extremes of emotion, and a rich orchestration of media, colors, and textures. When he visited France briefly in 1665, Bernini, the greatest exponent of this style, drew up designs for grand building projects for the Louvre in the center of Paris itself, incorporating all the features of the Italian Baroque. Although they were much admired, these plans were never implemented.

French taste leaned firmly toward more restraint. Jacques Sarrazin (1592–1660), *sculpteur et peintre ordinaire* to Louis XIII from 1631, professor at the Academie Royale de Peinture et de Sculpture from 1648 and rector there from 1654, was the most influential sculptor of the mid 17th century. He established a popular version of the Classical Baroque style in France, with his decorative secular sculpture for grand-scale interiors and garden decorative schemes. He trained a generation of French sculptors, but it is François Girardon (1628–1715) who is now considered to exemplify French Classical Baroque, for instance, in his tomb of Cardinal Richelieu (1675–77), his heroic equestrian statue of *Louis XIV* (1685–92), based on the Classical statue of Marcus Aurelius, and his masterpiece, *Apollo and the Nymphs of Thetis* (1666–75), commissioned as the centerpiece for the elaborate Grotto of Thetis at Versailles. Girardon closely based individual figures in the *Apollo* group on well-known Classical prototypes such as the *Apollo Belvedere*, while the pictorial effect depends more on the paintings of his contemporary Nicolas Poussin for its composition of figures within a tightly organized space. His rival Antoine Coysevox eventually overtook Girardon in royal favor with a succession of Italianate, dramatic, and exuberant decorations at Versailles, which heralded the development of a more fully Baroque taste in France beginning in 1679. After languishing for a long period without recognition from the court, Pierre Puget finally received royal affirmation during this period for the power and originality of his extraordinary sculptures. He spent most of his career in Marseilles and Genoa but achieved an outstanding success in 1683 when his intense, passionate statue of *Milo of Crotone* was unveiled at Versailles. Despite the patronage of the French minister, François Michel Letellier, marquis de Louvois, however, Puget's individual and assertive character did not fit into the large-scale coordinated teams supervised by Colbert that dominated the pattern of employment in the main art projects around Paris.

In 1679 the architect Jules-Hardouin Mansart began the (now destroyed) Château of Marly as a retreat for the king. Mansart laid it out in a coordinated pattern of interrelated little gazebos, parterres, and water features, with sculptures providing visual accents. As at Versailles, Coysevox and his nephews Guillaume I and Nicolas Coustou, together with sculptors from other French sculptural dynasties, worked on this project, producing allegories, Classical figures, and the most energetic and powerful group of all—the famous *Horses Restrained by Grooms* (1739–45). Although public funerary sculpture at the end of the 17th century depended more and more on restrained reference to Classical models in the work of Simon Guillan, François Anguier, and Gilles Guerin, a new naturalism began to assert itself in secular work for private patrons by Coysevox and members of his circle.

Rococo (*ca. 1700–ca. 1780*)

With the death of Louis XIV in 1705 and the gradual acceptance of naturalism by the French Academy, a lightness expressed through delicacy of proportion, humor, and narrative in subject and variety in texture became more acceptable in French sculpture. Similar changes emerged concurrently in architecture and painting. Direct dependence on Italian models almost disappeared; major artists took up commissions from private patrons, emphasis on individual characteristics rather than idealized forms developed, and in statuary the heroic male form gave way to a taste for sculptures of the female nude and of children.

Collectors at the beginning of the 18th century developed a taste for small bronzes of Classical figures, but by the middle of the century a preference for small terracottas also emerged. Madame de Pompadour, Louis XV's mistress beginning in 1745, became a major patron of the arts. Etienne-Maurice Falconet produced a large *Allegory of Music* (1751) for her château at Bellevue and received the directorship of the Sèvres porcelain factory (1757) as a reward. Jean-Baptiste Pigalle and Claude Michel, called Clodion, became famous for their figurines and small terracottas of playful or sensual subjects, although both sculptors were equally adept at creating life-size statues of modern heroes.

Great public projects still occurred, but these were not now necessarily commissioned by the crown for royal parks and residences. The comte d'Angiviller, *directeur-général des bâtiments du roi* (director of the king's buildings) from 1774 to 1791, for example, initiated a series of 27 statues of Great Men of France, figures not of military or political leaders but of intellectual men of letters who had established the character of French culture, such as *Corneille* (1779) and *Molière* (1787) by Jean-Jacques Caffieri, *Pascal* (1785) by Augustin Pajou, and *Nicolas Poussin* (1804) by Pierre Julien. One of the most impressive of the group is that of the author Racine, commissioned in 1783 from Louis-Simon Boizot and completed in 1787. Shown in the act of writing, Racine is slightly disheveled in his dress, with several of his completed works at his feet.

Even funerary sculpture—for example, the Monument to Cardinal Fleury (designed 1743) by Jean-Baptiste II Lemoyne (1704–78) and Jean-Baptiste Pigalle's more famous tomb of the maréchal de Saxe (1753–76)—introduced a degree of sentiment, portraying heroism tempered by pathos and demonstrating an explicit understanding of the modern human condition. The Saxe tomb represents a transition in both form and feeling from the Baroque to the Rococo in France. In contrast to the distinct zones of activity in Coysevox's tomb of Cardinal Mazarin (1689–93), the tomb of maréchal de Saxe unites the traditionally separate upper and lower areas of the tomb, which represent life and death, by depicting the maréchal striding down fearlessly from the battlefield to the grave, undeterred by the restraining hand of a grieving admirer.

French Rococo sculptors led 18th-century Europe in the development of portraiture, particularly through the example of Jean-Antoine Houdon. His lively, intimate interpretations of personalities from the French Enlightenment, executed in a wide range of materials, follow principles already evident in the portrait busts executed in a transitional style in terracotta, plaster, bronze, or marble by Jean-Baptiste I Lemoyne and his son Jean-Baptiste II Lemoyne. Lemoyne I's portrait of Mansart (1703) presents the architect as a public figure, dressed formally, wearing a wig; already, however, his expressive features are highly individualized. The appointment of Lemoyne I's son, the leader of the anticlassical group of sculptors, as director of the Academy of Painting and Sculpture indicates how far French taste had moved from the idealized grandeur of the Classical Baroque and from Italian influence. The academy continued to teach Le Brun's precepts concerning the categories of human expression and still sent their best students to study at the French Academy in Rome, but the interpretation of the human figure in French sculpture changed subtly from the heroic ideal toward variety and individuality. Lemoyne I's brilliant rendering in 1730 of the painter Noel-Nicolas Coypel's mobile features and impetuous move-ments contrasts strongly with the work of Edme Bouchardon, who continued to produce busts such as *Philipp Stosch* (1727) in a classicizing vein. Felix Lecomte and Pigalle even introduced such informality, individualism, and impression of characteristic movement into portraits of the royal family. However, the extreme realism of Pigalle's bold, unusual life-size nude statue of the aged *Voltaire* (1770) met with vigorous criticism, both at home and abroad, despite its claim to have been derived from Roman prototypes.

Houdon's brilliant images, which capture the most intimate glimpses of the private personality of his sitter, whether a member of his own or of the royal family, are the most memorable of the Rococo period. His ability to portray fleeting expressions parallels that demonstrated in the pastel portraits by his contemporary Maurice Quentin de La Tour. Critics throughout Europe admired Houdon's series of portraits of Voltaire (1779–81), in a variety of costume. Houdon also visited the United States in 1785 with Benjamin Franklin (of whom he sculpted a portrait bust) to prepare his famous public statue of George Washington (full-length figure, 1792; bust, 1801) in contemporary dress.

Neoclassical (*ca.* 1780–*ca.* 1815)

Many of the most prominent exponents of the Rococo in France adapted their style in the third quarter of the 18th century, when public taste turned back toward a more overt recognition of the Classical past. Publications of engravings of paintings, sculptures, and vases that had been excavated in Italy, at Ostia, Pompeii, and Herculaneum, created enormous interest among collectors. Patrons of the arts visited the sites, bought artifacts for their collections, and commissioned modern works in the new Classical style to decorate their homes, thereby stimulating the proliferation of workshops to produce small replicas, modern versions, and even forgeries. By using casts of Classical statues as models for students to admire and copy, academies that had sprung up throughout Europe set an authoritative seal of approval on the Neoclassical style.

Madame du Barry became the mistress of Louis XV in 1768, and her restoration of the Château of Louveciennes required sculptures in the most up-to-date style. The restoration matched paintings by Joseph Marie Vien, based on images from Herculaneum, with Neoclassical sculptures by Pajou, Pigalle, and Falconet. Characterized by more slender proportions than 17th-century figures, these female figures have tiny heads, delicate features, and softly modeled, compliant forms. In spirit they are close to secular Rococo female nudes; superficially remote and Classical, they are still expressive of human emotions. The most famous demonstration of this new sensibility is the sculpture by

Pajou of *Psyche Abandoned* (1785–90), a realistic life-size figure so overtly sensual that it caused public outrage when first exhibited. Julien made his *Goat Girl* (1787) acceptable and only marginally more classicized by adding a wisp of drapery and an attendant goat. François Joseph Bosio, although no longer highly regarded, was eminent in the academy and received royal commissions. Both he and Houdon produced sensitive sculptures of nude adolescents in Classical poses that expressed a vulnerability that was much admired by their contemporaries. The versatile Bosio also sculpted a huge, virile public statue of *Hercules Slaying Achelous* (1814–24, now in the Musée du Louvre, Paris) and the very different sensitive portrait in silver of *Henry IV as a Child* (1824).

The Italian sculptor Antonio Canova developed among both French and English sculptors a much more profound understanding and interpretation of the Roman Classical past. Napoléon recognized the utility of Canova's impressive heroic types as instruments of propaganda and commissioned a series of portraits of his family, although he judged Canova's heroic colossal nude of himself in the political role of *Mars Bringing Peace* (1803–9) to be too extreme. Canova's most admired and influential female statue for Napoléon was his nude of *Pauline Borghese Bonaparte as Venus Victorious* (1808). In the first decade of the 19th century, a series of works by French artists emulating Canova, including busts of the Empress Josephine by Joseph Chinard and Bosio, united the gravitas of Classical proportions with acute French realism. The emperor himself was persuaded to emulate Trajan by commissioning the huge bronze *Column Vendôme* (1873–74). This project, depicting the triumphs of his army on a frieze relief, employed 30 sculptors. For the next 50 years sculptors such as Augustine Dumas reverted to Classical models and represented Napoléon with the attributes of a Roman emperor.

The period of the First Empire (1804–14) saw a great expansion of public works; opportunities for sculptors to work on large-scale decorative schemes flourished under Napoléon. French sculpture continued to be completely dominated by the art of Greece and Rome in style and subject matter. The French Academy set exclusively either religious or Classical subjects for the *morceaux de réception* (final test piece) required of qualifying students. The academy continued to send the most successful students to further study Classical models firsthand at the French Academy in Rome.

Romantic (1815–1850)

A reaction against this classicizing tendency developed during the Bourbon Restoration (1815–30). François

Rude's famous monument to the emperor, *Napoléon Awakening to Immortality* (1845–47), demonstrates a quite different mood. This Romantic piece, poignantly situated at the breast of a hill, symbolizes the striving and achievements of France in its most glorious military period.

Gradually the academy introduced a greater range of models for study, including casts from the Renaissance, and it enlarged the system of training, reforming the curriculum. Although salon juries continued to be suspicious of less serious subjects taken from everyday life and resisted the placing of genre sculptures in the exhibitions, enterprising artists such as Rude found a ready market for their work among the wider public in the commercial production of statuettes. As was the case with painting, contemporary cultural and political events became the concern of 19th-century sculpture, and sculptors gradually experimented with materials, textures, and colors with increasing authority.

J. Patricia Campbell

See also **Anguier, François; Barye, Apollo Belvedere; Antoine-Louis; Bontemps, Pierre; Bouchardon, Edme; Clodion (Claude Michel); Colombe, Michel; Coustou Family; Coysevox, Antoine; Falconet, Étienne-Maurice; Francavilla, Pietro; Girardon, François; Goujon, Jean; Houdon, Jean-Antoine; Lemoyne Family; Pajou, Augustin; Pigalle, Jean-Baptiste; Pilon, Germain; Portrait; Puget, Pierre; Rude, François; Sarazin, Jacques**

Further Reading

The Age of Neo-Classicism: The Fourteenth Exhibition of the Council of Europe (exhib. cat.), London: The Arts Council of Great Britain, 1972

Beyer, Victor, *La sculpture française du XVIIe siècle: Au Musée du Louvre*, Gorle-Bergamo, Italy: Grafica Gutenberg, 1977

Blunt, Anthony, *Art and Architecture in France, 1500–1700*, London and Baltimore: Penguin, 1953; 5th edition, revised by Richard Beresford, New Haven, Connecticut: Yale University Press, 1999

Gaborit, Jean-René, et al., *Sculpture française*, 2 vols., Paris: Ed. du la Réunion des Musées Nationaux, 1998; see especially vol. 2

Haskell, Francis, and Nicholas Penny, *Taste and the Antique: The Lure of Classical Sculpture, 1500–1900*, New Haven, Connecticut: Yale University Press, 1981

Kalnein, Wend von, and Michael Levey, *Art and Architecture of the Eighteenth Century in France*, London: Penguin, 1972

Rosasco, Betsy Jean, *The Sculptures of the Château of Marly during the Reign of Louis XIV*, New York: Garland, 1986

Souchal, François, *French Sculptors of the 17th and 18th Centuries: The Reign of Louis XIV*, vols. 1–3, Oxford: Cassirer, 1977–87, and vol. 4, London: Faber, 1993

West, Alison, *From Pigalle to Préault: Neoclassicism and the Sublime in French Sculpture, 1760–1840*, Cambridge and New York: Cambridge University Press, 1998

FRANCE: mid–late 19th CENTURY

The motor of the development of sculpture in 19th-century France, as the generation of artists born in the 1840s came to understand, had been to change the status of the practice of sculpture from a position of dependence on the structures of power to one of concerted collaboration and relative autonomy.

In the 1830s the artists who formed part of the Romantic movement challenged the dominant Neoclassical mode in ways that remained inspirational for future generations. They believed that art practice should be based in the observation and closer rendering of nature; for example, Antoine-Louis Barye grounded his practice in the quasi-scientific study of animals, and François Rude and David d'Angers advocated working with the life model. In addition, these artists used sculpture as a medium to represent emotions and states of mind through the rendering of bodily movements and facial expressions, such as Rude in monumental historical narratives (*Departure of the Volunteers*; 1833–36), and Auguste Préault in personal visions (*Silence*; 1848). Also, while accepting that the process of articulating form involved a secondary commitment to the history of form, they shifted the interest from Classical antiquity; for example, Félicie de Fauveau revisited medieval culture, and Henri de Triqueti the quattrocento. James Pradier, however, reaffirmed the authority of the nude and Classical language (*Nyssia*; 1848) to express the concept of plastic beauty and contemporary sensibilities; through their work and teaching Eugène Guillaume and Paul Dubois maintained this tradition. Helène Bertaux appropriated this concept for emerging women sculptors (*Psyche*; 1889).

The major program of the urbanization of Paris undertaken by the Second Empire set the mode for the use of sculpture in relation to public architecture. The enlargement of the Louvre occupied 335 sculptors adapting their divergent aesthetics; drawing on 18th-century or Classical statuary, Albert-Ernest Carrier-Belleuse, Eugène Delaplanche, Eugène Lequesne, Auguste Ottin, Gabriel-Jules Thomas, Cordier, and women sculptors Claude Vignon and Marcello (Adèle d'Affry) all contributed to the decoration of cultural spaces, centers of trade, and commerce. Jean-Baptiste Carpeaux remained outstanding in his capacity to embed aesthetics research in public art, revitalizing the tradition of portraiture and inventing compositions that focused the debate on modernity (e.g., *Le Génie de la Danse*, 1866).

The explosion in the output of sculpture was a characteristic phenomenon of the French cultural scene. This may be partly explained in relation to French history and its upheavals—the revolutions of 1830 and 1848, the coup d'état of 1851, the Franco-Prussian War, and the Commune of 1871. In sponsoring vast programs of urbanization in which sculpture had a major role to play, successive governments sought to create an image of national and social unity, as well as to legitimize their claim for power. The July Monarchy (1830–40) undertook the sculptural program of the Palais Bourbon, seat of the National Assembly, featuring Pradier's *Public Education*. The Second Empire capitalized on the Catholic religion to control rural France; the cult of the Virgin Mary reanimated around large-scale sculptures (e.g., Joseph Fabisch's *Notre-Dame-de-Lourdes*, 1864). The Third Republic urbanized French cities as the state sought to take over the role of the Catholic church in controlling public imagination through its civic ceremonies and cultural rituals. The thoroughfare became appropriated for sculptural programs. The public saw Emmanuel Frémiet's *Joan of Arc* (1874), Aimé-Jules Dalou's *Triumph of the Republic* (1879–99), and Auguste Rodin's *Burghers of Calais* (1889), in their divergent styles, as defining civic and political virtues. Monuments to artists, men of letters, and scientists multiplied, often initiated by independent groups who employed locally born sculptors (e.g., Antoine-Jean Injalbert's *Molière*, 1896).

The Paris salons provided the main platform for aesthetic debate. The ideological notions of truth and science supported the changing modes of realism across the divide of avant-garde and academic art. While Edgar Degas recorded precise dance postures in three-dimensional forms (e.g., *Little Dancer, Fourteen Years Old*; exhibited 1881), Beaux-Arts artists Emmanuel Frémiet, Louis Ernest Barrias, Laurent Marquestre, Jean-Léon Gérôme, and Jean-Alexandre-Joseph Falguière sought to document the development of human civilization in time and in space. The representation of sexuality in Rodin's art was culturally legitimized under the ethos of naturalism by critics such as Gustave Geffroy, and the state commissioned Rodin's *The Kiss* in 1888. Sculptors pursuing a diverse political agenda in their representation of the heroism and hardship of industrial or rural work, including Dalou, Alexandre Charpentier, Jean Baffier, Henri Chapu, Camille Lefebvre, and Roger-Bloche, or redefining woman's social function, including Marie Cazin (*Science et Charité*, 1893) and Charlotte Besnard, developed L'Art Social.

In sponsoring Rodin's *The Gates of Hell* (1880–ca. 1900) the state provided institutional structures for the development of the most characteristic aesthetic movement of the late 19th century: intellectuality in art. In the 1890s Rodin, Albert Bartholomé, Camille Claudel, and Jules Desbois contributed complex works on the themes of death, aging, fate, sexuality, and mental suffering. From the mid 1880s through *Balzac* of 1898, Rodin's work engaged critics in fundamentally redefining the semantics, aesthetics, and cultural status of sculpture. Through the technique of modeling, spatial positioning, and combinations of figures, sculpture was understood to deploy its own system of signification that showed close parallels with the arts of language.

While the consciousness of the need for artists to take control of the diffusion and production of sculpture accelerated around Rodin's prestigious career, artists who undertook a greater part of the technical process, such as Claudel, Antoine Bourdelle, Aristide Maillol, or those who practiced direct carving, such as Paul Gauguin and Georges Lacombe, questioned the methods of production of sculpture, thus paving the way for the Modernist concept of "the autonomy of sculpture."

The creation of the Musée d'Orsay, opened in Paris in 1985, has stimulated a complete reappraisal of 19th-century sculpture and rehabilitation of historic collections.

CLAUDINE MITCHELL

See also **Barye, Antoine-Louis; Bourdelle, Emile-Antoine; Carpeaux, Jean-Baptiste; Carrier-Belleuse, Albert-Ernest; Claudel, Camille; Dalou, Aimé-Jules; David d'Angers; Degas, Edgar; Falguière, Jean-Alexandre-Joseph; Fauveau, Félicie de; Gauguin, Paul; Gérôme, Jean-Léon; Maillol, Aristide; Pradier, James; Rodin, Auguste; Rude, François**

Further Reading

De Caso, Jacques, "Bibliographie de la sculpture en France, 1770–1900," *Information de l'histoire de l'art français* (September 1963)

Fusco, Peter, and Horst W. Janson (editors), *The Romantics to Rodin* (exhib. cat.), Los Angeles: County Museum of Art, 1980

Le Normand-Romain, Antoinette, *Mémoire de marbre: La sculpture funéraire en France, 1804–1914*, Paris: Bibliotèque Historique de la Ville de Paris, 1995

Pingeot, Anne (editor), *La sculpture française au XIXe siècle* (exhib. cat.), Paris: Musées Nationaux, 1986

FRANCE: 20TH CENTURY– CONTEMPORARY

In the first decades of the 20th century, Paris attracted a dynamic international community of sculptors. They had been drawn from across Europe, as well as provincial France, by the teaching institutions such as la Grande Chaumière, the diversity of exhibition spaces, the annual salons, the studio facilities, and, in the case of some sculptors, the prospect of finding employment as *practicens* (sculptors' assistants) in a profession that had fast expanded in the age of Auguste Rodin.

The several generations of artists born in the period 1861–1910—and now often considered traditional—positioned their practice on some common ground. They defined sculpture as a material realization that required technical expertise and demanded patient labor: Joseph Bernard advocated direct carving; Aristide Maillol and Jane Poupelet experimented with methods of bronze casting and did their own chiseling. Second, they believed that formalist research could develop within representation. Third, they held that sculpture was a social function. This meant expanding the traditional outlets of the profession: Charles Despiau, Robert Wlérick, Chana Orloff, Anna Quinquaud, and Paul Belmondo diversified portraiture; François Pompon and Rembrandt Bugatti specialized in animal sculpture. Inspired by feminist issues, Poupelet and Yvonne Serruys subverted the practice of the nude. Antoine Bourdelle anticipated the future role of sculpture in urban developments with his designs for the Théâtre des Champs-Elisées in 1913. In the 1920s, most of these sculptors were employed in the production of memorials to World War I.

Many key figures of the Pan-European avant-garde established themselves in France for part or most of their careers: Pablo Picasso and Constantin Brancusi, who settled in Paris in 1904, and Jean Arp in the 1920s. Antoine Pevsner, Julio Gonzàles, Jacques Lipchitz, Max Ernst (who lived for 40 years in France), and Alberto Giacometti, were also based in France.

One of the representative characteristics of the avant-garde was the interdisciplinary nature of art practice, which was witnessed in sculptures by painters Henri Matisse, André Derain, and Joan Miró. The polychrome Cubist sculptures of Henri Laurens and Ossip Zadkine and the archetypal imagery in the sculptures of Ernst and Giacometti also reveal these characteristics. The literary, philosophical, and Freudian legacy advocated by writers such as Breton supported the formal experimentation of these sculptors. The collections of Breton and Picasso of African and ethnological art revealed the point of reference from which the avant-garde challenged the traditional values of Western art.

Although Picasso's constructions of 1912–15 using cardboard or cut-out metal negated the notion of sculpture as modeled or chiseled mass, the highly polished works of Brancusi maintained the value of craftsmanship within abstract art. All such oeuvres exemplified recurrent issues in Modernism—the autonomy of sculpture both in its function and its mode of signification, the relation to science in its fragmentation or its material, the dichotomy between what can be subjected to analysis or the sense of wholeness that defies verbal scrutiny, and the tension between abstraction and figuration. Henri Laurens, Henri Gaudier-Brzeska, Raymond Duchamp-Villon, and Etienne-Martin all addressed these issues.

The dominant figure of French 20th-century art remains Marcel Duchamp. His readymades of 1913–15—industrial objects appropriated and repositioned, many of which were redone in an edition of eight in 1964—became inspirational for Yves Klein and the sculptors of the 1960s who believed Duchamp had made intellectual inquiry the central purpose of art practice.

Today, in 21st-century Paris, two institutions reflect the divide between the traditional and the avant-garde, which art historians have often used to expound the development of sculpture. While the Musée des Années Trente, at Boulogne-Billancourt, highlights the tradition of figurative and Neoclassical art that constituted mainstream French sculpture until the 1950s, Modernism is prioritized at the revitalized Musée Nationale d'Art Moderne (MNAM) at the Centre Georges Pompidou. MNAM offers an account of the development of sculpture in terms of reactions, refusals, and ruptures taking place across the movements of Cubism, Surrealism, Dada, and Abstraction and points to their influences on the art of the post 1950s.

In the aftermath of World War II, research on the expressive qualities of material substances endowed the representation of the human figure with potent significance, as with the work of Germaine Richier. In the 1960s two influential concepts accelerated the transformation of sculptural practice. One was the idea of using the machines, tools, the technology of industry, or the debris of consumer society. César, who already worked with scrap metal, combining the technique of welding and assemblage, appropriated the new compressors of the demolition yard to produce colorful rectangular blocks. Arman's *Accumulations* consisted of refuse objects, categorized and placed in multiple in shallow boxes to be hung on a wall, or newly fabricated objects—such as parts of Renault cars—piled up, towerlike, to appropriate space. Niki de Saint Phalle incorporated plastic toys and domestic utensils in compositions that questioned the war in Algeria or the conditions of women. While Nicolas Schöffer used complex technology for his "sculpture-automobile" of the early 1970s, Jean Tinguely maintained the ethos of the absurd in his machinelike kinetic sculptures.

Another influential notion is that of sculpture as spatial organization. Etienne-Martin worked for more than 25 years on his series *Demeures* (first exhibited in 1960), which questioned the boundaries between private and public, outer and inner space. De Saint Phalle designed *Big Clarice*, 1970, and Jean Dubuffet designed *Closerie Falbala*, 1973, large-scale architectural environments for the open space. Anne Poirier and Patrick Poirier constructed imaginary archaeological sites (*Ostia Antica*, 1971). Jean-Pierre Raynaud's *Container zéro* (1974), or Marie-Ange Guillemot's *Paravent* (1997) functioned as mobile architectural environments.

Sculptural practice has long been centralized in France. The sculptural program for the permanent buildings of the Universal Exhibition of 1937, the Palais de Chaillot and Palais de Tokyo, exemplify how the French state envisaged sponsoring the arts. This project involved 50 artists promoted by the Académie (including Henri Bouchard, Alfred Janniot, and Paul Landowski) and artists who considered themselves *Indépendents* (such as Henry Arnold, Robert Wlérick, and Léon Drivier). However, the diverse manners in which these artists responded to commissions arising from the politics of the interwar period cannot be reduced to a single ideological position. The Ministère des Affaires Culturelles created by André Malraux in 1959 developed strategies to support contemporary art. The Centre National d'Art Contemporain was founded in 1967, and the Fonds Régionaux d'Art Contemporain (FRAC), founded in 1976, were to document, exhibit, and purchase new art. The commissioning of monumental sculpture was stimulated by declaring a mandatory expenditure for sculpture and painting of 1 percent of the budget for the construction of public buildings. Several Maillol sculptures were installed in the Tuileries gardens in 1964, and the first sculpture park opened at Vincennes in 1971. Under the socialist government, an unprecedentedly large budget enabled the ministry of Jack Lang to realize an ambitious program. While the FRAC organized innovatory temporary exhibitions across France, the policy to incorporate new sculptures in cities and in their historical sites was accelerated. In 1985–86 monumental works by Arman were installed at the Gare Saint-Lazare; by Daniel Buren and Pol Bury at the Palais Royal; and by Dubuffet at Issy. Jeanne-Claude and Christo also wrapped the Pont-Neuf at this time. The same period saw the creation of an increasing number of institutions for contemporary art.

Partially in response to such institutional structures, sculptors have appropriated the concept of mise-en-scène. Working with a wide range of material and processes and calling on personal and collective mythologies, artists "theatricalized" the gallery space. Work by Christian Boltanski at the Galerie Templon in 1970, Gina Pane's installation at MNAM in 1985, and the retrospectives of Annette Messager and Louise Bourgeois at the Musée d'Art Moderne de la Ville de Paris in 1995 consecrated the notion of spatial occupancy; Bourgeois's *Cells* set parameters to control the viewer's gaze, and Messager's *Parade* invaded the whole space to immerse the visitors. By using the notion of mise-en-scène, emerging sculptors such as Martine Aballéa, Françoise Dupré, Françoise Roc, Michel Blazy, and Sylvie Blocher seek alternative venues to expand the field of sculptural practice and its audience.

CLAUDINE MITCHELL

See also **Arman (Fernandez); Arp, Jean; Bourgeois, Louise; Christo and Jeanne-Claude; Duchamp, Marcel; Klein, Yves; Picasso, Pablo; Poupelet, Jane; Saint Phalle, Niki de; Tinguely, Jean**

Further Reading

Becker, Annette, *Les monuments aux morts*, Paris: Éditions Errance, 1989

Bony, Jacques, et al., *L'art sacré au XXe siècle en France*, Thonon-les-Bains, France: Albaron-Musée des Années Trente, 1993

Cowling, Elizabeth, and Jennifer Mundy, et al. (editors), *On Classic Ground: Picasso, Léger, de Chirico, and the New Classicism, 1910–1930*, London: Tate Gallery, 1990

Millet, Catherine, *L'art contemporain en France*, Paris: Flammarion, 1987; new edition, 1998

Qu'est-ce que la sculpture moderne? (exhib. cat.), Paris: Centre Georges Pompidou, 1986

FRANCESCO DI GIORGIO MARTINI
1439–1501 *Italian*

Giorgio Vasari praised Francesco di Giorgio as an excellent sculptor, but knew only three of his works. It remained for Paul Schubring in 1907 to recognize the artist as the author of five remarkable reliefs previously attributed to Andrea del Verrocchio and Leonardo da Vinci, and thereby to reestablish Francesco's reputation as a sculptor (see Schubring, 1907). Other recent attributions and the discovery of documentary evidence have further extended Francesco's sculptural oeuvre, but the chronology, patronage, and original settings of his works still remain poorly understood.

Francesco was the son of a civil servant of the commune of Siena. Nothing is known about his apprenticeship, but his unusually broad range of skills suggests he may have trained with several masters. He probably learned sculpture from Lorenzo Vecchietta and Antonio Federighi, the leading Sienese sculptors of the mid 15th century. His style and technique, particularly in bronze relief, however, are most profoundly indebted to Donatello, who lived and worked in Siena between 1457 and 1459. At the same time, Francesco's training as a painter (perhaps with Vecchietta or Sano di Pietro) developed his skills in drawing, visual narrative, and his understanding of antique art, all of which served him in the composition of narrative relief sculpture as well.

Francesco's first documented work as an independent artist is the life-size wooden statue of *St. John the Baptist*, completed in 1464 for the Sienese confraternity of San Giovanni Battista delle Morte (see Carli, 1949). The dramatic human figure marks the beginning of Francesco's life-long homage to Donatello. From 1468 to 1475, Francesco maintained a workshop together with Neroccio de' Landi, but it is unknown if they collaborated on sculpture as well as paintings. Works now attributed to Francesco in the early 1470s include a pair of elegant wooden angels in Florence (see Seidel, 1994) and a marble Madonna and Child in *rilievo schiacciato* (relief sculpture emphasizing light and shadow through carving methods) in Berlin (see Schubring, 1907). The life-sized terracotta *Lamentation* group from the monastery of Monteoliveto fuori Porta Tufi was most likely made about 1475, when the artist was working on the painted *Adoration* (Siena, Pinacotoca Nazionale) for the same monastery and on other projects for the Benedictines. Luciano Bellosi's new attribution of the bronze *gisant* (reclining figure) of Mariano Sozzini il Vecchio to the young Francesco contradicts evidence that it is by Vecchietta (see Bellosi, 1993).

By November 1477, Francesco had left Siena to work for Duke Federigo da Montefeltro of Urbino as engineer and architect, but evidently also as sculptor. The large bronze *Deposition* relief in S. Maria del Carmine in Venice features portraits of the Duke, his young son Guidobaldo, and other important members of the confraternity of Corpus Domini in Urbino. The variety of gestures of despair makes this relief one of the great *istorie* of mourning in the Albertian sense. But the technique is the crucial dramatic element in the composition, where surging, undulating surfaces flicker in light. The apparent *non-finito* (lack of finish) of the bronze may be deliberate (see Penny, 1994). Another tour de force in bronze relief, the Perugia *Flagellation*, appears to have been made in Urbino as well. Together the four bronze roundels of male saints now in Washington, D.C., Vaduz, and Berlin may have surrounded a devotional panel similar to the *Deposition* and *Flagellation* (see Pope-Hennessy, 1965). On a grander scale, Francesco designed, if not executed, the marble frieze of *The Arts of War* for the exterior of the Palazzo Ducale in Urbino. The 72 reliefs of machines are described by Vasari as painted.

It cannot be assumed, however, that all of Francesco's reliefs were Montefeltro commissions. The iconography and provenance of the so-called *Discordia* reliefs in Siena and London, for example, suggest a Sienese patron. Evidence that the artist had a number of other distinguished private patrons is furnished by his medals, which also diffused the artist's fame and style throughout Italy.

From the late 1480s until his death, Francesco once again lived in his native city of Siena, where, according

Deposition© Scala / Art Resource, NY

to Vasari, "his honors were as great as his profits." He enjoyed a salaried position in the Sienese commune, which frequently lent his services to foreign princes. Despite his frequent travels abroad during this period, he and his workshop produced sculpture for the private chapels of Sienese political leaders. Chief among Francesco di Giorgio's late works are the two monumental bronze angels in the Cathedral of Siena, commissioned in 1488 along with another pair by Giovanni di Stefano as part of the great Renaissance reformulation of the cathedral's high altar. Many of Francesco's bronze reliefs are often dated to the 1490s, as is *Man with a Serpent*, a fountain figure in Dresden attributed to him (see Schubring, 1907). The artist's status as a maker of small bronze statuettes, however, remains problematic.

At the time of his death, Francesco was *capomaestro* (chief architect) of the Cathedral of Siena and had begun bronze statues of apostles for the church. Two drawings in the Uffizi may represent his designs for this important project. His collaborator, Giacomo Cozzarelli, was the immediate heir to his unfinished commissions and dramatic style, but Francesco's achieve-

ments lived on in the Sienese sculptor-painter tradition, culminating in Domenico Beccafumi's exquisite bronze angels of 1548–51 for the Cathedral of Siena.

TRINITA KENNEDY

See also **Donatello (Donato di Betto Bardi); Vecchietta (Lorenzo di Pietro); Verrocchio, Andrea del**

Biography

Born in Siena, Italy, on or before 23 September 1439. Studied painting, sculpture, architecture, and engineering with several different masters, including probably Lorenzo Vecchietta, Antonio Federighi, Mariano Taccola, and Sano di Pietro; formed partnership with painter-sculptor Neroccio de' Landi, 1468; worked as painter at hospital of Santa Maria della Scala, Siena, 1471; employed as civic engineer in Siena, 1469–73; designed Church of the Madonna of Calcinaio, Cortona, 1474; dissolved partnership with Neroccio de'Landi, 1475; served Federigo da Montefeltro, Duke of Urbino, and his son as court artist, architect, military engineer, and diplomat, beginning *ca.* 1475; regained his Sienese citizenship, 1485; summoned to Milan to work for Duke Francesco Sforza and collaborated with Leonardo da Vinci in Pavia, 1490; invited to submit design for facade of the Cathedral of Florence, 1491; worked in Naples for Alfonso of Aragon, Duke of Calabria, in 1491, 1492, and 1494/95. Died at Volta di Fighille, near Siena, Italy, before 29 November 1501.

Selected Works

1464   *St. John the Baptist*; polychromed wood; Museo dell'Opera del Duomo, Siena, Italy

ca. 1470 Statues of two angels; polychromed wood; private collection, Florence, Italy

ca. 1470 *Madonna and Child*; marble; Staatliche Museen, Berlin, Germany

1474–77 *Deposition*: bronze; S. Maria del Carmine, Venice, Italy

ca. 1475 *Lamentation*, for Monastery of Monteoliveto fuori Porta Tufi, Siena, Italy; terracotta; Church of SS. Giacomo e Niccolò, Castelnuovo Berardenga, Siena, Italy

ca. 1475 *Saint Anthony Abbot*; bronze; private collection of the Prince of Liechtenstein, Vaduz, Liechtenstein

ca. 1475 *St. Jerome*; bronze; Staatliche Museen, Berlin, Germany

ca. 1475 *St. John the Baptist*; bronze; National Gallery of Art, Washington, D.C., United States

ca. 1475 *St. Sebastian*; bronze; National Gallery of Art, Washington, D.C., United States *ca.* 1477   *The Arts of War*; marble; Palazzo Ducale, Urbino, Italy

ca. 1480   *Discordia*; stucco; versions: Chigi Saracini Collection, Siena, Italy; Victoria and Albert Museum, London, England

ca.   *The Flagellation*; bronze; Galleria
1480–85   Nazionale dell'Umbria, Perugia, Italy

ca.   *St. Christopher*; polychromed and gilded
1488–90   wood; Musee du Louvre, Paris, France

1488–92   Two candelabrum-bearing angels; bronze; Cathedral of Siena, Italy

1490s   *Man with a Serpent*; bronze; Staatliche Skulpturensammlung, Dresden, Germany

Further Reading

Bellosi, Luciano (editor), *Francesco di Giorgio e il Rinascimento a Siena, 1450–1500* (exhib. cat.), Milan: Electa, 1993

Carli, Enzo, "A Recovered Francesco di Giorgio," *The Burlington Magazine* 91 (1949)

Penny, Nicholas, "Non-Finito in Italian Fifteenth-Century Bronze Sculpture," *Antologia di Belle Arti* 48–51 (1994)

Pope-Hennessy, John, *Renaissance Bronzes from the Samuel H. Kress Collection: Reliefs, Plaquettes, Statuettes, Utensils, and Mortars*, London: Phaidon Press, 1965

Schubring, Paul, *Die Plastik Sienas in Quattrocento*, Berlin: Grote, 1907

Seidel, Max, "Un colloquio con l'antichità: Il Giovane Francesco di Giorgio e la scultura romana," in *Umanesimo a Siena: Letteratura, arti figuratve, musica*, edited by Elisabetta Cioni and Daniela Fausti, Siena, Italy: Università degli Studi di Siena, and Florence: Nuova Italia, 1994

Toledano, Ralph, *Francesco di Giorgio Martini: Pittore e scultore*, Milan: Electa, 1987

Vasari, Giorgio, *Le vite de' più eccellenti architetti, pittori, e scultori italiani*, 3 vols., Florence: Torrentino, 1550; 2nd edition, Florence: Apresso i Giunti, 1568; as *Lives of the Painters, Sculptors, and Architects*, 2 vols., translated by Gaston du C. de Vere (1912), edited by David Ekserdjian, New York: Knopf, and London: Campbell, 1996

Weller, Allen Stuart, *Francesco di Giorgio, 1439–1501*, Chicago: University of Chicago Press, 1943

DAME ELISABETH FRINK 1930–1993

British

Dame Elisabeth Frink came to prominence in the British art world at age 22. While still a student at Chelsea Art School in 1952, she sold a sculpture (*Bird*) to the Tate Gallery in London. The next year she submitted an entry to the competition for the *Monument to the Unknown Political Prisoner*. Reg Butler won the competition, but Frink won a prize and the Arts Council bought her submission.

In the wake of Henry Moore's success, sculpture had entered the art scene mainstream in 1950s London. Frink was familiar with the wide range of sculptural experimentation at the time but her style was more naturalistic and expressionist than most of her immediate predecessors or contemporaries, such as Anthony Caro or Eduardo Paolozzi. Throughout her career her primary subjects were birds (the subject of the first Tate purchase and her submission to the Arts Council competition), animals, and humans. Her recognizable style and consistent subject matter earned her popular acclaim in Britain and a number of prestigious public commissions. Outside Britain, her work is less well known, and her only major show in the United States was a 1990 retrospective at the National Museum of Women in the Arts in Washington, D.C.

Frink developed her characteristic technique in art school. Like her contemporaries Alberto Giacometti and Germaine Richier, she did away with intermediary casts of clay by building her forms swiftly with plaster directly on a metal frame. Given the large scale of many of her works, this entailed very physical labor. She may have learned of Henry Moore's technique for finishing his works from her professor at Chelsea, Bernard Meadows, who had been Moore's assistant. Like Moore, Frink would often carve away from the plaster to create a more dynamic surface. The result could then be shellacked, as in the case of her early work, or cast in bronze as finances soon permitted.

The sense of vigor and emotional tension suggested by the surface of her sculpture suit the grand themes that preoccupied Frink. War and violence materialized in much of her work. The menacing birds of the 1950s and 1960s, such as the Tate purchase and *Harbinger Bird IV,* marked for her a place in the history of sculpture. Abstracted, predatory, and prone to flight, the birds represented a variety of postwar fascinations and fears. Frink herself lived in southwestern England during the bombing raids of World War II, and her father was a soldier.

Men were another frequent subject of Frink's art for personal and metaphorical reasons. Although she said she enjoyed the form of male bodies and their Classical implications, they represented well her concerns regarding "mankind." She was intrigued by their ability to simultaneously embody strength, ambition, and evil. These concerns were most fully realized in her giant heads of the late 1960s and 1970s, which are both absurd and dangerous. The *Goggle Heads* explore the blank faces of aggression, whereas the *Tribute Heads* and *Memorandums* read more like death masks and mark those who died for their beliefs. Some of these were produced for Amnesty International in order to contribute to the organization's protests against human rights violations. After the huge, ancient bronze Riace warrior statues were raised from the sea in the 1980s, Frink did a series of figures inspired by them. These warrior figures served as a suitable means

Goggle Heads
The Conway Library, Courtauld Institute of Art

to further probe the menacing possibilities of Classical heroism.

In all cases, Frink's subjects are pared down to their essential elements, but some, like her horses and dogs, are much more benign. Her aptitude for monumental and naturalistic figures that fit into the human landscape garnered her a number of commissions from Liverpool Metropolitan Cathedral, Salisbury Cathedral, and other major religious sites in England. A poem by Peter Levi describes the surreal experience of her innate figures in an organic landscape. Dogs that refuse to come when called and heroes frozen in their moment of glory seem all the more powerful outside the confines of the museum or gallery. Frink claimed that she enjoyed creating figures for an outside landscape because it encouraged viewers to develop a personal and intimate relationship with the sculptures. Deliberately on the same level as viewers, her men, dogs, and horses inhabit a shared space rather than a sacred and separate one. This can have a profound effect on their interpretation. The *Horse and Rider*, who sits in full view of the crowds of Piccadilly, London, at first seems like a noble equestrian subject. However, he has emerged in the wrong place at the wrong time. He is naked and too exposed in the middle of the big city to garner the respect the sculptural convention demands.

Throughout Frink's career, her driving themes and iconography remained the same. Some critics viewed this evolved consistency as indicative of her personal and artistic integrity and her ability to rise above shifting artistic trends. For others, the sameness precluded development and the chance to build on the promise shown in her early work. One critic referred to *Protomartyr* as indicative of how her work "often lapsed into academic dullness." Others complained of her complacency with surface at the expense of form. Some viewers have read her persistent concern with the dangers of masculine dominance as distinctly feminine. Her explorations into the underbelly of masculinity have resonated with feminist critics, but Frink usually described her preoccupations in abstracted and personal terms.

Frink found great financial success in sculpture and her concomitant interest in lithography. Although her first bird figure sold to the Tate for a mere £66, as of the 21st century her pieces have sold for tens of thousands of pounds.

SARAH WATSON PARSONS

Biography

Born in Thurlow, Suffolk, England, 14 November 1930. Attended Guildford School of Art, 1947–49, and Chelsea School of Art, London, 1949–53, under Bernard Meadows and Willi Soukop; taught at Chelsea School of Art, 1953–61, and at St. Martin's School of Art, London, 1954–62; won a prize in competition for *Monument to the Unknown Political Prisoner*, 1953; awarded Commander of the Order of the British Empire, 1969; elected associate of the Royal Academy, 1971; awarded Dame Commander of the Order of the British Empire, 1982; awarded doctorate by Royal College of Art, 1982; major retrospective exhibition at the National Museum of Women in the Arts, Washington, D.C., 1990. Died in Blandford Forum, Dorset, England, 18 April 1993.

Selected Works

1952	*Bird*; bronze; Tate Gallery, London, England
1961	*Harbinger Bird IV*; bronze; edition of nine: several locations
1966	Altar cross; bronze; Liverpool Metropolitan Cathedral, England
1969	*Goggle Head I*; bronze; edition of six: several locations
1974	*Horse and Rider*; bronze; edition of three: several locations, including Piccadilly, London, England
1975	*Tribute Head IV*; bronze; edition of six: several locations
1976	*Protomartyr*; bronze; edition of three: several locations

1989   *Riace IV*; bronze; private collection, artist's estate

Further Reading

Elisabeth Frink, Sculpture and Drawing 1950–1990 (exhib. cat.) Washington, D.C.: National Museum of Women in the Arts, 1990

Elisabeth Frink, 1930–1993, London: Beaux-Arts, 1997

Frink, Elisabeth, *The Art of Elisabeth Frink*, London: Lund Humphries, 1972

Gardiner, Stephen, *Frink: The Official Biography of Elisabeth Frink*, London: HarperCollins, 1998

Lucie-Smith, Edward, and Elisabeth Frink, *Frink: A Portrait*, London: Bloomsbury, 1994

Roberts, Emma, "Frink Again," *Women's Art Magazine* (London) 62 (January/February 1995)

Wilder, Jill (editor), *Elisabeth Frink, Sculpture: Catalogue Raisonné*, Salisbury, Wiltshire: Harpvale, 1984

KATHARINA FRITSCH 1956– *German*

Katharina Fritsch emerged as one of Germany's preeminent sculptors and Installation artists of the 1980s and 1990s. In a number of exhibitions both in Europe and in the United States, Fritsch initiated an international dialogue with the then-dominant Postmodern sculptural modes of simulationism and appropriation. In their exploration of color and form, her sculpture and installations engage significantly with photography and with a notion of the sublime derived from German Romanticism.

Two major themes—the focus on everyday objects or commodities and the interrelation between two- and three-dimensional representation—have characterized Fritsch's work since she began her studies at the Düsseldorf Kunstakademie in 1979. Her sculptural work retains the trace of her beginnings in the two-dimensional media of drawing and painting. *Eight Tables with Eight Objects*, exhibited as part of the group exhibition *von hier aus* (starting from here) in Düsseldorf of the same year, brought together individual pieces Fritsch had completed over previous years, such as a roughly life-size cheese wheel in yellow silicone. *Eight Tables with Eight Objects* is a precise and symmetrical arrangement of objects, some fabricated and some readymades, placed on the surface of a low octagonal table. Fritsch applied a careful formalist precision to these objects and their composition, which also referenced the display of objects in the domestic sphere or in the public space of the department store.

Two large-scale sculptural works shown in Germany in 1987 first brought Fritsch to the attention of the international art press: *Elephant*, shown at the Kaiser Wilhelm Museum in Krefeld, and *Madonna Fig-ure*, Fritsch's contribution to the Münster public sculpture program. Both works are life-size polyester or epoxy resin casts of found objects painted monochromatically. *Elephant* was cast from a taxidermy specimen in the collection of the natural history museum in Bonn, with the cast form featuring a great deal of detail. Fritsch installed the work in a whitewashed gallery perched on top of a high, white, oval-shaped plinth, which further accentuated the peculiar green color of the object. The *Madonna Figure* was also cast, although on an enlarged human scale, from a religious souvenir of the Virgin from Lourdes and painted a vivid yellow. The *Madonna Figure* was installed in a pedestrian area between a church and a shopping area in a primarily Catholic city of Münster. In applying an opaque, matte color to these cast objects, Fritsch counteracted their mass and flattened them visually into a sharply delineated, two-dimensional or pictorial image, a quality that photographic reproductions further emphasize. In addition, these original casts or copies are not linked to any singular and stable meaning as a referent but instead point to their function as an undetermined and almost abstract sign consisting of shape and color. The *Madonna Figure* had to be reconstructed as a stone casting after it was destroyed by vandals.

Fritsch used the *Madonna Figure* form on a smaller scale as a component of other pieces such as *Display Stand with Madonnas* of 1987–89, for which she arranged 288 small-scale yellow Madonna forms facing outward on a display stand with exactly 32 figures placed evenly on each of nine round surfaces. In these display works, Fritsch responds to appropriationist work, which similarly thematized the repetition of form and the modes of display practiced in retail shops. However, Fritsch's interest in color is unique, as is the level of tension she generates between the sacred and the secular mass-produced object. *Display Stand with Madonnas* also references both private space and that of public display, drawing upon the particular experiences of the viewer for its content.

Fritsch returned to large-scale installation in 1988 with *Company at Table*. In this work, she arranged 32 identical black-and-white cast figures symmetrically across from each other along a long table covered by a patterned tablecloth. The composition emphasizes the Renaissance pictorial structure of perspective and the convergence of orthogonals into a vanishing point, thus rendering these masses according to a pictorial order, an effect photographs of the work emphasize. The stark contrast of the black-and-white figures and the lack of detail of the repeated forms simplify them into patterned and receding shapes. It has been suggested that *Company at Table* may depict a totalitarian atmosphere of complete alienation, although Fritsch

Rat-King© CORBIS. Courtesy Matthew Marks Gallery, New York

has rejected any such fixing of a singular meaning for the work.

Her installations *Rat-King* and *Child with Poodles* return to explore the repetition of one element within a circular form and arguably also evoke terror or the sublime, standard concerns of German Romantic art of the early 19th century. Originally installed at the Dia Center for the Arts in New York, the basic unit of *Rat-King* is a matte-black polyester-resin form of a rat on a monumental scale (3 meters high by 1.5 meters wide), repeated 16 times in a circle with the forms facing outward. Not cast from any found original, Fritsch's rat form is slightly hunched forward and lacking in detail. The tails of the creatures were elaborately knotted together at the center of the circle; Fritsch would later realize this portion of the installation separately as *Knot*. *Child with Poodles* similarly manipulates black forms within the white gallery space: Fritsch arranged 288 black, inward-facing poodle forms into four concentric circles, in the center of which she placed a white infant form on its back, a quotation of the figure of the infant in Philipp Otto Runge's canonical Romantic painting *Morning* (1808; Kunsthalle, Hamburg). Fritsch continues to explore form through repetition in this installation: the rounded forms that dominate the poodle-unit of *Child with Poodles* transform the installation into an uninterrupted pattern of colored and flattened shapes. Although they intimate the sublime, Fritsch's recent sculptural forms militate against any attempt to fix their meaning absolutely into an illusionistic stability.

CLAUDIA MESCH

Biography

Born in Essen, Germany, 14 February 1956. Studied history and art history at University of Münster; at-tended drawing evenings at the Volkshochschule; moved to Düsseldorf in 1979; admitted to Düsseldorf Kunstakademie in 1979 to study with Fritz Schwegler; shifted focus to sculpture that same year, completed degree (Meisterschülerin), 1984; first one-person show at Galerie Johnen and Schöttle, Cologne, 1985; traveled to New York with a Dia Center for the Arts Fellowship, 1989–93; represented Germany at Venice Biennale, 1995; participated again in the Venice Biennale, 1999; solo show at Städtische Galerie Wolfsberg, Germany, same year. Lives and works in Düsseldorf, Germany.

Selected Works

1984   *Eight Tables with Eight Objects*; medium density fiberboard, steel, objects; Emanuel Hoffmann-Stiftung, on permanent loan to the Museum für Gegenwartskunst, Basel, Switzerland

1987   *Elephant*; polyester, wood, paint; collection of the artist

1987   *Madonna Figure*; epoxy resin, paint; Ydessa Hendles Art Foundation, Toronto, Ontario, Canada; Musée d'Art Moderne, Bordeaux, France

1987–89 *Display Stand with Madonnas*; aluminum, plaster of Paris, paint; edition of three and artist's proof: Staatsgalerie Stuttgart, Germany; Anette and Udo Brandhorst Collection, Cologne, Germany; La Caixa de Pensions, Barcelona, Spain; private collection, Boston, Massachusetts, United States

1988   *Company at Table*; polyester, wood, cotton, paint; Dresdener Bank, on permanent loan to the Museum für Moderne Kunst, Frankfurt, Germany

1991–93 *Rat-King*; polyester, paint; collection of the artist

1992–93 *Knot*; plaster of Paris, paint; Philadelphia Museum of Art, Pennsylvania, United States

1995   *Child with Poodles*; plaster of Paris, foil, polyurethane, paint; edition of two and artist's proof: Emanuel Hoffmann-Stiftung, on permanent loan to the Museum für Gegenwartskunst, Basel, Switzerland; collection of the artist

Further Reading

Baker, Kenneth (editor), *OBJECTives: The New Sculpture*, New York: Rizzoli, and Newport Beach, California: Newport Harbor Art Museum, 1990

Cameron, Dan, "Setting Standards," *Parkett* 25 (1990)

Harten, Jürgen, and David Ross (editors), *Binationale: German Art of the Late 80's/American Art of the Late 80's*, Cologne, Germany: DuMont, 1988

Heynen, Julie (editor), *Katharina Fritsch, 1979–1989*, Cologne, Germany: Verlag der Buchhandlung W. König, 1990

Katharina Fritsch (exhib. cat.), Basel, Switzerland: Museum für Gegenwartskunst, and San Francisco: San Francisco Museum of Modern Art, 1996

Schmidt-Wulffen, Stephan, "Low Fidelity: Notes on the Work of Katharina Fritsch," in *Robert Lehman Lectures on Contemporary Art*, edited by Lynne Cooke and Karen Kelly, New York: Dia Center for the Arts, 1996

GEORGE FULLARD 1923–1973 *British*

In 1974 a reviewer of Fullard's retrospective exhibition at the Serpentine Gallery in London remarked regretfully that, on seeing all the work together, he "suddenly and belatedly" realized that Fullard had been "a very considerable artist" (see Gosling, 1974). The memorial show attracted a plethora of adulatory reviews and tributes. However, such comments reveal that by the early 1970s Fullard's work had gone overlooked and undervalued. During the 1950s his work had been overshadowed by that of the British sculptors acclaimed by Herbert Read at the 1952 Venice Biennale. In the mid 1960s, Fullard's profoundly personal work was viewed as eccentric and idiosyncratic when set against the abstract self-referential work of the New Generation sculptors. However, as one of the few working in assemblage in the 1960s, Fullard represents an important alternative strand within postwar British sculpture. Furthermore, although the purposeful autobiographical element in his work may have distanced him from contemporary trends, it produced some of the most important and unusual war sculpture of the 20th century. The remarkable range, depth, and unity of his whole body of work is such that Fullard has of late become recognized as one of the most inventive British sculptors of the postwar generation.

Fullard's early social and political experiences, as well as growing up in a working-class family with strong communist connections, were important to his later drawings and sculpture. *War Game* displays a preoccupation with childhood games played in the labyrinthine terraces of Sheffield. However, it was Fullard's experience of war that became the central concern of his mature work. In 1959 he wrote in a personal notebook of his strong identification with a generation caught between two wars. He felt marked by the collective grief and war stories from his family's involvement in World War I. Images of the 1940 blitzkrieg on Sheffield feature in Fullard's student drawings. His experience of war was compounded when, as a trooper in the 17/21st Lancers, he was seriously wounded in the final battle for Monte Cassino in Italy in 1944. After he made a remarkable recovery, the notion of "survival" later acquired mythic significance for Fullard and provided the focus for the series of war assemblages he made in the 1960s.

Fullard emerged in 1947 from the Royal College of Art, where he had studies with Frank Dobson, with a reputation as a fine modeler. After a brief period in Paris, he returned to England and, for a time, shared a studio with painter Derrick Greaves at Fawcett Yard in London. At the time Fullard was working in clay, generally modeling large figures that he could not afford to cast into permanent materials. His abilities enabled him to obtain part-time teaching; he also secured a number of commissions for commercial projects, including the production of props for film and stage sets. However, he had little success in selling or showing his large figurative sculpture until the end of the 1950s. Works such as *Old Woman* and *Walking Man*, modeled in clay and cast into concrete, were concerned with the ordinariness of humanity and displayed a strong sense of social class. In the political environment of the Cold War, such work was received, described, and often denigrated, as "realist" and subsequently failed to engage acclaim in established critical circles. In 1955 the Marxist art critic for the *New Statesman*, John Berger, identified Fullard as one of a handful of young social realist artists who had become "famously unacceptable" for the kind of work they were making. After consistently supporting his work in various ways through the 1950s, in a review of Fullard's first solo exhibition at the Woodstock Gallery in London in 1958, Berger concluded that he was the best contemporary sculptor working in Britain at the time.

It was the artist's sudden turn to assemblage in 1958, however, that brought him wider critical acclaim and led to his being invited to become head of sculpture at the Chelsea School of Art in London. His first assemblages were figures—women, mothers, and children—made of bits of old cupboards, doors, and other debris gathered from bomb sites around his Chelsea home and studio. These meticulously assembled figures featured characteristically comic details, such as the footwear in *Woman*.

In assemblage Fullard discovered the perfect idiom for exploring the theme of war. One of his earliest assemblage pieces, *War Ghost*, brings together an exploration of the insanity of both world wars. In the war series, by putting together incongruous images and objects, Fullard explored the acute sense of the absurdity of his subject through irony and paradox. His war sculptures are assembled from various found objects, including toy tanks, toy soldiers, golf clubs, chair legs, and roughly carved offcuts of wood. Although Fullard's monstrous infants display the sculptor's sense of humor, their macabre aspect is tempered by a serious note. *The Infant St. George*, for example, might represent a woman pushing a child into battle, but it also resembles a ramshackle war machine, recalling the machinery of the trenches. *Death or Glory*, depicting an infant warrior with his toy sword, makeshift shield, and "steed," playfully ironizes the motto of Fullard's own regiment and introduces the recurring motif of a child's paper helmet-cum-boat.

After 1965 Fullard abandoned the subject of war but remained preoccupied with the child's view. Working in painted aluminum and sheet metal, he turned to nautical themes for his wall reliefs and constructed sculpture. In his adoption of color and new materials, there are affinities with the work of Anthony Caro and the New Generation of sculptors, but the work retains an idiosyncratic quality and displays Fullard's distinct facility to manipulate paradoxical elements. In *Forever*, a steamboat sinks on a still sea while the child's paper boat floats. These late works reflect Fullard's ethos that the artist should aim to recapture the untutored artistic creativity of the infant.

During his lifetime, Fullard showed in many major exhibitions of contemporary sculpture and had a number of solo shows, including one at the Marlborough New London Gallery in 1964. His early use of assemblage in the 1950s links his work to contemporaneous neo-Dada developments in Europe and the United States. Fullard died while his career was still developing, and his work had been overshadowed by a transatlantic trend for anonymous abstract sculpture as embodied in the coalition of Greenbergian theory and the work produced by Caro and followers, as well as by a pervasive conceptualism. However, late 20th-century art displays a continued preoccupation with assemblage techniques and with found objects. Additionally, Postmodernism and a receptivity to multiplicity has undermined the hegemony of the Modernist canon and has provided the impetus to research alternative art histories. Such trends have enabled a revaluation of Fullard's work and a renewed regard for the place of both realist sculpture and assemblage in historical accounts of sculpture.

GILLIAN WHITELEY

Biography

Born in Sheffield, England, 15 September 1923. Studied at Sheffield College of Arts and Crafts, 1937–42; war service with 17/21st Lancers, 1942–44; seriously wounded at Monte Cassino, Italy, May 1944; studied sculpture at Royal College of Art, Ambleside and London, 1945–47, under Richard Garbe and Frank Dobson; awarded travel scholarship to Paris in 1947 upon graduating from Royal College of Art; turned to as-

semblage and had first one-man show at Woodstock Gallery, London, 1958; held various part-time teaching posts in the 1950s, including St. Albans School of Art and the Royal College of Art, London; head of sculpture at Chelsea School of Art, London, 1963–73; associate of Royal Academy, 1973. Died in London, England, 25 December 1973.

Selected Works

1957   *Old Woman*; ciment fondu; Stoke-on-Trent City Museum and Art Gallery, England
1957   *Walking Man*; bronze; Sheffield Galleries and Museums Collections, England
1958   *Angry Woman*; bronze; Sheffield Galleries and Museums Collections, England
1958   *Infant with Flower*; bronze; Tate Gallery, London, England
1959   *Woman*; assemblage, wood; Arts Council Collection, Hayward Gallery, London, England
1960   *Head*; bronze; private collection, England
1961   *War Ghost*; assemblage, mainly steel; on loan from private collection to Sheffield Galleries and Museums Collections, England
1962   *War Game*; bronze; Sheffield Galleries and Museums Collections, England
1962–63 *The Infant St. George*; assemblage of wooden objects; on loan from private collection to Aberdeen City Art Gallery, Scotland
1963–64 *Death or Glory*; assemblage of various wooden objects; Tate Gallery, London, England
1964   *Captive*; boxed assemblage; Leeds City Art Galleries Collection, England
1969   *Forever*; painted steel and brass; Arts Council Collection, Hayward Gallery, London, England
1970–71 *Dream Day*; painted aluminium; on loan from private collection to Bristol City Art Gallery, England

Further Reading

Berger, John, "George Fullard," *New Statesman* (6 September 1958)
Brill, Fred, *George Fullard, 1923–1973* (exhib. cat.), London: Arts Council of Great Britain, 1974
Fullard, George, "Sculpture and Survival," *The Painter and Sculptor* 2/2, (summer 1959)
Gosling, N., "Belated Tribute," *The Observer* (28 July 1974)
Spalding, Julian, *George Fullard Drawings* (exhib. cat.), London: Arts Council of Great Britain, 1982
Whiteley, Gillian, *George Fullard—A Fastidious Primitive* (exhib. cat.), Wakefield, West Yorkshire: Yorkshire Sculpture Park, 1997

Whiteley, Gillian, "The Impact of the Survivor: The Sculpture of George Fullard (1923–1973)," *The Sculpture Journal* (1997)

Whiteley, Gillian, *Assembling the Absurd: The Sculpture of George Fullard*, London: Henry Moore Foundation/Lund Humphries, 1998

Whiteley, Gillian, "Playing with Paradox," in *Playing with Paradox: George Fullard, 1923–1973* (exhib. cat.), edited by Andrew Middleton, Sheffield, Yorkshire: Sheffield Hallam University Press, 1998

FUNERARY SCULPTURE

See **Tomb Sculpture**